D0079657

APPLIED INTERMEDIATE MACROECONOMICS

This textbook offers a complete course in applied macroeconomics at the intermediate level that emphasizes the application of economic theory to real-world data and policy. Topics covered include national and international income and financial accounts, business cycles, financial markets, economic growth, labor markets, aggregate supply and demand, inflation, and monetary and fiscal policy. The text is unique in developing a detailed toolkit of elementary statistics and graphical techniques for economic data. One strength is its detailed treatment of national and international financial markets and the institutions of monetary and fiscal policy, which makes it especially helpful in understanding recent economic crises. The website for the text is found at www.appliedmacroeconomics.com.

Kevin D. Hoover is Professor of Economics and Philosophy at Duke University. A graduate of the College of William and Mary, he received his doctorate from the University of Oxford. He developed his interest in applied macroeconomics early in his career while working at the Federal Reserve Bank of San Francisco. Before moving to Duke, Hoover taught economics at the University of California, Davis, and at Oxford. He is the author of *The New Classical Macroeconomics* (1988), *Causality in Macroeconomics* (Cambridge University Press, 2001), and *The Methodology of Empirical Macroeconomics* (Cambridge University Press, 2001) and has edited nine volumes and written more than one hundred academic articles on macroeconomics, monetary economics, econometrics, the methodology and philosophy of economics, and the history of economic thought. He is past chairman of the International Network for Economic Method, past president of the History of Economics Society, and a former editor of the *Journal of Economic Methodology*. He is currently the editor of the journal *History of Political Economy* and a Fellow of the Center for the History of Political Economy at Duke University.

APPLIED INTERMEDIATE MACROECONOMICS

KEVIN D. HOOVER
Duke University

CAMBRIDGE
UNIVERSITY PRESS

32 Avenue of the Americas, New York NY 10013-2473, USA

Cambridge University Press is part of the University of Cambridge.

It furthers the University's mission by disseminating knowledge in the pursuit of education, learning and research at the highest international levels of excellence.

www.cambridge.org
Information on this title: www.cambridge.org/9781107436824

© Kevin D. Hoover 2012

First published 2012
First paperback edition 2014

A catalogue record for this publication is available from the British Library

Library of Congress Cataloguing in Publication data

Hoover, Kevin D., 1955–
Applied intermediate macroeconomics / Kevin D. Hoover.
p.   cm.
Includes bibliographical references and index.
ISBN 978-0-521-76388-2 (hardback)
1. Macroeconomics.   I. Title.
HB172.5.H657   2011
339 – dc22   2011009806

ISBN 978-0-521-76388-2 Hardback
ISBN 978-1-107-43682-4 Paperback

Additional resources for this publication at http://www.appliedmacroeconomics.com

To
Joseph Bisignano
and
Andrew Graham,
my teachers and mentors in the quest to understand the economy,
not as we want it to be, but as it is.

Brief Contents

Contents

PART IX: MACROECONOMIC DATA

Acknowledgments

A vast number of people have helped me over the nearly fifteen years between when this book was first conceived and its finally appearing in print. I will certainly fail to recall them all or thank them as they deserve. I trust that any of those omitted will attribute it to the failures of my memory and my recordkeeping – which, in truth, are not all that they should be – rather than to a failure of gratitude; for my gratitude is boundless.

This book was first conceived in the mid-1990s when I engaged in a radical reformulation of my bread-and-butter Intermediate Macroeconomics course at the University of California, Davis – making it much more empirically oriented. None of the extant textbooks really suited my course. My first debt is to John Greenman, then a commissioning editor at Addison-Wesley. When he first proposed that I write a textbook, I expressed the reservation that the book that I wanted to write would be too unlike the market leaders, too much of a niche book to be commercially successful. Even so, he urged me to write a prospectus and offered me a contract. For various reasons, the work on the book was slow, and after a number of personnel changes, Addison-Wesley and I parted ways.

Fortunately, Cambridge University Press adopted my orphaned manuscript. This is the third book that I have published with Cambridge, each with the guidance and support of Scott Parris, who is the finest editor with whom it has ever been my pleasure to work. I am deeply in his debt. I also thank Adam Levine, editorial assistant at Cambridge, who has always been most efficient and helpful.

Without hundreds of macroeconomics students to motivate me, I would never have undertaken this project. Most of them offered me extremely useful comments and criticisms along the way. But to some of them I owe a special debt. I thank my research and teaching assistants Ryan Brady, Roger Butters, Michael Dowell, Jeanine Henderson, Gustav (David) Nystrom, and Piyachart Phiromswad. Heike McNaughton, in particular, read an early draft with the sensibility of an undergraduate just learning the material, but with the care of the best editor. In addition, I am grateful to the undergraduate tutors and readers who helped me in my course and who provided extremely valuable feedback on earlier drafts – from both their own experience and channeling the reactions of students in their sections. My thanks to Roman Alper, T. Andrew Black, Damien Charlety, Diane Chou, Perkin Chung, Courtney Deane, Marica Durica, Nma Eleazu, Sara Engle, Stephen Englert, Lou-Alan Fernandes, Brian Fields, Maria Fridman, Corrie Harrington, David Hodges, Lana Volk Ivanov, Dawn Johnson, Nishan Khoshafian, Phillip Lam, Rebecca Lee, Scott Levin, Gloria Li, Brian Mangold, Courtney McHarg, Nathaniel Moore, Amanda Robison, Steve Ross, Gursimran Sandhu, Leland So, Stephanie Stern, Michael Stewart, Jennifer Stivers, Jeannine Tchamourlian, Jacquelyn Walter, Chun Wang, Hope Welton, and Olga Zaretsky.

The two publishers engaged the assistance of a large number of economists to review the initial prospectus, as well as manuscripts in various stages. Most of these reviewers were anonymous. I thank them nonetheless; their reactions were important in shaping the book, and they saved me from many mistakes of fact and exposition. The few reviewers who are known to me by name – Manfred Keil, Axel Leijonhufvud, and Perry Mehrling – deserve special thanks, for they took special care with their reviews and tempered their criticisms with large measures of encouragement for the project. I especially note the help of Matthew Rafferty, my former Ph.D. student, and, more importantly, a critic who actually used the draft manuscript in his course and provided valuable field reports of its success. I am grateful as well to Mohammed El-Saka, who also used the manuscript to teach a course and provided frequent feedback. In addition, I thank my UC Davis colleague Thomas Mayer and another former Ph.D. student, Selva Demiralp, for advice on several points.

I have been a member of three departments while writing this book – Economics at UC Davis and both Economics and Philosophy at Duke University. My colleagues have provided me with great environments in which to work, and not a few have offered substantial encouragement along the way.

Throughout the seemingly endless process of writing this book, I have enjoyed the love and support of my wife Catherine and of our two daughters – Norah and Philippa ("Pippa"). Our daughters were but girls when I started this project, and are now quite grown and on their own. I thought of them as I worked on it; but, for better or worse, neither is destined to become an economist.

To the Student

The goal of economics is to make sense of the economy. *Applied Intermediate Macroeconomics* keeps that goal constantly in mind. It teaches macroeconomics as a tool of factual and interpretive understanding of the economy. It differs from most intermediate macroeconomics textbooks in its focus on applications to real-world data. The object is to prepare students to use economic theory and data to illuminate the information and policy debates that constantly bombard us in newspapers, on television and radio, and online. The strategy of the book is always to illustrate economic theory with data and detailed worked examples and to present the student with problems that involve the analysis and interpretation of actual data.

This strategy presupposes some facility with data manipulation and some familiarity with rudimentary statistics, such as constructing graphs, calculating growth rates, and taking means. The necessary level of statistical prowess is roughly things one can easily do with data using Microsoft's Excel or a similar spreadsheet *without* any special statistical add-ons. The text assumes a basic competence with Excel or another spreadsheet, and it gives frequent hints about particular applications. Most students will already have the necessary skills. But those who do not need to get quickly up to speed. The website www.appliedmacroeconomics.com, which is a resource for this book, contains some guidance on getting started with Excel.

The book does not assume that the student already knows any statistics. It teaches all the statistics required. The key resource is the chapter entitled *A Guide to Working with Economic Data* – usually referred to simply as the *Guide*. The *Guide* aims to be a self-contained reference – with clear, detailed explanations and numerous examples. It can be read profitably front to back or dipped into on an as-needed basis. Precise details often matter, so that even a student who is fairly familiar with basic statistics would be well advised to read the relevant sections of the *Guide* as a review. The main text contains numerous pointers to the sections of the *Guide* relevant to particular issues. And the instructions for the problems at the end of each chapter also note the relevant sections of the *Guide* that explain the techniques essential to doing the problems.

To master applied macroeconomics it is not enough just to read the text. The student must actively engage the material: pay close attention to the details of the worked examples, read the relevant sections of the *Guide*, and do the problems at the end of each chapter thoughtfully and carefully, always thinking about the way in which the theory in the text illuminates the data and the way in which the data illustrate, test, or challenge the theory. Remember that in the end, it is not about crunching numbers, but about analyzing, interpreting, and understanding the economy.

In addition to the *Guide*, the book contains other resources to aid the student:

- key concepts in each chapter are indicated in the text by bold-faced small capitals at the point of first use or best definition or discussion (e.g., ECONOMIC MODELS); other important terminology is indicated by bold-faced regular type (e.g., **production boundary**);
- all emboldened terms are defined in the Glossary;
- a list of Symbols used in the text is provided;
- a Summary of each chapter is broken down into succinct numbered points;
- Suggested Readings for each chapter provide sources for pursuing the subject of the chapter further;
- a Guide to Online Resources – mostly to sources of data – is provided.

The website www.appliedmacroeconomics.com provides essential supporting materials for the textbook and courses that use it. The website contains regularly updated data keyed to the end-of-chapter problem sets. It also includes hints for getting started with Excel, answers to selected end-of-chapter problems, and various other supplemental materials and links.

To the Teacher

The Problem and the Pedagogical Approach

This textbook has had a long gestation. It began in the mid-1990s when I taught intermediate macroeconomics at the University of California, Davis. I became increasingly dissatisfied that even very good students, students who had easily mastered the textbook materials, left our program with little factual knowledge of the economy and with little ability to make the theory that they had learned helpful in interpreting real-world macroeconomic issues. Even students who received A grades in Intermediate Macroeconomics often found it difficult to understand economic news and to use sound economic analysis to criticize the economic proposals of pundits, politicians, or central bankers.

I began to rethink my course – what its objects should be and how I should teach it. Most economics majors do not go on to further graduate study in economics. The greatest value-added for the typical student would be a macroeconomic education adapted to understanding the real world as filtered through the media and politics. Even those who go on to graduate study would be better prepared to appreciate the ultimate motivation of macroeconomic theory if they had first developed a good practical understanding of applied macroeconomics. This textbook is the fullest expression of that rethinking and is grounded in about fifteen years of teaching macroeconomics at UC Davis and at Duke University along these new lines.[1]

Current intermediate macroeconomics texts suffer from three common problems:

- *Theory is detached from the facts of the economy.* Textbooks often include boxed case studies to illustrate theoretical principles and illustrative graphs and tables

---

[1] A fuller account of the pedagogical philosophy behind my earlier courses and the book appears in Kevin D. Hoover, "Teaching Economics While Taking Complexity Seriously," in David Colander, editor, *The Complexity Vision and the Teaching of Economics*. Cambridge: Cambridge University Press, 2000, which can be downloaded from www.appliedmacroeconomics.com.

of current data. The numbers in the chapters on national income accounting are updated with each edition. Yet the facts of the economy are usually peripheral – not woven tightly into the main exposition. And it is common for students to emerge nearly as ignorant at the end of the course of the basic features of the economy as at the beginning.

• *Exposition of theory is not well adapted to the real world.* Macroeconomic news generally reports rates of change (e.g., growth rates, inflation rates), whereas typical textbooks focus on levels (e.g., the aggregate supply and demand curves determine the level of prices and GDP). The teacher knows how to translate from one context to the other, but the average student finds it difficult. Much of real-world macroeconomics is closely tied to the complexities of financial markets. Textbooks typically focus on "the" rate of interest as determined by the supply of and demand for money, leaving a richer analysis of financial markets to later money and banking courses.

• *There is too much stress on theoretical closure and advanced topics at the expense of first principles.* Many intermediate macroeconomics textbooks read like graduate textbooks without the mathematics.

In contrast, this book aims to avoid these common pitfalls through a complete integration of macroeconomic theory and statistical analysis and interpretation.

The goal of economics is to make sense of the economy. *Applied Intermediate Macroeconomics* keeps that goal constantly in mind. It teaches macroeconomics as a tool of factual and interpretive understanding of the economy. The key is that the textbook introduces elementary data analysis simultaneously with macroeconomic theory. Students apply these skills to the interpretation of actual U.S. economic data. Students develop competence to use economic theory and sophisticated back-of-the-envelope statistics as tools of analysis. They leave the course with both a well-grounded knowledge of the main features of the U.S. economy and the skills necessary to analyze any macroeconomy.

The textbook is structured around three parallel and interrelated streams:

• A clear presentation of the fundamentals of macroeconomic theory
• A practical introduction to elementary statistics
• A set of structured empirical exercises using actual macroeconomic data and the elementary statistical and graphical tools commonly available in modern spreadsheet software

The focus is on macroeconomics, not statistics. The only purpose in introducing the statistics is to give the student a foundation for applying the theory to actual data. Statistical topics are limited to those suitable for the task at hand, and are introduced only as needed to support the developing account of the macroeconomy. Consider each of the three streams in turn.

1. Macroeconomic Theory

The textbook has a clear theoretical point of view. It is Keynesian in the sense that recessions and cyclically high unemployment are regarded as (possibly remediable) deviations of the economy from optimal economic arrangements. Classical (and new classical) analysis in which all markets are regarded as clearing is seen as a limiting case, practically important for fully employed economies. Doctrinal disputes are largely ignored in the text, as they are more likely to confuse than to inform the neophyte.

Although the textbook concentrates on the practical core of macroeconomic theory, which is familiar to economists and is covered in other macroeconomics texts, it is distinguished from these texts by its emphasis on empirical applications of the theory. Some features that enhance the empirical relevance of the theory include:

- *Emphasis on fundamental economic ideas and their application.* Some examples: the distinction between real and nominal magnitudes, the distinction between *ex ante* and *ex post* points of view, the importance of expectations, opportunity cost and present value, supply and demand, arbitrage, and risk.
- *Richer than usual discussion of the structure and importance of financial markets for the macroeconomy.*
- *Orientation toward monetary and fiscal policy (including both aggregate effects and incentive effects) from the beginning of the book.* Relevant facts about policy can be gleaned from the earliest chapters on national accounting, through later chapters on factor markets and financial markets, and to the last chapters in which policy takes center stage.
- *Stress on a changing economy.* The analysis of economic growth and business cycles is integrated. The exposition is formulated so that the student can readily map the theory of the book onto the growth rates, inflation rates, and unemployment and utilization rates that dominate economic policy goals and popular economic commentary.

A symposium in the *American Economic Review* (May 1997) posed the question, "Is there a core of practical macroeconomics that we should all believe?" The approach in this book comes closest to the separate answers offered in that symposium by Robert Solow and Alan Blinder. Between them, Solow and Blinder identified the practical core as including: neoclassical growth theory, the IS curve, the Phillips curve, and Okun's law. Blinder observed the necessity for a more realistic treatment of financial markets that would downplay the analytical role of the LM curve (the instability of money supply and demand having rendered it virtually irrelevant analytically and as a guide to policy) and would provide an adequate account of the term structure of interest rates. A similar case for eliminating the LM curve from the macroeconomic model has been made by David Romer ("Keynesian Macroeconomics without the LM Curve," *Journal of Economic*

Perspectives, Spring 2000) and by Benjamin Friedman ("The LM Curve: A Not-So-Fond Farewell," National Bureau of Economic Research, Working Paper No. 10123, 2003).

The theory in *Applied Intermediate Macroeconomics* departs from some of the common elements of many macroeconomics textbooks to implement this vision of the core of macroeconomics. Although it relies on an aggregate demand–aggregate supply conception of the economy, one departure is that it makes no use of the apparatus of an aggregate demand and supply curve in price-output space. This apparatus is not easy to relate to data on the economy at the level at which undergraduates are equipped, nor do the aggregate demand and supply curves integrate well with discussions of long-term economic growth, Okun's law, or the Phillips curve.

Instead, the analysis of aggregate supply is developed using the aggregate production function, which is easily quantified, and which ties in directly to the neoclassical growth model and lends itself to discussions of productivity. Later the notions of the balanced growth path and productivity measures are easily related to Okun's law (which is given much stronger theoretical grounding in this text than is usually the case) and to the Phillips curve. The aggregate production function is also used to define a workable and data-relevant notion of potential output that is used throughout the book.

Another departure is that the core short-run macro model takes the form of three main elements: the IS curve, the Phillips curve, and the financial sector reflecting Federal Reserve interest-rate policy and the term structure of interest rates. These three elements are supplemented by Okun's law. The three-element approach is fundamentally the one advocated in the symposium on core macroeconomics cited earlier. It also closely reflects the approach to macro-modeling that now dominates thinking in the Federal Reserve and central banks around the world. This makes it especially easy to relate to current popular discussions of monetary policy.

Although the approach retains the IS curve as a key element in the analysis of aggregate demand, it omits the LM curve. I believe that the LM-curve analysis (1) is insufficiently rich to do justice to financial markets that play an increasingly prominent part in real-world macroeconomics; (2) overemphasizes the significance of the monetary aggregates, which are a tiny fraction of the asset base of the financial system; and (3) systematically misleads with respect to the actual conduct of monetary policy, which in most countries, including the United States (except for the 1979–1982 period), has been dominated by interest-rate targeting and, more recently in the crisis of 2008–2009, by credit-oriented monetary policy – the so-called quantitative easing. In place of the LM curve, the current text contains three chapters that provide a rich discussion of the domestic and international financial systems (tied through the flow of funds accounts to the national-income-accounting framework) and the behavior of interest rates, as well as a chapter on monetary policy that more closely reflects actual central-bank practices than one generally finds in textbooks at this level.

Some readers of earlier drafts have insisted on the importance of the LM curve. While I disagree, the LM curve and the IS-LM model are developed in the appendices to Chapters 7 and 13. An application of the IS-LM analysis (including the money-multiplier analysis) to the "monetarist episode" of 1979–1982 is provided in the appendix to Chapter 16.

2. Practical Statistics

Students will develop statistical skills in the service of economics. I have struggled over how best to incorporate statistical tools in the textbook. (It is practically much less of a problem in the actual conduct of a course.) In the end, it seemed most practical to present a comprehensive *Guide to Working with Economic Data* as a reference tool separate from the main text. Cross-references to particular parts of the *Guide* point out where statistical tools are relevant, and the end-of-chapter problems draw heavily on the skills taught in the *Guide*. (Each problem set notes the relevant sections of the *Guide*.)

The *Guide* aims to be a self-contained reference – with clear, detailed explanations and numerous examples. It can be read profitably front to back or dipped into on an as-needed basis. It is a subsidiary tool. My own practice has never been to try to teach a statistics course alongside an economics course. The *Guide* aims at basic competency in elementary statistics rather than proto-econometrics. Although many students will have already taken an introductory statistics course, it does not presuppose statistical knowledge. It gives a clear account from first principles that provides adequate background knowledge for the complete beginner and serves as a useful review for the better prepared student. The *Guide* uses only the most basic statistics – roughly things one can easily do with data using Microsoft's Excel spreadsheet *without* any of the statistical add-ons.

The *Guide* emphasizes three aspects of working with economic data:

- *General statistical methods.* The *Guide* begins with mundane, but too often neglected, topics, for example, units of measurement and the making of graphs and tables. It progresses to the simple but powerful statistical tools that are readily available in common spreadsheet packages, including descriptive statistics (means, variances, standard deviations, coefficients of variations, and correlation coefficients), trend fitting and single variable regression (as an option on scatter-plots), and moving averages.
- *Specifically economic methods.* For the most part, the *Guide* introduces statistical techniques that are particularly relevant to economics in the order in which they arise naturally in their economic contexts. These include: conversion of nominal to real (constant dollars); index numbers; ratios and percentage shares; calculation of growth (and inflation) rates, including annualization and compounding;

xxxviii
To the Teacher

calculation of doubling times; logarithms and their relationship to growth rates; and fitting linear and exponential trends.

- *Interpretive issues.* The end-of-chapter exercises stress the interpretive use of statistics. A number of formally difficult, sophisticated statistical issues are discussed in an informal manner, stressing their relevance to practical economic issues. These include the problem of spurious correlations resulting from common causes or common trends, instability over time, the direction of causation, unobserved expectations, and time aggregation.

3. Exercises

Problem sets at the end of each chapter typically include both theoretical and empirical exercises. Empirical exercises are dominant. Some can be done with a calculator, but most presume that the student will have access to a spreadsheet program. Microsoft's Excel is the model, although other spreadsheet programs may well be adequate. Although there is no systematic attempt to teach the fundamentals of Excel – my experience is that most students now have a rudimentary understanding before starting the class or can quickly come up to speed – there are numerous hints about how to apply Excel to particular problems.

The textbook is supported by a website (www.appliedmacroeconomics .com) containing, among other things, regularly updated data sets keyed to the empirical exercises for each chapter. The book and the website also contain a *Guide to Online Resources* that documents web-based sources of data. It is good for students to learn to find and use publicly available data sources. They should do so, for instance, for supplementary class projects. Nevertheless, there are many pitfalls, and experience shows that things work more smoothly if all students are using the same data for end-of-chapter exercises and do not have to struggle to find it in the right format.

Using the Text in a Course

The chapters of the book are arranged in a logical order – a little different perhaps from in other textbooks. In keeping with the empirical orientation of the book, the basic data of the economy – the national-income and product accounts, the balance of payments, and the flow of funds, as well as the descriptive analysis of business cycles (viewing economic data as having trend and cyclical components) – are all introduced early. Because of their key role in connecting aggregate supply and demand, the real economic content of the book begins with domestic and international financial markets. Aggregate supply – both in the aspect of long-term economic growth and the cyclical behavior of labor markets – is introduced next, followed by aggregate demand. Monetary and fiscal policy are integrated into the discussion of earlier chapters, but the book closes with a more detailed treatment of each.

Although the chapters are designed to be read straight through, they have sufficient independence that instructors who prefer to consider topics in various different orders should find that the chapters can be treated somewhat flexibly. Flexibility is reinforced by a comprehensive glossary and list of symbols used in the text, allowing students to fill in missing terminology or concepts. Key concepts in each chapter are indicated in the text by bold-faced small capitals at the point of first use or best definition or discussion; other important terminology is indicated by bold-faced regular type. All emboldened terms are defined in the glossary.

I have myself taught courses using the material in the book in different orders in both quarter and semester courses. The book is comprehensive in its treatment of most topics, so that some selection and omission are inevitable. The following table suggests a basic core course in domestic macroeconomics and notes several alternative or supplementary paths through the materials.

Possible Course Structures Using
Applied Intermediate Macroeconomics

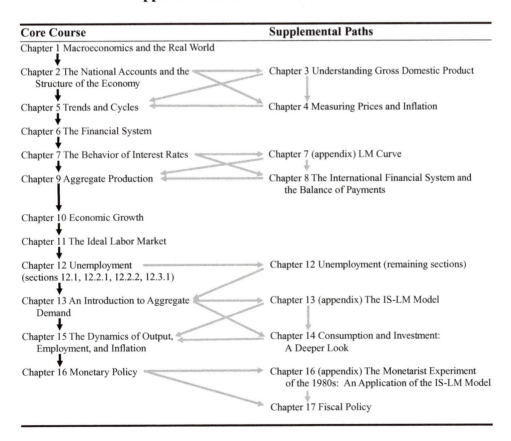

Core Course	Supplemental Paths
Chapter 1 Macroeconomics and the Real World	
Chapter 2 The National Accounts and the Structure of the Economy	Chapter 3 Understanding Gross Domestic Product
Chapter 5 Trends and Cycles	Chapter 4 Measuring Prices and Inflation
Chapter 6 The Financial System	
Chapter 7 The Behavior of Interest Rates	Chapter 7 (appendix) LM Curve
Chapter 9 Aggregate Production	Chapter 8 The International Financial System and the Balance of Payments
Chapter 10 Economic Growth	
Chapter 11 The Ideal Labor Market	
Chapter 12 Unemployment (sections 12.1, 12.2.1, 12.2.2, 12.3.1)	Chapter 12 Unemployment (remaining sections)
Chapter 13 An Introduction to Aggregate Demand	Chapter 13 (appendix) The IS-LM Model
Chapter 15 The Dynamics of Output, Employment, and Inflation	Chapter 14 Consumption and Investment: A Deeper Look
Chapter 16 Monetary Policy	Chapter 16 (appendix) The Monetarist Experiment of the 1980s: An Application of the IS-LM Model
	Chapter 17 Fiscal Policy

Essential supporting materials for the course are accessible through the website www.appliedmacroeconomics.com. The website includes regularly updated data sets for problems, hints for getting started with Excel, answers to selected end-of-chapter problems, and various other supplemental materials and links.

Part I

Introduction

1

Macroeconomics and the Real World

1.1 The Problems of Macroeconomics

Perhaps the most direct way to understand what *macroeconomics* is about is to sample the typical problems that it addresses.

Nothing focuses the mind on the economy more readily than an economic crisis. And when most of us think about an economic crisis, it is the macroeconomic aspects of the economy that spring to mind. The U.S. economy entered a recession in December 2007. Between then and the beginning of the recovery in June 2009, gross domestic product (GDP) fell by 3.7 percent – the largest fall during a recession since the Great Depression of the 1930s. To put that in perspective, GDP per head fell by $2,981 – that is, if the GDP had been evenly distributed across every person in the United States, each would have lost nearly $3,000 per year or nearly $4,500 over the eighteen-month recession (i.e., a family of four would have lost $18,000).

Of course, GDP is not evenly distributed and neither are the losses from a recession – many people are affected, but none suffer more than those who lose their jobs. Over this same period, 7,311,000 Americans lost their jobs – a fall of more than 5 percent of total employment. Looked at another way, the unemployment rate – the percentage of people who want to work but are not working – rose over this period by 4.4 percentage points to 9.4 percent. Nearly, one person in ten was out of work. Nor did the pain stop with the end of the recession. Employment continued to fall and the unemployment rate continued to rise for several more months. It is not for nothing that the recession of 2007–2009 is already widely known as the "Great Recession." The first central concern of macroeconomics is to understand MACROECONOMIC FLUCTUATIONS – that is, to understand why such calamitous situations arise and, possibly, to provide an intellectual foundation for doing something about them.

One should not conclude that macroeconomics is a gloomy field, concerned only with the malfunctioning economy. For a quarter of a century before the onset of the recession in 2007, the U.S. economy experienced growth punctuated by two mild recessions – one at the beginning of the 1990s and one at the beginning of the new millennium. Over the period from the end of the last big recession in November 1982 to the onset of the Great Recession of 2007, real GDP more than doubled; and, while population increased by 30 percent, total employment increased by more than 50 percent. People became richer. GDP per head rose by 75 percent or by nearly $19,000 per year or nearly $76,000 for a family of four (again on the unrealistic assumption that the gains were spread evenly). Over the course of U.S. history, the forward steps of rising GDP and rising employment have, in the end, overwhelmed the backward steps of recession. The second central concern of macroeconomics is to understand long-term ECONOMIC GROWTH – that is, to understand why such happy situations arise and, possibly, to provide guidance on how to foster them in the future.

1.2 What Is Macroeconomics?

1.2.1 Macroeconomics Defined

Macroeconomics is sometimes defined as the study of the relationships among aggregate quantities (or **aggregates**) such as GDP, employment, unemployment, inflation, interest rates, exchange rates, and the balance of trade. In contrast, *microeconomics* is sometimes defined as the study of the behavior of individual economic actors – individual people, households, and firms.

An alternative to this definition defines MACROECONOMICS as *the study of the economy taken as a whole*; whereas MICROECONOMICS is *the study of a part of the economy (particular people, households, firms, markets, and so forth), taking the remainder as given.*

The two definitions of macroeconomics are by no means identical, and the second definition is better. For example, the study of the market for personal computers is typically regarded as microeconomics, although it may use aggregated data – for example, the total sales of personal computers rather than the sales of a particular model by a particular manufacturer. Similarly, typical macroeconomic problems may be addressed – at least in theory – without aggregates. However, in most cases, the only practical way to study the economy as a whole is to use aggregates, so the two definitions will typically pull in the same direction.

The distinction between the study of the economy as a whole and the study of its individual parts, taking the rest of the economy as given, is an important one. Consider an analogy. A citizen of New Orleans might want to take the most efficient route to Baton Rouge. Normally, he would simply drive

Interstate Highway 10. In making that calculation, he assumes that other people will go about their own business in their ordinary ways. On the other hand, if there were a hurricane, and everyone tried to leave New Orleans by this route, the traffic jam would be enormous. The calculation that assumed that other people would act in their ordinary way would be misleading. And indeed, the problem arises mainly because many people act on that misleading calculation. The people who miscalculate in this way are guilty of a **FALLACY OF COMPOSITION** – *the assumption that what holds for a part must hold for the whole as well.*

Fallacies of composition also occur in economics. For example, when I say that I hold $2,935 worth of Google stock, what I mean is that the current price quoted on the stock exchange times the number of shares that I own equals $2,935. Because my few shares are only a tiny part of the outstanding Google shares, it is not unreasonable to think that I will be able to sell my shares for the going price without driving that price down. However, if the entire market decided that it was time to sell Google shares, their price would collapse. What is true of the individual is not necessarily true of the market as a whole.

The most famous fallacy of composition in economics was identified by the English economist John Maynard Keynes (1883–1946) and is discussed in Chapter 13: an individual can increase her wealth by saving, but the attempt of every individual simultaneously to increase savings will add nothing to the wealth of the economy as a whole. Individuals attempt to save more by reducing their consumption, which reduces the demand for goods, reducing the production needed to meet the lower demand, reducing the employment of workers needed in production, and, therefore, reducing their incomes and the amount of funds available for saving. Workers save at a higher rate relative to income, but that rate is multiplied by a smaller income. And, in the end, because their efforts to save lowers income, the amount that is successfully saved for the economy as a whole is just the amount needed to fund new investment, which did not change. (Of course, this is all conditional on no other sources of demand filling the void.) One goal of macroeconomics is to provide an analysis of the economy that does not commit fallacies of composition.

1.2.2 The Origins of Macroeconomics

Economics is an ancient field. Aristotle wrote on economic topics in the third century B.C. The origins of economics belong in equal measure to philosophy; the practical experiences of merchants, manufacturers, and government; and the law. What we now regard as macroeconomic problems are among the oldest in economics. For example, the relationship between the stock of money and the price level was addressed as early as the sixteenth century. The problem of the balance of trade concerned governments at least from the Renaissance and was widely discussed among economic commentators. Modern economics is usually dated to Adam Smith's *Wealth of Nations* (1776). Lacking a clear distinction, microeconomic and macroeconomic issues are run together in the *Wealth of Nations* and in the work of subsequent economists before the twentieth century.

Before the nineteenth century, economists had frequently addressed the problems of money, prices, trade, and the sources of economic growth. With the Industrial Revolution, business cycles – the difficult-to-understand alternation of good and bad times – became a central focus of economics. By the 1920s, economists had begun to reconceptualize business cycles as requiring a different sort of analysis from that appropriate to the behavior of consumers and firms. The Great Depression accelerated this reconceptualization.

Most famously, John Maynard Keynes's *General Theory of Employment Interest and Money* (1936) is widely credited with providing the foundations of modern macroeconomics. Whereas Keynes explicitly drew the distinction between the theory of the individual economic actor and the theory of the output and employment as a whole, it was not Keynes but the Norwegian economist Ragnar Frisch (1895–1973), winner of the first Nobel Prize in Economic Science in 1969, who in 1933 first coined the terms *microeconomics* and *macroeconomics*. Perhaps, more importantly, Frisch and the Dutch economist Jan Tinbergen (1903–1994), who shared the Nobel Prize with Frisch, set the stage for the way in which modern macroeconomics analyzes the economy. Tinbergen was originally trained as a physicist. And both Frisch and Tinbergen advocated the use of formal models as tools of data analysis to illuminate the workings of the macroeconomy. Frisch was the father of modern econometrics, whereas Tinbergen was the first to provide a complete macroeconometric model of the U.S. economy. These developments were possible only because, at about the same time, other economists, notably the Russian-American Simon Kuznets (1901–1985; winner of the Nobel Prize in 1971), the English Richard Stone (1913–1991; winner of the Nobel Prize in 1984), and the Australian Colin Clark (1905–1989), developed the modern system of national accounts that provides the basic data for macroeconomic analysis (see Chapters 2–4).

1.2.3 Positive versus Normative Macroeconomics

The Great Depression was a deep psychic wound to many who lived through it. Modern macroeconomics was born out of the desire to do something about it. Both Frisch and Tinbergen saw macroeconomic modeling as a tool for central planning. Keynes was not a central planner, but he also saw macroeconomics as a tool for government intervention to counteract recessions. He is often vilified by modern opponents of such intervention for having provided the intellectual justification for them.

Like most economists, Frisch, Tinbergen, and Keynes nonetheless understood the key distinction between the *positive* (how things are in fact) and the *normative* (how we want them to be). The goals of the policymaker are normative. What the policymaker can do to achieve those goals is positive. Two economists could agree on facts about how the economy works and its present condition – that is, they could agree on a positive account of the economy – and still disagree about what should be done. Some hope to use policy to guide the economy to better outcomes. Others wish to leave the economy to its own devices – which is itself a kind of policy. Either way, the goal of this book is to develop a sound positive account of how the economy works. Such an account provides vital information to inform policy, whichever direction policymakers, politicians, and citizens wish to take it.

One difficulty with a simple dichotomy between the normative and the positive – between policy and the way that policy actions work out in the economy – is that the government does not stand outside the economy, pushing a button here and pulling a lever there to guide it along. The government is part of the economy. It commands substantial economic resources, and it provides important services, as well as key elements of the institutional setting in which economic activity takes place. As a result, although a positive account of the economy does not endorse any particular policy, it must nevertheless take account of policies, what they aim to achieve, and how successful they are in their own terms in order to understand how the economy behaves in fact.

1.3 Doing Macroeconomics

1.3.1 Macroeconomics as a Science

Social Sciences versus Natural Sciences

Economics is a social science. The issue raised in the last section that positive economics must account for the normative goals and actions of policymakers is part of a general difference between social and natural sciences. Most natural sciences (with the partial exception of some aspects of biological sciences) deal with inert matter. Unlike human beings, molecules and planets and electricity do not hold beliefs, aim at goals, possess intentions, or make decisions. A reasonable hypothesis is that, at some level, we can find relatively simple rules describing the behavior of inert matter based on reasonably straightforward factual observations. It is hard to imagine social behavior being captured in the same way. Exactly how would a physicist account for something as basic as deciding to go to the store to buy a gallon of milk and the actions that follow it?

This is not to say that social life is inscrutable. Although a physicist using the tools of physics would find your trip to the store beyond the powers of his science, the same physicist as a human being may well be able to predict with considerable accuracy your route, means of movement (car or foot), the time it takes, and so forth simply by understanding your goals and the constraints that you face (for example, that it is too far to walk in a reasonable time). Nor need he know in detail what is inside your head. It will often suffice to understand what is typical about people. Of course, you might surprise him by having atypical characteristics or goals – prediction in social sciences is rarely certain or precise. We should be careful not to make too much of that. The relevant comparison is not with the precision that a natural science can achieve with respect to the motion of a planet or the measurement of a molecule. Rather we must ask whether the methods of the natural sciences or the methods of the social sciences, which take account of people's goals and constraints, give greater certainty or precision when applied to the behavior of human beings. On that front, the social sciences win hands down.

Rational Behavior

The distinction between positive and normative economics is sometimes described in the catchphrase "you can't derive *ought* from *is*." Scientific explanation in economics turns this prohibition on its head: in economics we frequently derive *is* from *ought*. Microeconomic explanations are typically of the form: "Given her preferences and the prices of fruit and what she has to spend, Louise would be more satisfied buying grapefruit than bananas (that is, Louise *ought* to buy grapefruit); therefore, Louise *does* buy grapefruit." This is the essence of the sometimes misunderstood economic premise: *people behave rationally*. Here "rationally" means only that people are assumed to adapt their actions efficiently to their own desires, whatever those desires are. It says nothing about the nature of the desires. And again, such explanations may turn out to be wrong in particular cases. But most economic explanations are not interested in particular cases anyway, but in what people do on average in markets or economies. Again, if we can appeal to what is typical – of people's desires and their behavior – then the insight that people typically try to fulfill their desires efficiently is helpful in understanding what happens in the economy.

The question of how macroeconomics is related to microeconomics has been debated for decades. For our purposes, it is sufficient to say that whatever happens in aggregate must be connected to the behavior of individual people. We do have to guard against fallacies of composition. Yet, as we shall see in subsequent chapters, we may frequently get some insight into the relationships of aggregate macroeconomic data from a careful analysis of how individuals should behave optimally. Such insights are never decisive. We must always check to see whether, and to what degree, the macroeconomic data reflect them.

Observation versus Controlled Experiments

One of the reasons that some physical sciences are more certain and precise than social sciences is that they are better able to run controlled experiments. Controlled experiments help to isolate causes and typically create situations that are much simpler to analyze than uncontrolled experiments or nonexperimental observation would allow. The difference is not perfectly sharp. Although experimental economics is now a recognized field, it mostly involves observing people in stylized market transactions or games. It provides genuine insight, for example, into how auctions work. But we cannot necessarily generalize from the experiment to real-world economic behavior. Similarly, not all natural sciences are experimental: astronomy, meteorology, and geology, for example, are no more – and perhaps less – susceptible to experiment than is economics.

Experiments of a type that would be most revealing are frequently not possible in economics. It is too hard, or we simply do not know how, to manipulate different aspects of the economy in the right way to achieve the right sort of controls. Experiments would also raise ethical problems. We can hardly test the effects of unemployment on inflation rates by intentionally creating mass unemployment just to see what happens. One of the great benefits of controlled experiments is that they simplify. They permit us to observe a situation in which everything other than the relationship of interest has been excluded. The economy is too complex to do such experiments on any large scale. We must instead simply observe the economy and try to infer its mechanisms through other means.

Another feature of experiments is that they can be repeated. Our confidence in what they show may be increased when scientists in other laboratories get the same results. In an earlier era, some scientific fields were called "natural history." The ecologist or wildlife biologist was a natural historian who might observe forests or seas or animals or plants in their natural environments. The geologist might drill, dig, measure, and map to try to determine the geological history of the earth. In all these cases, there is only a single history. The naturalist does not have the luxury of starting over and rerunning history to see if it works out the same. In this respect, economics is more like natural history than it is like physics or chemistry. Just as a wildlife biologist can observe different populations of, say, elephants in different areas, an economist might observe the economies of different countries. But neither the biologist nor the economist can observe the *same* population or the *same* economy with the *same* initial conditions. There may be similarities and general lessons to be drawn, but history moves on.

1.3.2 Models and Maps

Models as Maps

One approach to understanding phenomena that are both complex and hard to manipulate in their natural state is to construct models. Models are meant to represent known or conjectured relationships in a form that may allow us to experiment on the model, even when we cannot experiment on the thing that is modeled. These days models are often virtual, existing only on a computer. Originally, however, models were nearly always physical. Aeronautical engineers, starting with the Wright brothers, used models of airplanes in wind tunnels to discover how real airplanes will perform in flight. Civil engineers used models of river systems to learn about the hydrology of actual rivers.

Reasoning with models is analogical. We hope that when the analogies are close in some known respects, they will be close in some unknown respects. We may imagine that the more detailed the model, the more likely it is to be informative. That rarely turns out to be correct. Wind-tunnel models need to get the shape of the airplane correct. Yet it may be unnecessary – and even misleading – to try to mimic the internal structure. In what respects, and to what degree, a model needs to mimic the real thing depends in part on our purposes, in part on how the world is, and in part on the properties of the model itself that may not be related at all to what we are trying to model.

Maps are an example of a particular kind of model in which we can see that detailed copying of the world may be counterproductive. A "perfect" map on a one-to-one scale would be perfectly useless. Even a map on a much higher scale would be hard to use if it were cluttered with details that we do not need. A subway map (think of the iconic London Tube map) needs to show accurately which stations are connected by which subway lines. If the distances between the stations are even roughly proportional, it is a plus. But it would be utterly confusing and would defeat the purpose if it showed every building at the street level above the subway. The beauty of the map is that it accurately displays the information that is relevant to getting the rider on the right line and off at the right station.

Different maps might be employed in closely related activities. We may, for instance, want a subway map *and* a plan of the layout of a particular station. Different maps serve different purposes. It is not inaccuracy but different goals that allow one map to represent the subway station as a mere dot and another to represent it as made of platforms, corridors, stairs, and elevators. Each map is highly simplified. Each map has a specialized scope. And each map is useful for its purpose – sometimes on its own and sometimes in combination with other maps.

Economic models can be thought of as maps. In order to be tractable and useful, they are highly simplified. A good model does not misrepresent the economy, although it may represent only selective aspects of the economy. A good economic model, like a good map, helps us find our way in unfamiliar territory. Economics can be seen as the science of making economic maps.

Mathematical Models

Typically, economic models are not physical like wind-tunnel models, but are frequently graphical, like maps. Even more frequently, economic models are mathematical. Just as an equation can represent a circle or the fall of a ball, equations can be used to represent important economic relationships.

To take an example, the consumption function (see Chapter 13) is an equation that models the relationship of aggregate consumption to income. For example, a simplified consumption function might be written as

$$C = 0.95Y, \tag{1.1}$$

where C is a **variable** measuring consumption and Y is a variable measuring aggregate income (GDP). The coefficient 0.95 represents a behavioral fact about the economy – namely, how much consumption changes as GDP changes. The coefficient is a **parameter** – that is, a number that characterizes behavior or the relationship between variables in the model. By convention, in economic models equations are read from right to left: the independent variable Y *determines* (or *causes*) the value of the dependent variable C, such that if Y rose by 100, C would rise by 95.

Equation (1.1) represents the consumption relationship as linear. Many other more complicated – and possibly nonlinear – equations might represent consumption. The main question will always be, does an equation in the model truly represent reality to the level of precision good enough for our purposes? That depends both on how the world truly is and on our purposes.

If we take the equation to be a model of our small part of the economy, we would say that Y is an **exogenous variable** (i.e., *a variable whose value is determined outside of the model itself*) while C is an **endogenous variable** (*a variable whose value is determined by the model*).

Exogenous variables may sometimes also be random variables. A **random variable** is a variable whose value is not determined by any model. The value of a pair of tossed dice may be modeled as a random variable. "Fair" dice have a pattern: the only possible values are 2 to 12, and 7 is the most frequent value. In any particular toss, we cannot say in advance which of the 11 possible values will show up, although we know that some are more likely than others. It is doubtful that a consumption function, for instance, could be deterministic. We might then supplement our model with a random element:

$$C = 0.95Y + \textit{random error}, \tag{1.1'}$$

The random element is often referred to as an "error" because it is the deviation of the deterministic consumption function (1.1) from a perfect fit to the data.

The model (1.1) is a **static** model – that is, it represents a timeless relationship between the variables. Despite the random error term, even model (1.1') is static, because time is not involved in a fundamental way. But models can be **dynamic**. In a dynamic model, the current values of at least some variables depend on the past or expected future values of themselves or other variables. We might, for instance, have a particularly simple model of GDP in which GDP next year depends on GDP this year plus a random error:

$$Y_{t+1} = 300 + 0.7Y_t + \textit{random error}_t, \tag{1.2}$$

where the t subscript indicates at which time the variables occur (see the *Guide*, section G.1.1).

Notice that if equation (1.2) is regarded on its own as a model of GDP, Y, which was exogenous in the model (1.1), is now endogenous. Only the random-error term is exogenous. If equation (1.1) were combined with (1.2) to form a larger model, then again only the random-error term is exogenous. The current and future values of the variables are determined entirely by their past values and by the current and future random-error terms.

The Uses of Models

How can we use models? Two main uses are as measuring instruments and as tools for counterfactual experiments. To illustrate *models as measuring instruments*, suppose that we want to know how sensitive consumption is to income. Here is one way to answer this question. Collect data on consumption and income (for different countries or different time periods). We then model that data in a manner similar to model (1.1') except that we leave the parameter 0.95 free or unspecified. So, for example, we might have the model

$$C = \beta Y + \textit{random error}, \tag{1.1''}$$

where β is an unknown parameter. If we set β to some value (say, $\beta = 0.5$), then we can use equation (1.1'') to compute the value of the random errors:

random error $= C - 0.5Y$. Different choices for β will deliver errors of different sizes. We can then choose the value for β that, when all the errors are taken together, delivers – in some sense or other – the smallest errors. Statisticians have developed various methods for measuring the size of the errors. A very common method is known as *regression*. It chooses β such that the average of the errors is zero (i.e., positive errors always cancel out negative errors) *and* the variability of the errors is minimized (for example, a β for which the errors are on average close to zero is preferred to one in which they are far from zero, even if they cancel out in both cases). (Regression is explained in detail in the *Guide*, section G.15).

The other main use of models is to conduct counterfactual experiments. As we already saw, it is difficult to conduct controlled economic experiments and almost impossible to conduct controlled macroeconomic experiments on actual economies. A model, however, is completely within our control. A **COUNTERFACTUAL EXPERIMENT** is one in which we alter the facts represented in the model to be different from what they actually are in the world in order to answer a *what-would-happen-if* question. In a sense, the model allows us to create possible worlds different from our actual world, in much the same way that a designer may create a model of car that has never been built – and perhaps never will be.

To illustrate counterfactual experiments, suppose that we want to know what would happen if GDP fell from 1,000 to 900. Using model (1.1), consumption would fall from 950 to 855. Similarly, what would happen if people wished to consume only 80 percent of their incomes? The parameter would fall from 0.95 to 0.80. When GDP is 1,000, consumption would fall by 150.

For any counterfactual experiment, it is important to note which facts we alter or must allow to change because they are endogenous and which facts are held constant. In the first counterfactual experiment, in which GDP falls, we hold the equation itself (particularly its slope, the parameter 0.95) constant. We cannot, however, hold the endogenous variable C constant at the same time that we change GDP. In the second counterfactual experiment, in which the parameter falls, we hold GDP constant.

The point of changing one thing while holding others constant is to isolate the particular influence of the thing changed. This procedure is so common that economists frequently use the Latin phrase **ceteris paribus**, which means "other things equal," to clarify the natures of their counterfactual experiments.[1] In the second experiment we might then ask: "What would happen if *ceteris paribus* we reduced the parameter from 0.95 to 0.80?" We know then that we should hold constant every other parameter, exogenous

---

[1] *Ceteris paribus* is often abbreviated *cet. par.*

variable, and functional relationship, letting only the one parameter and the endogenous variable change.

Economists frequently use special types of counterfactual experiments:

- *Unconditional Forecasts.* Consider equation (1.2) taken on its own as a model of GDP, and suppose that we know that GDP in 2010 is 1,000 and that the random error term is 100. We can then make a forecast of the future path of GDP: $Y_{2011} = 1,070$; $Y_{2012} = 1,049$; $Y_{2013} = 1,034;\ldots;Y_{2025} = 1,000$. To make this forecast, we assume that future error terms are zero, because we do not have a crystal ball and cannot know what they will turn out to be. If our model is a good one, this will be true on average. Because there will be errors in the future, we would not expect the forecast to be perfectly accurate. Instead, the model generates a counterfactual forecast that tells us what would happen if there were no errors in the future, and it tells us what would happen on average if the errors of the future conform to the model and cancel out on average. Our forecast is *unconditional* in the sense that we merely let the model take the existing facts and process them.

- *Conditional Forecasts.* Suppose that we want to know what would happen to consumption if GDP were to rise by 10 percent per year. If GDP in 2010 were 1,000, then we would guess that it would rise in the following years to $Y = 1,100$; 1,210; 1,331,... If we model consumption with equation (1.1), then consumption would follow the path, starting in 2010 of $C = 950$; 1,150; 1,264;... This is a *conditional forecast* because we believe that the forecast of consumption is correct only to the extent that the assumption about the path of GDP turns out to be true. For example, if in 2012, we find out the GDP is actually 1,250 rather than 1,331 and if consumption is 1,188 rather than 1,264, our forecast is wrong but the model (1.1) is not falsified: garbage in, garbage out. However, if GDP turned out to be just as forecasted (1,331) and actual consumption turned out to be 1,150, it would count against the model. Similarly, if GDP turned out to be something different from what was forecasted (say, 1,500) but consumption failed to conform to the model (say, it was 1,200 rather than 1,425), that too would count against the model.

  A common problem is that the public and politicians treat conditional forecasts as if they were unconditional forecasts. Most economic forecasts are conditional. The economics may be right; but if the assumptions about the future turn out to be different from what the forecaster supposed, the conditional forecast will provide poor predictions of actual events. This issue arises frequently when the Congressional Budget Office (CBO) is asked to evaluate the budgetary effects of new laws. It is required to use the assumptions that Congress itself builds into the laws – for example, that an expenditure program will be canceled in five years. An outside observer may conclude that experience shows such programs are never canceled but roll over from year to year. A forecast conditional on that assumption may be more accurate than the CBO's forecast. The CBO is not trying to say what actually will happen, but merely what would happen if Congress kept its word. The failure of the budget to turn out as forecasted may not be the fault of the model, but the fault of Congress.

- *Mechanism Design.* Imagine that policymakers want to increase the level of aggregate savings. Their idea is that a tax credit will change people's behavior in a predictable way. If GDP is 1,000 and they want to increase savings by 100, they must lower consumption by 100. Using model (1.1) they might reason counterfactually, "If we give a big enough tax credit that the parameter 0.95 falls to 0.85, then consumption would fall from 950 to 850, just as we require." The model is being used in a manner similar to conditional forecasting, except that the focus is not on what happens to endogenous variables when exogenous variables change, but on what happens to them when parameters change. Such counterfactual experiments are important in designing policy mechanisms: how should the tax system be structured? What policy rule should the monetary authorities set? Such experiments recognize that policymakers typically determine the institutional background in which the economy works, but only in limited cases get to choose particular paths for exogenous variables. The government, for instance, does not choose the level of taxes that any individual pays. Instead, it sets income-, sales-, and other tax *rates* and then waits to see how much revenue these rates actually raise. Counterfactual experiments of this type help them to make sensible choices.

The Scope of Models

Whether a variable is exogenous or endogenous depends, just as the appropriateness of the functional form of the equation did, in part on the world and in part on the modeler. We do not get to choose which relationships are correct in the world. Yet, we do get to decide what it is that we want a model to illuminate; we get to decide the scope and purpose of our map. So, perhaps we want to add detail to the model. We might notice for instance that GDP consists of various components – in particular, consumption and investment (we ignore foreign trade and the existence of government). These are additional modeling choices, ones that are good for purposes of exposition but poor for actually representing the world. On these assumptions, GDP can be represented by another equation:

$$Y = C + I, \tag{1.3}$$

where I represents aggregate investment. Unlike in equation (1.1), taken to be a model on its own, Y is no longer an exogenous variable. A model that includes both equations (1.1) and (1.3) determines both Y and C endogenously. The new variable I is exogenous, and any change in I results in changes to both C and Y. To operate the model, we simply set I to its new value and solve the two equations.

Graphical or Diagrammatic Models

Many of the models in this book consist of one or more equations. Others consist of diagrams in which the lines or curves take the place of equations.

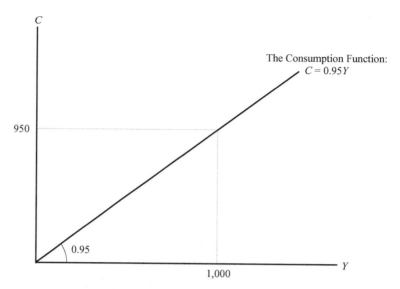

Figure 1.1. A Simple Economic Model. The exogenous variable (Y) determines the value of the endogenous variable (C), given the consumption function, the slope of which is determined by the parameter 0.95.

Sometimes we move back and forth between a model represented as equations and the same model represented in a diagram. The basic rules are the same. We use the models to answer questions by choosing the appropriate values of parameters and exogenous variables and then letting the model determine the values of the endogenous variables.

Model (1.1) is easily represented as a simple graph as in Figure 1.1. The model consisting of equations (1.1) and (1.3) is more complicated. The two equations involve three variables. This is no problem algebraically, because the variable I is exogenous and we do not need the model to determine it. But it is a problem to represent the equations on a two-dimensional diagram. A solution is to substitute (1.1) into (1.3) to get

$$Y = 0.95Y + I. \tag{1.4}$$

We now have a model consisting of three equations: (1.1), (1.3), and (1.4).

Figure 1.2 graphs the equations: Y is measured on the horizontal axis and C, I, and Y are measured on the vertical axis. The lower gray curve represents the consumption function. The black curve represents equation (1.3) – its slope is unity (or 45 degrees), because, in effect, it says $Y = Y$. The upper gray curve represents equation (1.4). Notice that it is parallel to the consumption function (i.e., they have the same slope, 0.95) and that its vertical intercept is I. This parallelism is not an accident. Equation (1.4) is not an independent relationship, but simply an intermediate step in the algebraic solution of equations (1.1) and (1.3). We cannot shift equation (1.1) while

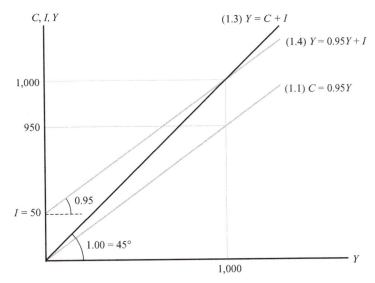

Figure 1.2. A More Complex Economic Model. The endogenous variables (C and Y) are jointly determined by equations (1.1) and (1.2), given the value of the exogenous variable (I). Equation (1.4) is not an independent relationship but an intermediate step in the algebraic solution of the model.

holding (1.4) constant. For instance, any change in the slope parameter of (1.1) will necessarily shift the slope of (1.4).

Assume that $I = 50$. The value of Y can be read off the horizontal axis below the intersection of the upper gray and the black curves. The value of C ($= 950$) can be read off the vertical axis at the point on the lower gray curve corresponding to the value of Y ($= 1,000$).

We can conduct a counterfactual experiment using the diagram. What happens if investment increases by 10? In this case, the intercept of the upper gray curve would shift up by 10, moving the intersection with the black curve to the right and increasing both Y and C. (We leave both the drawing of an appropriate diagram to represent this experiment and the algebraic solution to Problem 1.3).

The counterfactual experiment illustrates an important distinction when working with diagrammatic models – the difference between *shifting a curve* and *moving along a curve*. For example, in Figure 1.1 in which Y was exogenous, if we increase Y, the consumption function stays constant, and we move along the curve to find the new level of consumption. In contrast, if we were to model a change in consumption behavior that reduced the parameter 0.95 to 0.80, then we would have to shift the curve to reflect a shallower slope. In Figure 1.2, investment, because it is an exogenous variable, acts like a parameter. An increase in I shifts the intercept upward. In such a *ceteris paribus* experiment, we hold every other parameter and exogenous variable constant, so that the slope of the curve does not change and the

whole curve shifts, remaining parallel to an unchanged consumption function. Just as with Figure 1.1, because the change in I does not affect the
consumption function itself (I does not appear in equation (1.1)), we simply
move along the consumption function in Figure 1.2 to read off the new level
of consumption.

A general rule of thumb: *When a change is to an independent variable
that is represented on one axis with the dependent variable represented on the
other, the curve does not shift and we evaluate the change by moving along
the curve; when a parameter or an independent variable that does not appear
on the axis changes, then we evaluate the change by shifting the curve.*

It might appear that Figure 1.2 is an exception to this rule, because I is in
some sense represented on the vertical axis, and yet the change in I shifts the
curve. In fact, there is no exception. In equation (1.4) I is an independent,
not a dependent variable, and I is not represented on the horizontal axis. The
dependent variables represented on the vertical axis are actually C and Y. I
appears on the vertical axis only because it acts as a parameter, determining
the location of the upper curve. Graphically, I is merely a point rather than
a variable.

1.4 Where Do We Go from Here?

The models discussed in the previous section are not realistic. The point is
not that details are omitted; a model never represents every aspect of the
world. Rather the point is that these models make no claim to represent the
world except in the broadest strokes. The relationships are, perhaps, sug-
gestive of ones that we might find in the economy, but there is no claim that
they represent any actual economy, even at a low level of precision. The reason, of course, is that our purposes were pedagogical – to demonstrate how
models are used and manipulated and not to analyze an actual economy.
Such models bear the same relationship to the real world as a rubber-band-
powered balsawood airplane does to a Boeing 747 or a map of Tolkien's
Middle Earth does to a map of Europe.

Throughout this book we try to move beyond such toy models or fan-
tasy maps. The principles of economics are often surprisingly simple. The
difficulties are rarely with first principles. Rather most of the effort must
be directed to learning how to apply those principles to real cases. A person
who has studied maps of a strange city or an unfamiliar wilderness gains only
limited and, often highly theoretical, knowledge of what the city or wilderness is like. For a map or model to be useful, for it to serve as an instrument
of understanding, we must first get our bearings. We need data. And we need
to learn how the data relate to the conventions of the maps or the models.
It is one thing to see narrowly spaced isoclines on a topographical map; it

is quite another to read it as indicating a steep hill or pointing the way to the best path up the hill. A principal goal of this book is to use theoretical macroeconomic models in conjunction with actual economic data to learn how to read the economy in the same way that an experienced hiker reads a topographical map.

How do we begin to get our bearings? Here we must not take the analogy with maps too literally. A hiker can cross and recross the same ground. As we previously observed macroeconomics is not like that. It is more like natural history. Things happen exactly this way just once. Rather than a hiker crossing a wilderness with a premade map, a better analogy would be Lewis and Clark heading off into the American West for the first time and constructing their map as they went. The general principles of mapmaking would be helpful; and based on what they learned about geographical features in earlier parts of their journey, they might have been able to make useful predictions about what they might find across the next ridge. But surely there were many surprises.

Getting our bearings in macroeconomics involves becoming familiar with economic data and often with placing those data in historical context. A basic chronology of the economy may be a helpful tool. Table 1.1 presents one hundred years of the political and economic history of the United States. As well as recording key events (particularly major wars, which often have large economic consequences), it also provides a chronology of American presidents, the political makeup of Congress, and the leadership of the Federal Reserve System – some of the most influential actors in macroeconomic policy.

To develop our map of the macroeconomy, we begin in Part II with the most basic macroeconomic data – the national income and product accounts. At the beginning of this chapter, we noted that two sorts of problems dominate macroeconomics – growth and fluctuations. In Part III we see how these are reflected in a description of macroeconomic data that divides each time series into components identified as trend (i.e., growth) and cycle (i.e., fluctuations).

Because macroeconomics is the economics of the economy as a whole, we must address substantial attention to how its various parts are connected and coordinated. Microeconomics can frequently abstract from the monetary and financial systems. Macroeconomics can rarely do that. For it is precisely these monetary and financial systems that tie the various components of the economy together. As we will see in Part II, almost every transaction involving goods and services also involves a monetary flow. Nearly every act of savings involves a financial flow. The monetary and financial system, including the international financial system are examined more closely in Part IV.

Table 1.1. *Political and Economic Timeline of the United States*

Year	Presidents (White = Democratic; Gray = Republican)	Congress — Senate (White = Democratic Control; Gray = Republican Control)	Congress — House	Federal Reserve Chairs	Major Wars	Political and Economic Events
1911	Taft Mar. 1909–Mar. 1913					
1912						
1913	Wilson Mar. 1913–Mar. 1921					Federal Reserve created; income tax introduced
1914				C. S. Hamlin Aug. 1914–Aug. 1916		
1915						
1916				W. P. G. Hardy Aug. 1916–Aug. 1922		
1917					World War I (U.S. enters Apr. 1917)	
1918						
1919						Prohibition begins
1920						Women gain right to vote
1921	Harding Mar. 1921–Aug. 1923					
1922						
1923	Coolidge Aug. 1923–Mar. 1929			May 1923–Sept. 1927		
1924						
1925						
1926						
1927				Oct. 1927–Aug. 1930		
1928						
1929	Hoover Mar. 1929–Mar. 1933					Stock market crash; Great Depression begins
1930				Sept. 1930–May 1933		
1931						
1932						
1933	F. D. Roosevelt Mar. 1933–Apr. 1945			E. Black May 1933–Aug. 1934		New Deal; Great Depression continues; end Prohibition
1934				M. Eccles Nov. 1934–Jan. 1948		
1935						Social Security enacted
1936						
1937						
1938						

Great Depression ends

Bretton Woods agreement
Employment and Stabilization Act
Marshall Plan; GATT established

School segregation ruled illegal

Suez Crisis; Interstate Highways created
Sputnik launches space age

Berlin Wall built
Cuban Missile Crisis
President Kennedy assassinated
Kennedy/Johnson tax cut
Great Society program begins; Voting Rights Act;
Medicare and Medicaid begin

World War II
(U.S. enters Dec. 1941)

Korean War

Vietnam War

M. Eccles
Nov. 1934–Jan. 1948

T. B. McCabe
Apr. 1948–Mar. 1951

W. Mc. Martin
Apr. 1951–Jan. 1970

F. D. Roosevelt
Mar. 1933–Apr. 1945

Truman
Apr. 1945–Jan. 1953

Eisenhower
Jan. 1953–Jan. 1961

Kennedy
Jan. 1961–Nov. 1963

L. B. Johnson
Nov. 1963–Jan. 1969

1939
1940
1941
1942
1943
1944
1945
1946
1947
1948
1949
1950
1951
1952
1953
1954
1955
1956
1957
1958
1959
1960
1961
1962
1963
1964
1965
1966

(continued)

Table 1.1 (*continued*)

Year	Presidents (White = Democratic, Gray = Republican)	Congress — Senate (White = Democratic Control, Gray = Republican Control)	Congress — House	Federal Reserve Chairmen	Major Wars	Political and Economic Events
1967	Nixon Jan. 1969–Aug. 1974				Vietnam War	Six Day War
1968						M. L. King and R. F. Kennedy assassinated
1969						First moon landing
1970				A. Burns Feb. 1970–Jan. 1978		
1971						Wage-and-price controls imposed; Bretton Woods system unravels
1972						
1973						Yom Kippur War; first oil crisis begins; floating exchange rate system begins
1974						Nixon resigns
1975	Ford Aug. 1974–Jan. 1977					
1976						
1977	Carter Jan. 1977–Jan. 1981					
1978				G. W. Miller Mar. 1978–Aug. 1979		
1979						Iranian Revolution; second oil crisis
1980				P. A. Volcker Aug. 1979–Aug. 1987		
1981	Reagan Jan. 1981–Jan. 1989					
1982						
1983						
1984						Reagan tax cuts begin
1985						
1986						Tax Reform Act
1987				A. Greenspan Aug. 1987–Jan. 2006		Stock market crash
1988						

Years (left axis):
1989
1990
1991
1992
1993
1994
1995
1996
1997
1998
1999
2000
2001
2002
2003
2004
2005
2006
2007
2008
2009
2010

Presidents:
G. H. W. Bush
Jan. 1989–Jan. 1993

Clinton
Jan. 1993–Jan. 2001

G. W. Bush
Jan. 2001–Jan. 2009

Obama
Jan. 2009–

Federal Reserve Chairmen:
A. Greenspan
Aug. 1987–Jan. 2006

B. Bernanke
Feb. 2006–present

Wars:
Persian Gulf War

Afghanistan War
(Dec. 2001 on)

and

Iraq War
(Mar. 2003 on)

Events:
Berlin Wall falls; communism unravels
Bush tax increases/expenditures controls

NAFTA signed

Clinton impeached; Asian financial crisis
Asian financial crisis continues

9/11 terrorist attacks

Hurricane Katrina

Housing–market and financial crisis

The heart of the real economy is the production of goods and services that, directly or indirectly, are destined for consumption – the ultimate end of economic activity. A key element of economic mapmaking is the conceptual distinction between supply and demand. Wherever we can recast an economic problem as a question of supply and demand, we have begun to make headway in analyzing it. The distinction shows up in macroeconomics as the distinction between aggregate supply and aggregate demand. Part V focuses on aggregate supply, including a basic analysis of production and an analysis of economic growth. The treatment of aggregate supply also includes an analysis of the economics of the factors of production, especially of the factor closest to human interests – labor. Part VI focuses on aggregate demand, especially on consumption and investment.

By the end of Part VI most of the building blocks of our macroeconomic model are in place. We are finally ready to give an account of what governs the boom-and-bust cycle of the modern economy. Part VII aims to tie them together, to show how aggregate supply and demand interact to produce fluctuations in employment, unemployment, output, and inflation.

Finally, recall that a central impetus for the creation of macroeconomics as a distinct field, beginning in the 1930s, was policy. What might be done to help an economy emerge from the depths of a recession? What policies might prevent the recession from occurring in the first place? What policies might promote higher rates of long-term growth, which, as we have seen, historically tend to overwhelm the effects of macroeconomic fluctuations? The two major types of policy are **fiscal policy** (those policies concerned with government expenditure and taxation) and **monetary policy** (those policies concerned with the government's financial portfolio and the configuration of interest rates). Fiscal policy is largely the province of ordinary politics at the Federal, state, and local levels; while monetary policy is largely the province of the Federal Reserve, the U.S. central bank. Part VIII completes the book with an examination of the options for monetary and fiscal policy and their economic consequences.

Summary

1. The two most important practical concerns of macroeconomics are economic fluctuations and economic growth.
2. Macroeconomics can be defined as the study of the economy as a whole; whereas microeconomics is the study of a part of the economy, taking the remainder as given. Macroeconomics generally uses aggregate data.
3. Fallacies of composition – the often incorrect assumption that what is true of the parts is also true of the whole – are an important pitfall in extrapolating from microeconomics to macroeconomics.

4. Macroeconomics originated as a distinct field in the 1930s as a reaction to the Great Depression, created by economists who wished to intervene in the economy to resolve the depression and to prevent future recessions. Still, macroeconomics is a positive science that aims principally to understand how the economy works in a way that is neutral between those who advocate intervention and those who oppose it.

5. Economics is a social science. It is distinct from physical science principally in the fact that it involves human beings with beliefs, intentions, and desires rather than inert matter. This adds to the complexity of economics and makes experimentation difficult; it also supports prediction and explanation based on understanding typical people's reasons.

6. In the absence of experiments, macroeconomics principally tries to understand the economy through simple but insightful models.

7. Models can be used as instruments of measurement and as the basis for counterfactual experiments supporting conditional and unconditional forecasting and mechanism design or policy.

Key Concepts

macroeconomic fluctuations	parameter
economic growth	exogenous variable
macroeconomics	endogenous variable
microeconomics	counterfactual experiment
fallacy of composition	ceteris paribus
economic model	

Suggestions for Further Reading

Richard Carroll. *An Economic Record of Presidential Performance: From Truman to Bush*. Westport, CT: Praeger, 1995.

Problems

Data for this exercise are available on the textbook website under the link for Chapter 1 (appliedmacroeconomics.com). Before starting these exercises, the student should review the relevant portions of the *Guide to Working with Economic Data*, including sections G.1–G.3.

Problem 1.1. Provide some examples (economic or noneconomic) of fallacies of composition other than those in the text.

Problem 1.2. Consider equation (1.1) as a model of consumption, and begin with a GDP of 1,000. Algebraically *and* graphically (modifying Figure 1.1 as needed), analyze the counterfactual experiment of (a) raising GDP to 1,200; (b) lowering the sensitivity of consumption to GDP from 0.95 to 0.90. In both cases, indicate clearly what the effect *ceteris paribus* of these actions is on consumption.

Problem 1.3. Consider equations (1.1) and (1.3) together as a model of GDP and consumption. Algebraically *and* graphically (modifying Figure 1.2 as needed), analyze separately the counterfactual experiments of (a) raising investment from 50 to 60; (b) lowering the sensitivity of consumption to GDP from 0.95 to 0.90. In both cases, indicate clearly what the effect *ceteris paribus* of these actions is on consumption and GDP.

Problem 1.4. Consider equation (1.2) as a model of GDP. Assume that in 2010, $Y_{2010} = 800$ and *random error* $_{2010} = 50$. What unconditional forecast does the model imply for 2013?

Problem 1.5. Consider equations (1.1) and (1.3) to be a model of consumption and GDP. (a) What conditional forecast is implied by the model for consumption and GDP for 2012 when investment is 100? (b) When 2012 arrives, which of the following data would contradict the model?: (i) $I = 80$, $Y = 1,600$; (ii) $I = 90$, $C = 1,800$; (iii) $Y = 2,200$; $C = 2,090$.

Problem 1.6. Consider equations (1.1) and (1.3) to be a model of consumption and GDP. Imagine that government economists in 2010 estimate that the ageing of the population will lower the sensitivity of consumption to GDP from 0.95 to 0.85 by 2020. They also project that investment will remain at the same level $I = 100$. Conditional on this information, what does their model forecast the change in GDP to be?

Problem 1.7. People generally dislike both unemployment and inflation. An informal way of characterizing the state of the economy is the *misery index* = the inflation rate + the rate of unemployment. For each president in the post-World War II period, starting with Truman's second term (i.e., his only full term) calculate the *change* in the misery index between the first and last month of their terms. Construct a table with the presidents ordered by their success (or luck!) in lowering the misery index.

Part II

The National Accounts

2

The National Accounts and the Structure
of the Economy

Before we can understand the economy, we need to know how to describe and measure it. In this chapter we focus on gross domestic product (GDP), the most central quantity in macroeconomics. What is it? How is it created? How do we measure it? What is its relationship to other important quantities? How does it change over time?

2.1 How Big Is the Economy?

Since ancient days, bad times have followed good, and good times have followed bad. Since ancient days, people have looked to their leaders to promote the good times and soften the bad. In the Bible, Joseph predicts seven fat years to be followed by seven lean years, and advises Pharaoh to store grain against the coming famine. When agriculture dominated economies, the cycle of good and bad times mostly reflected the cycle between fair weather and drought or flood. In modern industrial economies, the causes of the cycle are not so readily visible. An important object of macroeconomics is to help us to understand these causes and to learn what policies might promote the good times and soften the bad. Economists may start with theories, but to apply those theories to actual economies and to judge whether they are really working as intended, we need some method of keeping score: how rich is the country (or how large is the economy)? How fast is it growing?

The news media constantly quote statistics that aim to answer these questions: The U.S. economy (i.e., the gross domestic product or GDP) fell by 5.4 percent per year in the first quarter of 2008. The U.S. economy in 2008 was 3.3 times larger than the Japanese economy (i.e., U.S. GDP was $14,260 billion and Japanese GDP was $4,329 billion). Most people understand that GDP and its growth rate report the economic score, yet few actually understand what they really mean. They are, in fact, the central quantities in macroeconomics. Almost every other quantity that might interest us is either a component of GDP (such as consumption, investment, wages, or profits) or connected to it through important economic relationships (such as unemployment or inflation).

We begin our study of macroeconomics with the national income and product accounts, the framework through which economists describe the economy as a whole. GDP is the central concept in the modern system of national accounts. According to the U.S. government's Bureau of Economic Analysis (BEA):

GROSS DOMESTIC PRODUCT (GDP) is *"the market value of the final goods and services produced by labor and property located" within the borders of a country within a definite period.*[1]

Almost every element of the bare definition of GDP hides some subtle conceptual issue. In Chapter 3, we shall take the definition apart and bring the most important subtleties to light. In this chapter we focus on putting the national accounts to work. We have already seen that GDP provides a quick measure that allows us to compare the economic performance of different countries. In the remainder of this chapter, we shall learn how the national accounts can be used to structure our thinking about the economy.

The national accounts are not in themselves economic analysis, but they provide us with the raw material from which to construct a richer understanding of how the economy works. To understand how we might use the national accounts, we need to understand the process through which GDP is created and distributed.

2.2 GDP and the Economic Process

2.2.1 Stocks and Flows

Before we start, we need to clarify the notions of INCOME and WEALTH. When we ask how rich a person is, there are at least two somewhat different measures. We might add up the value of everything that he owns (i.e., his wealth) or we might report his income. Wealth is measured as a certain number of dollars. Although it is measured at a particular time, the measurement itself does not involve time. Income is measured as a certain number of dollars per year (or week or month). It too is measured at a particular time, and it also involves time directly in the measurement. Wealth is what economists call a **stock**. A stock measures a quantity. Income is a **flow**. It measures a quantity per unit time. The definition of GDP refers to a specific

[1] Bureau of Economic Analysis, *NIPA Handbook: Concepts and Methods of U.S. National Income and Product Accounts*, pp. 2–7. (http://bea.gov/national/pdf/NIPAhandbookch1–4.pdf) downloaded 20 October 2009.

period, and GDP is a flow, measured as so many monetary units per unit of time (dollars per year, euros per quarter).

The terms "stock" and "flow" are hydraulic analogies. Think of a river that runs into a lake. The flow of the water into the lake is measured as so many gallons per minute (or acre-feet per day). The stock of water in the lake at any time is just a certain number of gallons. Of course, there may also be a river running out of the lake. If the rate of flow into the lake exceeds the flow out of the lake, then the stock of water in the lake rises. If the rate of flow out of the lake exactly matches the rate of flow into the lake, then the stock of water remains constant.

Wealth and income are related similarly. *Income* is the river running into the lake, *the flow of value into wealth* – so many dollars' worth per month. Notice that we said *value*, for the income need not take the form of actual money. It may be money deposited in a bank account. Equally, it may be the acquisition of a piece of land or a car or a boat or other valuable asset. The total of all these assets – monetary and nonmonetary – is the lake, the stock of *wealth*, and is measured in dollars without reference to time. Consumption expenditure (i.e., expenditure on items whose value vanishes with their immediate use) is the river flowing out of the lake. When the income flow is greater than the consumption-expenditure flow, the stock of wealth increases. It is, of course, perfectly possible to be rich in the sense of having large wealth, yet poor in the sense of having a small income. This is frequently the case of elderly people, farmers, or ranchers who own valuable real estate but have only a small income from a pension or the sale of agricultural products.

The sales of final goods and services generate all the individual incomes in the economy. GDP is the sum of these flows measured in dollars per year. Similarly, national wealth is the sum of the wealth of all the individuals in the economy measured in dollars. That part of income that does not flow away as consumption expenditure (called "savings") adds to wealth. While national accounts exist both for income and wealth, *income* accounts are more commonly used in macroeconomic analysis than wealth accounts.

2.2.2 The Circular Flow

The national income accounts provide a record of the income flows in the economy for a particular quarter or year. To understand what the accounts record, it helps to get a bird's-eye view of production and expenditure in the economy. We can think of the economy as comprising four sectors: the **Firm**, **Household**, and **Government Sectors**, and the **Foreign Sector** (or **Rest of the World**). The national accounts record the two-way exchanges between every pair of sectors.

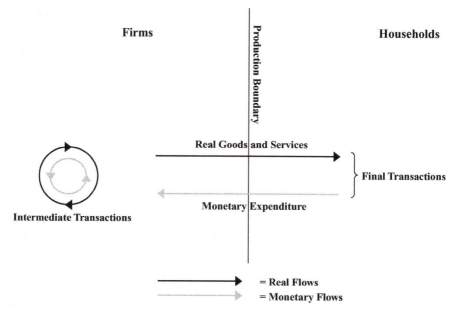

Figure 2.1. GDP Is Final Goods and Services. GDP comprises all *final* goods and services. To be final, production must leave the firm sector (i.e., cross the production boundary). Intermediate products are important to production, but do not leave the firm sector and do not count directly as GDP. The transfer of real production is in principle always matched to a monetary transfer of the same value. GDP can, therefore, be counted either by counting the value of goods or the value of expenditures crossing the production boundary.

The Domestic Private Sector

Our ideas will be clearer if we start with a simple economy and add complexity as we go along. Figure 2.1 shows an economy comprising only firms and households – for the moment we are assuming that it functions without a government and engages in no foreign trade.

Firms use labor, machinery, energy, raw materials, buildings, and the products of other firms as **inputs** to produce **outputs** in the form of various goods and services or products. Some of these products, known as **INTERMEDIATE GOODS AND SERVICES**, are sold to other firms and, therefore, remain in the Firm Sector. These are shown in the diagram as the closed loop in the Firm Sector. The remainder of the products is shown as flowing into the Household Sector. The line dividing the two sectors is marked **production boundary**. Only products leaving the Firm Sector *this period* – that is, goods and services that cross the production boundary – count as **final goods and services**. Intermediate products, which remain within the Firm Sector, are used up in the production process, and their value is incorporated into the final products.

Households own the various inputs to the production process directly (e.g., workers own their labor and sell it to firms for a wage or salary) or

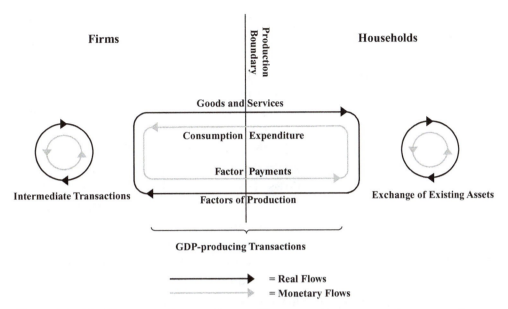

Figure 2.2. The Domestic Private Sector. Firms receive consumption expenditures in exchange for goods and services. Firms use the funds earned to purchase factors of production from households, so that household expenditures ultimately become household income. Similarly, firms use the factors of production to produce goods, so that the real services of households ultimately become the goods that they consume. GDP is equally well measured by the value of the goods and services produced (the expenditure on those goods and services) or by the value of the factors of production sold (the payments to the owners of those factors). Like intermediate transactions, the buying and selling of existing assets involves no crossing of the production boundary and so does not count in measuring GDP.

indirectly (e.g., one firm may sell a necessary input to another firm, but households as stockholders ultimately own the firms). The inputs to production are known collectively as **FACTORS OF PRODUCTION**. Figure 2.2 elaborates Figure 2.1, showing the flow of factors of production as the black arrow running from Households to Firms.

Effectively, Households exchange factors of production with Firms in return for final goods and services. Figure 2.2 emphasizes this exchange by joining the heads and tails of the factors-of-production arrow and the final-goods-and-services arrow to form a closed loop. Although we sometimes encounter direct barter ("will work for food"), most transactions involve money, so that the exchange of factors of production for final goods and services is indirect. Typically, workers sell their labor for wages and salaries paid in money. Other factors of production are also sold to Firms for money. Households, in turn, buy the products of the Firms for money. Effectively, Firms exchange money (**factors payments**) with Households for money (**CONSUMPTION EXPENDITURE**). These monetary flows are shown in Figure 2.2 as gray arrows. Again, connecting their heads and tails emphasizes the exchange through which the money of the Households becomes the money of the Firms and, then, is returned to the Households.

The economic process is essentially about people's enjoyment of the fruits of their labors. The real benefit of production is the consumption of the variety of final products. The real cost of production is the variety of work and physical resources needed to create those products. The outer, clockwise loop in Figure 2.2 captures these **real flows**. Each real arrow that crosses the production boundary must be matched by an arrow of equal value showing money crossing in the opposite direction. The inner, counterclockwise loop captures these **monetary flows**. Together the diagram shows that there are two circular flows. The real flow matters most to our lives. The monetary flow is, nonetheless, important. First, our economy is organized in such a way that disruptions to the monetary flow might cause disruptions to the real flow. (In Part IV [Chapters 6–8] we shall consider the monetary flows in more detail. And in Chapter 16, we shall consider how government monetary policy interacts with the real economy.) Second, it is not easy to measure the real flow directly. As we saw in section 2.1, money provides the common unit for measuring GDP.

The rule that every real flow must be matched by a monetary flow also applies to intermediate transactions as shown by the counterclockwise loop on the left side of Figure 2.2. For completeness, we ought also to note that households may engage in exchanges of existing assets themselves. When, for example, you buy a used car from a private owner, there is typically a monetary exchange. But that exchange does not add to GDP. The real good, the car, once crossed the production boundary and so counted as GDP in the period in which it was produced. But there is no *new* production when you purchase the car secondhand. It does not cross the production boundary again. Exchanges of existing goods and services are shown by the clockwise, real loop and the counterclockwise, monetary loop on the right-hand side of Figure 2.2.

The actual economy is more complex than the one shown in Figure 2.2. Yet, even in the actual economy, the relationship between Firms and Households is fundamentally important. Taken together these two sectors form the **Domestic Private Sector**. Starting with the Domestic Private Sector we can build up a more complete view by taking greater account of time and by introducing the Government and Foreign Sectors.

Investment Savings, Capital, and Time

If all production used only resources produced or supplied in the same period and all incomes were consumed in the same period, then the real flow of goods and services from Firms to Households would always exactly balance the real flow of factors of production from Households to Firms

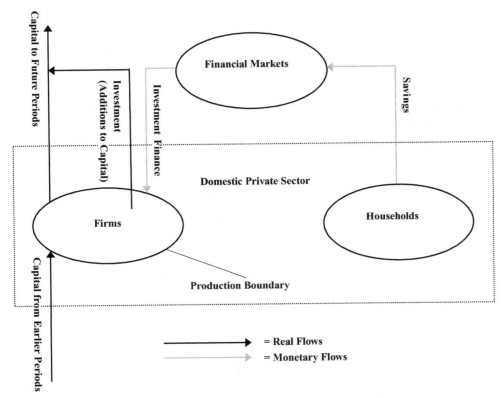

Figure 2.3. Savings, Investment, Capital, and Time. The diagram omits many details from Figure 2.2 to show that investment goods cross the production boundary this period and are added to the stock of capital used in production in future periods. Investment is matched by investment spending – in part taken from firms' own resources and in part transmitted from households and other firms through financial markets.

and, similarly, the monetary flow of consumption expenditure would always balance that of factor payments. In reality, they do not balance. As we shall see presently, the Government and Foreign Sectors account for some of the imbalance. Let us first consider the Domestic Private Sector itself.

Households earn income from the sale of factors of production. They do not necessarily wish to consume all of their income this period. In order to set aside purchasing power for future use, Households *save* – that is, they put their money in a bank (or a mattress) or they purchase financial (or, sometimes, real) assets, such as shares in a mutual fund (or a house). Consumption expenditure, therefore, falls short of income (purchases of factors of production); and, obviously, sales of goods and services to Households falls short of total production. **Savings** are shown in Figure 2.3 as a monetary flow away from the Domestic Private Sector.

Some physical means of production, such as energy and raw materials, are used up in the production process. Others, such as buildings, tools and machinery, and vehicles, known collectively as **capital**, are long-lived. The services supplied by capital are a factor of production. As shown in Figure 2.3, part of the stock of capital is inherited from the past and whatever remains useful after the current period of production is passed on to the future.

Additions to the stock of capital are called *investment*. **INVESTMENT** is *the flow of new physical means of production*. The word "investment" is used – quite properly – in financial markets to mean the purchase of financial assets. Similarly, "capital" is used to mean a monetary value tied up in a business. In economics, however, "capital" almost always refers to the stock of physical means of production, and "investment" to the flow that adds to that stock. Firms anticipating future needs purchase investment goods. This is shown in the diagram as the solid arrow flowing away from Firms. It is shown as crossing the production boundary and, therefore, as constituting part of GDP. Although investment goods remain within the Firm Sector, the fact that they are not used up this period, but transferred to a future period of production, makes them a final product *this period*.

Firms generally purchase investment goods from other firms. The outward real flow of investment goods is shown in Figure 2.3 as matched by an inward monetary flow of investment expenditure. This is shown in the figure as the gray line labeled "Investment Finance." Although it is not shown in the figure, firms may also purchase investment from retained earnings without resorting to borrowing. Where do the funds come from? Because ultimately all of the revenues of the Firms are owned by the Households, directly or indirectly Households must supply the needed funds. In making savings decisions, however, we do not generally consult the needs of firms. Financial markets (as shown in the figure) serve as a conduit directing the savings of Households to the investment expenditures of Firms. We shall consider financial markets in more detail in Chapter 6.

The Government Sector

Taking account of investment and saving complicated our initially simple picture of a circular flow of products and money. Now let us complicate it further with the addition of a Government Sector comprising all levels of government – national, state, and local. Figure 2.4 shows that to produce its output the Government too uses factors of production, mainly in the form of labor purchased from Households and goods and services purchased from Firms. The inputs are shown as real flows from the Domestic Private Sector matched by monetary flows (**GOVERNMENT EXPENDITURE**) and **wages** (and other factors payments) running in the opposite direction.

To pay for these real factors and products, the government must levy **TAXES**. Taxes (personal and corporate) are shown as monetary flows (labeled "Net Taxes") toward Government. Taxes are "net" because the

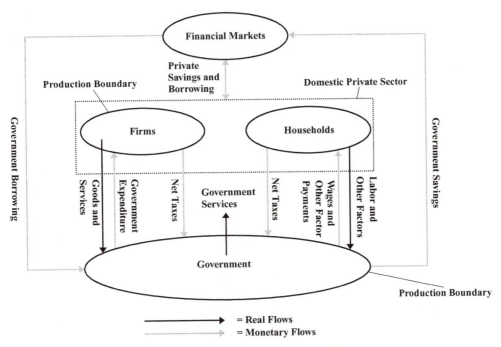

Figure 2.4. The Domestic Economy. The diagram omits many details from Figures 2.2 and 2.3 to show that goods and services sold to the government cross the production boundary and so form part of GDP. Government expenditure is the monetary flow that matches these goods and services. The government also purchases labor and other factors of production from firms. It uses both factors and goods and services to produce government services, which themselves cross the production boundary and form part of GDP. All government spending is financed through taxes or borrowing. Governmental units with excess revenue may also save.

government also sometimes makes **TRANSFER PAYMENTS** defined as *payments for which nothing of equal value is given in return*. Transfer payments include, among other things, Social Security payments, Medicare, welfare payments, and the interest on government debt. **Net taxes** equal *taxes less transfer payments*.

Sometimes government revenues from taxes exceed government expenditure on goods and services and transfer payments. The government then is said to run a **budget surplus**. State and local governments save their surpluses by purchasing private financial assets or by repaying loans or repurchasing previously issued bonds. The Federal government saves mainly through repurchasing or redeeming Treasury bonds. When expenditure exceeds revenues, governments must borrow through loans or the sale of bonds. Just as they do for Firms and Households, Financial Markets serve as a conduit directing private and government savings to the Government Sector.

For two reasons, Figure 2.4 shows the Government's output (**GOVERN-MENT SERVICES**) as an undirected arrow, neither flowing to Firms or Households nor as a counterpart to taxes. First, with some exceptions (e.g., when a municipal government runs an electric utility) most government services are not provided as part of a market exchange. We do not pay separately for legislative services by the bill (scandals to one side) or for military services by ordering up an hour's worth of an airborne battalion when we wish to be defended. Second, even though government services sometimes benefit particular people more than others, ideally they are aimed at the common good. The absence of market exchanges means that, unlike other parts of GDP, the value of government goods and services is not measured by the payments made for them but by their cost of production (see Chapter 3, section 3.5.2).

The Foreign Sector

The three sectors represented in Figure 2.4 taken together constitute the Domestic Economy. Some domestic production, known as **EXPORTS**, is sold to the rest of the world or Foreign Sector. Similarly, the Domestic Economy purchases goods and services, known as **IMPORTS**, from other countries. Figure 2.5 shows the real export and import flows as well as the corresponding monetary payments running in the opposite direction. In reality, these transactions occur between particular domestic and foreign firms, governments, or individuals. The figure suppresses these details and shows the transactions as if they were between the whole domestic economy and the world.

Exports and imports need not balance. If exports exceed imports, then monetary flows into the Domestic Economy (**export receipts**) exceed monetary flows out of the Domestic Economy (**import payments**). The economy then runs a **surplus** on the **current account** of the **balance of payments** Or, to put it another way, **net exports**, defined as *exports less imports*, is positive.[2] When imports exceed exports, the economy runs a **current-account deficit** or negative net exports. In 2008, the United States ran a balance-of-payments deficit of $706 billion. As a result, U.S. firms and consumers paid that amount to foreigners. The foreigners may, in turn, have held those dollars as dollars or used them to purchase their own currencies, to purchase dollar-denominated assets (such as U.S. government bonds or the stocks or bonds of U.S. corporations), or to buy foreign assets (such as German or U.K. bonds) from U.S. owners. The longer a country runs a balance-of-payments deficit, the more of its assets are acquired by foreigners or the more its holdings of foreign assets are reduced. These asset transactions are shown in Figure 2.5 as being transmitted through Financial Markets to the Domestic Economy.

---

[2] The current-account surplus and net exports are not, in fact, identical, because the current account includes net income flows (unrelated to exports and imports) and net transfers from abroad. These accounts are covered in more detail in Chapters 3 and 8.

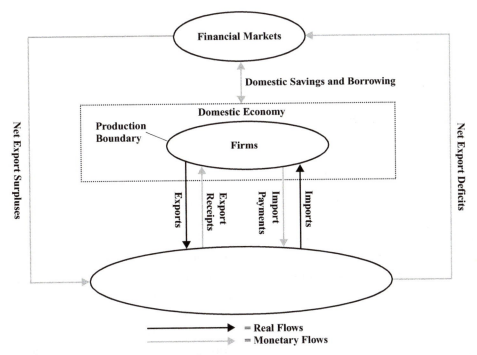

Figure 2.5. The Foreign Sector from the Perspective of the Domestic Economy. The diagram omits many details from Figures 2.2–2.4 to show that goods and services exported to foreigners cross the production boundary and so form part of GDP, whereas imports act as negative exports and reduce GDP. Exports and imports are matched by monetary payments in the opposite direction. If imports exceed exports then the domestic economy is short of monetary resources and must borrow them. Ultimately, the source of funds is the excess payments for imports that are lent indirectly through financial markets to the domestic economy. Similarly, if exports exceed imports, the domestic economy becomes a net lender to the foreign sector.

A Bird's-Eye View of the Economy

Figures 2.2–2.5 present a reasonably comprehensive view of the real and monetary flows in the economy. For all their complexity, the diagrams omit many details of the national accounts and most of the details of financial markets. Chapters 3 and 6 fill in some of these missing details.

The "circular" flow in the diagram is not a single, simple circuit. It is instead a set of interlocking real and monetary flows making for a complex circulation not unlike the circulation of blood in the body. If this circulation is to continue from period to period, then the flows must balance in at least three ways.

- First, every real and financial flow must be balanced by a monetary flow in the opposite direction.

- Second, the value of the flow of factors of production must equal the value of all of the expenditure on goods and services (consumption, investment, government, and foreign) or, equivalently, the value of all of the production must equal the value of all of the factor payments.
- Third, all of the monetary flows away from the Domestic Private Sector (savings, taxes, and import expenditure) must be matched by monetary flows toward it (investment, government, and export expenditure).

2.3 The National Accounting Identities

The circular flow of products and income and the property that real and monetary flows must balance give us a useful conceptual picture of the process of product- and income-creation. Practical macroeconomics, however, requires numbers. These are supplied by the NATIONAL INCOME AND PRODUCT ACCOUNTS (sometimes known by the acronym NIPA). The National Income and Product Accounts transform the flows and counter-flows of the circular flow of income and products into a series of double-entry accounts. They are "double-entry" because there is always a monetary, income counterpart to any real product, thus respecting the first balancing property of the circular flow mentioned at the end of the last section. (The principles of double-entry bookkeeping are described in more detail in Chapter 6, section 6.1.) GDP unifies the two sides of the books because it measures both all of the production of final goods and services in the economy and all of the income in the economy.

In the United States, National Income and Product Accounts are maintained by the Bureau of Economic Analysis (BEA) of the Department of Commerce. These accounts give us a detailed picture of the economy as a whole. They break GDP down into a large number of constituents on both product and income sides. When working with actual economic data, it is important to understand the details. When trying to form a useful picture of how the macroeconomy works, it is helpful to pass over many of the fine details and to paint with a broader brush. (Chapter 3, section 3.7, explains in detail how to read the national accounts and relate them to the simplified relationships developed in this section.)

2.3.1 The Production-Expenditure Identity

The relationships among aggregate product, aggregate expenditure, and aggregate income can be summarized in two simple identities. The first relates the value of production to expenditure. The value of the final goods and services available to the economy is what is produced (Y) plus whatever is imported (IM). Expenditure on these goods has four sources. The goods may be used for domestic consumption (C), domestic private investment (I), or government goods and services (G), or they may become exports (EX). The **product-expenditure identity** is then:

$$Y + IM \equiv C + I + G + EX. \tag{2.1}$$

The triple-barred equal sign ($\equiv$) indicates that the equation is an identity – its two sides are *necessarily* equal (i.e., equal by definition). The left-hand side indicates the size of the national income pie, while the right-hand side shows the way in which the pie is sliced. Subtracting imports (M) from both sides gives us another version of the identity:

$$Y \equiv C + I + G + (EX - IM). \tag{2.1'}$$

Defining $EX - IM$ as *net exports* (NX), this can be written as:

$$Y \equiv C + I + G + NX. \tag{2.1''}$$

The left-hand sides of equations (2.1') or (2.1'') can be thought of as production that generates income, and the right-hand sides as expenditure that purchases production.

Figure 2.6 portrays the production-expenditure identity using U.S. data for 2009: The pie itself represents the left-hand side of equation (2.1) – the goods and services available to the domestic economy. The inner circle represents GDP, while the outer ring represents imports. Each slice of the pie reflects one of the expenditure items on the right-hand side of equation (2.1). Consumption is by far the largest slice (70 percent of GDP), followed by government expenditure, investment, and exports.

2.3.2 The Disposable-Income Identity

The second accounting identity relates aggregate income to its uses. Because the value of all that is produced within a country comes initially to the workers, capitalists, and owners of factors of production in the form of income, GDP measures AGGREGATE INCOME just as it measures aggregate production and expenditure. Throughout this book we shall use the variable Y to represent all three: *production, expenditure, and income.*

Nothing, it is said, is certain aside from death and taxes. Not all the income earned is available for the purchase of goods and services. On the one hand, the government receives taxes (T) from income. On the other hand, the government makes transfer payments to the Domestic Private Sector (TR). DISPOSABLE INCOME (YD) is *income net of taxes and transfers.* In the broadest sense, people have only one decision with respect to their disposable income: spend it (C) or save it (S). The **disposable-income identity** is then

$$YD \equiv Y - T + TR \equiv C + S. \tag{2.2}$$

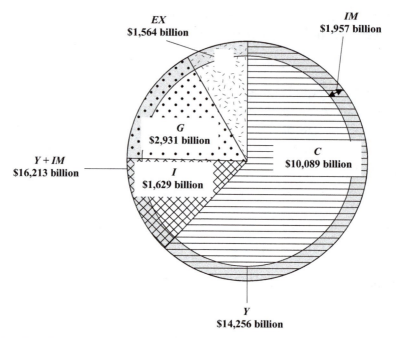

Figure 2.6. The Product-Expenditure Identity for the United States, 2009:

$$Y + IM \equiv C + I + G + EX$$

Source: Bureau of Economic Analysis.

Figure 2.7 portrays the disposable-income identity using U.S. data for 2009: The pie itself represents GDP. The ring formed by the outer and inner circles represents taxes, while the overlapping ring formed by the middle and inner circles represents transfer payments. The middle circle, therefore, represents disposable income (the left-hand side of equation (2.2)). The slices of the pie reflect the right-hand side of equation (2.2). Consumption, again, takes by far the largest slice (78 percent of disposable income). Household savings in the U.S. are notoriously low. Nonetheless, because savings in equation (2.8) corresponds to the savings not just of households, but of the whole private sector, including savings that is implicit in maintaining the stock of fixed capital (buildings, machinery, and so forth), the savings slice in the figure represents a high 22 percent of disposable income or 20 percent of GDP.

2.3.3 The Sectoral-Deficits Identity

Equations (2.1) and (2.2) are the two primary identities. We can derive two other useful identities from them. Subtracting the middle and right-hand

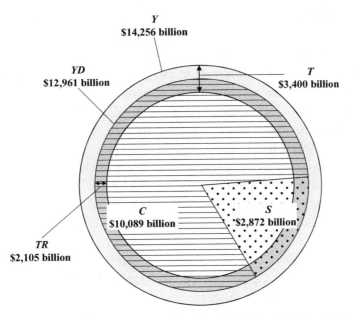

Figure 2.7. The Disposable-Income Identity for the United States, 2009:

$$Y - (T - TR) \equiv YD \equiv C + S$$

Source: Bureau of Economic Analysis.

terms of equation (2.2) from the right and left sides of equation (2.1) yields:

$$T - TR \equiv I + G + EX - IM - S.$$

Rearranging, we have the **sectoral-deficits identity**:

$$[G - (T - TR)] \quad + \quad [I - S] \quad + \quad [EX - IM] \quad \equiv 0$$
government budget deficit + private-sector deficit + foreign-sector deficit $\equiv 0$.
$$(2.3)$$

Each of the terms refers to one of the sectors that constitute the circular flow (taking Firms and Households together as the Domestic Private Sector). The first term in square brackets is the **government budget deficit** – that is, the excess of its expenditure over its revenue. Transfer payments can be regarded as negative taxes, and the term $T - TR$ is *net taxes*.

The second term can be thought of as the **private-sector deficit**. If Households consumed everything that Firms produced, the Domestic Private Sector would be in perfect balance. We know from the discussion of the circular flow (and the disposable-income identity) that Households typically save, consuming less than their incomes and, therefore, less than Firms produce. Equally, Firms purchase part of their own output as investment in long-lived capital. If savings is exactly enough to finance investment purchases, then the Domestic Private Sector is again in balance. But if savings falls short of investment, then the Domestic Private Sector runs a deficit.

The third term is the **foreign-sector deficit**. Looked at from the point of view of the domestic economy, this term is, of course, just net exports. A positive balance for net exports would constitute a current-account surplus for the United States. But because exports from the United States to the rest of the world can be thought of just as accurately as the imports by the rest of the world from the United States, the Foreign Sector will be in deficit exactly when U.S. net exports are positive.

The sectoral-deficits identity tells us that the financial balances of the three sectors are interconnected. Any one sector can run a deficit or a surplus (which is just a negative deficit), but the circular flow must be balanced overall: The deficits of the Government, the Domestic Private Sector, and the Foreign Sector must add up to zero.

To illustrate the identity, imagine that the private sector runs a deficit. Say that its investment exceeds its own savings by $3 billion, so that the middle term in equation (2.3) is positive. It must borrow the needed funds. But where do these borrowed funds come from? The equation tells us that they come either from the government or foreigners running a surplus (i.e., negative net exports for the United States). The equation must add up to zero.

If the government collects more tax revenues than it spends, it uses those revenues to retire its debt, freeing up funds that would otherwise be held in government bonds to be lent to corporations borrowing to make investments.

Similarly, if foreigners sell more to the United States than the United States sells to them, foreigners acquire dollars. The foreigners might use their dollars to finance the American investment directly by purchasing real property or capital (e.g., building a factory) in the United States, or indirectly by lending the funds to American companies through their own banks or through purchasing their corporate bonds or through purchasing other financial assets (such as U.S. Treasury bonds) from Americans, freeing up funds that can then be lent to the corporations.

Suppose, to carry on the example, that the government runs a $500 million surplus; the first term in equation (2.3) is negative. And suppose that foreigners run a $2.5 billion surplus (which is the same as saying that American net exports are in deficit); the third term is also negative. The national-income-accounting identity is fulfilled:

$$-\$0.5 \text{ billion} + \$3 \text{ billion} - \$2.5 \text{ billion} = 0.$$

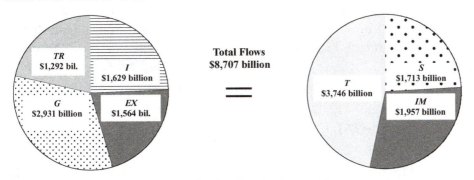

Inflows to the Domestic Private Sector

Outflows from the Domestic Private Sector

Total Flows
$8,707 billion

Figure 2.8. The Inflow-Outflow Identity for the United States, 2009:

$$I + G + TR + EX \equiv S + T + IM$$

Source: Bureau of Economic Analysis.

While any one or two of the three sectors can be in deficit at any time, one or two sectors must be in surplus (unless, against the odds, all three are in perfect balance). Every combination is possible so long as the identity adds up to zero. (See Box 2.1 for real-world examples of the variety of possibilities.)

2.3.4 The Inflow-Outflow Identity

A fourth identity focuses on monetary flows. Look again at the circular flow diagrams (Figure 2.2–2.5). They track both the flow of real goods and the flow of monetary payments. The Domestic Private Sector is the heart of the circular flow. Investment expenditure, government purchases, and export payments are all represented by monetary flows toward firms (i.e., toward the Domestic Private Sector). In contrast, savings, net taxes, and import payments are represented by monetary flows away from the Domestic Private Sector. Rearranging equation (2.3) gives us the **inflow-outflow identity**:

$$I + G + TR + EX \equiv S + T + IM.$$
$$Inflows \qquad \equiv \qquad Outflows \qquad (2.4)$$

The identity states that monetary flows into the Domestic Private Sector (**inflows**) must equal monetary flows away from the Domestic Private Sector (**outflows**). In some older textbooks, this identity was summarized memorably as stating that "injections" (inflows) must equal "leakages" (outflows) if the accounts are to balance.

Figure 2.8 portrays the inflow-outflow identity using U.S. data for 2009: The left-hand pie represents the total inflows of expenditure toward the

Box 2.1. The Twin-Deficits Problem and the Sectoral-Deficits Identity

In the 1980s, many people blamed the large current-account deficit on the large government budget deficits. This was the so-called twin-deficits problem. Early in the twenty-first century, the United States again faces the combination of large budget deficits and a large current-account deficit (i.e., a foreign-sector surplus). The data for 2009 for the sectoral-deficits identity (equation (2.2) follow (all values in billions):

$$[\$2,606 - (\$3,400 - \$2,228)] + [\$1,629 - \$2,632] + [\$1,669 - \$2100] \equiv 0^3$$
$$[G - (T - TR)] \quad + \quad [I - S] \quad + \quad [EX - IM] \quad \equiv 0$$

or

$$\$1,434 \quad + \quad -\$1,003 \quad + \quad -\$431 \quad \equiv 0$$

government budget deficit + private-sector deficit + foreign-sector deficit ≡ 0.

The twin-deficits argument claims that the reason net exports (foreign sector deficit) are large and negative is that the government budget deficit is large. If the government could balance its budget, net exports would rise (i.e., the foreign-sector deficit would get closer to zero). This argument misses two important points: First, there are three deficits. If the private sector is in deficit, net exports must continue to be negative, even if the government's budget is balanced. Second, an accounting identity is not itself an explanation of economic behavior. There is, in fact, no necessary connection between balance in the government's budget and foreign-sector balance. The following table demonstrates that every possible combination of surpluses and deficits that are theoretically possible are found at various times among the nations of the world:

Table B2.1. *The Sectoral-Deficits Identity for Selected Countries*

Country Unit	Year	Sectoral Deficit Government	Private	Foreign (net exports)[a]
United States	2003	309	186	−495
U.S. dollar, billions		deficit	deficit	surplus
Germany	2008	2	−180	178
euro, billions		deficit	surplus	deficit
United States	2009	1,434	−1,003	−431
U.S. dollar, billions		deficit	surplus	surplus
China	2008	−156	1,908	2,064
yuan, billions		surplus	deficit	deficit
South Korea	2008	−41,590	55,916	−14,326
won, billions		surplus	deficit	surplus
Finland	2008	−9	−5	4
euro, billions		surplus	surplus	deficit

Notes: Positive entries denote deficits and negative entries surpluses.
Entries in the last three columns sum to zero, because of the sectoral-deficits identity.
[a] The foreign-sector deficit is positive when the domestic net exports are positive.
Source: International Monetary Fund, *International Financial Statistics.*

[3] Savings include statistical discrepancy of $205 billion.

Domestic Private Sector. Each slice represents one of the sources of expenditure. The right-hand pie is necessarily the same size, and represents the outflows of funds away from the Domestic Private Sector. Each slice stands for one source of outflow.

2.4 Real Gross Domestic Product

The national accounts and the four accounting identities give us a snapshot of the economy at a particular time. An important part of macroeconomics concerns itself with changes in the economy over time. Before we can begin to understand why the economy changes or how policy might make it change for the better, we need to be able to describe the changing economy accurately. In this section we shall learn to describe changing GDP and in the next section changing prices.

2.4.1 Real and Nominal Quantities

In 1960, the grandparents of the typical American undergraduate were in the prime of their lives. U.S. GDP in that year was $526 billion. U.S. GDP in 2009 was $14,256 billion – more than 27 times greater. Is our economy really 27 times larger than our grandparents' economy? Of course not! We all know that a dollar today does not buy as much as a dollar did ten years ago, much less fifty years ago. The puzzle is how to account for that fact.

How much of the growth in GDP results from genuine increases in the final goods and services available to us and how much from rising prices (the falling value of the dollar)? A simple way to answer the question is to consider a representative commodity that has changed little, if at all, over the nearly fifty years. In 1960, a 12-ounce returnable bottle of Coca-Cola could be purchased from a vending machine for 10¢. In 2009, 12 ounces of Coke (now sold in a recyclable can) can be purchased for 75¢. The price of Coke has risen by seven and a half times.

To compare our GDP to our grandparents' GDP, we now have a choice. We can ask what would it cost us in today's money to purchase what our grandparents' purchased. In other words, what would 1960 GDP be in 2009 prices? The answer is easily found. If the price increase of Coke is typical, then each dollar in 1960 would buy seven and a half times what a dollar in 2009 would buy. We should, therefore, **inflate** the value of 1960 GDP by seven and a half times: $\$_{1960}526$ billion$\times 7\frac{1}{2} = \$_{2009}3,945$ billion. (The date subscripts on the dollar signs indicate this is the 1960 value of GDP expressed in the dollars of 2009 or, as it is usually put, *in constant 2009 dollars.*)

We could have put the question the other way round: What would it have cost our grandparents to purchase the final goods and services that we enjoy

Table 2.1. *Converting Nominal GDP to Real GDP Using the Price of Coca-Cola as the Deflator*

Year	Nominal GDP	Price of Coca-Cola (per 12 ounces)	Real GDP in Constant Dollars of Reference Year	
			1960	2009
1960	$526	$0.10	$526	$3,945
2009	$14,256	$0.75	$1,901	$14,256

today? In other words, what would 2009 GDP have been in 1960 prices? Since each 2009 dollar purchases only a fraction $(1/7\frac{1}{2})$ of what a 1960 dollar purchased, we **deflate** the value of 2009 GDP by seven and a half times: $\$_{2008}14{,}256$ billion $\div 7\frac{1}{2} = \$_{1960}1{,}901$ billion.

Table 2.1 summarizes the two ways of accounting for changing prices when comparing GDP in different years. Each line shows measured or nominal GDP (i.e., as it is recorded by the national accountants) for each year and its value expressed in the constant dollars of both 1960 and 2009. (Notice that 1960 GDP in 1960 constant dollars has the same value as measured GDP in 1960, and similarly for 2009 GDP in 2009 constant dollars.) Although it is misleading to compare measured GDP (second column), it is fair to compare GDP in constant dollars (compare the entries in either the second or the third columns). Either way we see that 2009 GDP is 3.6 times larger than 1960 GDP. That the U.S. economy should nearly quadruple in fifty years is itself a remarkable fact. But mere quadrupling seems paltry in comparison to the 2,600 percent increase in measured GDP. It is essential to account for changing prices.

Fundamentally, real GDP is the total disparate collection of final goods and services produced in some period. It is shoes, ships, sealing wax, and concert tickets, but not money. It is those goods and services and not money that actually fulfill our needs and desires. The important role of money is to provide a common denominator that allows us to add up the disparate goods and services according to their values. But now we see that the value of money itself changes and that we cannot compare monetary values unless we account for the change. "Real" in real GDP, therefore, has a second meaning. A **NOMINAL VALUE** is defined as *a value measured at current market prices.* A **REAL VALUE** is defined as *a value corrected for changing prices (i.e., a value expressed in constant units of money of a particular time).*

The second column of Table 2.1 shows the nominal values of GDP in 1960 and 2008, while the other columns show the real values. The table demonstrates that nominal and real values can sometimes coincide, although only in the **reference period** for the constant dollars (or other currency units in other countries). It also shows that real values are not unique. They can be

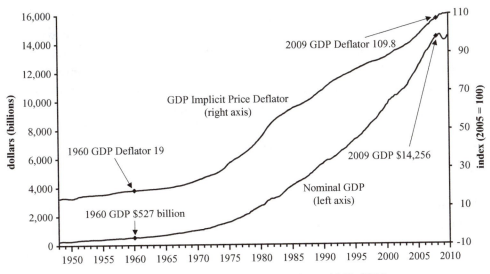

Figure 2.9. Nominal GDP and Prices, 1948–2009.

expressed in the constant dollars of any period, although valid comparisons can be made only if the same period is used for all values.

2.4.2 Converting Nominal to Real GDP

The price of Coca-Cola provided a straightforward way of separating real from nominal GDP. But do we have any reason to believe that the changing price of Coca-Cola is a good measure of the changing prices of all goods? Economists believe that it would be more accurate to track the changes in price of a bundle of goods more representative of what is actually produced and consumed. Typically, the price of such a bundle is converted to an index number that takes the value 100 in the reference period. An index number of 200 means that prices in general have risen 100 percent. An index number of 70 means that prices in general have fallen by 30 percent.

The national-income accountants publish a price index that reflects the goods and services in GDP. It is called the **GDP (IMPLICIT PRICE) DEFLA- TOR**. The term "deflator" reflects its use in converting nominal to real GDP – the pinprick that lets the hot air of high prices out of the GDP balloon. In Chapter 4 we shall consider the details of the construction of the GDP defla- tor and other price indices. Setting aside those intriguing details, in this chap- ter we shall use the GDP deflator both to convert nominal to real GDP and to measure the rate of inflation.

Figure 2.9 shows the time series for nominal GDP and the GDP deflator – the price index based on the bundle of goods and services that make up GDP as a whole. Each time series is marked with the average values at 1960 and at 2009. We can use this information to convert nominal GDP into the constant dollars of either 1960 or 2009. It does not matter which year we choose. But we must be consistent. The trick is exactly the same one we used with the prices of Coke. Find the factor by which prices have changed between the two years and, then, use that factor to inflate or deflate prices appropriately. (The *Guide*, sections G.8 and G.9, discusses the use of index numbers and conversions between nominal and real magnitudes.)

The general rule for calculating the **price factor** (pf) between any reference period and another period t is:

$$pf_t = p_{reference}/p_t. \tag{2.5}$$

To convert any nominal quantity X measured in the dollars of year t to those of the reference period, just multiply by the price factor:

$$\$_{reference}X_t = pf_t \times \$_t X_t. \tag{2.6}$$

The subscripts on the dollar sign indicate in which year's dollars X is measured. (For the time being we shall be careful to use time subscripts for currency. To keep things simple, in later chapters we will omit the time subscripts, whenever confusion between nominal and real quantities is unlikely.)

We can use formula (2.6) to convert 2009 GDP into 1960 constant dollars. Each 2009 dollar must be shrunk to reflect the loss in value owing to 49 years of inflation. The reference year is 1960, so using the values of the implicit price deflator from Figure 2.9:

$$\begin{aligned}
\$_{1960}Y_{2009} = pf_{2009} \times \$_{2009}Y_{2009} &= (p_{1960}/p_{2009}) \times \$_{2009}Y_{2009} \\
&= (18.6/109.8)\$_{2009} \, 14{,}256 \text{ billion} \\
&= (0.17)\$_{2009} \, 14{,}256 \text{ billion} \\
&= \$_{1960} \, 2{,}424 \text{ billion.}
\end{aligned}$$

Because prices are higher in 2009 than in 1960, the price factor for 2009, taking 1960 as the reference year, is $pf_{2009} = p_{1960}/p_{2009} = 0.17$ – a number less than one. It measures the decline in the value of the dollar over time.

GDP in 1960 could just as well be expressed in 2009 constant dollars:

$$\begin{aligned}
\$_{2009}Y_{1960} = pf_{1960} \times \$_{1960}Y_{1960} &= (p_{2009}/p_{1960}) \times \$_{1960}Y_{1960} \\
&= (109.8/18.6)\$_{1960} \, 526 \text{ billion} \\
&= (5.90)\$_{1960} \, 526 \text{ billion} \\
&= \$_{2009} \, 3{,}103 \text{ billion.}
\end{aligned}$$

Because prices are lower in 1960 than in 2009, the price factor for 1960, taking 2009 as the reference year, is $pf_{1960} = p_{2009}/p_{1960} = 5.90$ – a number

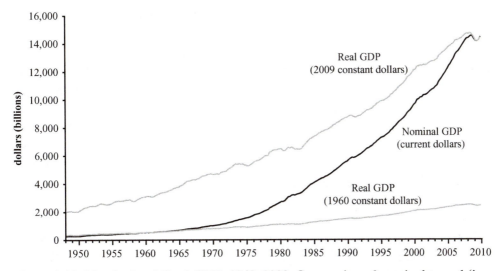

Figure 2.10. Nominal and Real GDP, 1948–2009. Conversion of nominal to real (i.e., constant dollar GDP based on data in Figure 2.9. Notice, first, that each real GDP series intersects the nominal GDP series in its base year; and, second, that each real GDP series is a fixed multiple of the others, so that the shape of the series in 2008 constant dollars is just a blowup of the shape in 1960 constant dollars. *Source:* Bureau of Economic Analysis.

greater than one. It measures the increase in the value of the dollar as we consider earlier times.

Figure 2.10 shows nominal GDP and real GDP expressed in the constant dollars of 1960 and 2009. The points at which the real GDP lines cross the nominal GDP line in Figure 2.10 are significant. Each represents the fact that real and nominal GDP are equal in the reference year. This is evident from the previous conversion formula, because, in the reference year, *reference = t* so that the price factor $p_{reference}/p_t = p_t/p_t = 1$.

Despite the numerical and visual difference, the two lines representing real GDP convey precisely the same information expressed in different units. The difference between them is of the same nature as the difference between speed measured in miles per hour and feet per second. It is just as correct to write $\$_{1960}526$ billion $= \$_{2009}3{,}103$ billion as it is to write that 100 miles per hour $= 147$ feet per second.

While every reference period is equally *correct*, one is often more *convenient* than another. For some purposes, we grasp the significance of 100 miles per hour more easily – say, when asking how long it might take us to travel by train from Washington to New York. For other purposes, 147 feet per second is clearer – say, when asking how far a model rocket will travel in five seconds. Similarly, current prices are more familiar than past prices. When a character in a television western pays 18¢ for a loaf of bread in 1876, has she been cheated or gotten a bargain? We usually could not say.

But if the price is converted to 2009 dollars (about $3.44), it is easier to see that this was a pretty expensive loaf of bread by today's standards. Equally, even for those who remember 1960, it is hard to keep a firm grasp on what the dollar bought five decades past. But current prices are not always the most convenient for particular problems. Constantly changing the reference period would make it hard to update time series with new data as they are released. Government agencies, therefore, usually choose a reference year and stick with it for some time. As the reference period recedes into the past, they usually update it to a more recent year and revise all of the past data to reflect the new reference year. At the time of writing this chapter, the official reference year for the National Income and Product Accounts was 2005.

We began section 2.4.1 by asking whether the U.S. economy was really 27 times larger in 2009 than in 1960. The answer, of course, is no. But we are now in a position to give a more accurate assessment. U.S. GDP was 4.6 times higher in 2009 than in 1960:

$$\$_{2009}14,256\,\text{billion}/\$_{2009}3,103\,\text{billion} = \$_{1960}2,424\,\text{billion}/\$_{1960}526 = 4.6.$$

A NOTE ON VARIABLE NAMES: *In sections 2.1–2.3, the variable names, Y, C, I, G, and so forth were allowed to stand for nominal quantities. In almost (but not quite) all cases, we are concerned with real quantities. Consequently, in the rest of the book, unless specific exceptions are made, dollar-denominated variables denote real or constant-dollar values. For simplicity, except where context demands it, the date subscript is omitted from the dollar sign ($). A dollar sign without a date indicates constant, reference-year dollars or, where context requires, current or nominal dollars.*

2.4.3 International GDP Comparisons

National income accounts not only allow us to compare GDP today to GDP in the past, they also allow us to compare GDP among countries. Because different countries use different currencies, comparisons first require conversion into a common currency using market exchange rates. But just as we cannot fairly compare 2003 dollars to 1960 dollars, because the value of the dollar itself has changed, we cannot compare a dollar in the United States to one converted into pounds sterling, because one dollar may buy more or less than its sterling equivalent (£0.69 or 69 pence in May 2010). As a result, fair comparisons require that national GDPs be converted into a common measure at **purchasing-power parity** – that is, taking account of the relative buying power of each currency. (The concept of purchasing-power parity is discussed in greater detail in Chapter 8.)

Table 2.2 shows the GDP in 2008 for three groups of countries: the so-called G-7 group of industrialized countries; the other (mainly important

Table 2.2. *GDP in 2008 for Selected Countries*

	Rank	GDP (billions, 2008 U.S. dollars at purchasing-power parity)
The G-7		
United States	2	14,260
Japan	4	4,329
Germany	6	2,918
France	9	2,128
United Kingdom	8	2,226
Italy	11	1,823
Canada	15	1,300
Other G-20		
European Union	1	14,910
China	3	7,973
India	5	3,297
Russia	7	2,266
Brazil	10	1,993
Mexico	12	1,563
South Korea	14	1,335
Indonesia	16	915
Turkey	17	903
Australia	19	800
Saudi Arabia	23	576
Argentina	24	574
South Africa	26	491
Selected Other Countries		
Thailand	25	547
Egypt	27	444
Ukraine	35	340
Hong Kong	40	307
Norway	41	275
Singapore	47	237
Israel	52	201
Ethiopia	80	69
Luxembourg	97	39
Nicaragua	130	17
Liechtenstein	165	4
Burundi	173	3
World		69,716

Source: Central Intelligence Agency, *The World Factbook 2008.*

developing countries) that, along with the G-7, constitute the G-20; and a selection of other countries. The economy of the United States is by far the largest in the world: three times larger than Japan, the next biggest G-7 country, and eleven times larger than Canada, the smallest G-7 country.

2.4.4 Population and Real per Capita GDP

One surprise, perhaps, in Table 2.2 is that China's economy, although smaller, is still more than half the size of the United States and larger than every other G-7 country including Japan. (In fact, the economies of India, Russia, Brazil, Mexico, and South Korea, as well as China, are larger than that of Canada, the smallest G-7 economy).[4] And yet China does not appear on the surface to be as rich a country as Germany or Canada or even as such small countries as Luxembourg or Singapore, in the sense that most of its people individually do not seem rich. And that is, of course, the key: the Chinese are not as rich person per person as the most developed countries in the world, but there are 1.3 billion Chinese. For some purposes, it is important to know the GDP of the economy. For other purposes, we want to know how much GDP on average each person has at his disposal – that is, how much is GDP per capita:

$$GDP \ per \ Capita = GDP/Population. \tag{2.11}$$

For China,

$$GDP \ per \ Capita = GDP/Population = \$7,973 \ \text{billion}/1.329 \ \text{billion people}$$
$$= \$6,000 \ \text{per head.}$$

Table 2.3 shows GDP per capita for the same group of countries in Table 2.2. It is clear that on an individual level, the Chinese are far below all the citizens of the G-7 countries. Economic well-being depends more on individual incomes, but economic and political power may often (although not always) depend on sheer size. Were China to develop to the same level of income per capita as now enjoyed by the United States, its GDP would be $62,330 billion. Its economy would be more than four times larger than that of the United States and only a little smaller than world GDP in 2008.

Using GDP per capita we can reconsider how the U.S. economy has grown since 1960 – this time from a more individual perspective. We already know that the economy of 2009 was more than four times larger than the economy of 1960. But since the population of the U.S. grew from 180 million in 1960 to more than 307 million in 2009 (an increase of about two-thirds), the increased GDP was spread over more heads. For the United States, GDP per capita in 1960 was $_{09}17,518 ($= \$3,103$ billion/177.135 million people), and in 2009 was $_{09}46,388 ($= \$_{09}14,256$ billion/307.322 million people). Although the U.S. economy is 359 percent larger, the average citizen is only 165 percent richer.

---

[4] Recently, Russia has been included in an expanded group, the G-8, more as a reflection of its continuing status as the successor to the former superpower, the Soviet Union, than of its economic importance.

Table 2.3. *GDP and GDP per Capita in 2008 for Selected Countries (ranked by GDP per capita)*

Countries	GDP (billions, 2008 U.S. dollars at purchasing-power parity)	Rank	GDP per Capita (2008 U.S. dollars at purchasing-power parity)	Rank
Liechtenstein			118,000	1
Luxembourg	39	97	81,000	3
Norway	275	41	59,300	5
Singapore	237	47	51,500	9
United States	14,260	2	46,900	10
Hong Kong	307	40	43,700	14
Canada	1,300	15	39,100	22
Australia	800	19	38,100	25
United Kingdom	2,226	8	36,500	32
Germany	2,918	6	35,400	34
Japan	4,329	4	34,000	37
European Union	14,910	1	33,700	38
France	2,128	9	33,200	39
Italy	1,823	11	31,300	41
Israel	201	52	28,300	49
South Korea	1,335	14	27,600	51
Saudi Arabia	576	23	20,500	59
Russia	2,266	7	16,100	73
South Africa	491	26	14,200	80
Mexico	1,563	12	14,200	81
Turkey	903	17	11,900	92
Brazil	1,993	10	10,200	101
Thailand	547	25	8,400	116
Ukraine	340	35	7,400	123
Argentina	574	24	2,600	125
China	7,973	3	6,000	132
Egypt	444	27	5,400	134
Indonesia	915	16	3,900	154
India	3,297	5	2,900	165
Nicaragua	17	130	2,900	167
Ethiopia	69	80	800	216
Burundi	3	173	400	226
World	49,000		10,400	

Source: Central Intelligence Agency, *The World Factbook 2008.*

It is important to be clear what this means. In Chapter 3 we shall see that real GDP is not an all-purpose measure of economic well-being; rather, it is a measure of the volume of final goods and services produced in the market economy. Real GDP per capita is simply how much of the real value of these goods and services could be enjoyed by each person *if* they were spread evenly across the population. Of course, not everyone gets the average. Some people get very little (6 percent of the population received less than $10,000 per year in 2005); others get a lot (in the same year 6 percent of the population received more than $150,000 per year).

Median income is a better indicator of what a typical person receives. **Median income** is *that income that marks the dividing line at which half the population receives more and half less than the median.* Population may be counted by individual or, more typically, by household. Median household income in the United States in 2009 was $49,777, well below the mean household income of $67,976.[5] This indicates that the distribution of income is positively skewd (see the *Guide*, section G.4.2). Imagine that the poorest household earned nothing and the richest household earned twice the median ($99,554); then the mean (or average) of the two households would equal the median. In fact, the richest household earns *much* more than twice the median, so the mean is higher than the median.

2.5 GDP through Time

Real GDP or real GDP per capita measures the income of the country or its average citizen. But whether we feel prosperous often seems to depend more on how fast income is growing rather than how high it is at the moment. As we shall see in Chapter 15, section 15.2, whether unemployment is rising or falling depends in large measure on whether the growth rate of real GDP is fast or slow. Although different times are involved, the answer to the question, "How much larger was the economy of 2009 than the economy of 1960?," is timeless. It is like the answer to the question, "How far is Chicago from New York?" As well as how far, we might also want to know how fast. "On your cross-country trip did you drive faster between New York and Chicago or between Chicago and Denver?" Similarly, we can ask questions of the economy such as, "Has the economy recently grown faster or slower than in the past?"

2.5.1 Visualizing Growth 1: Growth Rates

Figure 2.10 is not very helpful in answering questions about the speed of economic growth. On a graph of real GDP with a natural scale, a steeper slope corresponds to faster growth measured in dollars per unit time, but not necessarily to a faster growth rate measured as a *percentage* increase per unit time. The problem is that, as GDP grows, the base for computing the percentage change also grows.

A different way to visualize the speed of growth is to plot the rates of growth themselves. Figure 2.11 plots the (compound annualized) quarterly

---

[5] *Source:* U.S. Census Bureau, Current Population Survey, 2010 Annual Social and Economic Supplement.

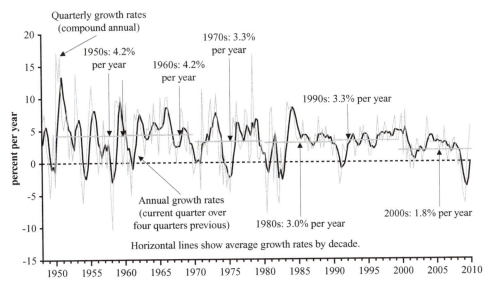

Figure 2.11. Real GDP Growth Rates (quarterly and annual), 1948–2009. Quarterly growth rates are highly volatile. Compounding makes this volatility more obvious. Annual rates are the geometric averages of quarterly rates and, like all averages, smooth out some of the variability. The average level of growth rates was highest in the 1950s and 1960s, and declined thereafter; while the volatility of growth rates remained high into the 1970s and declined after the mid-1980s during a period some- times called the "Great Moderation." *Source:* Bureau of Economic Analysis.

growth rate, the annual growth rate (current quarter over the same quarter one year earlier), and the average growth rate for each of the decades from 1950 to 2010 (shown as horizontal lines). (See the *Guide*, section G.10, for details on the calculation of growth rates, including com- pounding and annualization.)

A NOTIONAL CONVENTION: *Throughout this book a circumflex or "hat" over a variable indicates its rate of growth – for example,* $\hat{Y}$ *is the rate of growth of GDP.*

Notice that the compounded quarterly rate is the most variable of the three series. Compounding magnifies any small changes in GDP by rais- ing them to the fourth power. Annual growth calculations are somewhat less variable. They can be seen as averaging over four separate quarterly changes, finding their (geometric) mean, which is bound to be higher than the lowest annualized quarterly rate and lower than the highest. Even the annual rates are too variable to easily judge the typical rate of growth over any longish period. The decade averages, however, show clearly that the economy grew faster in the 1950s than in the 1980s.

2.5.2 Visualizing Growth 2: Logarithmic Graphs

Although it is relatively easy to see on Figure 2.11 that the average rate of growth is lower in the 1990s than in the 1950s, decades are arbitrary divisions

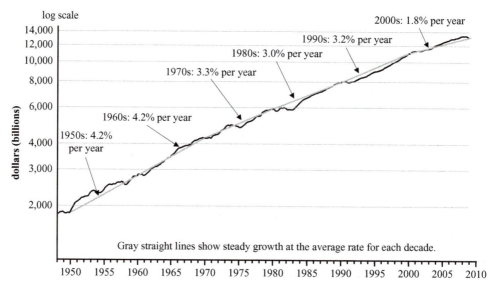

Figure 2.12. The Growth of Real GDP, 1948–2009. On a logarithmic scale, the slope of the line corresponds to the rate of growth. The straight segments of the gray lines in this figure correspond to the horizontal lines in Figure 2.11. The higher the horizontal lines in Figure 2.11, the steeper the segments of the gray lines in this figure. Again, we can see the large fall in the average rate of growth between the 1950s and 1960s and the 1970s through 2000s. *Source:* Bureau of Economic Analysis.

that do not necessarily correspond to significant economic, political, social, or historical divisions. It is unlikely that the growth rate of GDP dropped precipitously on New Year's Day in 1970. Can we locate the point at which the economy slowed down? The large quarter-to-quarter and year-to-year variation makes our task difficult. And we have already seen that it is no easier to read growth rates off of graphs of real GDP in natural units, such as Figure 2.10. Fortunately, we have another tool: the **logarithmic graph**. Because the slope of a logarithmic graph of any time series corresponds to its rate of growth (see the *Guide*, sections G.11.3–4), we are able to see the level of real GDP and its rate of growth simultaneously.

Figure 2.12 plots U.S. GDP on a logarithmic scale (black line). The slope of the gray line segments correspond to the horizontal lines in Figure 2.11 – that is, to the average growth rates for the decades between 1950 and 2010. The higher the horizontal segment in Figure 2.11, the steeper the corresponding segment in Figure 2.12.

2.6 Measuring Inflation

2.6.1 Inflation and Deflation

Until now, we have focused on real GDP. We used the GDP deflator principally as a tool to convert nominal into real GDP. Economists, policymakers, and the public also care about changing prices in their own right. General increases in prices are, of course, known as **INFLATION**. Inflation, measured by changes in a price index, corresponds to a falling **purchasing power of money**. The more the inflation, the less a dollar will buy. Because the price index can be made to take any value we like in its reference period, the actual value at any one time does not tell us whether prices are high or low. But changes in the value do tell us whether prices are higher or lower. And the rate of growth of the price index tells us whether prices are becoming higher or lower quickly or slowly. Inflation is measured as the growth rate of prices ($\hat{p}$) using all the same formulae as are used in computing the growth rates of real GDP (see the *Guide*, section G.10).

Anyone who holds assets valued as a certain number of nominal dollars has cause to dislike inflation. The holder of a dollar bill sees its ability to purchase goods waste away as prices increase. Similarly, recipients of private pensions or banks issuing mortgages lose purchasing power to higher prices. Inflation can produce winners as well as losers. Social Security or other U.S. government pensions are indexed to the price level, so that higher prices leave the real purchasing power of recipients unchanged. Borrowers (e.g., people who have bought houses using a mortgage) like inflation, because they are able to repay their loans with cheaper money. One person's gain is often another's loss. In the case of loans, what the borrower gains, the bank loses. Similarly, in the case of government debt, what the bond-holding public loses, the government gains. But, equally, what the Social Security recipient or the government pensioner gains, the government itself loses.

Through most of the past seven decades, inflation rates in most countries have been positive. But prices can fall. **DEFLATION** or **DISINFLATION** is *a fall in the general price level*. Like inflation, deflation produces winners (creditors) and losers (borrowers). The last serious deflation in the United States occurred during the Great Depression of the 1930s. The "okies" of John Steinbeck's *The Grapes of Wrath* were, in part, the victims of the deflation of the 1930s, as falling prices raised the real cost of the mortgages on their farms to levels they could not afford to pay. A book from the 1930s called *Inflation* begins with the statement, "The world sadly needs higher prices," a sentiment virtually unvoiced over the next 75 years.[6]

Japan provides a clear example of a prolonged period of mild deflation for more than a decade after 1994 (see Figure 2.13). During the same period, U.S. inflation rates (higher than Japanese rates throughout the period) fell, although they remain positive. In 2002 and 2003, inflation rates in the United States became low enough that monetary policymakers became genuinely concerned about deflation. But inflation picked up again until the recession that began in December 2007. In half of the eighteen months of that recession, prices as measured by the consumer price index (see Chapter 4,

---

[6] Donald B. Woodward and Marc A. Rose. *Inflation*. New York: McGraw-Hill, 1933, p. ix.

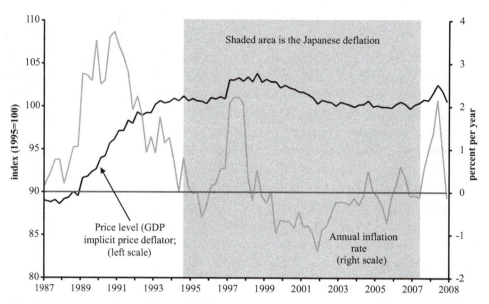

Figure 2.13. Japanese Deflation. Since the Great Depression, rising prices (inflation) rather than falling prices (deflation) have dominated the world economies. Japan in the 1990s and early 2000s presents a rare case of prolonged deflation in the post-Depression period. *Source:* International Monetary Fund, *International Financial Statistics.*

section 4.2) fell compared to the same month a year earlier. With the end of the recession, however, prices began to rise again. Deflation is sometimes more feared than inflation, because the losers to deflation (e.g., heavily mortgaged farmers in the 1930s or heavily indebted companies in Japan at the turn of the twenty-first century) are probably more vulnerable than the losers to inflation.

2.6.2 Measuring Inflation Using the GDP Deflator

In the opening years of the twenty-first century, the United States enjoyed low inflation rates reminiscent of the 1950s. Figure 2.14 shows both the annualized quarterly rate of inflation ($\hat{p}_t = (p_t/p_{t-1})^4 - 1$) and the annual rate of inflation ($\hat{p}_t = (p_t/p_{t-4}) - 1$). Notice that, as with growth, quarterly inflation is highly variable. Inflation rates were low in the 1940s and 1950s, increased throughout the 1960s and 1970s, reached their peaks in the early 1980s, and have generally fallen since then. Inflation in 2009 (annual rate) was 1.2 percent per year. Previously, we looked at GDP growth for the period 1960–2009. The average inflation rate over this same period was:

$$\overline{\hat{p}} = (p_{2009}/p_{1960})^{1/49} - 1$$
$$= (109.8/18.6)^{1/49} - 1 = 0.0369 \text{ or } 3.69 \text{ percent per year.}$$

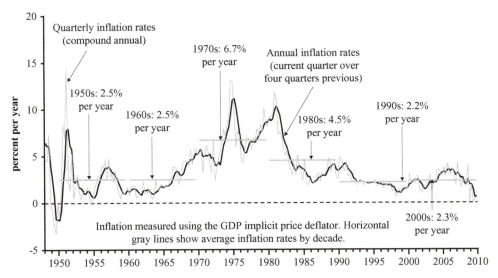

Figure 2.14. Inflation Rates (quarterly and annual), 1948–2009. Although quarterly inflation rates are more volatile than annual inflation rates because of averaging, comparison with Figure 2.11 shows that inflation is less volatile than real GDP growth rates. Inflation was low in the 1950s and 1960s, rose sharply in the 1970s and early 1980s, and has fallen back to lower average levels and lower levels of volatility in the 1990s and 2000s – another aspect of the Great Moderation. *Source:* Bureau of Economic Analysis.

One of the great successes of recent economic policy is often thought to be the taming of inflation, which is revealed by how far the current rate stands below past rates. Falling inflation rates over the past two decades were a worldwide phenomenon. But as Table 2.4 shows, many countries showed some acceleration of inflation in the run-up to the world economic crisis, beginning in 2008. One striking feature of the table is that the G-7 (large industrialized countries) typically – although not uniformly – report lower rates of inflation than the rest of the world.

2.7 Economic Behavior and the National Accounts: Aggregate Demand and Supply – A Prelude to Later Chapters

The national accounts give us a way of measuring the economy and presenting facts about it: How much is produced? How much of production is consumed? How fast is output growing? How fast are prices changing? Such descriptions are just a start. To understand not only what has happened, but why it has happened and what is likely to happen and how policy might affect the outcome, we must go much deeper.

The national-income-accounting identities remind us that the various parts of the economy are interconnected. What happens in one part of the economy has repercussions for other parts. The accounts have to add up.

Table 2.4. *Inflation Rates for Selected Countries (based on the GDP-implicit-price deflator)*

	Average of Rate of Inflation, 1998–2008 (percent per year)	Rate of Inflation, 2008 (percent per year)
The G-7		
Japan	–0.1	–1.4
Germany	1.6	2.6
France	1.8	2.8
Canada	2.3	2.4
Italy	2.4	3.3
United States	2.9	3.8
United Kingdom	2.9	4.0
Other G-20		
Saudi Arabia	1.4	9.9
China	1.7	5.9
European Union	2.2	3.3
South Korea	3.1	4.6
Australia	3.2	4.4
India	5.3	8.3
South Africa	5.3	9.9
Mexico	6.7	5.1
Brazil	6.9	5.7
Argentina	7.6	8.6
Indonesia	11.7	10.0
Russia	21.7	14.1
Turkey	29.6	10.4
Selected Other Countries		
Hong Kong	–0.7	4.3
Singapore	1.4	6.5
Norway	2.2	3.8
Israel	2.4	4.6
Luxembourg	2.4	3.4
Thailand	2.7	5.5
Egypt	6.7	18.2
Nicaragua	10.0	19.8
Burundi	10.0	24.0
Ethiopia	10.1	43.2
Ukraine	14.0	25.2

Source: International Monetary Fund, *International Financial Statistics.*

It is not possible, for example, to have a government budget deficit and, at the same time, to have both the Private sector and the Foreign sector in balance. The circular flow diagrams (Figures 2.2–2.5) also remind us that the economy has distinct parts. The chief executive officer of Westinghouse does not ask, "How large a surplus is the government running?" before deciding how much to invest. A worker at a John Deere factory in Des Moines, Iowa, does not ask, "How much will Westinghouse invest?" before deciding what to consume (and, therefore, what to save). A manager at Samsung in Korea does not ask, "How much does William McCormick, the worker in Des Moines, plan to save?" before shipping a DVD player to New York. Yet, somehow the accounts must add up. So, how is it that a hodgepodge of inconsistent plans nevertheless results in economic aggregates that fulfill the identities?

Economic behavior can be viewed from two perspectives. From the *EX ANTE* (or *before-the-fact* or *planning*) perspective, individual actors make independent decisions. That is not to say that they do not take anyone else into account in making their plans, only that complete and conscious coordination is not a precondition for economic action. From the *EX POST* (or *after-the-fact* or *realized*) perspective, the decisions of all economic actors must be consistent. And that is not to say that people must be happy with the way that things turn out, only that they cannot violate the constraints that the economy imposes on them. The national accounts add up – that is, they obey the four accounting identities – *ex post*. *Ex ante*, there is no reason for the plans of any two economic actors to be coordinated.

Two key institutions coordinate economic behavior – the monetary/ financial system and the price system. The monetary/financial system facilitates exchange, while at the same time, ensuring that people abide by their budget constraints. I can buy only if I have, or can borrow, the necessary funds. The price system directs people's choices by raising prices when demand exceeds supply and lowering them when supply exceeds demand. The details of these mechanisms belong more to courses in monetary and financial economics and to microeconomics than to intermediate macroeconomics. Yet, the principles involved are easily illustrated with economic aggregates.

Recall the inflow-outflow identity, repeated here as

$$I + G + TR + EX \equiv S + T + IM. \qquad (2.4)$$

Now imagine that the U.S. economy consisted only of consumers and firms (i.e., there was no government or foreign trade). The identity then collapses to $I \equiv S$ – realized investment must equal realized savings. Now, suppose that the consumers, with total disposable income of $6,000 billion, collectively planned to consume $5,400 billion and, so, to save $600 billion, while firms collectively planned to invest only $500 billion. Planned savings exceeds planned investment. What will happen to force savings and investment to equality *ex post* when they are unequal *ex ante*?

In the example, planned savings is too high relative to planned investment. Another way to put this is that consumers' plans to purchase goods fall short of firms' plans to supply those goods. An early sign that firms are selling less than they planned is that inventories begin to rise. Car dealers who normally stock cars in their lots equal to thirty days' worth of sales find that the unsold cars and the lower rate of sales increase their stock to thirty-five or forty days. The shelves in supermarkets and warehouses become fuller. Stocks of unsold goods (as well as stocks of raw materials and works in progress) count as part of capital, so that changes in these stocks or inventories count as investment. The increase of inventories is, therefore, recorded as additional investment in the national accounts. If the failure of consumers to purchase what firms had intended to sell leaves the firms holding $100 billion worth of inventories, investment has risen by $100 billion. Now the accounts balance: $S = \$600$ billion $= \$500$ billion (planned investment) $+ \$100$ billion (unplanned inventory investment) $= \$600$ billion $= I$.

The accounts balance *ex post* no matter what. Yet, in this case, the firms are not happy. Their plans have been thwarted. Unwanted inventories are building up and their profits are falling. This cannot be the end of the story. The typical firm finding itself with disappointing sales will not go on producing and adding to inventories. It may adjust its plans in at least two ways. It is likely to lower its prices in order to encourage sales. And it is likely to cut back on production, laying off workers. Production is brought more into line with demand. Of course, aggregate incomes also fall. The lower incomes force consumers to reduce their spending and/or their savings.

This too is not the end of the story. Both firms and consumers will continue to adjust their spending and production plans until planned investment and planned savings are brought back into line. This highly desirable state in which the plans of savers and the plans of investors are compatible is called **MACROECONOMIC EQUILIBRIUM**. When the economy is in equilibrium all the national accounting identities hold *ex post*, as they always do, and they hold *ex ante* as well ($I = S$ and $I^{planned} = S^{planned}$). Even without the simplifying assumptions of no government and no foreign trade, equilibrium is the situation in which the national-income-accounting identities (equations (2.1)–(2.4)) hold both *ex ante* and *ex post*. In equilibrium, because everyone's plans are realized, there are no incentives for further adjustments.

Macroeconomics is fundamentally about economic behavior, not about description or accounting. Still, the national accounts provide the framework within which we can investigate macroeconomic behavior. As we emphasized in section 2.2, the key distinction in the national accounts is between production (or supply) and expenditure (demand). Firms produce real goods, which become part of GDP when they are supplied across the production boundary. Households and other purchasers demand goods, directing a flow of monetary expenditure toward firms. Consider the product-expenditure identity, repeated here as

$$Y \equiv C + I + G + NX. \tag{2.1''}$$

The left-hand side of this equation can be thought of as production or **AGGREGATE SUPPLY (AS)**, while the right side can be thought of as expenditure or **AGGREGATE DEMAND (AD)**, so that the identity could be written as

$$Production \equiv Expenditure$$

or as

$$AS \equiv AD.$$

In the rest of this book, we will mainly try to understand economic behavior as the process of the coordination of economic planning decisions seen from the separate perspectives of aggregate supply and aggregate demand.

Summary

1. GDP, defined as the value of all the final goods and services produced within the borders of a country in a certain period, measures the size of the economy.
2. GDP is an example of a *flow*; that is, it measures the value of production *per unit time*. Wealth is an example of a *stock*; that is, it measures the value of asset holdings *at a certain time*.
3. The economy can be divided into four sectors: firms, households, government, and the foreign sector. Flows of real goods and services between sectors are matched by monetary/financial flows of equal value running the opposite direction.
4. Firms purchase factors of production (labor, land, capital, and raw materials) and use these to produce final goods and services. Only those goods that cross the production boundary – that is, those that firms sell to other sectors or to firms as investment goods to be used in other periods – count as final.
5. Financial markets direct funds from sectors with excess savings toward sectors whose spending exceeds their financial resources.
6. Government services are regarded as final (so that the government is regarded as a productive sector), even though they are not purchased service-by-service, but mostly paid for out of general tax revenues.
7. The foreign sector supplies goods (imports) to the domestic economy and receives part of its production (exports). Imbalances between exports and

imports result in net flows of financial assets that are directed through financial markets to sectors with excess expenditures.

8. Two primary identities organize the national accounts: (i) the product-expenditure identity ($Y \equiv C + I + G + NX$); and (ii) the disposable-income identity ($YD \equiv Y - T + TR \equiv C + S$). Two other useful identities can be derived from them: (iii) the sectoral-deficits identity ($[G - (T - TR)] + [I - S] + [EX - IM] \equiv 0$); and (iv) the inflow-outflow identity ($I + G + EX \equiv S + (T - TR) + IM$).

9. Reasonable comparisons of GDP between different times require an adjustment to account for the changing purchasing power of the dollar (i.e., inflation). The GDP price (implicit) price deflator provides a measure of that purchasing power. Real GDP is just nominal GDP (i.e., GDP measured at current market prices) expressed in the constant dollars of a selected year.

10. Real GDP measures the size of the economy, but individual welfare is more influenced by GDP per capita. There is little relationship between the size of GDP and GDP per capita. Some economically large countries have small GDP per capita, while some economically tiny countries have large GDP per capita.

11. Graphs of the growth rates of GDP or of the logarithm of GDP help us to make comparisons of growth over time. High after World War II, GDP growth in the United States slowed markedly, starting in the mid-1970s.

12. Generally rising prices are known as inflation; generally falling prices as deflation. The growth rate of a price index (e.g., the GDP price deflator) measures inflation. Inflation typically favors debtors and deflation creditors. Extended deflation is rare in the modern world, although since the early 1990s Japan provides one example.

13. The production of final goods and services (GDP seen from the view of firms) is aggregate supply. The purchase of that production (GDP seen from the view of the other sectors) is aggregate demand. The national accounts always balance so that aggregate supply and aggregate demand are equal *ex post*. But the plans of aggregate suppliers and aggregate demanders are not automatically coordinated *ex ante*. The substance of macroeconomics concerns the problem of coordinating those plans.

Key Concepts

gross domestic product (GDP)	transfer payments
income	government services
wealth	exports
intermediate goods and services	imports
factors of production	national income and product accounts
consumption expenditure	(NIPA)
investment	aggregate income
government expenditure	disposable income
taxes	nominal value

real value	*ex post*
GDP (implicit price) deflator	macroeconomic equilibrium
inflation	aggregate supply
deflation (disinflation)	aggregate demand
ex ante	

Suggestions for Further Reading

Eugene P. Seskin and Robert P. Parker. "A Guide to the NIPA's." *Survey of Current Business*, March 1998. (Available electronically from the U.S. Department of Commerce, Bureau of Economic Analysis: www.bea.gov/scb/account_articles/national/0398niw/maintext.htm).

Landefeld, J. Steven, Eugene P. Seskin, and Barbara M. Fraumeni. "Taking the Pulse of the Economy: Measuring GDP," *Journal of Economic Perspectives* 22(2), Spring 2008, 193–216. (Available electronically from the U.S. Department of Commerce, Bureau of Economic Analysis: www.bea.gov/about/pdf/jep_spring2008.pdf).

Problems

Data for this exercise are available on the textbook website under the link for Chapter 2 (appliedmacroeconomics.com). Before starting these exercises, the student should review the relevant portions of the *Guide to Working with Economic Data*, including sections G.1–G.4, G10, and G.11.

Problem 2.1. Figure 2.6 shows the shares of the various sources of aggregate demand (C, I, G, NX) in GDP (Y) for a particular year. How do these shares change over time? Using annual data and the product-expenditure identity in the form (2.1″), divide both sides of the identity by Y to yield: $1 \equiv C/Y + I/Y + G/Y + NX/Y$. The left-hand side is now the sum of the shares of the components, and the identity shows that they add up to 100 percent. Before making any calculations, write down your conjectures about the data: Do you guess that the rank order of the shares shown in Figure 2.6 are consistent over time? Would you guess that any of the shares trend up or down over time? Which shares do you think show the greatest fluctuations? Now calculate each of these shares from 1947 through the most recently available data. (Excel hint: Be sure to multiple by 100 so that your data displays as percentage points.)

   (a) Plot each series on the same graph.

   (b) Calculate the mean, standard deviation, and coefficient of variation for each share and present them in a table.

   (c) Using the information in (a) and (b), write a short description of the behavior of the shares over time and evaluate your conjectures in light of the evidence of your graph and descriptive statistics.

The following table supplies data that are used in the next three problems.

	1996	2000	2000
	Constant 1995 NZ$, Millions	Current NZ$, Millions	Constant 1995 NZ$, Millions
GDP	95,670		
Consumption		68,439	63,635
Savings	16,997		
Investment	21,336	22,783	21,184
Government Spending on Goods and Services		20,464	
Exports	27,084		38,386
Imports	26,570	39,252	36,497
Government Budget Surplus		−385	−358
Taxes	33,427		
Transfer Payments	11,865	14,361	13,353
Disposable Income	74,109		
Government Expenditure	28,574		32,380
	(1995 = 100)	(1995 = 100)	(1995 = 100)
GDP Price Deflator	101.64	107.55	
	millions	millions	millions
Population	3.65	3.78	3.78

Source: International Monetary Fund, *International Financial Statistics.*

Problem 2.2. Using the national-income-accounting identities and your knowledge of nominal-to-real conversions, fill in the missing data in the previous table.

Problem 2.3. Using the previous table as completed in Problem 2.2, verify that each of the four national-income-accounting identities holds in 2000 (in current dollars).

Problem 2.4.

(a) Compute the average growth rate of real GDP between 1996 and 2000.

(b) GDP in 1999 in current dollars was NZ$107,403 million and in 1995 dollars was NZ$103,621 million. What was the annual rate of growth of real GDP in 2000?

(c) What is the average rate of inflation between 1996 and 2000?

(d) What is the annual rate of inflation in 1996?

(e) What is the per capita income in 2000 current dollars? (Be careful with units; express results in NZ$/head.)

Problem 2.5. Figure 2.11 shows the growth rate of real GDP calculated at an annual rate (current quarter relative to the same quarter a year earlier) and at an annualized quarterly rate. The quarterly rate is obviously more variable than the annual rate. To put a number on the difference in variability, first use data for real GDP to calculate both series. Then, compute the variance and standard deviation of each series, starting in 1948:1. Does your calculation bear out the visual impression of Figure 2.11?

Problem 2.6. Figure 2.14 shows the inflation rate calculated at an annual rate (current quarter relative to the same quarter a year earlier) and at an annualized quarterly rate. The quarterly rate is obviously more variable than the annual rate. To put a number on the difference in variability, first use data for the GDP implicit price deflator to calculate both series. Then, compute the variance and standard deviation of each series, starting in 1948:1. Does your calculation bear out the visual impression of Figure 2.14?

Problem 2.7. The "baby boom" was one of the major demographic episodes of the twentieth century. It is generally agreed to have started at the end of World War II in 1945. Using any relevant calculations of growth rates or graphs of population, assign a date to the end of the baby boom. Explain your method and the reason for your choice.

Problem 2.8. Presidents get more blame and take more credit for the state of the economy than they deserve. Nevertheless, presidential terms make convenient reference points for thinking about history. Calculate and display in a table the average annual rates of real GDP growth and inflation (using the GDP implicit price deflator) for each presidential term starting with Eisenhower (refer to Table 1.1 in Chapter 1 for the dates of terms and update to the most recent president). Make another table listing the presidents from highest to lowest GDP growth and lowest to highest inflation (best to worst in each case). On the basis of these two tables, which president do you regard as most successful (or as the luckiest) economically? Explain your own balancing of real GDP and inflation as factors in your assessment.

Problem 2.9. The chairmen of the Federal Reserve System are often regarded as having more direct influence over the current economy than presidents. Repeat the exercise in Problem 2.8 substituting Federal-Reserve chairmen for presidents, starting with T. B. McCabe in 1948. (Again, consult Table 1.1 for their names and dates and update the information in the table to include any chairmen for dates later than shown on the table.)

Problem 2.10. The quarterly rate of real consumption (2005 constant dollars) in 2009:4 was $13,150 billion and in 2010:1, $13,255 billion. What is the rate of growth at a basic quarterly rate? At a compound annual rate?

Problem 2.11. Real GDP in Germany in 1980 was DM 1945 billion and in 1985 was DM 2062 billion. What are the compound average rates of growth for the period 1980–1985? If Germany had kept the same compound average growth rate, what would the level of real GDP have been in 2010?

Problem 2.12. Real GDP (1990 constant pounds) in the United Kingdom in 1998:4 was £636 billion, and in 1960:2 was £264 billion. What were the compound average rates of growth rate over this period?

Problem 2.13. Using nothing but the data given in the following table and your knowledge of growth rates, give your estimates of the missing data in the following table. Which of these estimates do you trust more? Explain.

Year	Canadian Real GDP (constant 1995 C$, billions)	Canadian Population (millions)
1991	657.55	
1992	662.58	
1993		28.95
1994	704.86	
1995	721.26	29.62

Source: International Monetary Fund, *International Financial Statistics.*

Problem 2.14. Using annual data for nominal GDP and the GDP implicit price deflator, create a graph of real GDP with two lines: one in the constant dollars of the year of your birth, one in the constant dollars of the current base year for official real GDP data. Plot the same data against a logarithmic scale. What do you notice about the gap between the two lines on the two graphs? Explain your findings.

Problem 2.15. Using the rule of 72 (see the *Guide,* section G.11.3), how long does it take per capita GDP to double at rates of growth of 0.33 percent per year, 1.5 percent per year, 3 percent per year, 13 percent per year? How long does it take population to quadruple at 0.25 percent per year, 1 percent per year, 2 percent per year? How long does it take population to halve at −0.25 percent per year, −1 percent per year?

Problem 2.16. This question is a preparation for Chapter 5. Real GDP growth is not steady. A recession is a prolonged slowdown in economic activity. A common rule of thumb identifies a period of two or more quarters of negative real GDP growth as a *recession* – by convention a recession is dated as running between a peak (the last quarter of positive growth) and the trough (the last quarter of negative growth after the peak). Using the quarterly data from 1947 on and this rule of thumb, identify the recessions in the U.S. economy. Are there any periods that this rule identifies that you would exclude as recessions? Any periods that it fails to identify that you would include? Explain your reasons. (Excel hint: Instead of looking at real GDP numbers directly, compute the first difference $\Delta Y_t = Y_t - Y_{t-1}$. Then one need only look for groups of negative numbers. It is also possible to write more clever formulae for identifying recessions, using Excel's $= if()$ function.)

3

Understanding Gross Domestic Product

In the last chapter we observed that GDP is subtle. In this chapter we clarify some of it subtleties. What conceptual problems arise in defining GDP and its components? How are GDP data collected and processed? How are the detailed national accounts related to the four accounting identities developed in Chapter 2?

How to measure the size of an economy is not straightforward. To reach our modern concepts took centuries of development. National income is not money. Fundamentally, it is all the goods and services that the nation produces. But how can we add up such disparate products as shoes, ships, sealing wax, cabbages, and concert tickets? This is, of course, an old problem known to every schoolchild from arithmetic class. We must find a common unit. So, even though the wealth of the nation does not consist of money, the money value of each product provides the common measure that permits us to add up disparate products. (As we saw in Chapter 2, section 2.4, even after we have expressed GDP in dollars, we have to account for the changing value of the dollar itself. In Chapter 8 we shall consider how to compare the GDPs of different countries that use different monies.)

At the beginning of Chapter 2 we quoted the definition of gross domestic product used by the U.S. Commerce Department's Bureau of Economic Analysis:

Gross domestic product is "the market value of all the final goods and services produced by labor and property located" within the borders of a country within a definite period.

We did not probe too deeply into this definition, although we did notice that virtually every element of the definition hid some subtlety. In this chapter we will explore some of those subtleties. Exactly what does, and what should, the national-income accountant count? How accurate are the national-income data?

3.1 What Is a Final Product?

3.1.1 *Quid Pro Quo*

We begin with the concept of GDP itself. If GDP is the value of the "final goods and services" (or final products), we should ask, what do "final" and "product" mean in this context? Start with "product." Earlier economists, such as Adam Smith (1723–1790), whose *Wealth of Nations* is the starting point of modern economics, argued that only tangible goods had real economic value: bread and beer were products, but the performance of a play or the lecture of a professor was not. This idea was even incorporated into the national accounts of the Soviet Union and other communist countries, which counted gross *material* product. National accounting in modern capitalist economies instead applies a simple test: a product is anything for which there is a market exchange or QUID PRO QUO (Latin for "something for something"). If you purchase a textbook, you give money in exchange, so the textbook is a product. Equally, if you purchase a shoeshine, you give money in exchange, so it too is a product.

The exchange, not the money, is critical. If you trade a motorcycle for a sailboat, there is a *quid pro quo*, so both are products. In contrast, if you give money to a beggar or an old coat to the Salvation Army, there is no *quid pro quo*. The coat or the money may be products, in that they have been involved in exchange previously, but the beggar or the Salvation Army does not supply a good or service in exchange for our donation. Instead, we have made a TRANSFER PAYMENT defined as *a contribution of a valuable good, service, or asset to another party without* quid pro quo. Gifts, payments of insurance policies, lottery winnings, interest payments, welfare payments, and Social Security are examples of transfer payments. Transfer payments are, of course, valuable to the recipient, but, because they do not involve a market exchange and there is no product given in return, they do not contribute to GDP. Transfer payments slice the GDP pie differently, but they do not change the size of the pie.

3.1.2 *Final and Intermediate Products*

Although GDP counts only products, not every product counts in GDP. Only final products are part of GDP. As we saw in the discussion of the circular flow in Chapter 2, section 2.2, a FINAL PRODUCT is *any good that leaves the firm sector (crosses the production boundary) in the period of measurement*. Final products include both **consumer goods** (and services) purchased for direct (and reasonably immediate) use and **capital goods** that are useful in production and are not used up, but endure for use in future periods.

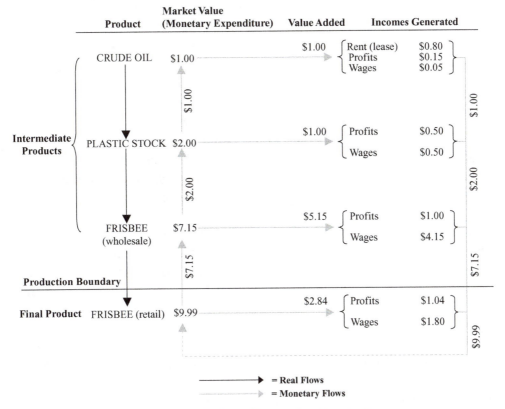

Figure 3.1. A Chain of Production for a Frisbee.

Investment *is the acquisition of newly produced capital goods.* In contrast, an **INTERMEDIATE PRODUCT** is *one that is used up in the process of producing other goods or services in this period.*

To get an idea of why the national accounts focus on final goods, consider the simplified chain of production for a Frisbee shown in Figure 3.1. Crude oil is tapped from a well and sold to a refiner for $1.00, who converts it into plastic stock. The plastic stock is sold to a toy manufacturer for $2.00, who makes a Frisbee and sells it at wholesale to a toy store for $7.15. The toy store sells it at retail to the public for $9.99.

Why should we not count the four distinct products (oil, plastic stock, wholesale Frisbee, retail Frisbee) equally as parts of GDP? The problem is summed up in the old adage "you cannot have your cake and eat it too." When the oil is turned into plastic, it is no longer available for other uses. It is incorporated into the plastic. To count both the oil and the plastic as contributions to GDP is to count the same good twice. Of course the plastic is something more than the oil. It is the oil processed. The extra $1.00 that the plastic sells for – above the cost of the oil input – is the **VALUE-ADDED** in the production of the plastic. Similarly, the toy manufacturer adds $5.15 in value, and the retailer another $2.84. If we counted the full value of each of the goods in GDP, then the production of a Frisbee would account for $20.14 (= $1.00 + $2.00 + $7.15 + $9.99). Yet, by the time that the Frisbee has been sold at retail, these earlier goods have been used up in its production. The value of the parts cannot exceed the value of the whole. The problem is that in reaching the value of $20.14, because oil has been incorporated into the plastic, the plastic into the Frisbee, and the wholesale Frisbee into the retail Frisbee, the value of the oil has been counted four times, the value of the plastic three times, and the value-added by the Frisbee manufacturer twice. Each should be counted only once. *Double-counting* occurs whenever the value of an intermediate good and the value of the good that it helps to produce are both counted.

If, instead of adding up the full value of each of the intermediate products and the final product, we add up only the incremental value at each stage of production (the value-added), double-counting is eliminated. The value-added of the oil production is $1.00. The value-added of the plastic is also $1.00 – that is, its value of $2.00 less the $1.00 spent on the oil input into its production process. The sum of all the values-added is $9.99 (= $1.00 + $1.00 + $5.15 + $2.84), which is exactly equal to the value of the final product. This is an important fact of national-income accounting: *The value of GDP is the sum of the value of all the final goods and services. It is also the sum of all the values-added in producing those goods and services.*

Intermediate goods are important to production, but only their value-added is ultimately incorporated into GDP. Another way to see why we should not count intermediate goods is to do a thought experiment. Fundamentally, national product is all the particular goods and services produced, and not their monetary values. Now, imagine that the Frisbee manufacturer bought the refinery that produces the plastic. The sale of the plastic would be eliminated from our chain of production because it would now be internal to the firm. It would no longer show up as a $2.00 sale. Total sales, which had been $20.14, would drop to $18.14. But domestic product could not have really changed because, in the end, there is no change in the products available to the public. A Frisbee worth $9.99 has still been produced.

The test of whether or not a product is final has nothing to do with the intrinsic qualities of the product itself, but with where it stands in the chain of production. A product must cross the *production boundary* as shown in Figure 3.1. A product has crossed the production boundary when it leaves the sphere of production *in this period*. It is either consumed (or exported to another country) or invested for use in a future period. A Frisbee is generally a final product, because most are sold to the public. But suppose that one is sold to another company to be used as a promotional gift. It is then part of the advertising expenses associated with the firm's final product and counts, therefore, as an intermediate product. When sold to the public, the Frisbee counts as GDP in that year; when sold as a promotional gift, it does not. Plywood sold to a homeowner to build a playhouse for his daughter crosses the production boundary and counts in GDP; plywood sold by the same lumber yard to a builder is an intermediate product and does not count. Electricity sold to a household counts as GDP; electricity sold to an aluminum smelter does not.

3.1.3 Existing Goods

Suppose that you sell your car. Does the sale add to GDP? Even though the sale stands outside of the sphere of production, your sale must be treated much the same as the sale of an intermediate good. The car does not cross the production boundary at the time that you sell it. When your car was first produced, it did cross the production boundary, and it was counted as part of GDP. To count it when you resell later would be to count the same production a second time.

But suppose that you started a business that bought an old Volkswagen Beetle in Southern California, where they are common and in good shape, shipped it to New York, where they are rare, and resold it. The cost of the car in California (an existing product) does not count in GDP. Yet the difference between the purchase price and the sale price, which includes the cost of the shipping (an intermediate product) and your profit (the return to your brokerage service), adds value to the car and counts in GDP. In a sense, your business is to use the existing Volkswagen-in-California to produce a new product, a Volkswagen-in-New-York.

Many businesses involve buying and reselling existing goods. The direct costs of the existing goods are not part of current GDP, but any brokerage or other value added in reselling such goods contributes to GDP. Buying and selling stocks, bonds, and other financial assets involve billions of dollars of transactions each day, but only a tiny fraction of the value of those transactions, representing the value-added of banks, brokerage houses, insurance companies, and other financial businesses, contributes to GDP.

3.2 Product and Income

The name "gross domestic product" emphasizes production, yet, as we saw in Chapter 2 (sections 2.2–2.3), GDP can be regarded equally as products, income, or value-added. Figure 3.1 again helps us to better understand the point. Starting with the market value of the final product, the upward arrows trace the payments made to earlier stages of production, and the rightward arrows show the value-added at each stage. Of the $9.99 earned by the sale of the Frisbee at retail, $7.15 must be paid to the wholesaler, and $2.84 is the value-added of the retailer. This value-added becomes the *income* of the various parties involved in its production. The diagram shows that the shareholders in the company (the owners of its capital) receive $1.04 in the form of **profit**, while the workers in the store receive $1.80 in the form of wages. The pattern is repeated at each stage of production. Part of the sale price pays for the goods received from an earlier stage of production, and the value-added is divided to form the incomes of the owners of the various FACTORS OF PRODUCTION (wages and salaries for labor, profits for capital, and rents for ownership rights in land, minerals, and intellectual property).

It is worth noting that "profit" is another tricky word. To an economist, profits are the payment to owners for the use of their capital. Profits are the revenues minus costs of firms. But these costs must include *imputed* or **opportunity costs** as well as measured costs. For example, if an oil wholesaler bought oil at $20 a barrel a year ago and sold it today for $30 a barrel, an accountant might report that the initial $20 earned a 50 percent return. But if the price at which the wholesaler could buy oil rose until today it stood at $28 a barrel, then the economist would impute the value of the capital (the stored barrel of oil) to have risen to its replacement cost. Then the profit is only $2 a barrel or 7.1 percent ($= 2/28$). In fact, if the wholesaler could have earned 4 percent interest on the $20 by using it to buy a government bond, then the opportunity cost (what is lost by tying up the funds in the form of oil) reduces the true economic profit to 2.9 percent ($= (2 - 0.06 \times 20)/28$). The national-income accounts make adjustments to accounting profits that bring them more into line with the economists' definitions. Similar adjustments are made for rental income as well.

We have already seen that the value of the final product is equal to the sum of the values-added at each stage of production. Looking again at Figure 3.1, we see that all incomes are generated from the value-added. Consequently, all of the incomes in the chain of production must add up to the value of the final product: rents ($0.80) + profits ($2.59 = $0.15 + $0.50 + $1.00 + $1.04) + wages ($6.50 = $0.05 + $0.50 + $4.15 + $1.80) = value of final product ($9.99).

What is true for the chain of production for a single good is also true for all the chains of production of all the goods and services in society added together to form GDP: *the value of all the incomes in a particular period is equal to the value of all the final products produced (GDP).* Of course, as we shall see in section 3.6, the values of incomes are not recorded as exactly equal to the value of final products in practice because of errors in measurement.

The fact that the value of the incomes generated in its production equals the value of the final product means that the owners of the various factors of production could, in principle, purchase all of the product that they helped to produce. This is shown in Figure 3.1 as the arrow that connects the incomes generated to the sale of the Frisbee. The last segment of this arrow is shown as dashed to indicate that the owners of the factors of production could afford to buy their own product, but need not actually do so. Though they may buy a Frisbee from time to time, typically they will want to buy groceries, gasoline, video games, and other goods and services produced by other owners of other factors of production. The arrow nonetheless reinforces an important point about the economy: *sales generate the incomes that pay for the sales.*

3.3 Domestic versus National Product

Until 1991, the Bureau of Economic Analysis, the U.S. government agency that keeps the national accounts, featured **GROSS NATIONAL PRODUCT (GNP)** rather than gross *domestic* product (GDP) in its press releases and public statements. What is the distinction? Gross domestic product counts all of the income generated *within the borders of a particular country.* Gross national product counts all the incomes *accruing to the residents of a particular country.*

Ford is a large American-owned automobile company. It is also a major producer of cars in Europe. Cars produced by Ford in, say Great Britain, are part of British GDP. Similarly, the wages earned by Ford workers in Britain count in the incomes paid for by British GDP. The profits of Ford's British operations, however, are paid to the American parent company and accrue mainly to American shareholders. Those profits are a factor-income flow into the United States. Of course, it works the other way as well. British Petroleum (BP) is a large oil company with operations in the United States. Its profits form an outflow from the United States into Great Britain. The Dutch, the British, the Japanese, and others own substantial interests in American operations, just as the Americans own substantial interests overseas.

For any country **NET INCOME FROM ABROAD** equals *income receipts from the rest of the world* less *income payments to the rest of the world.* A simple equation relates GDP and GNP:

$$GNP = GDP + net\ income\ from\ abroad.$$

GNP can be greater or less than GDP (see Table 3.1). The United Kingdom has substantial ownership of capital in foreign countries, which of course, earns significant income. Its GNP in 2008 was £1,474 billion – somewhat greater than its GDP of £1,443 billion. Its net income flows from abroad were 2.2 percent of its GDP. Many of the plantations and other industries in Costa Rica are owned by foreigners, who receive their profits. Its GNP in 2008 was 15,198 billion colones – significantly less than its GDP of

Table 3.1. *GDP versus GNP for Selected Countries, 2008*

Countries	GDP	Net Income Flows from Abroad		GNP
		Value	Percent of GDP	
The G–7				
Canada	1,602	–15	–0.9	1,588
France	1,950	13	0.7	1,963
Germany	2,488	41	1.6	2,529
Italy	1,570	–22	–1.4	1,548
Japan	507,371	16,735	3.3	524,106
United Kingdom	1,443	31	2.2	1,474
United States	14,441	142	1.0	14,583
Other Countries				0
Brazil	2,890	–72	–2.5	2,818
Costa Rica	15,610	–411	–2.6	15,198
Hong Kong	1,677	81	4.8	1,758
Kuwait*	39,788	2,720	6.8	42,508
Singapore	257,419	–7,031	–2.7	250,388
South Africa	2,284	–74	–3.2	2,210
South Korea	1,023,938	6,699	0.7	1,030,637
Thailand	9,103	–419	–4.6	8,684

Notes: Fourth column equals the sum of the first two. Except for column 4, data are in national currency units – billions, except millions where indicated by an asterisk.
Source: International Monetary Fund, *International Financial Statistics*.

15,609 billion colones. Its net income flows to foreigners were 2.6 percent of its GDP. Kuwait presents an extreme case. During the Gulf War of 1990, production in Kuwait (mainly oil) ceased, so its GDP fell to near zero. Yet, because Kuwait had used its oil profits to accumulate substantial assets in other countries, its GNP remained at about $3,500 per Kuwaiti resident. In 2008, net income flows from abroad were still 6.8 percent of GDP.

Is GDP or GNP a better measure of national product? For the United States, the two are so close that the question hardly arises. For countries in which the two diverge, it depends on what question one seeks to answer. For example, GDP is clearly more relevant to employment, because it measures production within a country, but GNP is more relevant to questions such as the distribution of income or public finance, because it measures all the income available to the economy.

3.4 Depreciation and Net Product

"Capital" has a number of useful, but sometimes incompatible, meanings. In macroeconomics CAPITAL is defined as *the physical means of production that endure from period to period*. A factory building or a stamping machine or a computer is a typical type of capital. As capital is used in the production process, we can think of it as supplying **capital services**. Capital goods generally have finite lives or require some expenditure on maintenance. The value of the wear and tear of capital, known as DEPRECIATION or CAPITAL CONSUMPTION, is a measure of the capital services it provides.

The most obvious example of capital depreciation is the physical wear and tear on machinery. A truck, a forklift, a milling machine, or a factory roof wears out with time and use. The maintenance needed to keep the means of production working efficiently is a measure of the depreciation. Some capital can be used virtually forever if it is properly maintained. Some modern highways in England run on the ancient Roman roads, and Roman aqueducts still supply water to some Italian towns. Other capital has a natural lifespan and becomes too worn to maintain at a reasonable cost.

Increasingly, however, there is another sort of depreciation – *technological obsolescence*. Computers provide a good example. A vintage IBM 8086 personal computer may still function in 2011 exactly as when new in 1985. Yet, economically, it has depreciated to the point that it is valuable only as scrap or a curiosity, or, perhaps, as a doorstop. The computer is not able to run up-to-date software or at the speeds needed for economically efficient applications. So, even though it is physically in nearly new condition, economically it has no value at all. Recent estimates place the depreciation rate of personal computers at about 50 percent per year: a four-year-old computer, then, is worth about 1/16th its original value.

An economy that did not replace or maintain its capital could achieve a higher level of production in the short run, but could not maintain it in the long run. As a result, a certain amount of the new production of capital goods each year must go simply to replace or maintain the worn-out capital stock.

Recall that the production and acquisition of new capital goods are known as *investment*. (We must be careful to distinguish the macroeconomist's use of "investment" from other uses, such as that of the financial world in which "investment" means the purchase of an asset, real or financial, new or existing.) Part of investment covers the depreciation of the existing capital, and only the remainder can be used to increase the stock of capital. **Gross investment** includes all investment goods, while **net investment** includes only those goods that add to the capital stock:

$$\textit{Net Investment} = \textit{Gross Investment} - \textit{Depreciation}.$$

Gross investment is part of GDP and GNP. Accounting for depreciation turns GNP into *net national product* (or *NNP*):

$$\textit{Net National Product} = \textit{Gross National Product} - \textit{Depreciation}.$$

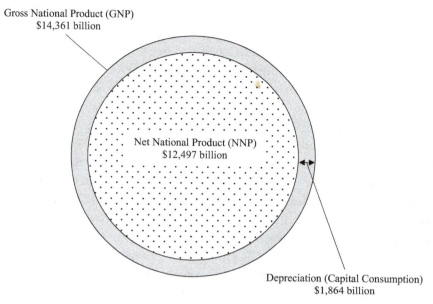

Gross National Product (GNP)
$14,361 billion

Net National Product (NNP)
$12,497 billion

Depreciation (Capital Consumption)
$1,864 billion

Figure 3.2. GNP and NNP for the United States, 2009. *Source:* Bureau of Economic Analysis.

Although the value of gross national product answers the question, "How much did the economy produce?," the value of net national product answers the question, "How much of that production can be consumed while keeping the productive capacity of the economy intact?" Figure 3.2 shows data on the relationship of GNP and NNP for the United States in 2009. Depreciation is a significant fraction of GNP – about 13 percent.

3.5 Limits, Judgments, and Puzzles

National accounting aims to reduce the myriad complexities of the economy into a few numbers. Any such reduction must involve some loss of information. Similarly, decisions must be made about exactly where to draw the lines among different categories – say, between intermediate and final goods or between consumption and investment goods. Reasonable people might design the national accounts differently, because they make these judgments differently or because they insist on highlighting some information instead of other information. Let us consider a few of the important cases.

3.5.1 Investment or Consumption?

The reason that we distinguish between investment and consumption is that investment goods become part of the capital stock. They endure from one period to the next and give up their services over time. Imagine that the national accountants treated an eighteen-wheeler tractor trailer rig with a useful life of twenty years as a consumption good – part of GDP in its year of production, but not part of the capital stock in later years. In later years, the big rig would in fact add to the productive capacity of the economy, but its services (and its depreciation) would not be measured. Producing more output with fewer measured inputs, the economy would appear more productive than it was in fact. And when the big rig was finally scrapped, the economy would in fact become less productive, even though the national accountants recorded no fall in the capital stock. Clearly, the big rig must be counted as investment and capital.

But if the big rig must be counted, why not your winter coat? It too endures for several years and delivers its services up over time. In fact, only a few goods or services are truly consumed in the instant: electricity or a live musical performance, perhaps. Most goods last for longer or shorter periods. GDP is typically measured on a quarterly or annual basis. Goods and services that are used up within the quarter – even if they are used up over days or weeks – can reasonably be regarded as pure consumption. These goods are examples of **consumer nondurable goods**. In contrast, goods that last many years, such as washing machines or cars (owned by households, rather than businesses), are **consumer durable goods**. Durable goods are really a sort of capital. National accountants nevertheless usually count only long-lasting goods owned by businesses as capital. (Owner-occupied housing is the lone exception to this rule in American practice.) Where should the line be drawn between nondurables and durables? This is a matter of pragmatic judgment. In the United States, goods that typically last less than three years are classified as nondurables, and longer-lasting goods as durables. Figure 3.3 shows that in the United States in 2009, goods made up only 32 percent of consumption (services made up the rest). Of those goods, about a third were durable and two-thirds nondurable.

Related judgments must be made in the business and government sectors as well. An intermediate good is used up in production, whereas a capital good endures, and only its services are used. Where should the line be drawn? Until recently, computer software was counted as an intermediate good in the national accounts. It is now recognized as a depreciating capital good.

If a health maintenance organization (HMO) builds a hospital or buys a new magnetic-resonance-imaging (MRI) machine, it counts as investment. In American practice until recently, if the Veterans Health Administration, a government agency, made identical expenditures, it would show up in the national accounts in exactly the same way as government expenditure on ink or meals for soldiers – that is, as government "consumption." Surely, the services of a government-owned hospital and a private hospital

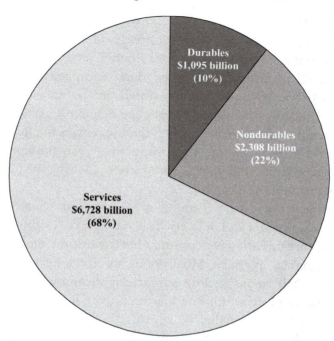

Figure 3.3. The Components of Consumption for the United States, 2009. *Source:* Bureau of Economic Analysis.

or a government-owned airplane and a private airplane are more or less the same – both add to the useful production of the economy, even if the services of the government-owned good are not sold in the market. The American national accounts now distinguish between *government consumption expenditures* and *government gross investment*. Figure 3.4 shows that government investment in the United States in 2009 was a relatively small, but still significant, part of total government spending on goods and services.

Investment generally involves expenditure on goods, not services. Yet, firms often spend large sums of money training workers. Similarly, education is a major item in government budgets, and individuals willingly pay for their own vocational and higher education. Because education results in enduring improvement to the productivity of workers and the capacity for enjoyment of consumers, it can be regarded as investment in **human capital**. National accountants typically ignore human capital and treat education as private or government consumption (or as a corporate intermediate service). Because it is difficult to make any accurate estimate of the monetary value of education, this practice is unlikely to change.

3.5.2 Nonmarket Production

Most of what is counted in GDP is involved in market transactions. In principle, even barter transactions are a kind of market transaction, and – although

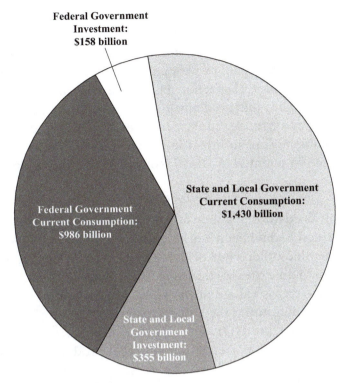

Figure 3.4. Government Spending on Goods and Services, 2009. *Source:* Bureau of Economic Analysis.

easy for official statisticians to miss – they should also be counted. Most non-market production is not counted.

Home Production

People often cook their own meals, clean their own houses, and mow their own lawns when they could in fact have paid someone else to do these jobs. The way GDP is currently measured, if a woman marries her gardener, measured GDP falls, even though the garden is tended just as carefully as before. And GDP rises if you pay your roommate to do your laundry and he pays you to do his laundry, even though just the same clothes are cleaned as before. The national accounts focus on market transactions, yet many non-market activities reflect valuable production.

Some economists and social activists advocate including the value of housework, including childcare, in GDP. In part, they wish to counteract the idea that the only valuable work is paid work and to raise the status of those (mostly women) who work in the home. Ignoring housework, it is thought, understates the national product. Yet, it cuts both ways. Say that a mother enters the paid labor force and pays for childcare. Apparently, GDP has risen by the additional paid income of the mother *and* the childcare worker. If housework is valued, however, the gain to GDP is only the income that the mother earns above and beyond her value in the home, measured in part by the salary of the childcare worker. Conventionally measured GDP would, in this case, overstate the value of homeworkers joining the workforce.

Leisure is a good thing and, as we shall see, in an important sense it is an economic *good* (Chapter 11, section 11.2). The cost of education includes the value of the leisure that students give up in order to attend classes and study. Just as firms surrender money to invest in physical capital, students surrender valuable leisure to invest in human capital. Should not the value of students' time be counted in GDP? Yet, where should we draw the line?

The Third-Party Test

Some economists advocate valuing all leisure time at the wage that a person could have earned had he been working. In a sense, you buy your leisure at the going wage, like other sales of final goods, and it ought to be included in GDP. Taken to an extreme, this suggestion is paradoxical. If every hour of every person's day is valued at the going wage, then measuring GDP is no different from measuring the average wage rate. One of the fundamental purposes of collecting GDP statistics is to distinguish production from nonproduction. If leisure is seen as a nonmarket product, that distinction is lost.

One way around the paradox is to apply a "third-party test": if an activity is one that people with higher incomes or in different circumstances might reasonably be expected to purchase, then this activity ought to be valued and included in GDP. By the third-party test, housework and cooking would be included, but highly personal things, such as personal hygiene or playing video games or other activities that would lose their essential character if done by a third party, would be excluded.

The third-party test means that whenever nonmarket activities are close substitutes for market activities, they should be counted. To do otherwise could be extremely misleading. For example, in many poor countries, large parts of the population have monetary incomes of less than one dollar per day. A moment's reflection should convince anyone that no one could live on what one dollar would buy. The poor in such countries may be subsistence farmers. They consume most of their crop themselves. Only the small "cash crop" might be recorded in official GDP statistics. Equally, in a developing country as production shifts from nonmarket to market production, a greater proportion of total production is typically counted, making the growth rate of GDP appear to be higher than it actually is.

Owner-Occupied Housing

Although a good case can be made that some sorts of home production ought to be included in GDP statistics, in fact most are not. Nevertheless, some nonmarket activities are too economically important to be omitted from the national accounts. If you rent a house, the housing services it provides are valued at your monthly rent. The rental is a market transaction. If you buy the very same house, you would receive the same housing services, but there would no longer be a market transaction. Owner-occupied housing in the United States was 68 percent of the housing stock in 2007, a huge part of the total capital stock.[1] New residential construction sold directly to home owners is an important part of investment. To leave the services of such housing out of GDP would make it a misleading measure of the production of economic goods. It would also make the GDP of countries such as Germany or France, in which substantially more people rent their housing, appear relatively higher. Who owns the title to a house or other capital good should not affect the value of the services it produces. The contribution of owner-occupied housing to GDP is measured by estimating what rent a property would command if it were in fact on the market. Although an estimate is always subject to error, it would be a greater error to ignore its contribution.

Government Services

Government services are another nonmarket activity that cannot be ignored. Although most government services do not involve direct payment for a particular service, some do. A government might own a *nationalized* corporation that sells its services like any other business. Although privatization of nationalized industries has been a worldwide trend for the past thirty years (and nationalization was always small in the United States), governments often own telephone companies, power companies, airlines, railroads, banks, or other industries. The contributions of such industries to GDP can be measured by their market sales of final goods and services. Governments sometimes also charge direct fees for, say, entry into a museum or a park. These fees are rarely the equivalent of true market prices and, so, understate the services provided.

Most government services, in contrast, are paid for through taxes or borrowing, and these payments are not in direct exchange for particular services. Everyone uses the roads or enjoys the protection of the police without a specific payment. Once again, so many resources are used by the government that to ignore these nonmarket contributions to the economy would seriously misrepresent the goods and services consumed. Unlike the case of housing, there are usually not market equivalents for government services that would provide good estimates of their contributions to GDP. Instead, the national-income accountants value government at the full cost of the

---

[1] U.S. Bureau of the Census, *American Housing Survey for the United States: 2007.*

resources that it uses on the ground that the final value of any good that can be produced on a sustained basis must cover all of its costs of production.

Only those parts of government expenditure that can be regarded as contributing to the production of goods and services count as part of GDP. By far the largest parts of government expenditure are direct payments to individuals that, even if they were provided by the private sector, would fail the *quid-pro-quo* test. Interest payments on government debt, Social Security, Medicare, Medicaid, government pensions, and welfare payments – large items in government expenditure – are transfer payments that do not contribute to GDP. Government transfer payments dominate government budgets in most developed countries. Payments for goods (such as aircraft carriers, paper, and computers), services (such as consultants' fees or research contracts), and the wages and salaries of civil servants constitute a much smaller part of total government expenditure. Only expenditures on real goods and services, and not transfers, are used to estimate the contribution of the government to final production and, therefore, to GDP.

3.5.3 *The Black Economy*

The sales of marijuana, cocaine, and other illicit drugs; the earnings of bookies and other promoters of illegal gambling; and prostitution where it is illegal (in the United States everywhere but Nevada) are examples of market transactions that rarely show up in government records and are not typically included in the national accounts. They – alongside other forms of remunerative, but illegal activities – are part of what is sometimes called the BLACK ECONOMY (also known as the *shadow*, *hidden*, *underground*, or *black-market economy*).

Not all the goods and services in the black economy are illegal in themselves. When a contractor installs your new bathroom and takes payment in cash, neglecting to report the income on his taxes, or when a waitress fails to report her tips, they too are part of the black economy. To some extent, the national accounts ignore the black economy *because* the activities are illegal. To record them might be seen to dignify and encourage them. The main reason for ignoring them is that it is too hard to know their true value, because the purveyors and customers of black-economy goods and services have strong incentives to hide them. Countries with high taxes and complicated bureaucracy and business regulation typically have larger black economies.

Ignoring the black economy can seriously understate GDP. Accurate estimates are, naturally, hard to obtain. Table 3.2 gives estimates for some selected countries in the 1990s. It shows that there is a huge variation in most regions of the world. Among industrialized economies, Italy and Sweden

Table 3.2. *The Black Economy in Selected Countries (as a percentage of GNP)*

Western Europe		Central Europe	
Greece Italy	27–30	Hungary Bulgaria	24–28
Spain Portugal Sweden	20–24	Poland Rumania	16–20
Norway Denmark	13–16	Slovakia Czech Republic Former Soviet Union	7–11
Ireland France Netherlands Germany United Kingdom	13–16	Georgia Azerbaijan Ukraine Belarus	28–43
Austria Switzerland	8–10	Russia Lithuania Latvia Estonia	20–27
Africa		**Asia**	
Nigeria	68–76	Thailand	70
Egypt Morocco	39–45	Philippines Sri Lanka Malaysia South Korea	38–50
The Americas			
Guatemala Mexico Peru Panama	40–60	Hong Kong Singapore	13
Chile Costa Rica Venezuela Brazil Paraguay Columbia	25–35	Japan	8–10
United States	8–10		

Source: Bruno S. Frey and Friedrich Schnieder, "Informal and Underground Economy," in Orley Ashenfelter, editor. *International Encyclopedia of Social and Behavioral Science*, vol. 12, *Economics*. Amsterdam: Elsevier, 2000.

are particularly high (20–30 percent of GNP), while the United States and Japan are low (8–10 percent of GNP). But some less developed economies, particularly in Central America, Africa, and Asia, have much larger black economies – as large as 70 percent of GNP for Thailand.

Both the United States and Italy make some effort to estimate the size of the black economy. Italians took substantial pride in *Il sorpasso*, the year 1987 when Italian national accountants first included the black economy in the official measures of GDP and Italy temporarily surpassed Great Britain as the fourth largest economy in the world.

3.5.4 Bads and Regrettables

GDP is the value of final *goods* and services. The term "good" here implies that we are counting things that we value. Electricity is a good. Unfortunately, the generation of electricity almost always involves the production of air pollutants or other undesirable by-products. Even solar or wind power may involve undesirable by-products from the manufacture of the solar cells or windmills. Most other goods and services also involve the production of **bads**. Sometimes these are clearly the costs of manufacture, and their negative value is built right into the price of the good. Sometimes, as with the pollution from electricity generation, some portion of the bad falls on society generally and is not reflected fully in the price of the good. Pollution is an example of what economists call a NEGATIVE EXTERNALITY. Some economists have argued that we should incorporate negative externalities into GDP by subtracting their value from the value of all the goods and services.

Natural resources present a similar case. To compute net national product (NNP) – which is the fraction of GDP that we can use up without impairing the ability of the economy to keep producing goods and services at the same rate – we subtract the depreciation of capital from GDP. The productive capacity of the economy depends not only on produced capital goods but also on limited natural resources. Properly, we should regard, for example, the using up of a finite supply of oil or the impairing of the quality of forest land as depreciation that must be deducted from GDP to compute NNP.

The official national accounts do not adjust either for bads or for the use of finite resources. This partly reflects the bias toward market transactions. It partly reflects the difficulties in obtaining uncontroversial estimates of their value. There is also a conceptual issue. As we shall see in Chapter 9, natural resources are not best thought of as a fixed quantity like a certain amount of water in a bucket. Their *effective* quantity depends on economic as well as physical considerations. There is, for example, an enormous amount of gold dissolved in seawater. Today it is too expensive to extract it commercially. If in the future the price of gold were to rise far enough, then it might become economically feasible to extract. It is hard, then, to say, when we have mined gold, either how close that we have come to the physical limit or what price we should place on unmined or unextracted supplies. How then should untapped gold be valued for the national accounts?

Regrettables are similar to bads. To fight rising crime rates, we hire more police. The national accounts treat the expenditure on the police as a government service. In a perfect world we would not have to have police. We regret the fact that we have to have them to protect us against crime. So, should they be counted as a final good? They might instead be thought of as an intermediate product. Even though, unlike the cost of private security guards, the cost of the police is not paid for specifically by producers and is not reflected in the price of particular goods, socially the police are merely an instrument that helps the economy to function rather than a final good.

The same argument would apply to military expenditure, pollution-control equipment, or any other sort of remedial expenditure. But where do we draw the line? Should expenditure on air conditioning or on heavy winter coats be omitted from GDP because people find them a necessary evil in dealing with climates that are too hot or too cold? Every "necessity" of life – including food, all clothing that is not strictly decorative, and housing – is to some extent regrettable. But how is the national accountant to separate those aspects of expenditure that are mere instruments from those that are truly final in the sense of fulfilling our wants and desires?

3.5.5 GDP and Welfare

Official national accounts often adjust for some nonmarket activities; they rarely adjust for bads or regrettables. Should they do more?

A crucial point is that we may have more than one purpose in mind. For instance, if we wish to compare the overall welfare of the United States to Norway or Mexico, we care about a great deal more than what can be bought and sold. The quality of life may depend on the distribution of GDP among the residents of a country as well as its level (see Chapter 2, section 2.4). And it may depend on such things as whether work is done in or out of paid employment, whether production creates negative externalities, or whether it depletes fixed resources and leisure time. Only if we account for a broad set of factors can we form a good picture of which country has a better life.

Many alternative measures of GDP or indices of quality of life have been suggested. The United Nations, for instance, computes its *Human Development Index*, which ranks countries not only by GDP per capita but factors in life expectancy, literacy, and school enrollment (see Table 3.3). There is a positive association between being rich and scoring high on the index. But it is only a rough one. Norway is number one on the index, four higher than

Table 3.3. *Quality of Life and National Income for Selected Countries*

	Human Development Index (rank)	GDP per Capita (rank)
The G-7		
Canada	4	22
France	8	39
Japan	10	37
United States	13	10
Italy	18	41
United Kingdom	21	32
Germany	22	34
Other Countries		
Norway	1	5
Luxembourg	11	3
Singapore	23	9
Hong Kong	24	14
South Korea	26	51
Mexico	53	81
Saudi Arabia	59	59
Russia	71	73
Brazil	75	101
Turkey	79	92
Thailand	87	116
China	92	132
South Africa	129	80
India	134	165
Ethiopia	171	216
Burundi	174	226

Source: United Nations, Human Development Indicators 2009.
Central Intelligence Agency, *The World Factbook 2008.*

its GDP-per-capita rank; while the United States is number thirteen on the index, three lower than its GDP-per-capita rank.

Some economists have also proposed adjusting GDP to account for the use of exhaustible natural resources or environmental damage. None of these adjustments has become widely accepted.

Human welfare is not always what we seek to measure. If we are interested in understanding the functioning of money in the economy, we care about transactions that involve money or that are closely related to ones that do. In that case, to include the value of the environment, literacy, or life expectancy, or to ignore military expenditure or pollution-control equipment might seriously distort our understanding of the pertinent issues.

Adjustments may pose difficult problems in gathering the basic data or producing commonly agreed estimates of key elements. Ultimately, our judgments must be pragmatic. What do we want the national accounts for? Can they usefully be made to serve that purpose? What we count depends greatly on what question we seek to answer. There is no reason to expect that one measure will suit all purposes equally well. It is also essential to remember that any measure, such as GDP, that reduces a large amount of information to a single number must lose some of the information. Sometimes this loss of information is actually positive. The old adage is that you cannot see the forest for the trees. Macroeconomics is about forests, not trees. Sometimes the information loss is clearly negative. And here we have a choice. One way of counting focuses our attention in one direction and, if we change the way of counting, we may cast light in another useful direction. An alternative is to give up the idea that we must reduce our information to a single number. It might be better, for example, to know that a 20 percent increase in electricity production adds $60 billion to GDP *and* 5 billion tons per year to greenhouse-gas emissions than to have the national-income accountants place a value on the costs of emissions (say $20 billion) and report only the adjusted addition to GDP ($40 billion).

GDP should not be considered the all-purpose measure of welfare. This is clearly true if we think of welfare as human happiness. Happiness is so more than getting and spending, buying and selling, owning and controlling. Recently, there have been a number of surveys about happiness. The survey reported in Table 3.4 adjusts the life expectancy in each country according to the subjective degree of happiness that its citizens report to create a measure of *happy life expectancy*. Again, although there is a positive association between happiness and high GDP per capita, it is not precise. The United States does quite well (13th in happiness), yet it is eclipsed by such rich countries as Switzerland and Canada, and even by substantially poorer ones like Malta. Costa Rica, Mexico, Brazil, and China are much happier than their GDP rank, while the African countries and the countries of the former Soviet Union appear to be fairly miserable.

The sources of human happiness and welfare are important questions for sociology, psychology, and statecraft. They may even be important questions for some parts of economics. Nonetheless, for most questions in macroeconomics, the conventional national accounts, which rely almost exclusively on market information, are generally adequate.

3.6 Measuring GDP

3.6.1 Sources and Methods

In principle the national accounting identities give us three alternative and largely independent ways of measuring GDP. (All three are displayed in

Table 3.4. *Happiness and National Income for Selected Countries*

	Happy Life Expectancy[a]		GDP per Capita
	Years	Rank[b]	(rank)[c]
The G-7			
Canada	64	5	22
United States	58	19	10
United Kingdom	57	22	32
Germany	55	26	34
Italy	54	30	41
France	53	35	39
Japan	51	41	37
Other Countries			
Costa Rica	67	1	95
Switzerland	65	4	18
Norway	62	8	5
Luxembourg	61	11	3
Mexico	60	15	81
Malta	56	24	53
Brazil	54	32	102
South Korea	47	57	51
China	46	59	133
Turkey	41	74	92
Russia	36	92	73
India	35	98	165
Ukraine	34	103	124
Moldova	33	106	171
South Africa	30	113	80
Nigeria	26	120	178

[a] *Happy life expectancy* is life expectancy multiplied by the average subjective degree of happiness in each country on a scale of 0 to 1.
[b] Ranks 148 countries.
[c] Ranks 227 countries.
Source: R. Veenhoven. *World Database of Happiness*, Erasmus University, Rotterdam. Available at: *worlddatabaseofhappiness.eur.nl*. Downloaded 31 October 2009.
Central Intelligence Agency, *The World Factbook 2008*.

Figure 3.1.) The **EXPENDITURE** (or **PRODUCT**) **METHOD** adds up the values of all the final goods and services. The **INCOME METHOD** adds up all the incomes. The **VALUE-ADDED METHOD** adds up all of the values added at different stages of production. Most countries use at least two methods. The United States uses the income and expenditure methods. Unlike the United States, many countries levy value-added taxes (VAT), for which firms are required to keep strict records of their payments to earlier stages of

Table 3.5. *Main Census Bureau Surveys Used in the NIPA Estimates*

Survey	Sample	Main Data Used	Main GDP Component Affected
Annual Retail Trade Survey	22,000 retail firms	Sales, inventories	Consumption of goods, inventory change
American Housing Survey	55,000 homes	Occupied housing, rents	Housing consumption, rental income
Current Population Survey	50,000 households	Occupied housing	Housing consumption, rental income
Service Annual Survey	30,000 service businesses	Sales	Consumption of services, software investment
Annual Survey of Manufactures	55,000 establishments	Shipments, inventories	Fixed investment, inventory change, capital consumption
Annual Wholesale Trade Survey	7,100 whole firms	Inventories	Inventory change
Annual Survey of Government Finances	All state and local governments	Miscellaneous	Government consumption and investment, consumption of services, indirect business taxes

Source: Joseph Ritter, "Feeding the National Accounts," *Federal Reserve Bank of St. Louis Review*, vol. 82, no. 2 (March/April 2000), p. 12.

production. Some of these countries (e.g., Great Britain) find it relatively easy to use all three methods.

Whichever methods are used, the national-income-and-product accounts compile information from a wide variety of sources. Although a few sources, such as the Annual Survey of Government Finances or Federal tax returns on corporations, provide essentially complete information on some components, most of the information takes the form of selected surveys – for example, the American Housing Survey of 55,000 homes. The surveys must, in turn, be scaled up to account for all those not actually surveyed in much the same way that political opinion polls extrapolate from a sample to the likely outcome of an election. Table 3.5 shows the main surveys used in annual NIPA estimates. Figure 3.5 presents a more systematic picture of the data sources for both the product and the income accounts.

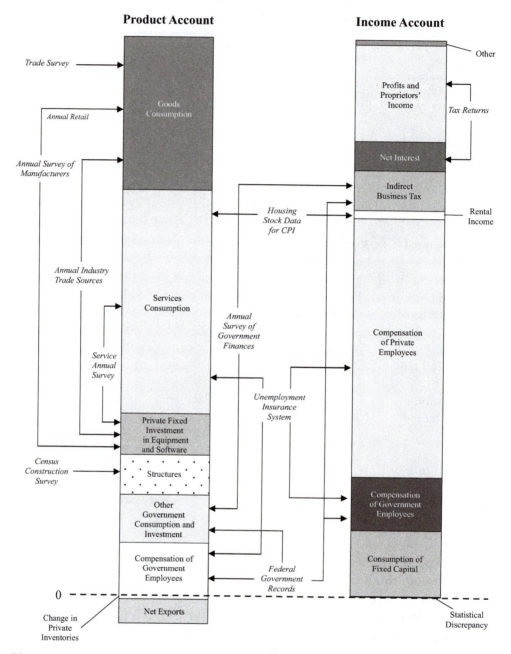

Figure 3.5. NIPA Data Sources, 2009. *Source:* Redrawn from Joseph Ritter, "Feeding the National Accounts," *Federal Reserve Bank of St. Louis Review*, vol. 82, no. 2 (March/April 2000), p. 15, figure 3; data updated to 2008.

Many of the data sources used in constructing annual estimates are not available more frequently. To produce quarterly NIPA estimates, the national-income accountants must impute the unobserved quarterly values. They use either less reliable, but more frequently reported, sources or they make educated guesses.

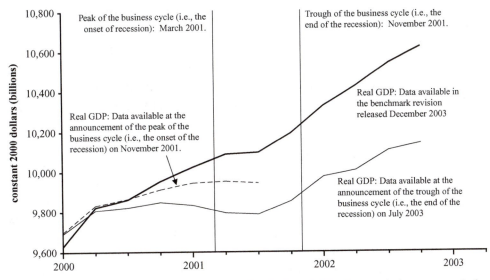

Figure 3.6. The Vanishing Recession of 2001. The NBER dated the onset of the recession in 2001 when it had evidence of only one quarter of falling GDP from an advance estimate. Its judgment appeared vindicated by final estimates showing a clear three quarters of falling GDP. But the comprehensive revision of 2003 showed that, while GDP slowed, it never fell in any quarter during the "recession." *Source:* Bureau of Economic Analysis.

Which method is best? Each can be used to cross-check the other. In principle, each should yield the same value for GDP. Of course, in practice they do not. It is impossible to catch and record or to estimate accurately every component of income or expenditure. The Bureau of Economic Analysis (BEA) believes that, overall, the expenditure method is the more accurate. As a result, the BEA presents the difference between the two estimates as a **statistical discrepancy** used to adjust the income accounts to make them agree with the expenditure accounts. The statistical discrepancy is typically on the order of 0.5 percent of GDP. Instead of assigning discrepancies to one side of the national accounts, the British present the average of the values determined by all three methods (including the value-added method) as the best estimate.

3.6.2 Revisions

The national accounts suffer not only from discrepancies among the different methods of counting, but they are also frequently revised – often by relatively large amounts. The recession of 2001 illustrates how such revisions can sometimes seriously cloud our understanding of the state of the economy (Figure 3.6). Normally, a recession involves two or more quarters of falling GDP. On 26 November 2001, the National Bureau of Economic Research (NBER) announced that the recession had begun in March of

2001. The starting date appeared peculiar because, based on the data available in November, GDP did not begin to fall until the third quarter of 2001. On 17 July 2003, the NBER announced that the recession ended in November of 2001. By that time, revised data appeared to vindicate their choice of March 2001 for the onset of the recession. The new data showed that GDP had indeed fallen for three quarters in all, starting in the first quarter of 2001. Within weeks, the peculiarity of the 2001 recession reemerged. The benchmark revisions to GDP released on 10 December 2003, showed, first, that GDP was markedly higher than previously thought in almost every quarter from 2000 through 2002, and that it did not fall in any quarter. If a recession requires falling GDP, the most recent revisions suggest that there was no recession at all in 2001. (The NBER would respond that its assessments are based on more information than just the GDP data. We shall consider recessions more fully in Chapter 5.)

The revision schedule reflects a difficult balancing act. Using macroeconomic policy to guide the economy is like a far-sighted captain trying to steer a ship while only looking out the stern. The things that are close are a bit blurry, but may give some information about what is in front of the ship. As things recede into the distance, they fall into sharper focus, but they also become less and less relevant to the ship's current situation. And, of course, what is actually in front of the ship right now is, at best, a guess. Similarly, the national accounts are always looking backward and are sliding into irrelevance just as they are coming into sharper focus. This pattern is clear in the case of the 2001 recession. The NBER did not announce the onset of the recession until eight months after it had begun – in fact, just about the time that it ended. And they did not announce the end of the recession until twenty months after its end date. If they had waited less than another month, they would have had the benchmark revisions of the national accounts to hand, which cast some doubt on whether there even was a recession.

There are three steps to the regular revision schedule. **Advance estimates** are released near the end of the first month after the end of the quarter (i.e., near the end of January, April, July, and October). The **preliminary estimates** for the same quarter are released near the end of the second month after the quarter ends (February, May, August, and November). The **final estimates** are released at the end of the third month (March, June, September, and December). As a result, new information about GDP is released every month.

"Final" estimates are not really final. Annual estimates are released each summer for the previous calendar year, along with revisions for the two years before that. The annual estimates are used to correct quarterly estimates for the years covered. Annual estimates use better sources of data and, for many components, replace judgments and extrapolations of trends

Table 3.6. *The Size of Revisions to the Growth Rate of GDP*

	Estimated Growth Rates			Revision of Estimates (percentage points)	
	Advance	Final	Comprehensive	Advance and Final	Advance and Comprehensive
Mean	2.64	2.81	3.27	0.19	0.63
Standard Deviation				0.81	2.13
66.67% range[a]				−0.62 to 1.00	−1.50 to 2.76
90% range[a]				−1.43 to 2.62	−3.63 to 4.89

[a] Based on estimated standard errors, 66.67 percent (2/3) or 90 percent of the revisions fall between the indicated upper and lower bounds.

Notes: Sample period 1968 (first quarter) to 2000 (second quarter).

Source: Adapted from Karen E. Dynan and Douglas Elmendorf, "Do Provisional Estimates Miss Economic Turning Points?" Division of Research & Statistics and Monetary Affairs, Federal Reserve Board, Finance and Economics Discussion Series, No. 2001–52 (November 2001), Table 3.

with actual data. About every five years, there is a **comprehensive** (or **benchmark**) **revision**. Comprehensive revisions typically incorporate methodological and statistical improvements and may make adjustments to the entire history of the accounts. The 2009 comprehensive revision made adjustments from 1929 through 2009.

Table 3.6 gives an idea of the size of the revisions for the growth rates of GDP on quarterly data. The first two columns show the different average growth rates calculated over the sample period using "advance" and "final" estimates of GDP. The third column shows the growth rate after any comprehensive revisions made before the end of the sample period. To get an idea of how large these revisions are, consider how long it would take GDP to double at each of those growth rates: for the advance rate, 26 years; for the faster final rate, 24.5 years; for the even faster comprehensive rate, 21 years. (See the *Guide*, section G.11.3, on calculating doubling times using the rule of 72.) Supposedly measuring the same thing, the different estimates produce substantially different results.

The fourth and fifth columns look at the revisions from another angle. The first line shows the average size of a revision between advance and final estimates and the second between advance estimates and comprehensive revisions. They show that earlier GDP estimates systematically underpredict the most up-to-date estimates. We could improve GDP estimates on average by adding two-thirds of a point to an advance estimate or a half point to a final estimate of GDP growth.

But it is more complicated than that. Although the average revisions are positive, individual revisions can be positive or negative, so to some extent the negative revisions cancel out the positive. The mean, then, gives a misleadingly low estimate of the typical revision. The second line reports the standard deviation of the revisions. From it, we can estimate the range of variation in the revisions (see the *Guide*, section G.4.3). The third line shows that about a third of the revisions are larger downward than 1.50 or larger upward than 2.76 percentage points, and about 10 percent are larger downward than 3.63 or larger upward than 4.89 percentage points. This implies that, in a fair number of cases, the absolute value of the revisions is greater than the initial estimates of the growth rates. In such cases, those initial estimates are nearly meaningless – we cannot be sure whether GDP growth rose or fell, much less how big it was.

Upward and downward revisions are not randomly distributed among the estimates. Not only are revisions positive on average, their direction varies with the state of the economy. When actual GDP has been rising and then begins to fall, early estimates tend to overpredict, and when it has been falling and then begins to rise, they tend to underpredict. It is easy to understand why the early estimates miss the **turning points**. If, for example, expenditures on residential improvements (such as remodeling kitchens) have been growing, the BEA will extrapolate that growth in its quarterly estimates. If, however, actual GDP, and therefore actual income, falls, then people are likely to spend less on residential improvements, and the actual value will fall below the trend estimate. Many other components of GDP are estimated through such extrapolations of trends. Knowledge of turning points would be the most valuable information that a policymaker could have. Unhappily, the thing that is most wanted is just what the early releases are worst at providing.

Stock and bond prices may rise or fall substantially depending on the estimates of GDP in the different releases. Looking at Table 3.6, markets should take the early releases with a grain of salt. Uncertainty about the true path of GDP takes considerable time to resolve.

3.6.3 Annualization and Seasonal Adjustment

Two final points about the presentation of the national accounts are worth noticing.

The first is that American NIPA data are **annualized**. GDP is measured over either quarters or years, and one might expect that adding up the four quarters of a year should give us the annual value. In fact, it gives us four times the true annual value. GDP is expressed as so-many dollars *per year*, even when it measures GDP only for a quarter. Measured GDP values are multiplied by four before they are published. (See the *Guide*, section G.1.2, on annualization.)

The second point is that the NIPA data are seasonally adjusted (see the *Guide*, section G.1.3). The idea of seasonal adjustment is simple, even though the adjustments are complicated to calculate. NIPA data interest policymakers and forecasters most when they behave in unexpected and unpredictable ways. But many of the changes in the economy are highly predictable. Retail sales usually rise significantly in December as Christmas approaches. A forecaster does not announce the dawn of good economic times just because retail sales are better in December than in November. A policymaker does not necessarily try to offset a drop in industrial production from June to July or a drop in housing construction from fall to winter. July is a peak month for vacations, so that factories typically produce less. Cold, wet, snowy weather often keeps construction workers off the site in winter. What matters more is whether sales this Christmas are higher than last Christmas or whether industrial production is unusually low for July or housing construction unusually low for winter.

Seasonal adjustment is a statistical method (actually a variety of methods) that estimates the usual variations. For example, seasonal adjustment of industrial production inflates the data (by differing amounts) for typically lower months (January, February, April, May, July, November, and December) and deflates the data for typically higher months (March, June, August, September, and October). The pattern of seasonal adjustments is not the same for industrial production and retail sales. It depends on the particular characteristics of each time series. The important point is that, once data have been seasonally adjusted, then month-to-month or quarter-to-quarter changes can be interpreted as economically significant. A forecaster may legitimately declare that good times are upon us when *seasonally adjusted* GDP rises, and the policymaker may wish to stimulate the economy when *seasonally adjusted* GDP falls. Many economic time series are published in both seasonally adjusted and nonseasonally adjusted versions, but only seasonally adjusted NIPA data are routinely published in the United States.

3.7 Putting It All Together: Reading the NIPAs

In the last section we examined some of main issues involved in compiling the national-income-and-product accounts. In the final section, we shall look at the accounts themselves and show how to relate them to the four national-income-accounting identities of Chapter 2. The official U.S. national-income-and-product accounts are presented in 148 separate tables. They are summarized in five interrelated tables, which can be regarded as more complicated versions of the national-accounting identities (2.1–2.3).

3.7.1 The National-Income-and-Product Account

The first account (Table 3.7) corresponds to the production-expenditure identity:

$$Y \equiv C + I + G + (EX - IM). \tag{2.1}$$

The right-hand side of the table is nearly identical to the right-hand side of the identity, except for some added detail. Most of the terms are familiar. Recall from Chapter 2 that inventories include stocks of unused raw materials, work in progress, and stocks of unsold finished goods (e.g., the food on the grocery shelf). Inventories are a form of capital, and a positive *change in private inventories* is a form of investment.

The left-hand side of Table 3.7 is the income side. Identity (2.1) lumps all income together, but we know from Chapter 2 and the discussion of Figure 3.1 (section 3.2) that income is paid to the factors of production in the forms of wages, profits, and rents. The table shows that income is paid in other forms as well.

- *Proprietors' Income.* Large firms are usually incorporated and owned by shareholders. Small firms are often owned and operated by the same person – the proprietor. Small businesses (for example, a small insurance agency, a convenience store, or a shoe-repair shop) are often proprietorships. Because the owner is also a worker in such businesses, his income combines what the economist regards as wages and profits in a way that is not easily sorted out. The national-income accountants lump them together in a category distinct from wages and profits.
- *Net Interest.* Firms pay part of their revenues as profits to the owners of their shares, but they also pay part to owners of corporate bonds or other debt in the form of interest. They may receive interest from individuals as well, so interest income is recorded as payments net of receipts.

The sum of wages and salaries (compensation of employees), proprietors' income, profits, and interest is known as NATIONAL INCOME (sometimes called NET NATIONAL INCOME AT FACTOR COST). It is more or less what people have to spend.

National income falls significantly short of total revenues. Revenues may be directed in four other ways:

- *Business Transfer Payments.* These include corporate gifts (such as BP's sponsorship of broadcasts by the Chicago Symphony Orchestra), personal injury payments, and taxes paid to foreign governments.
- *Taxes on Production and Imports Less Subsidies.* These include any taxes that can be treated as a business expense and incorporated into the price of the product (such as sales taxes or property taxes). Corporate income taxes are not included. This item must be adjusted for government subsidies (essentially a negative tax).

Table 3.7. National Income and Product Account for 2008

Line	Income		Line	Product	
1	**Compensation of employees**	**7,792**	29	**Personal consumption expenditures**	**10,089**
2	Wages and salaries	6,289	30	Durable goods	1,035
3	Supplements to wages and salaries	1,502	31	Nondurable goods	2,220
4	Employer contribution to pensions and insurance	1,044	32	Services	6,834
5	Employer contributions for social insurance	458	33	**Gross private domestic investment**	**1,629**
6	**Proprietors' income with inventory valuation and**	**1,041**	34	Fixed investment	1,750
	capital consumption adjustment		35	Nonresidential	1,389
7	**Rental income of persons with inventory valuation and**	**268**	36	Structures	480
	capital consumption adjustment.		37	Equipment and software	909
8	**Corporate profits with inventory valuation adjustment**	**1,309**	38	Residential	361
9	*Taxes on corporate income*	*292*	39	Change in inventories	−121
10	*Net dividends*	*690*	40	**Net exports of goods and services**	**−392**
11	*Undistributed profits*	*378*	41	Exports	1,564
12	**Net interest**	**788**	42	Imports	1,957
13	**National Income (Net National Product at factor cost)**	**11,198**	43	**Government consumption expenditures and gross investment**	**2,931**
14	**Taxes on production and imports less subsidies**	**964**	44	Federal	1,145
15	**Business transfer payments**	**134**	45	National defense	779
16	*To persons (net)*	*33*	46	Nondefense	366
17	*To government (net)*	*97*	47	State and local	1,786
18	*To the rest of the world (net)*	*5*			
19	**Current surplus of government enterprises**	**−8**			
20	**Consumption of fixed capital**	**1,864**			
21	Private	1,539			
22	Government	325			
23	**Gross National Income**	**14,152**			
24	Statistical discrepancy	209			
25	**Gross National Product**	**14,361**			
26	Less income receipts from the rest of the world	589			
27	Plus income payments to the rest of the world	484			
28	**Gross Domestic Product**	**14,256**	48	**Gross Domestic Product**	**14,256**

Note: Individual entries may not sum to totals because of rounding.

Source: Based on table A in Eugene P. Seskin and Robert P. Parker. "A Guide to the NIPAs." *Survey of Current Business*, March 1998, updated to 2008 from Bureau of Economic Analysis, National Income and Product Accounts.

- *Surpluses of Government Enterprises.* Like private corporations, public corporations (such as Amtrak or publicly owned utilities) may sell more than their expenses. Were the enterprises private firms, the surpluses would be counted as profits.
- *Consumption of Fixed Capital.* To maintain the capital stock intact, wear and tear (depreciation) must be made good.

The sum of national income and these four items is **gross national income** defined as *the total income received by the residents of a country.* In principle, gross national income should equal gross national product. In practice, there are measurement errors reflected in the *statistical discrepancy.*

To get *gross domestic product* (i.e., the total production of final goods and services generated within the borders of a country), we subtract *income receipts from the rest of the world* – that part of the income earned abroad (e.g., profits from U.S. ownership of a foreign factory or interest on foreign bonds) – and add *income payments to the rest of the world* (income generated from U.S. production but owned by foreigners). In other words, we work backward from GNP to GDP, where in the text we worked forward.

It may be helpful to explain some puzzling terms that appear in the table.

- *Inventory Valuation Adjustment* (lines 6, 7, and 8). If a firm counts the cost of using an inventory item at its historic purchase price rather than a higher replacement cost, it will record a profit from the use by an amount unconnected to current production and, therefore, to GDP. The adjustment corrects for the discrepancy.
- *Capital Consumption Adjustment* (lines 6 and 7). The adjustment corrects for differences between depreciation allowances as reported for tax purposes and economically based measures of depreciation.

Using 2009 data (billions of dollars), identity (2.1) is

$$
\begin{array}{ccccccccc}
Y & = & C & + & I & + & G & + & (EX & - & IM) \\
\$14,\!256 & = & 10,\!089 & + & 1,\!629 & + & 2,\!931 & + & (1,\!564 & - & 1,\!957). \\
\text{7-28} & & \text{7-29} & & \text{7-33} & & \text{7-43} & & \text{7-41} & & \text{7-42}
\end{array}
$$

(The numbers below the dollar values refer to the account number and line number from which the entry was drawn. For example, "7-28" means Table 3.7, line 28.)

3.7.2 The Personal-Income-and-Outlay Account

Table 3.8 is almost a rearrangement of the disposable-income identity:

$$YD \equiv Y - T + TR \equiv C + S. \tag{2.2}$$

Table 3.8. *Personal Income and Outlay Account for 2009*

Line	Outlays		Line	Income	
1	**Personal current taxes**	**1,102**	10	**Wage and salary disbursements**	**6,284**
2	**Personal outlays**	**10,459**	11	**Other labor income**	**1,503**
3	Personal consumption expenditure	10,089	12	**Proprietors' income with inventory valuation and capital consumption adjustment**	**1,041**
4	Interest paid by persons	214	13	**Rental income of persons with inventory valuation and capital consumption adjustment**	**268**
5	Personal transfer payments	156	14	**Personal income receipts on assets**	**1,793**
6	To government	92	15	Personal interest income	1,238
7	To the rest of the world	64	16	Personal dividend income	554
8	**Personal Savings**	**465**	17	**Personal current transfer receipts**	**2,105**
			18	*less* contributions to government social insurance	967
9	**Personal Income**	**12,026**	19	**Personal Income**	**12,026**

Note: Individual entries may not sum to totals because of rounding.
Source: Based on table A in Eugene P. Seskin and Robert P. Parker. "A Guide to the NIPAs."
Survey of Current Business, March 1998, updated to 2009 from Bureau of Economic Analysis,
National Income and Product Accounts.

To reconcile them, add taxes (T) to both the middle and the right-hand terms to give:

$$Y + TR \equiv \ T + C + S. \tag{3.1}$$

Subtract *personal transfer payments* from both sides of the table, so that *personal current transfer receipts* on the right-hand side can be regarded as *net* transfers. Similarly, subtract *interest paid by persons*, which is also a form of transfer payment from both sides, also combining it in net transfers. The right-hand side of the equation and the left-hand side of the table have the same form and vice versa.

There are two important differences. First, Table 3.8 refers only to the income and outlays of individual persons. Income (Y) and transfers (TR) include the receipts, and taxes (T) include the payments of the entire domestic private sector. Only individuals can consume, but savings in identity (2.2), unlike in Table 3.8, include the savings of businesses as well as the savings of individuals.

Second, the identities in Chapter 2 assumed that *TR* referred only to government transfer payments. The detailed accounts force us to notice other sorts of transfer payments from businesses, persons, and the foreign sector, as well as from government. We must be careful in computing the government budget deficit, $G - (T - TR)$, to count only those transfer payments originating with the government.

3.7.3 Three Sectors, Three Deficits

Tables 3.9–3.11 correspond roughly to the components of the sectoral-deficits identity:

$$[G - (T - TR)] + [I - S] + [EX - IM] \equiv 0. \qquad (2.3)$$

In each case some adjustments must be made to make the match complete. Except for some rearrangements, the major difference between the tables and the identities is that the identities ignore the difference between GNP and GDP. The derivation in the main text assumed that net income flows from abroad were zero and that no transfer payments were made to foreigners.

To account for this difference, some adjustments must be made to identity (2.2):

$$YD \equiv Y + NIA + TR - T - NTRA \equiv C + S. \qquad (3.2)$$

Identity (3.2) involves two new terms. *NIA* is *net income from abroad* – the difference between GNP and GDP. *NTRA* is *net transfer payments and taxes to abroad*. Transfer payments from business and individuals to other residents of the same country do not affect national income; they only redistribute it. But private transfer payments to foreigners act exactly the same way as a tax on the private sector, because the income is lost to domestic spending. *TR* remains transfers from the government to residents of the country. And *NTRA* includes government transfers to foreigners.

Subtracting (3.2) from (2.1) and rearranging yields

$$[G - (T - TR)] \quad + \quad [I - S] \quad + [EX + NIA - IM - NTRA] \equiv 0$$
$$\textit{Government Deficit} + \textit{Private Deficit} + \quad \textit{Foreign Deficit} \quad \equiv 0.$$

$$(3.3)$$

Identity (3.3) is similar to (2.3), except that the foreign deficit is no longer defined as the **TRADE BALANCE** (*net exports = EX – IM*), but as the **CURRENT-ACCOUNT BALANCE** ($EX + NIA - IM - NTRA$), which accounts for all

Table 3.9. *Government Receipts and Expenditure Account for 2009*

Line	Expenditures		Line	Receipts	
1	**Consumption expenditures**	**2,417**	14	**Current tax receipts**	**2,428**
2	**Current transfer payments**	**2,134**	15	Personal current taxes	2,102
3	To persons	2,072	16	Taxes on production and imports	1,024
4	To rest of the world	62	17	Taxes on corporate income	290
5	**Interest paid**	**379**	18	Taxes from the rest of the world	12
6	To persons and business	243	19	**Contributions for government social insurance**	**972**
7	To rest of the world	136	20	**Income receipts on assets**	**164**
8	**Subsidies**	**60**	21	Interest and miscellaneous	143
9	*Less* wage accruals less disbursements	0	22	Dividends	22
10	**Net government savings**	**−1,244**	23	**Current Transfer Receipts**	**189**
11	Federal	−1,225	24	From business (net)	97
12	State and local	−19	25	From rest of the world	92
			26	**Current surplus of government enterprises**	**−8**
13	**Current Government Expenditure and Surplus**	**3,746**	27	**Current Government Receipts**	**3,746**

Note: Individual entries may not sum to totals because of rounding.
Source: Based on table A in Eugene P. Seskin and Robert P. Parker. "A Guide to the NIPAs." *Survey of Current Business*, March 1998, updated to 2009 from Bureau of Economic Analysis, National Income and Product Accounts.

the monetary flows into and out of the country. The message is still the same: the sum of the government, private, and foreign deficits equals zero by definition.

The *net government savings* (line 10) in Table 3.9 is very nearly the government surplus defined as the negative of the deficit, $G - (T - TR)$. The difference is that Table 3.9 counts only government consumption expenditure (e.g., purchases of paper clips) and not government investment expenditure (e.g., building highways). To keep both sides of the account balanced, the addition of net government investment expenditure (government investment less consumption of government fixed capital) to line 1 must be offset by subtracting the same amount from line 10, making the current surplus or

Table 3.10. *Foreign Transactions Account for 2009*

Line	Receipts		Line	Payments	
1	**Exports of goods and services**	**1,564**	11	**Imports of goods and services**	**1,957**
2	Goods	1,038	12	Goods	1,575
3	Services	526	13	Services	381
4	**Income receipts**	**589**	14	**Income payments**	**484**
5	Wage and salary receipts	3	15	Wage and salary receipts	10
6	Income receipts on assets	586	16	Income receipts on assets	474
7	Interest	156	17	Interest	356
8	Dividends	203	18	Dividends	86
9	Reinvested earnings on U.S. direct investment abroad	227	19	Reinvested earnings on foreign direct investment in the U.S.	32
			20	**Current taxes and transfer payments to the rest of the world (net)**	**143**
			21	From persons (net)	64
			22	From government (net)	49
			23	From business (net)	30
			24	**Balance on current account**	**−430**
10	**Current Receipts from the Rest of the World**	**2,154**	25	**Current Payments to the Rest of the World**	**2,154**

Note: Individual entries may not sum to totals because of rounding.
Source: Based on table A in Eugene P. Seskin and Robert P. Parker. "A Guide to the NIPAs." *Survey of Current Business*, March 1998, updated to 2009 from Bureau of Economic Analysis, National Income and Product Accounts.

deficit more negative (i.e., shifting it toward a larger deficit). For 2009 (data in billions):

$$
\begin{array}{ccccc}
G & - & (T & - & TR) \\
\$2{,}606 & - & 3{,}400 & - & 2{,}228 \\
(9\text{-}1 + 11\text{-}2 - 11\text{-}10) & & (9\text{-}14 + 9\text{-}19) & & (9\text{-}2 + 9\text{-}5 + 9.8 - 9\text{-}9 \\
& & & & -9\text{-}20 - 9.23\text{-}9.26)
\end{array}
$$

$$
\begin{aligned}
&= \text{ \textit{Government Deficit}} \\
&= \$1{,}433. \\
&\quad [\text{-}1 \times (9\text{-}10 - 11.2 + 11\text{-}10)]
\end{aligned}
$$

Table 3.10 corresponds precisely to the modified foreign deficit in identity (3.3):

$$
\begin{array}{ccccccc}
EX & + & NIA & - & IM & - NTRA & = \textit{Foreign Deficit} \\
\$1{,}564 & + & 105 & - & 1{,}957 & - \quad 143 & = \qquad -430. \\
10\text{-}1 & & (10\text{-}4 - 10.14) & & 10\text{-}11 & 10\text{-}20 & 10\text{-}24
\end{array}
$$

Table 3.11. *Gross Savings and Investment Account for 2009*

Line	Investment		Line	Savings	
1	**Gross private domestic investment**	**1,629**	5	**Personal saving**	**465**
2	**Gross government investment**	**514**	6	**Wage accruals less disbursements (private)**	**5**
3	**Net foreign investment**	**−430**	7	**Undistributed corporate profits with inventory valuation and capital consumption adjustments**	**418**
			8	**Consumption of fixed capital**	**1,864**
			9	Private	1,539
			10	Government	325
			11	**Government current-account surplus**	**−1,244**
			12	**Statistical discrepancy**	**205**
4	**Gross Investment**	**1,713**	13	**Gross Savings and Statistical Discrepancy**	**1,713**

Note: Individual entries may not sum to totals because of rounding.
Source: Based on table A in Eugene P. Seskin and Robert P. Parker. "A Guide to the NIPAs."
Survey of Current Business, March 1998, updated to 2009 from Bureau of Economic Analysis,
National Income and Product Accounts.

Notice that the foreign deficit is referred to as *balance on current account* in Table 3.10.

Finally, Table 3.11 corresponds to the private-sector deficit, $I − S$. Three adjustments are needed. Because the variable I in (3.3) comprises only private investment, gross government investment (line 2) and net foreign investment (line 3) are eliminated from the left-hand side. (Recall that we had previously shifted government investment to Table 3.9.) Similarly, variable S also comprises only private savings, so that the *government current-account surplus* (line 11) is also eliminated. (Notice that business savings takes the form of wages that businesses owe but have not paid (line 6, "accruals less disbursements") plus undistributed profits (line 7) plus (importantly) consumption of fixed capital (line 8). This last item is savings because it counts that part of investment that firms use to make good the depreciation of their capital stocks – it is the difference between gross and net investment.

With these adjustments, the two sides of the account no longer balance. The difference between the right-hand and left-hand side is the private deficit (billions):

$$I \quad - \quad S \quad = Private\ Deficit$$
$$\$1,629 - \quad 2,427 \quad = \quad -798.$$
$$11\text{-}1 \quad (11\text{-}5 + 11\text{-}6 + 11\text{-}7 + 11\text{-}9)$$

In principle, the three deficits should sum to zero. But in fact,

$$Government\ Deficit + Private\ Deficit + Foreign\ Deficit = Statistical\ Discrepancy$$
$$\$1,433 \quad + \quad -798 \quad + \quad -430 \quad = \quad \$205.$$

The *statistical discrepancy* is, of course, the difference between adding up GDP from final goods and services or from incomes (and differs from that reported in Table 3.7, line 24 only because of rounding error).

There are 143 more accounts in the U.S. NIPA. Each adds additional detail or presents the basic data from a different angle. These five, however, provide the main data needed to begin our analysis of the macro-economy.

Summary

1. GDP is the value of all the final products in the economy.
2. A product is a valuable good or service for which there is a market exchange or *quid pro quo*. Transfer payments are valuables that are given without *quid pro quo*, and include gifts, welfare payments, and interest payments.
3. An intermediate product is one that is used up in the production process this period. A final product is one that crosses the production boundary (leaves the firm sector this period) and is available for either consumption or investment.
4. Only the value-added at each stage of production – that is, the value above and beyond the costs of production – adds to the value of the final product.
5. Sales of final products are distributed to the owners of factors of production in the form of wages, rents, and profits. In any period, the value of the sales of final products must equal the incomes generated, and the sum of the value added at every stage of production.
6. Gross national product (GNP) is GDP plus net incomes from abroad (payments to factors of production and transfer payments). GNP may be higher or lower than GDP, depending on whether payments from abroad are higher or lower than payments to foreigners.
7. Capital is long-lived physical means of production. Investment adds to the capital stock only after some of it is used to replace wear and tear (or obsolescence) of the capital stock, known as depreciation or capital consumption.
8. Some consumer goods known as consumer durables are long-lived and, therefore, are similar to productive capital. The division between durables and non-durables, consumer goods and capital, is not sharp. By convention, durables are goods that last more than three years.

9. Official GDP is mainly a market measure. Nonmarket production that is a close substitute for market production (e.g., owner-occupied housing is a close substitute for rental housing) may be included in the national accounts. Government services are also included. But other nonmarket production (e.g., cleaning one's own home) is not.

10. The black economy, various informal or illegal market transactions, should in principle be included in GDP, but often is not because information about them is necessarily hard to obtain. The black economy is a large fraction of GDP in many countries.

11. Many economists, as well as environmental and social activists, argue that GDP should be adjusted to account for many nonmarket activities – for example, upward for household production and additions to human capital and downward for environmental damage and social inequality. Such adjustments make sense when GDP is used as a measure of social welfare, but are inappropriate when it is used to capture the market economy and its close substitutes.

12. GDP data depend on a complex array of sources, leading to a tension between timeliness and accuracy. GDP data are frequently and substantially revised, sometimes long after their first release.

Key Concepts

quid pro quo
transfer payment
final product
intermediate product
value-added
factors of production
gross national product (GNP)
net income from abroad
capital
depreciation

capital consumption
black economy
negative externality
expenditure (or product) method
income method
value-added method
national income (or net national income at factor cost)
trade balance
current-account balance

Suggestions for Further Reading

Robert Eisner. *The Total Incomes System of Accounts*. Chicago: University of Chicago Press, 1989.

Eugene P. Seskin and Robert P. Parker. "A Guide to the NIPAs." *Survey of Current Business*, March 1998. (Available electronically from the U.S. Department of Commerce, Bureau of Economic Analysis: bea.gov/bea/an/0398niw/maintext .htm.)

Joseph Ritter. "Feeding the National Accounts," *Federal Reserve Bank of St. Louis Review*, vol. 82, no. 2 (March/April 2000), pp. 11–20. (Available electronically from research.stlouisfed.org/publications/review/00/03/0003jr.pdf.)

Joel Popkin. "The U.S. National Income and Product Accounts," *Journal of Economic Perspectives*, vol. 14, no. 2 (Spring 2000), pp. 215–224.

J. Steven Landefeld, Eugene P. Seskin, and Barbara M. Fraumeni. "Taking the Pulse of the Economy: Measuring GDP," *Journal of Economic Perspectives*, vol. 22, No. 2 (Spring 2008), pp. 193–216.

Problems

Data for this exercise are available on the textbook website under the link for Chapter 3 (appliedmacroeconomics.com). Before starting these exercises, the student should review the relevant portions of the *Guide to Working with Economic Data*, including sections G.1–G.4, G10, and G.11.

Problem 3.1. The following table contains data for the United Kingdom.

	2001	2002
Consumption	660	691
Government Expenditure on Goods and Services	191	210
Fixed Investment	167	170
Changes in Inventories	3	
Exports	272	273
Imports		305
GDP	994	
Net Income Flows from Abroad	8	20
Gross National Product		1,064
Net Transfers from Abroad	−3	−7
Savings	147	155
Capital Consumption	109	116

Units: Billions pounds sterling.
Source: International Monetary Fund, *International Financial Statistics.*

(a) Use your knowledge of the national accounts to fill in the missing values in the table.

(b) For each year, compute net national product (NNP), net investment, the trade balance, and the current-account balance.

Problem 3.2. Explain why or why not each of the following contributes to GDP: an antique dealer; a drug dealer; a worker at a charity (e.g., the Red Cross); a religious leader (e.g., a pastor, priest, rabbi, or imam); a dockworker; a psychologist. In what ways might the differences among these cases be puzzling? (Be specific.)

Problem 3.3.

(a) Who benefits most from a prosperous economy – workers or the owners of businesses? Table 3.7 shows that the main categories of factor income form an identity: *National Income ≡ Employee Compensation + Proprietors' Income + Rental Income + Profits + Net Interest.* Without consulting any source of information, answer the following questions (i.e., make your best guess). (i) What percentage of GDP is national income? (ii) What is the rank order from largest to smallest (as shares of GDP) of the differ-ent sources of national income? (iii) Which shares have trended upward, which downward, and which stayed more or less constant over the last fifty years?

(b) Compute national income and each of its components as a percentage of GDP for the post-World War II era. Present these data on a single graph.

(c) Using your answers to (b) and (c), reevaluate your answer to question (a). Are there any surprises?

Problem 3.4.

(a) Considering the income components in Problem 3.3 (same as the main components in Table 3.7), conjecture which sources of income are the most reliable.

(b) To check your conjecture, determine which income components show the greatest fluctuations? Compute the means, variances, standard deviations, and coefficients of variation for national income and each of its compo-nents expressed as a percentage of GDP for the post-World War II era and present the results in a table.

(c) Using the information from (b), compare your initial conjecture (a) with the evidence in (b). (Be explicit about which measure of variability you use and why.)

Problem 3.5. Table 3.1 shows that for the United States GNP was greater than GDP in 2008. Has this been true generally? Compute GNP as a percentage of GDP for each year since 1947. Calculate the minimum and maximum values of the resulting time series. What do your data imply about the typical relation-ship of GNP to GDP and of net income flows from abroad? Instead of calcu-lating the ratio of GNP to GDP, one could also have calculated the difference. Why would one method be preferred over the other?

Problem 3.6. Figure 3.2 shows that capital consumption (depreciation) was about 13 percent of U.S. GDP in 2008. Make a graph of the ratio of capital con-sumption to GDP (expressed as a percentage) for the post-World War II era. Describe your findings. Speculate on the causes of any patterns that you find.

Problem 3.7. Another take on the question in Problem 3.6: make a graph showing gross investment, net investment, and capital consumption as percentages of U.S. GDP for the post-World War II era. Split the sample in half and make a table displaying the mean values for each series in two halves of the sample. Describe their relative behavior over time. How much of any change can you attribute to changes in the typical share of gross investment and how much to changes in capital consumption?

Problem 3.8. Figure 3.3 shows that goods make up about a third of total consump-tion in the United States in 2009, with durable goods making up only about a tenth. Is this a permanent pattern? Make a graph of durable, nondurable, and service consumption as percentages of GDP for the post-World War II era. Describe the pattern over time. How might you explain it? Do you think that this pattern is likely to continue? Why?

Problem 3.9. Which level of government claims the largest share of GDP – Federal or state and local? Has the pattern changed over time? Make a graph of total government spending on goods and services in the United States, as well as its Federal and state and local components as percentages of GDP for the post-World War II era. Describe your findings. Speculate on the reasons for the patterns that you find.

Problem 3.10. To gain further insight into the differences between Federal and state and local spending, make a graph of U.S. Federal and state and local *investment* spending as a percentage of GDP for the post-World War II era. What historical events might account for the patterns that you find?

Problem 3.11. Yet more insight can be gained into the patterns of government spending by looking at the difference between defense and nondefense spending. Make a single graph of four U.S. Federal government expenditure series: (1) nondefense consumption; (2) nondefense investment; (3) defense consumption; and (4) defense investment. Express each as a percentage of GDP. Describe your findings.

Problem 3.12. The most familiar element of investment to most people is housing (investment in residential structures). How important an element of the economy is it? And how has it changed over time? On a single graph for the post-World War II era plot: investment as a percentage of GDP and residential investment as a percentage of total investment. Describe your findings. Try to place them into historical context.

Problem 3.13. Name two productive unpaid household activities – one that passes and one that fails the third-party test. Explain your choices.

Problem 3.14.

(a) Estimates of the size of the black economy are hard to come by and somewhat speculative because the participants try to hide their activities. One method used to estimate the size of the black economy starts with the observation that the ratio of U.S. cash (notes and coins) to the U.S. population is very high: more than $3,000 per person in early 2010. A second method starts with data on electricity use. Think about these data in relationship to the black economy. How might they be helpful in estimating its size? What problems might arise in using your suggested method?

(b) Suggest one or more other ways to estimate the size of the black economy.

Problem 3.15. Name the factors not counted in GDP that, in your view, most affect human welfare or happiness. How do you imagine that modifying GDP to account for these factors would raise or lower current U.S. GDP relative to earlier times or other countries? (Be specific in your references to time and country and provide reasons for your judgments.)

Problem 3.16. The data for this problem are found on the Bureau of Economic Analysis's (BEA's) website (www.bea.gov/) in the News Release Archive (www.bea.gov/newsreleases/relsarchivegdp.htm).

(a) Consider the quarter two before the current quarter. Go to the BEA website and locate the releases with the *advance, preliminary*, and *final estimates* of U.S. GDP for that quarter. For each release, identify or compute the GDP growth rate over the previous quarter (at a compound annual rate) and over the same quarter one year earlier. Make a table showing each growth rate for each release and the differences between the growth rates based on the advance versus the final estimates and on the preliminary versus the final estimates. Are these differences large or small? (How would you judge?)

(b) On the BEA website find the news release for the most recent *comprehensive revision* of GDP estimates. Choose a year about five years before the date of that revision. Compute or find the real GDP growth rate over the previous year in the comprehensive revision. Next find the earliest *annual revision* that covers that same year. Compute or find the same growth rate for the same year in that and the next three annual revisions. Record your results in a table that also reports the difference between each of the three annual revisions and the comprehensive revision. Are these differences large or small?

4

Measuring Prices and Inflation

As we have seen in the last two chapters, a measure of the general price level is needed to convert nominal quantities to real quantities and to estimate the rate of inflation. We begin this chapter with the question, how can information about millions of prices in the economy be reduced into a simpler, more manageable index? First, we look at the main types of price indices. How are they calculated? What are the advantages and disadvantages of each type? We conclude with a discussion of the price indices most commonly used in the formulation and execution of economic policy.

In Chapter 2, we used a **PRICE INDEX**, the GDP (implicit price) deflator, as the preferred measure of the general level of prices or the value of money. The GDP deflator is not the only price index. In this chapter we shall learn about a variety of price indices and how they are constructed.

The GDP deflator in Chapter 2 served two purposes. First, we typically care about *real* rather than *nominal* quantities: real GDP, real consumption, real investment, real government expenditure. In Chapters 2 and 3 we saw that real GDP and its components are not observed directly. Rather, the national-income accountants must first measure market or nominal GDP in current dollars and then use a price index to convert it into real or constant dollars. Second, we sometimes care about how fast prices are changing. The growth rate of a price index, the rate of inflation, provides a measure.

The construction of price indices is obviously important to the national-income accountant. A mistake in constructing the GDP deflator resulting in an overstatement of the rate of inflation by the very small amount of 0.1 percentage points would reduce the estimate of real GDP in 2008 by about $14 billion. Such errors can be costly to the government. For example, the government uses the consumer price index (CPI; see section 4.2.1) to adjust Social Security and government pensions for inflation. In 2008, each tenth of a percentage point overestimate of the CPI rate of inflation would have added about $500 million to the cost of Social Security. In 1996, the Boskin Commission estimated that the CPI rate of inflation was overstated by 1.1 percentage points. That would translate into \$5.5 billion in 2011 – a costly mistake. And such mistakes compound and accumulate year by year.

We are also often interested in the rate of inflation in its own right. One goal of monetary policy is to keep the rate of inflation low but not negative – as we saw in Chapter 2 (section 2.6), deflation (falling prices) is at least as undesirable as inflation. Zero inflation might, then, appear to be an optimal target for policy. But according to which index? Inflation rates are typically lower when measured using the GDP deflator than when using the CPI. If the GDP deflator were the better index, then achieving a zero rate of CPI inflation would imply deflation in fact. It is important to get the price index right or, at the least, to understand the differences among various price indices.

We begin with the general principles behind the construction of price indices and conclude with a description of the main indices used by economists, national-income accountants, and policymakers.

4.1 Constructing Price Indices

Why can the price of a single good (such as the can of Coca-Cola in Chapter 2, section 2.4) not serve as an accurate representation of all market prices? It would be perfect, provided that every price in the economy moved proportionately at all times. Alas, they do not. Although for more than half a century most prices in the United States have risen, they have done so at different rates, and the prices of some goods, such as a basic television set, have actually fallen. What we need is an average measure of prices. But a simple average (adding the prices of, say, a million goods and dividing by 1,000,000) would not be very satisfactory. The price of matches hardly matters to us, while the price of cars matters a great deal. A satisfactory measure needs to take account of the relative importance of different goods.

We can illustrate different approaches to estimating the GENERAL PRICE LEVEL with a simple, artificial example. The "couch-potato" economy produces only two goods – tortilla chips and beer. (The television and the couch can be considered to be natural resources.) Table 4.1 shows the prices and quantities of each for three years.

4.1.1 The Laspeyres (or Base-Weighted) Index

How much have prices risen, say, between 2010 and 2011? The price of tortilla chips has doubled, while the price of beer rose by 5/3. One approach to estimating the average is to weight these changes by how important each good is in total expenditure in 2010 (see the *Guide*, section G.4.2 on weighted means). Nominal GDP in 2010 is \$5.50 (= 5 tortilla chips × \$0.50/bag +

Table 4.1. *The Couch-Potato Economy*

		Tortilla Chips (bags)	Beer (cans)
2010	Price	$0.50	$0.75
	Quantity	5	4
2011	Price	$1.00	$1.25
	Quantity	4	5
2012	Price	$1.25	$1.40
	Quantity	3	6

4 beers × $0.75/can). Total expenditure on tortilla chips is $2.50 or 45.5 percent of nominal GDP (= $2.50/$5.50 = 0.455). Total expenditure on beer is 54.5 percent of GDP. The **BASE PERIOD** is *the period for which expenditure shares are calculated* – here 2010.

Using the expenditure shares in the base period as weights, the increase in general prices is measured by the **PRICE FACTOR**, defined as *the ratio of price levels* $(= p_{2011}/p_{2010})$ and calculated as

$$pf = 0.455 \times 2 + 0.545 \times 5/3 = 1.818.$$

The price factor shows that prices in general have risen faster than the price of beer, but slower than the price of tortilla chips.

The price factor can be used just as we used the relative increase in the price of Coke to deflate 2011 GDP and to express it in 2010 dollars. Nominal GDP in 2011 is $10.25. What is 2011 GDP in constant 2010 dollars?

$$\$_{2010} Y_{2011} = \$_{2011} Y_{2011} \div pf = \$_{2011} 10.25 \div 1.818 = \$_{2010} 5.64.$$

Real GDP has increased by 2.5 percent (= (5.64 − 5.50)/5.50).

To construct a price index, we start with a **REFERENCE PERIOD** in which the index is set to some arbitrary value – typically, to 100. If 2010 is the reference period, then by definition $p_{2010} = 100$. Because prices have increased in general by a factor of 1.818, the index for 2011 must be higher by the same factor: $p_{2011} = pf \times p_{2010} = 1.818 \times 100 = 181.8$. Using 2010 as the base year (i.e., using the expenditure shares of 2010), we could compute the price factor that measures how much prices increased between 2010 and 2012 and use it to compute the price index for 2012 (see Problem 4.3).

An index that weights price increases by the expenditure shares in the base period is known as a **BASE-WEIGHTED OR LASPEYRES INDEX** after the German statistician Ernst Louis Etienne Laspeyres (1834–1913), who invented it in the nineteenth century. The Laspeyres index is, perhaps, the most commonly used of all the many types of price indices. Such common indices as the consumer price index (CPI) and the producer price index

(PPI) are Laspeyres indices. (The *Guide*, section G.8.2, gives a general formula for computing a Laspeyres index.)

The base period (i.e., the period for which the weights are computed) and the reference period (i.e., the period in which nominal and real values coincide) are usually the same for a Laspeyres index, but they need not be. For example, we might have answered the question, what is the value of 2010 GDP in 2011 constant dollars, using the same Laspeyres index to *inflate* the dollars of 2010:

$$\$_{2011} Y_{2010} = \$_{2010} Y_{2010} \times pf = \$_{2010} 5.50 \times 1.818 = \$_{2011} 10.00.$$

Similarly, the price index could be arbitrarily set to 100 in 2011. Then, $p_{2011} = 100$ and $p_{2010} = 100/pf = 100/1.818 = 55.0$. Although the reference year is now 2011, the base year is still 2010, because the price factor is based on the 2010 expenditure shares.

The data in Table 4.1 tell a typical economic story. Notice that in 2010 the price of beer relative to tortilla chips is $0.75 per can of beer/$0.50 per bag of chips = 1.5 cans of beer per bag of chips. The price of chips rose faster than the price of beer, so that by 2011, the relative price of beer had fallen to 1.25 cans per bag. Table 4.1 shows that people bought more beer and fewer chips, illustrating a general rule: the principle of **substitution**: *When the relative price of a good falls, the quantity sold typically increases, while the quantity sold of the relatively more expensive good falls*. As a result, the Laspeyres index tends to overstate the average increase in prices. People tend to substitute those goods with slower than average increases in prices for those goods with faster than average increases. Typically, such substitution lowers the share in total expenditure of the goods with the faster increases in price. But because the weights of the Laspeyres index are fixed in the base period, neither the price factor nor the price index reflects the changes in consumer preferences and expenditure shares.

The overestimation of the rate of inflation because of fixed weights is called **SUBSTITUTION BIAS**. To mitigate substitution bias, the base period of a Laspeyres index must be updated from time to time. The weights for the CPI (a Laspeyres index) were updated historically about every ten years. Recently, the updating schedule has been accelerated, so that they are on average only about three years old. Even though the base period for the CPI has been updated several times, the reference period has remained 1982–1984 for some time.

A base-weighted price index can also overstate price inflation if it fails to account properly for quality change. The average price of a house in the United States has gone up substantially over the past fifty years, but so has its quality. For example, the average floor space of new houses in the United States more than doubled from 983 square feet in 1950 to 2,265 square feet in

2000. A price index that uses the price per house will find more inflation than one that uses the price per square foot of floor space. Similarly, a price index that measures prices of computers has not fallen as rapidly as the more relevant price of computing power – measured by such properties as the speed of the processor and the size of the memory – and contributes to overstating the rate of increase of prices in general.

Computers highlight another problem with base-weighted indices – NEW PRODUCT BIAS. In 2011, personal computers are an important element in general expenditure and carry a significant weight in the calculation of the general price level. Yet, in 1970 there were no personal computers. Weights must be updated from time to time to account for new goods.

4.1.2 The Paasche (or Current-Weighted) Index

One way of mitigating substitution bias is to update the weights. In 1874, Hermann Paasche (1851–1925), another German statistician, suggested replacing the backward-looking Laspeyres index with an index that used the current expenditure shares to weight different price changes. In Table 4.1, expenditure on tortilla chips in 2011 is 39 percent of GDP, and expenditure on beer is 61 percent of GDP. The price of tortilla chips in 2010 was half the price in 2011; the price of beer was 3/5. The price factor for the Laspeyres index expressed changes as the ratio of later prices to earlier prices. Because the **PAASCHE INDEX** (or **CURRENT-WEIGHTED**) **INDEX** looks forward, it expresses changes as the ratio of earlier prices to later prices. To put it on the same basis as the Laspeyres index, we must calculate the reciprocal of the weighted average:

$$pf = \frac{1}{0.39 \times 1/2 + 0.61 \times 3/5} = 1.783.$$

(The *Guide*, section G.8.2, gives a general formula for computing a Paasche index.) Real GDP in 2010 expressed in constant 2011 dollars is

$$\$_{2011}Y_{2010} = \$_{2010}Y_{2010} \times pf = \$_{2011}5.50 \times 1.782 = \$_{2011}9.80.$$

If the price index is set to 100 in the reference year 2011, then $p_{2011} = 100$ and $p_{2010} = p_{2011}/pf = 100/1.782 = 56.1$.

Although the Paasche index mitigates the substitution bias of the Laspeyres index, it suffers from a bias of its own – **QUALITY CHANGE BIAS**. When the price of one good rises we often substitute into less desirable goods: hamburger replaces steak, Budweiser replaces Heineken, a Toyota replaces a Lexus. The Paasche index undercounts the loss in satisfaction because of such substitutions. As a current-weighted index, the Paasche index also suffers from a major inconvenience. It must be recomputed each period because, typically, the weights change each period. Each time a Paasche index is recomputed, the whole history of the index could be revised using the new weights. In practice, however, the reference period is kept constant, and the new weights apply only to the calculation of the current level of the index.

4.1.3 The Fisher-Ideal Index

Is the rate of inflation in the couch-potato economy of Table 4.1 82 percent per year (according to the Laspeyres index) or only 78 percent (according to the Paasche index)? Whichever index we use, prices and quantities of chips and beer are the same. We are looking at the same underlying facts through different pairs of glasses. Is one pair better than the other? Unfortunately not. Each suffers from different biases.

There is no *true* price index. Price indices summarize the changes of millions of prices in a single number. Some information must be lost in the process. Different things are lost according to the weights placed on individual changes. The Laspeyres index more or less defines the upper bound for the change in the general price level, and the Paasche index defines the lower bound. There are, in principle, an infinite number of reasonable weighting schemes that lie between these bounds – each defines a different index. The great American economist Irving Fisher (1867–1947) suggested a compromise between the Laspeyres and the Paasche indices that he called "ideal," because of its many desirable properties. The price factor for the **FISHER-IDEAL INDEX** (pf^F) is the geometric average of the price factors for the Laspeyres (pf^L) and the Paasche (pf^P) indices:

$$pf^F = \sqrt{pf^L \times pf^P}. \tag{4.1}$$

The price factor for the Fisher-ideal index for the couch-potato economy for 2011 is $pf^F_{2011} = \sqrt{1.818 \times 1.782} = 1.800$. The price factor can be used in the usual way. If 2010 is taken to be the reference year, then the Fisher-ideal price index is $p^F_{2011} = pf^F_{2011} \times p^F_{2010} = 1.800 \times 100 = 180.0$.

(The *Guide*, section G.8.2, gives a general formula for computing a Fisher-ideal index.)

4.1.4 The Chain-Weighted Index

Most of the price indices used in compiling the national accounts in the United States are a variant of the Fisher-ideal type called the **CHAIN-WEIGHTED INDEX**. The first step in constructing a chain-weighted index is to calculate the price factors for the Fisher-ideal index for successive pairs of periods for which the base of the Laspeyres index is updated each period.

For example, using the data in Table 4.1, we already know that the Fisher-ideal index calculated for 2011, taking 2010 as the base of the underlying Laspeyres index, is $pf_{2011}^F = 1.800$. We also already know that, in 2011, 39 percent of expenditure went to tortilla chips and 61 percent to beer. Therefore, the Laspeyres price factor for 2012, taking 2011 as the base, is $pf_{2012}^L = 0.39 \times \frac{1.25}{1.00} + 0.61 \times \frac{1.40}{1.25} = 1.171$. The Paasche price factor is $pf_{2012}^P = 1.157$ (the student should confirm this value as an exercise). The Fisher-ideal price factor is then $pf_{2012}^F = \sqrt{1.171 \times 1.157} = 1.164$.

The price factors are then combined in a chain in which last period's index is multiplied by this period's price factor to construct the complete series. Taking 2010 as the reference year:

$$p_{2010}^C = 100,$$

$$p_{2011}^C = p_{2010}^C \times pf_{2011}^F = 100 \times 1.800 = 180.0,$$

$$p_{2012}^C = p_{2011}^C \times pf_{2010}^F = 180.0 \times 1.164 = 209.5.$$

$$\cdots$$

4.1.5 Price Indices and Real GDP

Table 4.2 shows the Laspeyres, Paasche, and chain-weighted price indices for 2010–2012 for the couch-potato economy and uses them to calculate real GDP. (The student should check to see that any entries not based on calculations in the text are correct.) The table illustrates two rules:

- *First, typically, the change in prices is greater when judged on the Laspeyres index than on the chain-weighted index, which is greater than on the Paasche index.*
- *Second, the higher the general price level, the lower any real quantity, so that the change in a real quantity appears larger when estimated using a Paasche index than a chain-weighted index, which in turn is larger than when estimated using a Laspeyres index.*

The first rule is reflected in inflation rates: the average rate of inflation between 2010 and 2012 measured by each index is: Laspeyres 45.9 percent > chain-weighted 44.7 percent > Paasche 43.6 percent. The second rule is reflected in the growth rate of real GDP: the average rate of real growth over the same period measured by each index is: Paasche 3.48 percent > chain-weighted 2.69 percent > Laspeyres 1.89 percent.

Although the numbers in the couch-potato economy exaggerate the differences among the three indices compared to what is typically observed

Table 4.2. *Converting Nominal GDP to Real GDP in the Couch-Potato Economy*

Year	Nominal GDP	Price Index			Real GDP in Constant Dollars Using								
		Laspeyres	Paasche	Chain-Weighted	Laspeyres Index			Paasche Index			Chain-Weighted		
					with reference year								
					2010	2011	2012	2010	2011	2012	2010	2011	2012
2010	$5.50	100.0	100.0	100.0	$5.50	$10.00	$11.85	$5.50	$9.81	$11.14	$5.50	$9.90	$11.52
2011	$10.25	181.8	178.2	180.0	$5.64	$10.25	$12.14	$5.75	$10.25	$11.64	$5.69	$10.25	$11.93
2012	$12.15	215.4	202.5	209.5	$5.64	$10.25	$12.15	$6.00	$10.70	$12.15	$5.80	$10.44	$12.15

Note: Data are based on Table 4.1.

Table 4.3. *Converting Nominal GDP to Real GDP Using the Implicit Price Deflator*

Year	Nominal GDP	Implicit Price Deflator (2005 = 100)	Real GDP in Constant Dollars of Reference Year	
			1960	2009
1960	$526	18.6	$526	$3,105
2009	$14,256	109.8	$2,415	$14,256

Source: Bureau of Economic Analysis.

in the real world, they illustrate the general pattern well. It is important to recall that, despite different inflation and growth rates, there is only one economy seen through different glasses. The faster growth rate based on the Paasche index does not give people in the couch-potato economy any more beer or tortilla chips than the slower growth rate based on the Laspeyres index. The faster inflation rate based on the Laspeyres index does not impose any more costs on them than the slower inflation rate based on the Paasche index.

4.1.6 The Implicit Price Deflator

Most of the components of U.S. GDP are converted into constant dollars or deflated using chain-weighted indices. A few components still use a fixed-weight index such as the Laspeyres or Paasche indices. Official estimates of real GDP are constructed from the deflated components. The ratio of nominal GDP to the estimate of real GDP gives an overall measure of the general price level known as the GDP **IMPLICIT PRICE DEFLATOR**:

$$p^{Implicit} = \frac{Nominal\ GDP}{Real\ GDP} \times 100.$$

Multiplying by 100 ensures that $p^{Implicit} = 100$ in the reference year for real GDP. The GDP implicit price deflator does not necessarily correspond exactly to any of the many price indices used to construct real GDP. Instead, it summarizes the net effect of their interaction. Implicit price deflators may be constructed for consumption and other components of GDP as well.

In Chapter 2, we asked how much bigger is the economy today than in 1960. It is now clear why that question is better answered using an appropriate price index than using the price of a can of Coca-Cola. The implicit price deflator in 1960 was 18.6 and in 2009, 109.8. On this measure, prices have risen 5.9 times over 49 years. Table 4.3 is similar to Tables 2.1 and 4.2 except that it uses this ratio to make the conversions of nominal GDP to the constant dollars of 1960 and 2009. Where using the price of Coke as deflator indicated that prices had risen about 7.5 times, using the Bureau of Economic Analysis's implicit price deflator shows a rise a little shy of 6 times. The slower pace of inflation as measured by the GDP implicit price deflator compared to the price of Coca-Cola also implies that real GDP has grown more as measured by the slower growing price measure: real GDP grew by 4.6 times between 1960 and 2009 as calculated using the implicit price deflator, compared to only 3.6 times measured using the price of Coke. What we believe is true about prices in general makes a big difference to what we believe about the size of the real economy.

4.2 Alternative Price Indices

Although the GDP deflator is used to convert nominal to real GDP, other price indices are generally used for other purposes. Monetary policymakers at the Federal Reserve (see Chapter 16) have recently preferred to use the **personal consumption expenditure (PCE) deflator** (i.e., the deflator defined as the ratio of nominal consumption to real consumption) to estimate inflation rates. One reason is that the GDP deflator reflects the prices of all of the components of GDP, yet significant parts of GDP (e.g., investment or government expenditure) are not consumed directly by individual people, and the welfare of people is the main aim of policy. The two most commonly cited price indices are not reported in the national accounts. These are the **consumer price index (CPI)** and the **producer price index (PPI)**. Both are constructed and published by U.S. Bureau of Labor Statistics (BLS).

4.2.1 The Consumer Price Index (CPI)

The CPI is a COST-OF-LIVING INDEX. Essentially, it is a Laspeyres index the weights of which reflect the relative importance of different goods and services in the consumption bundle of typical consumers. The CPI is based on surveys of what consumers actually buy. In fact, the CPI is not a single index; there are many CPIs. Each is distinguished by the basket of goods that is used to construct it. The most frequently quoted CPI is **CPI-U**, the consumer price index for all items for all urban consumers. This index reflects the purchasing bundles of the approximately 87 percent of the population living in urban areas.

More than 350 other CPI series are computed. There are indices for more than 200 particular types of goods (e.g., apples, airline fares, men's shirts, gasoline). These indices are combined into more than 120 broader indices (e.g., food and beverages, housing, medical care, energy, men's and boys' apparel), which are, in turn, combined into nine major groups (food and beverages, housing, apparel, transportation, medical care, recreation, education, communications, and other goods and services). And there are still broader

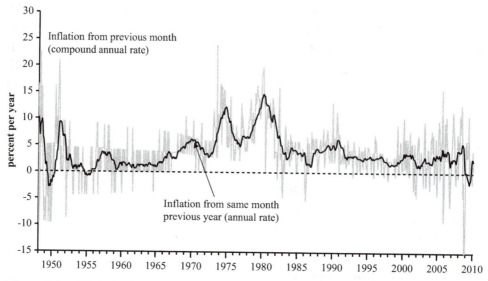

Figure 4.1. CPI Inflation (monthly and annual). *Source:* Bureau of Labor Statistics.

categories, such as durable goods, nondurable goods, and all items. In addition, separate CPIs are computed for major metropolitan areas, such as Los Angeles-Riverside-Orange County, California, or the Northeast Urban Census Region. A CPI series for a narrower group of urban wage earners and clerical workers (about 32 percent of the population) is called **CPI-W**. And the BLS is experimenting with a special CPI that uses a bundle appropriate to elderly people. Many of the various CPIs are published in both seasonally adjusted and nonseasonally adjusted versions (see the *Guide*, section G.1.3). Currently, the reference period for the CPI is set so that the average value in 1982–1984 is 100.

The CPI is the most timely and most frequently reported and cited measure of prices. Unlike the GDP price deflator, which is published quarterly and frequently revised, the CPI is published monthly and, once published, is not changed, even though the BLS makes frequent improvements to its methods of computing new data. Reports in the news media most often cite the monthly rate of inflation for CPI-U. Monthly CPI inflation is highly volatile (Figure 4.1). It is not uncommon for rapid growth one month to be followed by much slower growth the next. It is generally safer to look at annual rates of CPI inflation.

The CPI is the most widely cited of all price indices. It is particularly important because it is used to make cost-of-living adjustments, including those for Social Security recipients. The CPI has long been criticized for overstating the underlying rate of inflation. In the mid-1990s, the U.S. Congress commissioned a study of the CPI. The commission, headed by the economist Michael Boskin (Stanford University), noted several sources of bias in CPI estimates. In addition to the substitution, quality change, and new product biases discussed in section 4.1, it identified two other sources of bias: *Outlet-substitution bias* resulted from a failure of the BLS to account for consumers shifting their purchases of the same goods to cheaper outlets, such as Walmart. *Formula bias* occurred because of a technical problem in some BLS formulae, which affected historical CPI data although it had already been corrected by the time of the report. The Boskin commission estimated that the total bias averaged 1.1 percentage points (not counting 0.2 points for formula bias before 1996). It recommended a number of changes to the procedures of the BLS, including abandoning the Laspeyres formula, in favor of a so-called *superlative index*. A superlative index is similar in spirit to the Fisher-ideal index, although it relies on weighted-geometric, rather than arithmetic, averages to construct its root indices.

In the period since the Boskin report, the BLS has introduced many of its recommendations with respect to the treatment of new products, quality change, and outlet bias. The CPI remains essentially a Laspeyres index. It is not built up from individual prices, but from price indices for narrowly defined commodity groups. Some of these components are now superlative indices, while others remain Laspeyres indices. In 2002, the BLS also began publishing C-CPI-U, a chained CPI index based on the superlative formula. Unlike CPI-U, C-CPI-U is revised from time to time.

4.2.2 The Personal Consumption Expenditure Deflator

The PCE deflator (sometimes call the *PCE price index* or *PCEPI*) is the closest analogue to the CPI in the national accounts. In fact, the PCE deflator and the CPI use many of the same surveys as raw material. Yet, they differ in a number of ways. First, the PCE deflator takes a producer's-eye view. It tries to capture the prices of consumption goods produced in the domestic private sector, not the goods actually purchased by consumers. Among other things, it excludes foreign-produced goods. Second, it is a chain-weighted index, not a Laspeyres index. Third, it is revised as often as the national accounts are revised. In contrast, as already noted, once published, the CPI is essentially never revised. Finally, the PCE deflator is a quarterly rather than a monthly series. Table 4.4 summarizes the main differences between the PCE deflator and the CPI. Figure 4.2 compares annual rates of inflation measured by these two indices, as well as by the GDP deflator.

4.2.3 The Producer Price Index (PPI)

The PPI is the second most commonly cited price index in the United States. It is the oldest continuously computed price index in the United States,

Table 4.4. *Summary of the Differences between the CPI and the PCE Deflator*

Category	Differences
Formula	The CPI uses a fixed-weight Laspeyres formula, with weights determined by base-year expenditures.
	The PCE deflator uses a chain-weighted Fisher-ideal formula.
Scope	The PCE deflator is broader in scope.
	The CPI covers out-of-pocket expenditures by urban consumers [CPI-U].
	The PCE deflator also covers spending by rural consumers, nonprofit institutions that serve consumers, medical care and insurance funded by government and employers, and imputed financial services.
Weights	Weight differences reflect differences in: scope, item definition, and sources of expenditure data.
Prices	Although most of the detailed item prices in the PCE deflator are CPI indices, the PCE deflator relies on non-CPI price information for items not included in the CPI and items having substantially different coverage in the CPI and PCE deflator.
Treatment of Revisions	The CPI is essentially never revised, but the PCE deflator is continually revised.

Source: Adapted from Todd E. Clark, "A Comparison of the CPI and the PCE Price Index," *Federal Reserve Bank of Kansas City Economic Review*, vol. 84, no. 3 (3rd quarter), 1999, table 1, p. 21.

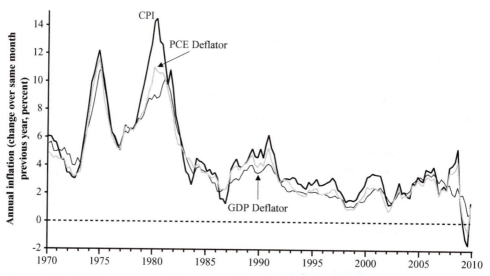

Figure 4.2. The CPI and National-Accounting Measures of Inflation. *Source:* CPI, Bureau of Labor Statistics; PCE and GDP deflators, Bureau of Economic Analysis.

having been first published by the BLS under its original name, the *wholesale price index*, in 1902. Like the CPI, the PPI is not one index but a family of indices that aim to capture the prices at which manufacturers and other producers sell their output. Producer price indices for more than 10,000 manufacturing and mining products in more than 500 industries are regularly published. In addition, there are more than 1,000 indices for service-sector outputs, and 3,200 indices grouped by type of product or end use.

Producer price indices are also published in groups divided according to *stages of processing*. Think back to Figure 3.1 in Chapter 3, which showed the production and sale of the Frisbee from crude oil through final product at retail. The various steps of Frisbee production correspond well to the three stages of processing used for the PPI. Crude petroleum at the well is an example of *crude materials for further processing*. Other examples include grains, livestock, metal ores, raw cotton, and construction sand and gravel. The plastic used in the production of the Frisbee is an example of *intermediate materials, supplies, and components*. This category also includes such products as flour, cotton yarn, lumber, diesel fuel, paper boxes, computer chips, and fertilizers. The finished Frisbee ready to be sold at wholesale is an example of *finished goods*. The prices recorded in the PPI refer to those received by the manufacturer, not the retail merchant, so that the final stage of the production and marketing of the Frisbee – sale to the consumer – is captured by the CPI rather than by the PPI. The PPI for finished goods is the most commonly reported PPI index. The PPI is reported monthly. Currently, the base for the PPI is set so that the average value in 1982 is 100.

For the most part the PPI refers to intermediate rather than final goods, which are not part of GDP. There are some exceptions: occasionally crude goods are consumed directly, and capital goods, which are considered final, are part of GDP. The stage-of-processing structure of the PPI is based on the idea that goods proceed in chains from crude to final. But, of course, the world is really more complicated. Some goods (say, tomatoes bought at a farmers' market) can move from the crude to the final consumer stage skipping all intermediate stages. Intermediate goods or final goods, for example containers or capital equipment, may be inputs to other intermediate or crude goods production. Putting these complications to one side, the stage-of-processing structure suggests that prices pass through as the outputs of one stage become the inputs for a later stage.

Much of the interest in the regular announcement of the PPI for finished goods derives from the idea that it is a harbinger of changes in the CPI. The linkage is loose. The PPI for final goods does not include services or imports, both of which are in the CPI, and does include capital equipment, which is not in the CPI. Figure 4.3 shows the relationship between inflation rates measured using the CPI-U and the PPI for finished goods. PPI inflation

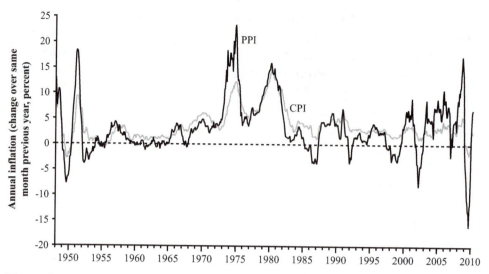

Figure 4.3. Consumer Price and Producer Price Inflation. Annual inflation: year over same month, previous year. *Source:* Bureau of Labor Statistics.

is somewhat more volatile than CPI inflation. Otherwise, they track each other quite well.

4.3 Core Inflation

4.3.1 The Core Rate of Inflation

Annualized monthly rates of CPI or PPI inflation tend to be highly volatile, which suggests that we might do better measuring inflation using true annual rates (current rate over twelve months previous). Even annual rates can be misleading, because the prices of some goods in the price index are more variable, not only month-to-month, but year-to-year as well. Food and energy prices are particularly variable. Oil prices rose sharply in the decade after 1973, only to collapse in the mid-1980s. In 2008, they set new record high levels. Food prices vary substantially with weather conditions (floods in the Midwest drive up the price of corn and corn-fed cattle; drought in California drives up the price of vegetables) and with international demand (good crop yields in Russia drive down the price of U.S. wheat). Food and energy prices carry a substantial weight in the CPI, but may behave differently from other prices and may convey little information about future trends. Policymakers often look to the inflation rate calculated using the CPI or the PPI less food and energy prices. Referred to as the **CORE RATE OF INFLATION**, these indices may be a better indicator of the general course of prices.

The gray line in Figure 4.4 shows the annual rate of CPI inflation, while the heavy black line shows the annual rate of core CPI inflation. Core CPI inflation is substantially smoother than CPI inflation. When the two lines

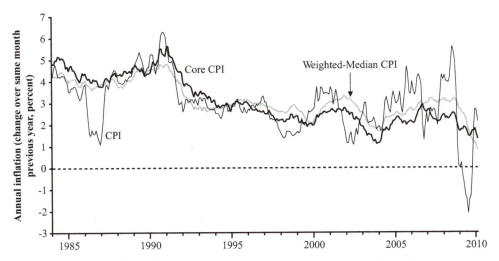

Figure 4.4. Core and Median Measures of CPI Inflation. Annual inflation: year over same month, previous year. *Source:* CPI and Core CPI, Bureau of Labor Statistics; Weighted-Median CPI, Federal Reserve Bank of Cleveland.

diverge, the prices of food and energy relative to other goods must be changing. If such divergences were permanent, policymakers who concentrated on core inflation would miss substantial changes in the underlying cost of living for consumers and would be misled over time about the general path of prices. But Figure 4.4 shows that, although the divergences often last for several years, core inflation tracks the overall CPI well over the longer term.

It is important to understand that excluding food and energy prices from core inflation is not to claim that they do not constitute genuine inflation. When oil prices rise, the consumer's bill for gasoline and home-heating oil rises, and the cost of living has gone up – sometimes painfully. For some purposes (say, for adjusting pensions), this is important. But monetary and fiscal policies aim to stabilize the overall rate of inflation of the general price level and cannot focus on any one price. If large fluctuations in energy or food prices are nearly always reversed, they represent changes in prices *relative* to the trend in the general price level and convey little information about the trend itself.

4.3.2 The Weighted-Median CPI

Because food production depends on highly variable weather conditions around the world, it seems likely that the volatility of food prices is a permanent feature of the economy. But is this necessarily true of energy prices as well? Most of the volatility in oil prices is the result of the particularly unstable nature of the political relationships of major oil exporters over the past forty or so years. This may or may not continue. And there is no reason to believe that other prices may not show similar episodes of volatility. The general rule is that in trying to judge the central tendency of price movements, less weight should be given to changes in prices that are volatile. This may sometimes mean discounting changes in energy prices, but it may also sometimes mean discounting changes in the prices of other types of goods.

Working at the Federal Reserve Bank of Cleveland, economists Michael Bryan and Stephen Cecchetti devised a CPI measure, called the **weighted-median CPI**, which discounts volatile price changes without assuming automatically that these must be food and energy prices. To construct the weighted-median CPI, they calculate the percentage changes of all the prices in the CPI bundle and then find the value that divides the prices into groups so that as many changes are above the value as are below it. An unusually large increase in an energy price or any other price will not change the median CPI at all unless it jumps from the group below the median to the group above the median. Even then, because it is just one of many prices in that group, it will not change the median very much. Only if most prices increase will the median increase noticeably.

The gray line in Figure 4.4 plots the weighted-median CPI. CPI-U, core CPI, and weighted-median CPI track each other fairly well. In the large run-ups in oil prices in the 1970s, early 1980s, and 2000s, as well as during the collapse in oil prices in 1986, there was a substantial deviation in the rate of inflation as measured by both the core and the median series compared to CPI-U. Median inflation is sometimes faster and sometimes slower than core inflation, reflecting the fact that food and energy prices are not always the most volatile prices.

Summary

1. Price indices are important for computing real quantities, for estimating inflation, and for making cost-of-living adjustments.
2. Price indices reduce large amounts of individual price information to a single number. There are many reasonable ways to do this and, so, many reasonable price indices.
3. The most common price index is the Laspeyres (base-weighted) index. It uses expenditure shares in a base period to form a weighted, arithmetic average of price changes.
4. The Laspeyres index suffers from substitution bias, as people typically reduce their expenditures on goods the prices of which increase relatively faster. It also suffers from new product and quality change biases, because base expenditure shares cannot reflect goods or new versions of goods that were not available in the base period.

5. The Paasche (current-weighted) index uses current expenditure shares to form a weighted average of price changes. It mitigates the biases of the Laspeyres index, but also suffers from a quality bias, as it underweights quality losses as people substitute inferior versions of goods to avoid rising prices.

6. The Fisher-ideal index is the geometric average of the Laspeyres and the Paasche indices. It aims to strike a happy medium between their conflicting biases.

7. In practice, the Fisher-ideal index is implemented as a chain-weighted index in which the base periods for the Laspeyres and Paasche indices are a period apart and are advanced each new period.

8. Estimates of real GDP are derived from nominal GDP, each component being deflated by an appropriate chain-weighted index. The ratio of nominal to real GDP expressed as a price index is called the GDP implicit price deflator. It measures the net effect of all the indices used to estimate real GDP.

9. The consumer price index (CPI) is the most commonly cited price index. It is essentially a Laspeyres index used to measure the cost of living for ordinary consumers. The CPI is economically important because many cost-of-living adjustments, including to Social Security payments, are based on it.

10. The personal consumption expenditure (PCE) deflator is the implicit price deflator for the consumption component of GDP. It uses much the same raw information as the CPI, but it is a chain-weighted index.

11. The producer price index (PPI) is the oldest U.S. price index. It measures prices for a large number of commodity groups and for various stages of processing from the point of view of the producer.

12. The core rate of inflation refers to CPI or PPI inflation, ignoring food and energy prices. These prices tend to track other prices over time, but are often highly volatile, so that month-to-month changes give little information about general price movements.

Key Concepts

price index	Paasche (current-weighted) index
general price level	quality change bias
base period	Fisher-ideal index
price factor	chain-weighted index
reference period	implicit price deflator
Laspeyres (base-weighted) index	cost-of-living index
substitution bias	core rate of inflation
new product bias	

Suggestions for Further Reading

Joseph Persky. "Retrospective: Price Indices and General Exchange Values," *Journal of Economic Perspectives*, vol. 12, no. 1 (Winter 1998), pp. 197–205.

Todd E. Clark. "A Comparison of the CPI and the PCE Price Index," *Federal Reserve Bank of Kansas City Economic Review*, vol. 84, no. 3 (3rd quarter), 1999, pp. 15–29.

Michael J. Boskin, et al. *Toward a More Accurate Measure of the Cost of Living.* Final Report to Senate Finance Committee from Advisory Commission to Study the Consumer Price Index, 4 December 1996.

Brian Motley. "Bias in the CPI: 'Roughly Right or Precisely Wrong,'" *Federal Reserve Bank of San Francisco Economic Letter*, 97–12, 23 May 1997.

Bureau of Labor Statistics. *BLS Handbook of Methods*, chapter 14 ("Producer Prices") and chapter 17 ("Consumer Prices"). Available on the BLS website: www.bls.gov/opub/hom/home.htm.

Problems

Data for this exercise are available on the textbook website under the link for Chapter 4 (appliedmacroeconomics.com). Before starting these exercises, the student should review the relevant portions of the *Guide to Working with Economic Data*, including sections G.1–G.4, G.6, and G.8–G.11.

Problem 4.1. The following information describes the "cop economy" in which the only two final goods are coffee and doughnuts.

	Coffee		Doughnuts	
Year	Quantity (cups)	Prices (dollars)	Quantity (number)	Prices (dollars)
2010	20	0.75	20	0.50
2011	30	1.00	18	0.75

(a) Compute the Laspeyres, Paasche, and Fisher-ideal indices for each year taking 2010 as the reference year ($p_{2010} = 100$).

(b) Compute real GDP for each year in constant 2010 dollars using the chain-weighted index.

(c) Compute real GDP for each year in constant 2011 dollars using the chain-weighted index.

Problem 4.2. Consider an economy completely described by the following goods and prices:

		Wine (bottles)	Hotel Accommodation (nights)	CDs (disks)
2009	price	$5	$100	$12
	quantity	50	5	10
2010	price	$6	$110	$15
	quantity	48	6	7
2011	price	$7	$120	$16
	quantity	45	7	8

(a) Taking 2009 to be the reference year ($p_{2009} = 100$) in each case, compute the Laspeyres (base-weighted) and Paasche (current-weighted) indices for each year.

(b) For each index compute the rates of inflation between 2009 and 2010, and between 2010 and 2011. Compute the average rate of inflation (expressed at a compound annual rate) between 2009 and 2011. Approximately how long will it take prices to grow fourfold if this rate of increase were to continue steadily?

(c) Using each index, compute real GDP for each year in constant 2009 dollars and the average rate of real GDP growth (compound annual rate) from 2009 to 2011.

(d) With reference to your computations in (a)–(c), explain the differences between the two indices.

(e) Calculate the chain-weighted price index for each year and use it to compute real GDP. Explain the relationship of these calculations to those in (a)–(c).

Problem 4.3. For the couch-potato economy of Table 4.1:

(a) Use 2010 as the base year (i.e., using the expenditure shares of 2010) to compute the price factor that measures how much prices increased between 2010 and 2012;

(b) Use the price factor to compute the price index for 2010 with a reference year of 2012 and for 2012 with reference year of 2010.

(c) Use the price index to compute the rate of inflation between 2010 and 2012 at a compound annual rate.

Problem 4.4.

(a) Show in detail how the Paasche and chain-weighted indices for 2012 were computed in Table 4.2.

(b) Using the chain-weighted index, show how real GDP for 2012 was computed in Table 4.2 for 2012 in the constant dollars of 2010, 2011, and 2012.

Problem 4.5. (This question draws on ideas from Chapter 3 as well as Chapter 4.) Elbonia is a country richly endowed with water and reeds, which are both free goods. It produces mud, *which is used exclusively for making bricks.* Bricks are baked in brick kilns and 10 percent of every batch of bricks must be used to keep the ovens in good repair. The Elbonians also produce funny reed hats. Here are the annual production figures and prices for Elbonia. Assume to begin with that Elbonia is a completely closed economy, completely owned by Elbonians.

		Mud (tons)	Bricks (number)	Hats (number)
2010	quantity	100	100,000	5,000
	price per unit (dollars)	810	1.00	20
2011	quantity	95	95,000	5,300
	price per unit (dollars)	891	1.10	21

(a) Calculate the following for each year: nominal GDP, the Laspeyres (base-weighted index), the Paasche (current weighted index), the chain index, and real GDP using the chain index. (For all price indices, take 2010 to be the reference year ($p_{2010} = 100$).

(b) Explain the difference between *gross* domestic product and *net* national product. Calculate the net national product for Elbonia at current prices in each year.

(c) Assume that all other things are the same as in the preceding table except that Elbonia opens trade with Italy. What would happen to nominal GDP and net exports in 2011 if Elbonia doubled its mud production and exported the entire additional amount in exchange for 100,000 Italian tiles priced at 0.50/tile?

(d) Assume that all other things are the same as in the preceding table, except that an American company buys half of the Elbonian hat-making industry in 2011. If the rate of profit is 10 percent of sales, what is the gross national product in 2010 and 2011?

Problem 4.6. The table gives actual expenditure shares and price indices for broad components of the CPI.

	Expenditure) Shares 2002 (percent)	Price Indices 2002 (1982–84 = 100)	Expenditure Shares 2010 (percent)	Price Indices 2010 (1982–84 = 100)
Food and Beverages	15.583	177.8	15.384	184.1
Housing	40.854	181.1	42.089	185.1
Apparel	4.220	121.5	3.975	119.0
Transportation	17.293	154.2	16.881	154.7
Medical Care	5.961	291.3	6.074	302.1
Recreation[a]	5.943	106.5	5.872	107.7
Education and Communication[a]	5.798	109.3	5.948	110.9
Other Goods and Services	4.350	295.6	3.776	300.2

[a] 1997 = 100 for these indices.

(a) Calculate the Laspeyres index for 2010, taking 2002 as the base and reference year.

(b) If the value of the CPI with 1982–1984 as the reference period ($p_{67} = 100$) was 180.9 in 2002, what is its value in 2010 based on your answer to (a)?

(c) The CPI is also reported with 1967 as the reference year ($p_{82-84} = 100$). If the value of the CPI with 1967 as the reference year was 541.9 in 2002, what is its value in 2010 based on your answer to (a)?

(d) Calculate the Paasche and Fisher-ideal indices for 2010 (taking 2002 as the reference year). Do your answers conform to the patterns discussed in section 4.1? If not, how do they differ? What might explain any differences?

Problem 4.7. Explain the advantages and disadvantages of the Laspeyres, Paasche, and chain-weighted indices.

Problem 4.8. Here are some actual prices of goods in past years, recorded in November of the indicated year: (i) Men's sport coat, $22.85 in 1960; (ii) Coffee (2 lbs.), $1.09 in 1965; (iii) Ford Sedan (Galaxie), $3,939 in 1972; (iv) Reclining Chair, $299 in 1981; Washing Machine, $349 in 1988. What are their prices in November 2011 constant dollars, using CPI-U as the price index?

Problem 4.9. Here are some actual prices of goods in the third quarter of 1998: (i) Vacuum Cleaner, $169; (ii) 10-piece Cookware Set, $299.99; (iii) Man's Sport Shirt, $24.99; (iv) 24" Television, $219.99; (v) Personal Computer, $604.00. What would their prices have been in the fourth quarter of 1980 and in the first quarter of 1948 constant dollars, using the GDP price deflator?

Problem 4.10. Here are some actual prices of past goods stated in 1992 constant dollars (using CPI-U): (i) One-Bedroom Apartment (Sacramento, California), $906 in 1960; (ii) Men's Necktie, $8.90 in 1965; (iii) Reclining Chair, $300.51 in 1972; (iv) Coffee (2 lbs.), $4.53 in 1981; (v) Ford Sedan (Galaxie), $11,809 in 1988. What would their prices have been in their year of sale?

Problem 4.11. (a) Calculate the difference between the annual rates of CPI and core CPI inflation reported in Figure 4.4. Visually, which is more variable? Calculate and report the mean, the variance, and the standard deviation of this difference.

(b) Using the calculation of the standard deviation, we can get an idea of how misleading CPI inflation might be for policymakers. Recall from the *Guide*, section G.6, that, if data are normally distributed, then about 62 percent of the time the data will be more than half a standard deviation above or below the mean; 32 percent of the time more than one standard deviation; and 5 percent of the time more than two standard deviations. Calculate the size of the difference (in percentage points) between CPI and core CPI at the 62, 32, and 5 percent reference points (i.e., how many percentage points of inflation correspond to 0.5, 1, and 2 standard deviations?). Would you judge that CPI inflation is very misleading or not very misleading relative to core CPI inflation for policymakers? Why?

Problem 4.12. The idea of categorizing producer prices by stages of processing is that crude prices pass on to intermediate prices, which in turn pass on to final producer prices. Compare the PPI at these three stages of processing using whatever graphics and calculations you deem appropriate. At which stage of processing are prices more variable? Is there any long-term trend for prices at one stage of processing to grow faster or slower than at other stages? Is there any evidence that prices at earlier stages predict prices at later stages?

Part III
Trends and Cycles

5

Trends and Cycles

The last three chapters focused on the measurement of key national accounting variables: GDP and prices. Although these are the centerpiece of macroeconomic analysis, there are thousands of other measures of the economy – most related in one way or another to GDP and its components. In this chapter, we begin a wider examination of the economy, shifting our focus to the question, how do GDP and a large variety of other economic variables behave over time? We begin by dividing their movements into longer run trends and shorter run cycles. We then ask, are the cycles in different variables closely related to an economy-wide business cycle? And, finally, what are the properties of the business cycle?

5.1 Decomposing Time Series

Look back at Figure 2.10 or 2.12. Each shows the path of U.S. real GDP over a period of about sixty years. Two characteristics of these graphs stand out. First, the dominant movement of U.S. GDP is upward. But, second, the movement is unsteady: there are frequent and, at best, roughly regular ups and downs. A large proportion of the thousands of economic time series that describe the economy behave similarly. Take three examples: Figure 5.1 shows the time series for personal disposable income (less transfers), industrial production, and employment. Each one resembles GDP; each displays a pattern of fluctuations around a dominant upward path.

The economist often finds it useful to distinguish the dominant path, known as the **TREND**, from the fluctuations, known as the **CYCLE**, because distinct factors explain each. Most of the later chapters of this book aim to explain the trend (especially Chapters 9 and 10) or the cycle (especially Chapters 13–15).

The upper panel of Figure 5.2 shows a stylized version of an economic time series, which cycles regularly about a smooth exponential trend. The time series may be decomposed in two steps: first, estimate the trend and, second, express the fluctuations as deviations from the trend. The lower panel shows the cycle, now measured as the difference between the time series and its

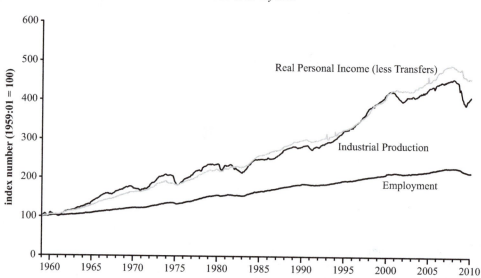

Figure 5.1. Trends and Cycles in Selected Time Series. Like real GDP, many economic time series show a pattern of fluctuations (a cycle) around an underlying growth path (a trend). *Source:* real personal income, Bureau of Labor Statistics; employment, Bureau of Economic Affairs; industrial production, Board of Governors of the Federal Reserve.

trend expressed as a percentage of the trend. Displaying the cycle as a percentage of the trend makes sense: although the fluctuations of an economic variable are likely to be *absolutely* smaller when its average value is small, there is no reason to believe that they will be *relatively* smaller than when its absolute value is large.

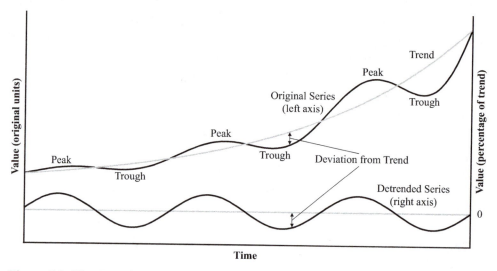

Figure 5.2. The Trend and Cycle of Stylized Economic Time Series. The detrended series is the difference between the trend and the original series expressed as a percentage of the trend. Peaks and troughs of the original series are also the peaks and troughs of the detrended series.

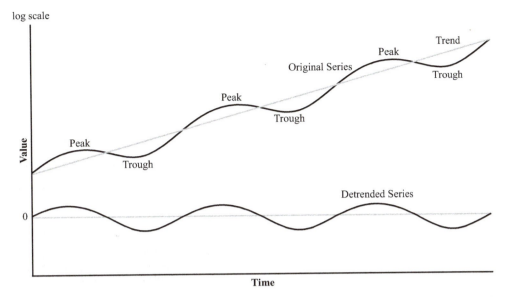

Figure 5.3. The Trend and Cycle of a Stylized Economic Time Series: A Logarithmic Version. The detrended series is the difference between the trend and the original series. Since the difference of logarithms is a ratio, the detrended series can be interpreted as a percentage of the original trend series. Peaks and troughs of the original series are also the peaks and troughs of the detrended series.

As we saw in Chapter 2, it is sometimes convenient to display economic time series on logarithmic graphs. Figure 5.3 displays the same information as Figure 5.2 using a logarithmic scale. The exponential trend becomes a linear trend. The lower panel shows the *difference* log(time series) – log(trend). Because the difference in logarithms is a ratio, just like a percentage difference, the lower panel is qualitatively identical to the lower panel in Figure 5.2. And, if we multiply by 100, it too can be read in percentage points. (See the *Guide*, section G.11, on logarithms and logarithmic graphs.) The key to decomposing any time series into its trend and cycle is the identification of the trend. (The *Guide*, section G.12, discusses some useful methods for estimating trends.)

In either the original or the logarithmic representation, a local high point is a **CYCLICAL PEAK** and a local valley is a **CYCLICAL TROUGH**. A complete cycle can be measured from peak to peak or from trough to trough. Sometimes the trend growth is referred to as **secular** change (or growth) to distinguish it from cyclical fluctuations.

Of course, Figures 5.2 and 5.3 are only stylizations. Compare Figure 5.2 to Figure 5.4, which shows actual real GDP and its trend in the upper part and the percentage deviations from trend below for the 1970s. The graphs of actual data are not as regular as the stylized graphs, but the overall similarity is clear.

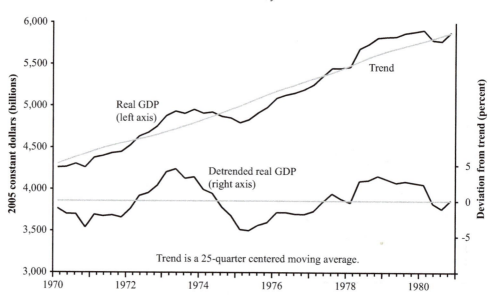

Figure 5.4. Real GDP: Trend and Cycle, 1970–1980. *Source:* Bureau of Economic Analysis.

5.2 The Business Cycle

5.2.1 The Language of Business Cycles

A careful look at Figure 5.1 shows that the ups and downs of the four series are closely related. When the data are detrended (Figure 5.5), the pattern is even more clear. This is not mere chance. The cyclical patterns of a large number of economic time series are closely related. The tendency of many

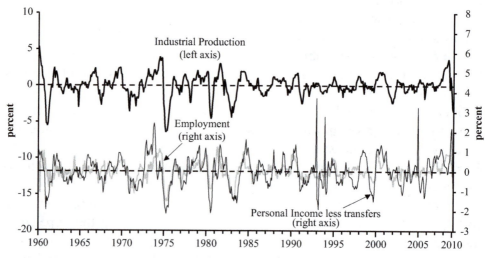

Figure 5.5. Selected Detrended Time Series. *Source:* real personal income, Bureau of Labor Statistics; employment, Bureau of Economic Affairs; industrial production, Board of Governors of the Federal Reserve.

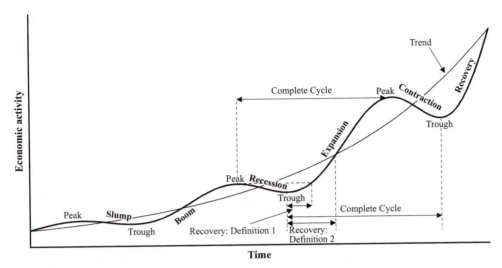

Figure 5.6. A Stylized Economic Time Series. The period from peak to trough is a *recession* (also known as a *slump* or *contraction*). The period from trough to peak is known as an *expansion* (also known as a *boom* or *recovery*). *Recovery* is sometimes used to indicate only a portion of the upswing, either: 1. the period from trough to the level of the previous peak; or 2. the period from trough to the level of the trend. A (*complete*) *cycle* is the period between a trough and the subsequent trough or a peak and the subsequent peak.

measures of economic activity to move in concert suggests that there are common driving forces and that we can think not just about the trends and cycles of the individual measures, but of a business cycle. A reasonable definition runs:

The **BUSINESS CYCLE** is *the alternation in the state of the economy of a roughly consistent periodicity and with rough coherence between different measures of the economy.*[1]

"Rough coherence" in this definition reflects the tendency of different economic time series to move up or down in closely related patterns. Saying that the economy-wide ups and downs are "roughly consistent" acknowledges the fact that, even though they are not evenly spaced, the pattern of ups and downs does not appear to be completely random: over the past 150 years, the average business cycle lasted four to five years; the shortest, less than two years; the longest, ten years.

As with cycles in particular times series, business cycles are identified by their peaks and troughs (see Figure 5.6). A specialized language has developed to describe business cycles. Key terms include:

- **RECESSION** (synonyms: **slump**, **contraction**): *the period between the cyclical peak and the cyclical trough, when economic activity is falling.*

---

[1] Occasionally, one still hears an older name of the business cycle: the *trade cycle*.

- **EXPANSION** (synonyms: **boom**, **recovery**): *the period between the cyclical trough and cyclical peak, when economic activity is rising.* "Recovery" is sometimes used in the more limited sense of the period between the trough and when the economy regains either (1) the level of activity experienced at the previous peak or (2) the level it would have experienced had it remained on trend (see Figure 5.6).
- **Depression**: *a particularly severe recession.* Originally, "depression" was a synonym – indeed, a euphemism – for a recession. Unfortunately, it became associated with the largest slump in U.S. and world economic history: the *Great Depression of 1929–1933*, in which real GDP fell 27 percent and the unemployment rate rose from a little more than 3 percent to just under 25 percent from the peak to the trough.[2] "Depression" is now largely reserved for a recession that is particularly severe in both scale and duration. Several of the contractions of the nineteenth century are considered depressions, but the Great Depression is the only example of the twentieth century.
- **Growth recession**: *a period of slower than trend growth, usually lasting a year or more.* During a growth recession, output continues to rise, but at so slow a rate that other aspects of the economy – particularly, employment – may stagnate or fall. A growth recession may be a harbinger of a proper recession.
- **(Complete) cycle**: *the period between a peak and the following peak or between a trough and the following trough.*

5.2.2 Dating the Business Cycle

The problem of dating business cycles is really just a matter of determining when the economy reaches its peaks and its troughs. With so ambiguous a notion as "the state of the economy," there is no unique way to identify the business cycle.

A common rule of thumb defines a recession as two consecutive quarters of negative growth in real GDP. The peak would then be marked at the quarter immediately before GDP begins to fall, and the trough at the quarter immediately before it begins to grow again.

Although it has no official status, the National Bureau of Economic Research (NBER), a private, nonprofit organization, is widely regarded in the United States as the arbiter of the beginnings and ends of recessions. The NBER explicitly rejects the two-quarter rule. According to the NBER, a *recession* is

a significant decline in economic activity spread across the economy, lasting more than a few months, normally visible in real GDP, real income, employment, industrial production, and wholesale-retail sales.[3]

---

[2] Although technically the trough of the Great Depression was reached in March of 1933, many economic historians regard the entire decade of the 1930s as depressed with recovery not secure until the United States entered World War II at the end of 1941.

[3] Quoted from the NBER website (www.nber.org/cycles.html); downloaded 15 December 2009.

Declining real GDP is, of course, typical of recessions, but the NBER Business-Cycle-Dating Committee regards it as an inadequate measure, because it is too narrow in its scope and calculated only quarterly. The NBER casts its net wider and looks closely at monthly, as well as quarterly, data. There is no formal rule. The NBER's judgment is based on its overall impressions of the movements of many series. The complete set of NBER business-cycle dates is given in Table 5.1.

The data that the NBER uses are often published only with a substantial delay, and the committee usually must wait to see whether a change in direction is reversed or confirmed by subsequent data. As a result, the dates of the peaks and troughs are not typically announced until six months to a year after they occur. A recession is usually nearly over before its onset is declared. An expansion is usually well underway before the end of the recession is known to the public.

In the 1992 presidential campaign, the delay in announcing the end of the recession allowed Bill Clinton to claim (with some plausibility) that the economy was in one of the longest recessions of the postwar period – which, of course, he blamed on the first President Bush. His catchphrase was, "It's the economy, stupid!" In fact, the recession of 1990–1991 was the second shortest in the postwar period: it lasted only eight months, and had ended by March of 1991 – twenty months before the election. In fairness to Clinton and the voters who agreed with his view of the economy, the unemployment rate did not begin to fall until June of 1992 (three months after the trough) and did not reach its level at the cyclical peak (6.8 percent) until August 1993 – more than two years after the recovery had begun. This is not unusual; the peak in the unemployment rate typically lags the cyclical trough. As we saw in Chapter 3 (section 3.6.2), the NBER did not announce that the economy had reached its cyclical trough in November 2001 until March 2003. And the Democrats again (and again with some plausibility) blamed President Bush the younger for an economy effectively in recession in the run-up to the 2004 election.

5.2.3 The Typical Business Cycle

How well do the NBER business-cycle dates capture the cyclical fluctuations in the U.S. economy? This is largely a question of how well they cohere with the movements of time series that can be taken to be good reflections of the general state of the economy. Economists have studied thousands of economic time series and classified their cyclical behavior. To try to give some feeling for the business cycle as a whole, the U.S. Department of Commerce created **indices of ECONOMIC INDICATORS**, similar to price indices. (Since 1995, the indices have been compiled by the Conference Board, a nonprofit

Table 5.1. *NBER Business-Cycle Dates*

| Business-Cycle Reference Dates | | Duration in Months | | | |
Peak[a]	Trough[a]	Expansion Trough to Peak	Contraction Peak to Trough	Cycle Trough from Previous Trough	Cycle Peak from Previous Peak
—	December (IV) 1854	—	—	—	—
June (II) 1857	December (IV) 1858	30	18	48	—
October (III) 1860	June (III) 1861	22	8	30	40
April (I) 1865	December (I) 1867	46	32	78	54
June (II) 1869	December (IV) 1870	18	18	36	50
October (III) 1873	March (I) 1879	34	65	99	52
March (I) 1882	May (II) 1885	36	38	74	101
March (II) 1887	April (I) 1888	22	13	35	60
July (III) 1890	May (II) 1891	27	10	37	40
January (I) 1893	June (II) 1894	20	17	37	30
December (IV) 1895	June (II) 1897	18	18	36	35
June (III) 1899	December (IV) 1900	24	18	42	42
September (IV) 1902	August (III) 1904	21	23	44	39
May (II) 1907	June (II) 1908	33	13	46	56
January (I) 1910	January (IV) 1912	19	24	43	32
January (I) 1913	December (IV) 1914	12	23	35	36

Peak		Trough					
August (III)	1918	March (I)	1919	7	44	51	67
January (I)	1920	July (III)	1921	18	10	28	17
May (II)	1923	July (III)	1924	14	22	36	40
October (III)	1926	November (IV)	1927	13	27	40	41
August (III)	1929	March (I)	1933	43	21	64	34
May (II)	1937	June (II)	1938	13	50	63	93
February (I)	1945	October (IV)	1945	8	80	88	93
November (IV)	1948	October (IV)	1949	11	37	48	45
July (II)	1953	May (II)	1954	10	45	55	56
August (III)	1957	April (II)	1958	8	39	47	49
April (II)	1960	February (I)	1961	10	24	34	32
December (IV)	1969	November (IV)	1970	11	106	117	116
November (IV)	1973	March (I)	1975	16	36	52	47
January (I)	1980	July (III)	1980	6	58	64	74
July (III)	1981	November (IV)	1982	16	12	28	18
July (III)	1990	March (I)	1991	8	92	100	108
March (I)	2001	November (IV)	2001	8	120	128	128
December (IV)	2007	June (II)	2009	18	73	91	81

Average, all cycles:

1854–2009	(33 cycles)			17	39	56	57[b]
1854–1919	(16 cycles)			22	27	48	49[c]
1919–1945	(6 cycles)			18	35	53	53
1945–2009	(11 cycles)			11	58	69	68

[a] Roman numerals indicate quarters; [b] 32 cycles; [c] 15 cycles.
Source: National Bureau of Economic Research.

Table 5.2. *Component Series of the Indices of Business-Cycle Indicators*

Index of Leading Indicators	Index of Coincident Indicators	Index of Lagging Indicators
1. Average weekly hours, manufacturing	1. Employees on nonagricultural payrolls	1. Average duration of unemployment[a]
2. Average weekly initial claims for unemployment insurance[a]	2. Personal income less transfer payments	2. Inventories to sales ratio, manufacturing and trade
3. Manufacturers' new orders, consumer goods and materials	3. Industrial production	3. Change in labor cost per unit of output, manufacturing[b]
4. Vendor performance, slower deliveries diffusion index	4. Manufacturing and trade sales	4. Average bank prime rate[b]
5. Manufacturers' new orders, nondefense capital goods		5. Commercial and industrial loans
6. Building permits, new private housing units		6. Consumer installment credit to personal income ratio
7. Stock prices, 500 common stocks		7. Change in consumer price index for services[b]
8. Money supply, M2		
9. Interest rate spread, 10-year Treasury bonds rate minus federal funds rate[b]		
10. Index of consumer expectations		

[a] Inverted series, a negative change in this component makes a positive contribution.
[b] In percent change form, contributions based on arithmetic changes.
Source: Conference Board.

business organization.) Each of the three indices (leading, coincident, and lagging indicators of the business cycle) is a weighted average of several monthly time series and is expressed as an index number based such that the average value for 2004 equals 100. Table 5.2 shows the component series for each index. At this stage, we are concerned only with the **index of coincident indicators** – a group of time series whose peaks and troughs should correspond to the peaks and troughs of the business cycle. (We will consider leading and lagging indicators later in section 5.3.) Figure 5.7 shows that the peaks and troughs of the (detrended) coincident indicators closely match the NBER cycle dates.

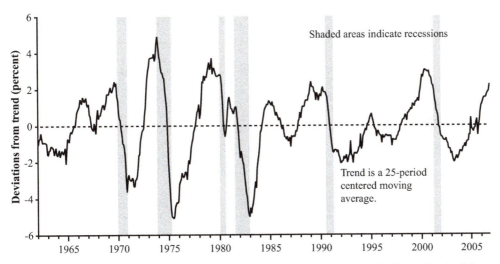

Figure 5.7. Coincident Indicators and the Business Cycle. The index of coincident indicators conforms well, though not perfectly, with the NBER business-cycle dates. Shaded areas are NBER recessions. Trend is a 25-period centered moving average. *Source:* Conference Board.

How can we characterize the typical business cycle? Figure 5.8 provides one answer with another view of the relationship between the coincident indicators and the NBER cycle dates. The figure is centered on the business-cycle peak, marked 0. The index of coincident indicators is rescaled to take the value of 100 at the business-cycle peak (see the *Guide*, section G.8.1). The figure shows twelve months before the peak (−1 to −12) and thirty-six months after (+1 to +36). The vertical lines indicate the NBER peaks and troughs. The black lines show average values for the eight recessions

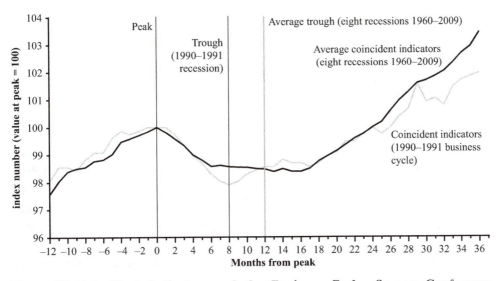

Figure 5.8. Coincident Indicators and the Business Cycle. *Source:* Conference Board.

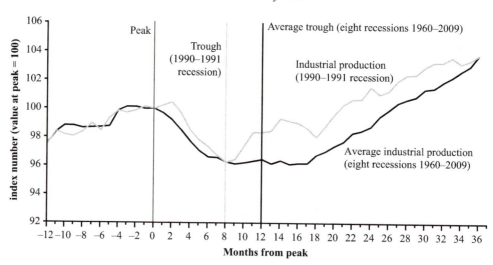

Figure 5.9(a). Industrial Production and the Business Cycle. *Source:* Board of Governors of the Federal Reserve System.

between 1960 and 2009, while the gray lines show the values for the 1990–1991 recession. (At the time of writing this chapter, the recession that began in December 2007 and ended in June 2009 was less than 36 months old. And as noted in Chapter 3, the recession of 2001 is somewhat unusual. Students are asked to examine it in problem 5.13.) The average index peaks exactly at the NBER peak. At +13 months, its trough is close to the average trough for the eight recessions 1960–2009 (+12). In 1990–1991 the coincident indicators track the NBER cycle dates exactly.

Figures 5.9 (a)–(c) examine the typical cyclical behavior of the three time series already displayed in Figure 5.1: personal income (less transfers), industrial production, and employment. These are three of the four components of the index of coincident economic indicators. The pattern of industrial production most strongly resembles that of the index of coincident indicators. Although the average series peaks at −3, it is virtually flat up to the point of the NBER business-cycle peak. Similarly, the actual trough at +9 is three periods ahead of the average NBER trough; the series is virtually flat through +17. And the data for 1990–1991 are nearly coincident.

The pattern for employment is similar for the average series, but the major losses in employment tend to come early in the recession, so that employment falls only slowly to its trough. The pattern of employment in the 1990–1991 recession is different: it peaks before the NBER peak, flattens out near the NBER trough, and begins a steady recovery only eight to ten months after the NBER trough. It was this anomalous pattern that supported the Democrats' claim that the economy was still in recession at the time of the 1992 election.

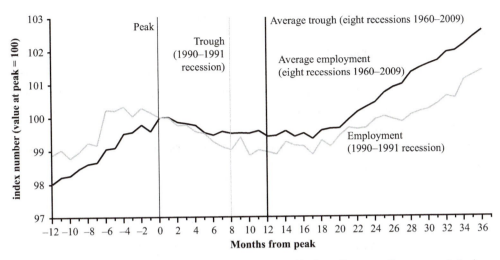

Figure 5.9(b). Employment and the Business Cycle. *Source:* Bureau of Labor Statistics.

The pattern of personal income less transfers is almost perfectly coincident at the peak; but for both the average series and the 1990–1991 series, it begins to recover before the NBER trough, though more rapidly after the trough.

Table 5.1 and Figures 5.7–5.9 give us a good picture of the history of recent U.S. business cycles. At least two characteristics are worth noting. First, the average recession in the post-World War II period lasted eleven months, while the average expansion lasted fifty months. Far from acting like the simple, symmetrical sine waves in the stylized graphs of Figures 5.2 and 5.3, business cycles are *asymmetrical*. The process of economic growth over the

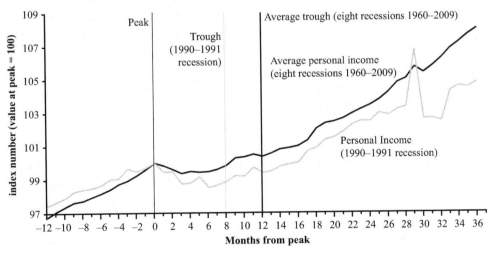

Figure 5.9(c). Personal Income (less transfers) and the Business Cycle. *Source:* Bureau of Economic Analysis.

last fifty years can be characterized as a pattern of five steps forward and one step back.

Second, the expansion that began in December of 1982 is the third longest on record, the expansion that began in April 1991 is the longest, and the recession that separated them is tied with the 2001 recession as the second shortest. Consequently, the typical college student in 2011 has lived through the longest sustained period of growth in U.S. economy history. Thus, the recession that began in December of 2007 is the first serious economic downturn that most students have faced.

5.3 The Business Cycle and the Economy

5.3.1 What Causes the Business Cycle?

The causes and proper analysis of the business cycle have been hotly debated by economists since it was first identified as a regular phenomenon in the nineteenth century. Economists have found it useful to distinguish two aspects of the cycle: IMPULSE and PROPAGATION MECHANISMS. A child on a swing follows a cyclical pattern. A mother who gives the child an occasional push provides the impulse. In this case, the cycle is caused by the propagation mechanism – that is, by gravity and the construction of the swing that limit its motion, guaranteeing that an outward motion reaches a peak, is reversed and reaches a trough on the backswing. Theories of the business cycle differ in whether they place the main emphasis on the impulse or the propagation mechanism.

One class of theories argues that the propagation mechanisms in the economy are – like the swing – intrinsically cyclical. Many of the cycles in nature, such as the tides or the paths of the moon and the planets, are intrinsic. Even a complex cycle, such as the vibration of a guitar string that needs impulses from time to time to continuing sounding, is mainly governed by its propagation mechanism. If the economy has an intrinsic cycle it is necessarily a highly complex one – more complex than the guitar string or the tides.

A second class of theories holds that the cycles in the economy are the result primarily of cycles in the impulse mechanisms themselves. In the nineteenth century, William Stanley Jevons (1835–1882) argued that variations in solar activity, correlated with sunspots, caused variations in agricultural harvests and, ultimately, caused the business cycle. Although Jevons' theory was never widely accepted, some economists today argue that exogenous cycles in technology cause the business cycle. Others believe that recurring recessions are induced by the actions of policymakers. If the Federal Reserve would just leave the economy to its own devices, and not raise

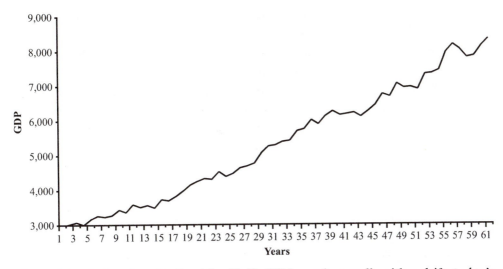

Figure 5.10. A Random Walk with a Drift. With random walk with a drift, today's value is yesterday's value plus a percentage growth term (the *drift*) plus a random term as equally likely to move up as down (the *random walk*). Such a series may appear to have a cycle (this one looks remarkably like the graph of real GDP), but there is no genuine regularity behind its fluctuations.

interest rates from time to time, advocates of this view believe that the economy would suffer few recessions.

A third class of theories argues that business cycles are ultimately irregular. Yes, there are ups and downs, but the patterns that we see in these ups and downs are illusory. Imagine that GDP tends to grow on average 2 percent per year, but that each year completely random good or bad events – events with no cycle – occur. Statisticians describe such a pattern as a **random walk** with a drift. (The drift is the 2 percent trend growth.) The pattern is called a "random walk" because it resembles the path that a drunken man might take after leaving the tavern: because each step is just as likely to go in one direction as another, the best average prediction of where the man will be after his next step is where he is now standing. Figure 5.10 shows a random walk with a drift that looks strikingly similar to graphs of real GDP (e.g., Figure 2.10). The apparent cyclical patterns in the figure are purely accidental and do not describe a genuine phenomenon in need of a theoretical explanation.

The jury is still out on which type of account of business cycles describes the actual economy: Are its ups and downs governed by laws as regular (if more complex than) those of physics and biology? Or are the ups and downs really just a reflection of the way in which the economy processes random influences? Or is there room for some combination of these mechanisms (e.g., random influences superimposed on underlying regular patterns)? We cannot hope to give definitive answers in an intermediate textbook. They are the agenda for cutting-edge economic research.

If the random-walk explanation is correct, then the cyclical behavior of the economy is an illusion. Economists who do not want to imply the strong notion of regularity that often attends the word "cycle" sometimes use *economic fluctuations* as a more neutral description than "business cycle." But there is something lifeless about this term; so, we shall continue to use "business cycle" throughout this book.

5.3.2 The Classification of Economic Indicators

Our definition of the business cycle had two parts: (1) alternation in the state of the economy; and (2) coherence among different measures of the economy. While economists continue to debate the ultimate sources of alternation, and even whether the patterns are truly recurring ones, they understand much better the nature of the coherence among different measures. Sometimes the connections are obvious. It takes workers to produce goods; therefore, it is not surprising that employment and industrial production follow similar patterns over time. It takes income to support expenditure; therefore, it is not surprising that consumption follows a similar pattern to income. Other connections are less obvious, and much of economic theory (and much of this textbook) aim to make them more clear. As a starting place, it is useful to have a good vocabulary to describe the relationships among different time series.

Economic indicators can be classified according to how they behave compared to the business cycle. We have already used the index of coincident indicators as a measure of the cycle. An indicator is said to be *coincident* if it reaches its peak at or near the peak of the business cycle and reaches its trough at or near the trough of the business cycle.

Economic indicators are classified by whether or not they generally move in the same direction as the main positive measures of the business cycle, such as GDP, industrial production, or employment. Indicators can be

- **procyclical**: they move in roughly the same direction as the business cycle (e.g., retail sales are procyclical);
- **countercyclical**: they move in roughly the opposite direction as the business cycle (e.g., the unemployment rate is countercyclical); or
- **acyclical**: they have no regular relationship to the cycle (e.g., agricultural production and population are acyclical).[4]

---

[4] Even though it has its own ups and downs, agricultural production follows the seasons and year-to-year fluctuations in the weather, rather than fluctuations in the economy as a whole. Agriculture now constitutes only 2.5 percent of the economy by total employment. In the past, when its share in the economy was larger, it would have been more closely related to the business cycle.

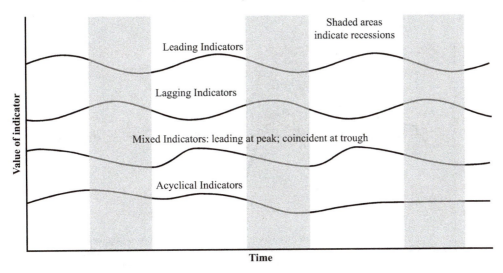

Figure 5.11 Classification of Economic Indicators. Shaded areas indicate recessions.

Indicators are also classified by their *phase relationship* to the business cycle – that is, according to whether their extreme points occur before, after, or at the same time as the extreme points of the business cycle. Some possibilities for procyclical time series are illustrated in Figure 5.11.

- A **leading indicator** reaches its peak and trough *before* the corresponding peak or trough of the business cycle;
- A **lagging indicator** reaches its peak and trough *after* the corresponding peak and trough of the business cycle;
- A **mixed indicator** follows a *regular* pattern different from either the leading or lagging indicator. The third series in Figure 5.11 shows a mixed indicator that leads the business-cycle peak at the peak, but is coincident at the business-cycle trough. There are many possible mixed patterns.

Countercyclical indicators can also be leading, lagging, or mixed indicators. The average duration of unemployment, for example, is a countercyclical, lagging indicator of the business cycle.

The U.S. Department of Commerce developed, and the Conference Board now maintains and publishes monthly, indices of leading, coincident, and lagging economic indicators. Table 5.2 shows the component series of these indices.

5.3.3 Is the Business Cycle Predictable?

The fact that a number of time series are consistent leading economic indicators suggests that it may be possible, to some degree, to predict the course

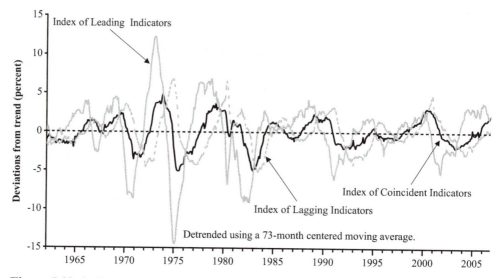

Figure 5.12. Indices of Business-Cycle Indicators. The three indices show closely related movements. As seen most easily at the peaks and troughs, the leading economic indicators anticipate the movements of the coincident indicators, which in turn anticipate the movements of the lagging indicators. *Source:* Conference Board.

of the business cycle. Figure 5.12 shows the three indices of economic indicators (detrended). Notice first the broad similarity of the fluctuations. All three series are procyclical, and they show the rough coherence that characterizes the business cycle.[5] Looking more closely, we see the expected pattern (especially clear at the peaks and troughs): the leading indicators move ahead of the coincident indicators, which, in their turn, move ahead of the lagging indicators.

How well can the relationships among the indicators be exploited to forecast the path of the business cycle? There are two questions: First, how long on average is the lead between the leading and coincident indicators? Second, how strongly related are the two indices? The second question can be answered by calculating the coefficient of correlation between the two indices. (See the *Guide*, section G.13, on the measurement of correlation.) The correlation between the leading and coincident indicators is 0.52, which is a moderate, positive correlation. But we should not really expect a strong correlation between the leading indicators today and coincident indicators today. We know that the leading indicators move ahead of the coincident indicators. We can instead calculate the correlation between the coincident indicators in each period and the leading indicators one or more months earlier. The correlation between the index of coincident indicators

[5] One of the component series of the index of leading indicators and one of the lagging indicators are actually countercyclical, but they are multiplied by −1 before being entered into the indices, so that all components tend to move in the same direction relative to the business cycle.

Table 5.3. *Correlations among Business-Cycle Indicators*

Number of Months Lead	Leading Indicator	Lagging Indicator
−12	−0.45	0.86
−11	−0.39	0.88
−10	−0.32	0.89
−9	−0.25	0.89
−8	−0.18	0.88
−7	−0.10	0.87
−6	−0.02	0.85
−5	0.06	0.81
−4	0.15	0.76
−3	0.24	0.71
−2	0.34	0.64
−1	0.43	0.56
0	**0.52**	**0.47**
+1	0.60	0.38
+2	0.67	0.30
+3	0.72	0.21
+4	0.77	0.13
+5	0.80	0.05
+6	0.83	−0.03
+7	0.85	−0.10
+8	0.86	−0.17
+9	0.86	−0.24
+10	0.85	−0.30
+11	0.83	−0.35
+12	0.81	−0.40

Entries represent the correlation coefficient between the current value of the indices of leading and lagging indicators and the value of the index of coincident indicators 1 to 12 months earlier and 1 to 12 months later.
Source: Conference Board and author's calculations.

and the index of leading indicators one month earlier is 0.60 – a little bit stronger.

Table 5.3 presents the results of such calculations for leads and lags of zero to twelve months. The first column shows the correlations between the coincident indicators and the leading economic indicators. The row labeled 0 is the correlation when both indices are measured in the same month. It is, as we already observed, 0.52. The row labeled +1 indicates correlation between the leading indicators and the coincident indicators one month later. It measures how well the leading indicators predict the later coincident indicators and, therefore, the business cycle. Again, we already have seen that the value is 0.60. Subsequent rows (labeled +2 to +12) show

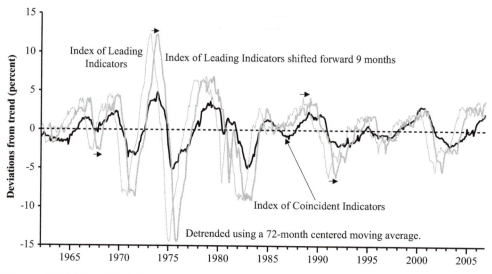

Figure 5.13. How Well Do the Leading Indicators Predict the Business Cycle? Shifting the leading economic indicators forward by nine months aligns them closely with the coincident indicators, giving some evidence of their ability to signal business-cycle fluctuations roughly three quarters ahead. *Source:* Conference Board.

the correlation between the leading indicators and the coincident indicators two, three, and up to twelve months ahead, as well as one to twelve months behind (−1 to −12). The second column shows a similar set of correlations between the lagging indicators and the coincident indicators.

The highest correlation between the coincident and leading indicators is 0.86 at +8 and +9 months lead (that is, roughly three quarters ahead). Such a strong correlation suggests that the leading indicators are a good, though imperfect, predictor of the future behavior of the business cycle. The point is reinforced visually in Figure 5.13, which is similar to Figure 5.12, except that the index of leading indicators has been shifted forward by nine months (i.e., the value for January is plotted at the following September and so forth). Once shifted, the leading and coincident indicators line up extremely well.

News reports frequently say that the index of leading economic indicators is the government's "main forecasting tool" and that the index signals downturns in the economy six to nine months ahead. The first claim is hyperbole. Most government forecasts are, in fact, generated from macroeconomic computer models of the economy in which tens, or even hundreds, of equations represent different aspects of the economy, and the index of leading economic indicators plays no part whatsoever. Also, as we noted earlier, the government has given over the maintenance of the business-cycle indicators to the private sector.

There is, nevertheless, good reason to believe that the index of leading indicators does have some predictive power for the business cycle. Notice that in Table 5.3 the correlation between the leading and coincident indicators is above 0.8 for each of the months between +5 and +12. This supports the idea that the leading indicators help to forecast recessions. A popular rule of thumb states that two months of consecutive declines in the leading indicators signals an imminent recession. This rule often works, but it also works too often: most recessions are predicted accurately, but sometimes a recession is predicted and none occurs. Others have suggested three months of decline, rather than two, to give more accurate predictions. In that case, however, there is necessarily less lead time between the signal and the onset of the recession.

One reason that the leading economic indicators are important is that, as we discussed in section 5.2.2, as well as in Chapter 3 (section 3.6.2), there is often considerable delay in getting relevant information about coincident indicators. One of the roles of the index of lagging economic indicators is to buttress the evidence that the economy actually entered or left a recession and to help to resolve the uncertainty that clouds all judgments about the state of the economy. Table 5.3 shows that the correlation between the lagging and the coincident indicators is highest at 0.89 with a lag of –9 to –10 months (roughly three quarters behind).

The consistent patterns of the leading, lagging, and coincident indicators demonstrate that there are facts about the business cycle that economists need to explain. They give some clues about the course of the business cycle. But they do not, in themselves, explain why the business cycle behaves as it does. In later chapters, we will try to understand the mechanisms that account for these patterns.

Summary

1. Many economic time series are dominated by fluctuations around a dominant tendency to grow. These may be decomposed into a trend, reflecting growth, and a cycle reflecting the fluctuations.
2. The high point of a cycle relative to trend is known as the peak; and the low point, the trough. A complete cycle is measured peak to peak or trough to trough.
3. The business cycle is the tendency of the state of the economy (measured by a wide variety of time series) to fluctuate in a roughly regular manner.
4. A complete business cycle includes a recession (the period from peak to trough) and an expansion (the period from trough to peak).
5. Business cycles are dated according to their peaks and troughs. The relevant information often arrives with a substantial delay.
6. The expansion phase of the typical post-World War II business cycle in the United States is about five times as long as the recession phase (50 versus 11 months).
7. Economists remain divided over the causes of business cycles. Some point to cycles in the extrinsic impulses to the economy. Others point to intrinsic

economic behavior that propagates cycles. Still others believe that the fluctuations are not true cycles, but random movements that merely suggest a cycle.

8. Whether cycles are genuine or not in the sense of possessing a deep regularity, economic behavior does explain common movements among economic time series. Series can be classified as moving with the business cycle (procyclical), against the cycle (countercyclical), or unrelated to the cycle (acyclical). They may also systematically lead, lag, or coincide with the business cycle, or have some more complex relationship to it.

9. The existence of patterns in which some time series are leading indicators for the business cycle implies that the cycle may itself be predicted. The index of leading economic indicators tends to lead the business cycle by about nine months.

Key Concepts

trend	recession
cycle	expansion
cyclical peak	economic indicators
cyclical trough	impulse mechanism
business cycle	propagation mechanism

Suggestions for Further Reading

National Bureau of Economic Research, Business Cycle Dating Committee website (*nber.org/cycles/main.html*) contains useful articles about its procedures and announcements of particular peaks and troughs.

Norman Frumkin. *Guide to Economic Indicators*. Armonk, NY: M. E. Sharpe, 1990.

F. M. O'Hara, Jr. and F. M. O'Hara, III. *Handbook of United States Economic Indicators*, revised edition. Westport, CT: Greenwood Press, 2000.

Problems

Data for this exercise are available on the course website under the link for Chapter 5 (appliedmacroeconomics.com). Before starting these exercises, the student should review the relevant portions of the *Guide to Working with Economic Data*: sections G.4, G.7, and G.13.

Problem 5.1. In Problem 2.16 you were supposed to have identified the peaks and troughs of the business cycle using the two-quarter rule. If you have not done this exercise already, do it now. Table 5.1 gives the NBER monthly dates in which peaks and troughs occurred. Convert these to the equivalent quarters and then construct a table that compares your results from Problem 2.16 to the NBER dates. Go the NBER's Business-Cycle Dating Committee's website (*nber.org/cycles/main.html*). Read the Frequently Asked Questions and other documents relating to their dating procedures. In light of the information provided by the NBER and your own understanding of the business cycle, explain how and why your dates differ from the official NBER dates.

Problem 5.2. (a) Using Table 5.1, construct your own table identifying by date and duration in months the shortest and longest booms, slumps, and complete cycles (peak to peak and trough to trough) for the period from 1946 to the present. Also identify by date and duration the median boom, slump, and complete cycle.

(b) Repeat the exercise in part (a) for the period before 1942.

(c) Does the business cycle have noticeably different characteristics before and after World War II?

Problems 5.3 and 5.4 generate data to be used in Problems 5.5 and 5.6.

Problem 5.3. Using quarterly real GDP data for the period since 1947, calculate the percentage change in GDP for each recession (peak to trough), expansion (trough to peak), and complete cycles (peak to peak and trough to trough) and enter them as separate time series on a spreadsheet. For each series calculate the mean and median values and report them in a table.

Problem 5.4. Using monthly unemployment rates for the period since 1947, calculate the change in unemployment rates (difference in percentage points, not percentage change) for each recession (peak to trough), expansion (trough to peak), and complete cycles (peak to peak and trough to trough) and enter them as separate time series on a spreadsheet. For each series calculate the mean and median values and report them in a table.

Problem 5.5. Using the data from Table 5.1 and the statistics reported in Problems 5.2, 5.3, and 5.4, describe the quantitative and temporal characteristics of the "typical" post-World War II business cycle.

Problem 5.6. There are a number of competing theories of the business cycle. One suggests that the seeds of the slump are sown in the boom, so that the higher the peak, the lower the subsequent trough. Another suggests that the economy is like a guitar string: the further it is plucked (the lower the trough), the more it rebounds (the higher the subsequent peak). Another holds that mild recessions are followed by strong recoveries. Yet another holds that adjacent recessions and expansions are essentially independent of each other. There are other possibilities. How could you state these four views in terms of correlations between the percentage changes in real GDP in adjacent recessions and expansions? (Hint: it is easier to think clearly if the falls in GDP during a recession are indicated by positive numbers, so multiply the change in GDP by -1.) Using the data you generated in Problem 5.3, test your hypotheses by calculating two correlations: 1. between expansions and the subsequent recession; and 2. between recessions and the subsequent expansion. Which of the four hypotheses (or which other pattern) do your calculations favor?

Problem 5.7. Instead of focusing on the size of changes as measured by GDP as in Problem 5.6, consider the same set of hypotheses using the duration of the recessions and expansions. Using the data in Table 5.1 for post-World War

II recessions and expansions (measured in months), repeat the calculations of Problem 5.6. Which of the four hypotheses (or which other pattern) do your calculations favor? Compare these results to those using GDP.

Problem 5.8. Use data on real GDP to establish the dates of the peaks and troughs of the Canadian business cycle. Explain your procedure. What is the typical Canadian business like measured by the size and durations of its recessions, expansions, and complete cycles? Do Canadian business cycles seem to be closely related to U.S. business cycles?

Problem 5.9. Use data on real GDP to establish the dates of the peaks and troughs of the Japanese business cycle. Explain your procedure. What is the typical Japanese business like measured by the size and durations of its recessions, expansions, and complete cycles? Should we characterize Japan as having experienced a *depression* in the 1990s?

Problem 5.10. How good are the leading indicators as predictors of recessions? One rule (see section 5.3.3) states that if the index of leading economic indicators turns down two months in succession, then a recession should be expected. Statisticians recognize two types of error. *Type I error* (false negative) occurs when a recession is not signaled, but one in fact follows. *Type II error* (false positive) occurs when a recession is signaled and none in fact follows. A recession signal occurs at every month in which the leading indicators turned down after having turned down in the preceding month (for a two-month rule) or two months (for a three-month rule). Use the time series of the index of leading economic indicators to identify all the recession signals and compare to the actual recession dates in Table 5.1. Count as follows:

- *Success:* a recession is successfully predicted if a recession follows within twelve months after a recession signal;
- *Type I error:* a recession occurs that was not preceded by a signal within twelve months;
- *Type II error:* a recession signal fails to be followed by a recession within twelve months.

(Note: (a) if a signal coincides with a month of a recession, do not count a successful prediction; (b) count only successful predictions of the same recession; (c) if the first signal in an unbroken series of months with signals fails to predict a recession but a later signal in the same series succeeds, count one Type II error and one successful prediction of that recession; (d) if every month in an unbroken series of months with signals fails to predict, count only one failure.)

Separately, apply a two-month and a three-month rule to the time series for the leading economic indicators and identify the successes and the errors by type, filling your results into two separate tables based on the following template table. How do the errors change for the two rules? Which rule is best? Why? Is the best rule useful as a predictor of recessions? Explain the reasons for your assessment.

Problem 5.11. Using whatever calculations and graphical analysis that you find helpful, examine the unemployment rate and identify its cyclicality; is it

Template Table for Problem 5.10

		Recession	
		Does Not Occur	Occurs
Leading indicators	**Do Not Signal Recession**	Leave this cell blank. Any case that does not fall into one of the other cells automatically belongs here.	**Type I Error**: Enter the number of times a recession occurred without having been signaled.
	Signal Recession	**Type II Error:** Enter the number of times a recession was signaled but failed to occur.	**Success:** Enter the number of times a recession was signaled and occurred.

procyclical, countercyclical, or acyclical? Is it a leading, lagging, or mixed indicator? (If mixed, give an accurate description of its properties.)

Problem 5.12. Read the *Guide*, Section G.12.3, on detrending using growth rates. Calculate the time series for the annualized quarterly rate of real GDP growth. Plot this series against the NBER business-cycle dates. Does your graph conform roughly to the stylized relationship between fluctuations in a level series and the rate-of-change series as shown in Figure G.12?

Problem 5.13. As observed in Chapter 3, section 3.6.2 (especially Figure 3.6), the 2001 recession appears not to have been a recession at all when judged by the revised data for real GDP. Using whatever data, calculations, and graphical analysis that you find helpful, does a wider range of data support the NBER's identification of a recession in that year? (You may have to find additional data on the web in order to answer this question.)

Part IV

Financial Markets

6

The Financial System

Money, which represents the prose of life, and which is hardly spoken of in parlors without an apology, is, in its effects and laws, as beautiful as roses.

Ralph Waldo Emerson

The first thing that comes to mind when most people think about the economy (or economics) is money: whence it comes, whither it goes. Probably no aspect of macroeconomics is more in the news than the financial system. We are deluged with daily reports of the state of the stock market, endless analyses of the Federal Reserve's monetary policy, speculations about expansions and consolidations among giant financial corporations, and stories about the financial solvency of foreign and local governments or industrial corporations. In this chapter, we examine the financial system's role in coordinating economic decisions and linking aggregate supply and aggregate demand. In the next chapter, we concentrate on the behavior of interest rates.

6.1 The Financial System and the Real Economy

6.1.1 The Role of Money and Finance

Money and financial assets are not direct sources of economic welfare. We cannot eat them or build houses with them. The Scottish economist/ philosopher/historian David Hume (1711–1776) wrote that money "is none of the wheels of trade: It is the oil which renders the motion of the wheels more smooth and easy."[1] We do not value a car for its lubrication system; we do not value an economy for its financial system. The financial system is important only because it affects the things that do govern our welfare: whether or not we have a job; how much we can consume now or in the future; how our government is financed; and the part that our country plays in the world. The lubrication system makes the complex parts of the car

---

[1] David Hume, "Of Money," in *Essays, Moral, Political, and Literary*, 1752.

function smoothly; the financial system simplifies consumption and production. The financial system is essential if complicated economic relationships are to be feasible. An economy without a financial system could hardly be more than a small village. Just as we often drive with no regard to lubrication, we conduct our daily economic transactions giving little thought to the financial system. But too little oil or a broken oil pump can bring the car to a standstill; and financial disorders can push an economy into a slump.

Real Flows and Financial Flows

The financial system is an important linkage between aggregate supply and aggregate demand. Firms use labor and other factors of production supplied by households to produce goods and services, which they in turn supply to households. In Chapter 2 this was shown as the circular flow of goods and services (see Figure 2.2 in which this real circulation is shown as the black clockwise loop crossing the production boundary in both directions). In a fundamental sense, the most economically significant action in the economy is this exchange of real factors of production for real goods and services. Nonetheless, only in rare cases do people work for food rather than money.

Any complex economy is more complicated than the circular flow of goods and services suggests. The workers and other suppliers of factors of production are unlikely to be satisfied with consuming only the product of the firms that employ them. You may work for a baker, but man does not live by bread alone. Workers demand the value of their labor in money to choose for themselves what to consume. And firms must, as a result, sell their products to a variety of people rather than barter them to their own workers. As a consequence, real flows in the economy are matched by counterflows of money (shown in Figure 2.2 as the gray counterclockwise loop crossing the production barrier twice in the opposite direction to the loop representing the real flows).

How much households decide to spend clearly depends on their money incomes; how much firms can pay in wages and other factor payments clearly depends on their money sales. Money does not itself directly provide utility to the consumer or resources to the firm, but any disruption in the monetary flow is bound to disrupt the real flows as well.

There is also another important monetary connection. In Chapter 2 (section 2.2.2) we saw that not all income is spent on consumption goods in the current period. Because the value of incomes must necessarily equal the value of production, the failure of households, for example, to use all their income for consumption could have disastrous consequences for the continuity of production, as firms would find themselves with stocks of unsold goods and, as a result, would cut back on production. Such dire problems could easily occur if households (or other savers) chose to keep their monetary savings in a cookie jar or under a mattress. But that is unlikely; most savers look for a safe place to lodge their savings and one that will provide them with interest or other return. As we saw in Chapter 2 (see Figure 2.3), FINANCIAL MARKETS serve to connect savers with excess purchasing power with borrowers with deficient purchasing power. Firms and individuals who borrow do so in order to spend. Investment and other spending using borrowed funds make up the shortfall in aggregate demand caused by savings.

Once again, in a monetary economy whenever money flows in one direction, something of equal value must flow in the opposite direction. When savers transfer money to financial markets, they receive in return a FINANCIAL INSTRUMENT – that is, *a record (paper or electronic) that specifies a claim to a current or future valuable good – for example, to the repayment of a debt or to the privileges of ownership.* There are a bewildering variety of financial instruments, although many are familiar to us all: checking accounts, savings accounts, corporate stocks, and government bonds. (The counterflow of financial instruments is not shown in Figure 2.3, but it is there in reality nonetheless.) Again, a disruption to the flow and counterflow of savings and financial instruments is likely to disrupt the flows of real goods and services that ultimately matter for our welfare. Even in a smoothly flowing economy, the terms on which people and firms borrow and lend, particularly the rate of interest, will affect not only how much is saved and borrowed, but who does the saving and the borrowing.

We have isolated two aspects of the financial system: the monetary transactions system and financial markets. We now look at each in more detail, starting with money.

The Monetary Economy

For economists, "What is money?," has long been a vexed question. There is no doubt that a dollar bill is money. But what else, if anything, counts as money? Traditionally, money has been defined by its functions:

1. **means of transactions:** we buy goods and services with money;
2. **unit of account:** values are expressed as so many dollars in our ledgers; and
3. **store of value:** we can save for future purchases by laying money aside.

The dollar bill and other **currency** (i.e., banknotes and coins) are the most familiar means of transactions. Yet currency is used in only about 20 percent of personal transactions (checks and credit cards taking the other 80 percent) and in even fewer business transactions (wire transfers between bank accounts dominating other transactions media). For now it is enough to note that MONETARY INSTRUMENTS (i.e., currency and other transactions media) are essential to the efficiency of a complex economy.

The alternative to a monetary economy is barter: for example, I supply you with labor and you, in turn, supply me with food. The labor I supply would necessarily be judged to be worth the food you supply. The national accounts would still balance: income equals output; output equals expenditure. Barter, however, requires coordination. Each party has to know not only what it wants to buy and sell but also what all the other parties want to buy and sell. A trade takes place only when my desire to buy coincides with your desire to buy *and* my desire to sell coincides with your desire to buy – a requirement sometimes referred to as the DOUBLE COINCIDENCE OF WANTS.

But an economy has to become only a little more complex than peasant farming before it becomes too complicated to keep track. One critical function of money is that it allows us to separate our plans from those of everyone else. All I need to know is what I want to sell (my labor) and what it earns and what I want to buy (food, shelter, and all varieties of things) and what it costs. (At each stage – buying and selling – there need be only a *single coincidence of wants*.) It is, for example, not important to me that my employer produce something that I want to consume. It is enough that I get paid and can buy what I want from some other producer. Money increases economic efficiency in part because it makes it easier to coordinate our individual plans.

The role of money as a unit of account may be as important – and perhaps more important – than its role as a means of transactions. Currency defines the unit in which the books are kept. Profits and losses, incomes and expenditures, are measured in dollars even when the currency itself is not directly involved. The ability to place values on vastly different real goods and services, to engage in bookkeeping, to account for economic performances, and to keep records that measure the successes and failures of economic enterprises, all in a common unit, is a fundamental building block of a modern economy.

Financial Instruments and Financial Intermediaries

Although currency and other monetary instruments can be used as stores of value, they are generally poor ones. Inflation eats away their value, and other assets typically earn more interest. Various financial instruments are better stores of value.

Each financial instrument represents the transfer of resources from a source of funds to a user of funds. The most common financial instruments are the various forms of **loans**. Each lender provides a resource (usually in a monetary form) in exchange for a promise from a borrower to repay on specified terms sometime in the future. The most primitive loans are created when one person gives another person money in exchange for an **IOU**.

Money plays a dual role. A loan can be thought of as the purchase of the financial instrument using money as a means of transactions. The loan is usually repaid using a monetary instrument. Some monetary instruments, such as checks, are themselves financial instruments in the sense that they are debt.

In most countries the **CENTRAL BANK** is a government-run bank whose customers are commercial banks. The **FEDERAL RESERVE SYSTEM** is the central bank of the United States.[2] Commercial banks have accounts with one of the district **Federal Reserve Banks** (branches of the System). *The funds in these accounts* are **CENTRAL-BANK RESERVES**.

Suppose that I write a check to you for $150 against my account at Wells Fargo Bank. When you deposit it at Chase Bank, your account is credited $150. Chase then turns the check over to the Federal Reserve (or to a private clearinghouse). When the check is presented to Wells Fargo, it transfers $150 of central-bank reserves to Chase and debits my account by $150. Once these central-bank reserves have been transferred, my debt to you is terminated. It is, then, your bank, not me, which owes you currency on demand or guarantees to honor your check up to the amount in your account by transferring central-bank reserves appropriately.

This illustrates another function of money:

4. **means of final payment:** *money terminates indebtedness.*

In our economy, only currency and central-bank reserves serve this function.[3]

Both the central bank and the commercial banks are examples of financial intermediaries – although the central bank is a special one, which is owned by the government and is not run principally for profit. A **FINANCIAL INTERMEDIARY** is *a firm whose business is buying and selling financial instruments or, equivalently, matching borrowers to lenders or savers to spenders.* Banks, mutual funds, insurance companies, investment trusts, stockbrokers, and pension funds are examples of the many types of financial intermediaries. Each financial intermediary specializes. Banks typically take business and personal deposits and make commercial and personal loans (e.g., mortgages, student loans, car loans, and credit cards). They can be seen as selling one financial instrument (checking and deposit accounts) to buy another (various loans).

---

[2] Legally the twelve banks that make up the district Federal Reserve System are private corporations owned by the commercial banks that are their members. Practically, the system as a whole is run by the Board of Governors in Washington, DC, which is a Federal Government agency. See Chapter 16 for more details.

[3] Before 1964, U.S. coins with denominations higher than 5 cents were silver and most U.S. currency was convertible into silver. The dollar bill was then a form of debt and not technically a final means of payment, though it was rare that anyone would demand payment in silver on a large scale.

The Flow of Funds

While money provides one source of efficiency (obviating the need for barter), the existence of specialized financial intermediaries provides another: the capacity of a monetary economy to separate the present from the future.

In a barter economy, if you want to consume more in the future than you earn (e.g., you would like to prepare for retirement), you must store particular goods – either ones that you are sure to want or ones that you think that you can trade. You have to have a detailed plan.

In a monetary economy, you can set aside money or financial assets (i.e., you can save) and delay the decision on exactly what to buy until the future actually arrives. Ultimately, all production is aimed at consumption. But in a monetary economy, we do not need a detailed plan for future consumption in order to prepare for it.

In a monetary economy the plans of different economic actors need not be coordinated. The various national-income-accounting identities of Chapter 2 show that the national-income-and-product accounts must add up *ex post*. For example, the deficits of all sectors must sum to zero (equation (2.3): $[G - (T - TR)] + [I - S] + [EX - IM] \equiv 0$.

Yet they need not be coordinated *ex ante*. A household does not attempt to discover firms' investment plans in order to make its own savings plans. The national accounts add up despite lack of coordination in part because they include *unplanned* investment. If a firm cannot sell everything it intends, it finds that its inventories of unsold goods, works-in-progress, or raw materials rise, adding to its capital stock. This unplanned investment was an important element in determining aggregate demand (see Chapter 2, section 2.7).

Most investment involves one firm purchasing capital goods from another firm. Funds must change hands. Where do firms get the needed funds? Households and other savers ultimately provide the funds, but how do they get to the investors? Typically households do not save by lending money directly to, say, General Electric or Microsoft to support a new factory or office building. For the most part, savers put funds into a bank or a 401K plan or individual retirement account (IRA) or some other financial asset. How do these funds find their way to the firms doing the investing?

Figure 6.1 shows a simplified picture of the FLOW OF FUNDS from savers (corporate and government, as well as private) to firms making investments or to others needing funds to finance expenditure. The figure can be viewed, in part, as an elaboration of the oval marked "Financial Markets" in Figures 2.3–2.5 (Chapter 2).

Just as in the Circular Flow of Income diagram, the Flow of Funds diagram emphasizes that economic transactions are based on *quid pro quo*

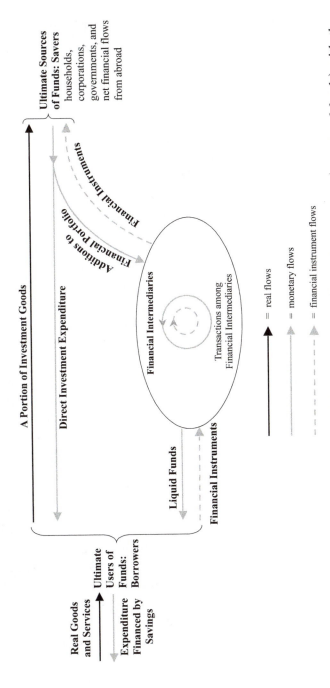

Figure 6.1. The Flow of Funds. The financial sector connects the ultimate savers (sources of funds) with the ultimate borrowers (uses of funds). Every transaction is the exchange of money for either a real good or service or for a financial instrument. No matter how convoluted the channels through a variety of financial intermediaries, ultimately savings finds its way to the purchase of real goods and services.

173

(see Chapter 3, section 3.1.1). The immediate **source of funds** feeding each monetary flow must receive something of equal value in return from the party that secures the **use of funds**. Every flow of monetary funds in the diagram must be matched by a counterflow of real goods or a financial instrument.

Money always flows from sources to uses (right to left in the diagram), whereas real goods and financial instruments always flow from uses to sources (left to right). At the top of the diagram, a portion of savings is shown as directly purchasing a portion of investment goods. For the most part, this corresponds to investment financed within firms themselves. If Caterpillar Company retains some of its profits (rather than distributing them to shareholders) to build a new engine plant, this is a form of corporate saving directly matched to a specific corporate investment. Similarly, if a household purchases a new automobile or puts a cash down payment on a new house, it both saves and directly invests. In either case, the savings *quid* is matched to the investment *quo*.

Most savings are channeled through the financial intermediaries shown on the lower portion of the diagram. Some financial intermediaries deal with both the ultimate savers and the ultimate borrowers. Others may lend to the ultimate borrowers but borrow only from other financial intermediaries or borrow from ultimate savers but lend only to other financial intermediaries. Still others may only borrow from and lend to other financial intermediaries. The interior flows in Figure 6.1 labeled "Transactions among Financial Intermediaries" only hints at the complexity of the financial system.

Although investment expenditure is probably the economically most important use for the funds generated from savings, there are other uses as well. When a consumer purchases an airline ticket on a credit card, he has in effect sold an IOU to the bank that issued the credit card. The funds that the bank pays to the merchant on his behalf are ultimately the savings of other consumers, firms, or governments. Similarly, although many governmental entities run surpluses and, so, are counted as savers, many others run deficits. Government purchases must be paid for, and the funds needed are raised by selling government IOUs – mostly to financial intermediaries – and receiving funds ultimately derived from savers in return.

6.1.2 The Flow of Funds Accounts

The Flow of Funds diagram (Figure 6.1) gives a reasonable schematic impression of the place of financial intermediaries in the macroeconomy. Practical economic analysis, however, requires numbers. The Federal Reserve collects these data for the United States in the **FLOW OF FUNDS ACCOUNTS**, which comprise 155 detailed accounts tracking the web of interrelationships among every type of financial intermediary. The flow of funds accounts do for financial markets what the national-income-and-product accounts do for the real economy.

As with other flow variables, the flow of funds can be likened to a stream of water. Savings flow through the network of financial intermediaries like the snowmelt from the high mountains running through a tangle of brooks and rivulets, creeks and rivers, until they reach the ultimate users like the water flowing into the sea. Stocks of financial wealth correspond to the standing waters – the lakes, ponds, pools, marshes, and reservoirs – along the way from mountain to sea. The particular financial instruments may keep turning over in the same way that the particular water molecules turn over in a lake. And just as the lake holds a standing stock of water, notwithstanding the turnover of the water molecules, individuals, productive firms, governments, and financial intermediaries retain standing stocks of financial assets. When the inflow of financial assets exceeds the outflow (that is, when the outflow of funds exceeds the inflow or lending exceeds borrowing), the stock of financial assets held by a particular person, firm, or other organization rises.

In order to understand the flow of funds accounts, it will help to examine briefly the nature of real and financial wealth and some elementary principles of accounting.

Real and Financial Wealth

If you hold a financial instrument, it forms part of your wealth. Wealth takes many forms. To ancient or primitive people, wealth was measured in real goods: houses, land, gold, cattle, slaves, wives, cowrie shells, wampum, stocks of foodstuffs. **REAL WEALTH** comprises things that provide direct utility or productive services. It is often tangible (a house, a car, a gold ring), but sometimes it is not – for example, ownership of a patent on a valuable invention is also real wealth. Real wealth is essentially a positive notion: you may own or not own a house or gold, but you cannot own less than nothing in the way of house or gold.

Financial wealth differs from real wealth in important ways. Financial instruments always involve two or more parties. They represent debt. For every owner of a financial instrument (the **creditor**), there must be someone who has promised to pay it off (the **debtor**). Unlike real wealth, financial wealth can be positive or negative. The creditor owns something of value; the debtor owes something. One's wealth is divided into **ASSETS** (positive wealth) and **LIABILITIES** (debts or negative wealth). Our assets include any real wealth owned and anything that others owe to us. Our liabilities include anything that we owe to others.

FINANCIAL WEALTH can be defined to be *claims to payment (or transfers) of something valuable at some future time.* Whereas real wealth comprises intrinsically valuable goods, financial wealth is not intrinsically valuable. It has a real value in the sense that we sell it and use the proceeds to obtain goods. But it provides no direct services of its own.

The fact that financial assets are always a claim on someone else (and financial liabilities, an obligation to someone else) gives a social character to the financial system. Notice that the net value of financial wealth is always zero. If Jane holds John's IOU, and Jane and John marry and consolidate their wealth, then Jane's asset cancels John's liability.

The future orientation of financial assets is critical to the way in which they promote economic efficiency. A worker who does not wish to consume as much as he can earn could lay away stocks of goods that he might need in the future. Aside from the difficulty of knowing just what he might need, it is costly and wasteful to keep real resources idle. Stocks of food deteriorate over time; clothes go out of style; and all goods must be stored, tying up space. It is easier to lodge savings with a financial intermediary and to purchase what is wanted later – billions of dollars will fit on a tiny microchip and those dollars are returned with interest.

Equally, the resources that might have been stored are available to others in the economy who need to use them now. The debtor needs real resources today and counts on being able to repay the value of those resources plus interest in future. The creditor needs real resources in the future and is willing to part with them today for the promise of repayment. The real resources are kept busier and more productive because of the financial system.

Accounting and Balance Sheets

How can we measure wealth? Anyone who has tried to borrow money from a bank (anyone who has applied for a student loan, a car loan, or a mortgage) has had to fill in an application. One part of the application consists of a form on which one lists one's assets (things owned) in column A and one's liabilities (things owed) in column B. The difference between column A and column B is one's wealth or NET WORTH. The idea of net worth is simple: if one sold all of one's assets and used the proceeds to pay all of one's debts, net worth is whatever is left. *Net worth* is defined in the FUNDAMENTAL IDENTITY OF ACCOUNTING as

$$Net\ worth \equiv Assets - Liabilities. \tag{6.1}$$

The loan application form is based on the rearrangement of this identity into the form

$$Assets \equiv Liabilities + Net\ Worth. \tag{6.2}$$

This equation can be represented as a **balance sheet**, which lists the assets and liabilities and calculates the net worth.

One form of the balance sheet – very much like the form on the typical loan application – is a table known as a **T-account**:

Assets	Liabilities and Net Worth
Things Owned	Things Owed
	Net Worth

The sum of the items in the left-hand column must add up to the sum of the items in the right-hand column, according to the fundamental accounting identity. It may at first seem odd to count net worth in the same column as liabilities; yet it is the standard practice. One way to think of it is that your net worth is what you owe to yourself.

The fundamental accounting identity refers to stocks of wealth. It can also be re-expressed in terms of flows:

$$\Delta Assets \equiv \Delta Liabilities + \Delta Net\ Worth. \tag{6.3}$$

This form provides the basis for **DOUBLE-ENTRY BOOKKEEPING**. The adjective "double-entry" refers to the fact that we cannot change one term in the fundamental identity (one entry on the balance sheet) without changing one (or more) other terms if things are still to add up. The double-entry rule forces us to maintain consistency in our accounts and to recognize, for example, that if we buy a car (adding to our assets) we are not richer: if we paid cash, our stock of money declined (reducing our assets); if we used a car loan to obtain the money to make the purchase, we added to our liabilities.

As simple as it seems, the principle of double-entry bookkeeping is one of those ideas (like the button and stirrups for horse riders – also products of the Middle Ages) that appeared only after thousands of years of civilization. The great German poet Goethe ranked it "among the finest inventions of the human mind."[4] And a recent scholar claims that "[i]n the past seven centuries bookkeeping has done more to shape the perceptions of more bright minds than any single innovation in philosophy or science."[5]

Flow Accounts

The Federal Reserve's Flow of Funds accounts come in two major types: flow accounts and level (i.e., stock) accounts. The flow accounts correspond most nearly to Figure 6.1. They start with the flow version of the fundamental accounting identity (6.3) although they recast it in terms of sources and

---

[4] J. W. Goethe, *Wilhelm Meister's Apprenticeship*, book I, chapter 10.
[5] Alfred W. Crosby, *The Measure of Reality: Quantification and Western Society, 1250–1600*. Cambridge: Cambridge University Press, 1997.

The Financial System

uses of funds. The change in assets is use and the change in liabilities and net worth is source, so that

$$\Delta Assets \equiv Use \equiv Source \equiv \Delta Liabilities. \tag{6.4}$$

Table 6.1 is a consolidated version of the more complex flow funds table called the Flow of Funds Matrix.[6] The main columns represent the various sectors of the economy, and the rows represent the changes to the real assets and financial instruments. Within each main column, there is a pair of subordinate columns – one for *uses* and one for *sources*. Each main column can be thought of as a T-account for a particular sector. The top four lines present gross flows for each sector. The next four lines give the details of the financial uses and sources.

For each sector, the accounts must balance in principle: sources must equal uses. In practice, because data collection is imperfect, the accounts do not balance. For example, the sources for the Household and Nonprofit Organizations sector (lines 1 and 4) are $1,724 billion − $194 billion = $1,530 billion; the uses (lines 2 and 3) are $1,359 billion + $301 billion = $1,660 billion. The difference, the *sector discrepancy*, is defined as *sources − uses* = −$130 billion. The sector discrepancy is reported as a use and, when added to the other uses, makes the accounts balance.

Similarly, for each instrument category sources must equal uses. The row sum for each instrument is reported in the main column labeled All Sectors. In principle the corresponding values in each of the two subordinate columns should be equal. In practice, they are not, and the difference is reported as the *instrument discrepancy* in the last column. The sum of all the sector discrepancies is equal to the sum of all the instrument discrepancies and is reported in the bottom right-hand cell – double-entry bookkeeping ensures that even the errors are consistent.

To see how the flow of funds accounts shed light on the complexity of the financial system, look at the data for the Household sector. In 2009, this sector saved $1,724 billion. Some of these funds went to purchase investment goods – largely residential property and durable goods such as cars and clothes driers (which count as investment in the flow of funds accounts, although they are reported as consumption in the national income and product accounts). Gross savings exceeds gross investment by $365 billion; so where did the funds that were not directed toward real investment go? Column 1, line 3 shows that households purchased $301 billion in financial assets. But that leaves $64 billion in savings. Line 4, column 2 shows that more than this amount (−$194 billion) was directed toward the

---

[6] The complete set of detailed flow of funds accounts is available from the Board of Governors of the Federal Reserve System at www.federalreserve.gov/releases/Z1/Current/default.htm.

Table 6.1. *Flow of Funds Matrix: 2009 Flows (billions of dollars)*

	Households and Nonprofit Organizations		Nonfinancial Businesses		Government		Financial Sectors		Rest of World		All Sectors		Instrument Discrepancy
	Use (1)	Source (2)	Use (3)	Source (4)	Use (5)	Source (6)	Use (7)	Source (8)	Use (9)	Source (10)	Use (11)	Source (12)	Use (13)
Gross Flows													
(1) *Gross Savings*	–	1,724	–	1,366	–	–953	–	293	–	424	–	2,854	–
(2) *Gross Real Investment*	1,359	–	1,081	–	521	–	153	–	–3	–	3,111	–	–257
(3) *Financial Uses*	301	–	198	–	395	–	–1,672	–	243	–	–535	–	391
(4) *Financial Sources*	–	–194	–	–4	–	1,718	–	–1,704	–	40	–	–144	–
Financial Flows													
(5) *Monetary Instruments*	–151	–	195	–	–67	–	–508	–	–401	–	–931	–	207
(6) *Debt Instruments*	–180	–237	15	–200	284	1,553	–776	–1,753	219	199	–438	–438	–
(7) *Corporate Equity and Business Credit*	469	49	–116	–166	23	80	54	731	196	73	627	767	140
(8) *Other Instruments*	163	–6	104	362	155	83	–443	–128	228	–60	207	251	44
(9) *Sector discrepancy*	–130	–	83	–	–151	–	108	–	223	–	134	–	134

Note: Table includes some inconsistencies due to rounding.
Source: Board of Governors of the Federal Reserve System, Flow of Funds, Quarterly Release Z.1. Entries consolidate detail.

repayment of debt. (The minus sign indicates that rather than raising funds to be spent, funds were directed to repayment.) This entry, however, explains too much, as the repayment exceeds the balance of savings (the $64 billion) by $130 billion. Where did the funds needed to repay this much debt come from? In fact, the Federal Reserve's accountants do not know precisely why this shortfall exists or which entries are incomplete or miscounted. If the accounts were perfect, gross savings plus financial sources would exactly equal gross real investment plus financial uses. There would be no short-fall, and everything would balance. As it is, the shortfall is exactly the *sector discrepancy* shown in column 1, line 9.

Notice that, at the same time as the Household sector was repaying debt (column 2, line 1), it also increased its own holdings of financial assets (column 1, line 3). The more detailed accounts show that households' largest purchases were of government bonds, shares in mutual funds, and stocks (corporate equities).

Together these flows illustrate that any one sector can change its holdings of financial assets in two ways:

- **NET ACQUISITION OF FINANCIAL ASSETS** *occurs when a sector saves more than it invests*;
- **PORTFOLIO REALLOCATION** *shifts funds from one financial instrument to another.*

Financial markets are always in flux, and both sorts of changes occur constantly.

A hypothetical example illustrates a pure portfolio reallocation. Suppose that you purchase a house worth $250,000, but that you have no net savings this year. How would you do it? And how would it show up in the flow of funds accounts? Your purchase would increase gross investment for the Household sector (column 1, line 2) by $250,000. To keep the accounts balanced, other entries must change by equivalent amounts. Suppose that you used $50,000 in your mutual fund for the down payment. This would show up as a negative entry in column 1, line 7 (also line 3). Then, if you borrowed the rest from a bank in the form of a mortgage, the entry in column 2, line 6 (also line 4) would rise by $200,000. The net effect of these transactions is that your total wealth remains unchanged. All that you have done is transform financial instruments into a real asset. Your wealth can rise only if you have gross savings.

Your house purchase also illustrates another important feature of the flow of funds accounts. The balance sheets of the different sectors are interdependent. For example, the fall in your mutual fund holding (a negative use) must also show up as a fall in the source of that instrument in the financial sector (column 8, line 7 and line 4). Of course, that is not the end of it: the accounts of the mutual fund (and the financial sector) must always balance and, so, must reflect the origin of the funds transferred to you. To give you $50,000, the mutual fund made other changes to its own portfolio – probably selling some of the stocks, bonds, or other financial instruments it holds. Similarly, the funds you raise through your mortgage must be provided by a bank, adding $200,000 to the debt assets of the financial sector (column 7, line 5); and the source of those funds will be reflected in other entries in the bank's balance sheet. The actions taken by the bank and the mutual fund to provide funds to you typically involved a chain of actions among many financial intermediaries that transmitted funds from the ultimate source to you, the ultimate use. The flow of funds table shows the net consequences of all of these changes.

Any one sector can, through borrowing, add to investment or build up its holdings of financial assets in excess of its gross savings. Yet, because every financial asset must be matched somewhere in the economy by an equal liability, when we add up across sectors, sources exactly equal uses and there can be no net acquisition of financial assets.

Adding up across sectors also ensures that savings equals investment. But investment is the acquisition of new real capital goods. Investment adds to real wealth. In contrast, financial assets zero out. This does not make them unimportant. It is the existence of financial assets that allows those with excess savings to shift resources to those whose savings fall short of their needs, even when they have no direct acquaintance with those people or their needs. The flow of funds account is thus an instrument for ensuring a flow of real resources into the parts of the economy that can use them most effectively. The financial system gives important support to economic growth and prosperity.

The Assets-and-Liabilities Accounts

The flow account (Table 6.1) traces the movements of financial instruments; the stock or assets-and-liabilities account (Table 6.2) shows the level of each instrument held by each sector. The flow account focuses on the rivers and streams, the stock account on the lakes and pools. The tables are related. For example, the positive entry for use of monetary instruments for nonfinancial businesses in Table 6.1 (column 3, line 5) implies that the holdings of monetary assets by these businesses ($2,490 billion in Table 6.2, column 3, line 3) were $195 billion higher than in 2008. Similarly any positive entry in a source column in the flow table is reflected in a change in the corresponding liability column in the assets-and-liability table. The flow tables tell us what happens to savings and how portfolios are changing. The assets-and-liabilities tables give us a snapshot of the financial portfolios of the economy.

Table 6.2. *Flow of Funds Matrix: 2009 Assets and Liabilities (billions of dollars)*

| | Households and Nonprofit Organizations | | Nonfinancial Businesses | | Government | | Financial Sectors | | Rest of World | | All Sectors | | Instrument Discrepancy |
	Asset	Liability	Asset	Liability	Asset	Liability	Asset	Liability	Asset	Liability	Asset	Liability	
	(1)	(2)	(3)	(4)	(5)	(6)	(7)	(8)	(9)	(10)	(11)	(12)	(13)
Gross Financial Position													
(1) *Total Financial Assets*	45,115	–	17,878	–	4,093	–	613,578	–	15,423	–	146,086	–	–6,544
(2) *Total Liabilities and Equity*	–	14,001	–	38,237	–	12,408	–	63,274	–	11,621	–	139,541	–
Financial Flows													
(3) *Monetary Instruments*	7,750	–	2,490	–	928	31	4,436	15,980	1,278	883	16,883	16,894	–69
(4) *Debt Instruments*	4,203	13,536	262	10,999	2,043	10,168	38,092	15,651	7,817	2,063	52,417	52,417	–
(5) *Corporate Equity Instruments and Business Credit*	12,783	444	2,725	14,819	451	900	12,732	11,577	2,931	4,162	31,623	31,903	
(6) *Other Instruments*	20,378	21	12,401	12,419	670	1,309	8,318	20,066	3,397	4,513	45,164	38,328	

Source: Board of Governors of the Federal Reserve System, Flow of Funds, Quarterly Release Z.1. Entries consolidate detail.

Some points worth notice in Table 6.2:

- First, the total volume of assets and liabilities (columns 11, row 1 and column 12, row 2) is huge – around ten times U.S. GDP.
- Second, the difference between total financial assets and total financial liabilities for households and nonprofit organizations – that is, the net worth of the sector – is huge: $33.1 trillion. In both the nonfinancial business and government sectors, liabilities exceed assets; while the rest of the world also shows positive net worth of $3.8 trillion. This makes sense. For-profit corporations are ultimately owned by people or organizations (e.g., colleges or the Red Cross) domestic or foreign, so that the asset value of any for-profit corporation is shown as a liability to the corporation and an asset to the Household or Rest-of-the-World sectors. In contrast, the financial sector is nearly in balance, showing a net worth of only $304 billion – about 0.5 percent of total assets of $64 trillion. Again, this makes sense, because the business of financial assets is to channel funds belonging to savers (shown as liabilities in column 8) to borrowers (shown as assets in column 7). The financial intermediaries' own stake in the process is *relatively* small.
- Third, the Government sector is a large net debtor. More detailed accounts (not presented here) show that most of the negative net worth of the sector in 2009 can be attributed to the Federal government. State and local governments were much closer to balance. About four-fifths of Federal government debt takes the form of Treasury securities (notes and bonds), which are included in the liabilities in column 6, row 4. Many of these bonds are held by households (included in the assets in column 1, row 4) state and local governments (included in the assets in column 5, row 4), but the lion's share are assets to the financial institutions (34 percent) and the rest of the world (48 percent) and are included in the asset columns for these sectors.
- Finally, all monetary instruments (row 3) are naturally the liabilities of the financial sector (including such governmental organizations as the Federal Reserve or the International Monetary Fund). Households hold nearly half of the monetary instruments, and the rest are distributed among the other sectors, including the financial sector itself (another bank or a mutual fund, for example, may itself have a bank account).

6.2 Principles of Valuation

A hydrologist might ask two questions about any natural water system: What forces move the water through it? What are the effects of that movement? Similarly, the economist should ask of the flow of funds: What forces govern the flows of financial instruments? What are the effects of these flows? Although we will study the answers to these questions in more detail in later chapters, we should give a preliminary answer here. The various players in financial markets allocate or reallocate their portfolios in search of the best combinations of risk and return (most often measured by interest rates). We shall study this process in detail in Chapter 7. The movements in financial assets affect the real economy because they affect expenditure decisions – both directly through the supply of funds and indirectly through the cost or opportunity cost of those funds (again most often measured by interest rates). The supplies of funds or the values of the various financial instruments are measured (e.g., in Tables 6.1 and 6.2) in dollars. Any financial instrument is a promise to provide something of value in the future, so the problem that arises immediately is how does the holder of an asset or the issuer of a liability or their accountants, the tax authorities, or anyone else know what value to place on any asset today.

6.2.1 Present Value

The Principle of Similarity and Replacement

The valuation of real assets is fairly straightforward. It follows the **PRINCIPLE OF SIMILARITY AND REPLACEMENT:** What a car or a machine is worth is simply what it would cost to *replace* it with another of the *same or similar* design and in the *same or similar* condition. Anyone who has wanted to place a value on a used car has probably looked at the *Kelley Blue Book* (in print or online). It gives current prices for used cars based on make, model, and condition. The point is to identify as closely as possible cars that have been sold recently with the car that one wants to sell to establish as close a similarity as possible. Real estate appraisers or the experts at Sotheby's or on the *Antiques Road Show* value even unique assets, such as a particular house or piece of land or a particular antique or painting, using the principle of similarity and replacement.

To say that this thing has the same value as that similar thing, which could replace it, is just a start. We can still ask, what determines the value of that other car or house or antique to which we compare *our* car or house or antique? Again, the universal answer to all economic questions is . . . *supply and demand*. The supply price of a car or a machine when new is just the cost of production (including profits). The price of land or an old painting is more problematic, as the supply is fixed and demand may frequently shift. In some cases, we can form a guess about the value, but we will never know *exactly* what some things are worth until they are actually sold.

The valuation of financial instruments also relies on the principle of similarity and replacement. Because they are identical and can perfectly replace each other, two 10-year government bonds must have the same value. And that value is determined by supply and demand. It is the same with two shares in General Motors or of any pairs of identical financial instruments.

Financial instruments pose a special problem, because the benefits they provide to the creditor and the costs they impose on the debtor occur in the future, while the costs they impose on the creditor, who provides the funds, and the benefits they confer on the debtor, who uses the funds, occur today. The problem is that valuation must compare costs and benefits today with benefits and costs in the future, and the future has not yet arrived. How is either party to a financial transaction supposed to know how to value the asset without a crystal ball?

Two Key Concepts: Opportunity Cost and Present Value

The answer depends on two of the most important ideas in economics: *opportunity cost* and *present value*.

The **OPPORTUNITY COST** *of any choice* is *the value of the best alternative choice that it forecloses*. Given the choice between cheesecake and chocolate mousse for dessert, if you choose the cheesecake, the opportunity cost is whatever value the chocolate mousse would have for you. For a chocolate lover, the opportunity cost is high. To someone allergic to chocolate, it may be zero. Here there is no explicit monetary value attached to the opportunity cost, but in many cases it would be easy to determine. If you choose to go to college rather than to work at Burger King for four years, the opportunity cost of going to college includes the wages you would have earned over the four years had you worked at Burger King instead.

The idea of opportunity cost can be applied easily to financial assets. If you buy shares in a mutual fund, the opportunity cost is the benefit you might have gained by buying some other financial asset. One measure of the benefit of holding an asset is the percentage **YIELD** or **INTEREST RATE**. If you put $100 into a bank account and, after a year, the account is credited with interest to the amount of $3, then the interest rate is 3 percent. Now suppose that instead of putting your $100 into the bank, you buy $100 worth of shares in a mutual fund. If the best alternative use of your funds were the bank account, then the opportunity cost of the shares would be 3 percent.

The idea of opportunity cost can be used to compare monetary values today with monetary values in the future. Imagine that a friend dates a check one year from today and writes it for the amount of $100 payable to cash. He then offers to sell the check (a simple 1-year bond) to you. What should you pay for it?

Assuming that the friend is trustworthy, the question is one of opportunity cost. You will pay an amount $X for the check in order to receive $100 in a year. During that year, your $X is tied up and cannot be used for other purposes. You have given up all the other opportunities it might have funded. If the best of those opportunities had been to earn, say, 6 percent in a bank deposit account, then 6 percent is the opportunity cost of lending the money to your friend. Unless the percentage yield on your $X is at least 6 percent, it would be better to put the money in the bank.

As a result, the most that you should be willing to pay for your friend's check is X, where the $100 received in a year is enough to pay you 6 percent more than you paid for the check. That is,

$$\$X + 0.06(\$X) = (1.06)(\$X) = \$100.$$

In words, X is the amount that, if you paid it, would make the $100 you are set to receive in a year 6 percent higher than what you paid. The second two terms of the expression can be solved to yield

$$\$X = \$100/1.06 = \$94.34.$$

You should be willing to pay no more than $94.34 for your friend's $100 check. And, because the bank account is your *best* alternative, your friend will accept no less. The present value of $100, one year in the future when a similar asset yields 6 percent, is $94.34.

The particular numbers in this example are not important. Instead of $100 let the future value be designated FV, and let the yield (or interest rate) on the best alternative asset be designated r. Then the previous equation can be written as a general formula for the present value (PV) of a value received one year in the future:

$$PV = \frac{FV}{1+r}. \tag{6.5}$$

In general, the **PRESENT VALUE** of an asset can be defined as *the value today of the future benefits it confers given the relevant opportunity cost.*

Think about some other examples. First, what is the present value of a Treasury bill that pays $10,000 one year from today, if the best alternative asset yields 4 percent? According to equation (6.5), $PV = \$10,000/(1.04) = \$9,615.38$.

But what would it be if the $10,000 were paid *two* years in the future? In that case, the purchase price of the bond would be tied up for two years and would have to earn 4 percent interest (compounded) for both years: $1.04(1.04)PV = (1.04)^2\$10,000$. Therefore, $PV = \$10,000/(1.04)^2 = \$9,245.56$. Again, the formula can be written more generally for the present value of a value received two years in the future:

$$PV = \frac{FV}{(1+r)^2}. \tag{6.6}$$

The same reasoning gives the general formula for the present values of a value received three, four, or more years in the future. If the number of years is m, then the present value is

$$PV = \frac{FV}{(1+r)^m}. \tag{6.7}$$

Present value, as expressed in this simple formula, *is the single most important concept in financial economics*. It is what permits us to make economically sensible comparisons of values at one time with those at another. And it arises (as we shall see in later chapters) in many contexts beyond the valuation of financial assets.

Four Properties of Present Value

Several general points about present value are implicit in equation (6.7):

1. Because interest rates are always positive, $1 + r$ is greater than one, and the present value of a future value is always less than the future value itself ($PV <$ FV).[7] In the case of a bond (or your friend's check), this means that one always pays less today than the future value of the bond. A future value is said to be purchased today at a **discount**. The computation of present values is sometimes referred to as *discounting*, and the yield that measures the opportunity cost as the **discount rate**. And, as a result, **present *discounted* value** is a synonym for "present value."

2. The fact that present value is less than future value has nothing to do with inflation. It is quite true that, when there is inflation, today's dollar will be less valuable tomorrow than it is today. But, discounting points to a different fact: *tomorrow's dollar is less valuable today than it will be tomorrow*. This is the result of opportunity cost, not inflation. The discount compensates the purchaser of the future value for the lost opportunity. (As we shall see in the next section, inflation and discounting interact, but it is important to distinguish the separate effects of each.)

3. The further a value is pushed into the future, the less it is worth today. In equation (6.7), as m becomes greater, PV becomes smaller. The longer you have to wait for your money, the less you should be willing to pay for it today.

4. The higher the opportunity cost, the greater the discount and the lower the present value. In equation (6.7) as r become greater, PV becomes smaller.

6.2.2 Real and Nominal Value

All the calculations of value so far have been conducted in nominal terms. By now, of course, we are familiar with the idea that – for the most part – it is *real* rather than nominal values that should guide economic decisions. Most financial instruments are contracts set out in nominal terms. How do we think about them in real terms?

Consider the case of a simple loan. You borrow $100 from a friend and repay him $105 in a year. What rate of interest did you pay? Clearly

---

[7] Near the nadir of the recent Japanese depression, some short-term government bonds were quoted with slightly negative interest rates. This appears to reflect the risk and trouble of holding the alternatives (currency, subject to loss or theft, or bank accounts, subject to bankruptcy) rather than a negative financial yield. The exception proves the rule.

5 percent. In general, the interest can be computed as $r_t = (FV_{t+1}/PV_t) - 1$, so that in the example of your loan

$$r_t = 105/100 - 1 = 5 \text{ percent.}$$

To figure the real rate of interest on the loan, we proceed by analogy and substitute the real or constant-dollar value of each amount in place of the nominal value. The real rate of interest (rr) is, therefore,

$$rr_t = \frac{RFV_{t+1}}{RPV_t} - 1, \tag{6.8}$$

where the R prefix indicates *real*. Recall that to convert any nominal quantity into the dollars of a reference year (year 0), we divide by the price level in the current year and multiply by the price level of the reference year (see Chapter 2, section 2.4.2, and the *Guide*, section G.9). Replacing each real quantity in equation (6.8) with the analogous nominal quantity converted to constant dollars gives

$$rr_t = \frac{FV_{t+1}\left(p_0/p_{t+1}\right)}{PV_t\left(p_0/p_t\right)} - 1. \tag{6.9}$$

Cancelling the base-period prices and rearranging terms yields

$$1 + rr_t = \frac{\left(\dfrac{FV_{t+1}}{PV_t}\right)}{\left(p_{t+1}/p_t\right)}. \tag{6.9'}$$

The numerator on the right-hand side of equation (6.9') is just the definition of one plus the nominal interest rate $(1 + r_t)$. The denominator is just one plus the rate of inflation $(1 + \hat{p}_{t+1})$. (Notice the timing implied in the subscripts. If a bond is purchased at time t, it is the inflation rate over the subsequent year – that is, the inflation rate for time $t + 1$ – that is relevant because the bond pays off at time $t + 1$.) Equation (6.9') can then be rewritten as

$$1 + rr_t = \frac{1 + r_t}{1 + \hat{p}_{t+1}} \tag{6.10}$$

or

$$1 + r_t = (1 + rr_t)(1 + \hat{p}_{t+1}). \tag{6.10'}$$

Going back to the example of your loan, imagine that the rate of inflation was 2 percent over the life of the loan; the equation (6.10) says that the real rate of interest

$$rr_t = (1.05)/(1.02) - 1 = 2.94 \text{ percent.}$$

A Useful Approximation

This last calculation is precisely correct, but equation (6.10) is more complex and cumbersome than it need be for many purposes. To simplify things, look at equation (6.10′) and multiply out the right-hand side:

$$1 + r_t = (1 + rr_t)(1 + \hat{p}_{t+1}) = 1 + rr_t + \hat{p}_t + rr_t(\hat{p}_{t+1}). \tag{6.11}$$

Because interest rates and inflation rates are typically small – much less than one (i.e., 100 percent) – their product ($rr_t \times \hat{p}_{t+1}$) is even smaller, and usually can be neglected with little error. Dropping the last term in equation (6.11) and subtracting one from each side gives

$$r_t \approx rr_t + \hat{p}_{t+1} \tag{6.11′}$$

or

$$rr_t \approx r_t - \hat{p}_{t+1}. \tag{6.11″}$$

We can use equation (6.11″) to calculate the real rate of interest on your loan as approximately $rr_t = 5 - 2 = 3$ percent.[8] The precise value is 2.94, so the error is 0.06 percentage points (i.e., $0.06/2.94 = 2$ percent of the true answer). For many purposes, such a small error does not matter. But the errors will be larger if the nominal interest rates or the inflation rates or both are high. What works well as an approximation in a low-inflation economy would be highly misleading in a high-inflation economy, for which the precise formula (6.10) is preferred.

The Ex Ante *versus the* Ex Post *Real Rate*

In the example, once your friend repays the loan, you can look at the CPI, compute the rate of inflation, and calculate the real rate of interest that you earned. As happens so often in economics, it is easy to calculate an important quantity after all of the action is past. This is the **EX POST REAL RATE OF INTEREST.** Unfortunately, the key economic decision is made when you agree to lend money to your friend, not after he repays the loan. What you really need is a guide to your decision before any of the action has started. You need to know the *ex ante* real rate.

If you had a crystal ball and could see the future precisely, the *ex ante* and the *ex post* rates of interest would be the same. Unhappily, none of us has a crystal ball. The best that we can do is form expectations of what the real rate will turn out to be. The **EX ANTE (OR EXPECTED) REAL RATE OF INTEREST** can, then, be indicated by a superscript e, so that $rr_t^e \approx r_t - \hat{p}_{t+1}^e$. The relevant nominal rate of interest is the market rate agreed to in the

---

[8] Another way to justify equation (6.13′) is to take logarithms of both sides of (6.12) to yield $\log(1 + r_t) = \log(1 + rr_t) + \log(1 + \hat{p}_t)$. Then, using the fact (see the *Guide*, section G.11.2) that, for small x,

$\log(1 + x) \approx x$, the expression can be rewritten $r_t \approx rr_t + \hat{p}_t$, which is the same as equation (6.13′).

loan contract and so is known with certainty. Only the rate of inflation is uncertain. The current price level is known, perhaps, but one can only guess the future price level.

The present-value formulae can all be transformed into real terms. Each nominal dollar-denominated quantity is converted to constant dollars, and each nominal yield is converted to a real yield. The *ex ante/ex post* distinction is important as soon as we consider unknown facts about the future. So, for example, equation (6.7) can be converted into an expression for real, *ex ante* present value:

$$RPV_t = \frac{RFV^e_{t+m}}{(1 + rr^e_t)^m},\tag{6.12}$$

where rr^e_t is the real opportunity cost expected to prevail over m periods starting at time t. Each present value calculation can be adapted as appropriate to apply to real values (*ex ante* or *ex post*). The key rule is: *do not mix and match*. When using real or constant dollar values, use real yields as the discount rate (opportunity cost). When using market or nominal values, use market or nominal yields.

6.3 The Main Financial Instruments

How can the general principles of valuation be applied to the different types of financial instruments? Tables 6.1 and 6.2 divide financial instruments into four broad categories – from largest to smallest: debt, other instruments, corporate equity, and monetary instruments (see Figure 6.2). The largest items in the category of "other instruments" are pension funds and life insurance reserves, which themselves mainly consist of debt or equity instruments, and the equity of noncorporate businesses. So if we understand the valuation of the other categories, we have gone a long way toward understanding these as well.

6.3.1 Debt

Debt instruments are promises to pay – IOUs. All debts are forms of loans. Some, such as ordinary bank loans (including mortgages) and credit card debt, reflect a direct relationship between the borrower and the lender for the life of the loan. In contrast, bonds are an impersonal form of loan in which the IOU is readily bought and sold on the open market.[9] In 2009,

---

[9] The line between bank loans and bonds has become blurred in recent years as mortgages and other loans have been sold by the original lender. Purchasers of loans through a process known as *securitization* sometimes pool the loans and use their income streams to pay the interest and principal on bonds sold on the open market. Securitization became infamous in the financial crisis of 2008–2009 when defaults on the underlying mortgages undermined the value of the bonds that they were supposed to secure.

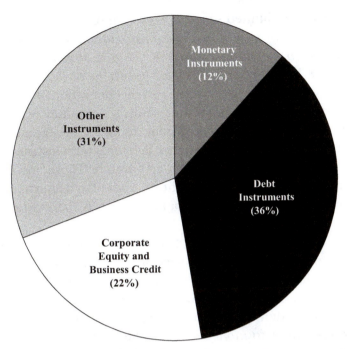

Figure 6.2. Financial Assets in 2009. *Source:* Board of Governors of the Federal Reserve System, Flow of Funds, Quarterly Release Z.1.

loans constituted about 14 percent of all financial assets or about 40 percent of the debt instruments shown in Table 6.2 and Figure 6.2; while bonds were similar in size at about 16 percent of all financial assets or about 44 percent of debt instruments. Although corporate equities (stocks or shares) constituted a similar share of financial assets (14 percent), the bond market raised more than four times the new funds than the stock market. It is easy to sympathize with Sherman McCoy, the protagonist of Tom Wolfe's novel *Bonfire of the Vanities*, who as a bond broker sees himself as a "Master of the Universe" but cannot get any respect at cocktail parties: bonds are bigger, but the stock market is sexier. Because of the financial crisis in 2009, only a very tiny amount of the new bond sales were corporate. Treasury bonds constituted the lion's share of new issues. But the situation is not the normal one. In more typical years, corporate bond issues swamp sales of newly issued stock.

What Are Bonds?

Like other debt, a bond is an IOU. Any debt may be represented as an IOU and, therefore, thought of as a bond. Your friend's postdated check in the last section was a primitive bond. A mortgage, a credit-card debt, or any loan could be thought of as a bond. The principles of valuation are the same whatever form the IOU takes. Still when we use the word "bond" we normally refer to financial instruments that are traded in highly organized markets. In this more limited sense, a **BOND** can be defined as *a promise to pay a definite stream of money in some fixed pattern, usually represented by a paper certificate or an entry in a broker's or government's books, that may be bought and sold on the open market.* A variety of financial instruments known by a bewildering array of names fit this definition: examples include short-term instruments such as Treasury bills, repurchase agreements, commercial paper, certificates of deposit, and bankers' acceptances; medium-term instruments, such as Treasury notes; and long-term instruments, such as debentures, Treasury bonds, and municipal bonds. These and other instruments differ in detailed ways that might be studied in a course on corporate or public finance or on money and banking, but at their core they all are similar.

Financial instruments traded on organized markets, especially longer-term instruments, are also known as **securities**. Hence, the U.S. government agency that regulates the trading of financial instruments is called the Securities and Exchange Commission (SEC). The market for shorter-term financial instruments is often referred to as the **MONEY MARKET**. When financial professionals refer to *money* or *cash*, they generally mean short-term, interest-bearing instruments traded on the money market, and not notes, coins, or checking accounts at banks.

Bonds are typically issued in uniform, fixed denominations so that they may be easily bought and sold. The ease of buying and selling, the so-called **LIQUIDITY** of the bond, helps to encourage people to make the loans.

The modern government bond market was created in Great Britain in the middle of the eighteenth century. Before that time, the government had financed its continental wars with loans from wealthy merchants and landowners, each one negotiated separately and on different terms. The national debt represented in these loans was consolidated and paid off with an issue of 3 percent perpetual bonds (known as "consols"). Because these bonds were issued in reasonably small denominations, the middle classes, as well as the rich, could afford to buy them, secure in the knowledge that they could be sold easily on the open market if the funds were needed.

The same principle applies to today's financial markets. Few could be persuaded to make private loans to the Ford Motor Company or to the Federal government. Yet, the same people may be willing to buy Ford or government bonds because they know that, if they need the funds, they will find a ready market.

The Mechanics of Bond Pricing

The price of a bond is just the present value of the future stream of income it delivers. The key to computing it is to know the stream of income and the relevant opportunity cost.

Most bonds are variations on the same general pattern. The key elements defining a bond are:

- The **face value** (*FV*): *the amount paid when a bond comes due or matures.* When bonds appear – as they do less and less frequently – in the form of a paper certificate, the face value is literally the value printed on the face of the certificate. The symbol "*FV*" is used both for future value and for face value, because the face value is, in fact, the future value of the bond at its maturity date.
- The **coupon** (**Cpn**): *regular payments to the holder of the bond (usually quarterly, semiannual, or annual).* In the past, bonds had small tags printed on their edges that indicated the amount and due date of one of these regular payments. To receive the payment, the bondholder would clip the coupon from the edge of the bond at the due date and send it to the issuer. As a result, wealthy people, who did not have to work but could live off the income from their financial portfolios, were sometimes known as "coupon clippers."
- The **coupon rate**: *the coupon expressed as a percentage of the face value – that is, the coupon rate = Cpn/FV.* If the face value of a bond is $5,000 and the coupon is $400 per year, then the coupon rate is $400/5,000 = 8$ percent. The coupon rate is just another way of expressing the value of the coupon. It is *not* the interest rate or yield that one earns on a bond unless one happens to pay the face value for the bond.
- The **market value** or **bond price** (*p_B*): *the actual price a bond commands on the current market.* The price of a bond is also its present value: $p_B = PV$.
- The **maturity**: *the date at which a bond pays off its face value and ceases to be a liability to its issuer or an asset to its holder.* Although the maturity is a date, we shall often wish to indicate **time to maturity** by the variable *m*, which measures the number of periods until a bond matures. For example, if a 10-year bond pays semi-annual coupons, then at the time of purchase $m = 20$. The maturity of a bond is not a fixed number, but falls as the bond gets older. By 2010, a thirty-year bond issued in 1990 has a maturity of only ten years.
- The **YIELD TO MATURITY** (*r*): *the rate of return earned if a bond is bought at the current market price and held until it matures and its face value is paid off.* Interest is received in the form of coupon payments and any premium of the face value over purchase price. The yield to maturity is expressed as a percentage of the purchase price. Because it is an interest rate, the yield to maturity is expressed as the variable *r*, the general symbol for a market rate of interest. The yield to maturity is also the opportunity cost of holding a bond. If there were sufficiently similar instruments with higher yields available, no one would hold the bond. And, if the bond had the higher yield, no one would hold the other instrument.

The different payments that are part of the bond contract – the coupons and the face value – are received at different times in the future. To figure the price today, each must be discounted to find its individual present value. For example, if today is time $t = 0$, the present value of a coupon payment received four years from now is $PV = Cpn/(1 + r)^4$. The present value of the face value received seven years from now is $PV = FV/(1 + r)^7$. The price of the bond is just the sum of the present values of each of the parts of the bond.[10] In general, then, the price of a bond that pays m periods in the future can be computed as

$$p_B = PV = \frac{Cpn}{1+r} + \frac{Cpn}{(1+r)^2} + \frac{Cpn}{(1+r)^3} + \cdots + \frac{Cpn}{(1+r)^m} + \frac{FV}{(1+r)^m}.$$

(6.13)

The general formula can be written more compactly as:

$$p_B = PV = \left[\sum_{t=1}^{m} \frac{Cpn}{(1+r)^t}\right] + \frac{FV}{(1+r)^m}.$$

(6.13′)

This formula applies equation (6.7) to each of the parts of the bonds separately. It assumes that the coupon payments are all the same value, and that the first coupon payment is received at the end of the first period.

Types of Bonds

The pricing of the two most common sorts of bonds is easily understood using the formula (6.13′). Most longer term government or corporate bonds are **coupon bonds**. Coupon bonds use the formula (6.13′) exactly.

In the last subsection, we considered the pricing of the Treasury bill. The Treasury bill is a common example of a **pure discount** (or **zero-coupon**) **bond**. A pure discount bond does not pay a coupon. The price of the pure discount bond is found by setting Cpn to zero in formula (6.4′) and setting m to the maturity of the bond. For example, the price of a one-year Treasury bill is:

$$p_B = \frac{FV}{1+r}.$$

(6.14)

The most common pure discount bonds are financial instruments such as Treasury bills and commercial paper whose maturities are less than one year. In recent years, however, dealers on the secondary markets have divided the coupon payment streams and the face values of government bonds and sold them separately. These are known as *Treasury STRIPS*.[11] Principal-only STRIPS have only a face value and so are priced as a pure discount

---

[10] In applying the formula in equation (6.4), the interest rate (yield to maturity) must be compatible with the frequency of the coupon payments. If coupon payments are received annually, then the interest rate is expressed at an annual rate. If the coupon payments are received semi-annually, then it must be expressed at a (simple) semi-annual rate: $r_{semi\text{-}annual} = r_{annual}/2$. Similarly, $r_{quarterly} = r_{annual}/4$, and $r_{monthly} = r_{annual}/12$.

[11] The name is an acronym for *S*eparately *T*raded *R*egistered *I*nterest and *P*rincipal *S*ecurities chosen to reflect the colloquial description of the process of dividing the interest and principal as "stripping" the bond.

bond.[12] When similar bonds yield 5.5 percent, a $5,000, 30-year principal-only STRIP would sell for $p_B = \$5,000/(1.055)^{30} = \$1,003.22$. In general, a pure discount bond, maturing m periods from today is priced as

$$p_B = \frac{FV}{(1+r)^m}. \tag{6.15}$$

In this chapter, we have looked only at the simplest sorts of bonds, which is enough for purposes of macroeconomic analysis. Courses in finance study different sorts of bonds in greater detail.

Prices and Yields

We observed earlier that the higher the opportunity cost measured by the interest rate on a similar asset, the lower the present value. This fact implies that bond prices and yields move inversely. This is obvious in equation (6.15). As r becomes higher, p_B becomes lower.

For example, when interest rates are 7.25 percent on similar assets, a $75,000 one-year certificate of deposit (a pure discount bond) would sell (using equation (6.5)) for $p_B = \$75,000/(1.075) = \$69,767.44$. But if the interest rate were to *rise* to 8 percent, it would sell for *less*: $p_B = \$75,000/(1.08) = \$69,444.44$.

Similarly, using equation (6.15), when competing interest rates were 9 percent, the price of a principal-only $1,000 Treasury STRIP maturing in 12 years would be: $p_B = \$1,000/(1.09)^{12} = \$355.53$. But if the interest rate were to *fall* to 8.75 percent, then it would sell for *more*: $p_B = \$1,000/(1.0875)^{12} = \$365.47$.

These examples presume that we know the yields on competing assets and use them to compute the price of the bond. We can also ask, given the price of the bond, what is its yield to maturity? Equations (6.14) and (6.15) can be solved for r:

$$r = \frac{FV}{p_B} - 1, \tag{6.16}$$

and

$$r = \sqrt[m]{\frac{FV}{p_B}} - 1. \tag{6.17}$$

In each of these formulae, as p_B rises (or falls), r falls (or rises). So, for example, if a one-year $10,000 Treasury bill costs $9,500, then its yield is given by equation (6.16): $r = (\$10,000/\$9,500) - 1 = 5.26$ percent. The yield, of course, moves inversely with price: if the price *rises* to $9,600, the yield *falls* to $r = (\$10,000/\$9,600) - 1 = 4.17$ percent.

---

12 The term "principal" refers to the original amount borrowed or the unpaid balance of a loan.

The same inverse relationship between bond prices and yields can be seen using equation (6.17). And, in fact, it applies to the more complicated general bond pricing formula. It is easy to see from equation (6.13′) that any increase in the yield would result in a fall in the bond price and vice versa. It is harder to compute the yield from the bond price, because the solution is a polynomial of order m. High-school students learn to solve quadratic equations, but there are no simple general formulae for higher-order polynomials. Nevertheless, the yields are readily computable using a spreadsheet program or a business calculator (see Problem 6.23).

The inverse relationship of bond prices and yields is so important that the general rule bears re-stating in a kind of mantra: *when bond prices rise, yields fall; when bond prices fall, yields rise; when yields rise, bond prices fall; when yields fall bond prices rise.*

Sometimes people – especially reporters in newspapers or on television – misunderstand the inverse relationship between bond prices and yields. Not infrequently, a reporter will say: "Interest rates rose today causing bond prices to fall." The connection is not causal. It is definitional. Given the face value, coupon structure, and maturity of a bond, if one knows the price, one can compute the yield, and if one knows the yield, one can compute the price. The price and the yield are just different ways of packaging the same information. A rise in interest rates does not cause a fall in bond prices; it is the very same thing as a fall in bond prices.

A pure discount bond must always sell for less (or at least no more) than its face value. If that were not true, it would not earn a positive yield. The situation is more complex with coupon bonds. Consider a two-year bond with a face value of $1,000 and a coupon rate of 5 percent paid annually. The coupon is $50 ($= FV \times coupon\ rate = \$1,000 \times 0.05$). If the yield on similar competing assets is 7 percent, the price is $p_B = \$50/(1.07) + \$50/(1.07)^2 + \$1,000/(1.07)^2 = \$963.84$. The bond sells at a discount over its face value.

What happens when the yield on competing assets falls to 4 percent? Then $p_B = \$50/(1.04) + \$50/(1.04)^2 + \$1,000/(1.04)^2 = \$1,018.86$. Now the bond sells for a **premium** over its face value. Does this violate the general rule that present value is always less than future value?

To see that it does not, notice that each of the individual parts of the payment stream – the coupons and the face value – obey the rule. Their present values are: $48.08, $46.23, and $924.56. To see why the sum of the parts is greater than the face value, think what income stream would be generated if the face value were placed in a bank account earning 4 percent interest. Each year the bank account would pay $40. But the bond pays $50 each year. The purchaser should be willing to pay more (i.e., pay a premium over face value) to receive the higher income stream.

Similar reasoning also explains why the bond sells at a discount when yields are greater than its coupon rate. When interest rates are 7 percent, a bank account would pay $70 a year on a $1,000 deposit. The bond pays only $40 per year, so the shortfall in yield must be made up by a face value greater than the purchase price – just as with a pure discount bond.

A special case occurs when the yield on similar competing assets is exactly equal to the coupon rate on the bond. In this case, the bond price is exactly equal to the face value. These relationships are summarized in the rule: *When the yield is equal to the coupon rate, a bond sells at its face value (i.e., at par); when the yield is greater than the coupon rate, it sells at a discount; when the yield is less than the coupon rate, it sells at a premium.*

6.3.2 Money

Monetary instruments (international and domestic) in the United States are a relatively small part of total financial assets – only about 13 percent in 2008. And money more narrowly defined as currency and checking deposits is less than 2 percent. Yet, as we have seen, money is important in that it defines the unit of account, facilitates a significant number of transactions, and acts as the final link in most chains of financial transactions.

Historically, money in most countries was gold or silver. The United States left the gold standard internally in 1933 and internationally in 1973. Until 1964, most American coins were silver, and paper dollars were promises to pay silver coin. The gold and silver standards are examples of COMMODITY MONEY. In contrast, the dollar and most paper currencies today are examples of FIAT MONEY. They are money because the government has decreed them to be **legal tender**, which means that, if any debt is denominated as a certain number of dollars, paper dollars must be accepted as the final means of payment.

It is relatively easy to understand why commodity money is valuable. Monetary commodities have alternative uses. Gold is used in jewelry and microchips, and silver in jewelry, cutlery, and photographic film. Both have many other uses. Despite the fact that old bills are turned into confetti for insulation or novelty gifts ("$1,000 in a jar for only $4.99!"), fiat currency has virtually no intrinsic value. It is valuable partly because it is in short supply and partly because everyone regards it as valuable.

An illustration of the self-reinforcing nature of the value of fiat money was provided by a civil war in the Congo (formerly known as Zaire). On overthrowing the government, the rebels repudiated the old currency and created a new fiat currency. They printed huge amounts of the new currency to pay their expenses. The value of the new currency fell rapidly, and many people would accept only the repudiated old currency in transactions – it was, after all, in limited supply and was familiar to them.

The government plays an important role in maintaining the value of a fiat currency. Contrary to the practice of the rebel government in the Congo, currencies are sound only when governments limit the supply so that it does not grow disproportionately to the need for hand-to-hand payments. Governments also reinforce the value of a fiat currency by paying their creditors in that currency or in assets immediately convertible into currency and by requiring that taxes be paid in the same way.

Hand-to-hand currency is the most familiar final means of payment. There is, however, another important one: central-bank reserves (see section 6.1.1). The value of central-bank reserves is tied directly to the value of currency. The Federal Reserve is always ready to exchange reserves for currency or currency for reserves. When a bank needs cash to fill its ATM machines, it withdraws the money from its account at the Federal Reserve in much the same way that you would at your local bank. One difference: it typically sends an armored car to cart the currency away.

For many years after a series of financial reforms in the wake of the Great Depression, it was illegal in the United States to pay interest on checking accounts. Although this is no longer the case, many checking accounts still do not pay interest – their owners finding that the transaction services that the accounts provide are adequate compensation. Other checking accounts and time and savings deposits, as well as money-market mutual funds, do pay interest. Those financial assets that are frequently counted among monetary instruments usually share two properties. First, they can be converted into currency either on demand or at relatively short notice. Second, they are *capital secure*: unlike a discount bond, which pays interest only implicitly from the fact that its price is below its face value, monetary instruments are always sold at their face values and any interest is paid explicitly.

Different financial instruments fulfill the traditional functions of money to different degrees. It is hard to know where to draw the line between money and nonmoney. The Federal Reserve, in fact, has three definitions of money or, as they are officially known, the MONETARY AGGREGATES. The narrowest focuses only on assets that serve as a final means of payment: the MONETARY BASE (MB) equals *currency plus central-bank reserves*. The other definitions focus on assets that can be held by the nonbank public and used in payments or turned quickly into assets that can be used in payments with increasingly less ease. The narrowest definition is known as M1. M1 equals *currency plus checkable deposits plus travelers' checks*. Table 6.3 gives the definitions of the monetary base, M1, and M2 monetary aggregates. A course in money and banking or financial economics would study these

Table 6.3. *The Federal Reserve's Monetary Aggregates*

Monetary Aggregate	Definition	Value as of 31 December 2009 (billions)
Monetary Base (MB)	= Reserves of depository institutions (including reserve balances with the Federal Reserve Banks and eligible vault cash) + Currency held by the nonbank public	**$2,075.4**
M1	= Currency held by the nonbank public + Travelers' checks + Demand deposits due to the nonbank public + Other checkable deposits	**$1,696.4**
M2	= M1 + Savings deposits (including money-market deposit accounts) + Small-denomination time deposits (less than $100,000) + Retail money-market mutual funds [M2 excludes balances in tax-free retirement accounts]	**$8,543.9**

Source: Board of Governors of the Federal Reserve System.

definitions and their uses carefully. In later chapters, we will refer only to the monetary base and, to a lesser extent, M1.[13]

6.3.3 Equity

What Are Stocks?

CORPORATE EQUITIES (also known as STOCKS or SHARES) are *fractions of the ownership of corporations.* The **corporation** is *an important legal structure in which the owners, the stockholders, have only limited liability.* This means that the shareholders are responsible for the actions of the corporation only up to the value of their shares. So, for example, if a corporation goes bankrupt, its shares may become valueless, and its shareholders would lose their equity. Although the firm's creditors could seize the firm's capital and financial assets in order to recoup their losses, they would have no claim on the shareholder's house, car, or other assets.

---

[13] In a historical perspective, the data in Table 6.3 are extraordinary because the monetary base exceeds M1, when typically M1 has been substantially larger. The reason is that banks received substantial central-bank reserves as part of the Federal Reserve's program of "quantitative easing" in response to the financial crisis of 2008–2009 (see Chapter 16, Box 16.1). Reserves are a part of the monetary base. Normally, a bank would lend out reserves in excess of reserve requirements, creating deposits, which in turn, expand M1 beyond the quantity of available reserves (see Chapter 16, Appendix, section 16.A.2). But in the crisis, banks have been content to hold reserves to protect their solvency.

Shares are not debt but a claim to the net worth of the firm. Shares carry the right to vote on the directors and senior management of the corporation, as well as on certain aspects of its legal structure. Most shareholders do not attend the annual meetings of firms or vote directly. Instead, they cede their right to vote by proxy to the management – or rarely, to an insurgent group that wishes to replace or redirect the management. Voting is important not because it is always exercised but because the threat always exists that it will be exercised if the management does not please the shareholders. Because of their voting rights, disgruntled shareholders can discipline the management either directly through their votes or indirectly by selling their shares to buyers who want to shape management decisions.

Corporations earn profits. These profits may be used to add to the capital stock or financial assets of the firm, in which case they are referred to as **retained earnings**. Or they may be distributed as **dividends** to the stockholders in proportion to the number of shares each holds. Most shares take the form of **common stock**, which carry full voting rights but no promise of any particular dividend payment. Sometimes companies issue **preferred stock**, which usually carries some guaranteed payment in exchange for some limitation on voting rights. Preferred stock is something like a cross between common stock and a corporate bond.

The Mechanics of Stock Pricing

In principle, the value of a share is equal to the present value of a firm divided by the number of shares outstanding (N). The present value depends on the expected profits of the firm (Π_t^e). Once again, financial markets (and economists) are hampered by the lack of a crystal ball. No one knows what profits firms will earn in the future. At best we can make educated guesses.

Ideally, the **stock price** (p_S) should follow a present value formula:

$$p_S = (1/N)\left[\sum_{t=1}^{\infty} \frac{\Pi_t^e}{(1+r)^t}\right]. \tag{6.18}$$

The term in square brackets is the present value of the firm: the profits expected in each future period are discounted appropriately and added together. Multiplying by $(1/N)$ turns this value into a value per share.

Although the stock-price formula is similar to the bond-price formula, there are some differences. First, instead of summing up returns over a fixed number of periods (m) as in equation (6.13′), the returns are summed up over an infinite future. There is no assumption that a corporation exists forever, only that the date of its demise is not known.[14] In any case, the discount

---

[14] Most businesses disappear or are absorbed into other businesses at some point. Some are nonetheless remarkably old. The oldest continuously functioning firm is the Japanese construction company

factor, $(1 + r)^t$, becomes very large as t becomes large, so that profits earned even moderately far in the future make only a small contribution to the stock price. For example, at an interest rate of 5 percent, one dollar thirty years in the future is worth only 23 cents ($= 1/(1.05)^{30}$), and one hundred years in the future, less than one cent. Little is lost if we ignore returns that accrue far in the future.[15]

The second difference is that the future income stream of bonds is known, whereas that of stocks is only expected. There is no absolute certainty, of course, that a bond will pay the contracted amounts, but what it promises is perfectly clear. If the market feels that a bond is at risk of not paying off, then the demand and the market price will be lower and, as we already know, the yield to maturity would be higher. There is no way to calculate *ex ante* the yield to maturity of stock, because the stock does not promise any definite payments. The most that can be said is that, *if* any profits are earned and *if* any are distributed, then they will be distributed in equal amounts per share.

One result of the uncertainty about future earnings of corporations is that the stock price can easily change with shifting assessments of a company's prospects. If a drug company discovers a new treatment for cancer, market expectations are likely to revise expected future profits upward – even if it will take several years for those profits to actually show up – and, according to equation (6.18) its stock price will rise.

And it works equally well the other way round. On 30 September 2004, the drug maker Merck announced that it was withdrawing its highly profitable Vioxx arthritis drug because of dangerous side effects. Merck's share price fell from $45 to less than $35 the same day and fell to less than $27 within a few days more. This was a reaction to the implications of its decision for *future*, rather than current, revenues and costs.

Similarly, it is the importance of *future* profits that explains why startup companies that have never made a dollar of profit may nevertheless have a high share price.

Stock Prices and Yields

Computing the yield of a bond *ex ante* is relatively easy because we assume that it will pay the coupons and face value in full at the promised time.

Kongo Gumi. Founded in 578, it is a family company that specializes in the construction of temples. Other old firms include: England's Faversham Oyster Fishery Company, founded in 1189; and the Swedish paper manufacturer Stora Enso, founded in 1288. Perhaps, the oldest firm structured from the beginning in a corporate form with shareholders is the Hudson Bay Company, founded in 1670 as a trading company and once master of substantial parts of what is now Canada (about 10 percent of the world's land area). It is now a department store.

[15] It is, of course, actually possible to add up the present values of an infinite number of future returns, provided that each present value is sufficiently smaller than earlier ones so that the series converges to a finite value. An example of summing a convergent series can be found with the case of the multiplier in Chapter 13, section 13.1.4.

Although it is easy to compute the yield of a stock *ex post* when the actual profits and prices are known, it is hard to compute it *ex ante*. The yield any stock market analyst, economist, or purchaser would assign depends on the expectations each holds for future profits, which cannot be known in advance. Still, some measures are widely cited in the financial press as indicators of stock yields.

A common measure is the **dividend yield**, defined as *the ratio of the annual dividend paid to the stock price*. The dividend yield is something like an interest rate, but it can be highly misleading. A corporation does not have to pay out all of its profits as dividends. It may choose to use retained earnings to invest in its own real capital or to purchase financial assets that would yield a better return for its shareholders.

Tax laws actually discourage firms from paying dividends. Corporate profits are taxed. If after the corporate taxes are paid, the firm distributes the profits as dividends, they are taxed a second time as personal income. To avoid this double taxation, the firm can pay a small dividend – or none at all. In the extreme case, a highly profitable firm could have a zero-dividend yield.

Even though the firm pays little or no dividend, the shareholder still benefits. Increasing profits raise the share price according to equation (6.18), so that anyone who buys a share at low price and sells it at a higher price earns a so-called **capital gain**.[16] Capital gains are taxable only when the stock is actually sold (the capital gain is then said to be *realized*). And, even then, it is taxed at a lower rate than ordinary income. Shareholders' preference for capital gains implies that the dividend yield is likely to be highly misleading as a measure of stock yield.

A somewhat better measure considers all of the profits (also known as **earnings**) – both dividends and retained earnings. The ratio of earnings to the share price provides a rough measure of the yield. The financial press typically refers to the inverse of the **earnings/price ratio**, the so-called **price/earnings** or **P/E ratio**. For example, if a corporation earns $2.30 per share on a share price of $34.50, then the earnings/price ratio is 6.67 percent, and the P/E ratio is 15 ($= 1/0.067$).

Although the earnings/price ratio provides a better measure of stock yields than the dividend yield, it is still imperfect. A startup company with no current earnings might nevertheless be expected to be highly profitable in time. Its earnings/price ratio would be zero, yet according to equation (6.18), its stock price could be large.

---

[16] "Capital" is used here in the sense common in the world of corporate finance to mean equity or net worth rather than, as we generally use it in macroeconomics, to mean the physical means of production.

Equation (6.18) is an ideal statement of the stock price. The object of operating a corporation is to earn profits for the shareholders, and the equation relates the stock price to this objective. Factors that are reasonably related to the prospects of the firm to earn profits are known as **FUNDAMENTALS**. Stock prices are highly volatile. Changing assessments of a firm's fundamentals explain much of this volatility. Values depend on expectations of future earnings, and expectations can shift rapidly. News that affects those expectations is often absorbed by market traders in a matter of minutes.

Nonfundamental factors may matter as well. Imagine that some participants in the stock market expect profits to improve and so bid up the price of a stock. Other traders, who may not agree with this assessment of the fundamentals, may nevertheless expect the price to rise because of the "irrational exuberance" (to borrow Alan Greenspan's famous phrase) of the optimistic traders. They would buy the stock in anticipation of the capital gain, and their demand would itself help ensure the increase in the stock price. Their expectation is not based on fundamentals, but is a self-fulfilling prophecy. When the prices of stocks or other assets are bid up independently of the fundamentals, the market is said to experience a **BUBBLE**. History provides a number of examples of rapid rises in the price of financial or real assets that some interpret to be out of proportion to the fundamentals. The most famous ones are probably the "Tulip Mania" and the "South Sea Bubble."

In Holland, in the middle of the seventeenth century, a fad for tulips resulted in some bulbs selling for the equivalent of hundreds of dollars, and one rare bulb trading for more than $20,000. The prices of tulip bulbs collapsed suddenly in 1637. The story generally concludes that many traders who had bought bulbs at high prices expecting to resell them at even higher prices were ruined, but the evidence on this point is disputed.[17]

The South Sea Company was a trading company formed in 1711. It was expected to profit from a monopoly on English trade with Spanish America, but never did. In 1720, its involvement in the finance of the British government's debt started a frenzy of trading in the company's shares, which rose from £100 to £1,000 per share in a matter of months. In September of 1720, the share price collapsed and many shareholders were ruined. Sudden collapse is characteristic of bubbles, because the high prices are sustained by expectations of capital gains ungrounded in fundamentals. If anyone believes that the price will fall, the best strategy is sell quickly, which of

---

[17] See Peter M. Garber, *Famous First Bubbles: The Fundamentals of Early Manias*. Cambridge, MA: MIT Press, 2001.

course brings on the very fall in prices that was feared. Capital losses as well as capital gains result from self-fulfilling expectations.

More recently, Japan experienced extraordinary rises in its stock market and property markets in the 1980s. Since the middle of the 1990s, the United States has experienced booms in property values (in the late 1990s until the recession of 2001) and again from about 2005 until the recession and financial collapse in 2008. P/E ratios rose to unprecedented heights, as stock prices in the United States outstripped earnings, only to collapse in 2000 and again, after a similar run-up, in 2008. Both episodes were widely regarded as bubbles. The run-up ending in 2000 was known as the *dot.com* bubble, because it particularly involved technology stocks tied to the internet boom. The financial collapse of 2008–2009 is generally thought to be the worst financial crisis since the Great Depression. It was directly related to the housing market, as a slowdown in the increase in housing prices and increases in interest rates on mortgages were factors that led to defaults on mortgages and the subsequent collapse of the value of various mortgage-backed securities. Many financial institutions with heavy exposure to such securities were threatened by bankruptcy. Some collapsed, while many others were rescued by the Federal Reserve and/or the Treasury or were taken over by stronger institutions.

Nevertheless, it is impossible to say with certainty that any particular run-up in asset prices is truly a bubble rather than the result of an optimistic assessment of the fundamentals. Some economists argue that all of the famous examples of bubbles floating to stratospheric heights and then bursting were really just radical reassessments of the fundamentals, not materially different from the collapse of Merck's share price on the news about Vioxx – clearly a fundamental.

Stock Market Indices

There are, of course, thousands of individual stocks. Some are traded on organized markets such as the New York Stock Exchange, the American Stock Exchange, or the National Association of Securities Dealers Automated Quotation System (NASDAQ). Others – usually the shares of small or "closely held" companies – are traded only privately. Macroeconomists are more interested in the common movements of stock prices than in the fate of any individual share price. Just as we capture such aggregate movements in the price indices for real goods, such as the CPI or PPI, stock prices are reflected in a variety of indices. The most famous index is the *Dow Jones Industrial Average*. In 1896, Charles Dow began publishing the average price of the shares of twelve industrial companies. Over the years, the group of companies contributing to the average has grown to thirty. Some companies have been added and others dropped from time to time.

And the exact method of calculation has changed. Dow Jones also calculates averages reflecting the share prices of transportation companies and utility companies.

There are other well-known averages and many less well-known ones. Among the most important are the *Standard and Poor's (S&P) 500*, which tracks the share prices of 500 large firms in the United States; the *New York Stock Exchange Composite Index*, which tracks every share on that exchange; and the *Russell 2000 Index*, which tracks the shares of two thousand smaller companies.

6.4 Financial Markets and Aggregate Demand

In most of this chapter we aimed to understand how financial markets work and how financial instruments are valued relative to the opportunity costs reflected in interest rates. This is just a beginning on which to build our understanding of the role of money and financial markets in the macroeconomy. The many rates of interest are clearly the key variables. We must understand in more detail what determines them and how they behave. This is the subject of Chapter 7. We also need to know how interest rates and the supply and demand for financial assets affect aggregate demand. Although this is the subject of most of the rest of the book, it may be useful to give a preview here.

Aggregate demand, as we already know, is the sum of investment, consumption, net exports, and government expenditure on goods and services. Consider the interaction between each of them and financial markets and interest rates in turn.

- *Investment.* If firms could always borrow freely, so long as they were willing to pay the price, then investment would represent a conceptually simple choice: which earns more, the capital good purchased through investment or a financial instrument purchased as an alternative? This is just a question of opportunity cost. When the opportunity cost, the relevant rate of interest is high, the firm is more likely to purchase the financial instrument; when it is low, the capital good. If firms cannot borrow freely – for example, if banks will lend them only a limited amount even at a high rate of interest for fear of bankruptcy – the firm's investment may also be limited. Then, any policy on the part of banks or the government that increases the available funds (increases the supply of financial instruments) increases the level of investment and aggregate demand. These issues are taken up in Chapters 13, 14, 16, and 17.
- *Consumption.* People frequently wish to consume in a pattern quite different from the pattern of their incomes. People may wish to consume more when young (e.g., paying for college) but earn more when old. Or people may wish to consume a relatively steady amount even though their incomes are variable month to month

or year to year. Just like firms with investment, if people could borrow and lend freely, then they would borrow when their incomes were relatively low with the intention of paying back when their incomes were relatively high. The interest rate affects consumption because it is the price of borrowing. But also like firms, many consumers find that they cannot borrow whatever they like even if they are willing to pay the price. In that case, the availability of funds (the supply of relevant financial instruments – e.g., credit-card debt) may determine whether people can consume as much as they like today. These issues are discussed in Chapter 14.

- *Net exports*. When the United States runs a balance-of-payments deficit, foreigners acquire American financial instruments. If after comparing U.S. interest rates to their own domestic interest rates, the foreigners are willing to hold the newly acquired assets, then the situation is sustainable. But if they find that U.S. interest rates are too low, then they will try to sell their assets, driving down their price (i.e., raising U.S. interest rates) and depreciating the exchange rate. This process stops only when everyone is happy with their portfolios. The change in the exchange raises the price of imports to Americans and lowers the price of American exports to foreigners, acting to reduce the balance-of-payments deficit. (International issues are discussed in Chapter 8.)
- *Government spending*. When the government runs a budget deficit, it must issue government bonds to pay for it. The increase in the supply tends to reduce the price of those bonds (raising their interest rates). Because other actors in the economy can buy these bonds, the higher interest rates represent higher opportunity costs for other real and financial assets. Government deficits may, therefore, affect investment, consumption, and net exports, and they may result in portfolio adjustments throughout the financial system that have more indirect effects. Government fiscal policy is discussed in Chapter 17.

In addition to any incidental effects, the government may deliberately use the financial system to affect the components of aggregate demand. It may choose its fiscal policy partly with an eye to the effect on interest rates. More directly, monetary policy involves the buying and selling of financial assets in order to change relative supplies and demands and, therefore, the interest rates of different financial assets with the object of altering aggregate demand. Monetary policy is discussed in Chapters 7 and 16.

Summary

1. The flow of all real goods and services (final and intermediate goods, as well as factors of production) is matched by a monetary counterflow.
2. Financial markets serve to connect savers (the ultimate sources of funds) with borrowers (the ultimate users of funds). Money flows from sources to uses and is matched by a counterflow of financial instruments that represent the indebtedness of the users.

3. Currency and, to different degrees, some other financial assets serve as monetary instruments. Money acts as a means of transactions, a unit of account, a store of value, and a means of final payment.

4. The central bank (in the United States, the Federal Reserve System) serves as a bank for banks. Funds held in the central bank known as central-bank reserves serve to settle debts among different banks – a means of final payment.

5. A financial intermediary is a firm whose business it is to buy and sell financial instruments, serving as part of the chain that connects savers to borrowers.

6. The Flow of Funds Accounts trace the financial interactions of the various sectors in the economy.

7. Financial wealth is held in the form of financial instruments. It differs from real wealth (both tangible and intangible goods that provide enduring services) in that for every positive holding (credit or asset) there must be a negative holding (debt or liability) somewhere in the economy, so that financial wealth always adds up to zero across the entire economy (including the foreign sector).

8. The fundamental identity of accounting states that *Assets* ≡ *Liabilities* + *Net Worth*. The identity can be represented in various ways, including in balance sheets and T-accounts. It is the basis of double-entry bookkeeping – so called because any change to a balance sheet must always be accompanied by one or more other changes in order to maintain the fundamental identity.

9. For any sector, flows of funds can either add to wealth (net acquisition of financial assets) or alter the forms in which wealth is held (portfolio reallocation). Adding up across all sectors, only additions to real wealth increase net wealth in the economy (i.e., there is no net acquisition of financial assets for the economy as a whole, including the foreign sector).

10. The principle of similarity and replacement states that when two goods are so similar that one can serve as a replacement for the other, then their values must be equal. Identical financial instruments must, therefore, have the same value, so that to value one we need only know the value of the other.

11. The opportunity cost of any choice is the value of the best alternative choice that it forecloses. The opportunity cost of a financial asset can be measured as the yield or interest rate on a closely related alternative asset.

12. The present value (PV) of any future value (FV) is the amount of money that would have to be placed in the alternative asset whose yield (r) measures the opportunity cost to give the same future value. For m periods in the future: $PV = FV/(1+r)^m$.

13. The real rate of interest is the nominal (or market) rate of interest adjusted for the rate of inflation. Approximately, $rr \approx r - \hat{p}$. The *ex ante* real rate uses the expected value of inflation; the *ex post* real rate uses the actual value of inflation.

14. A bond is an IOU in a standardized form that can be bought and sold on financial markets. Different bonds are distinguished by their issuer (governments or corporations) and their structure (coupon, face value, and maturity).

15. The bond price is the present value of the bond. Bond prices and yields always move inversely according to the formula for present value.

16. Money may take the form of commodity money (e.g., gold or silver) or fiat money, which refers to a set of financial instruments specialized for use in transactions. Different financial instruments are included in different official definitions of money. In the United States, the definitions run from the narrowest, the monetary base (currency plus central-bank reserves) to M1 (currency plus checkable deposits) to M2 (a wider definition that includes various short-term, interest-bearing, capital-secure financial instruments).

17. Corporate equity (stocks or shares) is the ownership rights in corporations that can be bought and sold on financial markets. Corporate equity is valued according to market expectations of the present value of the future profits of firms (the fundamentals). It may also sometimes be valued for the self-fulfilling expectation that it will increase in value (a bubble).

Key Concepts

financial markets

financial instrument

monetary instruments

double coincidence of wants

central bank

Federal Reserve System

central-bank reserves

financial intermediary

flow of funds

Flow of Funds Accounts

real wealth

assets

liabilities

financial wealth

net worth

fundamental identity of accounting

double-entry bookkeeping

net acquisition of financial assets

portfolio reallocation

principle of similarity and replacement

opportunity cost

yield (interest rate)

present value

ex post real rate of interest

ex ante (or expected) real rate of interest

bond

money market

liquidity

yield to maturity

commodity money

fiat money

monetary aggregates

monetary base (*MB*)

corporate equities (or stocks or shares)

fundamentals

bubble

Suggestions for Further Reading

Some Basic Sources:

Stephen D. Smith and Raymond E. Spudeck, *Interest Rates: Principles and Applications*. New York: Harcourt Brace, 1993.

Marcia Stigum and Anthony Crescenzi, *The Money Market*, 4th ed. New York: McGraw-Hill, 2007.

Introduction to Flow of Funds. Washington, DC: Board of Governors of the Federal Reserve System, 1980.

Some Historical Background on Financial Markets Is Found in:

Peter L. Bernstein, *Capital Ideas: The Improbable Origins of Modern Wall Street.* New York: Free Press, 1993.

The Existence of Financial Bubbles Has Been Hotly Debated for More Than 150 Years:

Charles MacKay, *Extraordinary Popular Delusions and the Madness of Crowds,* 1841.

Charles P. Kindleberger, *Manias, Panics, and Crashes: A History of Financial Crises,* 4th edition. New York: Wiley, 2000.

Peter M. Garber, *Famous First Bubbles: The Fundamentals of Early Manias.* Cambridge, MA: MIT Press, 2001.

Robert J. Schiller, *Irrational Exuberance,* 2nd edition. Princeton: Princeton University Press, 2005.

George A. Akerlof and Robert J. Schiller, *Animal Spirits. How Human Psychology Drives the Economy, and Why It Matters for Global Capitalism.* Princeton: Princeton University Press, 2009.

Problems

Data for this exercise are available on the textbook website under the link for Chapter 6 (appliedmacroeconomics.com). Before starting these exercises, the student should review the relevant portions of the *Guide to Working with Economic Data*, including sections G.1–G.4, and G.10–G.11.

Problem 6.1. Suppose that you buy a car for $12,000. Consider the effects on different balance sheets of alternative ways of financing your purchase. (Show your answers on a T-account and identify changes with a "+" or "−", the dollar value and the type of instrument – e.g., "+$1,800 stocks" or "−$500 credit card balance"). How is your balance sheet affected by financing your purchase through each of the following (remember balance sheets must always balance):

(a) a loan from your credit union?

(b) a check written on your bank account?

(c) $2,000 withdrawal from your money-market mutual fund and $10,000 charged to your credit-card account with your bank?

(d) winning the car in a raffle?

Problem 6.2. Consider the effects of the car purchase in the last problem on the balance sheets of financial intermediaries. What are the effects on the T-accounts of each financial intermediary in Problem 6.1 if the funds supplied to you are:

(a) raised by the credit union through additional deposits?

(b) raised by the bank by selling a $12,000 certificate of deposit (i.e., an interest-bearing IOU of the bank)?

(c) raised by the bank through a reduction in its reserves and by the mutual fund through the sale of some holdings of Treasury bills?

Problem 6.3. Suppose that you finance the car purchase in Problem 6.1 through a $12,000 loan from your father, who took the funds from his checking account. What are the effects on each of your T-accounts from your purchase? What would be the effect on your family's T-account – treating your father and yourself as a single unit?

Problem 6.4. Think about the economic activities of different financial actors. Create a T-account and list on the appropriate side the kinds of goods and financial instruments that are likely to appear as assets and liabilities of:

(a) households.

(b) a nonfinancial corporation (e.g., the Ford Motor Company).

(c) a bank.

Problem 6.5. Give three examples of different types of financial intermediaries and explain from whom they are likely to raise money (i.e., who is the source of their funds) and to whom are they likely to lend money (i.e., what is the use of their funds). In each case, what features make the financial intermediary different from other types of intermediaries?

Problem 6.6. Consider a flow-of-funds table like Table 6.1 but referring to a hypothetical 2010. Imagine that the Federal government ran a deficit of $500 billion. How would that deficit be reflected in the table (i.e., which cells would change – give the column and row numbers – by how much) if the deficit were financed by:

(a) foreign purchases of U.S. government debt?

(b) new savings by households held in mutual funds and purchases by the mutual funds of the U.S. government debt?

If the problem does not specify enough information to say exactly what happens, indicate the alternatives.

Problem 6.7. For each of the scenarios in Problem 6.6, take Table 6.2 as the starting point and state how the 2010 asset-and-liability table would be different (i.e., indicate the column and row numbers and dollar values of any cell that would have changed). If the problem does not specify enough information to say exactly what happens, indicate the alternatives.

Problem 6.8. Suppose that you earn $100 and decide to keep it in your non-interest-bearing checking account. Thinking of your actual situation, what would you regard as a good estimate of the opportunity cost of your action?

Problem 6.9. Using a spreadsheet and presenting your results on a single graph, calculate the present value of $1 for every year from the present (0) up to 100 years in the future, for each of the discount rates 0 percent, 1 percent, 5 percent, and 10 percent. What conclusions can you draw from your graph for the relationship of present value to: (i) how far in the future returns are received? (ii) the rate of discount? "Infinity is less than a lifetime." Comment with respect to your graph.

Problem 6.10. Using both the exact and the approximate formulae, what is the real rate of interest when:

(a) the market rate of interest is 7 percent and the rate of inflation is 2 percent?
(b) the market rate is 35 percent and inflation is 29 percent?
(c) the market rate is 4 percent and inflation is 2 percent?
(d) the market rate is 24 percent and inflation is 2 percent?

Comment on what your calculations suggest about when it is best to use the exact or the approximate formula.

Problem 6.11. Using the exact and the approximate formulae, what is the market rate of interest when:

(a) the real rate of interest is 2 percent and the inflation rate is 3 percent?
(b) the real rate is 2 percent and the inflation rate is 14 percent?
(c) the real rate is 10 percent and the inflation rate is 3 percent?
(d) the real rate is 3 percent and the inflation rates is 6 percent?

Problem 6.12. Using the exact and the approximate formulae, what is the rate of inflation when:

(a) the real rate of interest is 4 percent and the market rate of interest is 8 percent?
(b) the real rate is 4 percent and the market rate is 4 percent?
(c) the real rate is −1 percent and the market rate is 8 percent?
(d) the real rate is 4 percent and the market rate is 40 percent?

Problem 6.13. Using monthly data, measure the annual rate of CPI inflation *ex post* as $\hat{p}_t = (p_{t+12}/p_t) - 1$ and express your calculations in percentage points. Measure *ex ante* inflation using the Michigan Survey of Expected CPI Inflation (rate of inflation expected over the twelve months following the reported date). Using the market yield on a 1-year constant-maturity Treasury bond, compute both the *ex ante* and *ex post* real rates of interest and plot them on the same graph. How do they differ? What factors might account for the difference? Why is the difference important?

Problem 6.14. Redo Problem 6.13 but use the actual rate of inflation ($\hat{p}_t^e = (p_t/p_{t-12}) - 1$) over the preceding year *instead of the survey-based expectations* as the best estimate of expected future inflation when computing the *ex ante* real rate of interest. Are there important differences in this graph compared to that in Problem 6.13?

Problem 6.15. Redo Problem 6.14 using the 10-year constant-maturity bond rate and the actual rate of inflation over the preceding year as an estimate of the expected rate of inflation. How does the real rate on 10-year bonds compare to that on 1-year bonds? Note to compute the *ex post* real rate, the inflation rate must be the average rate over the ten following years: $\hat{p}_t = (p_{t+120}/p_t)^{(1/10)} - 1$.

Problem 6.16. Calculate the bond price of the following pure discount bonds:

(a) a $1,000 bond maturing in 1 year when yields on similar assets are 3 percent;
(b) a $1,000 bond maturing in 2 years when yields on similar assets are 5 percent;

(c) a \$5,000 bond maturing in 10 years when yields on similar assets are 11 percent.

Problem 6.17. Calculate the yield on the following pure discount bonds:
(a) a \$75,000 bond maturing in 1 year with a price of \$70,754.72;
(b) a \$1,000 bond maturing in 5 years with a price of \$862.61;
(c) a \$5,000 bond maturing in 10 years with a price of \$1,283.37.

For Problems 6.18 –6.23, recall that the yields are quoted at annual rates and that time and interest rates must be expressed in compatible units – see footnote 10.

Problem 6.18. U.S. Treasury bills are pure discount bonds sold with face values of \$10,000. Calculate the price for a Treasury bill that:
(a) matures in 3 months when yields on similar assets are 4 percent;
(b) matures in 6 months when yields on similar assets are 2 percent;
(c) matures in 9 months when yields on similar assets are 7 percent;
(d) matures in 1 week when yields on similar assets are 5 percent.

Problem 6.19. Calculate the yield on a 3-month Treasury bill sold at \$9,878.76.

Problem 6.20. Calculate (showing your work) the price of the following 2-year bonds when the yields on similar assets are 4 percent and the bonds have \$100 face values and annual coupons of:
(a) 3 percent;
(b) 4 percent;
(c) 5 percent.
Comment on the relationship between the prices that you calculate and the face values of the bonds.

Problem 6.21. Repeat Problem 6.20, but assume that the same coupons are paid in two semi-annual installments.

Problem 6.22. Using the *RATE* function in *Excel* (or the equivalent in another spreadsheet or business calculator), calculate the yield on a 10-year bond with a face value of \$100 and a semi-annual, 5-percent coupon purchased at prices of:
(a) \$108.18;
(b) \$100.00;
(c) \$92.56.
Comment.
[Excel hint: enter funds received by the bondholder (the coupon ($Cpn =$ Excel's *PMT*) and the face value (FV)) as positive numbers and funds paid out (the purchase price ($p_B = PV$)) as a negative number. The yield will be semi-annual and must be (simply) annualized before it is reported.]

Problem 6.23. Using the *PV* function in Excel (or the equivalent in another spreadsheet or business calculator), to calculate the relevant bond prices, what is the capital gain or loss from an initial yield of 5 percent on:
(a) a 5-year pure discount bond with a \$100 face value going to a yield of (i) 4 percent or (ii) 6 percent?
(b) a 5-year bond with a face value of \$100 and 5-percent annual coupons going to a yield of (i) 4 percent or (ii) 6 percent?

Comment.

[See the Excel hint for Problem 6.22.]

Problem 6.24. A *consol* (or *perpetuity*) is a bond that pays a coupon expressed as a percentage of its notional face value, but never matures (i.e., it pays its coupon forever). What is the value of a 3-percent consol with a face value of $1,000 when the yields on other long-term bonds are 4 percent? (Hint: use the bond-price formula, equation (6.13′), setting $m = \infty$. Notice that the term involving FV will be infinitely small and can be dropped. Then write out the equation, expanding the first few terms of the summation involving Cpn (of course, because it goes on forever you cannot write them all out). Now multiply the resulting expression (equation (1)) by $\frac{1}{1+r}$ to get equation (2). Subtract equation (2) from (1) noting which terms cancel out. You should get an equation with a finite number of terms that can be solved for p_B.) Can you write a general formula for the price of consol? Can you write a general formula for the yield of a consol, given its price?

Problem 6.25. Imagine that you are a shareholder in Orbit3, a company whose sole purpose is to win a prize for the first private spacecraft to orbit the earth three times. At the time that you purchase your shares, all the expenses of the firm up to the point of the prize mission have already been paid. If your firm wins, it earns $100 million. There are 1,000,000 shares. The relevant opportunity cost is 20 percent. Once the prize mission is over, the spacecraft becomes valueless and the firm will be disbanded.

(a) Based on fundamentals what should be the price of a share in Orbit3, assuming that it has no rivals and you are 100 percent confident of winning the prize one year from today?

(b) How would you expect the share price to change under the conditions in (a) as you get closer and closer to the date of receiving the prize? Be specific.

(c) How would you expect the price to change today if it were announced that another company, SpaceFirst, entered the picture and was generally regarded as having a 50–50 chance of beating Orbit3 to the prize?

(d) What would happen to the share price of Orbit3 if SpaceFirst's only ship blew up on the launch pad during a test, setting back their efforts by at least two years?

(e) What would happen to the share price of Orbit3 if SpaceFirst actually had a successful launch anytime during the current year?

Problem 6.26. Define *share price*, *dividend*, and *P/E ratio* of a firm. Record the actual values of these items for the last trading day before today for a firm listed on a major stock exchange. Provide an accurate citation of your source.

7

The Behavior of Interest Rates

Every six weeks or so, the financial news spends several days anticipating the announcement of the Federal Reserve's short-term interest-rate target and, once it has been announced, several days dissecting its policy implications. Whenever long-term bond rates rise or fall significantly, again it is a matter for intense financial commentary. Why? The short answer is that for anyone who borrows money to pay for college, buy a car, a digital camera, or any other good, every rise in interest rates makes things a little bit tighter, and every fall a little bit easier. A significant drop in mortgage interest rates can start a boom, not only in the real estate market but also in anything that might be financed with a home-equity loan. And equally, any significant rise can quickly cool these markets off. It is vitally important to macroeconomics to understand how interest rates behave: What determines their levels? What makes them change?

7.1 Five Questions about Interest Rates

Look at Figure 7.1, which shows the time series of five rates of interest: a short government rate (the 3-month Treasury-bill rate); a short private-sector rate (the 3-month commercial-paper rate); a long government rate (the 10-year Treasury bond rate); and two long private-sector rates for corporations with different degrees of riskiness (the Moody's Aaa and Baa bond rates). (The time series are a tangled skein, making the figure a little hard to read. But, as we shall see, the tangles themselves reflect an important fact about interest rates.) These five rates are chosen to represent the thousands of interest rates that are reported regularly. These thousands themselves represent the countless rates (one for each loan or debt instrument) recorded in the history of the economy. The figure reveals several consistent patterns in the interrelationships of the different rates and suggests at least five questions.

The most striking feature of Figure 7.1 is that all of the interest rates seem to follow the same broad pattern. Not only do they all start low at the end of

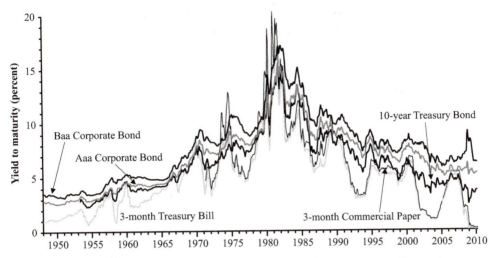

Figure 7.1. Selected Interest Rates. A selection of interest rates illustrates some common features: 1. Rates tend to move in similar broad patterns; 2. but they do not move perfectly together; 3. long-rates are usually (though not always) higher than short-term rates; 4. long-term corporate rates are higher than long-term government rates and short-term corporate rates are higher than short-term government rates. *Source:* Board of Governors of the Federal Reserve System.

the 1940s, rise to a global peak in the early 1980s, and then fall into a middle range by the turn of the twenty-first century but also their local peaks and troughs occur at more or less the same times. Yet despite the broad similarity, each series has a different history. In general, at any time, each series takes a distinct value. These observations point to the first two questions:

- *First, why do interest rates tend to move together?*
- *Second, why do they move only imperfectly together?*

There are further patterns in the data. Notice the two short-term interest rates (the rates on 3-month Treasury bills and on commercial paper) are typically, although not always, lower than the three long-term interest rates (on government and corporate Aaa and Baa bonds). Also notice that the Treasury-bill rate is typically lower than the commercial-paper rate and that the Treasury bond rate is uniformly lower than the two corporate bond rates. These observations suggest two more questions that can be seen as refinements of the second question:

- *Third, why do shorter maturity assets typically, but not uniformly, yield lower rates of interest than longer maturity assets?*
- *Fourth, why at each maturity do government assets yield lower rates of interest than private-sector assets?*

The first four questions address the relationship of each interest rate to the others. A final question highlights the whole structure of the rates:

• *Fifth, what determines the overall level of interest rates?*

This chapter aims to answer these five questions.

7.2 The Market for Financial Assets

7.2.1 Substitution and Arbitrage

Similarity and Replacement Again

In Chapter 6 (section 6.2.1) we explained the valuation of financial instruments through the principle of similarity and replacement. The value of one instrument was determined using a present-value formula with reference to the yield of another similar instrument. The yield (or opportunity cost) matters because the actors in financial markets are able to choose among competing instruments.

To one degree or another, all financial instruments are similar, but generally they are not identical. Each is issued by a different borrower with different chances of paying back the loan, each provides the lender with a different stream of income, and each may have its own special characteristics.

As a general rule, whenever *ceteris paribus* the price of any good rises relative to alternatives, people buy less of it and more of the alternative good. When the price of strawberry jam rises relative to marmalade, people typically buy less strawberry jam and more marmalade. Strawberry jam and marmalade are substitutes. Intuitively, goods are substitutes when they serve related functions. Economists, however, define substitutes more formally. Two goods are **SUBSTITUTES** if *when the price of the first good rises, the demand for the first good falls and the demand for the second good rises (and* vice versa *for price falls).*

When goods are effectively identical, even a very small difference in price can direct demand completely toward the cheaper good. For example, if identical bottles of beer (same brand, same size, same type) sit next to each other on the shelf, customers would not knowingly choose the more expensive bottle. Whenever the smallest price difference is enough to shift demand completely to the cheaper good, the two goods are known as **perfect substitutes**.

Goods may also be *complements*. Intuitively, goods are complements when the services of one are needed to complete the services of the other. Gasoline and motor oil are complements – both work together to make the car run. More formally, two goods are **complements** if *when the price of the* *first good rises, the demand for the first good falls and the demand for the second good also falls (and* vice versa *for price falls).*

Financial instruments are nearly always substitutes. Recall from Chapter 6 (section 6.2.1) that the price of a financial asset is inversely related to its yield or interest rate. Two financial assets are then SUBSTITUTES *when a fall in the yield or interest rate on the first asset (i.e., a rise in its price) reduces the demand for that asset and raises the demand for the other asset.* Identical instruments are perfect substitutes. Similar instruments are, to various degrees, imperfect substitutes. If all financial assets are substitutes to some degree, then the demand for each asset depends on the interest rate on all competing assets.

Supply and Demand

Consider two similar corporate bonds – say, bonds issued by Proctor & Gamble (P&G) and by Clorox. What determines their yields? As usual, the universal answer to all economic questions is...supply and demand. Unfortunately, "supply" and "demand" are tricky terms in financial markets. Their proper applications depend on what we think is being traded. For example, if you borrow money from the bank to buy a car, we normally say that the bank has supplied you a loan. On the other hand, if the government sells you a bond, we normally say that the government has supplied you a bond. In the first example, you are the borrower and the bank, called "the supplier," is the lender. In the second example, you are the lender and the government, called "the supplier," is the borrower. The usage is correct in both cases. In the first case, you are treated as using your liability to buy money. In the second, you are treated as using money to buy the government's liability. Because there are two sides to every transaction, both are correct. It is a matter of point of view.

To avoid confusion, we shall adopt the convention of always referring to the financial instrument itself as the object of trade. Borrowers use funds and *supply* the financial instrument; lenders are the source of funds and *demand* the financial instrument. In the case of the two bonds, the corporations are the suppliers, and the public are the demanders.

Reaching Equilibrium in a Financial Market

The markets for the two corporate bonds are shown in Figure 7.2. The yield to maturity of each bond is shown on the vertical axis and the number of bonds outstanding (or, equivalently, the total face value of the outstanding bonds) is shown on the horizontal axis.[1]

---

[1] Notice that, if the bonds are measured in terms of value, it is the face value and not the market value that is shown on the horizontal axis, because the market value changes with every change in yield according to the bond pricing formulae in Chapter 6 (e.g., equation 6.13′).

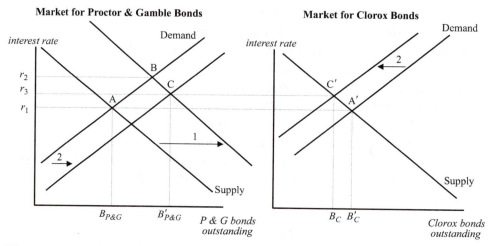

Figure 7.2. An Illustration of Arbitrage between Two Financial Markets. Initially, the markets are in equilibrium at points A and A', with a common interest rate, r_1. (1) An increase in the supply of Proctor & Gamble bonds shifts the supply curve rightward, which would *ceteris paribus* raise interest rates at point B to r_2. (2) Market participants move funds away from the lower yielding Clorox bonds toward the higher rate – a leftward shift of the Clorox-bond demand curve, lowering rates in that market, and a rightward shift of the Proctor-&-Gamble-bond demand curve, raising rates in that market. The process stops at points C and C' at which the rates are equal at r_3 in both markets.

Typical supply-and-demand curves for goods or factors of production refer to flows of valuable commodities – so many hours of labor or so many kilowatt-hours of electricity. Commodities are demanded or supplied with the object of being used. The supply and demand for a financial asset are for stocks – a timeless number of dollars. Financial assets are demanded or supplied with the object of being held. They are of course held for the valuable flow of funds that they generate; but, unlike electricity, which is used in the instant of its production, or apples, which spoil if not eaten and must be purchased frequently, a 30-year bond can fulfill a demand over the whole 30 years of its existence. The supply and demand for financial assets therefore depend on the entire stock of the assets outstanding (say, the stock of Clorox bonds) and not simply on the new issue of financial assets driven by the current need of the firm for funds.

The public's demand is shown in each panel of Figure 7.2 as an upward-sloping line. The higher the yield (the more each dollar lent earns), the more of either corporate bond the public is willing to purchase. The corporation's supply is shown in each panel as a downward-sloping line.[2] The higher the

---

[2] Notice that ordinary demand curves slope downward and ordinary supply curves upward. In contrast, here demand curves slope upward and supply curves downward, because we have expressed supply and demand as functions of interest rates, which are inversely related to bond prices. If we put bond

yield (the more each dollar borrowed costs), the less the corporation is willing to borrow. The interest rate is determined where supply equals demand in each market. And the rate is initially shown the same (r_1) in each market on the assumption that P&G bonds and Clorox bonds are perfect substitutes.

Now consider what happens if Proctor & Gamble decides to fund a major investment project through issuing new bonds. At each rate of interest its desire for funds will be higher, shifting its supply curve rightward (shift 1). All other things equal, the equilibrium would move from point A to point B, and the interest rate would rise from r_1 to r_2. The reason is that because more bonds are available, the only way the public can be enticed to hold them is for them to become cheaper. As their price falls, their yields rise.

Notice that with the market for Proctor & Gamble bonds at point B while the market for Clorox bonds is still at point A', the yield on the Proctor & Gamble bonds is higher than the yield on Clorox bonds. Because both bonds are assumed to be practically identical in the eyes of the public, why would people remain content to hold lower yielding Clorox bonds?

They would not. Some people would sell their (expensive) Clorox bonds and use the proceeds to buy the (now cheaper) Proctor & Gamble bonds. As a result funds would leave the Clorox bond market and enter the Proctor & Gamble bond market. At each level of interest rates, the demand for Clorox bonds would fall. The demand curve would shift leftward in the right-hand panel.

Similarly, at each level of interest rates, the demand for Proctor & Gamble bonds would rise, and the demand curve would shift rightward in the left-hand panel. (Both demand shifts are shown as shift 2.) This shifting of funds will continue so long as the yield on Proctor & Gamble bonds is higher than the yield on Clorox bonds. Eventually the yield on Clorox bonds is driven up (their price falls) and the yield on Proctor & Gamble bonds is driven down (their price rises) from point B until a new equilibrium is reached at a point like C.

More Proctor & Gamble bonds are outstanding at the new equilibrium ($B_{P\&G}$ increased to $B'_{P\&G}$). There are two effects. First, the rise in interest rates encouraged the public to buy more bonds. Second, the incipient difference between the yields in the two markets ($r_2 > r_1$) encouraged the public to shift from Clorox to Proctor & Gamble bonds until the yields were brought back into equality (B_{Clorox} fell to B'_{Clorox} and both bonds yield r_3). There are fewer Clorox bonds at the new equilibrium. Because of the higher rates, Clorox prefers less debt and so would lower it by not rolling over bonds as they mature and, even, by buying back outstanding bonds, which

prices on the vertical axis instead of interest rates, then the supply and demand curves for bonds would be just like the supply and demand curve for, say, apples.

are now cheaper. (This is only one of many possible examples. Other cases are addressed in Problem 7.1.)

Arbitrage

The process through which funds move between markets in search of higher yields is known as **ARBITRAGE**, which can be defined as *the simultaneous buying and selling of closely related goods or financial instruments in different markets to take advantage of price differentials*.[3] The person who engages in arbitrage, the so-called **arbitrageur**, buys the same good cheap in one market and sells it dear in another.

Actual financial markets are more complicated than the simple example of the two bonds. In reality there are many, many financial assets. They are almost all substitutes – sometimes extremely close substitutes. As a result, what happens in any market affects every market to some degree. The closer substitutes two assets are, the closer arbitrage drives their yields.

7.2.2 Efficient Markets

Inside and Outside Views of Financial Markets

Because there are large amounts of money at stake and because financial markets are well supplied with information, arbitrage is highly effective and works very quickly. In fact, the incentives reinforce the old adage, "He who hesitates is lost." As the market yield rises, the price of the bond falls. Anyone who fails quickly to sell the high-priced bond and purchase the low-price bond takes a capital loss. The value of his portfolio falls without any compensating gain in terms of the income stream – his bond yields the same coupons and has the same face value as before even though it is worth less on the market. As a result, the shift in demand happens quickly – often with very few trades being made and very few funds moving between markets. A bond seller immediately marks the price to where the equilibrium is anticipated to be, so that the yield jumps smartly to a value close to the final price, and the movements driven by actual flows of funds are relatively minor adjustments.

The effectiveness of arbitrage allows us to see financial markets from two perspectives. The first views the market from inside in terms of process. Highly motivated traders look for fleeting opportunities and exploit them quickly before they disappear. The process is complex, involving millions of trades every day.

---

[3] Some economists would restrict the definition to only those cases in which the profits are perfectly certain. But that would be a far narrower meaning than commonly encountered among financial professionals.

The market can also be viewed from the outside in terms of outcomes. Because arbitrage is highly effective, it is reasonable for many purposes to assume that it is complete. All profit opportunities are competed away so quickly that we can assume that they do not exist at all. From this second perspective, financial markets can be thought of as highly efficient processors of information. If anyone in the market learns anything relevant to the profitability of financial assets, asset prices change rapidly to reflect the new information. Studies show, for example, that a report of a cold snap in Florida is reflected in the market for orange-juice futures in a few minutes – and, indeed, the market typically anticipates the reports with great accuracy, so that only the small difference between the report and the expectation of what would be reported need be processed at all.

The Efficient-Markets Hypothesis

The outside view of the financial market as a highly effective processor of information is the critical element of the **EFFICIENT-MARKETS HYPO-THESIS**, which states *there are no* systematically *exploitable arbitrage opportunities based on information that is publicly available to financial markets*.

The efficient-markets hypothesis is sometimes illustrated with a lame joke: if you see a 100-dollar bill on the sidewalk, you should not bother to pick it up, because, if it were really there, someone would have picked it up already. The joke is misleading. The efficient-markets hypothesis does not say that arbitrage opportunities do not arise, only that they are not systematic. Systematic opportunities do not exist, *because* traders are ready and able to exploit them as quickly as they arise. If you see a 100-dollar bill on the sidewalk, you should pick it up quickly. It will not be there long. But having found the bill on the sidewalk at 34th and Vine, there is no reason to think that you will find another one there the next day.

The efficient-markets hypothesis says that no one can beat the market on average using publicly available information. In the 1980s comedy film *Trading Places*, the characters played by Dan Ackroyd and Eddie Murphy profit hugely through stealing the crop report for oranges and trading based on how the futures market was likely to react once the report was made public. Profiting from truly private information is consistent with the efficient-markets hypothesis.

Similarly, the efficient-markets hypothesis is consistent with some people beating the market and making enormous profits on financial trading. It does not rule out luck. On average, people who buy lottery tickets lose money. But someone wins the lottery – and sometimes for millions of dollars. Many traders, managers of mutual funds, and financial advisers believe that they can systematically outperform the market and can cite evidence of successive years of above-average returns. How could we tell if this were skill or luck? For any individual, it is impossible. The real test is: will the luck continue?

One test would be to divide the market into above-average and below-average performers for, say, one year and then to see whether the above-average continue to beat the below-average in the next year. Many careful studies have shown that an above-average performance one year does not predict an above-average performance the next year. Luck rules.

Some traders filter through reams of financial data and find patterns of mispriced assets that appear to present profit opportunities. In many cases, these apparent profit opportunities are too small to exploit. The brokerage and other costs of transactions exceed the gains from arbitrage. Such mispricing is also consistent with the efficient-markets hypothesis. Some of the opportunities are genuine and traders make a business of exploiting them. Such traders keep the markets efficient. The efficient-markets hypothesis does not say that traders cannot make their livings from such arbitrage activity. Rather, it says that the returns to such activity cannot on average exceed the amount that makes it just worth the traders' while to continue it. I could become a full-time hunter of mislaid 100-dollar bills, and I might even earn enough to eat from this activity. Yet if it were vastly more profitable than other occupations for the same time and effort, everyone would become bill hunters, and most of us would starve.

The efficient-markets hypothesis is the dominant theory of the functioning of financial markets, but there are many people who do not believe it. They point to people who have made millions, to statistical evidence of systematic, unexploited profit opportunities, and to psychological theories of herd behavior. Often they simply believe that they are just smarter than everyone else. A simple question will often silence someone who claims to be able to locate unexploited profit opportunities: "If you're so smart, why aren't you rich?" Some do turn out to be rich. John Maynard Keynes, the most important macroeconomist of the twentieth century, made fortunes both for himself and for King's College, Cambridge, of which he was investments bursar, through trading. Was this luck or skill? There is never an answer in the individual case, but if it is a skill, no one has ever shown how reliably to teach it to others. The statistical studies point more to luck than skill. The efficient-markets hypothesis remains the best account available of the working of financial markets.

Challenges to the Efficient-Markets Hypothesis

The considerations that should determine the value of an asset under the unrealistic assumption that people are perfectly informed are sometimes called market **fundamentals**. For example, if we had a crystal ball and knew exactly what the profit stream of a corporation would be for the infinite future, then its stock price should simply be the present value of those profits divided by the number of outstanding shares. Sometimes people confuse the efficient-markets hypothesis with the stronger hypothesis that market prices accurately reflect the fundamentals.

A new area of economics, *behavioral finance*, has applied psychological research on decision making to show that individual actors in financial markets do not always engage in rational calculation. They tend to be myopic, to weigh potential losses and more recent data too heavily relatively to potential gains and more complete data, and they systematically misjudge probabilities. It is not just that actors do not have a crystal ball – that is, do not make perfect forecasts – it is also that the forecasts that they make are systematically biased. These findings are sometimes taken as a direct challenge to the efficient-markets hypothesis.

The financial crisis of 2008–2009 is held out as a real-world illustration of the failure of efficient markets (and as validation of the insights of behavioral finance) as it appeared to be the result of valuations of real estate and stocks out of proportion to any sound judgments about fundamentals. Similarly, people appeared to have systematically underestimated the risk of various financial instruments – particularly of various so-called "derivatives," whose value ultimately depended on the returns and risk of pools of mortgages. How could financial markets be *efficient* when they managed to work themselves first, into an unreasonable boom ("irrational exuberance," as former Federal Reserve Chairman Alan Greenspan put it) and, then, into panic, chaos, and gridlock?

The question trades on an equivocation. "Efficiency" is taken to mean "functioning well." But in fact, "efficiency" in the efficient-markets hypothesis is defined more narrowly: markets are *efficient* when there are no profit opportunities that can be systematically exploited using publicly available information. Markets may be far away from their fundamentals and they may behave in ways that seem quite unreasonable and yet be efficient in this sense. It is perfectly possible, for example, for a "bubble" to be efficient in the sense of not presenting opportunities for arbitrage. We would, nonetheless, not think of a bubble as an example of a well-functioning market.

It is puzzling perhaps how markets could be approximately efficient when psychological studies show that individual people act in ways that undermine rational calculation and decision making. Yet, this would not be the only instance in which the behavior of the market as a whole would appear to diverge from the behavior of the individuals it comprises. For most purposes of macroeconomic analysis, we do not rely on markets being perfectly efficient, but only efficient to a good approximation.

Two Answers

We now have initial answers to the first two questions posed in Section 7.1:

- Interest rates tend to move together because financial assets are substitutes and profit-seeking traders engage in effective arbitrage;
- Interest rates do not move perfectly together because financial assets are not perfect substitutes.

These are only initial answers because they do not address some important issues. Substitution and arbitrage explain why, if yields move in some markets, yields in other markets tend to move sympathetically. They do not in themselves explain why the first yield moved. Similarly, imperfect substitutability can be regarded as just a name for the fact that arbitrage is ineffective in removing all differences in yields. It remains to explain why it is ineffective.

7.3 Risk

Bonds are not perfect substitutes because they are not perfectly alike. Even if two bonds have the same market price, they may have different structures. For example, some bonds do not have coupons and, even those bonds that do, have different coupon rates. Some bonds are callable; others are not. (A bond is *callable* when it is sold with the provision that it can be paid off before it matures.) Some bonds are exempt from Federal and/or state and local taxes; most bonds are not. There are other differences among bonds. In this section and the next, we focus on two of the most important: different bonds bear different degrees of risk, and different bonds have different maturities.

Risk is a complex business. We focus on two key elements: default risk and price or interest-rate risk.

7.3.1 Default Risk

Risk and Return

The individual, corporation, or other organization, such as a state or local government or a municipal utility district, that borrows funds through issuing a bond or taking out a loan might go bankrupt. In that case, the lender or bondholders face **DEFAULT RISK**: they might not get paid.

Some kinds of risk are more or less symmetrical. If I buy a share in Wal-Mart it may rise or fall. Some are asymmetrical. The typical state lottery ticket in most cases loses, but it costs only a dollar: there is a small *downside* risk. Although winning is rare, a win might bring millions of dollars: there is a large *upside* risk. Anyone who values the low probability of a large gain against the high probability of a small loss might rationally purchase a lottery ticket. Default risk is also asymmetrical. No matter how well the company does, the bond will pay off only what it promised; but, if the company fails, it may not pay off at all: there is downside, but no upside, risk.[4]

The chances of default on any particular bond are typically quite low. The chances of default on personal loans are generally much higher. Only a fool would choose a bond with a high risk of default over one with the same yield and a lower risk of default. If the high-risk bond were cheap enough – that is, if its yield were enough larger than that on the low-risk bond – it might become worthwhile to hold it. The additional yield or **risk premium** compensates for the higher risk.

A market player who purchases financial instruments that are more risky than the average market portfolio enjoys a higher yield but does not "beat the market." The advantages of the higher yield are offset by the disadvantages of higher risk: "no pain, no gain." Seen this way, the risk premium can be thought of as the price of risk. The higher average yield merely pays for the higher uncertainty of the yield from month to month or year to year.

Federal Government Bonds

Junk bonds stand at one extreme of the risk spectrum. U.S. Federal government bonds stand at the other. They are virtually free of default risk. Governments have a monopoly on taxation and, therefore, a ready source of funds to repay their debt. More importantly, the typical U.S. government bond is a promise to pay dollars – also a government-issued financial instrument. Because the federal government working with the Federal Reserve – effectively a government agency – can create as many dollars as necessary to fund its debt, it never has any reason to default.[5]

The key to its freedom from default risk is that federal government debt is denominated in dollars, which are within its control. Not every government is so favorably situated. State and local governments can default because they cannot print dollars. The debt of the central governments of other countries is equally free of default risk, as long as it is denominated in their national currencies.

Many developing countries find that they cannot borrow on international markets in their own currencies. Mexico, for instance, does not find it easy

---

[4] Notice that *shares* in the same company may have substantial upside risk – for example, if the management has "bet the firm" on a new product, the shareholders may make a fortune or lose their shirts.

[5] Strictly speaking, the government could default if it decided not to pay its debt even though it always has the ability to pay. In the Clinton Administration, the Treasury missed an interest payment by a few days, but markets did not treat it as a default. In 2011, however, Congress and the President agreed to raise the Federal debt ceiling only at the eleventh hour. Despite the subsequent downgrade of Treasury and Treasury-guaranteed debt by Standard & Poors, one of the three major rating agencies, default on dollar-denominated U.S. government debt could result only from a political decision (or political paralysis) and not from an *inability* to pay.

to sell peso-denominated bonds to foreigners, who usually prefer dollars, yen, or euros. Because Mexico cannot print dollars, its dollar-denominated bonds are just as subject to default risk as a corporate or municipal bond in the United States.

In the 1960s, the United States issued a small number of bonds denominated in Japanese yen. These were no different in principle from dollar-denominated Mexican debt; they carried some premium to cover default risk.

Rating Risk

Banks try to screen their personal and corporate borrowers to limit default. This is the reason that banks require borrowers to provide extensive information on their assets and liabilities and why they check borrowers' payment histories with credit information agencies such as TransUnion, Equifax, and Experian. Riskier customers pay higher interest rates on loans.

Default risk matters for bonds as well. Firms and government agencies who wish to sell bonds on organized markets are able to do so effectively only if they pay a bond-rating agency to rank the riskiness of their debt. These agencies (the three most important are Moody's, Standard & Poor's, and Fitch) use information – partly gathered from the firms themselves – to assign ratings similar to letter grades. The rating scale for Standard & Poor's (AAA to D) is shown in Table 7.1 (Moody's and Fitch use similar scales).

Bonds with ratings in the upper half of the rating scale (relatively low default risk) are referred to as **investment grade** and those in the lower half (high default risk) as **speculative**. The term **junk bond** became familiar starting in the 1980s. Although it sounds like a synonym for "worthless," junk bonds are just bonds below investment grade (i.e., below Moody's Baa or Standard & Poor's BBB). As such they carry a higher risk premium than safer bonds. The boom in the junk-bond market in the 1980s began with the financier Michael Milken and others who recognized that junk bonds were mispriced: their yields were too high relative to the actual risk reflected in their default histories. This presented the players in the market with an enormous arbitrage opportunity and made them extremely rich.[6]

The bond-rating agencies constantly monitor firms and municipalities. A downgraded rating adds substantial costs to borrowing. Critics worry that, because the firms pay to be rated, the agencies would accommodate them with higher ratings. Although there is a genuine risk, the importance of maintaining the reputation for impartiality on which their business depends may mitigate the tendency of the agencies toward inflating ratings. Any systematically biased rating should show up in default rates out of line with

---

[6] So rich in Milken's case that he was able to pay a $600 million fine for six violations of securities law and still have enough wealth to metamorphose into an important philanthropist.

Table 7.1. *Standard & Poor's Bond Ratings and Default Rates*

Grade	Description	Cumulative Default Rate[a] (percent)
	INVESTMENT GRADE	
AAA	Highest quality. Ability to pay interest and principal very strong.	0.67
AA	High quality. Ability to pay interest and principal strong.	1.30
A	Medium to high quality. Ability to pay interest and principal, but more susceptible to changes in circumstances and the economy.	2.88
BBB	Medium quality. Adequate ability to pay, but highly susceptible to adverse circumstances.	9.77
	SPECULATIVE	
BB	Speculative. Less near-term likelihood of default relative to other speculative issues.	24.51
B	Current capacity to pay interest and principal, but highly susceptible.	
CCC	Likely to default, where payment of interest and principal is dependent.	41.09
CC	Debt subordinate to senior debt rated CCC.	
C	Debt subordinate to senior debt rated CCC-D.	
D	Currently in default, where interest or principal has not been made as promised.	60.70

[a] Cumulative average default rates after 15 years from initial rating.
Source: "Long-term Rating Definitions," *Standard & Poor's Credit Week*, February 11, 1991, p. 128; *S&P Ratings Performance*, February 2003.

the risk ratings. The pattern in Table 7.1 seems consistent with the agencies doing a reasonable job.

Still, the rating agencies are not perfect, and are sometimes behind the curve. In the case of the energy trading company Enron in 2001, its stock price had collapsed over a period of months, but Moody's and Standard & Poor's cut Enron's bond rating from investment grade to junk status only four days before it announced bankruptcy. The case of WorldCom, the telecommunications giant, was similar, with the rating firms shifting from investment to junk ratings only shortly before bankruptcy in 2002. In the end, WorldCom bondholders received a mere 35.7 cents on the dollar.

In ordinary times, such mistakes by rating agencies may be the exceptions that prove the rule. Yet, rating agencies can also fail spectacularly. Many critics hold rating agencies responsible for underrating the risk to various mortgage-backed securities in the financial crisis of 2008–2009. Bonds and financial derivatives with an *ex ante* predictably high default risk were given high ratings, fueling rapidly rising prices in housing and stock markets. Many have called for congressional investigation and increased regulation of rating agencies in light of their failures in the financial crisis.

Default Risk and Interest Rates

Table 7.1 also shows the average cumulative default rates over a 15-year period for bonds in each risk class. Roughly speaking, we can interpret the default rate on a BBB bond of 9.77 percent as saying that such a bond has a nearly 10 percent chance of not paying off in full if held for 15 years.[7]

If default meant that the bondholder would receive nothing, then the expected yield would be $(1-default\ rate) \times r_{BBB}$. If bondholders did not care about risk for its own sake, but only about the expected rate of return, arbitrage would force that return to be equal to the return on a government bond of the same maturity.[8] Say that the government bond yield is $r_G = 5.00$ percent, then

$$(1 - default\ rate) \times r_{BBB} = (1 - 0.0977) \times r_{BBB} = 5.00 = r_G.$$

So that

$$r_{BBB} = \frac{r_G}{1 - default\ rate} = \frac{5.00}{1 - 0.0977} = 5.54 \text{ percent.}$$

A premium of 0.54 percentage points would be part of the arbitrageur's rational response to the level of risk typically experienced in holding BBB bonds.

This premium reflects the fact that the best estimate of the mean return of a BBB bond is lower than that of a risk-free government bond. But even if the BBB bond paid this rate, most bondholders would prefer the government bond because it not only pays the same return on average, but there is no chance that it will default (it has lower risk). Generally, the BBB bond will have to pay an additional risk premium to compensate bondholders for the uncertainty of it ever paying off.

The actual difference in yields for bonds of different default risk is reflected in Figure 7.1. The plot of the BAA bond rate (moderately low risk) typically lies about one percentage point above the plot of the AAA bond rate (very low risk), which in turn lies about 0.75 points above the plot of the government bond (virtually no default risk). The yield differentials between bonds in different risk categories are not constant. Default risks vary across the business cycle. The gap between high-risk and low-risk yields may widen in times of recession or economic crisis as market participants shift funds toward lower risk assets in a "flight to quality."

[7] In many defaults, bondholders do get repaid some fraction of what is owed.
[8] Our calculation assumes that both are zero-coupon bonds, which is unlikely. The result is, therefore, an approximation.

Table 7.2. *Market Interest Rates and Discount Bond Prices*

| | 5 | 4 | | 6 | |
			Market Interest Rates (percent)		
Maturity	Price	Price	Percentage Change vs. 5 Percent Rate	Price	Percentage Change vs. 5 Percent Rate
1-year	952.38	961.54	+0.96	943.40	−0.94
10-year	613.91	675.56	+10.04	558.39	−9.04
30-year	231.38	308.32	+32.25	174.11	−24.75

Note: Prices are for $1000 pure discount bonds.

7.3.2 Price or Interest-Rate Risk

We learned in the last chapter that the price or market value of a bond moves inversely with its yield. Consider, for example, a $1,000, 1-year discount bond when the market rate of interest on similar assets is 5 percent. Its price is $p_B = 1000/(1.05) = 952.38$. Now suppose that you purchased such a bond in the morning and decided by afternoon that you really needed the money and resold it. What would you get for it? That depends on the current rate of interest. If interest rates fell from 5 percent in the morning to 4 percent in the afternoon, then you could sell your bond for $p_B = 1000/(1.04) = 961.54$. You would have earned a **capital gain** of 0.96 percent ($= 961.54/952.38-1$). On the other hand, if rates had risen to 6 percent by afternoon, you would have taken a 0.94 percent **capital loss**.

The **PRICE** (or **INTEREST-RATE**) **RISK** *of holding a bond is the risk of capital gains or losses as a result of changes in interest rates between the point of purchase and the point of sale.* (The "price" in the term "price risk" refers to the bond price, p_B, and not to the general price level or to inflation.)

Price risk is greater for debt of greater maturity. Table 7.2 shows the percentage change in the price of discount bonds as interest rates fall or rise one point from a baseline of 5 percent. At a 1-year maturity the capital gains and losses are around one percent, whereas at 10-year maturity they are around 10 percent, and at a 30-year maturity between 20 and 30 percent. The reason for the difference is clear from the formulae for bond prices. The general formula for a discount bond (see equation (6.15)) is $p_B = FV/(1 + r)^m$. A given change in r results in a much larger change in the denominator when m is large (the maturity is long) than when m is small (the maturity is short). Although the numbers are different, the same is true for coupon bonds as well as for discount bonds.

All bonds, including federal government bonds, face price risk. Price risk explains at least some of the difference in yields for bonds of different maturities. Long bonds face greater price risk and, therefore, must earn a risk premium compared to short bonds. The longer the bond, the higher the risk premium. In Figure 7.1, the 3-month commercial paper rate is typically lower than the Aaa bond rate (a long commercial rate). The 3-month Treasury-bill rate (a short government rate) is typically lower than the long government bond rate. Some of this difference reflects a premium that compensates for price risk.

Risk premia – whether they compensate for default risk or for price risk – ensure that the returns to holding risky assets are higher than the returns to holding safer assets. If one is willing to hold a portfolio that is more risky than the average market portfolio, then one can earn returns systematically higher than those enjoyed by the market in general. Such returns do not violate the efficient-markets hypothesis. They are not the result of unexploited arbitrage opportunities. Rather they reflect the "price" of risk. The oldest example of pricing risk is, perhaps, insurance. Here too we talk about paying a premium to reduce risk. Many of the most important developments in financial markets – developments well beyond the scope of an intermediate macroeconomics textbook, but ones that might be studied in a course in corporate finance or money and banking – involve new ways to package, price, and trade various sorts of risk.

7.4 The Term Structure of Interest Rates

7.4.1 The Relationship of Interest Rates of Different Maturities

Look again at Figure 7.1. Although short rates are typically lower than long rates, they are sometimes (for example, in the early 1980s) higher. Figure 7.3 plots the 10-year government rate and the 3-month Treasury-bill rate and their difference. When the difference is negative, the short rate stands above the long rate. Something other than a premium for price risk must be at work.

To get a more detailed picture of the relationship of interest rates to maturity, plot the yield to maturity on the vertical axis of a graph and the time to maturity on the horizontal axis (Figure 7.4 does this for October of 2004 – a date in the middle of a business-cycle expansion). The black dots in Figure 7.4 mark the values at that date for the 3-month Treasury-bill rate and the 10-year government bond rate plotted in Figure 7.3 (where they are also marked by black dots). In a sense Figure 7.4 takes a vertical slice of Figure 7.3. But Figure 7.4 allows us to incorporate the interest rates on bonds of other maturities at the same date. These values are shown as open circles.

The smooth line connecting the various points on the graph is known as a **YIELD CURVE**. That the 10-year bond rate is above the 3-month Treasury-bill rate and, more generally, that longer rates exceed shorter rates are

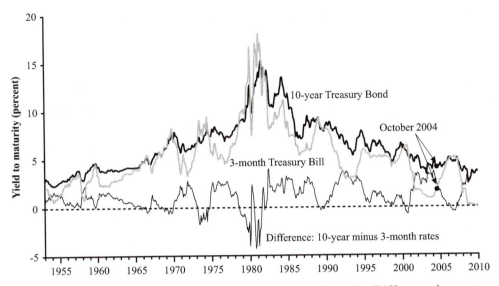

Figure 7.3. Yield and Maturity. Typically but not uniformly, *Difference* is greater than zero, indicating that the interest rate on long bonds is higher than on short bonds. *Source:* Board of Governors of the Federal Reserve System.

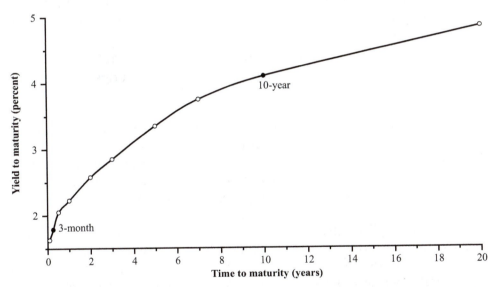

Figure 7.4. The Treasury Yield Curve for October 2004. The yield curve plots the interest rates on bonds against their time to maturity for a single time period. The black dots mark the yields at 3 months and 10 years and correspond to the black dots on the time series for 3-month Treasury bills and 10-year Treasury bonds in Figure 7.3. When *Difference* in Figure 7.3 is positive, the yield curve slopes up (at least between 3 months and 10 years); when it is negative, the yield curve slopes down. This yield curve is typical in that it slopes up. *Source:* Board of Governors of the Federal Reserve System.

reflected in the fact that the yield curve slopes up.[9] The relationship among the returns on bonds of different maturities is called the **TERM STRUCTURE OF INTEREST RATES**. The yield curve is one, particularly useful way of visualizing the term structure. Figure 7.3 offers another way. Whenever the difference in Figure 7.3 is positive, the yield curve slopes up (at least between 3 months and 10 years) and, whenever the difference is negative, the yield curve slopes down. To not confuse characteristics of interest rates related to maturity with those related to default risk, yield curves should be plotted only for bonds of similar default risk.[10]

7.4.2 The Expectations Theory of the Term Structure

Arbitrage across Different Maturities

How might we account for the term structure of interest rates? What explains the shape of the yield curve?

We must distinguish among bonds of different maturities. So, start with some notation: $r_{m,t}$ indicates the yield on a bond at time t that matures in m periods. For example, $r_{1,2001}$ is the yield in 2001 of a 1-year bond (i.e., it matures in 2002); $r_{5,(3\,\text{May}\,2008)}$ is the yield on 3 May 2008 of a 5-year bond (matures 3 May 2013); and $r_{0.25,t}$ is the yield at time t on a 3-month (0.25 year) bond (matures at $t + 3$ months).

Now consider a simple problem. You wish to put funds out at interest for two years. There are many ways that you can accomplish this, but consider two.

1. You might purchase a 2-year bond. In that case, for each dollar you put out, you would earn $1 + r_{2,t}$ for the first year on your principal, and another $1 + r_{2,t}$ for the second year on both your principal and the first year's interest. The total earned is $(1 + r_{2,t})(1 + r_{2,t}) = (1 + r_{2,t})^2$. For example, if the 2-year bond yields 11 percent per year, then each dollar is worth $(1.11)^2 = \$1.23$ at the end of two years.

2. Instead, you might purchase a 1-year bond. Then, for each dollar you put out, you would earn $1 + r_{1,t}$ on your principal at the end of the first year. Then you would have to decide what to do with the funds. One possibility is to purchase another 1-year bond. Of course, in the meantime, market interest rates may have changed. So, unlike the case of the 2-year bond, you cannot know at the beginning exactly what return you will receive over two years. It depends on what the interest rate turns out to be at the beginning of the second year. As so often in economics, we feel the want of a crystal ball. In trying to decide *ex ante* whether to buy a

---

[9] A "dynamic yield curve" at www.stockcharts.com/charts/yieldcurve.html allows you to watch the history of the yield curve as a moving picture.

[10] Variations in coupon structure also pose difficulties in comparing bonds. The most theoretically pure yield curves focus on zero-coupon (or pure discount) bonds.

1-year bond or a 2-year bond, we have to form an expectation of what the 1-year bond rate will be one year in the future. Call this expected rate $r^e_{1,t+1}$. Then our principal and the first year's interest are expected to earn $1 + r^e_{1,t+1}$ in the second year, and our best expectation of the total to be earned is $(1 + r_{1,t})(1 + r^e_{1,t+1})$.

Whether you should put your funds in the 1-year or the 2-year bond depends on what rate each bond yields and what rate a 1-year bond is expected to yield one year in the future. For example, consider the case in which $r_{1,t} = 10$ percent and $r^e_{1,t+1} = 9$ percent. Then, each dollar yields $(1 + r_{1,t})(1 + r^e_{1,t+1}) = (1.10)(1.09) = \$1.20$. This is less than the \$1.23 yielded by the 2-year bond, so you – and other market participants – should prefer the 2-year bond. The difference in the yield presents an arbitrage opportunity. New demand would be directed toward the 2-year bonds, and some owners of 1-year bonds would want to sell them in order to buy 2-year bonds. These flows of funds would tend to drive the price of 2-year bonds up (i.e., drive their yield down) and to drive the price of 1-year bonds down (i.e., drive their yield up). Funds would continue to flow until each of the two ways of holding your funds for two years had the same yield.

For instance, if the expectations of the future 1-year rate were unaffected by the flow of funds, so that $r^e_{1,t+1}$ remained 9 percent come what may, then a 1-year rate $r_{1,t} = 12$ percent and a 2-year rate $r_{2,t} = 10.5$ percent eliminate the arbitrage opportunity: $(1 + r_{1,t})(1 + r^e_{1,t+1}) = (1.12)(1.09) = (1 + r_{2,t})^2 = (1.105)^2 = \$1.22$.

The differences between the returns on different arrangements of your portfolio seem small – a penny or two. But remember that it is a penny or two per dollar placed in a particular bond. One-year Treasury bills are issued in \$10,000 denominations, so that a penny per dollar is \$100 in total. The large players in financial markets, such as banks, mutual funds, and insurance companies, shift millions of dollars at a time. Very small differences in yields make significant differences in their bottom lines. The profit motive is strong, so it is reasonable to assume that arbitrage is complete. Setting aside the particular numbers of the last example, the relationship $(1 + r_{1,t})(1 + r^e_{1,t+1}) = (1 + r_{2,t})^2$ is known as a **no-arbitrage condition**, which means that, when it holds, no profit opportunities are left to be exploited by arbitrageurs.

What works for two periods generalizes to three or more periods. To put funds out at interest for three years, you might buy a series of 1-year bonds or a single 3-year bond. If the actual and expected interest rates for each strategy fulfill the condition: $(1 + r_{1,t})(1 + r^e_{1,t+1})(1 + r^e_{1,t+2}) = (1 + r_{3,t})^3$, then there are no arbitrage opportunities. In general, the yield on an m-period bond over its life should equal the expected yields of m 1-period bonds:

$$(1 + r_{m,t})^m = (1 + r_{1,t})(1 + r^e_{1,t+1})(1 + r^e_{1,t+2}) \cdots$$
$$\cdots (1 + r^e_{1,t+m-2})(1 + r^e_{1,t+m-1}) \tag{7.1}$$

Solving for $r_{m,t}$,

$$r_{m,t} = \sqrt[m]{(1 + r_{1,t})(1 + r^e_{1,t+1})(1 + r^e_{1,t+2}) \cdots (1 + r^e_{1,t+m-2})(1 + r^e_{1,t+m-1})} - 1. \tag{7.2}$$

In words: the gross yield on an m-period bond (i.e., $1 + r_{m,t}$) is the geometric average of the gross yield on the m current and expected future 1-period bonds.

Equation (7.2) can be simplified for easier calculation. Taking logarithms of both sides and recalling that $\log(1 + x) \approx x$ when x is small (see the *Guide*, section G.11.2), equation (7.1) can be written as

$$m(r_{m,t}) \approx r_{1,t} + r^e_{1,t+1} + r^e_{1,t+2} \cdots + r^e_{1,t+m-2} + r^e_{1,t+m-1}$$

or

$$r_{m,t} \approx \frac{r_{1,t} + r^e_{1,t+1} + r^e_{1,t+2} \cdots + r^e_{1,t+m-2} + r^e_{1,t+m-1}}{m}. \tag{7.3}$$

In words: the yield on an m-period bond is approximately the arithmetic average of the yield on the m current and expected future 1-period bonds.

Expectations and the Shape of the Yield Curve

To understand what the no-arbitrage condition implies for the shape of the yield curve, consider an example in which the current and expected 1-year bond rates are:

$$r_{1,t} = 6 \text{ percent,}$$
$$r^e_{1,t+1} = 7 \text{ percent,}$$
$$r^e_{1,t+2} = 8 \text{ percent,}$$
$$r^e_{1,t+3} = 9 \text{ percent.}$$

If traders arbitrage perfectly, then equation (7.3) can be used to compute the rates on 1-year to 4-year bonds:[11]

$$r_{1,t} = 6 \text{ percent,}$$
$$r_{2,t} = (6 + 7)/2 = 6.5 \text{ percent,}$$
$$r_{3,t} = (6 + 7 + 8)/3 = 7 \text{ percent,}$$
$$r_{4,t} = (6 + 7 + 8 + 9)/4 = 7.5 \text{ percent.}$$

---

[11] All of these calculations are strictly approximations according to equation (7.3). It is more convenient, however, to write them as equalities.

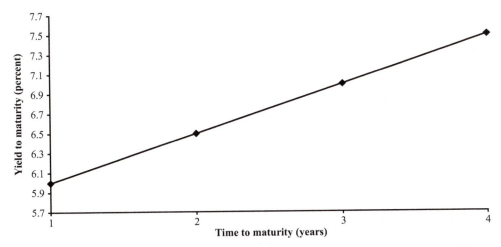

Figure 7.5. A Yield Curve Based on the Expectations Theory of the Term Structure of Interest Rates. The yield for each maturity is the average of the current and expected 1-year bond rates.

Figure 7.5 plots the yield curve for time t based on these calculations. Notice that the current and expected 1-year bond rates increase over time (between t and $t+3$) and that implies that the yield curve at t slopes up. If short rates decreased over time, the yield curve would slope down. The no-arbitrage condition is consistent with yield curves of any shape. Consider another example:

$$r_{1,t} = 8 \text{ percent},$$
$$r^e_{1,t+1} = 7 \text{ percent},$$
$$r^e_{1,t+2} = 9 \text{ percent},$$
$$r^e_{1,t+3} = 5 \text{ percent}.$$

The no-arbitrage condition, then, implies:

$$r_{1,t} = 8 \text{ percent},$$
$$r_{2,t} = 7.5 \text{ percent},$$
$$r_{3,t} = 8 \text{ percent},$$
$$r_{4,t} = 7.25 \text{ percent}.$$

(The reader should check these values using equation (7.3).) Figure 7.6 plots the yield curve implied in this example. It slopes down, then up, and then down again.[12] In actual financial markets, yield curves typically slope up, but downward-sloping and even humped or S-shaped yield curves are observed from time to time.

---

[12] The smoothing option in Excel's scatterplot option is used to interpolate the values between data points.

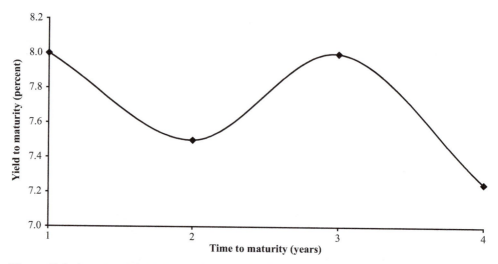

Figure 7.6. Another Yield Curve. Not all yield curves slope up. When short rates are expected to rise, yield curves slope up. When they are expected to fall, yield curves slope down.

The explanation of the shape of yield curves as an implication of the no-arbitrage condition is known as the **EXPECTATIONS THEORY OF THE TERM STRUCTURE OF INTEREST RATES**. In its simplest form, as here, it ignores risk. Presently, we shall consider the role of risk in the term structure.

Alternative Portfolio Strategies

Our account of the shape of the yield curve seems to support the common view that the expectations theory of the term structure explains long rates as the average of current and expected short rates. But this is not accurate. There is nothing in our account that says that the pattern of short rates *causes* the pattern of longer rates. What it really says is that, unless the no-arbitrage condition is fulfilled, there will be profit opportunities to be exploited and that exploiting them makes them disappear. There are many no-arbitrage conditions that must be simultaneously fulfilled. It is natural to look at equation (7.3) and think in terms of 1-year rates explaining *m*-year rates. But it could equally be thought of as 1-quarter (i.e., 3-month) rates explaining *m*-quarter rates. A 5-year bond rate would then be the average of twenty 3-month bill rates.

And it is more complex than that. For example, apply equation (7.3) to a 2-year and a 3-year bond at time *t*:

$$r_{2,t} = \frac{r_{1,t} + r^e_{1,t+1}}{2},$$

$$r_{3,t} = \frac{r_{1,t} + r^e_{1,t+1} + r^e_{1,t+2}}{3}.$$

The first expression can be rewritten as $2r_{2,t} = r_{1,t} + r^e_{1,t+1}$ and substituted into the second expression to yield

$$r_{3,t} = \frac{2r_{2,t} + r^e_{1,t+2}}{3}.$$

In words: a 3-year bond rate at t is the weighted average of a 2-year bond rate at t and the expected 1-year bond rate at $t + 2$. The student should check that the following relationship is also true:

$$r_{3,t} = \frac{r_{1,t} + 2r^e_{2,t+1}}{3},$$

the 3-year bond rate at t is the weighted average of the current 1-year bond rate at t and the expected 2-year bond rate at $t + 1$.

In fact, the expectations theory of the term structure implies that every sequence of bonds – of whatever maturities – that carry the owner from one particular time (t) to another ($t + m$) must have the same return. There are as many no-arbitrage conditions as there are pairs of available ways to get funds from t to $t + m$.

Implicit Expectations

Expectations are critical to the analysis. Yet expectations are not directly observable. On the assumption that the expectations theory of the term structure (ignoring risk) is true, we can work out what market expectations must be for future rates. Consider a simple example. At time t, let the yields on different maturity bonds be given as follows:

$$r_{1,t} = 2 \text{ percent,}$$
$$r_{2,t} = 3 \text{ percent,}$$
$$r_{3,t} = 5 \text{ percent,}$$
$$r_{4,t} = 7 \text{ percent.}$$

Now, say that we wish to know what the market expects the path of 1-year rates to be. The current 1-year rate is known: 2 percent. According to equation (7.3), $r_{2,t} = 3 = \frac{r_{1,t} + r^e_{1,t+1}}{2} = \frac{2 + r^e_{1,t+1}}{2}$. Solving for the unknown, $r^e_{1,t+1} = 2r_{2,t} - r_{1,t} = 2 \cdot 3 - 2 = 4$. The whole sequence of implied 1-year rates is then:

$$r_{1,t} = 2 \text{ percent,}$$
$$r^e_{1,t+1} = 4 \text{ percent,}$$
$$r^e_{1,t+2} = 9 \text{ percent,}$$
$$r^e_{1,t+3} = 13 \text{ percent.}$$

(Once again, the student should use equation (7.3) to prove that these values are correct.) What the market expects has been extracted from its observable actions *on the condition that the expectations theory of the term structure is correct.*

7.4.3 The Role of Risk

As we have already mentioned and as is clear from Figure 7.3, most of the time yield curves slope up. If the simple expectations theory of the term structure presented in the last section is true, this should be a puzzling fact. The expectations theory says that yield curves slope up when future short rates are expected to rise. So if yield curves slope up almost always, then short rates should be expected to rise almost always. A quick look at Figure 7.1 shows that such an expectation is unreasonable. Short interest rates rise *and* fall. If the people assumed that they would always rise, their expectations would be frequently disappointed. Although expectations are never perfect, one would like to believe that people would learn from their mistakes and recognize that rates do sometimes fall. So, is there some other explanation for the dominance of upward-sloping yield curves?

Recall that so far we have ignored the role of risk in the term structure. Also recall from section 7.3.2 that price risk is greater the longer the maturity of a bond and that generally markets require higher returns, a **term premium** (a kind of risk premium), to compensate for higher risk. The term premium is shown as a function of maturity because longer maturity bonds face greater price risk.[13] We can therefore modify equation (7.3) to add in the term premium:

$$r_{m,t} \approx \frac{r_{1,t} + r^e_{1,t+1} + r^e_{1,t+2} \cdots + r^e_{1,t+m-2} + r^e_{1,t+m-1}}{m} + term\ premium\ (m).$$

$$(7.4)$$

To see what affect the addition of a term premium has on the yield curve, consider a case in which current and expected short rates are constant at 6 percent, as shown in Table 7.3, and in which the term premium rises from zero for a 1-year bond by 0.25 point each year of maturity. Without term premia, the yield curve would be constant. With term premia, it is rising. Figure 7.7 shows the yield curve with and without the term premia. The gap between them at any maturity is the term premium.

---

[13] It is possible for term premia to become smaller at long maturities. Some bondholders might prefer long maturities to match future obligations, so that the risk to them is holding a short bond and having to repurchase another at an unfavorable price when it matures. The evidence supports the view that most people prefer shorter maturities.

Table 7.3. *An Illustration of the Term Structure of Interest Rates with and without Term Premia*

Current and Expected Short Rates		Current Rates on Bonds of Successive Maturities		
	Number of Years until Bond Matures	Term Premium at Each Maturity	Implied Rate at Each Maturity without Term Premium	Implied Rate at Each Maturity with Term Premium
$r_{1,t} = 6.0$	1	0.00	$r_{1,t} = 6.00$	6.00
$r^e_{1,t+1} = 6.0$	2	0.25	$r_{2,t} = 6.00$	6.25
$r^e_{1,t+2} = 6.0$	3	0.50	$r_{3,t} = 6.00$	6.50
$r^e_{1,t+3} = 6.0$	4	0.75	$r_{4,t} = 6.00$	6.75

7.5 Inflation and Interest Rates

7.5.1 The Effect of Inflation on the Supply and Demand for Bonds

The analysis in this chapter has concentrated entirely on market or nominal rates of interest. We learned in the last chapter that the market rate can be decomposed into the sum of a real rate of interest and the rate of inflation. Because inflation rates have varied considerably over time, it would be interesting to know how that variation might have affected interest rates. At first blush, one might think that the question is answered already in knowing the decomposition $r_t \approx rr_t + \hat{p}^e_t$. An increase in expected inflation increases the market rate of interest. But that moves too quickly. We cannot know how

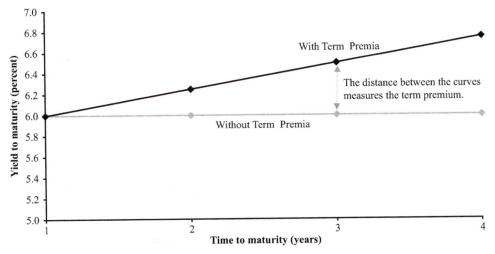

Figure 7.7. Yield Curves with and without Term Premia. The distance between the curves measures the term premium.

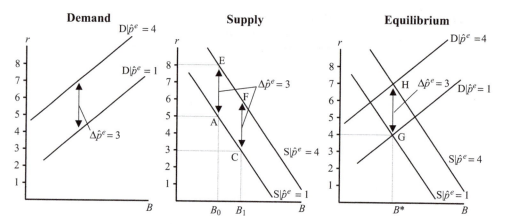

Figure 7.8. The Effect of a Change in the Expected Rate of Inflation on the Bond Market. Both the demand for and the supply of bonds and other loans depend on real rates of interest. If the rate of expected inflation increases (here by 3 percentage points), each real interest rate corresponds to a nominal interest rate higher by an amount equal to the change in the rate of inflation. As a result, both the supply and the demand curve for bonds must shift vertically up by the change in the rate of expected inflation, so that the equilibrium itself moves upward by the same amount and the volume of bonds remains unchanged.

any change in inflation affects nominal rates of interest until we know how it affects real rates of interest. For example, if real rates always fell by the same absolute amount when inflation rose, then nominal rates would stay constant. To decide what really happens requires us to think more carefully about the underlying economic behavior.

The key point is that rational people should not care about the nominal values of prices or interest rates. They should care about the real values, what their money will actually buy or what their savings will earn. Consider the market for a particular bond shown in Figure 7.8. The figure shows nominal interest rates (r) on the vertical axis as is customary. But if real interest rates are what is important to people, then we must know the expected rate of inflation $\hat{p}^e$. For example, suppose that $\hat{p}^e = 1$ percent. Then, both the demand curve (left-hand panel) and the supply curve (middle panel) are drawn conditional on that expected rate of inflation. A nominal rate $r = 5$ percent corresponds to a real rate $rr = 5 - 1 = 4$ percent. Similarly, a nominal rate $r = 3$ percent corresponds to a real rate $rr = 2$ percent. At the 4 percent real rate, the supply curve (point A) shows that borrowers wish to obtain B_0 in loans and, at the 2 percent real rate (point C), B_1.

What happens if the expected rate of inflation increases to $\hat{p}^e = 4$ percent? Because the users of funds care about real rates, they should be willing to supply exactly the same amounts at the same real rates. But now each real rate corresponds to a higher nominal rate. A nominal rate of 8 percent ($= rr + \hat{p}^e = 4 + 4$) corresponds to a real rate of 4 percent, and a nominal rate of 6 percent corresponds to a real rate of 2 percent. The whole supply curve, then, must shift vertically upward by exactly the change in the expected rate of inflation (i.e., by 3 percentage points), so that it lies parallel to original curve. At point E the nominal interest rate is higher than at point A, but because the real rate has not changed, the supply of bonds remains at B_0. Similarly, the supply of bonds remains unchanged between points C and F. The issuer of the bond is willing to pay higher rates of interest for the same funds, because he can pay them back with money that is losing its value faster because of the higher inflation.

An exactly parallel argument suggests that the demand curve should also shift vertically at every point by an amount equal to the change in the rate of inflation. The lender must charge higher rates of interest for the same loan to ensure that the real return remains the same in the face of money that is losing its value faster.

The combined effect of these two adaptations to higher rates of inflation is that both the supply and demand curves shift vertically by the same amount, so that the equilibrium (right-hand panel), which had been at 4 percent (point G), also shifts vertically to 7 percent (point H), and the equilibrium quantity of bonds (B^*) remains constant.

7.5.2 The Fisher Effect and the Fisher Hypothesis

The relationship between inflation rates and interest rates discussed in the last section is known as the Fisher effect, in honor of the great American economist Irving Fisher (1867–1947) who emphasized it in his analysis of interest rates. It may be useful to distinguish the Fisher effect from the Fisher hypothesis.

- The **FISHER EFFECT** can be defined as *a point-for-point increase in the market rate of interest that results* ceteris paribus *from an increase in the expected rate of inflation*. The *ceteris paribus* clause is important. The Fisher effect is a theoretical claim that may be difficult to observe in the world because other things are not always equal.
- The **FISHER HYPOTHESIS** can be defined as *the empirical phenomenon in which a change in market rates of interest is associated approximately point for point with a change in the actual rate of inflation*.[14]

The Fisher effect and the Fisher hypothesis do not simply recapitulate the decomposition of the nominal rate: $r_t \approx rr_t + \hat{p}_t^e$. This is just an (approximate) definition; and, like all definitions, it always holds. Fisher asserted something in addition to the definition – namely, that the real rate

---

[14] The terminology is not completely standardized. Different economists talk about the Fisher effect or hypothesis or relation or theorem sometimes as synonyms and sometimes drawing distinctions as we have done here.

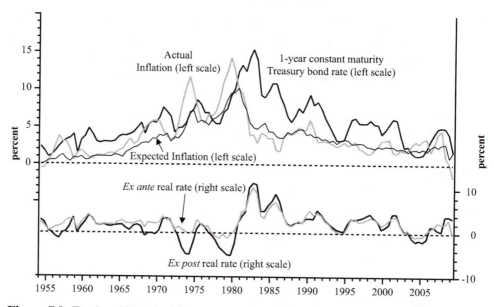

Figure 7.9. Real and Nominal Interest Rates. Expected inflation from the Livingston survey. *Ex ante* real rate = current interest rate − expected inflation rate over the following 12 months; *Ex post* real rate = current interest rate − actual inflation rate over the following 12 months. *Source:* bond yield, Board of Governors of the Federal Reserve System; expected inflation, Federal Reserve Bank of Philadelphia.

of interest and the expected rate of inflation are independent. In that case, an increase in inflation does not influence the real rate of interest and, as a result, the entire increase is passed on to the nominal rate of interest. To see the difference more clearly, suppose that the real rate of interest is 2 percent when the inflation rate is 3 percent and the nominal rate is 5 percent. The decomposition holds ($5 = 2 + 3$). Now imagine that the inflation rate increases to 4 percent and, as a result, the nominal rate rises to 6 percent. Then, the Fisher effect is correct, and the decomposition still holds ($6 = 2 + 4$). Now consider a different case in which the inflation rate increases to 4 percent but, as a result, the real rate falls to 1 percent. Then the nominal rate is unchanged. The Fisher effect is false, yet the decomposition *still* holds ($5 = 1 + 4$).

The upper panel of Figure 7.9 plots the 1-year Treasury bond rates alongside the year-over-year CPI inflation rate (actual and expected). The lower panel plots the real rates of interest implied by the data in the upper panel – *ex ante* ($rr = r - \hat{p}$) and *ex post* ($rr = r - \hat{p}^e$). If the Fisher hypothesis is true, then movements in the inflation rate should be mirrored in the nominal interest rate. If the Fisher hypothesis is true, then movements in the real rate in the lower panel should be uncorrelated with movements in the inflation rate in the upper panel. (On correlation see the *Guide*, section G.13.) The figure roughly conforms to the first pattern: the broad pattern of first rising then falling inflation rates is reflected (with a lag in a very similar pattern in interest rates). The figure does not support the second pattern so well: particular short-term rises or falls in inflation rates seem to be associated with simultaneous falls or rises in real rates of interest – that is, the series appear to be negatively correlated.

The evidence, then, is that the Fisher hypothesis – as Fisher himself was well aware – at best holds only roughly. One reason is that no inflation measure, such as the CPI, represents exactly the bundle that is relevant to the players in financial markets. Borrowers and lenders might have systematically different consumption bundles. Indeed, the relevant bundles need not be the same for all borrowers or all lenders.

A second reason is that taxes are levied on nominal interest payments. Higher interest rates, even if they are merely compensation for higher inflation rates, generate higher tax liabilities. Lenders would, therefore, require an extra increase in nominal interest rates to compensate for the loss of purchasing power due to inflation-induced increases in tax rates. In the United States, Federal income taxes have been indexed to inflation since 1985, so that standard deductions, tax brackets, and other features account for changing price levels. But not all states index or index completely, and not all taxes are indexed.

Finally, and probably most important, there is no reason to believe that expectations of future inflation are formed perfectly or are captured by the past behavior of inflation. It may take some time to adjust expectations to an unexpected increase or decrease in actual inflation. During the adjustment period, real rather than nominal rates would be affected. This is easily seen in Figure 7.9, the upper panel of which shows market interest rates on 1-year Treasury bonds. In the 1970s, when inflation accelerated, expectations of inflation lagged behind actual inflation, and *ex post* real interest rates (the difference between the market rates and the actual rate of inflation in the figure shown in the lower panel of Figure 7.9) fell. At some points *ex post* real rates became negative. In contrast, except for brief periods just below zero, *ex ante* real rates remained positive. After the mid-1980s, when inflation rates fell, again expectations lagged actual inflation and *ex post* real rates rose. A borrower equipped with a crystal ball would have found the mid-1970s to the mid-1980s to have been the best time to incur debt: reversing the normal course of things, lenders paid borrowers *ex post* in real terms to use the lenders' money. Absent a crystal ball, *ex ante* real rates were little different from the patterns of the previous twenty years. Most borrowers missed the opportunity because it was unexpected.

To calculate *ex ante* real interest rates, we used an estimate of expected inflation rates (the Livingston survey). Measuring expectations is a tricky business. Several alternative approaches are discussed in Box 7.1.

Box 7.1. Measuring Expected Inflation

Expected quantities are often central to economic analysis. But how can we measure them when they cannot be observed directly? Expected price inflation is a case in point. Economists have identified three broad strategies for measuring expected inflation: surveys, model-based estimates, and market estimates.

Surveys

Several groups conduct surveys of expectations of inflation. Two of the most important are the Livingston surveys and the surveys conducted by the University of Michigan Survey Research Center.

The oldest, continuously collected survey of inflation has been compiled since 1946 – first by Joseph Livingston, who was an economic columnist for the *Philadelphia Inquirer* newspaper. Livingston regularly surveyed professional economic forecasters, asking for their expectations of a number of variables, including consumer price inflation. The Federal Reserve Bank of Philadelphia assumed responsibility for the Livingston surveys in 1990.

While the Livingston survey refers to professional forecasters, the Michigan surveys ask households for their expectations of CPI inflation, among other measures of consumer sentiment about the state of the economy.

Economists are frequently suspicious of survey data because they focus on what people say rather than what they do and they do not capture the expectation at the actual moment in which economic decisions are made.

Model-Based Expectations

A common alternative to surveys is for economists to try to model how people *do* or *should* form their expectations. One form of such model-based expectations is known as *adaptive expectations*. We assume that people adapt current expectations to the mistakes of the past. For example, expectations of inflation might be modeled as

$$\hat{p}_{t+1}^e = \hat{p}_t + \lambda \left(\hat{p}_t - \hat{p}_t^e \right),$$

where $0 \leq \lambda \leq 1$. In words, this says that expected inflation next period is estimated to be actual inflation this period plus some fraction of the amount by which actual inflation differed from what was expected this period. Thus, if inflation were underpredicted this period, we would want to raise our expectations next period.

It is easy to show that adaptive expectations imply that current expectations are a weighted average of past actual inflation rates (see the *Guide*, section G.4.2, on weighted means). Economists frequently reject this or related models that give fixed weights to past actual inflation as inconsistent with rationality. For example, if actual inflation increases each period, expectations will always lag behind actual inflation: people are modeled as making the same underprediction every period. Typically, we expect people to learn from their mistakes.

Many economists, therefore, believe that it is better to model people as holding *rational expectations*. In a model with rational expectations – conditional on the information they are presumed to have – people are assumed to hold the expectations that are consistent with the predictions of the model. The key property then is that economists do not model people as making systematic mistakes. That is not to say that people do not make mistakes, but that the mistakes that they make are not *systematic* and, therefore, not easily correctible. If people, for example, always underpredicted inflation by differing amounts, but on average by 2 percentage points, then they could easily improve their forecasts by simply adding 2 points to whatever method they used to make them. There would often be a strong economic incentive to do this.

Advocates of rational expectations are fond of quoting President Lincoln's dictum: "You can fool ... all the people some of the time; ... but you cannot fool all of the people all the time." They sometimes forget the elided middle clause of his aphorism: "you can even fool some of the people all the time."

One disadvantage of rational expectations is that they assume that economists are working with a complete and approximately correct model of the economy in order to measure expectations accurately. We often want to have a measure of people's expectations when we are working with only a partial model of the whole economy or when some parts of the model are in doubt.

Market-Based Expectations

The bond market provides an alternative method of measuring expectations of price inflation. In addition to ordinary Treasury bills and bonds, the U.S. Treasury (as well as the governments of some other countries) issue **inflation-indexed securities**. These bonds differ from other Treasury securities in that their face value is adjusted for changes in consumer price inflation. For example, a dollar placed in a 1-year inflation-indexed bond

(continued)

Box 7.1 (*continued*)

at an interest rate r_I pays off $(1 + r_I) \times (p_{t+1}/p_t)$ dollars after one year. The *expected* yield to maturity in the dollars of one year in the future is thus $(1 + r_I)(p_{t+1}^e/p_t) = (1 + r_I)(1 + \hat{p}^e) \approx r_I + \hat{p}^e$. If markets work effectively to arbitrage between inflation-indexed and ordinary bonds, then the yield to maturity on a 1-year, noninflation-indexed bond (r) must equal that expected on an inflation-indexed bond. Thus, $r = r_I + \hat{p}^e$. And as a result,

$$\hat{p}^e = r - r_I.$$

That is, the difference between the market yields on an ordinary bond and the expected yield on an inflation-indexed bond is a direct measure of the expected rate of inflation. What is more, because the real rate of interest is defined in equation (6.11″) as $rr_t \approx r_t - \hat{p}_{t+1}$, r_I is itself a direct measure of the expected real rate of interest.

Surveys provide some measure of inflation a year or so in the future. Unfortunately, because the Treasury issues inflation-indexed securities only in long maturities, they can be used to calculate inflation only at horizons of five to ten years.

Different Measures Compared

Figure B7.1 compares four measures of expected inflation. Three are expectations one year ahead: the Michigan survey, the Livingston survey, and adaptive expectations with $\lambda = 0.5$. The fourth is market-based expectations based on the difference in yield between 10-year

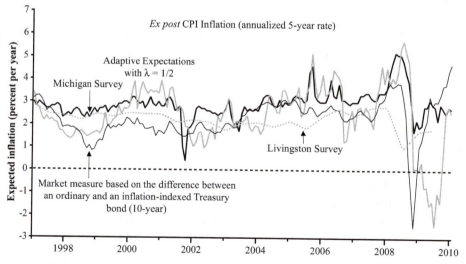

Figure B7.1. Measures of Expected CPI Inflation. *Source:* Livingston survey, Federal Reserve Bank of Philadelphia; Michigan survey, Survey Research Center, University of Michigan.

ordinary and inflation-indexed Treasury bonds. The expectations are broadly similar in terms of levels, although month-to-month changes vary considerably. For the most part, the Livingston data, based on the views of professional forecasters, show much smaller variability than the other series. There is a sharp collapse (quickly reversed) of expectations of inflation associated with the financial collapse of 2008, although the timing of the collapse differs among the different measures. Two key differences are: 1) that, unlike the other three measures, the expectations based on the Livingston survey never become negative (i.e., forecasters never expect deflation); and 2) the collapse in the adaptive expectations measure is later than the other three measures (early 2009), as is its recovery, reflecting the backward-looking character of fixed-weight measures.

7.6 The Level of Real Interest Rates

So far in this chapter we have tried to account for the relationships among different interest rates and between interest rates and inflation. If we had a starting place (that is if we knew one real rate of interest) we should be able in principle to use information about the maturity, coupon structure, risk, tax rates, and expected inflation rates to deduce the rates on all other bonds. But where do we find the starting place – the one real rate? Or, to put it another way, what determines the level of the real yield on any particular financial asset? There are two answers to this question, depending on whether we concentrate on short rates or long rates.

7.6.1 Monetary Policy and Short Rates

At the short end of the market, the interaction of monetary policy and expected inflation rates determines the real rate. We shall examine monetary policy more carefully in Chapter 16. For the time being, a brief account will suffice.

Central banks (in the United States, the Federal Reserve) typically buy and sell short-term assets (largely Treasury bills) on the open market. When the central bank buys, it pays by crediting funds to the accounts that commercial banks hold with it, creating central-bank reserves (see Chapter 6, sections 6.1 and 6.3.2). When it sells, it deducts funds from these accounts, eliminating reserves. In the United States, these reserves are known to financial markets as **Federal funds**.

Commercial banks are required to hold reserves in a certain proportion to their deposit liabilities. There is an active overnight market, the **Federal funds market**, in which banks with an excess of reserves over their requirements lend to banks with a shortage. The Federal Reserve can set the interest rate in this market, known as the **Federal-funds rate**, by raising or lowering the stock of available reserves through purchases or sales of short-term financial assets. Monetary policy today largely consists of setting a target for the Federal-funds rate.

The Federal funds target is officially a target for a nominal rate of interest. The Federal Reserve's concern, however, is the real rate of interest. It sets the Federal funds rate at a level that it hopes will influence longer term interest rates through the yield curve with the aim of influencing investment expenditure. Investment expenditure, as we will consider in detail in Chapters 13 and 14, depends inversely on real rates. So the Federal Reserve's nominal target must be set with some view about the market's expectations of inflation – that is, with some view of what the real rate should be.

The expectations theory of the term structure tells us that longer rates are the average of current and expected short rates. The rates that the Federal Reserve sets at the extreme short end of the yield curve affect the whole yield curve in a way that depends on what the markets believe the Federal Reserve will do in the future. Imagine that the Federal Reserve raised the (nominal) Federal-funds rate by 0.5 percentage point and markets believed that they would hold it at this higher level for all eternity. Then, every longer-term rate would rise by 0.5 point. At the other extreme, imagine that markets believed the 0.5-point increase would be reversed the next day. Then, the longer-term interest rate would be affected hardly at all. In reality, markets make constantly shifting guesses about the course of future monetary policy – the financial press is populated by numerous "Fed watchers" – and the conviction with which these guesses are held fades rapidly as the market players look further into the future.

7.6.2 Arbitrage to Real Returns

At longer maturities, bonds are substitutes for shares in corporations. If the real returns on bonds, after accounting for risk, are greater than the returns on stocks, then arbitrageurs will direct funds toward bonds, driving their rates down. Similarly, if the real returns on bonds are smaller, arbitrage will drive their rates up. The yields on stocks and bonds might be very different on average, but they should tend to move together over time.

Ultimately, the real yield on stocks – and, therefore, through arbitrage, the real yield on longer bonds – is determined by the profitability of corporations and the real return that they earn on their capital. It is useful to distinguish between physical and financial returns. (The return on *physical* capital includes here the return on the organization, management, and the so-called *human* capital – that is, the education, training, experience, and esprit de corps of the workforce.) Sometimes financial returns may differ substantially from the underlying physical returns on capital. In such a case, one would expect arbitrage to drive their returns together. Unlike arbitrage among financial assets, arbitrage between physical capital and financial instruments can be slow, especially if it involves investment and the expansion of the corporation. We shall consider the process of investment in more detail in Chapter 14. For now, it helps to reconcile a potential conflict in the determination of real rates.

How is it that real rates are determined both through monetary policy transmitted from the short end of the market through the term structure and simultaneously through arbitrage to the real returns on physical capital? Something has to give. That something is inflation.

Imagine that when the inflation rate is, say, 2 percent, the Federal Reserve sets short rates at 5 percent and intends to hold them there, so that the real rate on financial assets is 3 percent. But suppose that the real yield on physical capital is 5 percent. Arbitrage would then direct funds toward investment. If the economy had slack resources, aggregate demand and capacity utilization would rise. As the limits of capacity were reached, inflation would accelerate. If the Federal Reserve continued to hold interest rates at 5 percent, it would find that the real rate on financial assets was falling below its 3 percent target. Of course, as real rates fell further the incentive to invest in physical capital would increase, and inflation would accelerate further.

In the short run, the Federal Reserve might use a policy of holding real rates of interest on financial instruments below real rates of return on capital to stimulate an underemployed economy. In the long run, however, it would face accelerating inflation. Only by raising interest rates relative to the rate of inflation to set the yield on financial assets at about the same rate as the yield on physical capital could the Federal Reserve stop this inflationary process. Because the Federal Reserve does not directly observe the real rate of return on physical capital, this is largely a matter of trial and error. (The process of inflation and its interaction with monetary policy are more fully discussed in Chapters 15 and 16.)

7.7 The Five Questions about Interest Rates Revisited

We have covered many of the complexities of financial markets quickly. Let us conclude the chapter by taking stock of what we have learned about the five questions that motivated our investigations.

- *First, why do interest rates tend to move together?*
  Traders in financial markets seek the highest return on their available funds. All financial assets are, to some degree, substitutes. As a result any movement in the price or yield of any one financial asset opens up profit opportunities that are quickly arbitraged away. In the process of arbitrage, funds flow from

low-yielding assets (raising their yield) toward high-yielding assets (lowering their yield). Upward or downward movements of the yields of any one asset tend to draw the yields on other assets along in the same direction.

- *Second, why do they move only imperfectly together?*
  Although all financial assets are substitutes, they are not perfect substitutes. Even when the markets have taken advantage of every profit opportunity, differences in maturity, coupon structure, risk, and other features ensure that differences in yield usually remain. Changing economic circumstances may change the importance of these differences over time, so that the yield differentials are not necessarily constant.

- *Third, why do shorter maturity assets typically, but not uniformly, yield lower rates of interest than longer maturity assets?*
  Differences in maturity are a particularly important example of the imperfect substitutability of financial assets. The expectations theory of the term structure of interest rates assumes that arbitrage is highly effective. When arbitrage is complete, longer rates are the average of shorter rates plus a premium that reflects the added price risk of the longer asset. Long rates are higher than short rates whenever short rates are expected to rise or whenever an expected fall in short rates is not large enough to offset the risk premia.

- *Fourth, why at each maturity do government assets yield lower rates of interest than private-sector assets?*
  Governments whose debt is denominated in their own currencies have no reason to default on that debt, because they are always able to create the money necessary to pay the interest and principal. Any organization that cannot create its own money – state and local governments, agencies, and corporations – or whose debts are not denominated in its own currency faces some risk of bankruptcy, and its debt carries some default risk. A premium in the form of a higher yield must be paid to reflect this default risk.

- *Fifth, what determines the overall level of interest rates?*
  The two principal influences on real interest rates are monetary policy at the short end of the maturity spectrum and arbitrage with the yields on physical assets at the long end. Monetary policy typically targets nominal interest rates, but does so with an eye to the inflation rate and hence to real rates. To a first approximation, the Fisher effect determines nominal rates as the sum of the real rate and the expected rate of inflation.

Appendix: The LM Curve

For much of the past seven decades, macroeconomists have used the LM curve, which relates GDP to interest rates, to characterize financial markets. Although we argue later that the LM curve is too simple to represent all the features of financial markets that are important to macroeconomics, it is so widely used that it may be helpful to explain it more fully. LM-curve analysis is less complete than, but does not contradict, the analysis of this and the preceding chapter.

7.A.1 Money Supply and Money Demand

The Real Supply of Money

LM-curve analysis focuses on the narrow monetary instruments used by the public in conducting its transactions – in the United States typically on the Federal Reserve's M1 or M2 (see Chapter 6, Table 6.3). Whichever definition of money we might choose, call its nominal supply M^S. The real supply of money can be written as M^S/p, where p is, of course, the price level. An increase in the nominal supply of money *ceteris paribus increases* the real supply by raising the numerator in M^S/p. An increase in the price level *decreases* the real supply by raising the denominator in M^S/p.

Transactions Demand for Money

The most common use of narrow money is as a transactions medium. The higher the level of transactions in the economy, the more money would be needed.

For instance, holding real transactions constant, if the prices of every good and service were to double (nominal GDP would increase, but real GDP would remain constant), then twice as many dollars would be needed to move the goods and services. Although the nominal demand for money (M^D) has risen, the real demand (M^D/p) remains constant; both the numerator and the denominator in M^D/p change in the same proportion.

On the other hand, if real GDP doubles, more goods and services must be moved no matter what the price level. This is likely to require more real units of money. As a result, the real demand for money is likely to be an increasing function of real GDP.

Money Demand and Interest Rates

What is the opportunity cost of holding money? In other words, what alternatives do you have when you hold money? To keep things simple, assume that money is currency and non-interest-bearing checking deposits (roughly M1). If you hold a dollar in these forms, then you lose the interest that you might have earned from buying a government bond or placing your funds in a mutual fund. Call this rate of interest r.

Of course we ought to be concerned about the *real* and not the *nominal* return on any asset. The real return on our bond is $rr = r - \hat{p}^e$. To find the opportunity cost of holding money, we must compare this return to the rate of return on money itself. A dollar bill earns no interest. But if there is inflation then it loses its real value at approximately the rate of inflation (e.g., if inflation is 10 percent per year, the dollar yields –10 percent real returns). In general the real rate of return on money is $-\hat{p}^e$.

The opportunity cost of holding money is the difference in return between the next best alternative and the return on money itself. That is, the

opportunity cost of holding money = real return on the bond

− real return on money

$$= rr - (-\hat{p}^e) = (r - \hat{p}^e) - (-\hat{p}^e) = r.$$

In other words, even though we are interested in real (not nominal) rates of return, the true opportunity cost of holding money is measured by the *nominal* rate of interest on an alternative financial asset.

We would modify this analysis slightly to account for interest-bearing checking accounts or for wider concepts of money (e.g., M2) that include interest-bearing financial instruments. But so long as the rates of return on these interest-bearing components of the monetary aggregate are not perfectly correlated with those on the alternative financial instrument, a similar analysis will apply (see Problem 7.16).

Money is like other goods: the higher the opportunity cost, the less of it we want to hold. Consider, first, how the **transactions demand for money** (i.e., *the money held to facilitate purchases of goods and services*) is affected by higher interest rates. When the opportunity cost of money is high, we lose interest by holding more of it, so we find ways to hold less. For example, if interest rates are high enough, we might reduce the funds in our pockets and in our bank accounts and take funds out of interest-bearing mutual funds in smaller amounts more frequently. In other words, when interest rates rise, the transactions demand for money falls. Such close management costs us time and trouble, but the higher the opportunity cost, the more it will prove worth our while.

Because money is not subject to capital gains and losses as interest rates change, you can reduce the risk of your portfolio by including some proportion of money in it. You get lower risk, but at the cost of a lower return. Holding money for this purpose is known as the **speculative demand for money**. As interest rates rise, the cost to your portfolio of holding money rises (another expression of the opportunity cost), and you are likely to want to change the mix of the portfolio away from money toward higher yielding assets. In other words, when interest rates rise, the speculative demand for money falls.

The Money Demand and Supply Curves

Money supply (M^S) and money demand (M^D) can each be represented on a diagram with the real stock of money (M/p) on the horizontal axis and the interest rate (r) on the vertical axis.

Because money supply does not depend on interest rates, it is shown in Figure 7.A.1 as a vertical line above the real stock of money. An increase

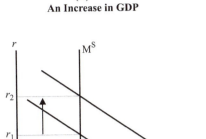
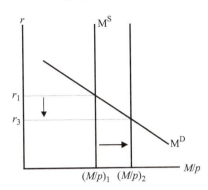

(A)
An Increase in GDP

(B)
**An Increase in the Nominal Money Supply
or a Fall in the Price Level**

Figure 7.A.1. The Money Market. The supply of money is independent of interest rates, so the real money supply curve is a vertical line that shifts rightward when the nominal money supply increases and leftward when the price level decreases. The demand for money slopes downward because higher interest rates correspond to a higher opportunity cost of holding money. Each real money demand curve is drawn for a particular level of real GDP. Panel A shows the effect of an increase in real GDP: more money is demanded at each level of the interest rate, the money demand curve shifts rightward, and the interest rate rises. Panel B shows the effect of an increase in the real supply of money: the money supply curve shifts rightward and interest rates fall.

in the nominal supply of money, holding prices constant, would shift this vertical line to the right. An increase in the price level, holding the nominal supply of money constant, would shift it to the left.

Because money demand is lower when the opportunity cost of money is higher and because the opportunity cost is measured by the nominal interest rate, the money demand curve is shown as a downward sloping curve (M^D). Of course, money demand is also an increasing function of real GDP. As a result, M^D is drawn for a particular level of GDP. When GDP increases, the demand for money increases at each interest rate (i.e., M^D shifts to the right).

In each panel of Figure 7.A.1, the interest rate is initially determined at the point at which money supply and money demand are equal: r_1. If real GDP increases, then money demand increases (M^D shifts rightward), and the equilibrium interest rate rises to r_2 (panel A). If the nominal money supply increases (or the price level falls), the real money supply increases (M^S shifts rightward), and the interest rate falls to r_3 (panel B).

7.A.2 The LM Curve

Deriving the LM Curve

The LM curve translates the information in the money supply/money demand diagram onto a diagram with real GDP on the horizontal axis and

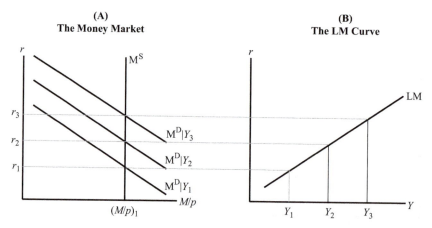

Figure 7.A.2. Deriving the LM Curve. The money demand curve shifts rightward as real GDP increases. For a constant real money supply, the interest rate must rise with each shift (panel A). The LM curve matches each of these interest rates to the corresponding level of real GDP (panel B). The LM curve is the set of all levels of real GDP (Y) and interest rates (r) for which the money market is in equilibrium – that is, real money supply equals real money demand.

interest rates on the vertical axis. Start in Figure 7.A.2 with GDP of Y_1. (The symbol $M^D | Y_1$ indicates that the money demand curve is drawn on the assumption that real GDP takes the value Y_1.) We see that Y_1 corresponds to the lowest money demand curve and the interest rate r_1 in panel (A). The point (Y_1, r_1) in panel (B) is the first point on the LM curve. Now consider a higher level of GDP: Y_2. This corresponds to the middle money demand curve in panel (A) and to the interest rate r_2. Thus, (Y_2, r_2) in panel (B) is a second point on the LM curve.

Obviously, we could look at other levels of income and their corresponding money demand curves and interest rates (not only (Y_3, r_3) but one for every level of real GDP). Connecting all such points gives us the LM curve. The **LM curve** can be defined as *the locus of all combinations of real GDP and interest rates (given the real supply of money) for which the money market is in equilibrium (i.e., for which the supply of money equals the demand for money)*. The position and shape of the LM curve clearly depend on both the money supply and money demand.

What Shifts the LM Curve?

A change in interest rates or a change in real GDP *ceteris paribus* corresponds by definition to movements along the LM curve. But the LM curve can shift as well.

Suppose that the nominal supply of money falls. In the left-hand panel of Figure 7.A.3, this is shown as a leftward shift of the vertical real money-supply curve. For each of the three money demand curves (each drawn for a

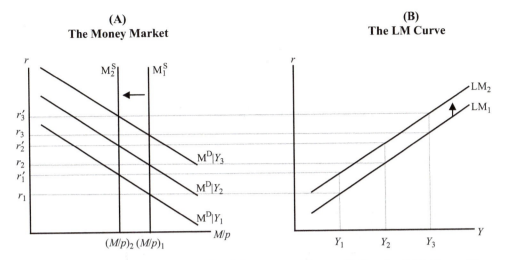

Figure 7.A.3. A Decrease in the Real Supply of Money Shifts the LM Curve Vertically. Panel (A) shows the money demand curve for three different level of real GDP. When the real money supply is M_1^S, these correspond to interest rates r_1, r_2, and r_3 and to LM_1 in panel B. When the real money supply is reduced (either because the nominal money supply is reduced or prices rise), the money supply curve shifts to M_2^S, which corresponds for each level of real GDP to the interest rates r_1', r_2', and r_3' and to LM_2 in panel B.

different level of real GDP), the interest rate rises: r_1 to r_1', r_2 to r_2', r_3 to r_3', and so forth. Translated to the right-hand panel, each level of real GDP now corresponds to a higher level of interest rates. In other words, the leftward shift of the real money supply curve results in an upward shift of the LM curve. Clearly, an increase in the price level, which reduces the real supply of money, has exactly the opposite effect (see Problem 7.17).

What Use Is the LM Curve?

The LM curve shows that an infinite number of combinations of interest rates and real GDP are compatible with equilibrium in the money market. It, therefore, does not tell us very much about the actual state of aggregate demand unless we can select a single point on it as the relevant one. For this we need another curve – the IS curve, which will be derived in Chapter 13. Even ahead of that, however, we can get an idea of what the LM curve is meant to tell us.

Start in Figure 7.A.4 in which the LM curve is LM_1 and the market interest rate is r^*. Then aggregate demand is given by the level of GDP at r^* – that is, by Y^*. Now suppose that the interest rate remains constant at r^* and, at the same time, the LM curve shifts downward (shift 1, due, e.g., to a fall in the price level) then aggregate demand would rise to Y_1. Of course, this could happen only if there were unused potential in the economy.

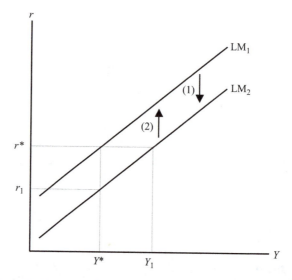

Figure 7.A.4. The LM Curve and Aggregate Demand. An increase in the nominal money supply shifts the LM curve downward (shift (1)). If the interest rate is held constant at r^* and if the economy is below its full potential so that aggregate supply is not a constraint, the aggregate demand rises from Y^* to Y_2. But if the economy is at full potential so that real aggregate supply cannot rise to meet the higher aggregate demand, then firms will have to raise prices. The higher price level reduces the real supply of money, shifting the *LM* curve upward (shift (2)) until the original equilibrium is reached at Y^*.

Consider another case, one in which the economy is already fully employed (at Y^*). Suppose that the LM curve shifts downward (perhaps due this time to an increase in the nominal money supply). There is pressure for aggregate demand to increase to Y_1, but that pressure cannot be realized because the economy is already at full potential. Firms find themselves with sales exceeding their production and so increase prices. The rising price level implies a falling real money supply, which results in an upward shift of the LM curve (shift 2). This process stops only when LM_2 has shifted all the way back to LM_1, and the interest rate has risen to r^* again at the original level of aggregate demand (Y^*).

Both of these cases are merely preliminaries to show how the LM curve works. We complete the analysis of the LM curve in the appendices to Chapters 13 and 16.

7.A.3 The Limitations of the LM Model

We have discussed the LM curve in some detail in this appendix because it is so widely used among macroeconomics textbooks. It does not, however, form a core part of the theory on which this book is based. It may be useful – without going into excessive detail – to say why. Mainly, it is because the

LM model of financial markets is too limited to address the full range of questions that interest us. To be more specific:

- The LM model overemphasizes monetary instruments. Table 6.2 (also Figure 6.2) shows that monetary instruments are only 12 percent of all financial assets. M1's share is even smaller – only 1.2 percent.
- The LM model considers only a single interest rate, but which one is it? Central banks typically target short-term rates and hope to use them to influence long-term rates. Investment most likely depends on longer-term rates. The relevant opportunity cost for the transactions demand for money may be a short-term rate, whereas the relevant opportunity cost for the speculative demand for money may be a long-term rate. To get at some really important economic issues it helps to consider multiple interest rates of different maturities connected through the yield curve.
- Monetary policy is usually analyzed in the LM model as movements of the supply of money, which raises two problems: (a) central banks do not directly control a monetary aggregate such as M1, but instead influence it through their control over the monetary base or central-bank reserves (we take this up again in Chapter 16, especially the appendix); and (b) most central banks most of the time use an interest-rate target, rather than a money-supply target, to guide monetary policy, so that the LM curve encourages us to look at monetary policy from a perspective quite different from the one natural to actual monetary policy (we consider an exception to this rule in Chapter 16, appendix).

Summary

1. There are countless interest rates in the economy, but they tend to follow some consistent patterns: (i) they move broadly together; (ii) but they are not perfectly correlated; (iii) short-term financial instruments typically (but not uniformly) have lower rates than long-term instruments; (iv) Federal government financial instruments have lower rates than corporate or state and local instruments of similar maturity; and (v) lower risk instruments have lower rates than higher risk instruments.
2. All financial instruments are, to varying degrees, substitutes. Arbitrage is the process of shifting funds among close substitutes in search of unexploited profit opportunities. Arbitrage tends to drive the yields on financial instruments as close together as their degrees of substitutability will allow.
3. The efficient-markets hypothesis states that there are no systematically exploitable arbitrage opportunities based on publicly available information.
4. Differences in risk, maturity, and payment structure explain differences in substitutability among financial instruments.
5. Default risk is the chance that a borrower will fail to pay off a loan.
6. Federal government debt is essentially free of default risk because the government's authority to tax and create money leaves it in a position always to pay off its debts so long as they are denominated in dollars.

7. Bond rating agencies classify firms and other borrowers according to the degree of anticipated default risk. Lower risk borrowers enjoy lower interest rates than higher risk borrowers.

8. Price risk (interest-rate risk) is the chance of capital gains or losses (change in the bond price) that occur as market interest rates move up and down. Price risk is greater the longer the maturity of the debt.

9. The term structure of interest rates is the pattern according to which interest rates vary with maturity. The yield curve is a graphical representation of the term structure that graphs the time to maturity on the horizontal axis and the yield to maturity on the vertical axis.

10. The expectations theory of the term structure of interest rates says that arbitrage will force interest rates into a pattern such that every way of moving funds from the current period to some future period through holding different chains of financial instruments of different maturities will have the same expected yield with an adjustment for a term premium that largely reflects price risk.

11. According to the expectations theory of the term structure, yield curves tend to slope up when short rates are expected to rise and to slope down when they are expected to fall. Yield curves slope up far more often than down; this bias is the result of the term premium rising with maturity.

12. Because people should rationally be concerned with real and not nominal returns, the nominal interest rate needed to justify either the supply of, or the demand for, any particular quantity of a financial instrument rises and falls point for point with changes in the rate of inflation. The theoretical point is known as the Fisher effect. The Fisher hypothesis is the claim that the Fisher effect characterizes financial markets pretty accurately in practice. The Fisher hypothesis may fail for various reasons – particularly, if expectations of future inflation are inaccurate.

13. The overall level of short-term interest rates is strongly affected by central-bank (Federal Reserve) monetary policies. The overall level of long-term interest rates is also affected through arbitrage to real rates of returns represented by the profits on capital invested in businesses.

Key Concepts

substitutes

arbitrage

efficient-markets hypothesis

default risk

price (or interest-rate) risk

yield curve

term structure of interest rates

expectations theory of the term
  structure of interest rates

Fisher effect

Fisher hypothesis

Suggestions for Further Reading

Some Basic Sources:

Stephen D. Smith and Raymond E. Spudeck, *Interest Rates: Principles and Applications*. New York: Harcourt Brace, 1993.

Marcia Stigum and Anthony Crescenzi, *The Money Market*, 4th ed. New York: McGraw-Hill, 2007.

The Efficient-Markets Hypothesis Has Provoked Some Lively Debate:

Burton G. Malkiel, *A Random Walk Down Wall Street*, 9th edition. New York: Norton, 2003.

Andrew W. Lo and A. Craig MacKinlay, *A Non-Random Walk Down Wall Street*. Princeton: Princeton University Press, 2001.

Robert J. Shiller, *Irrational Exuberance*. Princeton: Princeton University Press, 2001.

Stephen F. LeRoy, "Rational Exuberance," *Journal of Economic Literature*, vol. 42, no. 3 (September 2004), pp. 783–804.

George A. Akerlof and Robert J. Schiller, *Animal Spirits. How Human Psychology Drives the Economy, and Why It Matters for Global Capitalism*. Princeton: Princeton University Press, 2009.

An Up-to-Date Account of the Role of Credit-Rating Agencies, Particularly in Relation to the Credit Crisis of 2008–2009:

Lawrence J. White, "Markets: The Credit Rating Agencies," *Journal of Economic Perspectives*, vol. 24, no. 2 (Spring 2010), pp. 211–226

Problems

Data for this exercise are available on the textbook website under the link for Chapter 7 (appliedmacroeconomics.com). Before starting these exercises, the student should review the relevant portions of the *Guide to Working with Economic Data*, including sections G.1–G.4, G.7, G.10–G.11, and G.15.

Problem 7.1. Consider the scenario of section 7.2.1 (especially Figure 7.2).

(a) What would happen to the yields on P&G and Clorox bonds if Clorox decided to use extraordinary profits to buy back some of its bonds? Explain each step carefully.

(b) Assume that both Clorox and P&G bonds start with an AAA rating. What would happen to the yields on P&G and Clorox bonds if the bond rating on P&G bonds was reduced to BAA? Explain each step carefully.

Problem 7.2. A radio advertisement states that gasoline prices in the United States rise every summer and fall every winter, so that there is money to be made from buying gasoline futures in the winter and holding them until summer. (A future is a financial instrument that promises delivery of a commodity or the equivalent of its market price at a future date.) Is the underlying reasoning consistent with the efficient-markets hypothesis? Explain.

Problem 7.3. Differences in default risk should be reflected in interest rates as risk premia (section 7.3.1). To see how much, calculate the typical risk premia between the rates on 10-year constant-maturity U.S. Treasury bonds (as a measure of a bond free of default risk) and separately on Moody's Aaa and Baa corporate bond rates for the post-World War II period. Calculate and report the mean values for the yields on each bond and for the risk premia. (Save your data for the next two questions.)

Problem 7.4. How does default risk vary across the business cycle? Plot the risk premia for Aaa and Baa corporate bonds calculated in Problem 7.3 against the NBER recession dates. Comment on their cyclical properties.

Problem 7.5. Which is more risky: stocks, short-term bonds, or long term bonds? Which has the highest rate of return? Is there a clear trade-off between risk and return? Indices of total return measure both the direct yields and the capital gains to different assets on the assumption that interest payments or dividends are reinvested in the same asset. Calculate the *ex post* rate of total return for each month over a 1-year horizon for 3-month Treasury bills, 10-year constant maturity Treasury bonds, and stocks (S&P 500) as *rate of return*$_t = \frac{index_{t+12}}{index_t} - 1$. To get the real return, subtract the *ex post* rate of CPI inflation from the return ($\hat{p}_t = \frac{p_{t+12}}{p_t} - 1$). Based on these three real rates of return, calculate the mean real rates of return, the standard deviations, and the coefficients of variation, recording your data in a table. Answer the three questions at the beginning of the problem.

Problem 7.6. Suppose that the real rate of interest on a 1-year risk-free bond is constant at 2 percent. Suppose that people expect the following path for year-on-year inflation:

From Year to Year	Expected Rate of Inflation (percent)
2010 to 2011	2
2011 to 2012	3
2012 to 2013	4
2013 to 2014	5
2014 to 2015	6

Finally, suppose that people require a risk premium to hold bonds of longer maturities according to the following table:

Maturity	Risk Premium (percent)
1-Year	0.00
2-year	0.25
3-year	0.50
4-year	0.75
5-year	1.00

(a) Calculate what the yield to maturity should be for each bond purchased in 2010, starting with a 1-year bond purchased in 2010 maturing in 2011 up to a 5-year bond purchased in 2010 maturing in 2015. Sketch the yield curve and label the points.

(b) Calculate the expected yield on a 3-year bond purchased in 2012 maturing in 2015.

The next four problems are a related set.

Problem 7.7. For a recent business cycle, plot the yield curve for 1-, 2-, 3-, 5- 7-, and 10-year U.S. Treasury bonds at the NBER peak and trough of the same recession and for a date about midway through the expansion (preceding or following the recession). Depending on which business cycle you choose, two out of the three curves should slope upward. The third may slope up or down but, in any case, is likely to be flatter than the others. (Excel *hint*: (i) create a series of maturities in adjacent cells moving from left to right: 1, 2, 3, 5, 7, 10 and highlight these cells; (ii) select your dates and highlight the cells in adjacent columns containing the rates for each of these maturities at those dates; (iii) on the "Insert" menu, select "Chart" and insert a chart, selecting the scatterplot option with points connected by a smooth line.)

Problem 7.8. To get an idea of how the slope of the yield curve changes over time, create a series: *yieldslope = yield on 10-year Treasury bond rate – yield on 1-year Treasury bond rate*. When *yieldslope* is positive, the yield curve slopes up (at least between a maturity of 1 and 10 years), and when negative, it slopes down. Plot this series and indicate the NBER recession dates with shading. (Save the series for the next problem.)

Problem 7.9. To create a measure of the business cycle, first detrend industrial production using a 73-month moving average, expressing industrial production as a percentage of its trend. Then, create a scatterplot with detrended industrial production on the horizontal axis and *yieldslope* (created in Problem 7.8) on the vertical axis. (Recall from Chapter 5, section 5.2.3, especially Figure 5.9, that industrial production is an excellent coincident indicator.) Add a regression line and display its equation and R^2 (see the *Guide*, section G.12.2 on constructing a moving-average trend and section G.15 on regression and how to add the regression line).

Problem 7.10. Using the information from Problems 7.7–7.9, write a brief note on the relationship of the yield curve and the business cycle. (Both describe your findings and attempt to give an explanation of what you find.)

Problem 7.11. A 3-month Treasury bill rate should have a low (virtually no) price risk. Estimate the term premium for each maturity of Treasury bond by subtracting the time series for the 3-month rate from each of the others and calculating the mean. Present your results in a table. Comment on the relationship of term premia to maturity.

Problem 7.12. To see how well the Fisher hypothesis fits the data, estimate the *expected rate of inflation* using the actual past annual rate of CPI inflation ($\hat{p} = \frac{p_t}{p_{t-12}} - 1$). On separate graphs, plot the 1-year and the 10-year Treasury bond rates on the vertical axis against the inflation rates on the horizontal axis. (*Use all the available data.*) Add the regression line and display the equation and R^2 (see the *Guide*, section G.15, on regression and how to add the regression line). What does the Fisher hypothesis predict for the values of the coefficients in the equation? How well does the Fisher hypothesis match the data? What is the implied estimate of the average real rate of interest?

Problem 7.13. Has the success of the Fisher hypothesis changed over time? Repeat Problem 7.12 for the 1-year bond rate only using data for the last 15 years and separately for any other 15-year period in the data. Comment on the relative performance of the hypothesis in each period.

Problem 7.14. Past inflation may not give a good estimate of future inflation. Repeat Problem 7.12 for the 1-year bond rate for the past 15 years, but use the expectations of inflation series of the University of Michigan Survey of Consumers instead of the inflation rate calculated from CPI. Comment on the difference between your findings in the two problems. With respect to which set of data does the Fisher hypothesis work better?

Problem 7.15. The stock market is often cited as a leading indicator of the business cycle. Is it? Plot the time series of the S&P 500 stock-price index and indicate the NBER recession dates with shading. (Hint: use a logarithmic scale – why?) Comment on its cyclical properties. Discuss larger downturns in the stock market as an indicator of recessions. Consider both false negatives (type I error: recessions that were not preceded by a stock-market downturn) and false positives (type II error: stock-market downturns that were not followed by a recession) – see the *Guide*, section G.7.

Problem 7.16. In the Appendix we derived the money demand curve on the assumption that the real return on money was $-\hat{p}$. This was based on the assumption that currency and checking accounts do not bear interest. But, of course, some checking accounts do bear interest. Think about the case in which *all* money bears interest (perhaps we no longer use currency – just ATM cards). Then the *opportunity cost of holding money = real return on the bond – real return on money* $= (r_{bond} - \hat{p}^e) - (r_{money} - \hat{p}^e) = r_{bond} - r_{money}$.

What difference would this change make to the shape of the money demand curve? Would it still slope down? Would it be steeper or flatter? Consider two extreme cases: (i) r_{money} is fixed and does not vary when r_{bond} varies; and (ii) r_{money} varies point for point with r_{bond} so that their difference is constant. Which, if either, is likely to be closer to reality?

Problem 7.17. Explain in detail how and why the LM curve shifts when the price level increases.

Problem 7.18. Let real money demand be described by the equation:

$$\frac{M^D}{p} = 0.05Y - 0.5r$$

and nominal money supply by:

$$M^S = \overline{M}.$$

(a) Write down the general equation for the LM curve in terms of $Y, r, \overline{M}$, and p.

(b) If $\overline{M} = 10,000$ and $p = 100$, write down the specific equation for the LM curve and draw the curve.

(c) Using this last equation, if $r = 5$ percent, what is Y? (The equation presumes that r is measured in percentage points, so enter 5 – not 0.05.)

(d) If the money supply were increased to $\overline{M} = 10{,}050$, holding p and r constant, what would happen to aggregate demand (Y)? Sketch the change in the curve compared to the one drawn in (b).

(e) If the money supply were increased to $\overline{M} = 10{,}050$, holding p and Y constant, what would happen to interest rates (r)? Sketch the change in the curve compared to the one drawn in (b).

(f) If the money supply were increased to $\overline{M} = 10{,}050$, holding Y and r constant, what would happen to prices (p)? Sketch the change in the curve compared to the one drawn in (b).

8

The International Financial System
and the Balance of Payments

For good or ill, the world economy is interdependent and becoming more so. The financial system is increasingly able to direct savings in one part of the world toward its most profitable uses in some other part of the world. Yet, the financial crisis of 2008, which started in the U.S. domestic mortgage market, quickly spread to countries: interdependence introduces new risks. Robust foreign trade in goods and services is associated with economic strength and fuels the rapid development of many poor countries. Yet, dependence on trade allows a recession in one country to reduce demand and increase unemployment in other countries. Although these interconnections were introduced in the discussion of national accounts in Chapter 2 and of the financial system in Chapter 6, they present complications that we shall examine more closely in this chapter. In many ways, the world economy is just a bigger version of the national economy. Yet it is complicated by the fact that there are many barriers to international trade, especially in real factors of production, such as labor, and by the existence of different national currencies, which adds considerable complexity to financial markets.

8.1 The Global Economy

No component of GDP excites political passions to the degree of NET EXPORTS – not even government expenditure and its correlative, taxation. In recent years, advocates and opponents of **globalization** have frequently dominated headlines. "Globalization" generally refers to the increasingly free movement of goods, services, labor, and capital across national borders, increasing international financial integration and the rise of multinational corporations. Globalization has always excited passions.

Trade – even over very long distances – has existed since prehistoric times (cowrie shells, used as primitive money, have been found in African archaeological sites thousands of miles from the sea; a Chinese brass bell was found in the ruins of a Viking settlement in North America). Early trade was limited to easy-to-transport, high-value items such as gold and spices.

Trade grew along with the increasing sophistication of economies, but in Europe in the seventeenth and eighteenth centuries, the policies of

mercantilism typically highly regulated trade, imposing tariffs and quotas. Nations aimed to protect local industries and to gain monetary advantage over their neighbors. Mercantilism saw the gains of one nation as the loss of others.

The seminal document of modern economics, Adam Smith's *Wealth of Nations* (1776), was, to a great degree, an extended argument for free trade – both within and between nations. Smith (1723–1790) saw the growing wealth of nations and rising personal income as reaping the advantages of increased efficiency generated by the ever greater division of labor. Smith believed that the division of labor was limited by the extent of the market. Foreign trade expanded the market and, therefore, wealth and income for all parties. For Smith, all parties gain from trade.

David Ricardo (1772–1823) pointed out that world production is maximized if each nation can specialize in producing what it does relatively most efficiently, even if some nations do everything absolutely more efficiently than other nations. So, the United States may produce both airplanes and textiles absolutely more efficiently than Malaysia. Nevertheless, if the United States is relatively more efficient at producing airplanes than textiles and Malaysia relatively more efficient at textiles than airplanes, the United States should produce the airplanes and Malaysia the textiles. Of course, because the United States and Malaysia both need airplanes and textiles, trade between them is essential to this strategy, known as the **PRINCIPLE OF COMPARATIVE ADVANTAGE**.

The debate between mercantilists (under various names) and free-traders (known as *liberals* in the nineteenth century) has never been completely resolved. Free trade in goods and factors of production and financial integration, which is essentially free trade in financial assets, advanced in a first wave of globalization throughout the nineteenth century, so that by the beginning of the twentieth century, the world was highly economically integrated.

With World War I (1914–1918) the world said goodbye to all that. The response of many nations to the Great Depression of the 1930s – competitive, "beggar-thy-neighbor" tariffs and controls on the movement of financial capital – furthered economic disintegration. The response of the victorious Western Allies (especially the United States, Great Britain, and France) to the deep disruptions of World War II was to work toward a more harmonious international order based on increasingly free trade and cooperative international economic organizations, such as the International Monetary Fund (IMF) and the World Bank. From 1947 to 1995, a series of negotiations (known as "rounds") under the General Agreement on Tariffs and Trade (GATT) worked to lower tariffs and other trade barriers among the nations of the world. The Uruguay Round of GATT negotiations ended with the creation of the World Trade Organization (WTO) in 1995. The WTO is dedicated to governing free-trade treaties and resolving conflicts over trading rules, as well as promoting increasingly freer trade in the manner of previous GATT negotiations.

Various regional agreements on free trade have also been negotiated. The most famous of these is the European Union, which began in 1951 as the European Coal and Steel Community, a trade agreement among France, Germany, Italy, Belgium, the Netherlands, and Luxembourg, and which by 2008 had expanded to comprise 27 countries with nearly 500 million citizens and a combined GDP in 2008 of nearly $15 trillion – a little larger than the GDP of the United States. The North American Free Trade Agreement (NAFTA) signed in 1994 created a trading bloc that is less politically integrated than the European Union, but which is bigger in terms of GDP – about $17 trillion in 2008.

Perhaps because it is as much a political as an economic union, the European Union has not excited as much popular dissent as other trade agreements. In contrast, in the late 1990s and early 2000s, both the WTO and NAFTA were the focus of sometimes violent mass demonstrations from anti-globalization protesters, who blamed free trade for a variety of ills, including environmental damage, rising inequality, and violations of the rights of workers. Advocates of globalization counter that nothing has done so much to end world poverty and to promote rising standards of living as freer trade. And they seem to have won the argument economically, with the poorest nations of the world complaining vociferously about remaining barriers to trade. But by 2011, advocates of globalization were on the ropes politically, as calls for greater regulation of trade – or at least the slowing down of deregulation – under slogans such as "free trade but fair trade" had found political support in developed countries.

Be that as it may, there can be little doubt that we live in an increasingly economically integrated world. Figure 8.1 shows the growth of U.S. trade measured as the sum of imports and exports as a percentage of GDP. On this measure, if a country exported everything it produced and imported everything that it consumed – as it might nearly if it were a producer of some specialized raw material – it would have a trade of 200 percent of GDP. The striking thing about U.S. trade is its steady growth. In 1957, trade was a mere 10 percent of GDP, low enough that elementary economics textbooks sometimes treated the United States as a closed economy, isolated from the rest of the world. Although trade fell substantially in the recession of 2007–2009, its peak of 32 percent of GDP in 2008 was more than three times its 1957 level. Probably the most striking thing about this growth is its steadiness: the data tend to revert to an exponential trend rate of growth of 2.4 percent per year.

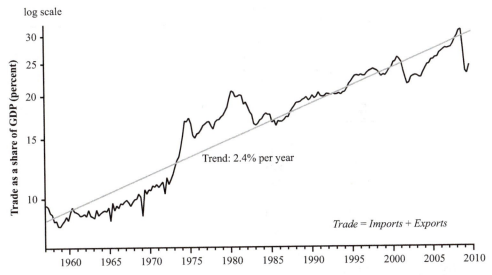

Figure 8.1. U.S. Foreign Trade. *Source:* International Financial Statistics. International Monetary Fund.

Despite the steady increase in the role of trade in its economy, trade forms a much larger share of GDP in many other economies. Nevertheless, the United States remains the largest trading nation in the world with 20 percent of world trade involving the United States as either an importer or exporter. Table 8.1 presents trade data for the G-7 and selected other countries with each group ordered by its share in world trade. Typically, the larger the country or trading bloc, the larger is its share in world trade, but the smaller is its trade relative to its own GDP. The United Kingdom, for instance, is a medium-sized nation, which accounts for only 7 percent of world trade; yet, trade is 38 percent of its GDP. In contrast, the United States and China each account for two to three times more total world trade than the United Kingdom but only 17 percent of GDP for the U.S. and 24 percent for China.[1] European Union trade (not shown in Table 8.1 because only older data were available at the time of writing) displays a similar in pattern: in 2007, European Union trade was 30 percent of world trade, but only 25 percent of its own GDP.

There are exceptions: within the European Union, Germany is an exporting colossus (just slightly behind China in exports and just behind the United States and China in total trade); yet it accounts for 17 percent of world trade, and trade is 73 percent of GDP. Ethiopia and Burundi, both desperately poor and economically small, are infinitesimally small parts of world trade, and yet trade little relative to their GDP.

---

[1] Astute readers will notice that U.S. trade as a percentage of GDP is lower in Table 8.1 than it is at the end of the period in Figure 8.1. Different sources and definitions of the U.S. Bureau of Economic Analysis (Figure 8.1) and the International Monetary Fund (Table 8.1) account for the difference.

Table 8.1. *World Trade, 2009*

	Trade (billions 2009 U.S. dollars at purchasing-power parity)			Total Trade	
	Exports	Imports	Total[a]	As Percent of World Trade[d]	As Percent of GDP
The G-7					
United States	995	1,445	2,440	20	17
Germany	1,121	931	2,052	17	73
Japan	516	491	1,007	8	24
France	457	532	989	8	47
United Kingdom	351	474	825	7	38
Italy	369	359	728	6	41
Canada	298	305	603	5	47
Selected Other Countries					
China	1,194	922	2,116	17	24
South Korea	355	313	668	6	49
Russia	296	197	493	4	23
Singapore	269	245	514	4	218
Hong Kong	317	345	662	5	219
Mexico	230	232	462	4	31
India	165	254	419	3	12
Brazil	159	136	295	2	15
Turkey	102	141	243	2	28
Thailand	151	132	283	2	53
Saudi Arabia	180	87	267	2	46
South Africa	68	70	138	1	28
Luxembourg	14	19	33	<0.05%	87
Ethiopia	2	7	9	<0.05%	12
Burundi	79[b]	318[b]	397[b]	<0.001%	34
World	12,020	12,092	12,056[c]	100	17

[a] *Trade = Exports + Imports.*
[b] Units millions.
[c] *World Trade = (Exports + Imports)/2.*
[d] Total trade shares for individual countries add up to 200 percent, because every export is some other country's import and each transaction, therefore, shows up twice in the complete accounting.
Source: Central Intelligence Agency, *The World Factbook 2009.*

Also worth noting are Hong Kong with trade of 219 percent of GDP and Singapore with trade of 218 percent of GDP. Both are so-called *entrepôt economies*, which import goods largely for reexport. Reexported goods add nothing to GDP (their contribution to net exports is definitionally zero), although brokers, shipping companies, and other businesses that service the trade contribute substantially to GDP in both economies.

Although the costs and benefits of trade are a vitally important economic issue, our principal purpose in this chapter is not to explore them – that is best left to specialized courses in the microeconomics of international trade. Rather we shall explore the international macroeconomics (sometimes known as international finance). Foreign trade, as we saw in Chapter 2 (section 2.2.2), opens another circuit in the circular flow of income. And just as with the domestic economy, a circular flow of real goods (exports and imports) is paired with a circular flow of money and financial assets running in the opposite direction. We want to learn how these international flows fit into the larger picture: How do the behavior of GDP, prices, and interest rates affect trade? And how does trade affect them and the things that they in turn influence, such as unemployment?

8.2 Balance-of-Payments Basics

As with other parts of the economy, before we can analyze foreign trade adequately, we need a good description; we need to learn how to count: How are the data organized? How are they related? What do they mean? Fortunately, we have already made a start in Chapter 2 (sections 2.2.2 and 2.3), where we discussed the roles of the foreign sector and the foreign-sector deficit (net exports) in the circular flow of income and production, and in Chapter 3 (section 3.7.3), where we introduced the current account of the **BALANCE OF PAYMENTS**. The balance of payments is a system of two related double-entry accounts: the **CURRENT ACCOUNT** tracks the flows of real goods and services and incomes among countries; the **CAPITAL ACCOUNT** tracks the flows of assets. We begin with a brief review of the current account.

8.2.1 The Current Account

The product-expenditure identity of the national accounts (equation (2.1″)) involves net exports defined as exports less imports: $NX \equiv EX - IM$. Exports and imports include both goods and services. Net exports are also referred to as both the **TRADE BALANCE** and the foreign-sector deficit. Net exports are the correct thing to look at it if we are interested in domestic production and the generation of domestic incomes. However, as we saw in Chapter 3 (section 3.7.3), if we are interested in disposable incomes, gross *national* product, or national income, we must also account for incomes that belong to citizens of a country but were generated abroad. The *current account of the balance of payments* tracks both trade generated from domestic production and income flows between countries. This wider notion of the foreign-sector deficit (see equation (3.3)) is typically called the *balance on* *the current account* or the **current-account balance** (*CA*) and is represented as an identity:

$$CA \equiv EX + NIA - IM - NTRA, \tag{8.1}$$

where in addition to exports and imports, *NIA* is net income flows from abroad, which include profits repatriated from domestically owned foreign business operations, payments of interest, dividends, and other factor incomes, as well as wage and salary receipts, and *NTRA* is net transfer payments from abroad – that is, payments without *quid pro quo* (see Chapter 3, section 3.1.1). The term *net* in the definitions of *NIA* and *NTRA* refers to the fact that payments from foreigners are offset against payments to foreigners.

The current account of the balance of payments is shown in Table 3.10 (Chapter 3). Net income and transfer flows are broken up into their component parts, and the balance on current account is shown, as net worth typically is (see Chapter 6, section 6.1.2), on the payments (liability side). Although recorded as a payment, the current-account balance should be thought of as a payment to the domestic economy itself, as if it were one of its own creditors. The reasoning that treats the balance on current account as a liability is exactly analogous to the reasoning that places net worth on the liabilities side of the balance sheet (see Chapter 6, section 6.1.2). As with all T-accounts, the two sides of the current account must always be equal, and any change to an entry on the account must be matched with at least one other change so that balance is always maintained.

8.2.2 The Capital Account

As the circular flow diagram (Figure 2.5) reminds us, every export from the United States generates a flow of monetary payments into the United States, and every import into the United States generates a flow of monetary payments to foreign countries. If exports happen to match imports (and if there are no other income flows), then the monetary flows are a wash. But what happens if, say, U.S. imports from China exceed exports to China, so that there is a bilateral current-account deficit? Then the Chinese acquire U.S. dollars – mostly in the form of dollar-denominated balances at banks. They may choose to sit on these balances, but generally they will get a better return by using them to purchase American real or financial assets. The Chinese have typically used their current-account surpluses with the United States – the precise counterpart of U.S. current-account deficits – to purchase U.S. Treasury bills and bonds. But lately they have also used them to acquire shares in U.S. corporations. The balance on the capital account of the balance of payments or, simply, the **capital-account balance** (*KA*) can be represented as an identity:

$$KA \equiv KR - KP, \tag{8.2}$$

where *KR* is capital receipts from the acquisition of domestic assets by foreigners, and *KP* is capital payments used to acquire foreign assets for the domestic economy.

The capital-account balance sometimes strikes students as counterintuitive, because additions of financial wealth to domestic portfolios show up as a negative balance. To see why, consider trade with China again. The capital-account balance exactly parallels the current balance in which exports generate receipts and imports generate payments. The only difference is that, with the capital account, it is the export and import of financial assets that are tracked. So, when the United States imports more goods and services from China than it exports to China, the money that China acquires is the export of a financial asset. This way exports (of goods and services plus financial assets) always equal imports (of goods and services plus financial assets), and the payments (current plus capital) always balance. To keep the accounts balanced, an American current-account deficit must always be offset by an American capital-account surplus. And such a surplus represents the net acquisition of American assets by foreigners.

Detailed capital accounts trace the flow of asset acquisition of each country against every other country and can be broken down into precise asset categories. Some of these details are already present in the flow funds accounts discussed in Chapter 6 (see especially Table 6.1). A consolidated summary of the capital account for the United States as prepared by the U.S. Bureau of Economic Analysis (BEA) is shown in Table 8.2. Some further explanation of its entries will help to illuminate the financial relationship between the United States and the rest of the world. Following guidelines for balance-of-payments accounting established by the IMF, the BEA divides the capital account into two subaccounts: **capital-account transactions** and the **financial account.**

Capital-account transactions are *"the acquisition and disposal of nonproduced, nonfinancial assets . . . , such as the rights to natural resources, and the sales and purchases of intangible assets, such as patents, copyrights, trademarks, franchises, and leases."*[2] In Table 8.2, capital-account transactions are represented by a single entry (line 1) on the receipts side, "net capital account transactions." The BEA could have recorded receipts and payments

---

[2] Federal Reserve Bank of New York, "Fedpoint: Balance of Payments," www.newyorkfed.org/aboutthefed/fedpoint/fed40.html, June 2004, downloaded 19 June 2008.

Table 8.2. *The Capital Account of the Balance of Payments, 2009*
(billions of dollars)

Line	Receipts (+indicates foreign acquisition of a U.S. asset)		Line	Payments (+indicates U.S. acquisition of a foreign asset)	
1	**Net Capital-Account Transactions**	−2	7	**U.S.-Owned Assets Abroad**	−237
2	**Foreign-Owned Assets in the United States, excluding financial derivatives**	435	8	U.S. Official Reserve Assets	−52
3	Foreign Official Assets in the U.S.	448	9	Other U.S. Government-owned Assets	542
4	Other Foreign Assets in the U.S.	−12	10	US. Private Assets	−727
5	**Net Financial Derivatives**	N/A	11	**Balance on Capital Account**	670
6	**Capital Receipts from the Rest of the World**	433	12	**Capital Payments to the Rest of the World** (including capital-account balance)	433

Note: Individual entries may not sum to totals because of rounding.
Source: U.S. Bureau of Economic Analysis, International Economic Accounts, table 1.

separately, but chose instead to net them out. It is only −$2 billion, a small entry compared to the more than $400 billion of total payments or receipts.

The rest of the table represents the financial account. Both foreign holdings of U.S. assets (line 2) and U.S. holdings of foreign assets (line 7) are broken down into official assets, which comprise the acquisition of assets by governments, including central banks, and nonofficial assets ("other foreign assets in the U.S.," line 4, and U.S. private assets, line 10). U.S. official assets are further subdivided into "official reserve assets" (line 8) and "other government-owned assets" (line 9). Official reserve assets comprise holdings of gold, special drawing rights and reserves at the IMF (which acts as a sort of central bank for central banks), and foreign currencies. These are all assets that can be used when the central bank or government intervenes directly in foreign-exchange markets. Other government-owned assets might include any acquisition of foreign financial assets by the government, but typically they would mainly be foreign government bonds.

The table shows that U.S. official capital-account transactions are small compared to private transactions. Foreign governments, however, have been more active, recently at least, in capital-account transactions than the U.S. government.

A more detailed presentation of the capital account would subdivide the acquisition of private assets into foreign direct investment, portfolio investment, and other investment. The classic case of **foreign direct investment** (frequently known by its acronym **FDI**) is the building of a new factory in a foreign country. The term is also used more widely to cover long-lasting investments in existing foreign companies through the purchase of their shares. The United Nations counts share acquisitions when the purchasing firm holds more than 10 percent of shares as FDI. The reasoning is that such a large share is likely to give the foreign investor genuine influence over the actions of the company. **Portfolio investment** is the sale or purchase of nonequity foreign financial assets, such as bonds, and shares short of the 10 percent threshold. Such investments are regarded as being made largely for passive financial gain, and not with an eye to exercising direction over a company. *Other financial assets* include foreign acquisition of bank deposits, currency, and other nonincome assets.

The BEA separates one final category out of private financial assets. *Net financial derivatives* are the net acquisition by foreigners of such financial assets as futures contracts on commodities or other financial assets, as well as more complicated derivatives such as various sorts of risk swaps. This too is a relatively small component of the capital account.

We have presented the capital account as if all the action were driven by current-account surpluses and deficits. Yet, even with no change in the current-account balance, it is possible for governments, firms, and individuals to change the compositions of their portfolios by trading financial assets with foreigners. For example, suppose that you sell a U.S. Treasury bill on the domestic market for $10,000 and use the proceeds to buy shares in the Japanese firm Matsushita. The domestic sale shows up elsewhere in the flow funds accounts (see Chapter 6, section 6.1.2), but not in the capital account for the United States. But the purchase of the Japanese shares shows up as an increase in U.S. private holdings of foreign assets (line 10 of Table 8.2). And the exactly equal payment of $10,000 shows up in an increase in the dollar holdings of the Japanese (line 4). The two sides of the account are bigger overall (lines 6 and 12 show an increase), but the balance on the capital account remains unchanged. Such portfolio adjustments constitute a large proportion of international financial trading.

8.2.3 The Balance-of-Payments Identities

For each country, every import or export is matched by a monetary flow, which is either held as money or converted into some other asset. As a result, any country with a current-account surplus must have an equal capital-account deficit, and every country with a current-account deficit an equal capital-account surplus. The relationship between the current and capital accounts can be summed up in the identity:

$$CA \equiv EX + NIA - IM - NTRA \equiv -(KR - KP) \equiv -KA. \qquad (8.3)$$

Table 3.10 in Chapter 3 shows the balance on the current account for the U.S. in 2008 to be −$707 billion; while Table 8.1 shows the balance on the capital account as $506 billion; yet equation (8.3) says that the two balances should be equal but of opposite signs. Because equation (8.3) is simply a fact about properly kept accounts, the national-income statisticians report the difference between the balances on the current account and the negative of the balances on the capital account ($201 billion) as a *statistical discrepancy*: some international transactions were recorded on one of the accounts while their counterparts on the other account were missed.

Trade between any two countries need not balance. For example, Japan has no domestic oil; Saudi Arabia produces little else for export; and Japan does not produce everything that Saudi Arabia wishes to import. Therefore, Japan may run a permanent current-account deficit with Saudi Arabia. Saudi Arabia uses its income from Japan to purchase the goods and services it wants to import, say, New Zealand lamb. New Zealand in turn may use its earnings from those exports to Saudi Arabia to purchase Japanese cars. Japan may, therefore, run a current-account surplus against New Zealand that partly makes up its deficit against Saudi Arabia. The critical point is that, because every import is the export for some other country, taking all countries together, total imports must match total exports. The current accounts of all countries must sum to zero:

$$\sum_{\text{all countries}} CA_i \equiv 0. \qquad (8.4)$$

And, because the capital accounts are equal in size, but opposite in sign, to the current accounts for all countries, the capital accounts of all countries must sum to zero:

$$\sum_{\text{all countries}} KA_i \equiv 0. \qquad (8.5)$$

Identity (8.4) implies that, if any country runs a current-account surplus, some other country or countries must run current-account deficits of an equal size. Identity (8.5) implies the same for capital accounts. A finance minister of a European country let his *bonhomie* outrun his economics when he declared "I look forward to the day when all countries can run current-account surpluses."

8.3 Exchange-Rate Basics

8.3.1 Exchange Rates as the Relative Price of Money

The Price of One Currency in Terms of Another

Each country's balance-of-payments accounts are reported in its home currency: the U.S. accounts in dollars, the British accounts in pounds sterling, the German accounts in euros, the Japanese accounts in yen. But not all of the trade among countries is conducted in its own currency. Typically, imports must be paid for in the currency of the exporting country. To buy a Chinese laptop, an American importer must obtain Chinese yuan.[3] (In a few cases, exports can be purchased in the importer's own currency or in the currency of a third country. For example, oil and other basic commodities are typically priced in dollars, wherever they are produced.) The values of imports in the balance-of-payments accounts must be converted into their dollar equivalents. This is possible because different national currencies are routinely bought and sold in international financial markets, establishing a relative price. The **EXCHANGE RATE** is *the price of one currency in terms of another currency*.

National currencies are not traded in centrally located marketplaces in the way that corporate equities, for example, are traded on the New York Stock Exchange. Rather they are traded through a disparate network of banks, brokers, and dealers known collectively as the **foreign-exchange market**.

The exchange rate is familiar to anyone who has traveled abroad. Banks, as well as kiosks in international airports, train stations, and most cities, offer to buy and sell a variety of currencies. A kiosk at San Francisco International Airport may post offers to sell pounds for dollars for $1.959 per pound sterling (£). A Scottish traveler may buy £200 worth of dollars: £200 × 1.959$/£ = $391.80. An American traveler, arriving at London's Heathrow Airport may wish to work the transaction the other way round and use $400 dollars to purchase pounds. If the Heathrow kiosk posts the price £0.510 per dollar, the traveler will obtain £204.19 = $400 × 0.510£/$.

The two exchange rates just quoted are in reality the same rate seen from a different point of view – the first is quoted as pounds in terms of dollars, the second as dollars in terms of pounds. The second rate is just the inverse of the first: 0.510£/$ = 1/1.959$/£. This is no different from quoting the price of lemons as 20 cents each or as five per dollar. Still, in working with exchange rates, one must always be careful to note which way they are quoted. As a general rule, the relatively more valuable currency is taken as the

---

[3] Frequently, also known as the *renminbi*, which means "people's currency." The renminbi is abbreviated as RMB, while the yuan is indicated by the symbol ¥, which is also used for the Japanese yen.

denominator. So, typically, because one pound is more valuable than one dollar, the exchange rate is quoted as dollars per pound sterling ($1.959/£ rather than £0.510/$) whether one is in San Francisco or London. The Japanese yen is less valuable than a dollar, so most frequently it is quoted as yen per dollar (¥106.157/$ rather than $0.00942/¥).

Some currencies – for example, the Canadian dollar, the U.S. dollar, and the euro – in some periods are close in value, and whichever is the more valuable may change over time. The euro (€) was introduced in 1999 at $1.18/€. It quickly fell to $0.82/€ in 2000, but by early 2010 it stood at $1.43/€. Since it was introduced as a currency more valuable than the dollar, the euro is most frequently quoted as dollars per euro. Still, extra caution is necessary when working with currencies that are close in value to make sure that the denomination is correctly understood.

Appreciation and Depreciation

In the example, we assumed that tourists on the same day at different airports would get the same exchange rate. Normally, however, a bank or dealer will purchase a foreign currency for a lower price than it will sell it. A kiosk at Heathrow may post that it buys dollars at $1.96/£ and sells them at $1.94/£. It may sell £1,000 worth of dollars to an English tourist on his way to the United States. The tourist receives $1,940 (= £1,000.00 × 1.94$/£). If another English tourist happens to return with just that amount of dollars, he may then purchase sterling from the same kiosk. He receives £989.80 (= $1,940/1.96$/£). The difference between the buying and the selling price, £10.20 (= £1000.00–£989.80) – equal to a little more than 1 percent of the initial purchase price – is profit to the dealer. In addition to the profit from buying cheap and selling dear, the dealer may also charge a commission.

Increasingly, tourists exchange money not at the retail dealers in airports or banks in foreign cities, but at foreign automated teller machines, using either a debit card or a credit card. The actual exchange of national currencies is made on their behalf between the foreign bank and their own bank – usually at a better rate than available through retail dealers.

Most foreign-exchange transactions do not involve tourists, but rather banks and nonfinancial companies engaged in foreign trade. We shall examine the foreign-exchange market in more depth in section 8.4 later in the chapter.

A currency **APPRECIATES** when *its value increases relative to another currency* and **DEPRECIATES** when *its relative value decreases*. The U.S. dollar appreciates about 1 percent when the dollar/sterling exchange rate *falls*, say, from $1.96/£ to $1.94/£. It appreciates about 15 percent against the yen, when the yen/dollar exchange rate *rises*, say, from ¥106/$ to ¥122/$. Because it feels more natural to associate appreciation with a rising currency and because this book is clearly oriented to the United States, we shall normally quote exchange rates henceforth as foreign currency per dollar. Then the dollar appreciates by about 1 percent when the sterling/dollar exchange rate *rises*, say, from £0.510/$ (= 1/1.96/£) to £0.515/$ (= 1/$1.94/£).

8.3.2 The Real Exchange Rate

The Real Price of a Foreign Good

Suppose that an Apple iPod costs €303 in Berlin and $400 in Washington. Who is getting the better deal – the Germans or the Americans? And how much better?

To make a fair comparison, we have to compare prices in the same currency – either convert the German price to dollars or the U.S. price to euros. If the exchange rate is 0.64 euros per dollar, then the euro price of the iPod in Washington is €256.00 (= $400×0.64€/$) and the dollar price in Berlin is $473.44 (= €303/0.64€/$). Either way, the iPod is about 18 percent more expensive in Germany than in the United States. In an obvious sense, a dollar buys more in the United States than does the euro equivalent of the dollar in Germany. Germans find the United States cheap; Americans find Germany dear.

Another way to look at this is to ask how purchasing power in United States compares to purchasing power in Germany. An iPod costs $400 in Washington and $400 is worth €256.00 in Berlin. So, an iPod in the United States will purchase only 0.84 iPods in Germany. The iPod exchange rate is then 0.84 iPods$_{Germany}$ per iPod$_{U.S.}$.

If purchasing power had been equivalent for each currency, then an iPod exchange rate would have been 1.00. Because the dollar has a lower purchasing power in Germany, it is *undervalued* by about 16 percent, and the euro is *overvalued*. The exchange rate 0.84 iPods$_{Germany}$ per iPod$_{U.S.}$ is called the **REAL EXCHANGE RATE** and may be defined as *that exchange rate that reflects the effective purchasing power of each currency*.

Of course, the real iPod exchange rate may not be equal to the real Mercedes exchange rate, or the real St. Pauli Girl beer exchange rate. The general rule for constructing real exchange rates is formed by analogy with the calculations using the prices of iPods:

$$RXR = XR\frac{p_{domestic}}{p_{foreign}}, \qquad (8.6)$$

where XR is the exchange rate and RXR is the real exchange rate. When the ratio of prices is exactly inverse of the exchange rate, $RXR = 1$ and funds needed to purchase a good in the domestic currency will purchase exactly the same quantity of the good when they are converted into the foreign currency.

Purchasing Power and Price Indices

In comparing purchasing power between countries, a firm might well be interested in the real exchange rate for particular goods. In contrast, tourists and government policymakers are typically more interested in (different) baskets of goods. This is just the problem of general price level multiplied to involve two currencies. One straightforward way of estimating a real exchange rate for the overall purchasing power of national currencies is to replace the particular prices of iPods, Mercedes, or beer in equation (8.6) with price indices.

There is a pitfall in such a move. The price indices for different countries refer to different baskets of goods and may be based on different times. Hence, when the German and the U.S. producer price indices (PPIs) are equal, it does not necessarily mean that their real prices are equal; and, as a result, a real exchange rate of one does not indicate equality of purchasing power. This is no problem if we care mostly about *movements* in the real exchange rate, because a rise will still indicate real appreciation of the domestic currency.

We might sometimes care about the absolute level of the real exchange rate and not just its relative movements. We could approximate the absolute real exchange rate if we could find a period for which we thought that there was independent evidence of equal purchasing power. Then we could rebase the price indices to take the same value at that date. There are various sorts of evidence about purchasing power, but the details of such calculations are beyond the scope of this book. (Note, however, that the data used for GDP for various countries in Table 8.1 are corrected for "purchasing power parity" – i.e., the statisticians have already made this sort of adjustment.)

Various government and private agencies sometimes calculate special indices to compare cost of living between countries on common baskets. For example, the U.S. General Services Administration compares a common basket for per diem compensation for government employees traveling on official business for a large number of American and foreign cities. The basket includes meals, hotel rooms, and related services. In June of 2008, the per diem rate for Berlin was \$491 and for Washington \$265, which implies a real exchange rate of 0.54.[4]

Since 1986, the British newspaper *The Economist* has published the *Big-Mac Index*, which estimates the real exchange rate and the over- or

---

[4] $RXR = XR/(\text{€/basket}_{\text{Berlin}}) \times \$/\text{basket}_{\text{Washington}} = \text{basket}_{\text{Berlin}}/\$ \times \$/\text{basket}_{\text{Washington}} = 1/(\$491 \text{ per basket}_{\text{Berlin}}) \times \$265 \text{ per basket}_{\text{Washington}} = 0.54.$

undervaluation of various currencies against the dollar by comparing market exchange rates and the relative price of the famous McDonald's hamburger. The Big Mac is not identical in every country – for example, in India the Big Mac (or "Maharaja Mac") is now made with chicken. Still, even though the Big-Mac index was originally calculated tongue firmly in cheek, it is a surprisingly good index of real exchange rates. First, it provides a good mix of various physical and service inputs, so it need not be viewed as a single commodity but as a bundle of goods. Second, despite small variations among different countries, it is reasonably homogeneous. As a result, it provides direct comparisons of purchasing power. When the producer price indices of two different countries are equal, it does not imply that the prices are the same in both countries – the indexed bundles are different and the base years are arbitrary. But when the price of a Big Mac is the same in both countries, then the prices are genuinely equal.

8.3.3 Effective Exchange Rates

An exchange rate, like any other price, expresses what one good, in this case a unit of currency, is worth in terms of the domestic currency. Just as we sometimes do not want to know the price of a particular good, but instead want to know the price of goods in general, we sometimes want to know the price of foreign currencies in general against the domestic currency. The trick with the general price level is to form an index of prices, such as the consumer price index (CPI) or the GDP deflator, which reflects the prices of a basket of goods. The same trick is used with exchange rates. Where price indices use expenditure shares to weight individual prices in the basket (see Chapter 4, section 4.1 and Guide G.8.2), the EFFECTIVE-EXCHANGE-RATE INDEX (often called the **trade-weighted exchange-rate index**) weights each bilateral exchange rate by the share each country takes in the foreign trade of the home country. Effective exchange rates can be *nominal* (or *market* rates) or *real* rates. The real effective exchange rate can be calculated using equation (8.6) with the exchange rate (XR) given by the nominal effective exchange rate, and the foreign price level ($p_{foreign}$) given as a weighted average (using the same trade weights) of individual foreign price levels. Real effective exchange rates are typically indexed to take a value of 100 in some reference period.

There can be many effective-exchange-rate indices for any country depending on which basket of currencies is thought to be relevant and how the weights are calculated. The Federal Reserve, among others, calculates a variety of indices for the United States. Figure 8.2 shows the Federal Reserve's nominal and real *broad effective-exchange-rate indices*. The baskets for these indices include the major U.S. trading partners. The largest

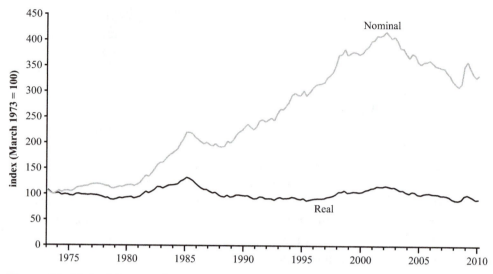

Figure 8.2. United States Effective Exchange Rate, Broad. *Source:* Board of Governors of the Federal Reserve System, Release H.10 Foreign Exchange Rates.

trading partners are the Euro Area countries, Canada, China, Japan, and Mexico – constituting more than 50 percent of U.S. foreign trade. Together with the next twenty-one largest trading partners, the currencies in the broad index are involved in more than 90 percent of U.S. foreign trade.

A subset of the countries in the broad index are regarded as having major currencies – that is, currencies that are widely traded in financial markets. These currencies are the euro, the Canadian dollar, the Japanese yen, British pound sterling, the Swiss franc, the Australian dollar, and the Swedish krona. In contrast to the countries in the broad index, all of the countries in the *major-currencies index* are highly developed countries with sophisticated financial markets. Not all of these countries are among the top trading partners, yet collectively they still constitute more than 50 percent of U.S. foreign trade. Figure 8.3 shows the nominal and real major-currencies effective-exchange-rate indices.

The two figures display important contrasts. Perhaps most striking is the strong appreciation of the dollar on the nominal broad index (Figure 8.2), whereas the real index fluctuates slowly, always reverting to a trend level of about 100. The divergence of these two rates reflects the fact that U.S. inflation rates have been lower than those of many of its trading partners and that the dollar has appreciated largely in line with these inflation differentials, keeping the exchange rate from trending too long in either direction. (See section 8.4.2 on the relationship between exchange rates and inflation.) In contrast, the real and nominal major-currency indices show very similar behavior – to each other and to the real broad index. This reflects both the broadly similar inflation histories of the major-currency countries as well as

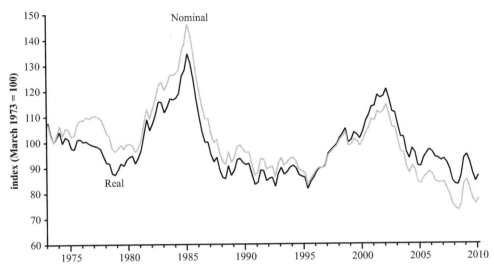

Figure 8.3. United States Effective Exchange Rate, Major Currencies. *Source:* Board of Governors of the Federal Reserve System, Release H.10 Foreign Exchange Rates.

the broad tendency of the exchange rate to reflect the real purchasing power of each currency.

8.4 The Foreign Exchange and Financial Markets

8.4.1 The Foreign-Exchange Market

Foreign Exchange and Real Trade

The retail end of the foreign-exchange market (those airport kiosks and foreign ATMs) is familiar to travelers. But most international transactions are conducted among various financial and nonfinancial corporations. What does the foreign-exchange market look like to them?

Imagine that an American distributor of fine chocolates wants to import Swiss chocolates worth CHF1 million.[5] The distributor places an order with the Swiss manufacturer, which probably ships the product and sends the distributor a bill denominated in Swiss francs. In order to pay the bill, the distributor would arrange, probably through its bank, to purchase Swiss francs. The bank would place a buy order with a foreign-exchange broker, perhaps specifying some minimum acceptable exchange rate (CHF/$). A broker, working on commission, would then try to match this order with parties who had placed sell orders (perhaps stipulating a maximum acceptable exchange rate). The exchange rate that allows the broker to find enough sellers to

---

[5] The symbol for the Swiss Franc, CHF, derives from the Latin name for Switzerland, *Confeoderatio Helvetica.*

supply the buyer, say CHF1.02/\$, is the exchange rate for that transaction. Publicly reported exchange rates are derived from such individual transactions. Once the parties are matched, instructions are sent to the distributor's bank to transfer (typically electronically) \$980,392 to a dollar-denominated account designated by the sellers of the Swiss francs, and instructions are sent to the seller to transfer the Swiss francs to a franc-denominated account designated by the distributor – most likely the bank of the chocolate manufacturer, which naturally settles the bill.

Foreign Exchange and Financial Trade

Although there would be no trade in foreign exchange were there no trade in real goods and services, the trade in foreign exchange dwarfs real trade. The *daily* volume of foreign-exchange transactions in 2007 was \$3.21 trillion, which translates (261 weekdays per year) into an annual volume of \$837.8 trillion or more than 60 times the value of world trade and more than 12 times world GDP (see Table 8.1). Why is trade in exchange rates so huge in comparison with trade in real goods and services?

To answer, it helps to consider the purchase of the Swiss chocolates a little further. After the distributor has paid his bill, the Swiss company is satisfied – it has received full payment in francs. The sale adds to Swiss exports, pushing its current account in the direction of surplus, and adds to American imports, pushing its current account in the direction of deficit. Similarly, the sellers of Swiss francs, who we will suppose are themselves Swiss, now possess dollars, which reflect a fall in the capital account equal to the rise in the current account. What should they do with these dollars?

Generally, bank accounts earn little or no interest. The Swiss holders may, therefore, wish to use those dollars to purchase American financial assets. They may, for example, purchase \$500,000 worth of shares in an American agribusiness and use the rest to purchase U.S. Treasury bonds. These transactions do not change the overall size of the capital accounts of either Switzerland or the United States, beyond the change already induced by the trade in chocolates, but they do change the mix between different items in the capital accounts.

Such portfolio changes, however, do not need to be tied to particular changes in current accounts – that is, to particular exports or imports. Even in the absence of trade, a Swiss company might decide that it wants to purchase the \$500,000 worth of shares in the American agribusiness. Then, it is in a similar position to the American chocolate distributor. It would have to use Swiss francs to buy dollars on the foreign exchange and then use those dollars to buy the shares on a U.S. stock exchange. The only difference between this transaction and the purchase of the chocolate is that it does not involve any change in the trade of goods and services, so that the

Table 8.3. *Currency Distribution of Foreign-Exchange Market, 2007*

Currency	Share of Foreign-Exchange Turnover (share (percent) of average daily turnover, April)
U.S. Dollar	86.3
Euro	37.0
Japanese Yen	16.5
U.K. Pound Sterling	15.0
Swiss Franc	6.8
Australian Dollar	6.7
Canadian Dollar	4.2
Swedish Krona	2.8

Note: Because each transaction involves two currencies, shares for all currencies (including ones not shown) total to 200 percent.
Source: Bank of International Settlements, *Triennial Central Bank Survey of Foreign Exchange and Derivatives Market Activity in April 2007: Preliminary Global Results*, table 3, September 2007, downloaded from www.bis.org/publ/rpfx07.pdf, 22 July 2008.

current account remains unchanged. All the action is on the capital account. Financial transactions are limited only by the willingness of different parties to exchange debt instruments or claims to real assets. Financial transactions are, at best, loosely connected to the underlying real transactions. Foreign-exchange transactions are just a particular type of financial transaction, so it is both possible and a fact that foreign-exchange transactions vastly exceed foreign trade.

Direct and Indirect Exchange

Although virtually all currencies are traded on foreign-exchange markets, some are more frequently traded than others. Table 8.3 shows the percentage of foreign-exchange transactions involving each of the eight currencies in the basket used by the Federal Reserve's major-currencies effective exchange rate (see section 8.3.3 and Figure 8.3). Because there are always two currencies involved in any foreign-exchange transaction, the individual entries (if the entire world's currencies were included) would add up to 200 percent. As it is, these eight currencies account for 175 percent of all foreign exchange transactions. The U.S. dollar is far and away the dominant currency, being involved in 86 percent of transactions, only slightly less than the 89 percent accounted for by the other seven currencies. Since 1997, the euro has established itself as an important international currency, although it is in second place, at less than half the share of the dollar. The euro's share is only about two percentage points higher than the combined shares in 1997

Table 8.4. *Foreign-Exchange Market Turnover by Currency Pair, 2007*

Currency Pair	Share of Foreign-Exchange Turnover (share (percent) of average daily turnover, April)
U.S. Dollar/Euro	27
U.S. Dollar/Japanese Yen	13
U.S. Dollar/U.K. Pound Sterling	12
U.S. Dollar/Australian Dollar	6
U.S. Dollar/ Swiss Franc	5
U.S. Dollar/Canadian Dollar	4
U.S. Dollar/Swedish Krona	2
U.S. Dollar/Other Currencies	19
Euro/U.K. Pound Sterling	2
Euro/Japanese Yen	2
Euro/Swiss Franc	2
Euro/Other Currencies	4

Note: Shares for all currencies (including ones not shown) total to 100 percent.
Source: Bank of International Settlements, *Triennial Central Bank Survey of Foreign Exchange and Derivatives Market Activity in April 2007: Preliminary Global Results*, table 4, September 2007, downloaded from www.bis.org/publ/rpfx07.pdf, 22 July 2008.

of the German deutsche mark and the French franc, the two most important currencies that it replaced.

One reason that the dollar is so dominant is that it is the world's principal reserve currency. Governments and central banks around the world hold foreign currencies (official reserves) to buttress the value of their domestic currencies. The dollar is the currency of choice, accounting for 63 percent of foreign-exchange reserves in 2007. The euro is increasingly also used as a reserve currency, accounting for 26 percent of reserves. The euro's gain has partly been at the expense of the dollar, but partly at the expense of other major currencies.

Another reason why the dollar is involved in so many foreign-exchange transactions is that not every currency is easily traded into every other currency. Markets for the currencies of smaller countries or countries with undeveloped financial markets are thin. It would be unbelievable luck to find someone who wanted to trade a large volume of Laotian kips for Bolivian bolivianos. Instead, one would normally have to go through a third currency: bolivianos for dollars and dollars for kips.

The dollar is the most common intermediate currency. Table 8.4 reports the shares of each particular bilateral currency pair in total foreign-exchange transactions. The exchange between dollars-euro pair is, by far, the most common (27 percent), followed by exchanges between the dollar-yen and the dollar-pound sterling pairs at about half that level. The dollar against the remaining currencies in the major-currency basket accounts for another 17 percent; exchanges of the dollars against all other currencies account for 19 percent. Exchanges of the euro against all other currencies except the dollar are only 10 percent. All other currency pairs are a mere 4 percent.

8.4.2 Exchange Rates and Relative Prices

Exchange rates are determined on foreign-exchange markets by the laws of supply and demand. When more people wish to exchange dollars for euros than euros for dollars, the price of the euro rises relative to the dollar – that is, the euro/dollar exchange rate falls; the dollar depreciates. The depreciation continues until the exchange rate finds a level at which the desire to exchange dollars for euros balances the desire to exchange euros for dollars. Supply and demand govern the foreign-exchange market, but the more interesting question is, what determines the supply and demand for currencies? What determines the rate at which traders are willing to exchange?

There are two dominant factors: the price level of one country relative to the other and the financial rates of return of one country relative to the other. Consider relative prices first.

The Law of One Price

In a free market, once we take account of transactions costs, two identical goods cannot sell for different prices at the same time. If, for example, oil sold for $102/barrel in New York and for $115/barrel in Los Angeles, it would be worth shipping oil from New York to Los Angeles. Such shipments would lower supply in New York, raising its price, and raise supply in Los Angeles, lowering its price. Shipments would continue until the Los Angeles price and the New York price were driven together.

Would they be exactly equal? Probably not. Because it costs to ship the oil across country, a price difference must be at least as wide as the shipping cost per barrel for it to be profitable to ship the oil. Thus, a differential no wider than the shipping cost per barrel could persist. In general, any costs associated with the movement of the oil from one place to another, costs such as insurance as well as transportation, are called **transactions costs** and would be reflected in the price differential.

Similarly, if California imposes taxes on oil, then the tax would also be reflected in the price – even in equilibrium – because a price that is higher because of taxes does not add to the revenues of the seller and so does not give any incentive to ship the oil. After accounting for transactions costs, taxes, and any other unavoidable differential costs, the oil price should be the same everywhere. This is another example of arbitrage familiar in financial markets: any certain profit opportunity will rapidly be competed away.

The consequence of commodity arbitrage is known as the LAW OF ONE PRICE.

Just as in a financial market, an actual shipment of goods is not typically necessary with commodities. Traders know that the price needs to be the same in all markets and move directly to the correct price. For if they fail to do so, they would lose an opportunity. Why would anyone in New York actually sell oil at $102/barrel knowing that the price was much higher in Los Angeles? Instead, the seller would immediately see that prices were too low in New York and ask for no less than the Los Angeles price. Of course buyers in Los Angeles would also see that the Los Angeles price was too high and would not agree to buy for more than the New York price. The actual price would quickly settle down somewhere in between. Differences as wide as $102 versus $115/barrel would never be allowed to open up in an organized and well-functioning market.

As it happens, oil is priced in dollars worldwide, so that international arbitrage is not really different from domestic arbitrage. But suppose that we are considering Australian and American wheat. A new consideration now enters if Australian wheat is priced in Australian dollars and the American wheat in U.S. dollars. To find the "one price" in the law of one price, we must convert to a common currency: $p_{Australia}/XR_{A\$/US\$} = p_{U.S.}$. Arbitrage, therefore, guarantees that internationally the law of one price takes the form:

$$XR = \frac{p_{foreign}}{p_{domestic}}. \tag{8.7}$$

Arbitrage does not tell us which of the three variables in this relationship must adjust. If only one good were ever traded, then the exchange rate could do all the adjusting. Because there are multiple goods, and the law of one-price must hold for many commodities, both prices and the exchange rate must take some of the burden of adjustment.

The case of wheat is unrealistic in the sense that Australia and the United States trade very little wheat with each other, because each country satisfies its domestic demand mainly from its domestic production and each country exports a substantial portion of its wheat to third countries. But the law of one price still holds. No country will pay more for Australian wheat than for American wheat. Suppose the wheat is exported to the Netherlands. Australian wheat is priced in Australian dollars and the American wheat in U.S. dollars. What a buyer in the Netherlands pays depends on the exchange rates:

$$p_{Australia} \times XR_{euro/A\$} = p_{U.S.} \times XR_{euro/US\$}. \tag{8.8}$$

Arbitrage also works in foreign-exchange markets. If one could get more Australian dollars by trading euros first for U.S. dollars and then for

Australian dollars than by trading directly for Australian dollars, a sure profit opportunity would open up, and currency traders would compete it away. As a result, the direct exchange rate between euros and Australian dollars ($XR_{euro/A\$}$) must equal the *cross* (or two-step) exchange rate through U.S. dollars ($\frac{XR_{euro/US\$}}{XR_{A\$/US\$}}$). Thus, $XR_{euro/A\$} = \frac{XR_{euro/US\$}}{XR_{A\$/US\$}}$, which can be rearranged to get $XR_{A\$/US\$} = \frac{XR_{euro/US\$}}{XR_{euro/A\$}}$. Using this last relationship, equation (8.8) implies

$$XR_{A\$/US\$} = \frac{p_{Australia}}{p_{U.S.}}, \tag{8.9}$$

which is just the law of one price once again, even though trade involved a third country.

Purchasing-Power Parity

Although the law of one price holds for goods that are nearly uniform in characteristics and quality and easily traded in nearly perfectly competitive markets, many – if not most – goods are not like that. Goods of the same general type may be differentiated in important ways: a Lexus LS and a Ford Focus are both cars, yet they are very different cars, and there is no reason that their prices should be identical. Nevertheless, because they do, at least in part, meet similar needs, an increase in the price of the Lexus relative to the Ford will shift some demand away from the Lexus and toward the Ford, with the effect of moderating the increase in the price of the Lexus and putting upward pressure on the price of the Ford. The two cars are substitutes, although not perfect substitutes (see Chapter 7, section 7.2.1).

Some goods may not be tradable at all. Because you cannot import a haircut from India, the price of a haircut in India and in Phoenix may be wildly different. Nontradable goods may be considered a special case of tradable goods in which the transactions costs are so high that no trade is profitable. Traditionally, many services were regarded as nontradable. Yet things change. For example, the advent of the internet and improved communication means that some services in the United States – such as bookkeeping or customer support – can now be supplied by workers in India.

In thinking about the relationship of exchange rates to prices, we are more interested in the prices as a whole than in the prices of any particular good. The exceptions to the law of one price – differentiated products, lack of perfect competition, nontradables – imply that the law of one price will not hold for each and every good. It may nonetheless hold approximately for goods in general. Instead of comparing prices of particular goods, we may compare the general price levels in the two countries. If there were only two countries in the world and if no other factors matter for the exchange rate, then the law of one price would hold for goods in general when the two price levels and the exchange rate took values such that trade was balanced between the two countries. Taking account of the product differentiation and the lack of perfect competition, neither country would have an overall price advantage over the other. In reality, because there are more than two countries in the world, it is possible that one country only imports from another country and only exports to still other countries, depending on what it needs and what it produces. So, bilateral trade may not be in balance country by country, even when exchange rates reflect prices relative to all trading partners. The test then would not be balanced bilateral trade, but balanced trade overall against the rest of the world.

The generalized law of one price is known as **PURCHASING-POWER PARITY**, which holds when the exchange rate and the general price levels of two countries (as opposed to the prices of individual goods) closely approximate the law of one price (equation (8.7)):

$$XR \approx \gamma \frac{P_{foreign}}{P_{domestic}}. \tag{8.10}$$

The new constant γ is an adjustment to account for the fact (already discussed in section 8.3.2) that the baskets of goods for each country's price level are not identical, so that, even if p took exactly the same level in each country, we would not believe that purchasing power was necessarily the same in them both.

The first important implication of purchasing-power parity can be seen by substituting (8.10) into the definition of the real exchange rate (equation (8.6)):

$$RXR = XR \frac{P_{domestic}}{P_{foreign}} \approx \gamma \frac{P_{foreign}}{P_{domestic}} \frac{P_{domestic}}{P_{foreign}} \approx \gamma. \tag{8.11}$$

In words, when purchasing-power parity holds, the real exchange rate is constant.

A second important implication can be seen by converting (8.10) into growth rates:

$$\widehat{XR} \approx \hat{\gamma} + \hat{p}_{foreign} - \hat{p}_{domestic} = \hat{p}_{foreign} - \hat{p}_{domestic}. \tag{8.12}$$

The right-most term omits $\hat{\gamma}$, because the growth rate of a constant is zero. Equation (8.12) says that the percentage rate of change of the exchange rate (i.e., its rate of appreciation) is approximately equal to the difference in the inflation rates between the two economies. Foreign inflation appreciates the currency; domestic inflation depreciates it.

The Mutual Adjustment of Prices and Exchange Rates

Like the law of one price, purchasing-power parity is an arbitrage relationship, yet the mechanism through which it is established is less direct.

Many commodities are traded on established exchanges similar to the stock exchange. For example, wheat, corn, and soybeans are sold on the Chicago Board of Trade; oil, gold, and copper on the New York Mercantile Exchange; and cocoa, rubber, and wool on the London Commodity Exchange. As we have already seen, in such efficient and highly competitive markets for undifferentiated products, arbitrage works very quickly and deviations from the law of one price are fleeting. But how does purchasing-power parity work when these ideal market conditions do not exist?

Consider the market for similar, but not identical, home-theater systems – the Danish brand Bang & Olufsen and the Japanese brand Sony. Suppose that the exchange rate is ¥23/DKK, that purchasing-power parity holds absolutely (e.g., on the Big Mac standard), and that net exports are close to zero in both Denmark and Japan. (DKK is the symbol for the Danish *krone*; plural *kroner*.) Now suppose that inflation picks up in Denmark, increasing the costs (in kroner) of manufacturing the Bang & Olufsen system faster than the costs (in yen) of the Sony system. If the exchange rate remains unchanged, the Bang & Olufsen system will also become relatively more expensive in Japan. As a result, fewer Bang & Olufsen systems will be sold in Japan, reducing Danish exports and net exports.

If the original price inflation in Denmark also extended to inflation of wages and salaries at the original exchange rate, the Danes would find themselves with more purchasing power over Japanese goods. They would import more Sony systems, increasing the imports of Denmark and the exports of Japan. With its imports rising and exports falling, net exports in Denmark would fall. It would, of course, be just the reverse in Japan: net exports would rise.

There are two effects of the shift in demand in favor of Japan. The direct effect is that the Japanese need fewer kroner and the Danes need more yen. The exchange rate (¥/DKK) will fall – that is, the kroner will depreciate.

The indirect effect is that with a fall in net exports, aggregate demand in Denmark will fall, putting downward pressure on the general price level (i.e., reducing inflation). Conversely, with a rise in net exports, aggregate demand in Japan would rise, putting upward pressure on the general price level.

Overall, there are, then, three adjustments to the initial increase in the inflation rate in Denmark. First, the exchange rate depreciates (direct effect). Second, the fall in Danish net exports, which reduces aggregate demand, draws the initial rise in Danish inflation back somewhat toward the original rate (indirect effect part 1). Third, the rise in net exports in Japan increases the inflation rate somewhat, in effect exporting some of the Danish inflation (indirect effect part 2). Each of these effects moves prices and the exchange rate back in the direction of purchasing-power parity.

Of course, the trade in home theater systems is small relative to the whole economies of Denmark and Japan. Yet, the situation is the same across the economy: Danish goods are disadvantaged relative to Japanese goods in instance after instance, broadening the base on which the adjustments to prices and exchange rates are made until purchasing-power parity is restored. Equally, the higher inflation in Denmark is likely to depreciate the kroner not only relative to the yen, but relative to any other currency with a lower inflation rate. In equilibrium, net exports would again be zero.

Although, the reestablishment of purchasing-power parity after a disturbance to the inflation rate is likely to operate less quickly than the law of one price, in principle it could work fairly fast. The foreign-exchange market is an efficient financial market similar to the highly organized commodities markets. In our example, once the inflation differential was clear, anyone holding kroner or kroner-denominated financial assets would want to sell them for yen, which would in itself work to depreciate the yen-kroner exchange rate.

As an arbitrage condition, purchasing-power parity merely says that exchange rates must be proportional to relative prices or there will be unexploited profit opportunities. It does not, in itself, say which is cause and which effect. Do exchange rates move because relative prices change? Or do relative prices change because exchange rates change? The answer is clearly both. Changes in relative prices result in changes in trade flows that change the balances of demand for a currency resulting in changes in its exchange rates against other currencies. But equally, movements of exchange rates relative to purchasing-power parity change the relative prices of foreign goods at home and domestic goods abroad, setting up changes in net exports that, in turn, affect prices through aggregate demand. Exchange rates are both cause and effect.

How Well Does Purchasing-Power Parity Work in Practice?

To begin to answer this question, look at Figure 8.4 comparing the exchange rate between the pound sterling and the dollar to the relative price levels in the United Kingdom and the United States. Equation (8.10) says that the exchange rate should be proportional to the relative prices, with a factor of proportionality γ to the exchange rate. The figure shows the time series for the exchange rate and relative prices ($\frac{P_{foreign}}{P_{domestic}}$). Prices are measured by each country's producer (or wholesale) price index. Producer prices are a better index than consumer prices for testing purchasing-power parity, because the producer price index excludes most nontradable goods. To make the two series, which have quite different units, easier to compare, they have each been converted to index numbers taking the value of 100 in March of

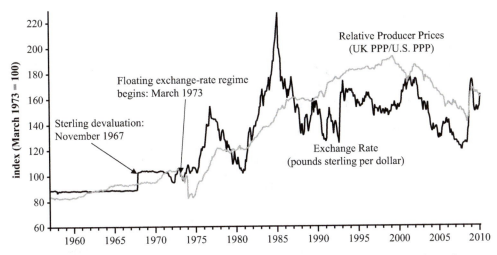

Figure 8.4. U.K. Pound Sterling/U.S. Dollar Purchasing-Power Parity. *Source:* International Monetary Fund, International Financial Statistics.

1973. This date is significant as it marks the end of the so-called "Bretton Woods System" of fixed exchange rates. After that date, exchange rates, with some exceptions, were free to move according to the dictates of supply and demand in the foreign-exchange markets.

If the two series are proportional, they should move together over time. And, in fact, they do in a rough-and-ready way. The exchange rate is much more volatile than relative prices. And the gap between the series widens and narrows too much for a strict proportionality. Still, the overall shape of the movements is quite similar. Purchasing-power parity seems, then, to hold roughly in the long run, though not closely at all in the short run.

Consider purchasing-power parity between another pair of countries – Japan and the United States. We could construct a figure similar to 8.4 (see Problem 8.9). Instead, in Figure 8.5, we take a different approach, basing our test on equation (8.11), which says that the real exchange rate should be constant. The figure plots the real exchange rate, calculated as $XR_{¥/\$} \frac{p_{U.S.}}{p_{Japan}}$, as well as its mean value for the floating exchange-rate period. The real exchange rate is certainly not constant, yet it shows no tendency to drift away from its mean. The large deviations of the real exchange rate from its mean imply that purchasing-power parity does not hold in the short run. But the fact that it keeps returning to its mean implies that it holds approximately in the long run.

The United Kingdom, Japan, and the United States are not special cases. Similar figures with similar results can be constructed for most pairs of countries. Purchasing-power parity, therefore, appears to be a good long-run approximation. The deviations from purchasing-power parity in the

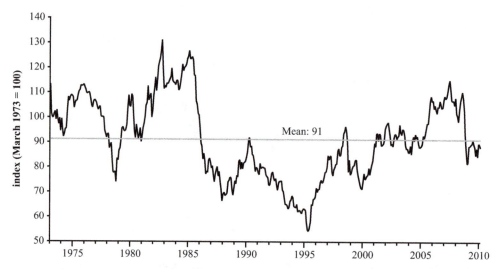

Figure 8.5. Japanese Yen/U.S. Dollar Real Exchange Rate. *Source:* International Monetary Fund, International Financial Statistics.

short run, however, are huge, and we must look elsewhere to explain short-run exchange-rate movements.

8.4.3 Exchange Rates and Interest Rates

The Exchange Rate, Capital Flows, and Interest Parity

To explain the shorter run deviations of exchange rates from purchasing-power parity, we must consider the capital account as well as the current account. Any deviation from purchasing-power parity opens up an opportunity for profitable trade. For example, if the dollar is overvalued relative to the yen, the Japanese may find it profitable to export laptop computers to the United States, pushing their current account in the direction of surplus and the U.S. current account in the direction of deficit. And of course, the Japanese find themselves holding dollars or dollar-denominated assets. If they were ready to give up yen for dollars at the initial exchange rate and if they are content to hold dollar-denominated assets, then there is no reason that the exchange rate should change at all as the result of the trade in laptops. The increase in the Japanese current-account surplus is matched by a increase in their capital-account deficit (i.e., an increase in their holdings of dollar-denominated financial assets).[6] It is only when the Japanese are unhappy with the new configuration of their financial portfolios that the exchange rate must change.

---

[6] Equivalently, the decrease in the Japanese capital-account deficit could reflect the transfer of American holdings of yen-denominated assets back to Japan.

If the Japanese feel that they have too large a share of dollar-denominated assets in their portfolios, then they may try to sell dollars and buy assets denominated in yen or some other currency, such as euros or Korean won. The effect will be to depreciate the dollar against the yen or these other currencies. Only when the exchange rates reach a point at which the Japanese no longer feel like they should sell dollar-denominated assets will the exchange rates stabilize.

Once again, it does not take any change in the current-account or capital-account balances to set off such a portfolio rebalancing. Any time holders of financial assets decide that in net they would prefer to hold different proportions of assets denominated in various currencies, exchange rates will have to adjust until every asset finds a home in some portfolio.

Are these portfolio decisions a matter of pure whimsy? Surely not. The same considerations matter in international as in domestic financial markets. In Chapter 7 (sections 7.2–7.3), we saw that once we accounted for risk and the time patterns of returns, financial assets could typically be regarded as perfect substitutes. Arbitrage would ensure that their risk-adjusted yields were equal. The only difference in international markets is that the various assets are denominated in different currencies.

To see what difference this makes, consider a bond trader in the United States. He could purchase, say, a 1-year U.S. Treasury bill with a yield of 5 percent or a 1-year Canadian Treasury bill with a yield of 6 percent. Which is better? Clearly, if the exchange rate were constant now and in the future, he would opt for the higher yielding Canadian bill. The shift of demand would lower the price (raise the yield) on U.S. bills and raise the price (lower the yield) on Canadian bills. The arbitrage opportunity would vanish as the two bills found a common yield between 5 and 6 percent.

But what happens if the exchange rate is not constant? The American trader must compare the yield on the U.S. Treasury bill to what the Canadian bill will yield in *U.S.* dollars. To buy the Canadian bill, he must convert each U.S. dollar into Canadian dollars. Suppose that the exchange rate is C$0.97/US$. Then, US$1 = 0.97C$. This will in turn, yield after one year $1.06 \times 0.97 = $ C$1.0282. Now this must be converted back into U.S. dollars.

The decision of whether to buy the Canadian bill must be taken today. It does not matter, therefore, what the exchange rate will actually be a year from now. What matters is what the trader today believes it will be a year from now; what matters is the *expected* exchange rate. Suppose our trader thinks that the U.S. dollar will appreciate over the coming year, so that the exchange rate will rise to C$0.99/US$. Then, one U.S. dollar placed in a Canadian bill today would deliver US$1.0386 (= 1.0282/0.99) or a yield of 3.86 percent. Because the U.S. Treasury bill yields 5 percent, the trader is actually better off purchasing the U.S. bill despite its lower nominal yield.

The expected depreciation of the Canadian dollar reduces the U.S. value of its yield.

And, of course, arbitrage will push up the price of U.S. dollars and push down the price of Canadian dollars until there is no arbitrage opportunity left. For example, if the U.S. bills yielded 4.8, Canadian bills 6.2 percent, the current exchange rate were C$0.98/US$, and the exchange rate expected one year from now 0.9931, the yield of the Canadian bill in U.S. dollars would be 4.8 percent: one U.S. dollar would convert to C$0.98, which would earn C$1.0408 (= 1.062×0.98), which in turn would be reconverted to US$1.0480 or a 4.8 percent gain. Because this is exactly equal to the yield on the U.S. Treasury bill, there is no arbitrage opportunity, and traders should be indifferent between holding U.S. and Canadian Treasury bills despite the higher Canadian yields.

Uncovered Interest Parity

The general rule for no-arbitrage is that the yields of assets must be equal once they have been converted to the same currency. It can be represented generally as

$$1 + r_{domestic} = \frac{XR_t(1 + r_{foreign})}{XR^e_{t+m}}, \tag{8.13}$$

where m = the maturity of the assets (one year for the Treasury bills in the example), and the superscript e indicates that the future exchange rate is expected (but not known with certainty) to take that value. Applying the formula to the example:

$$1 + r_{U.S.} = 1.048 = \frac{0.98(1.062)}{0.9931} = \frac{XR_t(1 + r_{Canada})}{XR^e_{t+1}}.$$

We can simplify the complicated rule in equation (8.13) by rearranging to give

$$\frac{XR^e_{t+m}}{XR_t} = \frac{1 + r_{foreign}}{1 + r_{domestic}}, \tag{8.13'}$$

which may, in turn, be expressed as

$$1 + \widehat{XR}^e_t = \frac{1 + r_{foreign}}{1 + r_{domestic}}, \tag{8.13''}$$

where $\widehat{XR}^e_t$ is the expected rate of appreciation (rate of growth) of the exchange rate over the maturity of the bond. Take logarithms of both sides and recall the approximation $\log(1+x) \approx x$, for small x gives:

$$\log\left(1 + \widehat{XR_t^e}\right) \approx \widehat{XR_t^e} = \log\left(\frac{1 + r_{foreign}}{1 + r_{domestic}}\right)$$

$$= \log(1 + r_{foreign}) - \log(1 + r_{domestic}) \qquad (8.13''')$$

$$\approx r_{foreign} - r_{domestic}.$$

(For the rules of growth rates and logarithms, see the *Guide*, sections G.10.4 and G.11.2.)

The no-arbitrage condition can thus be stated very simply as

$$\widehat{XR_t^e} \approx r_{foreign} - r_{domestic}. \qquad (8.14)$$

The relationship in equation (8.13) and its approximation (8.14) is known as the **UNCOVERED INTEREST-PARITY CONDITION**. It says that *there is no opportunity for arbitrage when the expected appreciation of the exchange rate is approximately equal to the difference between yields on foreign assets and domestic assets.*[7]

Exchange-Rate Risk

Uncovered interest parity should hold only when the two assets have similar maturity and risk characteristics. The necessary gap between the two interest rates may widen or narrow depending on the relative riskiness of the assets. Exchange rates also introduce another kind of risk. Just as interest-rate or price risk (see Chapter 7, section 7.3.2) is the risk of a capital loss from an unexpected change in market yields, **EXCHANGE-RATE RISK** is *the risk of a capital loss (measured in the domestic currency) of an unexpected appreciation of the exchange rate.*

In the example leading up to equation (8.13), traders expected an appreciation of the exchange rate of 1.34 percent ($= 0.9931/0.98 - 1$). That appreciation lowered the effective yield of the Canadian Treasury bill to that of the U.S. Treasury bill. But what if an American trader had purchased a Canadian Treasury bill and over the next year the exchange rate had

---

[7] The relationship is *uncovered* parity because the traders simply form their expectation of the appreciation of the exchange rate. Over the maturity of the asset, the actual appreciation may turn out to be different from what they expect. They could *cover* their position by purchasing a forward contract giving the right to purchase the domestic currency at an agreed exchange rate in the future. (People are willing to sell such contracts because they disagree with the buyer about the likely movement of the exchange rate, and so hope to profit from outguessing the buyer.) In this case, the forward exchange rate (FXR_t) can replace the expected future exchange rate in equation (8.13) to give the *covered interest-parity condition*: $1 + r_{domestic} = \frac{XR_t(1 + r_{foreign})}{FXR_{t+m}}$. Because forward exchange-rate contracts are traded in organized markets with efficient arbitrage and all relevant prices are known today, covered interest parity (similar to the law of one price for homogeneous commodities traded in organized markets) holds very closely.

appreciated *more* than expected to, say, C$1.00/US$? Then, equation (8.13) tells us that

$$1 + r_{U.S.} = 1.048 > 1.041 = \frac{0.98(1.062)}{1.00} = \frac{XR_t(1 + r_{Canada})}{XR^e_{t+1}}.$$

Although the expected yield had been equal for the two assets *ex ante*, the *ex post* yield of the Canadian bill in U.S. dollars is nearly a percentage point lower than the yield on the U.S. bill (4.1 vs. 4.8 percent).

Just as traders might demand extra yield to compensate for price risk in domestic markets, they might demand an **exchange-rate-risk premium** to entice them to hold a foreign asset. And, just as with other sources of risk, the necessary gap between the two interest rates may widen or narrow depending on the relative aversion to exchange-rate risk in the two economies. Expected appreciation and the interest-rate differential should nonetheless be associated even if uncovered interest parity does not hold precisely.

Interest-Rate Differentials and Short-Run Deviations from Purchasing-Power Parity

Interest parity – again, like the law of one price or purchasing-power parity – is a no-arbitrage condition and does not itself tell us the causal mechanisms that connect its terms. One practical difficulty, of course, is that market expectations of the appreciation of exchange rates are not directly observable. But as we saw in section 8.4.2, purchasing-power parity seems to hold in the long run. It is, therefore, not an unreasonable conjecture that, when real exchange rates are higher than their average level, the market will expect the exchange rate to depreciate sometime in the future. Of course, it is hard to say exactly when or how fast.

Despite the inexactness of the relationship, we can use the uncovered interest-parity condition to see, for example, how domestic monetary policy might affect the exchange rate. Without being very exact about time periods, we can think of the appreciation of the exchange rate as predicted by the relationship of the actual exchange rate to purchasing-power parity: $\frac{XR^e}{XR_t} \approx \frac{XR^{PPP}_t}{XR_t}$, where the superscript *PPP* indicates that the exchange rate is the rate that would hold if purchasing-power parity held. Then, we can reason from interest parity that

$$\frac{XR^{PPP}_t}{XR_t} \text{ is positively related to } r_{foreign} - r_{domestic}. \qquad (8.15)$$

In words, the deviation from purchasing-power parity should be related to the difference between foreign and domestic interest rates.

Taking the United States to be the domestic economy, consider a tighter monetary policy that raises U.S. interest rates, so that *ceteris paribus* the differential on the right-hand side of relations (8.14) and (8.15) narrows. Relation (8.15) implies that the left-hand side must also fall. Because the purchasing-power parity level of the exchange rate is assumed to be unchanged, the increase in the interest rate must raise the current value of the exchange rate (XR_t). And that, naturally, conforms to common sense in that the higher interest rate will raise the foreign demand for U.S. assets. The resulting inflows of foreign financial capital increase the demand for the dollar and put upward pressure on the exchange rate. What is less obvious to common sense, but true nonetheless, is that the appreciation of the current exchange rate portends a *smaller* future appreciation – maybe even a depreciation – as it raises the starting point from which appreciations are measured (the current exchange rate), while holding the finishing point (the expected future exchange rate) constant.

The same story can be told in terms of the real exchange rate. A real exchange rate above its purchasing power parity level ($RXR > \gamma$) indicates an expected depreciation. Thus,

$$RXR \text{ is negatively related to } r_{foreign} - r_{domestic}. \qquad (8.16)$$

Now when U.S. interest rates rise *ceteris paribus* and the interest-rate gap narrows, the real exchange rate must decrease. Given no change in prices, such a decrease requires a fall in the nominal exchange rate. A lower real exchange rate implies a smaller future adjustment to the nominal exchange rate in order to secure purchasing-power parity (i.e., the gap between RXR and γ has narrowed), so that in future the exchange rate would be expected to appreciate less (or to depreciate more).

Interest Parity in Practice

A simple test of uncovered interest parity is based on relation (8.16), which predicts a negative relationship between the real exchange rate and the interest rate differential. The regression line in the scatterplot in Figure 8.6 confirms the negative relationship for the U.K. pound sterling/U.S. dollar real exchange rate at the beginning of the 1980s through 2007. (The start date to account for the fact that markets might have taken some time to adjust to the transition between fixed and floating exchange-rate regimes was 1973.)

The black regression line in Figure 8.7 similarly confirms the negative relationship for the Japanese yen/U.S. dollar real exchange rate at the beginning of the 1980s through 1992. Before we jump to the conclusion that relation (8.16) is confirmed, notice that the gray regression line shows that after 1992, the relationship virtually vanishes or is even slightly positive. The break in the data corresponds to the onset of Japan's shallow, though long recession in the 1990s in which prices actually fell.

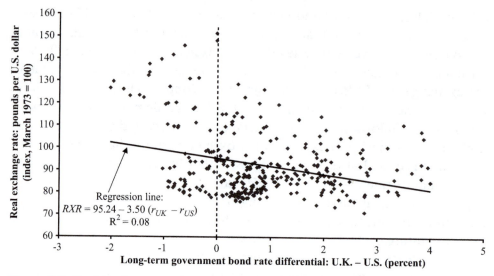

Figure 8.6. Real Exchange Rates and Interest Differentials: U.K. versus U.S., 1980–2007. *Source:* International Monetary Fund, International Financial Statistics.

Canada provides an even starker counterexample. Because the Canadian dollar floated against the U.S. dollar from the early 1950s, Figure 8.8 shows the same sort of scatterplot as for Japan and the United Kingdom from 1957 to 2007. Contrary to relation (8.16), the relationship is upward sloping. It turns out that this is true for most subperiods as well.

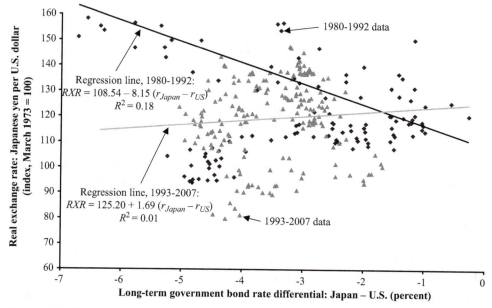

Figure 8.7. Real Exchange Rates and Interest Differentials: Japan versus U.S., 1980–2007. *Source:* International Monetary Fund, International Financial Statistics.

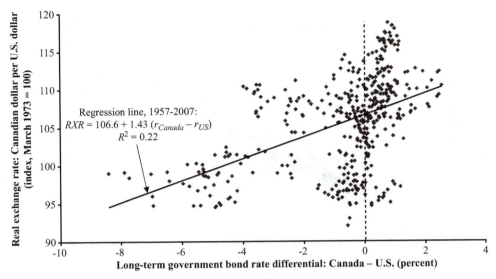

Figure 8.8. Real Exchange Rates and Interest Differentials: Canada versus U.S., 1957–2007. *Source:* International Monetary Fund, International Financial Statistics.

Although the data seem to point to interest-rate parity as a genuine force in determining exchange rates, they also suggest caution. A large number of factors affect exchange rates, and simple graphical methods are not powerful enough to account for them all at once. What is more, the relationship that we examine in these three figures is at best only roughly related to interest-rate parity. After all, what matters in equation (8.15) is the expected appreciation or depreciation rate of the exchange rate over the life of some particular bonds. Relations (8.15) and (8.16) are based on the assumption that the exchange will move toward purchasing-power parity – not over any precise period but *sometime*. It is perfectly possible that markets expect an overvalued exchange rate to fall sometime in the next five years and yet to rise over the next six months.

The Limits of Short-Run Exchange Rate Models

The fundamental problem with testing the interest-rate parity condition is that expectations are unobservable. Unobservability, combined with the fact that expectations in financial markets are determined by a huge variety of factors and may shift abruptly, explains why economists – even using much more sophisticated statistics – have found it hard to develop successful models for predicting short-run changes in exchanges rates.

In a famous article in 1983, Richard Meese of the University of California, Berkeley and Kenneth Rogoff, now of Harvard University, showed that theoretical models of the short-run behavior of exchange rates could not beat a

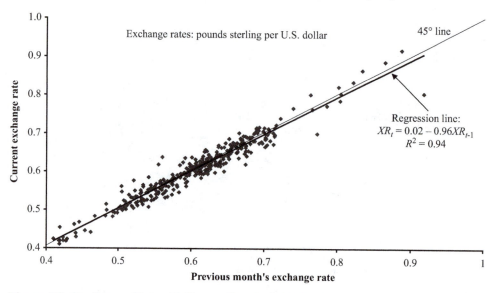

Exchange rates: pounds sterling per U.S. dollar

45° line

Regression line:
$XR_t = 0.02 - 0.96XR_{t-1}$
$R^2 = 0.94$

Figure 8.9. Exchange Rates Follow a Random Walk. *Source:* International Monetary Fund, International Financial Statistics.

simple statistical model – the random walk – that says that the best prediction of tomorrow's exchange rate is whatever today's exchange rate happens to be. Equivalently, the exchange rate is equally likely to rise or to fall from today's level. (See the discussion of the business cycle as a random walk in Chapter 5, section 5.3.1.)

To illustrate, Figure 8.9 plots each month's exchange rate (U.K. pound sterling/U.S. dollar) against its value in the previous month. The random-walk model predicts that the slope of this relationship will be a 45-degree line through the origin. The regression line and its equation (with a slope of 0.96, very nearly one) agree with the random-walk model. The close clustering of the data about the regression line is measured by the high R^2 (just a little less than unity).

Although the random-walk model fits very well – its R^2 is higher than for any other scatter plots involving exchange rates in this chapter – it provides no real explanation of exchange rates in the short run. What it says is just this: whatever factors happen to determine yesterday's exchange rate also determine today's exchange rate. Economic rationality tells us that exchange rates should adjust quickly to perceived profit opportunities. In the long run, these are apparently dominated by purchasing-power parity. In the short run, logic dictates that relative rates of return and risk aversion should dominate. But because economic decisions are forward-looking, it is the markets' *ex ante* perceptions of return and risk that matter, not what actually turns out to be true *ex post*. The *expected* exchange rate in equation (8.13) and the *expected* rate of appreciation in (8.14) acknowledge the importance of *ex ante* perceptions. Such perceptions are volatile and may be driven by sentiment or by attempts of each market trader to outguess the other rather than by observable economic facts. As a result, short-run changes in exchange rates may well be intrinsically impossible to predict with any precision, even when we have isolated factors that are *ceteris paribus* important – such as interest-rate parity.

Summary

1. International trade increases world production through the principle of comparative advantage: each country should produce the goods that it is *relatively* best at producing and trade for those goods that it is relatively less good at producing.

2. International trade has increased steadily since World War II as countries have worked through successive rounds of the General Agreement on Tariffs and Trade (GATT) and through the establishment of free-trade zones, such as the European Union (EU) and the North American Free Trade Agreement (NAFTA) to reduce barriers to international trade.

3. The balance of payments tracks the flows of international goods and services and incomes (current account) and monetary and financial assets (capital account) among countries.

4. The trade balance measures the difference between exports and imports of goods and services, whereas the current-account balance includes other income flows.

5. The capital-account balance measures net flows of financial assets into the home country: outflows less inflows.

6. For each country individually, the current-account balance plus the capital-account balance must equal zero. The sum of the individual current-account balances across every country in the world must equal zero. The sum of the individual capital-account balances across every country in the world must equal zero.

7. National currencies are traded on the foreign-exchange market. The price of one currency relative to another is the exchange rate. The exchange rate of one country appreciates when it becomes more valuable relative to that of another country, and depreciates when it becomes less valuable.

8. The real exchange rate is the exchange rate adjusted for the purchasing power of the national currencies. Such adjustments may be made for specific goods or, using price indices, for goods in general.

9. Effective-exchange-rate indices are measures of the appreciation or depreciation of one country's exchange rate against the exchange rates of a group of other countries. The group may be major trading partners or some broader or narrower selection of countries. Effective-exchange-rate indices may be based on market (nominal) exchange rates or on real exchange rates.

10. Foreign-exchange markets support both the exchange of real goods and services and of financial assets. Most currencies are actively exchanged only with

a few other currencies (the dollar, the euro, the yen, and the pound sterling are the most common major currencies into which others are traded). Exchange between minor currencies is typically a two-step process of trading a minor currency for one of the major currencies and then trading the major currency for the other minor currency.

11. The law of one price holds, that for any actively traded and reasonably homogeneous good, arbitrage should ensure that prices in different currencies cannot differ by more than the costs of transporting the goods between countries, where these costs include shipping, taxes and tariffs, insurance, etc. The principle of purchasing-power parity generalizes the law of one price to a variety of goods whether or not they are homogeneous or actively traded. Purchasing-power parity holds when the purchasing power of the national currency is the same at home or, converted into another national currency, in a foreign country. Equivalently, purchasing-power parity holds when the real exchange rate, adjusted for difference in the bases of the price indices, equals one.

12. Purchasing-power parity implies that changes in the exchange rate are proportional to changes in the relative price indices of the two countries. Equivalently, purchasing-power parity implies that the real exchange rate should be constant. Deviations from purchasing-power parity open up arbitrage opportunities in markets for goods and services that tend to move both exchange rates and price levels in each country toward parity. But in practice, purchasing-power parity holds approximately only in the long run.

13. Uncovered interest parity holds that interest rates adjusted for expected changes in exchange rates should be the same between countries. Failures of uncovered interest parity may reflect exchange-rate risk – that is, the risk of capital gains or losses owing to unexpected changes in exchange rates. Deviations from risk-adjusted uncovered interest parity open up arbitrage opportunities in financial markets that tend to shift demand for financial assets toward those with abnormally high returns, tending to push exchange rates and interest rates toward parity.

14. In practice, purchasing-power parity holds approximately only in the long run, and uncovered interest parity involves hard-to-observe expectations of exchange-rate appreciation or depreciation, so that predicting short-term exchange rates is extremely difficult. Few economic models of short-run exchange rates predict more accurately than the random walk: the best prediction of tomorrow's (or next year's) exchange rate is today's (or this year's) exchange rate.

Key Concepts

net exports
principle of comparative advantage
balance of payments
current account

capital account
trade balance
exchange rate
(exchange rate) appreciation

(exchange rate) depreciation

real exchange rate

effective-exchange-rate index

law of one price

purchasing-power parity

uncovered interest-parity condition

exchange-rate risk

Suggestions for Further Reading

Some Basic Sources:

Norman S. Fieleke, "What Is the Balance of Payments?" pamphlet, Federal Reserve Bank of Boston, 1995: http://www.bos.frb.org/economic/special/balofpay .pdf

Owen F. Humpage, "A Hitchhiker's Guide to Exchange Rates," *Economic Commentary*, 1 January 1998: http://www.clevelandfed.org/research/commentary/ 1998/0101.pdf

Two More Advanced Treatments of Exchange Rates:

Peter Isard, *Exchange Rate Economics*. Cambridge: Cambridge University Press, 1995.

Lucio Sarno and Mark P. Taylor, *The Economics of Exchange Rates*. Cambridge: Cambridge University Press, 2002.

Problems

Data for this exercise are available on the textbook website under the link for Chapter 8 (appliedmacroeconomics.com). Before starting these exercises, the student should review the relevant portions of the *Guide to Working with Economic Data*, including sections G.1–G.4.

Problem 8.1. Refer to Table 8.2 and indicate *ceteris paribus* which entries in the capital account would change and by how much under the following scenarios (recall that like all T-accounts both sides must always balance):

(a) The U.S. imports increase by $15 billion and the foreign recipients of these payments use them to purchase U.S. corporate bonds.

(b) A foreign company purchases a factory in the U.S. for $1 billion.

(c) A U.S. company sells a German factory for €3 billion and uses the proceeds to purchase German government bonds (assume that the exchange rate is $1.5/€).

(d) A U.S. company sells a foreign factory for €3 billion, converts the proceeds into dollars, and lodges them in its bank account in the United States.

(e) The People's Bank of China (the Chinese central bank) purchases $20 billion of U.S. Treasury bills, using U.S. dollars (cash).

(f) A Chinese company purchases $20 billion of U.S. Treasury bills, using the proceeds from sales of computers to the United States.

Problem 8.2. Here are some data for France in 2008: *exports* = $770 billion; *net income from abroad* = $36 billion; *net transfer payments from abroad* = −$35;

capital payments to foreigners = $373 billion; and the capital-account balance = $64 billion. Using your knowledge of the balance of payments, find the value of French *imports* and *capital receipts from foreigners.*

Problem 8.3. A U.S. bank buys Russian rubles at 30 rubles/dollar and sells rubles at 28 rubles/dollar. What is its profit as a percentage of its initial outlay if it exchanges $100 for rubles and then sells the same quantity of rubles in exchange for dollars?

Problem 8.4. A U.S. bank buys British pounds sterling at 1.64 dollars/pound and sells at 1.68 dollars/pound. What is its profit as a percentage of its initial outlay if it exchanges $100 for pounds and then converts the same quantity back into dollars?

Problem 8.5. If the exchange rate between the South African rand and the U.S. dollar is 7.39 rand/dollar and the exchange rate between the Mexican peso and the U.S. dollar is 12.66 pesos/dollar, what do you expect the peso/rand exchange rate to be? Explain why it makes sense to compute the peso/rand rate based only on knowledge of the rates of these two currencies against the dollar (i.e., what market forces ensure that your calculation is likely to be accurate?).

Problem 8.6.

(a) If one Indian rupee purchases 0.015 euros, what is the rupee/euro exchange rate?

(b) Starting with the rupee/euro rate as in (a), if the rupee appreciates 20 percent against the euro, what is the rupee/euro exchange rate?

(c) Taking the rupee/euro rate as in (a), if the rupee/dollar exchange rate is 45.64 rupee/dollar, what is the dollar/euro exchange rate?

(d) Starting with the configuration of exchange rates as in (c), if the dollar depreciates 5 percent against the euro, what is the dollar/euro exchange rate?

(e) Starting with the configuration of exchange rates as in (c), if the rupee appreciates 10 percent against the euro and depreciates 5 percent against the dollar, what are the rupee/euro, rupee/dollar, and dollar/euro exchange rates?

Problem 8.7. The same paperback best-selling novel can be purchased in the Toronto airport for C$19.99 and in the Fort Lauderdale airport for US$15.99. What is the implied Canadian dollar/U.S. dollar real exchange rate?

Problem 8.8. Consider the following data:

	Exchange Rate (S$/US$)	Consumer Price Index) (2005 = 100)	
		Singapore	United States
2005	1.66	100.0	100.0
2008	1.39	109.8	107.4

Suppose that purchasing-power parity held in 2005; what would the exchange rate have to have been in 2008 for it to continue to hold? If the initial assumption that purchasing-power parity held in 2005 were true, did it hold in 2008? What evidence would be needed to convince us that the initial assumption was true?

Problem 8.9. Using data for the United States and Japan, create a graph testing purchasing-power parity similar to that for the United States and United Kingdom in Figure 8.4. Does your graph tell the same story as the graph of the U.S./Japanese real exchange rate in Figure 8.5? Explain in detail.

Problem 8.10. Using data for United States and the United Kingdom, create a graph of the U.S./U.K. real exchange rate similar to that for the United States and Japan in Figure 8.5. Does your graph tell the same story as the graph testing U.S./U.K. purchasing-power parity in Figure 8.4? Explain in detail.

Problem 8.11. Using quarterly data, create graphs testing purchasing-power parity (similar to Figure 8.4) for:

(a) United States and Canada;

(b) United States and Australia;

(c) Australia and Canada.

In each case, comment on the success or failure of the purchasing-power parity hypothesis.

Problem 8.12. The euro was introduced in 1999. Consider the following pairs of members of the European Union:

(a) Germany (deutsche mark before 1999; euro thereafter) and Italy (lira before 1999; euro thereafter);

(b) Germany (deutsche mark before 1999; euro thereafter) and the United Kingdom (pound sterling before and after 1999);

On one chart for each country pair, create graphs of both the market (nominal) exchange rate and the real exchange rate, including data both before and after the introduction of the euro: Data for the period before 1999 should be converted to an index with 1998:12 = 100 and data after 1999 to an index with 1999:01 = 100. How does the real exchange rate differ from the behavior of the market exchange rate for the two country pairs? Explain the difference.

Problem 8.13. Suppose that a Lexus automobile costs \$45,000 in the United States and ¥4,914,000 in Japan. The exchange rate is 91 yen/dollar. Based on this one item, by how much (percentage) is the Japanese yen overvalued or undervalued relative to the dollar?

Problem 8.14. Suppose that the U.S./United Kingdom exchange rate is 1.64 dollars/pound sterling, and a Coca-Cola costs 50p (i.e., £0.50) in England and 75 cents in the United States. Based on this one item, by how much (percentage) is the British pound overvalued or undervalued relative to the dollar?

Problem 8.15. Would either the Lexus in Problem 8.13 or the Coca-Cola in Problem 8.14 provide an adequate standard for judging overall deviations from purchasing-power parity? Could any single good provide a reasonable standard?

Problem 8.16. Use the internet to find data on effective exchange rates for the United States (be careful to document your source). Based on this data, how much has the U.S. dollar appreciated or depreciated over the past year? Five years? Ten years?

Problem 8.17. Use the internet to find data on the interest rates on 1-year government bonds (Treasury-bill rates or other official rates) of similar maturity for this month a year ago for the United States, Canada, Germany, Japan, and the United Kingdom (3.45), as well as the exchange rates for the currencies of the other three countries against the dollar for today and for the same month a year ago. (If 1-year rates are not available, use a shorter rate such as a 3-month rate.) Based on the uncovered interest-parity condition, how would you have predicted these three exchange rates to move? How did they actually move? What factors may account for the difference?

Problem 8.18. Suppose that uncovered interest-parity holds and that the euro/U.S. dollar exchange rate is expected to rise by 10 percent over a year. If the 1-year Treasury bond rate for the United States is 4 percent, what is the 1-year German government bond rate?

Problem 8.19. Suppose that uncovered interest-parity holds and that the U.S. 5-year Treasury bond rate is 6 percent and the 5-year Danish government bond rate is 7 percent. If the current exchange rate is 6 Danish kroner/dollar, what exchange rate should be expected to hold five years from now?

Part V

Aggregate Supply

9

Aggregate Production

This chapter returns to the problem of explaining the real economy. We begin with aggregate supply. What determines how much GDP the firm sector wants to produce? What determines how productively the economy uses labor and physical inputs to production? How does the business cycle affect the use of inputs – especially the level of employment? An understanding of aggregate supply sets the stage for Chapter 10, in which we examine economic growth in the long term, and Chapters 11 and 12, in which we examine labor markets.

In Chapters 2–5 we learned what GDP and its components are, how they typically behave, and how they appear to be related to inflation, employment, industrial production, and other variables. It is now time to turn from description to explanation. Examples of the kind of questions that we would like to answer include:

- Why is GDP in the United States vastly higher in 2010 than in 1960 or 1910?
- Why is GDP in the United States higher than in any other country in the world?

Or, more specifically:

- What would happen to GDP if immigration rules were relaxed and 5 percent more workers joined the U.S. labor force?
- How much should we expect employment to fall in a recession or rise in a boom?

To begin to answer questions of this sort, recall from Chapter 2, section 2.7, that GDP can be seen through the eyes of producers (firms) as aggregate supply or through the eyes of purchasers (consumers, investors, government, foreigners) as aggregate demand. The national-income-accounting identities ensure that *ex post* aggregate supply equals aggregate demand. But aggregate supply and aggregate demand are different things, and *ex ante* they need not be equal. Aggregate demand is governed by the choices of spenders, given their incomes. Aggregate supply is governed by the choices of firms, given the available productive resources. In the end, it is these productive resources that set the upper limit to GDP.

Aggregate demand may fall short, and GDP may turn out to be less than it could be. But no matter how much aggregate demand rises, GDP cannot exceed the ability of the workers in factories, offices, and other worksites to produce. In this and the following three chapters we examine aggregate supply.

We know from our discussion of the circular flow of income and production (Chapter 2, section 2.2) that the firm sector purchases factors of production and transforms them into final goods and services. This is the heart of aggregate supply. The decisions that govern the production process are not made by the firm sector as a whole. Rather they are made by each individual firm. As a result, even though we are, in the end, concerned primarily with the aggregate product (GDP), looking at the production problem from the point of view of the firm is a valuable prelude to the main business of the chapter. It will help us to build up our intuitions and to cement essential terminology in our minds.

9.1 The Production Decisions of Firms

9.1.1 Production Possibilities

Technology

Consider a particular product, say, a barrel of gasoline. An oil refinery uses raw petroleum, energy, various chemicals, and various types of labor, among other INPUTS, to produce its OUTPUT – gasoline. The design of the refinery and its work practices embody a particular TECHNIQUE for producing gasoline. A technique is like a recipe for a cake. The inputs are the list of the ingredients used, the output (or possibly outputs) is the cake, and the recipe is the set of instructions for making the cake. Like the recipe, the technique is not the machinery or any of the physical inputs but the *knowledge* of how to make a certain sort of machinery or how to organize production. Technical knowledge guides the construction of machinery, the layout of a plant, the organization of the corporation, and the practices on the shop floor. Yet the technique is not any of these tangible things. It is the knowledge itself.

The process for producing gasoline is represented schematically in Figure 9.1. Notice that the process is incompletely specified. A few of the inputs have been listed. They are divided into different classes: material inputs, energy, services, and labor. Within each class various sorts of inputs are listed, but the recipe for making gasoline is very complicated, and these only hint at the complete description, which may or may not be recorded anywhere, even in the offices of the oil company. And, of course, the actual quantities needed are not listed.

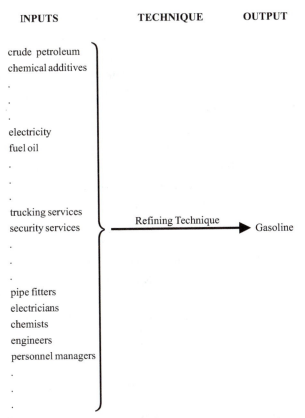

INPUTS   TECHNIQUE   OUTPUT

crude petroleum
chemical additives
.
.
.
electricity
fuel oil
.
.
.
trucking services   Refining Technique   Gasoline
security services
.
.
.
pipe fitters
electricians
chemists
engineers
personnel managers
.
.
.

Figure 9.1. A Schematic View of a Production Process. Production of individual commodities such as gasoline requires the use of particular techniques drawn from the available technology to convert (frequently large number of) inputs into an output.

Techniques are not usually unique. The same gasoline might be made with different inputs. During World War II, when its crude petroleum supplies were cut off, Germany developed a technology for turning coal into gasoline and other petrochemicals. South Africa used similar technologies to thwart the anti-apartheid embargoes during the twenty years before majority rule was established. The United States investigated technologies for extracting petroleum products from shale found in western states during the oil crises of the 1970s and early 1980s. **TECHNOLOGY** is *the set of available techniques*.

The Production Function

Which technique a firm chooses depends on the costs of the inputs, the productivity of the technique itself, and the selling price of the output. The techniques that produce gasoline from coal or shale are not usually cost effective. They have been adopted only in special circumstances in which the cost and availability of the crude petroleum input were prohibitive. But crude petroleum itself is not a single product; it comes in a variety of grades with different characteristics; and it takes a somewhat different recipe to convert each grade to gasoline. Which type of crude petroleum to buy and which recipe to use are key business decisions for oil companies, in which price and availability play an important part. California refineries, for instance, are specialized both in the type of crude that they process (North Slope crude from Alaska) and the type of gasoline they produce (a special formulation to meet California air pollution controls).

The producers themselves must have detailed understanding of the available technology, but this is much too complicated in most cases for the economist. Typically, economists work with a simplified picture of the production process. They summarize the wide variety of inputs in a few indicative categories – the **FACTORS OF PRODUCTION**. For example, all of the heterogeneous types of work that go into production are represented by a single category, **LABOR**, while all of the physical inputs are represented by another category, **capital services**. And the set of techniques (the technology) that govern the transformation of capital service and labor into output are represented mathematically by a **PRODUCTION FUNCTION**. For example, the refining process is represented as

$$gasoline = f(labor, capital\ services).$$

We can think about production even more abstractly. Instead of gasoline, consider any output – call it y. (The variable name y is chosen to echo the variable name for GDP (Y), because GDP is just the sum of the real dollar value of all the final production in the economy. We adopt a convention of writing variable names for the inputs and outputs of firms (microeconomic quantities) as lowercase letters, while writing the variable names for the analogous macroeconomic quantities as uppercase letters.) Similarly, instead of specialized labor and capital, think of general forms for labor and capital – call them l and k. A general production function can be written as

$$y = f(l, k). \tag{9.1}$$

Each point on the production function represents a particular technique: how a particular combination of capital and labor is transformed into a particular quantity of output. Not every technique is represented. If there are two techniques, each using the same quantities of inputs, but producing different quantities of output, the technique with the higher output *dominates* the technique with the lower output. No rational firm would ever choose a dominated technique. The production function represents the set of undominated techniques.

Measurement Issues

In principle, the production function $f(.)$ can be quantified. But measurement poses some tricky problems. The variable *gasoline* is measured in gallons, but what are the right units for the variables *labor* or *capital*? For any one kind of labor, it is natural to use the number of workers or the number of worker-hours as the unit. But some kinds of labor are more efficient than others, and some kinds of labor differ on other dimensions. The work of an electrician is qualitatively different from the work of a truck driver.

Similarly, what unit of measurement is appropriate for the wide variety of different physical inputs – electricity, petroleum, pipes, buildings, roadways, paper clips, computers, ovens, and so forth? We faced this same problem (see Chapters 2 and 3) in adding up final goods and services to measure real GDP. The solution was to find a common denominator – money. The same solution is applied to capital services, which are most often measured in real (or constant) dollars.

There is another difficulty in the case of capital services. The output of a production process (e.g., the gasoline) is a flow (so many gallons per unit time) and the inputs should also be flows. For labor this is relatively easy: number of workers per year or number of worker-hours per week. Some physical inputs are easily measured as flows. Electricity, for example, can be measured as kilowatt-hours per week. It is trickier for the flow of services from machinery or buildings or other long-lived capital goods. When a rental market exists, it may be easier – the rent on the floor space of an office measures the flow of property services to an accounting firm, or the lease price of an airliner measures the flow of aircraft services to an airline. But it is much harder to assess the exact flow of services from the machinery of an oil refinery or a hydroelectric dam as inputs to the production of gasoline or electricity.

Economists often take a shortcut to avoid the problem of measuring capital services. Instead of entering the contribution of physical inputs as a *flow* (capital services), they enter it as the *stock* of CAPITAL. Capital is typically measured in dollars without a time dimension. If the flow of capital services is roughly proportional to the stock of capital, then this shortcut provides a good approximation.

Like "investment," "capital" is one of the tricky words in economics. In ordinary life and often in business, "capital" means an amount of money tied up in a firm or a property. In macroeconomics, however, "capital" refers not primarily to money but instead to *the physical means of production*. Even though it costs money to buy the inputs to gasoline production, one cannot refine gasoline using money in the process. It is easy to get confused on this point because we generally measure the amount of capital in monetary

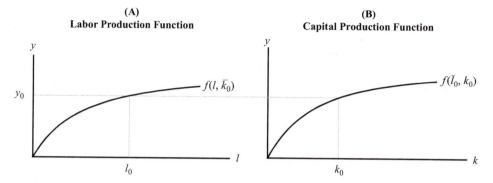

Figure 9.2. A Production Function. A production function in which output is related to two inputs, labor and capital, can be shown in two panels. In panel (A), the curve shows how output varies with the labor input provided that capital is fixed at $\overline{k}_0$. The bar over k_0 is a reminder that the curve presupposes that capital is fixed at that level. In panel (B), the curve shows how output varies with the capital input provided that labor is fixed at $\overline{l}_0$.

terms. In a simplified description of the production process, we refer to the total real monetary cost of the physical inputs. Still, we must not forget that it is the nonlabor inputs (not the money in which we measure them) that do the work.

Basic Properties of the Production Function

The production function (equation (9.1)) cannot be graphed in two dimensions. Instead, in Figure 9.2 we use two related graphs. Look first at panel (A). It shows the relationship of output (y) to a varying labor input (l) on the assumption that the capital input (k) is held to a constant value k_0. That is, it shows the relationship between output and labor *ceteris paribus*. The constancy of capital in panel (A) is indicated by the bar over the capital variable ($\overline{k}_0$). Panel (B) shows the same production function from a different point of view. The amount of output (y) is shown *ceteris paribus* (l held constant at $\overline{l}_0$) as an increasing function of capital (k). (For convenience, we refer to a graph of the production function with variable labor and constant capital as the *labor production function* and to one with variable capital and constant labor as the *capital production function*.)

  Why is the production function drawn in just this way? It is mainly a reflection of some commonsense ideas about production that can be summed up in three basic properties:

  Property 1: *If the inputs are zero, output is zero – that is, the production function goes through the origin* ("there's no such thing as a free lunch").
  Property 2: *The production function is increasing in each of the inputs – that is, it slopes up.* For a given amount of physical inputs more can be squeezed out

of them using more labor. For a given amount of labor, more can be produced using additional capital.

Property 3: *The production function displays* **DIMINISHING RETURNS TO FACTORS OF PRODUCTION** – *that is, each increase in any factor of production, holding other factors constant, raises output but at a slower rate than previous increases.* The production function is drawn as bowed (or concave) toward the horizontal axes to reflect diminishing returns.

A farm provides a classic illustration of these properties. Consider a farmer who has a fixed amount of land, tractors, fertilizer, seed, and other physical inputs. If he, his family, or any hired help did not work, there is no corn crop (the production function goes through zero). The more work they do, the bigger the crop will be. At first the returns are great. Each additional hour of work means more crop planted, fertilized, and tended, at least up to the point that the entire amount of seed and land have been used (the production function slopes up). But even after that, additional work in keeping down weeds, or more carefully monitoring the use of water, fertilizer, and pesticides produces some additional corn. But as more and more jobs are tended to, the jobs become less and less important to increasing the final harvest (the production function shows diminishing returns).

The story is exactly the same for capital. Consider the farm again, but this time imagine that every member of the family works a full day. If they use no land, tractors, seeds, fertilizer, and so forth, they get nothing. The more they plow and plant (the more tractors, plows, and seed they use), the more corn they grow at least until the entire farm is planted. Once the farm is planted, additional use of water, fertilizer, pesticides, tilling machines, and so forth adds to the final crop. But as more and more needs are met, the remaining needs become less and less important.

Look again at Figure 9.2. Notice that at the input values (l_0, k_0) the curves in both panels take the value y_0. Both curves represent the same production function, equation (9.1), from different points of view.

What would happen to the two curves if one of the factors of production changed? For example, in Figure 9.3, l_0 increases to l_1. Because capital remains fixed at k_0, this is a movement along the labor production function in panel (A) showing that output rises to y_1. Notice that in panel (B), the point (k_0, y_1) is not a point on the original production function. This is because that function was drawn on the condition that labor was fixed at l_0, but now there is a larger labor input. In general, the same amount of capital with more labor produces more output, no matter how much capital there is, so the curve must shift up. In fact, at k_0 it must pass through y_1, because this is the amount of output that the production function (equation (9.1)) assigns to (l_1, k_0) as is clear from panel (A). *A movement along one curve corresponds*

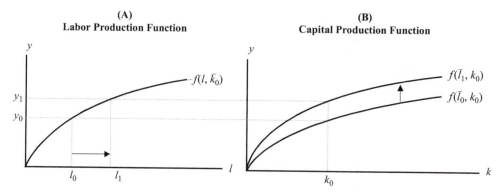

Figure 9.3. The Effect of an Increase in an Input. An increase in labor holding capital constant (panel (A)) is a movement along the labor production function. The increase of labor from l_0 to l_1 increases output from y_0 to y_1. Because labor has increased, the original capital production function (panel (B)), which was drawn on the assumption of labor at l_0 must shift upward so that it intersects the new level of output immediately above the unchanged level of capital.

to a shift in the other curve. Notice that the new curve in panel (B) is steeper, but essentially is the same shape as the old curve – in particular, it still must go through the origin. The student should work out the consequences for the diagram of a change in the capital input holding the labor input constant (see Problems 9.1 and 9.2 at the end of the chapter).

Returns to Scale

The thought experiment behind diminishing returns to a factor of production holds one input constant while increasing the other. What happens if both inputs are allowed to vary? Production functions are classified by how output responds to equal proportional increases in inputs. There are three possibilities: *when all inputs increase by the same proportion,* a production shows

- **CONSTANT RETURNS TO SCALE** *if output rises by the same proportion as the inputs;*
- **Increasing returns to scale** *if output rises by a greater proportion than the inputs;* and
- **Decreasing returns to scale** *if output rises by a smaller proportion than the inputs.*

Figure 9.4 illustrates *constant returns to scale.* The production function passes through the initial input-output combinations – (l_0, y_0) and (k_0, y_0). The **average product of labor** (abbreviated **apl**) is defined as *the number of units of output per unit of labor* (i.e., y/l). Notice that the slope of a ray from the origin through (l_0, y_0) is y_0/l_0. In other words, the slope of a ray from the origin to a point on the labor production function is the average product of labor. Similarly, the **average product of capital** (abbreviated **apk**) is defined

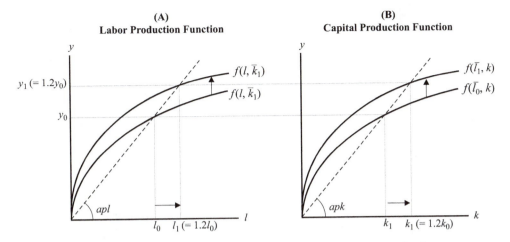

Figure 9.4. Constant Returns to Scale. A production function displays constant returns to scale when equi-proportional increases in all factors of production generate a proportionately equal increase in output. In this case, both labor and capital rise by 20 percent, as does output. The average product of labor ($apl = y/l$) and the average product of capital ($apk = y/k$) are indicated by the slope of a ray from the origin to the point of production. Constant returns to scale implies that the *apl* and *apk* remain constant as output expands: higher production points lie on the same ray from the origin as lower production points.

as *the number of units of output per unit of capital* (i.e., y/k). And it is indicated on the capital production function as the slope of a ray from the origin to the production point.

When a production function displays constant returns to scale, the average products remain constant as the inputs are increased by the same proportion. In Figure 9.4, both labor and capital are increased by 20 percent ($l_1 = 1.2l_0$ and $k_1 = 1.2k_0$). Given the increase in labor, the capital production function must shift upward; and given the increase in capital, the labor production function must also shift upward. But how far? A 20-percent increase in output would leave the point of intersection of each curve vertically above l_1 and k_1 on the same rays from the origin, so that $y_1 = 1.2y_0$.

Figure 9.5 illustrates *increasing returns to scale*. Again, each input is increased by 20 percent, but because output increases by more than 20 percent, each curve must shift upward so that the production points, (l_1, y_1) and (k_1, y_1), lie above the original rays from the origin. Rays from the origin to the new production points are steeper: increasing returns to scale raise the average product of each input. The student should analyze decreasing returns to scale using an analogous diagram (see Problem 9.3 at the end of this chapter).

It is important to remember that the thought experiment behind returns to a factor of production allows only one factor at a time to vary, whereas that behind returns to scale allows all factors to vary proportionally. The

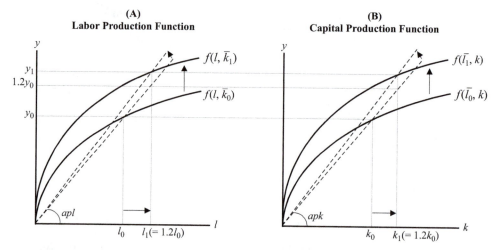

Figure 9.5. Increasing Returns to Scale. A production function displays increasing returns to scale when equi-proportional increases in all factors of production generate a proportionately greater increase in output. In this case, both labor and capital rise by 20 percent, but output rises by more than 20 percent. Because output rose faster than labor or capital, the slope of a ray from the origin to the new production point in each panel is steeper than one to the old production point, indicating that the average products of labor (*apl*) and capital (*apk*) rise as inputs rise equi-proportionately.

production functions in Figures 9.4 and 9.5 both display diminishing returns to labor and capital, while the first displays constant returns, and the second increasing returns, to scale.

9.1.2 Optimal Production

The production function displays the technological possibilities open to a firm. How does a firm choose which technique to use? Firms, of course, wish to make profits, so the question reduces to, how does the firm choose the level of output and the mix of labor and capital that generate the greatest profit?

Profit Maximization

Profit is defined as:

$$Profits = Revenues - Costs.$$

What happens if a firm produces more and more units of output? More output means more goods to sell, so revenues rise. But of course, more output requires more inputs, so costs rise as well. The question must be, which rises faster?

To analyze the firm's profit-maximization problem more carefully, consider a firm producing with a fixed stock of capital. What happens if the firm produces one more unit of output? The extra cost of the labor (or of any additional unit of an input) is known as the *marginal cost*. To economists, the word "marginal" means *having to do with a small additional increment*. So,

marginal cost (**MC**) is *the small increase in the cost of the factors of production attributable to a one-unit increase in output.*

The firm sells the marginal output:

marginal revenue (**MR**) is *the small increase in revenue attributable to the sale of a one-unit increase in output.*

It is worth increasing the labor input to the production process as long as the marginal revenue exceeds the marginal cost ($MR > MC$), because whenever this is true, the additional input means additional profits to the firm.

Imagine that we start off with a very low level of labor (say, on the farm in the earlier example). Each additional unit of output produced and sold adds revenue as well as labor costs. Typically, the first unit produced adds more revenue than costs. But recall the principle of diminishing returns to a factor. Each additional unit of output requires increasingly greater additions of labor – that is, *marginal costs tend to increase as the level of production rises*.

When a market is large relative to the producer (as a wheat market is relative to a wheat farm), the decision of an individual firm to produce or not produce will have no discernible effect on the price at which it sells its output. Such a firm is called a **price taker**. A market composed of such firms displays PERFECT COMPETITION. Because each additional unit of output earns the market price, the marginal revenue faced by a perfect competitor is constant.

When firms are large relative to their market, their output decisions affect market prices. (To sell more output, the firm must typically lower its prices.) Such firms are called **price setters**. A market composed of such firms displays **imperfect competition**. (Monopoly, duopoly, and oligopoly are forms of imperfect competition studied by microeconomists.) Typically, under imperfect competition each additional unit of output will sell for less than the previous unit, so the marginal revenue earned by the firm will fall.

Under either perfect or imperfect competition, as output increases, the gap between marginal revenue and marginal cost narrows, until eventually they are exactly equal. At this point, a profit-maximizing firm should stop expanding output and stop using additional inputs, because to go further would put marginal costs above marginal revenues and begin to cut into profits. The rule then is:

- *a firm maximizes its profits when it increases its use of any factor of production* ceteris paribus *up to the point that marginal revenue equals marginal cost:* MR = MC.

The same maximization rule applies to all forms of competition. To extend the analysis, we have to be more specific about the market organization. Because perfect competition is easier to analyze than imperfect competition and, in most cases, it provides a good approximation for macroeconomics, we focus on the profit-maximization problem for a perfectly competitive firm.

First, consider marginal revenue. A small increase in output can be indicated as Δy. Because the firm is a perfect competitor, it takes the market price of its output (p) as given beyond its control. Marginal revenue is, then, $MR = p\Delta y$.

Next, consider marginal cost. If capital is held constant, then the small additional amount of labor needed to produce the extra unit of output (Δy) can be indicated as Δl. If a firm takes the wage rate as given beyond its control at, say, w, then the marginal cost is $MC = w\Delta l$. The rule for profit maximization can now be reformulated:

- *a firm maximizes its profits when it increases its use of labor* ceteris paribus *up to the point that* $MR = p\Delta y = w\Delta l = MC$.

Marginal Products and Factor Prices

Look at the middle two terms in the maximization rule. Divide both by p and Δl to get

$$\Delta y / \Delta l = w/p. \tag{9.2}$$

This equation has a nice interpretation. The expression on the left-hand side, $\Delta y / \Delta l$, is the **MARGINAL PRODUCT OF LABOR (MPL)** defined as *the extra output produced* ceteris paribus *as the result of an additional unit of labor.* The expression on the right-hand side is the **REAL WAGE RATE (W/P).** In this case, it is the value of the wage rate expressed in terms of the output it will buy. (If a worker in a golf-ball factory is paid $12 per hour and golf balls sell for 50 cents each, then $w/p = 24$ balls.) We are, of course, familiar with converting other nominal quantities into real equivalents (see Chapter 2, section 2.4). When we do this with a price index such as the CPI or the GDP deflator, we implicitly express a number of dollars as the number of units of a bundle of commodities that those dollars will buy. In the firm's

Table 9.1. *Profit-Maximization Decision for a Golf-Ball Manufacturer*

Workers	Production (balls per hour)	Revenue: $p \times$ production (dollars/hour)	Cost: $w \times$ workers (dollars per hour)	Profit dollars	Marginal Product: $\Delta y/\Delta l$ (balls per hour)	Marginal Cost: w/p (balls per hour)
99	4,996	2,498	1,188	1,310	–	–
100	5,024	2,512	1,200	1,312	28	24
101	5,050	2,525	1,212	1,313	24	24
102	5,066	2,533	1,224	1,309	16	24

Note: Calculations assume that that the firm can hire workers at $12 per hour and sell golf balls at 50 cents each.

profit-maximization problem, it is not a bundle, but the single commodity produced by the labor that matters.)

Another way of expressing the rule for profit maximization is then:

- *a firm maximizes its profits when it increases its use of labor* ceteris paribus *up to the point that the marginal product of labor equals the real wage rate; that is, up to the point that*

$$mpl = \Delta y/\Delta l = w/p. \tag{9.3}$$

We can illustrate the rule with data for a hypothetical golf-ball manufacturer (Table 9.1). The table shows that each additional worker adds to total production, but at a decreasing rate. The last two columns show the marginal products and marginal revenues for different numbers of workers. Suppose that the firm started with 99 workers. An additional worker (the 100th) has a marginal product of 28 balls per hour, which is greater than the real wage of 24 balls per hour. Hiring that worker adds to profits. Similarly, hiring the 101st worker adds to profits. Notice, however, that for the 101st worker, the marginal product (24 balls per hour) equals the real wage. Hiring the 102nd worker is not a good idea: the marginal product is 16 balls per hour, which is less than the real wage rate, so the firm's profits would fall. The firm's optimizing decision is to hire 101 workers to produce 5,050 balls per hour. The third, fourth, and fifth columns confirm this choice. Revenues rise with each additional worker – in fact, they rise even with the 102nd worker. But up to 101 workers, revenues rise faster than costs; after 101 workers, revenues rise less quickly than costs. Profits reach their peak at 101 workers.

We can relate the maximization rule to the graphical presentation of the production function. In Figure 9.6 a small increase in labor is indicated by Δl and the resulting increase in output by Δy. Look at the line that passes

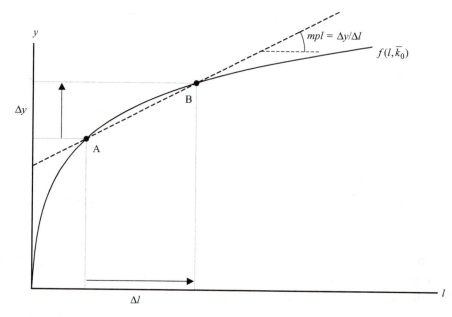

Figure 9.6. The Marginal Product of Labor for Discrete Changes. The marginal product of labor is the small increase in output (Δy) that results, holding other inputs to production constant, from a small increase in labor (Δl). The diagram shows only the labor production function. The slope of the line connecting the production points before and after the increase in labor (i.e., connecting point A to point B) measures the marginal product of labor ($mpl = \Delta y/\Delta l$).

through points A and B on the production function. Its slope is the rise (Δy) over the run (Δl) or $\Delta y/\Delta l$, which is the marginal product of labor.

When we think, as economists often do, in terms of calculus, we imagine Δl getting smaller and smaller until it is infinitesimally small. It is easy to visualize the line through A and B getting steeper as Δl gets smaller, with less and less of the production function lying above it until, in the limit it just touches the production function at point A. In the calculus we indicate discrete changes by Δ and infinitesimal changes by d. Figure 9.7 shows the result of letting Δl become infinitesimally small. The line is now tangent to the production function at point A, and the marginal product of labor is now expressed as the first derivative of the production function at point A: dy/dl.

This is a useful result: if we know the mathematical form of the production function, we can compute the marginal product of labor by taking the first derivative. The principle of diminishing marginal returns to labor can also be stated mathematically as the property that the marginal product of labor becomes smaller (dy/dl declines) as the labor input becomes larger (l increases). The rule for profit maximization can be restated:

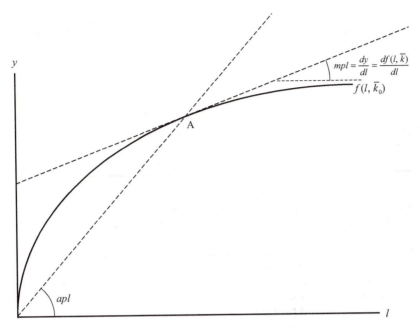

Figure 9.7. The Marginal Product of Labor for Infinitesimal Changes. If we imagine the discrete change in labor (Δl) in Figure 6.6 becoming smaller and smaller without limit, the line running through points A and B will eventually become tangent to the production function at point A. The slope of the tangent is the derivative of the production function at point A, so that the marginal product of labor is $mpl = dy/dl$. The slope of the tangent to the production function at any point is always less than the slope of ray from the origin to that point, indicating that always $mpl < apl$. This property reflects diminishing returns to a factor of production.

- *a firm maximizes its profits when it increases its use of labor* ceteris paribus *up to the point that the marginal product of labor equals the real wage; that is, up to the point that*

$$mpl = dy/dl = df(l,\overline{k})/dl = w/p. \tag{9.4}$$

Notice that the *mpl* at the profit-maximizing point of production is always less than the average product of labor ($mpl < apl$), another implication of diminishing returns: adding one more unit of labor adds output, but by less than the average of all preceding units.

With appropriate modifications, the same principles apply to capital, holding the labor input constant. We must think of capital services as something for which there is a market price, even if the firm owns its own capital. If a construction company hires a crane for a project, the **rental rate** measures the price of the capital service. If, instead, the company owns the crane itself, it should still regard the price that it would earn if rented on the market (its **IMPLICIT RENTAL RATE**) as its price, because the services that the crane

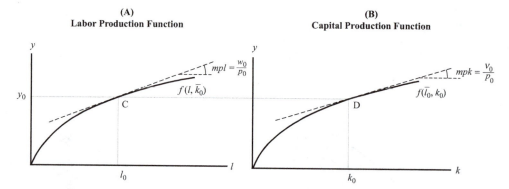

Figure 9.8. Optimal Output Adjusts to the Prices of Factors of Production. The firm maximizes its profits by hiring workers up to the point that the marginal product of labor is equal to the real price of each factor of production. Panel (A) shows that at the production point C (y_0, l_0), the marginal product of labor (the slope of a tangent to the production function at point C) is just equal to the real wage ($mpl = w_0/p_0$). Panel B shows that at the production point D (y_0, k_0), the marginal product of capital (the slope of a tangent to the production function at point D) is just equal to the real (implicit) rental rate ($mpk = v_0/p_0$).

provides are the same in either case. We designate the (implicit) rental rate of capital by the Greek letter v ("nu"). The rule for a profit-maximizing firm is then:

- *a firm maximizes its profits when it increases its use of capital services* ceteris paribus *up to the point that the **marginal product of capital** (MPK) equals the real (implicit) rental rate.* Mathematically, the profit-maximizing point occurs when

$$mpk = \Delta y/\Delta k = v/p \qquad (9.5)$$

or, for infinitesimal changes,

$$mpk = dy/dk = df(\overline{l}, k)/dk = v/p. \qquad (9.6)$$

Analogous to the case of labor, the marginal product of capital is always less than the average product of capital ($mpk < apk$) because of diminishing returns to capital.

Choosing Input Levels

How should a firm use the rules for profit maximization to choose the best mix of capital and labor? First, it must compute the real wage and the real (implicit) rental rate of capital services. Then it must find the combination of labor and capital that simultaneously sets the marginal product of labor equal to the real wage rate and the marginal product of capital equal to the real (implicit) rental rate. If we have a mathematical representation of the production function, this is easy to do. Diagrammatically, it is a little tricky, as it would involve a lot of trial and error. Figure 9.8, however, shows the

Labor Production Function

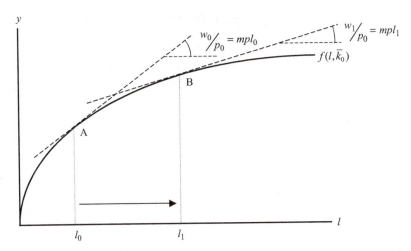

Figure 9.9. The Consequences of a Change in the Real Price of a Factor of Production. A firm that faces a real wage rate of w_0/p_0 would produce at point A, where the marginal product of labor is equal to that wage rate ($mpl_0 = w_0/p_0$). If the wage rate falls to w_1/p_1 and labor becomes cheaper, the optimal production point would correspond to a lower marginal product of labor. Because of diminishing returns to labor, a lower *mpl* lies to the right on the production function at point B where mpl_1 = w_1/p_1. To reach this point, the firm must hire more labor, increasing the demand for labor from l_0 to l_1.

end result in which the firm has chosen the best mix of labor and capital (l_0, k_0) given the wage rate (w_0), (implicit) rental rate (v_0), and product price (p_0) that it faces.

As the prices of factors of production change, the optimal mix of capital and labor also changes. Imagine that the wage rate falls because of an increase in the number of people willing to work, either from a natural boom in population twenty years before or increased immigration or increased participation in the labor force of teenagers or women. In that case labor would be cheaper to the firm, and the firm would use more of it. This is easy to see on Figure 9.9. Given the wage rate w_0, the firm initially hires labor of l_0. The real wage (w_0/p_0) is equal to the marginal product of labor (mpl_0) shown by the slope of the tangent line at point A on the production function. When the wage falls to w_1, the real wage also falls to w_1/p_0. The lower real wage must be set equal to a lower marginal product of labor. Because of diminishing returns to labor, the lower marginal product of labor must correspond to a higher total use of labor at a point to the right of A on the production function. This is shown by the flatter tangent line at point B where $w_1/p_0 = mpl_1$ and where the firm hires labor of l_1.

9.2 Aggregate Supply

9.2.1 The Aggregate Production Function

The individual firm is not the main concern of macroeconomics. We want to explain aggregate real GDP, not particular products such as gasoline, corn, or golf balls. Yet, the microeconomic prelude of the previous section provided valuable insights. If there is a relationship between individual inputs and output, there should also be a relationship between aggregate inputs (aggregate capital and aggregate labor) and aggregate output (real GDP). And we may be able to exploit important analogies between the more easily understood behavior of firms and the behavior of aggregate production.

We write the macroeconomic or AGGREGATE PRODUCTION FUNCTION by analogy to the microeconomic production function as

$$Y = F(L, K). \qquad (9.7)$$

Uppercase letters are used to show aggregates and lowercase letters are used to show micro-level quantities. The micro-quantities y, l, and k were placeholders for the particular output, labor, and capital of any firm we wanted to analyze. They were general algebraic variables that could be filled in for special cases. The output variable y, for example, could represent cars or bananas or blue jeans. Once we aggregate to the level of the whole economy, however, this is no longer true. Y is not a placeholder that can be filled in different ways; it is real GDP. Similarly, L and K are the labor and the capital inputs, not for particular firms, but for the whole economy.

Most of the properties of the microeconomic production functions were derived from a commonsense understanding of production processes and the behavior of firms. Many of these obviously carry over to the aggregate production function. The aggregate production function must pass through zero, because no GDP can be produced without inputs. And, it should slope up, because more inputs generate more output. But are there aggregate diminishing returns? Would the properties of the aggregate production function, derived from adding up the micro production functions for the whole economy, result in a curve with other predictable properties and shape?

It turns out that these questions are extremely difficult. They belong to an area of economics known as *aggregation theory*, and they are well beyond the scope of this book. Instead of trying to figure out the properties of the aggregate production function from first principles, our strategy will be to start with a conjecture that the economy can be described by a particular production function, one that shares important properties with microeconomic production functions. We will then test our conjecture empirically. If it seems to describe the data well, we shall be satisfied that it provides a useful approximation.

9.2.2 The Cobb-Douglas Production Function

Many mathematical functions have the properties we expect from a production function. A particularly useful one is the Cobb-Douglas production function. It was popularized in economics by Paul Douglas (1892–1976), a labor economist who later became a prominent U.S. senator, and Charles Cobb, a mathematician and Douglas's colleague at Amherst College in the 1920s. We shall first describe the Cobb-Douglas production function and some of its properties and then explain why it is a good one for elementary macroeconomic analysis.

The **Cobb-Douglas production function** can be written:

$$Y = F(L, K) = AL^{\alpha} K^{1-\alpha}. \tag{9.8}$$

A is a positive constant that can be interpreted as an index of the state of technology. It is often referred to as a measure of **total factor (or multifactor) productivity (TFP):** for the same labor and capital inputs, higher A implies higher GDP. The exponent α is a constant greater than zero and less than unity ($0 < \alpha < 1$). As we shall see shortly, it can be interpreted as labor's share of GDP, and its value will depend on the actual value of the labor share in the economy.

On a graph, the Cobb-Douglas production function has the same shape as the micro production function in Figure 9.2. (See the *Guide*, section G.16, for mathematical details and a numerical example of some of the useful properties of the Cobb-Douglas production function.) The Cobb-Douglas production function displays all three properties mentioned in section 9.1.1:

- **Property 1.** It is obvious from a glance at equation (9.8) that if both K and L are zero, Y is also zero – there is no "free lunch."
- **Property 2.** Similarly, it is obvious that if either K or L increases, Y increases.
- **Property 3.** To see that the Cobb-Douglas production function displays diminishing returns to factors of production, we must look at the marginal products. Each marginal product can be written in at least two equivalent forms (see the *Guide*, section G.16.2, for the derivation):

$$mpL = \alpha \left(\frac{\overline{K}}{L} \right)^{1-\alpha} = \frac{\alpha Y}{L}; \tag{9.9}$$

$$mpK = (1 - \alpha) \left(\frac{\overline{L}}{K} \right)^{\alpha} = \frac{(1 - \alpha)Y}{K}. \tag{9.10}$$

(Note that we write the marginal products with uppercase L and K as a reminder that we are working with aggregates.) Looking at the middle term in equation (9.9), it is obvious that the marginal product of labor gets smaller as L becomes larger. Equation (9.10) shows that the same is true for the marginal product of capital as K becomes larger.

In addition, the Cobb-Douglas production function displays three other important properties:

- **Property 4.** An increase in one factor of production raises the marginal product of the other factor of production. For example, raising $\overline{K}$, in the middle term of (9.9) raises mpL. Similarly, raising $\overline{L}$ in (9.10) raises mpK. (Graphically, when a Cobb-Douglas production function shifts up – while always going through the origin – the slope of each point must be higher than the slope of a point vertically below it on the original curve.)
- **Property 5.** An increase in the level of total factor productivity (A) raises both marginal products. An increase in A raises Y without changing labor or capital, which, looking at the right-hand terms of (9.9) and (9.10), must increase mpL and mpK.
- **Property 6.** The Cobb-Douglas production function displays constant returns to scale. (See the *Guide*, sections G.16.1 and G.16.2, for a numerical example and a proof.)

9.2.3 Does the Cobb-Douglas Production Function Provide a Good Model of Aggregate Supply?

What is the evidence that the Cobb-Douglas production function describes the economy of the United States? Any empirically acceptable production function must clearly fulfill properties 1 and 2. Although properties 3–6 appeal to our intuitions gained from thinking about the production functions of individual firms, it is not certain that they carry over to the aggregate economy. To provide some evidence that the Cobb-Douglas production function is a good description, we shall put it to a test. We derive an important joint implication of the Cobb-Douglas production function and the assumption that firms follow the maximization rules of perfect competition (see section 9.1.2). The test proceeds in two steps: first, we show that our assumptions imply that the labor and capital shares in GDP are constant; then, we show, to a good approximation, that those shares are in fact constant.

The Cobb-Douglas Production Function Predicts Constant Factor Shares

Real labor income (Y_L) is the real wage rate times the aggregate number of hours worked:

$$Y_L \equiv (w/p)L.$$

The **labor share** in real GDP is defined as

$$L\text{-}share \equiv Y_L/Y \equiv (w/p)\frac{L}{Y}. \tag{9.11}$$

Similarly, the **capital share** is defined as

$$K\text{-}share \equiv Y_K/Y \equiv (v/p)\frac{K}{Y}. \tag{9.12}$$

To move beyond these definitions, we use the assumption that the economy is approximately perfectly competitive. This allows us to use the profit-maximization rules from equations (9.3) and (9.5), replacing the lowercase y, l, and k with their macroeconomic analogues (uppercase Y, L, and K). The rules state that each real factor price is equal to the corresponding marginal product. Substituting the marginal products for the factor prices in (9.11) and (9.12) yields:

$$L\text{-}share = Y_L/Y = (mpL)\frac{L}{Y} \tag{9.13}$$

and

$$K\text{-}share = Y_K/Y = (mpK)\frac{K}{Y}. \tag{9.14}$$

On the assumption that GDP is produced according to a Cobb-Douglas production function, we can substitute the specific form of the mpL from (9.9) into (9.13) and for the mpK from (9.10) into (9.14) to yield:

$$L\text{-}share = Y_L/Y = \left(\frac{\alpha L}{Y}\right)\frac{L}{Y} = \alpha \tag{9.15}$$

and

$$K\text{-}share = Y_K/Y = \left[\frac{(1-\alpha)K}{Y}\right]\frac{K}{Y} = 1 - \alpha. \tag{9.16}$$

Because α is a constant, these equations show that the labor and capital shares are constant and equal to the exponents on L and K in the production function. (Henceforth, we shall refer to α as the *labor share of the Cobb-Douglas production function* and to $1 - \alpha$ as the *capital share*.)

Equations (9.15) and (9.16) demonstrate a key prediction: *if the economy is approximately perfectly competitive and if a Cobb-Douglas production function approximately characterizes aggregate production, then the shares of labor and capital in real GDP should be approximately constant.* Are they?

Are Factor Shares Constant?

Our Cobb-Douglas model assumes that GDP is paid exclusively to owners of labor and owners of capital. The actual national accounts provide a more complex picture of the distribution of factor incomes (see Chapter 3, section 3.7). Table 3.7 and Figure 3.5 divide income into a number of categories. Of the major categories, it is reasonable to classify profits, rents, and interest as

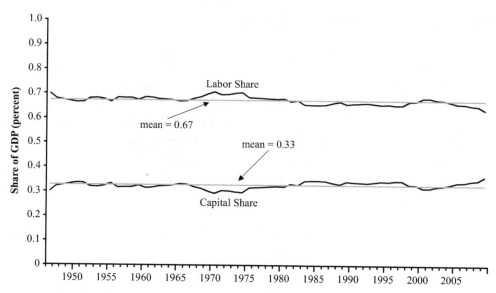

Figure 9.10. U.S. Labor and Capital Shares. The labor share in GDP is the proportion of GDP earned directly or indirectly by labor. The remainder is earned by capital. Both shares vary from year to year around a nearly constant mean. The mean labor share is used as an estimate of α, a key parameter of the Cobb-Douglas production function. *Source:* Bureau of Economic Analysis.

payments to capital. Similarly, compensation of employees is a payment to labor. National income itself differs from GDP by certain business-related items including consumption of fixed capital, which are reasonably assigned to capital.

Two items are harder to assign: proprietors' income and taxes on production (sometimes called "indirect business taxation"). Recall that proprietors' income accrues to the owners of small businesses, who supply both capital and labor. Similarly, some part of taxes on production falls on profits and some part is passed on to workers in the form of lower wages. To distribute the payments in these two categories, we assume that labor receives the same proportion of them as it does of other income (see the *Guide*, section G.16.3, for the exact formula).

Figure 9.10 plots the values of these shares for the United States in the post-World War II period.[1] The striking fact is that, while there is some variation, the variation is small and there is no trend. The approximate constancy of the labor share confirms the prediction of our model and provides a good reason to take the Cobb-Douglas production function as a reasonable approximation of aggregate supply in the U.S. economy.

---

[1] Students who did Problem 3.3 will already have seen that employee compensation as a share of GDP has no discernible trend in this period. But employee compensation does not capture all payments to labor.

The average labor share for the postwar period is $\alpha = 0.67$. Throughout this book we will use this value of the labor share as the key parameter in the Cobb-Douglas production function.

9.2.4 A Cobb-Douglas Production Function for the United States

For any quarter or year, we can formulate a Cobb-Douglas production function for the United States using readily available data on labor and capital, setting the labor share to its average value. The one unknown is the value of total factor productivity (A), which is not directly observable. One way to estimate A is set it to whatever level makes the two sides of the Cobb-Douglas production function equal. Using equation (9.8),

$$A = \frac{Y}{L^\alpha K^{1-\alpha}}. \tag{9.17}$$

For the U.S. economy in 2008, equation (9.17) can be filled in to yield

$$A = \frac{\$13,312 \text{ billion}}{(263,011 \text{ million worker-hours per year})^{0.67}(\$40,173 \text{ billion})^{0.33}}$$
$$= 9.63 \tag{9.17}$$

so that equation (9.8) can be written as

$$Y = 9.63 L^{0.67} K^{0.33}. \tag{9.18}$$

Equation (9.18) can be used to answer questions such as the one in the introduction to this chapter: what would GDP in 2008 have been if the United States had permitted immigration that expanded the workforce by 5 percent but made no additional investment?

Answer: If the new workers worked similar hours to existing workers, the labor input would grow by 5 percent to 276,162 million worker-hours per year. Then, GDP would be:

$$Y = 9.63(276,162 \text{ million})^{0.67}(\$40,173 \text{ billion})^{0.33} = \$13,756 \text{ billion},$$

an increase of 3.3 percent. In the rest of this chapter and in future chapters, we shall use quantified versions of the Cobb-Douglas production function to answer many other questions about the economy.

9.3 Productivity

Another thought experiment using the Cobb-Douglas production function highlights the importance of technology to aggregate supply. What would happen to GDP if technological improvements raised total factor productivity 5 percent?

Answer: A 5-percent increase in total factor productivity multiplies A by 1.05. Looking at equation (9.8), that would obviously raise Y by a factor of 1.05 as well. GDP in 2008 data, for example, would then rise by 5 percent from $13,112 billion to $13,768 billion.

Notice that an increase in total factor productivity is much more effective point for point in raising GDP than an increase in labor, for which a 5-percent increase resulted in only a 3.3-percent increase in GDP. Although numerically powerful, total factor productivity as represented by A does little to reveal the mechanisms of technological progress. And other measures of productivity are more commonly cited in economic and political discussions. Claims that productivity slowed markedly in 1970s compared to the period immediately after World War II or that it rose considerably in the late 1990s are usually supported by data on labor productivity rather than total factor productivity. In this section, we will examine productivity and the relationships among the various measures in more detail.

9.3.1 Alternative Measures of Productivity

Three Measures

Productivity measures try to answer the question of how much output results from a particular level of input. All take the form *productivity = output/ input*. Two measures correspond to the two main factors of production, and a third can be seen as a combination of the first two:

- **LABOR PRODUCTIVITY** is the amount of GDP per unit of labor. It is the macroeconomic equivalent of the average product of labor. We indicate it by the Greek letter "theta": $\theta = Y/L = apL$.
- **CAPITAL PRODUCTIVITY** is the amount of GDP per unit of capital. It is the macroeconomic equivalent of the average product of capital. We indicate it by the Greek letter "phi": $\phi = Y/K = apK$.
- **TOTAL FACTOR PRODUCTIVITY** is, as we have already seen in equation (9.17), the amount of GDP per unit of a bundle of capital and labor: $A = Y/L^\alpha K^{1-\alpha}$. The numerator in this expression can be regarded as the weighted geometric mean of labor and capital (see the *Guide*, section G.4.2).

The units of capital productivity are straightforward: dollars of GDP per dollar of capital. The units of labor productivity depend on how labor is measured. If labor is measured in hours of work, then labor productivity is measured as dollars of GDP per hour. If labor is measured in number of workers, then labor productivity is measured as dollars of GDP per worker. If the average hours per worker change (e.g., if overtime work increases), then labor productivity per worker may rise, even though productivity per hour remains constant. The units of total factor productivity are not very intuitive and depend on the units in which the variables from which it is calculated are measured – particularly, whether labor is measured in hours or workers.

Although we can easily calculate productivity in dollars of real GDP per unit of input, the official productivity data of the Bureau of Labor Statistics (BLS) are presented as index numbers (see the *Guide*, section G.8.1). The BLS does not compute the overall productivity data as we have. Instead, it computes indices for various subdivisions of the economy: the business sector, the manufacturing sector (overall, durable, and nondurable), non-financial corporations, nonfarm business sector, private businesses, private nonfarm business, as well as for a small group of particular industries. The coverage among these categories is incomplete and overlapping. Productivity data have improved their coverage in recent years to include many of the ever more important service sectors.

Productivity data are imperfect, mainly because they pose difficult measurement issues. The output measure that matters for any industry is the contribution to *final* goods and services. The BLS adjusts the data for interindustry trade to account for that part of the product that is an input into other production. But this is tricky. It is also often difficult to measure the real output of an industry at all. We saw in Chapter 3 (section 3.5.2) that the output of the government is generally measured by the inputs (wages paid and goods purchased) rather than by the value of what it produces. The reason, as we noted previously, is that final government services do not generally have market prices. Another important reason is it is hard to measure the intangible services that do not result in storable, easily countable physical products. The same problem applies to many service outputs in industry as well. Some economists have speculated that the reason that productivity measures show a slowdown in the late 1960s and early 1970s is that the economy was becoming more dominated by the hard-to-measure service industries. The slowdown might not have been genuine at all, but rather the result of poor measurement.

International Comparisons

Which countries are the most productive? Because capital stock data are generally more poorly developed, most cross-country comparisons rely on labor productivity rather than capital productivity or total factor productivity. Comparisons for 2008 among the G-7 and selected other countries of labor productivity measured both as output (GDP) per worker and output (GDP) per worker-hour are shown in Figure 9.11. Countries are ordered by increasing output per worker-hour. On both measures, the United States is

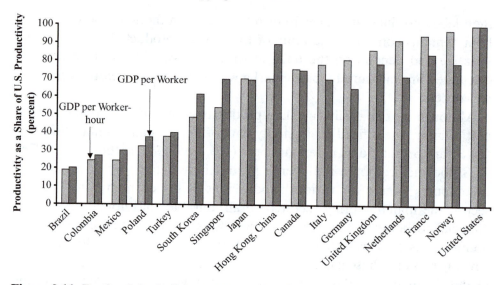

Figure 9.11. Productivity in Selected Countries, 2008. *Source:* Organization for Economic Cooperation and Development.

the productivity leader, data are reported as a percentage of labor productivity in the United States. For the less developed countries, output per worker tends to exceed output per hour. In contrast, for the G-7 and other highly developed countries, it is the other way round. The gap between the two measures is particularly striking for Norway, Germany, and the Netherlands. The gap reflects the fact that, although the developed countries approach U.S. levels of productiveness while workers are actually working, their workers work fewer hours per week and take more holidays and longer vacations than workers in the United States, so that each worker produces substantially less output overall.

How Are the Productivity Measures Related?

It is easy to see the relationship among the three productivity measures. Notice that $Y = Y^\alpha Y^{1-\alpha}$, for any α. Substituting this fact into equation (9.17), rearranging, and using the definitions of θ and ϕ yields:

$$A = \frac{Y^\alpha Y^{1-\alpha}}{L^\alpha K^{1-\alpha}} = \left(\frac{Y}{L}\right)^\alpha \left(\frac{Y}{K}\right)^{1-\alpha} = \theta^\alpha \phi^{1-\alpha}. \qquad (9.19)$$

In words: total factor productivity is a weighted geometric average of labor productivity and capital productivity, where the weights are the labor and capital shares in GDP. Total factor productivity cannot change unless at least one of labor or capital productivity changes. However, either measure of individual factor productivity could change without changing total factor productivity, provided the productivity of the other factor changed sufficiently in the opposite direction.

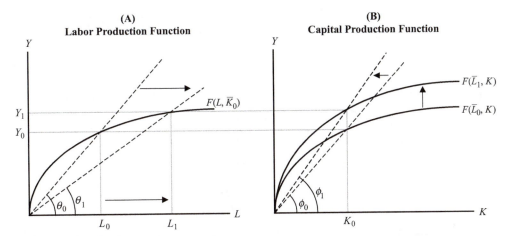

Figure 9.12. Factor Productivities Change in Opposite Directions When One Factor Production is Increased. Production initially takes place at (Y_0, L_0, K_0) at which point labor productivity is given by θ_0 and capital productivity by ϕ_0 – each is the slope of a ray from the origin to the production point. The increase of labor to L_1 raises GDP to Y_1 as the production point moves out along the labor production function to (Y_1, L_1). Diminishing returns to labor implies a fall in labor productivity to θ_1. Because the capital stock is unchanged, the capital production function must shift upward to intersect the new production point at (Y_1, K_0). The ray from the origin through this new point is steeper $(\phi_1 > \phi_0)$, indicating that capital productivity is now higher.

Diagrams may clarify the point. Figure 9.12 presents the production function in equation (9.8) graphically. Let us revisit the thought experiment of a 5-percent increase in labor *ceteris paribus* (see section 9.2.4). Initially, the economy uses inputs L_0 and K_0 to produce Y_0. Labor productivity (θ_0) is shown as the slope of the ray from the origin to the point (L_0, Y_0). Similarly, capital productivity (ϕ_0) is shown as the slope of the ray from the origin to (K_0, Y_0). The increase of labor to L_1 raises GDP to Y_1 – less than proportionally because of diminishing returns to labor. Clearly, labor productivity falls to θ_1. What happens to capital productivity? The capital production function must shift upward, because it was drawn on the assumption that labor was at L_0 and now labor is higher. Because capital has not changed, to be compatible with the labor production function, the curve must pass through (K_0, Y_1). At this point, capital productivity has risen to ϕ_1.

The thought experiment illustrates a general rule:

When one factor of production is used more intensely ceteris paribus, *its own productivity falls and the productivity of the other factors of production rises.*

Notice also that because the capital production function is steeper, its marginal product has also risen – see property 4 (section 9.2.2 and the *Guide*, section G.16).

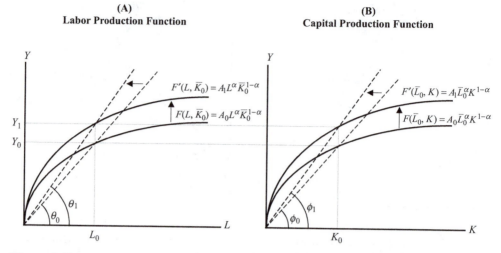

Figure 9.13. All Factor Productivities Rise When Total Factory Productivity Rises. Production initially takes place at (Y_0, L_0, K_0), where the production function is $F(L_0, K_0) = A_0 L_0^\alpha K_0^{1-\alpha}$. Initial labor productivity is given by θ_0 and capital productivity by ϕ_0 – each is the slope of a ray from the origin to the production point. The increase in total factor productivity to A_1 raises GDP to Y_1 at the original levels of labor and capital. The production function must shift up to intersect the new production point at (Y_1, L_0, K_0). As a result, the rays from the origin to the production point steepen, indicating a rise in labor productivity to θ_1 and in capital productivity to ϕ_1.

What happens to total factor productivity? Nothing. Figure 9.12 graphed equation (9.8) and the thought experiment assumed that other things were equal, including A constant. This means that the rise in capital productivity was exactly offset by the fall in labor productivity, keeping A constant.

We can distinguish changes in factors of production from changes in technology with a graphical analysis of the thought experiment that heads section 9.3: the effect of a 5-percent increase in technology (A) on GDP. In Figure 9.13, the economy initially uses inputs L_0 and K_0 to produce Y_0. Labor productivity is θ_0 and capital productivity, ϕ_0. The improvement in technology means that more GDP (Y_1) can be produced for the same level of inputs. The labor production function must, therefore, shift upward to pass through (L_0, Y_1). Labor productivity rises to θ_1. Similarly, the capital production function shifts upward to pass through (K_0, Y_1), and capital productivity rises to ϕ_1.

Again, the thought experiment illustrates a general rule:

When technology improves ceteris paribus, *the productivity of all factors of production rises.*

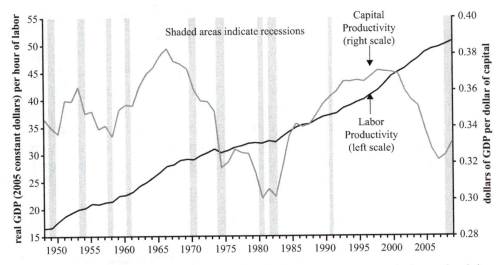

Figure 9.14. U.S. Labor and Capital Productivity. *Source:* capital productivity, Bureau of Economic Analysis and author's calculations; labor productivity, Bureau of Economic Analysis, Bureau of Labor Statistics, and author's calculations.

Notice also that because both the labor and capital production functions are steeper, the marginal products of both factors of production have also risen – see property 5 (section 9.2.2 and the *Guide*, section G.16).

9.3.2 Technological Progress

Factor Productivity over Time

One lesson of the last section is that any change in the relative use of labor and capital will alter factor productivities, even when technology is constant. Because relative use of labor and capital fluctuates with the business cycle, we should also expect factor productivities to fluctuate cyclically, which Figure 9.14 shows they in fact do. At the end of the 1990s, policymakers in the Clinton administration and the Federal Reserve debated endlessly whether sharp increases in productivity were permanent, secular changes or were the unsustainable result of using capital and labor too intensely. The one would have been cause for celebration; the other a rationale for restrictive monetary and fiscal policy. How can we tell the difference?

The thought experiments analyzed in the last section might suggest a test: a rise in total factor productivity is attributable to technology (as in Figure 9.13) and other changes are cyclical (Figure 9.12). But that does not work. Except in the cases in which changes in the relative use of labor and capital lead to exactly offsetting changes in factor productivities, equation (9.19) shows that any change in factor productivities also changes total factor productivity. Figure 9.13 shows that an increase in *A ceteris paribus* must increase θ and ϕ. But we cannot demonstrate the converse: that only if both θ and ϕ increase can A increase – sometimes other things are not equal.

Indeed, Figure 9.14 shows that labor productivity more than tripled (from \$16 per worker-hour in 1948 to \$51 per worker-hour in 2008). The trend in labor productivity is 1.9 percent per year, leading to doubling in a little less than 36 years. In contrast, capital productivity showed virtually no secular growth. Although both series are variable, when thinking about permanent technological change, we will not go very far wrong if we regard capital productivity as constant and labor productivity as growing strongly on trend.

Factor-Augmenting Technological Progress

According to (9.19), total factor productivity must grow to reflect the growth in labor productivity. But how can we reconcile the rise in A with the long-term constancy of ϕ in light of the thought experiment analyzed in Figure 9.13? Unlike the assumption of the thought experiment, capital in the United States did not stay constant, but in fact grew at a rate at which diminishing returns just offset the tendency of improving technology to increase capital productivity. The data suggest that technological progress does not affect factors of production equally.

Let us analyze this somewhat further. Technology is said to be **FACTOR-AUGMENTING** when technological progress has exactly the same effect on GDP as having more of the factor input. For example, a 2-percent increase in labor productivity, holding L constant, would have exactly the same effect on GDP as a 2-percent increase in the labor input, holding θ, constant. More specifically,

- Technology is said to be **labor-augmenting** when *an increase in technology is exactly the same as a proportional increase in the labor input.*
- Technology is said to be **capital-augmenting** when *an increase in technology is exactly the same as a proportional increase in the capital input.*

Suppose that all technology is factor-augmenting. Then we can rewrite the Cobb-Douglas production function as

$$Y = (A_L L)^\alpha (A_K K)^{1-\alpha}, \tag{9.20}$$

where A_L measures labor-augmenting technological progress and A_K measures capital-augmenting technological progress. Rearranging (9.20), we get

$$Y = \left(A_L^\alpha A_K^{1-\alpha} \right) L^\alpha K^{1-\alpha}. \tag{9.20'}$$

Comparing (9.20') to (9.8), it is clear that

$$A = A_L^\alpha A_K^{1-\alpha}. \tag{9.21}$$

In words, total factor productivity is the geometrically weighted average of labor-augmenting and capital-augmenting technological progress.

How does (9.21) relate to (9.19)? Where labor and capital productivity may change because of changes in the relative use of the factors of production (as in Figure 9.12), A_L and A_K change only as a result of technological change. Over long periods, when cyclical fluctuations cancel out, the average growth of labor productivity should equal the average rate of labor-augmenting technological progress $(\bar{\hat{\theta}} \approx \bar{\hat{A}}_L)$, and similarly for capital productivity and capital-augmenting technological progress $(\bar{\hat{\phi}} \approx \bar{\hat{A}}_K)$. The data for the United States show that the average growth of capital productivity is zero, so that $\bar{\hat{A}}_K \approx \bar{\hat{\phi}} \approx 0$.

9.4 Short-Run and Long-Run Aggregate Supply

9.4.1 Flexible and Inflexible Production Functions

Each point on the production function represents a different technique, using a different mix of labor and capital. Up to now we have assumed implicitly that firms were able to choose the technique and the level of production that maximized their profits for given real factor prices (w/p and v/p). We assumed that demand for the products of individual firms would always be sufficient to purchase whatever they found profitable to produce and that aggregate demand would always be sufficient to purchase planned or *ex ante* aggregate supply (see Chapter 2, section 2.7). We now consider what might happen if plans to purchase ($C + I + G + NX$) fall short of plans to produce.

In reality, falling aggregate demand is likely to be associated with changing relative prices – both of goods and of factors of production. For example, the oil shocks of the 1970s and 1980s, echoed by the rise in oil prices from 2003 culminating in a peak in 2008, increased the value of imports, thereby lowering net exports and aggregate demand. Firms had to adjust to both lower sales and the higher prices of oil products. Figure 9.15 shows the labor production function. Initially, the economy uses the whole labor force (LF) (and capital, not shown) optimally to produce Y_0. Now suppose that an oil price increase reduced aggregate demand to Y_1. It would be silly for firms to keep producing at the old level and building up stocks of unsold goods. The efficient course would be to move down the production function from point A to B. In addition, they would want to reduce their use of oil, and substitute the other now relatively cheaper energy inputs (such as coal or natural gas), as well as capital and labor for oil. This represents a change in technique. If technology were perfectly flexible, then this would be quick and easy.

Some capital is – like a child's Lego blocks – quite flexible. A power drill, a screwdriver, a pickup truck, or a personal computer is easily turned from one task to another. But other capital is highly inflexible – for example, a

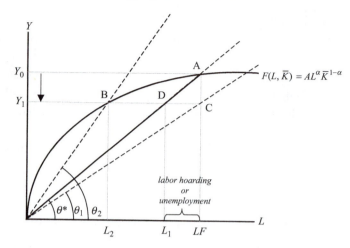

Figure 9.15. Short-Run Adjustment to a Fall in Aggregate Demand: Labor Productivity and Unemployment. Initially production occurs at point A where the whole labor force (*LF*) is used to produce Y_0. If aggregate demand falls to Y_1 firms would produce most efficiently if they could reduce production to point B lower on the long-run production function. But if technology is not flexible in the short run, then they will continue to use the same technique as at point A with labor productivity given at θ^*. The heavy segment of the ray from the origin to point A represents the short-run production function: the same technique is used with different levels of labor input. If firms hesitate to lay off redundant workers, then the actual production point would be C, and actual productivity would fall to θ_1. There would be labor hoarding. If firms used the minimum labor necessary to produce Y_1 at the original technique, they would produce at point D. Unemployment of $LF - L_1$ would result. If technology were more flexible, they would adopt a new technique at point B, raising labor productivity to θ_2. Greater unemployment would result.

hydroelectric dam. Other capital may fall in between – for example, an oil-fired power plant might be converted with some time and effort to use coal. Similarly, labor inputs may not be flexible: an airliner designed with a flight crew of three will not be easily run by two when wage rates are relatively high and will not benefit from a fourth member when they are relatively low. An airline facing higher wage bills might demand planes designed for smaller crews as it adds to, or replaces, its existing fleet, but that too takes time.

And that is the essential point: neither technology nor the organization of production can turn on a dime. When demand falls or relative prices change, it is not possible to move down the production function immediately to a new optimum. The production function should be regarded as the long-run production possibilities for the economy. Here **LONG RUN** refers to a planning horizon – a time sufficiently far in the future that a firm can regard its choice of technique as open and not fettered by past decisions about capital and organization. Like the horizon, the long run always recedes as we approach it. In the face of higher oil prices, a trucking firm may decide that a more fuel-efficient fleet is optimal. In the **SHORT RUN**, the here and now, it begins to scrap its oldest trucks and makes sure that new trucks are of the fuel-efficient type. If nothing else changed it would eventually converge to its new preferred fleet. But of course, before it is already there, other things are likely to change. In the short run, it must always make decisions aimed at the long run. But the long run is a moving target.

9.4.2 Productivity and Resource Use in the Short Run

What difference does it make to aggregate supply if technology is inflexible in the short run? Consider an extreme case, in which production techniques are absolutely fixed and no adjustments are possible. In Figure 9.15, the economy would have to keep exactly the same technique with exactly the same labor productivity (shown as the ray with slope θ^*). It could operate this technique at a lower level, but it could not choose another technique with another labor productivity. In effect, the segment of the productivity ray from the origin to point A (shown as a heavy line) would become the short-run production function.

What happens then if aggregate demand falls to Y_1? In the extreme short run, firms may simply hold onto their labor and produce at the lower level – producing at point C, which is off both the short- and long-run production functions. This is known as **LABOR HOARDING**. It might occur if the fall in demand is expected to be short-lived and if the costs of firing, rehiring, and training workers are substantial. Actual labor productivity would fall from θ^* to θ_1. Productivity falls not because firms have not adopted new techniques, but because some workers are idle. The degree of labor hoarding is measured by $LF - L_1$, where L_1 is the amount of labor truly needed to produce Y_1 using existing techniques.

If the fall is not expected to be short-lived, then firms would reduce their costs by laying off redundant workers. They would then produce at point D. Here labor productivity remains at θ^* but some workers are unemployed. If labor is measured by the number of workers, then $LF - L_1$ now represents **UNEMPLOYMENT**, because L_1 is now the amount of labor actually employed.

In reality, the economy would not remain at a point like D. If demand recovered quickly it might move back to point A on the production function at full employment. If demand remained low, firms would begin the process of adjusting to the new circumstances. For example, with demand at Y_1, point B on the production function, which uses labor of L_2, represents efficient techniques. Labor productivity is higher at point B (θ_2). But point B still represents a mismatch between the supply plans of firms and aggregate demand. Ideally, firms would find the new point on the production function that maximizes their profits in the face of new factor prices.

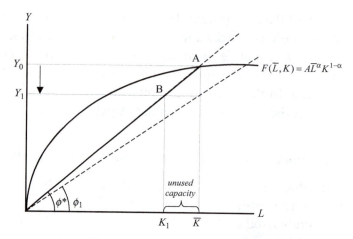

Figure 9.16. Short-Run Adjustment to a Fall in Aggregate Demand: Capital Productivity and Capacity Utilization. Initially, production occurs at point A where the whole capital stock ($\overline{K}$) is used to produce Y_0. If aggregate demand falls to Y_1 but technology is not flexible, firms would continue to use the same technique, so that the heavy segment of the ray from the origin to point A would describe the short-run production function. Firms producing at point B would still possess the capacity to produce at a higher level, and the portion of capital actually used (K_1) would produce with the original productivity (ϕ^*). Actual capital productivity (counting both the used and the unused portions of capital) would fall to φ_1 and $\overline{K} - K_1$ would be unused capacity. The existence of unused capacity permits a rapid rise in actual capital productivity when demand is restored to a higher level.

The situation with respect to capital in the face of the same fall in aggregate demand is a little different. Figure 9.16 shows the capital production function. Initially, the economy produces Y_0 optimally using $\overline{K}$ (and labor). Again, if the technique is fixed in the short run, then we can regard the segment of the ray from the origin to point A with a capital productivity of ϕ^* as the short-run production function.

Capital is not like labor – firms own it or lease it from other firms. Labor can be laid off – the resulting unemployment is a problem for the worker, but not for the firm. Capital cannot be laid off by the firm sector as a whole. It can be scrapped, but that would not be an economically sensible reaction in most cases, as it will be needed in future. Only the least productive capital is likely to be permanently scrapped when aggregate demand falls temporarily. Instead, what is not needed will sit idle. (When air travel fell dramatically after September 11, 2001, airlines and leasing agencies mothballed hundreds of aircraft in the deserts of California and Arizona. As demand picked up again, the idled planes were brought back into service.) In Figure 9.16, only K_1 units of capital are needed to produce Y_1. But because $\overline{K}$ units are actually available, measured capital productivity falls to ϕ_1. Unused (or excess) capacity is measured by $\overline{K} - K_1$.

As with labor, the extreme short run does not last long. If demand is not restored, then firms begin adjusting their capital to suit the new optimal techniques. Over time, through purchases of new types of machinery and depreciation, the capital stock is readjusted to move the economy back toward the new optimal point on the production function.

9.4.3 Measures of Resource Use

Labor Utilization

Economists have developed measures of the degree of idleness of the factors of production. Start with labor. The **labor force (*LF*)** is *the number of people who wish to be in paid employment*. If L is the actual number employed, then

- the **employment rate (*EMP*)** $= L/LF$ is *the fraction of the labor force employed*; and
- the **unemployment rate (*U*)** $= \frac{LF-L}{LF} = 1 - EMP$, is *the fraction of the labor force not employed*.

Employment and unemployment are examined in much greater detail in Chapters 11 and 12.

Capital Utilization

What unemployment is to labor, UNUSED, SPARE, OR EXCESS CAPACITY is to capital. In the United States, the Federal Reserve collects data from which it computes the **capacity-utilization rate**, which is the analogue of the employment rate.

Consider capacity at the level of the firm. Imagine that both capital and labor are used optimally according to a long-run production function. The point of optimal output on this production function measures the theoretical capacity of the firm's capital. In practice, a firm's decision about optimal production is a complex one. To collect data, the Federal Reserve asks managers of individual plants to estimate the sustainable maximum output – the greatest level of output a plant can maintain within the framework of a realistic work schedule, after factoring in normal downtime and assuming sufficient availability of inputs to operate the capital in place.[2]

Data for individual plants are combined into a large number of indices for more specific industrial groupings. These are, in turn, combined into various indices for larger industrial groupings and an overall *industrial capacity index*. The Federal Reserve also collects data on actual production for these

---

[2] Board of Governors of the Federal Reserve System, "Industrial Production and Capacity Utilization: Capacity Utilization Explanatory Notes," *Federal Reserve Statistical Release G.17*, www.federalreserve.gov/releases/g17/cap_notes.htm.

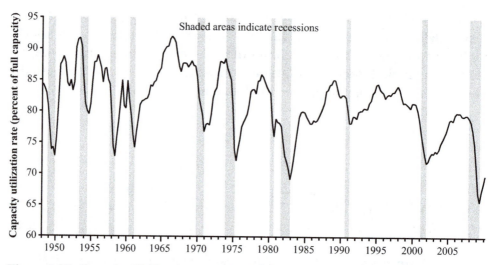

Figure 9.17. Capacity Utilization and the Business Cycle. Capacity use is the ratio of the index of industrial production to the industrial capacity index. It is a leading business-cycle indicator at the peak and a coincident indicator at the trough. *Source:* Board of Governors of the Federal Reserve System.

same industries and combines them into an **index of industrial production** and indices for various industrial groupings.

The capacity index does not cover all production in the economy, but concentrates on the physical output of manufacturing, mining, and electric and gas utilities. Actual and potential production are more difficult to measure in other sectors of the economy – especially in the increasingly important service sectors. Even so, as we saw in Chapter 5 (Figure 5.9), the index of industrial production is one of the best coincident indicators of the economy: it tracks real GDP very closely.

The *capacity utilization rate (CU)* is defined as

$$CU = \frac{index\ of\ industrial\ production}{capacity\ index};$$

that is, the capacity utilization rate expresses the level of output as a fraction of the economically optimal level of output of the physical plant and equipment in the economy.

Figure 9.17 plots the capacity-utilization rate for manufacturing against the business cycle.

Just as the unemployment rate does not fall to zero even in the best of times, the capacity utilization rate never reaches 100 percent. Just as the troughs of the unemployment rate gradually increased between the 1950s and the early 1990s, the peaks of capacity utilization have fallen from highs around 92 percent in the 1950s to the peak in the last complete business cycle of 85 percent. Effectively full capacity utilization is probably close to the most recent peak value.

The average levels of unemployment and capacity utilization may differ significantly among countries. In most years, since the mid-1980s, Germany and France, for instance, have had much higher average unemployment rates than the United States. These differences reflect differences in national labor, industrial, tax, and social welfare policies.

9.5 Potential Output

9.5.1 The Concept of Economic Potential

The fact that the unemployment rate is greater than zero and the capacity utilization rate is less than 100 percent suggests that the economy produces less than it could. A natural notion of **POTENTIAL OUTPUT** answers the question, *how much real GDP would be produced if the entire labor force and the entire capital stock were fully employed at their economically optimal levels?* The Cobb-Douglas production function provides an easy way to address this question. Substitute the whole labor force (LF) for (L) in equation (9.8) and assume that capital is fully employed to get:

$$Y^{pot} = A(LF)^\alpha K^{1-\alpha}, \tag{9.22}$$

where Y^{pot} is potential GDP.

Previously, we had assumed that capital was always fully employed. But if (9.22) defines potential GDP, then it would make more sense to adjust the capital stock to take account of unused capacity: capital in effective use is $CU \times K$. The production of real GDP could then be represented by the Cobb-Douglas production function written as:

$$Y = AL^\alpha(CU \times K)^{1-\alpha}. \tag{9.23}$$

Practically, the main difference between this equation and equation (9.8) is that the variability of capacity utilization was previously hidden in the variability of A, whereas now it is explicitly represented in its interaction with the capital stock.

9.5.2 Scaled Output

The measure of potential output based on full employment of labor and capital has a nice interpretation. Begin with real GDP as a fraction of potential output, calculated as

$$\tilde{Y} = \frac{Y}{Y^{pot}}. \tag{9.24}$$

Let us call $\widetilde{Y}$ *output scaled by potential output* or just **SCALED OUTPUT** for short.[3] Scaled output is a kind of generalized measure of capacity utilization that takes the rate of labor use, as well as the rate of capital use, into account. Scaled output can be expressed in terms of the Cobb-Douglas production function by substituting equations (9.22) and (9.23) into the definition:

$$\widetilde{Y} = Y/Y^{pot} = \frac{AL^{\alpha}(CU \times K)^{1-\alpha}}{A(LF)^{\alpha} K^{1-\alpha}} = \left(\frac{L}{LF}\right)^{\alpha} CU^{1-\alpha}. \qquad (9.25)$$

To simplify the notation, define $\widetilde{L} = L/LF$ and $\widetilde{K} = CU$. (We can call $\widetilde{L}$ **scaled labor** and $\widetilde{K}$ **scaled capital**.) $\widetilde{L}$ is, of course, another name for the employment rate, *EMP*, and $\widetilde{K}$ is another name for the capacity utilization rate, *CU*. Neither new name is necessary, but they help to distinguish the more generalized notions of factor utilization needed here from the actual data, which never correspond precisely to the ideal concepts of economic theory.

Equation (9.25) can be rewritten as

$$\widetilde{Y} = \widetilde{L}^{\alpha} \widetilde{K}^{1-\alpha}. \qquad (9.26)$$

Equation (9.26) has the same form as a Cobb-Douglas production function without the level of technological progress (total factor productivity), usually indicated by A. Technological progress is not omitted. Rather, it is incorporated into potential output in the calculation of $\widetilde{Y}$.

Figure 9.18 shows potential output, actual output, and scaled output against the business cycle. The usefulness of scaled output is already evident in the figure. Both actual and potential output trend upward as the economy grows. Similarly, labor and capital trend upward over time. And technology (measured by total factor productivity, A) also advances. But the calculation of scaled output uses factor inputs expressed as fractions of the available inputs, which can never exceed 100 percent, and technology cancels out. As a result, scaled output does not trend. Because the growth of the economy is factored into its calculation, it is easy to judge the state of the economy at different times, even though the economy is now much bigger than in the past.

The fluctuations in scaled output follow the business cycle closely. Scaled output is a leading-to-coincident indicator of the business-cycle peak and a clearly coincident indicator of the trough.

Although scaled output is based on a natural concept of potential output, it is not the only possible concept – see Chapter 16, Box 16.2, which examines some alternatives.

---

[3] The symbol "~" is known as a *tilde*, and the variable can be read as "*Y-tilde*."

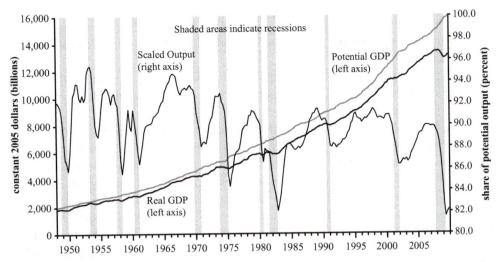

Figure 9.18. Output, Potential Output, and Scaled Output. Scaled output is the ratio of real GDP to potential GDP. Scaled output is a leading indicator of the business cycle at the peak and a coincident indicator at the trough. *Source:* Bureau of Economics Analysis and author's calculations.

9.6 Aggregate Supply: Questions Answered, Questions Raised

At the beginning of this chapter we posed some questions – three examples of the type of question that falls under the general heading of aggregate supply. This chapter showed that questions of that type can be answered using the aggregate production function and the assumption that firms are profit maximizers. Although these assumptions do not necessarily hold precisely in the economy, we saw that the Cobb-Douglas production function provides a good approximation. It allowed us to answer the most specific question ("What would happen to GDP if immigration rules were relaxed and 5 percent more workers joined the U.S. labor force?") with reasonable precision: *ceteris paribus* GDP would rise by 3.3 percent (see section 9.2.4).

The more general questions ("Why is GDP in the United States vastly higher in 2010 than in 1960 or 1910?" and "Why is GDP in the United States higher than in any other country in the world?") received only an implicit answer: GDP is higher when labor or capital inputs are higher or when technology is better. Our analysis would help us to calculate just how much of a change in labor, capital, or technology it would take to account for the differences in GDP over time or between countries. These questions are addressed in more detail in Chapter 10. Our analysis raises new questions: If factor inputs help to determine output, what determines factor inputs? This question is addressed in Chapters 11 and 12. If cyclical fluctuations in aggregate demand result in aggregate supply less than full potential, what determines aggregate demand? We examine that question in Chapters 13 and 14.

Summary

1. Aggregate supply is the combined effect of the production decisions of individual firms.

2. Production converts inputs (factors of production), broadly classified as labor and capital (i.e., nonlabor inputs), into outputs using particular techniques. Technology is the set of available techniques.

3. The production function represents the set of the best available techniques for producing each possible level of production. An acceptable production function shows no output when there are no inputs; increases as inputs increase; and displays diminishing returns to each factor of production (i.e., output increases at a decreasing rate as each factor increases *ceteris paribus*).

4. When all factors of production increase by the same proportion, the production function shows constant returns to scale, if it increases by the same proportion; diminishing returns to scale, if it increases by a lesser proportion; and increasing returns to scale, if it increases by a greater proportion.

5. The firm maximizes profits when it sets the level of production such that marginal cost equals marginal revenue ($MC = MR$). When firms are perfectly competitive, this rule can be expressed as: a firm maximizes profits when it uses labor up to the point that the marginal product of labor equals the real wage ($mpl = w/p$) and the marginal product of capital equals the real (implicit) rental price of capital ($mpk = v/p$).

6. The aggregate production function is the macroeconomic analogue of the firm's production function in which GDP (Y) replaces the output of a particular product, and aggregate labor and capital replace the individual firm's factors of production.

7. The Cobb-Douglas production function ($Y = AL^\alpha K^{1-\alpha}$) provides a useful representation of aggregate supply. Its properties are similar to those of microeconomic production functions. In addition, it shows other useful properties: constant returns to scale; an increase in a factor of production decreases the productivity of that factor but raises the productivity of other factors; and technological progress raises the productivity of all factors.

8. Under the assumption that firms are approximately perfectly competitive and that it describes the economy reasonably well, the Cobb-Douglas production function predicts constant labor and capital shares in GDP. This prediction agrees to a good approximation with the facts about the U.S. economy in the long run.

9. Productivity is measured as units of output per unit of input. The most common measures are labor productivity, capital productivity, and total factor productivity, which is the weighted geometric average of the first two.

10. Factor-augmenting technological progress occurs when technological progress can be represented as equivalent to adding more of the factor of production. Because labor productivity in the United States shows a strong trend, and capital productivity almost no trend, technological progress can be represented as labor-augmenting.

11. In the short run, it is not possible to adjust the choice of technique to changes in the level of demand or factor prices – technology is inflexible. But over time, if changes are long-lasting, techniques adapt. Short-run inflexibility leads to underutilization of factors of production (labor hoarding or unemployment and excess capacity).

12. The unemployment rate measures the underutilization of workers as a percentage of the labor force. The capacity-utilization rate measures the utilization of capital expressed as industrial production as a percentage of industrial capacity, so that a capacity-utilization rate less than 100 percent shows underutilization.

13. Potential output is the amount of GDP that would be produced if both labor and capital were fully utilized with the best choice of technique. The ratio of actual to potential output (scaled output) measures how intensely the economy is supplying GDP. Fluctuations in scaled output closely track the business cycle.

Key Concepts

input
output
technique
technology
factors of production
labor
production function
capital
diminishing returns to factors of
   production
constant returns to scale
perfect competition
marginal product of labor (mpl)
real wage rate (w/p)
implicit rental rate (v/p)
marginal product of capital (mpk)

aggregate production function
Cobb-Douglas production function
total factor (or multifactor)
   productivity (TFP)
labor productivity
capital productivity
factor-augmenting technological
   progress
long run
short run
labor hoarding
unemployment
unused, spare, or excess capacity
potential output
scaled output

Problems

Data for this exercise are available on the textbook website under the link for Chapter 9 (http://appliedmacroeconomics.com). Before starting these exercises, the student should review the relevant portions of the *Guide to Working with Economic Data*, including sections G.1–G.5, G.10–G.14, and G.16.

Problem 9.1. Imagine that Florida was an independent country and that a series of hurricanes destroyed 10 percent of its capital stock (while miraculously not harming any person). Use production function diagrams to show what this disaster would imply for (i) the level of GDP; (ii) labor productivity; and (iii) capital productivity. Assume that the labor force is fixed and fully employed.

Problem 9.2. Use a Cobb-Douglas production function for the United States, calibrated to the values of 2008 (see data in equation (9.17′)), to predict *ceteris paribus* the quantitative effects of a 10-percent fall in the capital stock on (i) the level of GDP; (ii) labor productivity; and (iii) capital productivity.

Problem 9.3. Use a diagram similar to Figure 9.4 or 9.5 to analyze the effects of a 20-percent increase in both capital and labor when production is subject to decreasing returns to scale. Particularly note the effects on labor and capital productivity.

Problem 9.4. Consider a production function that is like the Cobb-Douglas production function except that the exponents on the factors of production need not add up to one:

$$Y = AL^\alpha K^\beta$$

(Notice that if $\alpha + \beta = 1$, this is exactly the same as a Cobb-Douglas production function.) Show that, if $\alpha + \beta > 1$, this function displays *increasing returns to scale* (i.e., output rises more than proportionately to equi-proportional increases in factor inputs), and that, if $\alpha + \beta < 1$, it displays *decreasing returns to scale*. Think of economic situations in which each of these cases seems natural.

Problem 9.5. Use appropriate annual data for the United States to compute the time series (1948–2009) for total factor productivity (A), labor productivity, and capital productivity. (Assume that the labor share is constant at $\alpha = 0.67$.) Compute the average rate of growth of each (compound annual rates). What do your calculations suggest about the sources of productivity growth?

Problem 9.6.

(a) Using the same data and calculations from Problem 9.5, compute the implied real wage in 1948, 1978, and 2008.

(b) Compute the average growth rates of the real wage in (a) for 1948–2008, 1948–1978, and 1978–2008.

(c) Compare the result for 1948–2008 to your computation of the growth rate of labor productivity in Problem 9.5. Explain your finding.

(d) Before the recession of 2007–2009, the U.S. economy was often characterized favorably compared to European economies as a "job creation machine." What light do the data in parts (a) and (b) shed on the costs of this success? (Be careful to relate your conclusions to specific data.)

Problem 9.7. Detrend quarterly data for labor productivity in the United States from 1948 to the present (use the Bureau of Labor Statistics productivity index; see the *Guide*, section G.12, on detrending data. Explain your choice of detrending method.)

(a) Before attempting any data analysis, think about the business cycle using the models of this chapter. Explain how you might expect labor productivity to vary with the business cycle (e.g., do you expect productivity to be a leading, lagging, or coincident indicator; pro-cyclical or countercyclical?). State your reasoning carefully.

(b) Plot detrended labor productivity and indicate NBER recession dates using shading.

(c) Create a graph showing the typical cyclical behavior of labor productivity. First identify the segment of the data that run from 8 quarters before to 16 quarters after each of the last seven business-cycle peaks (excluding the most recent if there are not enough data). Convert each segment into an index taking the value 100 at the business-cycle peak. Average across all seven cycles. Plot the resulting series on the vertical axis against the values $-8, -7, \ldots, 0, 1, 2, \ldots 16$ (horizontal axis) – that is, against the number of quarters after the peak. (Your graph should be similar to Figures 5.8 and 5.9.)

(d) Based on your graphs, is there a clear cyclical pattern of either productivity series? Comment on the nature of the pattern. How well do these patterns agree with those you hypothesized in (a)? What might account for the differences between your expectations and the data?

Problem 9.8. Use quarterly data for the United States from 1948 to the present to compute capital productivity. Use this series to repeat steps (a)–(d) in Problem 9.7, substituting capital productivity for labor productivity where appropriate. (Because capital productivity does not have a significant trend, there is no need to use a detrended series in (b).)

Problem 9.9. Assume that the economy was fully employed and efficiently operating at the peak of the business cycle in 1990:3.

(a) Write down the equation of the short-run labor production function that corresponds to the segment of the ray from the origin to point A in Figure 9.15.

(b) Noting how far real GDP actually fell from the peak to the trough in 1991:1, use the function from (a) to compute the amount of labor needed to produce the 1991:1 level of output (i.e., the amount of labor that corresponds to point B in Figure 9.15). What level of capital productivity corresponds to that level of output assuming that capital had remained fixed at the 1990:3 level?

(c) What were the actual levels of labor, labor productivity, and capital productivity in 1991:1? Comparing these to the data and the computations from (b), how well does the short-run production function (Figures 9.15 and 9.16) describe the recession of 1990–1991? What might account for the difference between what it predicted and the actual outcomes?

Problem 9.10. Use quarterly data on real GDP and worker-hours to calculate labor productivity as Y/L. On the same graph, plot your series and (using a separate scale) the government's index of labor productivity. Compute the compound annual quarterly rate of growth for each series (to remove the trends), then calculate the correlation coefficient for the two series. Comment on how closely the two estimates of productivity are related. What might explain the differences between them?

Problem 9.11. Economists widely believe that sometime in the 1960s or 1970s, productivity growth slowed down and that sometime in the mid-1990s, it sped up again. Using the U.S. government's official productivity series and any appropriate statistical tool, determine the date or dates if any of a slowdown or speedup in labor productivity. Use these dates and calculate the average rates of growth of labor productivity for each of the periods that you have identified. Describe the pattern of your findings.

10

Economic Growth

To us in the twenty-first century, a growing economy is the norm. It was not always so. In the last chapter, we investigated the problem of aggregate supply: What determines the level of GDP produced? In this chapter, we use that analysis to ask the question: what makes GDP grow over time? Our analysis allows us to address questions like: Is it more factor inputs or using them better (technological progress) that explains the growth of the economy? How fast can the economy hope to grow in the long run? What effect will growth have on personal incomes? What factors promote or retard growth? Why have some economies grown rapidly and others stagnated?

10.1 Why Growth Is Important

Look at Figure 10.1, which shows the real GNP per capita of the United States from 1789 to 2009. Two features stand out: the pronounced business cycle and the secular trend, reflecting two centuries of strong **ECONOMIC GROWTH**. The ups and downs of the business cycle certainly matter. Booms add to human well-being; slumps are a substantial source of human misery. But economic growth is far and away the most important force shaping the face of the world in which we live.

To get a rough idea of what a difference two centuries of economic growth have meant to the United States, consider that U.S. GNP per capita in 1789 was about $638 (2008 constant dollars), which stands midway between the 2008 level of Burundi ($400) and Ethiopia ($800) – two of the poorest countries in the world (see Table 2.3). The poverty line for a single person in the United States in 2008 was a little more than $10,400 – about the per capita income of Brazil. Brazil is not rich as modern countries go, but neither is it poor. It is a middle-ranked country with a relatively advanced technology (e.g., it is an exporter of aircraft). Something economically important has happened when even to have less on average than such a country as Brazil defines poverty. When most of the poor have a refrigerator, a color television, and a washing machine, growth has changed the face of

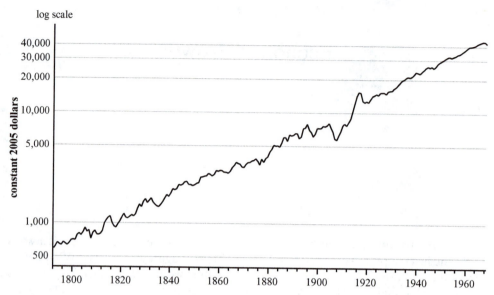

Figure 10.1. GNP per Capita in the United States. The history of U.S. per capita income fluctuates with the business cycle around the dominant upward trend. *Source: Bureau of Economic Analysis, Census Bureau, and Kevin D. Hoover and Mark V. Siegler, "Taxing and Spending in the Long View: The Causal Structure of U.S. Fiscal Policy After 1791," Oxford Economic Papers, vol. 52, no. 4, December 2000.*

Table 10.1. *Ownership of Durable Goods and Poverty Status in 2003*

	Percentage of People Owning Good Who Are:[a]		
Durable Good	Nonpoor	Poor	Total
Washing machine			92
Clothes dryer			89
Dishwasher			62
Refrigerator			99
Freezer			37
Television			99
Air conditioner			85
Stove			99
Microwave	97	89	96
VCR	92	75	90
Personal computer	67	36	63
Telephone:			
Landline	95	87	94
Cellular	67	35	63
Full Set of Appliances[b]	60	27	56

[a] In 2003, there were 111.2 million households in the United States, 13.9 million (12.5 percent) poor and 97.3 million (87.5 percent) nonpoor.

[b] A full set of appliances is defined as: washing machine, clothes dryer, refrigerator, dishwasher, and landline telephone.

Source: Annette L. Rogers and Camille L. Ryan, "Extended Measures of Well-Being: Living Conditions in the United States, 2003." *Household Economic Studies*. U.S. Census Bureau. P70–110, April 2007.

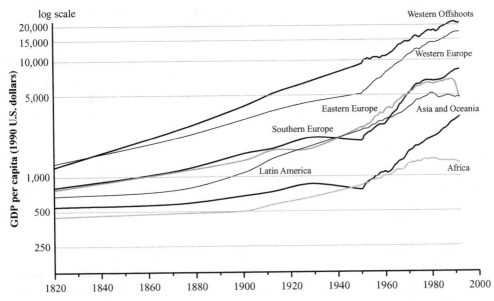

Figure 10.2. World Growth since the Industrial Revolution. *Notes:* Africa (56 countries); Asia and Oceana (56 countries) Eastern Europe (9 countries); Latin America (44 countries); Southern Europe (7 countries); Western Europe (23 countries); Western Offshoots (Australia, Canada, New Zealand, and the United States). *Source: Angus Maddison, Monitoring the World Economy, 1820–1992. Paris: OECD, Table G-3.*

poverty (see Table 10.1). Poverty in a rich country is less a matter of absolute material deprivation than of low *relative* economic and social position (see Table 10.1). A central question for macroeconomics is, how can we explain economic growth?

We take economic growth for granted. But through most of human history periods of economic growth have been rare. Although there were many technological differences, the ancient Greeks and Romans probably had as great economic resources as the Europeans who colonized the Americas 1,500 years later. A European peasant or a farm worker at the end of the eighteenth century was on average not much richer than a peasant in the Middle Ages, 500 to 800 years before. Sometime after 1750, the world changed. What is now called the Industrial Revolution accelerated the rate of technological progress and expanded the scope of organized production and markets. What is now the developed world embarked on 250 years of rapid economic growth.

Of course, this growth was not uniform across the world (see Figure 10.2). Great Britain industrialized first; the United States followed in close order. Western Europe and Japan grew rapidly by the end of the nineteenth century, while the so-called Newly Industrializing Countries (e.g., Taiwan, Korea, Malaysia, Brazil) began to grow rapidly only after World

Table 10.2. *The Importance of Growth Rates on Income per Capita*

Year	GNP per Capita		
	Level (2000 constant dollars)	Growth Rate from 100 Years Earlier (compound annual rate)	Level of GNP per Capita in 1990 if the Growth Rate in the Adjacent Column had been Sustained Constantly for 200 Years
1790	622		
1890	3,665	1.79	21,618
1990	32,397	2.20	48,302

Source: Kevin D. Hoover and Mark V. Siegler, "Two Centuries of Taxing and Spending: A Causal Investigation of the Federal Budget Process, 1791–1913," *Oxford Economic Papers*, October 2000; updated by author.

War II. Some, such as Singapore and Hong Kong, have caught up to U.S. and European levels of income per capita. Others are far behind but growing rapidly. Still others – many of them in sub-Saharan Africa – remain desperately poor. Understanding the process of growth and what makes one country industrialize successfully and another stagnate may be the most important knowledge that economists could hope to gain.

Although the United States has been the clear leader in growth for more than two centuries, the importance of growth is demonstrated by what might have been. During the one hundred years after 1790, the date of the first census, the average rate of growth of per capita income was 1.79 percent per year. It was higher over the next 100 years (2.20 percent). The difference appears small. Yet, consider (as the last column of Table 10.2 shows) that if each of these growth rates had been sustained steadily over the entire 200 years, income per capita would have been nearly 2.5 times as high at 2.20 percent than at the 1.79 percent. The small difference of less than 0.5 percentage point translates into a huge difference in outcomes – a splendid illustration of the power of compounding. The level of income per capita at the lower rate of conjectured growth is about two-thirds the actual level; whereas the level at the higher conjectured rate is about half again as large as the actual level.

An even more dramatic contrast can be seen if we consider the growth rate for income per capita between 1940 and 1970 – one of the faster thirty years of growth in U.S. history. If the growth rate over the 30-year period (2.91 percent) had been sustained from 1790 to 1990, the $622 of 1790 would have grown to $192,888. The massive increase in GDP (nearly six times the actual increase) would have resulted from an average rate of growth less than one percentage point higher than the actual average rate (2.00) over the 200 years. If economic policy could boost the average sustainable rate of

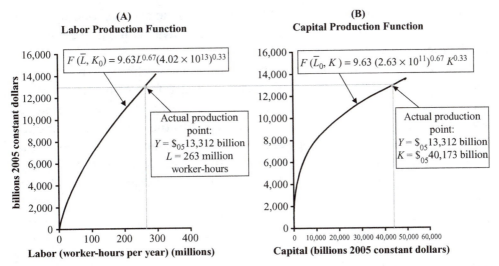

(A)
Labor Production Function

$$F(\bar{L}, K_0) = 9.63L^{0.67}(4.02 \times 10^{13})^{0.33}$$

Actual production
point:
$Y = \$_{05}13,312$ billion
$L = 263$ million
worker-hours

(B)
Capital Production Function

$$F(\bar{L}_0, K) = 9.63 (2.63 \times 10^{11})^{0.67} K^{0.33}$$

Actual production
point:
$Y = \$_{05}13,312$ billion
$K = \$_{05}40,173$ billion

billions 2005 constant dollars

Labor (worker-hours per year) (millions)

Capital (billions 2005 constant dollars)

Figure 10.3. A Cobb-Douglas Production Function for the United States, 2008.
Source: Bureau of Economic Analysis and author's calculations.

growth even by a quarter or half a percentage point, over decades it would substantially raise people's material well-being.

For the poor and the rich alike, economic growth has changed the face of our material world. As economists we need to understand that process better. In macroeconomics, we can think of this as applying the theory of aggregate supply over time. For the most part, we shall assume that aggregate demand is always adequate to the plans of firms to produce. This assumption amounts to ignoring the ever-present business cycle and acting as if the economy grew from peak to peak, always running at full potential, without intervening recessions.

10.2 Accounting for Growth

10.2.1 Production at a Point in Time and Production over Time

To understand the factors behind economic growth, it helps to look at the aggregate production function over time. In Chapter 9 we used the aggregate production function to provide a snapshot of the economy at a point in time. Equation (9.18), for example, described aggregate supply in 2008. We repeat it here as

$$Y = 9.63L^{0.67}K^{0.33}. \tag{10.1}$$

Figure 10.3 represents this equation. Only the one combination of labor and capital, one point on the graph of equation (10.1) – the point at which L and

K take their measured values for 2008 – describes the actual economy in that year. Every other point says what output would have been had the values of the factors of production been different.

Growth occurs when labor or capital increase or technology advances. If the growth of factors of production could by itself explain the growth of GDP, then equation (10.1) would be adequate. Growth would be modeled simply by plugging higher values for L and K into the equation. In practice, life is not so simple – technology changes too. For example, we can use equation (9.17) to calculate total factor productivity for 1948: $A = 4.40$. In other words, technology improved by 109 percent over 60 years. The production function for 1948 can be written as:

$$Y = 4.60 L^{0.67} K^{0.33}. \tag{10.2}$$

Not only do the factors of production change over time, the production function itself shifts. As equation (10.1) does for 2008, equation (10.2) provides a snapshot of aggregate supply in 1948. And just as in a movie, a series of snapshots builds up an image of the process of economic growth over time.

How is such a moving picture constructed? Figure 10.4 shows the relationship between the time series for GDP, labor and capital, and snapshots of their production functions. Panel (A) shows the time series for the three variables. We can consider vertical "slices" of the time series for the particular years 1948 and 2008. The appropriate values of the time series for these slices are connected to the snapshots by gray lines. The value for the coefficient A for 1948 is calculated from the first slice, and the resulting production function is shown as the lower curves in panels (B) and (C). Similarly, panels (D) and (E) show the production function for 2008. (Panels (D) and (E) are identical to Figure 10.3.) Figure 10.4 illustrates that the history of GDP over time is better described as a jumping from one point on a production function to another point on a *different* production function than as an upward movement along the same production function.

10.2.2 Decomposing Economic Growth

How much of the growth in GDP between 1948 and 2008 can be attributed to each factor of production and to technology? Some thought experiments help us answer the question. The overall change in GDP can be decomposed into three parts.

The basic data are given in Table 10.3. The 1948 aggregate production function is shown as the lower (black) curves in the two panels of

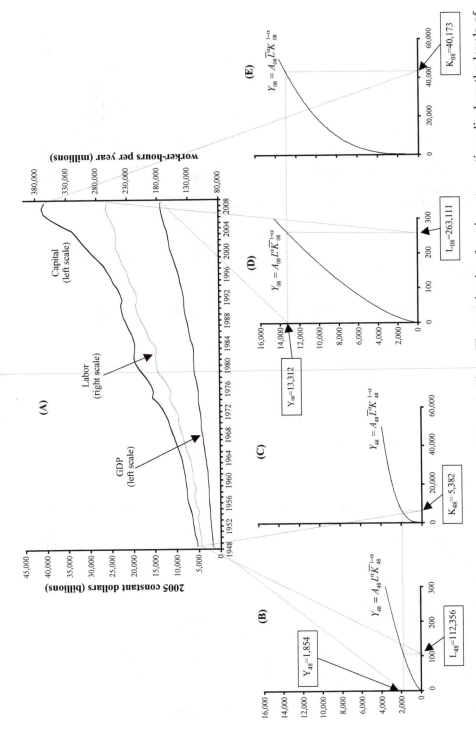

Figure 10.4. Production at a Point in Time and through Time. The production function at any time displays the levels of GDP that may be produced for different combinations of the factors of production. Only the production point shows what actually is; all the other points show what is possible. Because of technological progress, the production function shifts over time, so that the possibilities of 2008 are more extensive than those of 1948. *Source:* Bureau of Economic Analysis and author's calculations. *Source:* labor, Bureau of Labor Statistics; capital and GDP, Bureau of Economic Analysis.

359

Table 10.3. *Data for Growth Accounting*

Variable	1948	2008	Rate of Growth: 1948–2008
Y (billions 2005 constant dollars per year)	1,854	13,312	3.34%
A	4.60	9.63	1.24%
L (millions of worker-hours per year)	112,356	263,011	1.43%
K (billions 2005 constant dollars)	5,382	40,173	3.41%
α		0.67	

Note: Growth rates are calculated as average continuously compounded annual rates (see the *Guide*, section G.10.1).
Source: Bureau of Economic Analysis and author's calculations.

Figure 10.5. (These correspond to panels (B) and (C) in Figure 10.4.) The actual input/production points are marked as points A.

- **Thought experiment 1.** What would GDP have been in 1948 if *ceteris paribus* the 2008 labor input had been available?

To answer this question, we plug in the labor value for 2008, along with all the other values for 1948, into equation (10.2):

$$Y_{48}^{\dagger} = A_{48} L_{08}^{0.67} K_{48}^{0.33}$$

$$= 4.60(263{,}011 \text{ million worker-hours})^{0.67} (\$5{,}382 \text{ billion})^{0.33} \quad (10.3)$$

$$= \$3{,}276 \text{ billion}.$$

The superscript "dagger" on *Y* indicates that it is not actual GDP but **counterfactual** GDP – that is, *what GDP would have been if something* (in this case, the labor input) *had been different*. We can say that GDP would have been $1,422 billion (77 percent) higher in 1948 if the labor of 2008 had been available to the production process.

In Figure 10.5, the first thought experiment is shown as the movement from point A to point B along the original labor production function in panel (A), which raises GDP to $3,276. Of course, the capital production function in panel (B) must shift up so that production occurs at the original level of capital and the new level of GDP (point B on the gray, middle curve of panel (B)).

It would be easy to conduct a similar thought experiment:

- **Thought experiment 2.** What would GDP have been in 1948 if *ceteris paribus* the 2008 capital input had been available?

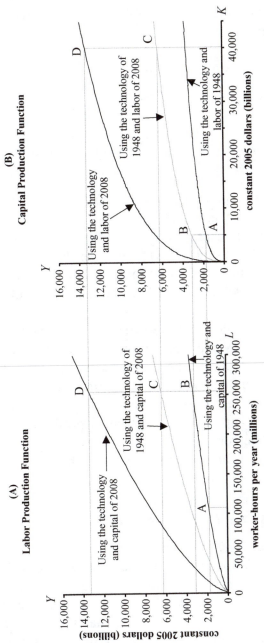

Figure 10.5. The Sources of Economic Growth. How much growth in GDP is due to growth in the factors of production and how much to changes in technology? The lower curves represent the actual production functions of 1948; the upper curves represent the actual production of 2008. The middle two curves in each panel are drawn with the technology (*A*) of 1948. The movement from point A to point B shows how much additional GDP is due to the increase in labor (*L*); from point B to C, the additional amount due to capital. The movement from point B to C, the additional amount due to capital. The distance between points C and D shows how much technology has added to GDP once changes in labor and capital are accounted for. *Source:* labor, Bureau of Labor Statistics; capital and GDP, Bureau of Economic Analysis.

We leave the answer of this experiment to Problem 10.2. Instead, let us turn to a different thought experiment:

- **Thought experiment 3.** What would GDP have been in 1948 if *ceteris paribus* both the 2008 labor and capital inputs had been available?

Using the appropriate values from Table 10.3:

$$Y^{\dagger}_{48} = A_{48} L^{0.67}_{08} K^{0.33}_{08}$$
$$= 4.60(263{,}011 \text{ million worker-hours})^{0.67}(\$40{,}173 \text{ billion})^{0.33} \quad (10.4)$$
$$= \$6{,}360 \text{ billion.}$$

Using both the labor and the capital inputs from 2008, GDP in 1948 would have been $4,506 billion (243 percent) higher in 1948.

In Figure 10.5, the increase in capital is shown as a movement along the capital production function in panel (B) from point B to point C. The increase in capital shifts the labor production function in panel (A) upward, so that output occurs at the 2008 level of labor and the new level of GDP (point C).

Even after both inputs have been allowed to take 2008 levels, GDP in 1948 would still fall substantially short of actual GDP in 2008. The difference between actual GDP in 2008 and the counterfactual GDP of the third thought experiment ($6,952 billion or 52 percent) provides a measure of the contribution of improved technology to economic growth. The upper (black) curves in Figure 10.5 represent the aggregate production function in 2008 (equation (10.2)). The vertical distance between points C and D in both panels represents the contribution of technological change to economic growth.

10.2.3 Accounting for Growth Rates

The three thought experiments help to clarify what we mean when we ask how much the three factors – labor, capital, and technology – contributed to economic growth. But the analysis is clumsy and can be greatly simplified. In 1957, Robert Solow, later the winner of the Nobel Prize in Economic Science for his work on economic growth, provided a classic analysis of this question. Solow's approach is easily implemented using the Cobb-Douglas production function.[1]

Start with the production function:

$$Y = AL^{\alpha} K^{1-\alpha}.$$

Using the algebra of growth rates and the notation that a hat ("^") over a variable indicates the percentage rate of growth (see the *Guide*,

[1] Any production function that shows constant returns to scale should support the same results.

Table 10.4. *Accounting for Real GDP Growth, 1948–2008*

Contributing Factor	Contribution to GDP Growth	
	Percentage Points	Fraction of Overall Growth Rate (percent)
Technological change	1.24	37
Growth in labor inputs	0.96	29
Growth in capital inputs	1.12	34
Total	3.34[a]	100

[a] Column does not sum to total because of rounding.
Source: Table 10.3 and author's calculations.

section G.10.4), the production function can be rewritten as

$$\hat{Y} = \hat{A} + \alpha\hat{L} + (1-\alpha)\hat{K}. \tag{10.5}$$

The equation says that the growth rate of output can be decomposed into a weighted average of three parts: the rate of technological change ($\hat{A}$ entering with a weight of one), the rate of growth of labor ($\hat{L}$, entering with a weight equal to labor's share of GDP, α), and the growth rate of capital ($\hat{K}$, entering with a weight equal to capital's share of GDP, $1-\alpha$).

We can compute each of the terms on the right-hand side of equation (10.2) to find out how many percentage points each of the factors contributes to the total rate of growth of GDP. Equally, we can divide both sides by $\hat{Y}$ to yield

$$1 = \frac{\hat{A}}{\hat{Y}} + \alpha\frac{\hat{L}}{\hat{Y}} + (1-\alpha)\frac{\hat{K}}{\hat{Y}}. \tag{10.6}$$

Each term on the right-hand side now gives the fraction of the total change attributable to one of the elements of the production function.

To account for the importance of each element in explaining growth from 1948 to 2008, use the data in Table 10.3 to calculate the average growth rates of each factor and GDP. Then plug these into equation (10.6). The results are shown in Table 10.4. Although a substantial proportion of the growth in output in the period after World War II can be attributed to the direct effect of increased inputs, the largest single factor is the fact that the technology used to convert those inputs into output improved by nearly 40 percent overall.

10.3 The Sources of Economic Growth

The decomposition of GDP growth rates into parts attributed to labor, capital, and technology tells us *what*. We next consider the *how* and the *why* behind each of the main determinants of economic growth, considering improvements in technology and the growth of the labor and capital inputs in turn.

10.3.1 Productivity and Technological Progress

The first determinant of economic growth, technological change, is the least well understood. There is no doubt that it is happening. And, as we saw in the previous section, we can measure its effects. But the exact mechanisms through which technological progress affects growth are not clearly understood and are widely debated.

Product Innovation

Technical change is evident. At the beginning of the twentieth century, steam and water ran factories, railroads and ships dominated long-distance transportation, and the telegraph was the premier mode of communication. The automobile, the airplane, and radio were in their infancies. Electric power and the telephone were barely in their adolescence. Nuclear power, television, and the electronic computer were not even the stuff of dreams. Within one lifetime, the technological landscape has changed almost beyond recognition.

Yet, despite the dramatic changes, the effects of technological development have been steady and incremental rather than revolutionary. Economic historians report that new inventions were typically introduced over many years, so that the new technology and the evidently inferior old technologies worked side by side for decades. The electric motor coexisted with steam-powered and water-powered, belt-driven tools. The railroad coexisted with canals. The tractor, available from earlier in the twentieth century, did not fully replace horses on American farms until after World War II.

The laser, one of the fundamental discoveries of the early 1960s, is now found in bar code readers, fiber-optic communication systems, medical instruments, and compact disc drives. Yet it was never patented, because for thirty years it did not appear to have economic applications.

The greatest puzzle of all is the computer itself. It clearly led to a *qualitative* change in modern life and opened up enormous possibilities in data processing, communication, design, education, and other areas. Yet until recently, economists were hard pressed to find a measurable increase in the productive capacity of the economy that could be directly attributed to the computer. Surely there is one, but it has not been easy to pin down. (In Problem 10.6, the student is asked to analyze this question in a growth-accounting framework using data from an economic study.)

Labor, capital, and total factor productivity (see Chapter 9, section 9.3) all aim to quantify a common feature of the economy: technological progress

makes it possible to do more with less. However we measure it, technological progress shows up as an upward shift of the production function.
Typically, we think of technological progress as reflected in different kinds
of machinery and different kinds of physical capital.

On the one hand, there has been a succession of innovative machinery,
either doing entirely new jobs (e.g., the radio) or doing old jobs better (the
automobile replacing the carriage or wagon). On the other hand, each of
these technologies has been improved – often by many orders of magnitude.
A famous example of steady improvement is Moore's law: the capacity of
computer chips doubles every 18 to 24 months. Intel's 4004 chip contained
2,300 transistors in 1971; its Quad-core Tukwila Itanium chip contained 2
billion transistors in 2008. (The average doubling time using these data is a
little more than 22 months.)

Process Innovation

To think of technological innovation only in the guise of new machines limits
our view. Processes are important too. In the early nineteenth century, Eli
Whitney – inventor of the cotton gin – was also the inventor, or at least an
early user, of the idea of interchangeable parts. Previously, the lock, stock,
and barrel were custom made by a gunsmith and fit only one particular musket. Whitney's idea was to make every part identical to close tolerances, so
that any part would fit any musket. This allowed him to fulfill a contract with
the U.S. Army for 10,000 muskets in two years – faster than any gunsmiths
of the time thought possible.

At the beginning of the twentieth century, Henry Ford combined the idea
of interchangeable parts with that of the assembly line to produce the Model
T – the first automobile cheap enough for ordinary workers to afford. Neither Ford nor Whitney relied on any radical innovation in the machinery.
Instead, they changed the way in which the machinery was used.

Similarly, in the late nineteenth and early twentieth centuries, the American efficiency expert Frederick Winslow Taylor observed, measured, and
timed the smallest tasks involved in production processes and then tried to
design "the one best way" for workers to perform each task. Taylorism lives
on in many modern firms – for example, McDonald's and the United Parcel
Service. In some contexts, it produces impressive gains in productivity and
quality control. Yet, it is often thought inhuman – reducing workers to cogs
in the machinery. It became the butt of satire in Charlie Chaplin's famous
silent movie *Modern Times*.

In the 1980s, American businesses became interested in Japanese methods
of production that were almost the opposite of Taylorism, in which workers took more responsibility for the whole production process. These were
reflected in ideas such as "quality circles" and "total quality management,"

in which workers were usually less specialized; and their own experience on the job, rather than the rules of an outside expert, guided process development. Similarly, "just-in-time inventory management" and new arrangements between firms and their suppliers were aimed at achieving productivity gains. These modern ideas, like Taylorism a century ago, do not introduce new types of machines so much as reorganize the work to generate productivity gains.

The net effect of all technical change is that we do more for less. An amusing observation that both illustrates substantial technical change and that, at the same time, points to some of its sources is that GDP is only a little larger now than it was in 1900 – *if we measure by the* weight *of output*. Economically, we obviously would not measure GDP this way. But how is it possible that our vastly larger GDP of today weighs little more than GDP of one hundred years past? One factor is that materials are used more efficiently. Recall Moore's law – very light computer chips replace heavier technologies, and they improved exponentially. Similarly, the productivity gains due to the organization of work are weightless. Perhaps the most important factor, however, is the shift of the mix of GDP from things to services. Cars, food, and clothing are heavy, but financial, medical, and educational services (the final goods, not the inputs needed to produce them) are weightless.

Research and Development

Some aspects of technological progress can occur nearly accidentally, as when a discovery in pure science or a casual observation turns out to have important economic uses. The laser, mentioned earlier, is an example of the first; the ability of a certain mold to kill bacteria that led to the development of penicillin is an example of the second. Economists refer to such cases as **exogenous technological progress**: a new technology arises independently of economic considerations. More important, however, is **endogenous technological progress**: a new technology is developed in response to economic incentives. The penicillin mold was discovered accidentally by the Scottish physician Alexander Fleming in 1926. But it was only as the result of a conscious decision to develop an antibacterial agent during World War II that researchers at Oxford University, Howard W. Florey and Ernst B. Chain, synthesized medical penicillin. (Fleming, Florey, and Chain shared the Nobel Prize for the discovery and development of penicillin.) The development of antibiotic drugs after the war was largely the result of targeted, large-scale **RESEARCH AND DEVELOPMENT (R&D)** – partly by universities and nonprofit research institutes, but largely by pharmaceutical companies in search of profits.

The development of antibiotics in many ways typifies endogenous technological progress. Most new ideas are not immediately useful, but must be developed in some way. Research and development creates a new idea without immediate economic payoff (as happened at Bell Laboratories with the laser); but often R&D borrows the root ideas from other sources and works to develop them in ways that will turn out to be profitable. This pattern is, no doubt, ancient. Yet, a modern innovation is that R&D has become a business in itself.

Thomas Edison's famous laboratory in Menlo Park, New Jersey, provides an early – if not the earliest – example of *systematic* research and development of technology for profit. There he invented the light bulb, the phonograph, the stock-market ticker, the carbon-button telephone microphone, and many other ubiquitous products. Some businesses – for example, some biotechnology or computer technology firms – operate on Edison's model, developing technologies that are licensed or sold to producers. Other businesses include their R&D arms within the productive enterprise. Either way, the central point is that much of the innovation in the modern economy is an intentional and focused response to profit opportunities, a response to changing relative prices and not simple good luck – endogenous rather than exogenous technological progress.

10.3.2 The Growth of Labor

The second determinant of economic growth is the growth of the labor input to production.

The Law of Motion of Labor

How fast the labor force grows depends on how fast the population was growing sixteen to twenty years before (the length of time it takes to get children up to the employable age) and how fast the rate of participation of potential workers in actual employment is changing. As we shall see in Chapter 11 (section 11.2.2), the participation rate in the United States has changed markedly since the middle of the 1960s; but it cannot keep changing at a high rate for very long, because participation can never exceed 100 percent.

The English economist Sir Roy Harrod (1900–1978), a pioneer of the economics of growth, referred to the long-term rate of growth of the labor force that resulted from population growth, rather than from temporary changes in participation rates, as the **NATURAL RATE OF GROWTH** – indicated by the constant n. A **LAW OF MOTION** describes the development of a quantity through time. The law of motion for labor can be written in terms of the natural rate of growth:

$$L_t = (1 + n)L_{t-1}. \qquad (10.7)$$

The stock of labor each period is *n* percent higher than the period before. If we pick a starting point, call it time 0, at which the stock of labor takes a known value, L_0, then the law of motion can also be written:

$$L_t = L_0(1 + n)^t, \tag{10.8}$$

where time *t* is measured as the number of periods after time 0.[2] The equation shows that labor grows exponentially at rate *n* (see the *Guide*, section G.11.3).

In many cases in macroeconomic analysis we are concerned about time horizons over which we can take the rate of population growth (and of the potential labor force) as outside of the influence of economic considerations. Although such an assumption is often a reasonable approximation, it may prove a poor one if we wish to explain growth in the long term or why different countries have grown at different rates.

Malthusianism

The rate of growth of the labor force or population was once the centerpiece of economic analysis. Given modern concerns for poverty in the developing countries and for the environment, many of those early discussions continue to resonate in popular discussions and policy debates. In the late eighteenth and early nineteenth centuries, economists such as David Ricardo (1772–1823) and T. Robert Malthus (1766–1834) argued that the rate of population growth was a function of the real wage.

Their idea was that when the real wage was high, workers were well nourished and could support larger families. They may have chosen to have more children; but, in any case, the children they did have were more likely to survive to adulthood. The increased number of workers increased the competition for work and drove the real wage back down. Now workers found themselves with inadequate resources. They and their families were likely to be malnourished and to become the victims of disease and early death. They might delay marriage or otherwise reduce the number of children conceived, and the population would fall. Equilibrium would be established at which the real wage was just large enough that the workers and the productive resources were in balance. The wage that maintains such equilibrium is called the **subsistence wage**. It was, in all probability, a poverty wage. Malthus's and Ricardo's pessimistic view of the economy was often called the **iron law of wages**.[3]

---

[2] Mathematically, equation (10.8) is the solution to the difference equation (10.7) when the value of labor at time 0 is given by L_0.

[3] Many economists and others believe that Carlyle's famous description of economics as "the dismal science" referred to the iron law of wages. In fact, it was a slur against economists (particular, John Stuart Mill) who opposed Carlyle's racist views. See David M. Levy, *How the Dismal Science Got Its*

Malthus is one of the two or three most famous economists of all time because of his **principle of population** from which the iron law of wages is derived. Malthus argued that, *unchecked*, population tends to grow exponentially, while food and other resources grow, at best, arithmetically. Consequently, population constantly threatens to outstrip resources. But, of course, it cannot actually outstrip resources, so one way or another population growth must be checked.

Contrary to both the modern critics and the advocates (often environmentalists) of modern Malthusianism, Malthus was not predicting *future* disaster. Instead, he was trying to explain current misery and to show that certain utopian ideas were not feasible. The key word is "unchecked." Malthus recognized two sorts of checks to population growth. *Positive* checks are the unpleasant consequences of insufficient resources: malnutrition, disease, and the resulting early death. He also recognized a *prudential* check: people wishing to maintain a standard of living taking steps to prevent their families from growing too large to support.[4]

Population could grow rapidly only if some extraordinary circumstance released these checks. The European discovery of the Americas, for example, made rapid population growth possible. In Malthus's view, given the development of their food gathering and farming technology, the native inhabitants had reached the limits of their population growth. But Europeans brought new farming technologies that allowed a higher level of production and, therefore, a higher level of population. In the transition from an initial low population to a new much higher equilibrium level, population could grow very rapidly.

Economic Development and the Stabilization of Population

Many modern commentators take the spectacular growth of population and real GDP over the past 200 years as proof that Malthus was wrong. But they misunderstand his analysis. True, the technological progress over these two centuries, especially the progress in agriculture, would have surprised Malthus – as indeed it has persistently surprised many. But given that progress, which removed the positive checks, Malthus would himself have predicted the population growth. Equally, the material prosperity (the increased real wages and income per capita) that have accompanied growth would have surprised Malthus. It would have been a pleasant surprise,

---

Name: Classical Economics and the Ur-text of Racial Politics. Ann Arbor: University of Michigan Press, 2001.

[4] There is substantial evidence that, even in Malthus's day, long before modern birth control, people could exercise considerable control over family size – through the delay of marriage, abstinence, and what we would now call "natural family planning." In 1800, the birthrate in the United States was 275 per 1,000 women aged 15–44. By 1960, the year in which the birth-control pill was first marketed, it had fallen by 57 percent to 118; by 2007, it fell another 41 percent to 69.

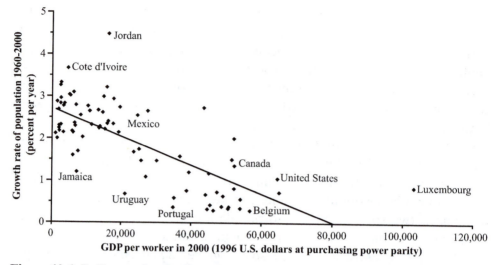

Figure 10.6. Is Prosperity the Best Contraceptive? Each point represents a country. Countries with higher GDP per capita tend to have lower rates of population growth. The slope of the regression line indicates that for each $10,000 in additional GDP per worker, the average population growth rate falls 0.3 percentage points. ($R^2 = 0.53$.) *Source:* Penn World Tables, version 6.1.

because Malthus had always hoped that workers would substitute the prudential check – a desire for a higher standard of living leading to smaller family size – for the misery of the positive check.

A cliché in the field of economic development is that prosperity is the best birth control. Richer countries tend to have lower rates of population growth. For example, the population of India (income per capita of $2,900 per year in 2008) is growing at 1.6 percent per year; while the population of Italy (income per capita of $31,300 per year) is growing at −0.05 percent per year. Figure 10.6 shows a strong negative relationship (correlation coefficient $R = -0.73$) between GDP per capita in 2000 and the average rate of population growth over the period 1960–2000. This would have appealed to Malthus's optimistic side.

Still, Malthus is ultimately correct that population must stabilize, whether at a high or low level of income per capita. And we can already see it happening. As the world becomes richer, the overall growth rate of population is slowing. Many demographers predict that the world population growth rate, 1.19 percent per year in 2008, will fall to less than 0.5 percent per year by 2050. And one way or another various checks must operate to bring population growth to a halt. The proof is simple: unchecked population growth must eventually exhaust the Earth's resources. At current rates of population growth, in approximately 2,400 years the weight of the entire mass of humanity would exceed the mass of the Earth itself.[5] Long before that, other

---

[5] This conclusion is based on the following calculation. The mass of the earth is 1.3228×10^{24} lbs. If the average person weighs 100 lbs, this is the equivalent of 1.3176×10^{22} people. In 2008, there were

checks would take hold. The message is not one of impending doom. There are good ways to slow down population growth (the low birthrates of Japan and Europe) and horrible ones (the epidemics of AIDS and the genocidal wars of central Africa).

10.3.3 The Growth of Capital

Although the growth of labor (and population) shows considerable inertia and responds to economic forces only in the long run, the factors that govern the growth of capital are the result of more immediate macroeconomic decisions. Recall from Chapter 2 (section 2.2.2) that, to an economist, "investment" is the acquisition of new physical means of production. Investment, like GDP, is measured as a flow of the dollar value of goods per quarter or per year. Investment adds to the stock of capital. The relationship can also be represented as a simple law of motion:

$$K_t = K_{t-1} + I_{t-1} - Depreciation_{t-1}. \tag{10.9}$$

Capital today is capital yesterday plus whatever investment is left over once we have made good the wear and tear on existing capital.

We should think of the stock of capital as measured at the beginning of each period, and investment and depreciation as carried on within the period. The variable I is sometimes referred to as **gross investment** (see Chapter 3, section 3.4). It is *the amount of GDP that is devoted to maintaining and increasing the stock of capital.* **Depreciation** is *the amount of capital that is lost during the production process.* It is the item referred to in the national-income-and-product accounts as "capital consumption." The last two terms in the equation are referred to as **net investment** (equals $I_{t-1} - Depreciation_{t-1}$), defined as *the amount of investment* net *of depreciation, the amount that investment adds to the stock of capital.* Subtracting K_{t-1} from each side allows us to relate investment to the change in the capital stock:

$$\Delta K_t = K_t - K_{t-1} = I_{t-1} - Depreciation_{t-1} = net\ I_{t-1}. \tag{10.10}$$

How fast capital grows is, then, a product of the economic decision of how much to invest and the technological fact that the capital stock depreciates, either through physical wear and tear or economic obsolescence.

What is the rate of growth of capital? Divide both sides of equation (10.10) by K_{t-1}:

$$\hat{K}_t = \Delta K_t / K_{t-1} = net\ I_{t-1} / K_{t-1}. \tag{10.11}$$

6.7 billion people on earth and the population grew at a rate of 1.19 percent per year. Using a standard growth equation, we get $1.3228 \times 10^{22} = (6.7 \times 10^9)(1.0119)^t$. To solve for t, first divide by (6.7×10^9) and then take logarithms (see the *Guide*, section G.11) to get $\log[1.3228 \times 10^{22}/(6.7 \times 10^9)] = t\log(1.0119)$. Solve for $t = \log[1.3228 - 10^{22}/(6.7 \times 10^9)]/\log(1.0119) = 2,393$ years.

Multiplying the right-hand side of equation (10.11) by Y_{t-1}/Y_{t-1} gives

$$\hat{K}_t = \left(\frac{net\,I_{t-1}}{K_{t-1}}\right)\left(\frac{Y_{t-1}}{Y_{t-1}}\right) = \left(\frac{net\,I_{t-1}}{Y_{t-1}}\right)\left(\frac{Y_{t-1}}{K_{t-1}}\right). \qquad (10.11')$$

The first factor on the right-hand side is the share of net investment in GDP, and the second term is capital productivity (ϕ). So, we can rewrite equation (10.11') as

$$\hat{K}_t = \left(\frac{net\,I_{t-1}}{Y_{t-1}}\right)\left(\frac{Y_{t-1}}{K_{t-1}}\right)\hat{K}_t = \phi_{t-1}\,net\,investment\,share_{t-1}. \qquad (10.11'')$$

Written in this form, the equation shows that the rate of growth of capital depends on the available technology (the capital productivity coefficient ϕ) and the economic choice of how much to invest. An increase in capital productivity or an increase in the rate of investment *ceteris paribus* boosts the rate of growth of capital; while an increase in the depreciation rate lowers net investment and, therefore, lowers the rate of growth of capital.

There is some evidence, however, that all things cannot in reality be held equal. More productive computer technology has been associated with a faster rate of economic obsolescence. The gain to capital growth from increased productivity would in that case be partly offset by the fall in net investment owing to higher depreciation rates. The key economic variable is the rate of investment (I). We shall examine the economic determinants of investment in Chapters 13 and 14.

10.4 The Neoclassical Growth Model

Now that we have looked at the factors that govern the growth of technology, labor, and capital, it is time to ask how they interact to determine the growth of GDP. A good starting place is the NEOCLASSICAL GROWTH MODEL. This term describes a family of models in which aggregate production is described by a constant-returns-to-scale production function (e.g., by the Cobb-Douglas production function) and in which the use of the factors of production can be adjusted quickly and flexibly to changes in relative prices so that full employment of resources is maintained at all times (i.e., there is no unemployment or labor hoarding, and capacity utilization is always 100 percent). Obviously, such a model cannot describe the business cycle, but it can describe the growth of potential GDP – the path of the economy from peak to peak. In the first subsection, we explore the process of economic growth using some of the general properties of the neoclassical growth model. In the following subsection, we develop a particular version of the neoclassical growth model – the Solow-Swan growth model – that can be used for a more detailed analysis.

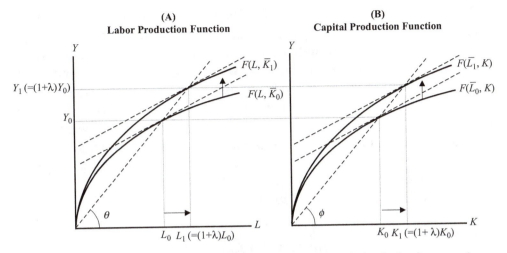

Figure 10.7. Balanced Growth. On a balanced growth path both the factors of production (L and K) and GDP (Y) grow at the same rate (indicated on the diagram as λ). All factor productivities (θ and ϕ) remain constant, shown by the production points lying along the same rays from the origin at higher as at lower levels of GDP. All marginal products (and, therefore, all factor prices) remain constant, shown by the fact that the tangents to the higher and lower production points are parallel.

10.4.1 The Process of Growth

Balanced Growth without Technological Progress

It is less complicated to start with the assumption that technology is not changing. Because aggregate production can be well described using a constant-returns-to-scale production function, one possible path for economic growth is to expand smoothly, so that the economy of 2010 is just a scaled-up version of the economy in 1910: labor, capital, and output are all bigger by exactly the same proportion. This idea of smooth or balanced growth is shown in Figure 10.7. The upper production functions represent an economy that is λ percent bigger than the economy of the lower production functions.

Under constant returns to scale and equal proportional increases in factors of production, the productivities of labor and capital remain constant – that is, the production points on the upper and lower production functions lie on the same ray from the origin (see Chapter 9, section 9.1.1). Notice that the **capital-labor ratio** (*the amount of capital per worker*) is $\kappa = K/L = \theta/\phi$. Because both labor productivity (θ) and capital productivity (ϕ) are constant, the capital-labor ratio is also constant. As the economy grows, there is more capital, but it is spread out over more workers. This is called CAPITAL WIDENING.

Also notice that in Figure 10.7, the slopes of the tangents at the production points for the upper curves are equal to those for the lower curves (they are parallel). This means that the marginal products of labor and capital remained constant as the economy grew. Because the rule for profit maximization (see Chapter 9, section 9.1.2) says that firms should use factors of production until the marginal product of each factor is equal to its real price, the real wage (w/p) and the real rental rate (v/p) must also be constant.

Taken together, these properties define **BALANCED GROWTH**:

An economy displays balanced growth without technological progress *when all real aggregates grow at the same constant rate (i.e., their ratios are constant) and when the marginal products of the factors of production and, therefore, factor prices remain constant.*

Balanced Growth with Technological Progress

As we saw in Chapter 9 (section 9.3.2), factor productivities could change either from shifting relative factor intensity with the same technology or from secular improvements in technology. Changes in factor intensities that are a result of a business cycle tend to cancel out over time, so that, in the end, productivity tends to follow technological developments. On average, labor productivity grows at the same rate as labor-augmenting technological progress ($\hat{\bar{\theta}} = \hat{\bar{A}}_L$) and capital productivity at the same rate as capital-augmenting technological progress ($\hat{\bar{\phi}} = \hat{\bar{A}}_K$). A factor-augmenting improvement in technology has exactly the same effect on GDP as an increase in the factor itself of the same proportion. For example, if the labor force grows at n and the rate of improvement in labor productivity due to labor-augmenting technological progress is $\hat{\bar{\theta}} = \hat{\bar{A}}_L$, then we can analyze the growth of GDP as if the labor force grew at $n + \hat{\bar{\theta}}$. Similarly, if the growth in capital productivity were due to capital-augmenting technological progress, GDP would grow as if the capital stock grew at $\hat{K} + \hat{\bar{\phi}}$. Balanced growth now requires not that GDP grows at the same rate as labor and capital, but that GDP grows at the same rate as labor and capital adjusted for technologically induced improvements in productivity.

Notice that the capital-labor ratio (K/L) will now be constant only if the growth rates of capital and labor productivity are the same. As we saw in Figure 9.14, capital productivity in the United States shows little secular growth, while labor productivity trends constantly upward. In that case, balanced growth requires the capital stock to grow rapidly to keep up with the growth of both labor and labor productivity – so the capital-labor ratio must rise at a trend rate approximately equal to $\hat{\bar{\theta}}$. (Problem 10.8 asks the student to supply a proof.)

Similarly, once there is technological progress, marginal products and factor prices will no longer remain constant. Recall that, according to equation

(9.9), the marginal product of labor for the Cobb-Douglas production function can be written as

$$mpL = \alpha \left(\frac{K}{L}\right)^{1-\alpha} = \frac{\alpha Y}{L} = \alpha \theta, \tag{10.12}$$

where we have used the definition of θ to eliminate Y/L to get the last term. The growth rate of the marginal product of labor can be written:

$$\widehat{mpL} = \hat{\alpha} + \hat{\theta} = \hat{\theta}. \tag{10.13}$$

The last term is implied by the assumption that α is constant, so that $\hat{\alpha} = 0$. Equation (10.13) shows that the marginal product of labor must grow at the same rate as labor productivity.

Because the real wage and the marginal product of labor are equal under perfect competition, the real wage should also grow at the same rate.

$$\widehat{\left(\frac{w}{p}\right)} = \widehat{mpL} = \hat{\theta}. \tag{10.14}$$

A parallel argument can be made to show that the marginal product of capital and the real rental rate should grow at the same rate as capital productivity.

According to the data used in Figure 9.14, from 1948 through 2008 labor productivity grew at an average rate of 1.9 percent per year, and capital productivity showed almost no growth. We should, therefore, have expected substantial growth in the real wage and almost no change in profit rates (the analogue of the real rental rate).

Putting the considerations of this section together leads to a modification of our earlier definition:

An economy displays balanced growth with technological progress *when real GDP grows at the same constant rate as labor and capital adjusted for factor-augmenting technological progress, such that the marginal products and prices of the factors of production grow at constant (but perhaps different) rates consistent with the relationship* n $+ \hat{\theta} = \hat{K} + \hat{\phi}$.

Unbalanced Growth

What happens if growth is not balanced? To keep things simple, we assume once again that there is no technological progress.

Consider the case in which labor grows faster than capital. In Figure 10.8 labor is governed by the law of motion for labor (equation (10.7)), so that at period t labor is L_t and one period later it is $L_{t+1} = (1 + n)L_t$. Capital grows so that $K_{t+1} = (1 + \hat{K})K_t$, but by proportionally less than labor: $\hat{K} < n$. The increase in GDP is greater than it would have been had both factors grown

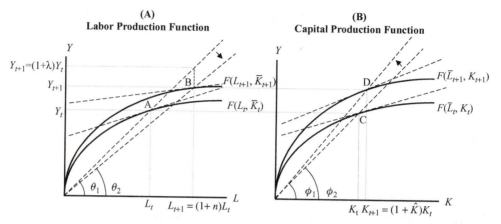

Figure 10.8. Unbalanced Growth. The diagram shows one of many unbalanced growth paths: here labor grows faster than capital. Output rises by a greater proportion than capital and by a smaller proportion than labor. The labor production function shifts up because of the increase in capital, but not by enough to offset diminishing returns to labor. The capital production function shifts up because of the increase in labor, but more than enough to offset diminishing returns to capital. As a result, labor productivity(θ) falls and capital productivity(ϕ) rises. The marginal product of labor and, therefore, the real wage fall, shown by the decreased slope of the tangent to the upper labor production function compared to the lower, and the marginal product of capital and the real (implicit) rental ratio rise.

at the slower rate $\hat{K}$ and smaller than if both had grown at the faster rate n. (The growth rate of GDP is an average of these two rates.[6])

In period $t + 1$, labor has become *relatively* more abundant. If firms could not adjust their production techniques in response to changing conditions, then the extra labor would simply remain unemployed – constrained by the fact that there is not enough capital, using the current technique, to outfit the new workers. But when, as we assume in the long run, firms can adjust, they respond to changing factor prices.

When the supply of anything rises, its *relative* price (here the real wage) falls. Point A on the production function for period t represents the original average product of labor (θ_1) and the original marginal product of labor. Because the real wage has fallen, firms want to hire more labor at a lower marginal product of labor. Their response to changing relative prices moves the production point along the labor production function; the increase in the capital stock shifts the production function upward. As a result, production shifts from point A to point B on the production function for period $t + 1$.

---

[6] Proof: $1 + \hat{Y}_t = \frac{Y_{t+1}}{Y_t} = \frac{A[(1+n)L_t]^\alpha[(1+\hat{K})K_t]^{1-\alpha}}{Y_t} = \frac{(1+n)^\alpha(1+\hat{K})^{1-\alpha}AL_t^\alpha K_t^{1-\alpha}}{Y_t} = \frac{(1+n)^\alpha(1+\hat{K})^{1-\alpha}Y_t}{Y_t} = (1+n)^\alpha$
$(1+\hat{K}_t)^{1-\alpha}$.

The product of the first two factors on the far right-hand side is the *weighted* geometric mean of $(1 + n)$ and $(1 + \hat{K})$ and must lie between them.

Here, not only is the marginal product of labor lower, the average product of labor has also fallen to θ_2.

In contrast, capital has become relatively scarce, so that the real rental rate rises. Instead of maintaining the old marginal product of capital and the old average products of capital (ϕ_1) at point C, firms economize on the now relatively more expensive capital, moving the production point to a steeper part of the production function for period $t + 1$ at point D, where the marginal product of capital is higher to match the higher real rental rate. As a result, the average product of capital rises to ϕ_2.

There is no unemployment or excess capacity in this example precisely because the market responds to the changing factor prices by choosing a technique more appropriate to the new relative factor supplies. Notice that as we move from period t to period $t + 1$, the capital labor ratio κ ($= K/L = \theta/\phi$) falls, because θ falls and ϕ rises.[7]

We could just as well have considered the case in which capital grew faster than labor. Although the details are left as an exercise (see Problem 10.9), it is intuitively obvious that the capital-labor ratio would rise in this case, instead of falling as in the previous example. The capital-labor ratio provides a measure of **capital intensity** defined as *the amount of capital per unit of labor*. Along a balanced growth path, the economy experiences capital widening, but capital intensity remains constant. Along an unbalanced growth path, firms respond to changes in relative factor supplies, so capital intensity changes. When capital grows faster than labor, capital intensity increases, which is known as CAPITAL DEEPENING: *there is more capital available for each worker to use*. We have already seen that capital deepening will occur when the rate of labor-augmenting technological progress exceeds the rate of capital-augmenting technological progress.

It is not just the mix of broad categories such as capital and labor that changes in response to changing prices, but as we saw in Chapter 9 (section 9.1.2), the detailed mix of all the inputs to the production process and the technologies needed to support that mix changes as well. This process of adjusting the mix of inputs to changing supplies is essential to keeping the economy growing smoothly (see Box 10.1).

Convergence to Balanced Growth

So far, we have considered only what happens when factors grow in an unbalanced manner for a period or two. What happens over longer periods?

---

[7] These changes in θ and ϕ do not contradict our initial assumption of constant technology as they must occur in a manner that holds total factory productivity (A) constant. Changes in these average products correspond to selecting different techniques from the available set represented by the production function, rather than a new technology that would offer new techniques and a new production function.

Box 10.1. Relative Prices in the Growth Process

The genius of the market economy is that prices convey information more subtle than the most comprehensive planner with the largest computer could ever hope to process. When computer chips are in short supply their prices rise, rationing their sale to those most willing to pay the higher prices and signaling a profit opportunity to manufacturers that says both, "ramp up production if possible" and "add capacity if necessary." When oil is plentiful, its price is low, signaling producers to cut back on pumping and refining and to lower capacity and to slow down on developing new oil fields. Prices are central in conveying information about the technologies that support growth. They provide signals that guide producers on the substitution among the factors of production. The neoclassical growth model assumes that the price system works smoothly and rapidly.

In 1972, the Club of Rome, an international think-tank, issued a famous report entitled *The Limits to Growth*. They predicted shortages of many key commodity inputs – such as oil, natural gas, industrial metals, and foodstuffs – as well as increasing unemployment throughout the world as the result of economic growth. Four decades later, their predictions have not been realized. It is instructive to see why.

Although their predictions were based on a complex model, its core was a growth model that did not allow substitution among the factors of production: a model based on production functions similar to the *short-run, inflexible* production function of Chapter 9 (section 9.4.1). As we have seen, when an economy has such a production function, unemployment of labor and other resources is possible. And, in fact, if techniques could not adjust to changing factor prices, then each successive period would take such an economy further away from the balanced growth path, leading to greater and greater unemployment or to exhaustion of nonreproducible resources. Of course, we argued that production techniques were inflexible only in the short run. Any model similar to the Club of Rome's model in which inflexibility in production is permanent was sure to predict disaster.

Contrast the Club of Rome's predictions with those from a neoclassical growth model in which substitution is possible. In such a model, as unemployment develops and real wages fall, firms substitute labor for capital – reducing unemployment. When titanium or copper or rubber is in short supply, raising its real price, firms change their technologies to economize on the more expensive good. While a balanced-growth path may never be attained, the economy keeps adjusting in its direction, guided by price signals.

In 1980, the well-known biologist and environmentalist Paul Ehrlich made a famous bet with the economist Julian Simon. In his book, *The Population Bomb* (first published in 1968 with several later editions), Ehrlich warned of impending environmental and economic disaster if economic and population growth were allowed to continue unchecked. Because he viewed natural resources as finite, Ehrlich, consistent with the production functions that do not permit substitution, predicted massive shortages of industrial metals and many other commodities. He predicted that their real prices would rise astronomically. Simon, consistent with the neoclassical production function, predicted that higher prices would signal users to substitute other inputs for the metals and producers of metals to search out new sources and to improve the efficiency of mining and refining technologies. He predicted that their real prices would not rise – and, indeed would most likely fall because of technological progress. Ehrlich and Simon bet $10,000 on the prices of five metals over ten years. In 1990, Ehrlich paid Simon. In fact, far from rising in price, the five metals were below their 1980 price. The following table gives the details.

Metal	1980 price (1980 dollars)	1990 price (1980 dollars)	Percentage change
Copper (195.56 lbs)	$200	$163	−18.5%
Chrome (51.28 lbs)	$200	$120	−40.0%
Nickel (63.52 lbs)	$200	$193	−3.5%
Tin (229.1 lbs)	$200	$56	−72.0%
Tungsten (13.64 lbs)	$200	$86	−57.0%

Source: Brian Carnell.

Recall that labor may temporarily grow faster than population for two reasons. First, there is a lag between any slowdown in births and the resulting decline of the labor force, so that the labor force may grow faster than population until the labor shortage begins to take hold after sixteen to twenty years, when the missing population would have joined the labor force. Second, the proportion of the population that wishes to work may increase. Because the proportion of the population working cannot exceed 100 percent – and, in fact, will stop far short of that limit – any faster growth from increasing participation must be temporary. In the long run, the growth of the labor force must be its natural rate, n.

If production is flexible, we can demonstrate that in the long run the growth rate of capital must adapt to the natural growth rate of the labor force. The demonstration begins with one form of the law of motion for the capital stock (equation (10.10)) in which both sides have been divided by

K_{t-1} to give an expression for the rate of growth of capital:

$$\hat{K}_t = \frac{\Delta K_t}{K_{t-1}} = \frac{I_{t-1} - depreciation_{t-1}}{K_{t-1}}. \tag{10.15}$$

We make two simplifying assumptions. First, investment is taken to be a fixed proportion ι (the lowercase Greek letter "iota") of real GDP, so that $I = \iota Y$. Second, depreciation is taken to be a fixed proportion δ (the lowercase Greek letter "delta") of the capital stock, so that *depreciation* $= \delta K$. Equation (10.15) can be rewritten as

$$\hat{K}_t = \frac{\Delta K_t}{K_{t-1}} = \frac{\iota Y_{t-1} - \delta K_{t-1}}{K_{t-1}} = \iota \phi_{t-1} - \delta. \tag{10.16}$$

We have already seen that when capital grows faster than labor, capital productivity (ϕ) falls; and, when labor grows faster than capital, capital productivity rises. Equation (10.16) shows *ceteris paribus* that when ϕ falls, capital grows more slowly and, when it rises, capital grows more quickly. An important consequence of this fact is that over time the economy displays **CONVERGENCE** toward a balanced growth path. If capital starts out growing faster than labor, its rate of growth will fall, and if it starts out growing slower than labor its rate of growth will rise.

Equation (10.16) implies that if population growth were ever to stop, the economy would converge to a rate of growth given by $\hat{\theta}$. At that point, gross investment is just enough to offset depreciation. And GDP can increase only because quality improvements in investment (or education or the organization of production) make labor more effective.

Equation (10.16) also implies that, by increasing the rate of investment, the economy can secure a higher rate of capital growth and, therefore, of output growth in the short run, even though it will converge to the natural rate of growth in the long run. But will it converge to the same balanced growth path?

The answer is no. An increase in the rate of investment (ι) raises the rate of growth of capital; and, as we know, ϕ falls as a result. The fall in ϕ, of course, results in capital deepening (i.e., $\kappa = K/L = \theta/\phi$ rises). With more capital for each worker, more GDP per capita is produced in the economy. In the long run, the economy does not grow any faster, but it is more productive. Figure 10.9 shows a stylized growth path for an economy after an increase in the rate of investment. At the point at which the rate of investment increases, the economy begins to grow more rapidly than the initial balanced growth path. Over time growth converges to the natural rate (n), and output approaches the new balanced growth path asymptotically.

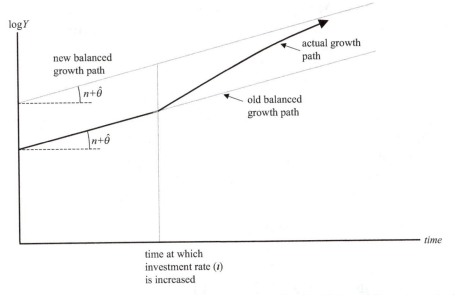

Figure 10.9. The Growth Path after an Increase in the Rate of Investment. An increase in the rate of investment raises the level of GDP at every period but does not change the growth rate along the balanced growth path. Initially, GDP grows faster than the steady-state growth rate in order to move to the new higher balanced growth path. As GDP approaches the new path asymptotically, its rate of growth converges to the original rate.

The Speed Limit

The fact that an economy has a tendency to adjust in the direction of a balanced growth path implies that there is a long-term *speed limit* on economic growth. When there is excess capacity, an economy can grow very fast indeed. But when the economy is fully employed it can grow no faster in the long run than the sum of the rate of growth of the labor force (equal to the rate of growth of population in the very long run) and the rate of growth of labor productivity.

High rates of investment in capital might increase growth, but the identity $n + \hat{\theta} \equiv \hat{K} + \hat{\phi}$ reminds us that unless the increased capital stock has the effect of raising the growth rate of labor productivity ($\hat{\theta}$), what is gained from higher investment will necessarily be offset through lower growth in capital productivity ($\hat{\phi}$) itself. Anyone who argues for a *sustained* rate of growth much higher than those reported at full employment must face this fact: either they argue for faster population growth (higher births or immigration) or faster technological development that generates growth in labor productivity. While economic considerations may influence either factor to some extent, neither is subject to delicate control or easy political direction.

Because there is virtually no secular growth in capital productivity in the economy of the United States and because capital adapts to labor, the speed limit, the balanced growth path for the U.S. economy, is given by $n + \hat{\theta}$ – the rate of population (long-term labor force) growth supplemented by the rate of growth of labor productivity.

10.4.2 The Solow-Swan Growth Model

In the 1950s, the American economist Robert Solow (winner of the Nobel Prize in Economic Science in 1987) and the Australian economist Trevor Swan independently developed a particular form of the neoclassical growth model, now known as the **SOLOW-SWAN GROWTH MODEL** or often in the United States, somewhat parochially, as the **Solow model**.

A Model with Labor-Augmenting Technological Progress

We shall develop a version of the Solow-Swan model with a Cobb-Douglas production function. For simplicity, we shall continue to assume that investment is a fixed share of real GDP ($I = \iota Y$) and that depreciation is a fixed proportion of the capital stock (*depreciation* $= \delta K$).[8]

Begin with the Cobb-Douglas production function: $Y = AL^\alpha K^{1-\alpha}$. We saw in Chapter 9 (equation (9.21)) that total factor productivity can be written as the geometrically weighted average of labor-augmenting and capital-augmenting technological progress: $A = A_L^\alpha A_K^{1-\alpha}$. We also saw (Figure 9.14) that capital productivity varies about a constant mean, so that there is on average no capital-augmenting technological progress – that is, $\hat{A}_K$ is zero. If we choose our units of measurement, so that $A_K = 1$ at some point, the fact that it does not grow means that it equals one always. Then we can write: $A = A_L^\alpha$.[9] Substituting that into the Cobb-Douglas production function yields

$$Y = A_L^\alpha L^\alpha K^{1-\alpha} = (A_L L)^\alpha K^{1-\alpha}. \tag{10.17}$$

The term $A_L L$ is known as **effective labor**. Imagine that when we first begin to measure at time 0, we choose units so that $(A_L)_0 = 1$ and the number

---

[8] We write the first assumption, as before, as $I = \iota Y$. It is more frequent in the growth literature to use the fact that, in an economy without government or foreign trade, savings equals investment: $S = I$. Instead of $I = \iota Y$, these models write $I = S = sY$, where s is the average rate of saving in real GDP. Although this substitution is correct in a model in full equilibrium in which the national-income-accounting identities hold both *ex post* and *ex ante*, it asks us, counterintuitively, to focus on savings behavior rather than on the investment behavior of firms. Surely investment behavior is more closely connected to the growth of capital, especially when consumers and firms fail to coordinate their plans.

[9] We have used the facts about U.S. productivity to justify the assumption that all technological progress is labor-augmenting. It is also a fact that capital-augmenting technological progress is not compatible with a balanced growth path. Along any balanced growth path, the rate of growth of capital must by definition be constant. But if there is capital-augmenting technological progress ($\hat{A}_K > 0$), then ϕ grows over time relative to any particular level of capital. Equation (10.16) shows that this would imply a constantly changing rate of growth of capital ($\hat{K}$), violating the definition of a balanced growth path.

of workers $L_0 = 1,000$. If the labor force grows at $n = 2$ percent per year and technological progress grows at $\hat{A}_L = 3$ percent per year, then at time 1 effective labor would be 1,050. In reality, there would be only 20 more workers, but each of the 1,020 workers would be 3 percent more effective, so that it would be just like having 1,050 workers.

As we know, the Cobb-Douglas production function shows constant returns to scale: we can multiply or divide L and K by any common value, and Y will change by the same proportion. We can therefore write the production function as

$$\frac{Y}{A_L L} = \left(\frac{A_L L}{A_L L}\right)^\alpha \left(\frac{K}{A_L L}\right)^{1-\alpha} = (1)^\alpha \left(\frac{K}{A_L L}\right)^{1-\alpha} = \left(\frac{K}{A_L L}\right)^{1-\alpha}. \qquad (10.18)$$

We can read the left-hand side of equation (10.18) as GDP *per effective labor unit*. It is convenient to give this its own symbol: $\breve{Y} \equiv \frac{Y}{A_L L}$. We will consistently use a "smile" over a variable to indicate that it is *adjusted for technology*. Notice that $\breve{Y}$ can be written as $\breve{Y} \equiv (Y/L)/A_L = \frac{\theta}{A_L}$, which is output per worker (i.e., labor productivity (θ)) adjusted for the level of technology. We call $\breve{Y}$ **adjusted output** for short. Obviously, $\theta \equiv A_L \breve{Y}$.

The bracketed term on the far right-hand side of (10.18) is capital per effective labor unit: $\breve{K} \equiv \frac{K}{A_L L}$. We call $\breve{K}$ **adjusted capital** for short. Notice that $\breve{K}$ can be written as $\breve{K} \equiv (K/L)/A_L = \frac{\kappa}{A_L}$, which is the capital-labor ratio (κ) adjusted for the level of technology. Obviously, $\kappa \equiv A_L \breve{K}$.

Using these definitions, we can rewrite (10.18) in effective labor units as

$$\breve{Y} = \breve{K}^{1-\alpha}. \qquad (10.19)$$

A production function expressed in effective labor units is said to be written in **intensive form**. A graph of equation (10.19) has the same general shape as the usual graphs of the Cobb-Douglas production function and inherits almost all of the same properties. It does have one distinct advantage: it can be drawn in a single panel.

When there is labor-augmenting technological progress, balanced growth occurs when GDP and capital both grow at the same rate as effective labor, so that $\breve{Y}$ and $\breve{K}$ are constant. To find a balanced growth path, we focus on capital. We need to find a situation in which $\breve{K}$ is not changing. Using the algebra of growth rates, $\hat{\breve{K}} = \hat{K} - \hat{L} - \hat{A}_L$. Ignoring time subscripts and substituting in equation (10.16) and the fact that, in the long run, labor grows at rate n, yields

$$\hat{\breve{K}} = \hat{K} - \hat{L} = \frac{\iota Y - \delta K}{K} - (n + \hat{A}_L). \qquad (10.20)$$

The absolute change in $\breve{K}$ can be written as $\Delta \breve{K} = \hat{\breve{K}} \breve{K}$, so that equation (10.20) can be rewritten as

$$\Delta \breve{K} = \hat{\breve{K}} \breve{K} = \breve{K} \left(\frac{\iota Y - \delta K}{K} \right) - (n + \hat{A}_L) \breve{K}$$

$$= \left(\frac{K}{A_L L} \right) \left(\frac{\iota Y - \delta K}{K} \right) - (n + \hat{A}_L) \breve{K}$$

$$= \iota \breve{Y} - (\delta + n + \hat{A}_L) \breve{K} = \iota \breve{K}^{1-\alpha} - (\delta + n + \hat{A}_L) \breve{K}. \quad (10.21)$$

Clearing out the intermediate steps, equation (10.21) can be written as a simple law of motion for capital per effective labor unit:

$$\Delta \breve{K} = \iota \breve{K}^{1-\alpha} - (\delta + n + \hat{A}_L) \breve{K}. \quad (10.22)$$

This law of motion for capital lies at the heart of the Solow-Swan model.

Balanced Growth and Convergence

The **STEADY STATE** of a law of motion occurs when the quantity that it governs stops changing. The steady state of equation (10.22) occurs when $\Delta \breve{K} = 0$. At that point, capital grows at the same rate as effective labor, so the economy is on a balanced growth path. To determine the steady state or balanced growth path of equation (10.22), set it equal to zero and rearrange to get

$$\iota \breve{K}^{1-\alpha} = (\delta + n + \hat{A}_L) \breve{K}. \quad (10.23)$$

We can visualize the condition for a balanced growth path using Figure 10.10. The upper curve in the figure is just the intensive form of the Cobb-Douglas production function, given in equation (10.19). The left-hand side of equation (10.23) is shown as the lower curve concave to the $\breve{K}$-axis. The right hand is shown as the ray from the origin with slope $\delta + n + \hat{A}_L$. Equation (10.22) is fulfilled at point A. Here the value of capital per effective labor unit is $\breve{K}^*$ and effective GDP per capita can be read off the production function at $\breve{Y}^*$.

One way to interpret Figure 10.10 is to see that the ray, $(\delta + n + \hat{A}_L)\breve{K}$, measures the amount of capital needed to cover the depreciation of the existing capital stock and to support capital widening for the increasing population. The lower curve $(\iota \breve{K}^{1-\alpha})$ measures the amount of investment that must be divided between depreciation and capital widening, on the one hand, and capital deepening, on the other.

The distance between the upper curve and the lower curve measures the amount of output per worker that is not invested. If we assume, for

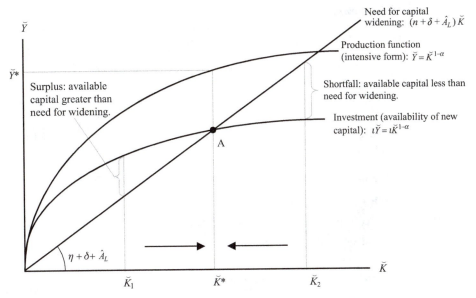

Figure 10.10. The Solow-Swan Model of Economic Growth. The steady state of the Solow-Swan model occurs where the need for capital to cover population growth, depreciation, and labor-augmenting technological progress (capital widening) just absorbs the available capital (point A). When there is a surplus of capital, the adjusted capital stock grows (capital deepening) and when there is a shortfall it falls, so that there is always a tendency to converge on the steady state and the balanced growth path for the economy.

simplicity, that there is no government and no foreign sector, the national-accounting identities tell us that this is the amount of consumption per worker.

What happens when the economy is away from a balanced growth path? Consider $\breve{K}_1$ in Figure 10.10, which is lower than $\breve{K}^*$. Here $\iota \breve{K}^{1-\alpha} > \delta + n + \hat{A}_L$, so that $\Delta \breve{K}$ in equation (10.21) is positive. The amount of capital available exceeds that needed for capital widening and depreciation, so capital becomes deeper: $\breve{K}$ increases. Similarly, at $\breve{K}_2$, which is higher than $\breve{K}^*$, $\iota \breve{K}^{1-\alpha} < \delta + n + \hat{A}_L$, so that $\Delta \breve{K}$ in equation (10.22) is negative. The amount of capital available falls short of what is needed for capital widening and depreciation, so capital becomes less deep: $\breve{K}$ decreases. Together these facts confirm what we had already discovered in our earlier examination of balanced growth paths: whenever $\breve{K}$ is away from $\breve{K}^*$, the capital-labor ratio adjusts until the economy regains a balanced growth path.

The process of converging to a balanced growth path need not be quick, and the economy is constantly being shocked and moved away from the balanced growth path. The best assumption, then, is that a balanced growth path is an "attractor" – a path toward which the economy tends if left to its own devices – but not something generally attained in reality.

Table 10.5. *Parameters for Calculating U.S. Steady-State Capital Stock*

Parameter (1997–2007 average)	Value	Units
Population growth rate (n)	1.0	percent per year
Labor productivity growth rate ($\hat{\theta} = \hat{A}_L$)	2.8	percent per year
Depreciation rate (δ)	4.2	percent of the capital stock
Investment rate (ι)	16.7	percent of GDP

Source: Author's calculations based on data from the Bureau of Economic Analysis, Bureau of Labor Statistics, Census Bureau.

Is the United States on a Balanced Growth Path?

To determine whether a country is on its balanced growth path, we need to compare its steady state with the actual data. First, solve equation (10.23) for the optimal adjusted capital-labor ratio:

$$\breve{K}^* = \left(\frac{\delta + n + \hat{A}_L}{\iota} \right)^{(-1/\alpha)} . \tag{10.24}$$

Table 10.5 gives data for the key parameters based on averages of values taken from the U.S. national-income-and-product accounts and labor statistics from 1997 to 2007. On the basis of this data, we can calculate steady-state adjusted capital for the United States:

$$\breve{K}^* = \left(\frac{\delta + n + \hat{A}_L}{\iota} \right)^{(-1/\alpha)} = \left(\frac{4.2 + 1.0 + 2.8}{16.7} \right)^{(-1/0.67)} = 3.00. \tag{10.25}$$

To see what equation (10.25) means, we need to find A_L. Solving equation (10.17) and using data for 2008, we get:

$$A_L = \frac{\left(\frac{Y}{K^{1-\alpha}} \right)^{(1/\alpha)}}{L} = \frac{\left(\frac{13{,}312 \times 10^9}{(40{,}173 \times 10^9)^{(1-0.67)}} \right)^{(1/0.67)}}{136{,}777{,}000} = \$56{,}489 \text{ per worker.}[10]$$

$$\tag{10.26}$$

Because by definition $\breve{K} \equiv \frac{K}{A_L L} \equiv \frac{\kappa}{A_L}$, the steady-state capital-labor ratio is $\kappa^* = A_L \breve{K} = 56{,}489 \times 3.00 = \$169{,}467$ per worker. The actual capital-labor ratio is $\kappa = \$40{,}173$ billion/136,777 thousand $= \$293{,}712$ per worker. The U.S. economy then has a capital-labor ratio higher than its steady state and is not on its balanced growth path. According to Figure 10.10 and equation (10.22), this implies that adjusted capital and, along with it, adjusted GDP must fall. If technological progress is fast enough, actual GDP per

---

[10] These data differ from those used in equation (9.17′) only in that we use the number of workers rather than the number of worker-hours to calculate an alternative measure of labor productivity.

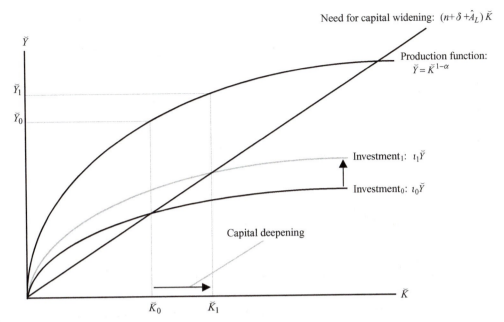

Figure 10.11. The Effect of an Increase in the Rate of Investment. An increase in the rate of investment raises the available capital at the original steady state above the needs of capital widening, which permits capital to be used to increase capital per worker (capital deepening) until the economy converges on a new steady state with more adjusted capital per worker and higher adjusted GDP per worker.

worker $(\theta = Y/L = A_L \breve{Y})$ may not fall, but it must grow more slowly than at the steady state in order to regain the balanced growth path.

How Does the Steady State Shift?

The Solow-Swan growth model is useful in analyzing how changing economic behavior or changing policy affects the long-run tendencies in the economy. We consider two of many possible scenarios.

- **Scenario 1.** Imagine that, because of economic policy or a change in the expectations of firms, the share of investment in the economy rose (i.e., ι became larger). How would this affect the economy?

The scenario is laid out in Figure 10.11. Initially, the economy grows along a balanced growth path at the rate $\delta + n + \hat{A}_L$. with adjusted capital at $\breve{K}_0$. When the rate of investment rises from ι_0 to ι_1, the new balanced growth path has a capital-labor ratio of $\breve{K}_1$. To get from the old balanced growth path to the new one requires capital to grow faster than labor. At $\breve{K}_0$, $\iota \breve{K}^{1-\alpha} > \delta + n + \hat{A}_L$, so that $\Delta \breve{K}$ is positive ($\breve{K}$ is increasing) and will continue to do so until the new balanced growth path is reached. Again, this is the process of capital deepening. Growth is faster than $\delta + n + \hat{A}_L$ in the transition

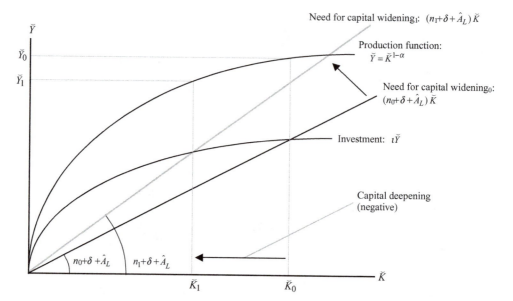

Figure 10.12. The Effect of an Increase in the Rate of Population Growth. An increase in the rate of population growth raises the need for capital to fit out new workers (capital widening), so that there is a shortfall relative to investment at the original steady state. As a result, capital per worker begins to fall (negative capital widening) until the economy converges on a new steady state with less adjusted capital per worker and a lower adjusted GDP per worker.

between the balanced growth paths – exactly as in Figure 10.9 – but it is the same (rate $\delta + n + \hat{A}_L$) along each balanced path. The benefit of additional investment in the long run is not a faster rate of growth (even though growth is faster in the short run), but a higher level of adjusted GDP (the increase from $\breve{Y}_0$ to $\breve{Y}_1$) and the higher income per capita and real wages that go with it.

- **Scenario 2.** How would an increase in the long-run rate of growth of population and the labor force affect the economy?

The scenario is laid out in Figure 10.12 and shows the initial balanced growth path at $\breve{K}_0$, where the rate of growth of labor is n_0. The increase in the growth of labor is shown as the steepening of the ray from the lower slope, $\delta + n_0 + \hat{A}_L$, to the higher, $\delta + n_1 + \hat{A}_L$. The new balanced growth path is at $\breve{K}_1$, where the rate of growth of labor is n_1. The economy could move directly to this new balanced growth path, but it does not make sense to throw capital away. The economic thing to do is to continue to use the current capital but to invest at a lower rate, so that enough capital is absorbed through depreciation and capital widening (more quickly now, because the labor force is growing more quickly) until the capital-labor ratio falls to the

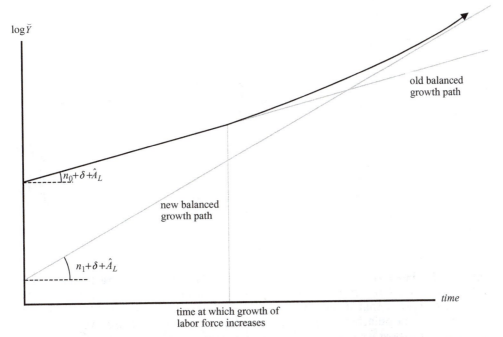

Figure 10.13. The Growth Path after an Increase in the Rate of Population Growth. An increase in the rate of population growth raises the level and growth rate of adjusted GDP at every period. At first, as investment is diverted into capital widening, GDP grows more slowly than the faster growth rate along its new balanced growth path. Its growth rate accelerates as it converges asymptotically to its new steady state and balanced growth path.

desired $\breve{K}_1$. At $\breve{K}_0$, $\delta + n + \hat{A}_L$, so that $\Delta \breve{K}$ is negative ($\breve{K}$ is decreasing) and will continue to be negative until the new balanced growth path is reached. Figure 10.13 shows the transition to the new balanced growth path. Along the new path, adjusted capital is lower (the opposite of capital deepening), as is adjusted GDP, as well as income per capita and the real wage rate.

We can use the Solow-Swan model to consider a variety of other scenarios to guide our thinking about the long-run path of the economy. (Some other cases are taken up in Problems 10.12–10.14.)

10.5 What Accounts for Differences in the Growth of Nations?

10.5.1 Catching Up

The Importance of Technology

Why is the whole world not rich? As we saw in Table 2.3 the GDP per capita of the United States is more than 72 times and that of Luxembourg is more than 97 times that of Burundi. The Solow-Swan model directs us to look

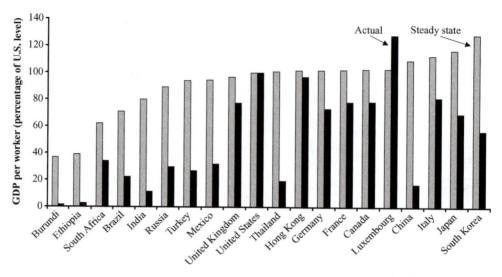

Figure 10.14. How Does Technology in Other Countries Compare to the United States? For each country the steady-state value of GDP per worker is calculated on the assumption that it has the same technology as the United States, but different rates of population growth and investment shares (data are averages 1997–2007). The steady-state values of GDP per worker are compared to the actual values. The difference between steady state and actual shows the degree to which the technology in each country falls short or exceeds that of the United States. Data are ordered from low to high according to steady-state values. Many countries have higher steady-state values than the United States due to higher investment shares or lower population growth rates, but only Luxembourg has a higher actual value. *Source:* Penn World Tables, version 6.3 and author's calculations.

at three factors to account for the differences in GDP per worker (closely related to GDP per capita) among countries:

- technology reflected in the production function, including the level of technological progress (A_L), its growth rate ($\hat{A}_L$), and the rate of depreciation (δ);
- the rate of gross investment in the economy (ι); and
- the long-term rate of growth of the labor force (or population).

It is easy to see that technology is the most important of these three factors. Figure 10.14 compares the steady-state GDP per worker for the same countries as in Table 2.3 on the assumption that they have identical levels and rates of technological progress as the United States. The differences are only the different rates of investment and population growth. The figure also compares the actual GDP per worker for these countries. Each comparison is expressed as a ratio of the country's value to the value for the United States. If the only factors that mattered were population growth rates and investment shares, then the two ratios would be the same.

No country except the United States, for which the two ratios are equal by construction, shows anywhere near the same ratios. These wide disparities

Table 10.6. *Speed of Convergence to Steady State*

Fraction of U.S. Steady-State Adjusted Capital Stock ($\breve{K}/\breve{K}^*$) (percent)	Growth Rate of Adjusted Capital Stock (percent per year)	Doubling Time of Adjusted Capital Stock (years)	Time to Catch up to the U.S. Steady State	
			90 Percent of the Way (years)	99 Percent of the Way (years)
100	0.0			
75	1.5	46.8	20	68
50	4.1	16.8	36	84
25	10.7	6.4	46	95
10	26.1	2.6	52	100

Source: Author's calculations based on equations (10.19) and (10.23) and the parameters from Table 10.5 in text.

confirm that technology (broadly conceived) is the dominant factor distinguishing standards of living among countries. Many countries have higher *steady-state* values than the United States. This says that if the United States had, for example, the high investment share and low population growth rate of Japan, it would have a higher GDP per worker. Only one country, Luxembourg, has a higher *actual* value. This says that only Luxembourg has an intrinsically more productive economy.

The Speed of Convergence

Imagine two countries – one with a low level of technology and one with a high level of technology but with the same rates of investment and population growth. According to equation (10.24), both would have the same steady-state adjusted capital. But the high technology country would have a much higher level of the actual steady-state capital-labor ratio ($\kappa^* = A_L \breve{K}^*$) because it has a much higher A_L.

Now imagine that suddenly the poorer country suddenly acquired the technology of the richer country. (Obviously, it never happens quite that way in the world, but the situation resembles the position of East Germany when it was reunited with a richer West Germany in 1989.) The poorer country would now be well below its steady state, because $\breve{K}^* = \frac{K}{A_L L}$ and A_L rose sharply while K and L were unchanged. The country would be in the situation already described in Figure 10.10 as $\breve{K}_1$. A country in that situation should grow faster than the balanced growth rate and eventually converge to steady state.

Convergence is faster the further a country is out of steady state. Table 10.6 is based on equation (10.22), using the values of the parameters from Table 10.5 to show how fast a country just like the United States but below its steady state would converge. For example, line 3 shows that if the country's adjusted capital-labor ratio were half that of the United States, its capital would grow initially at 4.1 percent per year. To get an idea of how fast that is, the third column reports the doubling time at that rate as close to 6.5 years (see the *Guide*, section G.11.3). Unfortunately, that rate of convergence cannot be maintained, because the closer the country's capital-labor ratio gets to steady state, the slower it grows (compare line 3 to line 2). The last two columns account for this slowdown. They report the number of years it would take for each starting capital-labor ratio to reach 90 percent and 99 percent of the way to the steady state. Convergence is slow. For the country that starts at half steady state, it takes 36 years to get to 90 percent and 84 years to get to 99 percent. Even for a country that is already 75 percent of the way there, it takes 20 years to reach 90 percent and 68 years to reach 99 percent.

Do Countries Converge?

Among other things, improvements in communication and the increasing economic linkages among countries (so-called *globalization*) spread technology. Once upon a time, it may have made sense to think of each country as having a separate technology, so that each would reach its own steady state – some high, some low. One way to interpret differences in growth rates is to view the poorer countries as countries that acquire access to much better technology. This never happens as completely or rapidly as the data in Table 10.6 assume. Still, the spread of technology should promote faster growth in the countries furthest away from the steady states of the most technological advanced countries. The Solow-Swan model predicts convergence.

Japan (Figure 10.15) after the Meiji Restoration in 1868 began to converge on the growth path of the United States – especially rapidly after World War II – until reaching near equality in GDP per capita by the early 1990s. The story is the same for other technologically advanced countries. Figure 10.16 plots the average growth rate of each member country of the **Organization of Economic Cooperation and Development (OECD)** over the period 1960–2000 against its GDP per worker in 1960. The relationship is strongly negative (the correlation coefficient $R = -0.76$), which shows that the poorer the country in 1960, the faster it grew over the next forty years. Poor countries in the OECD appear to catch up rapidly to the rich.

In the opening years of the twenty-first century, China, rather than Japan, is often seen as the economic juggernaut. Judged by GDP per capita China is much poorer than the United States: $6,000 per person versus $46,900 per person (see Table 2.3). But China is growing rapidly: over the three years 2006 through 2008, GDP per capita grew at an average rate of

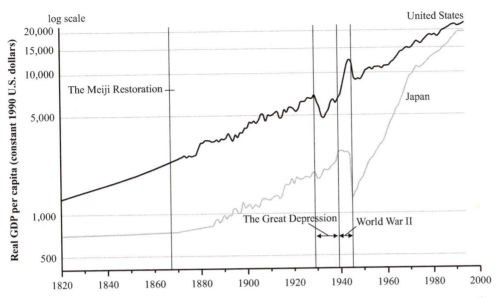

Figure 10.15. Japanese Convergence. *Source: Angus Maddison, Monitoring the World Economy, 1820–1992.* Paris: OECD, Table D-1a.

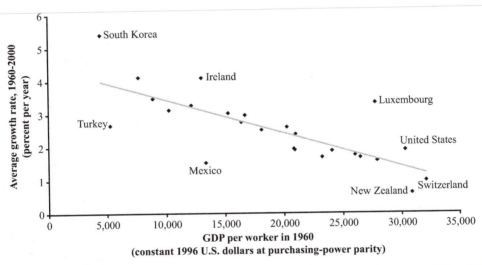

Figure 10.16. OECD Countries Converge. Each point represents one of the 25 countries of the Organization of Economic Cooperation and Development, a club of richer countries. OECD countries display strong convergence. Countries that had high GDP per worker in 1960 typically showed slower growth over the next forty years than those with low GDP per worker. The regression line shows that on average, if two countries differed in GDP per worker by $10,000, the poorer country grew 1 percentage point faster over the next forty years. The correlation between labor productivity in 1960 and the average growth rate is $R = -0.76$. *Source:* Penn World Tables, version 6.1.

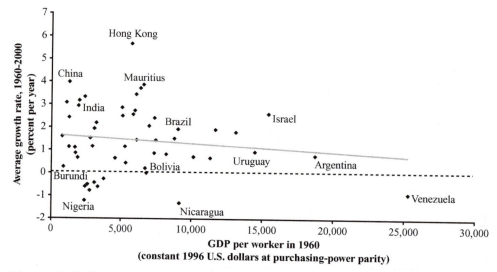

Figure 10.17. Non-OECD Countries Show Little Evidence of Convergence. Each point represents a non-OECD country. These countries shows little evidence of convergence. Some countries that were poor in 1960 show rapid growth over the next forty years, while others actually went backward. Some countries that were relatively rich in 1960 continued to grow rapidly, while others lost ground. Although the regression line indicates that on average, if two countries differ in their GDP per worker in 1960 by $10,000, the poorer country grew faster over the next forty years by 0.4 percentage points, unlike the case of the OECD countries in Figure 10.16, the data do not cluster around the regression line. The correlation between labor productivity in 1960 and the average growth rate is $R = -0.12$ – a low rate. The data provide weak evidence of, at best, weak convergence. *Source:* Penn World Tables, version 6.1.

10.5 percent per year. If such a rate could be sustained, China would catch up to 2008 U.S. GDP per capita in about twenty-one years. Of course, the United States is likely to continue to grow at close to the balanced growth rate over that period – that is, at approximately 1.5 percent per year – moving the bar forward. It would take China about twenty-five years to catch up to this higher level. These calculations assume that Chinese growth could be sustained at that high level. But the neoclassical growth model suggests that Chinese growth rates will slow down. China may catch up to the United States, but it is likely to take much more than a quarter-century. China may even surpass the United States, but only if it captures technological leadership.

Sadly, unlike the OECD countries, many non-OECD countries – among them the poorest countries in the world – are apparently not converging toward the per capita incomes of the developed countries. Figure 10.17 presents the same data for some non-OECD countries. There is no strong negative relationship (the correlation coefficient $R = -0.11$). There is little evidence of catching up for many countries.

10.5.2 Which Factors Promote Growth?

How can we explain the difference between countries that grow rapidly and catch up and those that do not? At a broad level, it comes down to three factors: technology, investment rates, and population growth rates. High levels of technology growth raise the steady state. High investment rates not only raise the steady state but also can speed up the rate of convergence (see equation (10.22)). High rates of population growth rate raise the steady-state *rate* of GDP growth but lower the steady-state *level* of GDP per worker.

Economists have investigated a large number of factors that explain the relevant differences among countries. Cultural differences may be important. The sociologist Max Weber (1864–1920) introduced the idea of the *Protestant work ethic* to explain why northern European countries were wealthier than Roman Catholic, southern European countries. These differences appear largely to have vanished, but there is some evidence of a *Confucian work ethic*: countries with a high proportion of followers of Confucius (largely ethnically Chinese) tend to have higher growth rates.

Why should such factors matter? Particular religious beliefs may, for example, promote high rates of investment or social organizations that promote trust and cooperation in business or a greater readiness to adopt outside technology or business practices. (It is important to recall that technology is not just the level of technological advancement of capital; it is also the social arrangements of productive workplaces and societies.) Other factors that are frequently cited as promoting growth are:

- openness to foreign trade, which may increase exposure to technology;
- sound social and legal institutions, such as honest police and courts, high regard for civil liberties, and low levels of official and business corruption;
- a peaceful environment with low levels of wars and domestic unrest, ethnic factionalization, or linguistic or religious divisions;
- high levels of education at primary and higher levels, including education of women;
- developed financial institutions, which help to foster entrepreneurial enterprises;
- favorable geography (some economists believe that backwardness in Africa is the result of much of the continent providing a perfect environment for tropical diseases).

While economists continue to investigate these and many other factors, there is no universal consensus on which are the most important in explaining differences in either the levels of GDP per capita or the growth rates of different countries.

10.5.3 Endogenous Growth

As Figure 10.15 shows, Japan converged rapidly on the U.S. growth path. In the late 1980s, many commentators extrapolated this rapid growth and predicted that Japan would soon have a higher GDP per capita, and perhaps not long after, a higher GDP than the United States. The notion was that Japan possessed a superior manufacturing technology, exemplified in its world-beating automobiles, electronics, and cameras. But this did not happen. Japan spent much of the 1990s in a prolonged recession, and it never fully recovered during the opening decade of the twenty-first century. Partly, this was the usual cyclical fluctuations. More importantly, however, the recession exposed institutional weaknesses in the nonmanufacturing sectors and in the organization of Japanese business – especially in its financial institutions and their relationship to the government. Looked at more broadly, perhaps Japan's technology was not superior after all.

The concerns of the 1980s are being replayed with respect to China, with the popular press worrying that China will soon surpass the United States economically. Given its large population and rapid economic growth, it seems likely that China will surpass the United States in terms of the level of GDP in the not-too-distant future – it is already the second largest economy in the world (see Table 2.2).[11] As we have already seen, however, it is likely to take much longer for China to reach U.S. levels of GDP per capita. The considerations of the last section suggest that the path may require fundamental economic and political reforms that may not prove easy for a country with limited political freedom and substantial intervention in the economy from the ruling Communist Party. It is striking that every country in the world with a GDP per capita in 2008 higher than $20,000 was either a democracy or owed its high income almost exclusively to oil extraction. One-party rule may not be compatible with a level of economic performance on par with the most developed countries.

Some economists suggest another factor that might explain why it is difficult for a rapidly converging economy such as Japan's to surpass the leading country and why some countries, despite growth, never converge at all. Their idea is known as **ENDOGENOUS GROWTH**: *fast growth begets fast growth*.

The neoclassical growth model does not display endogenous growth. The fundamental pattern is one of convergence to a steady state. In the previous section, we saw a number of social and economic factors that might promote investment and the development or integration of technology. But we did not suggest that the level of investment or the capital stock or GDP altered

---

[11] Discounting the European Union, which is not a single country.

the technological possibilities open to the economy. *Growth is endogenous when growth itself causes the technological possibilities to expand.*

Economists have suggested several mechanisms that might generate endogenous growth. One is known as **learning-by-doing**. Studies of aircraft manufacturer showed that the more planes a manufacturer assembled, even when the factories and machinery were essentially the same, the higher the labor productivity. If learning-by-doing were general across the economy, then as more GDP were produced, it would be produced more efficiently. Technological progress would advance the most in countries that produced the most and would keep them ahead. It is not clear, however, that the particular experience of manufacturing generalizes easily to the whole economy (remember the experience of Japan).

Another suggested mechanism concentrates on the production of the knowledge that forms the backbone of technological progress. Ideas depend on people, their numbers, and their education. Ideas are cumulative and do not wear out. And ideas are easily shared. A bigger, more successful economy may have more ideas.

To see the implications of this notion, consider the neoclassical growth model. It displays constant returns to scale. An economy could have the same technology as the United States but only half its capital and labor. It would produce half as much, but would have the same per capita income – on average its people would be as rich as Americans. And there would be no advantage from the individual point of view in increasing capital and labor to become the same absolute size as the American economy.

If economically important ideas are more common and more commonly implemented when there are more people in the right educational and business environments, then any increase in the scale of the economy would not leave technology constant as it does in the neoclassical growth model. As GDP increased, ideas would increase, and technology would advance. There would be increasing returns to scale: doubling the capital and labor would more than double GDP because ideas would also increase, so that technology would improve endogenously.

Models of endogenous growth are at the forefront of economic research. The neoclassical growth model provides substantial insights into the process of economic growth. Whether models of endogenous growth deepen those insights remains an open question.

10.6 Economic Growth: Achievements and Prospects

Economic growth is the dominant fact of world history over the past 250 years. It has utterly transformed the lives of rich and poor alike. Increasing population, capital (investment), and technology are the mainsprings of growth. Of these the most important is technological progress – both in the sense of it having accounted for most of the actual growth and in the sense that only technological progress holds any hope of sustaining growth permanently. Technology must be broadly conceived. It is not just the marvelous development of machines but also the organization and practices of the workplace and of the larger society. The growth models discussed in this chapter demonstrate a strong tendency of an economy to converge to its balanced growth path and of different economies to converge to similar balanced growth paths within the limits of their technology broadly conceived. That some countries have failed to keep pace, or have even fallen behind economically, can be attributed mainly to a failure of the best technology (including economic and political freedom) to diffuse evenly throughout the world. The knowledge that reforms are possible holds out the transforming promise of economic growth even to the most backward economies.

The analysis of this chapter presumed that the smooth operation of the price system would maintain the continuous full employment of the factors of production. In the next chapter we will examine more deeply the mechanisms that govern the availability of the factors of production – especially labor. In Chapter 12, we will consider what happens when the assumption of smooth operation fails. Instead of the economy growing with continuous full employment of the factors of production, we return to the real world of business cycles and the problem of unemployment.

Summary

1. Rapid economic growth is rare in human history, but has changed the face of the world over the past 250 years. Small differences in growth rates compounded over long periods of time make profound differences in per capita incomes.

2. Growth is best modeled as governed by a production function that shifts over time with changing technology. The production function can be used to decompose growth into three sources: technological progress, increases in population, and investment in capital. All three have contributed to growth in the United States, but technological progress is the most important.

3. Technology comprises not only innovations to particular tools and products, but also the organization of production in firms and industries and, to some extent, social and political organization more generally. Technology has developed both fortuitously (exogenously) and as a result of directed research and development (endogenously).

4. In the long run, the growth of labor is approximately equal to the growth of population. Economic forces help determine the growth of population – positively, as more resources may promote procreation and the survival of

offspring (Malthusianism), and negatively, protection of higher standards of living demands smaller families (the richest countries have the slowest population growth rates).

5. The rate of growth of capital depends on capital productivity and the rate of investment.

6. The neoclassical growth model assumes that a smoothly functioning price system directs the factors of production to their most profitable uses, maintaining full employment at all times.

7. A balanced growth path occurs when real GDP grows at the same constant rate as labor and capital, each adjusted for factor-augmenting technological progress. Along a balanced growth path, investment is devoted entirely to depreciation and to fitting out new workers with the capital needed to maintain the current level of capital intensity (capital widening). The rate of growth along a balanced growth path depends on the rate of population growth and the rate of technological progress. The rate of output per worker depends also on the rate of investment.

8. Along an unbalanced growth path, changes in the relative prices of capital and labor induce changes in the choice of techniques. An increase in the rate of investment results in greater capital intensity (capital deepening) and a temporarily faster rate of growth. Changes in capital productivity ultimately push the economy *ceteris paribus* back to the balanced growth path.

9. The Solow-Swan model is a useful version of the neoclassical growth model. The Solow-Swan model allows us to calculate the steady-state values of the capital-labor ratio and of GDP per worker. These values will obtain when the economy has converged to its balanced growth path. The model can be used to determine the effects of different changes in background conditions (e.g., changes in population growth rates or changes in policies that affect the rate of investment).

10. The Solow-Swan model shows that the rate of convergence of an economy to its balanced growth path is faster the further it is away from its steady state. Thus, the model predicts that a poor economy that gains access to the technology of a richer economy should converge rapidly at first and, then, more slowly toward similar levels of output per worker and income per capita.

11. In practice, some countries in fact have shown rapid convergence toward the richest countries in the post-World War II period. But many other countries have not. The main reason is that they do not, as assumed by the model, share the technology of the richer countries, taking technology in a broad sense to include social and political organization.

12. The Solow-Swan model predicts that the richest countries will tend to grow the slowest, but this is also not always true. One possible explanation is that technological progress is not exogenous but is itself faster in richer countries because of learning-by-doing or increasing returns to scale in technical knowledge. Endogenous growth remains an open area for economic research.

Key Concepts

economic growth	capital deepening
research and development (R&D)	balanced growth
natural rate of growth	convergence
law of motion	Solow-Swan growth model
neoclassical growth model	steady state
capital widening	endogenous growth

Suggestions for Further Reading

Charles I. Jones, *Introduction to Economic Growth*, 2nd edition. New York: Norton, 2001.

N. Gregory Mankiw, "The Growth of Nations," *Brookings Papers on Economic Activity*, no. 1, 1995, pp. 275–310.

William J. Baumol, Sue Ann Batey Blackman, and Edward N. Wolff, *Productivity and American Leadership: The Long View*. Cambridge, MA: MIT Press, 1989.

Robert J. Barro, *The Determinants of Economic Growth: A Cross-country Empirical Study*. Cambridge, MA: MIT Press, 1998.

Kevin D. Hoover and Stephen J. Perez, "Truth and Robustness in Cross-country Growth Regressions," *Oxford Bulletin of Economics and Statistics*, 2004.

Problems

Data for this exercise are available on the textbook website under the link for Chapter 10 (appliedmacroeconomics.com). Before starting these exercises, the student should review the relevant portions of the *Guide to Working with Economic Data*, including sections G.1–G.5, G.10–G.11, G.13, and G.16.

Problem 10.1.

(a) Use the data in Table 2.3 to compute the rates of growth of real GDP per capita that would be needed for Burundi, Ethiopia, and Russia (countries mentioned in the introduction to section 10.1) to catch up to the 2008 level of GDP per capita in the United States in 100 years. In 200 years.

(b) Find the current rates of growth of GDP per capita for each of these countries. If these actual levels could be sustained, how long will it take these countries to reach the level of the United States in 2008? (It could be helpful to review logarithms before answering this question – see the *Guide*, section G.11.)

Problem 10.2. In section 10.2.2, we quantified the effect of technological change by using the values for capital and labor for 2008 in the production function of 1948 and comparing the resulting output with the actual output in 2008. The reverse exercise should also be informative. Write down the production function for 2008 (use the estimate for $A = 9.63$ from equation (9.17′)) and use this function to estimate what 1948 real GDP would have been with 2008 technology. Compare your answer to the actual level of real GDP in 1948.

Problem 10.3. How much has technology changed in your lifetime? Repeat the counterfactual experiment in Problem 10.2 *and* the one in section 10.2.2 for the year of your birth and 2008.

Problem 10.4. In a well-known study in 1992, Alwyn Young tried to understand the growth experience of two rapidly developing countries, Hong Kong and Singapore, using a growth-accounting exercise like that in section 10.2.3. The table presents a small part of Young's data (note that percentage changes are not yet annualized):

| Country | Percentage Change 1970 to 1990 of: | | | Average Labor Share (α) |
	Output	Labor	Capital	
Hong Kong	147.2	54.9	159.9	0.616
Singapore	154.5	82.5	240.2	0.533

Source: Alwyn Young. (1992) "A Tale of Two Cities," *NBER Macroeconomics Annual 1992*. Cambridge, MA: MIT Press, pp. 13–53; Table 5, p. 35.

On the basis of the information given in the table, compute the contribution of labor, capital, and technological change as a percentage of the growth rate in output for each economy. How do the sources of their growth differ? Do you find the results surprising? Why? Comment on the sustainability of the growth rates in the two countries in the long run.

Problem 10.5. Capital productivity is defined as output per unit of capital, $\phi = Y/K$. Given the information that Y is increasing at 5.2 percent per year and K is increasing at 4.8 percent per year, use the algebra of growth rates to compute the rate of growth of capital productivity.

Problem 10.6. A recent study by two economists at the Federal Reserve Board, Stephen Oliner and Daniel Sichel, tried to assess the importance of computer technology for economic growth through an extension of the growth-accounting framework. They divided the capital stock into four groups: computer hardware, software, communications equipment (such as modems and internet routers), and all other capital. An extended Cobb-Douglas production function can then be written as: $Y = A L^{\alpha} K_H^{\beta H} K_S^{\beta S} K_C^{\beta C} K_O^{\beta O}$, where the subscripts H, S, C, and O refer to hardware, software, communications equipment, and other capital; and the superscripts $\beta H, \beta S, \beta C, \beta O$ are the shares of the income attributed to each type of capital in nonfarm business output (a narrower notion of income output than real GDP). The following table presents data from Oliner and Sichel's paper:

	Period		
	1974–1990	1991–1995	1996–1999
Growth rate of output (percent per year)			
Income shares	3.06	2.75	4.82
Hardware (βH)	0.010	0.014	0.018
Software (βS)	0.008	0.020	0.025
Communications equipment (βC)	0.015	0.019	0.020
Growth rates of inputs (percentage points)[a]			
Hardware	31.3	17.5	35.9
Software	13.2	13.1	13.0
Communications equipment	7.7	3.6	7.2

[a] Average difference of logarithms $\times\, 100$.

Source: Stephen D. Oliner and Daniel E. Sichel "The Resurgence of Growth in the Late 1990s: Is Information Technology the Story?" *Journal of Economic Perspectives*, 14(4), Fall 2000, pp. 3–22.

Using the analogy to the calculations described in equation (10.6) and Table 10.4, compute for each period the percentage of the total rate of growth of output that can be attributed to each type of computer-related capital separately and collectively. How important is the growth of computer technology in explaining growth, and especially the acceleration of growth at the end of the 1990s? Are these conclusions surprising?

Problem 10.7.. So far, our growth-accounting exercises focused on the growth of real GDP. But real GDP per capita is probably more important for people's well-being. To shift the focus to real GDP per capita, first, divide both sides of the Cobb-Douglas production function by L to get $\frac{Y}{L} = AL^{\alpha-1}K^{1-\alpha}$. Notice that the left-hand side is labor productivity $\theta = Y/L$, which is not the same as GDP per capita but will obviously be closely related to it as GDP per hour of work (or GDP per worker). Next, use the algebra of growth rates to write down the appropriate analogue to equation (10.6) decomposing the growth of labor productivity into parts attributable to technology, labor, and capital. Then, use the data in Table 10.3 to quantify the importance of each factor. (Be especially careful about the *sign* of the factors.) Explain the differences between your results and those in Table 10.4.

Problem 10.8. Suppose that labor productivity grows at a steady rate $\bar{\theta}$ and capital productivity is constant on average ($\bar{\hat{\phi}} = 0$). Prove that the capital-labor ratio (κ) must grow at $\bar{\theta}$.

Problem 10.9. In the discussion of unbalanced growth in section 10.4.1, we considered the case in which labor grew faster than capital. Now analyze a case in which capital grows faster than labor using a diagram analogous to

Figure 10.8 and noting particularly what happens to labor and capital productivity and to capital intensity (the capital-labor ratio). What will happen to the growth rate of the capital stock as a result of this unbalanced growth? Left to its own devices, will the economy persist on the unbalanced growth path? Explain carefully why or why not.

Problem 10.10. As we saw in section 10.4.1, the balanced growth path for an economy is a sort of long-term "speed limit." Consider whether the speed limit has changed recently. An economy is more likely to be close to its balanced growth path at the business-cycle peak than at other times. Identify the last three business-cycle peaks (see Table 5.1). Use the average growth of labor productivity peak-to-peak to approximate the growth rate of labor-augmenting technological progress ($\hat{A}_L$). Use the rate of growth of the labor force to approximate the rate of growth of the relevant population (n). Then, compute the growth rate along the balanced growth path ($n + \hat{A}_L$) for each of the two periods defined by the three business-cycle peaks. Make a table including the relevant data, the balanced growth paths, and the actual rate of growth of real GDP for each period. Has the "speed limit" changed? How does the actual growth rate compare to the balanced growth path?

Problem 10.11. Repeat the last problem, but use the rate of population growth instead of the rate of growth of the labor force for n. Why are the results different? Under what circumstances might population growth be a more meaningful measure than labor-force growth for estimating the balanced growth path?

Problem 10.12. Assume that there is no technological progress. Explain carefully, using the neoclassical growth model (the Solow-Swan model), the short-term and long-term effects on GDP per worker, capital per worker, and the rate of growth of GDP of (i) a decrease in the rate of investment and (ii) a decrease in the rate of population growth.

Problem 10.13. Some economists have suggested that the adoption of computer technology involves faster rates of capital depreciation. Assume that there is no technological progress (aside from the change in the depreciation rate). Using the neoclassical growth model (the Solow-Swan model), what would you expect to happen to the rate of balanced growth, the amount of capital per worker, and the real GDP per worker if the rate of depreciation (δ) of capital increased? Explain carefully.

Problem 10.14. Using the neoclassical growth model (the Solow-Swan model), what would be the effect on adjusted output (i.e., output adjusted for technological progress or $\breve{Y}$), adjusted capital ($\breve{K}$), and the rate of balanced growth of an increase in the rate of labor-augmenting technological progress ($\hat{A}_L$)? Would such an increase be good or bad for workers? Explain carefully (think about the difference between quantities expressed in natural units and in units adjusted for technological progress).

Problem 10.15.
  (a) What relationship do you expect between the rate of investment and the average rate of growth of GDP per capita? Explain.

(b) Separately for OECD and non-OECD countries: calculate the average growth rates of GDP and the average investment shares for a 10-year period, using the most recently available data for each country; plot them on a scatter diagram; and calculate their correlation coefficient.

(c) Does the evidence in (b) support your expectation in (a)?

11

The Ideal Labor Market

Labor is the most important factor of production. Most of us are workers and derive our main source of income from labor. In this chapter, we investigate the labor markets when they are working well. Some of the questions considered are: How much labor do firms want to hire? How many people want to work? For how long? How do taxes, technological progress, and immigration affect real wages? In the next chapter, we consider the problem of unemployment.

In the last two chapters we investigated the determination of aggregate supply. The key question was, looking at the economy from the point of view of the firm sector, what determines the amount of GDP produced? The simple answer was technology and factor inputs. That answer is only partial in the sense that it immediately raises the question, what determines technology and factor inputs? Although we touched on this question in the earlier chapters, our answer – especially with respect to factor inputs – was limited. We have a special interest in the answer because ordinary people provide the labor input and it forms the basis for most incomes in the economy. In this chapter we ask what in ideal circumstances (i.e., when the economy is running smoothly and all markets are in equilibrium) determines the amount of labor available to production. The analysis can be applied with appropriate modifications to capital as well. We concentrate on labor because of its overwhelming importance to the typical person.

The nearly universal answer to all economic questions is *supply and demand*. If we wish to know why a certain amount of labor is available and used in the production process, a good starting place is to notice that firms demand labor and workers supply it. Our analysis, then, has three parts: (1) What factors govern the decisions of firms to hire labor? (2) What factors govern the willingness of workers to supply it? (3) How do the decisions of firms and workers interact to determine the amount of labor used in production?

11.1 Labor Demand

11.1.1 The Firm's Demand for Labor

Deriving the Firm's Labor-Demand Curve

As we saw in Chapter 9 (section 9.1.2), firms decide how much labor to hire (their **LABOR DEMAND**) based on the conditions for profit maximization. Here we take the straightforward step of translating that earlier analysis into a form that is easy to use in our analysis of the labor market.

The **labor-demand curve** shows *the amount of labor a firm would optimally choose to hire* ceteris paribus *at each real-wage rate*. We already know the general relationship between real-wage rates and the demand for labor. Recall the rule for profit maximization: *a firm hires labor until the marginal product of labor is equal to the real wage* ($mpl = w/p$). Because of diminishing returns to a factor of production, the relationship between real-wage rates and the marginal product of labor is inverse: a firm can profitably hire more labor only if the real wage falls enough to match the fall in the marginal product.

To determine the relationship between the real wage and the firm's demand for labor more precisely, we must apply the profit-maximization rule to the production function to derive a labor-demand curve (see Figure 11.1). The labor production function is shown in the upper panel. We want to derive the relationship between the real wage and labor in the lower panel.

Imagine that the firm with a given stock of capital (perhaps the golf-ball producer of Chapter 9, section 9.1.2) faces a real wage of $(w/p)_1$. The optimal production point is found where the marginal product, shown as the slope of a tangent to the production function at point A, takes the value $(w/p)_1$. This point corresponds to a particular level of labor – call it l_1. The combination $(l_1, (w/p)_1)$ forms point A$'$ in the lower panel and is one point on the labor-demand curve. If the firm paid its workers anything more than $(w/p)_1$ to produce at A, it would reduce its profits because the marginal worker produces only $(w/p)_1$.

But what would the firm do if it faced a lower wage, say $(w/p)_2$? Now it can afford to produce at a point with a lower marginal product. Because the marginal product falls as the firm adds workers and moves rightward along the production function, the new optimal production point will be at a point like B. Here the marginal product is lower than at A and corresponds to the now lower real wage. At B the firm uses the higher amount of labor, l_2. The combination $(l_2, (w/p)_2)$ shown as point B$'$ in the lower panel is another point on the firm's labor-demand curve

Other combinations of real wages and labor inputs can be associated in the same way. The labor-demand curve connects A$'$, B$'$, and every other

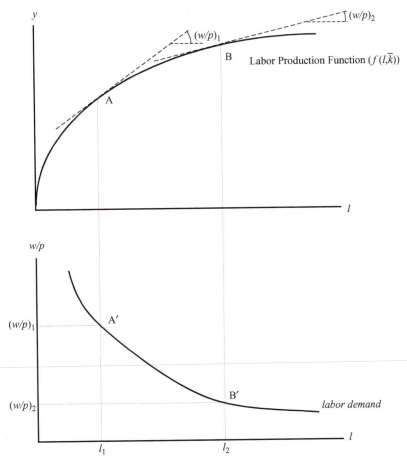

Figure 11.1. Deriving the Labor-Demand Curve. To derive the labor-demand curve (lower panel), start with a real wage; consistent with the rule for profit maximization, find the level of labor that corresponds to that real wage on the production function (upper panel) to form one point on the labor-demand curve; repeat for various real-wage rates to find other points on the curve. Because the production function displays diminishing returns to labor, the falling marginal product as labor increases translates into a downward-sloping, labor-demand curve.

profit-maximizing point. It is downward sloping because of diminishing returns to labor.

Factors That Shift the Labor-Demand Curve

The labor-demand curve shows that *ceteris paribus* an increase in real wages (a movement along the curve) reduces the firm's demand for labor. Whenever two variables are related by a mathematical function or "curve," we should always ask not only what factors move us along the curve but also what happens when other things are not equal: what factors cause the curve to shift? The labor-demand curve is not independent of the production

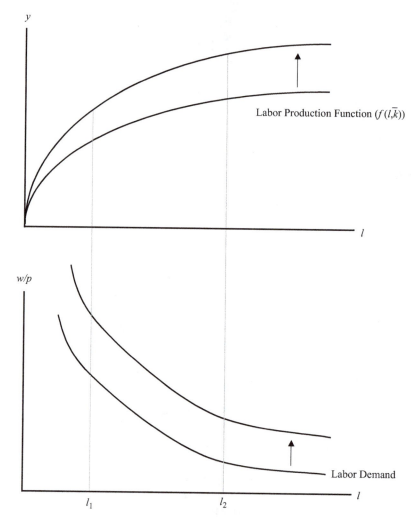

Figure 11.2. A Shifting Production Function Shifts Labor Demand.

function. In fact, it just translates the production function from a graph in which the axes represent labor and output to one in which they represent labor and real-wage rates. As a result, anything that shifts the production function will, in general, shift the labor-demand curve, and the labor-demand curve cannot shift unless the production function also shifts.

We already know from Chapter 9 (section 9.3.2) that technological progress or an increase in the capital stock shifts the production function upward. Consider an increase in the capital stock. How does it shift the labor-demand curve?

We already know that an increase in capital raises the marginal product of labor at every level of labor (shown as the upward shift of the production function in Figure 11.2, where the tangent to each point on the upper production function is steeper than the tangent to the lower production function vertically below it). The higher marginal product means that the profit-maximizing firm can afford to pay a higher real wage at each level of labor. This implies that each level of labor is associated with a higher real wage in the lower panel of Figure 11.2, so that the labor-demand curve shifts vertically upward.

Why would the firm pay workers more for a particular level of labor when additional capital raises their marginal products? Why does the firm not just pocket the windfall? The answer: competition. When the marginal product rises, each firm tries to hire more workers because additional workers would add to their profits at the current wage rate. But because we have assumed that markets are all in equilibrium, all available workers are already employed, and it is only by paying higher wages that the firm can attract them. It is willing to do so until the real wage rises to equal the marginal product. Further rises past that point would cut into their profits.

11.1.2 The Aggregate Demand for Labor

In macroeconomic analysis we are, of course, more concerned with the aggregate demand for labor – that is, how total labor in the economy is related to wages – than with the labor demands of individual firms. If all firms produced the same products and if all workers were alike, then aggregation from the firm to the economy as a whole would be easy. We would simply look at each real-wage rate in turn and ask how much labor each firm would choose to hire at that rate and then add up across every firm to get the total (see Figure 11.3). Unfortunately, it is not that simple.

The first problem is that all firms are not producing the same product. Recall from the example of the golf-ball producer (Chapter 9, section 9.1.2) that the real wage from the point of view of the firm is measured in units of the firm's own output (in that example, the real wage at the optimum production point was 24 golf balls/hour, which was the monetary equivalent of $12 per hour). When different firms produce different goods, we must find a common unit of measurement. Just as with GDP, we can replace the price of a unit of output with a price index. The appropriate index might be the PPI or the GDP deflator (see Chapter 4, section 4.2). This question is discussed further in section 11.3.1.

The second problem is that not all workers are alike. There are many different kinds of workers with different training and skills. Most workers can easily do more than one job, but none can do every job. Different kinds of workers may face different wage rates – jobs that many workers are able to do generally pay less as competition is greater – and, therefore, have different marginal products at the optimum. At any time, there is a wage

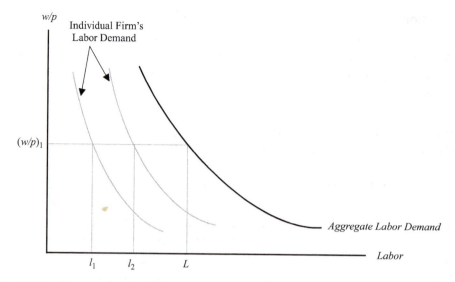

Figure 11.3. The Aggregate Labor-Demand Curve. If all firms produced a homogeneous output, then the aggregate labor-demand curve would be the horizontal sum of all the individual firms' labor-demand curves at each real wage. Here there are only two firms. The aggregate demand for labor at the wage $(w/p)_1$ is $L = l_1 + l_2$. Each point on the aggregate labor-demand curve is derived in the same way. In the actual economy, millions of individual firms' labor demands would contribute to aggregate labor demand.

structure with, for example, day laborers paid low wages and brain surgeons paid high wages. For our purposes, the wage structure can be summarized in the average wage rate. When the entire wage structure moves up or down, the average wage rate follows. It provides an imperfect index of the movements of the wage structure. It is imperfect because the average can change not only because the whole structure moves up and down but also because, even when every individual wage rate remains unchanged, the number of workers in jobs paying different wage rates may change. This imperfection is just another example of what we already noted in Chapter 4 (section 4.1.3): any time a lot of information is summarized in a single number, some information is lost. Here the aggregate real-wage rate loses detailed information about the wage structure itself.

We saw in Chapter 9 (section 9.2.3) that the Cobb-Douglas production function provided a good approximation of aggregate supply in the economy. We will continue to use it here, so that the aggregate labor-demand curve can be derived in just the same way as the individual firm's labor-demand curve in Figure 11.1. To go from the firm to the aggregate, we replace y with real GDP (Y) and l with aggregate labor (L) in the upper panel and we measure the real wage (w/p) not in units of output but as the average real wage measured in the dollars of a base year, where prices (p)

are measured by a price index that appropriately reflects the composition of the output of firms in aggregate. At the optimum production point for the economy as a whole, we regard the marginal product of the aggregate production function as equal to the average real wage.

11.2 Labor Supply

Firms demand labor; workers supply it. We now turn to the factors behind labor supply. Again, although we are mainly concerned with the aggregate supply of labor, it helps to look first at the supply decision of the individual worker. In Chapter 9 we saw that labor could be measured either in hours of work or number of workers. Each measure was useful for different purposes. The two measures reflect two aspects of the worker's labor-supply decision: (1) participation – that is, whether to work or not work; and (2) intensity – that is, how many hours to work. It is easiest if we consider intensity first: conditional on having decided to work, what factors govern the worker's choice of how many hours of work to supply?

11.2.1 The Worker: Choosing Hours of Work

The Price of Leisure

People work for a variety of reasons. The most obvious is to earn the income with which they buy their groceries, pay their rent, finance their cars, and purchase every other necessity or luxury of life. Many people – although not all – find their work fulfilling and interesting. Still, even those people would generally prefer another hour of leisure to another hour of work if it involved no loss of income. It is, therefore, reasonable to assume that leisure is a good. We can consume an hour of leisure exactly as we can consume a loaf of bread, a night in a hotel, a ride in a car, a day in jeans and a tee-shirt, a vacation, or other goods or services.

Goods generally have a price. Yet there is no market for leisure that, for example, seems comparable to the market for cars or meals in a restaurant. (Which is not to say that there is no market for leisure activities such as base-ball games, skiing, or visits to art museums.) Even though there is no explicit price, there is an implicit price or opportunity cost. Recall from Chapter 6, section 6.2.1 that the **OPPORTUNITY COST** *of any choice is the value of the best alternative choice that it forecloses.* The implicit price of leisure is its opportunity cost. If you take an hour of leisure, you forgo the opportunity to work for an hour. What you lose is an hour's wage. Money is not valuable in itself. What you really lose is what an hour's money wage would purchase in consumer goods, which is measured by the real wage (w/p). Here the price level (p) measures the prices of the basket of consumer goods that you would purchase if you had the money. If, for example, you are the typical American urban consumer, this might be measured by CPI-U (see Chapter 4, section 4.2.1).

The Labor-Leisure Choice

Once we see leisure as a good and the real-wage rate as its price, it is easier to understand the choices a worker faces. There are 168 hours in a week. If a worker chooses not to work at all, he enjoys 168 hours of leisure, but forgoes the income needed to buy any other goods. If the worker instead takes fewer hours of leisure, he supplies labor $l = 168 - $ *hours of leisure*, and he gains the ability to purchase goods worth $w/p \times l$. The problem for the worker is to choose the hours of labor (l) that at the margin makes the psychic value of a small further loss of leisure time (i.e., a small increase in labor time) exactly equal to the psychic value of the small gain in consumption goods that would be purchased by that labor.

To make this concrete, suppose that the wage rate is $15 per hour and, after balancing the marginal benefits of consumption and leisure, you decide to supply 20 hours of labor per week (consume 148 hours of leisure). What happens when the real-wage rate rises to, say, $16 per hour? Do you supply more or less labor? There are two aspects of the increased wage rate: first, if you continue to work 20 hours per week, it raises your income from $300 to $320 per week; second, it increases the opportunity cost of leisure. Although these are both aspects of the same change in the wage rate, we can analyze them separately through two thought experiments.

- **Thought experiment 1.** *How would your supply of labor change if you could receive the income that results from the increased wage rate without facing a changed opportunity cost of leisure?*

To make sense of this thought experiment, imagine that the wage rate stayed at $15 per hour, but that you instead inherited a small legacy that paid $20 per week whether you worked or not. Would you work more or less?

As a general rule, an increase in income *ceteris paribus* increases the demand for all goods.[1] The extra $20 per week would permit you to buy more goods, including as much as one hour and fifteen minutes of extra leisure without reducing your purchases of other goods. Typically, you would buy some additional goods *and* some additional leisure – that is, you would reduce your supply of labor by a small amount. *The reduction in the supply of labor as the result of an increase in income* is called the **INCOME EFFECT**.

---

[1] Students who have studied microeconomics will, of course, recognize that this applies to so-called "normal" goods only. An increase in income may reduce the demand for "inferior goods."

- **Thought experiment 2.** *How would your supply of labor change if you faced a higher wage rate, but no change in your income?*

To make sense of this thought experiment, imagine that the wage rate rose to $16 per hour, but that the government levied a lump-sum tax (i.e., a tax that each person must pay regardless of income) of $20 per week. Now your weekly income when you are working 20 hours per week is still $300, but your wage rate is higher. Would you work more or less?

As a general rule, whenever *ceteris paribus* the price of anything rises relative to alternatives, the demand for it decreases. When the price of strawberry jam rises relative to marmalade, people typically buy more marmalade. Here the price of leisure (its opportunity cost) has risen relative to the price of other goods, including both jam and marmalade. Typically, you would buy more jam, marmalade, and other goods and less leisure – that is, your supply of labor would rise. The change in the wage rate encourages you to substitute the now cheaper goods for the now more expensive leisure. *The increase in the supply of labor as the result of an increase in the price (or opportunity cost) of leisure* is called the **SUBSTITUTION EFFECT**.

Although we can separate them conceptually, any actual change in real-wage rates always has both an income effect, which encourages us to reduce our supply of labor, *and* a substitution effect, which encourages us to increase it. What happens to our labor supply as the result of a change in wages depends on which effect is stronger.

The Labor-Supply Curve

How might we represent the individual's labor supply on a graph in a manner analogous to the firm's labor-demand curve?

Figure 11.4 represents the worker's labor-supply decision. Look first at panel (A). Suppose that at point A, where the real wage is $(w/p)_1$, the worker decides that providing l hours of work balances the advantages of a little more consumption against a little more leisure at the margin. Now consider what happens when the real wage rises to $(w/p)_2$. There is a substitution effect shown by the arrow pointing to the right, which encourages the worker to supply more labor. The size of the substitution effect is measured by the length of the arrow.

There is also an income effect shown by the arrow pointing to the left, which encourages the worker to supply less labor.

The net effect is measured by the difference between the substitution and income effects shown at point B. As shown in the figure, the substitution effect is stronger than the income effect, so that an increase in the wage rate increases the worker's supply of labor to l_2 to the right of l_1. If the substitution effect is always stronger, then the labor-supply curve slopes upward.

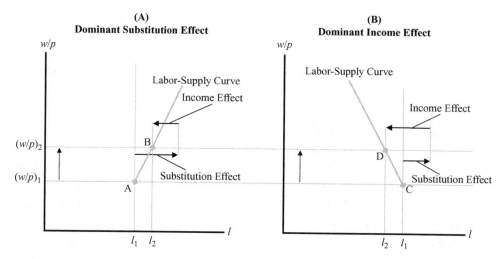

Figure 11.4. The Slope of the Labor-Supply Curve. When the real-wage rate rises, the substitution effect encourages people to supply more labor because the opportunity cost of leisure has risen, and the income effect encourages people to supply less labor because they can now afford more leisure. If the substitution effect is stronger, the labor-supply curve slopes upward. If the income effect is stronger, the labor-supply curve slopes downward.

The whole labor-supply curve can be constructed in the same manner by considering different real-wage rates and looking for the net consequence of the substitution and income effects.

Substitution effects are not necessarily stronger than income effects. Panel (B) shows the construction of the labor-supply curve, starting from point C, when income effects are stronger than substitution effects. When the real-wage rate increases from $(w/p)_1$ to $(w/p)_2$, the dominant income effect overwhelms the substitution effect, and labor supply (point C) falls from l_1 to l_2. If income effects are stronger for all wage rates above $(w/p)_1$, then the labor-supply curve will slope downward toward point C: higher real-wage rates lower labor supply.

Although the labor-supply curve can slope downward toward a point like C, it is not reasonable to believe that it could slope downward for every possible wage rate. What would happen if it did? As the real-wage rate fell from $(w/p)_1$ toward zero, the worker would supply more and more labor, so that at zero he would supply more labor than at any positive wage rate. But that makes no sense. People will not normally work for nothing except as a charitable act.

Instead, at very low wage rates it is more reasonable to suppose that, with very low incomes, the worker's need for food, clothing, shelter, and other "essential" goods is so acute that the income effect is weak and the substitution effect strong. We should, therefore, expect the labor-supply curve to be upward sloping when wage rates are low.

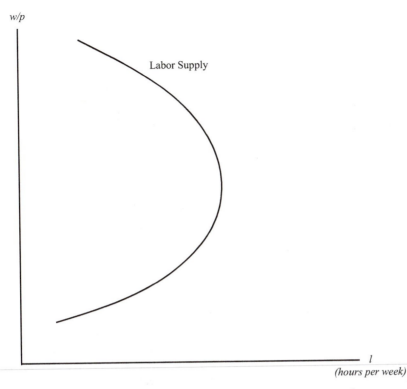

Figure 11.5. Backward-Bending Labor-Supply Curve. At low real-wage rates, it is likely that substitution effects are stronger than income effects, so that the labor-supply curve slopes upward. As real-wage rates rise, income effects may become relatively stronger, producing a steeper curve or even one that bends backward.

On the other hand, it is also unlikely that as wage rates get ever higher, a worker would continue to value goods so much and leisure so little at the margin that he would supply more and more hours of labor. At some point, the marginal value of free time will surely overwhelm the lost increment of consumption. Then the income effect would begin to counterbalance the substitution effect, turning the labor-supply curve back on itself. Figure 11.5 shows a **backward-bending labor-supply curve**, one in which income effects are weak when wages are low and become stronger when wages are high.

Adding Realism: Taxes

Our derivation of the labor-supply curve omits many features of the economy that might affect the behavior of actual workers. But the analysis is easily modified to account for some of the neglected features. We shall look at two omissions in detail – taxes and the standard workweek.

One of the great disappointments to any teenager receiving a first paycheck is the discovery that the government takes a sizeable chunk of a

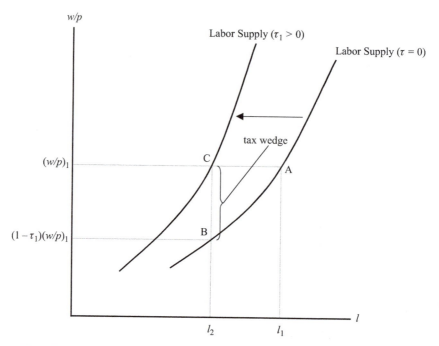

Figure 11.6. The Effect of a Tax Increase on Labor Supply. If the substitution effect outweighs the income effect, an increase in marginal tax rates shifts the labor-supply curve left. Because taxes are proportional, the effect is greater at high real-wage rates than at low, which steepens the curve as it shifts left.

worker's earnings in the form of income taxes and Social Security contributions. The U.S. tax code is complicated. So, to analyze the effect of taxes on labor supply, we must simplify. The worker's decision – like most economic decisions – is made at the margin. The important question is, what are the gains or losses from working a little more or a little less? The question with respect to taxes is, how does the tax code affect the income from a little more or a little less work? To answer this question we must know the marginal tax rate. The **marginal tax rate** is defined as *the fraction of an additional dollar of income that is paid as taxes*. To keep things simple, assume that all income is taxed at the same flat rate – call it τ (the Greek letter "tau"). In this case the marginal tax rate must also be τ, which takes a value between zero and one. If a worker earns a real wage w/p for an hour of work, the government takes $\tau(w/p)$ as taxes and leaves the worker $(1 - \tau)(w/p)$ as the **after-tax real wage**.

Because the worker actually receives the after-tax real wage, it – rather than the wage paid by the firm to the worker – is the true opportunity cost of leisure. Any increase in the marginal tax rate represents a decrease in the opportunity cost of leisure. If substitution effects are stronger than income effects, then any increase in marginal tax rates reduces the supply of labor as shown in Figure 11.6.

The labor-supply curve with no taxes is shown on the far right of the figure. At a real wage $(w/p)_1$, the worker supplies labor l_1. If a tax of τ_1 is imposed, what happens to labor supply? The after-tax real wage is $(1 - \tau_1)(w/p)_1$. The worker should react exactly as if he paid no taxes but suffered a cut in his wage rate to this level. This is shown as a movement along the right-hand curve from point A to point B where labor supply has fallen to l_2. But of course the wage rate did not really fall; the employer still pays $(w/p)_1$. This means that the combination $(l_2, (w/p)_1)$ is the labor supply (point C). Because the same argument would apply for any real-wage rate, every point on the original curve shifts to the left. Because the tax rate is proportional, its absolute effect is greater, as is the shift in the labor-supply curve, at high wage rates, resulting in a steepening of the curve. The new labor-supply curve is drawn on the assumption that the tax rate is τ_1. Any further increase in the tax rate to, say, τ_2, would shift the labor-supply curve further to the left. (In Problem 11.5, the student is asked to work out the effect of an increase in tax rates on a backward-bending labor-supply curve.)

The length of the line segment $\overline{BC}$ in Figure 11.6 measures the **TAX WEDGE** between the real wage paid by employers and the after-tax real wage received by workers. The larger the tax wedge, the larger the leftward shift of the labor-supply curve and the greater the reduction in labor supplied at any real wage.

We have assumed that the only relevant taxes are income taxes, but the tax wedge also includes any difference between the value of the marginal product paid by the firm and what the worker can actually choose to spend that varies with the number of hours the worker supplies.

For example, an increase in an indirect tax, such as a sales tax, acts similarly to an increase in income tax rates. If workers spend all of their income on taxable consumption goods, a one-point increase in the sales tax reduces their effective purchasing power by 1 percent, lowering the opportunity cost of leisure. Of course, the exact effect is complicated by the fact that sales taxes rarely apply to all goods (e.g., some states exempt food) and may also be avoided if workers choose to save rather than spend their earnings. Even income taxes are more complicated than we have suggested because of the various ways to avoid paying them (such as 401Ks and other tax-deferred savings accounts). Although the exact size of the tax wedge is variable and hard to measure, the qualitative effect is clear.

The idea that tax increases lower labor supply, and conversely that tax cuts increase labor supply, was a major tenet of the so-called **supply-side economics** popular in the early 1980s. President Ronald Reagan and his advisers used it to argue that cuts in marginal tax rates would stimulate people to work harder and to earn larger incomes. Conceivably, the increase in incomes could be large enough to offset the lower tax rates, so that total tax revenues would actually rise. Whether this happens in practice depends on whether substitution effects are large enough, not only to outweigh income effects, but to increase labor supply by a greater proportion than the fall in tax rates.

The evidence appears to confirm some supply-side effects of the tax cuts made in Reagan's first term, although, in the event, the effects were not large enough to increase revenues. Although laying less stress on either the labor market or the self-financing possibilities of tax cuts, President George W. Bush revived the supply-side policies in his first term.

Adding Realism: A Standard Workweek

Another way in which the simple analysis of labor supply is unrealistic is that many workers are not given an option about the number of hours they work. Although people work part-time and overtime, either may be voluntary or mandatory. The Federal law that requires firms to pay wage workers (as opposed to salaried supervisory or professional employees) "time and a half" for overtime provides a disincentive for them to permit overtime. Despite exceptions, the 40-hour week is the norm in the United States.

Let us take a small step toward realism by assuming that workers are not permitted to work more than 40 hours a week – although they can work less. Figure 11.7 is similar to the backward-bending labor-supply curve in Figure 11.5 except that it includes a constraint shown as a vertical line at 40 hours. If the worker were permitted to choose freely, then the labor-supply curve would be the curve running through points A, B, C, D, and E. At points A, D, and E, the worker wants to supply less than 40 hours, so the constraint is not binding. But the gray segment of this curve to the right of the constraint shows points that are not allowed. At point B the worker wants to supply more than 40 hours, but is permitted to supply only 40, so that the constraint forces point B to shift leftward to point F. Similarly, desired labor supply at point C is too high, and it shifts to point G where the worker supplies only 40 hours. The overall effect is to reshape the labor-supply curve as indicated by the black curve with the vertical segment that runs through points A, F, G, D, and E. Any worker on this vertical segment is constrained.

The Individual Labor-Supply Curve in Practice

What does the individual labor-supply curve look like in reality? It is difficult to answer such a question, because in reality we can observe only one point (one combination of labor and a real-wage rate) on the labor-supply curve for a single worker at a particular time. All the other points are conjectures about what the worker *would* supply if faced with different wage rates. If we imagine that on average workers are substantially similar, we might

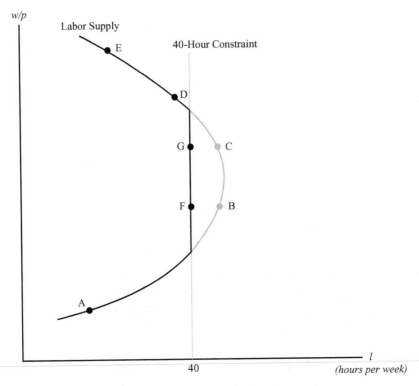

Figure 11.7. Labor Supply with a Statutory Workweek.

nonetheless get some idea of what the individual labor-supply curve might look like.

The National Longitudinal Survey (Youth) has catalogued the work histories of a large sample of individuals starting at a young age. Figure 11.8 plots the real-wage rates and average weekly hours of labor for about 10,000 male workers from this survey for a single period. The best fitting flexible line through these points is fitted using the "Add Trendline" option in the Excel spreadsheet package. This is the so-called "nonlinear regression line." (See the *Guide*, section G.15, for an introduction to regression as a statistical tool.) The regression line serves as our empirical estimate of the labor-supply curve for these workers.

Notice the close similarity between this figure and Figure 11.7. The regression line traces out a shape very like the backward-bending labor-supply curve with a 40-hour constraint. What looks like a vertical line above 40 hours is not really a solid line at all but a reflection of the fact that about 7,500 of the 10,000 workers in the sample supply 40 hours per week at a variety of wage rates. The labor-supply curve traces out a segment above the 40-hour point that corresponds to the constraint.

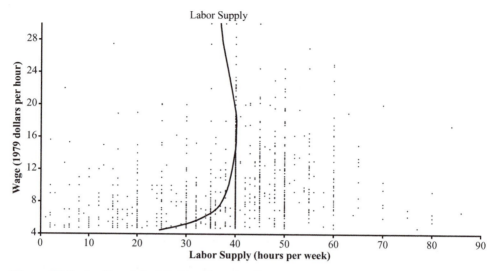

Figure 11.8. An Empirical Labor-Supply Curve. Each of the 10,036 points represents one (male) worker's weekly hours of work supplied and hourly wage rate. The labor-supply curve is the best fitting nonlinear regression line. *Source:* Bureau of Labor Statistics, *National Longitudinal Survey of Youth 1979*.

There are points to the right of 40 hours. This is reasonable because, in the real world, workers do work overtime – either because they are supervisors or professionals or because employers offer them the legally mandated time-and-half wage rate for overtime.

The fit of the regression line is far from perfect; points lie on both sides of the line. We should interpret it as a snapshot of the behavior of the *typical* worker. But of course, the typical worker is not any actual worker in particular.

11.2.2 The Worker: Choosing to Participate

So far, we have examined only one aspect of the worker's labor-supply decision: how many hours to work for a given real wage. We now take up the second aspect: participation – that is, whether or not to work at all.

A labor-supply curve that starts at the origin and slopes upward for at least a portion of its length suggests that even if the wage were very low – say, 1 cent per hour – the worker would work a little bit. That is clearly unrealistic: no one would work at all for 1 cent per hour. What factors determine how high the wage must be to induce a person to participate in the labor market?

The **labor-force participation** decision is, once again, a question of opportunity cost. Idleness has its charms. Before anyone enters the labor force, the wage rate must be high enough to overcome them. Working has costs that do not depend on the number of hours one works. A worker may need special clothes, a car or other transportation, or child- or eldercare just to be in the position to take a job even for one minute. The *opportunity cost of participating in the labor force* is the sum of

- the implicit value the worker places on complete idleness;
- the explicit costs of working compared to not working (such as clothing, transport, childcare); and
- the explicit losses from working (for instance, housework not done).

The opportunity cost is thus partly psychological and partly material.

If people were completely independent of each other and never had the support of any other person, the worker might place a lower value on the opportunity cost of participation. For then the choice might literally be between work and starvation. But most people are not completely independent. For many (e.g., teenagers living at home or a spouse providing a second income) whether or not to participate in the labor force could be a genuine choice and would depend on the real wage.

The **RESERVATION WAGE** is defined to be *the opportunity cost of working compared to not working – that is, the real wage that is high enough to make it just worthwhile for a worker to participate in the labor force.*

Taking account of the opportunity costs of participation affects the shape of the labor-supply curve shown in Figure 11.9. As long as the real wage is below the reservation wage $((w/p)^R)$, the worker supplies no labor at all. This is shown as the black segment on the vertical axis. Above the reservation wage there is a normal labor-supply curve.

Figure 11.9 captures the two stages of the labor-supply decision: First, at low wages, the worker will not supply any labor at all, and small increases in wages have no effect. But, second, as soon as the wage rises enough for the worker to bite the bullet and join the labor force, the minimum labor supplied will be well above zero, and the worker will decide how many hours to supply above this minimum through the usual process of balancing the opportunity cost of leisure against the desire for consumption goods.

11.2.3 Aggregate Labor Supply

The Aggregate Labor-Supply Curve

How can we move from the microeconomics of the labor supply back to an aggregate relationship usable in macroeconomic analysis? If workers were essentially alike, the problem would be easy.

As we have seen, labor supply has two dimensions – participation in the labor force and choice of hours of labor. We can derive aggregate labor-supply curves by focusing on each dimension. Take the participation

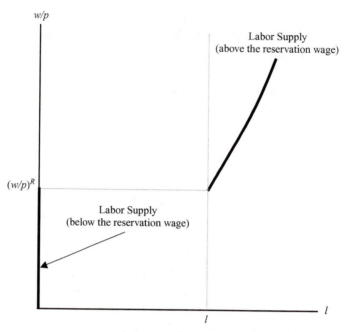

Figure 11.9. The Effect of the Participation Decision on Labor Supply. Each worker has a reservation wage – the minimum wage rate that overcomes the explicit costs and opportunity costs of beginning to work. At a wage rate below the reservation wage, no labor is supplied, producing a discontinuity in the labor-supply curve.

decision first. If all workers were alike except for differences in their reservation wage, then we could rank them from lowest to highest reservation wage. We can then ask: What would happen if the real-wage rate started at zero and began to rise? The result is shown in Figure 11.10. At a wage rate of zero, no one participates, and labor supply is zero. As the wage rate rises, it meets and then exceeds more and more people's reservation wages, so that more and more people participate. The aggregate labor-supply (participation) curve is strictly upward-sloping.

Of course this is too easy. Just as we observed in deriving the aggregate labor-demand curve, workers are not all alike, but differ in knowledge and skills, in tastes and opportunity costs. They face different real-wage rates and have different reservation wages. Once again we must interpret the vertical axis of Figure 11.10 as measuring the average real wage that, at best, provides a kind of index for the level of the wage structure. An individual worker might have a reservation wage well below the prevailing average real wage and yet actually be offered only a wage below his reservation wage. That worker will not join the labor force.

The problem remains the same when we turn to the choice of hours. Workers are all different and face a structure of wages. For each worker individually there is a jump from supplying zero to supplying some positive

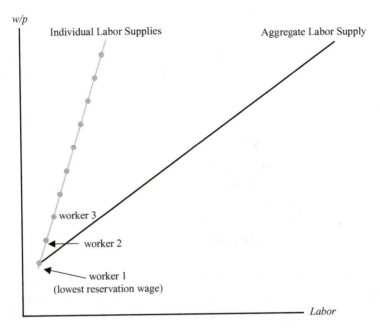

Figure 11.10. Derivation of the Aggregate Labor-Supply Curve. If every individual is alike except for their reservation wages, then each has the same labor-curve for the points above the reservation wage. Each dot on the individual labor-supply curve marks a higher reservation wage. The aggregate labor-supply curve starts when the wage reaches the lowest reservation wage. As the wage rises, the labor supply of more and more workers contributes to the aggregate labor supply as they enter the labor force in turn.

number of hours when his own wage rate surpasses his reservation wage. But in aggregate we are unlikely to see such a jump. Not only are there a variety of wages offered at any time, but reservation wages differ. As a result, at any average wage rate some workers are supplying labor. As the wage structure shifts upward, average real wages rise, and individual workers move upward along their labor-supply curves. Individual workers may have backward-bending segments on their individual labor-supply curves, but the level of wages at which the curves start to bend backward differs among workers. If, as seems likely, at any average real wage most workers find themselves on the upward-sloping or vertical segments of their individual labor-supply curves, then increases in average wages will be associated with increases in labor supply. Then the aggregate labor-supply (hours) curve will slope upward just as the participation curve (Figure 11.10) did.

A curve like Figure 11.10 can be used to display either the participation decision or the hours decision, but not both at the same time. The horizontal axis of aggregate labor-market diagrams in this book is marked with an uppercase L. For many purposes, there is little harm in shifting between workers and worker-hours as measures of the labor supply. The two meanings are not completely independent: by definition, *workers* $\equiv$ $\frac{aggregate\ worker\ hours}{average\ hours\ per\ worker}$. When no confusion is likely, we will let L stands for worker-hours (as it generally did in Chapters 9 and 10) or for workers (as it often will in Chapters 12 and 15, as well as later parts of this chapter). When working with actual data, however, we must be more scrupulous in making our meaning clear.

The Participation Rate and Average Hours

What do empirical evidence and the microeconomic analysis of labor supply tell us about the shape of the aggregate labor-supply curve? Aggregate labor supply is the result of millions of individual decisions. The factors that are important for each individual worker affect the aggregate; although, as always in macroeconomics, their manner of operation is not necessarily simple or straightforward.

The two critical aspects of the worker's labor-supply decision – whether to participate in the labor force and, conditional on participation, how much to work – carry over to aggregate labor supply. Because workers' tastes, skills, opportunity costs, and reservation wages are different, workers face different wage rates, and each has a different labor-supply curve. The regression line in Figure 11.8 reflects, at best, the typical behavior of the surveyed workers – all people who had chosen to participate – but again the typical worker is no worker in particular.

Let us look first at the aggregate participation decision. The aggregate number of workers who have decided to participate is known as the **labor force**. The *civilian labor force older than 16 years of age* in the United States in 2009 was 154,369,600 workers. This number excludes uniformed members of the armed services and the small number of workers younger than 16 years old. The labor force, of course, has grown right along with population. The **participation rate (PR)** measures *the labor force as a ratio to the relevant population: participation rate* $= \frac{labor\ force}{relevant\ population}$. The *civilian noninstitutional population older than 16* in 2009 was 235,801,000 ("noninstitutional" excludes people, for example, in prison or in homes for the aged). Therefore, the PR = 154,369,600/235,801,000 = 65 percent – just a little less than two-thirds of the potentially available population are in the civilian labor force.

The aggregate number of hours worked is not as easy as the participation rate to relate to the individual workers' choices. If every worker had the same labor-supply curve (say, Figure 11.7), we would have to know the wage offered to each one to calculate the total number of labor hours supplied. In reality, workers are not all alike. Labor-supply curves may vary systematically according to the sex, age, ethnic group, education, experience, or other social or economic characteristics of the workers. And within any group, the labor-supply curves of individuals are likely to vary.

In principle, if we had a good statistical estimate of the typical distribution of the wages (what are the relevant groups and what proportion of workers in each group received each possible wage), we could make a reasonable calculation. But statisticians at the Bureau of Labor Statistics (BLS) do not try to calculate the labor supply in this way. Instead, they count the number of hours that workers actually work and the *average* wages and salaries they are paid. As usual for aggregate data, much of the interesting variation among workers is lost in these calculations. Some of it is regained when the BLS calculates average wages and hours for different occupations, economic sectors, industries, sexes, and racial and ethnic groups.

The total hours of labor in the United States in 2009 were 251,885 million. The average hours of work using the labor force estimate quoted earlier were 251,885 million/154,369,600 = 1,632 hours per year = 32.6 hours per week (assuming a 50-week year). This number is about one-fifth below the full-time 40-hour week, which makes sense because it averages over full-time, part-time, and overtime workers.

Table 11.1 places the U.S. data into an international context. Relatively more Americans work: participation rates are higher (sometimes substantially higher) in the United States than in most other countries – well above both the OECD average and the average of European OECD countries. However, Canada, the Netherlands, and the United Kingdom all have higher participation rates than the United States. Americans also work more hours than people in most countries, although they do not work the most: average annual hours of work in the United States are similar to Japan and Italy; below Korea, Turkey, Poland, and Mexico; and substantially above France, Germany, and the Netherlands.

Is the Labor Supply Stable over Time?

Statistics on participation rates or average hours for a particular month or year are snapshots of the labor market. Only one point on each worker's labor-supply curve is observed. How should we think of the labor supply over time? The real wage has risen by several orders of magnitude over the history of the United States. Can we analyze the effects of that increase on the labor market under the assumption that the labor-supply curves of workers remain essentially stable?

If the labor-supply curve of typical workers were stable and were essentially like that in Figure 11.9, participation rates should have risen over time. Different people no doubt have different tastes and different reservation wages, but as the average real wage rises, it should surpass the reservation

Table 11.1. *Labor Supply in 2008*

	Participation Rate (percent of persons 15–64 years old)	Average Annual Hours of Work (per actual person employed)
The G-7		
Canada	78.6	1,727
France	69.7	1,542
Germany	75.9	1,432
Italy	63.0	1,802
Japan	73.8	1,772
United Kingdom	76.8	1,653
United States	75.3	1,792
Other Countries		
Australia	76.5	1,721
Belgium	66.3	1,568
Ireland	71.9	1,601
Luxembourg	67.8	1,555
Mexico	62.2	1,893
Netherlands	78.4	1,389
Poland	63.8	1,969
South Korea	66.0	2,316[a]
Spain	73.7	1,627
Turkey	50.6	1,918[b]
OECD Europe	69.0	N/A
Total OECD	70.8	N/A

[a] 2007 datum; [b] 2004 datum.

Source: Organization of Economic Cooperation and Development, *Employment Outlook, 2004.*

wage of more and more people encouraging them to enter the labor force. Data on participation rates in the United States appear to support this conjecture; Figure 11.11 shows the overall civilian participation rate trending upward from the early 1960s (although falling slightly since the recession in 2001).

Unfortunately, the behavior of participation rates probably does not reflect the effect of rising real-wage rates on stable labor-supply curves. People's tastes and reservation wages (opportunity costs) are likely to depend on age, sex, and possibly other factors. The overall participation rate reflects in part the average effect of these various factors and in part the effect of changing real-wage rates. The overall participation rate may be hard to interpret, because it mixes men and women, young and old, skilled and unskilled. To isolate the effect of real wages, it would be better to look at more homogeneous groups. Figure 11.11 also shows the participation rate

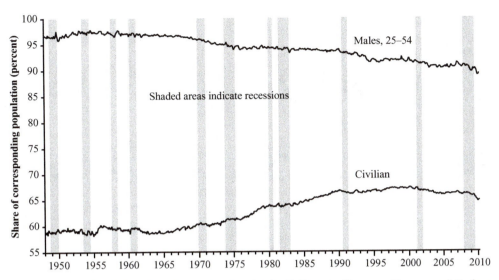

Figure 11.11. Participation Rates in the United States. *Source:* Bureau of Labor Statistics.

for one such group: **prime-age males** – that is, *men in their peak working years, 25–54*. Their participation rate fell very slowly from a high around 98 percent in the early 1950s to around 91 percent in the early 2000s. Their participation fell somewhat more sharply to a little less than 90 percent in the aftermath of the recession of 2007–2009. (A more detailed analysis of the differences in participation rates by sex is left for Problems 11.9 and 11.10.)

What explains the fall in prime-age male participation rates? For several years, economists and politicians have debated whether real wages – properly computed – rose or fell from the early 1970s to the mid-1990s. The fall in the prime-age male participation rate is consistent with a constant distribution of reservation wages and a falling real wage. But the reservation wages were not necessarily constant. The fall in participation rates is also consistent with an increasing reservation wage that could have resulted from changing demographics and social relations (e.g., the average number of children in families or the proportion of wives in the labor force).

The two relatively stable periods, before 1970 and after 1990, also challenge the idea that labor-supply curves were stable. Real wages increased over both periods, which should imply increased participation rates. This may provide further evidence that reservation wages vary over time, perhaps because workers' relative taste for leisure over consumption adjusts to the levels of consumption to which they become accustomed. For example, if a real wage of $8 per hour was enough to induce a worker to enter the work force in 1970 and, by 2012, real wages had risen to, say, $24 per hour, then that worker, who is now used to the higher wage, might stop participating if the real wage falls to $21 per hour. A young but otherwise similar

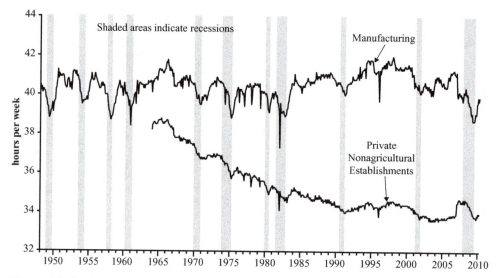

Figure 11.12. Average Weekly Hours of Work in the United States. *Source:* Bureau
of Labor Statistics.

worker might not wish to enter the labor force unless the real wage was
more than $24 per hour. Such shifting tastes and *relative* preferences are
also consistent with the notion that poverty is a matter of relative, rather
than absolute, material deprivation (see Chapter 10, section 10.1, especially
Table 10.1).

Turning to the choice of hours of labor, it is harder to draw a definite prediction from our analysis. If we imagine that Figures 11.8 and 11.9 describe
typical individual labor-supply curves, where any individual worker finds
himself on the curve depends on the distribution of wage rates offered by
firms. If the average real wage rises over time, we would expect the whole
wage structure to shift up. Workers on the low end of the wage spectrum are
likely to supply more hours, workers at intermediate wage rates would supply the same number of hours (the statutory 40 per week), and workers at the
higher end, who find themselves on the backward-bending segment, would
supply fewer hours. But how do these changes affect the aggregate number
of hours supplied? That depends on how many people are on each segment
of the typical labor-supply curve. If many people are on the lower, upward-
sloping segment, then the rise in average real-wage rates should increase
average hours supplied. If, as seems likely from the data behind Figure 11.8,
many workers find themselves constrained to supply 40 hours per week, then
average hours would not be too sensitive to changes in wages rates. Only
if many workers were on the backward-bending segments might we expect
average hours to fall. What actually happened?

Average weekly hours of work for all persons in private industry fell
steadily between the mid-1960s and the early 1990s, flattening out somewhat after that (Figure 11.12). But, as with the data on civilian participation

rates, these data mix a wide diversity of workers. Figure 11.12 also shows the average hours for a single sector in which workers may be more homogeneous: manufacturing. These are highly variable around a steady mean of about 40 hours per week up to the mid-1980s.

Steady average hours could have several explanations. One possibility is that income effects could exactly offset substitution effects. A second is that workers generally wish to work more hours but are constrained to work the normal 40-hour week by their employers. The first explanation seems unlikely. Precisely offsetting income and substitution effects would make the labor-supply curve in Figure 11.9 vertical, but would not remove the discontinuity at the reservation wage. So, although hours supplied would remain steady on average, rising wages would over time be accompanied by rising participation rates. But, as we saw, participation rates tend to be constant or falling.

Given the statutory 40-hour week, the rising trend in average hours in manufacturing since the mid-1980s must be the result of overtime. The explanation for increased overtime is unlikely to be a change in taste on the part of workers. Surely, many of those who work a 40-hour week would work more if the employers would let them. But the rule of time-and-a-half for overtime means that there is a large jump in marginal costs at 40 hours per week. A firm will allow overtime on a continuing basis only if it is cheaper to pay some workers overtime than to hire more workers on straight time. The explanation for rising overtime surely must be sought in some change in the structure of labor costs in firms rather than in changes in the tastes of workers.

The interpretation of average hours is complicated. To get behind the aggregate data, the economist needs to pay attention to demographics, social organization, the distribution of worker skills, and other factors. These are the domain of a specialized field, *labor economics*, and outside the scope of a macroeconomics course. Still, the evidence points to some general conclusions about aggregate labor supply. The fact that many workers are constrained to work 40-hour weeks plus the empirical observation that participation rates do not vary much despite massive increases in real wages (Figure 11.11) suggest that aggregate labor-supply curves are likely to be relatively steep – that is, large changes in average real-wage rates cause only small changes in participation rates or average hours worked.

11.3 Labor Market Equilibrium

11.3.1 Market Clearing

Now that we have both labor-supply and labor-demand curves, we can use them to describe a smoothly functioning, ideal labor market. When both curves are plotted on the same diagram, the crossing point defines the equilibrium real-wage rate and the equilibrium level of labor employed.

There is one complication. The real wage looks different from the point of view of the firm and the worker. For the firm, the relevant real wage is the **product-real wage** defined as *the number of units of the firm's good that the wage will purchase* $(= \frac{w}{price\ of\ product})$. For the worker, the relevant real wage is the **consumption-real wage** defined as *the number of typical consumption baskets that the wage will purchase* $(= \frac{w}{price\ of\ consumption\ basket})$. For aggregate analysis, we might use the PPI or the GDP deflator to approximate the product price and the CPI to approximate the consumption price.

For many purposes, the distinction between product-real wage and consumption-real wage can be ignored. In those cases, we will speak simply of the real wage without qualification. But it is easy to see that it could matter. Suppose that the product-real wage and the consumption-real wage in Figure 11.13 start out with the identical value $(w/p)^*$ at the market-clearing point A. Now suppose that Japanese cars are a large portion of the typical worker's consumption basket and that *ceteris paribus* the price of Japanese cars rises sharply. This means that the real wage from the point of view of the consumer falls to $(w/p_{CPI})_1$ at point B on the labor-supply curve (L^S), so that the worker would want to supply less labor (L_1).

But that is not the end of the story. How does it look from the point of view of the firms? The rise in the price of Japanese cars has no effect on the price of their products. Nevertheless, they see a reduction of labor supply at the original market-clearing wage. It is as if the labor-supply curve has shifted to the left to $L^{S'}$, which passes through $(w/p)^*$, L_1 at point C. At the original wage rate, labor demand exceeds labor supply, so firms raise wages in an effort to attract workers until they reach the new market-clearing wage at point D where they pay $(w/p_{PPI})^{**}$ for labor of L^{**}. The rise in the price of Japanese cars has the effect of raising the wages that firms must pay and reducing labor employed. Higher wages partly compensate workers for the higher costs of consumption, but firms can afford to pay those higher wages only if marginal products rise as a result of their using less labor. The rise in wage rates is not enough to compensate workers fully, so the consumption-real wage in equilibrium is $(w/p_{CPI})^{**}$ at point E.

The alert student will notice that the shift in the labor-supply curve induced by the increase in price of Japanese cars follows from exactly the same logic as the shift induced by an increase in tax rates (see Figure 11.6). We can think of import prices as a tax levied on consumers and of an increase in import prices as widening the tax wedge.

Unless the issue that we want to analyze depends on the difference between product- and consumption-real wages (e.g., in Problem 12.6 in the

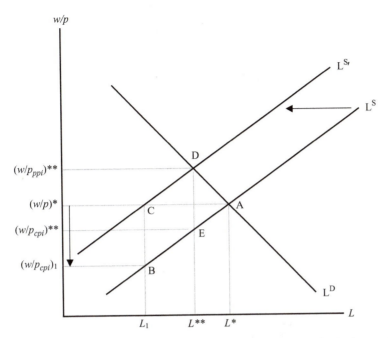

Figure 11.13. An Increase in the Price of Consumption Goods Relative to the Price of Output. Assume that the market clears at point A, where the prices of consumption goods and output are the same. If the price of consumption goods rises (e.g., due to a rise in the price of imported goods), the consumption-real wage falls *ceteris paribus* to $(w/p_{cpi})_1$ – a movement along the labor-supply curve to point B. Viewing the labor market through the production-real wage, this appears to firms as a shift of the labor-supply curve to $L^{S'}$, which passes through point C (the same labor supply (L_1) as at point B but with the unchanged production-real wage). Point B is not an equilibrium. Firms are willing to increase wages to $(w/p)^{**}$ in order to reach the new equilibrium at point D. Equilibrium labor is reduced to L^{**} and the increased wage rate is not enough to compensate workers fully for the cost-of-living increase as the equilibrium consumption-real wage $(w/p_{cpi})^{**}$ (point E) remains below the original real wage at $(w/p)^*$.

next chapter), we will treat the real wage as the same for both labor supply and labor demand.

11.3.2 Analyzing Ideal Labor Markets

The aggregate labor-supply/labor-demand diagram provides us with a powerful tool. To illustrate the use of our new tool, we now analyze three important macroeconomic issues: (1) the effect of tax cuts on employment; (2) the effect of technological progress on the well-being of workers; and (3) the effect of immigration on existing workers. We remain within the framework of the ideal labor market in which aggregate demand is always sufficient to keep the economy at its full potential and the labor force fully employed.

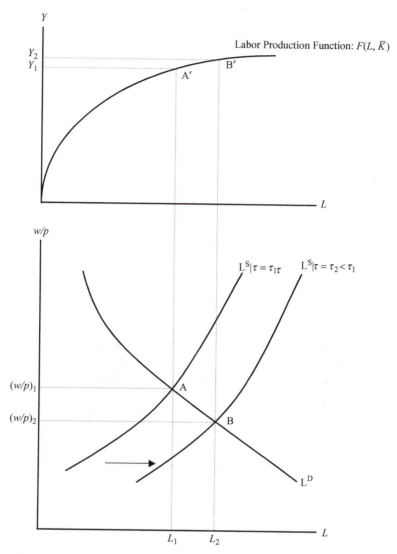

Figure 11.14. Issue 1: The Effect of a Cut in Marginal Tax Rates.

Issue 1. Tax Cuts

What are the effects of a cut in marginal income-tax rates on employment and the level of GDP in the economy?

Recall from section 11.2.1 that a lower marginal income-tax rate increases labor supply at each real wage (a rightward shift of the labor supply). Labor market equilibrium moves from point A to point B in the lower panel of Figure 11.14. Notice that the amount of labor available to firms increases, so that firms move production from A' to B' on the labor production function in the upper panel. Real GDP rises. Also notice that the real wage falls from $(w/p)_1$ to $(w/p)_2$.

We must be careful in interpreting the fall in real wages. The vertical axis measures the *before-tax real wage*. Because the cut in taxes increases the number of workers willing to work at each wage, the labor market would be in excess supply if the wage rate did not fall. The lower real wage is what encourages firms to hire more workers and produce more. But workers care about their take-home pay – that is, about their *after-tax real wage*. And the after-tax real wage must have risen or else the workers would not have wanted to work more, and there would have been no excess supply and no fall in the before-tax wage in the first place. This is perfectly consistent: the new after-tax real wage, $(1 - \tau_2)(w/p)_2$, can be greater than the old after-tax real wage, $(1 - \tau_1)(w/p)_1$, as long as the rise in the take-home share $(1 - \tau)$ is proportionately greater than the fall in the before-tax real wage (w/p).

The analysis depends on substitution effects dominating income effects, which they probably do in aggregate, if not for every worker. So the supply-siders of the Reagan years are correct in principle. How much output will increase depends on how large the substitution effect is. If most people work a standard 40-hour week, the effect could be quite small, and the increase in output might also be very small in practice.

Issue 2. Technological Progress and Worker Welfare

Are technological progress and the increasing use of machinery and other capital beneficial for workers?

Many people intuitively believe that technological progress or greater mechanization harms workers. The argument seems obvious: if machinery or new technology allows firms to produce the same amount of output with fewer workers, then it encourages them to get rid of the some workers, which is surely a bad thing for workers.

This argument has nearly always persuaded most people. In the early nineteenth century, masked handloom weavers in the North of England rioted and used the cover of darkness to destroy newly introduced steam-powered and water-powered textile mills, which they feared would displace them. They were said to have been led by King Ludd or Ned Ludd, although he is likely a mythical figure. Ever since, people violently opposed to technological change or capital accumulation have been known as "Luddites."

To see why the Luddites are wrong – at least for clearing labor markets – recall that technological progress and increased capital both shift the labor-demand curve upward (see Figure 11.2). The lower panel of Figure 11.15 shows that the effect of the increased demand for labor is to increase total employment and the real wage. Firms can pay a higher real wage because the additional capital or technological progress increases the marginal product of labor.

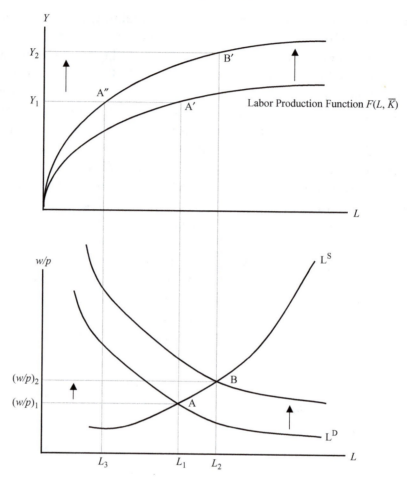

Figure 11.15. Issue 2: The Effects of Technological Progress.

The Luddites' mistake is most easily seen in the upper panel. The Luddite argument assumes that fewer workers will produce the same total output. Production starts at A′ using L_1 workers to produce Y_1. After the upward shift in the production function, the same output could be produced using less labor (L_3) at point A″. The problem is that A″ is not an equilibrium. At that point, the marginal product of labor is higher than the original real wage, so a profit-maximizing firm would want to expand production. To do this they must hire more labor than L_3; and, indeed, they find it profitable to hire more labor than the original L_1. The only way actually to increase labor is to raise the real-wage rate above its original level. Technological progress, therefore, favors workers by increasing employment and wages.

The Luddites' mistake is known as the **LUMP-OF-LABOR FALLACY**. They assume that a fixed pool of workers has a fixed amount of work to do. If firms find a more productive way to do the work, then the only option is for them to idle some members of the pool. In reality the available work depends on what the firms find profitable, and technological progress makes *more* work profitable. The available labor depends on the real-wage rate. Technological progress not only makes it possible for firms to pay higher wages, because marginal products are now higher, but also the pool of workers itself is not fixed but expands as wage rates increase. All consumers, including workers, benefit from the increased supply of goods and the higher real wage.

Early in the nineteenth century, handwoven cloth was very expensive, and a worker was lucky to own the clothes on his back and a spare set for church on Sunday. Textiles were one of the first industries to benefit from the Industrial Revolution, so that by the end of the nineteenth century, machine-made fabrics and mass production made decent clothing in larger quantities accessible to most of the population of the more developed countries. Similar progress has been made in most forms of production: agricultural production, which at the turn of the twentieth century absorbed half the labor force, now absorbs less than 3 percent while producing more food more cheaply than ever. Automobiles, which were an extravagant luxury good a hundred years ago, are now an essential commodity; and motor-vehicle production in the United States approximately doubled between 1960 and 2002 while employing only about 20 percent more production workers.[2]

We must be careful not to dismiss the Luddites as altogether foolish. Although new technology, especially over decades, has proved to be a net gain for workers in general, the Luddites were in fact correct that their way of life was threatened. Independent weavers became factory hands; unskilled workers, increasingly women and often children, replaced skilled craftsmen; and factory work often involved long hours in brutal conditions. The wider society reaps the benefits of technological change, while a narrow group sometimes disproportionately bears its costs. Our analysis also assumes that markets generally clear. The implicit assumption is that displaced workers move on to new jobs, possibly in other forms of production. Markets may have a tendency to clear in the long run, yet workers may find themselves displaced in the short run, say, over the course of a business cycle. We will consider this problem further in Chapter 12.

Issue 3. Immigration, Jobs, and Real Wages

How does an increase in the labor force through immigration or natural population growth affect labor and GDP?

One of the emotional issues associated with U.S. immigration policy – particularly toward low-wage workers from Mexico – is the idea that immigrants

---

[2] U.S. Census Bureau, *Statistical Abstract of the United States 1963* and *2003*. Washington: Government Printing Office.

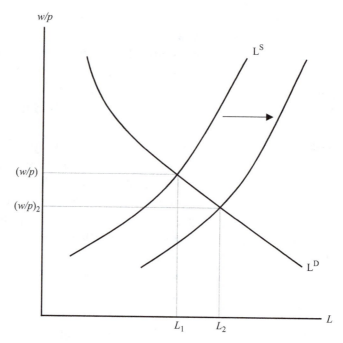

Figure 11.16. Issue 3: The Effects of Immigration. An increase in immigration or natural population growth shifts the labor-supply curve rightward, increasing labor and lowering the real wage.

take jobs away from native workers. We might be tempted to dismiss this fear as another example of the lump-of-labor fallacy. Yet there is a sensible intuition behind the argument. An increase in the labor force – due either to immigration or to higher population growth rates – can be represented as an outward shift of the aggregate labor-supply curve as shown in Figure 11.16. Employment increases, but real wages fall. It is not, then, that immigrants take jobs away from natives. Rather they compete for jobs, putting downward pressure on real wages.

Again, we must exercise care in interpreting the analysis. The diagram assumes that workers are homogeneous and are paid the same wage. But remember that aggregate labor and average wage rates hide many details of the labor process. The incomes of the new immigrants create demand for the new production that they make possible. Workers, in reality, present a variety of skills and are paid a variety of wages. And immigrant workers (at least those – whether legal or illegal – who have become the focus of the most intense political debate) are likely to possess fewer skills than natives. The net effect is that the increased demand for goods and services generated by immigrants is likely to increase the demand for skilled (and largely native) workers relative to their supply and, so, to increase real wages of skilled workers. Low-skilled immigration may lower the real wage for farm workers; but, if anything, it would raise the real wage for computer programmers.

11.3.3 The Labor Market in Practice

The labor-supply/labor-demand picture runs the risk of making the labor market appear to function too smoothly to be believable. The analysis of immigration provides a good illustration of why it is important not to use our analytical tools mechanically and why it often helps to recall particular market details hidden in the aggregates and averages.

Both the labor-supply and labor-demand curves were derived under the rules of perfect competition. Each supplier and each demander are regarded as too small to affect market prices: both workers and firms are modeled as *price takers* (see Chapter 9, section 9.1.2). The rules of perfect competition are most closely approximated in markets in which homogeneous commodities are auctioned. Natural gas on the New York Mercantile Exchange or soybeans on the Chicago Board of Trade are sold in such a manner that every potential supplier or demander can observe *the* market price. Labor markets are quite unlike auction markets.

As we already observed, labor is extremely heterogeneous. Some unskilled work can be done by virtually anyone – carrying bricks, serving hamburgers, collecting garbage. Other jobs require specialized skills – master mason, *haute cuisine* chef, environmental engineer. An increase in the supply of unskilled workers is likely to lower the wages of all types of unskilled workers. An increase in the supply of environmental engineers is unlikely to affect the wages of chefs. Skilled jobs define separate markets, whereas unskilled jobs, to some extent, form a single market. Another way to put this is that there is high substitutability among unskilled jobs and low substitutability among skilled jobs.

Even among skilled jobs, substitutability is a matter of degree and may be higher in the long run than in the short run. Many skills are job-specific, but a person with a strong general background may relatively easily move with some training from teacher to journalist or from corporate personnel manager to social worker, although it may be next to impossible to move from electrical engineer to brain surgeon without starting one's education over essentially from scratch. Existing workers have more vested interest in their current job, whereas new entrants (e.g., students choosing initial career paths) may be more flexible and display greater substitutability. The different markets for skilled labor overlap each other to some degree. Conditions of excess supply or demand in one market affect those in other markets to a degree and with a delay determined by the amount of overlap.

Markets for skilled labor also bear an asymmetrical relationship to markets for unskilled labor. Attachments to a profession – if not to a particular job – are likely to be long term, whereas attachments to unskilled jobs are likely to be looser. A temporarily unemployed worker may be able, if need be, to easily work in an unskilled job, whereas an unskilled worker cannot work in a skilled job at all.

A distinction is sometimes drawn between **PRIMARY LABOR MARKETS**, which comprise skilled work preferred by those qualified to do it, and **SECONDARY LABOR MARKETS**, which comprise unskilled jobs that anybody can do. Excess supply in primary labor markets might affect wages in secondary labor markets, but excess supply in secondary markets will have little or no influence on primary markets.

The image of perfect competition is that every firm must pay the same wage for the same work or else all the workers would quit the low-paying firms and move to the higher-paying firms. Knowing this, the firm would never let its wage differ from the market. Although this image captures a genuine tendency for markets to keep wages in related jobs from getting out of line, it overstates the efficiency with which they work. Distinct labor markets imply that there is a variety of wage rates, and these are unlikely to be known to one and all. Firms cannot simply observe the "market wage rate," but must often invest resources in consultants and other sources of information to discover appropriate wage structures – ones that do not pay workers too much (i.e., more than their labor adds to the profits of firms at the margin) nor too little (i.e., not enough to keep them from decamping for the firm's competitors).

The main messages of the model of perfect competition point in the right directions. This is why they form the backbone of the analytical framework for macroeconomics. Yet, sometimes they overlook details and suggest that the world works more smoothly than it actually does. In Chapters 12 and 15 we shall see that to understand some issues in macroeconomics it is crucial to have knowledge of these details and of the "frictions" that prevent the world from working as smoothly as the model of perfect competition.

Summary

1. An ideal labor market is one in which there is perfect competition and smooth wage and price adjustment so that the market remains in constant equilibrium.
2. Firms demand labor according to the rule for profit maximization: hire labor until the marginal product of labor is equal to the real wage rate. The labor-demand curve plots the firm's or the economy's demand for labor against the real wage. The labor-demand curve slopes downward because of diminishing

returns to labor. Anything that shifts the production function, changing the marginal product, shifts the labor-demand curve.

3. Workers make a two-dimensional choice in supplying labor: whether to participate in the labor force and, if so, how many hours of work to supply. In each case, the worker must balance the benefits of leisure against its opportunity cost (the real wage and what it will buy).

4. When real wage rates rise, the substitution effect increases the supply of labor in response to a higher opportunity cost of leisure, whereas the income effect decreases the supply of labor as the worker can now afford more leisure. The actual change in labor supply may be positive or negative depending on whether the substitution or income effect is dominant.

5. The labor-supply curve plots labor supply against the real wage. When substitution effects are dominant, it slopes upward. When income effects are dominant, it slopes downward. Individual labor-supply curves may start off upward sloping and at higher wages bend backward.

6. An increase in income taxation typically reduces labor supply as the worker's after-tax real wage falls, lowering the opportunity cost of leisure.

7. Legal and institutional constraints may prevent workers from supplying the amount of labor they would like at a given wage. For example, many workers are restricted to working a 40-hour week when they would prefer to work more. The constraint adds a vertical segment to the labor-supply curve – both in theory and practice.

8. The reservation wage is the minimum wage that would overcome the disincentives to work and induce a worker to join the labor force.

9. The aggregate labor-supply curve plots the total labor, measured either as workers or as worker-hours, against the average real wage rate.

10. In equilibrium, tax cuts increase employment, output, and after-tax real wages.

11. In equilibrium, technological progress increases employment, output, and real wages.

12. In equilibrium, immigration increases employment and output, but lowers real wages.

Key Concepts

labor demand	reservation wage
opportunity cost	lump-of-labor fallacy
income effect	primary labor markets
substitution effect	secondary labor markets
tax wedge	

Suggestions for Further Reading

Mark Killingsworth, *Labor Supply*. Cambridge: Cambridge University Press, 1983.

Daniel Hammermesh, *Labor Demand*. Cambridge: Cambridge University Press, 1996.

Problems

Data for this exercise are available on the textbook website under the link for Chapter 11 (appliedmacroeconomics.com). Before starting these exercises, the student should review the relevant portions of the *Guide to Working with Economic Data*, including sections G.1–G.4, and G.16.

Problem 11.1. Use the production function and the rule for profit maximization to show graphically how to derive the labor-demand curve. What effect would an increase in the stock of capital *ceteris paribus* have on labor demand? What effect would a decrease in real wage rates have on labor demand?

Problem 11.2. A car manufacturer in 2010 produced a single model that it sells for $12,900. It pays a wage of $42,500/year. The CPI in 2010 was 217 (1982–1984 = 100). What is the value of the product-real wage and the consumption-real wage? (Be careful to specify the units precisely.) When is each of these measures of real wages relevant?

Problem 11.3. The U.S. tax code assumes that each taxpayer begins to pay taxes only after having achieved a certain minimum income (*the standard deduction*). Use the labor-supply analysis of this chapter to conjecture what effect raising the standard deduction by $1,000 would have on the labor supply of a relatively high income taxpayer, who already pays $10,000 a year in income taxes. How would your answer differ for a taxpayer who, although liable for tax before the change, owed no tax after the change? (Hint: your answer should be formulated in terms of income and substitution effects and the likely behavior of taxpayers with different levels of income.)

Problem 11.4. Conjecture the effect of an increase in the marginal rate of taxation on labor supply of each of the two taxpayers as in Problem 11.3.

Problem 11.5. Assume that the labor-supply curve is backward-bending as in Figure 11.5. Show graphically the effect of an increase in marginal tax rates on this labor-supply curve.

Problem 11.6. Conjecture how winning $1 million from the state lottery would affect a worker's labor supply.

Problem 11.7. Conjecture what the effects would be on labor supply of an earned-income credit paid as a 10-percent premium on the wages of low-income workers.

Problem 11.8. Unemployment compensation pays a fixed amount to workers who have been laid off from their jobs.

(a) Assume (which is not generally true in the United States) that there is no time limit to receipt of unemployment compensation for those workers who report themselves as seeking work. Conjecture how an increase would affect participation rates and unemployment rates.

(b) In the United States, unemployment compensation generally runs for 13 weeks. In recent recessions, Congress has extended the coverage period to 26 weeks or more. Conjecture how such extensions might affect participation rates and unemployment rates.

Problem 11.9. As Figure 11.11 shows, between the 1950s and the early 2000s, the participation rate for all civilian workers steadily increased, even as that for prime-age male workers steadily declined. Before doing any data analysis, conjecture what might account for this difference. Then plot the time series of the participation rates for males, females, and teenagers (16–19–year-olds, male and female) and indicate NBER recession dates with shading. Is your conjecture supported by the data? If so, how? If not, modify your conjecture and explain how the data support your new view.

Problem 11.10. Referring to the data plotted in Problem 11.9, describe the differences in the secular (i.e., long-term) and cyclical behavior of participation rates. How do they differ by age and sex? What social and economic factors might account for the differences?

Problem 11.11. Plot average weekly hours of work for males, females, and teenagers (16–19–year-olds, male and female) and indicate NBER recession dates with shading. Describe and compare the secular and cyclical behavior of hours for the three groups. What social and economic factors might account for their common characteristics and their differences?

Problem 11.12. Use the data and the (Cobb-Douglas) functional forms of equations (9.17′) and (9.18) in Chapter 9 and assume that the economy is and remains fully employed:

(a) Compute the real wage consistent with the actual hours of employment.

(b) How much would the real wage have to change to justify an increase of 1 percent in the total number of hours employed?

(c) How much would the hours of labor change if the real wage increased by 1 percent?

(d) How much would the real wage change if total factor productivity increased by 1 percent holding hours constant?

(e) How much would hours change if total factor productivity increased by 1 percent holding real wages constant?

Problem 11.13. The production function referred to in Problem 11.12 (and in Chapters 9 and 10) measured labor in hours of work. It is sometimes convenient to measure it in numbers of workers. In 2008, total employment in the United States was 137,588,000 workers. Recompute the Cobb-Douglas production function analogous to equation (9.18) in Chapter 9 for 2008 replacing worker-hours with the number of workers, but otherwise using the data in equation (9.17′).

Problem 11.14. Repeat Problem 11.12 (a) using the information in Problem 11.13 and replacing hours of labor with the number of workers wherever applicable. Would the answers to Problem 11.12 (b)–(e) be the same or different using this new information? Explain.

Problem 11.15. During the Iraqi occupation of Kuwait (1990–1991), substantial parts of the Kuwaiti capital stock were destroyed. Use labor-supply/labor-demand analysis to conjecture the effects this would have had on employment and real wages provided that full employment was maintained at all times.

Problem 11.16. In the Middle Ages, the "Black Death" killed one-third of the population of Europe. Use labor-supply/labor-demand analysis to conjecture the effects this would have had on employment and real wages provided that full employment was maintained at all times.

Problem 11.17. The state of Alaska gives an annual rebate of oil revenues to each of its citizens – a flat dollar amount (approximately $3,300 in 2008) independent of income or personal characteristics. Assume that Alaska can be treated as a separate economy from the rest of the United States. Use labor-supply/labor-demand analysis to conjecture the effects that the introduction of such a rebate would have on employment and real wages provided that full employment was maintained at all times (i.e., compare the situation with and without a rebate).

12

Unemployment and the Labor-Market Process

If the typical recession were nothing more than a 2–3 percent fall in real GDP, most people would probably shrug it off as a nuisance. But recessions are typically associated with a sharp rise in unemployment, so that the costs are painfully concentrated on a narrow segment of the population. Why the economy should suffer from recurring bouts of unemployment is one of the great puzzles of macroeconomics. In this chapter, we explore the concept and causes of unemployment and lay the groundwork for macroeconomic policies that might reduce it.

12.1 The Concepts of Employment and Unemployment

One implication of the perfectly competitive model of the labor market as we described it in the last chapter is that everyone who wants to work at the market wage is able to find work at that wage. To put another way: there is no involuntary unemployment. Yet, every month the government announces that some significant percentage of the labor force is unemployed. An important question, then, is, why is there unemployment?

Before we attempt to answer that question, it will help to understand what unemployment means. In this section, we shall consider labor markets out of equilibrium. Our goal is to define some important concepts. We return to the question of *why* the labor market is out of equilibrium in the next section.

Where the labor-supply and demand curves cross in Figure 12.1 determines the market-clearing level of employment (L^*) and the real-wage rate $(w/p)^*$. Because the question that interests us here is whether people are working or not working, it is best to think of L as measuring the number of workers rather than aggregate hours of work.

Consider what would happen if the market wage rate were higher than the market-clearing rate at $(w/p)_1$. At this wage rate, labor supply (L^S) exceeds labor demand (L^D). Because firms cannot be forced to hire workers whose marginal product would not cover their wage, the actual amount of labor employed is determined by labor demand ($L = L^D$). The market

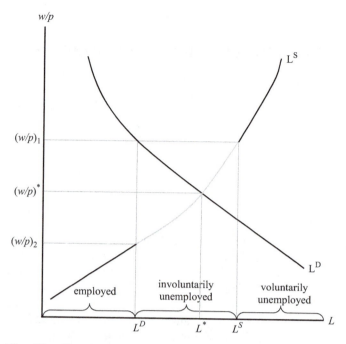

Figure 12.1. The Classification of Unemployment. At a $(w/p)_1$, a wage above the market-clearing level, the difference between labor supply and labor demand is involuntary unemployment (people corresponding to the gray segment of the labor-supply curve). Voluntary unemployment consists of people who do not wish to work at $(w/p)_1$ (upper black segment). Employment corresponds to labor demand at $(w/p)_1$ (lower black segment). The real wage $(w/p)_2$ indicates the lowest real wage that workers would accept and still supply just the labor demanded at $(w/p)_1$. It measures the amount the firms would overpay workers at $(w/p)_1$. When the real wage is at $(w/p)^*$, labor demand and supply are equal and there is no involuntary unemployment.

wage rate and labor demand divide the labor-supply curve into three segments: *Employment* comprises every worker to the left of L^D. The remaining workers are unemployed. The wage rate $(w/p)_1$ divides the unemployed into two groups: **VOLUNTARY UNEMPLOYMENT** comprises those workers whose reservation wage is greater than $(w/p)_1$ (i.e., those to the right of L^S); **INVOLUNTARY UNEMPLOYMENT** comprises those unemployed workers whose reservation wage is lower than $(w/p)_1$ (i.e., those between L^D and L^S, corresponding to the gray segment of the labor-supply curve). For the voluntarily unemployed, the real wage is not high enough to overcome the opportunity cost of working. They are not now part of the labor force; but, if their wage were higher, they might reassess their situation and choose to participate. The involuntarily unemployed want to work at the market wage (and all but the marginal worker would be willing to work even at a wage *below* the market wage), but firms will not hire them because the market real wage exceeds their marginal product.

Notice that when markets clear and labor supply equals labor demand, involuntary unemployment vanishes. The market-clearing level of employment is also known as **FULL EMPLOYMENT**, *a state in which every worker who wants to work at the going wage has a job*. It does not mean every worker capable of working is employed. And it does not set an upper bound on total employment. Even at full employment, voluntary unemployment persists; if the real wage were higher, some people would leave voluntary unemployment to join the labor force.

It is easy to conflate "voluntary" with "good" and "involuntary" with "bad." Some might argue that voluntary unemployment raises no policy issue: the voluntarily unemployed have chosen to be out of work and, if they wished to do so, could lower their reservation wage to a point that firms would hire them. This argument is wrong. A choice may be made voluntarily and nonetheless be undesirable. A thief puts a gun to your head and says, "Your money or your life," and you give him your money. It a voluntary choice in the important sense that it is the product of reflection and assessment of the options rather than a mere reflex. Yet it is not a choice that you desire to make, and it is one that public policy (the law and the police) tries to protect you from having to make. Similarly, if a financial manager finds that he could gain employment only at half the salary he has come to expect, he may voluntarily choose not to work. He may have made the best choice under the circumstances; yet, once again, it is a choice he wished not to make. Economic policy may legitimately want to direct the economy in a way that prevents him from having to make such a choice. Although policy may have a role to play in reducing voluntary unemployment – that is, in increasing the real-wage rate and the participation rate – we shall see later in the chapter that it takes different sorts of policy to affect voluntary and involuntary unemployment.

12.2 Measuring the Labor Market in Theory and Practice

12.2.1 Labor Market Data

In the United States, the Bureau of Labor Statistics (BLS) conducts two surveys from which it constructs most of its labor market data. The first is the so-called **Household Survey**. Conducted monthly as part of the *Current Population Survey*, the Household Survey employs trained interviewers to contact about 60,000 households and is used to generate data on the employed and unemployed – both overall and classified by age, sex, race, marital status, occupation, industry, and other characteristics. It also generates data on the past work experiences of people who are not in the labor force. The Household Survey is the source for the most commonly published measure of the U.S. unemployment rate.

The second survey is known as the **Establishment Survey**. It is part of a regular electronic survey (*Current Employment Statistics*) in which employers provide information on nonfarm wage and salaried employment, average weekly hours, average hourly earnings, and average weekly earnings, both nationally and for smaller geographic areas. The survey contacts about 160,000 businesses and government agencies, which pass on information about 440,000 worksites. The active sample includes around one-third of all nonfarm payroll workers.

The two surveys are complementary. Only the Household Survey can be used to generate unemployment rates, but both surveys provide estimates of total employment. Because its sample is so much larger, the Establishment Survey has generally been regarded as the more reliable guide to employment rates, although recently that has been called into question (see Box 12.1).

12.2.2 The Unemployment Rate

Theoretically, the **UNEMPLOYMENT RATE** can be defined as $U = \frac{L^S - L^D}{L^S}$. The numerator is the amount of involuntary unemployment, and the denominator is the number of workers whose reservation wages are at or below the market wage rate. It would be reasonable to assume that near the peak of the business cycle the economy is as close to full employment as it is going to be. Figure 12.2 plots the official unemployment rate for the United States (the shaded areas show recessions). Surprisingly, the data show that the lowest unemployment rate ever achieved in the United States over the past 60 years was not zero but 2.5 percent (May and June of 1952). But the unemployment rates achieved near the peaks of the business cycle are typically much higher that this (as high as 5.7 percent in May of 1979). Why is it that there is so much measured unemployment even when the economy is "as good as it gets" near the peak of the business cycle?

There are at least three complementary explanations.

Mismatched Definitions

To estimate the unemployment rate, the Bureau of Labor Statistics asks its sample households the following two questions: "Are you currently working?" and, if not, "Are you actively seeking work?"[1] Anyone answering

---

[1] More precisely, the BLS asks (1) "Did you do any work as a paid employee, proprietor of a business or farmer, or 15 hours or more of unpaid work in a family business? Or were you temporarily absent from such work because of illness, bad weather, vacation, labor-management disputes, or similar personal reasons?" (2) "If the answer to (1) is, 'no,' were you available for work during the survey week and did you take a specific action to contact a potential employer within the past four weeks? Or were you waiting to be recalled to a job after being laid off within the last six months?"

Box 12.1 A Jobless Recovery?

The U.S. Bureau of Labor Statistics reports two broad measures of overall employment: *civilian employment* from the Household Survey and *nonfarm employment* from the Establishment Survey. Generally, the two series track each other well. But in the recovery from the recession of 2001, they told quite different stories (Figure B12.1). Each of the candidates in the 2004 U.S. presidential election pointed to the series most helpful to his electoral prospects. Because nonfarm employment never regained its pre-recession peak, John Kerry stigmatized George W. Bush as the first president since Herbert Hoover on track to end his term with fewer people employed than when he began. Pointing to civilian employment, Bush took credit for the recovery in employment by October 2003 and the addition of two million more jobs in the following year up to the time of the election.

Who was right remains a puzzle. The Household Survey is generally regarded as more noisy – reflected in the *jagged* appearance of the time series for civilian employment in the figure. The Establishment Survey, which uses a much larger sample, is typically considered more accurate – reflected in the much *smoother* time series for nonfarm employment. The difference between the series after the recession, however, is not a question of month-to-month fluctuations but of a more prolonged divergence. Proponents of the Household Survey argue that many of the jobs created since 2001 were either self-employment or in new (and often small) firms. The Household Survey would pick up these kinds of jobs, whereas the Establishment Survey, which adds new firms only slowly, may miss the new firms and may miss self-employment altogether.

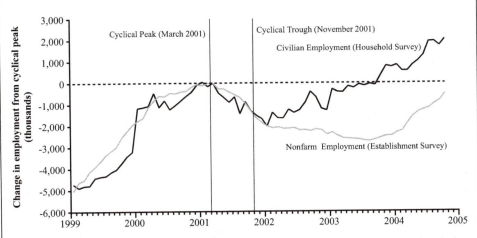

Figure B12.1. Two Measures of Employment. *Source:* Bureau of Labor Statistics.

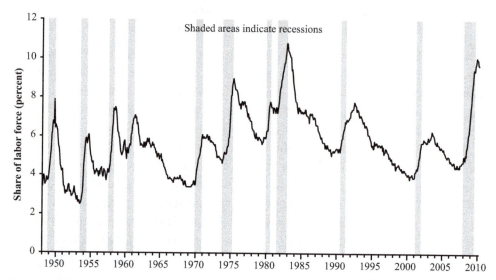

Figure 12.2. Unemployment Rate in the United States. Unemployment rates are countercylical. In the past they were coincident indicators at the peak and slightly lagging indicators at the trough. In the past three recessions the lag after the trough has lengthened. *Source:* Bureau of Labor Statistics.

"yes" to the first question is counted as employed and in the labor force (no distinction is made between full-time and part-time employment). Anyone answering "yes" to the second question is counted as unemployed and in the labor force. Everyone else is counted as not in the labor force. Based on these data the BLS calculates the unemployment rate as

$$U = \frac{labor\,force - employment}{labor\,force}$$

and the participation rate as

$$PR = \frac{labor\,force}{population\,over\,16\,years\,of\,age}.$$

These survey questions are not ideal in light of macroeconomic theory. An economist would prefer to replace the BLS's second question with: "Are you willing to work *at the going wage for the kind of work that you are actively seeking and qualified to do?*" It is possible for a person to answer the BLS's second question "yes" and this question "no."

The economist would not count someone as involuntarily unemployed whose reservation wage was higher than the wage currently offered in the market. The BLS could. Similarly, the economist would not count someone as unemployed who sought a job for which he was not qualified. The BLS could. I should not be counted as unemployed because the University of California Davis Medical Center will not hire me as a surgeon or because the Washington Redskins will not hire me as a quarterback.

Some workers who are essentially unemployable because of high reservation wages or unrealistic assessments of qualifications will count as "unemployed" according to BLS definitions. In fact, they should count as "out-of-the-labor-force" according to economically ideal definitions. Some such incorrectly measured unemployment will persist even at the peak of the business cycle.

There are practical reasons why the BLS does not use the economist's ideal definitions. Because labor is heterogeneous and paid a variety of wages, it is difficult to determine what "the going wage" is without really detailed information about firms.

Similarly, workers are heterogeneous both in skills and in tastes. A worker may be qualified for a number of different sorts of jobs that pay different wages and yet be willing to work only at some subset of those jobs. In a sense, the worker is involuntarily unemployed with respect to some jobs and voluntarily unemployed with respect to others.

Finally, there is a large measure of subjective judgment about a worker's qualification for a particular job. It is not a fact that can necessarily be easily ascertained through a survey. In the event, the worker and the employer have to agree about qualifications only when a worker is actually hired. And, even then, hiring may be on a trial basis in order to discover whether the judgment was correct. What qualifications are required and how willing a firm is to train a worker vary not only from firm to firm but also from time to time, depending on how tight the labor market is. No practical survey could address such nuanced questions even if there were a sharp answer in every case. The BLS survey is a compromise with practicality.

Transitional Unemployment

Heterogeneity in employment provides a second explanation of the persistence of unemployment even at the peak of the business cycle in another way. Because firms grow at different rates and experience different rates of technological improvement, there are always some firms reducing and other firms increasing the sizes of their work forces. **Transitional unemployment** refers to the fact that inevitably it takes time to find new jobs: a shorter time when times are good; a longer time when times are bad; yet always, some time. Some segment of the labor force is always between jobs.

In most cases, people laid off from one job and searching for another are probably involuntarily unemployed. Even in cases in which people quit a job voluntarily, they may still be involuntarily unemployed in the sense that they are willing to work at the going wage at some other job. In some cases, however, workers actively engaged in job searches are voluntarily unemployed because their reservation wage is higher than the going wage. Generally, as time passes and such searches prove unfruitful, workers lower their reservation wages and enter the ranks of the involuntarily unemployed.

Whether voluntary or involuntary, the key point is that, even in a growing and successful economy, transitions between jobs are normal and are captured in the unemployment statistics. The failure of the unemployment rate to ever fall to zero is no surprise; it would be a miracle if it did.

A Real-Wage Floor

A third explanation for unemployment persisting even near the peak of the business cycle depends on the existence of a **real-wage floor** defined as *a lower bound to how far the real wage can fall*. If, for any reason, the real wage for any job is higher than the market-clearing real wage, firms will hire fewer workers than the market-clearing number.

For example, **minimum-wage laws** require firms to pay no less than a certain wage rate. (The U.S. minimum wage in 2009 was $7.25 per hour.)[2] A firm that hired a worker the value of whose marginal product was less than the minimum wage would reduce its profits. Some low-productivity workers may be employable only at a wage below the minimum. Even at the peak of the business cycle, firms will not hire them. (Minimum wage laws are discussed more fully in section 12.3.1.)

Another example of a real-wage floor occurs when firms themselves believe that their profits would suffer if they were to set wage rates too low. The REAL EFFICIENCY-WAGE HYPOTHESIS argues that workers paid real wages above the market-clearing rate are more productive or efficient than workers paid at the market-clearing rate. There are many reasons why this may be true.

First, a real wage above the market-clearing rate marks out a job as a good job. Workers work harder at jobs that they regard as good – either because of the favorable psychological effect or because it raises the opportunity cost of losing the job and having to find another, less good job.

A firm may care that workers regard their jobs as good, because workers have a great deal of discretion in how well they serve the firm. An illustration is provided by the tactic of "work-to-rule." Many (particularly, but not exclusively, unionized) jobs are subject to contract. Often if workers follow their contracts to the letter and do not adjust their service flexibly in ways that contravene contractual terms, the firm cannot deliver its product effectively. Even so, the firm has no legal grounds for complaint.

For example, in the spring and summer of 2000, pilots at United Airlines, while bargaining for a new contract, decided to abide precisely by the overtime rules of the existing contract. Because the airline relied on pilots

---

[2] A "subminimum wage" (sometimes called a "training wage") of $4.25 per hour is allowed for workers younger than age 20 for the first 90 days of their employment.

working overtime in situations that the contract did not allow, schedules were badly disrupted – passengers were stranded and flights cancelled. Not only did United ultimately have to accept the pilots' terms, it had to issue a public apology and give its best customers extra frequent-flyer miles in an attempt to rebuild goodwill.

A second reason why firms might want to pay higher than the market-clearing wage is that they often incur certain fixed costs when they hire a worker, so that a high wage, which reduces the attractiveness of other jobs and lowers turnover costs, may actually raise their profits. Firms have a strong incentive to reduce turnover. The cost of replacing and retraining a worker has been estimated to be typically 1.5 year's salary. These costs matter less in some occupations than others. Just as the minimum wage is likely to affect unskilled jobs in the secondary labor market, efficiency wages are more likely to be paid in the high-skilled, primary labor market.

Even if firms rationally desire to pay a higher wage, they still should not hire workers at a wage greater than their marginal products. An efficiency wage, therefore, implies that firms will hire fewer workers at higher marginal products. At higher rates, more people want to work, but fewer are hired.

Whatever its source, a real-wage floor means that some workers will not be hired even when the market wage is above their reservation-wage rates: there is involuntary unemployment.

Frictional Unemployment

Measured unemployment never falls to zero. Whatever the reason (mismatched definitions, transitional unemployment, or various real-wage floors), we summarize the phenomenon using the term **FRICTIONAL UNEMPLOYMENT** defined as *the unemployment that persists even at the peak of the business cycle*. Just as lubrication can make a wheel turn more smoothly yet not completely eliminate friction, good economic times can reduce unemployment yet not eliminate frictional unemployment.

12.2.3 *Other Dimensions of Unemployment*

The unemployment rate is the most widely reported measure of unused labor resources. Yet, like other aggregate measures, it paints only part of the picture of unemployment. In addition to the questions from which it constructs the unemployment rate, the BLS asks a variety of questions that provide a much richer canvas.

Part-Time Employment

The official unemployment rate treats workers as either in or out of the labor force with no recognition of degrees of participation or degrees of

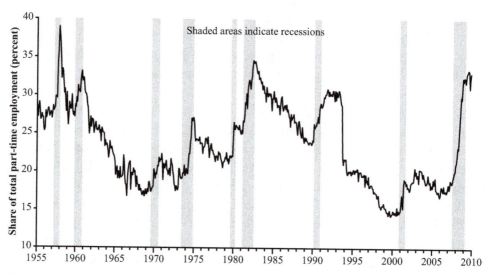

Figure 12.3. Ratio of U.S. Involuntary Part-Time Employment to All Part-Time Employment. The involuntary component of part-time employment rises sharply in recessions. *Source:* Bureau of Labor Statistics.

employment. Since the mid-1950s, part-time employment has accounted for between 11 and 20 percent of the labor force. Some of the part-timers work their desired number of hours. They can be regarded as partial participants, whose nonworking hours are voluntary. Some of the part-timers, however, want to work full time. They should be regarded as partially unemployed. Figure 12.3 shows that involuntarily part-time employment as a percentage of all part-time employment rises sharply in recessions and falls steadily in recoveries.

Overtime Employment

Wage workers must generally be paid 1.5 times their usual wage for work beyond the statutory 40-hour week. Some union contracts call for double time or more. Such regulations were introduced in the 1930s to encourage employers to abide by the standard workweek and to hire more workers rather than to work fewer employees more intensely. Even with such a disincentive to use overtime, manufacturing workers averaged around three hours of overtime per week from the mid-1950s through the early 1980s. Average overtime then climbed throughout the 1980s and has stabilized around 4.5 hours per week since the early 1990s. Overtime in other sectors of the economy is surely less than in manufacturing, because the average workweek for all workers is only about 35 hours.

A fall in the opportunity cost to firms of hiring overtime workers may partly explain the rise in overtime in the 1980s. At that time, an increasing part of worker compensation was shifted to tax-free benefits, such as health insurance and pensions, rather than to direct wages. Because the time-and-a-half rule applies only to the explicit wage, overtime wage rates are less than 1.5 times wages including benefits. And they become proportionately less the larger benefits become relative to explicit wages. Some firms find it more profitable to increase the hours of existing workers than to incur, for example, the fixed costs of training and health insurance for new employees.

Overtime, like part-time employment, may be voluntary or involuntary. As we saw in Chapter 11, section 11.2.1, workers may want to work more than the statutory 40 hours per week, but be constrained by their employers to work only 40. In that case, an offer of overtime may be welcome. In some cases, a worker will not want to work overtime (at least not of the required amount). Then, overtime is voluntary only in the sense that the worker has a choice between accepting the mandatory overtime or leaving the job altogether. Even in the case in which he accepts mandatory overtime, the worker may still be constrained from adjusting labor supply at the margin (i.e., an hour more or less). In that sense, a worker may agree to the overtime and, at the same time, it may be partially involuntary.

Loosely Attached Workers

Just as part-time and overtime indicate different degrees of employment, there can be different degrees of unemployment. Imagine the unlikely situation in which measured unemployment fell to zero. Would that put an absolute limit on additional labor supply? Most likely not. Where would the additional labor supply come from? First, existing workers can be asked to work overtime. Second, employees who are involuntarily working only part-time can be used full-time. Third, with labor in short supply, real wages would rise and would attract new participants into the labor force (including some voluntarily part-time workers shifting to full-time work). Beyond these three sources of labor, current measurement practices may exclude people from the ranks of the unemployed who are effectively in the labor force.

Since the mid-1990s, the BLS has tracked marginally attached and discouraged workers. **Marginally attached workers** are *people who indicate that they desire to work, are ready to work, and have looked for work sometime in the recent past, but who are not now working or actively seeking work.* **Discouraged workers** are *a subset of the marginally attached who offer a job-market related reason for not seeking work, such as believing that current employment prospects are so poor that a search would be fruitless.*

The BLS now calculates six measures of underutilization of the labor force, called U-1 to U-6 (see Table 12.1). U-3 is identical to the usual unemployment rate, while the other Us measure different aspects of unemployment. Figure 12.4 shows the historical relationships among these measures since 1994.

Table 12.1. *Concepts of Underutilization of Labor*

Concept	Definition
U-1	Persons unemployed 15 weeks or longer as a percent of the civilian labor force.
U-2	Job losers and persons who completed temporary jobs as a percent of the civilian labor force.
U-3	Total unemployed as a percent of the civilian labor force (i.e., the official unemployment rate).
U-4	Total unemployed, plus discouraged workers, as a percent of the civilian labor force plus discouraged workers.
U-5	Total unemployed, plus discouraged workers, plus all other marginally attached workers, as a percent of the civilian labor force plus all marginally attached workers.
U-6	Total unemployed, plus all marginally attached workers, plus total employed part-time for economic reasons (i.e., voluntarily part-time workers) as a percentage of the civilian labor force plus all marginally attached workers.

Source: Bureau of Labor Statistics. "The Employment Situation," table A.7.

The narrowest of these indicators (U-1), which essentially measures long-term unemployment of those who continue to identify themselves as in the labor force, is less than one-third of the official unemployment rate (U-3). In contrast, the broadest measure of underutilization (U-6) is almost double the official unemployment rate.

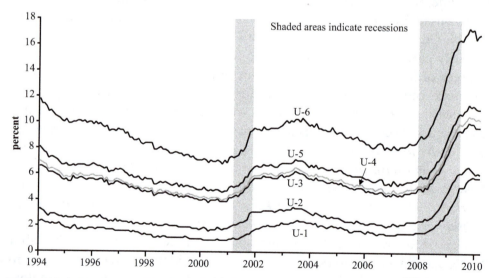

Figure 12.4. Measures of Underutilized Labor in the United States. Wider measures of the underutilization of labor are substantially higher than narrower measures, but all measures tend to move together. *Source:* Bureau of Labor Statistics.

The ratios of the different indicators are very stable. The gaps between U-1 and U-2 and the official unemployment rate narrowed a little after the recession of 2001, but the gaps between U-4, U-5, and U-6 were nearly constant. Overall, the co-movement of the six measures is so strong, that, even though the official unemployment rate may not give the full picture of the underutilization of labor, it gives a good index of whether it is becoming more or less severe.

Underemployment

Another aspect of underutilization of the labor force is much more difficult to measure: the mismatch between the skills of the jobholder and those needed to perform the job. In the primary-employment sector, firms place a premium on getting this match right. Turnover is expensive. The firm obviously does not want to squander training on an unqualified worker, and an *overqualified* worker is unlikely to stay when times are good. It is less important for the secondary-employment sector, in which training costs are low and rapid turnover is the norm.

UNDEREMPLOYMENT occurs when workers who are laid off from primary-sector jobs take jobs below their ability and their potential value-added – particularly, jobs in the secondary sector. An unemployed engineer may work as a taxi driver; an unemployed accountant may work at McDonald's. When the recovery gets underway, not only do the unemployed get hired, the underemployed move on to jobs that better match their skills. Their productivity rises. The existence of underemployment helps to explain why, even at low levels of unemployment, output can rise faster than employment. Instead of working more, people work better.

International Comparisons of Underutilization of Labor

How do U.S. labor markets measure up in international comparisons? Table 12.2 shows unemployment rates and rates of part-time employment (by sex) for selected countries in 2008, a year in which the United States experienced the first stages of the long recession (December 2007 to June 2009). Although the unemployment rate was higher than a year or two earlier, it was nonetheless well below the peak of more than 10 percent that it would reach later in the slump. At that point, only Japan and the United Kingdom among the G-7 had lower unemployment rates than the U.S. rate of 5.8 percent (and they were close). The other large European countries (France, Germany, and Italy) reported unemployment rates from one to two points higher. And U.S. rates were much lower than average European rates, although just below the OECD average of 6.0 percent.

Table 12.2. *Underutilization of Labor in Selected Countries, 2008*

	Unemployment Rate (percentage of labor force)	Part-Time Employment (percentage of employment)	
		Male	Female
The G-7			
Canada	6.1	11.3	26.4
France	7.8	5.2	22.7
Germany	7.3	8.2	38.6
Italy	6.8	6.6	31.0
Japan	4.0	9.9	33.2
United Kingdom	5.6	10.2	33.7
United States	5.8	7.5	17.0
Other Countries			
Australia	4.2	12.3	37.7
Belgium	7.0	5.9	33.8
Ireland	6.3	8.2	36.0
Luxembourg	4.9	1.8	27.3
Mexico	4.0	N/A	N/A
Netherlands	2.8	16.2	59.9
Poland	7.2	5.3	14.1
South Korea	3.2	6.5	13.2
Spain	11.4	3.8	21.1
Turkey	9.4	4.6	19.2
OECD Europe	7.9	6.8	28.5
Total OECD	6.0	7.7	25.3

Source: Organization of Economic Cooperation and Development, *Employment Outlook, 2009.*

Table 12.2 shows huge variability among countries in part-time employment. This is not surprising as part-time employment sometimes reflects involuntary underemployment of labor and sometimes highly desirable flexibility in labor markets. Part-time employment of males (7.5 percent) in the United States was a little below the European average and 1.5 points above the OECD average. In contrast, the United States shows one of the lowest part-time employment rates for females (17.0 percent) – about two-thirds the OECD and European averages.

12.3 The Labor-Market Process

Let us now return to the question postponed in the last section: How is it that labor markets remain out of equilibrium? How is it that unemployment can persist? Unemployment is fundamentally a mismatch between the supply of, and the demand for, labor. The problem is, then, why do labor markets not adjust quickly to bring supply and demand back together?

Up to now we have assumed that aggregate demand always adjusted to the level of aggregate supply. In this section, we drop that assumption. Aggregate demand determines how much firms can sell and, therefore, affects their demand for labor. We must, therefore, take the possibility of a mismatch between aggregate demand and supply into account.

12.3.1 Why Do Wages Not Fall?

The Unemployment Puzzle

To an economist, unemployment is a puzzling phenomenon. In the face of a pool of unemployed workers, why do firms not reduce the wages that they pay to their workers with the threat that they will fire them and hire unemployed workers in their places?

Look back at Figure 12.1. Recall that the wage $(w/p)_1$ is higher than the market-clearing wage $(w/p)^*$, so that there is involuntary unemployment. The number of workers who wish to work at that wage exceeds the number that firms wish to hire. In Figure 12.1, every employed worker is willing to work at the wage $(w/p)_2$ or less. So, why would firms not follow the rules for profit maximization and simultaneously increase their use of labor to L^* and reduce the wage to $(w/p)^*$? Or, if they thought that they could not sell this extra output, why would they not lower the wages of existing workers to $(w/p)_2$?

Notice that the problem is to lower the *real* wage. A cut in real wages may or may not mean a cut in the *nominal-wage rate*. Because $\widehat{(w/p)} = \hat{w} - \hat{p}$, the real wage will fall whenever wage inflation is less than price inflation, even if both are positive. A falling real wage is compatible with either rising or falling nominal wages and prices.

Also notice that the issue is not whether real wages ever fall in the face of unemployment. They often do. The issue is instead why they might not fall far enough or fast enough to guarantee that every worker who wants a job gets one without spending an extended period unemployed. The persistence of unemployment, and the failure of wages to adjust properly to clear labor markets, is, perhaps, the single most vexed problem in macroeconomics over the past eighty years. Many explanations have been offered, many may contain some part of the answer, but none has gained universal acceptance. This question remains a focus of cutting-edge research.

No one doubts that a god or a magician who could choose each price and wage rate in the economy could ensure that the labor market and all other markets cleared. An old axiom of economics known as **Say's law**, after the French economist Jean-Baptiste Say (1767–1832), says, "*Supply creates its own demand.*" In this context, Say's law means that firms could cut real wages and expand production, and the additional incomes generated from the larger level of employment and the higher profits would be enough to purchase the newly produced goods. In other words, there is no barrier to full employment. Of course, believers in Say's law are not blind. They too can see that measured rates of unemployment can be high. Most would argue that high unemployment results from some "unnatural" impediment to the smooth operation of markets. Some would go further to claim that measured unemployment is, in reality, largely voluntary, so that an apparently underemployed economy is really at full employment after all.

A more reasonable approach stresses the fact that production and labor are complex and heterogeneous. The simple analysis of the aggregate labor-supply/labor-demand diagram may be misleading. There is a **fallacy of division** (the opposite of a fallacy of composition): *what is true of the whole is not necessarily true of the parts*. Here what is true in aggregate is not true for the individual firms. Yes, if a god or a magician could arrange it just so, the economy could always move to full employment. But imagine how things appear to a single firm paying $(w/p)_1$ and employing L_1 workers in Figure 12.1 (in your mind, convert the aggregate uppercase L to the firm-specific lowercase l).

Suppose it sells all that it produces, but experiences no excess demand for its product. If it increases employment to L^*, who is going to buy the extra output? Of course, our knowledge of the national income and product accounts (Chapter 2) tells us that aggregate output equals aggregate income. And things would work fine in this case if the workers took some portion of the very goods they had produced as their wage. (Similarly, a firm's suppliers of raw materials would have to be willing to be paid in kind.)[3] But most firms are specialized, and they rarely produce the goods that individuals want to consume. A steelworker's marginal product is measured in tons of steel per hour. Yet the steelworker does not want to be paid in cold-rolled sheet steel. He does not want to be paid his literal marginal product. He wants to be paid the *value* of his marginal product *in money*.

The problem for the firm is that it can pay its workers in money only if it is able to sell its product and realize its value. If it fails to sell the product, the output is added to the inventory of the firm and counts as income to its owners, as if the firm had sold the goods to itself. The national accounts still balance, but the "income" arrives in a form that does not motivate the firm to produce more. Nor will it cover the money wages the firm must pay to the workers. If each and every firm could simultaneously expand its

---

[3] In the Soviet Union and initially in post-Soviet Russia, the absence of well-structured markets and financial systems encouraged many firms to attempt to conduct business through barter of their products for necessary inputs. It proved to be an extremely inefficient and cumbersome system – an element in the collapse of the Soviet Union and an impediment to the growth and development of the Russian economy.

employment and output, it would be possible to reach full employment for the economy. Unfortunately, none of the gods or magicians of the real world has volunteered to take on the job of economic coordinator. And without such a coordinator, each firm must wait until demand increases before it is able to expand production and employment.

Just pointing out the possibility of a **DEMAND FAILURE** does not eliminate the puzzle; it merely changes its form. Look at Figure 12.1 once more. The marginal product of labor at the employment level L_1 is the same as the wage rate on the labor-demand curve $(w/p)_1$ while firms' marginal labor cost measured on the labor-supply curve is lower at $(w/p)_2$. Every currently employed worker would be willing to work for a real wage of $(w/p)_2$ or lower. The difference would be pure profit. Even if demand were insufficient to justify higher production, why would firms not lower the wages they pay? A benefit of lower wages and higher profits is that firms could afford to lower prices to stimulate demand. If they were successful, the economy would move toward full employment. Yet, this does not seem to be how firms actually behave.

The puzzle of unemployment can be restated: why is it that workers are sometimes involuntarily unemployed and yet the real wage does not show a tendency to fall fast enough or far enough to clear the labor market, eliminating the unemployment? Firms appear to be missing profit opportunities. Economists are rarely satisfied with economic analysis that suggests that there is an unexploited profit opportunity. We shall look at three explanations for the failure of wages to adjust: efficiency wages, unions, and government actions.

Cutting Wages or Raising Prices

To lower the real wage, a firm could cut its own nominal wage or it could allow relatively faster inflation to erode the real value of the nominal wage – that is, *collectively* firms might raise prices faster than nominal wages.

Because it is the product-real wage $(= \frac{w}{price\ of\ the\ firm's\ own\ product})$ that should matter to labor demand, one might think that the firm could achieve the same effect by raising its own price irrespective of what others firms do. Once again, there is a fallacy of division. An increase in the price of its own output, if other firms do not go along and raise their prices, will reduce demand for the firm's product – especially relative to its direct competitors – which would not be helpful in increasing employment. If all prices rise simultaneously, relative prices are unaffected. And, if the reason for a higher general price level is an increase in *nominal* aggregate demand larger than the increase in prices (which is likely when there are unused resources), *real* aggregate demand will rise, moving the economy in the direction of full employment.

In contrast to the firms, which care about a single price (or no more than a few prices), workers care about the average price level for the basket of goods that they typically consume. A higher general price level that reduces the real wage also lowers the size of the labor force as the economy moves down the labor-supply curve. The unemployment rate falls both because firms hire more workers and because relatively fewer people want to work.

Real-wage adjustment strictly through price inflation (i.e., with the nominal wage fixed) is usually a slow process. For example, if the real wage is 10 percent above its market-clearing level and the inflation rate is 5 percent per year, it would take two years of persistent unemployment to close the gap. Unlike the general price level, which is beyond the control of the individual firm, its own nominal-wage rate is within its control. So why does the firm not just lower it to a more profitable level? Once again, what might work for all firms taking coordinated action might be unprofitable for any one firm.

Efficiency Wages

Previously in Section 12.2.2, we considered efficiency wages as placing a floor below which the real wage could not fall. The *real efficiency-wage hypothesis* is not, it turns out, helpful for the problem at hand. Real wages need to fall to clear the market, and the real efficiency-wage hypothesis says that they will not. It is not just that the nominal wage will not be cut. If workers experience general price inflation, the firm would have to *increase* the nominal wage to keep the real wage constant at the efficient level.

Another version of the efficiency-wage hypothesis may be helpful nonetheless. The important point is that worker productivity is affected by the wage rate. George Akerlof (winner of the Nobel Prize in Economic Science, 2001) and Janet Yellen (former president of the Federal Reserve Bank of San Francisco) and various colleagues have stressed the idea that productivity is connected to workers feeling fairly treated, and that *nominal* wages may be an important measure.[4] Workers might measure fairness against various benchmarks.

- First, in addition to their purchasing power, which depends on the real wage, workers might care about their relative social position, and judge it against similar workers in other firms. For example, the relative real wage between United and American Airlines is $\frac{(w_{United}/p)}{(w_{American}/p)} = \frac{w_{United}}{w_{American}}$. Because the price-level terms cancel out, relative *real* position and relative *nominal* position are identical. Each airline would be reluctant to be the first to cut its nominal-wage rate, because that would shift the relative wage against its own employees and make them less efficient. Of course, each airline has to strike a balance. The savings in direct costs of a nominal wage cut may sometimes be greater than the value of lost efficiency. In that case,

---

[4] George A. Akerlof and Janet L. Yellen, *Efficiency Wage Models of the Labor Market.* Cambridge: Cambridge University Press, 1986.

the airline would cut the nominal-wage rate. Any case in which the efficiency of workers depends on the nominal wage might be called the **NOMINAL EFFICIENCY-WAGE HYPOTHESIS**. The **relative efficiency-wage hypothesis** is one example of a nominal efficiency-wage hypothesis, as well as an example of Akerlof and Yellen's **fair-wage hypothesis**.

- Second, workers may judge their positions relative to workers in their own firms. Truman Bewley, an economist at Yale University, conducted extensive interviews with employers, union officials, and job-placement professionals during the recession of the early 1990s.[5] He argues that both workers and firms have relatively poor information about compensation and working conditions at other firms and base their judgments about fairness on the conditions in their own firms.

  An example that predates Bewley's research is found in the case of the London newspaper printers' union. The union struck the *Times of London* for ten and a half months beginning in November of 1978.[6] One cause of the strike was a narrowing in the relative wage differential between its members and janitorial staff. The union would have been just as satisfied with a cut in the janitors' wages as with an increase in the wages of its own members.

  Academic labor markets provide another example. New assistant professors are paid whatever the competitive wage is in the year that they are hired. Once they are hired, their wage often rises more slowly than market wages, so that the last hired is often the best paid. Department chairs and deans are familiar with the cries of "unfair" from the more senior assistant professors.

- Third, workers may judge their wage relative to their own past wages. Bewley's survey indicates that workers generally regard any cut in their nominal wage as unfair, even if they do not know the wages of other workers. The economic psychologist Daniel Kahneman (winner of the Nobel Prize in Economic Science in 2002) and his colleagues studied worker reactions to wage cuts.[7] Workers typically found a 5-percent cut in the nominal wage when the inflation rate was zero to be unfair, but they did not object to a 7-percent increase in the nominal wage when the inflation rate was 12 percent. Yet both scenarios represent a 5-percent cut in real purchasing power. Economists typically stigmatize such behavior as irrational. Workers are said to suffer from **money illusion** – that is, to not understand the equivalence of the two situations. Of course, workers may sometimes suffer from money illusion – even relatively simple economic reasoning is not inborn. Still, greater concern for a nominal-wage cut than for a price-level increase is not necessarily irrational.

  Workers may rationally care about what their bosses think of their performance and may take psychic pleasure from a good appraisal and feel psychic pain from a poor one. Talk is cheap. Decisions about wages may convey the boss's feelings more persuasively than words could do. If workers recognize that individual firms

---

[5] Truman F. Bewley, *Why Wages Don't Fall in a Recession*. Cambridge, MA: Harvard University Press, 1999.

[6] *Wall Street Journal*, 22 October 1979, p. 23.

[7] Daniel Kahneman, Jack L. Knetsch, J., and Richard Thaler. "Fairness as a Constraint on Profit Seeking: Entitlements in the Market." *American Economic Review*, vol. 76, no. 4, 1986, pp. 728–741.

have little control over, say, the CPI, they will take their signal from the nominal-wage rate. What is more, workers may not monitor the CPI closely at all, so that a change in their paycheck provides a far more direct signal than a change in the real wage could.

Prices typically change continuously, whereas nominal wages change infrequently – often only annually. The real wage then is constantly changing. It would be inconvenient and costly for workers to monitor their real wages daily and to adjust their behavior in direct proportion. It is far more practical to focus on the discrete changes in the nominal wage.

Cognitive psychology plays a part here. It is said (although this may be a science legend) that a frog dropped into hot water will immediately jump out; but, if dropped into cold water that is then heated gradually, it will allow itself to be poached. To some extent, people are like that. We more easily notice a discrete, relatively large drop in real purchasing power owing to a cut in nominal wages than its gradual erosion owing to inflation.

Whether the workers' concern for nominal wages is rational or irrational, Bewley's survey confirms that employers are reluctant to cut them. Even when the alternative is cutting everyone's wages (and/or hours of work) and maintaining employment levels, firms would generally prefer to maintain wages (and hours) and lay off redundant workers. A smaller work force with the goodwill attributed to the higher wages typically offsets any cost savings that might be gained from lowering the wage.

Unions

The actions of unions provide a second explanation for wages not falling in the face of unemployment. Unionized members typically work under a contract. During the life of the contract, the wage rate can be lowered only with the agreement of the union. If the agreement is for a nominal-wage rate, inflation may nonetheless erode the real wage and move the economy toward market-clearing. Often, especially in times (such as the 1970s) when inflation rates are high and variable, unions negotiate cost-of-living adjustments (COLAs) into their contracts. The COLA ties the nominal wage to a price index, such as the CPI. A contract with a COLA is effectively a contract for a definite real wage.

Why do firms enter into such contracts? To a large degree, firms deal with unions because the law says that they must. Still, the same considerations that go into efficiency wages may matter for contracts as well. Workers under contract with a known wage may work more reliably and productively than workers without such contracts.

One might think that unions would have an interest in increasing employment. But the situation is more complicated than that. Generally, only workers who are employed, on temporary layoff, or on strike are members of the union. The members or *insiders* may prefer high wages for themselves,

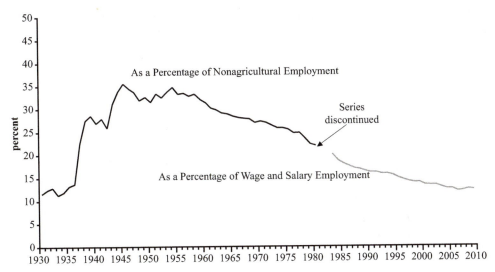

Figure 12.5. Unionization of Labor in the United States. Union membership in the United States as a proportion of the labor force hit a peak at the end of World War II and has declined ever since. *Source:* Bureau of Labor Statistics.

even if it means that the unemployed or *outsiders* remain unemployed. The **INSIDER/OUTSIDER MODEL OF UNEMPLOYMENT** is often thought to explain relatively high levels of unemployment in Europe compared to the United States over the past quarter-century. The situation could easily arise in the United States as well, but, in contrast to Europe, only a small and shrinking share of the labor force in the United States is unionized.

Union membership, which grew significantly after the Great Depression, peaked at about one-quarter of the workforce in the mid-1950s and has fallen steadily since then (Figure 12.5). In 2009, union membership was just 12 percent of wage-and-salary employment. What is more, government workers form a larger share of union membership than in the past, leaving a small number of unionized private-sector workers concentrated in a limited number of trades. Unionization may, then, explain some part of the failure of wages to adjust, although not a large part.

In contrast, unionization rates in most European countries are half again to nearly six times higher than in the United States (Table 12.3). Unionization in France is actually lower than in the United States at 8 percent, whereas in Sweden it is massively higher at 71 percent. Most European countries also have social and labor legislation that gives workers (unionized or not) extensive rights with respect to dismissal, severance pay, maternity leaves, and so forth. Many economists, as well as domestic critics, have argued that the designs of many of these programs discourage flexibility in the labor market and actually contribute to higher unemployment rates as firms are reluctant to hire and incur the risks of not being able to adjust

Table 12.3. *Unionization Rates in Selected Countries, 2007*

	Union Members (percentage of all employees)
The G-7	
Canada	29
France	8
Germany	20
Italy	33
Japan	18
United Kingdom	18
United States	12
Other Countries	
Australia	18
Austria	32[a]
Belgium	53
Denmark	69
Finland	70
Ireland	32
Netherlands	20
New Zealand	22[a]
Norway	54
Sweden	71
Switzerland	19[a]

[a] 2006 value.

Source: Organization of Economic Cooperation and Development; data for France, Ireland, and Italy from the European Industrial Relations Observatory.

their use of labor downward in future. The countries that appear to have the most flexible labor markets in Europe, such as the United Kingdom and the Netherlands, also have relatively low unemployment rates – although they are still high compared to the United States. Germany, which has a similar level of unionization to these countries but extensive labor-protection laws, has consistently had a high unemployment rate in recent years.

Government Actions

A third explanation for the failure of wages to adjust in the face of unemployment points to the actions of the government. In one sense the power of the unions is the result of government action. Without the National Labor Relations Act, employers would not have to recognize the right of unions to represent workers.[8] Aside from providing the legal basis for unions, the government intervenes more directly in wage setting.

---

[8] The National Labor Relations Act is known as the Wagner Act of 1935, as amended by the Taft-Hartley Act of 1947 and the Landrum-Griffin Act of 1959.

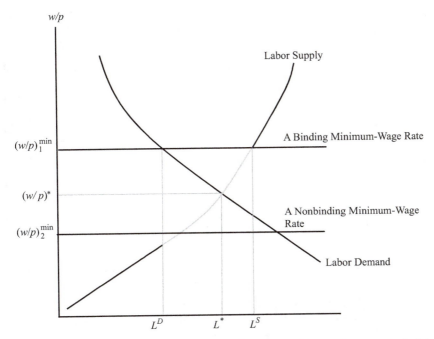

Figure 12.6. The Effect of the Minimum Wage on Unemployment. A binding minimum-wage rate (e.g., $(w/p)_1^{\min}$) sets the real wage above the market-clearing wage $(w/p)^*$, where labor supply exceeds labor demand and results in involuntary unemployment (gray segment of the labor-supply curve) of $L^S - L^D$. When the minimum-wage rate is set below the market-clearing rate (e.g., at $(w/p)_2^{\min}$), it has no effect on unemployment as firms are willing to pay the market-clearing wage.

The best-known instance is the minimum-wage law. A required minimum wage means that firms cannot profitably hire any worker whose marginal product is less than the minimum wage. Figure 12.6 shows the labor market. When wages are set freely, the market clears at $(w/p)^*$. But when the government imposes a minimum wage above the market-clearing rate at $(w/p)_1^{\min}$, labor supply exceeds labor demand and $L^S - L^D$ workers are unemployed. Firms would willingly hire more workers, and workers would willingly accept lower wages, but the law prohibits them from going below the minimum.

Minimum-wage rates are set in nominal terms and updated only infrequently. Over time inflation may erode the real value of the minimum wage, so that it falls in the direction of, or even below, market-clearing real wage. The real wage $((w/p)_2^{\min}$ in Figure 12.6) is an example of a *nonbinding minimum-wage rate*. When the minimum-wage rate is nonbinding, firms will offer higher wages (in this case, the market-clearing rate, $(w/p)^*$). Figure 12.7 shows the real and nominal value of the minimum wage in the United States *and* the percentage of workers actually paid at (or below) minimum wage. The fact that the real minimum wage does not trend upward as

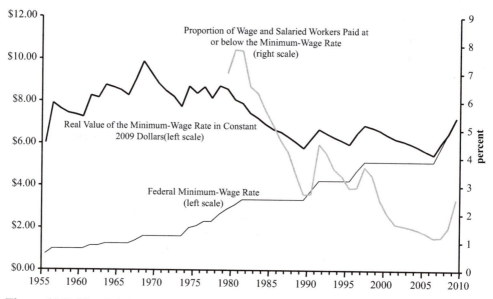

Figure 12.7. The Minimum Wage in the United States. While the minimum-wage rate has risen over time, its real value has mainly fallen since the late 1960s, and fewer and fewer workers are actually paid at or below minimum wage. *Source:* Bureau of Labor Statistics.

average real wages have in the United States and the fact that the number of workers subject to minimum wage has trended downward together suggest that, for most jobs, the minimum wage is nonbinding.

Economic theory predicts that minimum-wage laws will raise unemployment rates unless they are nonbinding. Any worker who remains employed benefits from an increase in the wage rate, but these benefits are offset to some degree by the income lost to those who are fired, or who are never hired, because of a binding minimum wage. It is useful to remember that jobs and workers are heterogeneous. The minimum wage (at least at the rates that have prevailed over the past five decades) is relevant only for the most unskilled workers. If the labor-demand curve for occupations that pay minimum wage is very steep, then even a large change in the minimum-wage rate would have little effect on unemployment.

In the 1990s, the economists David Card (University of California, Berkeley) and Alan Krueger (Princeton University) unleashed a vigorous debate about the minimum wage with a study that appeared to show that an increase in the minimum-wage rate in New Jersey had actually raised employment.[9] For economists, this was a man-bites-dog story, and Card and Krueger's methods and evidence were quickly challenged by other economists.[10]

[9] David Card and Alan B. Krueger, *Myth and Measurement: The New Economics of the Minimum Wage.* Princeton, NJ: Princeton University Press, 1995.

[10] One of the many opposing studies is Richard V. Burkhauser, Kenneth A. Couch, and David Wittenburg, "Who Gets What from Minimum Wage Hikes: A Replication and Re-estimation of Card and Krueger," *Industrial and Labor Relations Review*, vol. 49, no. 3, April 1996, pp. 547–552.

Although the controversy continues, now that the dust has settled, there is little evidence that overall employment would increase by much if the minimum wage were cut or that overall unemployment would rise by much if the minimum-wage rate were raised moderately. Both negative and positive effects would likely be concentrated on particular groups, such as teenagers.

Another example of government regulation of wage rates is provided by the Davis-Bacon Act, first adopted in 1931. The act requires that firms pay workers on federal construction projects at prevailing union-wage rates for those trades in those areas, whether or not the workers are unionized. The act extends the influence of unions in preventing wage cuts to a wider group of workers.

There have been numerous proposals from time to time to establish **comparable-worth laws** that would categorize jobs according to some standard other than the supply and demand for workers of a particular type. The proponents of such legislation argue that certain types of jobs have been regarded as "women's work" and pay less than jobs that are in some sense just as valuable. Compared to plumbers, for example, nurses might require more education and face life-and-death responsibilities and yet be paid less. A comparable-worth law might, therefore, judge that nurses should be paid more than plumbers. Any increase in the wage for plumbers – for example, as the result of an increase in demand – would have to be met by a proportionate increase in the wage for nurses to maintain comparable worth, even if that increase raised the wage above its market-clearing level and reduced the demand for nurses, adding to their unemployment.

So far comparable-worth legislation in the United States has been restricted to a few states and applied only to state and local employees. Comprehensive extension to the private sector seems unlikely politically (few politicians wish to support central planning) and economically (setting wage rates independent of supply and demand interferes with their ability to transmit information important to economic efficiency).

12.3.2 The Labor-Supply Process

Job Search

Unemployment is a stock variable, similar to other stock variables such as capital and wealth. We likened stock variables to a lake or a pool into which some correlative variables (investment for capital and savings for wealth) flow in and some (depreciation and dissavings) flow out. Unemployment may also be envisaged as a pool in which laid-off or newly entering workers are streams flowing in and the newly employed or workers leaving the labor force are streams flowing out. A richer analogy would be, perhaps, that the economy is a mansion with many rooms (firms or workplaces) and many hallways. Those out of the labor force are outside the house. The unemployed wander the hallways in search of the appropriate room. The firms determine how many workers may stay in a room, rather like a game of musical chairs in which the firms determine the number of chairs. The house is a busy place.

Obviously, in a recession, the halls teem with workers searching for rooms with empty chairs. The number of chairs falls short of the available workers. Still, some workers find chairs. The halls become less crowded in the late stages of a business-cycle expansion, but even then there are plenty of workers about. Different firms grow at different rates. Technological improvements may reduce the need for workers in particular firms, while rising demand increases the need for workers in other firms. Some firms are bankrupted and close their doors even when times are generally good. And workers more readily leave their jobs voluntarily when they believe that it will be easier to find another.

Not all rooms can be adjacent. A worker searching for the right match may aim for an upper floor (a high-paying job). If the search goes on, the same worker might have to settle for a lower floor. The willingness to adjust one's reservation wage downward may depend on how crowded the halls are (the unemployment rate). When they are teeming, workers may take whatever they can get, even if it means going straight to the basement.

The search for employment is not quite like the game of musical chairs because some workers do not fit some chairs. Workers look for positions that match their skills. The unemployment that results when jobs remain vacant even though some workers are still unemployed because of mismatch is sometimes called **structural unemployment**. Structural unemployment is not a mutually exclusive category with respect to voluntary and involuntary unemployment. Rather, it is a form of extreme frictional unemployment in which the cause of the friction is highlighted. Structural unemployment is likely to be high in particular areas facing large-scale changes to dominant industries. When deep coal mining declined in the eastern states, the unemployed miners, whose skills were now redundant or obsolete, could have been considered to be structurally unemployed, even though other jobs were vacant elsewhere in the country.

Employment Status and Job Flows

Statisticians can count the number of people in each employment state: *out-of-the-labor-force, unemployed, employed*. Such statistics fail to convey the fact that the labor market is never quiescent. People are constantly changing their employment state. The changes of the different employment states are the net results of inflows and outflows between the different pairs of states. Figure 12.8 shows a typical boom month (May 2006). Employment rose in

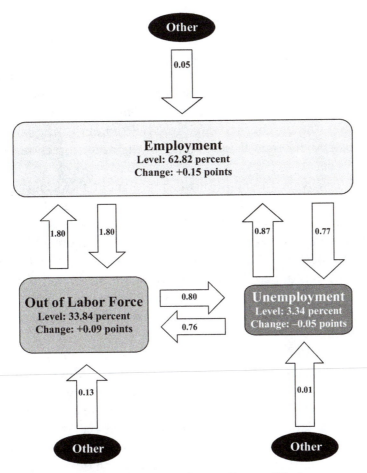

Figure 12.8. Typical Employment Flows in the Boom. Workers move constantly between employment states. The differences between the numbers moving in and out of any state are usually small. The difference between a boom and a slump is typically a small tipping of the balance toward employment as slightly more unemployed workers are hired than lose their jobs in each month. Added up over many months, employment rises and unemployment rates fall. In this month (May 2006), an equal number moved in each direction between out of the labor force and employment; a slightly larger number moved from out of the labor force to unemployment – that is, to looking for a job. Levels are expressed as a percentage of the civilian population older than 16 years of age; changes are expressed in percentage points. *Source:* Bureau of Labor Statistics, Household Survey.

that month by 0.15 percentage points of the working-age population. Part of that rise can be attributed to 0.10 points more people moving off the rolls of the unemployed than lost their jobs that month. The remainder is attributed to the category "other," which is mainly new entrants to the working-age population – either young people reaching the age of sixteen or immigrants. Of the people in the "other" category, some go directly into work; a much smaller number join the ranks of the unemployed; a much larger number are not seeking work and are counted among those out of the labor force. Transitions between employment states are unceasing, and the gross flows are often an order of magnitude greater than their net effects. For example, in May of 2006 the number of people quitting or losing a job and yet not looking for another one (i.e., joining those out of the labor force rather than those unemployed) was relatively large at 1.80 percentage points. Yet, the number moving directly from out-of-the-labor-force to a new job exactly matched those moving in the other direction, so that the net effect was zero.

Figure 12.9 provides a snapshot of employment flows during a typical month in a slump (May 2001). Again, there are relatively large transitions between each pair of employment states and relatively small net effects. Indeed, comparing the size of the flows to those in Figure 12.8 reveals that the differences between the boom and the slump are not really very large. But the balance has tipped slightly toward greater flows out of employment and greater flows into unemployment, so that the smaller net effects are those typical of a recession: lower aggregate employment; greater aggregate unemployment.

Figures 12.8 and 12.9 present snapshots of the labor market. To gain historical perspective, Figure 12.10 plots the time series for net job flows against the business cycle. Net flows are the difference between the outward flows and the inward flows for each of the employment states. The figure confirms our picture of the labor market as continuously active. At every stage of the business cycle there are significant net flows among employment states. The net flows shift toward employment as the expansion develops. The net flow between unemployment and employment tends to be highest early in the expansion, while the net flow between out-of-the-labor-force and employment tends to be highest late in the expansion. Both turn sharply negative in the recession. In contrast, the net flow between out-of-the-labor-force and unemployment tends to rise sharply in recessions and to turn negative only in the middle of the subsequent expansion.

Notice that flows between out-of-the-labor-force and both unemployment and employment affect participation rates. In a typical recession flows from out-of-the-labor-force to unemployment rise, which *ceteris paribus* raises the participation rate; while flows from employment to out-of-the-labor-force also rise, which *ceteris paribus* lowers the participation rate. The net effect can go either way, so that it is hard to predict the cyclical behavior of participation rates. A look back at Figure 11.11 shows that they do not behave consistently across different recessions.

Changes in the participation rate correspond to changes in the size of the labor force. The fact that the size of the labor force is not fixed is often overlooked in popular discussions of labor markets; yet both Figure 12.8 and 12.9

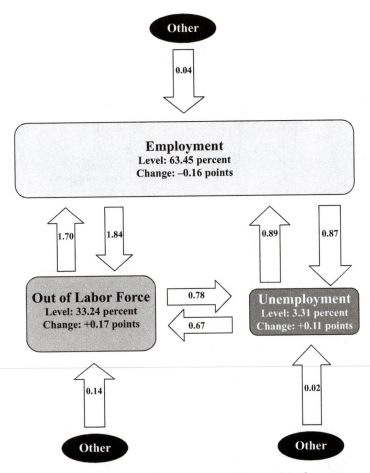

Figure 12.9. Typical Employment Flows in the Slump. Workers move constantly between employment states. The differences between the numbers moving in and out of any state are usually small. The difference between a slump and a boom is typically a small tipping of the balance toward unemployment as slightly fewer unemployed workers are hired than lose their jobs in each month. In this month (May 2001), employment shrank more by workers leaving the labor force than moving to unemployment; unemployment rose more from workers previously out of the labor force beginning to look for work. Added up over several months, employment falls and unemployment rises. Levels are expressed as a percentage of the civilian population older than 16 years of age; changes are expressed in percentage points. *Source:* Bureau of Labor Statistics, Household Survey.

show that flows into and out of the labor force can dwarf the flows between employment and unemployment. They also account for a not uncommon situation in which both employment and the unemployment *rate* fall. Recall that the unemployment rate is the ratio of unemployment to the labor force. If a large enough number of the unemployed – perhaps because they are discouraged at the prospects of finding work – leave the labor force, then the

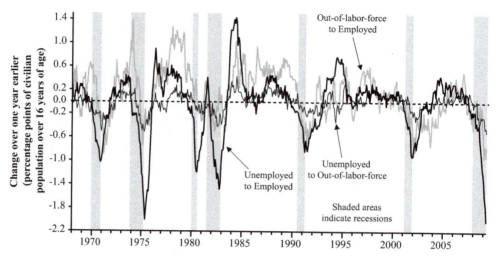

Figure 12.10. Net Flows between Employment Statuses in the United States. *Source:* Bureau of Labor Statistics, Household Survey and author's calculations.

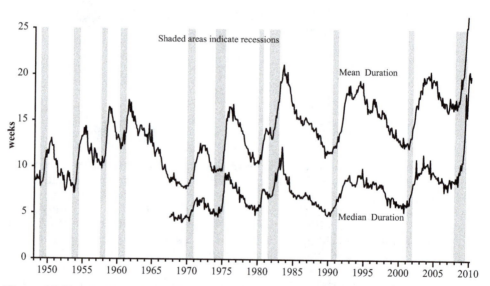

Figure 12.11. The Duration of Unemployment in the United States. Mean duration exceeds median, implying that many are unemployed for a short time and fewer for a long time. Duration is countercyclical. *Source:* Bureau of Labor Statistics.

ranks of the unemployed can shrink faster than the labor force, lowering the unemployment rate.[11]

---

[11] For example, suppose that the working-age population is 100 of which 54 are employed, 6 are unemployed, and 40 are out of the labor force. The unemployment rate is 10 percent $= \frac{6}{54+6}$. If employment drops by 2 and at the same time 2 of the unemployed leave the labor force, then the unemployment rate falls to 7.1 percent $= \frac{4}{52+4}$.

The Duration of Unemployment

Returning to the metaphor of the labor market as a mansion, the unemployment rate tells us how bustling the hallways are, but it does not tell us how fast the inflow or outflow is nor how rapidly the denizens of the hallways turn over. At the same time, even if the unemployment rate is relatively high, unemployment is less of a problem when the typical unemployed worker is out of work only for a short time than when he is out of work for a long time. In either case, the economy has some unused resources. But when unemployment spells are short, some of the costs are spread over more workers, so that each suffers less. A high turnover rate may also indicate that unemployment is largely frictional and, therefore, virtually impossible to eliminate.

Figure 12.11 shows the mean and median duration of unemployment (measured in weeks) in relation to the business cycle. The mean is uniformly higher than the median, which implies that a lot of people are unemployed for a short time and a few for a *much* longer time (i.e., the distribution of durations is positively skewed; see the *Guide*, section G.4.2). The duration of unemployment is a leading or coincident indicator of the recession, reaching its lowest level at or near the cyclical peak, and a lagging indicator of the recovery, peaking after the cyclical trough.

The lag is easily explained. In a recovery, the first to be hired are usually those who have been unemployed only a relatively short time – regular employees on temporary layoff and those whose skills are the freshest. This, in itself, skews the remaining pool of workers toward the longer-term unemployed, who themselves increase the lengths of their individual periods of unemployment, further skewing the pool while they wait for the recovery to progress.

The number of those unemployed for more than 15 weeks reached a high of around 4 percent of the workforce in the double-dip recessions of the early 1980s. In the 1950s, it was sometimes lower than 0.5 percent, but in the last thirty years it has been substantially higher. Even in the strong recovery at the end of the century, it remained near 1 percent. The long-term unemployed workers are in special danger of losing their skills and becoming ever less employable. They represent a problem for economic policy somewhat different from that posed by the short-term unemployed.

Another measure of the inflexibility of European labor markets relative to those of the United States is shown by the incidence of long-term unemployment (Table 12.4). In the United States in 2008, only about one-fifth of the unemployed were out of work for more than six months, compared to about 40 percent for the OECD and more than 50 percent for Europe. Similarly, in the United States about 11 percent of the unemployed were without work for more than a year, compared to 26 percent in the OECD and 37 percent in Europe. The incidence of long-term unemployment is highest

Table 12.4. *Long-Term Unemployment in Selected Countries, 2008*

	Incidence of Long-Term Unemployment (percentage of employment)	
	6 Months and Longer	12 Months and Longer
The G-7		
Canada	14.7	7.1
France	55.6	37.9
Germany	68.9	53.4
Italy	62.3	47.5
Japan	46.9	33.3
United Kingdom	43.0	25.5
United States	19.7	10.6
Other Countries		
Australia	26.7	14.9
Belgium	68.3	52.6
Ireland	48.2	29.4
Luxembourg	63.3	38.6
Mexico	4.2	1.7
Netherlands	52.5	36.3
Poland	46.7	29.0
South Korea	9.7	2.7
Spain	40.2	23.8
Turkey	42.6	26.9
OECD Europe	53.2	36.8
Total OECD	38.9	25.9

Source: Organization of Economic Cooperation and Development, *Employment Outlook, 2009.*

in Germany and Italy. A likely explanation is the relatively more generous unemployment benefits in Europe compared to the United States that keep the opportunity cost of work in Europe high, encouraging workers to maintain high reservation wages.

12.3.3 The Labor-Demand Process

Job Creation and Destruction

The net flows between employment states in the last section quantified the labor market process from the point of view of the worker. Once again using the mansion as a metaphor for the labor market, we can take a different perspective. Instead of tracing the movements of people from rooms to hallways and out the door, let us trace the placement of chairs (i.e., jobs) among the rooms (firms). Any time a firm opens a place for a worker (adds a chair to the room) a job is created. Any time it eliminates a place (removes a chair) a job is destroyed. **JOB CREATION (gains)** and **JOB DESTRUCTION (LOSSES)**

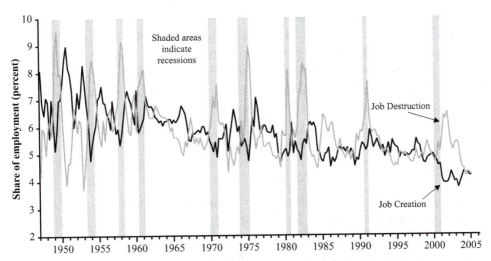

Figure 12.12. Job Creation and Destruction in Manufacturing. *Source:* Steven J. Davis, R. Jason Faberman and John Haltiwanger. "The Flow Approach to Labor Markets: New Data Sources and Micro-Macro Links," *Journal of Economic Perspectives*, vol. 20, No. 3 (Summer, 2006), pp. 3–26.

may be incremental (add a job here, remove one there) or wholesale (open a new factory, shut down an old one). The absolute magnitudes of job creation and job destruction determine how active the labor market is (whether the halls of the mansion are crowded or empty). The net balance between job creation and destruction determines whether employment is rising or falling (and, in large measure, whether the mood in the hallways is optimistic or dispirited).

The U.S. Census Bureau has recently begun publishing data on U.S. job gains and losses going back to 1990. Earlier data are available, but only for manufacturing (Figure 12.12). Several facts stand out. First, both job creation and destruction are high at all stages of the business cycle. The average level of job creation is less than 5 percent of employment, while the average level of job destruction is a little more than 5 percent. Second, job creation is less variable than job destruction. Job creation ranges from a minimum of about 3 percent to a maximum of about 6 percent, while job destruction ranges from about 3 percent to about 10 percent. Third, job destruction is markedly countercyclical. It rises rapidly in recessions and falls rapidly in expansions. In contrast, job creation is probably best described as acyclical. It falls in some recessions and rises in others, and it shows little marked pattern in expansions.

The data paint a picture of the business cycle in manufacturing as waves of job destruction imposed on a background of steadier job creation. The fact that average rates of job destruction exceed those of job creation implies a secular decline in manufacturing jobs as a share of total employment, although not – it must be emphasized – a decline in manufacturing output.

The picture of the manufacturing sector is, in the main, reflected in the data for the whole economy with an important exception. Unlike with manufacturing, job creation for the economy as a whole exceeds job destruction on average. We do not have enough data to be sure, but the acyclicality of job creation may also be peculiar to manufacturing. The peculiarities of manufacturing may result from its relatively high rate of technological progress, which is related to its relative decline as a share of total output. It is worth thinking a little more deeply about this.

Technological Progress and the Reallocation of Labor

When using the common tools of macroeconomic analysis, it is easy to think of the economy in a much too neat and simple way. The aggregate labor-supply/labor-demand diagram encourages us to think of *the* labor market, and the production function with a single measure of productivity growth encourages us to think of *homogeneous* output produced by a *single* underlying technology. Yet we know that both labor and output are heterogeneous and that technological progress varies widely among different sectors of production. The metaphor of the mansion is meant to emphasize the heterogeneity of the labor market.

Rates of technological progress that vary across industries encourage high rates of job destruction. The point can be clarified with a simple example. Imagine an economy in which there are two goods: massages and video games. All workers are alike. And initially each worker can deliver either 20 massages or 20 video games. The workers, who are also consumers, always wish to consume equal numbers of massages and video games. Starting with 1,000 workers, 500 are devoted to giving massages and 500 to producing video games. Real GDP of the economy is 10,000 massages and 10,000 video games. Each worker's consumption bundle is 10 massages and 10 video games.

Massages are not subject to technological progress, because each requires the work of a masseuse for a fixed amount of time. In contrast, we find cleverer and more efficient ways to build video games, just as we have done for all electronic goods. Imagine that there is technological progress in the video-game industry so that each worker can produce 30 instead of 20 video games (a 50-percent increase in productivity). Because workers still wish to consume equal numbers of video games and massages, 500 workers can now produce more video games than the demand warrants. Some workers must shift from video-game production to giving massages. What is the economic mechanism behind the shift?

The increased productivity in the manufacture of video games raises the marginal product of workers in that sector, as well as their wages and incomes. Video-game workers do not themselves wish to buy all their potential new output. Some of the new demand spills over into the massage sector, raising wages there. The failure of the new demand to keep up with production encourages video-game firms to lay off some workers. (To boost their sales, they may lower the price of video games, which raises the product-real wage, so that firms must cut production to get a marginal product of labor to match the higher real wage.)

Massage firms raise wages to attract more workers to meet higher demand. Higher consumption-real wages are possible even though the marginal physical product of workers in the massage sector did not rise, because massage firms raise their prices in the face of higher demand. If the nominal wage were not increased, then the higher price of massages would lower the product-real wage below the marginal product of labor. But of course, the fact that the product-real wage would be lower is exactly the signal the firm needs both to expand production of massages and to hire more masseuses. In the face of higher demand, massages became more expensive, while video games became cheaper (reflecting the higher productivity in their production). Workers in both industries end up with the same real wage.

When all the adjustments are done, 600 workers will produce 12,000 massages and 400 workers will produce 12,000 video games. Each worker's consumption bundle will be 12 video games and 12 massages. Technological progress has in this case destroyed 100 jobs in the video-game industry and created 100 jobs in the massage industry.

The central message of this contrived example is important for understanding the growth of the economy. In general, jobs must flow from the sectors in which productivity grows quickly, such as manufacturing, into sectors in which productivity grows more slowly. It is not possible that productivity can grow perfectly evenly. For example, how could productivity grow in the childcare industry? All productivity growth could mean would be more children per childcare worker. But we would regard that as a degradation of quality rather than an increase in efficiency.

Nor is it possible that the patterns of demand will stay constant over time. Adam Smith (1723–1790), the father of modern economics, made this point in his famous book *The Wealth of Nations*:

The desire of food is limited in every man by the narrow capacity of the human stomach; but the desire of the conveniences and ornaments of building, dress, equipage, and household furniture, seems to have no limit or certain boundary.[12]

As people become richer, they devote a smaller proportion of their income to food.[13] And although there may be no bound for goods in general, one

---

[12] Adam Smith, *The Nature and Causes of the Wealth of Nations*, book I, chapter XI, part II.

[13] This regularity was formulated by the Prussian economist Ernst Engel (1821–1896) and is known to economists as *Engel's Law*.

can use only so many cars or stereos or shoes. A growing economy must shift production constantly from one product to another to reflect the changing patterns of demand.

Many people are puzzled over the fact that in the best of economic times, when unemployment rates are low, the television, radio, and newspapers frequently report massive layoffs. Some take this as evidence that there is a hidden weakness in the economy and that all is not as good as the unemployment statistics report. But, as we have seen, such job destruction is an essential part of adapting a more productive economy to patterns of demand that change as income per capita rises.

Job destruction is often dramatic and newsworthy. In a good economy it is most likely to take the form of an obsolete, unproductive factory being shut down in its entirety or a badly run business going bankrupt. Job creation in a booming economy will be a mixture of incremental additions to existing plants or firms and, from time to time, opening new facilities. Employment at new facilities generally starts off at a moderate level and grows slowly as the business prospers. Job destruction, then, is like the crash of an airliner: it affects a large number of people in a short time, generally in a highly unpleasant manner. Job creation is often like incremental improvements in airliner safety: it is hardly noticed at the time, but its cumulative effect is to raise employment steadily, just as airliners have become steadily safer. News reports of airline crashes tend to convince people that flying is far more dangerous than it really is. News reports about the labor market tend to convince people that it works against the interest of workers far more than it really does.

Recall from Chapter 10 (equation (10.14)) that the growth of real wages (and real incomes generally) depends on the growth of labor productivity. It is tempting to react to the fact that job destruction outweighs job creation in the high-productivity sectors by wanting to stop the process (remember the history of the Luddites). At the same time, people often rail against what they regard as stagnant real wages. One cannot have it both ways. The growth of real wages and job destruction and creation are two aspects of the same growth process.

Wage gains owing to productivity growth are not uniform across all employment. Wage rates depend on education, job-specific skills, relative supplies and demands for specific types of labor, the risks involved in different occupations, and other factors. Still, productivity gains in one sector typically benefit workers in all sectors.

The parable of the video games and the massages applies generally in the actual economy. The prices of manufactured goods have tended to fall rapidly over time. A television in 1960 or a computer in 1980 may have had the same – or, sometimes, even higher – *nominal* price (and, therefore, a much higher *real* price) than the equivalent television or computer today. Yet, the services of a doctor, lawyer, or childcare worker may be much more expensive in real terms now than twenty or forty years ago. These relative price adjustments serve to match demand to unevenly increasing productive capacities and to spread the benefits of those increasing productive capacities throughout the economy. The constant hum of job destruction and creation is the music to which economic growth marches.

Employment Policy

Once we understand how the labor market works, we can get an idea of what sort of policies are likely to be successful in improving economic outcomes. Policies that attempt to regulate job destruction are likely to be counterproductive, because moving workers between sectors is essential to economic growth. Macroeconomic policies that increase aggregate demand when there is cyclical involuntary unemployment may be helpful. Yet, despite pleas for expansionary monetary and fiscal policies during times of low unemployment, such policies cannot reduce voluntary unemployment and are likely to have little effect on true structural unemployment.

The key to reducing structural unemployment is to improve the match between workers and employers – through training to develop the skills most in demand, through better dissemination of information about where workers and jobs are to be found, and possibly through tax or other incentives to encourage firms to locate in areas with relatively high unemployment.

Even voluntary unemployment may sometimes be a policy concern. Among the voluntarily unemployed are the retired and women (and, increasingly, men) rearing children. A case could even be made that as a society we work too much, that it would be better to consume more leisure and fewer goods. Just as with structural unemployment, reducing voluntary unemployment is not a matter of increasing aggregate demand. Instead, it requires changing incentives and opportunities for individual people – a more microeconomic than macroeconomic approach.

Summary

1. Workers are voluntarily unemployed when the real wage is lower than their reservation wage, so that they choose not to participate in the labor market. They are involuntarily unemployed when the real wage is at or below their reservation wage, so that they are willing to work but do not have a job.

2. The unemployment rate ideally is the ratio of involuntary unemployment to the labor force. In practice, the unemployment rate never falls to zero, even at

the peak of the business cycle, because of measurement problems, workers in inevitable transitions between jobs, and real-wage floors (e.g., due to minimum-wage laws or to firms finding that workers paid above the market-clearing wage are more efficient).

3. The unemployment rate fails to measure all dimensions of employment. Workers may be employed part-time or overtime. They may be loosely attached or discouraged (i.e., not reported as unemployed, but easily drawn into the labor force when demand is high) or underemployed (i.e., working at a job below their potential productivity).

4. The central puzzle of unemployment is why real wages do not fall far enough or fast enough to eliminate unemployment.

5. The nominal efficiency-wage hypothesis explains the failure of wages to fall sufficiently through the observation that the efficiency of workers may depend on the nominal wage (either because they mistake nominal for real wages (money illusion) or because they regard nominal wage cuts as a signal of disapproval from employers or because they care about relative economic position rather than just purchasing power). Firms may be reluctant to be the first to cut nominal wages in order to secure a fall in real wages, knowing that a cut will reduce worker efficiency.

6. Unions may inhibit wage adjustments. Insiders to unions may care more about the income effects to the employed (the insiders) than about the incentives to firms to hire the unemployed (outsiders).

7. Government regulations – minimum-wage and prevailing-wage or comparable-worth laws – may inhibit wage adjustments.

8. Workers and jobs are heterogeneous, so that the labor market is constantly engaged in a process of matching workers to appropriate jobs and workers are constantly moving between jobs and between labor market states: out-of-the-labor-force, employment, and unemployment. Recessions correspond to times when the net flows are into unemployment from the other two states. Expansions correspond to times when the net flows are into employment. In a recession the time the unemployed must typically spend looking for work is longer, even for the same rate of unemployment, than in an expansion.

9. Firms create and destroy jobs as they shift production to match changing demand and differential rates of productivity growth in different industries. Recessions are times when job destruction rises relatively to job creation. Job destruction may also be high in expansions, but job creation is relatively higher.

10. Workers must be constantly shifted from industries with high rates of technological progress to those with low rates. This process spreads the benefits of productivity growth among all workers as demand grows disproportionately for the labor of workers in low-productivity industries.

11. Macroeconomic (monetary and fiscal) policies may help to reduce involuntary unemployment, but they cannot eliminate voluntary unemployment. Policies that interfere with the process of job creation and destruction are likely to be counterproductive because growth requires constant reallocation of labor.

Key Concepts

voluntary unemployment
involuntary unemployment
full employment
unemployment rate
real efficiency-wage hypothesis
frictional unemployment
underemployment

demand failure
nominal efficiency-wage hypothesis
insider/outsider model of
  unemployment
job creation (job gains)
job destruction (job losses)

Suggestions for Further Reading

Bureau of Labor Statistics, *BLS Handbook of Methods*; Chapter 1, "Labor Force Data Derived from the Current Population Survey" and Chapter 2, "Employment, Hours and Earnings from the Establishment Survey" (www.bls.gov/opub/hom/).

Truman F. Bewley, *Why Wages Don't Fall in a Recession*. Cambridge, MA: Harvard University Press, 1999.

George A. Akerlof and Janet L. Yellen, *Efficiency Wage Models of the Labor Market*. Cambridge: Cambridge University Press, 1986.

Steven J. Davis, John C. Haltiwanger, and Scott Schuh, *Job Creation and Destruction*. Cambridge, MA: MIT Press, 1996.

Problems

Data for this exercise are available on the textbook website under the link for Chapter 12 (appliedmacroeconomics.com). Before starting these exercises, the student should review the relevant portions of the *Guide to Working with Economic Data*, including sections G.1–G.4, G.8–G.9, and G.16.

Problem 12.1. The following are selected data for Australia:

Year	Labor Force (thousands)	Employment (thousands)	Population (millions)
1998	9,343	8,618	18.73
1999	9,470	8,785	18.95
2008	11,186	10,712	21.07

(a) Calculate the unemployment rate for 2008 and the participation rate for 1998.

(b) If employment is converted to an index number for employment that takes the value of 100 in 1998, what is the value of this index in 1999?

Problem 12.2. Use the labor-supply/labor-demand diagram to show how an economy that starts at full employment would generate unemployment through adopting a minimum wage above the market-clearing wage. Discuss how the quantitative effects of the minimum wage depend on the steepness of the labor-supply and labor-demand curves. To what economic features of firms or workers does the relative steepness of each curve correspond? How might this simple analysis tell less than the whole story about minimum-wage increases?

Problem 12.3. Calculate and plot the minimum-wage rate as a share of the average hourly wage rate. Discuss the relationship of the two rates over time. Is there anything in the data that would suggest that the importance of the minimum-wage rate for unemployment might have changed over time?

Problem 12.4. Figure 12.3 shows involuntary part-time employment as a share of all part-time employment. Examine part-time employment in more detail by plotting involuntary and voluntary part-time employment as separate series, indicating the NBER recession dates with shading. Compare and discuss their cyclical and secular behavior.

Problem 12.5. Plot average overtime hours (available only for manufacturing industries) and indicate NBER recession dates with shading. Discuss the cyclical and secular behavior of overtime.

Problem 12.6. Recently, it has been argued that workers have fared poorly and that real wages have not grown much since the early 1970s. In particular, it has been claimed that workers have not shared in large increases in labor productivity. To investigate that claim, using quarterly data, first, start with the time series for *total compensation* (which includes benefits as well as wages and salaries) and convert it to *real* total compensation in two different ways: a) use the CPI to get an estimate of the *consumption*-real wage; and b) use the PPI to get an estimate of the *product*-real wage. Next, convert each of the series and the time series for labor productivity (output per hour) to an index number, taking 1950:1 as the base period (i.e., 1950:1 = 100 for each series). Plot the three series on a single graph. Review the relationship among profit maximization, real wages, and productivity in Chapter 10, section 10.4.1 (especially equation (10.14)) and Chapter 11, section 11.3.1. If firms raise wages proportionately to higher productivity, their labor costs per unit of output will not rise. But this proposition is based on the *product*-real wage, whereas workers' complaints are based on the *consumption*-real wage. Consider your graph of the relationship of the two measures of real wages and labor productivity: Have workers fared well or poorly since 1970? Does it matter whether we take the firms' or the workers' point of view? If so, explain the difference.

Problem 12.7. Consider three scenarios for annual wage increases and rates of inflation: (1) inflation is zero and wages fall by 5 percent; (2) inflation is 5 percent and wages stay constant; (3) inflation is 10 percent and wages rise at 5 percent.

(a) Before doing any calculations, choose which scenario you would prefer. Comment on your reasons.

(b) Ask three friends to do the same.

(c) For each scenario, calculate the change in the *real* wage. Comment on the results of (a) and (b) in light of your calculations.

Problem 12.8. Plot the data on unemployment by duration (i.e., unemployed for less than 5 weeks, 5–14 weeks, 15–26 weeks, and more than 27 weeks all expressed as a percentage of total unemployment) and indicate the NBER recession dates with shading.

(a) How does turnover of the unemployment pool vary with the business cycle?

(b) Has the nature of unemployment experiences changed over time?

Problem 12.9. Diffusion indices compare the number of industries increasing to the number decreasing employment. More precisely, the index is the percentage of industries increasing employment plus one-half the percentage with unchanged unemployment. An index of 50 means that increases and decreases exactly balance. Indices differ according to the period over which the change in employment is measured. Plot the diffusion index for manufacturing firms for a 12-month change in employment and indicate the NBER recession dates with shading. Comment on the cyclical behavior of the diffusion index. Compare the diffusion index to the data on job creation and destruction in Figure 12.12. Do these two variables tell essentially the same story about employment and the business cycle?

Problem 12.10. Repeat Problem 12.9 using the diffusion index for all nonagricultural firms. Note any salient differences.

Problem 12.11. Section 12.3.3 discusses the relationship of employment to productivity and the relative prices of goods. Make three charts: (1) plot the productivity indices for nonfarm business (as a proxy for productivity in services), durable goods manufacturing, and nondurable goods manufacturing; (2) plot the CPI for all items, durables, nondurables, and services; (3) calculate and plot employment in durable, nondurable, and service industries as a percentage of employment in nonfarm establishments. How well do the data conform to the analysis of Section 12.3.3?

Part VI

Aggregate Demand

13

An Introduction to Aggregate Demand

The central question of macroeconomics is what determines the level and growth rate of GDP. In Part V we looked at the economy from the side of aggregate supply. How did the producers decide how much to produce? And how did they decide how many workers and how much capital to employ in the process? Of course, producers can profit only if they are able to sell their output. So in this and the next three chapters, we look at the economy from the side of aggregate demand. How do people decide how much to spend?

13.1 A Simple Model of Aggregate Demand

Our objective in this chapter is to understand the general principles governing aggregate demand. The national income and product accounts (see Chapters 2 and 3) provide a good starting point. The accounts must always balance; the four national-income-accounting identities (equations (2.1)–(2.4)) must always hold *ex post* or in people's plans. Macroeconomic equilibrium occurs when they also hold *ex ante*: everyone's plans are simultaneously fulfilled.

Think back to Chapter 2. The product-expenditure identity (equation 2.1″) is reproduced here as:

$$Y \equiv C + I + G + NX. \tag{13.1}$$

We can think of Y in the equation as the level of aggregate demand. Our focus will be to explain the different elements on the right-hand side. In this chapter, we take the bird's-eye view: How do spending plans of the different households, firms, the government, and the foreign sector become coordinated? That is, how does the economy reach equilibrium – if in fact it does reach equilibrium? What determines the actual values of GDP and other aggregates in equilibrium? And how does the economy behave away from equilibrium? To keep sight of the big picture, this chapter focuses on how the different elements of aggregate demand interact to determine the total. In later chapters, we examine each of the different elements in more detail.

13.1.1 Consumption Behavior

Consumption is the largest component of aggregate expenditure (see Figure 2.6 and Problem 2.1). We can make a start at understanding aggregate demand by understanding consumption.

The Consumption Function

Many factors determine how much people consume. (We consider consumption in detail in Chapter 14.) One factor stands out above all the others: typically, people consume more if they have more income. In his *General Theory of Employment, Interest and Money* (1936), John Maynard Keynes famously put it this way:[1]

> The fundamental psychological law, upon which we are entitled to depend with great confidence both *a priori* from our knowledge of human nature and from the detailed facts of experience, is that men are disposed, as a rule and on the average, to increase their consumption, as their income increases, but not by as much as the increase in their income. (p. 96)

This means that if you receive an additional dollar of income, you will increase your expenditure, but by less than one dollar. The amount that you increase your expenditure is known as the **MARGINAL PROPENSITY TO CONSUME** (or **mpc**) and is defined as *the rate at which consumption increases when (disposable) income is increased by a small increment.*

The mathematical relationship between consumption and the factors that determine it is known as the **CONSUMPTION FUNCTION**. A simple linear consumption function captures Keynes's point:

$$C = c_0 + cYD. \tag{13.2}$$

C is, of course, consumption; YD is disposable income; and c_0 and c are parameters that must be determined from data. Figure 13.1 portrays the function. Its slope is the marginal propensity to consume: $\Delta C / \Delta Y = c$ (or, using derivatives, $dC/dY = c$). Keynes's fundamental psychological law can be restated: $0 < c < 1$ – the marginal propensity to consume lies between zero and one.

---

[1] Keynes (1883–1946) is by most reckoning the most influential economist of the twentieth century. (His surname rhymes with "trains" not with "beans.")

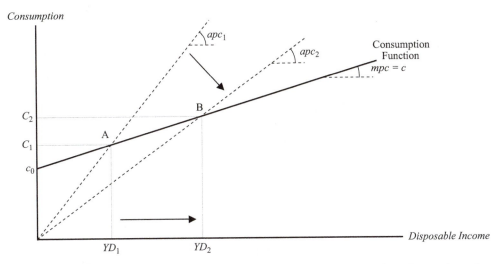

Figure 13.1. The Consumption Function. The consumption function shows the relationship between disposable income and consumption. The slope of the consumption function is the marginal propensity to consume (*mpc*) – the amount of additional consumption that results from a small increase in disposable income. The average propensity to consume (*apc*) is the ratio of total consumption to total disposable income, shown by the slope of a ray from the origin to the consumption point. When disposable income increases from YD_1 to YD_2, consumption rises from C_1 to C_2. The *mpc* remains constant, but the *apc* falls from apc_1 to apc_2.

The Shape of the Consumption Function

The marginal propensity to consume tells us how much is consumed out of the "last dollar" received. But it does not tell us how much is consumed on average. The **AVERAGE PROPENSITY TO CONSUME (apc)** is given by C/YD where the marginal propensity to consume is given by $\Delta C/\Delta YD$ or dC/dYD. Figure 13.1 shows that a disposable income YD_1 results in consumption C_1 at point A on the consumption function. A ray from the origin to point A has the slope C_1/YD_1. In other words, the slope of a ray from the origin measures the *apc*.

The ray to point A is steeper than the consumption function itself. This reflects a general property:

- *The average propensity to consume is greater than or equal to the marginal propensity to consume* (apc ≥ mpc).

When the consumption function is linear (as in Figure 13.1), the marginal propensity to consume is constant, because the slope of the consumption function is constant. But the average propensity to consume is not constant. To illustrate, look what happens if disposable income increases to YD_2. The marginal propensity to consume at point B is just the same as at point A; but the average propensity has fallen from apc_1 to apc_2.

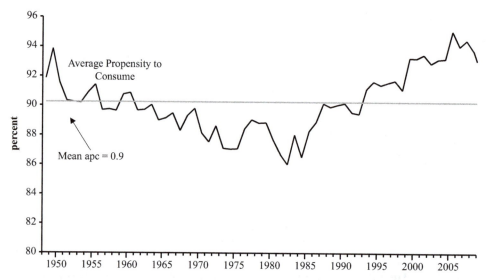

Figure 13.2. The Average Propensity to Consume for the United States. The average propensity to consume (*apc*) declines somewhat over the first 40 years of the sample and rises thereafter, but there is no clear declining trend as predicted by a linear consumption function with a marginal propensity to consume (*mpc*) less than the *apc*. Consequently, a reasonable first approximation to an empirically relevant linear consumption function may be one with the *mpc* = *apc*, here approximated by a mean of 90 percent.

Must the average propensity to consume fall as income rises? Not necessarily. When $c_0 = 0$, the consumption function goes through the origin in Figure 13.1. Because every ray from the origin would then lie along the consumption function itself, the *apc* would be constant and would have the same value as the *mpc*. In equation (13.2), if $c_0 = 0$, then $apc = C/YD = c$ – that is, $apc = mpc$ and, of course, *mpc* is constant in the simple linear consumption function.

As it turns out, a constant average propensity to consume is not a bad approximation to reality. In fact, Figure 13.2 shows that the average propensity to consume for the United States fell until around 1980 and then rose (with some ups and downs) after that. But there is no consistent, long-term downward trend. Thus, for the U.S. data, we can approximate the consumption function as:

$$C = 0.90YD. \tag{13.3}$$

This is a rough-and-ready approximation. The behavior of the actual average propensity to consume is hard to reconcile in detail with the simple linear consumption function. We will put off discussion of more complicated functions until Chapter 14.

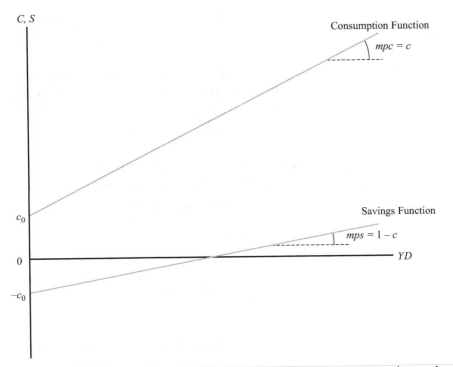

Figure 13.3. Linear Consumption and Savings Functions. The consumption and savings functions are different ways of packaging the same information. If a linear consumption function is written as $C = c_0 + cYD$, then the savings function can be written as $S = YD - C = -c_0 + (1 - c)YD$. The marginal propensity to consume ($mpc = c$) is the slope of the consumption function, while the marginal propensity to save ($mps = 1 - c$) is the slope of the savings function; and $mpc + mps = 1$.

The Savings Function

Sometimes it is helpful to think in terms of what is not consumed, *savings* (S), rather than in terms of what is (C). The two notions are connected through the disposable-income identity (equation (2.2)) – repeated here as

$$YD \equiv Y - T + TR \equiv C + S, \tag{13.4}$$

which states that disposable income is divided between consumption and saving. Substituting equation (13.2) into (13.4) and rearranging gives us the **savings function**:

$$S = YD - (c_0 + cYD) = -c_0 + (1 - c)YD. \tag{13.5}$$

The savings function and the consumption function describe exactly the same behavior from different perspectives.

Both functions are graphed in Figure 13.3. Both are straight lines. The slope of the consumption function is $mpc = c$. The slope of the savings function is $1 - c$. This slope measures the **marginal propensity to save (mps)** defined as *the rate at which savings increases when (disposable) income is increased by a small increment.*

Notice that $mps = (1 - mpc)$ or, equivalently, that $mpc + mps = 1$. This says that, if you receive an extra dollar, part goes to consumption and the remainder goes to saving. For example, suppose that $mpc = 0.92$, then $mps = 1 - 0.92 = 0.08$. If you receive an extra dollar, 92 cents goes to consumption and 8 cents goes to savings.

If equation (13.3) were a good first approximation of a consumption function for the United States, then the savings function can also be approximated by setting $c_0 = 0$ and $c = 0.90$ in equation (13.5):

$$S = 0.10YD. \tag{13.6}$$

13.1.2 Tax Behavior

Net Taxes

Consumption and savings depend on disposable income; disposable income depends on GDP, taxes, and transfers. The disposable-income identity (equation (13.4)) can be rearranged:

$$T - TR \equiv Y - C - S. \tag{13.7}$$

It is convenient to treat transfer payments as *negative taxes* and to drop TR as an explicit variable, so that equation (13.7) can be rewritten as:

$$T \equiv Y - C - S. \tag{13.7'}$$

Taxes (T) cover every kind of deduction (explicit taxes) or contribution (transfer payments) from every level of government – Federal, state, and local – from GDP. The variable T represents not just personal taxes but taxes of every kind – any net flow of funds to the government that opens a gap between GDP, the ultimate source of income, and consumption and saving. (Saving here is not just personal saving, but saving of firms and governments as well – see Chapter 3, section 3.7.)

The government does not levy taxes simply by making up tax bills and sending them to citizens. Mr. Fernandez does not receive a bill from the Internal Revenue Service saying "Please pay $15,000" nor does Ms. Chung receive a bill saying "Please pay $8,980" independent of any action they have themselves taken. Instead, taxes depend on our economic choices – the amount we earn (income taxes), the amount we spend in general (sales taxes), the amount we spend on particular things such as gasoline or cigarettes (excise taxes) – or on our economic fortunes (inheritance taxes).

The government sets the rates, not the actual levels of the revenues that they generate. The top rate of Federal income tax in 2009 was, for example, 35 percent. How much revenue this rate generates depends on how much taxable income people earn.

Transfer payments also depend to some degree on people's incomes. Roughly three-quarters of the Federal budget goes to transfer payments: Federal pensions, Social Security, Medicare, Medicaid, assorted welfare programs, and interest on the Federal debt. State and local governments also spend considerable amounts on transfers. Some of these payments depend only on unchangeable facts about the recipient – for example, having retired from the Federal government. Others depend on the state of the economy. When times are good and GDP is relatively high, welfare payments fall. Transfer payments would, then, appear to vary inversely with the state of the economy.

Yet not all transfer payments act the same way. Interest payments are more complex. When times are good, interest rates tend to rise, which would raise the governments' interest payments. On the other hand, when times are good, governments tend to run smaller deficits or even surpluses, which are used to pay off part of their debt, lowering interest payments.

On balance, transfer payments are probably countercyclical – rising in bad times and falling in good times – acting to offset explicit taxes so that the rate of net taxation is lower.

The Tax Function

The Federal tax code is tremendously complex, involving many different rates for corporations and individuals at different levels of income and for different family structures, different exemptions, as well as many different indirect taxes. And, of course, each state and locality adds its own complicated tax code. It would be impossible to capture all the detail in a model that we could easily grasp.

Fortunately, for our purposes a simple linear **tax function** will be a good enough approximation:

$$T = \tau_0 + \tau Y. \tag{13.8}$$

Here τ is the **marginal tax rate** – a number between zero and one that expresses the fraction of an additional dollar of income that goes to taxes. The intercept, τ_0, is probably negative, because income taxes generally start only after a certain threshold level of income is reached and some forms of transfer payments are highest when incomes are lowest. Figure 13.4 graphs the function. Only the portion above the Y axis is relevant, because taxes cannot be negative. An important message of this function is that the level of taxation rises as the economy grows.

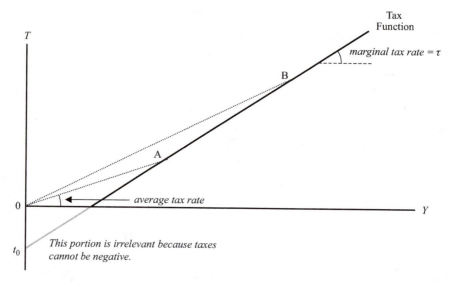

Figure 13.4. The Tax Function. A linear tax function has a constant slope (marginal tax rate) and may intersect the vertical axis below zero if low-income people are not taxed. The average tax rate is given by the slope of a ray from the origin to the tax function. It rises with rising income, unless the function starts at the origin in which case the marginal and average tax rates would be equal.

Also notice, by analogy with *apc* and the consumption function, that the slope of a ray from the origin measures the **average tax rate** (T/Y). The particular function illustrates two general characteristics of tax functions. Because the intercept (τ_0) is negative, the slope of a ray from the origin to any point on the tax function is flatter than the function itself:

- *the average rate of taxation is typically lower than the marginal rate of taxation.*

Also notice that the ray to point B is steeper than the ray to point A:

- *the average rate of taxation typically rises with increasing income.*

The Shape of the Tax Function

As with the consumption function, we can use data to pin down a good enough approximation for the tax function. Figure 13.5 plots the average tax rate for the United States, taking into account all levels of government – Federal, state, and local. There is considerable variation from year to year, and there is a clear but slow upward trend, which is sharply reversed after 2000. We can, once again in a rough-and-ready way, treat the average tax rate as a constant. As with the consumption function, this would make sense only if the average and marginal tax rates were the same so that the tax function goes through the origin. The mean value for the average tax rate

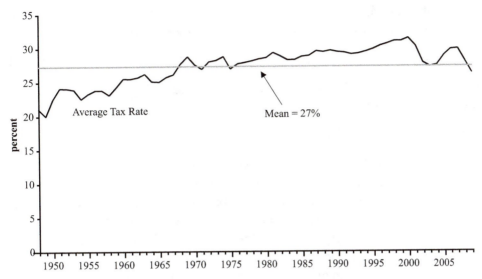

Figure 13.5. The Average Tax Rate for the United States. The average tax rate shows a clear but small upward trend until about 2000, after which there is a distinct fall. A linear tax function with the marginal tax rate equal to the average tax rate, therefore, is not precisely correct, but may nonetheless be a reasonable first approximation. *Source:* Bureau of Economic Analysis.

in the figure is 27 percent. So setting $\tau_0 = 0$ and $\tau = 0.27$, equation (13.8) becomes

$$T = 0.27Y. \tag{13.9}$$

Tax and transfer rates have, of course, not been either simple or constant since the end of World War II, but the success of equation (13.9) as a reasonable approximation says that constant and complicated adjustments to the various tax codes and transfer programs have had a simple net effect: to hold net taxes in aggregate to about 27 percent of GDP for many years.

13.1.3 What Determines the Level of Aggregate Demand?

The Model

To answer the question what determines the level of aggregate demand, we combine the economic behavior captured in the consumption and tax functions with the national-income-accounting identities to form a simple model of aggregate demand. Macroeconomic equilibrium occurs when the choices of people represented in the two functions make the identities hold *ex ante* as well as *ex post*.

The inflow-outflow identity (equation (2.4)) is repeated here as:

$$I + G + EX \equiv S + (T - TR) + IM. \tag{13.10}$$

If we subtract *IM* (imports) from both sides and treat transfer payments (*TR*) as negative taxes included in *T*, we can rewrite this as:

$$I + G + NX \equiv S + T, \tag{13.11}$$

where $NX \equiv EX - IM$. We then substitute in the savings function (13.5) and the tax function (13.8) to get

$$I + G + NX = (1 - c)YD + \tau Y, \tag{13.12}$$

where for simplicity we have set c_0 and τ_0 equal to zero, which is both realistic and will not change any important conclusions (a point addressed in Problem 13.1). Notice that when we substituted the savings and tax functions into the national-income-accounting identity (13.11), we also replaced the triple-barred identity sign with the double-barred equal sign. Equation (13.12) is no longer an identity, but now reflects economic behavior: the *ex ante* plans of consumers and not just the *ex post* national accounts.

It is helpful to treat the variables on the left-hand side of equation (13.11) as a group, which we shall call **autonomous expenditure**: $Au \equiv I + G + NX$. Substituting in this definition, as well as the definition of disposable income ($YD \equiv Y - T$), and the tax function gives us

$$Au = (1 - c)(Y - \tau Y) + \tau Y = [1 - c(1 - \tau)]Y. \tag{13.13}$$

Rearranging terms gives us a simple model of aggregate demand:

$$Y = \frac{1}{1 - c(1 - \tau)} Au. \tag{13.14}$$

To understand this model, it is helpful to recall the distinction made in Chapter 1 between an **endogenous variable** (*a variable determined within a particular system of the economy or within a model that represents that system*) and an **exogenous variable** (*a variable determined outside that system or model*). In this model, the autonomous variables (*Au* and its components *I*, *G*, and *NX*) are exogenous, as are the parameters *c* (the marginal propensity to consume) and τ (the marginal tax rate). In equation (13.14) only *Y* is endogenous, but the model also includes the consumption, savings, and tax functions, so that *C*, *S*, and *T*, as well as *YD*, are also endogenous as well.

Equilibrium and Convergence to Equilibrium

There are two natural steps in understanding any economic model. The first is to solve it for its equilibrium values; the second to investigate how those values change when the exogenous variables change. We take a graphical approach to the first step.

Figure 13.6 is based on equation (13.12). We can think of the left-hand side of the equation as representing *inflows* to the domestic private sector,

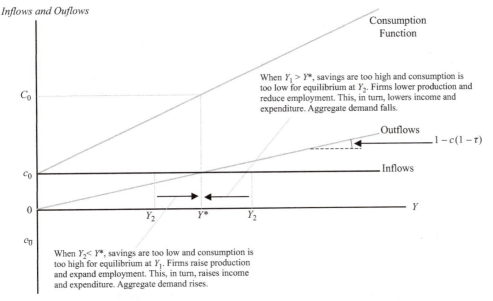

Figure 13.6. The Determination of Aggregate Demand.

while the right-hand side represents *outflows* – in each case, these interpretations follow naturally from the inflow-outflow identity (equations (2.4) and (13.10)) on which equation (13.12) is ultimately based. Because the inflows are exogenous (and thus not affected by income) in the model, the left-hand side is represented as the horizontal *Inflows* curve at the expenditure level Au. The right-hand side is represented by the upward-sloping *Outflows* curve. Its slope is $1 - c(1 - \tau)$, which is the coefficient on Y in equation (13.12). The equilibrium for the model is given at the crossing point of the two lines: Y^*.

The level of aggregate demand, Y^*, is an equilibrium because, at that level of income, the planned savings and taxes generated in the economy (the planned outflows) are exactly enough to balance the planned investment, government expenditure, and net exports (the planned inflows). As a result, Y^* is the level of aggregate demand that coordinates the plans of consumers with those of the other sectors of the economy.

But what happens if aggregate demand is at some other level? Imagine that aggregate demand stood higher than Y^* at Y_1. Savings (adjusting for taxes) would be greater than investment (adjusting for government expenditure and net exports) or, to put it differently, consumers would wish to consume too little for equilibrium at that level of income. (This is the case that we already examined in Chapter 2, section 2.7.) Firms would find themselves with increasing stocks of unsold goods and would lower prices to promote demand and cut back on production to reduce oversupply of their products. For the sake of simplicity, we have assumed for this model that firms do not

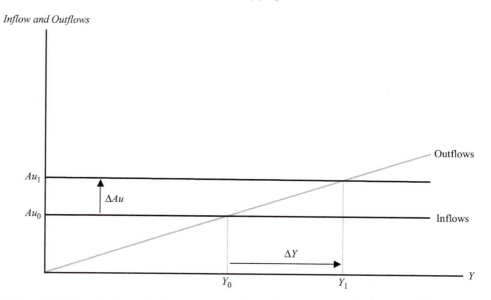

Figure 13.7. An Increase in Autonomous Spending Increases Aggregate Demand.

adjust prices so all the adjustment must take the form of reduced production. Reduced production, of course, requires fewer workers, which generates lower incomes, which lowers both savings and consumption. Aggregate demand falls as expenditure falls. As long as income exceeds Y^*, the natural adjustments in the economy push aggregate demand downward toward Y^*.

A similar adjustment takes place when aggregate demand stands below equilibrium, say, at Y_2. Here investment exceeds savings or, to put it differently, consumers wish to spend more than firms planned to supply. In such a case, firms would find their stocks of inventories falling. If they could raise their prices to choke off demand, they would. They would increase production and, therefore, employment, raising both output and incomes. The increased incomes would increase both savings and consumption expenditures. The additional expenditures increase aggregate demand. As long as income falls short of Y^*, the natural adjustments in the economy push aggregate demand upward toward Y^*.

The Effect of Changes in Autonomous Expenditure on Aggregate Demand

The second step is to ask what happens when autonomous spending changes. For example, what happens if firms increase their levels of investment by $1 billion? Figure 13.7 shows an increase in autonomous expenditure as the upward shift of the inflow curve from Au_0 to Au_1. Its point of intersection moves up along the outflow curve, raising equilibrium aggregate demand from Y_0 to Y_1. In general, the same size increase in government expenditure or in net exports would have exactly the same effect on aggregate demand, as each raises autonomous spending by the same amount. And a cut in autonomous spending would reduce aggregate demand.

13.1.4 The Multiplier

The Static Multiplier

When autonomous expenditure rises by $1 billion (or even by $1), how much does aggregate demand rise? To answer that question we need to know the value of the ratio of the increase of GDP (indicated in Figure 13.7 by the horizontal arrow) to the increase in autonomous expenditure that caused it (indicated by the vertical arrow). This quantity ($\Delta Y / \Delta Au$) is known as the **CONSUMPTION MULTIPLIER** (frequently just abbreviated to **multiplier**) and is indicated by μ (the Greek letter "mu"). If $\mu \equiv \Delta Y / \Delta Au$, then $\Delta Y = \mu \Delta Au$. The trick to answering our question is knowing what value μ takes.

In the real world finding μ may require complex analysis. In our simplified model, it takes just a bit of algebra, which we have already done and reported in equation (13.14). We can rewrite that equation in terms of changes as

$$\Delta Y = \frac{1}{1 - c(1 - \tau)} \Delta Au, \tag{13.15}$$

so that the multiplier is

$$\mu = \frac{\Delta Y}{\Delta Au} = \frac{1}{1 - c(1 - \tau)}. \tag{13.16}$$

(We would get the same result for infinitesimal changes by defining the multiplier as $\mu \equiv dY/dAu$ and taking the derivative of equation (13.14).)

A Numerical Example

A numerical example may clarify the model and the multiplier formula. Using the average values for the marginal propensity to consume ($c = 0.90$) and the marginal tax rate ($\tau = 0.27$) estimated in sections 13.1.1 and 13.1.2, the multiplier is:

$$\mu = \frac{1}{1 - 0.90(1 - 0.27)} = 2.9. \tag{13.17}$$

An increase in autonomous expenditure of $1 billion would, therefore, yield an increase in aggregate demand of $2.9 billion.

The Size of the Multiplier

What determines the size of the multiplier? Notice that the denominator of the multiplier in equation (13.16) is the slope of the outflow curve in

Figure 13.7. The steeper the outflow curve, the smaller the increase in GDP (ΔY) for a given increase in autonomous expenditure (ΔAu). The outflow curve will be steeper the larger the denominator in the multiplier formula. The denominator becomes larger when the marginal propensity to consume (c) is smaller or when the marginal tax rate (τ) is larger.

Consider some extreme cases:

- If $\tau = 0$, then $\mu = \frac{1}{1-c}$. For the values in our numerical example $\mu = \frac{1}{1-0.90} = 10$ – that is, more than triple its value compared to when $\tau = 0.27$.
- If $\tau = 1$ (which says that any additional dollar is completely absorbed in taxes), then $\mu = 1$ – that is, the only effect of an increase in autonomous expenditure is the direct effect. A \$1 million increase in government expenditure adds \$1 million to aggregate demand, but has no multiplied effect.
- If $c = 0$, then once again $\mu = 1$, and there are only direct but no multiplied effects.
- If $c = 1$, then $\mu = \frac{1}{\tau}$. For the values in our numerical example $\mu = \frac{1}{0.27} = 3.70$ – that is, about one-third larger than when $c = 0.90$.

These extreme cases illustrate the rules:

- *The multiplier is larger, the higher the marginal propensity to consume*; and
- *The multiplier is smaller, the higher the marginal tax rate.*

The Multiplier Process

The multiplier seems magical. Every time the government increases its expenditure or every time firms sell more products abroad or purchase investment goods, aggregate demand in the economy increases by much more than the initial expenditure. But is it magical?

Not really. The process behind the multiplier is based on one of the oldest ideas in economics: the butcher's purchases become the baker's income, the baker's purchases become the candlestick maker's income, and so on, in a circle coming back around to the butcher.

During the Great Depression of the 1930s, many people suggested that the government should spend more on roads, schools, hospitals, and other public works to "prime the pump." A small increase in government spending on roads would not only give income to the road builders; it would also give income to their landlords, grocers, and clothiers, whose subsequent expenditures would give income to many others.

The English economist A. C. Pigou (1877–1959) was unimpressed by this commonsense idea, and offered a *reductio ad absurdum* argument against it. If this process were effective, Pigou argued, then a single penny's worth of extra expenditure would eventually cascade into greater and greater incomes until, eventually, those incomes would be great enough to purchase the entire output of the economy. But Pigou believed that such an outcome was ridiculous, so the very notion that incomes could be expanded in this manner must be wrong.

Another English economist, Richard Kahn (1905–1989), responded to Pigou in an article written in 1931. Kahn developed a multiplier formula similar to equation (13.16) not to show that the process was powerful, but rather to show that it was not *absurdly* powerful – that it had a limit.

To understand why the multiplier works and why it is not magical after all, it helps to see it as a process. Imagine that the Boeing Aircraft Company purchased $1,000 worth of tools from a specialist supplier. Let's trace out the process through which $1,000 increases aggregate demand.

Assume that anyone who receives income as a result of Boeing's expenditure faces the same tax rate (27 percent) and the same marginal propensity to consume (90 percent). These numbers reflect the average rates used in the multiplier formula (13.17). Anyone who receives income, then, can dispose of only 73 percent ($= 100 - 27$), so that only 66 percent of the income ($= 0.73{\times}0.90$) is consumed. On these assumptions what is the effect of Boeing's $1,000 purchase on aggregate demand?

Boeing's initial purchase is a form of investment, and so adds $1,000 directly to aggregate demand. The specialist supplier uses Boeing's payment to purchase inputs and to pay its wages and salaries, profits, and rents. Each of the recipients of this income will, after tax, spend 66 percent. So the initial $1,000 also results in an indirect, second-round expenditure by the recipients of the factor incomes of $660. Now these second-round expenditures may be paid-for groceries or rent or to make mortgage payments or to buy clothes or any number of other things. Ultimately, they too form the incomes of people. And those people will after tax make third-round expenditures of 0.66×$660 = $436.60. The process continues to the fourth round, where consumption expenditures are 0.66×$436.60 = $287.50; and so on for round after round. At each round, additional consumption expenditures become smaller. The process effectively stops when the amount available to spend is less than a penny.

Let's add up the total effects on aggregate demand:

$$\Delta Y = \underset{\textit{direct effects}}{1,000.00} + \underset{\textit{indirect effects}}{660.00 + 436.60 + 287.50 + \cdots}$$

This would be easier to analyze if we were specific about the relationships among the different terms. Each is 0.66 times the preceding term, so that

$$\Delta Y = \underset{\textit{direct effects}}{1,000} + \underset{\textit{indirect effects}}{0.66(1,000) + 0.66^2(1,000) + 0.66^3(1,000) + \cdots}$$

$$= 1,000(1 + 0.66 + + 0.66^2 + 0.66^3 + \cdots). \tag{13.18}$$

To solve this, multiply both sides by 0.66 to yield

$$0.66\Delta Y = 1{,}000(0.66 + +0.66^2 + 0.66^3 + 0.664\cdots). \qquad (13.19)$$

Subtracting equation (13.19) from (13.18) gives us

$$(1 - 0.66)\Delta Y = 1{,}000. \qquad (13.20)$$

Each term in parentheses on the right-hand side of (13.18) except for the initial "1" is cancelled by one of the terms on the right-hand side of (13.19) all the way out to infinity. We can solve (13.20) to get

$$\Delta Y = \frac{1{,}000}{1 - 0.66} = 2{,}941. \qquad (13.21)$$

Boeing's initial purchase results in an increase in aggregate demand nearly three times the initial purchase. Except for rounding in the calculation, this is the same multiplier as in equation (13.17). And in fact, whatever the values for c, τ, and ΔAu, the sequence in which purchases become incomes become purchases become incomes...always results in a total effect given by the multiplier formula (13.16). (Problem 13.2 asks for a general proof of this proposition.)

Looking at the multiplier as the outcome of a sequence of purchases generating incomes reminds us of the importance of the notion of the circular flow of income and expenditures (see Chapter 2, section 2.2.2, and Chapter 3, section 3.1.2, especially Figure 3.1). It also makes it clear that the multiplier is not instantaneous, but unfolds over time. The calculation assumes rounds of expenditures. How long a round is depends on how fast the income received is spent. Although individual people are paid at various intervals – some daily, more weekly, and probably most biweekly or monthly – they spend constantly. In reality, the multiplier traces out an average effect. Each round could on average be as short as a day or, quite reasonably, a week or more. The multiplier process is not quick. If each round expends 66 percent of the round before it, then it takes 18 rounds for the expenditure to fall below one dollar and 29 rounds to fall below one cent. If each round takes a day these correspond to a little more than two and a half weeks to reach a dollar and more than four weeks to reach one cent. But if each corresponds to a week, then they correspond to four and a half and seven months.

Even though *complete* adjustment takes many rounds, most of the changes occur in the early rounds. Half of the final effect occurs by round 3, three-quarters by round 4, and 90 percent by round 6.

13.2 Fiscal Policy

In Chapter 12 we saw that aggregate demand may be insufficient in some cases to guarantee full employment of labor or to keep the economy operating at its full economic potential. To combat unemployment, the government could try to raise the level of aggregate demand through monetary or fiscal policy. (We will see in Chapter 15 that it may also want to reduce aggregate demand to combat inflation.) We postpone the main discussion of monetary policy until Chapter 16, but the simple model of aggregate demand developed in this chapter gives us the basis for a preliminary discussion of fiscal policy (elaborated in Chapter 17).

Fiscal policy (see Chapter 1) is *the set of actions that determine the levels of government spending and taxes and that together determine the size of the government budget deficit.* FISCAL POLICY can be DISCRETIONARY (i.e., deliberately chosen to achieve a particular result) or AUTOMATIC (i.e., built into the design of the tax code and spending programs). We first consider discretionary fiscal policy.

13.2.1 Discretionary Fiscal Policy

Choosing the Level of Government Spending

If the government finds the level of aggregate demand to be too low, it can raise it through increasing government spending. This is easily seen as a special case of the scenario described in Figure 13.7. An increase in government spending (G) is just one of many ways that autonomous spending can be raised, and each has a multiplied effect on aggregate demand. But exactly how much should spending be raised?

To guide their fiscal actions, policymakers have built detailed models of the economy. Surprising as it may seem, these complex models (often involving hundreds of equations) are largely constructed according to the same principles that have guided us in this chapter. So even without the hundreds of equations, the simple model and the static multipliers provide a great deal of insight into how economists and policymakers actually design fiscal policies.

An Illustrative Model: Benchmark. Start with a simple, artificial example. Imagine an economy without foreign trade and with taxes, but no transfer payments. Consumers' behavior is described by the consumption function:

$$C = 0.8(Y - T). \tag{13.22}$$

The government levies a simple "flat tax":

$$T = (1/6)Y. \tag{13.23}$$

Initially, government expenditure $G = 500$ and investment $I = 500$.

The first question is, what is the equilibrium level of aggregate demand? We solve for it, beginning with the inflow-outflow identity (2.4 or 13.11) with *EX*, *IM*, and *TR* set to zero:

$$I + G = S + T. \tag{13.24}$$

From equations (13.5) and (13.22), we know that savings $S = (1 - 0.8)(Y - T)$. Substituting this and equation (13.23) into (13.24), as well as the values for *I* and *G*, gives

$$500 + 500 = 1,000 = (1 - 0.8)(Y - (1/6)Y) + (1/6)Y = (1/3)Y \tag{13.25}$$

or

$$Y = 3,000.$$

(You should use this value and the tax and consumption functions to check that the national-income-accounting identities hold.)

The *government's budget deficit* is $G + TR - T$. Here, it is *deficit* $= 500 + 0 - (1/6)3,000 = 0$. In words, the budget is balanced.

An Illustrative Model: Case 1. Now, imagine that the government believes – perhaps because there is unemployment – that the level of aggregate demand is too low. It believes that, if it can raise aggregate demand to 3,600, it can eliminate unemployment. How much does it need to increase *G*?

One way to find *G* is to go back to the simple model (e.g., in equation (13.25)), replace the 500 that represents government expenditure with the variable *G*, and replace the variable *Y* with the value 3,600, then solve for *G*. Another way is start with the multiplier formula (13.16) with the values $c = 0.8$ and $\tau = 1/6$ given in the example:

$$\mu = \frac{\Delta Y}{\Delta Au} = \frac{1}{1 - c(1 - \tau)} = \frac{1}{1 - 0.8(1 - (1/6))} = 3. \tag{13.26}$$

Because the government wants to raise *Y* from 3,000 to 3,600, $\Delta Y = 600$, and $\Delta Au = \Delta Y / \mu = 600/3 = 200$. Any change in autonomous spending of 200 would raise aggregate demand the required amount. The government can achieve its goal by increasing government spending so that $\Delta Au = \Delta G = 200$.

Our solution to the government's fiscal planning problem is quite similar to how actual governments evaluate fiscal policy, although their models are more realistically detailed.

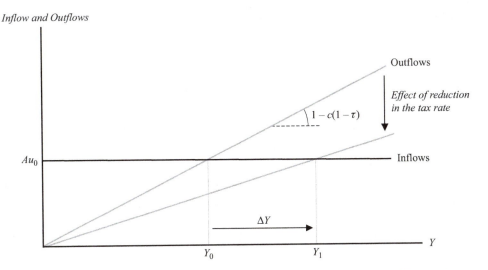

Figure 13.8. Cutting the Marginal Tax Rate Increases Aggregate Demand.

Setting Tax Rates

The government may prefer to stimulate aggregate demand through a tax cut rather than through an increase in government expenditure. As we mentioned in section 13.1.2, governments do not levy taxes in arbitrary amounts; instead they set rates that together with the levels of income or other economic activity determine the total tax take. Taxes are then *endogenous*; tax rates are *exogenous*. So the question that the government has to answer is, what tax rate is needed to raise aggregate demand to the right level?

The principle is fairly straightforward: lower tax rates raise disposable incomes with a multiplier effect. Figure 13.8 shows that a decrease in tax rates flattens the outflow curve, raising aggregate demand from Y_0 to Y_1. But again, how would the government find the particular tax rate that achieved its goal for aggregate demand?

An Illustrative Model: Case 2. One way is to go back to the simple model, replace the tax rate of one-sixth with the variable τ and the variable Y with the target level of GDP (3,600), then solve for τ. This will give us the same result as using the solution to the simple model given in equation (13.14) with $Y = 3,600$, $c = 0.8$, and $Au = G + I = 500 + 500 = 1,000$:

$$3,600 = \frac{1}{1 - 0.8(1 - \tau)}1,000, \qquad (13.27)$$

which can be solved for the tax rate that delivers the desired level of aggregate demand:

$$\tau = 9.72 \text{ percent.}$$

Targeting the Level of Taxes. A politician may believe that the citizens are overtaxed, and coming into office may promise a tax cut of a particular amount – in our model, say, 100. What tax rate would the government have to choose in order to achieve that level of taxation? The problem here is that now the target level of taxes is fixed, whereas the tax rate must be adjusted to achieve it. The level (T) is now exogenous while the rate (τ) is endogenous. The previous solution to the model (equation (13.14) and the multiplier formula (13.16) assumed just the opposite, so they no longer apply. Instead we must solve the model again under the new assumptions.

We start with the inflow-outflow identity (13.8 or 2.4), letting autonomous spending $AU \equiv I + G + NX$. We substitute in the savings function (13.5), setting $c_0 = 0$ for simplicity, and the definition of disposable income, $YD \equiv Y - T$ (where, as before, we treat transfer payments as negative taxes). This gives us

$$Au = (1 - c)(Y - T) + T = (1 - c)Y + cT \tag{13.28}$$

or

$$Y = \frac{1}{1 - c}Au - \frac{c}{1 - c}T. \tag{13.28'}$$

There are now two multipliers (distinguished by subscripts):

- the **tax multiplier** is *the amount that aggregate demand changes* ceteris paribus (here holding *Au* constant) *for a change in taxes*:

$$\mu_T \equiv \frac{\Delta Y}{\Delta T} = -\frac{c}{1 - c}; \tag{13.29}$$

- and the **autonomous expenditure multiplier** is *the amount that aggregate demand changes* ceteris paribus (here holding *T* constant) *for a change in autonomous spending*:

$$\mu_{Au} \equiv \frac{\Delta Y}{\Delta Au} = \frac{1}{1 - c}. \tag{13.30}$$

The tax multiplier is, of course, negative, because taxes are an outflow from the domestic private sector. But notice that it is also smaller in absolute value than the autonomous expenditure multiplier. If, as in our numerical example, $c = 0.8$, then $\mu_T = -4$ and $\mu_{Au} = 5$. An easy way to see why is to remember that while each of the components of Au is a direct contributor to GDP *and* has indirect multiplier effects, taxes and transfer payments do not contribute directly to GDP; although, because they change disposable income, they still have multiplier effects. So if we look again at the multiplier process in equation (13.18) and imagine that the stimulus was not $1,000 of additional investment spending, but a $1,000 tax cut or a $1,000 increase in transfer payments, then we would have to drop the first term (the initial

$1,000 representing the direct effect) and start with 0.66(1,000), which is of course $c\Delta Y$. Every term then is smaller by the factor c; so the tax multiplier itself is smaller in absolute value by the factor c.

Also notice that the autonomous expenditure multiplier is larger than the earlier consumption multiplier: $\mu_{Au} = \frac{1}{1-c} > \frac{1}{1-c(1-\tau)} = \mu$ for all positive tax rates. In fact, μ_{Au} is exactly μ with $\tau = 0$. That makes sense: when the government targets the level of taxes (T), it makes that level independent of the marginal tax rate; it is as if the marginal tax rate had been set to zero.

An Illustrative Model: Case 3. Now let us return to our problem. What happens in our illustrative model if the government cuts taxes so that $\Delta T = -100$? Using the tax multiplier,

$$\mu_T \equiv \frac{\Delta Y}{\Delta T} = \frac{\Delta Y}{-100} = -\frac{c}{1-c} = -\frac{0.8}{1-0.8} = 4.$$

Solving for the change in aggregate demand:

$$\Delta Y = -4 \times -100 = 400.$$

Even though the government has a fixed tax target in this example, it still must implement its target by choosing a tax rate. What rate should it choose? The tax function (13.8) can be solved for the marginal tax rate (setting the intercept $\tau_0 = 0$):

$$\tau = T/Y. \tag{13.31}$$

Originally taxes in our illustrative model were 500, but now they have fallen to 400. And originally GDP was 3,000, but now it has risen to 3,400. So the tax rate, which had been $1/6$ ($= 16.67$ percent), is now lower at

$$\tau = T/Y = 400/3,400 = 11.76 \text{ percent.}$$

The Balanced-Budget Multiplier

In the benchmark version of the illustrative model, the budget is balanced. What happens to the deficit in *Case 1* in which government spending is increased by 200 to 700, which in turn has a multiplied effect on aggregate demand, increasing it from 3,000 to 3,600? Taxes increase so that $T = \tau Y = (1/6)3,600 = 600$. And the deficit then becomes

$$deficit = G - T = 700 - 600 = 100.$$

What if the government found a deficit unacceptable? Could it increase spending and taxes in such a way as to keep the budget balanced *and* increase aggregate demand?

Once again, this is a case in which the level of taxes (T) is exogenous: to keep the budget balanced, it must be that $T = G$, whatever level government spending takes. So the tax rate (τ) must be adjusted endogenously to deliver the appropriate level of taxes.

Once again, we go back to the inflow-outflow identity and substitute in the savings function as in equation (13.28). But this time, we use the fact that $T = G$ to eliminate T. It is also helpful to write out the components of Au:

$$I + G + NX = Au = (1 - c)(Y - G) + G = (1 - c)Y + cG \quad (13.32)$$

or

$$Y = \frac{1}{1 - c}(I + NX) + G. \quad (13.32')$$

There is no longer a tax multiplier, because taxes are not a decision variable but are always fixed to be the same as government expenditure. The multipliers for investment and net exports are just the same as the autonomous expenditure multiplier when taxes are exogenous. The extraordinary thing is that an increase in government expenditure increases aggregate demand, but only by exactly the amount that it increases itself. The **BALANCED-BUDGET MULTIPLIER** (i.e., *the amount that aggregate demand increases for an increase in government expenditure while adjusting taxes to keep the budget balanced*) is unity:

$$\mu_G^{BB} = \frac{\Delta Y}{\Delta G} = 1. \quad (13.33)$$

One might think that the increase in taxes needed to keep the budget balanced would set up a negative multiplier process that would offset the positive process started by the increase in government expenditure, so that the balanced-budget multiplier was zero. But that is wrong.

There are two processes, each with a separate multiplier. Because the increase in taxes is a fixed amount (exactly equal to the increase in government spending), taxes are exogenous, so equations (13.29) and (13.30) give the appropriate multipliers. The net effect is the sum of the two individual effects:

$$\mu_G^{BB} = \mu_{Au} + \mu_T = \frac{1}{1 - c} + \left(\frac{-c}{1 - c}\right) = \frac{1 - c}{1 - c} = 1. \quad (13.34)$$

The offset is not perfect – so the balanced-budget multiplier is not zero – because, as we saw earlier, the tax multiplier is smaller in absolute value than the autonomous expenditure multiplier. The tax multiplier process cancels out the *indirect* multiplier effects of the increase in government expenditure, but leaves the *direct* effect intact.

Illustrative Model: Case 4. Suppose that the government wants to increase aggregate demand by 600 to 3,600, as in *Case 1*, but wants to leave the budget balanced. The fact that the balanced-budget multiplier is unity means that to do so it must raise government spending by just as much as it wants aggregate demand to increase – that is, by 600.

Taxes must also increase by 600 to 1,100. What tax rate must be set to achieve the balanced budget?

$$\tau = T/Y = 1,100/3,600 = 30.56 \, \text{percent},$$

an extraordinarily steep increase!

13.2.2 Automatic Stabilizers

The flows of funds away from production (other than to savings) are sometimes known as **AUTOMATIC STABILIZERS**, because they attenuate the fluctuations in aggregate demand. Consider the multiplier in equation (13.17): When $c = 0.90$ and $\tau = 0.27$, $\mu = 2.9$. However, when the automatic stabilizer of taxes is removed (i.e., $\tau = 0$), then $\mu = 10$. Say that firms raised investment by $10 billion. In the first case, aggregate demand would increase by $29 billion and, in the second, by $100 billion. Similarly, say that people purchased more foreign goods so that imports increased by $5 billion (a fall in net exports). Then, in the first case, aggregate demand would fall by $14.5 billion and, in the second, by $50.0 billion. Without the automatic stabilizer the fluctuations are more extreme and may give rise to a more immediate need for an offsetting policy action. On the downside, increases in unemployment would be larger, and on the upside increases in inflation would be larger. In all events, GDP would be more variable.

To see why taxes act as an automatic stabilizer, look at Figure 13.9. Initially, the economy is in equilibrium at the intersection at point B of the lower Inflows curve and the black Outflows curve (whose slope is $1 - c(1 - \tau)$). Aggregate demand is Y_0. Now say that exports increase, which is an increase in autonomous spending, shifting the Inflows line upward and moving the equilibrium to point C, where aggregate demand is Y_1. (The ratio of the change in aggregate demand to the increase in autonomous spending is the multiplier.)

The increase in aggregate demand can be thought of as having two parts. The first is an increase in demand because of the multiplier without any automatic stabilizers. This is indicated by the shallower, gray Outflows curve (slope $1 - c$, because no stabilizer means $\tau = 0$). If this were the true Outflows curve, then equilibrium would be at point D and aggregate demand at Y_2. But it is not. The extra aggregate demand generates taxes. These taxes can be thought of as increasing outflows for each level of aggregate demand,

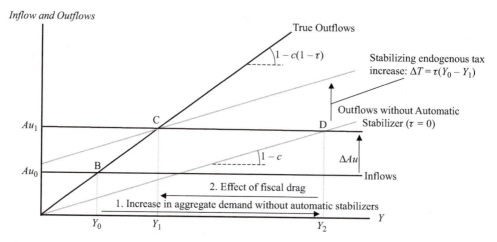

Figure 13.9. The Action of Automatic Stabilizers. The effect of an increase in autonomous spending can be broken down into: 1. the multiplied increase in aggregate demand that would occur if outflows such as taxes did not increase automatically with increasing income; and 2. the fiscal drag (or automatic stabilizer) that results from the endogenous increase in taxes.

shifting the lower gray Outflows curve vertically upward by the amount to the new tax generated ($\Delta T = \tau \times (Y_1 - Y_0)$), so that it intersects the actual equilibrium at point C with aggregate demand of Y_1.

The negative multiplier induced by this tax increase is sometimes referred to as **fiscal drag**. The tax system acts like the tail on a kite, slowing down its movements, but also stabilizing its fluctuations.

It is easy to see how automatic stabilizers got their name. When the economy enters a recession, the government often acts to expand aggregate demand. It may increase government expenditure or transfer payments, cut taxes, or take steps to promote investment. Similarly, when an economy is booming and the government fears that too much demand might promote inflation, it may take the opposite actions to reduce aggregate demand. The automatic stabilizers act in just the same way. As the economy goes into recession, taxes and transfers rise; as it goes into a boom, they fall. It is just as if the policymakers had taken a deliberate action to fight the recession (i.e., to "stabilize" the economy). While deliberate fiscal policies must be proposed and debated and, once implemented, work through the economy slowly, the automatic stabilizers act immediately without any political or bureaucratic delay.

13.3 Investment and Aggregate Demand

So far we have examined the role of the consumption and savings decisions of households and the fiscal policies of the government in determining aggregate demand. Next we turn to the investment decisions of firms.

13.3.1 What Determines the Level of Investment?

The Opportunity Cost of Investment

Investment is the purchase of new capital goods – the physical means of production. Firms invest in order to produce, sell, and make profits. Investment is forward-looking. The costs come immediately; the profits come only sometime later. In this sense, the purchase of an investment good is analogous to the purchase of a bond or other financial asset (see Chapter 6, section 6.2.1). And just as with a financial asset, the choice to invest is a good one when the returns generated using the investment good are higher than the returns that would have been paid on any alternative use of the funds.

The opportunity cost of investment can be measured by the difference between the real returns to an alternative financial asset, such as a bond, and the returns to the investment. We can summarize the real rate of return on investment by the variable ρ – the Greek letter "rho." (We discuss the measurement of ρ in more detail in Chapter 14.) The opportunity cost is then

opportunity cost of investment = real return on the bond

– real return on investment

$$= rr - \rho.$$

When the opportunity cost is positive, purchasing a bond (or other financial asset) is more lucrative than purchasing an investment good or engaging in an investment project. Real investment is more attractive the more negative the opportunity cost and less attractive the more positive the opportunity cost. Different investments will, of course, have different rates of return and, therefore, different opportunity costs. Taking the economy as a whole, for given rates of return, the higher the real rate of interest, the fewer different investment projects prove to be more lucrative than purchasing bonds and the lower the level of investment will be. Investment expenditure should therefore be inversely related to real interest rates.

Figure 13.10 shows the **INVESTMENT FUNCTION** as a downward-sloping relationship between the real interest rate (rr) and real investment (I). Because investment also depends on the real returns to investment, the curve must be drawn for a particular level of ρ. The lower curve is drawn for ρ_0 and shows that, when the real rate of interest is rr_0, the level of investment is I_0. If returns to investment rise to ρ_1, then the opportunity cost is lower for each level of the real interest rate, so investment must be higher and the curve must shift upward. Now at rr_0, investment is higher at I_1.

Investment and Risk

Investment also depends on the risks involved. Compare two projects. One has a guaranteed return of 14 percent per year. The second has a 50-percent

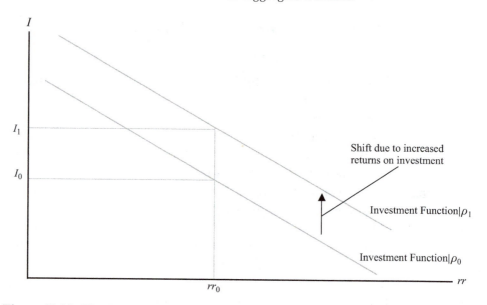

Figure 13.10. The Investment Function. The investment function is a downward-sloping relationship between investment and the real rate of interest for a given level of real returns to investment. An increase in real returns shifts the function upward and results in an increase in investment for each level of real rates of interest.

chance of earning 7 percent per year and a 50-percent chance of earning 21 percent per year. Its expected return is also 14 percent ($0.5 \times 7 + 0.5 \times 21 = 14$), but it is more risky – the firm could hit it big or do pretty poorly. In general, the less risky project will appear worthwhile at a lower rate of interest than the more risky project. More risky projects must give higher returns than less risky projects for the same opportunity cost if the investment is to appear attractive to the firm. Investment is then inversely related to risk. The higher the risk, the lower the investment for each real rate of interest. An increase in risk shifts the investment function downward.

Investment and Finance (and Other Factors)

Capital markets are *perfect* when firms (or people) can borrow as much as they like at the market rate of interest. When capital markets are perfect, investment should be determined entirely by its opportunity cost and risk. In practice, however, not all firms have unfettered access to lending. Banks may reduce their own risk by limiting the amount that they are willing to lend even if the firm would willingly pay a higher rate of interest to borrow more. Firms with lower credit ratings may have a limited ability to raise funds through the sale of bonds to take the place of rationed bank loans. As a result, how much the firm invests may depend on the availability of credit. If monetary policy actions make banks more willing to lend, and more of the pent-up demand for loans can be satisfied, firms may invest more. Greater availability of finance shifts the investment curve upward at each real rate of interest.

In the recession of 2007–2009 – and especially after the financial crisis that started in the fall of 2008 – interest rates were very low and yet banks were unwilling to lend freely as they hoarded funds to guard against possible defaults on the parts of their borrowers. Many businesses – large and small – found themselves deprived of their usual sources of funds, and investment plans were sharply curtailed, despite the low rates of interest. The Federal Reserve provided substantial funds to the banks, both to make them more secure and in the hope that these funds would ultimately encourage banks to lend more freely, bolstering investment and, thereby, initiating a multiplier process that would raise aggregate demand and pull the economy out of recession.

In principle, nothing else aside from opportunity cost, risk, and access to finance should matter to investment. But notice that, because all of the action with any investment project is in the future, the return and risk cannot be observed directly. Neither the firm nor the economist has a crystal ball, and each must form guesses about the future. As a result, investment will also be correlated with anything that helps to predict future returns or risk. Current GDP or the current level of the capital stock or current profits or other measures of economic activity or indicators of where the economy is in the business cycle might help to predict future returns and risk.

13.3.2 The Investment Function in Practice

Figure 13.11 plots the time series for real investment and for the real interest rate for the United States. There is a striking difference between the two series. Real interest rates are approximately stationary; they vary within a narrow range and display no long-term trend. In contrast, real investment is nonstationary; it grows steadily on trend. (See the *Guide*, sections G.5.2 and G.14, on stationary and nonstationary data and on relations between them.) These properties of the data imply that investment cannot be represented by a simple function of the form $I = f(rr)$. Real interest rates frequently return to similar levels. Such a function would imply that investment too should return to the corresponding levels. But in fact, a particular level of real interest rates is associated with a much higher level of investment late in the sample than it is early in the sample.

A reasonable way of dealing with the relationship between the two series is to recognize that the importance of investment depends on the size of the economy. A level of real investment that is large in a small economy will be small in a large economy. We can easily capture this difference by expressing investment as a share of potential output – that is, as scaled investment $\tilde{I}$.

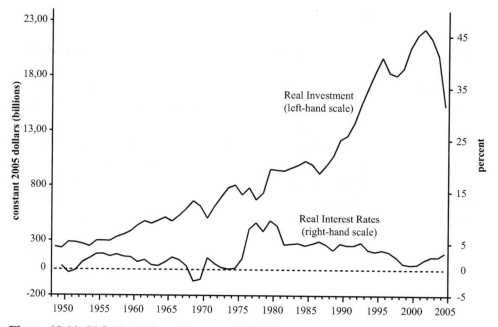

Figure 13.11. U.S. Real Investment and Real Interest Rates. Real interest rates are 10-year Treasury bond rates less annual inflation based on the GDP implicit price deflator. *Source:* Real Investment, Bureau of Economic Analysis; interest rate, Board of Governors of the Federal Reserve System; and author's calculations.

(See Chapter 9, section 9.5.2, for the construction of scaled variables.) Because scaled variables are, of course, bound between 0 and 100 percent, they cannot grow on trend. The investment function could then be expressed as $\tilde{I} = f(rr)$: the higher the real rate of interest, the lower scaled investment.

13.3.3 The IS Curve

To integrate investment behavior into our simple model of aggregate demand, we translate the inflow-outflow diagram (e.g., Figure 13.6) into a diagram with aggregate demand on the horizontal axis and the real rate of interest on the vertical axis. In keeping with the conclusion of the last section, we express aggregate demand as a share of potential GDP (scaled output $\tilde{Y}$).

Deriving the IS Curve

The top panel of Figure 13.12 is essentially the same as Figure 13.7. However, now we will regard investment not as an exogenous component of autonomous spending, but as a decreasing function of real interest rates. The bottom panel shows real interest rates (rr) on the vertical axis and aggregate demand ($\tilde{Y}$) on the horizontal axis. Consider three real rates in ascending order: $rr_1 < rr_2 < rr_3$. Say that at the lowest real rate (rr_1), investment is

Inflows and Outflows

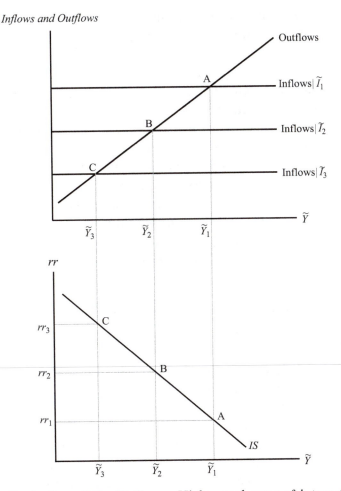

Figure 13.12. Derivation of the IS Curve. Higher real rates of interest (rr) correspond to lower levels of investment, resulting in successively lower Inflow curves in the upper panel. For a given Outflow curve, each results in a lower equilibrium level of aggregate demand ($\tilde{Y}$). The IS curve (lower panel) is the locus of each combination of real rates and aggregate demand corresponding to these equilibria.

$\tilde{I}_1$. It contributes to the inflows to the domestic private sector indicated by the upper horizontal line in the top panel. (The line is marked Inflows $|rr_1$ to show that it is the level of inflows that would be produced when scaled investment takes the value ($\tilde{I}_1$) compatible with the real rate taking the value rr_1.) The equilibrium is at point A with aggregate demand $\tilde{Y}_1$. The combination of rr_1 and $\tilde{Y}_1$ is shown on the bottom panel – also as point A.

When the real rate rises to rr_2, investment falls to $\tilde{I}_2$. If government expenditure and exports remain unchanged, the fall in investment shifts the Inflows curve down to the middle line. The equilibrium moves to point B, at the reduced aggregate demand $\tilde{Y}_2$. Again, this corresponds to point B in the lower panel ($\tilde{Y}_2$, rr_2). A further increase in real rates of rr_3 results in a further fall in investment to $\tilde{I}_3$, a further shift of the Inflows curve, and a further shift of the equilibrium to point C in both the top and bottom panels.

Clearly, any increase in real rates will result in lower investment and a lower equilibrium aggregate demand. Each equilibrium in the top panel can be mapped onto a point in the lower panel. The line that connects all such points in the lower panel is known as the *IS curve*. (The IS curve apparently takes its name from the initial letters of *I*nvestment and *S*avings. The first IS curve is due to Sir John Hicks (1903–1989), winner of the Nobel Prize in Economics in 1972.) The **IS curve** can be defined as *the locus of all combinations of real rates of interest and aggregate demand for which plans to invest, given other flows of funds into the domestic private sector (government spending, transfer payments, and exports), are compatible with plans to save, given other flows of funds away from the domestic private sector (taxes and imports).*

An Increase in Autonomous Spending Shifts the IS Curve to the Right

The IS curve in Figure 13.12 was drawn for given levels of autonomous spending and for given marginal propensities to consume and marginal (net) tax rates. What happens to the IS curve when any of these given values change? Consider first an increase in autonomous spending (e.g., an increase in government spending or a rise in exports).

Figure 13.13 shows the effect of an increase in autonomous spending on the derivation of the IS curve. The black lines correspond to those in Figure 13.12, where each horizontal line represents the different level of autonomous spending that results from the level of investment changing with the real rate of interest. If autonomous spending rises, say by ΔAu, then each of these lines would shift upward to the corresponding gray lines as shown. For example, the top two lines in the upper panel represent inflows when the real interest rate is rr_1 before and after the increase in autonomous spending. The equilibrium in both the upper and lower panels shifts from B to B' (raising aggregate demand from $\tilde{Y}_1$ to $\tilde{Y}_1'$).

Exactly the same thing happens with the Inflows lines that correspond to other interest rates: the equilibrium point C shifts to C' and D to D'. A new IS curve (shown as a gray line) connects all such equilibrium points in the lower panel. It lies to the right of the original IS curve. An increase in autonomous spending results in a rightward shift, and a decrease in a leftward shift, of the IS curve.

An Increase in the Rate of Return on Investment Shifts the IS Curve to the Right

Figure 13.12 was drawn on the assumption that the return to investment, ρ, was constant, so changes in real rates of interest were the only source of

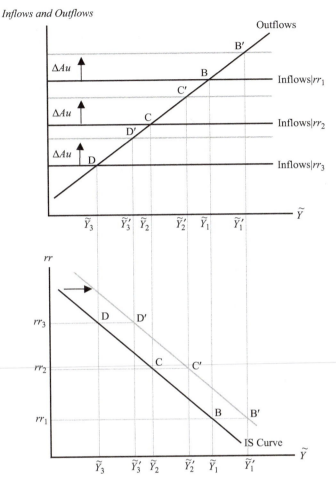

Figure 13.13. An Increase in Autonomous Spending Shifts the IS Curve to the Right.

changes in the desirability of investment relative to other opportunities. Any increase in ρ, holding rr constant, results in an increase in investment. Such an increase in investment at a constant real rate results in exactly the same sort of vertical shift of the Inflows curve in Figure 13.13 as an increase in government expenditure or net exports. It has exactly the same effect on the IS curve, shifting it rightward.

An Increase in Marginal Tax Rates Pivots the IS Curve Downward

Figure 13.14 shows the effect of an increase in the marginal tax rate (τ). Again, the black lines correspond to those in Figure 13.12. We know from Figure 13.8 that an increase in τ steepens the Outflows curve. The black Outflows curve corresponds to the lower tax rate, while the gray line corresponds to a higher tax rate. The intersection of the Inflows and the Outflows curves when the real rate of interest is rr_1 at the lower tax rate was at point B.

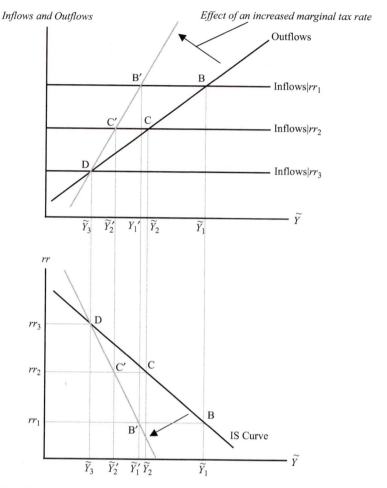

Figure 13.14. An Increase in the Rate of Taxation Steepens the IS Curve. An increase in the marginal rate of taxation, steepens the Outflow curve and the IS curve.

When the tax rate rises, it moves to point B'. Exactly the same thing happens with equilibrium point C, which shifts to C'. (It makes the diagram easier to read to treat point D as the pivot point.)

Each new equilibrium point corresponds to a lower level of aggregate demand for the same real rate of interest. The new IS curve (gray line) connects all such equilibrium points in the lower panel. It lies to the left of, and is steeper than, the original IS curve. An increase in the marginal rate of taxation results in a leftward shift, and a decrease in a rightward shift, of the IS curve.

An Increase in the Marginal Propensity to Save

Because the slope of the Outflows curve is steeper not only when taxes are higher, but when the marginal propensity to save is higher, an increase in the marginal propensity to save (i.e., a decrease in the marginal propensity to consume) would result in a leftward shift and a steepening of the IS curve. A decrease in the marginal propensity to save would result in a rightward shift and a flattening of the IS curve.

The IS Curve and the Multipliers

At any given real rate of interest, the horizontal shifts in the IS curve correspond exactly to the changes in aggregate demand implied by the various multipliers. The movement along the IS curve corresponding to a change in the real rate of interest corresponds exactly to the resulting change in investment times the consumption multiplier. The principal difficulty with using the IS curve is this: one must know the real rate of interest to know where along the curve the economy finds itself. Earlier in Chapter 7 (section 7.6), we showed that real rates depend on the interaction of monetary policy, financial markets, the profitability of real capital investment, and inflation. (We return again to some of these issues in Chapter 16, which concerns monetary policy.)

Numerical Examples

It is easy to understand the IS curve through an extension of the illustrative model discussed in earlier sections. Start with the benchmark model of section 13.2.1. But now we will assume that potential GDP is $Y^{pot} = 4{,}000$ and re-express all the levels as percentage shares of scaled output (e.g., if $G = 500$, then $\widetilde{G} = 500/4{,}000 = 12.5$ percent).

Illustrative Model: Case 5. Now, however, let investment behavior be described by a linear equation in which ρ is assumed to be 3 percent:

$$\widetilde{I} = i_0 - i(rr - \rho) = 8.75 - 1.25(rr - 3). \qquad (13.35)$$

(Notice that the real rate and ρ are measured in percentage points, so that 3 percent is written "3" and not "0.03".)

If in equation (13.25) we replace one of the values of 500 with the investment function (13.35) and the other value of 500 with the variable G, we obtain

$$8.75 - 1.25(rr - 3) + \widetilde{G} = (1 - 0.8)(\widetilde{Y} - (1/6)\widetilde{Y}) + (1/6)\widetilde{Y} = 1/3\widetilde{Y}.$$

Solving for $\widetilde{Y}$ yields the IS curve:

$$\widetilde{Y} = 26.25 + 3\widetilde{G} - 3.75(rr - 3). \qquad (13.36)$$

(Contrary to the common practice of mathematics, the IS curve is typically drawn with aggregate demand ($\widetilde{Y}$) on the horizontal axis, even when, as here, it is written as the dependent variable in the equation.)

To see how the IS curve works, start with a simple case in which $\tilde{G} =$ 12.5 percent and $rr = 0$. According to equation (13.35), investment $\tilde{I} = 12.5$ percent; and, according to the IS curve, aggregate demand $\tilde{Y} = 75$ percent. This is closely related to the earlier *Case 1* in Section 13.2.1: when investment is at the same level as in *Case 1*, aggregate demand is also the same (because 75 percent of 4,000 is 3,000).

Illustrative Model: Case 6. What happens if real rates of interest increase, say, to 5 percent? Then, according to equation (13.35), investment falls to $\tilde{I} =$ 6.25 percent; and, according to the IS curve, aggregate demand falls to $\tilde{Y} =$ 56.25 percent. The drop in aggregate demand corresponds to a movement along the IS curve. Notice that the consumption multiplier is $\mu = \frac{1}{1-c(1-\tau)} = \frac{1}{1-0.8[1-(1/6)]} = 3$. The increase in interest rates results in $\Delta \tilde{I} = -6.25$ percent and $\Delta \tilde{Y} = 75 - 56.25 = -18.75$, exactly as predicted by the multiplier.

Illustrative Model: Case 7. Another case: keep real rates at 5 percent, but increase government spending by 100 (i.e., 2.5 percent), so that $\tilde{G} = 15$ percent. Aggregate demand rises by 7.5 percent to $\tilde{Y} = 63.75$ percent. Because the consumption multiplier is the same for both investment and government expenditure ($\mu = 3$), this is again just what the multiplier predicts. The increase in government expenditure corresponds to a rightward shift of the IS curve at each real rate of interest. (In Problem 13.11 you are asked to demonstrate that an increase in the marginal (net) tax rate (τ) results in leftward shifts of the IS curve.)

13.4 Aggregate Demand and the Current Account

13.4.1 Some Pitfalls

In principle, international trade is already accounted for in our analysis of aggregate demand in the sense that net exports are included in autonomous spending. We should, however, look at the role of the current account more carefully, because its major components behave quite differently. The current account is essentially the difference between inflows of funds associated with exports and income from investments abroad and outflows of funds associated with imports and income from domestic investments paid to foreigners. As a composite, its movements are bound to be complex. The temptation to explanatory shortcuts poses two common pitfalls.

The first pitfall is the glib explanation of the current account that points to the sectoral-deficits identity in the national accounts (equation (2.3) in Chapter 2) to justify the claim that government deficits cause current account deficits (see Box 2.1). The so-called "twin-deficits" problem notes that the government's budget deficit plus the private-sector deficit must equal the foreign-sector deficit (i.e., the current-account deficit). Thus, the story goes, when the government runs a budget deficit the economy must necessarily also run a current-account deficit.

The argument is correct in its assumption that national accounting identities must hold, so that the three deficits must adjust to each other. But there are three deficits in the identity. The argument ignores the private-sector deficit and it assumes that adjustment must run from the government deficit to the current-account deficit, when the influence could just as well run the other way. Generally, this explanation paints the current account too passively as simply the balancing item for the other deficits. Adjustment among the three deficits is mutual. As always, accounting identities must hold, but deep explanations must identify the mechanisms that ensure that they do.

The second pitfall is nearly opposite in spirit, painting the current account as too active rather than too passive. The capital account is sometimes regarded as simply the balancing item for the current account. Yet, as we have already seen, the capital account has a life of its own as traders pursue the highest rates of return in internationally integrated financial markets. The financial flows reported in the capital account can affect exchange rates and interest rates directly and, affect relative prices indirectly. These, in turn, can affect aggregate demand and trade flows. Thus, current-account imbalances set up financial flows to which financial markets must adjust; but, equally, capital-account imbalances set up flows of goods and services to which the real economy must adjust. We considered the capital account in some detail in Sections 8.2.2. We now turn to the current account, investigating its main components – imports and exports.

13.4.2 The Behavior of Imports and Exports

From the laws of supply and demand, we know that the main determinants of production and expenditure – internationally, as well as domestically – are income and relative prices. As incomes rise, consumers purchase more goods, including foreign goods, and imports should rise along with other purchases. Exports also should depend on incomes, albeit foreign incomes rather than domestic.

The data confirm the role of domestic incomes. Both imports and exports show strong upward trends, so Figure 13.15 plots *detrended* U.S. imports against the NBER business-cycle dates. Imports are strongly procyclical. They fall sharply with the fall of incomes at the onset of a recession, typically reaching their nadir somewhat after the cyclical trough and then growing rapidly toward the cyclical peak as incomes recover.

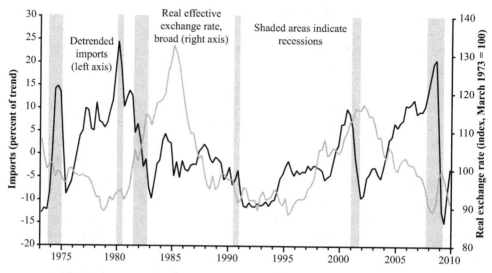

Figure 13.15. U.S. Imports, Aggregate Demand, and Real Exchange Rates. *Sources:* Imports, Bureau of Economic Analysis; Exchange Rates, International Monetary Fund, *International Financial Statistics.*

In contrast, Figure 13.16 shows no clear relationship between U.S. exports and the domestic business cycle. Exports rise during some recessions and fall during others. The absence of clear cyclicality in exports is to be expected, because demand depends on foreign rather than domestic incomes.

As we saw in Section 8.3.2, relative prices are complicated by the need to convert foreign and domestic prices into a common currency. The real exchange rate accounts for both relative price levels and for the nominal

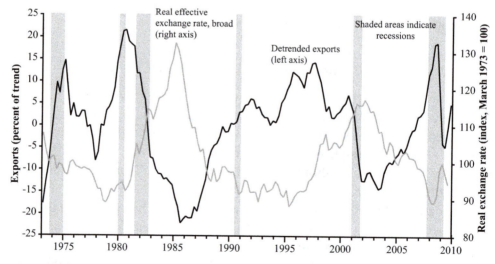

Figure 13.16. U.S. Exports, Aggregate Demand, and Real Exchange Rates. *Sources:* Imports, Bureau of Economic Analysis; Exchange Rates, International Monetary Fund, *International Financial Statistics.*

exchange rate. Because a high real exchange rate implies that domestic goods are expensive relative to foreign goods, we should expect imports to rise and exports to fall when the real exchange rate rises. There are, however, possible complications. An important one is that many goods produced in the United States and other developed countries use imports, which – in the short run at least – may not be easily replaced. Not only do developed countries import large volumes of raw materials, production of complex products may involve a global supply chain. The new Boeing 787 "Dreamliner" is manufactured from subassemblies from many countries: the wings from Japan, the horizontal stabilizers from Italy, the ailerons and flaps from Australia, and so forth. A low real exchange rate raises the cost of these parts to Boeing while making it easier for foreigners to acquire the dollars needed to purchase the airplane. An increase in exports owing to a lower real exchange rate may require a complementary increase in imports to manufacture the goods for export in the first place.

Figure 13.15 confirms the conjecture for the United States that real exchange rates have a smaller influence on imports than might appear on first consideration. There is no consistent relationship. The correlation between the two time series is nearly zero: 0.02.

In contrast, Figure 13.16, as predicted, shows a clear inverse relationship between exports and the real exchange rate. The correlation is negative and larger than for imports: −0.42. Typically, orders for exports are placed in advance, so that a change in the real exchange rate is likely to act with a lag. Visual inspection of Figure 13.16 suggests that if the curve for the real exchange rate were shifted forward by a year, it would more closely track the exports. In fact, the correlation between exports and the 1-year lagged real exchange rate at −0.76 is larger in absolute value than the correlation for the unlagged series, confirming both the importance of relative prices and the delay between changes in the real exchange rate and its maximum effect.

13.5 The Limits to Aggregate Demand Management

What lessons should we draw from our understanding of aggregate demand? At first blush, it might seem that the multipliers or the IS curve gives us a recipe (in former President Clinton's infelicitous phrase) to "grow the economy." Any increase in government expenditure apparently raises aggregate demand, so why not just keep increasing expenditure until GDP is as large as we like?

Recall also that any increase in the marginal propensity to consume results in a larger multiplier. So why not encourage people to consume more and save less to raise aggregate demand? Such suggestions are often heard when economies are deeply depressed, as, for example, the Japanese economy was through most of the 1990s and into the new millennium. Similar sentiments were sometimes expressed during the severe recession in the United States in 2007–2009.

13.5.1 The Paradox of Thrift

Consider a different illustrative model. (We are once again working with the levels of real variables rather than their scaled equivalents.)

Illustrative Model: Case 8. Initially, let the consumption function be $C = 0.9YD$, investment $I = 500$, and government spending $G = 500$ (net exports and transfer payments are both zero). And, to keep things simple, let the tax rate $\tau = 0$. The consumption multiplier (see equation (13.16)) is $\mu = \frac{1}{1-c(1-\tau)} = \frac{1}{1-0.9(1-0)} = 10$, equilibrium aggregate demand is $Y = 10,000$, and savings is $S = (1 - c)Y = 1,000$.

Now imagine that the government is concerned with increasing resources available for investment. Because $Y = C + I + G$, the government reasons that by cutting back on consumption and, therefore, by raising savings rates additional investment could be financed. So the government exhorts the population to reduce the marginal propensity to consume. Assume that the marginal propensity to consume falls from $c = 0.9$ to $c = 0.8$. The multiplier falls from $\mu = 10$ to $\mu = 5$, and aggregate demand falls from $Y = 10,000$ to $Y = 5,000$. What happens to savings? Answer: nothing! Before savings $S = (1 - 0.9) \times 10,000 = 1,000$. Now $S = (1 - 0.8) \times 5,000 = 1,000$.

This situation is known as the **paradox of thrift:** *higher rates of savings reduce aggregate demand without increasing the resources available for investment, even though consumption is reduced.* The flip side of the paradox is that an increase in the marginal propensity to consume (say to $c = 0.95$) appears to promote higher GDP with no loss to the resources available for investment.

It is too good to be true.

13.5.2 Resource Constraints

Remember that GDP is determined by the interaction of aggregate demand and aggregate supply. In this chapter, we have largely ignored aggregate supply. All of our models presume that aggregate supply was not a constraint in the sense that anything demanded would be supplied in any quantity without any increase in prices. (We address what happens when this is not the case in more detail in Chapter 15.) Such an assumption is reasonable when there are spare resources in the economy. In a recession, for instance, there are unemployed workers and idle plant and equipment. More demand can easily be supplied. Additional government expenditure or a cut in interest rates that promotes additional investment can then have a multiplied influence on aggregate demand, and supply rises as the unused resources are put to work.

But what if an economy is working at full capacity – the unemployment rate is low and plant and equipment are running at full tilt – as it might be near the peak of the business cycle? In that case, more resources – particularly, more physical capital – must be added to the economy or else supply cannot rise to meet the demand. An expansion of government expenditure or a cut in interest rates at such a juncture would stimulate demand, but GDP could not rise. Where would the increased demand go? Some of it would be absorbed in the mismatch between the plans of firms and the plans of consumers. Firms would find themselves running their inventories down (unplanned disinvestment). This is unlikely to be satisfactory, so they will also look for ways to expand production – that is, ways to invest. Of course, in the face of high demand, firms can raise prices, which will itself reduce some of the demand. And some of the demand may spill over into imports, so that foreigners supply the increase.

The paradox of thrift – like all true paradoxes – only appears to be contradictory. Investment and economic growth require additional resources, and those resources must be saved if they are to be used. Yet the attempt on the part of consumers to supply those resources results in lower aggregate demand and unchanged savings.

The resolution of the paradox brings us back to the observation of Chapter 2, section 2.7: the plans of the different actors in the economy are not necessarily coordinated. When savers increase their rates of saving, more resources are made available to firms, but only if the firms choose to take advantage of them and to invest. In our example, if firms had raised the level of investment at the same time that households increased their savings, aggregate demand would have increased. Even if households maintain an *unchanged* marginal propensity to consume, any time investment increases, savings also increase, because the same fraction of a higher aggregate demand yields a higher level of savings. The higher level of investment lays the groundwork for the increased capacity of the economy to supply goods and services.

Aggregate demand can never expand beyond the limit set by available resources; but aggregate demand can fall short of that limit. Any negative shock to aggregate demand can start a multiplier process that draws the economy below its productive capacity. Similarly, when the economy is already below its productive capacity, any positive shock to aggregate demand can start a multiplier process that pushes the economy back toward full capacity. Any attempt to push aggregate demand beyond the available

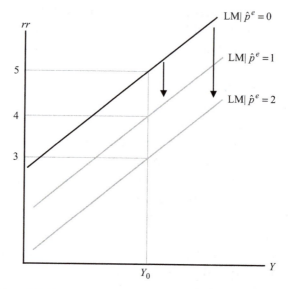

Figure 13.A.1. The LM Curve and Expected Inflation. Although naturally drawn with nominal rates of interest on the vertical axis, the LM curve can be translated onto a diagram with real rates instead. A particular level of aggregate demand (say, Y_0) corresponds to a particular nominal interest rate. The black curve shows that when the expected rate of inflation is zero, the nominal and real rates coincide and Y_0 corresponds to 5 percent (nominal and real). When expected inflation rises to 1 percent, a nominal rate of 5 percent corresponds to a real rate of 4 percent, and the LM curve shifts down by one point. Similarly, when expected inflation rises to 2 percent, a nominal rate of 5 percent corresponds to a real rate of 3 percent, and the LM curve shifts down two points.

resources can result only in rising prices, falling inventories, and a widening trade deficit. Once resources are fully used, further increases in real GDP require additional resources, and not a stimulus to boost aggregate demand.

Appendix: The IS-LM Model

The IS curve can be combined with the LM curve (Chapter 7, Appendix) on a single diagram to provide a complete model of aggregate demand.

13.A.1 The LM Curve and Expected Inflation

We have drawn the IS curve as a function of real interest rates and the LM curve as a function of market (nominal) interest rates. To put the curves onto a single diagram one or the other must be re-expressed. For our purposes, it is easier to re-express the LM curve as a function of real interest rates. The top line in Figure 13.A.1 shows the LM curve when expected

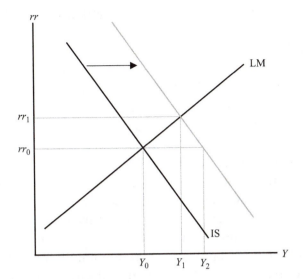

Figure 13.A.2. The IS-LM Model: An Increase in Government Spending. An increase in government spending shifts the IS curve to the right, raising aggregate demand and real interest rates. The standard multiplier effect is shown by the increase in aggregate demand to Y_2 with real interest rates constant at rr_0. But the endogenous rise in interest rates reduces investment, producing an offsetting multiplier effect that reduces aggregate demand partly to Y_1.

inflation is zero ($\hat{p}^e = 0$). In this case, real and nominal interest rates coincide: $r = rr + \hat{p}^e = rr + 0 = rr$.

Consider what happens when expected inflation increases, say, to 1 percent per year. On any point along the LM curve, a particular level of aggregate demand corresponds to a particular *nominal* interest rate. For example, Y_0 corresponds to $r = 5$. If expected inflation rises by 1 point, then $r = 5$ corresponds to a real rate of 4 ($= r - \hat{p}^e = 5 - 1$). Thus, when the expected inflation rate rises by 1 point, the whole LM curve (drawn with real rates of interest on the vertical axis) must shift down by 1 point as shown by the middle LM curve. Similarly, if expected inflation were to rise by 2 points, the LM curve would shift down by 2 points as shown by the lower curve.[2]

13.A.2 Working with the IS-LM Model

Figure 13.A.2 shows the IS and LM curves on the same diagram. (For expositional convenience, we have written Y rather than $\widetilde{Y}$. Nothing important in the analysis will be affected if we switch back to $\widetilde{Y}$, except the units of measurement.) The crossing point determines both the levels of aggregate

---

[2] Instead of drawing the LM curve on a graph with real rates on the vertical axis, we could have drawn the IS curve on a graph with nominal interest rates. In that case, the IS curve would shift vertically upward point for point with expected inflation.

demand and the real rate of interest. Anything that shifts either curve shifts the equilibrium levels of these variables. Consider a few illustrative cases. (Additional cases are considered in Problems 13.13–13.15.)

An Increase in Government Expenditure

As we know from section 13.3.2, any increase in autonomous expenditure (including an increase in G) shifts the IS curve to the right as shown in Figure 13.A.2. We can see immediately that aggregate demand rises (from Y_0 to Y_1), as we already knew to expect. The IS-LM model also suggests that the real interest rate will rise (from rr_0 to rr_1). The mechanism is that the increased aggregate demand increases transactions demand for money. But because the supply of money is assumed to be fixed, nominal interest rates must rise to keep the supply and demand for money in equilibrium. For a given level of expected inflation, a rise in nominal interest rates is equivalent to a rise in real interest rates. Higher real interest rates reduce investment, which has a negative multiplier effect that partly offsets the positive multiplier from increased government spending.

We can relate the IS-LM model to the analysis of the IS curve in section 13.3.3. There when we considered an increase in government expenditure, we assumed that real rates of interest would remain constant at rr_0, so that aggregate demand would rise to Y_2. The increase in aggregate demand $(Y_2 - Y_0)$ is the fully multiplied effect of ΔG. In the IS-LM model, however, real rates of interest are not held constant, but are endogenous. The increase in aggregate demand $(Y_1 - Y_0)$ is the multiplied effect of ΔG less the offsetting multiplied effect of the fall in investment as a result of the induced rise in real rates.

An Increase in the Money Supply

As we know from Chapter 7, section 7.A.2, an increase in the nominal supply of money *ceteris paribus* increases the real supply of money and shifts the LM curve to the right. As shown in Figure 13.A.3, aggregate demand rises (from Y_0 to Y_1), and real interest rates fall (from rr_0 to rr_1). With a higher stock of money, the supply would exceed the demand. In order to restore equilibrium to the money market, the nominal rate of interest must fall until the demand is equal to the supply. At a constant expected rate of inflation, this fall in nominal rates translates into a fall in real rates, which, in turn, stimulates investment. The additional investment has a multiplied effect on aggregate demand.

An Increase in the Rate of Inflation

As we saw in section 13.A.1, an increase in the rate of inflation shifts the LM curve downward point for point. Figure 13.A.4 shows that this results in an

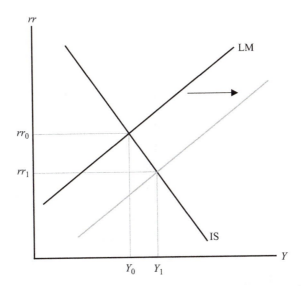

Figure 13.A.3. An Increase in the Money Supply. An increase in the supply of money shifts the LM curve to the right, raising aggregate demand and lowering real interest rates.

increase in aggregate demand (from Y_0 to Y_1) and a fall in real interest rates (from rr_0 to rr_1). Although the LM curve shifts, the action is not in the money market (the shift is just an accounting fact that results from our having drawn the LM curve on a graph with real interest rates instead of the more natural nominal interest rates). The increase in the rate of inflation for a fixed

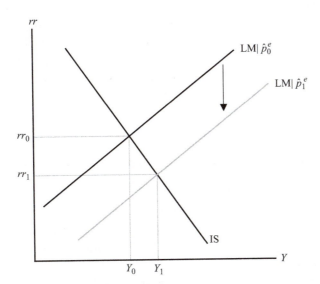

Figure 13.A.4. An Increase in the Rate of Inflation. An increase in the expected rate of inflation ($\hat{p}_0^e > \hat{p}_1^e$) shifts the LM downward, raising aggregate demand and lowering real interest rates.

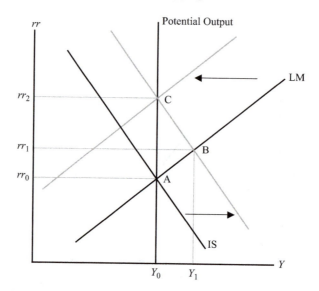

Figure 13.A.5. An Increase in Government Spending at Full Employment. When the economy is already at full employment, an increase in government spending, shifting the IS curve to the right, would ordinarily shift the equilibrium from point A to point B with higher aggregate demand ($Y_1 > Y_0$) and a higher real rate of interest ($rr_1 > rr_0$). This cannot be sustained because aggregate demand would exceed aggregate supply (Y_0). Full equilibrium requires higher prices, which reduce the real money supply, shifting the LM curve leftward until it intersects the IS curve at the level of potential output (point C). At this point, all markets are in equilibrium; the economy is producing at full potential; and the higher real rate of interest reduces investment, freeing up resources for the increased level of government spending.

nominal rate of interest reduces the real rate of interest point for point. The lower real rate stimulates investment, which has a multiplied effect on aggregate demand. The surprising result that higher anticipated inflation stimulates demand is sometimes known as the *Mundell-Tobin effect* named for Robert Mundell of Columbia University (winner of the Nobel Prize in 1999) and the late James Tobin (1918–2002) of Yale University (winner of the Nobel Prize in 1981).

13.A.3 The IS-LM Model at Full Employment

Each of the cases considered in the last section assumed that aggregate supply was not a constraint on aggregate demand – that is, that the economy was at less-than-full employment. What happens when the economy is already fully employed and aggregate demand increases? Just to take one case, consider once again an increase in government expenditure. Figure 13.A.5 shows the initial equilibrium at point A (Y_0, rr_0). The vertical line through point A indicates the full-employment level of aggregate supply – that is, potential output.

An increase in government expenditure shifts the IS curve to the right. If aggregate supply were not a constraint, the equilibrium would shift to point B (Y_1, rr_1). But point B is not feasible because at that point aggregate demand exceeds aggregate supply. In such a situation, firms raise prices (section 13.4). An increase in the price level reduces the real supply of money, shifting the LM curve to the left (Chapter 7, section 7.A.2). To restore equilibrium, the increase in the price level must be great enough to move the intersection of the LM curve with the new IS curve back to equality with aggregate supply at point C. Here the original level of aggregate demand is restored to Y_0 and the real interest rate is even higher at rr_2.

At the new equilibrium, the economy is no bigger than before, but output is distributed differently. Because the size of the pie is unchanged, the increase in government expenditure must be at the expense of some other sector. Here the increased real rate of interest reduces the level of investment by exactly enough to fund the additional government spending. This phenomenon is sometimes referred to as the *crowding out* of private spending by government spending. Crowding out is discussed in more detail in Chapter 17.

Summary

1. GDP is determined by the interaction of aggregate supply and aggregate demand. The components of aggregate demand are given by the right-hand side of the product-expenditure identity: $Y \equiv C + I + G + NX$. A theory of aggregate demand explains the economic behavior behind each of the components. Equilibrium occurs when the plans of all the economic actors are compatible.

2. Consumption depends on many factors. The consumption function relates consumption to its most important determinant – disposable income. The marginal propensity to consume (mpc) is defined as the small increase in saving that results from a small increase in (disposable) income and is the slope of the consumption function. The mpc is greater than zero and less than one. In theory, the mpc is less than or equal to the average propensity to consume (apc).

3. Data for the United States suggest that a good approximation of consumption behavior sets the mpc equal to the apc, so that the consumption function passes through the origin.

4. Taxes are generally a function of income. The marginal tax rate is greater than zero and less than one. Data for the United States suggest that a good approximation for the tax function sets the marginal tax rate to a constant equal to the average tax rate.

5. A simple model of aggregate demand substitutes the consumption and tax functions into the national-income-accounting identities. In such a model, an increase in autonomous spending on investment, government goods and services, or net exports raises GDP by a multiplied amount. The initial spending

or inflow becomes income for consumers, who in turn spend some and save some, creating income for other consumers. The pattern repeats until the initial spending is absorbed in increased savings or other outflows. The consumption multiplier measures the ratio of the increase in GDP to the initial increase in autonomous spending.

6. The consumption multiplier is larger the higher the marginal propensity to consume. It is smaller the higher the marginal tax rate (or other rates of outflow).

7. A model of aggregate demand can be used to guide fiscal policy – that is, government policy with respect to spending and taxes. Increases in spending boost aggregate demand by an amount given by the autonomous expenditure multiplier; increases in taxes lower it by an amount given by the tax multiplier.

8. The autonomous expenditure multiplier is larger than the tax multiplier. An increase in autonomous spending has a direct effect, because it is a component of GDP itself, and indirect or multiplied effects. A tax increase has only indirect effects, because taxes and transfers are not part of GDP. As a result, a balanced-budget increase in which autonomous spending and taxes rise by exactly the same amount adds to GDP just the amount of the increase in autonomous spending (i.e., the direct effect). The indirect effect of autonomous spending is offset by the indirect effects of the tax increase. The balanced-budget multiplier is, therefore, unity.

9. Governments usually set tax rates, not tax levels. As a result, any stimulus to aggregate demand that increases GDP generates additional tax revenue that itself begins a negative multiplier process, partially offsetting the initial stimulus. Offsets due to taxes or other endogenous outflows are known as automatic stabilizers because they reduce the variability of GDP.

10. The rate of investment is determined by the difference between the real rate of interest and the returns on investment, which measures the opportunity cost of investment, the risk involved in the investment, and the availability of borrowed funds when firms are cash constrained. Higher real interest rates, higher risk, and lower borrowing facilities lower the rate of investment.

11. The IS curve is the locus of all combinations of real rates of interest and aggregate demand for which plans to invest, given other flows of funds into the domestic private sector (government spending, transfer payments, and exports), are compatible with plans to save, given other flows of funds away from the domestic private sector (taxes and imports). The IS curve summarizes the state of aggregate demand for given levels of real interest rates.

12. On a graph with real interest rates on the vertical axis and real GDP on the horizontal axis, the IS curve is downward sloping. An increase in autonomous expenditure shifts the IS curve to the right, increasing GDP at a constant rate of interest. An increase in tax rates pivots the IS curve down and to the left, decreasing GDP at a constant rate of interest.

13. Multiplier processes can increase GDP only when the economy is operating below its full potential. Any increase in aggregate demand at full potential must be absorbed in higher prices or higher outflows from demand – for example, higher imports or negative inventory investment.

Key Concepts

marginal propensity to consume

consumption function

average propensity to consume

savings function

consumption multiplier

discretionary fiscal policy

automatic fiscal policy

balanced-budget multiplier

automatic stabilizers

investment function

IS curve

Suggestions for Further Reading

John R. Hicks, "Mr. Keynes and the Classics," in *Critical Essays in Monetary Theory*. Oxford: Clarendon Press, 1967.

Robert A. Mundell, *Monetary Theory, Inflation, Interest, and Growth in the World Economy*. Pacific Palisades, CA: Goodyear Publishing Co., 1971.

Michel De Vroey and Kevin D. Hoover, editors. *The IS-LM Model: Its Rise, Fall, and Strange Persistence*. Durham, NC: Duke University Press, 2005.

Problems

Data for this exercise are available on the textbook website under the link for Chapter 13 (appliedmacroeconomics.com). Before starting these exercises, the student should review the relevant portions of the *Guide to Working with Economic Data*, including sections G.1–G.5, G.12, and G.15.

Problem 13.1. The multiplier formula (13.17) was derived on the assumption that the consumption function passed through the origin – that is, it took the form given in (13.2) with the intercept c_0 set to zero. Assume that $c_0 \neq 0$ and, following the same steps as the text, derive the three equations analogous to (13.14), (13.15), and (13.16). Note the similarities and differences between these equations and your derivations. What do they tell you about the relationship of the multiplier, the consumption function, and the marginal propensity to consume?

Problem 13.2. In the subsection of section 13.1.4 *The Multiplier Process*, we showed using a particular example that the process of spending becoming income becoming spending becoming income and so on ultimately resulted in the same multiplier as the static multiplier given in equation (3.16). Prove that this is true in general. Instead of the $1,000 investment expenditure of Boeing, assume that there is an arbitrary increase in autonomous expenditure (ΔAu); instead of the assumption that the marginal propensity to consume $mpc = 0.75$, assume that $mpc = c$; and instead of the tax rate of 0.27, assume that the marginal tax rate is τ. Derive the analogous expression to (13.21). What is the multiplier?

Problem 13.3. Although the average propensity to consume in the United States (Figure 13.2) does not trend uniformly downward over the whole post-World War II period, it does trend down until the early 1980s and sharply upward after that. We might obtain a better estimate of the marginal propensity to consume if we use detrended data. Detrend real consumption and real disposable income. (Explain your method and your reasons for choosing it.) Make a scatterplot of detrended consumption against detrended disposable income. Add the regression line and the regression equation. The slope coefficient is an estimate of the marginal propensity to consume. Compare your estimate to that in the text. Use your estimate and $\tau = 0.27$ to compute the multiplier. How does it differ from the estimate in the text?

Problem 13.4. Are the marginal propensity to consume and the multiplier stable over time? Look again at Figure 13.2. Choose a date that divides the sample into two parts – one in which the apc is trending downward and one in which it is trending upward. Using the procedure in Problem 13.3 (or just using the calculations that you have already made for that problem), create a scatterplot and obtain the regression lines and equations for each of your subsamples. How does the mpc change between the two periods? Use your estimate and $\tau = 0.27$ to compute the multiplier (using equation (13.16)) for each subperiod. Comment on your results.

Problem 13.5. Consider an economy with no foreign trade and no transfer payments whose consumption function is given as

$$C = 100 + 0.9(Y - T).$$

(a) Initially let $G = 800$, $T = 800$, and $I = 300$. What is the level of Y? Assuming that taxes follow the simple function, $T = \tau Y$, what is τ?
(b) Holding τ constant, what is the effect on Y of increasing G by 100 to 900?
(c) What is the effect *ceteris paribus* on Y of decreasing T by 100? At what value must the government set τ to achieve this tax cut?
(d) Explain why the effects in (b) and (c) are different.
(e) Suppose that the government wanted to maintain a balanced budget and increased both G and T by 100. What would be the effect on Y? What τ would it need to choose to keep the budget balanced?

Problem 13.6. Consider an economy with no foreign trade whose consumption function is given as

$$C = c(Y + TR - T).$$

Taxes are determined as

$$T = \tau Y$$

and transfer payments are determined as

$$TR = tr_0 - tr Y,$$

where tr_0 and tr are positive constants.

Suppose that initially $c = 0.9$, $\tau = 0.2$, $tr_0 = 666.67$, $tr = 0.05$; $I = 500$, and $G = 1,000$.

(Note that some of the results are very sensitive and identities may deviate by rounding error.)

(a) Sketch the transfer-payment function. Are transfer payments procyclical or countercyclical?

(b) Derive a general formula for the autonomous expenditure multiplier and compute its specific value for this economy. (Note: this multiplier will differ from equation (13.16) because it includes endogenous transfer payments.)

(c) Show that the budget is balanced under the initial conditions. If the tax rate is cut from $\tau = 0.2$ to $\tau = 0.15$, how much will aggregate demand (Y) change as a result? What is the surplus or deficit after the tax cut?

(d) Starting from the initial conditions stated earlier in which the budget is balanced, suppose that the government wishes to keep it that way. Compare the following policies. Do any of them improve "welfare" (i.e., the social good) more than the others? In particular, consider how the policies affect consumption, GDP, and the government's budget deficit:

(i) An increase of government expenditure of 100 accompanied by a decrease in transfer payments of 100, holding T constant. Find the new tr (assuming tr_0 constant), the new τ, and the change in Y.

(ii) An increase of government expenditure of 100 accompanied by an increase of taxes of 100, holding TR constant. Find the new τ, the new tr (assuming tr_0 constant), and the change in Y.

(iii) A decrease in taxes of 100 accompanied by a decrease in transfer payments of 100. Find the new tr (assuming tr_0 constant), the new τ, and the change in Y.

Problem 13.7. Consider an economy in which aggregate demand is described by the following equations:

$$C = 200 + 0.9(Y + TR - T)$$
$$I = 200 - 25rr$$
$$T = \tau Y.$$

(Note that the real rate of interest (rr) is measured in percentage points, not as a natural fraction.) Initially, $G = 400$, $TR = 100$, the market rate of interest (r) is 6 percent, and the expected rate of inflation ($\hat{p}^e$) is 2 percent.

(a) Assuming that the budget is balanced, what are the values of aggregate demand and the tax rate?

(b) Starting with the initial conditions and tax rate calculated in (a), all other things equal, what is the effect of an increase of 50 in transfer payments on aggregate demand and the government deficit?

(c) Under the conditions in (b), what would be the effect on aggregate demand of an increase of 50 in transfer payments if the tax rates were adjusted to keep the budget balanced? What tax rate would be necessary to achieve a balanced budget?

(d) Starting with the initial conditions and tax rate calculated in (a), all other things equal, what would be the effect on aggregate demand of a 1 percentage point increase in market interest rates?

(e) Starting with the initial conditions and tax rate calculated in (a), all other things equal, what would be the effect on aggregate demand of a 1 percentage point increase in the expected rate of inflation?

Problem 13.8. Consider an economy in which aggregate demand is described by the following equations:

$$C = 100 + 0.9(Y + TR - T)$$
$$I = 300 - 20rr$$
$$G = 400$$
$$TR = 200$$
$$T = \tau Y$$
$$NEX = 100$$

(Note that the real rate of interest (rr) is measured in percentage points, not as a natural fraction.)

(a) Initially if $rr = 6$ percent and $\tau = 0.14285$ (i.e., 14.285 percent), what is Y? If you have calculated this correctly, the budget will be balanced.

(b) Starting from the situation in (a), what would be the effect on Y of an increase of 100 in transfer payments? How would the government budget deficit be affected?

(c) Starting from the situation in (a), what would be the effect on Y of a decrease of 100 in G while keeping the government budget balanced? What tax rate (τ) would the government have to set to achieve this?

Problem 13.9. For the same economy as described in Problem 13.8:

(a) Write down the equation for the IS curve. Sketch the curve.

(b) Starting from the situation in Problem 13.8(a) show that the IS curve implies that Y is what you calculated in Problem 13.8(a).

(c) What would be the effect on Y and the budget deficit of an action by the monetary authorities that cut rr by 1 percentage point?

(d) Again, starting from the situation in Problem 13.8(a), what would be the effect of a cut in the tax rate to $\tau = 0.12$? Calculate the value of Y and the budget deficit, and sketch the shift in the IS curve.

Problem 13.10. Any outflow from the domestic private sector that rises in the boom and falls in the slump might act as an automatic stabilizer. As well as taxes, candidates include transfer payments, imports, and inventory investment.

(a) To get an idea of which of these act as automatic stabilizers, express each as percentage of potential GDP (i.e., form scaled variables $\widetilde{T}, \widetilde{TR}, \widetilde{M}, \widetilde{InvI}$). This removes the trends and, because potential output is acyclical, does not itself contribute to the cyclicality. Plot each series and indicate the NBER recession dates with shading to determine its cyclicality. Do the series show the right cyclicality to be automatic stabilizers?

(b) Assess the effectiveness of the automatic stabilizers in light of your investigation.

Problem 13.11. Using the illustrative model in the text (see section 13.3.3, case 5), work out a numerical example and a diagram to show that an increase in the marginal tax rate results in a leftward movement of the IS curve.

Problem 13.12. How do the following affect the IS curve?

(a) A decrease in exports;

(b) A decrease in imports;

(c) An increase in the marginal propensity to import (i.e., the rate at which imports increase with an increase in GDP);

(d) An increase in investment risk;

(e) An increase in the savings rate;

(f) A decrease in the expected returns to investment;

(g) An increase in payments of interest on the government debt.

Problem 13.13. Use the IS-LM model and assume that the economy is at less than full employment to determine how each of the cases in Problem 13.12 would affect aggregate demand and the real interest rate.

Problem 13.14. Use the IS-LM model and assume that the economy is at less than full employment to determine how each of the following affect aggregate demand and the real interest rate.

(a) A cut in the money supply;

(b) An increase in the speculative demand for money;

(c) The substitution of ATM cards for cash and check transactions.

Problem 13.15. Use the IS-LM model and assume that the economy is at full employment to determine how a 10-percent increase in the supply of money would affect the price level and the real rate of interest. Be specific about the quantitative effects.

14

Consumption and Investment: A Deeper Look

Consumption and investment are the two largest components of GDP and aggregate demand. In the last chapter we gave a rough-and-ready account of the factors that govern them. Now we probe deeper. The choices of both consumers and investors are, in fact, closely analogous to portfolio choices in financial markets. In this chapter we develop that analogy, consider complicating factors, and examine how the individual choices play out for aggregate consumption and investment and aggregate demand.

The domestic private sector accounts for roughly 85 percent of U.S. GDP: consumption about 70 percent, investment about 15 percent (see Figure 2.6). In Chapter 13, we explained the determination of aggregate demand mainly through simple models of the determination of consumption and investment. But these components are so important that it is useful to give each of them a more careful look.

PART A. CONSUMPTION

14.1 Simple Consumption Functions and the Real World

In Chapter 13, we worked the consumption function presented in equation (13.1) and repeated here (with subscripts to indicate time) as

$$C_t = c_0 + cYD_t, \tag{14.1}$$

in which real consumption (C) is a simple, linear function of disposable income ($YD = Y - (T - TR)$). The simple consumption function is like a roughly sketched map. Such a rough map can be useful; but if taken too literally, it gives stark and unsubtle directions. We can easily get lost if we follow it slavishly. It is important not to get lost. As we have seen, the effect of fiscal policy on GDP in the short run depends largely on consumption behavior (see Chapter 13, section 13.1). If we misunderstand consumption behavior, we will misjudge the effect of policy actions.

Some of the starkest predictions derivable from the simple consumption function concern the average propensity to consume out of disposable income ($apc = C/YD$). Dividing both sides of equation (14.1) by YD yields:

$$apc_t \equiv \frac{C_t}{YD_t} = \frac{c_0}{YD_t} + c, \qquad (14.2)$$

which predicts that as disposable income increases, c_0/YD and, therefore, the *apc* itself become smaller. We already saw this prediction graphically in Figure 13.1. What is more, equation 14.1 predicts that the correlation between changes in disposable income and changes in consumption should be very high. Indeed, if equation (14.1) fit perfectly and if c_0 were zero – we saw evidence in Chapter 13 (section 13.1.1) that it was very small – then the correlation should be +1. (See the *Guide*, section G.13, on correlation.)

These stark predictions apply equally to short-run and long-run changes in disposable income. We know that disposable income has grown with considerable fluctuations along a strongly rising trend. So, if equation (14.1) truly fit the economy, we should expect average propensity to consume:

1. to move inversely with disposable income in the short run (i.e., to fall in the boom and rise in the slump); and
2. to move inversely with disposable income in the long run (i.e., to fall on trend as disposable income grows).

In addition, the correlation between consumption and disposable income should be:

3. strong in the short run; and
4. strong in the long run.

Are these predictions supported by the data?

Figure 13.2 showed that the average propensity to consume is not constant. But it does not appear to drift very far from its mean, and there is no permanent tendency to fall on trend – evidence against the second prediction.

Let us approach the predictions more directly. Figure 14.1 plots the average propensity to consume, marking the NBER recessions. In most recessions, the apc rises for some significant part of the recession, although this is not true in every case. Overall, the evidence of countercyclical movements in the apc is equivocal.

The long run introduces some additional complications. If each individual were governed by a personal consumption function similar to equation (14.1), then we would expect the aggregate average propensity to consume to fall if the typical consumer had a higher disposable income. On the other hand, if the population grew without altering the distribution of income,

Figure 14.1. The Average Propensity to Consume and the Business Cycle. *Source:* Bureau of Economic Analysis and author's calculations.

then *aggregate* disposable income would rise, because there would be more people earning incomes; yet, the typical consumer's average propensity to consume would not change. We must, therefore, distinguish between increases in aggregate disposable income owing to a larger population and those owing to consumers becoming individually richer. An easy way to do this is to express the aggregate consumption function in *per capita* terms, specifying an equation analogous to equation (14.1) in which the main variables are scaled by population (*POP*):

$$\frac{C_t}{POP_t} = c_0 + c\frac{YD_t}{POP_t}. \tag{14.2}$$

Figure 14.2 provides an estimate of the long-run *per capita* consumption function by plotting C/POP against YD/POP for quarterly data from 1947 to 2009, and fitting the regression line. The resulting equation is:

$$\frac{C_t}{POP_t} = -726 + 0.94\frac{YD_t}{POP_t}. \tag{14.3}$$

The *negative* intercept term ($c_0 = -726$) distinguishes this relationship from the consumption function graphed in Figure 13.1, and suggests, contrary to our prediction, that the average propensity to consume *rises* as disposable income becomes larger. We probably should not make too much of this result because the intercept is not very large relative to the scale of disposable income and consumption and may be truly zero except for the random variation in the data.

The relationship between consumption and disposable income is very tight. Their correlation is high: $R = \sqrt{R^2} = \sqrt{0.99} \approx 1$. Of course, the close

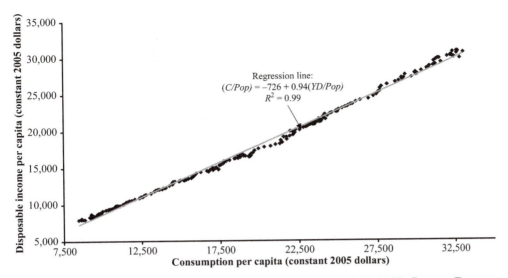

Figure 14.2. The Long-Run U.S. Consumption Function, 1947–2009. *Source:* Bureau of Economic Analysis.

apparent relationship between two strongly trending variables may be an example of a *nonsense correlation* (see the *Guide*, section G.14.1). But that is unlikely for two reasons: First, we have every reason to believe from our own day-to-day experience that consumption and disposable income should be closely related – we must pay for our consumption somehow. Second, the fact that the ratio of consumption to disposable income does not show a strong trend, even though both the numerator and the denominator do, is evidence of a genuine relationship (again, see the *Guide*, section G.14.2).

The balance of evidence, then, supports the hypothesis, implicit in equation (14.1) that there is a high correlation in the long run between consumption and disposable income, but contradicts the hypothesis that the average propensity to consume falls on trend.

Looking again at the short run, if we lag equation (14.2) by one period and subtract it from the original equation, we get a consumption function expressed in changes:

$$\Delta\left(\frac{C_t}{POP_t}\right) = \frac{C_t}{POP_t} - \frac{C_{t-1}}{POP_{t-1}} = c\left(\frac{YD_t}{POP_t} - \frac{YD_{t-1}}{POP_{t-1}}\right) = c\Delta\left(\frac{YD_t}{POP_t}\right).$$

(14.4)

Equation (14.4) predicts a strong correlation between changes in consumption per head and disposable income per head; and adds a fifth prediction:

5. the marginal propensity to consume (c) should be the same as in equation (14.2), while the intercept should be zero.[1]

---

[1] Because c_0 is constant, it disappeared when we took first differences of equation (14.2) to get (14.4).

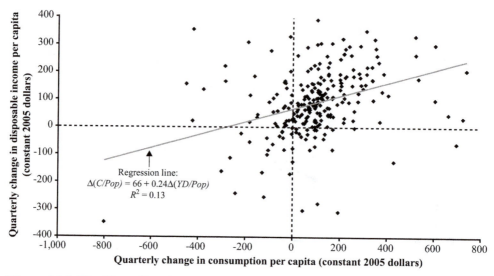

Figure 14.3. The Short-Run U.S. Consumption Function, 1947–2009. *Source:* Bureau of Economic Analysis.

Figure 14.3 plots those two series and fits a regression line. Its equation is

$$\Delta\left(\frac{C_t}{POP_t}\right) = 66 + 0.24\Delta\frac{YD_t}{POP_t}. \qquad (14.5)$$

The marginal propensity to consume in equation (14.5) is much lower than in (14.3) ($c = 0.24$ versus $c = 0.95$), and the intercept is not zero (although, again, we should probably not make too much of this last point). More importantly perhaps, the correlation between the changes in consumption per head and disposable income per head is much weaker than between the levels ($R = \sqrt{0.13} = 0.36$ versus $R \approx 1$), suggesting that, in the short run, the relationship is tenuous at best.

Revisiting the five predictions of the simple consumption theory, we find:

1. the short-run evidence for the countercyclical movement of the average propensity to consume is *mixed*;
2. *contrary* to the prediction, the apc *does not* move inversely with disposable income in the long run; rather it remains approximately constant;
3. *contrary* to the prediction, the correlation between consumption and disposable income is *weak* in the short run;
4. *consistent* with the prediction, the correlation between consumption and disposable income is *strong* in the long run;
5. *contrary* to the prediction, the marginal propensity to consume (c) is not the same in the short-run equation (14.5) as in the long-run equation (14.3).

Taking stock, we can conclude that it is unlikely that the *same* consumption function describes the economy in both the short and long runs. Our simple map of consumption behavior appears to give an inaccurate picture of the layout of the economy and to leave too many byways uncharted. We need a better map.

14.2 The Permanent-Income/Life-Cycle Hypothesis

14.2.1 Consumption Smoothing

To begin to build a better map, consider whether – as the simple consumption function implies – we should really expect consumption to vary with every variation in income. Some thought experiments will illuminate the issues:

- **Thought experiment 1.** An extreme stylization. Imagine that you had an income of $50,000 per year in odd-numbered years and of $100,000 per year in even-numbered years. Would you double your consumption in odd-numbered and halve it in even-numbered years? That seems unlikely. Most people would likely smooth consumption by spending less than their income in even-numbered years and more in odd-numbered years, setting their consumption levels in proportion, not to the current income, but to the average income of $75,000.

  Although this is an extreme stylization, real-world cases may approximate it. Schoolteachers, for example, are often paid only for nine months' work each year. Typically, we would expect that they would save about a quarter of their income each month to carry them over the summer months with approximately the same level of consumption. Similarly, people who work on commission or for tips are aware that some seasons of the year (say, Christmas for a salesman or summer holidays for a waitress in a resort town) are likely to be more lucrative; and they are likely to save some of the income from these periods to boost consumption in slower times.

- **Thought experiment 2.** You earn $50,000 per year. And then you win $500,000 in the state lottery. Do you spend it all at once, say, in a massive party? Most people probably would not do so. Were you to take the $500,000 and purchase an interest-bearing financial asset (say, you put your money in a mutual fund), you could spend only the interest for the rest of your life, leaving the principal intact. If the market rate of interest were, say, 5 percent, then your lottery winnings would generate $25,000 per year, raising your income *permanently* to $75,000 per year. Any unexpected windfalls can be treated in much the same way.

- **Thought experiment 3.** Despite being an impecunious 20 year old, your grandfather leaves you a legacy of $2 million. He loves you but does not trust your youth and inexperience, so he stipulates that you must be 35 before you actually receive the money. Must you wait fifteen years to spend your inheritance? No, there are financial intermediaries who will lend you money to be repaid when your inheritance comes due. If we suppose that the market interest rate is 5 percent, then the present value of your legacy is $962,034 ($= $2 \text{ million}/(1.05)^{15}$). If you are truly as bad as your grandfather fears, you can spend it all before you are 35 (this is a classic theme in Victorian novels); but if you are as sensible as he hopes, then, just as with the lottery winnings in the second thought experiment, you might purchase an interest-bearing financial asset. At the same market rate of interest, your legacy earns \$48,102 ($= 0.05 \times \$962,034$) per year forever. As in the second thought experiment, the purchase of a financial asset allows you to convert a lumpy income stream into a smooth one and to smooth out your consumption from that income.

The legacy is just one example of the shifting of income over long periods of one's life. Anyone who takes out a student loan to pay for college with the intent of paying it off during the years of peak earning or anyone who builds up assets in middle age in order to spend them during retirement engages in the same sort of income shifting. The point, in every case, is to make consumption patterns smoother than they would be if consumption were governed entirely by current income.

In each of these thought experiments, one premise is that people desire consumption streams that are smoother than their income streams. The first thought experiment suggests that *predictable* short-run fluctuations in income can be smoothed by adjusting consumption to the average level of income – saving when income is high and dissaving when income is low. The second thought experiment suggests that unpredictable, transitory fluctuations in income can be smoothed by saving (adding to wealth) and consuming only the earnings from that wealth. These two experiments are the basis for the **PERMANENT-INCOME HYPOTHESIS**, first articulated by the American economist Milton Friedman (1912–2006, winner of the Nobel Prize in Economic Science in 1976). The third thought experiment suggests that long-term changes in income can be smoothed in the same way. It forms the basis for the **LIFE-CYCLE HYPOTHESIS** most closely associated with the Italian-American economist Franco Modigliani (1918–2003, winner of the Nobel Prize in 1985).

14.2.2 Consumption, Income, and Wealth

At first blush, the two hypotheses seem to explain different phenomena: the permanent-income hypothesis focuses on responses to short-run or transitory fluctuations in income; the life-cycle hypothesis focuses on planning consumption over a lifetime. But in fact, the underlying analysis of the two hypotheses is fundamentally the same, and modern economics treats them simply as different expositions of a common model of consumption behavior. For convenience, we will refer to the permanent-income/life-cycle hypothesis simply as the permanent-income hypothesis.

Recall that the present value of any financial asset is found by discounting the income streams that it generates by the (risk-adjusted) market rate of interest (see Chapter 6, section 6.2). Real assets can be thought of in the same way. The value of a house is the series of incomes that it generates – the (actual or implicit rent) discounted back to the present. The permanent-income hypothesis sees each of us as similar to a real asset. Over our lifetime we have a certain earning potential, and our **human wealth** is *the present value of our expected future earnings discounted back to today.*

Life-cycle wealth can be defined to be *the present value of all human, real, and financial wealth.* If we indicate the income expected at some period t from our human wealth (i.e., from future earnings or other sources not associated with our current wealth – real or financial) as y_t^e, then our *life-cycle wealth (lcw)* today (period 0) can be defined to be:

$$lcw_0 = \sum_{t=0}^{\infty} \frac{y_t^e}{(1+rr)^t} + current\ wealth_0. \tag{14.6}$$

Notice that discounting uses the *real* rate of interest (assumed to be a constant) on the ground that income and current wealth are themselves measured in real dollars. Also notice that the summation runs from the current period to infinity. We do not assume that people live forever, but merely that we cannot specify the date of their deaths. The value of y_t^e for any period after one's death is zero, and so contributes nothing to life-cycle wealth.

Permanent income may be defined to be *the income stream generated from the earnings of life-cycle wealth* or equivalently as *the maximum flow of income that can be withdrawn from life-cycle wealth without reducing the value of the stock of life-cycle wealth.* Formally, permanent income is interest income from our life-cycle wealth:

$$y_0^P = rr \times lcw_0. \tag{14.7}$$

The ideal permanent-income consumer takes every bit of current income earned, saves it in the form of financial or other assets, and allows the earnings from those assets to govern his consumption.

To return to the hydraulic analogies invoked in our discussion of financial assets in Chapter 6 (section 6.1.1), we may conceive of income as a variable stream of water. The simple consumption function places a T-valve into the income pipe, diverting some portion toward consumption and the rest toward savings. The stream of consumption necessarily varies just about as much as the incoming stream of income. In contrast, the permanent-income hypothesis directs the income stream into a holding tank in which additional income flows in proportion to the level of the tank (the equivalent of interest). A pipe from the bottom of the tank allows an outflowing stream. If its valve is set correctly, the stream is steady – unlike the variable income stream – and the level of water in the tank may fluctuate somewhat, but it is not allowed to fall steadily. The water in the tank is, of course, life-cycle wealth, and the outflowing stream is the now smoothed flow of consumption.

How is it that a variable income is transformed into a smooth flow of permanent income and consumption? Where does the variability end up? The answer is implicit in the smoothing process. When current income is above its permanent level, there is net savings (the water rises in the tank); when it is below its permanent level, there is net dissavings (the water falls in the tank). Savings buffers or absorbs the fluctuations in current income, allowing permanent income to flow in a steady stream. Savings becomes more variable to the inverse degree that permanent income and consumption become smoother.

Although it is easiest to explain the permanent-income hypothesis on the assumption that people smooth their consumption through savings and dissavings from financial assets, wealth may be real as well as financial. The lottery winner in the second thought experiment may well have bought a house rather than a financial asset. If he rented out the house, the rental income would provide the permanent-income flow from his lottery windfall. And even if he decided to live in the house, the flow of housing services it generates – treating himself in effect as both the renter and the landlord – can be regarded as income flow.

What is true of a real asset such as a house, as we saw in Chapter 3 (section 3.5.2), is also true of any consumer durable good. Consumer durables are a form of wealth, and the acquisition of consumer durables is not consumption but savings or investment. Consumer durables are consumed, not as they are purchased, but as they are used up. The distinction between durables and nondurables is essential for stating the permanent-income hypothesis accurately. For like other forms of savings, purchases of consumer durables absorb part of the variability of current income. A worker who receives a bonus at work may save that bonus in the form of a purchase of a washing machine or a television set or a car. The permanent-income hypothesis thus implies relatively smooth consumption of nondurables and relatively variable purchases of durables.

14.2.3 The Aggregate Permanent-Income Hypothesis

From the Individual to the Economy as a Whole

So far, we have examined the permanent-income hypothesis from the point of view of an individual consumer. In macroeconomics, we naturally work with the aggregate analogues to the individual relationships. *Aggregate* life-cycle wealth is defined by analogy with equation (14.6):

$$LCW_0 = \sum_{t=0}^{\infty} \frac{Y_t^e}{(1+rr)^t} + current\ wealth_0, \qquad (14.8)$$

where LCW_0 is aggregate life-cycle wealth today, and Y_t^e is expected GDP at time t. Similarly, *aggregate* permanent income is defined by analogy with equation (14.7):

$$Y_0^P = rrLCW_0. \tag{14.9}$$

The difference between current GDP and permanent income is **TRANSITORY INCOME** (Y^T) so that

$$Y \equiv Y^P + Y^T. \tag{14.10}$$

The permanent-income hypothesis can be stated in yet another way: *transitory income is saved; consumption is governed by permanent income.*

Some versions of the permanent-income hypothesis assume that all permanent income is consumed: *nondurable consumption* $= Y^P$. This implies that life-cycle wealth is increased only by transitory windfalls or by reassessments of future income streams. At the individual level, each consumer leaves his heirs a legacy equal to the entire value of his life-cycle wealth. In his original version of the permanent-income hypothesis, Friedman assumed that there was a simple consumption function, $C = cY^P$, where the marginal propensity to consume had the usual properties: $0 < c < 1$. Friedman's hypothesis implies that there is savings out of permanent income, so that life-cycle wealth rises through time. At the individual level, each consumer has built up a legacy for the next generation.

Modigliani's original life-cycle hypothesis assumed that consumers formed a steady consumption plan that would zero out wealth over the lifetime. They would consume not only their permanent income but their wealth as well. In later versions, they are assumed to target some particularly desirable legacy between nothing and the maximum of their lifetime wealth. Because middle-aged people would be building up their wealth while younger and older people were running theirs down, the life-cycle hypothesis implies that the age distribution of the population matters to aggregate savings (and consumption). These differing assumptions are all variations on the same permanent-income principle, and whether any of them (or some other assumption) is correct is an empirical question.

One difficulty with the notion of permanent income is that it depends on future income; and, as we have frequently lamented in earlier chapters, both consumers and economists lack a crystal ball. The best that consumers can do is form an expectation or educated guess about future income. Economists are then stuck with trying to assess what consumers typically expect. Sometimes they rely on models of how consumers do, in fact, or should form expectations. Sometimes they rely on surveys that ask what people expect. Yet, whether or not we can form good estimates of consumers' expectations, the permanent-income hypothesis has some strong implications.

Consider a transitory shock to GDP – say an unexpected increase of $100 million in exports. According to the simple consumption function, the initial boost to consumption would be the marginal propensity to consume times the shock. If the marginal propensity to consume were 0.9, the export shock would initially boost consumption by $90 million. In contrast, consider the version of the permanent-income hypothesis in which people consume their entire permanent incomes. The transitory boost to GDP accrues to people who save it in one form or other. Permanent income – and therefore, consumption – rises only by the real rate of interest times the export shock. If the real rate of interest were 5 percent, then consumption would rise initially only by $5 million. The other $95 million would be absorbed in savings – both in additions to financial assets and to real wealth, including to consumer durables. We should, therefore, expect savings to fluctuate substantially more than nondurable consumption. In our example, the fluctuations will be nineteen times as large.[2]

A permanent increase in GDP has a much different implication than a transitory shock. Imagine that a new energy source is discovered that provides $100 million worth of additional electricity every year forever. Because GDP does not rise just this year but every year into the indefinite future, the present value of the discovery is actually worth $100 million/$rr$, and the permanent income generated by this addition to life-cycle wealth is, in fact, $100 million per year. (The proof is left as an exercise; see Problem 14.4.) Nondurable consumption, therefore, rises by $100 million. Additional savings is unnecessary, because the loss to life-cycle wealth owing to this year's additional consumption is made good by this year's additional income, and this is repeated each year into the future.

Permanent income need not be constant. Any unanticipated addition or subtraction to GDP changes permanent income. A transitory loss, such as a temporary cold snap that limits construction and other industries for a short time, reduces permanent income by roughly the real rate of interest times the loss. Such windfall losses (or gains) may come frequently or infrequently. While the permanent-income hypothesis predicts smoothing of consumption in response to transitory fluctuations in income, it predicts proportionate change with respect to permanent changes in income. The discovery of a large, new oil field in the Gulf of Mexico adds roughly the entire annual value of the production to permanent income.

How the Permanent-Income Hypothesis Explains the Data

We are finally in a position to see just how the permanent-income hypothesis explains the empirical findings in section 14.1. When we look at longer runs

---

[2] $= \$95/\$5 = \frac{1-rr}{rr} = \frac{1-0.05}{0.05}$.

of data, transitory fluctuations average out to zero. This is definitional. It is the point of the decomposition of current income into a permanent and a transitory component in equation (14.10). The long-term trend in measured GDP is, therefore, essentially an estimate of the long-term trend in permanent income. The permanent-income hypothesis predicts that consumption will change in proportion to permanent income. This fits the relationship shown in Figure 14.2 very well.

Because the trend rate of growth of GDP changes only slowly, taking the first difference of GDP is essentially a detrending method. The first-differenced data can be regarded as estimating transitory income. Because the permanent-income hypothesis predicts that consumption is governed by permanent, rather than transitory, income, it also predicts that there should be little correlation between changes in consumption and transitory income. To a first approximation, that *is* the message of Figure 14.3. The low R^2 indicates that the correlation is weak.

The puzzle posed by the data for the simple, linear consumption function is no puzzle at all for the permanent-income hypothesis. It is, rather, just about what one should expect if the permanent-income hypothesis were true.

14.2.4 The Permanent-Income Hypothesis and Fiscal Policy

The idea that the government can boost or retard aggregate demand through changes in its expenditure or tax policy (i.e., fiscal policy) depends on consumption behavior. For example, in Chapter 13, the effect of a boost to government expenditure on GDP was determined by the autonomous expenditure multiplier (equation (13.16)) – repeated here as

$$\mu_{Au} = \frac{\Delta Y}{\Delta Au} = \frac{1}{1 - c(1 - \tau)}. \tag{14.11}$$

To analyze a boost in expenditure, we set $\Delta Au = \Delta G$; and, naturally, we could write μ_G, because government expenditure is the particular form that autonomous spending takes here. The permanent-income hypothesis, however, suggests that our analysis was incomplete.

Recall that we can think of the multiplier as a process, in which the expenditure of one person becomes the income of another; and some part of that income is, in turn, spent and some part saved. If the permanent-income hypothesis is true, then we must distinguish between permanent and transitory income because each implies different expenditure patterns and, therefore, different subsequent income patterns.

If a fiscal-policy action is a permanent increase in government expenditure, then the whole of the initial income that it generates will also be regarded as permanent by the individuals who receive it. Their permanent income will rise by the full amount of the expenditure, and their personal marginal propensities to consume will govern their consumption/savings decision. In that case, we can apply the usual multiplier formula in equation (14.11) to figure out the effect of the government's expenditure on GDP.

But what if the expenditure is transitory – for example, a stimulus such as President Obama and the Democrats enacted in early 2009, explicitly stating that it was temporary? Of course, the public has to decide whether it actually believes that the stimulus is temporary or, despite political protestations, permanent. If people believe that it is all transitory, then the initial reaction to the government's expenditure will be to save it and to raise their own expenditure only in proportion to the income to be earned off of the saving. In effect, the boost to income is not $\Delta Au = \Delta G$ but $\Delta Au = rr\Delta G$. How much this will reduce the effectiveness of the fiscal policy can be demonstrated with an example.

According to the Congressional Budget Office, the stimulus of 2009 was roughly \$862 billion. Suppose that it is regarded as a permanent increase in government expenditure, and that the initial expenditure all goes to purchasing goods and services. Let the marginal propensity to consume be $c = 0.94$, which is the value from Figure 14.2; let the tax rate be $\tau = 30$ percent, which is a very rough estimate of the average marginal tax rate (not to be confused with the average tax rate, which is lower); and let the real interest rate be $rr = 5$ percent. According to equation (14.11), the multiplier is

$$\mu_{Au} = \frac{\Delta Y}{\Delta Au} = \frac{1}{1 - c(1 - \tau)} = \frac{1}{1 - 0.94(1 - 0.30)} = 2.92 \quad (14.12)$$

and the \$862 billion stimulus will raise aggregate demand by

$$\Delta Y = \mu \Delta Au = 2.92 \times \$862\,\text{billion} = \$2{,}517\,\text{billion}, \quad (14.13)$$

which is approximately 20 percent of U.S. GDP in 2009 – a very effective stimulus indeed.

Contrast this case with one in which the stimulus is regarded as wholly temporary. To see the contrast more clearly, it is helpful to look again at the case of a permanent increase in government expenditure and to think of the multiplier process in which we distinguish between the direct and indirect effects of autonomous expenditure (see equation (13.18)). The initial expenditure is the direct effect that forms the initial incomes in the economy, so that in the first round $\Delta Au = \Delta G = \$862$ billion. Part of those incomes is taxed and part is saved, so that the recipients of the direct expenditure themselves spend $(1 - \tau)c\Delta G$, which forms the incomes ΔAu in the second round of the multiplier process. The indirect effect is the multiplied value of that secondary expenditure. Following this logic, we can rewrite the calculation in equation (14.13) as

$$\Delta Y = \Delta G + \mu_{Au}(1 - \tau)c\Delta G = \$862 \text{ billion} + 2.92(1 - 0.3)$$
$$\times 0.94 \times \$862 \text{ billion}$$
$$= \$2{,}518 \text{ billion}. \tag{14.14}$$

(The difference between (14.13) and (14.14) in the final digit is rounding error.)

Now consider what happens when the government's expenditure is temporary. Again, there is a direct effect: all the initial expenditure goes to goods and services and, therefore, directly adds its whole amount to aggregate demand. Thus, $\Delta Au = \Delta G$ in the first round. And again, there is an indirect effect, but this time only the permanent part of the first-round income is spent. As before, taxes are levied and savings are made out of permanent income, but only $rr\Delta G$ is regarded as permanent income, and therefore, in the second round $\Delta Au = (1 - \tau)c(rr\Delta G)$. So, in this case, the effect of the multiplier process is

$$\Delta Y = \Delta Au + \mu_A(1 - \tau)c(rr\Delta G)$$
$$= \$862 \text{ billion} + 2.92 \times (1 - 0.3) \times 0.95 \times (0.05 \times \$862 \text{ billion})$$
$$= \$945 \text{ billion}, \tag{14.15}$$

which is a little more than one-third of the effect when the increase in GDP is permanent. Indeed, if we calculate the government expenditure multiplier as $\mu_G = \frac{\Delta Y}{\Delta G}$ and fill in these numbers the multiplier would be

$$\mu_G = \frac{\Delta Y}{\Delta G} = \frac{945}{862} = 1.10 \tag{14.16}$$

– a dramatic collapse of the powerful fiscal policy implied by equation (14.12).

A temporary tax cut would also have a small effect if the permanent-income hypothesis were correct. For example, a tax rebate that left tax rates unchanged but just made a direct payment to taxpayers would not have a first-round effect at all, because taxes and transfers are not parts of GDP, but would have a second-round effect with the same multiplier as the second round in equation (14.14). Permanent-income consumers would save virtually all of a temporary tax cut, adding it to wealth by buying real assets, including consumer durables, buying financial assets, or paying off debts. An $862 billion tax rebate would result in a gain of only $83 billion: a tax multiplier of only $\mu_T = \frac{83}{-862} = -0.1$.

This analysis of President Obama's stimulus is entirely conjectural – at the time of writing this chapter, not enough time had passed to possess the necessary perspective. However, economists have analyzed an earlier attempt by President George W. Bush to stimulate the economy, which will serve as both a test of the permanent-income hypothesis and an example of its application to fiscal policy (see Box 14.1).

14.3 Borrowing Constraints, Rules of Thumb, and Consumption

A consumer following the permanent-income hypothesis must be able to adjust his portfolio of real or financial assets. A relatively rich person can do that fairly easily at a nearly constant opportunity cost. For example, someone with a large holding in mutual funds finds it straightforward to add windfalls to the funds and to use the funds to make up for shortfalls, keeping consumption streams even.

The situation is likely to be quite different for poor people. Generally, the poor face a large difference between the rates at which they can borrow and lend. Payday lenders charge high rates of interest. Banks usually charge high rates of interest on credit cards, and the poor much more than the rich are less likely to pay off the balances every month. On the other hand, even when the poor have something to save, they may not have enough to meet minimum-balance requirements for a mutual fund, much less to buy stocks or bonds, and so may be limited to low-interest savings accounts at banks. The poor face an asymmetry: On the one hand, the cost of debt is high. In fact, they may find it practically impossible to borrow at all, except perhaps from Freddie, the loan shark. On the other hand, the returns to saving are low, so that the opportunity cost of spending is low, which favors consumption over saving. A poor person unable to borrow or lend very easily is said to face a **LIQUIDITY** or **BORROWING CONSTRAINT**. Borrowing constraints favor a strategy of living hand-to-mouth over a strategy of smoothing consumption over time. A borrowing-constrained consumer does not follow the permanent-income hypothesis.

Sometimes, of course, poorer consumers have managed to get into debt. Then, because of the high interest rates they face, saving a windfall – that is, paying off some of the debt – has a high return. And if lenders are willing to let them take on more debt at the margin, they would in fact be able to smooth consumption, though on vastly more unfavorable terms than richer people face. In practice, however, when one is already deeply in debt, lenders are reluctant to extend further credit, but will readily accept repayment out of a windfall. So, we would not expect the indebted to mimic the consumption-smoothing behavior of those with substantial assets.

Box 14.1. Testing the Permanent-Income Hypothesis: A Natural Experiment

Economic upheavals may be bad news for consumers, but they may also generate "natural experiments" by means of which we can test economic theories. Temporary stimulus packages provide just such a test for the permanent-income hypothesis.

In response to the "Great Recession" that started in December of 2007, the Obama administration passed an unprecedentedly large stimulus package – a mixture of additional government spending and tax cuts that, according to the Congressional Budget Office, ultimately amounted to $862 billion. Christina Romer, Chair of the President's Council of Economic Advisers, estimated that the multiplier was about 1.6, so that the stimulus would add, in the end, to about $1.4 trillion to GDP. It is too early, at the time this is being written, to judge whether or not she was correct. But history gives us another recent stimulus package that can be examined for clues.

In early 2008, anticipating a slowing economy, George W. Bush's administration proposed a $152 billion stimulus. More than two-thirds of the stimulus consisted of direct payments (tax rebates) to 130 million American households. Most received between $300 and $1,200 with the payments phasing out for richer households. Almost all the payments were received between May and July 2008. Such a stimulus provides a test case for consumption theory. The stimulus was an unexpected, transitory addition to current income. The permanent-income/life-cycle hypothesis suggests that such an increase should be largely saved.

Two economists, Matthew Shapiro and Joel Slemrod (both of the University of Michigan), analyzed a survey in which households were asked (both before and during receipt of the tax rebates) how they planned to use the money.[3] The results are in Table B14.1. Of those who both

Table B14.1. *Responses to 2008 Rebate Survey*

Intended Disposition of Tax Rebate	Percentage of Respondents Receiving Rebates[a]
Mostly spend	19.9
Mostly save	31.8
Mostly pay off debt	48.2
Total	100.0

[a] Entries do not sum to 100 because of rounding.
Source: Shapiro and Slemrod (2009).

(continued)

[3] Shapiro, Matthew D., and Joel Slemrod. "Did the 2008 Tax Rebates Stimulate Spending?" *American Economic Review*, 99(2), May 2009, pp. 374–379.

Box 14.1 (*continued*)

Table B14.2. *Disposition of the 2008 Tax Rebate and Age*

Age Group	Percent of Survey Respondents Planning to "Mostly Spend" the Rebate
29 or younger	11.7
30–39	14.2
40–49	16.9
50–64	19.9
Age 64 or younger	17.0
Age 65 or older	28.4

Source: Shapiro and Slemrod (2009).

responded to the survey and received a rebate, only about a fifth intended mostly to spend the money. The remainder intended either to save it or to use it to pay off debts, which is itself a form of saving. And of course, any spending used to purchase durable goods also counts as savings (and investment) according to the permanent-income hypothesis. The survey is thus broadly consistent with the permanent-income hypothesis.

The permanent-income/life-cycle hypothesis also suggests that older consumers will increasingly spend the funds that they saved in their youth. The survey confirmed that plans to spend increase with age (see Table B14.2).

Looking at aggregate data, Shapiro and Slemrod observed that the personal savings rate, which had been nearly zero before the stimulus, increased markedly as the tax rebates were delivered and then fell again. The increase in savings was only slightly smaller than the size of the stimulus. This pattern is consistent with consumers saving the lion's share of the stimulus, just as the permanent-income hypothesis predicts.

Shapiro and Slemrod estimated that overall the marginal propensity to consume out of the stimulus was about one-third. Using equation (14.11) on the assumption that the marginal tax rate is 30 percent, the autonomous expenditure multiplier would be

$$\mu_{Au} = \frac{\Delta Y}{\Delta Au} = \frac{1}{1 - c(1 - \tau)} = \frac{1}{1 - 0.33(1 - 0.30)} = 1.30,$$

a value lower than the Obama administration's estimate, but one that still suggests a nontrivial stimulus to GDP. Of course, the Bush administration's stimulus package was short-lived. After the stimulus in the early summer of 2008, government spending fell back to its old pattern – an offsetting negative stimulus in its own right. And, as we know now, the economy slipped into the deepest recession since World War II despite the stimulus.

Although based on a simple idea, actually following the permanent-income hypothesis requires both a certain insight about rational planning and the ability to form at least educated guesses about future income. This may be psychologically unlikely for many people. Rather than thinking about their consumption as a future-oriented planning problem, they may simply follow a rule of thumb that has worked for them in the past: say, save 10 percent of one's income and leave it at that. Interpreted as a description of individual behavior, the simple consumption function of Chapter 13 (section 13.1) is exactly that sort of rule of thumb.

Whether owing to borrowing constraints or rules of thumb, some consumers almost surely do not follow the permanent-income hypothesis. The question is just how many do not. In a well-known study, economists John Campbell and N. Gregory Mankiw (both currently of Harvard University) estimated that about half of consumers followed the permanent-income hypothesis, while the other half based consumption on current income in the manner of the simple consumption function.[4] The aggregate consumption function should, then, be approximately the average of the multipliers in equations (14.12) and (14.16) – that is, $\mu_G = 0.5(2.92 + 1.10) = 2.01$, a diminished but not insignificant multiplier.

Although the numbers used in our example are not unreasonable, they are back-of-the-envelope numbers and not careful, empirically justified estimates. For several reasons, our calculations may suggest that the multiplier is more powerful than it is in fact. The assumed marginal propensity to consume may, perhaps, be too high, as may the real interest rate. If either or both were in fact lower, the multiplier would be smaller. The outflow of income from the domestic private sector in the form of imports acts like a tax and, therefore, would also lower the multiplier. Reliable estimates of the multiplier can be established only through more careful economic research; we can see as a matter of logic that the multiplier weakens in proportion to the number of consumers who follow the permanent-income hypothesis.

PART B. INVESTMENT

14.4 An Asset-Based View of Capital and Investment

The permanent-income hypothesis views people in effect from two perspectives – each of us is simultaneously a consumer and a worker. The worker can be regarded as an asset that generates a stream of income over the future; and the consumer can be regarded as the owner of that asset, who can decide

---

[4] John Y. Campbell and N. Gregory Mankiw. "Permanent Income, Current Income, and Consumption," *Journal of Business Economics and Statistics*, vol. 8, no. 3, July 1990, pp. 265–279.

how to manage its present value. Seen this way, much of what we already know about financial assets illuminates consumption. Physical capital and investment can also be analyzed through the analogy with financial assets. We have already made a step in this direction in the last chapter when we treated the investment decision as related to an opportunity cost represented by a market rate of interest. In this part, we elaborate that analysis.

14.4.1 Evaluating an Investment Project

The Present Value of an Investment Project

Investment, as reported in the national accounts, is a flow – the acquisition of the real physical means of production per unit time. And as we saw in Chapter 10 (section 10.3.3), the purpose of investment is to increase the capital stock and thereby add to the productive capacity of the economy. Equation (10.10), repeated here as

$$\Delta K_t = K_t - K_{t-1} = I_{t-1} - Depreciation_{t-1} = net\ I_{t-1}, \quad (14.17)$$

shows that the change in the capital stock is determined by net investment. But this is simply an accounting fact. What we really want to understand is what explains the particular level of investment. We can begin by asking – from the point of view of the firm – why it seeks some particular level of capital.

By definition, capital is the physical means of production. It may be long-lived or short-lived, but it must not be used up in the production process of the current period. Because capital does its work over time, we are faced – just as we were in evaluating financial assets or permanent income – with the problem of assessing values that accrue at different times on a common basis: the evaluation of a capital project is a present-value problem.

Firms acquire capital in order to reap profits. Profits (Π) can be defined simply as

$$\Pi_t = Revenue_t - Cost_t. \quad (14.18)$$

Consider a rental car company that wants to decide whether to buy a Ford Focus to add to its rental fleet – its capital stock. Suppose that the car costs $15,000, and that the rental car company intends to operate it for two years. It believes that it can sell it on the used car market for $12,000. The final sales price is often referred to as the **scrap value** – "scrap" to the rental company, although anything but scrap to the buyer of the used car. It estimates, considering the number of days per year it can rent it out and the maintenance costs of keeping it in good shape, that it will net $3,000 for each of the two years that it serves in its fleet. To make the problem simpler, we assume unrealistically that it receives the $3,000 at the end of each year as a lump sum. What is the car worth to the firm? What that really means is, what is the present value of the car given an appropriate opportunity cost? Suppose that the firm can earn 5 percent on a purchase of $12,000 of additional financial assets. The present value is then

$$PV = \frac{3,000}{1.05} + \frac{3,000}{(1.05)^2} + \frac{12,000}{(1.05)^2} = \$16,463, \qquad (14.19)$$

which is a net return in terms of present value of $1,433 (= $16,433 – $15,000). The car, then, returns more than its cost; it is a worthwhile investment.

We can generalize the example: the present value of any capital acquisition today (period t) is

$$PV_t = \sum_{m=1}^{M} \frac{\Pi^e_{t+m}}{(1+rr)^m} + \frac{scrap\ value^e}{(1+rr)^M}, \qquad (14.20)$$

where M is the number of periods until the capital is scrapped. We have used the real interest rate (rr) as the measure of the opportunity cost, which implies that we have calculated the *real* present value and therefore need to measure PV, Π, and scrap value conformably in constant-dollar terms. (Naturally, we could also calculate *nominal* present value using a market interest rate and *nominal* values for the other variables.) Present value is, of course, a forward-looking notion; so we add the superscript e to indicate that we do not know the future income stream with certainty but must form expectations or guesses of the values of its components.

The general rule is:

- *a firm should invest when the present value of a capital project exceeds its cost of acquisition.*

The investment problem is sometimes posed equivalently in terms of **net present value** – that is, in terms of *NPV ≡ PV – initial costs*. Then equation (14.20) becomes:

$$NPV_t = PV_t - initial\ cost_t = \sum_{m=1}^{M} \frac{\Pi^e_{t+m}}{(1+rr)^m} + \frac{scrap\ value^e}{(1+rr)^M} - initial\ cost_t.$$

$$(14.20')$$

The general rule then becomes:

- *a firm should invest when the net present value of a capital project is greater than zero.*

Internal Rate of Return

Firms generally have many potential investment projects involving different initial outlays and different profit streams. They may need to rank them on a common basis to determine just how efficient a particular capital project is at generating revenue. For this purpose, they can look at the present-value problem in a different way. Think of the capital tied up in a project as a bond. Its market price ($15,000) is the cost of purchase. It pays a series of coupons over its lifetime (here, the profits of $3,000 each year, although the profits in other cases may accrue less regularly). And it has a face value (the scrap value of the car, $12,000). With these facts, we can evaluate the "yield to maturity" of the purchase of the car in exactly the same way that we would the yield to maturity of a bond by fitting the data into the bond-pricing formula (equation (6.13′)):

$$\$15{,}000 = \frac{3{,}000}{1+\rho} + \frac{3{,}000}{(1+\rho)^2} + \frac{12{,}000}{(1+\rho)^2}, \tag{14.21}$$

where we have written the opportunity cost as ρ – the *discount rate*. In the present-value problem, the unknown was PV, which we then compared with the acquisition cost. Here, the acquisition cost is written on the left-hand side of the equation; and it is ρ, the equivalent of the yield to maturity, that is unknown. This is the same yield on investment that we treated less formally in Chapter 13 (section 13.3.1). The solution to (14.20) is $\rho = 10.5$ percent. (This is easily confirmed by substituting 1.105 for $1 + \rho$ in (14.20) and checking that the right-hand side equals $15,000. As with yield to maturity, calculating discount rates is not generally easy to do by hand, but any spreadsheet program or business calculator incorporates functions that solve for them readily.)

The discount rate (ρ) is known as the **INTERNAL RATE OF RETURN**, which can be defined as *that rate of discount that makes the future stream of income generated by a capital project just equal to its cost of acquisition.* To put it in terms of a formula, the *internal rate of return* is

$$\rho \text{ such that } cost\ of\ acquisition_t = \sum_{m=1}^{M} \frac{\Pi^e_{t+m}}{(1+\rho)^m} + \frac{scrap\ value^e}{(1+\rho)^M}. \tag{14.22}$$

The higher the value of ρ, the higher the internal rate of return of the capital project, the more desirable it is to the firm. Of course, whether a firm should invest in a project depends on the opportunity cost (*rr*). The general rule is:

- *a firm should invest when the internal rate of return of a capital project exceeds the opportunity cost ($\rho > rr$).*

For the car rental firm, $\rho = 10.5$ percent > 5 percent $= rr$. Therefore, the firm should invest; the firm earns a higher rate of return from buying the car than it would from buying a bond.

The present-value calculation in equation (14.20) and its associated investment rule and the internal rate of return calculation in (14.22) and its associated investment rule use the same information but package it in different forms. The difference is exactly the difference encountered with financial assets between calculating the price of a bond and its yield to maturity. The internal rate of return is preferred when we wish to compare a capital project to its opportunity cost expressed as a market interest rate or yield to maturity, because the two values share a common unit facilitating a valid comparison.

Investment and Risk

We already saw in the last chapter that two investment projects might have the same expected return on average but present different levels of risk (Chapter 13, section 13.3.1). How might we build risk into the formal assessment of capital projects?

Two aspects of risk that might concern us are price risk and default risk. In the case of financial assets, price risk was the risk that changing market rates of interest might imply capital losses. We found that price risk was particularly salient when considering the term structure of interest rates – risk generally rising as the maturity of bonds became longer. Markets build in a risk premium into the market yield on longer bonds to compensate for price risk.

An obvious way to deal with price risk in the context of real investments is to choose an opportunity cost of an appropriate maturity. In the rental car example, a 2-year bond matches the maturity of the investment. A project in which the returns accrue over longer periods should be compared to a bond that matures over a similar period. If, for example, a construction firm were to consider an investment in a dump truck with an expected service life of ten years, a 10-year bond would provide an appropriate measure of the opportunity cost.

Some capital projects yield their returns over very long periods – consider a hydroelectric dam, a canal, or a road. These might call for comparison to bonds of longer maturities than are readily available in the market. But this is unlikely to pose a problem because, as we have seen previously, the present value of money received even thirty years in the future is typically so small that it can be neglected. The present value at 5 percent of $1 thirty years in the future is 23 cents; one hundred years in the future, less than 1 cent. The present value of $1 received each year for thirty years is $15.37; each year for one hundred years, $19.84; and each year forever, $20.

Given how little the distant future contributes to present value and given how closely the present value for a long, but finite, maturity conforms to an infinite maturity, we will not go far wrong using the yield on bonds with the longest available maturities as the appropriate opportunity cost.

What about default risk? We saw in Chapter 7 that bonds are rated according to their default risk, and that the riskier bonds had to pay a premium in terms of a higher yield over less risky bonds (see section 7.3.1, especially Table 7.1). The equivalent of default risk for a particular physical investment is just that it fails to pay off or fails to pay off to the expected degree.

Returning to the rental car example, suppose that, instead of earning profits of $3,000 for the two years before scrapping, there is a 50–50 chance that the car earns only $2,500 each year. If these lower returns were certain, then the internal rate of return would turn out to be 7 percent. The expected return taking both possibilities into account is then 8.75 percent $(= (10.5 + 7.0)/2)$. Although this return is greater than the 5-percent opportunity cost that we previously assumed, that estimate of the opportunity cost may well be too low if it does not incorporate a risk premium. If the real return on the investment is judged to be as risky as, say, a 2-year BB-rated bond and such a bond yields 11 percent, then $\rho = 8.75 < 11 < rr$. The firm would earn a better return at the same risk by *not* investing in the car and buying the bond instead.

The assessment of risk is more complicated than in this simple example. Ideally, the investor should find a financial asset with identical risk characteristics to the investment to use as the measure of opportunity cost. In practice, finding perfectly identical financial assets is not often possible. As a result, firms in practice may make a more rough-and-ready judgment, basing the estimate of ρ on their best expectations as in equation (14.21), but requiring a subjectively assessed risk premium before committing to a new capital project. Their rule in practice is:

- *invest if $\rho >$ rr + risk premium.*

However the rule is formulated, it is clear that the riskier the investment, the higher the internal rate of return must be to justify it. And if assessments of risk increase because of changing economic circumstances, fewer capital projects will generate big enough returns to justify the investment. Investment, therefore, *ceteris paribus* moves inversely to risk.

14.4.2 *The Rate of Investment*

An astute student might object to the discussion in the previous section, saying that we had answered a different question than the one that motivates this part: we examined what determines a desirable *stock* of capital, not what determines a desirable *flow* of investment. In other words, we have failed to account for the rate at which capital goods are added to the existing stock. The objection is correct but easily repaired in principle. A detailed formal analysis is too complex, but the main points are easily made with examples.

A commonplace among engineers and project managers runs, "You can build it cheap; you can build it fast; you can build it right; ... pick any two of the three." Let us assume that all of our investments are built right; then the commonplace statement points to a trade-off between fast construction and cheap construction. If we take time on a construction project, we can plan the work so that different workers do not interfere with each other; we can shop for the necessary materials, looking for the best price, even if this means waiting longer to get them; we are less likely to make costly errors because we can check out each step carefully before moving on to the next one. So, in general, slower construction is cheaper construction.

Conversely, the slower we go, the farther off we push the profits of the project into the future. And we know that future returns are discounted – the farther in the future, the more heavily – so that slow construction reduces the present value of a project. To decide how fast to build, the benefits of slower construction must be balanced against its costs.

A simple example illustrates the point. Suppose that Arianespace, the European rocket-launching company, wants to decide whether to invest in a new rocket used to place a satellite into orbit. To keep the problem simple, assume that the rocket can be used only once and will earn €1 million for a successful launch. Assume that Arianespace may choose to build the rocket over a period of one year at a cost of €960,000; two years at €900,000; or three years at €875,000. And assume that although the expenditures are paid out evenly each year of the period of construction, the funds must be deposited at the start of construction.

The internal rate of return for the project uses equation (14.22) suitably adapted to the details of the problem:

$$cost\ of\ acquisition_t = \frac{\Pi^e_{t+M}}{(1+\rho)^M}. \tag{14.23}$$

Because the profits are all accrued at the date of completion of the project, the summation sign is omitted (and the subscript and exponent m changed to its final value M); and, because the rocket is destroyed in the launch, there is no scrap value. The returns for each speed of construction are then easily computed. For example, if construction takes three years, the problem is to find ρ such that

$$875,000 = \frac{1,000,000}{(1+\rho)^3}. \tag{14.24}$$

The solution is

$$\rho = \sqrt[3]{\frac{1,000,000}{875,000}} - 1 = 4.5 \text{ percent.} \qquad (14.25)$$

Call this internal rate of return ρ_3. The internal rates of return for years one and two are calculated analogously: $\rho_1 = 4.2$ percent; $\rho_2 = 5.4$ percent.

The maximum internal rate of return over the possible building periods is $\rho^* = \rho_2 = 5.4$ percent. _If_ Arianespace decides to build the rocket, its best strategy is to build it in two years. But should it build the rocket? That depends, of course, on the opportunity cost. Say that the relevant market rate of interest is 3 percent, then $\rho^* = 5.4 > 3 = rr$, and the rocket should be built. The rate of investment is €450,000 per year (= €900,000/2).

Realistic examples are more complex. The simple example, however, is enough to show that considerations of internal rate of return and opportunity cost govern both the desirability of a particular capital project and the rate of investment, provided that we take account of the way that costs change with the time involved in carrying out the investment.

14.4.3 _Investment and the Stock Market_

All of the examples used so far assume that the relevant opportunity costs of investment are found in the bond market, but this need not be the case. The stock market also provides an alternative to physical investment and, therefore, a potentially relevant opportunity cost.

Students sometimes believe that the stock market is important to investment because firms sell shares in order to raise funds for purchasing capital goods. Firms sometimes do sell new shares in what is called a **public offering**. When firms first "go public" – that is, when they first allow their stock to be sold freely on the market – they make an **initial public offering** or **IPO**. Public offerings are important sources of finance to firms – especially when they are just starting out. But public offerings, initial or otherwise, are very small relative to the huge volume of existing shares that are bought and sold daily and, in fact, are not an important influence on the rate of overall investment.

The real influence of stocks on investment, just like the real influence of bonds on investment, is through the mechanism of opportunity cost. A firm has a choice between purchasing physical capital and using those same funds to purchase a financial asset – shares, just as much as bonds. And it is the relative returns of these choices that determine whether a firm should make the investment.

Stocks are usually held both for their dividend flow and for capital gains – that is, for the hope that their price will appreciate. Stocks do not have a definite maturity, but we can estimate their expected yield over any particular period – that is, the expected **HOLDING-PERIOD YIELD** $(r^e_{S,t})$ – as

$$r^e_{S,t} = \frac{dividend_t}{p_{S,t}} + \hat{p}^e_{S,t}, \tag{14.25}$$

where the first term on the right is the dividend yield and the second term is the rate of growth of the stock price expected between period t and $t + 1$ – that is, the percentage capital gain. The holding-period yield can be used directly in place of the yield to maturity on a bond as the opportunity cost in evaluating an investment.

There is another way to look at the influence of the stock market on investment decisions. Consider a drug company whose patents are nearing the end of their terms. When the patents expire, the drug becomes generic. Although the company may still manufacture it, other firms can do so too, and competition is likely to drive the price and the profitability down. Anticipating reduced future profits, the company has a choice: it can invest in the research and development of new drugs, or it can purchase shares (or even a controlling stake) in another drug company whose patents are farther from expiration. The question it faces is, which is the cheaper alternative?

When the share price of the target company is high, buying all or part of it is a relatively costly way to acquire the profits from drugs. In that case, the first drug company would find it more lucrative to invest in its own production. But when the share price is low, the target company is a bargain, and the first drug company would find it best to forgo investment and purchase the existing assets of the target company. A real-world example: in 2009, Pfizer Pharmaceutical purchased another large drug company, Wyeth, to form the largest pharmaceutical company in the world. The purchase allowed Pfizer to capture Wyeth's pharmacopoeia, saving it some investment in new drugs.

The general rule:

- *high-share prices promote real investment; low-share prices promote the purchase of existing shares.*

This rule is completely consistent with the idea that stock-market yields drive investment. As with bonds, share prices and yields are related inversely. As we have already seen, high yields or opportunity costs reduce investment, and high yields are equivalent to low-share prices.

The firm's decision criterion is sometimes summarized in a variable called Tobin's q. It is named for the winner of the 1981 Nobel Prize in Economic Science, James Tobin (1918–2002), although a similar idea is found in John Maynard Keynes's (1883–1946) *General Theory of Employment, Interest, and Money* (1936). **Tobin's q** is defined as *the ratio of the market value of* a firm (measured by the value of its outstanding shares) to the replacement cost of its physical assets. Thus, if $q > 1$, it would be cheaper to build an equivalent firm from scratch, and if $q < 1$, it would be cheaper to buy the existing firm. Because q will be higher, the higher the share price, high-share prices promote investment.

14.5 Aggregate Investment

14.5.1 Factors Governing Aggregate Investment

The discussion of investment in Section 14.4 was entirely from the point of view of the individual firm. Aggregate investment, of course, comprises the individual investment decisions of the diverse firms that make up the productive sector of the economy. Understanding individual firm behavior provides insight into how we expect aggregate investment to behave. Recall the general rule for investment: *a firm should invest when the internal rate of return of a capital project exceeds the opportunity cost* ($\rho > r$), where the internal rate of return is defined in equation (14.22), repeated here:

$$\rho \text{ such that } cost\ of\ acquisition_t = \sum_{m=1}^{M} \frac{\Pi^e_{t+m}}{(1+\rho)^m} + \frac{scrap\ value^e}{(1+\rho)^M}. \quad (14.22)$$

We shall consider what the investment rule suggests for the behavior of aggregate investment with respect to five factors.

1. Opportunity Cost

Whether we measure the opportunity cost of physical investment by an interest rate or by the expected yield on stocks or some other financial asset, we expect that investment will be an inverse function of the opportunity cost – a fact that we already encountered in Chapter 13 and represented as the downward-sloping investment curve in Figure 13.10. In Chapter 13 we also derived the IS curve (e.g., Figure 13.12) – in part from the investment curve. Figure 14.4 presents an investment curve, and Figure 14.5 an IS curve. A change in the opportunity cost, represented in these diagrams by the real rate of interest (rr), results in movements along the curves.

The investment curve and the IS curve are drawn *ceteris paribus* – that is, holding other factors that might affect investment constant. That the data of the actual economy, naturally, are not generated similarly holding other factors constant is evident in Figure 14.6, which plots investment as a percentage of potential GDP (scaled investment) against an estimate of the real interest rate and the NBER recession dates. It is difficult to discern any clear relationship between the investment series and the interest-rate series.

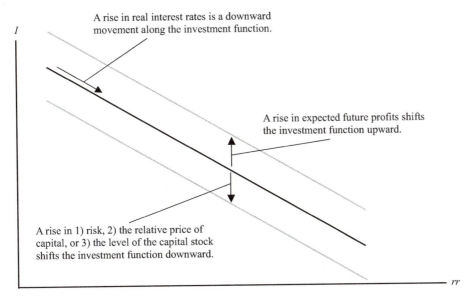

Figure 14.4. Factors Shifting the Investment Function.

This is not surprising, because a variety of other factors are changing at the same time.

To take one example, notice that both investment and real interest rates typically fall during some part of most recessions and typically rise (at least relative to trend) during substantial parts of expansions – the opposite of the inverse behavior that should hold *ceteris paribus* in theory. We might think of the behavior of each series as being driven by GDP. Rising GDP,

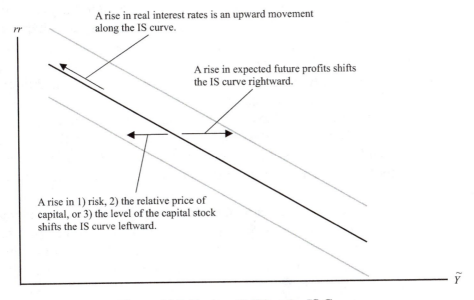

Figure 14.5. Factors Shifting the IS Curve.

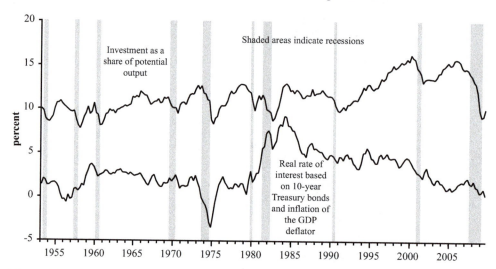

Figure 14.6. Investment, Real Rates of Interest, and Business Cycles. *Source:* Investment, GDP, GDP deflator, Bureau of Economic Analysis; interest rates, Federal Reserve; and author's calculations.

for example, may cause people to revise their expectations of future profits upward, raising the internal rate of return and promoting investment. Rising GDP may also raise interest rates through at least two mechanisms. First, monetary policymakers typically increase short-term interest rates in the boom to suppress inflation and reduce them in the slump to fight unemployment; and, as we saw in our discussion of the term structure of interest rates in Chapter 7 (section 7.4), expected increases in short rates tend to raise long rates as well. Second, firms tend to borrow more in a boom to finance additional investment, which raises their demand for bank loans, as well as the amount of new bonds that they issue, again driving up interest rates. Thus, even if investment would be lower when interest rates are higher *holding* GDP constant, when GDP is not held constant, both investment and interest rates can change in the same direction. The problem is a general one: when two variables are both affected by a common cause, we must control for the common cause to isolate the direct relationship between them. That requires more sophisticated statistical techniques than are appropriate to the level of this book. (However, see the discussion of causation in the *Guide*, section G.13.)

Another consideration is that capital construction generally takes many months or years, and firms build in a premium into the internal rate of return to account for the risk of changing interest rates. Thus, although our rule says that *any* time the firm's estimate of the internal rate of return rises above the relevant opportunity cost, it should invest, in practice firms require an internal rate of return considerably higher than the relevant opportunity cost before embarking on a long-lived project. This premium provides a

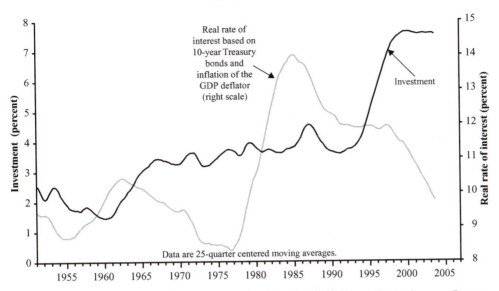

Figure 14.7. Investment and Real Rates of Interest in the Long Run. *Source:* Investment, GDP, GDP deflator, Bureau of Economic Analysis; interest rates, Federal Reserve; and author's calculations.

cushion, so that small rises and falls in the interest rate are unlikely to bring the opportunity cost above the internal rate of return. As a result, short-term fluctuations in interest rates are not likely to affect investment very much.

Long-lived changes in interest rates should, in contrast, have a more noticeable effect. To capture long-lived changes, Figure 14.7 plots a centered moving average of real interest rates against the moving average of scaled investment. (The period of the moving average is 25 quarters, which approximates the typical length of U.S. business cycles – see Chapter 5, section 5.2.3, and the *Guide*, section G.12.) The data show a broad, if imprecise, tendency to move inversely to one another – falling interest rates are associated with rising investment and rising with falling – which is what theory predicts.

We previously noted that interest rates are not the only possibly relevant opportunity cost of investment. Figure 14.8 plots the 1-year holding-period yield on stock against scaled investment. The most striking feature of the graph is that almost every instance in which stock returns are actually negative (i.e., periods in which stocks are becoming cheap relative to physical capital) is associated with sharp falls in investment – again perfectly consistent with our investment theory.

2. Expected Future Profits

For any given internal rate of return (ρ), an increase in one or more of the expected profit terms (Π^e_{t+m}) results in an increase in the present value represented by the right-hand side of equation (14.22). If the cost of acquisition of the capital goods is unaffected, then the equation requires that the present value *not* increase. As a result, the internal rate of return must rise. And a

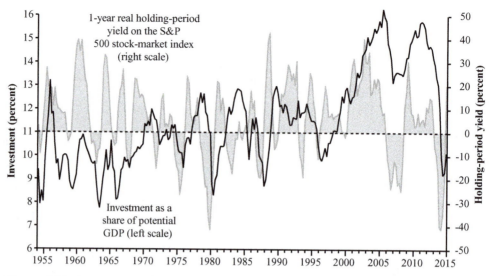

Figure 14.8. Investment and Real Stock-Market Yields. *Source:* Investment, GDP, GDP deflator, Bureau of Economic Analysis; S&P's 500 index and dividends, Standard & Poor's; and author's calculations.

higher internal rate of return is more likely to exceed the opportunity cost, thus promoting investment. As a result, if expected profits increase for most firms in the economy, we can expect aggregate investment to increase. At each level of *rr* in Figure 14.4, the investment curve would shift upward. Similarly, the IS curve in Figure 14.5 would shift to the right.

Investors may or may not have a firm basis for their expectations of future profits. Keynes famously argued that investment in common with "a large proportion[of our positive activities depend[s] on spontaneous optimism . . . " or "animal spirits – . . . a spontaneous urge to action rather than inaction." On this view, estimates of future profits are apt to shift rather easily, and investment is likely to prove more volatile than, say, consumption. Booms may be fueled by unreasonable hopes and slumps by unreasonable fears:

if the animal spirits are dimmed and the spontaneous optimism falters, leaving us to depend on nothing but a mathematical expectation, enterprise will fade and die; – though fears of loss may have a basis no more reasonable than hopes of profit had before. . . . In estimating the prospects of investment, we must have regard, therefore, to the nerves and hysteria and even the digestions and reactions to the weather of those upon whose spontaneous activity it largely depends.[5]

Keynes's view implies that the investment curve and the IS curve should not be thought of as relatively stable but as fluttering up and down or left and right fairly easily.

[5] John Maynard Keynes, *The General Theory of Employment, Interest, and Money*. London: Macmillan, 1936, ch. 12, section VII.

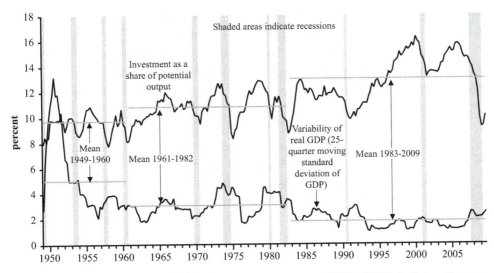

Figure 14.9. Investment and Risk. *Source:* Investment, GDP, GDP deflator, Bureau of Economic Analysis; and author's calculations.

3. Risk

The relevant opportunity cost should reflect the riskiness of an investment. If risk in the economy rises, investments should be evaluated using a higher measure of opportunity cost or – what amounts to the same thing – a larger premium on that internal rate of return needed to justify an investment. A higher opportunity cost *ceteris paribus* implies that fewer investment projects will be undertaken. The investment curve should shift down, and the IS curve should shift to the left.

How could we measure the aggregate risk in the economy? An economy would seem riskier if GDP were more variable and less predictable. The standard deviation of GDP growth rates provides a measure of its variability (see the *Guide*, section G.4.3). Because we would like to measure how that variability changes over time, we can calculate a moving standard deviation analogous to a moving average.

The lower time series in Figure 14.9 plots the 25-quarter moving standard deviation. We see that these divide naturally into three distinct periods: 1) from the end of World War II through the Eisenhower administration (i.e., through 1960); 2) from the beginning of the Kennedy administration through 1982 (a date that marks the end of the first phase of Federal Reserve Chairman Paul Volcker's effort to combat inflation, which induced two recessions in three years; and 3) 1983 through 2007, ending with the severe recession that started in December of 2007. The horizontal lines indicating mean variability of GDP over this period stair-step downward from a mean standard deviation of 5.7 percentage points in the earliest period to only 2.0 percentage points in the latest period. The data thus reflect the fact that GDP growth

over the last twenty-five years has been much smoother than in the immediate post-World War II period. The later period is sometimes referred to
as the "Great Moderation." It is a period in which investors would rightly
have judged macroeconomic risk to be substantially lower than in the preceding three decades and lower, of course, than in the dark days of the Great
Depression.

The upper time series in Figure 14.9 plots the 25-quarter moving average
of scaled investment. The horizontal lines indicate its mean value for each
of the same three periods. These are the mirror image of the means of the
volatility of GDP growth rates: as volatility falls the average rate of investment stair-steps upward from 9.9 percentage points in the first period to 12.9
percentage points in the third period. The inverse relationship of investment
and risk is consistent with the predictions of our investment theory.

4. The Relative Price of Capital Goods

If the cost of acquiring new physical capital becomes cheaper, the left-hand
side of equation (14.22) becomes smaller; and to keep the equation balanced, the internal rate of return (ρ) must increase. A higher internal rate of
return of course raises the likelihood that any investment project will exceed
its opportunity cost by a large enough margin to justify the investment. Naturally, the process works the other way as well, so that an increase in the cost
of physical capital *ceteris paribus* would decrease investment at each interest
rate, shifting the investment curve down and the IS curve to the left.

One area of investment in which the costs have fallen rapidly – especially
relative to quality or productivity – is information processing, both computer
hardware and software. The data in Problem 10.6 show that various types of
information-processing capital grew in importance over the last quarter of
the twentieth century – consistent with the lower relative price promoting
investment.

5. The Level of the Capital Stock

Firms acquire additional capital in pursuit of what they believe to be profit
opportunities. They may, of course, be overly optimistic in that they may
believe that demand for their product will be higher than it turns out to be.
They may also fail to take into account the actions of competing firms. For
example, the early 2000s were a boom time in Las Vegas. Various firms built
casinos and hotels – each chasing the same demand. For some period, all
the investment was useful. Eventually, there proved to be too much capital. Though the fall accelerated with the onset of the severe recession in
December of 2007, which brought a fall in absolute demand, it had set in
even earlier. Firms built more hotel rooms than the still high level of visitors

would warrant, and investment in hotels and casinos collapsed. An increase in the level of the capital stock, because it represents the fulfillment of the very needs that investment aims to target, reduces the need for investment. The investment curve shifts downward, and the IS curve shifts to the left.

Figure 14.9 (equivalently, Figure 14.6) provides good evidence of the phenomenon in the aggregate data. Investment invariably rises strongly in the expansion. But notice that in every case, it peaks some time before the NBER business-cycle peak – that is, it is a leading indicator of the recession. A shallow decline then accelerates into a collapse during the recession itself. The initial fall in investment as the result of levels of capital outstripping demand provides a downward stimulus to the multiplier process and may in large measure account for the onset of the recession and for the subsequent collapse in investment. Overinvestment is probably a critical element in what seems to be the inevitable recurrence of recessions, suggesting that they are driven by an internal dynamic and not only by outside forces.

The role of the misalignment of the capital stock with aggregate demand is borne out by the behavior of capacity-utilization rates. Look back at Figure 9.17 (Chapter 9). Capacity-utilization rates are also leading indicators of recessions and follow a pattern closely related to the pattern of investment itself. Higher levels of the capital stock add to productive capacity. In the boom, rising aggregate demand may outstrip additions to capacity, and capacity-utilization rates rise. When investment continues apace even as the growth of aggregate demand levels out, the economy acquires too much capital, and capacity-utilization rates begin to fall – well before the business-cycle peak. They collapse once the recession sets in.

14.5.2 The Accelerator

A recurrent theme of the previous subsection is that investment appears empirically to be related to income in complicated ways. We already learned in Chapter 13 (section 13.1) that changes in investment could cause changes in aggregate demand (income) through the multiplier; but income also seems to be a cause of investment. In principle, *current* GDP should have little to do with current investment. The message of our analysis of the firm's investment decision is that it is *future* expected profits rather than any current fact that largely determine the desirability of acquiring new capital. Yet, the role of current income in the data is unlikely to be accidental.

As we already know, GDP in most countries has tended to grow – with some significant fluctuations, to be sure – around more or less steady long-term trends. Over any period as long as a complete business cycle, growth dominates cyclical fluctuations. On average a large part of any quarterly increase in GDP represents a permanent contribution to growth rather than a transient boomlet soon to be reversed. Profits – as we saw when we calibrated the Cobb-Douglas production function in Chapter 9 (section 9.2) – are empirically a fairly constant share of GDP. Thus, although it is future profits, not current GDP, that should matter to investment, a rising level of GDP is generally associated with rising profits, presaging higher future profits. Any increase in GDP can be permanently maintained only if there is sufficient capital to generate higher output. Higher GDP on balance implies profitable investment. If investment falls short, capital will be inadequate and rising aggregate demand will spill over into imports or be cut off by increasing inflation.

Capital productivity (ϕ) is determined by the interaction of firms' investment decisions and the available production technology. To produce additional output at the same level of productivity, the firm must add capital in proportion to the increase in its output. Turning to the aggregate, recall that in Figure 9.14 we saw that there is no long-term trend in capital productivity for the United States. Any permanent increase in GDP must be supported by a proportionate increase in aggregate capital. How much is needed? Recall the definition of aggregate capital productivity: $\phi = \frac{Y}{K}$. Therefore, for any level of GDP, $K = \frac{Y}{\phi}$ and $\Delta K = \frac{\Delta Y}{\phi}$. Of course $\Delta K = net\ investment$, so

$$net\ I = \frac{\Delta Y}{\phi}. \tag{14.26}$$

Equation (14.26) is called the **INVESTMENT ACCELERATOR**. To see why, recall that on average ϕ for the United States is about 0.4. This implies that production of each unit of GDP requires about 2.5 units of capital ($1/\phi = 1/0.4 = 2.5$). Consequently, the necessary increase in capital must be *faster* than the increase in GDP – it is accelerated.

The investment accelerator interacts with the investment multiplier. Suppose that aggregate demand rises for reasons unrelated to investment. The accelerator implies that investment will rise by a larger amount than GDP itself, although in practice capital takes some time to build, so that the increase in investment will be distributed over some time. Additional investment is, of course, an inflow into the domestic private sector and has a multiplied effect, thus adding even more to GDP. This addition to GDP must itself be met by higher investment and so forth in a self-sustaining process. The investment accelerator can increase the effectiveness of the multiplier process. Of course, it works in reverse as well. If capital is too high relative to the permanent level of GDP, each fall in GDP must be met by disinvestment in excess of the fall. If some part of a fall in GDP is regarded as permanent, the accelerator could exacerbate the fall.

14.5.3 Investment and Fiscal Policy

Investment has a dual effect: it adds through the multiplier process to aggregate demand, and it adds through capital formation to productive capacity. To promote one effect or the other or both, governments not infrequently resort to fiscal policy.

Governments levy taxes on all sorts of income. The corporate income tax, for example, can be regarded as a tax on profits. The denominator (Π_t^e) in equation (14.20) or (14.22) is best regarded as *after-tax* profits. An increase in the corporate income-tax rate essentially reduces the after-tax profits expected over the life of an investment and, consequently, reduces the internal rate of return of the investment. As with anything that reduces the internal rate of return, an increase in corporate income-tax rates reduces investment. Likewise, a cut in corporate income-tax rates raises the internal rate of return and promotes investment.

Governments sometimes try to promote investment through more focused measures. Capital has a finite life. Even long-lived capital such as a bridge or a major building will survive only if continuing investments make good the wear and tear of use and age. Quite reasonably tax authorities often treat depreciation, the wear and tear or maintenance of capital, as a cost that can offset the revenues that the capital generates, reducing the taxable profits.

If a large truck that initially cost $80,000 has a useful life of twenty years, the government might treat one-twentieth of its purchase price ($4,000 per year) as a cost. In order to encourage investment, a government might allow firms to claim *accelerated* depreciation, acting as if the useful life of the truck were only, say, ten years, so that the cost of depreciation were higher (say, $8,000 per year). Such a fictional accounting lowers the taxable profits on the truck – while not lowering actual profits – in the early years, which, of course, are the years that matter most to the present value of the investment. The effect is to raise the internal rate of return of the truck or other capital, promoting investment.

Efforts to promote investment may be even more specific. For example, a government may promote a policy of "green" energy by offering a tax credit – that is, a direct reduction of a firm's tax bill – if the firm invests in wind generators. Social policy is sometimes promoted in a similar manner. A firm may get a tax credit for building factories in an area with high unemployment. From the firm's point of view, tax credits boost after-tax profits, increase the internal rate of return, and therefore promote investment. Critics, of course, object that artificially promoting investment in projects that otherwise would not be profitable is neither wise nor effective. But that is a political argument that can be left to another day.

Whereas a tax credit for a wind generator aims mainly to shape the structure of production, tax policy sometimes aims to promote investment for its effect on aggregate demand. More generalized tax credits are sometimes offered as anti-recessionary policies. Recall that the purchase of consumer durables or houses is essentially investment on the part of consumers that can be analyzed similarly to investment by firms. In the recession of 2007–2009, the U.S. government promoted its "cash-for-clunkers" program that offered a direct credit to purchasers of new cars and a first-time homebuyers' program that offered a direct credit to purchasers of new houses. Both programs were focused on particular industries, and the cash-for-clunkers program had the additional goal of improving the environment (the credit was conditional on replacing a car with low fuel efficiency by one with high fuel efficiency); yet, the main point was to stimulate aggregate demand.

Both programs were successful in the sense that purchases of new cars and houses rose. But they also illustrate another point. We saw that in the case of consumption a transitory stimulus, such as a temporary income-tax cut, would have little effect if consumers followed the permanent-income hypothesis. With investment, the effect is just the opposite. A temporary tax cut, which is, after all, what the tax credits effectively are, may stimulate a larger increase in investment than a permanent tax cut. The reason is simple: use it or lose it. Because the cash-for-clunkers program was temporary, people who might have planned to buy a car in a year or eighteen months found a strong incentive to accelerate their purchase to benefit from the credit. The internal rate of return for a purchase now would be much higher than a year from now. A permanent tax cut also raises the internal rate of return, but it does not favor the present over the future quite so strongly.

The downside to the acceleration of investment owing to a temporary tax credit is just that: temporary. Car sales skyrocketed while the cash-for-clunkers program was in place and collapsed as soon as it was removed. Many of the purchasers would have purchased the cars anyway – if not immediately, over the next year or two. But having purchased cars early, they had no need to purchase them later. A permanent tax cut may have less flash, but may raise aggregate demand over a longer period.

Summary

1. The simple linear consumption function predicts that the average propensity to consume (apc) falls as disposable income rises (1) in the short run and (2) in the long run; that the correlation between consumption and disposable income per capita is strong (3) in the short run and (4) in the long run, and (5) that the consumption function is the same in the short run and the long run. The

data support (1) and (4), but not (2), (3), or (5), suggesting a need for a richer account of the determinants of consumption.

2. Income often arrives irregularly. It may fluctuate period to period in an expected way and consumers may progress from a predictably lower income in youth to a peak income near the end of their working lives to a reduced income in old age. And consumers may receive unexpected windfalls and shortfalls. Life-cycle wealth is the income stream notionally generated from the present discounted value of current and expected future income.

3. The permanent-income hypothesis and its close relative, the life-cycle hypothesis, state that transitory deviations of income (expected and unexpected) are saved in the form of real or financial assets and that consumption is proportioned to permanent income – i.e., to the yield from life-cycle wealth. Expenditure on consumer durables counts as a type of investment or savings under the permanent-income hypothesis.

4. Most versions of the permanent-income consumption function assume that the marginal and average propensities to consume are equal. They predict (1) that because in the long run most changes in income are permanent (transitory changes cancel out), the apc will be constant; (2) that, in the short run because changes in income are more transitory (and do not cancel out), consumption rises less with a transitory than with a permanent increase, reducing the apc; (3) that the long-run correlation between income and consumption (dominated by permanent income) is strong; (4) that the short-run correlation (dominated by transitory income, which is mostly saved) is weak; and (5) that the consumption function is the same in the short run and the long run, although it is very different from the simple, linear consumption function. The permanent-income hypothesis accounts for the data better than the simple, linear consumption function.

5. The permanent-income hypothesis predicts that temporary fiscal policies, which alter only transitory income, will display weak multiplier effects; whereas permanent fiscal policies, which alter permanent income, will display strong multiplier effects.

6. The permanent-income hypothesis requires that consumers be able to borrow and lend at similar interest rates without constraint. Consumers with low income or poor credit may be liquidity (or borrowing) constrained. Equally, the permanent-income hypothesis requires consumers to form expectations of future income. Some consumers may simply follow rules of thumb. Both liquidity-constrained and rule-of-thumb consumers are likely to let their consumption fluctuate more closely with income than the permanent-income hypothesis predicts.

7. When some consumers are liquidity constrained or follow rules of thumb, consumption multipliers are likely to be an average of the small permanent-income multiplier and the larger standard multiplier.

8. Investment may be valued in the same manner as a financial asset by calculating the present value of its future income stream. An investment in a capital project is profitable if its present value exceeds its cost.

9. Like bonds, one can calculate the analogue to the yield to maturity of an investment project – its internal rate of return, defined as that rate of discount that makes the future stream of income generated by a capital project just equal to its cost of acquisition. An investment is worth undertaking if its internal rate of return exceeds the opportunity cost of the funds (e.g., the yield on a bond). More capital projects will be worth undertaking the higher their internal rate of return or the lower the opportunity cost of funds.

10. Risky investments should be evaluated using a measure of opportunity cost that reflects a similar risk premium.

11. The optimal *rate* of investment, the speed with which a capital project is brought online, is determined by the trade-off of lower costs from slower construction against the lower present value from deferring the profits it generates to later dates.

12. The yields on corporate shares (stocks) are also a relevant opportunity cost for investment evaluation. The decision can be seen as a choice between using funds to make a physical investment that adds to a firm's productive capacity and using the same funds to acquire the profits from the existing productive capacity of another firm. More physical investments will be worth undertaking the higher the price of corporate shares (i.e., the lower their yield) and the higher the internal rate of return on the investment.

13. The following reduce the level of aggregate investment: increases in (1) opportunity costs (higher interest rates or lower share prices); (2) risk (uncertainty about profitability); (3) the relative price of capital goods; and (4) the level of the capital stock. Increases in expected future profitability of investment raise the level of aggregate investment.

14. Expected profitability of the capital stock rises *ceteris paribus* with rising income, providing an incentive for investment to be roughly proportioned to the level of GDP. Because the desirable ratio of capital to GDP is greater than one, trend increases in GDP encourage investment of similarly greater proportions than changes in GDP itself – a phenomenon known as the investment accelerator.

15. Reduced taxes or tax credits may boost investment through raising its profitability and internal rate of return. Temporary tax reductions or tax credits may have very large, though temporary, effects, as they provide an incentive to shift investment that would have been made in the future into the current period.

Key Concepts

permanent-income hypothesis
life-cycle hypothesis
life-cycle wealth
permanent income
transitory income

liquidity or borrowing constraint
internal rate of return
holding-period yield
investment accelerator

Problems

Data for this exercise are available on the textbook website under the link for Chapter 14 (appliedmacroeconomics.com). Before starting these exercises, the student should review the relevant portions of the *Guide to Working with Economic Data*, including sections G.1–G.4 and G.12–G.15.

Problem 14.1. Use quarterly data to create a table of the mean values of total consumption (C), personal disposable income (YD^P), personal savings (S^P), and total savings (S). Express each variable as a share of potential GDP. What proportion of personal disposable income is consumed on average? How large is the difference between personal and gross savings? Why are they different?

Problem 14.2. Plot the time series of the variables C, YD^P, S^P, and S as defined in Problem 14.1 and indicate the NBER recession dates with shading. Comment on their cyclical behavior and their relationships to each other.

Problem 14.3. Using quarterly data, calculate the coefficient of variation of detrended personal disposable income (YD^P), consumption (C), consumption of durables (C^D), and consumption of nondurables plus services (C^{NDS}). (Use real data and detrend the original data, not the data expressed as a share of potential GDP as in Problems 14.1 and 14.2. A 25-quarter, centered moving average is one reasonable method of detrending.) Comment on the relative variability of these series. To what degree, if any, are these data supportive of the permanent-income hypothesis or of the idea that some consumers are liquidity- or borrowing-constrained? Explain.

Problem 14.4. In section 14.2.3, we asserted that a new energy source that generates $100 million per year forever to the economy adds $100 million/$rr$ to life-cycle wealth and, therefore, $100 million per year to permanent income. Prove this result by using the definition of life-cycle wealth. (The trick is to sum the infinite series in a manner analogous to computing the multiplier in Chapter 13, equations (13.18)–(13.21).)

Problem 14.5. Investment consists of a variety of different sorts of capital goods. Use quarterly data to express aggregate investment and some of its subcomponent (residential investment, nonresidential structures, equipment [including software], and consumer durables) variables as a percentage of potential GDP. Plot these six series and indicate the NBER recession dates with shading. Comment on their cyclical behavior. Changes in investment might be a cause of changes in GDP and they might be caused by changes in GDP. Describe the mechanisms and processes that might make each of these relationships true and relate them to the typical behavior of investment over the business cycle.

Problem 14.6. Economic theory suggests that investment and real interest rates should be related inversely *ceteris paribus*. Use quarterly data on 1-year and 10-year Treasury bonds and inflation rates calculated from the GDP deflator (current quarter over the same quarter in the previous year) to calculate the real rate of interest. Then, create a scatterplot of each investment variable created in Problem 14.5 (vertical axis) separately against the most appropriate real rate of interest (explain your choice) and add a regression line. In each case, how well do these data conform to the theoretical expectation? Conjecture explanations for why some of the variables do not seem to conform. And conjecture what might distinguish those variables that do from those that do not conform. (The evidence developed in Problem 14.5 and Figure 14.6 may bear on your answer.)

Problem 14.7. Consider the example of a present-value calculation in equation (14.19) in which a car that costs the rental car company $15,000 is expected to earn $3,000 per year for two years and to be sold at the end of two years for $12,000. When the relevant market interest rate is 5 percent, its present value is $16,463. Consider this to be the base case. Consider the following variations from the base case – compute the present value and state whether the rental car company should invest in the car.

(a) All else as in the base case except that the car is expected to earn only $2,000 per year;

(b) All else as in the base case except that the car is expected to be sold for $11,000 at the end of two years;

(c) All else as in the base case, except that the initial purchase price of the car is $16,000.

Problem 14.8. Use the same information as the base case in Problem 14.7 to show that the internal rate of return is 10.5 percent (show your work).

Problem 14.9. Use the information in Problem 14.7 to calculate the internal rate of return for the base case and each of the cases (a)–(c). [Excel hint: use the function *IRR*, enter the initial cost in the top cell of a column as a negative number and enter *all* the income flows for each succeeding year in successive lower cells (i.e., the rental income and the scrap value that accrue in the same year belong in the same cell).] If the market interest rate is 5 percent, in which cases will the rental car company invest in the car? How do your answers compare to your answers in Problem 14.8? How does your answer change if market interest rates rise to 8 percent?

Problem 14.10. What general lessons can you draw about investment based on the results in Problems 14.7–14.9?

Problem 14.11. A power company has to decide whether to build a nuclear reactor. It estimates that it will take ten years to build at a cost of $250 million per year; it will earn $300 million per year net of operating costs for the thirty years following its completion; and it will cost $100 million to decommission in the year following those thirty. Use either present-value or internal-rate-of-return analysis to determine whether or not the company should invest in the reactor, when relevant market interest rates are 5 percent. Or 8 percent. What considerations relevant to the investment decision may have been left out of consideration? [Excel hint: see Problem 14.9 for a hint on using the *IRR* function to calculate internal rates of return. For present-value calculations use the *NPV* function: arrange data in a single column with negative entries for costs and positive entries for earnings, one cell for each year; the interest rate should be entered as a natural number (e.g., 3 percent is entered as 0.03).]

Problem 14.12. When fully operational, a semiconductor factory is expected to generate $30 million in net revenue per year for fifteen years. There is no cost or scrap value in winding up the plant at the end of its useful life. The plant can be built in one year at a cost of $250 million; in two years at a cost of $100 million per year; or in three years at a cost of $65 million per year. Should the company invest in this plant when interest rates are 6 percent? When interest rates are 9 percent? In each case, over how many years? How, if at all, would your answer change if the company required a premium on its return to investment of 5 percent over the market rate of interest to cover risk? (See the Excel hints in Problems 14.9 and 14.11.)

Problem 14.13. Use your knowledge of the factors that govern aggregate investment to discuss the likely effects of the following on both aggregate investment and aggregate demand (note that in some cases there may be effects working in opposite directions):
(a) a war in an oil-producing region of the Middle East;
(b) a shortage of steel resulting in a large increase in its price on international markets;
(c) a decrease in the taxes on corporate profits;
(d) a prolonged period of low investment during a deep recession;
(e) controls on the prices at which firms can sell their products.

Problem 14.14. In Chapter 13, you saw how government spending or tax cuts might have a multiplied effect on aggregate demand. Governments sometimes seek to "prime the pump" – in other words, to use a small stimulus to generate response from the private sector greater than the government expenditure multiplier itself would warrant. Use your knowledge of the multiplier and the investment accelerator to explain how priming the pump might work. Consider the role of "animal spirits" in this process. How might a related process explain especially deep recessions?

Part VII

Macroeconomic Dynamics

15

The Dynamics of Output, Unemployment, and Inflation

We judge the economy – as we judge many areas of life – as much by how it is changing as by its current state. We want to know whether GDP, unemployment, and inflation are rising or falling, not just whether they are high or low. In this chapter we examine what determines whether the key variables – unemployment, output, and inflation – are rising or falling at different stages of the business cycle. In earlier chapters, we examined aggregate demand and supply separately. Here we consider how they work together to change output, unemployment, and inflation.

15.1 The Interaction of Aggregate Supply and Aggregate Demand

An easy way to distinguish supply factors from demand factors starts with the definition of **output scaled by POTENTIAL OUTPUT (SCALED OUTPUT)** developed in Chapter 9 (section 9.5.2): $\widetilde{Y} = \frac{Y}{Y^{pot}}$. The theory of growth – that is, the theory of aggregate supply in the long run – is really a theory of the development of potential output. The theory of aggregate demand is a theory of output relative to potential. A *pure aggregate-supply factor* can therefore be thought of as one that changes potential output while holding scaled output ($\widetilde{Y}$) constant. A *pure aggregate-demand factor* can be thought of as one that changes scaled output while holding potential output constant.

Although actual economic factors often mix supply and demand aspects, let us first look at the pure cases.

15.1.1 Supply Fluctuations

Adjustments to Supply Factors When Wages Are Flexible

An economy at full employment (i.e., with a clearing labor market) is not necessarily at the peak of the business cycle. Growth can continue, but only if the economy can use more capital or labor or use it more effectively because of technological improvement. Any of these sources of growth might be called **SUPPLY FACTORS**.

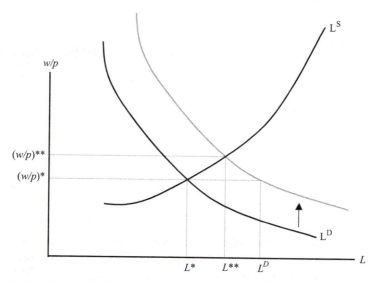

Figure 15.1. The Effect of a Favorable Shift in Aggregate Supply on the Labor Market. A favorable shift in aggregate supply (an upward shift of the labor-production function) raises the marginal product of labor and shifts the labor-demand curve upward. At the original real wage $(w/p)^*$, the demand for labor exceeds the supply. If wages are flexible, firms compete to attract labor through higher market-wage rates, raising the real wage to $(w/p)^{*\prime}$ at which point labor supply again equals labor demand and the size of the labor force has increased from L^* to L^{**}.

Starting from full employment, a favorable movement of supply factors other than labor (i.e., an increase in the capital stock or a technological improvement) would shift the production function and the labor-demand curve upward. Figure 15.1 shows just the shift in the labor-demand curve. The level of full employment increases from L^* to L^{**}. At the original real wage $(w/p)^*$, labor demand (L^D) exceeds labor supply. Firms must raise wages to $(w/p)^{**}$ to attract more workers. Higher labor or greater labor productivity, of course, translates into higher real GDP – the expansion continues.

A less likely scenario in the United States, but one not historically unknown, is a fall in labor supply.[1] The analysis of this case, in which the labor-supply curve shifts inward, is taken up in Problem 15.1.

Adjustments to Supply Factors When Wages Are Inflexible

If labor markets were flexible and always cleared (as we assumed in Chapter 11, section 11.3), then the analysis of an unfavorable change in supply factors

---

[1] Because of death and emigration, the population of Ireland, which was about 8.4 million at the beginning of the Potato Famine in 1844, fell to 6.6 million by 1851. Emigration and low birthrates continued into the twentieth century, so that at independence from Great Britain in 1921, its population was about half of its level before the famine. Similarly, the outbreak of bubonic plague in the fourteenth century known as the "Black Death" reduced the population of Europe by about one-third over the five years from 1347 to 1352.

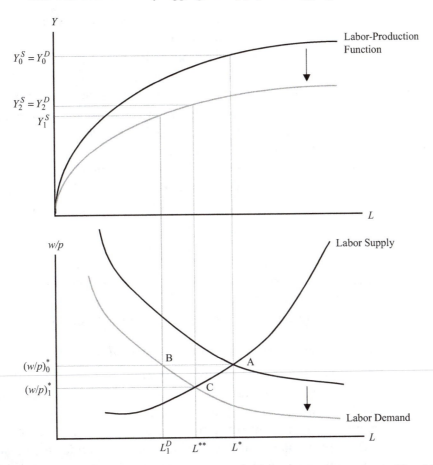

Figure 15.2. An Unfavorable Shift in Aggregate Supply. An unfavorable shift in aggregate supply is shown as the downward shift of the labor-production function, resulting in the fall of the marginal product of labor and the downward shift of the labor-demand curve. At the original real wage $(w/p)_0^*$, labor supply exceeds labor demand. If wages are flexible, the real wage will fall to reestablish equilibrium at point C. If wages are not flexible, then prices must rise (as aggregate demand (Y_0^D) exceeds aggregate supply $(Y_1^S)_0$ until the real wage falls to $(w/p)_1^*$, again reestablishing equilibrium at point C, where there is full employment, but a smaller labor force and less output than at the original equilibrium (point A).

would just be the reverse of a favorable one. If nominal wages do not fall rapidly to clear markets (see Chapter 12, section 12.3.1), then the situation is more complicated.

It is helpful to distinguish clearly between aggregate demand (the expenditure side of GDP), indicated by a superscript D, and aggregate supply (the production side of GDP), indicated by a superscript S. In Figure 15.2 at full employment at point A with a real wage $(w/p)_0^*$ and employment (L^*), aggregate demand (Y_0^D) equals aggregate supply (Y_0^S). A negative supply shock shifts the production function and the labor-demand curve downward. To maintain full employment, the real wage would have to fall. If it remains at $(w/p)_0^*$, then labor demand falls to L_1^D, while labor supply remains at L^*. Firms lay off workers and the unemployment rate increases.

If nominal wages are not sufficiently flexible, then the real wage may be lowered and equilibrium restored by a relative increase in prices: price inflation must exceed wage inflation until the new full employment real wage $(w/p)_1^*$ is established. What makes prices rise?

The lower panel shows that the fall in the labor-demand curve at the original wage would generate labor demand at point B of L_1^D, which (in the upper panel) would produce aggregate supply of Y_1^S. At this level, aggregate demand exceeds aggregate supply ($Y_0^D > Y_1^S$). In such circumstances firms raise their prices – in this case, faster than the rate of wage inflation – which lowers the real wage. Increasing prices and falling employment reduce labor income and, therefore, real aggregate demand. The adjustment is complete when aggregate demand and supply are equal once again at ($Y_2^D = Y_2^S$), corresponding to the new equilibrium in the labor market at point C(L^{**}).

Technological Progress and Capital Obsolescence

When we think of capital or technology generically, it is hard to think of circumstances in which they would fall and generate a decline in output and rising prices. Recall, however, that *capital* is a portmanteau term that includes every nonlabor input into the production process. A large change in relative prices of particular factors of production may render the existing mix of physical inputs inappropriate and encourage firms to economize on them.

In earlier chapters we regarded capital and labor as **SUBSTITUTES IN PRODUCTION** – that is, *if the price of one of them rose, its demand would fall, and the demand for the other one would rise.* This is almost certainly true in the long run. But in the short run, labor and capital are likely to be **COMPLEMENTS IN PRODUCTION** – that is, *if the price of one of them rose, its demand would fall, and the demand for the other one would also fall.* When inputs are complements in production, we can look on a firm's retrenchment in the face of higher input prices as *either* an effective reduction in its capital *or* as a reduction in its productivity. Either way, the labor production function shifts downward.

Similarly, technological innovations or shifts in demand may render particular capital inputs obsolete. The introduction of audio compact discs (CDs) virtually eliminated the value of machinery specialized in making long-playing, vinyl records (LPs). The technological innovation reduced the effective capital stock. When the physical instruments of production remain unchanged, economic statistics do not necessarily reflect such economic losses to capital accurately. If capital is measured as still available, even though it is obsolete, measured capital productivity will fall. Either way, the labor-production function shifts downward.

Cost-Push Inflation

The price inflation that results from firms trying to adjust to increases in their underlying costs owing to shifting supply factors is sometimes called COST-PUSH INFLATION. Costs, seen as originating outside the firms, are passed through and push prices upward from below. Cost-push inflation is usually considered a key element in the so-called **stagflation** (*stag*nation + in*flation*) of the 1970s: both unemployment and inflation were high, and the economy grew slowly even when it was not actually in recession.

Macroeconomists and economic historians offer a variety of explanations for stagflation. One of the most popular points to the large, unexpected increases in the prices of imported commodities in the early 1970s, and in oil prices after late 1973, as having initiated a series of negative **supply shocks** – that is, *unfavorable (and unexpected) shifts in supply factors*. This explanation is likely to be a significant part of the truth. Still, we should also recognize that demand factors might have been involved as well. The United States – and, indeed, most of the developed world – is a net importer of oil. A sudden increase in oil prices also raises import expenditure so that net exports decline – a fall in aggregate demand.

15.1.2 Demand Fluctuations

To isolate pure supply factors, we assumed that either wages or prices or both move in such a way that aggregate demand was always adjusted to keep it equal to a shifting aggregate supply that was itself always equal to potential output. To isolate pure **DEMAND FACTORS**, we assume that potential output is constant, so that changes in aggregate demand open up a gap between expenditure plans and output plans. In that sense, aggregate demand may be smaller or larger than (planned) aggregate supply or potential output.

When Aggregate Demand Falls Short of Aggregate Supply

When we turn to aggregate-demand fluctuations, we must work backward through the diagrams. We start with the level of aggregate demand and ask, given the technology, how much labor would it take to produce the required output? Although potential output is unaffected, the actual output supplied, in this case, adjusts to aggregate demand.

In Figure 15.3, aggregate demand is initially at Y^{D*}. At this level, the labor market clears at point A with a real wage $(w/p)^*$ and employment L^*. A reduction in demand to, say, Y_1^D reduces the demand for labor to L_1^D.

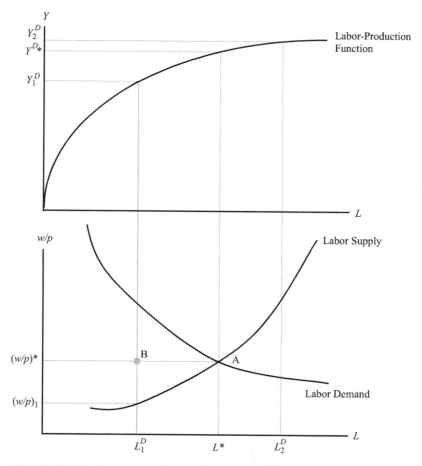

Figure 15.3. Shifts in Aggregate Demand. A reduction in aggregate demand to Y_1^D reduces the demand for labor-generating unemployment at the going wage (point B). Workers would be willing to supply labor to meet labor demand (L_1^D) at a wage below market clearing $(w/p)_1$, but a fall in the real wage to this level will not restore full employment unless aggregate demand also increases. An increase in aggregate demand to Y_2^D is infeasible because workers require a higher real wage than firms can profitably pay to meet demand for labor (L_2^D). Firms that offer higher money wages to attract workers and pass on the prices to consumers ultimately increase the general price level and reduce real aggregate demand back to its market-clearing level.

If the wage does not adjust, the fall in aggregate demand creates involuntary unemployment at point B. Firms are off their labor-demand curves, and workers are off their labor-supply curves. That this situation could persist is, of course, the puzzle of unemployment discussed in Chapter 12 (section 12.3.1).

At the lower level of aggregate demand (Y_1^D), firms could apparently increase their profits by reducing the real wage to $(w/p)_1^*$. Yet such an action would not, in itself, reestablish full employment. Only an increase in aggregate demand will increase employment.

When Aggregate Demand Exceeds Aggregate Supply

Any attempt to increase aggregate demand above the full employment point is infeasible. Look again at Figure 15.3. At a higher level of aggregate demand, Y_2^D, firms wish to employ a larger number of workers (L_2^D) than want to work at the market-clearing wage. Because slavery is illegal, they can attract additional workers only by bidding up the money wage.

But, of course, because workers are already being paid their marginal products, profit-maximizing firms would have to pass on the additional costs in the form of higher prices for their output, which would hold down the product-real wage. The net result of firms across the economy raising their product prices would be an increase in the general price level, reducing the consumption-real wage and, in general, the purchasing power of any given level of nominal income. Real aggregate demand must fall back to the full employment point.

This is an extremely important result:

- *Increases in aggregate demand cannot push the economy beyond the point of full employment; instead they drive up the general price level.*

Inflation that results from increases in aggregate demand beyond the levels compatible with full employment is sometimes referred to as **DEMAND-PULL INFLATION**: the forces of demand, standing above firms, are seen as pulling prices upward.

Distinguishing the Types of Inflation

Cost-push and demand-pull inflation are fundamentally different. Cost-push inflation arises because prices must rise *relative* to wages in order to adjust to a change in the underlying supply conditions. The inflation that results is temporary and lasts only long enough to move the price level sufficiently to obtain the new market-clearing real-wage rate.

In contrast, demand-pull inflation results from aggregate demand exceeding potential output. All prices (including wage rates) must rise in order to reduce expenditures to a level at which aggregate demand and supply are again compatible.

15.2 Unemployment and Output Fluctuations

So far we have focused on snapshots of the economy in order to isolate pure supply and demand factors. In reality, these factors are generally mixed together, and we would like to understand how they interact. Economic growth is not a smooth process. Recessions and accompanying increases in unemployment punctuate a generally upward trend. We now turn to trying to understand the *process* behind these fluctuations – to construct a moving picture rather than a snapshot. We begin with unemployment: what determines the fluctuations of unemployment over time?

15.2.1 What Changes the Unemployment Rate?

Start with the definition of the unemployment rate (see Chapter 9, section 9.4.3, and Chapter 12, section 12.2.2). Writing LF for the *labor force* as a function of time and L for *the number of workers actually employed*, the unemployment rate at a particular time (t) is

$$U_t = \frac{LF_t - L_t}{LF_t} = 1 - \frac{L_t}{LF_t} = 1 - EMP_t. \tag{15.1}$$

The *employment rate, EMP* ($= L/LF$), in the right-hand term is the complement of the unemployment rate (i.e., $U + EMP = 1$ by definition).

How does the unemployment rate change through time? The growth rate of the employment rate is $\widehat{EMP} = \hat{L} - \widehat{LF}$. As is intuitively obvious, the employment rate increases and, therefore, the unemployment rate decreases when employment grows faster than the labor force, and *vice versa*. These relationships follow immediately from the definition of unemployment, but do not explain much economically. We need to dig deeper.

The first step is to make the previous observations more precise. Rewrite equation (15.1) as

$$1 - U_t = \frac{L_t}{LF_t}. \tag{15.1'}$$

Expressed in growth rates, equation (15.1') becomes

$$\widehat{(1 - U)} \approx \frac{\Delta(1 - U_t)}{1 - U_t} = \hat{L} - \widehat{LF}.$$

Notice that because 1 is a constant in the numerator, the middle term can be rewritten as $-\Delta U_t$. Substituting in this expression and multiplying the middle and right-hand side by $-(1 - U_t)$ gives

$$\Delta U_t \approx (1 - U_t)(\widehat{LF} - \hat{L}). \tag{15.2}$$

The second term in parentheses on the right-hand side of this equation is just the difference in the growth rates of the labor force and employment. It tells us what we already knew: the unemployment rises when the labor force grows more quickly than employment and falls when employment grows more quickly than the labor force. The employment rate $(1 - U_t)$ acts as a scaling factor that indicates the base on which the growth rates operate.

It varies across the business cycle, although usually within a relatively narrow range. (The post-World War II maximum employment rate for the United States was 97.5 percent and the minimum was 89.2 percent, although in only three recessions did the employment rate fall below 92 percent.)

15.2.2 The Modified Balanced Growth Path

Although equation (15.2) is more precise, it still adds little to what we already knew. The next step is to explain the two growth rates. Recall that labor productivity was defined in Chapter 9 (section 9.3.1) as $\theta = Y/L$, so that $\hat{\theta} = \hat{Y} - \hat{L}$ or $\hat{L} = \hat{Y} - \hat{\theta}$. The participation rate was defined in Chapter 12 (section 12.2.2) as $PR = LF/POP$, where POP is the working-age population, so that $\widehat{PR} = \widehat{LF} - \widehat{POP}$ or $\widehat{LF} = \widehat{PR} + \widehat{POP}$. Substituting these facts into equation (15.2) gives

$$\Delta U_t \approx (1 - U_t)(\widehat{PR}_t + \widehat{POP}_t - \hat{Y}_t + \hat{\theta}_t)$$
$$= (U_t - 1)[\hat{Y}_t - (\widehat{PR}_t + \widehat{POP}_t + \hat{\theta}_t)]. \tag{15.3}$$

The far right-hand expression is derived from the middle expression by rearrangement and by multiplying both middle terms by -1.

It is helpful to define $\hat{Y}^* \equiv \widehat{PR} + \widehat{POP} + \hat{\theta}$. Then equation (15.3) can be rewritten as

$$\Delta U_t \approx (U_t - 1)(\hat{Y}_t - \hat{Y}_t^*). \tag{15.3'}$$

Notice that the term $U_t - 1$ is negative, because U_t must lie between zero and one.

Equation (15.3'), then, says that there is a critical rate of growth: $\hat{Y}_t^*$. Whenever the growth rate of the economy is above this rate, unemployment falls; whenever it is below this rate, unemployment rises. What is more, we know what determines the critical rate. It is the sum of the growth rates of participation, population, and labor productivity. The faster any one of these three is growing, the higher the critical rate.

Recall from Chapter 10 (section 10.4.1) that along a balanced growth path $\hat{Y} = n + \hat{\theta}$, where n is the rate of growth of population. The participation rate cannot grow indefinitely, because, by definition, it cannot exceed 100 percent; in practice, it cannot even come close to 100 percent. So, in the long run, the rate of growth of the labor force is equal to the rate of growth of population ($\widehat{LF} = \widehat{POP} = n$). The long-run equality notwithstanding, the participation rate may change considerably over the business cycle or, as has been true over the past sixty years, even over longer periods. The critical rate of growth $\hat{Y}_t^*$ may therefore be seen as a **MODIFIED BALANCED RATE OF**

GROWTH: *the growth rate sustainable along a balanced growth path modified for a changing participation rate.*

The modified balanced rate of growth carries both a promise and a challenge. Imagine that the economy is at full employment – a low, but nonzero, measured rate of unemployment. If GDP grew at exactly $\hat{Y}_t^*$, then the unemployment rate would remain constant at that full-employment rate. (Even if the unemployment rate is higher, if GDP grows at $\hat{Y}_t^*$, the unemployment rate remains constant.) The *modified* balanced rate of growth acts as a kind of speed limit for the economy (in just the same way as we observed in Chapter 10 (section 10.4.1) that the balanced growth path acted as a speed limit).

To raise that speed limit, one of the elements that make up $\hat{Y}_t^*$ (i.e., one of the growth rates of the participation rate, population, or labor productivity) must increase. The promise is that, if one of these elements – especially labor productivity – can be increased, the economy can sustain higher rates of growth of GDP (and, as we have seen in Chapter 10 (section 10.4), higher rates of growth of GDP *per capita*). The challenge is that the higher modified balanced growth path raises the bar. When it was lower, a lower rate of growth would have been enough to keep the unemployment rate low. When it is higher, the same lower rate of growth would be associated with rising unemployment.

15.2.3 Okun's Law

Equation (15.3′) is written as an approximation. If the time interval over which we measure the change in unemployment were to shrink to an instant, then the equation would be exact. Each of the substitutions made to convert equation (15.2) into (15.3) are based on the definitions (rather than fallible estimates) and are exact for instantaneous change. Real data, however, are not sampled instantaneously but, in this case, at monthly, quarterly, or annual intervals.

Even if the average levels of $\widehat{PR}$, $\widehat{POP}$, and $\hat{\theta}$ were constant, which they are not over long periods of time, their cyclical variation would ensure that equation (15.3′) did not fit exactly. For example, labor productivity tends to decline in recessions (see Chapter 9, Problem 9.7). The fall in labor productivity (a negative $\hat{\theta}$) would lower $\hat{Y}_t^*$. All other things equal, a lower $\hat{Y}_t^*$ would reduce the rise in the unemployment rate associated with the recession.

Over time, as the average levels of the elements of $\hat{Y}_t^*$ change, so will its value. For example, the growth in the participation rate, which had been substantial in the United States after the mid-1960s, seems recently to have slowed, which should depress $\hat{Y}_t^*$. Similarly, the growth of labor productivity, which had slowed in the 1960s, picked up substantially after 1995, which should raise $\hat{Y}_t^*$.

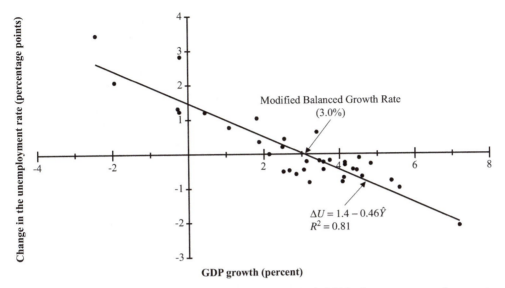

Figure 15.4. Okun's Law for the United States, 1974–2009. *Source:* unemployment, Bureau of Labor Statistics; GDP, Bureau of Economic Analysis; and author's calculations.

Using annual data for the United States, we can form a direct estimate of $\hat{Y}^*$ from data on the growth rate of real GDP and the change in the unemployment rate. (The omitted time subscript indicates that we estimate the *average* value rather than the period-specific value.) Figure 15.4 is a scatterplot of these data for the period 1974 to 2009. The period is chosen to reflect the fact that long-term GDP growth appeared to slow down significantly after the first oil crisis beginning in late 1973.

The regression line in Figure 15.4 can be described by an equation with the general form:

$$\Delta U_t = a + b\hat{Y}_t + error_t.$$

Multiplying and dividing the first two terms on the right-hand side by b yields

$$\Delta U_t = b(\hat{Y}_t + a/b) + error_t. \tag{15.4}$$

Because the slope of the regression line is negative, b is also negative, while a is positive.

Equation (15.4) can be rewritten

$$\Delta U_t = -\gamma(\hat{Y}_t - \hat{Y}^*) + error_t, \tag{15.4'}.$$

where $\gamma = -b$ and $\hat{Y}^* = -a/b$. An empirical relationship in this form is known as **OKUN'S LAW**, named for Arthur Okun (1928–1980) who developed the analysis while serving on President Kennedy's Council of Economic Advisers. $\hat{Y}^*$, of course, measures the modified balanced rate of growth. The parameter γ measures how quickly deviations between the

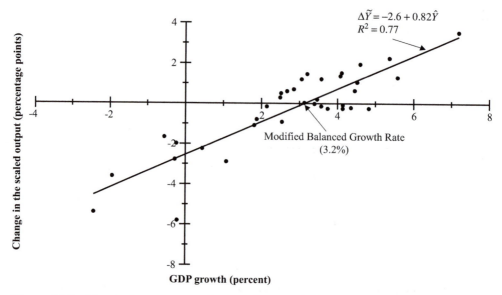

Figure 15.5. Okun's Law for the United States, 1974–2009 (using scaled output). *Source:* GDP growth, Bureau of Economic Analysis; scaled output, Board of Governors of the Federal Reserve System and Bureau of Labor Statistics; and author's calculations.

actual rate of growth and $\hat{Y}^*$ are translated into changes in unemployment rates.

The actual estimated equation for the regression line in Figure 15.5 is $\Delta U_t = 1.4 - 0.46\hat{Y}_t + error_t$, so that the parameters can be calculated: $\gamma = 0.46$ and $\hat{Y}^* = -\frac{1.4}{-0.46} = 3.0$ percent per year. Okun's law for 1974–2009 is then

$$\Delta U_t = -0.46(\hat{Y}_t - 3.0) + error_t. \tag{15.5}$$

Notice that when $\hat{Y}_t = \hat{Y}^*$, $\Delta U_t = 0$. Therefore, we can read $\hat{Y}^*$ directly from Figure 15.4: it is the point at which the regression line crosses the horizontal axis.

To give an example, imagine that in a recession real GDP growth falls 0.5 percent over a 1-year period. Equation (15.5) predicts that the rate of unemployment will rise: $\Delta U_t = -0.46(-0.5 - 3.0) = -0.46(-3.5) = 1.6$ percentage points over the course of that year.

A more positive example: if in the middle of an expansion, real GDP grows at a rate of 4.5 percent per year, equation (15.5) predicts that the rate of unemployment will fall: $\Delta U_t = -0.46(4.5 - 3.0) = -0.46(1.5) = -0.7$ percentage points over a year.

Okun's law clarifies the phenomenon of **growth recessions** in which the economy grows, so that technically there is no official recession, but slowly enough that unemployment rises. Any GDP growth rate greater than zero but less than $\hat{Y}^*$ results in a rising unemployment rate, even though there is no recession.

Okun's law is an empirical relationship that does not explain every aspect of changing unemployment. That is why there is an error term. It is, nevertheless, one of the most robust empirical relationships in macroeconomics. With an $R^2 = 0.81$ in equation (15.5), changes in the growth rate of real GDP account for 81 percent of the variance of changes in the unemployment rate. This corresponds to a correlation between the two time series of 0.90 – which is high.

15.2.4 The Dynamics of Resource Utilization

The unemployment rate is a measure of the degree of utilization of the labor force. Output scaled by potential output ($\tilde{Y}$) provides a more general measure of resource utilization in the economy. Just as with unemployment, we can ask what determines the changes in scaled output. The analysis is based on Figure 15.5.

The figure plots the change in scaled output against the growth rate of real GDP. In contrast to the case of unemployment (Figure 15.4), the regression line is upward sloping. Scaled output is procyclical; unemployment is countercyclical. Good economic times are associated with high scaled output and low unemployment.

Translated into the form of Okun's law, the equation for the regression line in Figure 15.5 is

$$\Delta \tilde{Y}_t = 0.82(\hat{Y}_t - 3.2). \tag{15.6}$$

The modified natural-growth rate is $\hat{Y}_t^* = 3.2 \ (= 2.6/0.82)$ per year. This estimate for $\hat{Y}_t^*$ is only a little higher than the estimate formed using the usual approach to Okun's law, which equation (15.5) gave as 3.0 percent per year. The R^2 for the regression is 0.77, which is only slightly lower than the $R^2 = 0.81$ for equation (15.5). Either estimate will make little difference to our understanding of the potential of the economy for growth in the medium term.

15.3 Inflation and Unemployment

Okun's law is useful because it gives us some idea about how aggregate demand and supply interact to determine changes in the rates of unemployment or resource utilization. Unfortunately, it does not tell us everything we might want to know about the dynamics of macroeconomic aggregates. Because it focuses on changes, it does not tell us what level of unemployment we might expect. For that we need a starting place. If we know the level, we can predict how demand will change it. If the growth rate of aggregate demand ($\hat{Y}$) is equal to the growth rate of aggregate supply (i.e., to the modified balanced growth path, $\hat{Y}^*$), the rates of unemployment and resource utilization remain constant – whatever their levels. We would also like to know what determines the levels. Equally, Okun's law focuses on the *real* economy. And we would like to know what determines *nominal* quantities, such as the rate of inflation. Thinking about how prices get set in aggregate sheds light on both the level of unemployment and the determination of the rate of inflation.

15.3.1 Pricing Behavior

As is often the case, the behavior of individual firms provides some insight into aggregate outcomes. We know from microeconomics (discussed in Chapter 9, section 9.1.2) that, theoretically, a perfectly competitive, profit-maximizing firm takes the price at which it can sell its output, and the wages and other prices it must pay for its inputs, as given. Competition ensures that the price it can charge will just cover its costs, including normal profits, and will be the same as that charged by its competitors.

From the point of view of the buyer of its output, the important thing is not the nominal price of the output but the real price – that is, the price of the good relative to the price of other goods. Call p_j the price of a particular good j. The price of other goods can be summarized in a price index (call it p), so that the real price or relative price of good j can be expressed as p_j/p. If demand and supply conditions are constant, then the real price will itself be constant. An increase in demand or a decrease in supply (e.g., because of rising costs of materials or other factors of production) will raise the real price of the good.

Although perfect competition is a good approximation for many purposes – and we have relied heavily on it in discussions of growth and labor markets in previous chapters – it is rare to find strict perfect competition in actual economies. In reality, goods are not exactly alike: an increase in the price of a Honda sedan does not drive every customer to buy a Nissan instead – as it should if the market were perfectly competitive. Nor is there an auction market in which Honda and Nissan can observe the going price for sedans before they make their supply decisions.

In reality, many actual markets are **imperfectly competitive**. Car companies – and producers of most goods – must choose both the price at which they sell their goods and the amounts they wish to supply at that price. This does not mean that firms have a free hand. What a firm charges is clearly limited by demand. And it is limited by its competitors. I may prefer a Honda, but if Honda charges too high a price, I will choose the Nissan instead, despite the fact that I do not like its features quite so much.

Imperfect competition is difficult to analyze – and usually best left to a course in microeconomics. The rules of perfect competition help us to analyze actual economies in many cases, because the competition between firms is great enough that their supply decisions are close to what perfect competition suggests. Nevertheless, strict application of the rules of perfect competition is sometimes misleading. In particular, to understand aggregate inflation, it is best to think of firms as choosing their own prices.

The question, then, is how to set the price. When supply and demand conditions remain unchanged, firms should set a constant real price (p_j/p). Of course, if there is general price inflation, then the price of the particular good would have to rise at the rate of inflation in order to keep the real price constant. The growth rate of the real price is $\hat{p}_j - \hat{p}$; it is zero when $\hat{p}_j = \hat{p}$.

Decisions in economics are necessarily forward-looking. A firm may, for instance, set its prices at monthly, quarterly, or even annual intervals. To do so, it must anticipate how general prices will change over the month, quarter, or year – that is, it needs to form an expectation about future prices and needs to change its own price in line with expected inflation ($\hat{p}^e$), not with past inflation. If supply and demand conditions remain unchanged, then the firm should follow the rule: $\hat{p}_{j,t} = {}_{t-1}\hat{p}_t^e$. This rule says that a firm at the end of the previous period ($t-1$) forms an expectation of what general price inflation will be during the current period (t), and adjusts the price of its own good to inflate at the same rate.[2] (Of course, this is an approximation to firm behavior, because most firms will not find it convenient to change prices continuously, but may in fact select a single price such that the average price over the period grows at the appropriate rate.)

Demand and supply conditions are unlikely to be constant. If demand increases during the period, a firm would want to raise its real price. To do so, the price of its good must rise more quickly than general price inflation. Similarly, if real factor prices rise or if conditions of production become unfavorable (e.g., a drought would reduce agricultural productivity), then a firm would also want to raise its real price. This suggests that the price-setting rule should be modified to account for these factors:

$$\hat{p}_{j,t} = {}_{t-1}\hat{p}_t^e + f(\textit{demand factors}) + g(\textit{supply factors}). \qquad (15.7)$$

The two functions $f(.)$ and $g(.)$ determine how demand and supply factors affect the pricing decision. For the time being, we let them remain indefinite, general functions.

---

[2] The expectation could equally be thought of as being formed at the very beginning of a period with the decision governing the changes of prices during the period.

15.3.2 The Phillips Curve

Equation (15.7) applies to a single firm. If we average over all firms, the variable on the left-hand side will become the general rate of inflation $\hat{p}_t$. Demand and supply factors that are unique to particular firms or products will tend to average out. What will be left are factors that affect the economy as a whole. The result of averaging can be written:

$$\hat{p}_t = {}_{t-1}\hat{p}_t^e + f(\text{aggregate-demand factors}) + g(\text{aggregate-supply factors}).$$
$$(15.8)$$

The expected inflation term in equation (15.7) was the individual firm's expectation of general price inflation. In equation (15.8) it is the average expectation of general price inflation for all firms. The function $f(.)$, in the terminology of section 15.1, captures demand-pull inflation, while the function $g(.)$ captures cost-push inflation.

Equation (15.8) is known to economists as the **EXPECTATIONS-AUG-MENTED PHILLIPS CURVE** (or just the **PHILLIPS CURVE** for short). It is named for the New Zealand economist A. W. H. Phillips (1914–1975), who in 1958 published an important empirical study of the relationship of wage inflation to the unemployment rate in the United Kingdom from which other versions of the Phillips curve have descended.

To apply the Phillips curve to actual data requires definite measures for the aggregate-demand and aggregate-supply factors and definite functional forms for $f(.)$ and $g(.)$. Since the first Phillips curve in 1958, the usual measure of aggregate demand has been the rate of unemployment. We know that unemployment is a strongly countercyclical variable – high in recessions, when we expect demand to be low, and low in expansions when we expect demand to be high. Other measures of demand could equally well be used, as we shall see in the next section.

On the assumption that the relationship between demand and unemployment is linear, we can write

$$f(\text{aggregate demand}) = a + bU.$$

The coefficient b is assumed to be negative, because demand and unemployment are inversely related. Substituting into equation (15.8) yields

$$\hat{p}_t = {}_{t-1}\hat{p}_t^e + a + bU_t + g(\text{aggregate supply}_t). \qquad (15.8')$$

15.3.3 The Natural Rate of Unemployment and NAIRU

The Concept of the Natural Rate

Assume for the moment that aggregate-supply factors can be ignored. What rate of unemployment would make *actual* inflation $\hat{p}_t$ equal to *expected* inflation $_{t-1}\hat{p}_t^e$? That is, what rate of unemployment would leave firms satisfied that their pricing strategies were correct? Expressed algebraically, the question is when does

$$\hat{p}_t - {}_{t-1}\hat{p}_t^e = a + bU_t = 0?$$

Indicate the solution by U_t^*, so that

$$U_t^* = -a/b.$$

U_t^* is known as the **NATURAL RATE OF UNEMPLOYMENT** and can be defined as *that rate of unemployment that, if maintained, would result in an actual rate of inflation equal to the average expected rate of inflation.*

As long as a and b remain constant, U_t^* will itself remain constant and can be indicated by U^* without a time subscript. The two coefficients are not necessarily constant. The function $f(.)$ represents the relationship between aggregate-demand factors and the relative pricing decisions of firms, which may depend on the detailed structure of the production process. The relationship between the unemployment rate and aggregate demand may itself depend on the organization of labor markets. Changes in either sets of relationships may result in changes in a and b and, therefore, in changes in the natural rate of unemployment. We shall consider the variability of the natural rate further in a later subsection. For now we assume that it is constant.

Using the natural rate of unemployment, the Phillips curve (equation (15.8′) can be rewritten

$$\hat{p}_t - {}_{t-1}\hat{p}_t^e = -\beta(U_t - U^*) + g(\textit{aggregate-supply factors}_t), \quad (15.9)$$

where β (the lowercase Greek letter "beta") $= -b$. (β is assumed to be positive, and the minus sign helps to remind us that the relationship is inverse.) Equation (15.9) says that when the unemployment rate is below the natural rate, inflation tends to rise faster than expected and when the unemployment rate is higher than the natural rate, it tends to rise slower than expected.

An Estimate of the Natural Rate of Unemployment

Empirical macroeconomists have estimated Phillips curves for many periods and many countries. They use sophisticated econometric techniques to take account of the variety of demand and supply factors that might influence prices. As valuable as such sophisticated studies are, there is much to be learned from simpler approaches.

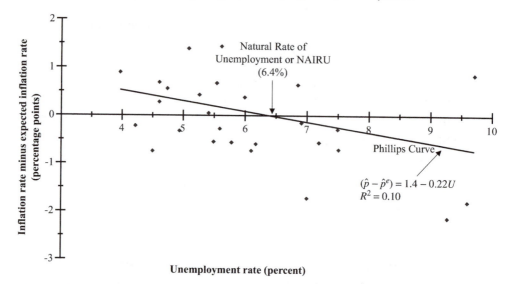

Figure 15.6. The Expectations-Augmented Phillips Curve, 1981–2009 (expectations based on surveys of expected inflation). *Source:* Inflation (CPI-U) and unemployment rates, Bureau of Labor Statistics; expected annual inflation rates, Livingston Survey, Federal Reserve Bank of Philadelphia.

To estimate β and U^*, we must have data on the expectations of inflation. Fortunately, several surveys provide such data. Figure 15.6 is based on equation (15.9). The vertical axis measures the difference between the actual inflation rate for each year and the rate expected at the end of the previous year by professional forecasters (who, of course, advise firms) for inflation over the year. The horizontal axis measures the rate of unemployment. The forecast data are available only from 1981. The equation of the regression line is

$$\hat{p}_t - {}_{t-1}\hat{p}^e_t = 1.4 - 0.22 U_t + error_t.$$

We assume that aggregate-supply factors can be ignored. In terms of the equation, this is the equivalent of setting $g(aggregate\text{-}supply\ factors_t)$ to zero. In terms of the regression, it means that any deviations of $g(aggregate\text{-}supply\ factors_t)$ from zero show up as part of the error – that is, in the fact that the points in the scatterplot do not lie exactly on the regression line.

Multiplying and dividing by -0.22 transforms the equation into the form of equation (15.9):

$$\hat{p}_t - {}_{t-1}\hat{p}^e_t = -0.22\left(U_t - \frac{1.4}{0.22}\right) = -0.22\left(U_t - 6.4\right). \qquad (15.10)$$

The adjustment parameter is $\beta = 0.22$, and the natural rate of unemployment is $U^* = 6.4$ percent. Analogously to Okun's law, when $U_t = U^*$, $\hat{p}_t - {}_{t-1}\hat{p}^e_t = 0$, and we can read the natural rate (U^*) directly from Figure 15.6 as the point at which the regression line crosses the horizontal axis.

NAIRU and the Formation of Expectations

Surveys have not always been available; and, in any case, economists are often skeptical of survey data. More often than not, macroeconomists eschew surveys of expected inflation and try instead to model the process through which expectations are formed. (See Box 7.1 on measuring the expectations of inflation.)

Although there are many ways to model expectations of inflation, the most simple, and perhaps the most common, way is to assume that whatever rate of inflation was *actually* observed last period is expected to obtain this period: $_{t-1}\hat{p}_t^e = \hat{p}_{t-1}$. Substituting into equation (15.9) yields

$$\hat{p}_t - \hat{p}_{t-1} = \Delta\hat{p}_t = -\beta(U_t - U^*) + g(\textit{aggregate supply}_t). \quad (15.11)$$

Here an unemployment rate below the natural rate increases the rate of inflation, while an unemployment rate above the natural rate reduces it.

The inflation rate is the (percentage) change in the price level, so the change in the inflation rate is the *acceleration* in the price level. Equation (15.11) says that when the actual and natural rates of unemployment are equal, the price level will not accelerate (or decelerate). Consequently, the natural rate estimated from such an equation is frequently known as the NON-ACCELERATING *I*NFLATION *R*ATE OF *U*NEMPLOYMENT (or **NAIRU**).[3]

Some economists distinguish between NAIRU and the natural rate of unemployment. Milton Friedman (1912–2006, winner of the Nobel Prize in Economics in 1976) and Edmund Phelps (of Columbia University, winner of the Nobel Prize in 2006), who independently developed the expectations-augmented version of the Phillips curve in the late 1960s, thought of the natural rate as the equivalent to full employment. In addition, they thought of markets as having a strong tendency to return to full employment if left alone. "Natural rate" was a clever coinage aimed at converting us to faith in the smooth functioning of markets and to the view that full employment is what generally occurs in markets if they are left to their own devices.

One reason to prefer the term "NAIRU" to the "natural rate of unemployment" is that NAIRU is the more ideologically neutral term. Although virtually every economist would agree that there is some level of aggregate demand (and, therefore, some level of unemployment) that at any time implies a stable rate of inflation, there is considerable disagreement about whether that rate is stable over time and whether the economy has any strong tendency to return to it.

---

[3] Properly speaking, NAIRU is misnamed because it is the *price level* that accelerates. The rate of inflation rises or falls, but does not accelerate. Be that as it may, the term *NAIRU* is now cast-iron idiom among macroeconomists.

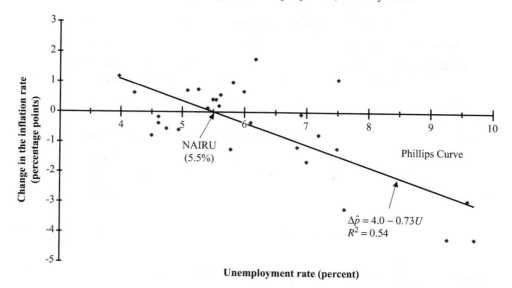

Figure 15.7. The Expectations-Augmented Phillips Curve, 1981–2009 (expectations based on past inflation rates). *Source:* Bureau of Labor Statistics.

An Estimate of NAIRU

Instead of using survey estimates of expectations, we can use equation (15.11), which forms expectations based on past inflation. Figure 15.7 measures the *change* in the inflation rate ($\Delta \hat{p}_t = \hat{p}_t - \hat{p}_{t-1}$) on the vertical axis and the rate of unemployment on the horizontal axis. The equation for the regression line is

$$\Delta \hat{p}_t = 4.0 - 0.73 \, U_t + error_t.$$

The adjustment parameter is $\beta = 0.73$ and NAIRU is $U^* = 5.5$ percent.

As before, this may be transformed into the form of a Phillips curve – this time into the form of equation (15.10):

$$\Delta \hat{p}_t = -0.73 \left(U_t - \frac{4.0}{0.73} \right) = -0.73 \, (U_t - 5.5) . \qquad (15.12)$$

To understand what the estimated Phillips curve means, consider an example. Suppose that the inflation rate is 7.5 percent and that the unemployment rate is 8 percent. Substituting the unemployment rate for U_t in equation (15.12) gives us $\Delta \hat{p}_t = -0.73(8.0 - 5.5) = -1.8$ percent per year. So after a year of a steady 8 percent rate of unemployment, on average one would expect the inflation rate to fall from 7.5 to 5.7 percent per year. The relatively poor fit of the estimate on which this prediction is based should remind us that particular forecasts may often be wrong and hardly accurate to two decimal places. Many other factors matter, and the result is likely to hold on average and not for each particular year.

Both the estimates based on surveys of expectations and on the past rate of inflation follow the general pattern of a Phillips curve: high unemployment is associated with falling rates of inflation (decelerating prices), and low rates of unemployment with rising rates of inflation (accelerating prices). There are two caveats. First, the regression line in Figure 15.6, equation (15.10), explains only a small fraction of the variation in prices as measured by R^2; while that in Figure 15.7, equation (15.12), explains only a moderate fraction. Second, the estimates of NAIRU and the adjustment parameter are different between the two estimates. What should we make of these caveats?

The low to moderate fits show that supply factors – or other factors not adequately captured by the unemployment rate – are relatively important. The tendency of high demand to accelerate prices and low demand to decelerate them is definitely an enduring fact about the economy, but there are important nondemand factors as well.

The difference in the estimates is to be expected. We do not know for certain whether the survey data or the past inflation rates provide a more accurate estimate of actual expectations of inflation. Detailed research into the Phillips curve displays a wide variety of estimates of NAIRU. Such uncertainty may arise because the true relationship between demand and inflation may not be linear as the regression line suggests.

Our empirical estimates also implicitly assume that NAIRU is constant during the estimation period. This assumption is not true in general, although it may be approximately true for particular periods. Economists using more sophisticated statistical techniques have estimated a NAIRU that changes over time. Figure 15.8 shows one such estimate – prepared by the Congressional Budget Office (CBO). The value of NAIRU changes slowly over time. Nonetheless, the average value for the period 1981–2009 is 5.5 percent. Not only is that average nearly the same as the mean value for 1948–2009 shown on Figure 15.8, it is the same as the estimate based on Figure 15.7 for the 1981–2009 period.

Changing demographics explain much of the change in NAIRU. In particular, variations in the proportions of teenagers in the labor force account for much of the rise and fall of NAIRU. Because teenagers typically have a higher unemployment rate than prime-age employees – whatever the state of the economy – the greater the proportion of teenagers, the higher the unemployment rate that corresponds to a given level of aggregate demand.

The Phillips Curve and Resource Utilization

The unemployment rate has traditionally been used as the measure of aggregate-demand factors in the Phillips curve. It is not, however, necessarily the best measure, and another is readily available: *output scaled by potential output* ($\tilde{Y}$).

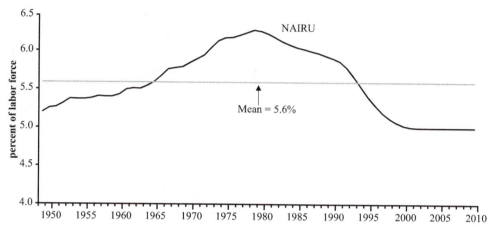

Figure 15.8. The Non-Accelerating Inflation Rate of Unemployment for the United States. *Source:* Congressional Budget Office.

Figure 15.9 estimates a Phillips curve using scaled output instead of unemployment for the period 1974–2009. Because scaled output is a procyclical variable while the unemployment rate is a countercyclical variable, the Phillips curve slopes up. Translated into the standard Phillips curve form, its equation is

$$\Delta \hat{p}_t = 0.61(\widetilde{Y}_t - 88.5). \tag{15.13}$$

The point at which the Phillips curve crosses the $\widetilde{Y}$ axis indicates NAIRU – but now we must redefine NAIRU as the *Non-Accelerating Inflation Rate*

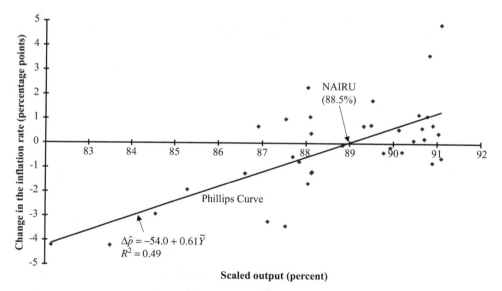

Figure 15.9. The Expectations-Augmented Phillips Curve for the United States, 1981–2009 (using scaled output). *Source:* Inflation (CPI-U), Bureau of Labor Statistics; scaled output, Bureau of Labor Statistics, Board of Governors of the Federal Reserve System; author's calculations.

of Resource Utilization equal to about 89 percent of potential GDP ($= 54.0/0.61$). The simple Phillips curve relationship fits roughly the same using scaled output ($R^2 = 0.49$) as it does using unemployment ($R^2 = 0.54$) as a measure of demand pressure.

Scaled output is a more general measure of inflationary pressures than the unemployment rate alone. Recall that scaled output can be thought of as a geometrically weighted average of the employment rate and the capacity-utilization rate (Chapter 9, section 9.5.2, equation (9.25)). Capacity-utilization and employment rates tend to move broadly together. Yet, at some points of the cycle they pull in different directions.

Late in the boom, capacity-utilization rates are typically below their peaks (see Chapter 9, Figure 9.17) and work to offset some of the inflationary pressure of tight labor markets. Capacity-utilization rates typically peak in mid-expansion because firms invest more heavily to accommodate increased demand. Their plans are not coordinated with those of their competitors; so, it generally happens that they invest more than demand requires. With more capacity than demand, capacity-utilization rates fall. Low rates of utilization are less profitable and firms hold prices down to stimulate demand. Tight labor markets are met by the relatively slack use of capital, which moderates – or even offsets – the acceleration in prices.

NAIRU and Full Employment

Should we think of NAIRU as the equivalent of full employment? Probably not. Recall that the labor market is heterogeneous – a large number of overlapping, but somewhat independent labor markets (Chapter 12, section 12.3). Equally, product markets are themselves heterogeneous. As aggregate demand rises, it will not be spread evenly across all product markets. Certain industries and certain labor skills will have high demand and others somewhat less. As unemployment falls toward its full employment level, some markets will find themselves short of labor sooner than others. They will raise their prices earlier and faster than in markets in which demand is lower and unemployment rates higher. As a result, prices accelerate *before* the economy as a whole reaches full employment, and the rate of unemployment consistent with stable prices is likely to be *higher* than the rate corresponding to full employment. If the economy stabilizes at NAIRU, then some people will remain involuntarily unemployed; if it stabilizes at true full employment, then inevitably there will be some (possibly rising) inflation.

This gives us another reason, besides its ideological neutrality, to prefer "NAIRU" to the "natural rate." The term "natural rate" suggests a kind of equilibrium, so that it is easily but mistakenly identified with full employment in the sense of labor supply equaling labor demand.

15.3.4 Inflation and Supply Factors

Wage Inflation and Labor Productivity

A profit-maximizing, perfectly competitive firm produces at the point that the real wage equals the marginal product of labor. If a Cobb-Douglas production function describes the firm, this rule is expressed as $w/p = \alpha\theta$, where α is the labor share and θ is labor productivity (see Chapter 10, section 10.4.1). Because α is nearly constant, this can be written in growth rates as $\hat{w} - \hat{p} = \hat{\theta}$ or $\hat{w} = \hat{\theta} + \hat{p}$. The message of this relationship is that as long as wages rise no faster than price inflation plus the rate of growth of labor productivity, firms can continue to produce at profit-maximizing rates. At this rate of wage inflation, real wages rise at the rate of labor-productivity growth, and firms can afford to accommodate these real wage increases without loss.

What happens if unions or the government act to make wages inflate faster than $\hat{\theta} + \hat{p}$? Firms then face an increase in real **unit labor costs** defined as *the real wage (and other compensation and benefits) per unit of output*. If nothing is done, their profits would fall. A firm whose competitive position permitted it to set prices would pass these costs on to the consumer. Even though perfectly (or even highly) competitive firms cannot pass the costs on directly because they cannot successfully charge a higher price than their competitors, the losses would cause some firms to leave the market, lowering supply and raising prices.

If firms successfully pass through the increased costs of production in the form of higher prices, then real wages do not rise. Unions that once pushed wages higher might be tempted to try to do so again, trying to establish a real wage higher than firms found sustainable. And again, firms would try to raise prices to compensate. Such a pattern of competitive inflation was in the 1950s and 1960s frequently discussed under the name **wage-price spiral**. It is less likely to be relevant in a time when unions are relatively weaker.

Supply Shocks

Increased real wages provide only one example of aggregate-supply factors that might affect inflation. In general, firms might pass on changes in the real prices of any factor of production. Ideally, of course, much of the increased cost would be mitigated through factor substitution – choosing a technological mix better adapted to new relative prices. Such adaptation is unlikely to occur in the short run and, even in the longer run, is not unlimited.

Increases in real factor prices may be permanent or transitory. If they are permanent, the technological mix will adapt over time. Even if they are transitory, the effects on prices may last for some time for at least two reasons.

First, if the higher inflation gets built into the firms' expectations of future inflation, as the version of the Phillips curve represented by equation (15.7) suggests that they will, there will be a sort of ratchet effect raising the underlying inflationary trend. Working against the upward push, however, is the fact that higher prices caused by aggregate-supply shocks will reduce aggregate demand unless nominal incomes rise proportionally. Real output would then fall, and unemployment would rise.

Similarly, to the extent that firms are unable to pass the costs on, they would reduce employment in the face of higher real wage rates. According to the Phillips curve, higher unemployment rates would moderate the acceleration of prices to some extent. Policymakers might resist the rising unemployment through actions designed to raise aggregate demand. So the second reason that supply shocks might have long-lasting effects is that they encourage aggregate-demand-management policies that, in effect, ratify the increase in the inflation rate.

The 1970s provide a possible illustration of the way in which real price increases translated into general inflation. The rising commodity prices in the early years of the decade and the oil-price increases following the Yom Kippur War added to inflation in the United States and induced a recession. Monetary and fiscal policy acted to offset the recession, which to some extent limited the inflation-moderating influence of the higher unemployment.

Macroeconomists and economic historians vigorously debate the causes of the stagflation of the 1970s and 1980s; the possibility that policymakers raised the rate of inflation and slowed down desirable adjustments to higher oil prices by using demand management to combat the decline in output is real. Japan adopted a less expansionary policy response to the oil price shock – even though it was more dependent on foreign oil than the United States – and displayed a smaller increase in its inflation rate.

15.3.5 Stagflation and Credibility

The expectations-augmented Phillips curve helps us to understand how high levels of inflation are compatible with high levels of unemployment as observed in the 1970s and early 1980s. Throughout the long expansion of the 1960s demand was high, pushing the unemployment rate below NAIRU. Prices accelerated so that firms came to expect high levels of general price inflation and, therefore, inflated their own prices at similarly high rates. Once such an expectation is embedded in the economy, it is hard to dislodge. It may take a concerted effort over a long time to reduce aggregate demand (and raise unemployment rates) in order to reduce inflation to moderate levels.

The supply shocks of the early 1970s and the subsequent inflation, of course, entrenched expectations of future inflation. There were severe recessions in the 1970s, but these were not enough to reduce inflation and entrenched expectations of inflation back to the levels of the 1950s and 1960s. So, high inflation coexisted with high unemployment – this was the period of *stagflation*. No policymaker was willing to bear the real costs of even higher unemployment and lost output in order to reduce inflation.

The expectations-augmented Phillips curve singles out firms' expectations as a critical factor in the control of inflation. The fact that firms understood the reluctance of policymakers to reduce aggregate demand meant that they were unlikely to revise their expectations of inflation downward. When inflation was finally reduced in the 1980s, the process began with the two severe recessions of 1980–1982. It was made easier by the CREDIBILITY of Paul Volcker and Alan Greenspan, the two chairmen of the Federal Reserve System, who were widely seen as single-minded in their determination to use monetary policy to reduce inflation.

When firms believe that policymakers will act successfully to reduce inflation, they revise their expectations downward, and this makes it easier for the policymakers to succeed with a smaller loss to output and unemployment. A reputation as an inflation fighter is self-fulfilling. Volcker's and Greenspan's successes are the reverse side of the policy problem of the 1970s. When no one believed that policymakers would truly pay the price for reducing inflation, high inflation was a self-fulfilling prophecy, and the costs of reducing it were increased.

15.4 Another Look at the Limits of Demand Management

We will study the details of aggregate-demand management and macroeconomic policy in Chapters 16 and 17. For now, it is enough to recognize that the government (including the Federal Reserve or other central banks) can use the tools of monetary and fiscal policy to affect the level and the growth rate of aggregate demand. Okun's law tells us that higher growth rates of aggregate demand reduce unemployment, so why would the government not exploit Okun's law to eliminate unemployment altogether? Or, to put it differently, what limits might there be on government demand-management policies?

Think about the estimate of Okun's law given in equation (15.5). Imagine that the unemployment rate is 6 percent and the government wants to reduce it to 2 percent. To do so, it engineers a growth rate of aggregate demand of, say, 4.5 percent per year. At this rate, we would expect the unemployment rate to fall at 0.7 percentage points per year ($= -0.46(4.5 - 3.0)$). To fall from 6 percent to 2 percent unemployment would then take a little less than 6 years ($= (6 - 2)/0.7$). So, why not do it?

One problem can be easily seen by consulting the Phillips curve. Consider equation (15.12), where NAIRU is estimated to be 5.5 percent. So inflation is likely to rise once the unemployment rate falls below NAIRU (in the first year of the policy!). By the end of the fifth year, we would expect the inflation rate to rise by 2.6 percentage points per year ($= -0.73(2.0 - 5.5)$). Continuation of such a policy for a long period of time would result in a very high inflation rate. Not wanting to increase the rate of inflation so much, policymakers are unlikely to persist in the attempt to lower the unemployment rate so far.

The desire of policymakers to avoid deliberately raising the inflation rate too much is not the only limit on the useful effects of an expansionary policy. The 2 percent unemployment rate in the example is below what anyone reasonably believes economically full employment to be. Because workers may choose not to work, once *involuntary* unemployment has been eliminated, the unemployment rate cannot fall further. Except for frictional unemployment, involuntary unemployment is effectively zero at some *measured* rate of unemployment well above 2 percent. There is, then, a limit to the scope of Okun's law.

In the end, real aggregate demand cannot exceed real aggregate supply. How is the attempt to push aggregate demand above aggregate supply thwarted? At least three elements are important.

- First, if policy actions push *nominal* aggregate demand upward faster than prices are rising, real aggregate demand will rise. But if this results in accelerating prices, the increase in *real* aggregate demand will be moderated.
- Second, if real aggregate demand exceeds production, firms will supply the demand from stocks of goods already produced. Such inventory disinvestment is itself a fall in *ex post* real aggregate demand.
- Finally, if demand cannot be met from domestic production, people will increase imports (and reduce exports). The resulting fall in net exports again reduces real aggregate demand.

15.5 Aggregate Supply and Demand: Putting It Together

15.5.1 A Steady State

We can summarize what we have learned in this chapter about the interaction of aggregate supply and demand by combining two diagrams: Figure 15.10 stacks the IS curve above the Phillips curve – both expressed as functions of scaled output. The point $\widetilde{Y}_N$ indicates NAIRU. Let the middle, black IS curve represent the initial state of aggregate demand and rr_N, a long-term

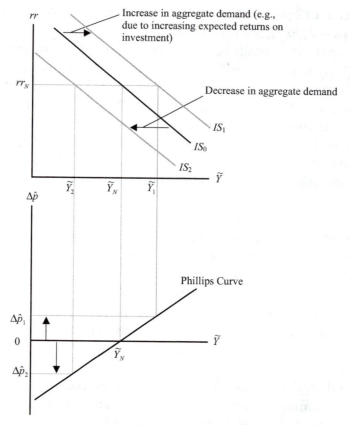

Figure 15.10. The Output and Price Effects of Shifting Aggregate Demand. Shifts in aggregate demand (e.g., due to changing expected returns on investment across the business cycle) shift the IS curve back and forth. The level of real interest rates rr_N holds aggregate demand at NAIRU and the inflation rate steady when the IS curve is IS_0. Increases in aggregate demand (rightward shifts of IS) *ceteris paribus* increase rates of resource utilization ($\widetilde{Y}$) and accelerate prices ($\Delta \hat{p}$). Decreases in aggregate demand have the opposite effect.

real rate of interest that is compatible with NAIRU. This configuration represents a halcyon economy – a steady state:

- the rate of resource utilization (scaled output) is constant because both aggregate demand and aggregate supply are growing at the modified balanced growth rate $(n + \hat{\theta} + \widehat{PR})$;
- the unemployment rate is itself constant; and
- prices are inflating at a constant rate.

To maintain such a steady state, the economy must be harmonized on three margins:

- first, aggregate demand must equal aggregate supply;
- second, financial and real markets must be compatible – in particular, the long-term real rate of interest must be right; and

- third, government policy must be compatible with private-sector plans – fiscal policy must not shift the IS curve in either direction; monetary policy (typically operating through short-term interest rates) must not push long-term interest rates up or down.

15.5.2 Shifts in Aggregate Demand

Shifts in aggregate demand or supply will upset the steady state. Let us first look at aggregate demand. Anything that shifts the IS curve, while not disturbing the underlying growth path of potential output, is a pure aggregate-demand factor. One such factor that is likely to be important over the course of the business cycle is the rate of return on investment (ρ). As we saw in Chapter 13 (section 13.3), an increase in ρ lowers the opportunity cost of investment and shifts the IS curve to the right. One factor that may initiate the recovery from recession is an increase in the return on investment. This is shown in Figure 15.10 as the rightward shift of the IS curve to IS_1. If financial markets are unaffected (and monetary policy holds steady), the real rate of interest remains constant at rr_N. Scaled output rises to $\widetilde{Y}_1$: the unemployment rate will fall and capacity-utilization rates will rise. And the inflation rate will increase by $\Delta \hat{p}_1$ per year. These are, as we have seen in earlier chapters, the typical patterns of the upswing of the business cycle.

As the recovery continues, the best investment opportunities tend to be played out or more than optimal amounts of resources are directed toward them, and the rate of return falls, raising the opportunity cost of further investment. As a result, the IS curve shifts leftward, perhaps as far as IS_2. The economy slumps. Scaled output falls to $\widetilde{Y}_2$: the unemployment rate rises and capacity-utilization rates fall. The inflation rate declines by $\Delta \hat{p}_2$ per year. And, once again, these are the typical patterns of the downswing of the business cycle.

Fluctuations in the rate of return on investment are only one possible cause of business-cycle fluctuations. Anything that shifts the IS curve – cycles in government spending, consumption, foreign trade, or in long-term interest rates (either endemic to financial markets or the result of monetary policy actions) – could equally well generate similar patterns.

15.5.3 Shifts in Aggregate Supply

Supply shocks affect potential output (Y^{pot}). Because scaled output is defined as $\widetilde{Y} = \frac{Y}{Y^{pot}}$, a fall in potential output for the same level of aggregate demand (Y) increases scaled output. All other things equal, at the same level of real interest the IS curve must shift to the right as shown in

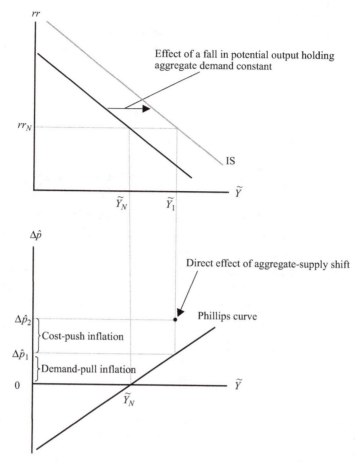

Figure 15.11. The Output and Price Effects of Shifting Aggregate Supply. A fall in aggregate-supply shock shifts the IS curve rightward as potential output falls relative to unchanged aggregate demand. Prices accelerate as aggregate demand exceeds NAIRU. There is also a transient direct effect (shown as the point off the Phillips curve). The price level must rise to reduce the real wage in response to the now lower marginal product of labor. The transient effect disappears as soon as this adjustment is complete.

Figure 15.11 because aggregate demand *relative* to potential output is now higher. The fact that the fall in potential output shifts the IS curve shows that changes in aggregate supply do not typically have only a supply-side effect, but also have an induced effect on aggregate demand.

Notice that despite the higher level of resource utilization, the induced increase in aggregate demand is not a good thing. At the same level of real interest rates, scaled output is higher, but the full-employment point now corresponds to a lower level of GDP; full-employment real-wage rates must be lower, so that the labor supply and the level of full employment will fall. Although fewer people are working at NAIRU, the actual NAIRU rate of unemployment may not be any higher. With the old level of aggregate demand, aggregate demand is greater than NAIRU ($\tilde{Y}_1 > \tilde{Y}_N$), so that prices accelerate.

Although the resulting rise in prices is cost-push inflation, we can think of the acceleration in prices having two parts. The *direct effect* is any additional increase in the price level that can be attributed to the supply shock itself. So, for example, when oil prices rise, and oil is one of the prices in the major price indices, then those indices increase. The direct effect is shown by point A, lying above the Phillips curve. There is also an *indirect effect*: the mismatch of the old level of aggregate demand with the now lower level of aggregate supply leads prices to accelerate by $\Delta \hat{p}_1$. The indirect effect acts exactly like demand-pull inflation except that it burns itself out automatically: as prices rise, the existing nominal aggregate demand corresponds to a lower and lower real aggregate demand until NAIRU is restored. The direct effect ($\Delta \hat{p}_2 - \Delta \hat{p}_1$) is strictly temporary and disappears as soon as real wages have adjusted to the new supply conditions.

Summary

1. Supply factors alter potential output, holding aggregate demand constant; demand factors change aggregate demand relative to potential output.

2. Changes in aggregate supply generally result in a change in relative prices (particularly of the general price level relative to the wage rate) even at full employment. Shortfalls in aggregate demand lead to unemployment (of workers and other resources) with or without price changes; increases in aggregate demand above potential output lead to inflation.

3. Changes in the general price level that result from the relative price adjustments owing to supply factors are known as *cost-push inflation*; changes owing to demand factors are known as *demand-pull inflation*. Cost-push inflation is strictly transitory. Demand-pull inflation can continue as long as pressure exists pushing aggregate demand above potential output.

4. The unemployment rate rises whenever the growth rate of the labor force exceeds the growth rate of employment. This situation will occur whenever the growth rate of aggregate demand falls short of the *modified balanced growth rate* defined as $\hat{Y}^* \equiv \widehat{PR} + \widehat{POP} + \hat{\theta}$. This is the balanced growth rate adjusted for changes in participation rates. The relationship between changes in the unemployment rate and the growth rate of aggregate demand is known as *Okun's law*.

5. An Okun's-law-like relationship also exists between output scaled by potential output ($\tilde{Y}$) and the growth rate of aggregate demand. Empirical estimates of $\hat{Y}^*$ are similar whether based on changes in the unemployment rate or changes in scaled output.

6. Price-setting firms choose optimal prices relative to the general price level. In order to achieve the desired relative price, they must set prices in anticipation of future inflation. The relative prices of the goods they produce are likely to be modified to take account of cost pressures (supply) or demand pressures.

7. The (expectations-augmented) Phillips curve aggregates the price-setting behavior of firms to find a relationship between inflation, relative to expected inflation, and a measure of aggregate demand (aggregate-supply factors may also be considered). Aggregate demand (relative to aggregate supply) is often measured by the unemployment rate. The Phillips curve may be written as: $\hat{p}_t - {}_{t-1}\hat{p}_t^e = -\beta(U_t - U^*) + g(\textit{aggregate-supply factors}_t)$, where U^* is the *natural rate of unemployment*, defined as the rate that keeps actual and expected inflation in agreement.

8. Expectations are frequently measured on the assumption that this period's inflation rate will be the same as last period's. Then the Phillips curve may be written as: $\Delta\hat{p}_t = -\beta(U_t - U^*) + g(\textit{aggregate supply}_t)$. In this version, U^* is frequently referred to as *NAIRU*, the non-accelerating inflation rate of unemployment.

9. Other measures of aggregate demand relative to supply can be used in the Phillips curve, such as scaled output. Then *NAIRU* would be interpreted to mean non-accelerating inflation rate of resource utilization.

10. NAIRU (or the natural rate of unemployment) is not constant over time, but may vary with changes in real factors, such as demographics or the organization of labor markets.

11. The role of expectations in the Phillips curve highlights the importance of credibility in demand-management policy: reducing inflation is less costly in terms of unemployment or other unused resources if the public believes that policy-makers will actually be successful in reducing it.

12. Although Okun's law suggests that growth in aggregate demand can reduce unemployment any amount over enough time, in fact full employment (labor supply equals labor demand) sets a limit. Any attempt to breach the full-employment level results in rising prices (reducing real aggregate demand for a constant nominal level), falling inventories, and falling net exports (both reducing real aggregate demand).

Key Concepts

potential output

scaled output

supply factors

substitutes in production

complements in production

cost-push inflation

demand factors

demand-pull inflation

modified balanced rate of growth

Okun's law

Phillips curve

expectations-augmented Phillips curve

natural rate of unemployment

non-accelerating inflation rate of unemployment (NAIRU)

credibility

Suggestions for Further Reading

James Tobin, "Okun's Law: How Policy and Research Helped Each Other," in *Full Employment and Growth: Further Keynesian Essays on Policy*. Cheltenham, UK: Edward Elgar, 1996; pp. 56–65.

A. W. H. Phillips, "The Relation between Unemployment and the Rate of Change of Money Wage Rates in the United Kingdom, 1861–1957." *Economica NS* 25, no. 2 (1958): 283–299.

Milton Friedman, "The Role of Monetary Policy." *American Economic Review* 58, no. 1 (1968): 1–17.

"Symposium: The Natural Rate of Unemployment," [with contributions by various authors] in *Journal of Economic Perspectives* 11, no. 1 (1997): 3–108.

Kevin D. Hoover, "The Phillips Curve," in David R. Henderson, editor. *The Concise Encyclopedia of Economics*. Indianapolis, IN: Liberty Press.

Problems

Data for this exercise are available on the textbook website under the link for Chapter 15 (appliedmacroeconomics.com). Before starting these exercises, the student should review the relevant portions of the *Guide to Working with Economic Data*, including sections G.1–G.5, G.10–G.11, and G.15.

Problem 15.1. Imagine the unfortunate event of a new plague that kills a quarter of the population of a country. Use labor-supply/labor-demand analysis to analyze the effects of such a misfortune on real wages, employment, and real GDP.

Problem 15.2. Think of some concrete examples of cases in which particular economic developments lower the economic stock of capital while leaving the physical stock of capital intact.

Problem 15.3. The growth rates of labor productivity and participation rates are important elements in determining the modified balanced rate of growth ($\hat{Y}^*$). How they change over time will determine how $\hat{Y}^*$ changes. The mid-1970s seems to mark a point at which participation rates and the behavior of labor productivity seemed to depart from past experience. Based on your understanding of these data, how do you conjecture that $\hat{Y}^*$ is likely to have changed from before to after the mid-1970s? To check this, estimate Okun's law, following the example of Figure 15.4, by making a scatterplot for ΔU versus $\hat{Y}$ for the periods 1948–1973 and 1974–2008, fitting a regression line to each scatterplot, and calculating the implied $\hat{Y}^*$. Do your estimates change in the way that you anticipated?

Problem 15.4. Calculate the average growth rates for labor productivity, participation rates, and working-age population and use them to calculate $\hat{Y}^*$ for each of the periods in Problem 15.3. How close do these estimates come to estimates based on the regression of changes in unemployment on growth rates?

Problem 15.5. It has been argued that labor productivity has risen substantially in the late 1990s. Use a scatterplot and regression line (as in Problem 15.3) for U.S. data after 1992 to estimate $\hat{Y}^*$. Has the "speed limit" been raised? By how much? Is there any reason to believe your estimates might systematically over- or underestimate the true modified balanced growth path? (Hint: think about how labor productivity behaves over the business cycle and where in the business cycle your data come from.)

Problem 15.6. Reestimate Okun's law for each of the subperiods identified in Problem 15.3 using the change in scaled output in place of the change in unemployment. Put each equation into standard form. Compare your estimates to those in Problem 15.3. In particular, how do your estimates of the modified natural rate of growth differ from the earlier estimates?

Problem 15.7. Using data for each of the G-7 countries for the period 1995–present, estimate Okun's law and report in a table the estimates of the modified balanced growth rate ($\hat{Y}^*$), the speed-of-adjustment parameter (γ), and the fit of the regression equation (R^2). How do the estimates for the other six countries compare to those for the United States? What factors account for the difference? Suggest what further investigations that you might undertake to test your conjectures.

Problem 15.8. Assume that equation (15.5) is the true Okun's law for the U.S. economy today. Locate the most recent GDP and unemployment data (http://www.bea.gov for GDP and http://www.bls.gov for unemployment). Based on the growth rate of GDP for the most recent quarter over the same quarter a year before, what does Okun's law predict for the change in unemployment for the last month of the most recent quarter over the same month a year earlier? What has in fact happened? Discuss any disparity.

Problem 15.9. To get some idea of how well surveys perform relative to past inflation rates as estimates of expected inflation, calculate two series: (1) the *ex post* or actual rate of inflation calculated as the rate of CPI inflation between the current year and the following year; and (2) the lagged rate of inflation calculated as the rate of CPI inflation between the previous year and the current year.

(a) Plot these two series on the same graph as the Livingston CPI Inflation Survey data used in Figure 15.6.

(b) Create two new series of forecast errors by subtracting the actual rate of inflation from each of the expectations series. Plot the two new series on a graph. Present a table with the mean, median, and standard deviation for each of the new series.

(c) Based on your charts and calculations, which of the expectations series predicts current inflation best? Do either or both systematically underpredict or overpredict for any relatively long period? If so, can you speculate on why this might occur? (For example, is it likely to be that the measurements do not capture people's true expectations or is it likely that people make systematic errors? And, if they make systematic errors, is there any pattern to their mistakes?)

Problem 15.10. Estimate Phillips curves for the United States like that in Figure 15.7 for the periods 1950–1970, 1971–1986, and 1987–present. (Calculate the inflation rate as the change in the current CPI over the previous year.) Write the equation for each in standard form. Create a graph similar to Figure 15.8, plotting the Congressional Budget Office's (CBO's) estimate of NAIRU (i.e., the natural rate of unemployment) and your own estimate as a horizontal line at your estimated value for each period. Compare your estimates of NAIRU to those of the CBO in Figure 15.8. How well do they agree?

Problem 15.11. Reestimate the Phillips curve using scaled output instead of unemployment for each of the subperiods identified in Problem 15.10. Write each equation in standard form. What are your estimates of the non-accelerating inflation rates of scaled output?

Problem 15.12. To get some idea of why NAIRU might shift over time, make two charts. On the first, plot the participation rates of prime-age men, women, and teenagers in the labor force for the United States and, on a separate scale on the same chart, plot the CBO's estimate of NAIRU. On the other chart, plot the unemployment rates for prime-age men, women, and teenagers and the CBO's estimate of NAIRU. Calculate and report in a table the average values of each of these seven series for each of the subperiods in Problem 15.10. Based on these data why do you think NAIRU shifts over time? Relate your reasons carefully to the data.

Problem 15.13. Some researchers have suggested that one way to account for changing demographics in the Phillips curve is to use the unemployment rate for a demographically homogeneous group of workers. Use the unemployment rate for prime-age males to estimate the Phillips curve for the two periods 1971–1986, and 1987–present. Write each equation in standard form. Compare the two estimates of NAIRU to those based on the entire working population for these same periods in Problem 15.10. Do the curves using the whole population or only prime-age males fit better as judged by R^2? Which pair of curves delivers the more stable estimate of NAIRU?

Problem 15.14. The CPI is tailored to consumer expenditure and may not be the best measure of inflation overall. To see how a broader measure would affect the analysis of inflation, estimate a Phillips curve using the GDP deflator in place of the CPI for the period 1987–present and write it in standard form. Compare it to an estimate using the CPI for the same period. In particular, are there any significant differences in the estimate of NAIRU?

Problem 15.15. Using CPI and unemployment data for each of the G-7 countries (1995–present), estimate a Phillips curve and report in a table the estimates of NAIRU (U^*), the speed-of-adjustment parameter (β), and the fit of the regression equation (R^2). How do the estimates for the other six countries compare to those for the United States? What factors account for the difference? Suggest what further investigations that you might undertake to test your conjectures.

Problem 15.16. What light does Okun's law shed on the actual path of the economy? Taking the actual unemployment rate in 1990 and the actual rates of GDP growth, use equation (15.5) to generate a series of predicted changes in the unemployment rate. Start with the *actual* unemployment rate in 1990 and add to it the predicted change for 1991 to form the predicted rate for 1991; then add the predicted unemployment rate for 1992 to your *predicted* unemployment rate for 1991 to form the predicted unemployment rate for 1992; and so forth to the end of the sample to build up a predicted time series for unemployment. Graph your predicted series against the actual unemployment rates. How well do your predictions match the actual data?

Problem 15.17. Repeat Problem 15.16 using scaled output rather than unemployment in Okun's law (equation (15.6)). Comparing your results with those in Problem 15.16, which version of Okun's law does a better job at prediction?

Problem 15.18. What light does the Phillips curve shed on the actual path of the economy? Taking the actual inflation rate in 1990 and the actual unemployment rates, use equation (15.12) to generate a series of predicted changes in the inflation rate (based on the CPI). Start with the *actual* inflation rate in 1990 and add to it the predicted change for 1991 to form the predicted rate for 1991; then add the predicted change in the inflation rate for 1992 to your *predicted* inflation rate for 1991 to get the predicted inflation rate for 1992; and so forth to the end of the sample to build up a predicted time series for the inflation rate. Graph your predicted series against the actual inflation rates. How well do your predictions match the actual data?

Problem 15.19. Repeat Problem 15.18 using scaled output rather than unemployment in the Phillips curve (equation (15.13). Comparing your results with those in Problem 15.19, which version of the Phillips curve does a better job at prediction?

Part VIII

Macroeconomic Policy

16

Monetary Policy

The chairman of the Board of Governors of the Federal Reserve System Ben Bernanke is frequently called the "second most powerful man in the United States." His immediate predecessors, Alan Greenspan and Paul Volcker, were similarly regarded in their days. How is it that an unelected public servant should be widely regarded as having an influence over the state of the nation second only to the president of the United States? Our goal in this chapter, indirectly, is to answer that question. The short answer is straightforward: the chairman of the Federal Reserve stands at the center of monetary policymaking in the United States. But that just raises other questions: Why is monetary policy so important? How does monetary policy work? To answer those questions is the main business at hand.

16.1 Monetary and Fiscal Policy

Monetary policy is one of the two main types of macroeconomic policy. In Chapter 13 (section 13.2) we defined the other type, *fiscal policy*, as comprising those government actions that aim to influence macroeconomic performance through the manipulation of government revenue (taxes) and government spending (both on goods and services and on transfer payments). **MONETARY POLICY** *comprises those government actions that aim to influence macroeconomic performance through the financial system.* Although we touched on monetary policy in the discussion of the financial system in Chapter 7 (section 7.6.1), a complete picture needs much more detail. The main discussion of fiscal policy is in Chapter 17. Nonetheless, because monetary and fiscal policies are not independent, we shall consider their relationship in this section.

16.1.1 The Government Budget Constraint

Like all agents in a free-market economy, the government must pay for the goods and services it receives. When tax revenues fall short of expenditure (i.e., it runs a deficit), the government must raise the money some other way. Most often, it does so by selling government bonds, which adds to the stock of government debt held by the private sector (B^G). There is another possibility: instead of borrowing, the government can "print money." Sometimes, it is literally true that governments finance their spending by printing more currency. More often, this phrase refers to the central bank (in the United States, the Federal Reserve) purchasing some of the government bonds. They pay for these bonds with CENTRAL-BANK RESERVES – that is, by *credits to the accounts of commercial banks with the central bank.* As we saw in Chapter 6 (section 6.3.2), the MONETARY BASE (MB) equals *currency plus central-bank reserves.*

Because it is simply a matter of adding numbers to the reserve accounts of the commercial banks, there is in principle no limit to the amount of monetary base the Federal Reserve can create. In fact, the Federal Reserve does not ever make a gift of reserves. Sometimes it lends a bank reserves, so that the Federal Reserve's books show both a liability (the reserves) and an offsetting asset (the loan to the commercial bank). Although in a few extraordinary cases – the financial crisis of 2008–2009 serving as the prime example – such lending has been extensive, in normal times, it is typically small; and most reserves are created when the Federal Reserve purchases government bonds. Such purchases increase the monetary base. When the Federal Reserve purchases bonds, they are removed from the hands of the public and, for most purposes relevant to macroeconomics, effectively extinguished.

The GOVERNMENT'S BUDGET CONSTRAINT shows the financing options for a deficit:

$$G - (T - TR) = \Delta B^G + \Delta MB. \tag{16.1}$$

The left-hand side of equation (16.1) is the government's budget deficit (see Chapter 2, section 2.3.3). The equation says that this deficit (a flow variable) must be financed either by adding to government debt or to the monetary base. The stock of debt (B^G) and the monetary base (MB) are just the sum of all the past changes (ΔB^G and ΔMB).

The left-hand side of equation (16.1) reflects fiscal policy – the revenue and expenditure decisions of the government. The right-hand side reflects monetary policy – the management of the government's financial portfolio. The equal sign shows that fiscal and monetary policies are closely related.

An example of a *pure fiscal policy* would be a tax cut exactly offset by a cut in expenditures (a cut in either G or TR). Although two (or even all three) variables on the left-hand side changed, the deficit would remain unchanged, and there would be no need to adjust the financial portfolio. A *pure monetary policy* would change the right-hand side while leaving the left-hand side unchanged. The Federal Reserve could purchase a government bond, in effect exchanging monetary base for government debt. The term ΔMB would be positive and the term ΔB^G negative and of equal magnitude.

Most policy is not pure. Typically, the government runs a deficit. It sells enough bonds to finance the deficit. The Federal Reserve then has to choose its monetary policy. The case in which the Federal Reserve does nothing is an example of a **debt-financed deficit**. The case in which the Federal Reserve purchases the entire increase in the stock of debt (increasing the monetary base, extinguishing the new debt, and leaving $\Delta B^G = 0$) is an example of the **monetization of the deficit** – the classic case of the government's "printing money" to finance its expenditure (for a more detailed discussion see Chapter 17, section 17.2.1). In most cases, it chooses an intermediary policy in which both monetary base and outstanding debt adjust to the deficit.

At the turn of the twenty-first century – as for much of the nineteenth century – the Federal government ran a surplus. With a surplus, all the same policy questions arise in reverse. Should the debt be retired or should the monetary base be reduced or both?

16.1.2 Monetary Policy and the Real Economy

In Chapter 13 (section 13.1), we learned that fiscal policy can be used to stimulate or retard aggregate demand through the multiplier process. Fiscal policy (the left-hand side of the government's budget constraint) clearly matters to GDP, unemployment, and the other real outcomes that matter to us. But how and why does monetary policy (the right-hand side of the government's budget constraint) matter? There are two main channels through which monetary policy affects the real economy: the opportunity-cost channel and the credit channel.

First, when the Federal Reserve buys and sells government debt, it changes the supply of bonds available to the public, which in turn affects their price or yield. And because financial assets are typically substitutes, yields of other assets move in the same direction as the yields on government bonds (see Chapter 7, section 7.2.1). As we have seen in Chapters 13 and 14, a fall in the yield on financial assets reduces the opportunity cost of acquiring new capital and encourages firms to invest. This is the **OPPORTUNITY-COST** (or **INTEREST-RATE**) **CHANNEL**, discussed in more detail in section 16.3.

The second channel depends on the interaction of the Federal Reserve's portfolio with that of the commercial banks. When the Federal Reserve buys government bonds, commercial banks find themselves holding more central-bank reserves. These reserves allow them to make additional loans to businesses and consumers, independent of any effect that the Federal Reserve's action may have on bond yields. The new loans, in turn, finance additional consumer spending or investment. This is the **CREDIT CHANNEL** discussed in more detail in section 16.4.

In addition to these two main channels, monetary policy can also influence the economy through a third channel – its effects on the foreign-exchange markets and international trade. We shall examine this channel in section 16.6.

Before we examine these two major channels, we must look more carefully at the mechanics of monetary policy.

16.2 The Federal Reserve and the Banking System

16.2.1 The Central Bank

Some History

Commercial banking is very old. The ancient Greeks and Romans had a type of bank. Banks very similar to modern banks were first established in Venice in 1135 AD. Central banking is more recent. The Sveriges Riksbank (the **CENTRAL BANK** of Sweden), founded in 1668, is the oldest central bank in the world. As with the Bank of England (founded 1694) and the Bank of France (1800), the original mission of the Riksbank was to help manage government debt.

Under the leadership of the first Secretary of the Treasury Alexander Hamilton (c. 1755–1804), whose portrait graces the ten-dollar bill, the United States created the First Bank of the United States in 1791. Its charter lapsed after twenty years. Five years later in 1816, the Second Bank of the United States was also chartered for twenty years. The failure in 1836 to renew the charter of the Second Bank was considered a triumph for the decentralized democracy advocated by the first populist president Andrew Jackson (1767–1845). The populist attitudes that led to the demise of the Second Bank are still common in the United States and help to explain why American banking is more fragmented and decentralized than banking in other industrialized countries.

In the nineteenth century, central banks began to function as the anchors of an increasingly complex financial system. The British Empire dominated the world economy, and London was its financial center. The financial system suffered periodic commercial crises. At those times, the Bank of England became the **lender of last resort** for commercial banks in Britain (and indirectly throughout the world), which, despite solidly positive net worth, lacked sufficient cash on hand to cover the immediate demands of skittish depositors. Monetary policy in the nineteenth century, up to the Great Depression of the 1930s, focused mainly on the stability of the financial system. As long as the financial system was anchored by gold and silver money, the central bank had limited power to affect the real economy.

After the demise of the Second Bank of the United States in 1836, the United States lacked any central bank. During the balance of the nineteenth century, a series of financial panics was managed by the financial might and

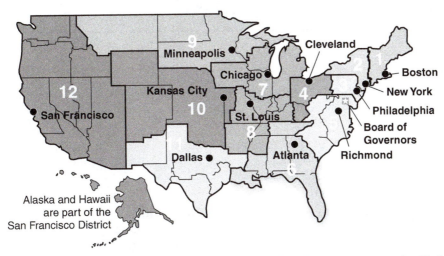

Figure 16.1. The Federal Reserve System. *Notes*: Numbers represent the Federal Reserve Districts and cities indicate the location of the Federal Reserve Bank for each district. The Board of Governors is located in Washington, DC.

goodwill of the great private bankers. The financial panic of 1907 strained the ability of a consortium of bankers, led by John Pierpont Morgan (1837–1913), to stem the tide of the crisis and avert the total collapse of the financial system. The Federal Reserve System was created in 1913 as a direct reaction to the financial panic of 1907. It was charged to serve as a lender of last resort and an "elastic" supplier of currency adequate to the needs of a growing, and increasingly complex, financial system.

The Structure of the Federal Reserve System

The Federal Reserve Act divided the country into twelve districts, each with a **Federal Reserve Bank** (Figure 16.1). The locations of the banks are a legacy of the distribution of economic activity, population, and, perhaps more importantly, the balance of political power in Congress in 1913. Were the Federal Reserve to have been created early in the twenty-first century, it is unlikely that two Federal Reserve Banks would be located in Missouri (St. Louis and Kansas City).

Formally, each Federal Reserve Bank is a private corporation owned by the member banks in its district. Practically, the Federal Reserve Banks are government agencies. For example, except for a fixed dividend paid to the member banks, the profits of the Federal Reserve Banks are paid to the Federal government; and, although the district banks have some freedom in their day-to-day operations, all important matters of monetary policy and banking regulation are guided by the **Board of Governors of the Federal Reserve System** in Washington, DC. The Federal Reserve System (the Board plus the twelve district banks) is by its own description "an

Table 16.1. *The Balance Sheets of the Federal Reserve and the Commercial Banks*

Federal Reserve		Commercial Banks	
Assets	Liabilities	Assets	Liabilities
Government bonds	Banknotes held by nonbank public	Reserves	Transactions accounts
Discount loans	Reserves (reserve balances and eligible vault cash)	Loans	Savings and large and small time deposits
Coins held by Federal Reserve		Government and commercial bonds and other assets	Discount loans
Foreign exchange		(Federal funds lent)	(Federal funds borrowed)
Gold	Net worth		Net worth

independent entity within the government, having both public purposes and private aspects."[1] The system as a whole – taking the district banks and the Board together – is colloquially known as **THE FED**.

The Board is run by seven governors appointed to fourteen-year terms by the president and confirmed by the Senate. Ben Bernanke, first appointed in 2006, is the current (as of 2011) chairman of the Board of Governors. The most important aspects of monetary policy are controlled by the **FEDERAL OPEN MARKET COMMITTEE** (**FOMC**). The FOMC comprises the seven governors, the president of the Federal Reserve Bank of New York, and four of the eleven presidents of the other district banks as voting members on a rotating basis.[2] When the news media report that the Fed raised or lowered interest rates, they are reporting a decision of the FOMC.

16.2.2 Bank Balance Sheets

The relationship between the Fed and the commercial banks is easy to see from their balance sheets (Table 16.1).

The Fed's Balance Sheet

The left-hand panel refers to the Fed. Despite being a "government entity," the Fed's balance sheet is usually disaggregated from that of the rest of the Federal government. Thus, its main asset is shown as its holdings of

---

[1] Downloaded on 15 February 2005 from: www.federalreserve.gov/generalinfo/faq/faqfrs.htm5.

[2] At the time of writing this chapter, proposals are being mooted to revise the structure of the FOMC in light of the financial crisis of 2008–2009.

government bonds. These holdings do not amount to debt in the usual sense. Practically, one part of the Federal government holds the debt of another. (Almost all of the profits on government bonds held by the Federal Reserve are returned to the Treasury.)

The other items on the asset side are of less immediate concern. **Discount loans** are *short-term loans of reserves that the Fed makes to commercial banks*. Just as the Fed can buy and sell government bonds, it can also buy and sell foreign currencies (**foreign exchange**). Most foreign-exchange operations are conducted by the Treasury rather than the Federal Reserve. They are most relevant to exchange-rate policy; although, as we shall see (see section 16.6), they may also act as a channel between monetary policy and the economy. The monetary gold on the Fed's balance sheet is a legacy of the period before 1973 when gold was the instrument of settlement of international accounts. Gold transactions are no longer important for monetary policy. Coins held by the Fed are also treated as assets. The Fed acts as a distribution center for coins needed by banks.

Turn now to the Fed's liabilities. Take a look at a dollar bill. Along the top edge is printed "Federal Reserve Note." Technically, banknotes (or paper currency) are liabilities of the Federal Reserve. Before 1964, a dollar bill was a liability in the sense that it was convertible on demand into silver coin. Now a dollar bill is, at best, convertible into a newer, crisper dollar bill or into coins, which are themselves merely tokens and no longer valued for their metal content or (for banks) into central-bank reserves. It remains a liability of the Fed for accounting purposes.

Notice that the entry on the liability side of the Fed's balance sheet refers only to currency in the hands of the nonbank public. Currency held by banks in their vaults, at their tellers' windows, and in their ATM machines is called **vault cash** and counts as part of banks' reserves. When you withdraw $100 from an ATM, the currency item on the Fed's liabilities rises and the reserve item falls.

Reserves are another liability of the Fed. Reserves take the form either of balances in the accounts of commercial banks at a district Federal Reserve Bank or of vault cash. Reserves – especially when they are traded among commercial banks – are commonly known as **Federal funds**.

Commercial Bank Balance Sheets

Every financial liability must be someone's asset. Reserves – the liability of the Fed – are an asset to the commercial banks (shown on the right-hand side of Table 16.1). The most profitable assets to banks are loans, which take many forms, among them credit-card lending, mortgages, home equity loans, automobile loans, and commercial and industrial loans. Banks may also own other assets, such as government and corporate debt.

Where do banks get the funds that they lend? The sources are shown on the liability side of the banks' balance sheet, mostly as various forms of deposits. **Transactions accounts**, which include demand deposits (the common checking account) as well as some other easily transferred types of accounts, are an important component of M1, the monetary aggregate that most nearly corresponds to the idea of money as means of transactions (see Chapter 6, sections 6.1.1 and 6.3.2). **Savings** and small **time deposits** are familiar to the ordinary customers of banks. Large time deposits generally take the form of short-term bonds known as **negotiable certificates of deposit (CDs)**.

When customers withdraw funds from bank accounts or when banks are asked to honor checks written against their accounts or directed to wire funds to other banks, they lose reserves. In order to cover such outflows of funds, prudent banks would voluntarily choose to hold some reserves. With or without prudence, the banks face a legal RESERVE REQUIREMENT: they must hold reserves equal to 10 percent of their transactions accounts. Currently, savings and time deposits are not subject to reserve requirements.[3] Reserve requirements are generally set well above the demands of prudence and serve more as a tool through which the Fed can manipulate bank lending than as security for depositors (see section 16.2.3).

If banks find themselves short of reserves, they can acquire more. The most immediate way is to borrow them. They could for instance borrow them from the Fed as discount loans. Traditionally, the Fed discourages such borrowing, and, if a bank borrowed much or borrowed frequently, regulators might look more closely at its books. The threat of such unwanted scrutiny keeps discount loans small. Recently, the Fed has begun to lend more freely, provided that the bank is in good standing and provides good collateral, although at a rate above market rates.

The bank may also borrow from another bank that happens to have reserves surplus to its requirements. (Specialized brokers help to arrange these loans.) These Federal funds transactions are shown on both sides of the balance sheet. Because the balance sheet consolidates the individual balance sheets of each bank, all interbank transactions would normally cancel out. *Federal funds lent* would exactly match *Federal funds borrowed*. They are shown in Table 16.1 in parentheses to emphasize that these transactions remain important even though they must net to zero for the banking system as a whole.

---

[3] Before 1990, time and savings accounts were also subject to reserve requirements, albeit lower ones than transactions accounts. And the transactions accounts of smaller banks are currently subject to a lower (3 percent) reserve requirement than that charged to larger banks (see www.federalreserve .gov/monetarypolicy/reservereq.htm).

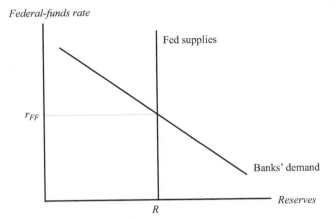

Figure 16.2. The Federal Funds Market. The supply of reserves depends largely on the past open-market operations of the Fed, and is insensitive to the level of the Federal-funds rate. The demand for reserves depends on the opportunity cost to banks of holding them, which is a negative function of the Federal-funds rate: a bank that holds a dollar of reserves loses the interest it could have earned by lending it on the Federal funds market, but gains not having to go to the market itself to borrow if it finds itself unexpectedly short of reserves. Equilibrium is, naturally, where supply equals demand, and it determines the Federal-funds rate.

Federal funds lending is literally overnight lending – loans made one day are usually repaid the next. The **FEDERAL-FUNDS RATE**, the rate of interest charged on one of these overnight loans, is the yield on the shortest maturity bond (or loan) typically reported. The Federal-funds rate is particularly important because it is the target rate for U.S. monetary policy.

16.2.3 The Mechanics of Monetary Policy

To understand how monetary policy works, we must first understand the structure of the market for bank reserves (Federal funds). In 2008, the Fed began to pay interest on reserves held at Federal Reserve banks.[4] This is a major change in the operation of monetary policy. It will be easier, however, if we first consider how the Federal funds market operated for most of the period since World War II when the Fed paid no interest on reserves. We shall then consider the recent change.

The Classic Federal Funds Market

The **FEDERAL FUNDS** (or **RESERVE**) **MARKET** can be described in a simple supply-and-demand diagram. In Figure 16.2, the Fed's supply of reserves to

---

[4] This change was announced on 6 October 2008, the twenty-ninth anniversary of another famous change in the Federal Reserve operating procedures – the introduction of nonborrowed-reserve targeting, which heralded Fed Chairman Volcker's "monetarist experiment" on 6 October 1979. See the appendix to this chapter for a discussion of that episode.

the market is shown as a vertical line above R. The supply is determined mostly by the Fed's purchases of government bonds and does not change no matter how the Fed-funds rate (r_{FF}) may change.[5]

Banks demand reserves to fulfill their legal reserve requirements and their prudential needs. Unhappily for the banks, under its "classic" operating procedures, the Fed paid no interest on reserves. Nevertheless, under the classic operating procedures a bank can profitably lend its excess reserves to other banks that need them. Each bank must consider the opportunity cost of holding an extra dollar of reserves.

On the one hand, if the bank holds the dollar, it loses what it could earn from lending it – that is, the interest, measured by the Fed-funds rate (r_{FF}).

On the other hand, if the bank holds the dollar of reserves, that dollar remains available in case it is needed to honor an outstanding check or electronic funds (or wire) transfer. What is the value of that? If the bank did fall short, it would itself have to borrow the dollar and pay the Federal-funds rate. As is generally true with economic decisions, the bank must choose its course of action without knowing the outcome. It may decide to hold the dollar and yet, in the end, not need it. Then the bank loses the interest with certainty. But there is some probability (call it *prl* for "probability of reserve loss") that the bank will be called on to use the dollar; then holding it avoids the need to borrow to meet its commitments. The value of this insurance is the probability of reserve loss times the cost of borrowing at the Federal-funds rate: $prl \times r_{FF}$.

The opportunity cost of holding a dollar of reserves is then the certain loss of not lending it out less the probabilistic gain of avoiding having to borrow:

$$opportunity\ cost = r_{FF} - prl(r_{FF}) = (1 - prl)r_{FF}.$$

Notice that as the Fed-funds rate rises, the opportunity cost itself rises. When the opportunity cost is higher, a bank wishes to hold fewer reserves. As a result, the demand for reserves for the banking system should be downward sloping in Figure 16.2. Notice also, that as the probability of reserve loss increases, the lower the opportunity cost. So, at each Fed-funds rate, the banks would demand more reserves, and the reserve-demand curve would shift to the right.

All of the reserves outstanding must be held by one bank or another. Any bank unwilling to hold them at a particular Fed-funds rate will try to lend

---

[5] This is a simplification because banks may also borrow reserves from the Fed (discount loans). Such borrowing becomes more attractive than borrowing from other banks whenever the discount rate is lower than the Federal-funds rate. Recognizing this gives the reserve-supply curve a more complicated shape. But under classic Fed rules, the Fed sets the discount rate above the Federal-funds rate, so there is very little discount borrowing; thus, we can usually ignore these complications.

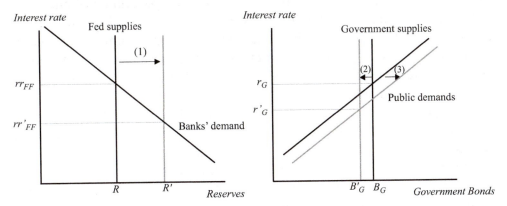

Figure 16.3. An Open-Market Purchase. An open-market purchase consists of the Fed using reserves to buy government bonds. This increases the supply of reserves (shift 1), and reduces the supply of government bonds (shift 2). In addition, because reserves and government bonds are substitutes, the demand curve for government bonds also shifts to the right in response to the fall in the Federal-funds rate. The net effect is that the stock of reserves rises, the stock of government bonds fall, and the interest rates on both instruments fall.

them, and any bank that wants more at that rate will try to borrow them. Thus, the Fed-funds rate must adjust until it reaches the value determined by the intersection of the supply and the demand for reserves.

Open-Market Operations

The Federal Reserve can manipulate the stock of reserves and the Fed funds rate by buying or selling some asset. In practice, the Fed normally restricts itself to government bonds. Such purchases and sales are known as **OPEN-MARKET OPERATIONS**. The FOMC determines the Fed's policy. During most of the period since World War II, open-market policy has been directed toward controlling interest rates. And since 1980, the policy has involved an explicit target (or target range) for the Federal-funds rate.[6]

The FOMC meets in Washington (usually eight times a year) to assess the state of the economy and to determine monetary policy until the next meeting. Its policy is summarized in an instruction to the **Open Market Desk**, the office in the Federal Reserve Bank of New York that deals with selected government-bond brokers. Each day, the Open Market Desk monitors the Federal-funds rate and decides the level of reserves it needs to supply to hit the FOMC's target. It is usually able to do so with great accuracy.

Imagine that the FOMC wishes to reduce the Fed-funds rate. Figure 16.3 shows how this can be achieved through an **open-market purchase** of

---

[6] From the end of 1979 through 1982, the FOMC set so wide a range for the Federal-funds rate target that it was effectively not binding. This period is discussed in more detail in the appendix to this chapter.

government bonds. The left-hand panel is similar to the Federal funds market in Figure 16.2. The right-hand panel shows the government-bond market. The supply of government bonds is shown as the vertical line at B^G. It is determined by the history of the deficits and by the government's choice of maturity structure. The public's demand to own government bonds is shown as an upward-sloping line: the higher the yield (the lower the price), the more they wish to hold.

When the Fed purchases the government bonds, it credits the banks with more reserves. The banks, in turn, credit those who sold the government bonds to the Fed with more money in their checking accounts. The increase in the supply of reserves is shown as the shift of the reserve-supply curve (1) from R to R'. This drives the Fed-funds rate down from r_{FF} to r'_{FF}. Of course, the Fed's purchase of government bonds reduces the supply in the hands of the public dollar for dollar.

The shift of the government-bond supply curve (2) is shown as *relatively* smaller than the shift of the reserve curve, because the government-bond market is much larger than the Fed funds market, so implicitly the units of measurement on the bond axis of the right-hand panel are coarser than those on the left. Economically, the *direct* reduction of the government-bond rate is likely to be smaller than that of the Federal-funds rate.

There is also an *indirect* demand effect to consider. Fed funds and government bonds are substitutes in bank portfolios. As we saw in Chapter 7 (section 7.2.1), when the yield on one financial instrument (here, Fed funds) falls, the demand for the other financial instrument (here, government bonds) increases. This is shown as a rightward shift in the public's demand for government bonds (3), which further reduces the government-bond rate. The combined direct and indirect effects are shown as the fall in the bond rate from r_G to r'_G.[7] An open-market purchase is an example of **EXPANSIONARY** (also called **looser or easier**) **MONETARY POLICY**: lower interest rates stimulate expenditure and aggregate demand.

An **open-market sale** of government bonds works exactly the reverse of a purchase: the Fed decreases the stock of reserves, raising the Fed-funds and government-bond rates. An open-market sale is an example of a **CONTRACTIONARY** (also called **tighter** or more **restrictive**) **MONETARY POLICY**. Using open-market operations, the Fed is able to set the Fed-funds rate at pretty much any level it chooses.

Open-Mouth Operations

We saw in Chapter 7 that the demand for financial assets is not a purely mechanical thing but depends crucially on expectations of the future, which

---

[7] In principle, the demand curve for reserves could also shift in response to changes in the yield on government bonds, but we have ignored this shift as it is likely to be small.

are affected by ever-changing information. The Fed funds market is no different. Where the Fed wants the Federal-funds rate to be is probably the most relevant information. For many years, the FOMC kept its deliberations and its target secret until long after its meetings. Even so, a profession of "Fed watchers" learned to guess with a fair degree of accuracy what the Fed's target actually was. In 1994, the Fed began publishing its target on the day of the FOMC meeting.

The market tends to use the Fed-funds target as a focal point for its demand. As a result, once the target is known the demand curve tends to shift immediately to the target rate without the Fed actually engaging in open-market operations. Because just saying it, in effect, makes it so, target changes are sometimes referred to as **OPEN-MOUTH OPERATIONS**. It is not that open-market operations are unimportant. Rather, they now serve as a threat. Knowing that the Fed can force a change in the Federal-funds rate, arbitrage forces the market to the target rate without actual open-market operations. To see why, think what would happen if the Fed lowered its target rate. No bank would be willing to borrow at a higher rate, because the Fed had committed to reducing the rate through open-market operations if need be. And competition between lending banks would drive actual rates down to the level that borrowing banks would be willing to pay. A credible threat of enforcing a target through open-market operations would provide all the incentive that both borrowers and lenders need to focus on the target rate. Although the Fed does not directly target the Treasury bill rate, a similar process works in the markets to keep Treasury-bill rates in their proper relationship to the targeted Federal-funds rate.

Figure 16.4 shows how an open-mouth operation simplifies Fed-funds-rate targeting. The Fed announces its reduction of the Fed-funds target from r_{FF} to r'_{FF}. The banks' demand curve immediately shifts (1) until it intersects the unchanged reserve-supply curve at the new Federal-funds rate. Because no reserves were actually bought or sold, the supply of government bonds is unaffected, but the public's demand for government bonds increases (2) because of arbitrage. The government-bond rate falls from r_G to r'_G.

Interest-Bearing Reserves

Although a bank borrowing reserves must pay the Federal-funds rate to the lending bank, banks that simply held reserves with a Federal Reserve Bank traditionally earned no interest. Under the new operating procedures, banks earn interest on reserves held with the Fed at a rate a little below the Federal-funds target rate.[8] The effect of this policy is to reduce the

---

[8] The exact rate (as of March 2010) for **required reserves** is 10 basis points (= 0.10 percent) below the average target rate for the two-week reserve accounting period and for **excess reserves** 75 basis points below the minimum target rate for the accounting period. (A **basis point** = 1/100th of a percentage point.)

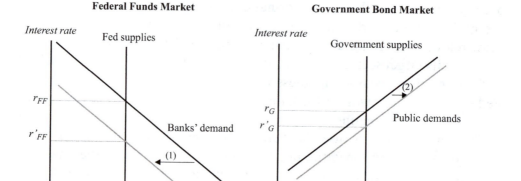

Figure 16.4. **An Open-Mouth Operation.** An "open-mouth" operation occurs when the Fed announces a new target, which becomes a focal point for the Fed funds market. If the Fed announces a new, lower target rate, the banks' demand for reserves shifts (1) to the left and the Federal-funds rate falls, even though the supply of reserves remains unchanged. Because reserves and government bonds are substitutes, the public's demand for government bonds increases in response to the lower Federal-funds rate (shift 2), reducing the government bond rate as well.

opportunity cost for a bank holding reserves and, therefore, to reduce the bank's incentive to lend them to other banks.

To see what this means consider Figure 16.5, which is a modification of Figure 16.2. The rate at which the Fed pays interest on reserves (r_{floor}) places

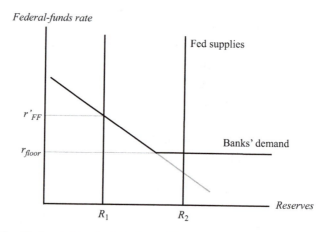

Figure 16.5. **The Federal Funds Market.** When the Federal Reserve pays interest on reserves held by banks at Federal Reserve banks, it sets a floor (r_{floor}) or lower bound to market interest rates, as no bank would lend Federal funds to another bank at less than the r_{floor}. In effect, it puts a kink into the banks' demand curve. At a reserve supply of R_1 the floor is not binding, and the Federal funds market behaves in the classic manner. But at a reserve supply of R_2 the floor is binding and the Federal-funds rate is determined by the floor – itself determined by the Fed's own target for the Federal-funds rate.

a floor below market rates. No bank would lend reserves below that rate. As a result, the demand curve for holding reserves, which looks exactly the same as in Figure 16.2, above the floor rate has a kink and becomes horizontal at r_{floor}. If the total reserve supply is at a level such as R_1, then the floor is not binding, and the analysis of the market is exactly the same as in the classic case. On the other hand, if the total reserve supply is at a point such as R_2 at which it intersects reserve demand to the right of the kink, the floor is binding, and the Federal-funds rate is determined by r_{floor}.

When the floor is binding, the new policy gives the Fed greater control over the reserve market. Whereas under the classic procedures, any fluctuation in the banks' demand for reserves would change the Federal-funds rate, under the new procedures the Federal-funds rate can be targeted more exactly – it is determined by the floor. And if the Fed wishes to change the Federal-funds rate, it can do so simply by raising or lowering its target rate, which in turn changes the floor rate.

Discount-Window Policy

The open-market operation is far and away the most important tool of recent monetary policy. But the Fed does have other arrows in its quiver. The next in line is **discount policy**. The Fed can determine the **discount rate**, that is, *the interest rate that a bank pays to borrow reserves from its district Federal Reserve Bank*. The institutional mechanism through which the Fed makes discount loans is referred to as the **Discount Window**.

Before the Great Depression, discount lending was the major source of reserves to the banking system. From the 1930s until the financial crisis of 2008–2009, discount lending was typically tiny. In the month before the onset of the recession in December of 2007, discount lending was about $366 million – less than 0.5 percent of outstanding bank reserves. For most of the post-World War II period, the Fed had set the discount rate below the Fed-funds rate. In principle, such a policy should have encouraged banks to borrow from the Fed rather than from other banks. Yet, as was mentioned earlier, the Fed frowned upon frequent or large discount borrowing and, in fact, maintained regulations that discouraged it. Recently, however, the Fed has changed its policy. It sets the discount rate for most borrowers above the Federal-funds rate (so that banks would generally want to borrow from the Fed only in an emergency), but it also welcomes borrowing from banks in good standing with good collateral.

Despite its minor importance in day-to-day monetary policy in normal times, discount lending still plays an important part when the Fed is called upon to act as a lender of last resort. In the wake of the attack on the World Trade Center, when the normal bank-clearing mechanisms in New York were physically disrupted, discount lending shot up from $156 million before

September 11th 2001 to $6.6 billion immediately after. Emergency measures soon restored the necessary infrastructure, and three weeks later discount lending fell back to $612 million and five weeks later was actually about half its pre-September 11th value.

The financial crisis of 2008–2009 provides the single most striking example of the Fed acting as a lender of last resort through the discount window. To protect the liquidity of the banking system, the Fed increased discount lending by more than 1,100 times over the level in November of 2007 to a level of $403 billion in November of 2008.

Reserve Requirements

The Fed can also change reserve requirements. An increase in reserve requirements is equivalent to a rightward shift of the reserve-demand curve in Figure 16.2. It would raise the Federal-funds rate much the same as an open-market sale of government bonds. Reserve requirements were changed frequently in the 1950s and 1960s. Since then, the Fed has largely abandoned changing requirements as a tool of monetary management. Reserve requirements on transactions accounts, for example, have remained constant at 10 percent since 1992.

16.3 The Opportunity-Cost or Interest-Rate Channel of Monetary Policy

Monetary policymakers seek to improve macroeconomic outcomes by stimulating or restraining aggregate demand using short-term interest rates as their primary tool. There are two steps in this process:

1. Changes in interest rates affect investment, but capital is typically a long-lived real asset, so the appropriate opportunity cost is a long-term, not a short-term, rate of interest. Somehow the Fed must use the Fed-funds rate to control longer rates of interest.
2. Interest-rate policy affects nominal rates of interest, but real investment and real aggregate demand depend on real rates. Monetary policy must take account of the expected rate of inflation when choosing the appropriate nominal interest rate.

16.3.1 Using Short Rates to Control Long Rates

Scenario 1: A Credible Permanent Change in the Federal-Funds Rate

According to the expectations theory of the term structure of interest rates (see Chapter 7, section 7.4.2), long-term interest rates can be seen as the average of current and expected future short rates. If the Fed alters the

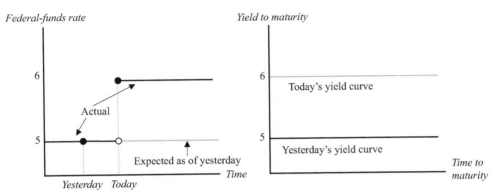

Figure 16.6. The Effect of a Permanent Increase in the Federal-Funds Rate on the Yield Curve. An unexpected, a permanent increase in the Federal-funds rate shifts the yield curve vertically upward.

Federal-funds rate, it will affect the entire term structure of interest rates. Figure 16.6 presents an ideal case.

The left-hand panel shows the path of the Fed-funds rate. Imagine that for a very long time it had been held at 5 percent and that, until yesterday, the public had expected it to be held at 5 percent for the foreseeable future. If we ignore risk, then it is easy to calculate (as we did in Chapter 7, section 7.4.2) that bonds of every maturity would also have to yield 5 percent – otherwise there would be arbitrage opportunities. *Yesterday's yield curve* in the right-hand panel reflects this flat-term structure.

Now imagine that today the Fed surprises the public by raising the Federal-funds rate to 6 percent and announcing its intention to hold it at that rate indefinitely. *Today's yield curve* shows that bonds of every maturity would have to rise quickly to 6 percent to cut off new arbitrage opportunities. In an ideal case, the Fed can use a single interest rate of the shortest maturity to control rates at every longer maturity.

Scenario 2: The Public Believes the Change in the Federal-Funds Rate is Temporary

Scenario 1 makes monetary policy look too easy. Unfortunately, the Fed never announces its intention to hold the Federal-funds rate constant forever. And, even if it did, anyone who looked at the history of a widely fluctuating Federal-funds rate would have no reason to credit the Fed's intention. It is not the Fed's actual intentions that matter to the yield curve, but rather what the public *believes* the Fed's intentions to be.

The left-hand panel of Figure 16.7 shows the Fed attempting to follow the same policy as in scenario 1. But in this case, the public believes that the Fed will raise the Federal-funds rate by one point to 6 percent, hold

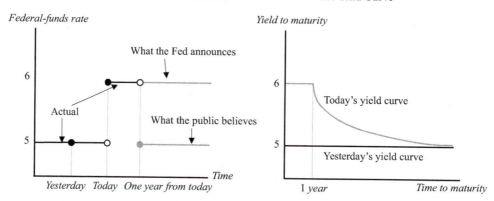

Figure 16.7. The Effect of a Permanent Increase in the Federal-Funds Rate on the Yield Curve. An announced permanent increase in the Federal-funds rate will not necessarily result in a vertical, parallel shift of the yield if the public does not believe the announced policy. In the diagram, the public believes that the Fed will reverse its policy after one year. The result is that the yield curve shifts up by the full amount of the increase in the Federal-funds rate for maturities between 0 and 1 year, and for smaller amounts for every longer maturity. Because longer maturities are an average of expected future short rates, the longer the maturity the smaller the weight given to the first year's Federal-funds rate and the lower the current yield.

the new rate in place only for one year, and then return to the old rate of 5 percent. As a result, using the expectations theory of the term structure, every bond from a 1-day to a 1-year maturity must yield 6 percent. This is shown as the flat section on the left-hand side of the upper, gray curve in the right-hand panel. Notice that the 2-year rate is the average of the current 1-year rate and the 1-year rate expected next year: $(6 + 5)/2 = 5.5$. The 3-year rate is the average of the current 1-year rate and the expected 1-year rates for the next two years: $(6 + 5 + 5)/3 = 5.33$. And so on. The yield curve implied in this scenario slopes downward for all maturities longer than one year. It is always higher than 5 percent, but at long maturities it lies only a little above yesterday's yield curve. Under scenario 2, monetary policy would reduce aggregate demand only a little, because it would not raise long rates by much.

Credibility

Both scenario 1 and 2 are extreme cases. The FOMC does not attempt to hide the fact that it adjusts its target for the Federal-funds rate in response to changing economic conditions and never announces that any change is permanent. But the two scenarios do highlight the fact that it is not just the Fed's intentions that matter; it is also the degree of faith that the public puts in the Fed's policies.

For example, the following would produce exactly the same yield curve:

(i) the Fed announces that the Federal-funds rate will increase by one point for one year and then return to its old level, and the public believes the Fed;
(ii) the Fed announces that the Federal-funds rate will increase by one point permanently, but the public firmly believes that the Fed will reverse course and lower the rate by one point in a year's time.

In the first case, the Fed gets the pattern of interest rates it wants. In the second case, it wants long rates to rise by the full increase in short rates; but, lacking **CREDIBILITY**, its policy is thwarted.

In the 1970s, the public – especially financial markets – came to believe that it could not trust the Fed to follow a policy of fighting inflation by restraining aggregate demand through higher interest rates. Whether this belief was justified or not, the Fed's policies lacked credibility, which compromised its ability to use the Federal-funds rate to raise or lower longer rates. The chairmen of the Federal Reserve, Paul Volcker (1979–1987) and Alan Greenspan (1986–2007), were widely praised for restoring the Fed's influence over macroeconomic outcomes. Volcker and Greenspan demonstrated that they were willing to raise the Federal-funds rate to very high levels if necessary, tightening monetary policy and reducing inflation, even at the cost of higher unemployment. Once the Fed's credentials as an inflation-fighter were restored, once Volcker and Greenspan had established credibility, then smaller increases in the Federal-funds rate could achieve the desired effect.

16.3.2 Long Rates, Real Rates, Output, and Inflation

If the Federal Reserve could successfully use the Federal-funds rate to set long rates of interest, what level of long rates should it choose?

A Stable Inflation Rate

Investment depends in part on its opportunity cost (Chapters 13 and 14, section 14.5.1). We measured the opportunity cost as the difference between the *ex ante* real rate of return on a bond (rr^e) and the real rate of return on real capital (ρ): $rr^e - \rho = (r - \hat{p}^e) - \rho$ (Chapter 13, section 13.3.1). The term in parentheses reminds us that the real rate is the nominal rate corrected for expected inflation. To set a particular real rate, the monetary policymaker has to pay attention to the rate of inflation. The policymaker's problem can be displayed using the combined IS/Phillips curve diagram from Chapter 15 (e.g., Figure 15.10).

Imagine that the Fed was prepared to accept the current rate of inflation ($\hat{p}_0^e$), but wanted to prevent it from accelerating and was unwilling to

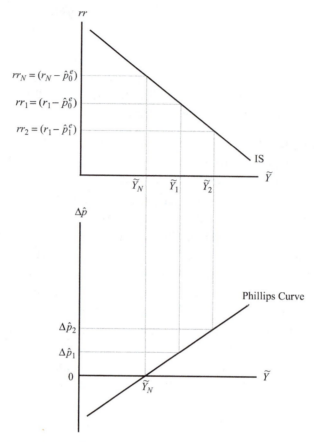

Figure 16.8. A Cumulative Process. Aggregate demand is represented by the IS curve. In order to maintain NAIRU, the real rate of interest must be set where aggregate demand equals NAIRU ($\tilde{Y}_N$). The Fed aims for a Fed-funds rate that delivers a nominal long-term rate (r_N) that, for the initial rate of inflation $\hat{p}_0^e$, achieves a real rate of rr_N. If monetary policy results in a lower real rate of interest, then aggregate demand exceeds the natural rate and prices begin to accelerate. The increase in the inflation rate for the same nominal rate reduces the real rate further, and prices accelerate faster and faster.

let output fall (or unemployment rise) to reduce it. Where should it set the nominal rate of interest? The lower panel of Figure 16.8 shows that NAIRU is $\tilde{Y}_N$. The upper panel shows that a real rate of rr_N is needed to achieve the NAIRU level of aggregate demand. Given the current rate of inflation, the Fed should try to achieve a long rate of interest of $r_N = rr_N + \hat{p}_0^e$.[9]

An important lesson of Figure 16.8 is that whether a monetary policy is tight or loose cannot be judged on the basis of a market interest rate

---

[9] Both the Swedish economist Knut Wicksell (1851–1926) and the English economist John Maynard Keynes (1883–1946), in his *Treatise on Money* (1930), referred to a rate such as r_N that holds the inflation rate constant as the *natural rate of interest*. In fact, Milton Friedman coined the term the *natural rate of unemployment* through a conscious analogy to Wicksell's usage.

alone – neither from the Federal-funds rate nor from a longer-term rate. For example, a rate of 6 percent may be tight when expected inflation is 1 percent (so that the real rate is 5 percent), but it is very likely loose when the expected inflation rate is 5 percent (and the real rate 1 percent).

A Cumulative Process

Recall from Chapter 15 (section 15.3.3) that NAIRU (expressed as an unemployment rate) is usually somewhat higher than full employment defined as the point at which the supply of labor and the demand for labor are equal. With the economy at NAIRU, monetary policymakers who care about unemployment might be led into temptation. If they were to lower long rates a little, say to r_1, and if expected inflation were unaffected, then the real rate in Figure 16.8 would fall to $rr_1 = r_1 - \hat{p}_0^e$. Output would rise to $\tilde{Y}_1$, and unemployment would fall. That's the good news.

The bad news is shown in the lower panel. The Phillips curve shows that the increase in aggregate demand causes prices to accelerate. When expectations have fully adapted, the new expected inflation rate is higher ($\hat{p}_1^e = \hat{p}_0^e + \Delta \hat{p}_1$), and the real rate even lower ($rr_2 = r_1 - \hat{p}_1^e$), even though the Fed has held the nominal rate constant at r_1. The fall in the real rate pushes aggregate demand still higher to $\tilde{Y}_2$. And that, of course, causes a further acceleration of prices. The initial reduction in the nominal interest rate has set off a **CUMULATIVE PROCESS** in which higher aggregate demand leads to accelerating prices and higher inflation, which lead to even higher aggregate demand, and so on.

Accelerating prices are the natural consequence of trying to push the economy below NAIRU. That fact does not imply that the effort is futile. Depending on how rapidly expectations adjust and how willing the Fed is to accept the inflationary consequences, the economy may enjoy additional output and lower unemployment for some time. But it does show that there is a cost to adopting such a policy. Eventually, the distaste for inflation will outweigh the desire for fuller employment, and the policy will have to be reversed. The further prices are allowed to accelerate, the harder and more costly it will be to wring inflation out of the system.

The Effective State of Monetary Policy Depends on the State of the Economy

Even if the Fed chooses an interest-rate policy that holds inflation constant, it must remain vigilant and ready to respond flexibly to changing circumstances. For example, toward the end of a boom, the real rate of return on capital tends to fall as firms have used up the best profit opportunities and very likely overinvested (easily seen as the fall in capacity utilization at a time when GDP growth is still strong). This fall in ρ results in lower

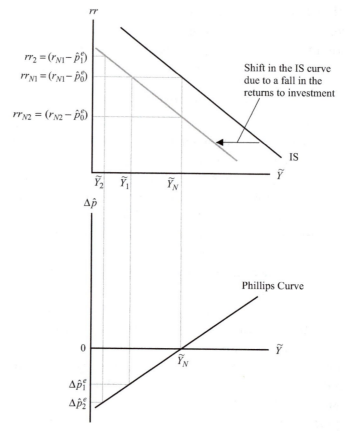

Figure 16.9. A Fall in the Return on Real Capital Decelerates Prices. Starting at NAIRU ($\widetilde{Y}_N$) where the real interest rate is rr_{N1}, inflation is constant. A fall in the real return on investment shifts the IS curve to the left, reducing aggregate demand and decelerating prices at the rate $\Delta\hat{p}_1$. The lower inflation rate raises the real rate of interest, for a constant nominal rate, which further reduces aggregate demand, further decelerating prices. The process is cumulative unless monetary policy is able to reduce nominal long-term interest rates by enough (to rr_{N2}) to restore NAIRU.

investment at every real rate of interest – that is, in a leftward shift of the IS curve as shown in Figure 16.9.

Initially, aggregate demand is at NAIRU with an interest rate of r_{N1}, corresponding to a real interest rate of rr_{N1}. To hold the economy at NAIRU in the face of the shift in the IS curve, the Fed should aim for a lower long rate of r_{N2} yielding a real rate of rr_{N2}. What happens if the FOMC is inattentive and holds the long rate at r_{N1}?

That rate corresponded initially to the real rate of rr_{N1}; but on the new IS curve that rate implies scaled output below NAIRU at $\widetilde{Y}_1$, which leads, according to the Phillips curve, to a deceleration of prices ($\Delta\hat{p}_1 < 0$). The new rate of inflation is $\hat{p}_1 = \hat{p}_0 + \Delta\hat{p}_1$. If the nominal rate continues to be held at its original level and expectations adapt to the now lower rate of inflation, the real rate rises to $rr_2 = r_{N1} - \hat{p}_1$, which further reduces investment and aggregate demand and further decelerates prices ($\Delta \hat{p}_2 < 0$).

Without taking any direct action, the Fed has allowed monetary policy to tighten. Just as in the previous case, the shift in the IS curve has set off a cumulative process – but this time in the opposite direction: lower aggregate demand leads to decelerating prices and lower inflation, which lead to even lower aggregate demand, and so on.

16.4 The Credit Channel

In addition to the opportunity-cost (or interest-rate) channel, monetary policy may also affect the real economy more directly through a *credit channel*.

16.4.1 The Narrow Credit Channel

If the Federal Reserve lowers the supply of reserves through an open-market operation, some banks will find themselves with fewer reserves than needed to fulfill their reserve requirements. When one bank is short, it can borrow on the Federal funds market. When the whole banking system is short, there are insufficient funds to satisfy all the banks. In the scramble for reserves, the banks will drive the Federal-funds rate up. This should affect the economy through the interest-rate channel, but it does not solve the banks' problem – they are still short of reserves.

There are two possibilities. First, the banks raise more reserves through issuing more liabilities. Large banks may be able to sell negotiable certificates of deposit (CDs) that compete with commercial paper, Treasury bills, and other short-term bonds. These CDs do not face reserve requirements.

Second, the banks may be able to shift some of their profitable assets into reserves. Loans of various sorts form the largest entries on the asset side of commercial-bank portfolios. Some are payable on demand, but it is usually bad business to call loans early. Banks also hold government and commercial bonds. These have a ready market. In the short run, banks can sell these bonds and hold the proceeds as reserves.

In the slightly longer run, banks can reduce their loan portfolios. Every day banks receive some repayments of interest and principal on outstanding loans. If they hold these funds and do not turn around and lend them again, then their reserve balances rise. To implement such a policy, the bank tightens its lending standards: it sets a higher standard of creditworthiness for its new customers; it demands higher collateral and higher down payments; it insists on smaller average loan amounts; it engages in **credit rationing**, even if it does not charge a higher interest rate.

These actions would appear to improve the reserve position of any one bank, but because the stock of reserves is fixed, they do not in themselves improve the reserve position of the banking system. But as banks shift their asset portfolios away from loans toward reserves, deposits will also fall for the banking system as a whole. This is easiest to see when, say, a car loan is paid off: if I send the bank a check, the bank deducts its value from my checking account (the deposit liabilities of my bank fall); and, if the bank does not lend the funds it received to another customer, the bank's loan assets fall as well. With lower deposits, the system's need for reserves is reduced.

When credit rationing becomes widespread in the banking system, there is a **credit crunch**, and economic activity slows. A builder may not be able to bid on a contract because the bank has reduced his credit line below the point needed to purchase supplies and meet payroll. A software firm may have to lay off employees and curb its expansion plans. A restaurant on the edge of breaking even may have to close its doors. Similarly, a couple may not be able to find an adequate mortgage to finance their first house. A recent graduate may delay buying a new car.

It is often easiest to think of credit as rationed only by price: when it is in high demand or short supply, interest rates rise; when it is low demand or high supply, interest rates fall. Whatever the rate, firms or people can borrow as much or as little as they like at that rate. It is only the opportunity cost that enters their calculation. This is an ideal case of the so-called **perfect capital market**. The real world is imperfect. Real people and real firms cannot borrow as much as they like. Lenders consider the risk of the loan and the collateral of the borrower. It is easier and cheaper to borrow to buy a house than to finance a party. If the borrower defaults on a mortgage, the bank can always seize the house and recover at least a good part of its money.

The credit channel as described so far is sometimes known as the **narrow credit channel**. Monetary policy can operate through it even if interest rates do not change much.

16.4.2 *The Broad Credit Channel*

A monetary policy that does change interest rates may also operate through a **broad credit channel**, which reinforces the opportunity-cost channel.

The broad credit channel works through changes in the value of the financial portfolios of firms. As we know from Chapter 6 (section 6.2), rising interest rates reduce the market value of financial assets in firm portfolios – both interest-bearing bonds and, because of substitution and arbitrage, stocks. They also raise the cash that must be devoted to debt service. If the amount that banks or financial markets are willing to lend to any firm depends on the strength of its financial portfolio, then the deterioration of its balance sheet and cash flow reduces its borrowing opportunities and may lead to downgrading of its credit rating. Risk premia (measured, e.g., by the spread between yields on corporate and government bonds of similar maturities) rise as default risk increases. Even if firms are able to borrow, their opportunity costs have risen; so, they invest less.

Narrow or broad, the credit channel operates only because of market imperfections. If a bank, for example, can easily raise funds through selling negotiable CDs, it does not have to reduce its lending in the face of lower reserves. Financial markets are less accessible to small banks than to large banks. Similarly, if banks are reluctant to extend credit, a large firm with a good credit rating can often turn to bond markets – especially to the short-term commercial paper market. Thus, in normal times, the credit channel is likely to operate more through smaller banks and smaller or less creditworthy firms. A credit crunch hits some parts of the economy harder than others.

Times are not always normal, as the financial crisis of 2008–2009 amply demonstrated. The crisis was striking in that the biggest, and previously strongest banks, suddenly faced doubts about their solvency and found it difficult to raise funds. Similarly, AAA-rated corporations found the commercial paper markets to have completely dried up. To counter the crisis and the recession that contributed to it, the Fed drove the Federal-funds rate to zero. With no expansionary power left in the opportunity-cost channel, and the entire financial system and corporate-sector liquidity constrained, the credit channel – normally a minor mode of monetary policy – became the Fed's principal instrument (see Box 16.1).

16.4.3 The Operation of the Credit Channel

Narrow or broad, the credit channel operates through shifting the IS curve. Starting from NAIRU ($\widetilde{Y}_N$), with the real rate of interest at rr_N and the inflation rate constant, Figure 16.10 shows a credit crunch: tighter monetary policy as indicated by a fall in reserves relative to GDP (or potential GDP) reduces some firms' access to finance, lowering their investment at each level of real interest rates, and shifting the IS curve to the left. This policy may, of course, also result in a higher real interest rate, say, at rr_1.

The *narrow credit channel* is indicated by the fall in scaled output to $\widetilde{Y}_1$ at the original interest rate, resulting in a fall in the inflation rate of $\Delta \hat{p}_1^e$. The rise in interest rates, if it occurs, will have the usual opportunity-cost effect. The *broad credit channel* is operative if any part of the shift in the IS curve occurs only because of the rise in real-interest rates. The combined effect of

Box 16.1. The Monetary Policy Response to the Financial Crisis of 2008

The financial crisis that started in October of 2008 has been blamed on many factors. The economy had already been in recession for nearly a year. Housing prices had increased out of proportion to other prices, to the growth of GDP, and to historical precedent – some called it a "bubble." Some blamed the Fed for holding interest rates low for too long after the 2001 recession, encouraging all sorts of borrowing and making lenders eager to secure the higher yields offered by less creditworthy borrowers. Some blamed regulatory regimes that promoted mortgage lending on little collateral to ever lower-income and riskier borrowers. Some blamed financial innovations that bundled mortgages into pools financed by bonds backed by these mortgages. When housing prices began to fall, reducing borrowers' collateral, and when the interest rates on adjustable rate mortgages (ARMs), initially offered at low "teaser" rates, began to be reset to market rates, many homeowners found themselves unable to repay their loans. Banks that had purchased credit-default swaps – essentially insurance against the failure of the mortgage-backed bonds in their portfolios – discovered that more such instruments had been sold than could be honored, and the values of the assets on their balance sheets collapsed. With considerable doubt about whether particular firms were solvent, stock prices collapsed and routine borrowing on short-term money markets (e.g., sales of commercial paper) dried up. Unable to finance ordinary operations through the usual channels, the recession accelerated as businesses – large and small – laid off workers and many firms went bankrupt.

The Federal Reserve responded in the single greatest exercise of its lender-of-last-resort function in its nearly 100-year history. Initially, the Fed propped up the collapsing investment bank Bear Stearns, first by making it emergency loans; and then, using its regulatory powers, by forcing a sale at an extremely low price to JP Morgan Chase, another investment bank. The Fed made large emergency loans to AIG, an insurance company that was the largest provider of credit-default swaps. In September, perhaps to discourage other institutions from counting on Fed support, the Fed allowed another investment bank, Lehman Brothers, to go bankrupt. Financial markets were spooked by the collapse of Lehman and the stock market. Many count the collapse of Lehman Brothers as the hinge of the crisis, and many question the wisdom of the Fed's decision not to rescue the company.

Aiming to stimulate the economy and add liquidity to the financial system, the Fed cut the Federal-funds rate to nearly zero, and other short-term interest rates followed suit. Such monetary easing had little effect and, with such low interest rates, further cuts were impossible. The Fed then adopted a policy that came to be known as *quantitative easing*.

Essentially, quantitative easing amounted to purchasing a wider range of assets – both longer maturities and private, rather than Treasury, assets. In November of 2007, the month before the start of the recession, 51 percent of the Fed's holdings of Treasury assets had a maturity of less than one year and 81 percent less than five years. By March of 2010, only 11 percent had a maturity less than one year and 46 percent had a maturity more than five years. In addition, where before the crisis, the Fed held few private assets, by February of 2010, close to half of the Fed's portfolio consisted of private assets: mortgage-backed securities, commercial paper, and the assets taken as collateral from Bear Stearns, AIG, and other troubled banks.

The point of quantitative easing was partly to reduce longer rates of interest by operating directly at the long end of the yield curve. It also functioned to provide the banking system with large amounts of reserves – in effect attempting to operate the credit channel of monetary policy on a massive scale. Ten-year Treasury bond rates, which had stood at 4.10 percent in November of 2007, hit a low of 2.42 percent in December of 2008 and remained at well below 4 percent in early 2010. Bank reserves grew astronomically 2,500 percent between the onset of the recession and early 2010, when they stood at more than $1 trillion. Federal Reserve assets other than bonds backing reserves – for example, direct loans to troubled financial institutions – came to roughly another $1 trillion.

The Treasury backed the Fed's actions when Congress authorized $700 billion for the Troubled Asset Relief Program (or TARP), which provided loans to financial firms holding mortgaged-backed securities of uncertain value.

The recession ended in June of 2009, although by early 2010 the recovery was still weak. The Fed now faced an unprecedented monetary-policy problem: how to unwind its massive monetary stimulus without causing a second recession. The policy of paying interest on reserves is part of the Fed's proposed solution, as banks have less of an incentive to lend interest-bearing than non-interest-bearing reserves.

the broad credit channel and the opportunity-cost channel is shown in the additional fall of scaled output to $\tilde{Y}_2$ with the accompanying additional fall in the inflation rate of $\Delta \hat{p}_2^e$.

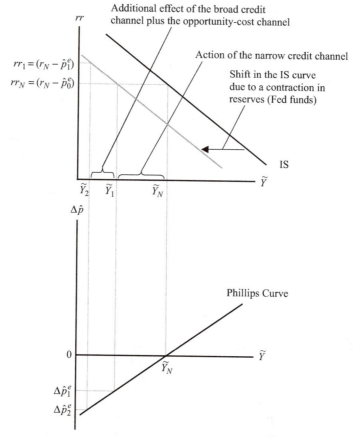

Figure 16.10. The Credit Channel of Monetary Policy. The credit channel operates through nonprice rationing of loans by banks in the face of changing reserves. Here a fall in reserves (credit crunch) reduces bank lending, which in turn reduces investment and consumption expenditure financed by loans, shifting the IS curve leftward. The narrow credit channel refers to the fall in aggregate demand and deceleration of prices that result even at an unchanged interest rate. The broad credit channel adds the further effect of rationing of loans as a result of the fall in net worth of firms and households when interest rates rise.

16.5 The Conduct and Limits of Monetary Policy

16.5.1 The Goals of Monetary Policy

Inflation and Employment

The Humphrey-Hawkins Act of 1978 requires that the Fed pursue a policy aimed at securing "maximum employment, stable prices, and moderate long-term interest rates." The Fed's legal mandate is a difficult one. The monetary policymaker is rather like Cinderella trying to satisfy the impossible demands of her stepsisters: "Go up into the attic, go down into the cellar – you can do them both together, Cinderella." If unemployment is the

Fed's cellar and inflation its attic, the Phillips curve assures our monetary-policy Cinderella that she cannot do them both together.

The Fed's problem may be even more difficult than having to decide the most desirable trade-off between inflation and unemployment. Most economists believe that, in the long run, monetary policy (and aggregate-demand policies generally) can affect only inflation, and not output, employment, or other aspects of the real economy. In Chapter 13 (section 13.4), we saw that an economy cannot be pushed past full employment, although full employment may imply a measured unemployment rate less than NAIRU. Once at full employment, further growth is possible (as we saw in Chapters 9 and 10) only if the capital stock or labor force grows or technology improves. Barring that, an expansionary monetary policy (as we saw in Figure 16.8) must be absorbed by higher prices.

Some economists go further and argue that monetary policy mainly affects inflation even in the short run. They often point to the 1960s and 1970s as evidence. Then, they say, the Federal Reserve tried to push the unemployment rate below NAIRU. Inflation accelerated and, because of unfavorable supply shocks, real output actually fell. The result was stagflation.

This argument makes two key assumptions. The first is that the economy is either always quite near full employment or, if driven away from it, is essentially rapidly self-correcting. On this assumption, increased aggregate demand has nowhere to go but into higher prices. The assumption, however, could be true only if the price system adjusts smoothly and quickly. It may do so in the market for wheat, or even for cars, but (as we saw in Chapter 12) it is unlikely to do so in the labor market. And there may be other markets in which prices are sticky as well.

The second assumption is that expectations of inflation adapt very quickly to changes in actual inflation. If this were not the case, then the economy could run for some time above NAIRU, as both workers and firms suffered from **money illusion** – that is, *the confusion of nominal for real values*. Each would believe that real (relative) prices had shifted in their favor and would willingly supply more labor and output when, in reality, the general price level had risen. Figure 16.11 shows that, although actual and expected inflation track each other roughly, there are long periods of persistent difference.

Hot or Cold Monetary Policy

It seems unlikely that either assumption is true – and even less likely that both are. At the least, the economy might find itself in a slump for some prolonged period. And then, monetary policy could be helpful in pushing it back toward full employment. Indeed, it may be possible to run the economy "hot" – that is, above NAIRU – for some time, provided that the monetary policymakers were prepared to accept the eventual acceleration of prices.

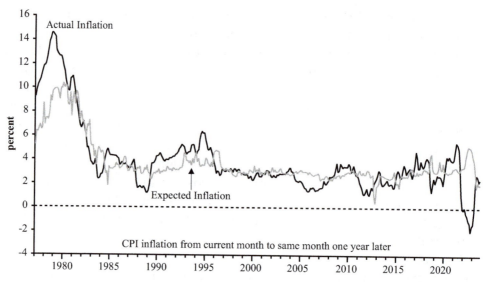

Figure 16.11. Actual and Expected Inflation. *Source:* CPI, Bureau of Labor Statistics; expected inflation, University of Michigan Survey.

Many economists believe that no good could come from such a policy. They appeal to another debatable assumption – namely, that the factors that govern growth and the factors that govern the business cycle are independent. But are they?

An expansionary monetary policy operating through the interest-rate channel and, to some degree, through the credit channel raises aggregate demand by increasing investment. That same investment, however, adds to the capital stock and, potentially, to long-term growth. It may also increase productivity. Even if there were no new technological innovations, the newer capital is likely to be more productive than the oldest capital in use. A higher proportion of new capital, then, implies higher aggregate productivity. Beyond that, it is also likely that true technological innovation accelerates in a boom. (The fall in measured capital productivity [ϕ] near the end of a boom [see Chapter 9, section 9.4.2 and Problem 9.8] is likely to be the result of capital investment outpacing aggregate demand, rather than of a true decline in technology.) In these ways, increased aggregate demand could induce an increase in aggregate supply that, in its turn, helped to mitigate some of the acceleration in prices. Similarly, running the economy "cool" to keep inflation under control could have the opposite effects and perpetuate a tendency to long-run stagnation.

Balancing the Risks

Before drawing the simplistic conclusion that monetary policy should run the economy hot, consider the risks. Even if it has real benefits for growth and employment, the cost of such a policy is accelerating prices. Once the inflation rate gets to an unacceptably high level, monetary policymakers will have to opt for tighter policy. It is hard to get the policy just right and to achieve the so-called "soft landing." If policy is too tight, the Fed may push the economy into recession. A "stop-go" policy – switching between policy-induced booms and policy-induced recessions – is likely to be bad for long-term growth as it raises uncertainty over the course of the economy, making it hard for businesses to plan and periodically bankrupting some of them. (See Chapter 14, section 14.5.1 on the negative effects of risk and uncertainty on investment.)

There is, perhaps, a happy medium in which the central bank aims to hold inflation to a moderate level in the boom, but stands prepared to fight the slumps. This, more or less, has been the policy of the Federal Reserve since World War II. One chairman of the Federal Reserve, William McChesney Martin (1906–1998), is said to have quipped that the Fed's duty was to "take away the punch bowl just when the party was getting going." That probably states the goal too negatively. Its duty might be better described as making sure that the punch is not spiked so much that the police have to be called. Martin also (and more aptly) described the Fed's policy as "LEANING AGAINST THE WIND" – that is, *loosening when the economy was slowing and tightening when it was booming.*

The Fed's official goals have long been both full employment and low inflation. Other central banks differ in whether and how they take the real economy into account. The Reserve Bank of New Zealand and the European Central Bank (ECB), for example, pursue inflation targets exclusively. Before the advent of the euro, the Bundesbank (the German central bank), driven by memories of the great German hyperinflation of the 1920s, also pursued a single-minded policy of defending the purchasing power of the deutschemark. The Bank of England is required to pursue price stability (defined as a 2.5 percent inflation target); although, not unlike the Fed, this goal is explicitly seen as laying the groundwork for sustained growth and high employment.

16.5.2 Rules versus Discretion

A long-standing debate among monetary economists and policymakers is whether central banks should use their **DISCRETION** to direct monetary policy toward whatever goal appears to be best today or whether instead they should establish a fixed **POLICY RULE** and follow it come what may. The argument for discretion is straightforward. Situations change. Information changes. A policymaker who fails to adapt to new situations or to reassess both the situation and policy in light of new information must surely miss opportunities to foster better economic outcomes.

The argument against discretion and in favor of fixed rules is more complex. Advocates of rules make at least four interrelated arguments.

(i) Ignorance

Policymakers are ignorant about the data. Only a few variables, such as interest rates, are available daily. A small number are available weekly. Most are available only monthly (e.g., unemployment) or quarterly (e.g., GDP). In Chapter 3 (section 3.6.2) we likened policymaking in the face of such delays to steering a ship while looking out the stern. If it reacts to every movement in reported GDP, the Fed could easily adopt exactly the wrong policy – for example, to tighten monetary policy when the economy has already entered a recession (running the ship aground). Rather than risking a systematically ill-timed policy, the Fed might do better to follow a rule set to average conditions.

Aside from delays in the collection and publication, we also saw in Chapter 3 (section 3.6.2) that GDP data are frequently revised by relatively large amounts. Most other economic data are also revised – sometimes many times.[10] We saw in Chapter 12 (section 12.2.2) that the unemployment rate does not perfectly reflect the economist's ideal definition of unemployment. The policymaker, then, must decide whether a decrease in unemployment truly reflects an improving economy or whether it is driven by other factors. Again, the same problem applies to other economic data.

Policymakers may also be ignorant about the details of how the economy works. Although economists mostly agree on the broad picture, a discretionary monetary policy requires an accurate calculation of the detailed processes. Generally accepted *detailed* models of the economy are almost nonexistent. A policy that looks perfect according to one model may be disastrous according to another. A simple rule of thumb that is second best under both models could give better average outcomes than putting all of the policy eggs in one model's basket.

(ii) Policy Lags

Monetary policy operates with a three-part **POLICY LAG**. First, the **recognition lag** is *the delay between an actual change in the economic situation and its*

---

[10] The Federal Reserve Bank of Philadelphia maintains a *real-time* macroeconomic database that records data as they were actually published. This allows economists to trace the revisions of the data, but more importantly allows them to see the actual data to which policymakers were reacting, rather than the final data that did not become available until many years later (www.phil.frb.org/econ/forecast/reaindex.html active on 9 March 2010). Using this data, Athanasios Orphanides (formerly an economist with the Board of Governors of the Federal Reserve and currently the governor of the Bank of Cyprus) has argued that monetary policy in the 1970s was not as misguided as later economists have supposed, but merely informed by poorer-than-usual-quality real-time data (see Orphanides, "Monetary Policy Rules Based on Real-Time Data," *American Economic Review*, vol. 91, no. 4 (September 2001), pp. 964–985.)

being perceived by the policymaker. Although the recession of 2001 started in March, economic commentators debated through much of the summer and fall over when, if at all, the downturn would come. The National Bureau of Economic Research (NBER) announced the date of the recession only in November of 2001 – eight months after it began. Similarly, the NBER announced the date of the 2007 recession only in December of 2008 – a year after it began. As we saw in Chapter 5 (section 5.2.2), the lag in the NBER announcing the end of the 1990–1991 recession may have influenced the 1992 presidential election.

Once the need for a change in policy has been assessed, the policymakers must act. This second lag is the **implementation lag**. Typically, the implementation lag for monetary policy is short. The FOMC meets monthly, and has the option of having telephone meetings between the regularly scheduled meetings.

The recognition and implementation lags are sometimes known collectively as the **inside lag**, because they refer to delays within the policymaking process. The distinction between the two lags is not sharp. The FOMC often changes the Federal-funds rate in a series of small quarter- or half-percentage point steps. These slow steps reflect the policymakers' uncertainty about their assessment of the state of the economy. The slow implementation results from the struggle to recognize the true state of the economy.

The effects of any policy action are not immediate. This third lag is the **transmission lag**, also sometimes known as the **outside lag**, because it is the lagged response of those outside the circle of policymakers to the policy action. A decrease in interest rates, for example, quickens the pace of investment only after firms have had time to reassess their capital plans, arrange their financing, place their orders, and commence construction or begin to take delivery of new equipment. It is often said that the lags in monetary policy are "long and variable."

In some sense, the problem of lags is just another version of the problem of ignorance. If data were perfectly timely and perfectly accurate, there would be no recognition lag. If the effects of monetary policy were perfectly predictable, there would still be an implementation lag, but it would not matter, because the right policy could be set in advance to account for it. A rule may be preferred in the absence of such perfection – second best may be all that is practically possible.

(iii) A Stable Economic Environment

While the monetary policymaker reacts to the economy, firms and households react to the policy. A discretionary policy is likely to change in unpredictable ways as it seeks to adjust to each new circumstance. A firm finds it easier to plan its investment or production if it can make an accurate guess about the course of real interest rates. The more unpredictable they are, the more uncertain the firm will be, and the greater the risk that it will make a poor choice. Risk, of course, raises the firm's opportunity costs and discourages investment. It should be easier to predict the actions of a central bank following a rule. And it may help to make the business environment more predictable and less risky. Stability is probably better promoted through simple, easily understood, and easily monitored rules than through complex rules, no matter how scrupulously the monetary policymakers adhere to them.

(iv) Time Consistency

Without a rule, the policymaker finds it hard to stick to the right course of action. Consider a noneconomic example. Both a professor and his students should care about students' learning. The professor may say that a homework assignment is due on Friday. When the day comes and a student asks for an extension, the professor may reason that the loss in learning to the student is high relative to the cost to the professor in accepting the paper late. So, he gives the extension. Word gets around, and more and more students successfully appeal to the same cost-benefit calculation and are allowed to turn in the homework late.

Eventually the cost to the professor rises sufficiently that grade-point penalties are put into place. The penalties may be adjusted to produce a number of late homework assignments that, in the professor's eyes, balances the marginal cost to him of getting work late against the marginal educational benefit of allowing the students extra time to work. This situation is probably much worse than one in which no one turns in the homework late. The problem is that the professor who always uses discretion and adjusts to the situation at hand, finds it hard to say no to a request for an extension when the marginal cost to him is low and the gain to the student high.

A situation in which one policy is announced because it looks good (turn in the homework on Friday), but is (predictably) not enforced in the event, because it looks less good from a later perspective (on Friday extensions are preferred to grade penalties) is said to be TIME- (or DYNAMICALLY) INCONSISTENT. A rule may also be time-*consistent*. A professor who announces a rule of absolutely no extensions and, despite his pangs of pity, is willing to penalize students heavily for missing assignments may find that almost no one actually misses them. The rule reaches the best outcome, while discretion leads to a bad outcome.

The same argument can be applied to monetary policy. Ideally, the central bank would like to achieve price stability and low unemployment. So, it announces a policy aimed at NAIRU. Recall that an economy at NAIRU may not be fully employed in the sense that there is no involuntary unemployment. This is a temptation for a benign policymaker, because an expansionary monetary policy may lower unemployment for a time and the cost in higher inflation may be trivial. Eventually, however, the policy produces a high rate of inflation. If it becomes too costly to let prices accelerate further, then unemployment most be forced back up to NAIRU and the economy is in the unpleasant situation of high inflation for no gain in unemployment.

The original policy of low and constant inflation was dynamically inconsistent. It is sometimes argued that it might have been better never to start down this road. But to keep the central bank from being tempted, it must be fettered by a rule. New Zealand, for instance, not only requires its central bank to pursue only an inflation target, it also ties the compensation of the governors of the bank to their success in hitting the target.

16.5.3 How the Federal Reserve Behaves

Discretion or Rules?

A monetary-policy rule might be simple: hold the real Fed-funds rate at 2 percent. A rule also might be complex and allow for many contingent outcomes. On the one hand, a very complicated rule begins to look very much like discretion and, being less intelligible, it may fail to promote stability.

On the other hand, discretion sometimes begins to look very much like a rule. We all know that to get the water temperature right in the shower, it helps to turn the handle a little, to wait for the temperature to adjust (even in plumbing there is a variable lag), and then to turn it a little more. Big steps usually alternate between freezing and scalding. This sort of tempered discretion also applies in monetary policy.

The policy of leaning against the wind (raise interest rates when inflation accelerates, lower interest rates when GDP growth slows) could be characterized either as a loosely specified rule or as a kind of moderate discretion. If the policy proceeds in small steps, it may capture many of the advantages of a rule without being strict. A quick glance at Figure 16.12 shows that when the Fed tightens or loosens monetary policy, the Federal-funds rate is raised or lowered in a series of small steps – usually 0.25 or 0.50 percentage points.

The Taylor Rule

When Ben Bernanke testifies to Congress each February and July, his rhetoric is the rhetoric of discretion. When the FOMC meets, all the latest data are reviewed, and ostensibly it chooses the best policy based on its assessment of the state of the economy. Yet, there appears to be rule-like patterns in its behavior. John Taylor, a Stanford economist and former

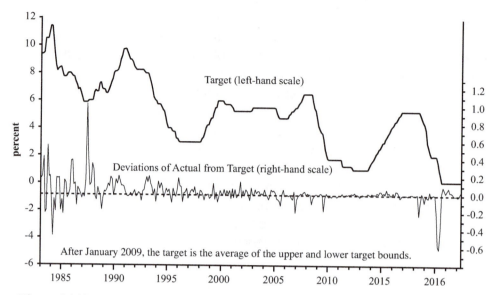

Figure 16.12. Actual and Target Federal-Funds Rate. *Source:* Federal Reserve.

Treasury official, argued that the Fed's policy between 1987 and 1992 could be characterized by a simple rule for setting the Federal-funds rate (r_{FF}):

$$r_{FF} = \overline{rr} + \hat{p} + 0.5(\hat{p} - \hat{p}^*) + 0.5gap. \qquad (16.2)$$

How does the **TAYLOR RULE** work? The rule says that the Fed-funds rate is set with the average real rate of $\overline{rr}$ in mind, but that there are adjustments when actual inflation deviates from its target rate of $\hat{p}*$ and when GDP deviates from potential GDP. (The variable *gap* is the percentage difference between actual and potential GDP, usually measured using the estimates of potential GDP produced by the Congressional Budget Office (CBO) or a similar series in which actual output can exceed potential output. Box 16.2 compares the CBO concept of potential to that developed in Chapter 9, section 9.5, and used throughout this book.)

Taylor assumed that both $\overline{rr}$ and $\hat{p}*$ are 2 percent. Then the rule can be written:

$$r_{FF} = 2 + \hat{p} + 0.5(\hat{p} - 2) + 0.5gap. \qquad (16.2')$$

Imagine that inflation is exactly 2 percent and that actual GDP equals potential GDP, so that *gap* is zero. Then the Federal-funds rate would be set to 4 percent, and the real rate would be 2 percent ($= r_{FF} - \hat{p} = 4 - 2$).

What if inflation picked up to 3 percent, while *gap* remained at zero? Then the Fed would increase the Federal-funds rate by 1.5 points to 5.5 percent ($= 2 + 3 + 0.5(3 - 2)$). The rise in the implied real rate to 2.5 percent ($= 5.5 - 3$) would tighten monetary policy.

Box 16.2. Concepts of Potential Output

Economists frequently use a different concept of potential output than one used throughout this book (see Chapter 9, section 9.5). Several organizations – governmental (e.g., the Congressional Budget Office), international (e.g., the International Monetary Fund and the Organization for Economic Cooperation and Development), and commercial (e.g., Data Resources Incorporated) – have estimated the potential real GDP of the U.S. economy using a different concept. The CBO's estimate is typical. The CBO defines *potential output* as *the level of output attainable when the economy is operating at a high rate of resource use consistent with a stable rate of inflation.*[11] Where we had previously defined potential output as a ceiling that the economy cannot breach, the CBO defines it as a certain desirable level of output.

Although the CBO's method for estimating potential output is sophisticated – in particular, it looks at the rate of resource use in several sectors of the economy independently – its essence is simple. It starts with a Cobb-Douglas production function. Total factor productivity (the coefficient A in the Cobb-Douglas formula) rises in booms and falls in slumps. The CBO abstracts from these cyclical fluctuations to generate a series that grows smoothly from peak to peak. It assumes that the capital stock is always able to deliver its full potential of capital services. The key element in the estimates is that the CBO sets the labor input to the production function equal to the fraction of the labor force that would be available if the economy were operating at NAIRU. This can be written as $(1-NAIRU) \times LF$. The idea is that when labor is at NAIRU, the inflation rate will remain stable. Their method results in the following equation in which the superscript *pot* indicates "potential":

$$Y_t^{pot} = A_t^{pot} [(1 - NAIRU_t)LF]^\alpha \, K_t^{1-\alpha}. \qquad (\text{B16.1.1})$$

In contrast, our definition of potential output in equation (9.22) is repeated here as:

$$Y^{pot} = ALF^\alpha K^{1-\alpha}. \qquad (9.22)$$

The difference in the two approaches rests on whether we regard the entire labor force as contributing to potential production or only that fraction that does not contribute to accelerating inflation.

(continued)

---

[11] Congressional Budget Office, "CBO's Method for Estimating Potential Output," CBO Memorandum, October 1995, p. 1. (The report is available at the CBO website at: ftp://ftp.cbo.gov/3xx/doc312/potout.pdf.)

Box 16.2 (*continued*)

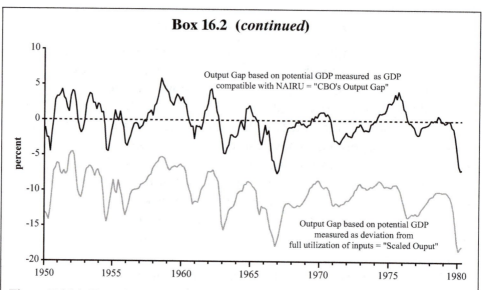

Figure B16.1. Two Concepts of Potential Output. *Source:* Various components from Bureau of Economic Analysis, Congressional Budget Office, the Federal Reserve; Bureau of Labor Statistics; and author's calculations.

Approaches similar to the CBO's have become the most common methods of estimating potential output. Yet, they strain intuition and the natural usage of "potential," which the dictionary defines as "ability or capacity for use or development."[12] Because the actual unemployment rate can stand above or below NAIRU, actual output may sometimes exceed potential output. Clearly, such a concept of potential understates the economic capacity of the economy. In normal usage, "potential output" should express a ceiling.

Rather than computing scaled quantities, we can compute the difference between actual and potential GDP using either definition of potential and expressed as a percentage of potential output. The difference is known as the **output gap**, the **GDP gap**, or the **inflationary gap** and may be defined as: *output gap* $= \frac{Y_t - Y_t^{pot}}{Y_t^{pot}}$. When using the CBO's definition of potential, a positive output gap implies an unemployment rate below NAIRU and, therefore, accelerating prices, whereas a negative output gap implies an unemployment rate above NAIRU and decelerating prices.

Figure B16.1 plots the output gaps using both concepts of potential output. Notice that the CBO gap is sometimes positive and sometimes negative, while gap based on potential as ceiling is always negative – we never live up to potential. The correlation between the two series is high ($R = 0.87$), which suggests that, for many purposes, the difference between the two series will be unimportant.

[12] *Oxford American Dictionary.*

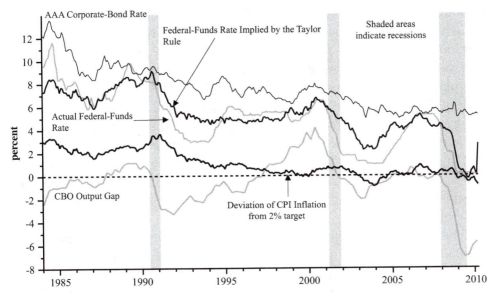

Figure 16.13. Monetary Policy, the Taylor Rule, and Market Interest Rates. *Source:* interest rates, Board of Governors of the Federal Reserve System, CPI, Bureau of Labor Statistics; output gap, Congressional Budget Office; and author's calculations.

Similarly, if inflation were constant, but the *gap* became −2, as it might in a recession, then the Fed would lower the Federal-funds rate to 3.5 percent, and the real rate would fall to 1.5 percent: monetary policy becomes expansionary.

Taylor originally offered the rule as a description of actual Fed behavior. Since then, a number of economists have argued that a Taylor rule (perhaps with different weights on inflation and the *gap*) might also be an economically optimal rule. Even when not an official rule, central banks around the world have used calculations based on a Taylor rule to provide a benchmark against which to measure their actual policy decisions.

Does the Fed Follow a Taylor Rule?

How does the Taylor rule fare as a description of actual Fed policymaking? Figure 16.13 compares the Federal-funds rate implied by the Taylor rule to the actual Federal-funds rate from 1985 to 2010. It also shows the output gap and the gap between actual inflation and its target to give an idea of the forces behind the Taylor rule, and the long-term corporate AAA bond rate to show the reaction of the financial markets to monetary policy. Even though the Federal-funds rate does not conform perfectly to the Taylor rule, it is reasonably close in levels and most of the changes are in the same direction.

The Taylor rule advised a tightening of monetary policy in the three boom periods and a loosening in the three slumps, and actual Fed policy followed suit. The lower two series show that tighter policy in 1980s was driven more by immediate and relatively high inflation, whereas tighter policy in the 1990s was driven by high rates of resource utilization – anticipating and heading off accelerating prices. In both the 1990–1991 recession and the 2001 recession, the Fed cut the Federal-funds rate faster than advised by the Taylor rule. Similarly, in the "Great Recession" of 2007–2009, the Fed cut the Federal-funds rate rapidly to near zero, reacting to a massive fall in the output gap. The Taylor rule, in fact, suggested a negative Federal-funds rate – although, of course, a negative nominal interest rate is impossible. What is striking – and opened the Federal Reserve to much criticism – is that the Taylor rule suggested increasing the Federal-funds rate in the immediate aftermath of the recession to between 2 and 3 percent; yet, the Fed held it at zero for many months.

Finally, notice the relationship between monetary policy and longer rates of interest. The broad pattern of the AAA bond rate is similar to the Federal-funds rate. When monetary policy is tightened near the end of the boom, however, the gap between the two rates narrows considerably. This is the flattening of the yield curve characteristic of the end of a business-cycle expansion, familiar from Chapter 7 (Problems 7.7–7.10). It also confirms the point made in Section 16.3.1 that theory suggests that longer rates of interest will move much less than shorter rates in response to monetary-policy actions, which are rarely regarded as permanent.

The Limits of the Taylor Rule

The Taylor rule implicitly accepts that shocks to aggregate demand are the main challenge to economic stability. How would the economy fare against a shock to aggregate supply (see Chapter 15, sections 15.1.1 and 15.3.4) that raised inflation and lowered GDP when the policymakers followed the Taylor rule?

The increase in the general price level in this case is likely to be permanent, but the increase in the inflation rate merely temporary. Even so, the inflation-target term in equation (16.2′) suggests that the Federal-funds rate should rise. If capital and productivity are properly measured, a supply shock should reduce potential as well as actual GDP, so that *gap* may be affected relatively little. If not measured properly, then *gap* is likely to be negative, and the output-gap adjustment term will suggest a fall in the Federal-funds rate – partially offsetting the rise resulting from inflation. Still, on balance, the Fed-funds rate may well rise. Surely, the last thing that the economy needs in the face of a supply shock is a tight monetary policy adding aggregate-demand insult to aggregate-supply injury – all in reaction to a temporary increase of inflation that accompanies a necessary and permanent adjustment in prices and real wages.

The lesson here is that, although the simple Taylor rule may be a good description of Fed behavior and may offer good policy advice in the right circumstances, it is not the right rule for all circumstances. The Fed may broadly follow a rule, but it also needs to adapt to some shocks by ignoring its rule. In 1987, when the stock market crashed, the Fed ignored its rules and its goals of stable prices and low unemployment and temporarily followed an extremely loose monetary policy to stabilize the financial system. It acted, as it was charged to do in its original charter, as the lender of last resort. The Fed behaved similarly in the immediate aftermath of the terrorist attacks on New York and Washington on September 11, 2001. The most carefully thought-out rule will always need to leave room for this sort of discretion.

16.6 Monetary Policy and International Finance

Although American policymakers and commentators sometimes treat monetary policy as if it involved only domestic considerations, this is the illusion of a large country with a *relatively* small exposure to foreign trade. For any small country, the interaction among monetary policy, its exchange rate, and its foreign trade is likely to be the most important monetary policy issue. Even in the case of the United States, it is well to recall that trade (imports + exports) is a significant fraction of GDP. Monetary policy significantly affects foreign-exchange markets, and they, in turn, affect monetary policy. As mentioned earlier, in addition to the standard opportunity-cost and credit channels of monetary policy, there is also a foreign-exchange channel.

16.6.1 *Controlling the Exchange Rate*

Direct Intervention

If the government desired to control the exchange rate, how would it do it? The most obvious method is to intervene directly. If the United States wants the dollar to appreciate, the Treasury, which controls exchange-rate policy, would direct the Federal Reserve Bank of New York to use official foreign-exchange reserves (its stock of foreign currencies) to buy dollars. It might target a specific currency, say, by buying dollars with Japanese yen – the equivalent, naturally, of selling yen for dollars. Although the proximate effect would be to raise the yen-dollar exchange rate, the overall scarcity of dollars is likely to make them more valuable against a wider range of currencies. And, of course, the government could sell a broader spectrum of currencies.

Under floating exchange rates, direct interventions are rare and generally occur only when the Treasury becomes convinced that currencies are seriously misaligned. The Treasury intervened a mere ten days between 1995 and 2006. Official intervention is typically tiny compared to the ordinary flows on foreign exchanges. The stock of foreign currencies held by the Federal Reserve at the end of 2008 was worth only $25 billion – less than 2 percent of the *daily* volume of foreign-exchange transactions in the world.

Although the Federal Reserve could quickly exhaust its supply of foreign currencies trying to appreciate the dollar, there is no clear limit to direct interventions to depreciate the dollar. Because the Federal Reserve can create dollars, it could buy an unlimited amount of foreign currencies (incidentally adding to official reserves), raising their value and lowering the value of the dollar. Because of this asymmetry, foreign-exchange interventions may be coordinated with other countries. Because the European Central Bank, for example, has an unlimited ability to create euros, it is less constrained than the Federal Reserve in actions to appreciate the dollar against the euro.

Some countries do hold very large foreign-exchange reserves. At the end of 2009, China had the biggest stockpile: $2.4 trillion. Although thirty times larger than U.S. official reserves (including gold and reserves held as special drawing rights or on account with the International Monetary Fund), Chinese official reserves are still roughly half of the daily foreign-exchange volume and could easily be exhausted in direct intervention.

The Treasury and Federal Reserve are aware of their limitations. The Fed's purchases or sales of dollars are small compared with the total volume of dollar trading; they cannot shift the balance of supply and demand directly by very much. Instead, the Fed regards direct intervention "as a device to signal a desired exchange rate movement," through which they hope to affect the present and future behavior of foreign-exchange traders.[13] The idea is to let the markets know that the government believes that exchange rates should be aligned differently. Such interventions work on market expectations, not unlike "open-mouth" operations in domestic monetary policy, by providing markets with a focal point for foreign-exchange transactions. The markets do not always take the hint.

Foreign Exchange and Monetary Policy

The relationship between the exchange rate and monetary policy is two-way. On the one hand, foreign-exchange interventions affect domestic monetary policy. Using newly created dollars to purchase foreign currencies adds to the U.S. monetary base – most of the dollars ending up as additional reserves for the banking system. Essentially, transactions on the foreign exchanges are just another form of open-market operation, using foreign assets rather than Treasury securities as the instrument. These reserves allow banks to expand lending and increase the stock of bank deposits and, therefore, the M1 monetary aggregate.

To avoid monetary expansion resulting from foreign-exchange interventions, the Federal Reserve normally conducts **sterilized interventions**. At the same time as it buys or sells foreign currencies, adding or subtracting

---

[13] "Fedpoint: U.S. Foreign Exchange Intervention" (www.newyorkfed.org/aboutthefed/fedpoint/fed44 .html, active 9 March 2010).

reserves to the banking system, it conducts an offsetting open-market operation. If it has bought foreign currency, it sterilizes the purchase by selling government bonds to the same amount, reabsorbing the newly created reserves. And if it has sold foreign currency, it sterilizes the sale by buying government bonds, replacing the newly depleted reserves. Sterilization restores the *status quo ante* in the banking system.

Conversely, domestic monetary policy may be used to influence the exchange rate – that is, to intervene on foreign-exchange markets indirectly. Indirect intervention is practically more important than direct intervention. Tighter monetary policy (raising U.S. interest rates) is likely to encourage appreciation of the dollar as financial markets around the world pursue higher rates of return.

Changes in the exchange rate may in turn redound on the domestic economy. In fact, the **exchange-rate channel** provides yet another mechanism through which the actions of the monetary authorities manipulate the economy. The appreciation of the exchange rate, owing to tighter monetary policy, has a direct effect: some foreign goods immediately become cheaper measured in dollars, temporarily reducing the rate of inflation. The direct effect may be attenuated for the United States, because a large proportion of its imports are actually invoiced in dollars. Over a longer horizon, foreign firms nonetheless may lower the dollar price of such goods. For example, any dollars earned through selling an Airbus, which is invoiced in dollars, would translate into a greater number of euros; Airbus could set a more competitive dollar price without loss of euro profits.

An indirect effect reinforces the direct effect of tighter monetary policy along the exchange-rate channel. If the increase in the market exchange rate also raises the real exchange rate, the current account is likely to shift in the direction of deficit as U.S. imports expand relative to exports. The fall in net exports reduces aggregate demand and puts downward pressure on inflation.

16.6.2 Exchange-Rate Regimes

Fixed versus Floating Exchange Rates

Up to now, we have assumed that exchange rates are determined on freely operating foreign-exchange markets. Look at Figure 8.4 (Chapter 8). Since 1973, the sterling/dollar exchange shows considerable month-to-month variability, typical of a free market. In contrast, before 1973, there are long periods in which the exchange rate is constant. March 1973 marks the point at which, for most major currencies, a **floating exchange-rate regime** replaced a **fixed-exchange-rate regime**.

The international gold standard, which flourished before World War I and collapsed in the 1930s, represents the ultimate fixed exchange-rate regime. The primary currency of most countries was a gold coin of a specific weight and fineness. The exchange rate was simply the ratio of the pure gold content of these coins. In the 1870s, a British gold sovereign coin worth £1 contained 0.2354 Troy ounces of pure gold; a French gold Napoleon coin worth 20 francs contained 0.1867 ounces of gold. The exchange rate was, therefore, F25.22/£.[14]

Under the gold standard, the central bank was obligated to convert paper banknotes into gold coin on demand. Sometimes – for example, in World War I – governments used monetary expansion to finance expenditure so that the outstanding banknotes vastly exceeded the gold that was supposed to back them. To stanch the outflow of gold as foreigners sought to convert paper money into gold, the major combatants suspended convertibility – that is, they temporarily abandoned the gold standard in favor of unbacked (or *fiat* money). Despite various attempts, the gold standard was never again reestablished for long on the same footing as in the nineteenth century.

In the aftermath of World War II, the **Bretton Woods Agreement** (named for the resort in New Hampshire where it was signed in 1944) established a nearly worldwide system of fixed exchange rates, as well as the World Bank and the International Monetary Fund, institutions that originally aimed to support the exchange-rate system. The Bretton Woods system was a sort of modified gold standard. The U.S. dollar was defined as 1/35 ounce of gold, and other currencies were defined in terms of the dollar. The dollar supplanted gold and the British pound sterling as the world's major reserve currency. Countries agreed to coordinate direct intervention in the foreign-exchange markets to maintain stable exchange rates.

The Bretton Woods system came under great strain toward the end of the 1960s when U.S. inflation resulted in a seriously overvalued dollar (i.e., an exchange rate well above purchasing-power parity). As a result, some foreign holders began to convert dollars into gold, and doubts arose about the ability of the United States to maintain convertibility at $35 per ounce of gold. In 1971, the dollar was revalued to $38 per ounce; in early 1973, to $44 per ounce. Finally, in March of 1973, the link between the dollar and gold was broken entirely, and major currencies were allowed to float freely against one another. For practical purposes, gold ceased to be money at this point, although holdings of monetary gold are still reported as items in official foreign-exchange reserves.

Varieties of Exchange-Rate Management

The period since 1973 is most simply described as a floating-exchange-rate regime; yet few countries have allowed the markets to determine exchange rates with no intervention whatsoever. In fact, there are a variety of

[14] $F25.22/£ = \dfrac{0.2354 \frac{oz.}{£}}{(0.1867/20)\frac{oz.}{F}}$

exchange-rate regimes from truly fixed rates on one end to truly freely floating on the other.

- *Dollarization.* An extreme form of a fixed exchange rate occurs when a country simply adopts the currency of another country (usually, but not always, the U.S. dollar) as one's own. In Panama, for example, the U.S. dollar is legal tender. Panama's own currency, the balboa, is defined as one U.S. dollar. Unofficial dollarization is also common, especially in countries with high inflation rates. For example, in Turkey before the currency reform of 2005 it was common to maintain dollar-denominated bank accounts and to express the prices of high-value goods, such as real estate, in dollars, even though the dollar had no official status. Informal dollarization often recedes once inflation rates are brought down and confidence in the domestic currency is reestablished.
- *Currency Boards.* Another form of fixed exchange rate occurs when a country declares that its currency will trade at a fixed exchange rate and empowers a currency board to issue banknotes that are 100 percent backed by foreign-exchange reserves. The Hong Kong dollar (as of March 2010) is defined as 7.8 U.S. dollars. And the currency board can issue additional Hong Kong dollars only as it acquires and holds U.S. dollars. Some countries operate currency boards with exchange rates fixed against the pound sterling (e.g., the Falkland Islands) or against the euro (Estonia).
- *Formal Pegs.* The Bretton Woods system formally pegged currencies to the U.S. dollar. Although similar, a formal peg may differ from a currency board, because there is no guarantee of a one-to-one correspondence between currency issued and foreign exchange. With a formal peg, the exchange rate can be sustained so long as the central bank can meet actual claims on foreign-exchange reserves. This does not always work. For example, in 1967, after years of current-account deficits, foreign holdings of pounds sterling exceeded British reserves. When traders began to convert these holdings into foreign currencies, the British faced the prospect of exhausting their reserves. To stanch the outflow, sterling was devalued (i.e., depreciated in a discrete step) from $2.80 per pound to $2.40. The devaluation, which is clearly visible in Figure 8.4, amounted to raising the sterling price of the dollar. At the higher price, traders were less willing to use their sterling to buy dollars. Because the values of other currencies were defined against the dollar, the reduction of the sterling/dollar exchange rate amounted to devaluation against every currency in the Bretton Woods system (except those, like the Irish pound, that were pegged to the pound sterling itself). Periodic devaluations and revaluations were a characteristic feature of the Bretton Woods system. Although the worldwide system of fixed exchange rates has vanished, a number of countries maintain formal exchange-rate pegs. China maintained a formal peg of ¥8.27 per dollar from 1997–2005.
- *Informal Pegs.* Countries may manage their currencies as if they had fixed exchange rates without declaring a formal peg. A number of countries in the European Union but not (yet) part of the Euro Area, such as Denmark and the Baltic states, informally peg their currencies to the euro.

- *Managed Float.* Many countries try to stabilize the movements in their exchange rates – to prevent short runs swings, while allowing longer run appreciation or depreciation. They may target the exchange rate against a particular currency or the value of the currency against a basket of other currencies. After abandoning its peg against the dollar, the Chinese have managed the yuan, targeting a basket of currencies, with an overall trend toward appreciation. In practice, managed floats often target fairly wide bands of exchange rates, say, a target rate ±15 percent.

There is no sharp line between managed floating and freely floating, because even the freest floaters sometimes intervene to stabilize foreign-exchange markets. Equally, there is no sharp line between fixed and floating exchange rates, because fixed exchange rates can become unsustainable, usually as the result of overvaluation, and devalued or revalued to align them better with purchasing-power parity. Sharp line or not, the market-determined exchange rate system of today is very different from the Bretton Woods system before 1973.

Fixed versus Floating: Advantages and Disadvantages

Why should a country prefer one exchange-rate regime to another? Consider the matter under three headings:

- *Disequilibrium.* A system of fixed exchange rates compels policymakers to choose "correct" rates. If they fail to do so, especially where the rates represent significant overvaluation, a country is likely to experience a current-account deficit and a drain on its reserves. The solution is either to make frequent adjustments to the fixed rate, in which case it may as well be floating, or live with unbalanced trade for long periods and to make larger, less frequent adjustments, disrupting economies with classic balance-of-payment crises. Under a system of floating exchange rates, the market finds the right rate and adjustment can be rapid and more incremental. Because there is no fixed rate to defend, there is no drain of official foreign-exchange reserves, even when the current account is in substantial deficit. But, as we already saw in Chapter 8 (section 8.4.2), a market-determined exchange rate need not reflect purchasing-power parity (real exchange rates are typically not constant) nor move in such a way as to keep the current account in constant balance. In addition, markets may tolerate substantially overvalued currencies for long periods of time and then suddenly turn against them. Such speculative attacks result in rapid depreciation that may be every bit as disruptive as large discrete changes in fixed exchange rates.
- *Exchange-Rate Risk.* As we saw in the discussion of uncovered interest parity (Chapter 8, section 8.4.3), floating exchange rates introduce a new kind of risk into financial markets – *exchange-rate risk*, the capital gains and losses to holdings of assets denominated in foreign currencies that result from movements in the exchange rate. An advantage of fixed exchange rates is that they support stable calculation of international values. They reduce exchange-rate risk, because

they increase the chance that the exchange rate will not change over the holding period of any foreign bond. Such reduction in risk should promote the integration of financial markets between countries, allowing, for example, traders in the United States to treat German, British, and Japanese assets as no different from American assets and promoting greater diversification of other sorts of risk. Fixed exchange rates may reduce such risk, but they do not eliminate it altogether, because devaluations or revaluations are always possible. And, indeed, there may be speculative attacks against a currency with a fixed exchange rate.

The Asian currency crisis of 1997 started in just this way. Speculators came to doubt whether the exchange-rate of the Thai baht, which was pegged to the U.S. dollar, could be sustained. Fearing devaluation, they shunned the baht, forcing Thai authorities, first, to intervene heavily to defend the peg, draining foreign-exchange reserves and, finally, to abandon it altogether, resulting in a rapid 45-percent depreciation. Fear of devaluation spread to other pegged currencies in the region. The Indonesian rupiah, the South Korean won, the Philippine peso, and the Malaysian ringgit all depreciated substantially as a result. The Hong Kong currency board was able to defend the Hong Kong dollar with massive interventions, while the Singapore dollar was more gradually devalued against the U.S. dollar. Even the floating Japanese yen suffered a large depreciation because of Japan's deep ties to the economy of the region. The disruptions in the foreign-exchange markets spread to other financial markets and the real economy, with many firms declaring bankruptcy and the growth rates of GDP collapsing.

Fixed exchange-rate regimes may, therefore, be subject to large, infrequent, hard-to-predict risks, whereas floating-rate regimes are subject to smaller, more frequent, but possibly more predictable risks.

- *Macroeconomic Policy.* Fixed exchange rates subordinate domestic macroeconomic policy to the policies of dominant countries. If the United States runs an inflationary policy of high aggregate demand, unfulfilled demand spills over into imports, which are naturally the exports of other countries. Increases in net exports represent a stimulus to demand in those countries, moving their economies in an inflationary direction. The United States, in this case, has exported its inflation. For a less dominant country than the United States, a similar high-demand policy and consequent current-account deficit might provoke an unsupportable outflow of official foreign-exchange reserves and a balance-of-payments crisis. To avoid the crisis, the government must shift policy into a deflationary direction. A balance-of-payments crisis may then lead to a policy-induced recession – the international crisis is translated into a domestic crisis.

In contrast, a floating exchange-rate regime insulates domestic macroeconomic policy from the policies in other countries. If exchange rates move to maintain purchasing-power parity, then high U.S. inflation would lead to a depreciation of the dollar rather than to higher demand in other countries. With no fixed rate to defend, the state of official foreign-exchange reserves would not constrain domestic macroeconomic policies. However, as we know well by now, although floating exchange rates typically do move in the direction of purchasing-power parity, they do not move all that quickly, so domestic policies are not fully insulated from international conditions. In any case, we may not want them to be. For some countries, the discipline of international markets may usefully constrain overly expansionary tendencies.

The other man's grass is always greener. After three and half decades of floating exchange rates, a number of economists have argued for the virtues of a return to Bretton Woods or even to the gold standard. Whatever the abstract virtues of a comprehensive system of fixed exchange rates, such a regime can succeed only if national macroeconomic policies are disciplined and coordinated enough to avoid placing too much strain on the system. If it is politically impossible for each major country to act in the interests of the whole, then differential inflation rates, payment imbalances, and frequent devaluations will follow. We should remember that the system of floating exchange rates was adopted, not because it was thought to be superior, but because the Bretton Woods system collapsed, as had every attempt to reestablish a comprehensive gold standard since 1914.

Currency Areas

Under the Bretton Woods system or in the various islands of dollarization, currency boards, and formal pegs that survive in the world in which most major currencies float, each country has its own currency, and can in principle alter its exchange rate against other currencies. This is even true for a country such as Panama that allows the U.S. dollar to pass as legal tender. A more extreme case of fixed exchange rates occurs when different countries adopt a common currency. The Central African franc is used by six African countries, whereas the West African franc is used by eight – mostly former French colonies. Both currencies were originally pegged to the French franc and are now pegged to the euro.

The most famous common-currency area is the Euro Area (or Eurozone), introduced in 1999. In 2010, the Euro Area consists of sixteen of the twenty-seven members of the European Union (EU) that have adopted the euro in place of their national currencies. In addition, the euro is used in five other countries with or without formal agreements with the European Union. A number of other EU member states intend to adopt the euro eventually.

Although the Euro Area is the most famous common-currency area today, it is easy to forget that the United States is itself a common-currency area, a common dollar having replaced a variety of state currencies after the signing of the Constitution. The United States illustrates some of the characteristics that make a common-currency area workable and beneficial.

First, common-currency areas make sense when economies are highly integrated in the sense that labor and capital, including financial capital, move freely among them. As well as establishing the common currency, the Constitution also created the world's largest free-trade area – states were forbidden to impose tariffs or restrictions on each other's goods or to inhibit the free movement of workers. States regulated banks and other financial intermediaries quite differently at first, but over time a mainly national system of regulation emerged, so that the United States also has a highly integrated financial market.

Second, a common-currency area works best when a common macroeconomic policy suits all of its constituents. This will be true if shocks to the system are symmetrical. But what if they are not? Suppose that world demand for cars falls at the same time as world demand for computers rises. The Michigan car industry might benefit from an expansionary macroeconomic policy, while the California computer industry might prefer a more moderated policy. If they each had a separate currency, then each could follow its own policy and the exchange rate would adjust between them. Labor and capital mobility, of course, makes up for some of this lost independence. But it is a slow process moving former Michigan autoworkers to the computer industry in California. As a result, the fiscal policy that suits one state does not suit another, and if the needs of California dominate, Michigan may suffer. Fiscal transfers from the Federal government – for example, unemployment insurance or funds for economic redevelopment – may mitigate some of the pain.

Common macroeconomic policy may be required throughout a currency area. Because monetary policy is controlled centrally, only fiscal policy can differ from state to state. Without the chance of monetizing deficits, however, there are limits to state spending. Voters may resist excess taxation, and bond markets will drive up the interest rate on excess state borrowing because of default risk.

How does the Euro Area stack up to the United States as a common-currency area? The European Union has essentially free trade in goods. Neither capital nor labor is practically as mobile in the Euro Area as in the United States. But EU regulations are working toward ever greater integration. The monetary policy of the Euro Area is concentrated in the European Central Bank in Frankfurt, Germany. Although fiscal policy is mostly set country-by-country, in principle Euro Area governments have to conform to EU guidelines on the size of government deficits and the ratio of debt to GDP that aim to reduce the sort of conflicts that might make separate currencies and shifting exchange rates attractive. The countries of the Euro Area are routinely hit by asymmetrical shocks – the economies of Finland and Greece, for example, are very different. And the European Union has only limited mechanisms for fiscal transfers that would compensate the countries that lose from the elimination of exchange-rate adjustments.

So far, however, the threat of differential shocks has not placed unbearable strain on the Euro Area.[15] But there is still a risk. In the United States, the question of seceding from the dollar area was definitively decided by the outcome of the Civil War. In Europe, the member states retain their individual sovereignty and, if the common currency proved too disadvantageous, could in principle act to readopt a national currency. What should be remembered is that the United States has been a common-currency area for more than two hundred years, whereas the Euro Area is only somewhat more than a decade old. The dollar has itself been an instrument of deeper economic integration, and there is reason to believe that the euro will further such integration in the Euro Area. The longer the euro remains in place, the less likely any member state is to defect. The economic integration is already seen in financial markets. Before the introduction of the euro, interest rates varied considerably between the member states of the European Union. After the formation of the Euro Area, rates have converged substantially.[16]

Appendix: The Monetarist Experiment of the 1980s: An Application of IS-LM Analysis

For more than half a century, U.S. monetary policy (with the exception of one short period) has been framed in terms of interest rates. During the period, sometimes known as the "monetarist experiment," from 6 October 1979 to about the end of 1982, the Federal Reserve pursued a policy of targeting the monetary aggregates. This period provides a natural opportunity to apply IS-LM analysis because, first, the LM curve explicitly models the market for money; and, second, sophisticated versions of the IS-LM model were key parts of the Fed's macroeconomic models and informed its thinking throughout this period.

16.A.1 The Situation in 1979

The Problem and Paul Volcker

The 1970s were the decade of stagflation. The unemployment rate, which had been dropping throughout the recovery of the late 1970s, began to rise again toward the end of 1979. The *lowest* unemployment rate of that expansion (5.6 percent) was only slightly below the *highest* point of the 2001 recession and its recovery (6.3 percent). GDP growth, which had been strong, fell by the end of 1979 to a limping 1.3 percent per year. The second

---

[15] Fiscal crises in Greece, Ireland, and, possibly also in Portugal and Spain in 2010 and 2011 pose the most severe test of the system to date. As of July 2011, the outcome remains in doubt.

[16] Although they have diverged again for the countries involved in the 2010–2011 fiscal crisis (see footnote 15).

oil crisis, associated with the Iranian Revolution, delivered a significant supply shock. But the worst was the inflation rate: up past 11 percent per year for the first time since the first oil crisis (1973–1974). Interest rates followed suit, with long rates more than 10 percent, much to the chagrin of home buyers and businesses.

At the time, G. William Miller, the chairman of the Board of Governors of the Federal Reserve, was widely regarded as a hapless steward of monetary policy. When Miller resigned in 1979, President Carter appointed Paul Volcker, the president of the Federal Reserve Bank of New York and a former Treasury official, to be the new chairman. Volcker was highly respected on Wall Street. And, what was perhaps as important, he that he had a mandate to use monetary policy more aggressively to rein in rising inflation.

Monetarism and the Fed

The economic doctrine of **monetarism** had increasingly come to influence the policy debates of the 1970s. There is genuine doubt whether Federal Reserve policymakers were ever strict monetarists, but it is clear that monetarist thinking helped to frame their decisions. Monetarism, a doctrine associated especially with Milton Friedman, Karl Brunner (1916–1989), and Alan Meltzer of Carnegi-Mellon University, rests on two major claims. First, in the long run, expansions of the money supply have no real effects but are translated entirely into higher prices. This, as we saw in Chapter 13 (Appendix), is exactly what the IS-LM model would predict in a fully employed economy. Second, and in striking contrast, changes in the money supply are the major source of real fluctuations in the short run.

To avoid short-run fluctuations (deemed pointless because they cannot be sustained in the long run), the monetarists advise the policymaker to adopt a monetary rule in which the money supply grows steadily. Such a rule, they argue, will produce a steady rate of inflation given by the difference in the growth rate between money and potential output: $\hat{p} = \hat{M} - \hat{Y}^{pot}$. Ideally, if the growth rate of the money supply is equal to that of potential, prices will be constant. Figure 16.A.1 shows an IS-LM diagram with scaled output on the horizontal axis. On this diagram, $\hat{M} = \hat{Y}^{pot}$ would result in a constant LM curve.

16.A.2 Implementation

An IS-LM Analysis

In broad outline, the Fed under Volcker acted to implement the monetarist advice of trying to stabilize the growth of the money supply – particularly, as measured by the monetary aggregate M1. In the long run, Volcker hoped to produce a lower, steadier inflation rate.

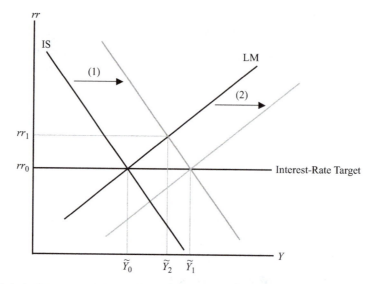

Figure 16.A.1. Monetary Targeting versus Interest-Rate Targeting. Under an interest-rate target, when the IS curve shifts unexpectedly, monetary policy aims to shift the LM curve to maintain the original interest rate. Under monetary aggregate targeting, monetary policy aims to hold the LM curve constant. This results in a higher interest rate, but a smaller change in aggregate demand, than under interest-rate targeting.

But in the short run, he hoped to end unnecessary fluctuations in GDP. The mechanism can be seen clearly in Figure 16.A.1. Under a policy of targeting interest rates (at rr_0), a shock to the IS curve (e.g., an unexpected export boom) would shift it to the right (1) and *ceteris paribus* would raise interest rates to rr_1. The Fed, however, would conduct open-market purchases to supply reserves and expand the money supply in order to shift the LM curve to the right (2) by enough to keep the interest rate at its target. Aggregate demand increases from $\tilde{Y}_0$ to $\tilde{Y}_1$.

In contrast, under a monetary-aggregate target, the LM curve would not shift at all. The shift in the IS curve would be allowed to increase interest rates somewhat, but aggregate demand would increase only to $\tilde{Y}_2$. Demand fluctuations are smaller under monetary-aggregate targeting than under interest-rate targeting.

Reserve Targeting

The technical problem with monetary-aggregate targeting is that the Fed does not control the money supply directly. Take M1 to be the relevant aggregate. Minor components aside, it is the sum of currency and demand deposits:

$$M \equiv Cu + D, \qquad (16.A.1)$$

where M is money measured as M1; Cu is currency; and D, demand deposits. The Fed could, in principle, limit the supply of currency, but in practice it allows the public to convert its assets into any level of currency the public can afford. The Fed cannot control the level of demand deposits, but it can influence them through reserve requirements and the supply of reserves.

When a bank uses reserves to make a loan, it typically credits its customer's checking account with the amount of the loan. The bank's assets (the loan) and its liabilities (the deposits) rise by equal amounts. The bank is, of course, limited in the amount of loans that it creates as it must keep enough reserves to meet the reserve requirements on its new deposits. The customer, in turn, typically wants to spend the money – otherwise why borrow it? When the money is spent by check and the check deposited in another bank, that bank returns it to the original bank and receives reserves in exchange. Now the second bank has reserves that it can lend out, and the process begins again. At each stage, some reserves are held to meet reserve requirements. This money-multiplier process means, first, that any new reserves will result in an increase in deposits; and, second, that the Fed has a mechanism for influencing the volume of deposits.

To use the money-multiplier process to control the stock of deposits, the Fed must first quantify it. Start with the definition of the monetary base:

$$MB \equiv Cu + R, \tag{16.A.2}$$

where MB is the monetary base, and R, reserves. Dividing both sides of equation (16.A.1) by (16.A.2) yields

$$\frac{M}{MB} \equiv \frac{Cu + D}{Cu + R}. \tag{16.A.3}$$

This can be rewritten as[17]

$$M \equiv \left(\frac{1 + Cu/D}{Cu/D + R/D} \right) MB \equiv mMB, \tag{16.A.4}$$

where Cu/D is the public's desired ratio of currency to demand deposits; R/D, the banks' required reserve ratio; and $m = (\frac{1+Cu/D}{Cu/D+R/D})$, the **monetary-base multiplier**. The monetary-base multiplier tells us how a dollar of monetary base will translate into more M1.

Equation (16.A.4) is an identity. It becomes a useful equation for prediction if we can assume that the monetary-base multiplier (and the two ratios that lie behind it) are constant or at least stable enough to be predictable. Then the Fed's strategy is straightforward. First, it estimates the monetary-base multiplier. Then it uses it to decide the path that the monetary base must take to achieve the growth in M1 consistent with its target. Next, it uses

---

[17] To get the second expression, divide the numerator and denominator of equation (16.A.3) by D.

past behavior to estimate the public's likely demand for currency. With that knowledge, it can decide how many reserves it must supply through open-market operations to obtain the right path for the monetary base. This, in a nutshell, is the **reserve operating procedure** that Volcker announced to the world on 6 October 1979.[18]

The success of the Fed's new operating procedure depended crucially on two things:

- first, the stability of the relationship between the monetary base and M1 – on this hung the Fed's ability to control the money supply;
- second, the stability of money demand – the Fed needed to control the shifts in the LM curve using the money supply, but (as we saw in Chapter 7, appendix), the LM curve can also shift because money demand shifts.

16.A.3 Post-Mortem

Expectations and Outcomes

Did it work? The Fed expected monetary-aggregate targeting to deliver two positive outcomes: (1) a lower, and less variable, inflation rate and (2) a less variable growth rate of real GDP. It expected the cost to be a somewhat larger variation in interest rates.

What actually happened? Figure 16.A.2 shows what happened to interest rates. Both long and short rates were *much higher* on average during the period of monetary-aggregate targeting and suffered wild fluctuations. This was, perhaps, the most deeply unpopular consequence of the policy.

Table 16.A.1 considers three subsamples (the period of monetary-aggregate targeting and periods about five years before and after) and, for each subsample, reports the mean growth rate of GDP and the mean inflation rate and their standard deviations, as a measure of variability. Contrary to the Fed's intentions, during the period of monetary-aggregate targeting, the inflation rate was higher and more variable and the GDP growth rate lower and more variable than in either of the periods of interest-rate targeting before or after. On the basis of this dismal record, monetary-aggregate targeting was abandoned by the end of 1982.

What Went Wrong?

We cannot, of course, do a complete analysis of this episode, but we can conjecture why the policy was a failure. First, the Fed appears to have over-estimated its ability to control M1. Figure 16.A.3 plots the monetary-base

---

[18] Technically, he announced a *nonborrowed* reserve operating procedure, taking account of the fact that banks can obtain reserves through discount borrowing as well as through open-market operations. But this is a detail in the main story.

Table 16.A.1. *Did the Monetary-Aggregate Targeting Regime Stabilize the Economy?*

Period	Growth Rate of Real GDP[a]		CPI Inflation Rate[b]	
	Mean	Standard Deviation	Mean	Standard Deviation
January 1975– September 1979	3.93	4.28	7.58	3.03
October 1979–December 1982	−0.18	5.22	8.38	5.18
January 1983–December 1987	4.39	2.39	3.38	2.47

[a] Annualized quarterly growth rate. [b] Annualize monthly growth rate of CPI-U.
Source: GDP, Bureau of Economic Analysis; CPI-U, Bureau of Economic Analysis.

multiplier (*m*) over the three subsamples used in Table 16.A.1. The multiplier, which had been falling on trend in the period before 6 October 1979, reversed course just as reserve targeting was introduced. It also became more variable. Table 16.A.2 shows that in the period before monetary-aggregate targeting, the multiplier declined at an average rate of 1.22 percent per year with a standard deviation of 3.94. During the period of monetary-aggregate targeting, it hardly changed on average, but (with a standard deviation of 8.25) it was twice as variable. After the return to interest-rate targeting, the multiplier began to grow at more than 1 percent per year while its variability declined.

With an unstable multiplier, it was hard for the Fed to choose the right level of reserves to hit its target for M1. Yet, even if it had been successful, this may not have stabilized the LM curve. We can get a rough idea of

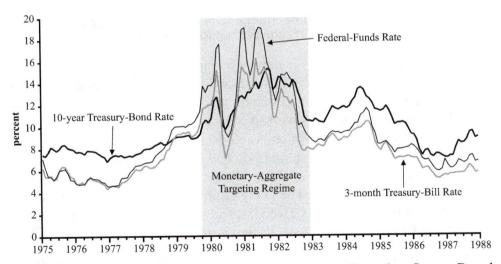

Figure 16.A.2. Interest Rates under Monetary-Aggregate Targeting. *Source:* Board of Governors of the Federal Reserve System.

Table 16.A.2. *Were the Monetary Conditions Stable in the Monetary-Aggregate Targeting Regime?*

	Monetary-Base Multiplier[a]		Transactions-Demand for Money[b]	
Period	Mean	Standard Deviation	Mean	Standard Deviation
January 1975–September 1979	−1.22	3.94	−4.08	3.53
October 1979–December 1982	0.09	8.25	−1.77	7.10
January 1983–December 1987	1.07	5.11	2.49	6.00

[a] $= M1/MB.$ [b] $= M1/nominal\ GDP.$

Source: M1 and Monetary Base (MB), Federal Reserve; GDP, Bureau of Economic Analysis.

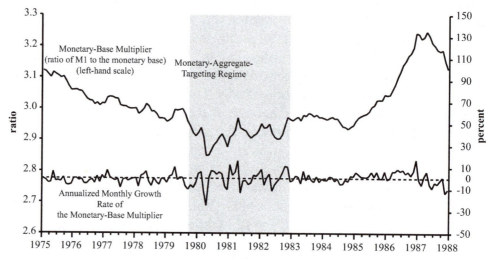

Figure 16.A.3. The Monetary-Base Multiplier under Monetary-Aggregate Targeting. *Source:* Board of Governors of the Federal Reserve System.

the behavior of the demand for money by plotting the ratio of M1 to nominal GDP, which approximates the transactions-demand for money (Figure 16.A.4).[19] This ratio had been falling on trend in the period before 6 October 1979; but it too suddenly reversed course in the middle of the monetary-aggregate-targeting regime. Again, Table 16.A.2 reports its growth rate and standard deviation for each subperiod. The key point is that it was nearly twice as variable during the monetary targeting period as before, and that the variability fell back after. The Fed's assumption that money demand was stable proved to be erroneous. Even if it had succeeded in setting the money supply, the LM curve would have shifted unpredictably.

---

[19] This figure is the inverse of the *income-velocity of money* – that is, the number of dollars of GDP per dollar of M1, which indicates roughly how fast money must circulate to keep up with the circular flow of income and expenditure.

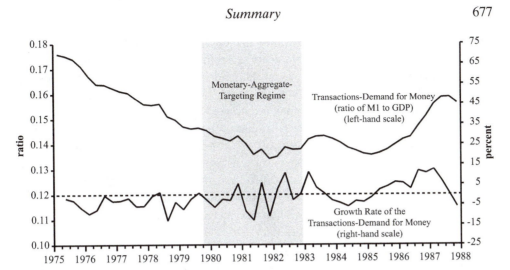

Figure 16.A.4. The Transactions-Demand for Money under Monetary-Aggregate Targeting. *Source:* Board of Governors of the Federal Reserve System.

Was monetary-aggregate targeting really a failure or just a victim of bad luck? This is much harder to say. The short period contained two recessions in such rapid succession that they virtually blended into one. Was monetary policy to blame? Perhaps, but there were other culprits. The Fed could not control the oil-price shocks of 1979 and 1980. And, in early 1980, President Carter introduced credit controls, which may have contributed to the recession and that certainly complicated monetary policy. On top of all of this, the early 1980s was a period of rapid innovations in banking and finance that witnessed, among other things, the introduction of interest-bearing checking accounts, interstate banking, and electronic access to retail bank accounts (e.g., ATM machines). Some of the shifts in the demand for money reflect these developments. They made it much harder for the Fed to predict the demand for M1. But whether the policy was really a failure or not, it was abandoned; and, after 1982, interest-rate targeting has dominated monetary policy in the United States.

Summary

1. Monetary policy consists of actions by the government that aim to influence the macroeconomy through the financial system. Monetary policy is usually conducted through the central bank. In the United States, the Federal Reserve System (Fed) is the central bank, and the Federal Open Market Committee is its principal monetary policymaking body.

2. The government's budget constraint expresses the fact that monetary and fiscal policies are connected, because government deficits must be financed either through selling debt to the public or through the creation of the monetary base (currency plus central-bank reserves).

3. The balance sheets of the Fed and the commercial banks are related. Most important is the fact that reserves are a liability to the Fed and an asset to the banks. Banks hold reserves to meet demands for payment and to fulfill reserve requirements against transactions accounts. The Fed can affect bank portfolios by changing the volume of available reserves.

4. Banks borrow and lend reserves to each other in the Federal funds (reserve) market. The Fed buys and sells government bonds, paying or receiving reserves in return. These open-market operations change reserves available to banks and directly influence the Federal-funds rate (and, indirectly, other rates). Open-market purchases increase reserves and reduce interest rates: they are expansionary monetary policy. Open-market sales reduce reserves and increase interest rates: they are contractionary.

5. Market demands for assets may move in response to announced or surmised Federal Reserve interest-rate targets, ahead of or without any actual open-market operation to avoid any capital losses (or to capture any capital gains) associated with the change in rates. Such responses are known as open-mouth operations.

6. The opportunity-cost (or interest-rate) channel of monetary policy involves, first, an increase in the Federal-funds rate transmitted to longer-term nominal rates of interest. The change in nominal rates will, for a given inflation rate, also change real rates (the opportunity cost of investment) and, hence, aggregate demand (a shift in the IS curve). The change in aggregate demand may change real output and the rate of inflation, according to the Phillips curve. Any change in the rate of inflation will itself change real interest rates in the same direction as the original policy action, leading to a cumulative acceleration or deceleration of prices, unless nominal interest rates are further adjusted to offset it.

7. The credit channel operates through the balance sheets of banks. The *narrow credit channel* operates even if real rates of interest are constant: an expansion of reserves may allow a bank to make more loans. If firms or consumers are credit rationed, then the additional loans increase investment and consumption, increasing aggregate demand (shifting the IS curve outward). The *broad credit channel* requires changes in interest rates: when interest rates rise, the net worth of borrowers falls, and banks' willingness to lend to them may fall. If so, investment and consumption are curtailed, reducing aggregate demand.

8. Central banks must balance the advantages of higher output against the costs of accelerating prices. If NAIRU is above the unemployment rate that corresponds to true full employment, then the advantages are real; but monetary policy can never push the economy above its actual potential output. Different economists and central banks differ on what weight to give to output and employment versus inflation.

9. Monetary policy may be guided either by discretion (always adjust policy to new circumstances to reach the best outcome) or by policy rules. Four factors support rules: (i) ignorance about the true state of the economy at the time of the decision; (ii) lags in recognizing and implementing policy; (iii) rules provide

a more stable background for private economic decisions; and (iv) rules overcome the problem of dynamic consistency. Complex rules that account for many contingencies are, in fact, hard to distinguish from discretion.

10. The actual behavior of the Federal Reserve is reasonably well described by the Taylor rule, which sets the Federal-funds rate to the rate of inflation plus positive factors for inflation above target and output above potential (as measured using a concept of potential output for which exceeding potential is possible).

11. Governments may influence the exchange rate directly through buying and selling foreign currencies or indirectly through monetary policies that affect interest rates or rates of inflation.

12. Interventions in foreign-exchange markets affect monetary policy because purchases and sales of foreign exchange act like other open-market operations to change the stock of central-bank reserves. The Fed may "sterilize" such changes to the reserve base through offsetting open-market operations in government bonds.

13. Exchange-rate movements in response to policy affect the relative prices of domestic and foreign goods and, therefore, net exports, which offer another channel from monetary policy to the real economy.

14. In earlier times, the foreign-exchange values of national currencies were determined by their prices in terms of gold. From the end of World War II until 1973, their values were determined by international agreement – a system of fixed exchange rates. Since 1973, currencies have largely "floated" relative to each other – their values determined by supply and demand in foreign-exchange markets. Governments have weighed the costs and benefits of fixed exchange rates and floating exchange rates differently. As a result, although floating currencies are the norm, for various currencies and at various times over the past forty years, governments have intervened to manage their currencies to various degrees from the extreme of pegging them to other currencies to intervening directly or indirectly in the market, that determines their values.

15. The extreme version of fixed exchange rates is a common currency for different countries. The United States can be seen as a common-currency area, with the states playing the role of countries. The Euro Area is the most important recent common-currency area. The success of any common-currency area depends on the harmonization of economic interests among its members. Free trade among members, mobility of factors of production, integrated financial markets, common macroeconomic shocks, and coordinated monetary and fiscal policies all promote such harmony.

Key Concepts

monetary policy
central-bank reserves
monetary base (MB)
government's budget constraint

opportunity-cost (or interest-rate)
 channel
credit channel
central bank

Federal Reserve System (the Fed)	open-mouth operations
Federal Open Market Committee (FOMC)	credibility
	cumulative process
reserve requirement	"leaning against the wind"
Federal-funds rate	discretion
Federal funds (or reserve) market	policy rule
open-market operations	policy lag
expansionary monetary policy	time- (or dynamically) inconsistency
contractionary monetary policy	Taylor rule

Suggested Readings

Alan S. Blinder. *Central Banking in Theory and Practice.* Cambridge, MA: MIT Press, 1998.

The Federal Reserve: Purposes and Functions. Washington, DC: Board of Governors of the Federal Reserve System, 1994.

Milton Friedman and Anna Schwartz. *A Monetary History of the United States, 1867–1960.* Princeton: Princeton University Press, 1963.

Charles. A. E. Goodhart. *The Evolution of Central Banks.* Cambridge, MA: MIT Press, 1988.

Robert L. Hetzel. "The Taylor Rule: Is It a Useful Guide to Understanding Monetary Policy?" Federal Reserve Bank of Richmond *Economic Quarterly*, vol. 86, no. 2, Spring 2000, pp. 1–33.

Alan Meltzer, *A History of the Federal Reserve, volume 1: 1913–1951.* Chicago: University of Chicago Press, 2003.

Ann-Marie Meulendyke. *U.S. Monetary Policy and Financial Markets.* New York: Federal Reserve Bank of New York, 1998.

Problems

Data for this exercise are available on the textbook website under the link for Chapter 16 (http://appliedmacroeconomics.com). Before starting these exercises, the student should review the relevant portions of the *Guide to Working with Economic Data*, including sections G.1–G.4, G.13, and G.15.

Problem 16.1. Go the website of Board of Governors of the Federal Reserve.
   (a) What is the most recent daily Federal-funds rate?
   (b) Find the most recent FOMC policy statement in which a change in the target for the Federal-funds rate is announced. How big was the change? What is the current target?
   (c) Read the policy statement. Briefly summarize how it characterizes the goals and the monetary policy action taken. Does it mention any other tools of monetary policy besides the Federal-funds rate?

Problem 16.2. On the same website as in the previous problem, find the most recent statistical release H.3 "Aggregate Reserves of Depository Institutions and the Monetary Base." For the most recent month available: What fraction of the monetary base is held as currency and reserves? What fraction of reserves is held as vault cash or commercial bank accounts with Federal Reserve Banks?

Problem 16.3. The monetary aggregates are defined in Chapter 6 (Table 6.3). On the same website as in the previous problem, find the most recent statistical release H.6 "Money Stock Measures." For the most recent month available: What fractions of M1 are currency and demand deposits? What fractions of M2 are M1, savings deposits, time deposits, and retail money funds?

Problem 16.4. Indicate on a pair of balance sheets similar to Table 16.1 the effects on the portfolios of the Federal Reserve and the commercial banks of the following actions. (Recall that balance sheets must always balance; make the minimum changes consistent with the question; if the question does not give enough information to complete the balance sheet, make a reasonable assumption to complete it, and explain your assumption.)

(a) An open-market sale by the Fed of $100 million of government bonds;

(b) $10 million of discount borrowing by the commercial banks;

(c) $1 billion of new loans by the commercial banks;

(d) $5 million borrowed by one bank on the Federal funds market from another.

Problem 16.5. Use a diagram like Figure 16.3 to show the effects of an open-market sale of government bonds on the reserves, the stock of government bonds, the Federal-funds rate, and the yield on government bonds.

Problem 16.6. Use a diagram like Figure 16.4 and assume that open-mouth operations are effective to show the effect on the Federal-funds rate and the government-bond rate of an increase in the Federal-funds-rate target. If open-mouth operations were not effective, what actions would the Fed have to take to secure the same pattern of interest rates? Would these actions have any effects different from the open-mouth operation?

Problem 16.7. Use diagrams similar to Figure 16.6 and 16.7 and ignore the effects of risk to show the effects on the time-path of the Federal-funds rate itself and the yield curve of:

(a) a 1-point cut in the Federal-funds rate that is credibly believed to be permanent;

(b) a 1-point cut in the Federal-funds rate that is credibly believed to be held for five years and then returned to the original rate;

(c) an announcement of the same policy as in (b) that the public believes will, despite the official announcement, be reversed in only 1 year.

Problem 16.8. Find the last time the Federal Reserve changed its target for the Federal-funds rate (see Problem 16.1). Use a daily-yield curve from the *Wall St. Journal* or another source or construct it yourself from data available on the Board of Governors of the Federal Reserve's website (release H.15), and compare the yield curves for four dates: (1) one month before the target change,

(2) one day before, (3) one day after, and (4) one month after. What does the pattern of these yield curves suggest about the ability of the Federal Reserve to change market interest rate through its target for the Federal-funds rate? Would whether the Fed's policy action was expected or unexpected make any difference to how you might expect the yield curves to change? Explain.

Problem 16.9. How effective are the linkages connecting monetary policy to the economy? Create the following scatterplots; add regression lines and R^2:

  (i) the change in the 3-month Treasury bill rate (vertical axis) on the change in the Federal-funds rate (horizontal axis);

  (ii) the change in the 10-year Treasury bond rate on the change in the Federal-funds rate;

  (iii) the change in the Moody's Aaa corporate bond rate on the 10-year Treasury bond rate.

Look at the regression coefficients. Consider a 1-point rise in the Fed-funds rate. On average, how much would you expect the yields on 3-month Treasury bills and 10-year Treasury bond rates to rise as a result? How would it affect the overall shape of the yield curve? Consider a 1-point rise in the 10-year Treasury bond rate. On average, how much would you expect the yield on Aaa corporate bonds to rise as a result? The difference between these two rates measures the risk premium of corporate over government debt. How would you expect the risk premium to change as a result? Comment on the fit of your regressions. How does it affect your confidence in the results?

Problem 16.10. Repeat Problem 16.9 using the annual change (current month over 12 months previous) in each interest rate. How do the results differ? Can you explain the difference in terms of typical Federal Reserve behavior (e.g., Figure 16.12 is relevant) and in terms of the importance of credibility in monetary policy?

Problem 16.11. The difference between the Moody's Aaa bond rate and the 10-year Treasury bond rate is a measure of the risk premium of corporate over government debt. Calculate and plot this time series and indicate the NBER recession dates with shading. What are the cyclical characteristics of this series? Do they suggest a channel of monetary policy related to the broad credit channel? Explain.

Problem 16.12. Use a diagram like Figure 16.8 to explain the effects of a monetary policy action that results in an increase in long-term interest rate (r_N) – that is, the nominal interest rate that, at the current rate of inflation, raises the real interest rate (rr_N) above the value compatible with NAIRU.

Problem 16.13. Use a diagram like Figure 16.10 to explain the effects of an increase in reserves operating through the credit channel. Indicate clearly which effects can be attributed to the narrow credit channel and which to the broad credit channel.

Problem 16.14. The development of financial markets from the mid-1970s through the recession of 2007–2009 improved the access of firms and households to credit. For example, mortgage applications were simplified and made accessible through the internet; and mortgage lenders competed heavily for business among households, tailoring repayment patterns, maturities, and down payments to borrower preferences. Would you expect the credit channel to have become more or less important over time as a result of such developments? Explain your reasons carefully. How might these changes have been related to the financial crash of 2008?

Problem 16.15. Does the Federal Reserve follow a policy of "leaning against the wind" in its management of the Federal-funds rate?

(a) Make a diagram, similar to Figure 5.8 (in Chapter 5) for the Federal-funds rate: For each business cycle for which enough data are available, express the values for the 12 months before and the 24 months after the cyclical peak relative to the value at each peak (i.e., let each peak take the value 100). Average these values across business cycles to form a typical profile of the Fed's management of the Federal-funds rate over the business cycle.

(b) Calculate and plot the *ex post* real Federal-funds rate (use annual CPI inflation, $\hat{p}_t = \frac{p_{t+12}}{p_t} - 1$), indicating NBER recession dates with shading.

(c) On the basis of your two diagrams, summarize the evidence for or against the Fed in fact "leaning against the wind." Describe the conduct of Fed policy over the business cycle – both their intentional actions in managing the Federal-funds rate and the outcome in terms of the *real* Federal-funds rate. Are the data consistent with the idea that monetary policy is the cause of, or at least a leading indicator of, recessions?

Problem 16.16.

(a) Estimate the IS curve. Using annual data, calculate the real 10-year Treasury bond rate (explain your choice of variables and method of calculation). Create a scatterplot of scaled output (vertical axis) on the real rate (horizontal axis); add the regression line, equation, and R^2. (Note that the axes are reversed from Figure 16.8; why? – see the *Guide*, section G.15.3.)

(b) What real interest rate does your equation imply is compatible with the NAIRU (see equation (15.12) in Chapter 15 for an estimate of NAIRU)?

(c) Starting at an interest rate compatible with NAIRU, what does your equation in combination with equation (15.12) imply will be the effect on inflation of reducing the real rate of interest by 1 point and holding it there for a year?

Problem 16.17. How important are the inflation-target and output-gap terms in the Taylor rule? Calculate and plot three series 1984–present using quarterly data: (1) Use equation (16.2′) to calculate a target series for the Federal-funds rate; (2) repeat (1) but set the coefficient on the deviation from the inflation target to zero; (3) repeat (1) again, but set the coefficient on *gap* to zero. (Inflation should be calculated as the annual growth rate of core CPI (current quarter over same quarter a year earlier).) Does the advice given by the Taylor rule differ in any systematic way depending on which of the two factors are included? For example, is monetary policy typically made tighter or looser by the inclusion of each factor?

Problem 16.18. Use the internet to find the current CBO output gap and the current CPI inflation. Use them to calculate a target for the Federal-funds rate according to the Taylor rule (equation (16.2′)). Find today's actual Federal-funds rate. How do they compare? Find the last time the Federal Reserve changed its Federal-funds rate target (see Problem 16.1). Was it in the direction of closing the gap between the Taylor rule target and the actual Federal-funds rate?

Problem 16.19. Describe how a loose monetary policy might be transmitted through the exchange-rate channel to the real economy.

Problem 16.20. At the time of writing this book (late 2010), the Euro Area was in turmoil as the result of a series of crises concerning excessive government debt in Greece and Ireland (and possibly in Portugal and Spain as well). Many feared that one or more countries might abandon the use of the euro and reestablish its national currency. Use the internet or other resources to research and write a brief note updating the history of this crisis. How did things turn out? Describe current currency arrangements of the European Union.

17

Fiscal Policy

How much should the government spend? How should it pay for it? Are higher taxes needed to balance the budget or will they merely stifle economic growth? Do deficits raise interest rates? Is the debt a burden to future generations? These and related questions concern fiscal policy. Directly or indirectly they are the main topics of political economic debate. In Chapter 13, we explored the role of fiscal policy in the determination of aggregate demand. In this chapter, we go into greater depth to investigate fiscal policy in the long and short runs.

In the United States, monetary policy is relatively independent of politics. The Federal Reserve was created by Congress, and Fed chairmen testify regularly before congressional committees about the state of monetary policy. Nevertheless, the Federal Reserve has been structured to be free of day-to-day political control. Central banks are not independent in every country, but the idea that they should be independent has steadily gained support throughout the world over the past quarter century.

In contrast, fiscal policy is the warp and woof of politics. The word "fiscal" is derived from the Latin word *fisc* meaning the emperor's privy purse or the public treasury. More political heat is generated on questions about filling or depleting the purse – on getting and spending – than on any other question.

Ronald Reagan, in his successful presidential campaign in 1980, argued simultaneously for a smaller government and a balanced budget. He argued that lower tax rates and less government would encourage private-sector growth and help to balance the budget, as revenues rose in response to higher incomes, despite the lower tax rates. In fact, while growth increased, so did deficits. Republicans at the turn of the twenty-first century are still the party of tax cuts.

The Democrats under President Clinton argued that the balanced budgets actually achieved at the end of the 1990s contributed to the longest business-cycle expansion on record. They argued that lower Federal borrowing led to lower interest rates, which in turn spurred private investment. The Democrats were left in a puzzling position when the recession developed

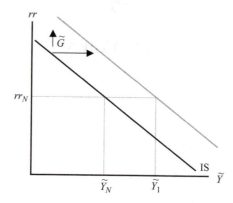

Figure 17.1. Fiscal Stimulus. If monetary policy maintains a constant real rate of interest, then an increase in government expenditure shifts the IS curve to the right and increases aggregate demand by a fully multiplied effect to $\tilde{Y}_1$.

in 2001. It was politically expedient to blame it on George W. Bush's tax cuts and the reemergence of a budget deficit. But their rhetoric was inconsistent with their own economic analysis: interest rates did not actually rise, and no politician wanted to raise taxes and cut spending at the bottom of the recession, knowing that the resulting fall in aggregate demand would worsen unemployment. Despite having excoriated Bush and the Republicans over budget deficits during the 2008 campaign, President Obama and the Democrats raised spending and widened the deficit after 2009.

The point, however, is not to take sides in past (if recent) political debates. Rather, those debates illustrate just how politically charged fiscal policy can be. Macroeconomists should contribute constructively to the public discourse by clarifying how fiscal policy works.

The recent debates highlight two questions. First, how might fiscal policy help to push the economy out of recession or to restrain recrudescent inflation? Second, what effect does fiscal policy have on the long-run prospects for economic growth?

17.1 Countercyclical Fiscal Policy

17.1.1 *Fiscal Responses to Aggregate Demand and Supply Shocks*

Active and Passive Fiscal Policy

Some of the key features of fiscal policy have already been discussed in Chapter 13. There we saw that changes in taxes, transfers, and government expenditure have multiplied effects on aggregate demand. Fiscal policy can be either discretionary or automatic (section 13.2): AUTOMATIC FISCAL POLICY is *built into the design of the tax code and spending programs*; DIS-CRETIONARY FISCAL POLICY is *deliberately chosen to achieve a particular result.*

Figure 17.1 uses the IS curve and the long-term interest rate to illustrate
a particular discretionary fiscal-policy action: an increase in government
expenditure. (Problem 17.2 considers other types of discretionary fiscal policy.) Automatic fiscal policy is embodied in the shape and location of the IS
curve and in the degree to which a nonpolicy factor, such as a change in net
exports or the marginal propensity to consume, shifts or rotates the IS curve
(i.e., on the multipliers).

The most straightforward illustration is shown in Figure 17.1. As in Chapters 15 and 16, GDP and its components are scaled by potential output in
the figure. An increase of government expenditure ($\widetilde{G}$) shifts the IS curve
rightward. At a fixed real interest rate, aggregate demand rises from $\widetilde{Y}_0$ to
$\widetilde{Y}_1$. As we saw in Chapter 13 (section 13.3.3), the magnitude of the rightward
shift is given by the autonomous expenditure multiplier times the change in
government spending: $\mu \Delta \widetilde{G}$.

Aggregate-Demand Shocks

If the economy always grew on a perfectly steady path, the policy problem
would be simple. Unfortunately, events at home and abroad can knock the
economy off course. In Chapter 15 (section 15.1), we classified events into
those that affect aggregate expenditure, called **aggregate-demand shocks**,
and those that affect potential output, called **aggregate-supply shocks**.

The currency crisis and accompanying recession in the East Asian newly
industrializing countries (NICs) in the period 1997–1999 provide a real-life
example of an aggregate-demand shock to the United States: the NIC's
imports of American goods fell from the highest level in 1997 to the lowest level in 1999 by 38 percent. This, of course, contributed to the continuing
fall in U.S. net exports during this period.

In Figure 17.2, starting at NAIRU, the aggregate-demand shock is shown
as a leftward shift of the IS curve. At the same real interest rate, GDP falls
from $\widetilde{Y}_N$ to $\widetilde{Y}_1$ and prices begin to decelerate with the change in the inflation rate falling from 0 to $\Delta \hat{p}_1$. As we saw in Chapter 16 (section 16.3.2), a
movement away from NAIRU can start a spiral of cumulatively decelerating
prices and aggregate demand: if left alone, GDP and inflation rates will fall
and unemployment will rise at increasing rates.

Of course, the East Asian crises were not the only things going on in the
U.S. economy at the time. Figure 17.2 shows the effect of the aggregate-
demand shock *ceteris paribus*. But other factors more than counteracted
this negative one (in sum preventing the IS curve from falling and, perhaps,
pushing it to the right of NAIRU), so that the period 1997–1999 was, in reality, one of strong growth and low unemployment. Some of the countervail-
ing factors may have been offsetting positive aggregate-demand shocks or
monetary or fiscal policy actions. In principle, a fiscal action (an increase in
government spending or transfer payments or a cut in taxes) could stimulate

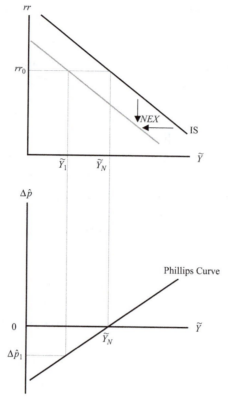

Figure 17.2. An Aggregate-Demand Shock. An aggregate-demand shock (here a fall in net exports) shifts the IS curve leftward, reducing aggregate demand below NAIRU and decelerating prices.

spending. If the policy action were properly designed, the IS curve would shift back to its original position, offsetting the negative shock.

Aggregate-Supply Shocks

Supply shocks affect potential output (Y^{pot}). Recall that scaled output is $\tilde{Y} = \frac{Y}{Y^{pot}}$. If potential output falls, then, *for the same level of aggregate demand* (Y), scaled output will rise. All other things equal, the IS curve must *initially* shift to the right as shown in Figure 17.3. It is important to recall (Chapter 15, section 15.5.3) that this rightward shift *does not* correspond to an increase in real GDP. Rather, the old level of aggregate demand is now suddenly higher relative to the now lower level of potential output. The acceleration in prices that results ($\Delta\hat{p}_1$) ultimately reduces relative aggregate demand back to its NAIRU level (a leftward shift in the IS curve back to its original position). Because of the fall in potential output, NAIRU now corresponds to a lower level of GDP with lower real-wage rates (because the labor-production function shifted down, reducing the marginal product of labor). With lower real-wage rates, labor supply and the level of full employment will fall. Although fewer people are working at NAIRU, the

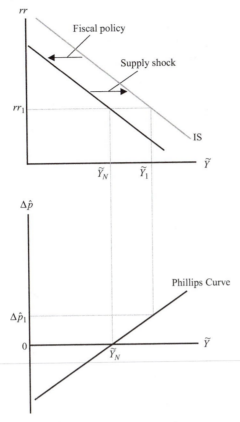

Figure 17.3. An Aggregate-Supply Shock. A negative aggregate-supply shock shifts the IS curve rightward as potential output falls in the face of unchanged aggregate demand. Prices accelerate as aggregate demand exceeds NAIRU. A fiscal-policy action can shift the IS curve back to its old position to offset the inflationary effect of the supply shock.

actual NAIRU rate of unemployment may not be any higher, because the labor force may have become smaller as participation rates fall.

Mixed Shocks

In the real world, pure aggregate-demand or pure aggregate-supply shocks are rare. The massive rises and falls of oil prices in the 1970s and 1980s, as well as after 2005, mixed both kinds of shocks. Consider a large increase in oil prices. The aggregate-demand effect is negative: the United States (like Japan and most of western Europe) is a net importer of oil. If the demand for oil is relatively inelastic in the short run, the big price increase translates into a big increase in the dollar value of imports.

The aggregate-supply effect is also negative: the immediate result of an increase in the price of oil relative to other sources of energy and other goods is that the economy is producing with machinery that was adapted to the old relative prices, so that it must be economically less efficient under the new relative prices (see Chapter 9, section 9.4.1). Potential output must fall.

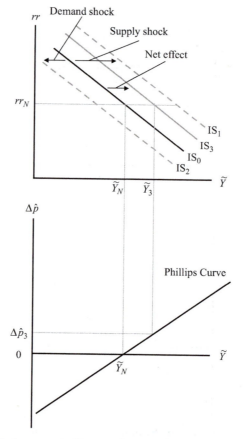

Figure 17.4. A Mixed Aggregate-Demand and Aggregate-Supply Shock. A mixed supply and demand shock (e.g., an oil-price shock) has two effects. The supply shock alone would shift the IS curve rightward as potential GDP falls in the face of the original demand. The demand shock alone would shift it leftward. The net effect is shown as IS_3 on the assumption that the supply shock is larger than the demand shock. A contractionary fiscal policy would shift the IS curve back to IS_0, realigning aggregate demand with now lower aggregate supply and stopping the price acceleration. If potential output is mismeasured, the fiscal authorities may believe that the actual IS curve is IS_2 (i.e., they recognize only the fall in demand). They might then adopt a fiscal policy that would try to close the gap between IS_2 and IS_0. But such an expansionary fiscal policy would only add to price acceleration and not restore the lost potential output.

Figure 17.4 shows each aspect of the oil-price increase separately. The original IS curve is IS_0. The supply shock is shown as a rightward shift of the IS curve from IS_0 to IS_1. IS_1 is not an actual IS curve, but a virtual IS curve that represents what would have happened to the IS curve if *only the supply shock* had been operative. Similarly, the demand shock is shown as the leftward shift from IS_0 to IS_2. IS_2 represents what would have happened if *only the demand shock* had been operative.

The actual shift of the IS curve is the sum of both shocks. In the figure, the aggregate-supply shock is shown as bigger, so that the net effect is to shift the IS curve rightward to IS_3. (Of course, if the demand shock had been greater, then IS_3 would lie to the left of IS_0.)

If there were no policy action, then prices would accelerate at $\Delta \hat{p}_3$. A fiscal policy that aimed to stabilize prices would adjust spending or taxes to shift the IS curve back to IS_0. At that point, the economy would still suffer a loss of real GDP, owing to the supply shock, but the acceleration of prices would be checked. Left alone, higher prices would, as in the case of a pure aggregate-supply shock, eventually reduce the real value of aggregate demand, shifting the IS curve back to NAIRU.

The Cost of Misperception

In principle, fiscal policy can offset the collateral damage to inflation operating through aggregate demand. In practice, it is not usually so easy. Unlike GDP itself, potential output and, hence, scaled output ($\widetilde{Y}$) and the output gap are not observed directly. They must be calculated from a model as we saw in Chapter 9 (section 9.5.1). The data on the capital stock or the productive capacity of firms that lie behind these calculations are updated less frequently than GDP data and, even when updated, do not always accurately reflect the changes in the economic efficiency of capital implied by a supply shock.

As a result, the policymaker is likely not to recognize the full extent of the supply shock as shown by IS_1. To see the problem, consider what would happen if the supply shock resulted in no revision at all of the potential output data, despite the fact that, economically, potential output had really changed. Then the policymaker would ignore the supply shock altogether, as if the shift corresponding to IS_1 had not happened. Then the net effect would not be IS_3. Instead, the policymaker would take account only of the aggregate-demand shock and would regard IS_2 as the true post-oil-price-shock IS curve.

Suppose that the policymaker tried to use fiscal policy to offset the shock. A fiscal stimulus big enough to move the *apparent* IS curve (IS_2) back to the original location (IS_0) would shift the true IS curve (IS_3) away from, not toward, the original IS curve. Of course, the result would be to push aggregate demand further past NAIRU and to accelerate prices even further. Such perceptual mistakes may well have contributed to the rapid inflation of the 1970s and early 1980s.

17.1.2 The Limits of Countercyclical Fiscal Policy

In the two decades immediately after World War II, monetary policy was widely regarded as ineffective and fiscal policy was ascendant. Fiscal policy was credited with a substantial part of the recovery from the Great Depression of the 1930s. Many economists thought that fiscal policy fostered the long expansion of the 1960s. They believed that the tax cuts of 1964, at the least, had prevented a recession from developing and had allowed the economy to grow steadily in what proved to be the then-longest business-cycle expansion in history (surpassed only recently by the 1991–2001 expansion). Opinions differed about the roots of the economic growth of the 1980s, but many economists credited it to the fiscal stimulus of the tax cuts in 1981 through 1986 under Ronald Reagan's administration.[1]

From the late 1980s through 2008, monetary policy was ascendant. Despite the appeals of George W. Bush's administration for a fiscal stimulus in the 2001 recession, *systematic* countercyclical fiscal policy had few advocates. The reason was not that fiscal policy was thought not to be powerful. Rather, it was thought to be too unwieldy. The Obama administration embraced fiscal policy wholeheartedly in 2009 when it sought to check the recession with the largest fiscal stimulus in U.S. history – $862 billion.[2] Whether the stimulus will illustrate the unwieldiness of fiscal policy or instead demonstrate its effectiveness remains to be seen (in mid-2011).

The Lag in Fiscal Policy

Like monetary policy, fiscal policy acts with a tripartite lag – recognition, implementation, and transmission lags (see Chapter 16, section 16.5.2). The recognition lag is similar for both monetary and fiscal policy. No countercyclical actions can take place until the policymakers have assessed the changing situation. Such assessments are as difficult and time-consuming for fiscal policy as they are for monetary policy.

In contrast, the implementation lag is likely to be much longer for discretionary fiscal policy than for monetary policy. The reason is that in the United States – as in all democracies – there is no fiscal policymaker in the same sense that the Federal Reserve or other central banks can be thought of as monetary policymakers. The Federal Open Market Committee has twelve voting members, yet the committee directs monetary policy with a unified voice. The same cannot be said for fiscal policy.

Federal tax and budget policies are the subject of complex negotiations within Congress and between Congress and the White House. Even after legislation establishes the main outlines of a policy, the Internal Revenue Service (IRS) or spending agencies may have been left with further detailed decisions to make: Exactly how should a tax rule be written? Exactly where

---

[1] The details of the tax reforms of 1981, 1986, as well as some smaller adjustments in 1982 and 1984 are complicated; see U.S. Treasury, "Fact Sheet on the History of the U.S. Tax System" (www.ustreas.gov/education/fact-sheets/taxes/ustax.shtml) for a concise history.

[2] Congressional Budget Office estimate, March 2010.

should a highway be sited? The process is bound to be a slow one. So slow, in fact, that the combination of the recognition and implementation lags is typically longer than the length of the average recession.

Discretionary fiscal policy is not only likely to be too late, but by the time it is finally implemented, it may push the economy in the wrong direction altogether. And it is not possible to know in many cases exactly what the policy action was. Congress and the president, just like everyone else, may forecast the dollar value of a particular tax increase based on the rate schedules and other assumptions about the economy, but they cannot say with precision "taxes were raised today by $100 million." In contrast, the Federal Reserve can raise the Federal-funds rate and hold it within a small fraction of a point of where it chooses.

Although long dormant, discretionary fiscal policy was reinvigorated with the adoption of President Obama's stimulus package in February of 2009. The details of the package do illustrate some of the difficulties with such policies. By the time that the stimulus passed Congress and had been signed into law, the recession was already nearly fourteen months old. And the stimulus – a combination of increased spending and decreased taxes – came on slowly. The Congressional Budget Office estimated that by the end of 2009, only 31 percent had been implemented.[3] According to news reports, the Obama administration expected 70 percent of the stimulus to come online within a year and half. The recession itself ended in June of 2009. Discretionary countercyclical fiscal policy is clearly not nimble, although the jury is still out on whether it was an effective response to the most severe recession since the Great Depression.

In contrast, nondiscretionary fiscal policy – the automatic stabilizers – does not suffer from either the implementation or recognition lags. Without the notice or special care of the policymakers, they quietly dampen fluctuations in aggregate demand. The design of adequate and effective stabilizers is an important role for the policy planner.

The transmission lag is likely to be shorter for fiscal policy than that for monetary policy. Consumer spending is closely related to incomes. Higher paychecks, because of tax cuts or new incomes generated by increasing employment, translate relatively quickly into rents paid, groceries and luxuries bought. Lower interest rates translate into increased investment, but often only after a recognition and implementation lag within firms themselves. The shorter transmission lag was one of the reasons that fiscal policy was so frequently advocated thirty or forty years ago. The advocates failed to grasp that the ponderous political processes of a democratic government

---

[3] Congressional Budget Office, "Estimated Impact of the American Recovery and Reinvestment Act on Employment and Economic Output from October 2009 through December 2009," February 2010 (www.cbo.gov/ftpdocs/110xx/doc11044/02–23-ARRA.pdf downloaded 10 March 2010.)

ensure that the implementation lag typically swamps any advantage gained from the shorter transmission lag.

Permanent versus Temporary Policies

In Chapter 14 (sections 14.2 and 14.5.3) we saw that it was necessary to distinguish between permanent and temporary incomes and opportunity costs. For those consumers (probably about half the population) who are able to borrow and lend relatively freely, a temporary increase in income results in little extra consumption. The rational consumer saves the windfall and, at most, consumes the interest it earns – perhaps only 1/20th of the increase. For consumers, then, tax cuts or increases in government expenditure that are believed to be long-lived should have a much higher multiplier and a bigger ultimate effect on aggregate demand than do transitory policy actions.

How does it work out in practice? President George H. W. Bush provided a case study in 1992 when, as a stimulus measure, he directed the IRS to reduce tax withholdings from paychecks, with no change in tax rates. More cash was placed in people's pockets immediately. The permanent-income/life-cycle hypothesis of Chapter 14 (section 14.2.4) suggests that this policy would have almost no effect. Come April 15th, when tax returns must to be filed, the taxpayer would have had to write a check for any shortfall in the tax bill. The policy did not increase anyone's income, but it temporarily shifted personal cash flows. Yet, if some consumers were liquidity constrained or myopic (Chapter 14, section 14.3), then consumption might in fact rise somewhat.[4]

One study of this episode concluded that liquidity effects were unimportant; that 43 percent of the taxpayers displayed myopia and treated the change in withholding as genuine income; and the net direct stimulus to consumption was about $11 billion or 0.2 percent of 1992 GDP.[5] The ultimate effect, of course, depends on the multiplier. If the multiplier were as large as 2.9 (Chapter 13, equation (13.17), then the effect would have been relatively large at $43 billion or 0.6 percent of GDP. Most economists estimate the multiplier to be much lower. President Obama's Council of Economic Advisers assumed a multiplier of about 1.6 while planning the 2009 stimulus, and other economists have estimated that the multiplier is actually significantly less than one.

Congress has frequently proposed temporary tax credits for firms engaged in investment. In contrast with consumption, as we saw in Chapter 14, these should be relatively powerful in the short run. The payoff to a long-lived

---

[4] See Chapter 14, Box 14.1 for a similar analysis of the effects of the younger President Bush's 2008 stimulus.

[5] Matthew Shapiro and Joel Slemrod, "Consumer Response to the Timing of Income: Evidence from a Change in Tax Withholding," *American Economic Review*, vol. 85, no. 1 (March 1995), pp. 274–283.

investment project is generally not very different if it started now or a year from now. If the government offers a tax credit for this year only, the firm has a reason to move the start date of the project forward. A relatively small incentive might have a large effect on investment spending today. The effect is likely to be larger than for a permanent tax credit, because firms know that the opportunity is fleeting – "make hay while the sun shines."

Still, temporary tax credits generally prove to be ineffective. When the tax credit is removed the next year, the incentive for further front-loading investment is removed. What is more, many investment projects that would have been started next year have already been started, so that there could be a large fall in new investment next year, reversing the gains of the current policy.

Fiscal policy is likely to be more effective if it is permanent. Yet, discretionary fiscal policy is never truly permanent. It may not even be long-lived. Ronald Reagan oversaw large tax cuts in 1981 and 1986 that he clearly intended to be permanent. Some tax rates were increased even during the Reagan administration. Reagan's successor, the elder George Bush, campaigned on a pledge of fiscal stability ("Read my lips...NO new taxes"). The fact that he reneged on that promise was an important element in his defeat at the next election. His defense was the reasonable one that, as circumstances change, the right policy surely changes. That is just the point: consumers, workers, and firms are well aware that circumstances change and that whenever they have changed in the past, fiscal policy has also changed. Tax cuts are not *time-consistent* (see Chapter 16, section 16.5.2). The younger George Bush successfully pushed Congress to cut estate taxes. He preferred that the tax cut be permanent, but in fact Congress explicitly limited it to ten years. And President Obama and a Democratic Congress chose not to extend the cuts, so that estate taxes return to their previous levels starting in 2011.

State and Local Budgets

Fiscal policy is often described as if it involved only the Federal government. State and local governments account for about half of all government spending in the United States. State and local governments do not typically conduct countercyclical fiscal policy. One reason is that the states are so interconnected that fiscal actions in one state would spill over into the other states and, as a result, may have little direct effect on employment in the originating state. The same problem could, of course, occur for small countries with open economies – especially if, as many countries of the European Union now do, they share the same currency. State fiscal actions may nonetheless matter to the U.S. macroeconomy even if they are not used intentionally to smooth the business cycle.

Just as at the Federal level, state tax and transfer policies are part of the economy's automatic fiscal policy. Unfortunately, they may often act as automatic *destabilizers*. When Federal expenditures outstrip revenues, the Federal government sells bonds to make up the difference. States are not in the same position. According to their constitutions, most states must – within some limits – balance their budgets. States do sometimes borrow, although their borrowing is typically restricted to capital expenditure and frequently requires direct approval (sometimes with a two-thirds majority) from the voters. The consequence is that when a state goes into recession and revenues fall, it is forced either to raise taxes or to cut expenditures. Both tend to reduce aggregate demand and exacerbate, rather than offset, the recession.

17.2 Fiscal Policy in the Long Run

17.2.1 Monetary Policy as Fiscal Policy

Seigniorage

In Chapter 16 (section 16.1.1), we saw that monetary and fiscal policy are closely connected through the government's budget constraint (equation 16.1) repeated here as

$$G - (T - TR) = \Delta B^G + \Delta MB. \tag{17.1}$$

Any fiscal policy that results in a deficit on the left-hand side of the equation must be financed through additions to government liabilities on the right-hand side of the equation. Financing through the creation of monetary base is known, as we already learned (Chapter 16, section 16.1.1), as MONETIZA-TION OF THE DEFICIT.

Historically, monetization has had a bad name. In older times when money was virtually all gold and silver, kings would often issue new coins with less of the precious metal (and perhaps more of some base metal to maintain the weight and size) but with the same face value. If the king used 8 million old coins to produce 10 million new coins, the difference of 2 million formed part of his revenue and could help to finance his wars or his finery. The increase in the king's expenditure without any reduction in the expenditure of his subjects increased demand relative to supply, and prices rose. The fall in the real value of their nominal wealth is exactly what financed the king's additional expenditures. The *debased* coinage acted as a hidden tax, an INFLATION TAX, on his subjects.

Even when the king did not debase the coinage, it was usual for him to require that his subjects give more gold or silver bullion at the mint than would be returned to them as coins. The surplus, known as SEIGNIORAGE (from the French *seigneur* meaning "lord"), was pure profit.

Debasement was a dishonest practice that counted on the king's subjects accepting a coin at its face value when it was really worth less. In contrast, people would willingly pay a moderate seigniorage because coined metal was easier to handle and more easily valued than bullion – it really was worth a small premium.

In modern times, the value of the paper that goes into a dollar bill or even the value of the base metals that go into our coins is small relative to the face value of the money. The potential for seigniorage would seem huge. In addition, when the government issues monetary base, unlike when it sells bonds, it does not have to pay interest. Why then does the government not simply monetize the deficit?

To some extent it does. The monetary base grows over time. However, if it grows relatively fast compared to GDP or to other financial assets, it tends to depress interest rates, stimulating aggregate demand. If the economy is near full employment, the natural result is increased inflation. Just like the kings of old, it has debased the currency. Monetary cranks frequently complain about the Federal Reserve doing the same thing. In fact, seigniorage is generally a small part of government revenue. For example, in 1993, which until the financial crisis of 2008–2009 was the year in which the monetary base grew the fastest since World War II, it covered only 2.6 percent of government outlays. The financial crisis showed that seigniorage may still be a major source of revenues. In Chapter 16 (Box 16.1) we saw that the reserve component of the monetary base increased massively in 2009. But purchases of private securities, which do not directly provide seigniorage, accounted for more than three-quarters of the increase. Even so, purchases of Treasury securities provided seigniorage of about 9 percent of Federal government outlays.

Risks of Hyperinflation

Seigniorage often forms a much larger portion of government revenue in countries with ineffective or mismanaged fiscal regimes. If a government finds it hard to levy taxes or to sell bonds, "printing money" may be its only alternative. In Argentina, for example, seigniorage financed 47 percent of the government's outlays in 1991. Economies that rely on seigniorage are prone to bouts of high inflation. Argentina's inflation rate in 1991 was 172 percent per year.

Fiscal disorders, including the reliance on seigniorage for substantial revenue, *sometimes* pave the way for **hyperinflation** (often defined as inflation rates more than 50 percent per month). The most famous hyperinflation of all time occurred in Germany in the aftermath of World War I. The victorious allies demanded reparation payments far beyond the scope of ordinary sources of revenue. The German government literally turned to the printing press. Between August of 1922 and November of 1923, the average German

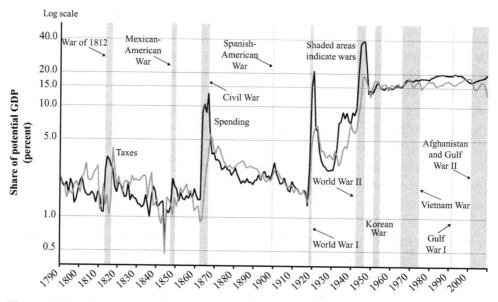

Figure 17.5. U.S. Federal Taxes and Spending, 1790–2009. *Source:* Kevin D. Hoover and Mark V. Siegler, "Taxing and Spending in the Long View: The Causal Structure of U.S. Fiscal Policy After 1791," *Oxford Economic Papers,* vol. 52, no. 4, December 2000.

inflation rate was 322 percent per month. The inflation rate in October of 1923 rose to 41 percent per day! It took wheelbarrow loads of cash to buy a loaf of bread or a pack of cigarettes.

17.2.2 Deficits and the Debt through Time

Fiscal policy has long-term as well as cyclical consequences. Government spending, taxation, transfers, and the deficit are all flows. Government debt is the stock counterpart to the government's budget deficit. Through most of U.S. history, the Federal government has regarded a balanced budget, and no borrowing, as the ideal goal of fiscal policy. The history of Federal fiscal policy is reflected in Figure 17.5, which shows expenditures and revenues as a share of GDP over a period of more than two hundred years.

It is striking that both expenditures and revenues start low at the beginning of the republic and increase in a series of stair steps – each step is associated with a national cataclysm – the Civil War, World War I, the Great Depression/New Deal, and World War II. The pattern was the same throughout the nineteenth century – it even applies to the smaller wars (War of 1812, the Mexican-American War, and the Spanish-American War).

Nineteenth-century wars called for extraordinary expenditures. These were financed through the sale of government bonds. After each war, the government on average ran a surplus and used the surplus to repay the debt. The same pattern can be seen in the case of World War I, but it breaks down with the Great Depression/New Deal and World War II. From the 1930s, the Federal government has generally run a deficit. For twenty-five years after the end of World War II, revenues and expenditures were never far out of line; but, since about 1970 (around the time of the Vietnam War), expenditures have largely outstripped revenues. Only for a brief period at the end of the 1990s up to the recession of 2001 did the Federal government run a significant surplus.

The evolution of the debt through time depends both on past and present actions. When it sells bonds, the government is committed to pay interest on them. Other parts of government expenditure – including so-called entitlements – are to different degrees discretionary. It is useful to decompose the government deficit into two parts: $(G + TR) - T = the\ Primary\ Deficit + Interest\ Payments$. The **PRIMARY DEFICIT** is the difference between *non-interest* expenditures and revenues. Where interest payments represent the inherited obligations of the past, the primary deficit represents present choices.

The evolution of the debt can, then, be represented by an equation:

$$B_t^G = B_{t-1}^G + r_{t-1}B_{t-1}^G + PD_t, \qquad (17.2)$$

where the stock of debt at the end of the current period (B_t^G) is the sum of the past stock (B_{t-1}^G), the flow of interest payments contracted in the past and paid this period $(r_{t-1}B_{t-1}^G)$, and the current primary deficit (PD_t).

Further insight into the growth of the debt can be gained by dividing both sides by B_{t-1}^G and rearranging to get

$$\frac{B_t^G}{B_{t-1}^G} - 1 = r_{t-1} + \frac{PD_t}{B_{t-1}^G}. \qquad (17.3)$$

The left-hand side is, of course, the growth rate of the debt, so the equation can be rewritten as

$$\hat{B}_t^G = r_{t-1} + pd_t, \qquad (17.3')$$

where pd_t is the ratio of this period's primary deficit to the previous stock of government debt $(pd_t \equiv PD_t/B_{t-1}^G)$ – that is, the ratio of newly incurred to existing obligations. Where the interest rate represents the flow of expenditures related to the old obligations, the primary deficit ratio represents the flow of expenditures related to the new obligations.

Figure 17.6 shows the growth rate of debt, the interest rate paid on the debt, and the primary debt ratio for the post-World War II period. Notice that before 1970, the primary debt ratio was often negative – that is, the Federal government would have run a surplus except for the need to meet interest payments. In the 1990s, the primary debt ratio became negative in 1994. Over the next three years, an increasing primary surplus acted to

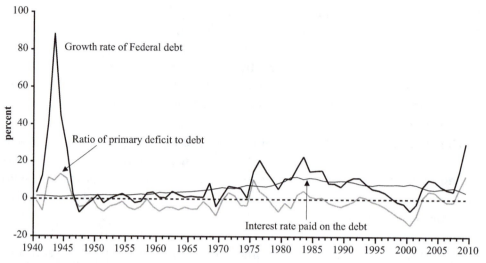

Figure 17.6. Growth of the Federal Government Debt. The growth rate of the debt
is the sum of the interest paid on the debt and the ratio of the primary deficit to the
debt. The primary deficit is expenditures minus interest payments. The current level
of the debt can be understood, then, as the legacy of past fiscal policy (interest) plus
the current fiscal policy (primary deficit). *Source:* debt and interest rate, Bureau of
the Debt; deficit, Bureau of Economic Analysis; and author's calculations.

counteract relatively steady interest payments, finally offsetting them completely, arresting the growth, and initiating the short-lived reduction in the
Federal debt. This reduction, of course, corresponds to the budget surpluses
at the end of the Clinton administration.

17.2.3 Crowding Out

Functional Finance

The majority of the public and probably the majority of politicians believe
that balanced budgets (zero deficits) and no public debt represent an eco-
nomical – and perhaps, moral – ideal. The constitutions of many states
require balanced budgets – at least for ordinary operating expenses. Not
many years ago, talk of a balanced-budget amendment to the U.S. Constitution was widespread. The strong preference for balanced budgets just
seems like common sense. After all, if any of us routinely spent more than
we earned, we would be courting financial disaster.

The notion that a balanced personal budget is ideal has deep cultural
roots. In Charles Dickens' (1812–1870) great novel *David Copperfield*,
the eponymous narrator recounts the wisdom of the jovial n'er-do-well,
Mr. Micawber:

He solemnly conjured me, I remember, to take warning by his fate; and to observe
that if a man had twenty pounds a-year for his income, and spent nineteen pounds

nineteen shillings and sixpence, he would be happy, but that if he spent twenty pounds one he would be miserable.

Many people implicitly agree with Polonius in Shakespeare's *Hamlet*, who tells his son, "Neither a borrower nor a lender be." (It is sometimes forgotten that Polonius was a fool.)

Most of us would doubt the wisdom of borrowing $250,000 to throw a party; few would argue that borrowing the same amount to purchase a house was misguided until we had further information. Similarly, borrowing to go to college may be the smartest thing that many of us have done.

Like personal borrowing, government deficits must be judged according to the circumstances. **FUNCTIONAL FINANCE** is the term that the economist Abba Lerner (1903–1982) gave to the view that government budgets and financing decisions should not be judged by whether or not they balance, but by what effects they have on the economy. Some issues that are relevant from the perspective of functional finance are:

- How does a deficit affect aggregate demand? (A question we addressed in Section 17.1.)
- How does government expenditure interact with private expenditure?
- Do government financing decisions (tax or debt-management decisions) re-distribute wealth or income in favorable or unfavorable ways?
- Do government financing decisions alter incentives in favorable or unfavorable ways?

In short, to judge the soundness of fiscal policy we need to look, not at the national accounts or the national balance sheet, but at the effects of the policy on the real things we care about: output, employment, and the distribution of income and wealth – that is, on the real economy. We shall consider some of these issues in the remainder of this chapter.

Zero-Sum Crowding Out

A persistent fear among the critics of government involvement in the economy is that fiscal policy will *crowd out* the private sector. **CROWDING OUT** has been used to refer to many things. The least controversial is what might be called **ZERO-SUM CROWDING OUT**: *if an economy is fully employed, then any time the government takes more resources, those available to the private sector must fall.*

The point is obvious from the production-expenditure identity (Chapter 2, equation (2.1'')): $Y \equiv C + I + G + NX$. At full employment, Y is constant (the pie has a fixed size). So, any increase in the government's slice (G) must result in smaller slices for consumers (C), investors (I), or foreigners (NX). It is a zero-sum game.

Zero-sum crowding out refers only to the government's outlays on real goods and services (G) and not to its outlays on transfer payments (TR), such as interest, Social Security, or welfare. Transfer payments only shift the ownership of resources among the members of the private sector, so that their direct effect is to leave the relative size of the private sector unchanged. Transfers may, of course, have indirect effects.

Crowding Out or Crowding In?

Although increases in the government's share necessarily crowd out the private sector's share, the story is more complex if we think, not of shares, but of the actual level of real resources. Shares refer to the division of the pie. But what if government actions can change the size of the pie? Recall from Chapter 13 (section 13.1.4) that, when the economy is below full employment, an increase in government expenditure increases GDP through a multiplier process.

Even at full employment, government fiscal actions may affect the size of GDP positively or negatively. Imagine a country – much as the United States was in the nineteenth century – rich in resources but poor in infrastructure. A government that built canals, railroads, and telegraphs would have promoted private industry. GDP would be larger and the absolute resources commanded by the private sector would be larger, even though the government's share itself was larger.

In fact, infrastructural development in the United States was a mixture of government and private actions. Often the government promoted private development – for example, land grants to railroads. Because of the indirect channels of its policies, the government's role in the economy was understated in the national accounts. In other countries, government policies were more direct, and the government share in the economy higher.

In modern times, government involvement in the development of the internet and in the construction and maintenance of roads, airports, schools, hospitals, and public transportation contributes not only directly to GDP, but indirectly provides services essential to the private sector. Such indirect benefits are referred to as **positive externalities** in contrast to the negative externalities of Chapter 3 (section 3.5.4). In recent years, there has been a lively debate about the level and the importance of the external benefits of government expenditure. Some economists have argued that infrastructural investment increases the rate of economic growth. Far from crowding out, they argue that such investment offers a case of CROWDING IN: the government expenditure increases the resources available to the private sector. The jury is still out on this debate.

Although roads, schools, and other infrastructure are typical examples of government investment, the private sector itself sometimes provides virtually every type of infrastructural investment. The government, however, also provides services that are rarely, if it all, provided privately: the police, the courts, and health-and-safety regulation, to name a few. These services also exhibit positive externalities. The questions – which services are best provided by the government and which by the private sector, and how large should the government sector be? – are central to the field of economics known as *public economics* or *public finance*. We cannot address these issues in any detail in this course. It is enough for us to notice that the question of whether additional government expenditure is positive or negative for the economy is not simple and requires further study.

Displacement of Private Expenditure

Another kind of crowding out may occur when government expenditures displace previously private expenditures. For example, before the middle of the nineteenth century, governments typically did not mandate or provide public schooling for children. Yet, many children attended private schools. When governments assumed the duty of public education, citizens were free to reduce their private expenditures on schools without loss to their children.

Similarly, before Social Security was initiated in 1936, U.S. citizens had to save for their own retirement unless their employer provided a pension (and few did). Of course, private pensions are now common, and many people still have substantial private savings for retirement. Nevertheless, some economists believe that the currently low personal savings rates in the United States are partly the result of the presence of Social Security and that increases in Social Security provisions would result in further reductions in savings rates.

Deficits and Interest Rates

The financial press often mentions another form of zero-sum crowding out. Recall from Chapter 2 the sectoral-deficits identity (2.3) repeated here as

$$[G - (T - TR)] + [I - S] + [EX - IM] = 0. \qquad (17.4)$$

If the government's budget deficit (the left-most term in square brackets) becomes larger while savings, the foreign deficit, and net exports (the third term) remain constant, then investment must be "crowded out."

Although, as a matter of accounting, an increase in the budget deficit must be balanced by some other item in the identity, it is by no means clear that investment is the only thing that would adjust, and it is unlikely that it would adjust one-for-one. Fiscal policy cannot be described merely by the size of the deficit. To achieve a particular deficit, the government chooses the levels of discretionary expenditure, predicts the amount of interest it must pay on its debt, and sets the *rates* of entitlement expenditures and taxation.

Tax and transfer rates and interest rates affect economic behavior. These rates, as well as other economic factors such as the level of GDP, the real

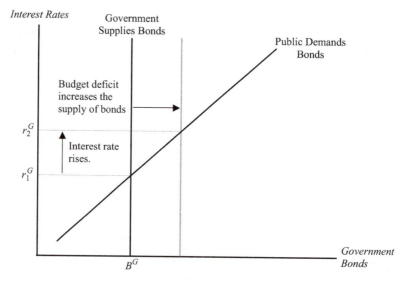

Figure 17.7. Deficits and Interest Rates. A bond-financed budget deficit increases the stock of bonds, shifting the bond supply curve to the right. In order to induce the public to demand the additional bonds, the interest rate must rise.

return on capital, and the exchange rate, affect the public's saving, investment, and import behavior as well as foreigners' demand for domestic exports. The budget deficit may affect them as well, but only indirectly. In particular, investors do not first look at the size of the budget deficit or the pool of savings and then decide how much new capital to install. Instead, each investment decision is based on the expected returns and opportunity costs that the firm faces. There is no direct connection between savings and investment or between the budget deficit and investment.

Interest rates provide one channel through which government fiscal actions are often thought to crowd out private investment. An increase in the deficit is financed through additional debt, increasing the supply of government bonds. To sell these additional bonds, their yield must rise (i.e., their price must fall) as shown in Figure 17.7 by the movement along the public's demand curve for government bonds. For a given rate of expected inflation, the real interest rate rises, which discourages some investment, and through a multiplier process reduces GDP.

Crowding out through interest rates has long been the fear of those who demand a balanced budget. Robert Rubin, Secretary of the Treasury under President Clinton, carried the argument further by maintaining that surpluses, which reduced the debt, lowered interest rates enough to account for a significant part of the economic boom of the 1990s.

On Rubin's scenario, the move toward a balanced budget "crowded in" private investment. Although a crowding-out mechanism operating through interest rates seems straightforward (more debt implies higher interest rates implies lower investment implies lower GDP), it is incomplete.

As we saw in Chapter 7 (section 7.2.1), the demand for financial assets depends not only on the direct influence of the own-rate of interest but also on the yields of other financial assets, and arbitrage tends to push returns toward a stable relationship. In particular, monetary policy tends to determine market interest rates at the short end of the term structure and expected inflation and returns on real capital at the long end of the term structure.

For shorter rates, then, whether or not deficits raise interest rates depends in large part on whether the monetary authorities allow them to do so. For longer rates, arbitrage tends to bring the real return on long bonds back into its usual relationship with real returns on stocks. The returns on stocks are, of course, related to the profitability of firms and, therefore, in a complicated way to investment.

A process of arbitrage that involves investment may be slow, so that, in the short run, deficits may increase market interest rates, but unless deficits affect real returns on capital or inflation rates, these effects should wash out in the long run. How big the short-run effects are is an empirical question on which there is no generally agreed answer.

17.2.4 Wealth Effects

Are Government Bonds Net Worth?

There is no doubt that fiscal policies affect the real economy. How much and what kinds of real expenditures the government chooses clearly matter, as do (as we shall see again in the next section) various taxes and incentives. But does the size of the deficit in itself matter, independent of the way in which it is financed? One way it might matter is that larger government debt corresponds to larger private wealth.

Recall from Chapter 6 (section 6.1.2) that the private sector as a whole cannot become wealthier through its members borrowing and lending among themselves. If you lend to me, the loan shows up as your asset and my liability. When we aggregate our balance sheets to obtain the balance sheet for the whole private sector, these entries cancel out. The same is *not* true if either of us holds government debt. A government bond is your asset and the government's liability. When we aggregate the *private* sector only, the government bond remains as an asset on the aggregate private balance sheet. It appears to be wealth. But is it really?

David Ricardo (1772–1823), an important English economist, provided a counterargument. Imagine that the government wants to increase consumption through a tax cut. It does not change any of its other plans for government expenditure or transfer payments. Suppose that your share of the tax cut is $100. To provide you with that $100, the government must increase its debt. Say that it sells a 1-year bond for $100 to make up its shortfall.

After one year, it will pay off the bond with interest. If the interest rate is 7 percent, then after one year it will have to increase taxes by $107 to pay off the debt created by your share of the bond. Imagine that you anticipated that exactly that amount would be your share of the future taxes; would you then raise your consumption in the face of the current tax cut?

The answer is no. If, in fact, you were happy with your consumption plans before the tax cut, there is no reason to change them after the tax cut. What are your choices? If you spend the entire $100, then you must lower your consumption next year by $107. But you can also save the money. In fact, you could yourself buy the government bond for $100. If you do, the government will pay you $107 next year, which is just the amount of the increase in your tax bill. By buying the bond, your consumption does not change either this year or next.

Because the increase in your holdings of government bonds – apparently increasing your wealth this year – did not result in any change in your consumption, then the bonds failed to act like true wealth. In fact, using the logic of the permanent-income/life-cycle hypothesis (see Chapter 14, section 14.2), it is easy to see that the tax changes do not change life-cycle wealth. The present value of the tax cut and the future tax increase that pays for the bond is: $PV = -T + \frac{T(1+r)}{1+r} = -100 + \frac{107}{1.07} = 0$. The government bonds, which are the positive counterpart to the tax cut, appear to be net wealth only when the future tax consequences of issuing the bonds are ignored.

The proposition that government bonds are not net wealth or that the government's choice between debt finance and tax finance has no real consequences is known as **RICARDIAN EQUIVALENCE**. Ricardian equivalence is sometimes misunderstood. It does not say that the level of government expenditure does not matter. Rather, it says that the manner in which a *given* level of government expenditure is financed (taxes or debt) does not matter.

The Limits of Ricardian Equivalence

Given fixed plans for government expenditure, if Ricardian equivalence holds, then it does not matter whether or not the government runs a deficit or balances its budget. Given the assumptions we made in the tax-cut scenario, the logic of Ricardian equivalence is unimpeachable. But are the assumptions correct?

Surprisingly, Ricardo himself did not think so. First, he believed that people were myopic, so that even though debt would eventually be paid off, some people would not grasp that this would mean higher taxes and so would fail to save the whole tax cut in order to have funds to pay future taxes. Second, he believed that some people would take the benefits of a tax cut and then emigrate, leaving their compatriots with the tax bill. Emigration from

England in the nineteenth century was substantial, but that hardly seems relevant to the United States or most developed countries in the twenty-first century.

There is, however, another kind of emigration. In the illustration, we have assumed that bonds must be paid off after a year. But, of course, the debt may be financed with long-term (say, 30-year) bonds. And, even then, when these bonds come due, new bonds may be issued to pay off the old, so that the repayment of the debt is pushed far into the future. In the meantime, the original beneficiaries of the tax cuts may die. In effect, they have emigrated into the past. If they had anticipated that taxes would not be raised to repay the bonds until after they are dead, they could have taken the tax cut as a definite gain and regarded the corresponding government bonds as net wealth.

One reply to this argument is that people who care about their heirs will not chose to leave them with the tax burden. Instead, when bonds are issued in their lifetime, they will save enough to cover the implied future taxes on their heirs. Economists (especially Robert Barro of Harvard University) have shown that Ricardian equivalence continues to hold – even when debt survives the initial beneficiaries of the tax cut – but only if people foresee having heirs and systematically account for the way inheritance and taxes affect the behavior of those heirs. It pushes the assumption of rationality too far to assume that they do this with the necessary precision. What is more, the assumption that the debt must be paid off at any horizon is suspect. What is to keep the government from issuing new debt to repay the old forever?

Like the permanent-income/life-cycle hypothesis of Chapter 14 (section 14.2), Ricardian equivalence assumes that people can borrow or, in this case, lend at the government's rate of interest to any degree necessary. This is a strong assumption. As we saw in Chapter 14 (section 14.3), a significant number of people are *liquidity constrained* – that is, unable to borrow or lend at favorable rates – and so live more or less hand to mouth. A tax cut eases this constraint and is likely to be spent, despite its future tax consequences. Similarly, even those who do borrow face higher rates of interest than the government pays. A tax cut allows them to reduce their high-interest borrowing and to repay the benefit at the lower government rate of interest sometime in the future. A tax cut, therefore, provides a net benefit, and at least a portion of the corresponding government bonds ought to be regarded as net wealth.

In summary, although consumers may take some account of the future taxes implied by new government debt, they are not likely to take complete account. They are, therefore, not likely to save the entire amount of a tax cut, and they are likely to regard the bonds that are issued to finance any tax cut as an addition to their net worth. What fraction of the market value of the bonds should be regarded as net wealth is a much debated, empirical question.[6]

17.2.5 Taxes and Incentives

What if Ricardian equivalence held completely? Would that imply that fiscal policy was unimportant in the long run? Absolutely not!

First, Ricardian equivalence addresses only the government's choice between tax and debt finance. The level of government expenditure on goods and services as a share of GDP, which measures the government's share of national resources, remains important. Equally important is just what the government does with those resources. Similarly, even though transfer payments do not represent direct pressure of the government on national resources, transfer programs such as Social Security or Medicare may confer substantial benefits (and possible costs) not only on the recipients but, indirectly, on the economy as a whole. Second, fiscal policy works not only through the levels of taxation and spending but also through the rates.

Average and Marginal Tax Rates

In earlier chapters we have emphasized that important economic decisions are made "at the margin." On the simple tax function in Chapter 13 (Figure 13.4), the slope of the function represents the *marginal tax rate*, and the slope of a ray from the origin to the function represents the *average tax rate*. Figure 17.8 is essentially the same diagram, except that now it refers to an individual taxpayer – personal income rather than GDP is shown on the horizontal axis. The figure depicts a **flat tax** – that is, one with a constant marginal rate. Because the function intersects the income axis to the right of the origin, rays to the function become steeper as income rises: the higher the income, the higher the average tax rate. *A tax code in which average tax rates rise with income* is called **PROGRESSIVE**; one in which *average tax rates are constant* is called **NEUTRAL**; and one in which *average tax rates fall with income* is called **REGRESSIVE**.

Figure 17.9 shows the actual income-tax schedule (marginal tax rates) for a single taxpayer in 2010. It is clearly not a flat tax. The average tax rate is systematically lower than the marginal rate (as we would expect from Figure 17.8). It rises with income, which shows that the tax schedule is progressive. Is the tax code progressive across all taxpayers? That turns out to be a

---

[6] John J. Seater, "Ricardian Equivalence," *Journal of Economic Literature*, vol. 31, no. 1 (March 1993), pp. 142–190, provides a pro-Ricardian survey. T. D. Stanley, "New Wine in Old Bottles: A Meta-Analysis of Ricardian Equivalence," *Southern Economic Journal*, vol. 64, no. 3 (January 1998), pp. 713–727, provides a statistical reevaluation of 27 separate studies, and concludes that Ricardian equivalence does not hold.

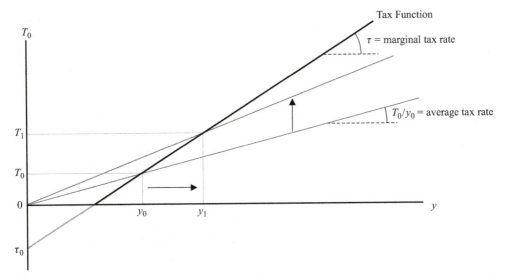

Figure 17.8. Average and Marginal Tax Rates. The marginal tax rate is the slope of the tax function. The average tax rate is the slope of a ray from the origin to a point on the tax function. Taxes are progressive when the average tax rate increases with income.

complex question, because the tax rates are calculated for adjusted gross income, which includes many deductions and adjustments to actual income (such as mortgage interest and medical deductions) that alter the actual tax bill. The tax code is further complicated by different tax schedules for married couples filing together or separately. In all, it is extremely complex.

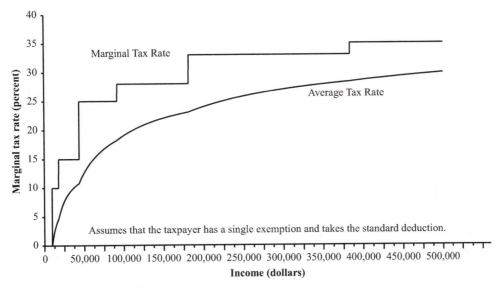

Figure 17.9. Federal Tax Rates for a Single Taxpayer, 2010. *Source:* Internal Revenue Service.

Income taxes are not, of course, the only relevant taxes. People pay a variety of indirect taxes (e.g., sales taxes or excise taxes on alcohol or gasoline). And, for many lower income workers in the United States, the most significant tax is not the income tax but the payroll taxes that fund Social Security and Medicare. These are truly flat taxes – although, in the case of Social Security, only up to a ceiling level of income.

When asking questions about the distribution of taxes, the average tax rate is important: when taxes are progressive, the rich pay a greater proportion of their incomes in taxes than do the poor. In contrast, when asking questions about the efficient allocation of resources it is the marginal tax rate that matters. In Chapter 11 (section 11.2.1) we saw that, to a worker, an income tax reduces the effective real-wage rate. In principle, we would expect a decrease in the tax rate (raising the effective real-wage rate) to increase the supply of labor somewhat.

Transfers act like negative taxes. A decrease in the marginal transfer rate should act much like an increase in the marginal tax rate. Because many transfers fall with increasing income, recipients (e.g., welfare recipients) may face extremely high *net* marginal tax rates. When a welfare recipient takes a job, not only does she face taxes on the income, she also may lose all or most of her welfare payments, so that the net marginal tax rate for the first dollar earned may actually be higher than 100 percent. Recognizing the problem, governments sometime introduce further complications into the tax code (such as the earned income credit in the United States) that aim to mitigate disincentives to work.

As we saw in Chapter 14 (section 14.5.3), corporate income tax rates matter as well. They can be regarded as a tax on the returns to investment. The lower the tax, the higher the return, and the more likely a firm is to invest.

Supply-Side Economics

Generally, lower marginal tax rates encourage people to supply labor and firms to invest. Increasing factors of production, of course, raise potential output and the rate of economic growth. **SUPPLY-SIDE ECONOMICS** is *the economic doctrine that lower tax rates promote growth substantially*. Supply-side economics was popularized during the Reagan administration (1981–1989). Rightly or wrongly, it is often seen as a conservative political ideology. As a matter of apolitical economics, there is no question that *qualitatively* its key idea is sound. The real question – which remains important for economic research – is whether tax-incentive effects are *quantitatively* large and whether they are associated with politically unacceptable distributional consequences.

The most zealous advocates of supply-side economics went further and argued that large cuts in tax rates would be self-financing, because the

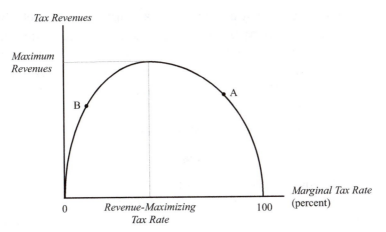

Figure 17.10. The Laffer Curve. The Laffer curve shows the relationship between marginal tax rates and revenues. Because a tax rate of zero would generate no revenue and a tax rate of 100 percent would also generate no revenue (because no one would work for no gain), there must be an intermediate rate that maximizes revenue. If the economy were on the Laffer curve at point A, a cut in tax rates would raise revenue. At point B an increase of tax rates would raise revenues.

growth in taxable income would be more than proportional to the cut in tax rates. The government would get less on each dollar, but make it up in volume. This optimistic supply-side scenario was buttressed by a common-sense observation. At a tax rate of zero, the government gets no revenue. At a tax rate of 100 percent, the government also gets no revenue: who would produce knowing that the government would take everything? Therefore, somewhere between 0 and 100 percent, there is a tax rate that maximizes government revenue.

Figure 17.10 displays this observation in the form of a graph of tax rates against revenue. This graph is named the **LAFFER CURVE**, after the economist who introduced it, Arthur Laffer. The high point of the graph shows the revenue-maximizing tax rate. Suppose that the economy were at point A. A tax cut would then actually raise revenue. But if the economy were at point B, a tax cut would decrease revenue.

Unfortunately, the commonsense observation that there is *some* revenue-maximizing tax rate cannot tell us whether the economy is actually at a point like A or like B. For that, we would need a Laffer curve that accurately represented the economy. Or we can – as the Reagan administration did in the 1980s – conduct the experiment of cutting taxes. The economy boomed, which is consistent with supply-side economics. (Of course, it is also consistent with a tax multiplier in an economy well below full employment.) Yet, revenues did not keep up with government expenditure, and deficits widened substantially.

Most economists agree that fiscal policy has supply-side effects, but there is considerable disagreement on how important they are. One study concludes that the tax cuts of the 1980s probably raised GDP through higher labor supply by less than 1.5 percent.[7] Of course, there are supply-effects on capital as well as labor. Whether or not, this number should be higher, it is clear that the most zealous supply-siders were too optimistic in thinking that tax cuts would be self-financing – at least in the short run.

Costs of Complexity

In addition to the indirect incentive effects of taxation, fiscal policy imposes a direct cost on the economy – the cost of compliance. Clearly, taxes have to be collected; the Internal Revenue Service and various state tax boards are not free. What is more, the tax code is exceedingly complex and becomes more complex over time. The Tax Foundation, a think tank, estimates that the number of words in the U.S. Internal Revenue Code nearly quadrupled between 1955 and 2000, growing on average at more than 3 percent per year.[8] And complexity imposes costs of its own.

First, a large industry of specialized tax accountants and tax preparers, tax software, tax lawyers, and financial advisers has grown up around the tax code. Although this provides employment, expenditures of this type fall under the heading of *regrettables* (Chapter 3, section 3.5.4). Specialized tax services are not primary sources of good in anyone's eyes, but are necessary given the structure of the tax code.

Second, the complexity of the tax code not only forces individuals and firms to turn to experts for help in filing tax returns, it encourages them to find ways to alter their behavior to limit their tax exposure. Sometimes this is exactly what fiscal policy intends. For example, Congress may offer a tax break for solar-power generation with the hope of reducing pollution. Such policies are always debatable, but such debates are the stuff of political discourse.

Sometimes, however, the tax code has unintended consequences and encourages people and firms to make economic choices that use resources unwisely, lowering productivity. There are legitimate arguments over how complex a fair and efficient tax code should be. The current Federal tax code in the United States, however, is jerry-rigged and so complex that even the

---

[7] M. A. Akhtar and Ethan S. Harris, "The Supply-Side Consequences of U.S. Fiscal Policy in the 1980s," *Federal Reserve Bank of New York Quarterly Review*, Spring 1992, p. 16.

[8] Data on tax complexity and compliance in this section are taken from Scott Moody, "The Cost of Tax Compliance," Tax Foundation, February 2002 (www.taxfoundation.org/research/show/306.html) and Tax Foundation, "Tax Data," 26 October 2006 (www.taxfoundation.org/research/show/1962.html), both downloaded 10 March 2010.

agents of the IRS are at a loss to know just what it requires. Compliance with Federal taxes is estimated to have cost $324 billion in 2010 or about 2.5 percent of GDP.

17.3 The Burden of the Debt

Among politicians and the popular press, the government debt is persistently characterized as a burden – a burden on the public, because taxes must service the interest payments, and a burden on future generations, because our children and our children's children must pay off the principal. Obviously, if Ricardian equivalence held, the debt would be no burden in itself. Government expenditure may be a burden, but how it is financed would be quite irrelevant. In previous sections, however, we have given reason to doubt that Ricardian equivalence holds. And, so, we must ask, is government debt a burden?

17.3.1 Debt and Growth

Debt and Income

The dollar amount of a debt is a poor measure of its burdensomeness. A new high-school graduate, earning $20,000 a year, would find a $15,000 car loan to be a serious burden. A corporate manager earning $125,000 a year would find it manageable. Similarly, a country with a GDP of $10 trillion can bear a debt of $3 trillion more easily than a country with a GDP of $500 billion could bear a debt of $700 billion. The debt must be measured relative to the size of the economy.

A simple measure is the ratio of debt to GDP (B^G/pY). (The price level (p) in this last expression can be thought of as converting real GDP (Y) to nominal GDP, so that it is the ratio of nominal debt to nominal GDP (pY); or it can be thought of as converting nominal bonds to real bonds (B^G/p), so that it is the ratio of real debt to real GDP.)

How can we judge whether debt is large or small relative to income? What should we compare it to? One possibility is to compare it to the experience of other countries. Table 17.1 shows the ratios of debt to GDP for a selection of OECD countries. In 2008, U.S. debt was about two-fifths of U.S. GDP – although it has been growing rapidly after 2009. This was a lower ratio than any G-7 country, except Canada, and lower than most of the selection of non-G-7 countries in the table. It is only about one-third the rate of Italy, and about one-fifth the rate of Japan. Another obvious comparison is between current and past levels of debt. This is addressed in Problem 17.17.

Table 17.1. *Debt Ratios for Selected Countries, 2008*

	Ratio of Central Government Debt to GDP (percent)
The G-7	
Canada	29
United States	40
Germany	46
United Kingdom	56
France	69
Italy	114
Japan[c]	197
Other Countries	
Luxembourg	11
China[a]	13
Mexico	14
South Korea	18
Turkey[c]	25
Thailand[b]	27
South Africa[a]	46
Russia[a]	49
India[c]	58
Singapore[b]	84
Ethiopia[a]	101
Burundi[a]	184

Notes: [a] 2001 value; [b] 2005 value; [c] 2007 value.
Source: OECD Statistics Portal for the United States, Japan, Germany, France, United Kingdom, Italy, Canada, South Korea, Mexico, Turkey, and Luxembourg; World Bank *World Development Indicators* for China, India, South Africa, Singapore, Ethiopia, Burundi, Russia, and Thailand.

Outgrowing Debt

Such simple comparisons, however, do not present the full picture. A medical resident may earn $45,000 and have student loan debts of $120,000 and yet not be worried, because she knows that in a few years she will be earning $170,000 per year. As with the doctor, sometimes, the economy can outgrow the public debt. The growth rate of the debt ratio can be expressed as

$$\left(\widehat{\frac{B_t^G}{p_t Y_t}} \right) = \hat{B}_t^G - \hat{p}_t - \hat{Y}_t. \tag{17.5}$$

Substituting from equation (17.3′), this can be rewritten as

$$\left(\widehat{\frac{B_t^G}{p_t Y_t}} \right) = r_{t-1} + pd_t - \hat{p}_t - \hat{Y}_t = (r_{t-1} - \hat{p}_t) + pd_t - \hat{Y}_t. \tag{17.6}$$

If the primary deficit (PD_t) is constant (or even grows sufficiently slowly), then the primary debt ratio ($pd_t = PD_t/B_t^G$) will fall toward zero as the economy grows. In that case, the growth rate of government debt is the difference between the *ex post* real rate of interest ($r_{t-1} - \hat{p}_t$) and the rate of real GDP growth. On the one hand, if the real rate of interest is low relative to the overall economic growth, then debt will become less burdensome over time, even if it never falls in its dollar value. On the other hand, if economic growth is slow, only a surplus on the primary deficit could reduce the debt as a share of GDP.

Inflation and the Debt

What is the effect of inflation on the debt? Notice that if there is a Fisher effect (see Chapter 7, Section 7.5.2) and if the inflation were anticipated, then any increase in the inflation rate would be matched point for point by an increase in the interest rate. The real rate ($r_{t-1} - \hat{p}_t$) would be unchanged and the debt ratio would be unaffected.

However, if the Fisher effect was incomplete or the inflation was unanticipated, then the real rate would fall and reduce the debt ratio, easing the government's financial burden. Unanticipated inflation, in effect, provides the government with a hidden source of revenue, closely related to the inflation tax discussed in section 17.2.1.

17.3.2 Capital and Consumption Spending

The number one cliché of long-term public finance is "the public debt is a burden on future generations." But must it be? The cliché implicitly assumes that government expenditure as a pure loss. Imagine that a family purchases a house for $400,000 financed by a $320,000 mortgage. Is the mortgage debt a burden? The transaction, in itself, does not alter the family's net worth – equal entries appear on both sides of its balance sheet. The real question is whether the net return on the house (the implicit rental services it provides) is higher or lower than the cost of servicing the debt, and whether purchasing those services is a good idea in itself, taking account of the family's income.

The same considerations arise with respect to government debt. The Interstate Highway System was a massively expensive capital investment – mostly in the 1950s and 1960s. It continues to be a valuable asset returning important services. Equally, airports, hospitals, schools, college campuses, public libraries, public parks, and other government-financed amenities are public capital that offset the debt. The right questions to ask are: How does the real rate of return on these public investments compare to the interest paid on the debt that financed them? And do these investments generate the services that are the most beneficial to the citizenry? If such investments were made prudently, the corresponding debt should hardly be thought of as burden on future generations. Far from it; having failed to make such investments would have been far more burdensome.

Even debt incurred for noncapital expenditure may be well justified. Sometimes present needs are so important for public welfare that they must be met, even if it means borrowing. As we saw in Figure 17.5, America's wars have all been debt financed. Clearly, it was better to borrow to win World War II than not to have fought it. The risk, of course, is that politicians will be tempted to claim that all manner of current expenditure falls into the same category as necessary wars.

17.3.3 Domestic and Foreign Debt

If the number one cliché of long-term public finance is "the public debt is a burden on future generations," number two is surely the cheerful, but equally hackneyed thought, "the debt is really no burden at all, because we owe it to ourselves." Like most clichés, this one contains an element of truth. Repayment of the interest and principal on the government debt is a transfer payment that does not affect real GDP directly. It may, of course, raise distributional issues: if the benefits of the expenditure financed by the debt accrue to different people than those who pay the taxes to service it, there is a net real transfer among them, which may or may not be desirable.

The cliché "we owe it to ourselves" assumes that government debt is purchased only by citizens of our own country. The assumption is false: in September of 2009, 29 percent of the national debt ($3,497 billion) was held by foreigners. The interest on their holdings transfers a substantial part of U.S. GDP to foreigners. In fact, "we owe it to them."

Is indebtedness to foreigners necessarily bad? For one thing, it is a two-way street. The United States holds the public and private assets of foreign countries as well, generating largely offsetting income flows. (Recall that these net flows are the difference between GNP and GDP; see Chapter 3, section 3.3.)

Borrowing frequently contributes to good economic outcomes. It is easier to see with private debt. American railroads in the nineteenth century were largely built with foreign finance. True, we had to repay the debt with real transfers of income, but we also got the railroads, the jobs they produced, and the services they provided. Today, states go out of their way to attract foreign investment in car factories, hotel complexes, or other industries.

It is harder to see, but the same point applies to foreign holdings of government debt. One way or another, if expenditures exceed revenues, the debt will be sold. If it is not sold abroad, interest rates must rise until it is attractive enough to be sold at home. If it is sold abroad, the domestic funds that might have purchased the government debt are turned toward private financial markets, where they help to finance domestic investment. The profits and labor incomes connected with this investment are taxed in part to service the government debt. The flow of funds to foreigners arises just as much from productive investment in the U.S. economy when the foreigners own government debt as when they own private debt.

17.4 Summing Up: Functional Finance Again

The main message of this chapter is that the simple ideas that government budgets should always be balanced, that government debt is a burden on future generations, and that debt is costless after all because we owe it to ourselves are useless as sensible guides to fiscal policy. Instead, we have adopted the perspective of functional finance. The key notion behind functional finance is that we must look past the accounts to the effects of fiscal actions on the economy. We must look to the way that particular fiscal actions affect the level of unemployment and capacity utilization, incentives to produce or to supply factors of production, and the distribution of income and wealth. These aspects of fiscal policy do not bear any simple relationship to either the size of the government's current budget deficit or to the size of its debt.

Summary

1. *Fiscal policy* concerns government tax and spending decisions. It is more politicized than monetary policy.
2. Short-run or *countercyclical fiscal policy* can be passive (automatic stabilizers, such as countercyclical tax and transfer rates, are built into the existing law and regulations) or active (the government alters tax or spending plans in light of economic developments).
3. Generally, to maintain full employment and stable prices, fiscal policy should stimulate in the face of negative aggregate-demand shocks and contract in the face of positive-demand shocks. Fiscal policy has little ability in the short run to alter the real effects of supply shocks. However, an aggregate-supply shock that reduces potential output – *at the same level of aggregate demand* – acts on prices effectively like a positive aggregate-demand shock and can be offset through a contractionary policy. Fiscal stimulus in that situation would only accelerate prices.
4. A disadvantage of discretionary fiscal policy is that there are often long lags between recognizing the need, making appropriate political decisions, and taking the fiscal actions with the result that the implementation of the policy can be badly mistimed.

5. If consumers are fully rational, temporary fiscal policies would have little effect as they do little to alter permanent income. *Temporary* fiscal policies should have large current effects on investment because firms can often easily alter the timing of investment. *Permanent* policies work in the opposite way. In practice, consumers appear to form a mixture from fully rational to highly myopic or liquidity constrained, so that temporary policies have greater effects on consumption than theory might predict.

6. Balanced-budget requirements in state constitutions often force states to adjust spending procyclically and taxes countercyclically – in effect creating *automatic destabilizers*.

7. Monetary and fiscal policy are connected through the *government's budget constraint*. Deficits may be partly or completely *monetized*. Countries with inadequate institutions for levying taxes may instead "print money," levying an inflation tax. Such a fiscal strategy is often associated with particularly high inflation – sometimes called *hyperinflation*.

8. The growth of the debt depends on the legacy of past fiscal policy, reflected in *interest payments*, and current fiscal policy, reflected in the *primary deficit* (the difference between current non-interest spending and current receipts). Reducing or eliminating the current primary deficit generally slows the growth rate of the debt.

9. *Functional finance* is the view that deficits and debts should not be evaluated by their size in an accounting sense, but by their effects on the real economy.

10. *Crowding out* refers to a number of phenomena in which government spending reduces private economic activity. Zero-sum crowding out occurs at full employment, when any increase in the government's share of GDP must be met with a reduction of some private party's share. Government may also displace particular expenditures, as when private-school spending falls as the result of the creation or expansion of public schools. Government spending financed by borrowing may raise real interest rates and, therefore, reduce private investment.

11. *Ricardian equivalence* is the claim that a debt-financed tax cut does not increase current private wealth, because the present value of the future taxes needed to pay off those bonds exactly offsets the current addition to wealth. Ricardian equivalence may fail to hold if taxpayers are myopic and fail to understand the implications for future taxes or if the burden of those taxes can be shifted away from the current beneficiaries toward either other current parties or future generations. Whether Ricardian equivalence holds in fact is still hotly debated.

12. Taxes have both distributional and incentive effects. The distributional effects of tax systems are classified *progressive* if average tax rates rise with income; *neutral* if they are constant; and *regressive* if they fall. Marginal tax rates modify effective real prices or yields. For instance, higher marginal income-tax rates reduce effective real wages, typically lowering labor supply; higher corporate income-tax rates reduce the yield on capital, typically lowering investment.

13. *Supply-side economics* is the doctrine that lower tax rates substantially raise growth rates by encouraging greater supplies of labor and capital. The *Laffer*

curve relates tax rates to the level of tax revenue. The Laffer curve must have a maximum value between a 0 and 100 percent tax rate. Some supply-side advocates argue that the economy is past the maximum, so that a cut in tax rates would actually increase tax revenues. Evidence for the United States does not support this view. Evidence does support the existence of genuine supply-side effects of tax rates on real GDP.

14. The ratio of the debt to GDP is one measure of its *burden*. The change in this ratio depends on the real interest rate, the ratio of the primary deficit to the existing debt, and the growth rate of the economy. Typically, if the rate of growth of GDP is greater than the real interest rate, a low primary deficit results in a falling burden of the debt.

15. A substantial share of U.S. public debt is held by foreigners. In assessing its cost, however, the benefits of the real expenditure it financed must also be counted.

Key Concepts

automatic fiscal policy	zero-sum crowding out
discretionary fiscal policy	crowding in
monetization of the deficit	Ricardian equivalence
inflation tax	progressive tax
seigniorage	neutral tax
primary deficit	regressive tax
functional finance	supply-side economics
crowding out	Laffer curve

Suggested Readings

Robert Barro, "The Ricardian Approach to Budget Deficits," *Journal of Economic Perspectives*, vol. 3, no. 2 (Spring 1989), pp. 37–54.

Kevin D. Hoover, *The New Classical Macroeconomics*. Oxford: Blackwell, ch. 7, 1988.

Abba Lerner, "Functional Finance and the Federal Debt," *Social Research*, vol. 10, no. 1 (1943), pp. 38–51.

John Taylor, "Reassessing Discretionary Fiscal Policy," *Journal of Economic Perspectives*, vol. 14, no. 3 (Summer 2000), pp. 21–36.

Problems

Data for this exercise are available on the textbook website under the link for Chapter 17 (appliedmacroeconomics.com). Before starting these exercises, the student should review the relevant portions of the *Guide to Working with Economic Data*, including sections G.1–G.5, G.9–G.11, G.13, and G.15.

Problem 17.1. The distinction between *aggregate-supply factors* and *aggregate-demand factors* was already made in Chapter 15. Aggregate-supply and aggregate-demand *shocks* suggest a special case in which the factor changes by a large and unexpected amount. Give some particular examples of recent events that might be classified as aggregate-demand or aggregate-supply shocks. Try to think of both positive and negative shocks. Explain your reasoning. If an event is a mixed shock, explain which aspects of it contribute to aggregate supply and aggregate demand.

Problem 17.2. Figure 17.1 uses the IS curve with a market real rate of interest to show the effect of a fiscal-policy action: an increase in government expenditure. Use the same apparatus to show the effect of other fiscal-policy actions:

(a) an increase in marginal tax rates;

(b) an unanticipated across-the-board tax rebate (e.g., a $1,000 payment to every taxpayer).

Problem 17.3. Figure 17.2 analyzes a negative aggregate-demand shock. Identify a positive-demand shock and use a similar diagram to analyze its effects, noting its effect on output, employment, unemployment, and inflation. Describe particular fiscal-policy actions that would maintain (or restore) NAIRU in the face of the shock. (Be specific about the policymakers' actions; do not just describe the shifting of curves.) What assumptions have you made about the conduct of monetary policy?

Problem 17.4. An unexpected rise in productivity would count as an aggregate-supply shock: positive or negative? Use a diagram or other analysis to show how such a shock would affect output (relative to potential) and inflation. How should fiscal policy respond? What happens if policymakers fail to perceive the true nature of the shock?

For Problems 17.5–17.9 use annual data.

Problem 17.5. For the U.S. Federal government, plot total expenditures and expenditures on goods and services, transfer payments, and interest payments, all as a percentage of GDP for the post-World War II period. How have these shares changed over time? Write a brief essay discussing these changes in relationship to the political, economic, and social history of the United States. (Chapter 1 is relevant to your answer, but further research may be necessary.)

Problem 17.6. For the U.S. Federal government, plot current and capital (i.e., investment) expenditures as a share of GDP for the post-World War II period. On a separate graph, plot military and nonmilitary expenditures as a share of GDP. Relate any large changes in the series on either graph to particular presidential administrations. Write a brief essay on the changing role of the Federal government in the economy. (Additional research may be helpful.)

Problem 17.7. For the U.S. Federal government, plot total revenues and revenues due to each of the main tax sources (personal taxes (e.g., income taxes), corporate taxes, customs and excise taxes, and contributions to social insurance) as a share of GDP for the post-World War II period. Describe the pattern of Federal revenues as a share of GDP over time. (What are they on average?

Do they show a distinct trend?) Write a brief descriptive note on the changing importance of different revenue sources.

Problem 17.8. For the post-World War II period, plot U.S. Federal government revenues and state and local revenues as a share of GDP. Compare to Figure 13.5. How have the level and composition of taxes in the U.S. economy changed during this period?

Problem 17.9. For the post-World War II period, plot U.S. Federal government expenditure, total state and local expenditure, and each of the categories of state and local expenditure (on goods and services, on transfer payments, and on interest) as shares of GDP. Write a brief essay commenting on any changes in the economic role of the Federal versus the state and local governments suggested by these data. (If you have done Problems 17.6 or 17.7, incorporate your findings into the essay.)

Problem 17.10. Are state and local fiscal actions stabilizing or destabilizing? To investigate, plot quarterly state and local expenditures and revenue as shares of potential GDP, indicating the NBER recession dates with shading. Write a brief note summarizing the evidence about the stabilizing or destabilizing effects of state and local fiscal actions.

Problem 17.11. How might a strict balanced-budget amendment to the U.S. Constitution affect the actions of the automatic stabilizers in the economy?

Problem 17.12. In 2010, the Social Security payroll tax in the United States was 6.20 percent on income up to $106,800 and zero thereafter; the Medicare payroll tax was 1.45 percent on income with no limit. Make two (quantitatively accurate graphs): one of the payroll tax function (i.e., the combined taxes as a function of income analogous to Figure 17.8) and one showing the marginal and average tax rates (analogous to Figure 17.9). Are the combined payroll taxes progressive, regressive, or neutral?

Problem 17.13. High deficits are sometimes blamed for high *real interest rates*.

(a) Explain why.

(b) Plot the U.S. Federal government budget deficit (scaled by potential output) and the *ex post* real interest rate (10-year government bond rate less the inflation rate calculated as $\hat{p}_t = \frac{p_{t+1}}{p_t} - 1$). Do the data appear to be stationary? Does your graph suggest either a short-term or a long-term connection between the two series? (See the *Guide*, sections G.5.2, G.14, and G.15.4.)

(c) If the two time series in (b) appear to be stationary, make a scatterplot of the real interest rate (vertical axis) against the scaled deficit (horizontal axis); add a regression line, displaying the equation and R^2. If they do not appear stationary, then make this graph *and* an additional graph in which the two series are transformed by taking differences. Again, add a regression line, displaying the equation and R^2.

(d) Write a brief note summarizing the evidence in your graphs for and against deficits causing high real interest rates. (Be as specific and quantitative as possible.) How compelling is the evidence? What pitfalls might you face in drawing such inferences?

Problem 17.14. High deficits are sometimes blamed for high *inflation rates*.

  (a) Explain why.

  (b) Plot the U.S. Federal government budget deficit scaled by potential output and the *ex post* CPI inflation rate (i.e., the inflation rate calculated as $\hat{p}_t = \frac{p_{t+1}}{p_t} - 1$). Do the data appear to be stationary? Does your graph suggest either a short-term or a long-term connection between the two series? (See the *Guide*, sections G.5.2, G.14, and G.15.4.)

  (c) If the two time series in (b) appear to be stationary, make a scatterplot of the real interest rate (vertical axis) against the scaled deficit (horizontal axis); add a regression line, displaying the equation and R^2. If they do not appear stationary, then make this graph *and* an additional graph in which the two series are transformed by taking differences. Again, add a regression line, displaying the equation and R^2.

  (d) Write a brief note summarizing the evidence in your graphs for and against deficits causing inflation rates. (Be as specific and quantitative as possible.) How compelling is the evidence? What pitfalls might you face in drawing such inferences? (Hint: think about the connection between inflation and tax revenues. See the *Guide*, section G.13.5.)

Problem 17.15. Think of examples currently under discussion in political circles (whether or not they have any realistic chance of being implemented) of government expenditures that might displace particular private expenditures. (See section 17.2.3 in the main text.) Can you think of examples of proposals to eliminate government expenditures that might have the opposite effect?

Problem 17.16. The U.S. Social Security Trust Fund is underfunded in the sense that the present value of its current and expected revenues falls short of the present value of its current and future commitments to retirees. Compare three policies to address this question: (1) raise the Social Security payroll tax by enough to bring the present value of revenues up to that of commitments; (2) sell enough government bonds to build up the trust fund to a level to meet expected needs; (3) do nothing right now. Under all three policies, assume that the government remains committed to paying benefits as currently scheduled and that no one doubts that they will do so. Write a brief essay on the economic effects of these policies on interest rates, inflation, and output assuming, first that Ricardian equivalence holds and, second, that it does not hold.

Problem 17.17. With the return of U.S. Federal budget deficits in 2001 after a brief period of surpluses, political discussion turned again to the growth of the Federal debt. To put it in perspective:

  (a) Of course, nominal quantities are usually misleading, so convert the Federal debt to real terms (explain your conversion) and plot from 1948 to the present.

  (b) The burden of the debt is probably better measured by its size relative to national income, so express the debt as a share of GDP and plot from 1948 to the present.

(c) Write a brief essay relating the main features of your two plots to the economic and political history of the United States. What light does this history shed on the current situation with regard to the debt? (Chapter 1 is relevant to your answer, but further research may be necessary.)

Problem 17.18. The theory of financial markets suggests that it is the *level* of the debt (relative to the size of the economy), rather than the deficit that ought to be related to real interest rates. Using whatever data and statistical techniques you believe to be appropriate, investigate this question. Write a note describing your data, your procedures, and your answer to the question: does a larger debt imply higher real interest rates?

Part IX

Macroeconomic Data

A Guide to Working with Economic Data

This *Guide* provides information about various statistical and data-handling techniques that are useful in understanding the text and working the problems at the end of each chapter. Although the *Guide* can be read straight through, the sections are relatively self-contained, so that it may be consulted on particular points as necessary. Cross-references to the *Guide* are provided in the main text and at the beginning of each problem set.

G.1 Economic Data

G.1.1 Variables

Economic data are represented by variables that name a particular economic concept. For example, Tables G.1 and G.2 report data for the G-7 countries corresponding to the concept "Real GDP" and "Employment." These may be designated by variables: real GDP by $Y_{i,t}$ and employment by $E_{i,t}$. The subscript i indicates to which unit the data refer (here a G-7 country: Canada, France, etc.), and the subscript t indicates the time period (here 1991, 1992, etc.). For example, $Y_{Japan,1996} = \$1,560$ billion; $E_{France, 2000} = 23,262,000$. Variables are sometimes written as functions rather than with subscripts; so that $Y(i,t) = Y_{i,t}$. For example, $Y(\text{Italy}, 1997) = \$426$ billion.

Units, of course, need not be countries. They could be states, families, firms, individual people, particular financial assets, or, in fact, any category that can be measured. Time may be divided, as here, into years; but also, commonly, into quarters, months, weeks, days, or larger or smaller divisions. Measurements may be made at a particular period (e.g., the last day of the quarter) or as an average across the period.

Months are frequently indicated by the year followed by a colon and a number: 01 for January up to 12 for December. Quarters are frequently indicated similarly: 1 for the first quarter, 2 for the second, and so forth. For example, July of 2001 is indicated as 2001:07; the third quarter of 1992 is indicated as 1992:3.

Table G.1. *Real GDP in the G-7 Countries (1996 constant U.S. dollars [Chain indexed] at purchasing-power parity)*

	Canada	France	Germany	Italy	Japan	United Kingdom	United States
1991	277	444	764	422	1,455	474	3,027
1992	274	429	764	425	1,475	463	3,115
1993	281	403	738	400	1,477	467	3,216
1994	299	434	748	402	1,486	492	3,431
1995	310	407	758	411	1,502	510	3,548
1996	316	451	760	416	1,560	528	3,699
1997	336	419	765	426	1,602	555	3,911
1998	355	477	782	438	1,567	577	4,087
1999	376	454	808	451	1,561	594	4,289
2000	401	520	837	462	1,591	617	4,558

Source: Penn-World Tables, 6.1, Table G.2, and author's calculations.

Typically, an economic variable tracks different units over a single time period or the same unit over different time periods. Data for which time is held fixed and each point refers to a separate unit are called **cross sections**. The fourth line in Table G.1 is the cross section of G-7 real GDP for 1994. When context makes it clear that a cross section is intended, then, to avoid clutter, the variable usually omits the t subscript. For example, Y_i is adequate notation for the last cross section, so long as we keep in mind that it applies to 1994.

Data for which time is held fixed and each point refers to a separate unit are called **time series**. The third column in Table G.2 is the time series of employment in Germany. When context makes it clear that a time series is intended, then the variable usually omits the i subscript. For example, E_t is

Table G.2. *Employment in the G-7 Countries (thousands)*

	Canada	France	Germany	Italy	Japan	United Kingdom	United States
1991	12,916	22,316	37,445	21,595	63,690	26,400	116,877
1992	12,842	21,609	36,940	21,609	64,360	25,812	117,598
1993	13,015	20,705	36,380	20,705	64,500	25,511	119,306
1994	13,292	21,875	36,075	20,373	64,530	25,717	123,060
1995	13,506	20,233	36,048	20,233	64,570	26,026	124,900
1996	13,676	22,311	35,982	20,320	64,860	26,323	126,709
1997	13,941	20,413	35,805	20,413	65,570	26,814	129,558
1998	14,326	22,479	35,860	20,618	65,140	27,116	131,463
1999	14,531	20,864	36,402	20,864	64,623	27,442	133,488
2000	14,910	23,262	36,604	21,225	64,464	27,793	136,891

Source: International Monetary Fund, *International Financial Statistics.*

adequate notation for the last time series, as long as we keep in mind that it applies to Germany.

G.1.2 The Dimensions of Data

Keeping Track of Units

The units in which data are measured are an essential part of economic variables and must be tracked. Often units are abbreviated where it causes no confusion. For example, in the last section, Japanese real GDP in 1996 was reported as $1,560 billion: the stated unit is "billions of dollars," where the true unit is "billions of 1996 constant U.S. dollars (chain indexed) at purchasing-power parity." Writing that every time would be clumsy; nevertheless, we must always be careful to make such relevant information available (as it is in the title of Table G.1).

Dimensions follow the same algebra as variables themselves. Suppose that we wish to compute real GDP per capita: $YH_{i,t} = Y_{i,t}/E_{i,t}$. Its units are just the units of real GDP divided by the units of employment, so that $YH_{Canada,1998} = \$355$ billion$/14{,}326$ thousand $= 0.024780 \frac{billion\ dollars}{thousand\ people}$. Here, as often happens, the units that follow naturally from the calculation are awkward, and may be restated in a more convenient form. Usually, scientific notation is helpful: $YH_{Canada,1998} = (\$355 \times 10^9)/(14{,}326 \times 10^3$ people$) = 0.024780 \times 10^6 \frac{dollars}{person} = 24{,}780 \frac{dollars}{person}$. Or, to put it more naturally, $YH_{Canada,1998} = \$24{,}780$ per person (or per capita or per head).

Example G.1: What are the units of the price of a Mercedes car and what are the units of the proceeds from selling 10 Mercedes at $50,000 each?

Answer: Units of price: dollars/car; units of proceeds: (dollars/car) × cars = dollars.

Example G.2: If 50,000 workers each work 2,000 hours over the course of a year, what is the rate of total work expressed in correct units?

Answer: 100,000,000 worker-hours per year.

Stocks and Flows

A **stock** is a quantity measured at a point in time, so that its units are the units of the quantity; a **flow** is a quantity per unit time. As a result a *flow* × *a period of time* has the dimensions of (quantity/time) × time = quantity. Water flowing through a faucet at 5 gallons per minute for 5 minutes adds 25 gallons to the stock of water in a bathtub. The distinction between stocks and flows is particularly important in economics and is discussed in detail in Chapter 2 (section 2.2.1).

Annualization and Aggregation

Even when time is measured in units of, say, months or quarters, it is often convenient to convert the results to units of years. Such conversion is called **annualization** and is no different in principle than converting the speed of a sprinter from seconds per quarter mile to miles per hour: for example, 55 second per quarter mile = 16.36 miles per hour. To take an economic example, real GDP in the United States is measured quarterly, but annualized before it is published: the quarterly number is simply multiplied by 4. For example, real GDP in the fourth quarter of 2004 was $2,748.33 billion per quarter = $10,993.3 billion per year. (In the United States, only the annualized figure is published. In some other countries, GDP data are published at quarterly rates.)

Example G.3: The officially published nominal GDP for the United Kingdom for the third quarter of 2004 was £290.7 billion per quarter. What is it annualized?

Answer: £1,162.8 billion per year.

Often, we want to know the average flow of a quantity over a period larger than its **frequency of observation**. For example, we may want to know real GDP for 1993 – that is, for the whole year, not for one quarter annualized. Moving from *higher frequency data* (i.e., data observed more often) to *lower frequency data* is called **temporal aggregation**. With British GDP data, because it is not annualized, the problem is straightforward: add up each quarter. With American data, each point has already been multiplied by 4, so that just adding them up would produce a number four times too big. We must, therefore, add them up and divide by 4.

Example G.4: U.S. real GDP for the four quarters of 2004 was: $10,697.5, $10,784.7, $10,891.0, $10,993.3 (each measured in billions at an annual rate). What is real GDP for 2004?

Answer: ($10,697.5 + $10,784.7 + $10,891.0 + $10,993.3)/4 = $10,841.6 billion.

Example G.5: U.K. nominal GDP for the four quarters of 2003 was: £277.6, £276.2, £282.3, £286.5 (each measured in billions at a quarterly rate). What is nominal GDP for 2003?

Answer: £277.6 + £276.2 + £282.3 + £286.5 = £1,122.6 billion.

Percentages and Percentage Points

Percent refers to a fraction or share expressed in hundredths. In fact, the percent sign (%) is a stylization of "/100," the denominator of a fraction in hundredths. Any *natural* fraction or decimal can be read properly as a percentage: 0.047 *is* 4.7 percent, just as 12 inches is 1 foot.

Percentage point refers to the unit one hundredth (1/100). Although one may properly read a fraction either as a natural number or a percentage, when making calculations a natural fraction must be multiplied by 100 to convert it into percentage points. Such a conversion is not part of the fundamental calculation but merely a way of selecting preferred units. (In this book, this unit-conversion step is always omitted. It cannot, however, be omitted in making calculations. [Excel hint: To express fractions as percentages, either multiply by 100 or click "Format," "Cell," and then click "Percentage" on the "Number" tab].)

Special care must be taken not to confuse *percent* and *percentage point*. For example, an interest rate is expressed as a percentage of the principal – say, 5.2 percent per year. If the interest rate rises to 6.4 percent per year, it has risen by 1.2 percentage points ($= 6.4 - 5.2$) but it has risen by 23 percent ($= (6.4 - 5.2)/5.2 = 0.23$).

G.1.3 Seasonal Adjustment

Many economic series vary according to the time of year in a regular way. Sometimes we are interested in this variation in which case we use **seasonally unadjusted** data. In other cases, this variation is confusing. For example, if we are concerned about whether the economy is entering a recession, then the fact that seasonally unadjusted GDP slows in the first quarter every year would confuse our judgment. What we really want to know is whether it has slowed *more than usual* this year. **Seasonally adjusted data** transform the seasonally unadjusted data to account for the usual seasonal variation. There are many ways of seasonally adjusting data, each differing by how they determine what is "usual."

Typical seasonal adjustment is displayed in Table G.3, which shows the CPI for food for 2001 in its seasonally adjusted and seasonally unadjusted forms. The third column shows the **seasonal factor** – that is, the number that converts seasonally unadjusted to seasonally adjusted data according to the formula:

$$seasonally\ adjusted\ variable = seasonally\ unadjusted\ variable$$
$$\times\ seasonal\ factor. \tag{G.1}$$

For example, food prices tend to be high in January, when many fresh foods are out of season, so that a seasonal factor less than one adjusts the value down. The downward adjustment is 0.29 percent as shown in the fourth column. Similarly, from midsummer to late autumn (July to November) food prices tend to be low as fresh food production is high, so that the seasonal factors greater than one adjust the values upward. The main differences

Table G.3. *An Illustration of Seasonal Adjustment: Consumer Food Prices in 2001*

Month	Seasonally Adjusted	Nonseasonally Adjusted	Seasonal Factor	Percentage Adjustment
January	170.4	170.9	0.997	−0.29
February	171.2	171.3	0.999	−0.06
March	171.6	171.7	0.999	−0.06
April	172.0	171.9	1.001	+0.06
May	172.5	172.5	1.000	0.00
June	173.0	173.0	1.000	0.00
July	173.6	173.5	1.001	+0.06
August	174.0	173.9	1.001	+0.06
September	174.2	174.1	1.001	+0.06
October	174.9	174.9	1.000	0.00
November	174.9	174.6	1.002	+0.17
December	174.7	174.7	1.000	0.00
Total	2077	2077	12.000	−0.01[a]

[a] Does not sum to zero due to rounding error.
Note: CPI-U food (1982–1984 = 100).
Source: Bureau of Labor Statistics.

between different methods of seasonal adjustment are (1) how they estimate the seasonal factors and (2) whether they use multiplicative factors (as most do) or additive adjustments.

Notice that the sum of the seasonally adjusted and seasonally unadjusted prices in Table G.3 is the same and that the seasonal adjustments factors add to 12, the number of months. Both reflect the fact that methods of seasonal adjustment generally reallocate data across a year, but do not change it year to year. The annual sum of prices is not an economically meaningful number, but in other cases (e.g., GDP) this is a very important property.

G.2 Graphs

Spreadsheets generally support a large variety of types of graphs. Here we consider only some representative examples. (*Chart, figure, plot* are among the terms that are commonly used as synonyms for *graph*.)

G.2.1 Cross-Sectional Graphs

Univariate Cross-Sectional Graphs

A *bar chart* is a typical means of displaying a single (*univariate*) cross section. Figure G.1 shows G-7 employment in 1995; it plots one line from the Table G.2. Other univariate cross-sectional graphs include the *pie chart*, especially useful for emphasizing relative shares (see, e.g., Chapter 2, Figure 2.8). There are a large number of other types, each helpful in stressing particular

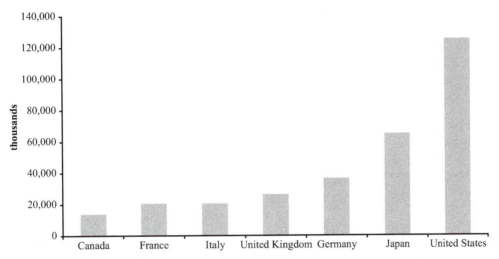

Figure G.1. G-7 Employment in 1995. *Source:* International Monetary Fund, *International Financial Statistics.*

aspects of the data. (Excel hint: To make a graph, highlight the data, then click "Insert," "Chart," and choose from among the menu of chart types.)

Multivariate Cross-Sectional Graphs

"[T]he relational graphic – in its barest form, the scatterplot and its variants – is the greatest of all graphical designs."[1]

Related cross sections can be displayed in a variety of graphical forms. The most important is the **scatterplot**. Figure G.2 plots the data displayed in Figure G.1 for employment against real GDP for the G-7 countries in 1995 (i.e., one line from Table G.2 against the corresponding line from Table G.1). The scatterplot not only allows us to see the different levels of real GDP and employment in each country, it also shows clearly that there is a strong upward association: the higher the real GDP, the higher the level of employment. Which is cause and which effect is not clear (see sections G.13.5–7).

G.2.2 Time-Series Graphs

Time-Series Plots

The most common way of displaying a time series is to plot it with time on the horizontal axis and the time series on the vertical. If time is considered to be a variable then the **time-series plot** is just a scatterplot of a variable against time. A single variable or several variables may be plotted either

---

[1] Edward Tufte, *The Visual Display of Quantitative Information*, 2nd edition. Chesire, CT: Graphics Press, 2001, p. 47.

Figure G.2. A Scatterplot of Real GDP and Employment in the G-7 Countries in 1995. *Source:* employment, International Monetary Fund, *International Financial Statistics*; GDP, Penn-World Tables, 6.1, Table G.2; and author's calculations.

against a common or separate vertical scales. Figure G.3 plots real GDP and employment for Canada. Because units of measurement are incommensurable, real GDP is plotted against the left-hand vertical scale and employment against the right-hand scale. When two series are plotted against separate scales, their relative changes may remain economically meaningful, but the vertical location (including whether and where they cross) does not: the series can be moved up or down by changing the vertical scale.

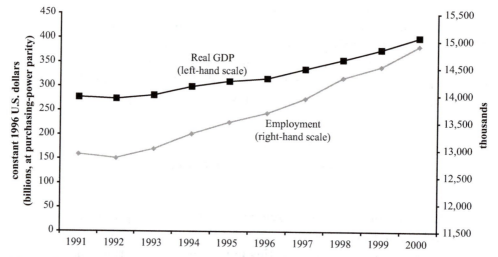

Figure G.3. A Time-Series Plot: Canadian Real GDP and Employment. *Source:* employment, International Monetary Fund, *International Financial Statistics*; GDP, Penn-World Tables, 6.1, Table G.2; and author's calculations.

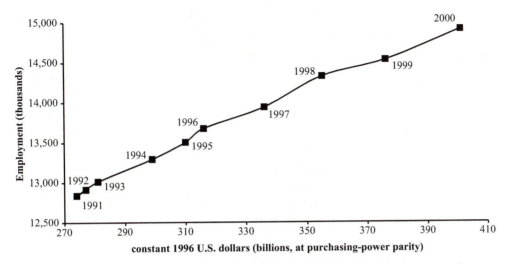

Figure G.4. Time-Series Scatterplot: Canadian Real GDP and Employment. *Source:* employment, International Monetary Fund, *International Financial Statistics*; GDP, Penn-World Tables, 6.1, Table G.2; and author's calculations.

It is typical, but not required, to connect the points on a time-series plot. The squares and diamonds in Figure G.3 mark the only observed data. Any information read off of lines that connect these markers is an **interpolation** or conjecture. Frequently, the markers themselves are omitted.

Time-Series Scatterplots

Two time series may also be displayed in a scatterplot. Figure G.4 presents the same data as Figure G.3, but this time employment is plotted against real GDP rather than against time. Time is shown in the labels. The scatterplot again shows clearly that both real GDP and employment are growing over time; yet, rather than emphasizing the time dimension, it highlights the fact that higher employment is associated with higher real GDP (i.e., what was true for the G-7 in a single year [see Figure G.2] is also true for Canada over the last decade of the twentieth century). Because of the focus on the relationships between the variables, time-series scatterplots frequently omit time labels and lines connecting observed points.

G.2.3 Guide to Good Graphics

Graphs serve two main functions: to communicate and to support empirical analysis. To do these well, graphs should be (1) informationally rich; (2) clear and self-contained; and (3) aesthetically pleasing.

A Good Graph Is Informationally Rich

Each graph is created for a particular purpose; it has a point of view. The point of view determines in large measure the type of graph created (e.g., scatterplot, pie chart, time-series plot). A good graph includes as much information relevant to that point of view as possible. A good graph not only presents the facts in such a way that it supports a conclusion that we wish to communicate, it also presents a full enough set of facts that readers can explore the data relationships on their own. In many cases, we create a graph as a tool for data exploration – not because we know what it will show, but precisely because we do not yet know. The more information that is displayed, and the more effectively it is displayed, the more likely we are to see a relationship among data that might have eluded us otherwise.

Of course, graphs cannot and should not contain everything. The point of view guides our choice not only of what to include but of what to omit. A good graph is not dishonest: it does not portray false data; it avoids misleading psychological effects. For example, if the variations of a series in a range between 90 and 100 are of primary interest, a graph that used a scale of 0 to 100 would *appear* to display a flatter line with less variation – a psychologically misleading presentation even if every data point were placed accurately.

A Good Graph Is Clear and Self-Contained

The nature of the information displayed in a graph should be clear to anyone looking at it without essential reference to an accompanying text.

- Every graph should have a descriptive title.
- Its axes should be clearly labeled with the units of measurement and, where appropriate (as in a scatterplot) the name of the variable to which it refers. (An exception may be made for the horizontal axis in a time-series plot. If the fact that the scale refers to dates is obvious, then labeling the axis with "date" or "years" or other units is usually not necessary.)
- When a graph has multiple lines, they should each be made clear and distinct through the use of different weights, styles (solid, dashed, etc.), and markers. (Before using colors, consider whether the graph is likely to be printed or copied in black and white by you or a subsequent user.) Each line should be clearly labeled.
- Graphs should indicate the source of the data.
- Explanatory notes should be kept to a minimum, but used where needed to describe the contents of the graph fully and accurately.

A Good Graph Is Aesthetically Pleasing

A good graph should not add to the ugliness of the world; there is too much already. There are two aspects: utility and taste.

With respect to utility:

- All lines (not only data plots, but also axes, arrows, and so forth) should be dark and clear.
- Fonts should be large enough to be easily read.

- Legends identifying the data plots outside the graph (an Excel default) should be avoided in favor of labels near each line inside the graph: legends force the reader to continually go back and forth between data plot and legend to assign the correct variable name.

Taste is in the eye of the beholder – although generally some people are held to have better taste than others. My personal taste suggests:

- Use white backgrounds (not the gray backgrounds that are the Excel default).
- Avoid data markers (squares, diamonds, etc.) in time-series plots – especially when the data are dense.
- Avoid gridlines unless essential to an accurate reading of the graph or on logarithmic graphs, where they help to reinforce the reader's appreciation of the nonlinear scale.
- Do not put graphs in a box (i.e., leave the top and right side (where there is no scale) open.
- Select scales to use available space to show, except in cases where it would be misleading from a reasonable point of view, the maximum variation of a data plot.
- Use proportional, serif fonts (e.g., Times New Roman or Book Antiqua) rather than nonproportional fonts (e.g., Courier) or sans serif fonts (e.g., Arial, the Excel default), as they are easier on the eye.

The Golden Rule of Graphics

No list of rules is complete. What constitutes a good graph depends, in part, on the circumstances and, in part, on personal taste. Some graphs are clearly better than others. Compare Figure G.5 (which is, more or less, the graph that Excel creates using its default settings) to the same data displayed in Figure G.3. Which is the better graph? An excellent source of guidance and inspiration on how to make graphs effective and pleasing is found in a series of lovely books by the political scientist Edward Tufte (see Suggested Readings at the end of the *Guide* for the references).

The golden rule of graphics is *be respectful of the reader*: create only graphs that you yourself would find useful, effective, and pleasing to the eye. The object is not to follow an arbitrary set of rules, but to communicate and support empirical analysis effectively. Any rule can be broken if it helps to make a more effective graph.

G.3 A Guide to Good Tables

Many of the rules and considerations discussed in the previous section that govern good graphics also apply to good tables. There is no need to repeat them all here. Some rules are particular to tables:

- Make the relationships between headings and subheadings clear.
- Align numbers in columns consistently (on the decimal point if there is one) clearly below the appropriate heading.

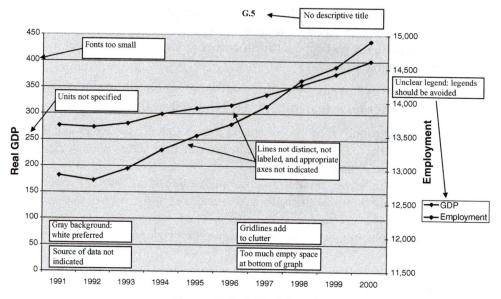

Figure G.5. A Bad Graph.

- Avoid vertical rules or grids.
- Use horizontal rules sparingly to indicate the beginning and end of tables or sections of tables, and to group headings in a logical manner.
- Units should be indicated in the headings; avoid attaching units directly to entries in the table itself. (For example, if the units are percentages, put that in the heading, and enter, say, 6.8 rather than 6.8%, as data in the table.)

Tables G.1 and G.2, and other tables in this book, provide reasonable models to follow.

G.4 Descriptive Statistics

The main problem with data is that there is too much of it: we cannot see the forest for the trees. Statistics are tools for economizing on information, for describing a mass of data more simply, so that we can see the essential relationships among them.

G.4.1 Histograms and Frequency Distributions

Some data are *discrete*; they must take integer values. If we count the number of M&Ms of each color in a bag, there are only six categories (blue, brown, green, orange, red, yellow). We could make a bar chart with each color corresponding to one column and the height of the column to the number of M&Ms in the bag. Such a chart is called a **histogram**; it displays

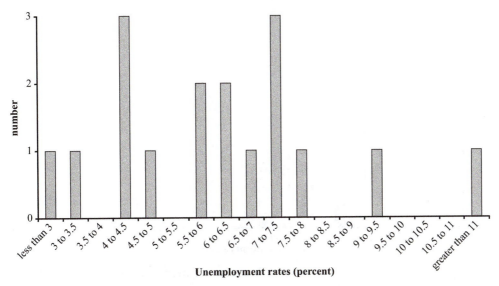

Figure G.6A. A Histogram: Unemployment Rates (selected countries). *Source:* Table 12.2.

graphically the **frequency distribution** (how many of each type) of M&Ms in the bag.

Most economic data are not discrete. For example, look at Table 12.2 (Chapter 12), which reports the unemployment rates for selected countries in 2008. The unemployment rates are *continuous*; they can take any real value between 0 and 100 percent. In fact, nearly every value in Table 12.2 is unique. A histogram running from the minimum value (2.8) to the maximum (11.4) by units of 0.1 would count one entry for 16 values corresponding to each of the 17 countries for which values are reported with Japan and Mexico sharing the same value. Such a histogram would offer no economy of information.

To do better with continuous data, we can divide the possible values into intervals. For example, Figure G.6.A shows a histogram for the data in Table 12.2 that counts the data falling into eighteen ranges or bins: less than 2, between 2 and 2.5, between 3.5 and 3, and so forth up to greater than 11. With more bins than data points, this histogram is not particularly informative: no bin receives more than three entries. Figure G.6.B shows that we gain economy of description if we reduce the number to six wider bins: less than 2, 2 to 6, 6 to 8, 8 to 10, and greater than 10. Fewer, broader bins means that we lose some of the detail in the original data, but the overall pattern is now clearer: most of the unemployment rates fall in the 4 to 8 range with a bias toward the higher side; and very high rates are rarer. In general, histograms or other descriptions of frequency distribution involve a trade-off between the fine detail of the data and the overall pattern (the big picture).

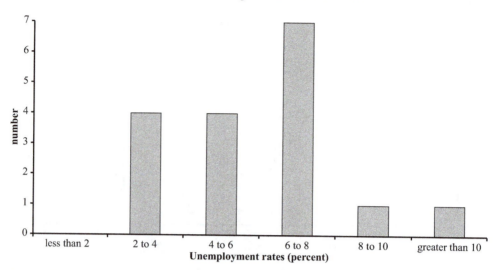

Figure G.6B. A More Informative Histogram: Unemployment Rates (selected countries). *Source:* Table 12.2.

G.4.2 Measures of Central Tendency

Even more economy can be gained if we can summarize the data in a few numbers that characterize its frequency distribution. The most important summary measures fall into two categories: measures of central tendency and measures of variation (or dispersion).

The (Arithmetic) Mean

The word *average* is sometimes used as a synonym for any measure of central tendency (i.e., for a measure of the middle of a frequency distribution). More commonly, it refers to a specific measure: the **arithmetic mean**, usually abbreviated simply as **mean**. The mean starts with a set of data and answers the following question: *If every data point were to be replaced by ones that all took the same value, what value would they have to take to be equal to the same total as the original data?*

Example G.6: What is the mean of a set of data: 4, 2, 7, 1?

Answer: The total is 14. If every data point took the value 3.5 ($= 14/4$), then we would have the same total.

The general formula for the mean of a variable X_i, where i indicates one of N data points, is:

$$\overline{X} = \frac{\sum\limits_{i=1}^{N} X_i}{N}.$$

(G.2)

The bar over the variable (without a subscript) indicates the mean.

Example G.7: What is the mean of the unemployment data in Table 12.2?

Answer: $\overline{U} = \dfrac{\sum\limits_{i=1}^{17} U_i}{17} = \dfrac{103.8}{17} = 6.1$ percent.

Excel hint: the command for the mean is: =AVERAGE(number1, number2,...).

The Weighted Mean

Sometimes different data points have different degrees of importance. What if we wanted to know the mean unemployment rate for the United States and Canada taken together? Applying equation (G.2) to the data in Table 12.2 yields 6.95 percent $(= (5.8 + 6.1)/2)$. But if we want to use the average unemployment rate as a measure of the chance that a randomly chosen person from the United States and Canada is unemployed, we should take account of the fact that the United States has about ten times the population of Canada (301.6 vs. 33.2 million – both for July 2008), so that many more people face the lower unemployment rate than the higher. We can adjust the formula (G.2) to form a **weighted mean** in which population provides the weights (w_i) :

$$\overline{X} = \frac{\sum\limits_{i=1}^{N} w_i X_i}{\sum\limits_{i}^{N} w_i}. \tag{G.3}$$

Example G.8: What is the weighted mean of U.S. and Canadian unemployment rates taking the populations of the countries as weights?

Answer: Using formula (G.3), the weighted mean unemployment for the United States and Canada is: $\overline{X} = \frac{301.6 \times 5.8 + 33.2 \times 6.1}{301.6 + 33.3} = 5.83$. This is much closer to the U.S. value than to the Canadian value and lower than the unweighted mean, because the U.S. value receives a far larger weight.

The Median

The arithmetic mean can be thought of as choosing the point that puts an equal weight of the frequency distribution on each side. Visually, imagine the histogram in Figure G.6.B flipped over so that the bars hung down from the horizontal axis. The question the mean answers is, where along the horizontal axis should we attach a string if the histogram is to hang perfectly level?

The mean can be misleading. For example, if we want to know the center of the distribution of income in the State of Washington, then Bill Gates's billions of dollars get a very heavy bar in the histogram with bins representing different income levels on the horizontal axis. We would have to move the string far to the right to make it hang level. But at that point, the vast majority of Washingtonians are situated far to the left of the mean. The mean does not give us a good idea of what is typical. The **median** asks a different question: *What value divides the distribution into an equal number above and below that value?* In answering this question, despite his billions, Bill Gates counts as one person above the median with an equal weight to a person who is just one above the median.

Example G.9: What is the median of the unemployment data in Table 12.2 and Figure G.6?

Answer: 6.1 percent. Eight countries have unemployment rates higher than this level and eight lower.

Notice that in this last example, the median is actually one of the points in the data set: it is the value for Canada. Whenever there is an odd number of data points (here 17), the median will be an element of the data set itself. By convention, if there is an even number of data points, the median is reported as the arithmetic mean of the highest value in the lower half of the sample and the lowest value in the higher half of the sample.

Example G.10: Using the same data set as in Example G.9 but supplemented with an additional observation for Elbonia with an unemployment rate of 53 percent, what is the median?

Answer: 6.2 percent. Canada (6.1 percent) now has the highest unemployment rate of the lower nine countries and Ireland (6.3 percent), the lowest of the highest nine countries: $(6.1 + 6.3)/2 = 6.2$.

When a distribution is *symmetrical* – that is, the left-hand and right-hand sides of the histogram are mirror images of each other, the median and the arithmetic mean coincide. When a distribution is **positively skewed** (i.e., its weight is shifted to the right as in Figure G.6.B), *the mean is greater than the median.* When it is **negatively skewed** (i.e., more weight is in the left-hand side of the histogram), *the mean is less than the median.*

Example G.11: Consider 14 people: 1 has an income of $1,000; 5 of $2,000; 4 of $3,000; 2 of $4,000, 1 of $5,000. What are the mean and the median? Is the distribution of income skewed? If so, which way?

Answer: *Mean* $= [1(1,000) + 5(2,000) + 4(3,000) + 2(4,000) + 2(5,000)]/ 14 = \$2,929$. Since the number of items is even, the median equals the mean of the highest value of the lowest seven ($3,000) and the lowest value of the highest seven (also $3,000); so the *median* then is $3,000. Because the mean of the 14 people is less than the median, the data are *negatively skewed.*

Excel hint: the command for the median is: =MEDIAN(number1, number2,…).

The Geometric Mean

Just as the arithmetic mean is a natural measure for data that are related as a sum, the **geometric mean** is a natural measure for data that are related as a product. The geometric mean starts with a set of data and answers the following question: *If every data point were to be replaced by ones that all took the same value, what value would they have to take to be equal to the same product as the original data?*

The general formula for the geometric mean is:

$$\overline{X} = \sqrt[N]{\prod_{i=1}^{N} X_i} = \left(\prod_{i=1}^{N} X_i \right)^{1/N},$$ (G.4)

where $\prod$ (uppercase Greek letter "pi") is the product sign, which says, "multiply each term together," just as $\sum$ (uppercase Greek letter "sigma") is the summation sign, which says, "add each term together." We use the bar over the variable (without subscript) to indicate the geometric mean, relying on context to keep us from confusing it with the arithmetic mean.

Suppose that GDP in the country of Elbonia has grown over three successive years at 16 percent, 5 percent, and 9 percent. A growth rate of 16 percent means that GDP is 1.16 times the level of GDP the year before; 5 percent means 1.05 times; 9 percent, 1.09 times. The total after three years is the *product* of each of these factors times the level of GDP the year before the first year of growth. What is the average rate of growth over these three years? Applying the formula: the geometric mean is $(1.16 \times 1.05 \times 1.09)^{1/3} = 1.10$, a growth rate of 10 percent.

Example G.12: You are given a set of data that appear to be growing steadily, but one observation is missing: 1.1, 2, X_3, 8.1, 16.3, where X_3 is the missing observation. What is a good guess for the value of X_3?

Answer: This is a problem of interpolation. One strategy is to take the average of the adjacent values: 2 and 3.9. Because the data are growing fairly steadily, and growth is a multiplicative process, the geometric average is preferred. Applying formula (G.4), $\overline{X} = \sqrt[2]{2 \times 8.1} = 4.0$. Notice that the arithmetic mean is 5.0, which is, in context, a very different value.

Excel hint: the command for the median is =GEOMEAN(number1, number2,…).

As with the arithmetic mean, some individual data points may be more important than others, suggesting a **weighted geometric mean**. With an

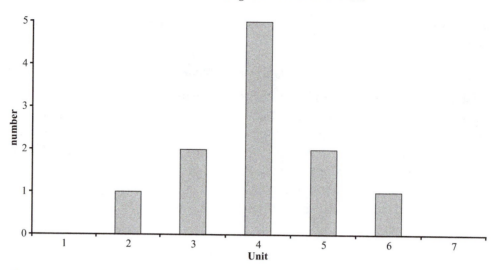

Figure G.7A. A Histogram with Relatively Low Dispersion. The mean, median, and mode of these data are all 4, as in Figure G.7.B, but they have a lower variance.

arithmetic mean, the weights enter multiplicatively; with a geometric mean, they enter as powers. The formula is:

$$\overline{X} = \ ^{(\Sigma w_i)}\!\sqrt{\prod_{i=1}^{N} X_i^{w_i}} = \left(\prod_{i=1}^{N} X_i^{w_i}\right)^{(1/\sum w_i)}. \tag{G.5}$$

Example G.13: A bank offers a special account that earns 7 percent for the first five years and 5 percent thereafter. Interest accrues in the account. If you hold the account for 20 years, what is your average yield?

Answer: Interest acts like a growth rate: 7 percent interest, for instance, implies that each year the account becomes larger by a growth factor of 1.07. Applying formula (G.5) gives us: *average growth factor =* $^{(5+15)}\!\sqrt{1.07^5 \times 1.05^{15}} = \sqrt[20]{2.92} = 1.055$, which corresponds to an interest rate of 5.5 percent.

G.4.3 *Measures of Variation*

Variance

The mean and median are all measures of the center of a frequency distribution. We might also want to know how spread out a distribution is. Figure G.7.A shows a histogram of the data set $A = \{2, 3, 3, 4, 4, 4, 4, 4, 5, 5, 6\}$ and Figure G.7.B of the data set $A = \{1, 2, 2, 3, 3, 3, 4, 4, 4, 4, 5, 5, 5, 6, 6, 7\}$. Both data sets have the same mean and median – all 4. Yet, the set B is clearly more spread out than set A.

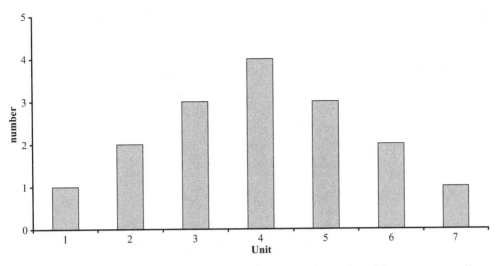

Figure G.7B. A Histogram of Data with Greater Dispersion. The mean, median, and mode of these data are all 4, as in Figure G.7.A, but they have a higher variance.

One way of measuring the spread would be to take the mean as the center of the distribution and to measure the deviations from the mean. The mean of these deviations would measure the variation. So, for example, the first deviation in set A would be -2 ($= 2 - 4$); whereas the last deviation would be $+2$ ($= 6 - 4$). The problem with this idea is that when we add up the deviations to take their mean, the positive and negative ones would cancel out. Because both data sets are symmetrical, the cancellation would be complete, and the measure of variation would be zero for both – not at all capturing the obvious fact that data set B is more spread out than A. Instead, we could take the absolute value of the deviations and add them up. That suggestion works, and is sometimes used as a measure of variation: *mean absolute variation.*

More commonly, variation is measured as the **variance**, calculated as:

$$\text{var}(X) = \frac{\sum_{i=1}^{N} (X_i - \overline{X})^2}{N - 1}. \tag{G.6}$$

The term in parentheses on the right-hand side of formula (G.6) defines each deviation from the mean. Because all squared numbers are positive, every deviation contributes positively to the sum.

The total is averaged over $N - 1$, rather than over N (as might seem more natural). To understand why, consider the variance formula if there were only a single observation. The mean ($\overline{X}$) would equal that one observation, and there would be no variation around it. If we then add a second observation, we would supply only one additional piece of information. If the denominator in formula (G.6) were N, then we would appear to have jumped discontinuously from no deviations from the mean to two distinct deviations. But that is not right. If we know the mean, the sum of the deviations around the mean, and one of the deviations, we can calculate what the other deviation must be; it is not an *independent* piece of information. So, with two observations there really is only one independent piece of information about the variation; with three observations, two; with four observations, three; ...; and with N observations $N - 1$. Dividing by $N - 1$ properly accounts for the actual number of independent pieces of information. (This is known as a *degrees-of-freedom correction*.)

Example G.14: What is the variance of $\{1, 2, 3, 4, 5\}$?

Answer: The mean is 3; $N = 5$. The deviations from the mean ($X_i - \overline{X}$) are $\{-2, -1, 0, +1, +2\}$. Applying formula (G.6) yields $\text{var}(X) = [(-2)^2 + (-1)^2 + 0^2 + 1^2 + 2^2]/4 = 10/4 = 2.5$.

Example G.15: Which is more spread out, data set A or data set B in the text above and in Figure G.7.A and B?

Answer: Applying formula (G.6), var(data set A) = 1.200 and var(data set B) = 2.667, confirming our visual impression that B is more spread out than A.

Excel hint: the command for the variance is: =VAR(number1, number2,...).

Standard Deviation

A disadvantage of the variance is its units are difficult to interpret. For example, suppose that we calculated the variance of real GDP in Table 2.2. The units of the original data are *billions 2008 U.S. dollars at purchasing-power parity*. The units of the variance are (*billions 2008 U.S. dollars at purchasing-power parity*)^2. It is hard to know what that means. It is, therefore, often convenient to transform the variance into the **standard deviation**, defined as

$$\text{stdev}(X) = \sqrt[+]{\text{var}(X)}. \tag{G.7}$$

The standard deviation has the same units as the original data.

Example G.16: What are the standard deviations of data sets A and B (see Example G.11).

Answer: Applying formula (G.7), stdev(data set A) = $\sqrt{1.200} = 1.095$ and stdev(data set B) = $\sqrt{2.667} = 1.633$, again confirming our visual impression that B is more spread out than A.

Excel hint: the command for the standard deviation is: = STDEV(number1, number2, ...).

Coefficient of Variation

Sometimes the variance or the standard deviation can be quite misleading about the degree of variability. Imagine a population of mice in which variations of an ounce around the mean weight of a mouse were common. Compare that to a population of elephants in which variations of 5 pounds (80 ounces) were common. The variance and standard deviation of the weight of the elephants are much larger than that of the mice. Yet, there is a clear sense in which *relative to their normal weight*, the mice show more variation. To capture this sense, we can calculate the **coefficient of variation**, which expresses the standard deviation as a share of the mean:

$$cv(X) = \left| \frac{stdev(X)}{\overline{X}} \right|. \tag{G.8}$$

We take the absolute value of the share because means can be positive or negative, and the coefficient of variation is always reported as a positive number. The coefficient of variation is generally expressed in percentage points; therefore, do not forget to multiply by 100 when making calculations.

Example G.17: Relative to their means, which is more variable, unemployment rates among the G-7 countries or the non-G-7 countries in Table 12.2?

Answer: This table gives the coefficients of variation and the elements from which it is calculated using formula (G.8):

	G-7	non-G7
Standard deviation (percentage points)	1.26	2.78
Mean (percent)	6.20	6.00
Coefficient of variation (percent)	20.00	46.00

With a coefficient of variation of 46 percent, real GDP in the non-G-7 countries is more than twice as variable as in the G-7 countries (20 percent).

G.5 Making Inferences from Descriptive Statistics

G.5.1 Homogeneity

We can always calculate various descriptive statistics, but whether they are meaningful depends on how we choose to use them. For example, imagine that you plan to take a group of sixth graders on a balloon ride. There are

10 children in the group, but the balloon can hold up to 15 children weighing not more than 1,600 lbs. in total. If the mean weight of the sixth graders is 100 lbs., then your group is easily accommodated. Now suppose that you want to add 5 more children from another class: will the balloon accommodate them? If you cannot weigh the children, then you might reason that because the average weight of your group was 100 lbs., adding five more will on average only add 500 lbs., leaving 100 lbs. as a margin of safety for the balloon. Your reasoning is fine – provided that the children you are going to add are typical of the children in your original group. If they come from a class of sixth graders, this may be a good assumption. But what if they come from a class of twelfth graders, who, on average, weigh 135 lbs.? The balloon would then be overloaded ($10 \times 100 + 5 \times 135 = 1,675$ or 175 lbs. above the weight limit).

The point of the story is that we often calculate descriptive statistics for the purpose of *projecting* them beyond the data set that we have observed – that is, to make inferences about unobserved data from observed data. This works only if the observed and unobserved data are, on relevant dimensions, alike or homogeneous.

We may also require **homogeneity** within a data set as well as between data sets. If we claim that a mean or other descriptive statistic is *typical* of the data, it should be typical of any subset of the data. For example, consider a group of first graders on a field trip with their parents – one parent per child. We can calculate the mean weight of the group. But if parents have a mean around 150 lbs. and first graders have a mean of around 50 lbs., then the mean for the whole data set will be around 100 lbs.: not typical of either the parents or the children, and for most purposes of little use.

Data are *homogeneous* when *every reasonably sized subset displays similar descriptive statistics*. Statisticians have developed a number of formal tests of homogeneity, which are beyond the scope of this book. But frequently, commonsense reflection on a problem and examination of some subsets of the data will give us a good idea of whether the data are homogeneous enough for our purposes.

Example G.18: Are unemployment rates among the G-7 countries in Table 12.2 homogeneous?

Answer: There is no unequivocal answer to this question; it depends partly on our purposes. But notice that we can readily divide the G-7 into two subsets: Japan, the United Kingdom, and the United States with low unemployment rates (mean = 5.1 percent); and Canada, France, Germany, and Italy with higher unemployment rates (mean = 7.0). For some purposes we would reject the homogeneity of G-7 unemployment rates.

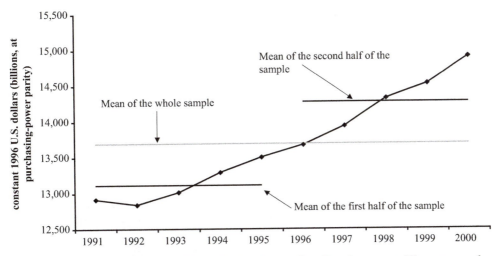

Figure G.8. A Nonstationary Time Series: Canadian Employment. The mean of a nonstationary time series is not constant over time. *Source:* International Monetary Fund, *International Financial Statistics.*

G.5.2 Stationarity

Figure G.8 shows the same Canadian employment data as Figure G.3. If we divide the data into two halves, the means for each subset (shown as horizontal lines in the figure) are clearly different: the data set is clearly not homogeneous even though it refers to a single economic unit, Canada, rather than to the different economic units in the last section. Although the order of observations in a cross section is arbitrary, the order in a time series follows the natural succession of dates. Canadian employment, like many economic time series, trends upward: later segments typically have higher means than earlier segments. The Canadian data illustrate a particular type of nonhomogeneity. A time series is **stationary** when *every reasonably sized subperiod displays similar descriptive statistics*. The Canadian data are **nonstationary**. Projecting the level of Canadian employment in the later period based on its mean for the earlier period would have led to a substantial underprediction. To do better, we would have to take account of the fact that the mean was constantly increasing.

Statisticians have developed formal tests of stationarity, but these are beyond the scope of this book. Informally, we judge a time series to be stationary when it frequently crosses its sample mean. Obviously, a series that is trending strictly upward or downward, such as Canadian employment, will cross its sample mean only once. But a series need not trend strictly in one direction to be nonstationary.

For example, Figure 13.2 (Chapter 13) shows that the average propensity to consume in the United States crosses its mean only five times in fifty years and drifts fairly far away from it at times, so it should be regarded

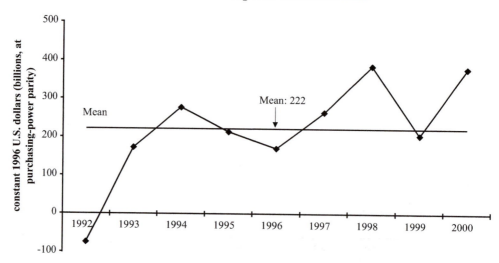

Figure G.9. Tranformation of a Nonstationary to a Stationary Time Series: Canadian Employment. The first difference of a nonstationary time series (here Canadian employment from Figure G.8) is often stationary. *Source: International Monetary Fund*, International Financial Statistics.

as *nonstationary*. In contrast, Figure 5.5 (Chapter 5) shows that detrended industrial production, personal income, and employment cross and re-cross their means many times. These three series could be regarded as *stationary* (which, of course, is the point of detrending).

A time series that follows a random walk (see Chapter 5, section 5.3.1), with or without a drift (which is a kind of trend), is also a nonstationary time series. Unlike a trending series, a random walk without a drift does not typically move dominantly in one direction. Nevertheless, it crosses its mean infrequently, so that descriptive statistics appropriate to stationary data should not be applied to it.

A nonstationary time series may be transformed into a stationary one in various ways. If a series has a clear trend, a detrended version will usually be stationary (see section G.12). Also, the **first difference** of a nonstationary series ($\Delta X_t = X_t - X_{t-1}$) or the growth rate ($\hat{X}_t$) (see section G.10) is frequently stationary.

Example G.19: Can Canadian employment data be transformed into a stationary series?

Answer: Figure G.9 shows the first difference of Canadian employment data and its mean. It is much more like a stationary series than the level data in Figure G.8.

The previous example illustrates that it may be hard to judge whether a series is stationary or not in a short sample. In general, we are more likely to perceive stationarity over long time horizons than over short ones. The data

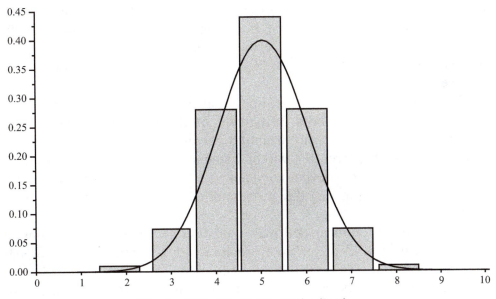

Figure G.10. The Normal Distribution.

for the real rate of interest in Figure 7.9 might appear to be stationary over the whole 50-year period of the plot, but would appear to be nonstationary were we to look only at the decade of the 1980s. This is not an illusion or a mistake, but the result of the data adjusting slowly to deviations from the mean – a property called *persistence*. To predict the course of real interest rates from 1986 to 1990, the downward trend of the apparently nonstationary data of the early 1980s would generally be more relevant. But over a longer horizon, say, predicting data for the early 2000s on the basis of data up to 1985, we would usually do better to project the apparently stationary mean of the longer period such as 1953–1985.

The importance of stationarity becomes even clearer in Section G.14.

G.6 The Normal Distribution

Many data in the world have (or can be transformed to have) a **normal frequency distribution**. Figure G.10 shows a histogram of normally distributed data. The smooth bell curve that is superimposed on the histogram shows what the curve would become if we had a large amount of data and chose narrower and narrower bins until they were infinitesimally small. Where the histogram is a *discrete* distribution; the bell curve is the *continuous* version of the normal distribution. When a teacher says that students will be "graded on a curve," the usual assumption is that the grades are at least approximately normally distributed.

The normal distribution is common because of a remarkable result in statistics known as the *central limit theorem*. Roughly, the central limit theorem says that the frequency distribution of the average of a number of independent distributions tends to be normal even when the original distributions are very far from normal (i.e., their histograms do not have a bell shape). If data display random variation as the result of a large number of unmeasured, independent causes, then the net effect of those causes tends to have a normal distribution.

The normal distribution has an important property: whatever the mean or standard deviation, about 38 percent of the observations lie within 0.5 standard deviation of the mean; 68 percent within 1 standard deviation; and about 95 percent lie within 2 standard deviations. These benchmarks – especially the 2-deviation-equals-95-percent benchmark – are often used as a way of expressing the measure of our uncertainty about random data.

For example, a political poll may state that 48 percent of the sample approves of the president's job performance with a "margin of error of ±3 points." How do we interpret this information?

Margin of error in the case of opinion polls almost always refers to a two-standard-deviation criterion. Suppose that another poll were conducted with a similar number of people in the sample on the same population. Even if 48 percent were the true value, any particular poll would probably come up with a different number. If 100 polls were taken, we would expect 95 of them on average to find a value between 45 and 51 percent. Suppose that a second poll produced a value of 49 percent. We would typically believe, given the uncertainty of the first poll, that this number is consistent with it and would not show that opinion had shifted. On the other hand, if a poll produced a value of 60 percent (and we did not believe that it was poorly conducted), there would be two possibilities: (a) it could be one of those (5 percent on average) cases in which the true value was 48 but the measured value fell outside the margin of error (more than two standard deviations away from the mean) or (b) opinion had really changed, so that the difference was a real one and not random variation. The reason for using a 95 percent criterion, instead of say a 50 percent criterion, is to try to reduce the times when explanation (a) applies. Usually, with such a large difference people would conclude (b), the change was genuine.

G.7 Type I and Type II Error

In the last section, we gave the example of trying to judge when two political polls reflect a genuine shift in opinion. This illustrates a common problem in statistical and nonstatistical reasoning. Suppose that we have a rule: *whenever the index of leading economic indicators turns down two months in a row, predict a recession within six months.* Is this a good rule?

It would be perfect if every time the index turned down two months in a row, a recession followed *and* every time it did not turn down two months

Table G.4. *Type I and Type II Error*

	The Hypothesis is Really	
	False	True
We infer that the hypothesis is		
False	Success	Type I Error
True	Type II Error	Success

in a row, no recession followed. The rule can fail in two different ways: the index does not turn down, but there is a recession anyway (this is known as a *false negative*). or the index does turn down, but no recession follows (this is a *false positive*).

Statisticians classify these errors in another way. If we have a hypothesis (there is a recession), denying it when it is true (false negative) is called **type I error**. Affirming it when it is false is called **type II error**. Table G.4 shows the relationship between the truth and these two types of error.

Generally, there is a trade-off between type I and type II error. For example, suppose that a man is on trial. Ideally, if he really committed the crime, we would like to convict; and, if he really did not, we would like to acquit. If he really did commit the crime, but we acquit him we have committed type I error. To minimize it, we could adopt the rule: always convict. Then, no criminals would ever get away. But, of course, some noncriminals would be unjustly sent to prison. If he really did not commit the crime, but we convict him anyway, we have committed type II error. To minimize, it we could adopt the rule: always acquit. No one would go to prison unjustly. But, then again, no criminal would ever go to prison either. To balance the possibilities of type I against type II error, we must choose some intermediate rule. Which way it leans depends, of course, on which type of mistake is more costly in the particular case.

A similar problem arises with the two opinion polls in the last section. What we want to decide is whether the poll that reports 60 percent really reflects the same opinion as the poll that reports 48 percent. The rule is to deny that the polls are the same if the second poll (60 percent) is outside the margin of error of the first poll (two standard deviations), which it is. The two-standard-deviation rule essentially says that there is a 5 percent chance of making a type I error following this rule. We could employ an even tighter standard to further reduce the chances of type I error, but then we would increase the chance of type II error: that is, of treating the polls as the same when they are really different.

The two-standard-deviation rule is a statisticians' rule-of-thumb for balancing type I against type II error. But without further analysis, a precise measure of type II error is not usually known.

G.8 Using Index Numbers

G.8.1 Index Numbers

An **index number** transforms a data set from its natural units into one that uses one of its values as a reference point. For example, suppose that we have a time series that takes the value 5 in 2003, 10 in 2004, and 12.5 in 2005. Index numbers are always stated by choosing a reference value and setting it to a base value for the index, usually (but not necessarily) 100. Here let the **reference value** be 5 in 2003 (this is usually stated 2003 = 100). So the index series takes the values 100 in 2003, 200 in 2004 (because 10 is twice the reference value) and 250 in 2005 (because 12.5 is 2.5 times the reference value).

The general formula for an index number is:

$$XI_t = \left(\frac{X_t}{X_0}\right) Z, \qquad \text{(G.9)}$$

where XI is the value of X expressed as an index (the suffix I indicates that a natural variable (X) has been turned into an index number); X_t is the value of the natural variable at time t; X_0 is the reference value (i.e., the natural value of whichever data point is taken to be the reference value), with the subscript 0 indicating the reference period or unit (e.g., a country in a cross section), whenever or whichever that might be; and Z is the scale factor that determines the value that the index will take in the reference period. Typically, $Z = 100$, so that the index = 100 at the reference date. But it could be chosen to be some other number: 1 and 10 are sometimes used; other values are rare. In effect, the formula says *set the value of X_0 to Z at date 0 and adjust all other values of X_t proportionately*.

The reference value need not be the value of a particular observation. Usually with monthly data, the average value over the 12 months of a year, and with quarterly data, over the 4 quarters of the year, is taken to be the reference value (X_0). Sometimes a longer period is chosen: the reference value for the consumer price index (CPI) is 1982–1984 – the average over 36 months.

Example G.20: Restate French employment data in Table G.2 as index numbers with reference periods of 1991, 1995, and 1998–1999.

Answer: The reference value 1991 is 22,316; for 1995, 22,311; for 1998–1999, 21,670.5 (= 22,479 + 20,864)/2). The three index numbers are shown in Table G.5.

Commonly, we indicate the units of an index number by stating the reference period and the value of Z. For example, for the first index in Table G.5,

Table G.5. *Index Numbers: Employment in France*

	Original Data	Index Numbers with Reference Periods		
	Thousands	1991 = 100	1995 = 100	1998–1999 = 100
1991	22,316	100.0	110.3	103.0
1992	21,609	96.8	106.8	99.7
1993	20,705	92.8	102.3	95.5
1994	21,875	98.0	108.1	100.9
1995	20,233	90.7	100.0	93.4
1996	22,311	100.0	110.3	103.0
1997	20,413	91.5	100.9	94.2
1998	22,479	100.7	111.1	103.7
1999	20,864	93.5	103.1	96.3
2000	23,262	104.2	115.0	107.3

Source: International Monetary Fund, *International Financial Statistics.*

the units are stated as $1991 = 100$, and for the third index as $1998–1999 = 100$. The units of the CPI are $1982–1984 = 100$. The units of the S&P 500 stock market index are $1941–1943 = 10$ (i.e., X_0 = the average value over the 1941–1943 period and $Z = 10$ – a rare case of $Z \neq 100$). With cross-sectional data, we might say, for example, Canada $= 100$.

Index numbers express data as a percentage of the reference value. In effect, they are a way of converting changes into levels. They are particularly useful when we wish to emphasize comparisons. Index numbers are most commonly used with time series, but not exclusively: Figure 9.11 (Chapter 9) displays a cross section of national productivity levels, taking the U.S. level as the reference value.

Index numbers are also useful when we want to display a variety of data with incommensurable units: Figure 5.1 (Chapter 5) plots the time series for personal income (units: billions of dollars), employment (units: thousands of people), and industrial production (units: an index with $1997 = 100$), all against the same axis, by converting each to an index number with $1959:01 = 100$.

Once an index number has been calculated, it may be rebased by treating the index itself as the original data set and applying formula (G.9).

Example G.21: Using the index for French employment ($1998–1999 = 100$) in Table G.5, find the index number for 1993 with the reference period $2000 = 100$.

Answer: From the table we know that the value for 1993 is 95.5 and for 2000, 107.3. Using formula (G.9), $EmploymentI_{1993} = (95.5/107.3)100 = 89.0$.

This is exactly what we would get using the original data: 20,705 for 1993 and 23,262 for 2000: $EmploymentI_{1993} = (20{,}705/23{,}262)100 = 89.0$.

G.8.2 Price Indices

Price indices are a weighted average of individual prices, expressed as an index number. Chapter 4 (section 4.1) provides a detailed discussion about the construction of price indices, concentrating on the choice of the weights for the **price factor**. The price factor takes the place of the term in parentheses in formula (G.9). Here we present the detailed formulae for the price factors for the main indices.

Laspeyres (or Base-Weighted) Index

Number each good (j) from 1 to n. Then p_{jt} is the price and q_{jt} is the quantity of good j in period t. Let $t = 0$ indicate the **base period** (that is the period for which the expenditure shares would be calculated). A simple formula for the price factor for Laspeyres index is

$$pf_t^L = \frac{\sum\limits_{j=1}^{n} p_{jt} q_{j0}}{\sum\limits_{j=1}^{n} p_{j0} q_{j0}}. \tag{G.10}$$

It is easy to show that this formula, in fact, weights the changes in the price of individual goods by their shares in total expenditure in the base period just as in Chapter 4 (section 4.1.1). Notice, first, that the denominator is total expenditure in the base period (i.e., base period GDP if the basket is all the final goods and services in the economy). Multiplying and dividing by p_{jt} in the numerator and rearranging yields

$$pf_t^L = \frac{\sum\limits_{j=1}^{n} p_{jt} q_{j0}}{\sum\limits_{j=1}^{n} p_{j0} q_{j0}} = \sum\limits_{j=1}^{n} \left(\frac{p_{jt}}{p_{j0}}\right) \left(\frac{q_{j0} p_{j0}}{\sum\limits_{j=1}^{n} p_{j0} q_{j0}}\right). \tag{G.10'}$$

The first term on the right-hand side of (G.10′) is the price factor for the good j. The numerator of the second term is expenditure on good j in the base period. Consequently, the second term as a whole is the share of expenditure on good j in the base period. The price factor is then the sum of each price change times its share in expenditure in the base period.

Example G.22: What is the Laspeyres price index for 2009, 2010, and 2011 in the couch-potato economy in Table 4.1?

Answer: Using (G.10′) and taking 2009 to be the base year and calling tortilla chips good 1 and beer good 2, then the price factor for 2009 is:

$$pf_{2009}^L = \frac{\sum_{j=1}^{2} p_{j2009}q_{j2009}}{\sum_{j=1}^{2} p_{j2009}q_{j2009}} = \frac{0.50 \times 5 + 0.75 \times 4}{0.50 \times 5 + 0.75 \times 4} = 1.000,$$

for 2010:

$$pf_{2010}^L = \frac{\sum_{j=1}^{2} p_{j2010}q_{j2009}}{\sum_{j=1}^{2} p_{j2009}q_{j2009}} = \frac{1.00 \times 5 + 1.25 \times 4}{0.50 \times 5 + 0.75 \times 4} = 1.818,$$

for 2011:

$$pf_{2005}^L = \frac{\sum_{j=1}^{2} p_{j201}q_{j2009}}{\sum_{j=1}^{2} p_{j2009}q_{j2009}} = \frac{1.25 \times 5 + 1.40 \times 4}{0.50 \times 5 + 0.75 \times 4} = 2.118.$$

Using these price factors and taking 2009 to be the reference year (i.e., $p_{2009}^L = 100$), the values of the Laspeyres index for each year are:

$$p_{2009}^L = p_{2009}^L \times pf_{2009}^L = 100 \times 1.000 = 100.0,$$

$$p_{2010}^L = p_{2009}^L \times pf_{2010}^L = 100 \times 1.818 = 181.8,$$

$$p_{2011}^L = p_{2009}^L \times pf_{2011}^L = 100 \times 2.118 = 211.8.$$

These calculations are equivalent to substituting the price factors for the term in parentheses in formula (G.9). They also agree with the example in Chapter 4 (section 4.1.1).

Paasche (or Current-Weighted) Index

The formula for calculating the price factor for the Paasche index is:

$$pf_t^P = \frac{\sum_{j=1}^{n} p_{jt}q_{jt}}{\sum_{j=1}^{n} p_{j0}q_{jt}}. \tag{G.11}$$

Because the Paasche is a current-weighted index, the base period is now period t, and the price factors express the ratio of prices in the current period

(t) to those of some earlier period (0). It is easily shown to be the inverse of the sum of the individual price changes weighted by their shares in current expenditure. Notice that the numerator is total expenditure in the current period.

$$pf_t^P = \frac{\sum_{j=1}^{n} p_{j1}q_{j1}}{\sum_{j=1}^{n} p_{j0}q_{j1}} = \sum_{j=1}^{n} \frac{1}{\left(\dfrac{p_{j0}}{p_{j1}}\right)\left(\dfrac{p_{j1}q_{j1}}{\sum_{j=1}^{n} p_{j1}q_{j1}}\right)}. \tag{G.11'}$$

The first term in the denominator on the right-hand side of (G.11') is the individual price factor for good j, and the second term is the share of expenditure on good j in the current period.

Example G.23: What is the Paasche price index for 2009 and 2010 in the couch-potato economy in Table 4.1?

Answer: Using formula (G.11') and taking 2009 as the reference year, then, by definition, the price factor for 2009 is 1.000. For 2010:

$$pf_{2010}^P = \frac{\sum_{j=1}^{2} p_{j2010}q_{j2010}}{\sum_{j=1}^{2} p_{j2009}q_{j2010}} = \frac{1.00 \times 4 + 1.25 \times 5}{0.50 \times 4 + 0.75 \times 5} = 1.783.$$

So, the price indices are:

$$P_{2009}^P = P_{2009}^P \times pf_{2009}^P = 100 \times 1.000 = 100.0,$$

$$P_{2010}^P = P_{2009}^P \times pf_{2010}^P = 100 \times 1.783 = 178.3,$$

which agree with the calculations in Chapter 4 (section 4.1.2).

Because the Paasche index uses new weights for each current period, the price factors and the values of the price index will differ if a later year, say 2011, were taken to be the current period. Whereas Laspeyres indices are very common, Paasche indices are used most often as a step in the calculation of chain indices, where the shifting base is a desired feature.

The Fisher-Ideal Index

The Fisher-ideal index is the geometric average of the Laspeyres and the Paasche indices as shown in Chapter 4 (section 4.1.3). The Fisher-ideal index is almost always used as a step in computing chain indices in which the base is updated each period. In this context, the base period for the Laspeyres component is period $t - 1$, whereas the base period for the Paasche component is period t. A general formula for the price factor of a Fisher-ideal index is then:

$$pf_t^F = \sqrt{pf_t^L \times pf_t^P} = \sqrt{\frac{\sum\limits_{j=1}^{N} p_{jt}q_{jt-1}}{\sum\limits_{j=1}^{N} p_{jt-1}q_{jt-1}} \times \frac{\sum\limits_{j=1}^{N} p_{jt}q_{jt}}{\sum\limits_{j=1}^{N} p_{jt-1}q_{jt}}}. \qquad \text{(G.12)}$$

Example G.24: What is the Fisher-ideal price index for 2009 and 2010 in the couch-potato economy in Table 4.1?

Answer: Using formula (G.12), the price factor for 2010:

$$pf_t^F = \sqrt{\frac{\sum\limits_{j=1}^{2} p_{j2010}q_{j2009}}{\sum\limits_{j=1}^{2} p_{j2009}q_{j2009}} \times \frac{\sum\limits_{j=1}^{2} p_{j2010}q_{j2010}}{\sum\limits_{j=1}^{2} p_{j2009}q_{j2010}}}$$

$$= \sqrt{\frac{1.00 \times 5 + 1.25 \times 4}{0.50 \times 5 + 0.75 \times 4} \times \frac{1.00 \times 4 + 1.25 \times 5}{0.50 \times 4 + 0.75 \times 5}}$$

$$= \sqrt{181.8 \times 178.3} = 1.800,$$

which agrees with the results of Chapter 4 (section 4.1.3). If 2009 is the reference year, then by definition $p_{2009}^F = 100$. And the value for 2010 is $p_{2010}^F = p_{2009}^F \times pf_{2010}^F = 100 \times 1.8000 = 180.0$.

G.9 Real and Nominal Magnitudes

G.9.1 Conversions between Real and Nominal Magnitudes

Converting Nominal Data to Real

Fundamentally, a nominal or market value is a number of dollars; a real value is the number of units of a good that those dollars will buy. If Big Macs cost $3.69, the $100 is a nominal value equivalent to the real value of 27.1 Big Macs ($= 100/3.69$). Price indices are typically based on a basket of goods. If we knew the dollar cost of the basket, then we could convert any dollar value into a real value measured as a number of baskets. But price indices are generally published only as index numbers and, as we saw in section G.8.1, index numbers are really a way of turning relative changes into levels. We can use index numbers (see Chapter 2, sections 2.4.1 and 2.4.2) to restate the value of a nominal quantity in the dollars of one year into the *constant dollars* of another year. This is similar to creating an index number as in section G.8.1, except that, instead of taking the reference value to be 100, we take the reference value to be the nominal value in the reference period. The general formula for converting any nominal monetary value X to a real value is:

$$\$_R X_t = (\$_t X_t)(p_R/p_t), \tag{G.13}$$

where the subscript R refers to the reference period, and the subscript on the dollar sign indicates in which period's money the quantity is measured.

Example G.25: Mexican exports in 2003 were 165,396 million pesos. If the consumer price index (2000 = 100) was 18.56 in 1990 and 116.80 in 2003, what was the real value of Mexican exports in 2000 pesos? In 1990 pesos?

Answer: Using formula (G.13) and, of course, substituting pesos for dollars, $\text{Pesos}_{2000}Exports_{2003} = (\text{Pesos}_{2003}Exports_{2003})(p_{2000}/p_{2003}) = 165,396$ $(100.0/116.80) = \text{Pesos}_{2000}141,606$ million. Similarly, $\text{Pesos}_{1990}Exports_{2003} = (\text{Pesos}_{2003}Exports_{2003})(p_{1990}/p_{2003}) = 165,396(18.56/116.80) = \text{Pesos}_{2000}26,282$ million.

Converting Real Data to Nominal

To convert real data to nominal, we simply work this last process backward. Starting with equation (G.13), solve for the nominal value to yield:

$$\$_t X_t = (\$_R X_t)(p_t/p_R). \tag{G.14}$$

Example G.26: U.S. real GDP in the fourth quarter of 2004 was $12,303.5 billion in constant 2005 dollars. If the implicit price deflator for 2004:4 was 97.86, what was nominal GDP?

Answer: Using formula (G.14),

$$\$_{2004:4}Y_{2004:4} = (\$_{2005}Y_{2004:4})(p_{2004:4}/p_{2005}) = 12,303.5(97.86/100.00)$$
$$= \$_{2004:4}12,040.2 \text{ billion}.$$

Converting Real Data of One Reference Period to That of Another Period

If data are already expressed in constant dollars of one reference period ($R1$), we can convert them to the constant dollars of another reference period ($R2$) using the following formula:

$$\$_{R2} X_t = (\$_{R1} X_t)(p_{R2}/p_{R1}). \tag{G.15}$$

Example G.27: According to Example G.21, the real value of Mexican exports in 2003 was $\text{Pesos}_{2000}26,282$ million in 1990 constant pesos. Using this value and the fact that the Mexican CPI was 18.56 in 1990 and 100 in 2000, what was the real value of Mexican exports in 2000 constant pesos?

Answer: Using formula (G.15) and, of course, substituting pesos for dollars, $Pesos_{2000}Exports_{2003} = (Pesos_{1990}Exports_{2003})(p_{2000}/p_{1990}) = 26{,}282$ $(100.0/18.56) = Pesos_{2000}141{,}606$ million. Naturally, this is the same value as when we converted nominal exports in 2003 to 2000 constant pesos; the calculation is different because we started here with real (i.e., constant peso) values rather than nominal (i.e., current values).

G.9.2 Real Values Using Chain-Weighted Indices

The construction of chain-weighted indices from underlying Laspeyres and Paasche indices, as well as the calculation and use of indices to convert nominal to real values, is described in Chapter 4 (section 4.1.4). Chain-weighted indices provide the best method for comparing the levels of a given series at different times. Unfortunately, because of the shifting weights used in their construction, chain-weighted price indices have some undesirable properties.

Table G.6 shows nominal GDP and its components, as well as their real counterparts in (chain-weighted) 2005 constant dollars for 2001, 2005, and 2009. Notice that using nominal values for any of these years the identity $Y = C + I + G + NEX$ holds exactly. Of course, in 2005 real and nominal values are the same, so that the identity also holds for real values in 2005. But notice that for real values in 2001, $C + I + G + NEX = \$11{,}352$ billion $>$ $\$11{,}347 = Y$. The difference is shown as the residual: -5. (It is easy to check that the identity also fails in 2009.) The general rule that the whole is the sum of its parts fails when chain-weighted indices are used to calculate real values. In contrast, fixed-weight indices preserve the rule.

The difference between the real value of GDP and the sum of the real values of its components is reported (as it is in the tables of the national-income-and-product accounts (NIPA)) as a *residual*. The residual is usually small – often small enough to ignore altogether.

The residual can cause problems. For instance, suppose that we ask, how has the proportion of GDP that is absorbed by government expenditure changed over time? Because both income and expenditure are, in fact, conducted in the current dollars of the day, the correct answer to this question is easily calculated from the nominal (or market) values. The true share for 2001 is Nominal G_{2001}/Nominal $Y_{2001} = 1{,}846/10{,}286 = 17.9$ percent. Suppose, however, that we tried to calculate this share using (chain-weighted) constant values. Then, the share for 2001 would be Real G_{2001}/Real $Y_{2001} = 2{,}178/11{,}347 = 19.2$ percent. Table G.7 shows the shares for each of the years in Table G.6 using nominal and real values. In 2005, of course, the shares are the same either way. But in every other year, the real shares are systematically different.

Table G.6. Nominal and Real (Chain-Weighted) GDP and Its Components

	Nominal (billions)					Real (billions chain-weighted 2005 constant dollars)					
	GDP	Consumption	Investment	Government Expenditure	Net Exports	GDP	Consumption	Investment	Government Expenditure	Net Exports	Residual
2001	10,286	7,149	1,662	1,846	−371	11,347	7,814	1,832	2,178	−472	−5
2005	12,638	8,819	2,172	2,370	−723	12,638	8,819	2,172	2,370	−723	0
2009	14,256	10,089	1,629	2,931	−392	12,987	9,235	1,528	2,565	−356	16

Source: Bureau of Economic Analysis.

Table G.7. *Shares in GDP Calculated Using Nominal and Chain-Weighted Real GDP*

	Percentage of Nominal GDP				Percentage of Chain-Weighted Real GDP			
	Consumption	Investment	Government Expenditure	Net Exports	Consumption	Investment	Government Expenditure	Net Exports
2001	69.5	16.2	17.9	−3.6	68.9	16.1	19.2	−4.2
2005	69.8	17.2	18.8	−5.7	69.8	17.2	18.8	−5.7
2009	70.8	11.4	20.6	−2.7	71.1	11.8	19.8	−2.7

Source: Table G.6.

A similar problem occurs in computing the contribution of different components of GDP to the growth rate of GDP (or, equally, the contribution of the components of any series to the growth rate of the whole). Great care must be exercised whenever comparisons are made between different chain-weighted real time series. These calculations become more and more misleading the further away they are from the reference year. In computing shares, it is best to use the nominal values. How to calculate the correct contributions of real components to the growth of the whole is well understood, but somewhat complex. Fortunately, NIPA includes supplemental tables that make the necessary calculations appropriately. The NIPA also includes supplemental tables that use a variety of reference years to facilitate accurate real comparisons.

G.10 Growth Rates

G.10.1 *The Essentials of Growth Rates*

Simple Growth Rates

A **growth rate** is *the proportionate (or percentage) rate of change per unit time.* A simple growth rate is calculated like a simple percentage change:

$$\hat{X}_t = X_t / X_{t-1} - 1. \tag{G.16}$$

Throughout this book we shall use the circumflex or "hat" (ˆ) over a variable to indicate a growth rate.

Example G.28: In 2002, U.S. real GDP (in 2005 constant dollars) was $11,553 billion and in 2003, $11,841 billion. What was the growth rate of GDP?

Answer: $\hat{Y}_{2003} = 11{,}841/11{,}553 - 1 = 0.025$ or 2.5 percent per year.

Note that the two ways of writing the answer (in *natural units* as 0.025 or *percentages* as 2.5 percent) are equivalent. Generally, in reporting results one should use percentages. In many cases, natural units are preferred for calculations. (Excel hint: to ensure that calculations show as percentages, either multiply the answer by 100 or on the *Number* tab of *Format Cells*, click *Percentage*.)

Compound Annualization

If data are observed annually, then the simple growth rate is annual (per year). If they are observed monthly or quarterly, then the simple growth rate is per month or per quarter. It is easier to understand growth rates and to make comparisons between them if they are all **annualized** or re-expressed in annual units. The general rule is:

$$\hat{X}_t = (X_t / X_{t-1})^m - 1, \qquad \text{(G.17)}$$

where m is the number of periods per year (4 for quarterly data; 12 for monthly; and so forth).

For example, to convert a quarterly rate of growth to a **compound annual rate**, we apply the following formula:

$$\hat{X}_t = (X_t / X_{t-1})^4 - 1. \qquad \text{(G.17')}$$

Example G.29: U.S. real GDP in the fourth quarter of 2003 was $12,042.8 billion and in the first quarter of 2004, $12,127.6 billion. What was the compound annualized growth rate of GDP in the first quarter of 2004?

Answer: $\hat{Y}_{2004:1} = (12{,}127.6/12{,}042.8)^4 - 1 = 0.028$ or 2.8 percent per year.

To annualize monthly rates of growth, replace the power 4 with the power 12.

Annual Growth Rates

It is still possible to compute annual (not annualized) rates of growth from monthly or quarterly data. To use quarterly data to compute an **annual rate** of growth, use the formula:

$$\hat{X}_t = X_t / X_{t-4} - 1. \qquad \text{(G.18)}$$

Example G.30: U.S. real GDP in the first quarter of 2003 was $11,645.8 billion. What was the annual rate of growth in the first quarter of 2004 over the same quarter in 2003?

Answer: $\hat{Y}_{2004:1} = (12{,}127.6/11{,}645.8) - 1 = 0.041$ or 4.1 percent per year.

To use monthly data to compute annual rates of growth, replace $t - 4$ with $t - 12$ in the formula. As Figures 2.11 and 2.14 (Chapter 2) show, the time series of annual rates are smoother than those of compound annualized quarterly (or monthly) rates.

Average Growth Rates

We sometimes want to know the **average rate of growth** – in other words, *that rate of growth that if steadily maintained would carry a time series from a starting value to a finishing value in the time that separates them.* The formula is just a variation on the compound annual growth rate formula:

$$\overline{\hat{X}_t} = (X_t / X_{t-k})^{1/k} - 1, \qquad \text{(G.19)}$$

where k is the interval in time between the beginning point $(t - k)$ and the end point (t), measured in years; and the bar over the growth rate indicates that it is an average.

Example G.31: U.S. real GDP in the second quarter of 1999 was $10,684.0 billion and in the third quarter of 2003 was $11,935.5 billion. What was the average rate of growth over this period?

Answer: The period is 4.25 years, so $\overline{\overline{Y}} = (11{,}935.5/10{,}684.0)^{1/4.25} - 1 = 0.026$ or 2.6 percent per year.

G.10.2 When Should Growth Rates Be Compounded?

Compound growth rates make sense when the growth of one period is added to the stock, and the addition itself, as well as the original stock, grows the next period. They are, therefore, natural when considering the growth of real GDP, population, employment, and most other macroeconomic variables. However, sometimes the growth of one period is siphoned off, and each period starts with the same base.

For example, suppose that you have $100,000 in a bank account that bears 1 percent interest per quarter. Each quarter you receive $1,000. If you left that money in the account and let it grow alongside the original principal, then compounding would be natural. But suppose that each quarter you spend the $1,000. Then what is your *annual* rate of interest? It is just four times your quarterly rate of interest, because in one year you earn $4,000 or 4 percent on your principal. This is an example of **simple annualization**: quarterly rates of growth are multiplied by four, monthly by twelve, and so forth.

The most common application of simple annualization in macroeconomics and finance is the formulae used to price debt and compute payments (e.g., mortgage payments). Interest rates are general quoted as simple annual rates. To find the monthly rate, for example, they are divided by twelve.

Example G.32: A bank account pays interest at 7.30 percent per year paid each month. If you put $200 in the account and hold it for one year, letting the interest be held in the account: (a) what is the compound rate of interest on your account, and (b) how much will you have at the end of a year?

Answer: The simple monthly rate of interest is 0.608 ($= 7.30/12$) percent. The compound annual interest $r_{annual}^{compound} = (1 + r_{monthly}^{simple})^{12} - 1 = (1.00608)^{12} - 1 = 7.54$ percent. The value of your holding at the end of the year is $200(1.0754) = \$215.09$.

The general formula relating the simple to compound annual rates is:

$$\hat{X}_{annual}^{compound} = \left(1 + (\hat{X}_{annual}^{simple}/m)\right)^m - 1, \qquad (G.20)$$

where $m =$ the frequency of compounding: 4 for quarterly, 12 for monthly; 52 for weekly, and so forth.

Example G.33: In example G.32, how would the compound annual rate of interest have differed if the bank had compounded daily instead of monthly?

Answer: Using formula (G.20), the annual rate compounded daily would be $r_{annual}^{compound} = (1 + (r_{annual}^{simple}/365))^{365} - 1 = (1 + (0.073/365))^{365} - 1 = 7.57$ percent, which is higher than 7.54 percent, the annual rate compounded quarterly in Example G.32.

G.10.3 Extrapolation

The compound average annual rate of growth for real GDP in the United Kingdom for the nine years from 1991 to 2000 (see Table G.1) is 2.97 percent $(= (617/474)^{1/9} - 1)$. What would real GDP be in 2008 if this rate of growth continued steadily? This is a problem in **extrapolation**. A general formula for extrapolating time-t data k periods into the future is:

$$X_{t+k} = X_t(1 + \overline{X})^k, \qquad (G.21)$$

where $\overline{X}$ is the average rate of growth *expressed in the same time units as* k (e.g., if k is measured in quarters, $\overline{X}$ must be the *quarterly* compound average rate). Using the formula, real GDP in the U.K. in 2005 would be $Y_{2008} = X_{2000}(1 + \overline{X})^8 = 617(1 + 0.0297)^8 = \$780$ billion.

Example G.34: Employment in Italy grew at a 1.54 percent compound annual rate between 1997:4 and 2002:4. Employment in 2002:4 was 21,757,000. If growth continued at a steady rate, what would be the level of employment in 2009:1?

Answer: First, we need the average compound quarterly rate of growth: $\overline{E} = (1 + 0.0154)^{1/4} - 1 = 0.38$ percent. Then, 2009.1 is 25 quarters ahead of 2002:4, so that $k = 25$. Using formula (G.21), we get $E_{2009:1} = E_{2002:4}(1 + \overline{E})^{25} = 21,757,000(1.0038)^{25} = 23,920,970$.

G.10.4 The Algebra of Growth Rates

Because growth rates are closely linked to logarithms, they follow rules analogous to the rules governing the use of logarithms (see section G.11.2):

$$\text{If } z = xy, \quad \text{then } \hat{z} \approx \hat{x} + \hat{y}. \tag{G.22}$$

$$\text{If } z = x/y, \quad \text{then } \hat{z} \approx \hat{x} - \hat{y}. \tag{G.23}$$

$$\text{If } z = x^y, \quad \text{then } \hat{z} \approx y\hat{x}. \tag{G.24}$$

$$\text{If } z = \sqrt[y]{x}, \quad \text{then } \hat{z} \approx \hat{x}/y. \tag{G.25}$$

These rules hold only approximately. The approximations are excellent when the growth rates are small, but become worse as they grow larger.

Example G.35: Suppose that nominal wages are growing at 5 percent per year and inflation as measured by the CPI is 2 percent per year. How fast are real wages growing?

Answer: *real wage* $= (w/p)$, so that according to rule (G.23), *the growth rate of the real wage* $= \hat{w} - \hat{p} = 5 - 2 = 3$ percent per year.

Application of the other rules is straightforward.

G.11 Logarithms

G.11.1 What Are Logarithms?

The Concept of the Logarithm

In the days before electronic calculators, personal computers, and spreadsheet programs, logarithms (first developed by Scottish mathematician John Napier (1550–1616)) were an important tool for calculation. Today they remain useful as tools of analysis.

A **logarithm** *of a number is the power (or exponent) to which a given base must be raised to produce that number.* So, for example, the base 10 logarithm (notated as $\log_{10}$) of 100 is:

$$\log_{10}(100) = 2, \text{ because } 10^2 = 100.$$

Similarly,

$$\log_{10}(1000) = 3, \text{ because } 10^3 = 1{,}000.$$

Logarithms are not restricted to integer powers:

$$\log_{10}(43) = 1.633, \text{ because } 10^{1.633} = 43.$$

(Check this with a pocket calculator.)

Base 10 logarithms are known as **common logarithms**. Generally the button on a calculator marked "log" computes the common logarithm. There is, however, nothing mathematically special about base 10:

$$\log_2(43) = 5.426, \text{ because } 2^{5.426} = 43.$$

The Antilogarithm

If we know the logarithm, we can calculate the original number by raising the base to the power of the logarithm. So, for example, if we are given a common logarithm of 3.478, we can calculate the original number as

$$10^{3.478} = 3,006.076.$$

This is referred to as taking the **antilogarithm**. For common logarithms it is sometimes notated as antilog$_{10}$ and sometimes as log^{-1} (read as "log inverse"), so that

$$\text{antilog}_{10}(3.478) = \log_{10}^{-1}(3.478) = 3,006.076.$$

The antilogarithm *undoes* or reverses the logarithm and vice versa.

The Natural Logarithm

Common logarithms are convenient for expositional purposes, because everyone is familiar with the powers of 10. Base 10 was the most frequently used base in the past when logarithms were commonly used for calculation; hence the name "common logarithm." In many scientific applications, however, another – and, at first sight, quite strange – base is preferred. This base is given the name e, and is defined as $e = 2.71828.$ ... The ellipsis marks indicate that e is an irrational number (like π) that cannot be expressed as a ratio of integers, and, therefore, never terminates or repeats. Logarithms to base e follow the same rules as logarithms to base 10 or any other base. For example, $\log_e(17) = 2.83321$, because $e^{2.83321} = 17$; antilog$_e$ is often written exp, so that antilog$_e(2.83321) = \exp(2.83321) = e^{2.83321} = 17$.

Logarithms to base e are called **natural logarithms**. This name and the explanation for the strange value of e arise because the base e logarithm is involved naturally in the solution to important problems in mathematics. One such problem arises in the integral calculus: what is the area under the rectangular hyperbola $y = 1/x$ between $x = a$ and $x = b$?[2] Mathematicians have proved that the answer is $\log(b) - \log(a)$. But this answer will be correct numerically only if the logarithms are expressed to the base $2.71828.$ ... In other words, $\log(a) = \log_e(a)$ and so forth.

In the main text of this book, only natural logarithms are used. Natural logarithms are indicated by several different notations. The most common

[2] For those familiar with the integral calculus, the problem is to evaluate $\int_a^b (1/x)dx$.

are $\log_e$, ln, and log. Frequently ln is used on calculators and in spreadsheets (including Excel) to avoid confusion with common logarithms. Unfortunately, in many contexts, the lowercase "l" in ln can be mistaken for the numeral "1." We shall indicate natural logarithms as log, without any subscript, which has the virtue of suggesting its correct pronunciation.

G.11.2 Calculating with Logarithms

Logarithms convert multiplication problems into addition problems, which are generally easier to solve (at least by hand). To see how this works, consider multiplying 10,000 by 1,000,000. Of course, this is easy to do, but it illustrates the principle. We can write the problem as

$$10{,}000 \times 1{,}000{,}000 = 10^4 \times 10^6.$$

The rules of exponents tell us that we can rewrite the right-hand term as

$$10^4 \times 10^6 = 10^{4+6} = 10^{10}; \text{ that is, we sum the exponents. So,}$$

$$10{,}000 \times 1{,}000{,}000 = 10^4 \times 10^6 = 10^{10} = 10{,}000{,}000{,}000.$$

The exponents are, of course, just the common logarithms. Adding the exponents is just like adding the logarithms. Therefore, another way of approaching the problem would be to say:

$$\log_{10}(10{,}000) = 4$$
$$\log_{10}(1{,}000{,}000) = 6$$
$$4 + 6 = 10$$
$$\text{antilog}_{10}(10) = 10^{10} = 10{,}000{,}000{,}000.$$

Logarithms reduce the level of complexity of many calculations: they convert multiplication problems into addition problems; division into subtraction; raising to powers into multiplication; and taking roots into division. The main rules for (natural) logarithms are:

$$\text{If } xy = z, \quad \text{then } \log(x) + \log(y) = \log(z). \tag{G.26}$$

$$\text{If } x/y = z, \quad \text{then } \log(x) - \log(y) = \log(z). \tag{G.27}$$

$$\text{If } xy = z, \quad \text{then } y\log(x) = \log(z). \tag{G.28}$$

$$\text{If } \sqrt[y]{x} = z, \quad \text{then } \log(x)/y = \log(z). \tag{G.29}$$

If x is a natural number, then antilog(log(x))
$$= \log^{-1}(\log(x)) = \exp(\log(x)) = e^{\log(x)} = x. \tag{G.30}$$

If y is a logarithm, then $\log(\exp(y)) = \log(\log^{-1}(y)) = \log(e^y) = y$. (G.31)

$$\text{For small } x, \log(1 + x) \approx x. \qquad\qquad (G.32)$$

Example G.36: Use logarithms to calculate (a) $1{,}356 \times 43{,}119$; (b) $317 \div 48$; (c) 211^{14}; (d) $\sqrt[4]{12{,}591}$; (e) x, when $\log(x) = 0.57$; (f) y, when $\exp(y) = 8.22$; (g) $\log(1.024)$.

Answer: Using rules (G.26)–(G.32) in turn:

(a) $\log(1{,}356) + \log(43{,}119) = 7.2123 + 10.6717 = 17.8840$; $\exp(17.8840) = 58{,}468{,}576$;

(b) $\log(317) - \log(48) = 1.88770$; $\exp(1.88770) = 6.6042$;

(c) $\log(211^{14}) = 14\log(211) = 14(5.35186) = 74.92604$; $\exp(74.92604) = 3.4671 \times 10^{32}$;

(d) $\log(\sqrt[4]{12{,}591}) = \log(12{,}591)/4 = 9.44074/4 = 2.36018$; $\exp(2.36018) = 10.5929.$

(e) $\exp(0.57) = 1.0587$;

(f) $\log(8.22) = 2.1066$;

(g) without calculation (applying formula (G.32)) $\log(1.024) \approx 0.024$; more exactly $\log(1.024) = 0.0237.$

Rules (G.26)–(G.29) are strongly analogous to the rules governing the algebra of growth rates in Section G.10.4.

G.11.3 Logarithms and Growth

Logarithmic Derivatives and Percentage Changes

Start with a fact that is demonstrated in any standard calculus textbook:

$$\text{if } z = log(x), \quad \text{then } dz/dx = d\log(x)/dx = 1/x.$$

Recall that a derivative is the rate of change of a function. So, if we want to know how much z changes for a small change in x, we must multiply the *rate* at which z changes for any change in x times the *change* in x itself: $dz = (dz/dx)dx$. In the case of $z = \log(x)$, this is

$$dz = (dz/dx)dx = (d\log(x)/dx)dx = (1/x)dx = dx/x.$$

Notice that for small changes $dx \approx \Delta x$, so that

$$dz \approx \Delta x/x = \text{the percentage change in } x.$$

That is: *a small change in the logarithm of a variable (dz) is approximately equal to the percentage change in the variable itself.*

Example G.37: Suppose that the price level in one month is $p_t = 123$ and the next month it is $p_{t+1} = 124$. What is the percentage change?

Answer: Using logarithms, $d\log(p)/dt \approx \log(124) - \log(123) = 4.82028 - 4.81218 = 0.0081$ or 0.81 percent. This is the same as direct calculation: $(124/123 - 1) = 0.0081$.

The next example illustrates an important caveat: the logarithmic approximation works *only* for *small* changes:

Example G.38: Suppose that the price level in one month is $p_t = 123$ and the next month it is $p_{t+1} = 275$. What is the percentage change?

Answer: Using logarithms, $d\log(p)/dt \approx \log(275) - \log(123) = 5.54908 - 4.81218 = 0.7369$ or 73.69 percent. But the exact result from direct calculation is very different: $(275/123 - 1) = 0.\ 1.2358$ or 123.58 percent. The difference in logarithms understates the actual percentage change by almost half.

Logarithms and Growth Rates

Consider a time series x. We can think of x as a function of time t. So, for example, when we plot GDP on a graph, the equation that describes GDP might be $z = Y(t)$. Take the logarithm of each side of this expression: $\log(z) = \log(Y(t))$. What is the derivative of $\log(z)$ with respect to time? Using the rule for the derivative of a logarithmic function and the chain rule:

$$d\log(z)/dt = d\log(Y(t))/dt = [1/Y(t)][d(Y(t))/dt].\qquad\text{(G.33)}$$

The first term in square brackets is the original logarithmic derivative. The second term in square brackets follows from the chain rule: it is the derivative of the function within the function.

We can interpret the right-hand side of (G.33) in a practical way. Rearranging the terms gives us $\frac{dY(t)/Y(t)}{dt}$. Remembering that for small changes $dx \approx \Delta x$, we see that

$$d\log(z)/dt = [1/Y(t)][d(Y(t))/dt] = \frac{dY(t)/Y(t)}{dt}$$

$$\approx \frac{\Delta Y(t)/Y(t)}{\Delta t}.\qquad\text{(G.34)}$$

The numerator of the right-hand side is the percentage change in Y. (Here time t rather than the more common time $t - 1$ is taken to be the base period. This difference will not matter as long as all the changes are small.) The denominator is a small change in time. The whole expression can be read as *the percentage change per unit time*, which is, of course, the definition of the *rate of growth*. The general rule, then, is:

$$\frac{d \log(z)}{dt} = \frac{dz/z}{dt} \approx \frac{\Delta z/z}{\Delta t}.$$

For small changes $= \hat{z} = the\ percentage\ change\ in\ z\ per\ unit\ time$ (G.35)

or *the rate of growth of z*,

where the circumflex or "hat" ($\hat{}$) over a variable indicates the rate of growth. The derivative of a function measures the slope of its graph. We have, therefore, proved mathematically that *the slope of a logarithmic time-series graph of a variable is the rate of growth of the variable.*

Similarly, we can demonstrate why there is a strong analogy between the rules for logarithms ((G.26)–(G.32)) and the algebra of growth rates in Section G.10.4.

Example G.39: What is the growth rate of $z = xy$?

Answer: $\hat{z} = d \log(z)/dt = d \log(xy)/dt = d \log(x)/dt + d \log(y)/dt = \hat{x} + \hat{y}$, which is just rule (G.22).

The other rules of the algebra of growth rates are derived similarly.

Continuous Compounding

Look again at the formula for compound growth in equation (G.17). The ultimate compound annual growth rate depends on the frequency of compounding. Going from quarterly ($m = 4$) to monthly ($m = 12$) to weekly ($m = 52$) to daily ($m = 365$), the compound growth rate increases as the time interval between compound increments becomes smaller. Any standard calculus book proves that as m becomes infinitely large, so that the time interval between compound increments becomes infinitesimally small, the compound growth formula converges to:

$$X_{annual}^{compound} = \exp(X_{annual}^{simple}) - 1. \tag{G.36}$$

Example G.40: In Examples G.32 and G.33, how would the compound annual rate of interest differ if the bank had compounded continuously instead of daily or quarterly?

Answer: Using formula (G.36), the annual rate compounded daily would be $r_{annual}^{compound} = \exp(r_{annual}^{simple}) - 1 = \exp(0.073) - 1 = 7.57$ percent, which is higher than the annual rate compounded quarterly, 7.54 percent, but the same as the rate compounded daily. The equivalence is the result of rounding. If we carry the calculation to enough decimal places the continuously compounded rate would exceed the daily compounded rate slightly.

Look again at the extrapolation problem in equation (G.21). If we replace $1 + \overline{X}$ with its continuously compounded equivalent, $\exp(\overline{X})$, we get

$$X_{t+k} = X_t[\exp(\overline{X})]^k. \tag{G.37}$$

Taking logs of both sides gives

$$\log(X_{t+k}) = \log(X_t) + k\overline{X},$$

and rearranging

$$\overline{X} = \frac{\log(X_{t+k}) - \log(X_t)}{k}. \tag{G.38}$$

Equation (G.38) says that we can compute the continuously compounded average rate of growth as the difference in logarithms (a percentage change) divided by the number of periods over which that difference is taken (k). The units of k determine time units of $\overline{X}$ – for example, if k is measured in years, $\overline{X}$ will be an annual rate; if k is measured in months, a monthly rate.

Example G.41: Real GDP in Sweden in 1995:3 was 403.39 constant 1995 krona and in 2004:1, 553.41 krona. What is the average compound rate of growth over this period at (a) a quarterly rate; and (b) an annual rate?

Answer: Use formula (G.38). Measured in quarters the time between the two dates is $k = 34$ quarters; in years, $k = 8.5$ years. So (a) $\overline{Y} = \frac{\log(Y_{2004:1}) - \log(X_{1995:3})}{34} = \frac{\log(553.41) - \log(403.39)}{34} = 0.93$ percent per quarter; and (b) $\overline{Y} = \frac{\log(Y_{2004:1}) - \log(X_{1995:3})}{8.5} = \frac{\log(553.41) - \log(403.39)}{8.5} = 3.72$ percent per year, which is, of course, four times the quarterly rate.

Further Examples

Here are three further examples using the fact that the difference in the logarithms in different time periods is approximately the continuously compounded rate of growth:

Example G.42: In 1997.2, real GDP in the U.S. was \$7,236 billion; in 1997.3 it had grown to \$7,311. What is the quarterly growth rate of real GDP?

Answer: $\hat{Y} \approx \log(7{,}311) - \log(7{,}236) = 0.0103$ or 1.03 percent per quarter. To annualize this at a compound rate, multiply by 4 to get $\hat{Y} \approx 4.12$ percent. How accurate is the approximation? Compare to the annualized compound quarterly growth rate calculated using the formula given in equation (G.17′).

Example G.43: In 1990.4, the GDP price deflator was 95.1 and, in 1991.4, 98.3. What is the annual rate of inflation?

Answer: $\hat{p} \approx \log(98.3) - \log(95.1) = 0.033$ or 3.3 percent per year. Again, check the accuracy against the percentage change calculated using formula (G.16).

Example G.44: In 1980, the population of the United States was 227,225,000 and, in 1998, 267,636,000. What is the average annual rate of growth?

Answer: $\hat{pop} \approx [\log(267,636,000) - \log(227,225,000)]/18 = 0.009$ or 0.9 percent per year. Again, check the accuracy using formula (G.19) for the average compound annual rate of growth.

The Rule of 72

Is a particular growth rate fast or slow? It often helps to have a rough-and-ready guide. An easy one is the **rule of 72**: *the doubling time of any growing quantity is 72 divided by its growth rate expressed in percentage points.*

Example G.45: If the inflation rate is 12 percent per year, how long will it take the price level to double?

Answer: The doubling time is approximately $72/12 = 6$ years.

Why does the rule of 72 work? Consider a quantity X and ask, how long does it take for it to double at a continuously compounded rate of growth, that is, to reach $2X$ at a rate of growth $\overline{X}$? Substitute these values into equation (G.38):

$$\overline{X} = \frac{\log(2X) - \log(X)}{k} = \frac{\log(2X/X)}{k} = \frac{\log(2)}{k}.$$

Solving for k gives

$$k = \frac{\log(2)}{\overline{X}} = \frac{0.69}{\overline{X}}. \tag{G.39}$$

The growth rate in equation (G.39) is measured in natural units, but if we want to measure it in percentage points, then it becomes

$$k = \frac{100\log(2)}{\hat{X}} = \frac{69}{\hat{X}}. \tag{G.39'}$$

Using the numbers in Example G.45, $k = 69/12 = 5.75$ years, which is a more exact doubling time than the 6 years estimated previously. So, the rule of 72 is really a *rule of 69*. Why not state it that way?

The answer goes back to the initial assumption: we need a *rough-and-ready* guide to the speed of growth. The number 69 has four integer factors {1, 3, 23, 69}. In contrast, 72 has twelve integer factors {1, 2, 3, 4, 6, 8, 9, 12, 18, 24, 36, 72}. Seventy-two is, therefore, an easier number to use for mental arithmetic, and the errors will not matter much if we apply it to low growth rates and do not require a precise answer. Whenever it is easier, any other number close to 69 (68, 69, 70) will work just as well or better than 72. These four numbers have 23 distinct factors among them.

G.11.4 Logarithmic Graphs

Figure 2.12 shows real GDP on a **logarithmic scale**. The logarithmic scale is also called a **ratio scale**. The reason can be seen on the vertical axis. On a normal scale, the distance between $2,000 billion and $4,000 billion is the same as the distance between $4,000 billion and $6,000 billion. Notice that on the logarithmic scale, the second distance is substantially closer than the first distance. Also notice that the distance between $2,000 billion and $4,000 billion is the *same* as the distance between $4,000 billion and $8,000 billion. The rule for a logarithmic scale is *equal distances represent equal ratios*. $4,000 billion is double $2,000 billion, so it is the same distance between them as it is between $4,000 billion and its double, $8,000 billion. Similarly, the distance between $1 billion and $3 billion is the same as that between $1 and $3 or $100 billion and $300 billion or $2,000 billion and $6,000 billion, because all stand in a 3:1 ratio.

The constant-ratio property of logarithmic graphs is the direct result of the property of logarithms of turning division (i.e., forming ratios) into subtraction (i.e., computing linear distances).

The logarithmic scale is convenient whenever we wish to plot data with a very wide range of values on the same graph or when we want to highlight their ratios. Growth can be thought of as a ratio: 100 percent growth is 2:1; 50 percent growth is 1.5:1; 10 percent growth is 1.1:1. A graph in which the vertical axis is logarithmic and the horizontal axis measures time allows us to see the growth rate as a ratio per unit time or, equivalently, as a growth rate. The slope of a graph is the rise over the run. In this case, the rise is a percentage change, because that is what a ratio is, and the run is a number of units of time. The slope is, therefore, a direct measure of the growth rate. If the line is steeper at 1955:1 than it is at 1985:3, then, unlike the case of a graph on a normal scale, it is correct to conclude that the rate of growth was faster at 1955:1.

Figure G.11 shows two series, each growing perfectly steadily: one at 10 percent per period, the other at 20 percent per period. In panel A, both are graphed on a natural scale; and, in panel B, on a logarithmic scale. On

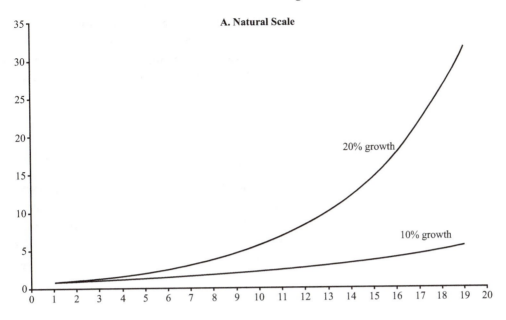

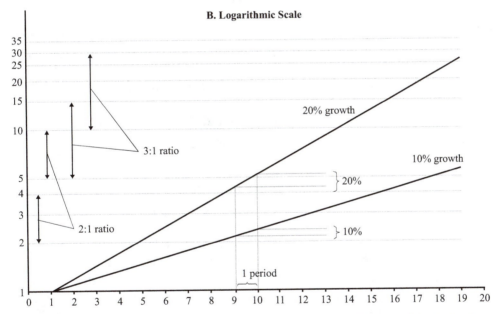

Figure G.11. The Logarithmic Graph (A) Natural Scale, (B) Logarithmic Scale.

the logarithmic scale both series become straight lines. The steeper line corresponds to the faster rate of growth.

G.12 Detrending

The distinction between trend and cycle is not given in nature. There is
no one right way to detrend a time series. The question is not one of right

or wrong, but of useful or not useful. Does it help us to see more clearly what is happening in the economy? In this book, we will use three of the many methods of detrending: 1. constant trends (section G.12.1); 2. moving-average trends (section G.12.2); and 3. differences or growth rates (section G.12.3).

G.12.1 Constant Trends

Using Constant Trends

Constant trends correspond to an equation with fixed coefficients, and include linear and exponential trends. If we believe that, despite cyclical fluctuations, the average growth rate of a series does not change much over a long period, then it is reasonable to assume that the trend has a constant rate of growth and can be described by an equation

$$trend = a(1 + b)^t$$

or

$$trend = a\exp(bt),$$

where t is time, and a and b are constants. Each equation describes exponential growth at a constant rate, b. The trend line in Figure 5.2 (Chapter 5) can be described by these equations.

The difference between the time series and the trend is

$$deviation\ from\ trend = time\ series - trend$$
$$= time\ series - a(1+b)^t$$

or

$$deviation\ from\ trend = time\ series - trend$$
$$= time\ series - a\exp(bt).$$

At each period, there is a different deviation from trend (see Figure 5.2).

If we knew the values of the constants a and b, we could calculate the values of each of the deviations and the variance of those deviations (section G.4.3). Different values for a and b would give us different sets of deviations and different variances. One rule for choosing the trend is to pick values for a and b that maximize the part of the change in the time series attributed to the trend, minimizing the part attributed to the cycle. This is equivalent to estimating a regression equation (see section G.15).

If a time series grows at a steady proportionate rate, then log(*time series*) will grow at a steady absolute rate as in Figure 5.3 (Chapter 5). The trend is then described by a linear function, not an exponential function:

$$trend = a + bt.$$

The method of finding the trend by choosing a and b to minimize the variance of the deviations remains the same. Linear trends arise naturally when we consider the logarithms of steadily growing data, but may also be appropriate even for natural data that do not grow exponentially.

Linear Trends

Excel (and other spreadsheet programs) allow a variety of trend lines to be added to a time-series chart: in Excel click on Chart, Add Trendline, Choose Trend/Regression Type, and then click on the type you want (for the trends in this book usually Linear or Exponential); click OK and the chart will display a trend. It is usually a good idea to display the equation of the trend line: before clicking OK, click on the Options tab and check the box that says Display Equation on Chart. (Note that the Options tab also allows you to extrapolate a trend forward or backward on your chart.)

The equation is useful in forming the **detrended series** or the deviations from the trend: *deviations from the trend = time series − trend.* Once you have the equation of the trend, add a column to your worksheet that starts with 1 for the first period in the sample over which the trend was formed, 2 for the next, and so on to the end. Say that this is column C (although it could be any column) and that 1 is placed in cell C2. The equation for a linear trend will be reported on your chart as $y = bx + a$, where b and a are numerical coefficients and x stands for time measured starting from 1, just like your entries in column C. The value of the trend for period 1, then, can be entered into some other cell (say, D2) as "$= b^*C2 + a$." The value for period 2 would be entered in D3 as "$= b^*C3 + a$," which can, of course, be implemented by simply dragging down the cell D2 using Excel's autofill feature. Excel does not recognize an equation cut from the chart and pasted into the spreadsheet, so you must copy the numbers for a and b by hand. Once you have all the trend values, then the detrended values are easily computed. (*A test that your computation is correct*: plot your computed trend on the same chart as your added trend line; they should be indistinguishable.)

Example G.46: Suppose that the equation of a linear trend line is given as $y = 0.4896x + 11.699$ and the value of original time series in period 7 is 23.06507. What is the value of the trend and the detrended series at period 7?

Answer: Assuming that your time data are in column C with C2 $= 1$, then period 7 corresponds to row 8. The *trend at period* $7 = 0.4896(7) +$ 11.699 (which is equivalent to entering $= 0.4896^*C8 + 11.699$ into a cell) $= 15.1172$. The *detrended value of the series at period* $7 = 23.06507 -$ $15.1172 = 7.947874$.

Exponential and Other Constant Trends

The procedures for exponential and other constant trends are similar except that the equations describing the trend take a different form.

Example G.47: Using the same original series as in Example G.46, suppose that the equation of an exponential trend line is given as $y = 22.785e^{0.0086x}$. What is the value of the trend and the detrended series at period 7?

Answer: Assuming that your time data are in column C with C2 = 1, then period 7 corresponds to row 8. The *trend at period* 7 = 22.785 exp(0.0086(7)) (which is equivalent to entering = 22.785*exp(0.0086*C8) into a cell) = 24.19878. The *detrended value of the series at period* 7 = 23.06507 − 24.19878 = −1.13371.

Note the big difference between the trend and detrended values in Examples G.46 and G.47. *The method of detrending matters.* In most cases in macroeconomics that involve growing data, exponential trends are preferred to linear trends. If data have been transformed by taking logarithms of the original time series, linear trends are preferred (another example of how logarithms reduce a more complex problem to a simpler one).

G.12.2 Moving-Average Trends

The Moving-Average Trend

In Chapter 2 (especially Figures 2.11 and 2.12) we saw that average growth rates were not constant decade by decade. In such cases, a constant trend may not be appropriate. We could perhaps use the average growth rate each decade to approximate the trend. But that would imply, wrongly, that decades were somehow natural breaks. Instead, we can calculate a **centered moving average**. Suppose that we have annual data on real GDP from 1960 to 2006. A five-year centered moving average would start in 1962 and average the value for 1962 with the values for two years before and two years after:

$$trend_{1962} = \frac{Y_{60} + Y_{61} + Y_{62} + Y_{63} + Y_{64}}{5}.$$

In 1963, the moving average would drop Y_{60} and add Y_{65}:

$$trend_{1963} = \frac{Y_{61} + Y_{62} + Y_{63} + Y_{64} + Y_{65}}{5},$$

and so on until 2004.

One disadvantage, of course, is that the centered moving average cannot start right at the beginning of the sample and must end before the end of the sample in order to accommodate the leading and lagging terms. Centered moving averages should have an odd number of terms, to preserve symmetry. The narrower the *window* (i.e., the number of periods in the average), the more fluctuations the trend will display. There is no one right choice of window, but for detrending economic time series, a fairly long window is usually appropriate. The 25-quarter window used in Figure 5.4 (chapter 5) approximates the average length of the U.S. business cycle, ensuring that the trend averages both upswings and downswings at every point.

Calculating Moving-Average Trends

Excel will fit a *trailing moving-average trend*. In this book, however, we use only *centered moving-average trends*. These are easily constructed from Excel functions. If the original series is in column B, then a centered moving-average trend with N leading and N lagging terms can be constructed in another column as AVERAGE(Bc-N:Bc+N), where c is the row number of the current cell.

Example G.48: What is the 15-period centered moving average of data in column B at the time corresponding to row 47?

Answer: The current cell $c = 47$. To have a 15-period average, $N = 7$, because the leading terms plus the lagging terms plus the current period equals the total $(2N + 1)$. So, at row 47, the moving average = AVERAGE(B40:B54).

Dealing with the Endpoint Problem

The *endpoint problem* arises with the moving-average trend because we do not have enough data to calculate a $(2N + 1)$-period moving average for any cell less than $N + 1$ cells from the beginning or the end of the sample. For many purposes it is acceptable to ignore the troublesome cells and to just not compute any value for those dates. But sometimes we *must* have a value, in which case there are various "fixes" that might be made. One simple one is to adjust the original series before calculating the moving average by adding N terms to the beginning and end of the sample, where each term takes the value of the mean of the first or last N terms of the original sample.

So, in the last example, if the mean of the last 7 terms were 16.5, we would add 7 cells with 16.5 to the end of the sample. Now when we calculate the moving average – stopping on the last row of the *original* data – the AVERAGE function will find the needed seven additional cells to average over 15 values altogether. (The approach would be the same working with the beginning of the sample, except we would use the average of the first 7 rather than the last 7 terms.)

The last 7 terms of the moving average are not then the same as terms in the middle of the sample. Instead they are a weighted average of the current

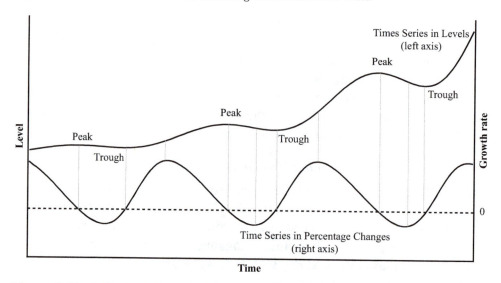

Figure G.12. A Stylized Time Series and in Levels and Percentage Changes. Plotting the growth rate of a time series shifts its phase: the peaks and troughs of the original series occur when the growth rates are zero, whereas the fastest positive and negative growth rates (the peaks and troughs of the growth-rate series) occur one-quarter cycle later in mid-expansion and mid-recession.

and 7 trailing terms with the average value of the last 7 terms. As we get closer to the endpoint, the weights shift more heavily toward the average.

This is not a perfect solution to the endpoint problem, but it should be good enough for many purposes.

G.12.3 *Differences or Growth Rates*

The previous two methods truly decompose the trend and the cycle into separate parts. Sometimes we may not really care about the trend but just want to focus on fluctuations. This is easily done by taking the **first difference** of the data:

$$\Delta X_t = X_t - X_{t-1}.$$

More commonly, we calculate the proportional first difference, which is just the growth rate:

$$\hat{X}_t = \frac{\Delta X_t}{X_{t-1}} = \frac{X_t - X_{t-1}}{X_{t-1}}.$$

Figure G.12 shows a time series that has been detrended by calculating growth rates. Notice that differencing a time series (or calculating a growth rate) causes a *phase shift*: when the original time series is falling, its growth rate is negative; when the level time series is rising, the growth rate is positive. The growth rate reaches its peak one-quarter cycle ahead of the original series. This makes sense. When the level is exactly at its peak or exactly at its trough it is neither rising nor falling, so its growth rate must be zero. After one of these extreme points, it changes faster for a while and then slows down to no change just at the next extreme point. Its growth rate must, therefore, reach its fastest absolute value between the peak and the trough of the level series. What this means economically is that we cannot judge the peak or trough of economic activity from the peak or trough of the growth rate of GDP, but instead from noting when that growth switched from positive or negative or back to positive. Growth rates should be fastest somewhere in the middle of economic expansions and slow to nothing at the cyclical peaks and troughs, and should reach their most extreme negative rates somewhere in the middle of recessions.

G.13 Correlation and Causation

G.13.1 The Nature of Correlation

Data that move together systematically are said to be *correlated*. The left-hand side of Figure G.13, panel A, shows two perfectly positively correlated series plotted against time. They have different means and different amplitudes, but a 20 percent rise in X is matched by a 20 percent rise in Y, and a 3 percent fall by a 3 percent fall, and so on. The **correlation coefficient** (R) measures the degree of conformity between the series. A correlation coefficient of $R = +1$ indicates perfect correlation. Look at the data another way. The right-hand side of panel A, which shows the same two series plotted against each other rather than against time, illustrates the hallmark of perfect correlation: the points lie on a straight line.

The correlation coefficient takes the value $R = -1$, when series are perfectly negatively correlated. Then each movement of X would be matched by a proportional movement of Y in the opposite direction. It takes the value $R = 0$, when there is no relationship between the series. Besides these extreme points, values in the intervals $0 < R < 1$ and $-1 < R < 0$, indicate different degrees of conformity between fluctuations between series.

Panel B shows two highly, but imperfectly, correlated series ($R = 0.9$). For the most part the series fluctuate together. Once in a while they move in opposite directions, and, when they move together, it is not always with a constant proportion. The right-hand side of Panel B shows that the scatter-plot forms a cloud of points. The more oblong this cloud, the closer it comes to a straight line, the higher the correlation.

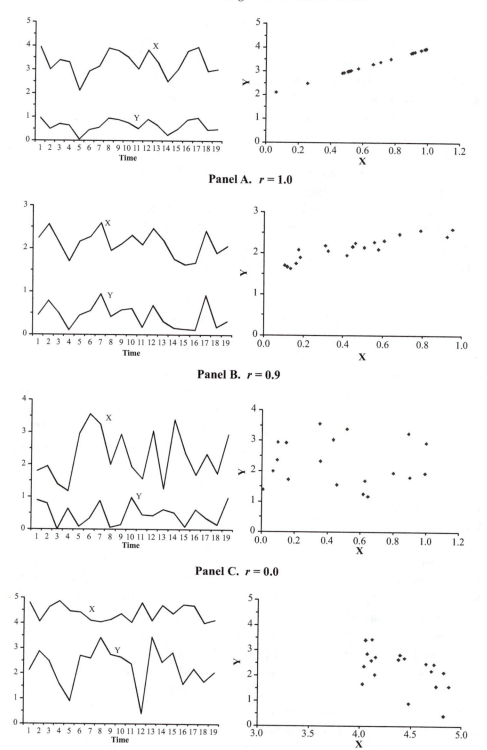

Panel A. *r* = 1.0

Panel B. *r* = 0.9

Panel C. *r* = 0.0

Panel D. *r* = –0.5

Figure G.13. Correlations between Time Series.

Panel C illustrates a case of zero correlation ($R = 0$). Here there is no common pattern to the movements of the time series. The cloud of points are scattered in a diffuse oval rather than tightly grouped along a line. Panel D shows a moderate negative correlation ($R = -0.5$). The points in the scatterplot form an obviously downward tilting cloud – neither as diffuse as panel C nor as tight as panel B.

Although the illustrations are all time series, the correlation coefficient can also measure the conformity among cross-sectional data. We can equally calculate the correlation between GDP growth rates and inflation rates for the United States since the 1970s or for the G-7 countries in 2004.

Like other summary statistics, the coefficient of correlation is interpretable only for stationary data. The *Guide*, section G.14.1, discusses **nonsense correlation**, which arises when data do not have constant means. Two trending series will generally have a high correlation coefficient. Yet, there may or may not be a genuine relationship between them. It is important to detrend nonstationary time series before calculating the coefficient of correlation.

G.13.2 Covariance

The **covariance** of two sets of data provides a measure of the degree to which they move together:

$$\text{cov}(X, Y) = \frac{\sum_{i=1}^{N} (X_i - \overline{X})(Y_i - \overline{Y})}{N - 1}. \tag{G.40}$$

First, compare this formula to the formula for the variance, equation (G.6). If X and Y took exactly the same values, $\text{cov}(X, Y)$ would equal $\text{var}(X) = \text{var}(Y)$. But in most cases, series are different. If X tends to be *above* its mean when Y is *above* its mean, the products to be summed will tend to be positive on average, and the covariance will be *positive*. If X tends to be *below* its mean when Y is *above* its mean and vice versa, then the products to be summed will tend to be negative on average and the covariance will be *negative*. If there is no relationship between the two variables, then the products will sometimes be positive and sometimes negative, so that when they are summed up they will cancel and be zero on average.

G.13.3 The Correlation Coefficient

Like variance, the actual size of the covariance depends, in part, on the units of measurement. Correlation expresses the covariance as a share of the geometric mean of the variances of the two variables in order to produce a unit-free measure of association:

$$R = \text{cor}(X, Y) = \frac{\text{cov}(X, Y)}{\sqrt{\text{var}(X)\text{var}(Y)}} = \frac{\frac{\sum_{i=1}^{N}(X_i - \bar{X})(Y_i - \bar{Y})}{N-1}}{\sqrt{\frac{\sum_{i=1}^{N}(X_i - \bar{X})^2}{N-1}\frac{\sum_{i=1}^{N}(Y_i - \bar{Y})^2}{N-1}}}$$

$$= \frac{\sum_{i=1}^{N}(X_i - \bar{X})(Y_i - \bar{Y})}{\sqrt{\sum_{i=1}^{N}(X_i - \bar{X})^2 \sum_{i=1}^{N}(Y_i - \bar{Y})^2}}. \tag{G.41}$$

Formula (G.41) shows that if there were no relationship between the two variables, so that the covariance was zero, then the correlation coefficient (R) would itself be zero. Similarly, if the two series were identical, then both numerator and denominator (most easily seen in the expression after the second equality) would be equal to the variance, so that $R = 1$.

What value would R take if the two series moved perfectly together but were not identical? For example, let $X_i = \{1, 2, 4, 1, -1, -8, \ldots\}$ and $Y_i = \{0.5, 1, 2, 0.5, -0.5, -4, \ldots\}$, then $Y_i = \frac{1}{2}X_i$. We can see the answer more clearly by considering two variables each with mean zero, so that $\bar{X} = \bar{Y} = 0$, and $Y_i = bX_i$. Then

$$R = \text{cor}(X, Y) = \frac{\text{cov}(X, Y)}{\sqrt{\text{var}(X)\text{var}(Y)}} = \frac{\sum_{i=1}^{N}(X_i)(Y_i)}{\sqrt{\sum_{i=1}^{N}(X_i)^2 \sum_{i=1}^{N}(Y_i)^2}}$$

$$= \frac{\sum_{i=1}^{N}(X_i)(bX_i)}{\sqrt{\sum_{i=1}^{N}(X_i)^2 \sum_{i=1}^{N}(bX_i)^2}} = \frac{b\sum_{i=1}^{N}(X_i)^2}{\sqrt{b^2}\sqrt{\left(\sum_{i=1}^{N}(X_i)^2\right)^2}} = \frac{b}{\sqrt{b^2}}. \tag{G.42}$$

If b is any positive number then, the last term in equation (G.42) equals one: *if any two series move perfectly directly proportionally to each other, then $R = 1$.* If b is any negative number, then the last term is negative one: *if any two series move perfectly inversely proportionally to each other, then $R = -1$.*

It is messier to demonstrate, but equally true, that the same results hold if the relationship between X and Y is the more general linear function: $Y_i = a + bX_i$ – in which case one or both variables would have different nonzero means.

Generally, two variables will not move perfectly together, so that we rarely find $R = 1$ or -1 unless, first, we have made a mistake or, second, the two variables are connected as identities. But the more closely the movements in variables conform to each other (directly or inversely), the larger the absolute value of R.

Variables that have low, but nonzero correlations may be either (a) truly, but weakly, related or, (b) unrelated. The second case is always possible with random data. For example, if we keep track of the number of heads and tails of a fair coin over many thousands of flips, at any point we will not typically have an equal number of heads and tails, even though the average will get closer and closer to 0.5 (calling heads 1 and tails 0) as the number of flips increases. There are formal statistical tests, beyond the scope of this book, for deciding between option (a) or (b). At this level, the soundest procedure is not to use a very low correlation as positive evidence *by itself* for a real, but weak relationship. But if we have *independent evidence* that a relationship is real, then a low correlation does give some idea of its strength. In that case, a low correlation might suggest that there are other important factors that we have not considered.

Excel hint: the function for calculating correlation is CORREL(array1, array2), where array1 and array2 refer to the range of cells for two variables.

G.13.4 Two Important Properties of Correlations

Correlation Is Symmetrical

The correlation of X with Y is exactly the same as the correlation of Y with X: *correlation is symmetrical*. Look at equation (G.41). If we were to switch X and Y every place they occurred, it is easy to see that the functions would all take the same values. This is easily proved in a spreadsheet as well. Calculate the correlation between two series using, for example, Excel's CORREL function. Now reverse the order of the variables in the function; you should get exactly the same number.

Correlation Is Not Transitive

A relationship such as "larger than" is transitive. If X is larger than Y, and Y is larger than Z, then X is larger than Z. But *correlation is not transitive*. If X is correlated with Y, and Y is correlated with Z, it does not then follow that X is correlated with Z.

Example G.49: Consider two sets of random data chosen to have a very low correlation: $X = \{0.53, 0.14, 0.2, 0.75, 0.65, 0.22, 0.75, 0.08, 0.75, 0.48\}$ and $Y = \{0.8, 0.81, 0.83, 0.75, 0.2, 0.66, 0.57, 0.34, 0.7, 0.82\}$. A third variable is the sum of the two, $Z = X + Y = \{1.33, 0.95, 1.03, 1.5, 0.85, 0.88, 1.32, 0.42, 1.45, 1.3\}$. Use these variables to show that correlation is not transitive.

Answer: It is easy to calculate the correlations on a spreadsheet. $\text{Cor}(X,Z) = 0.76$, which is reasonably high; $\text{cor}(Z,Y) = 0.59$, which is still moderate. So, clearly X is correlated with Z, and Z is correlated with Y. But $\text{cor}(X,Y) = 0.06$, which is very low; so, we can conclude that X is not correlated with Y. Correlation is not transitive.

G.13.5 Causation versus Correlation

The Nature of Causation

When we say that X causes Y we typically mean something like, if we could control X we could control Y. An old adage holds that *correlation does not prove causation*. There may be a correlation between the number of police in various towns and their crime rates. It is doubtful that the police are the cause of the crime. A genuine correlation – that is, one that is not just a statistical fluke – *does* suggest that variables are causally connected: either (a) one causes the other; or (b) there is some more complex causal connection between them, involving other variables. But a correlation cannot tell us whether it is (a) or (b).

Properties of Causation

The key properties of causes are the opposite to those of correlation (see the previous section). Where correlation is symmetrical, *causation is asymmetrical*. If X causes Y, in general, Y does not cause X. (Mutual causation is possible, but it is not the general case.) Where correlation is intransitive, *causation is transitive*. If X causes Y and Y causes Z, then X causes Z. Even if a correlation indicates a causal connection between X and Y, it cannot tell us which is cause and which is effect or whether some other cause or causes connect them.

G.13.6 Causal Structure

Mutual and Cyclical Causes

Although generally cause is asymmetrical, there could be cases of *mutual* or *simultaneous* cause. Imagine two ladders leaning against each other to form an A-frame. Each ladder could be seen as the cause of the other ladder's standing upright. Equilibrium relationships in economics could display mutual causation. For example, the arbitrage relationship between interest rates of different maturities (see Chapter 7, section 7.4) is an equilibrium relationship. Anything that alters the value of an interest rate on a bond of one maturity will generally alter the value of rates of a bond of another maturity and vice versa.

Causes may also be sequenced cyclically through time. Think about the multiplier process described in Chapter 13, section 13.1.4. Anything that initially changes consumption will raise income in a later period, which will in turn raise consumption in a still later period, and so on as the multiplier converges to its final value.

Direct and Indirect Causes

Because causes are transitive, we can distinguish between *direct* or *immediate* causes and *indirect* causes. Some economists argue that increases in the stock of money cause inflation. Some economists argue that increases in government deficits cause inflation. These two theories could be consistent if, for instance, deficits were financed by increases in the money stock, which in turn caused the inflation. Money would be the direct cause, and deficit finance the indirect cause.

The same cause might have both direct and indirect effects, and they need not act in the same direction. An increase in aggregate demand may, for example, be a positive cause of an increase in the rate of capacity utilization. It may also be a positive cause of an increase in investment. But because an increase in investment adds to the capacity of the economy, it could be a negative cause of capacity utilization. The net effect of aggregate demand on capacity utilization must balance off the positive direct effect against the negative indirect effect.

Common Causes

A causal connection between two variables explains their correlation. But two variables may be genuinely correlated and yet not causally connected in the sense that *any* change in one of the variables would necessarily be transmitted to the other. Gasoline prices may be highly correlated with the price of plastic. The best explanation is not that one causes the other, but that both are derived from petroleum, so that the price of crude oil is causally connected to each of the other two prices.

G.13.7 Causal Inference

Correlations are important evidence that some causal structure connects variables. But how can we sort out cause from effect and direct cause from indirect and common causes? This is an interesting problem for advanced statistics and scientific methodology. But there are some considerations that are helpful even at a fairly elementary level.

Time Order

Aside from science fiction (and perhaps some arcane areas of physics), we typically believe that causes cannot be later than their effects. They may, however, as in the examples in section G.13.6, be simultaneous. Time order is often a good clue to which is cause and which is effect, but it can still be tricky. Consider the example of oil prices as a common cause of gasoline and plastic prices. Changes in oil prices may act more quickly on gasoline prices than on plastic prices, so that it would appear that, not only are gasoline and plastic prices correlated, changes in gasoline prices always precede changes in plastic prices. Still, we should not conclude that gasoline prices cause plastic prices.

Time order is especially treacherous when we casually assess movements in time series. If both X and Y vary in a rough cycle but are not coincident, then which is the leading and which is the lagging series? A visual examination of the two variables (e.g., in a time-series plot) may be inconclusive. We do sometimes find that the correlation of X_t with Y_{t+1} is stronger than the correlation of X_{t+1} with Y_t. This could suggest that X_t causes and leads Y_{t+1}. But of course, if both correlations are relatively large, there may be cyclical causation in which each variable causes the other with a lag.

Economic Theory and Common Sense

Common sense can sometimes tell us which of a pair of correlated variables is likely to be the cause and which the effect. For instance, we know that the Federal Reserve can set the Federal-funds rate very close to any target level and we know that the 3-month Treasury bill rate is highly correlated with the Federal-funds rate. We are justified in thinking that the Federal-funds rate is likely to be the direct cause of the Treasury bill rate, because it is the rate that is directly controlled – that is, we know that it is Fed policy that determines it and, therefore, that it is independent of any other factors that might change the Treasury bill rate. Notice, however, that the Treasury bill rate could still be an indirect cause of the Federal-funds rate. If the Fed's policy was to use the Federal-funds rate to hold the Treasury bill rate to target, then any factor that tended to change the Treasury bill rate would directly cause the Fed's policy action, which would indirectly cause a change in the Federal-funds rate.

Economic theory can sometimes also serve the same role as common sense. We know, for instance, that changes in stock-market prices are a leading indicator of changes in GDP. There may be several mechanisms at work. One mechanism is discussed in Chapter 6 (section 6.3.3). Stock prices are based on the discounted value of *expected* future profits. If GDP is higher in the future, it is likely to be a cause of an increase in future profits. If people use this causal connection to more or less correctly predict future profits,

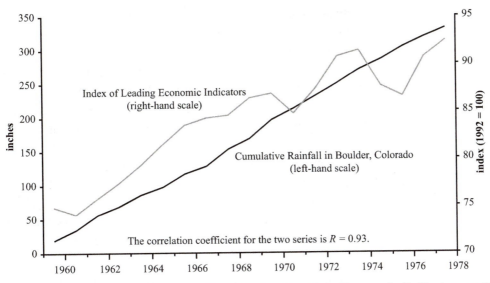

Figure G.14. Two Nonstationary Time Series: Leading Economic Indicators and Cumulative Rainfall. *Source:* leading indicators, Conference Board; rainfall, U.S. Weather Service.

then stock prices will rise today in anticipation of future profits. As a result, changes in stock prices will be correlated with future changes in GDP, even though the future does not cause the past. Our knowledge of economic theory will help us to sort out such a potential confusion about causal direction.

G.14 Relationships between Stationary and Nonstationary Time Series

G.14.1 Nonsense Correlations

It is easy to misuse correlation and, as a result, to reach wrong conclusions about the reality and the strength of economic relationships. A simple demonstration illustrates the problem.

Figure G.14 plots the index of leading economic indicators and cumulative rainfall in Boulder, Colorado, from 1959 to 1977. Both series trend upward. The correlation coefficient, $R = 0.93$, is very high. The great statistician George Udny Yule referred to such relationships as **nonsense correlations** defined as *a correlation that is high despite an absence of a genuine relationship between the variables*. The example is clearly a nonsense correlation as the history of rainfall in one town can hardly have any deep connection to the leading economic indicators. If they are nonsense, why do such correlations occur?

Notice that the correlation coefficient is based on the means, variances, and a covariance (equation (G.41)). We know from section G.5.2 that these are easily interpreted only for stationary time series. But both the index of leading economic indicators and cumulative rainfall are strongly trending series – that is, they are nonstationary (they do not cross their own means frequently). The current value of an upwardly trending series is always above its mean, and its mean rises each period. The product terms for two upwardly trending series in the correlation formula (G.41) will both be positive, and so R will also necessarily be positive and will get closer to one over time. (If both are negatively trending, R will still be positive; if one is downwardly trending, R will be negative; but, in every case, R will get closer to one in absolute value over time.) These results say nothing for or against a genuine relationship. They occur simply because the data have trends.

The first lesson is: *do not calculate correlation coefficients for trending data; they are meaningless*. A corollary is: *do not calculate correlation coefficients for other types of nonstationary data; they are equally meaningless*.

G.14.2 Genuine Relationships between Nonstationary Time Series

Given the problem of nonsense correlations, how do we distinguish genuine from spurious relationships between nonstationary time series? Relationships may exist in the short run or the long run (roughly the distinction between trend and cycle in Chapter 5, section 5.1). We take each case in turn.

Short-Run Relationships

The idea is simple: if we first detrend each series, so that each is stationary, then it is appropriate to apply the correlation coefficient as a measure of their association and to interpret a high correlation as indicative of some (perhaps complicated) relationship.

Example G.50: Is there a genuine short-run relationship between the index of leading economic indicators and cumulative rainfall in Boulder, Colorado?

Answer: There are many ways to detrend (see section G.12). Figure G.15 shows one of them: the first differences of trending data in Figure G.14. These data look stationary. The correlation coefficient between the detrended series is $R = 0.03$, which is very low and suggests that there is no genuine relationship.

Although the relationship in this example supports the characterization of nonsense correlation, the next example considers a more reasonable economic relationship.

Example G.51: Is there a genuine short-run relationship between the Canadian employment and GDP per capita data in Tables G.1 and G.2?

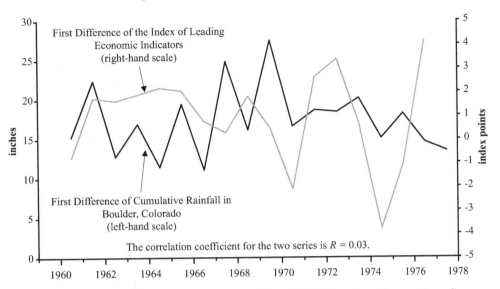

Figure G.15. A Nonsense Correlation Does Not Hold Up under Detrending. *Source:* leading indicators, Conference Board; rainfall, U.S. Weather Service.

Answer: Figure G.16 plots the growth rates of the data (see Figure G.3 for the levels). It is hard to make secure judgments of stationarity with short runs of data (here we have only 9 periods). Nevertheless, these are certainly more stationary than the original data. The correlation coefficient of the two time series is $R = 0.94$, which suggests a genuine tendency to move directly together in the short run.

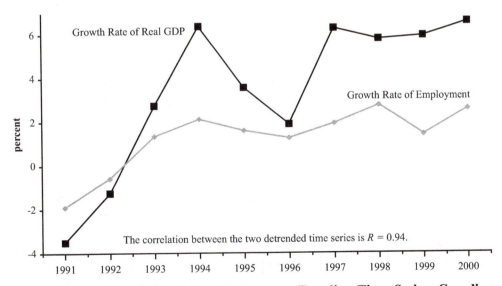

Figure G.16. A Genuine Relationship between Trending Time Series: Canadian Real GDP and Employment. *Source:* employment, International Monetary Fund, *International Financial Statistics;* GDP, Penn-World Tables, 6.1, Table G.2; and author's calculations.

Long-Run Relationships

Any time one transforms data, information may also be lost. Just because trending series are vulnerable to nonsense correlations does not mean that all genuine relationships must show up in data transformed through differencing or other forms of detrending. There may be important economic relationships between the levels of variables. For example, the main reason that consumption is higher in 2010 than in 1800 is that GDP is higher. This would be true whether or not the quarter-to-quarter or year-to-year change in consumption was highly correlated with the quarter-to-quarter or year-to-year change in GDP. The relationship between them is not a nonsense correlation.

Sometimes the long-term relationship between two time series takes a simple form.

Example G.52: Is there a genuine long-term relationship between GDP and capital in the United States?

Answer: Figure 9.14 shows that capital productivity (i.e., the ratio of GDP to capital) shows no trend around its mean of 0.35. (Although it is not trending, it is most likely not a genuinely stationary series, crossing its mean too few times. Nevertheless, it suggests that, in the long term at least, the relationship between GDP and capital is genuine.)

What if we apply the same technique to a case of nonsense correlation?

Example G.53: Is there a genuine long-term relationship between the index of leading economic indicators and cumulative rainfall in Boulder, Colorado?

Answer: Figure G.17 shows that the ratio of the two time series is itself a trending (nonstationary) series. The ratio provides no evidence in favor of a genuine long-term relationship.

The last example reinforces our belief that the rainfall/leading indicator example is nonsense, but that is partly because we have other evidence to support that view. Although a stable ratio suggests a genuine relationship, the failure to find a stable ratio could result either from a nonsense relationship or from a genuine, but more complicated relationship.

Example G.54: Is there a genuine long-term relationship between Canadian employment and Canadian GDP per capita?

Answer: Figure G.18 shows the ratio of GDP per capita to employment appears to be trending (nonstationary). Nevertheless, the relationship is likely a genuine one. The trend arises because the relationship is more

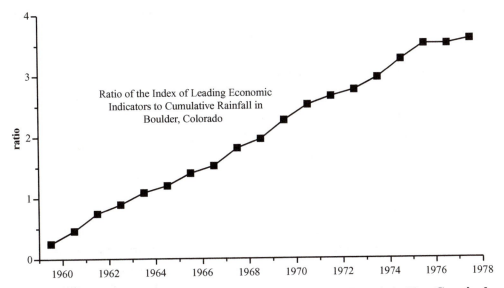

Figure G.17. The Ratio of Nonstationary Time Series That Are Not Genuinely Related Is Itself Nonstationary. *Source:* leading indicators, Conference Board; rainfall, U.S. Weather Service.

complicated, involving labor productivity as well as the two series on the graph (see Chapter 10, section 10.4).

This example reinforces another important lesson: *statistical calculations alone rarely, if ever, tell us which relationships are genuine or not; they are*

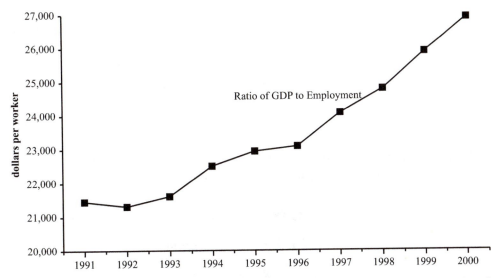

Figure G.18. The Ratio between Trending Time Series That Are Genuinely Related May Also Be Nonstationary: Canadian Real GDP and Employment. *Source:* employment, International Monetary Fund, *International Financial Statistics*; GDP, Penn-World Tables, 6.1, Table G.2; and author's calculations.

part of the evidence, but must be applied with economic understanding, taking all the evidence into account.

G.14.3 Do Not Mix Stationary and Nonstationary Time Series

Two stationary time series may or may not have a genuine, simple relationship. The same is true for two nonstationary time series. But a stationary and a nonstationary time series certainly do not have a genuine, simple relationship. For example, there can be no genuine, simple relationship between the level of prices in the United States and the unemployment rate. The level of prices (Figure 2.9) has grown almost steadily since World War II, rising by more than 700 percent. And while the level of unemployment (Figure 12.2) may not be technically stationary (it appears to have long periods with higher or lower means), it clearly has kept within a much narrower bound than prices (minimum 2.5 percent; maximum 10.8 percent; mean 5.7 percent), so that it can for some purposes be thought of as stationary about that mean. Suppose that prices were a function of the unemployment rate: $p = f(U)$. Consider a point early in the sample (say, 1960) when the price level was 18.6 and the unemployment rate 5.5 percent. Because unemployment is stationary, it is likely that at some later time the unemployment rate will be at or near 5.5 percent again – as it was, for example, about 1996. The equation, of course, predicts that prices should also return to their earlier level. But of course, at that date, because prices are strongly trending upward they are in fact at the much higher level of 83.0. Clearly, no equation of this type can describe the relationship.

This is not to say that there is no relationship between prices and unemployment. In Chapter 15 (section 15.3), we derive an important relationship between the change in the inflation rate (the growth rate of prices) and the unemployment rate. But in that case, prices have been transformed into an inflation rate, and the first difference of the inflation rate is stationary, so we no longer have an impermissible relationship between a stationary and a nonstationary time series.

So the final lesson of this section is: *do not look for a genuine, simple relationship between a stationary and a nonstationary time series.*

G.15 Regression

G.15.1 Linear Regression

The Regression Line

We frequently want to summarize the general relationship between two sets of economic data (time series or cross section) in a simple way. For example, Figure G.19 shows a scatterplot of some artificial labor-supply data. Each point plots the labor supply for one worker against the worker's real-wage

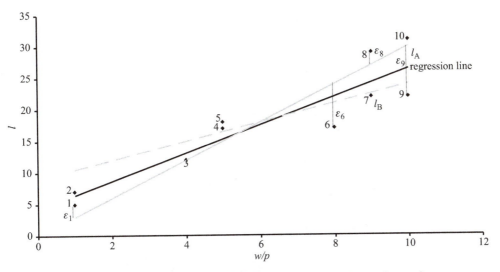

Figure G.19. Regression of l (labor) on (w/p) (the real wage).

rate. The general tendency of the data is to move up and to the right. But how can we summarize it more compactly? The solid gray line (line A) was chosen arbitrarily. Its equation is:

$$l_A = a + b(w/p) = 0 + 3(w/p).$$

How can we measure how well it fits? Look at point 1. The length of the dashed vertical line between it and line A is a measure of its error, which we can call ε_1. We can calculate this error as

$$\varepsilon_1 = l_1 - l_A = l_1 - (0 + 3(w/p)).$$

Similar errors can be calculated for each point on the scatterplot. The errors for points 6, 8, and 9 (i.e., ε_6, ε_8, and ε_9) are shown on the scatterplot. We calculate their values in the same manner. In fact, we can calculate the value of the errors at every point on the scatterplot (see Table G.8).

Obviously if the fit were perfect, each point would lie exactly on the line. If the points cluster tightly around the line, then the fit would be good. And if they scatter loosely around the line, it would be poor. Variance measures how tightly or loosely data cluster together (see section G.4.3). Table G.8 reports the variance of the errors around line A as 19.2.

But is that number big or small? We can know only if we have something to which to compare it. Line B is another arbitrary line whose equation is:

$$l_B = a + b(w/p) = 9 + 1.5(w/p).$$

Using this equation, we can calculate a new set of errors as well as their variance. This is reported in the table as 18.3. The lower variance shows that line B fits the data better than line A.

Table G.8. *How Well Do Different Lines Fit the Data?*

| Observation Number | Data | | Fit for Alternative Choices of Coefficients | | | | | |
| | Real Wage (w/p) | Labor (l) | Line A | | Line B | | Regression Line | |
			$l_A = 0 + 3(w/p)$	Error ε_A	$l_B = 9 + 1.5(w/p)$	Error ε_B	$l_R = 2.2 + 4.2(w/p)$	Error ε_R
1	1.0	5.0	3.0	2.0	10.5	−5.5	6.4	−1.4
2	1.0	7.0	3.0	4.0	10.5	−3.5	6.4	0.6
3	4.0	12.0	12.0	0.0	15.0	−3.0	13.0	−1.0
4	5.0	17.0	15.0	2.0	16.5	0.5	15.2	1.8
5	5.0	18.0	15.0	3.0	16.5	1.5	15.2	2.8
6	8.0	17.0	24.0	−7.0	21.0	−4.0	21.8	−4.8
7	9.0	22.0	27.0	−5.0	22.5	−0.5	24.0	−2.0
8	9.0	29.0	27.0	2.0	22.5	6.5	24.0	5.0
9	10.0	22.0	30.0	−8.0	24.0	−2.0	26.2	−4.2
10	10.0	31.0	30.0	1.0	24.0	7.0	26.2	4.8
Variance of the dependent variable (l)		72.2	Variance of errors	19.2		18.3		11.9

Note: The errors for each fitted line are calculated as $\varepsilon_i = l - l_i = l - (a + b(w/p))$, where i indicates line A, line B, or the regression line.

We could continue to try different lines by trial and error, looking for the one with the lowest variance. Fortunately, statisticians have developed a formula for calculating the coefficients (a and b) that deliver the lowest variance. Spreadsheets such as Excel (using the Add Trendline tool on the Chart menu) calculate the best coefficients automatically. The equation of the black line on the scatterplot, known as the **regression line**, uses the best coefficients:

$$l_R = a + b(w/p) = 2.2 + 4.2(w/p).$$

The table shows that its variance is 11.9, much lower than those of lines A or B.

When a computer program or spreadsheet calculates a regression, it finds the "best" values for the coefficients a and b of the equation

$$Y_i = a + bX_i + error_i, \tag{G.43}$$

where the error terms cannot be observed, but must be estimated depending on the choice of the coefficients, and "best" is defined to mean the values that minimize the variance of the error terms. The formulae for these best estimates are:

$$b^* = \frac{\text{cov}(X, Y)}{\text{var}(X)}$$

$$a^* = \bar{Y} - b^*\bar{X}, \tag{G.44}$$

where the star on the coefficient indicates that it is an estimate.

As we shall see in the next section, regression and correlation are closely related. They are useful for different things. Correlation measures the strength of association between variables. Regression helps us to put a mathematical form on the association by giving us coefficient values that allow us to say how much one variable will change when another changes.

Goodness of Fit

But how well does the regression line fit absolutely? We can think of the regression line as an effort to give a simple *explanation* of the relationship between real wages and labor supply. The variance of labor is reported in the table as 72.2. The variance of the error term (11.9) is 16.5 percent of that value. We interpret that to mean that real wages *explain* 83.5 ($= 100 - 16.5$) percent of the variance of labor supply. This is an example of a common measure of goodness-of-fit, which is calculated as

$$R^2 = 1 - \frac{variance\ of\ errors}{variance\ of\ dependent\ variable}. \tag{G.45}$$

The second term on the right-hand side is the variability of the error terms expressed as a proportion of the variability of the dependent variable – that is, as a proportion of the thing to be explained. Because the error terms are that part of the variation of the dependent variable that is not explained by the independent variable, this term is the "unexplained" fraction of the variance; the whole right-hand side (one minus this fraction) is the proportion of the variability of the dependent variable that is "explained" by the independent variable. R^2 is thus the ratio of explained to unexplained variability of the dependent variable.

Although we will not provide the derivation, (G.45) is equivalent to

$$R^2 = \frac{\text{cov}(X, Y)^2}{\text{var}(X)\text{var}(Y)}.^3 \tag{G.46}$$

This measure is called R^2 because $\sqrt{R^2} = R$, which is the correlation coefficient (see the *Guide*, section G.13.3). Equation (G.45) shows that the lower the variability of the data around the regression line – that is, the lower the variance of the errors – the higher is R^2. In the example, $R = \sqrt{0.835} = 0.914$, which shows that the data are highly correlated.

G.15.2 Nonlinear Regression

The various lines on the scatterplot (Figure G.19) are straight (i.e., linear). The same reasoning can be applied to lines with other shapes. For example, we might think that the relationship is quadratic. In that case, the spreadsheet would try to find the values for the coefficients (a, b, and c) that deliver the lowest variance for an equation such as $l = a(w/p)^2 + b(w/p) + c$. In Figure 11.8 (Chapter 11), Excel was used to fit a sixth-degree polynomial. Such a complex form was chosen because it allows the possibility of bending backward, which our theoretical discussion suggested was a real possibility, but which the simple linear regression line could never do.

G.15.3 The Direction of Regression

Correlation is symmetrical (section G.13.3); regression is asymmetrical: in general, the regression of Y on X is not equivalent to the regression of X on Y. Consider an equation like (G.43) but with X and Y switched:

$$X_i = c + dY_i + error_i. \tag{G.47}$$

---

[3] The proof uses equation (G.35) and the definitions of b^* and a^* to define the estimated errors. It then calculates their variance in terms of the variances and covariances of X, Y, substitutes this result into (G.45), and simplifies.

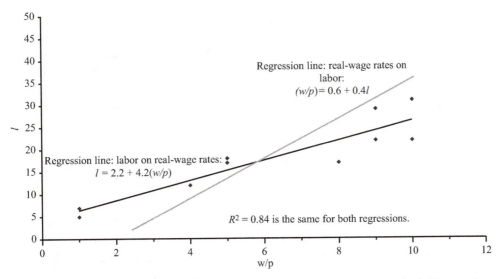

Figure G.20. The Direction of Regression, Regression is asymmetrical. Regression equations are different depending on which variable is treated as dependent and which as independent. The direction of regression should correspond to the direction of causation if that is known.

If the error terms were zero, then a little algebra shows that $d = 1/b$. Ordinary equations are symmetrical. But when the error terms are not zero, this is no longer true. The regression estimate of d is

$$d^* = \frac{\text{cov}(X, Y)}{\text{var}(Y)}. \tag{G.48}$$

Obviously, $d^* \neq 1/b^*$.

To visualize this result, Figure G.20 shows the same scatterplot and regression line as in Figure G.19. That line reports the regression of labor (l) on the real wage (w/p). In addition, Figure G.20 also shows the reverse regression of the real wage on labor. The two lines are clearly different.

Unlike correlation, regression has a direction. How should we choose which way to run a regression? The rule is simple in principle: *regression equations should be written with causes on the right-hand side (the horizontal axis of a scatterplot) and effects on the left-hand side (the vertical axis).* In that case, the coefficient on the independent variable can be interpreted as the strength of the causal connection between the independent and dependent variables, and the error terms can be interpreted as unobserved (and perhaps unobservable) causes of the dependent variable. This rule is not always easy to apply in practice, because we do not always have good evidence – or intuitions – for which is cause and which is effect (see sections G.13.5–7). Here, as in other cases, more sophisticated statistics than appropriate to an intermediate course might be helpful.

G.15.4 Nonsense Regression

Regression and correlation are closely connected. Look again at equation (G.41), which defines the correlation coefficient and equations (G.44) and (G.48), which define b^* and d^*, the regression coefficients. They are built up out of the same variances and covariances. And, of course, the higher the correlation between two variables (R), the better fitting the regression (R^2).

An important lesson to be drawn from this close connection is that just as we must guard against drawing conclusions from nonsense correlations (section G.14.1), we must also be on guard for **nonsense regressions**. The regression of one trending variable on another will have a high R^2, but cannot be easily interpreted as expressing a genuine economic connection. Just as with correlations, we must transform data into stationary forms through detrending, differencing, taking growth rates, or ratios before estimating regression equations. And, just as it makes no sense to posit a simple, genuine relationship between a stationary and a nonstationary variable, it makes no sense typically to estimate the regression of a stationary variable on a nonstationary variable or vice versa.

When there is a genuine relationship between nonstationary data (see section G.14.2), the regression line may sometimes capture that relationship. Usually, the data must be far apart in time to allow the long-term relationship to dominate the short-term relationship (or lack thereof). Be sure to note that the regression equation in such a case reflects the long-run tendency of the two series to move together and should not be used to predict month-to-month, quarter-to-quarter, or year-to-year changes, because adjustment to the long-run relationship is typically slow.

G.16 The Cobb-Douglas Production Function

G.16.1 The Properties of the Cobb-Douglas Production Function: An Example

The properties of the Cobb-Douglas production function are easily illustrated with simple numerical examples. (In the next section, we derive them using calculus.)

To apply the Cobb-Douglas production function in equation (9.8) to the data of the actual economy, we would have to have estimates of the key parameters, A and α. To illustrate its properties, however, we can just make up some numbers. Let $A = 1$ and $\alpha = 0.75$. Then the production function can be written as

$$Y = L^{0.75} K^{0.25}.$$

To illustrate the properties of this function, we calculate the values of Y for different levels of the inputs, L and K. The table below shows sixteen different combinations – four levels of L matched with four levels of K.

Value of Output (Y) for Different Combinations of Inputs (L and K)

			L		
		0.0	1.0	1.1	1.2
	0.0	0.0	0.0	0.0	0.0
K	1.0	0.0	1.0000	1.0741	1.1465
	1.1	0.0	1.0241	1.1000	1.1742
	1.2	0.0	1.0466	1.1242	1.2000

The student should plug some of the values of L and K into the production function to check that they are correct.

Using the table, we can prove the six properties in Section 9.2.2.

- **Property 1** *(GDP increases with each factor of production* ceteris paribus.*)*: Each row shows what happens to Y as L is increased, holding K constant. As we read across any row, Y increases. Similarly, each column shows what happens to Y as K is increased, holding L constant. The values of Y increase in both directions.
- **Property 2** *(The production function goes through the origin)*: GDP is zero for every entry in the first row (capital zero) and the first column (labor zero) – "there's no such thing as a free lunch."
- **Property 3** *(diminishing returns to each factor of production)*: Looking at the second row ($K = 1.0$), Y increases by 0.0741 as L increases from 1 to 1.1 and by a smaller amount, 0.0724, as L increases from 1.1 to 1.2. The small increase in Y is the marginal product of labor. The student can confirm that the same pattern of the second equal increase in L corresponding to a smaller increase in Y is true for the other rows as well. Similarly, holding L constant and looking down the columns, the same pattern holds for equal increases in K.
- **Property 4** *(an increase in one factor of production* ceteris paribus *raises the marginal product of the other factors)*: Looking at the row with $K = 1$, the marginal effect of adding 0.1 units of labor (from $L = 1$ to $L = 1.1$) is $\Delta Y = 1.0741 - 1.0000 = 0.0741$, so that the marginal product of labor is $\Delta Y / \Delta L = 0.741$. Looking at the row with $K = 1.1$, the same change in labor yields a higher $\Delta Y = 1.1000 - 1.0241 = 0.0759$, so that the marginal product of labor is also higher ($\Delta Y / \Delta L = 0.759$). The student can confirm that the same sort of result applies to capital, holding labor constant by looking down the rows.
- **Property 5** *(an increase in technology raises the marginal product of each factor of production)*. The student should recompute the values in the table on the assumption that $A = 2$ instead of $A = 1$. Comparing the new table to the old, every nonzero cell will have a higher value.

- **Property 6** (*constant returns to scale*): The last two cells along the main diagonal correspond to equal percentage increases in each of the factors (10 and 20 percent) compared to the second cell ($K = 1$, $L = 1$). Notice that Y increases by the same percentage in each case.

G.16.2 The Mathematics of the Cobb-Douglas Production Function

No Free Lunch

The Cobb-Douglas production function can be written as

$$Y = AL^\alpha K^{1-\alpha}, \tag{G.49}$$

where $0 < \alpha < 1$.

It follows immediately from the formula that if either input (L or K) is zero, output is zero. Graphically, this shows that *the Cobb-Douglas production function goes through the origin*.

More Inputs, More Output

The marginal product of labor is the small extra output that is produced from a small increase in the labor input, holding other inputs constant. Expressed in the terminology of the calculus, it is the derivative, dY/dL. Because Y is a function of more than one variable, this is properly a problem in multivariate calculus. We can, however, treat the other variables just as we would constant terms (indicated by a bar over the variable), so that we act as if Y were a function of L only, and then apply the power rule of ordinary calculus:

$$mpL = \frac{dY}{dL} = \alpha AL^{\alpha-1}\overline{K}^{1-\alpha} = \alpha AL^\alpha L^{-1}\overline{K}^{1-\alpha}$$
$$= \frac{\alpha AL^\alpha \overline{K}^{1-\alpha}}{L} = \frac{\alpha Y}{L}. \tag{G.50}$$

Another useful way to write this would be

$$mpL = \frac{dY}{dL} = \alpha AL^{\alpha-1}\overline{K}^{1-\alpha} = \alpha A\left(\frac{\overline{K}^{1-\alpha}}{L^{1-\alpha}}\right) = \alpha A\left(\frac{\overline{K}}{L}\right)^{1-\alpha}. \tag{G.51}$$

Similarly, the marginal product of capital is

$$mpK = \frac{dY}{dK} = (1-\alpha)A\overline{L}^\alpha K^{-\alpha} = (1-\alpha)A\overline{L}^\alpha K^{1-\alpha}K^{-1}$$
$$= \frac{(1-\alpha)A\overline{L}^\alpha K^{1-\alpha}}{K} = \frac{(1-\alpha)Y}{K}. \tag{G.52}$$

And, again, this can be written as

$$mpK = mpK = \frac{dY}{dK} = (1-\alpha)A\bar{L}^{\alpha}K^{-\alpha} = (1-\alpha)A\left(\frac{\bar{L}^{\alpha}}{K^{\alpha}}\right)$$

$$= (1-\alpha)A\left(\frac{\bar{L}}{K}\right)^{\alpha}. \tag{G.53}$$

Because inputs cannot be negative, except in the case that one or both is zero, the marginal products are necessarily positive. Graphically, this means that *the Cobb-Douglas production function slopes up*.

Diminishing Returns to Factors of Production

Looking at the right-most term of equation (G.51), it is obvious that as L becomes larger, mpL becomes smaller. In other words, the Cobb-Douglas production function shows *diminishing returns to labor*. Diminishing returns can be demonstrated mathematically by taking the derivative of mpL, which shows the rate at which it changes as L increases. The first derivative of mpL is the same as the second derivative of Y. Using the third term in equation (G.51) as the expression for the mpL:

$$d(mpL)/dl = d^2Y/dL^2 = d(\alpha AL^{\alpha-1}K^{1-\alpha})/dL = (\alpha-1)\alpha AL^{\alpha-2}K^{1-\alpha}. \tag{G.54}$$

Because $\alpha < 1$, the first term on the right-hand side is negative. The rest of the expression is positive, so that the whole expression is negative. Equation (G.54), therefore, says that the marginal product of labor declines as L increases. Graphically, *the production function is concave toward the labor axis*.

Similar results can be derived for capital through the same procedures making appropriate modifications.

Example G.55: Using the data from Chapter 9, section 9.2.4, for 2008: $\alpha = 0.67$, capital is \$40,173 billion, labor is 263,011 million worker-hours per year, and real GDP is \$13,312. What are the marginal products of labor and capital? Prove that they are diminishing.

Answer: Using equation (G.50) $mpL = \alpha(Y/L) = 0.67(13,312 \times 10^9)/(263,011 \times 10^6) = \$51/\text{hour}$; using equation (G.52) $mpK = (1-0.67)(13,312 \times 10^9)/(40,173 \times 10^9) = 0.11$ dollars of output/dollar of capital. The value of A can be computed from the other information as in equation (9.17′) to be 9.63. Using equation (G.54), $d(mpL)/dl = (\alpha-1)\alpha AL^{\alpha-2}K^{1-\alpha} = (0.67-1)0.67(9.63)(263,011 \times 10^6)^{(0.67-2)}(40,173 \times 10^9)^{(1-0.67)} = -4.47 \times 10^{-20} < 0$; the equivalent expression for capital would be

$$d(mpK)/dl = -\alpha(1-\alpha)AL^{\alpha}K^{-\alpha-1} = -0.67(1-0.67)(9.63)(263{,}011 \times$$
$$10^6)^{0.67}(40{,}173 \times 10^9)^{(-0.67-1)} = -1.82 \times 10^{-15} < 0.$$

Because the derivatives of each of the marginal products are negative, each is getting smaller as the input gets larger – that is, returns are diminishing.

Increasing Returns to Scale

Suppose that we increase the inputs of the two factors of production by the same proportion; call it λ. How much will output increase? Replacing K and L in the right-hand side of equation (G.49) with λK and λL gives us:

$$A(\lambda L)^{\alpha}(\lambda K)^{1-\alpha} = A\lambda^{\alpha}L^{\alpha}\lambda^{1-\alpha}K^{1-\alpha} = \lambda^{\alpha+(1-\alpha)}AL^{\alpha}K^{1-\alpha} = \lambda Y. \quad (G.55)$$

In words, an equi-proportional increase in the two factors of production results in an equi-proportional increase in output. Mathematicians refer to this property as *homogeneity of degree one*. Economists refer to it in this context as **constant returns to scale**.

G.16.3 Estimating Labor's Share (α) of Output from Data

Labor's share in GDP is, in principle, just the income of workers divided by GDP. A problem arises because the national-income-and-product accounts recognize a variety of classes of income. Wages and salaries are clearly labor income, while profits, interest, and dividends are clearly capital income. But what about proprietors' income? Proprietors are the owners of businesses in which they are, themselves, also among the principal workers, so that proprietors' income is a mixture of labor and capital income. To distribute proprietors' income, we assume that it can contain the same proportion of labor income as the rest of GDP.

The labor share in GDP, excluding proprietors' income, is

$$\alpha = \frac{compensation\ of\ employees}{GDP - proprietors'\ income - indirect\ business\ tax\ and\ nontax\ liability}.$$

The term *indirect business tax and nontax liability* is needed because proprietorships, like other businesses, pay taxes at a stage of production before their incomes are reported.

The share α used in the text (0.67) is the average of annual estimates over the period 1946 to 2008.

Suggestions for Further Reading

B. S. Everitt, *The Cambridge Dictionary of Statistics*. Cambridge: Cambridge University Press, 1998.

Darrell Huff, *How to Lie with Statistics*. New York: Norton, 1993.

Bernard Lindgren, *Statistical Theory*, 3rd ed. New York: Macmillan, 1976.

Edward Tufte, *The Visual Display of Quantitative Information*, 2nd edition. Chesire, CT: Graphics Press, 2001.

Edward Tufte, *Visual Explanations: Images and Quantities, Evidence, and Narrative*. Chesire, CT: Graphics Press, 1997.

Edward Tufte, *Envisioning Information*. Chesire, CT: Graphics Press, 1990.

Symbols

Special Symbols

In addition to the common algebraic symbols, the following are used in the text.

$\$_{\text{date}}$ dollars of the subscripted date

| indicates that the value of what precedes it is conditional on the values of what follows it

Δ change in, difference, or first difference (i.e., difference between current and immediately preceding period)

$\equiv$ identity; equal by definition

$\approx$ approximately equal

Functions and Operators

antilog   inverse natural logarithm

antilog_x inverse logarithm to base x

exp   exponential; inverse natural logarithm

$f(.)$ generic function

$F(.)$ generic function

$g(.)$ generic function

log   natural logarithm $= \log_e$

$\log_x$ logarithm to base x

Subscripts

A variety of subscripts are used to identify the entity or concept to which a variable applies. Their meaning is generally clear in context and they are not listed here.

0	initial or reference value
e	base of the natural logarithms $(2.71828\ldots)$
M	number of periods to maturity
N	(1) natural rate; (2) number of observations
t	time or date

Superscripts

A variety of superscripts are used to identify the entity or concept to which a variable applies. Their meaning is generally clear in context and they are not listed here.

*	(1) equilibrium or optimum value; (2) estimated value
†	counterfactual
$'$, $''$, $'''$	alternative value or version
e	expected
m	number of periods to maturity
P	permanent
pot	potential
T	transitory

Accent over a Variable

^	(circumflex or "hat") growth rate of quantity
—	(bar) (1) mean (arithmetic or geometric); (2) value of variable or variable held fixed
⌣	("smile") variable measured in effective labor units
~	(tilde) scaled (percentage of potential or full capacity value)

Variables, Parameters, and Labels

α	labor's share in GDP (natural fraction) $= Y_L/Y$
β	speed of adjustment parameter in the Phillips curve
δ	(lowercase Greek "delta") depreciation rate (depreciation as a share of capital)
ϕ	(lowercase Greek "phi") average product of capital $= apK$
γ	(1) factor of proportionality between the exchange rate and relative national price levels (see equation (8.10)); (2) speed of adjustment parameter in Okun's law
ι	(lowercase Greek "iota") investment rate (investment as a share of GDP)
κ	(lowercase Greek "kappa") capital-labor ratio $(= K/L)$

μ	(lowercase Greek "mu") (consumption) multiplier
ν	(lowercase Greek "nu") rental rate (factor payment for capital services)
θ	(lowercase Greek "theta") average product of labor $= apL$
ρ	(lowercase Greek "rho") internal rate of return on investment (real return on investment)
τ	(lowercase Greek "tau") marginal tax rate
τ_0	(lowercase Greek "tau") intercept in tax function
Π	(uppercase Greek "pi") profits
A	total-factor productivity
A_L	labor-augmenting technical progress
A_K	capital-augmenting technical progress
Au	autonomous expenditure
AD	aggregate demand ($= Y^D$)
apc	average propensity to consume
apl	average product of labor for a firm
apL	aggregate average product of labor
apk	average product of capital for a firm
apK	aggregate average product of capital
AS	aggregate supply
B	bond
BB	balanced budget
c	marginal propensity to consume ($= mpc$)
c_0	intercept in consumption function
C	(1) consumption; (2) chain index
CA	current account
Cpn	coupon (on bond)
Cu	currency
CU	capacity-utilization rate
D	(1) demand; (2) demand deposits
EMP	employment
EX	exports
F	Fisher-ideal index
FF	Federal funds
FV	future value or face value (of a bond)
G	(1) government spending on goods and services; (2) government
gap	gap between actual and potential output as a percentage of potential output
GDP	gross domestic product
GNP	gross national product
I	investment

$\tilde{I}$	scaled investment (investment scaled by potential GDP $= I/Y^{pot}$
IM	imports
implicit	implicit price deflator
k	capital input of a firm
K	aggregate capital
$\tilde{K}$	scaled capital (capital in use as a share of total capital $= CU$)
$\check{K}$	capital in effective labor units ($\check{K} \equiv {K}/{A_L L}$)
KA	capital account
KP	capital payments
KR	capital receipts
l	labor input of workers to a firm
L	(1) aggregate labor; (2) Laspeyres (base-weighted) price index
L^S	supply of labor
L^D	demand for labor
$\tilde{L}$	scaled labor (labor employed as a share of the labor force $= L/LF$)
lcw	individual life-cycle wealth
LCW	aggregate life-cycle wealth
LF	labor force
m	(1) number of periods to maturity; (2) money multiplier
M	(1) number of periods to maturity; (2) money
M^D	money demand
M^S	money supply
MB	monetary base
MC	marginal cost
mpc	marginal propensity to consume ($= c$)
mpk	marginal product of capital for a firm
mpK	aggregate marginal product of capital
mpl	marginal product of labor for a firm
mpL	aggregate marginal product of labor
mps	marginal propensity to save
MR	marginal revenue
n	rate of population growth ($n = \hat{L}$)
N	(1) number of observations; (2) natural rate
NIA	net income from abroad
$NTRA$	net transfer payments from abroad
NX	net exports ($EX - IM$)
p	price (specific price or index)
P	(1) permanent; (2) Paasche (current-weighted) price index
p_B	bond price
p_S	stock price
$\hat{p}$	the rate of inflation (growth rate of prices)

pd	ratio of primary deficit to the stock of government debt ($pd = PD/B^G$)
PD	primary (government budget) deficit (deficit net of interest payments)
pf	price factor
POP	population
PR	participation rate
prl	probability of loss (of central-bank reserves)
PV	(discounted) present value
q	Tobin's q (the ratio of the market value of a firm to the replacement cost of its physical assets)
r	(market or nominal) interest rate, yield, yield to maturity
R	(1) *as statistic*, correlation coefficient; (2) central-bank reserves (Federal funds); (3) reservation (wage)
r_S	holding-period yield for a corporate share (stock)
R^2	*as statistic*, squared correlation coefficient (measure of goodness of fit)
RFV	real future value or face value (of a bond)
RPV	real (discounted) present value
RXR	real exchange rate
rr	*real interest rate*
S	(1) savings; (2) supply; (3) (corporate) share or stock
s	savings rate
T	(1) tax; (2) transitory
tr	marginal transfer rate
tr_0	intercept in transfer function
TR	transfer payments
U	unemployment rate
w	wage rate
X	generic variable
XR	exchange rate
y	output of a firm
Y	gross domestic product (GDP)
$\tilde{Y}$	scaled output (GDP scaled by potential GDP $= Y/Y^{pot}$)
$\breve{Y}$	GDP in effective labor units ($\breve{Y} = Y/A_L L$)
Y^D	aggregate demand ($= AD$)
y^e	individual expected income
Y^e	aggregate expected income
Y_L	value of labor's share of GDP
Y_K	value of capital's share of GDP
y^P	individual permanent income

Y^P	aggregate permanent income
Y^{pot}	potential GDP
Y^S	aggregate supply ($= AS$)
Y^T	transitory income
YD	disposable income

Glossary

Entries correspond to terms emboldened in the main text – both those in ordinary font and small capitals. Bold entries in definitions indicate cross-references; numbers in square brackets refer to the section of the text in which the term is defined, explained, or first appears.

A

acyclical [5.3.2] having no regular relationship to the business cycle, usually said of a variable or time series.

adjusted capital [10.4.2] capital expressed in units of effective labor.

adjusted output [10.4.2] output expressed in units of effective labor.

advance estimates (of the U.S. **NIPA** accounts) [3.6.2] the earliest available estimates; released near the end of the first month after the end of the quarter (i.e., near the end of January, April, July, and October); compare **preliminary** and **final estimates**.

after-tax real wage [11.2.1] value of the real wage after income taxes have been withdrawn.

aggregate [1.2.1] a quantity calculated by summation over the whole economy or major sector.

aggregate demand [2.7] sum of all expenditures on goods and services for the whole economy.

aggregate-demand shock [17.1.1] exogenous change to the demand side of the economy – for example, from a change in profitability of investment or export demand.

aggregate income [2.3.2] sum of all incomes in the whole economy.

aggregate production function [9.2.1] the mathematical representation of the relationship between inputs to the production process and outputs, given technology, for the whole economy.

aggregate supply [2.7] sum of the value of all the output of goods and services for the whole economy.

aggregate-supply shock [17.1.1] exogenous change to the supply side of the economy – for example, from a change in the prices of a factor of production or technology.

annual rate of growth [G.10.1] percentage change of a quantity over a 1-year period or the percentage change over a longer or shorter period expressed as an annual equivalent.

annual rate of growth, compound [G.10.1] a growth rate annualized in such a way that increments to growth in one period are accounted for as themselves growing in subsequent periods.

annualization, simple [G.10.2] conversion of a rate expressed at a frequency less than or greater than one year to a rate per year by multiplying by an appropriate factor; for example, a monthly rate of interest is simply annualized by multiplying by 12.

annualized (annualization) [3.6.3, G.10.1] **1.** conversion of any flow expressed in time units shorter or greater than a year into the equivalent in time units of a year (e.g., $1 billion per quarter is *annualized* to $4 billion per year; **2.** specifically of growth rates, conversion of any growth rate into an annual growth rate of growth.

antilogarithm [G.11.1] inverse of a logarithm (e.g., $\text{antilog}(\log(x)) = x$).

appreciation (appreciate) [8.3.1] of a foreign exchange rate, an increase in the value of a currency relative to the value of the currency of another nation.

arbitrage [7.2.1] simultaneously buying and selling of closely related goods or financial instruments in different markets to take advantage of price differentials.

arbitrageur [7.2.1] one who engages in arbitrage.

arithmetic mean [G.4.2] a measure of central tendency in which values are summed and divided by their number; often simply called the **mean** or *average*.

asset [6.1.2] valuable thing (real or financial) owned; positive wealth, as opposed to **liability** or *debt*.

automatic (fiscal) policy [17.1.1] automatic stabilizers built into the design of the tax code and spending programs.

automatic stabilizers [13.2, 13.2.2] mechanisms that without conscious action tend to increase spending in a recession and decrease spending in an expansion, especially those built into the tax code or spending programs.

autonomous expenditure [13.1.3] expenditure exogenous to a model of aggregate demand: $Au \equiv I + G + NX$.

autonomous expenditure multiplier [13.2.1] ratio of the increase in aggregate demand to an increase in autonomous expenditure ($\mu_{Au}^{BB} = \frac{\Delta Y}{\Delta Au}$).

average product of capital [9.1.1] number of units of output per unit of capital (i.e., y/k or Y/K); synonym, **capital productivity**.

average product of labor [9.1.1] number of units of output per unit of labor (i.e., y/l or Y/L); synonym, **labor productivity**.

average propensity to consume [13.1.1] fraction of disposable income absorbed in consumption (i.e., C/YD); abbreviated apc.

average rate of growth [G.10.1] that rate of growth that, if steadily maintained, would carry a time series from a starting value to a finishing value in the time that separates them.

average tax rate [13.1.2] fraction of GDP taken by the government as taxes (i.e., T/Y).

B

backward-bending labor-supply curve [11.2.1] supply curve for labor that becomes negatively sloped at higher real-wage rates.

bad [3.5.4] opposite of *a good* – that is, a product that is undesirable.

balance of payments [2.2.2, 8.2] **1.** difference between payments into and out of a country; **2.** refers to *balance-of-payments accounts*, which record exports, imports, income, and asset flows of a country relative to foreign countries.

balance sheet [6.1.2] record of the assets, liabilities, and net worth of an economic entity or organization (household, firm, government, etc.).

balanced-budget multiplier [13.2.1] ratio of the increase in aggregate demand to an increase in government expenditure when taxes are adjusted to keep the budget balanced ($\mu_G^{BB} = \frac{\Delta Y}{\Delta G}|_{G=T}$).

balanced growth [10.4.1] **1.** in general: a growth path for an economy in which major quantities grow at steady and sustainable rates. **2.** in the absence of technological progress, a growth path in which all real aggregates grow at the same constant rate (i.e., their ratios are constant) and when the marginal products of the factors of production and, therefore, factor prices remain constant. **3.** in the presence of technological progress, growth path in which real GDP grows at the same constant rate as labor and capital adjusted for factor-augmenting technological progress, such that the marginal products and prices of each factors of production grow at constant (but perhaps different) rates consistent with the relationship: $n + \bar{\theta} = \hat{K} + \bar{\phi}$.

base period (of a price index) [4.1.1, G.8.2] the period for which expenditure shares are calculated.

base-weighted index [4.1.1] price index in which each rate of change of price of a component good is weighted by the share of expenditure on that good in a base period; synonym, **Laspeyres index**.

basis point [16.2.3] unit of measure of yields or interest rates equal to one-hundredth of a percentage point.

benchmark revision (of the U.S. **NIPA** accounts) [3.6.2] a   revision   conducted approximately every five years that updates sources and methods to produce new estimates, frequently making revisions for every period covered from the beginning of the accounts to the present; synonym, **comprehensive revision**.

black economy [3.5.3] economic transactions that are not directly reported to, or recorded by, government authorities because they are either illegal in themselves or involve the illegal avoidance of taxation or regulation (also known as the *shadow, hidden, underground,* or *black-market economy*).

Board of Governors of the Federal Reserve System [16.2.1] U.S.   government agency that together with the regional Federal Reserve Banks constitutes the central bank of the United States.

bond [6.3.1] a type of financial instrument – particularly, a promise to pay a definite stream of money in some fixed pattern, usually represented by a paper certificate or an entry in a broker's or government's books, that may be bought and sold on the open market.

bond price [6.3.1] actual price a bond commands on the current market; the present value of a bond; synonym, **market value** (of a bond).

boom [5.2.1] the period between the cyclical trough and cyclical peak, when economic activity is rising; synonym, **expansion**.

borrowing constraint [14.3] limitation on consumption resulting from an inability to borrow as much as a consumer would like at the current rate of interest; synonym, **liquidity constraint**.

Bretton Woods Agreement [16.6.2] international treaty that established a nearly worldwide system of fixed exchange rates; named for the resort in New Hampshire where it was signed in 1944.

broad credit channel (of monetary policy) [16.4.2] mechanism through which changes in monetary policy that affect market interest rates result in changes in balance sheets that, in turn, induce banks to ration credit quantitatively to firms or households; contrast **narrow credit channel**, **opportunity-cost (interest-rate) channel**, **exchange-rate channel**.

bubble [6.3.3] increase in the price of an asset out of proportion to the fundamental determinants of value; the situation in which an asset appreciates only because it is expected to appreciate further.

budget surplus (government's) [2.2.2] excess   of   government   revenue (taxes) over expenditures (expenditures on goods and services plus transfer payments).

business cycle [5.2.1] **1.** alternation in the state of the economy of a roughly consistent periodicity and with rough coherence between different measures of the economy; synonym, **cycle**; **2. complete**... [5.2.1] the period between a business-cycle peak and the following peak or between a trough and the following trough.

C

capacity-utilization rate [9.4.3] the ratio of aggregate (or sectoral) output to the productive capacity of the economy (or sector); synonym **scaled capital**.

capital [2.2.2, 9.1.1] physical (nonlabor) means of production that endure for more than one period; usually, long-lasting physical means of production; often refers to aggregate capital goods.

capital account (of the balance of payments) [8.2] record of the exchanges and other transfers of assets in to and out of a country.

capital-account balance [8.2.2] difference between acquisition of foreign assets and transfer of domestic assets to foreigners.

capital-account transactions [8.2.2] international transactions involving nonproduced, nonfinancial assets, including the rights to natural resources, and the sales and purchases of intangible assets (e.g., patents, copyrights, trademarks, franchises, and leases).

capital-augmenting technical progress [9.3.2] a form of technical progress indistinguishable from simply increasing the quantity of the capital input, holding technology constant.

capital consumption [3.4, 10.3.3] the amount of capital that is lost during the production process (the process of losing the value of capital through time); synonym, **depreciation** (**depreciate**).

capital deepening [10.4.1] increase in capital per worker.

capital gain [6.3.3, 7.3.2] increase in the market value of an asset.

capital good [3.1.2] individual instrument of production that is not used up in the current period, but endures for use in future periods.

capital intensity [10.4.1] amount of capital per unit of labor.

capital-labor ratio [10.4.1] amount of capital per worker.

capital loss [7.3.2] decrease in the market value of an asset.

capital productivity [9.3.1] output (or GDP) per unit capital; synonym, **average product of capital**.

capital, scaled [9.5.2] capital in actual use as a fraction of capital available; synonym, **capacity-utilization rate**.

capital services [3.4, 9.1.1] flow of useful services from the stock of capital goods.

capital share [9.2.3] portion of income or GDP in a production process attributed to the capital input.

capital widening [10.4.1] increase in total capital, holding capital per worker constant.

centered moving average [G.12.1] average of the current value of a time series with an equal number of lagging and leading values.

central bank [6.1.1, 16.2.1] bank (typically government-run) whose customers are commercial banks, other branches of government, or foreign entities – usually charged with maintaining clearing operations between banks, regulation of banks and other financial intermediaries, and monetary policy; in the United States, the **Federal Reserve System**.

central-bank reserves [16.1.1] credits on the accounts of commercial banks with the central bank plus **vault cash**.

ceteris paribus [1.3.2] Latin phrase meaning "other things equal" used to indicate that a change in an exogenous variable (or combination of exogenous variables) holds other exogenous variables and basic relationships constant while observing the induced changes in endogenous variables.

chain-weighted index [4.1.4] price index, typically a Fisher-ideal index, in which the base period for weights based on expenditure shares is updated each period, although the reference period remains constant.

Cobb-Douglas production function [9.2.2] specific mathematical form of a production function; in its aggregate form, written as $Y = AL^\alpha K^{1-\alpha}$, where $0 < \alpha < 1$.

coefficient of variation [G.4.3] standard deviation expressed as absolute ratio to the mean: $cv(X) = \left| \frac{stdev(X)}{\overline{X}} \right|$.

coincident indicator [5.2.3] time series that typically reaches its own peaks at or near the business-cycle peaks and reaches its own troughs at or near the business-cycle trough.

commodity money [6.3.2] money the value of which is embodied in a physical commodity (usually gold or silver); as opposed to *token money* or **fiat money**.

common logarithms [G.11.1] the exponent of 10 needed to express a given number – e.g., common logarithm of $57 = \log_{10}(57) = 1.756$, because $10^{1.756} \approx 57$; compare **logarithm, natural logarithm**.

common stock [6.3.3] fractional ownership shares in a corporation that entitle the owner to a share of the residual value of a company after all debts and contractual commitments to preferred stockholders have been settled (compare **corporate equities, preferred stock, shares, stock**).

comparable-worth laws [12.3.1] laws that dictate that wages and salaries in professions (usually dominated by women) must be equal to wages and salaries in other professions (usually dominated by men) that are regarded to be "comparable."

complements [7.2.1] pair of goods such that, when the price of the first good rises, the demand for the first good falls and the demand for the second good also falls; typically, complementary goods are ones that are used together – for example, bread and jam.

complements in production [15.1.1] complementary factors of production; a pair of factors of production such that, when if the price of one of them rises, its demand falls, and the demand for the second one also falls.

complete (business) **cycle** [5.2.1] the period between a business-cycle peak and the following peak or between a trough and the following trough.

compound annual rate of growth [G.10.1] a growth rate annualized in such a way that increments to growth in one period are accounted for as themselves growing in subsequent periods.

comprehensive revision (of the U.S. **NIPA** accounts) [3.6.2] a revision conducted approximately every five years that updates sources and methods and produces new estimates, frequently making revisions for every period covered from the beginning of the accounts to the present; synonym, **benchmark revision**.

constant returns to scale [9.1.1, G.16.1] a characteristic of a production function in which an equi-proportional change in factor inputs results in a change in output of the same proportion.

consumer durable goods [3.5.1] long-lasting goods (in U.S. national accounts lasting more than three years); a form of capital owned by consumers.

consumer goods (and services) [3.1.2] products aimed at purchase and consumption by individual people.

consumer nondurable goods [3.5.1] short-lived consumer goods (in U.S. national accounts lasting less than three years).

consumer price index (CPI) [4.2] base-weighted price index aimed to capture the price of the consumption bundles of typical consumers.

consumption expenditure [2.2.2] expenditure on consumer goods.

consumption function [13.1.1] relationship between consumption and (disposable) income or GDP; complement of the **savings function**.

consumption multiplier [13.1.4] ratio of the change in GDP to any of a number of changes in exogenous variables whose effect is transmitted through the consumption function – that is, the **autonomous expenditure multiplier** or the **government spending multiplier**; (abbreviated **multiplier**).

consumption-real wage [11.3.1] real wage defined as the number of typical consumption baskets that the wage will purchase: $(= \frac{w}{price\ of\ consumption\ basket})$.

contraction [5.2.1] period between the cyclical peak and the cyclical trough when economic activity is falling; synonyms, recession, **slump**; compare **depression, expansion**.

contractionary monetary policy [16.2.3] monetary policy aimed at reducing aggregate demand (synonyms, **restrictive** or **tight** monetary policy).

convergence [10.4.1] of economic growth, the process of the rates of GDP growth in different countries with common technology reaching a common level of GDP per worker (or per capita).

core rate of inflation [4.3.1] rate of inflation measured on a price index that excludes prices of food and energy.

corporate equities [6.3.3] fractional ownership shares in a corporation (synonyms, **stocks**, **shares**; compare **common stock**).

corporation [6.3.3] legal structure of firms in which the owners (i.e., the stockholders) have only limited liability.

correlation coefficient (R) [G.13.1] measure of the degree of conformity or covariation between data series, in which $R = +1$ indicates that changes in the series are perfectly positively proportional; $R = -1$, perfectly negatively proportional; $R = 0$, no systematic relationship; and any other value for R between -1 and $+1$, different degrees of conformity (a particular scaling of the **covariance**).

cost-of-living index [4.2.1] a price index that intends to reflect the expenditures of typical consumers.

cost-push inflation [15.1.1] inflation originating in changes in **supply factors**, especially in exogenous changes to the prices of factor inputs; compare to **demand-pull inflation**.

countercyclical [5.3.2] of time series, moving in the opposite direction to the business cycle – rising in recessions, falling in expansions.

counterfactual [10.2] adjective indicating that a situation is analyzed that did not in fact actually occur but is what *would* have occurred had things been different in specific ways.

counterfactual experiment [1.3.2] analysis in which specific facts are represented in a model to be different from what they actually are in the world in order to answer a *what-would-happen-if* question.

coupon [6.3.1] regular payments to the holder of a bond (usually quarterly, semiannual, or annual).

coupon rate [6.3.1] the coupon of a bond expressed as a percentage of the face value.

covariance [G.13.2] a measure of degree of conformity or covariation between data series analogous to the **variance** of a single series and related to the **correlation coefficient**.

CPI-U [4.2.1] consumer price index for all urban consumers.

CPI-W [4.2.1] consumer price index for wage earners.

credibility [15.3.5] of monetary or fiscal policy, trust that the public places in policymakers to carry through an announced or implied policy.

credit channel (of monetary policy) [16.1.2] mechanism through which changes in monetary policy that result in changes in balance sheets that, in turn, induce banks to ration credit quantitatively to firms or households; compare **broad credit channel** and **narrow credit channel**.

credit crunch [16.4.1] a tight monetary policy in which firms and households find it difficult to obtain credit even if they are willing to pay market interest rates for loans.

credit rationing [16.4.1] limitation by banks and other lenders of amount of credit available to borrowers, usually independently of the rate of interest borrowers are willing to bear.

creditor [6.1.2] a lender; the holder of a financial asset; compare **source of funds**.

cross-section [G.1.1] variable that ranges over various units (e.g., different people, countries, or firms) at particular time.

crowding in [17.2.3] a situation in which an increase in government expenditure results in higher private expenditure, especially higher investment spending; antonym, **crowding out**.

crowding out [13.A.3, 17.2.3] a situation in which an increase in government expenditure results in lower private expenditure, especially lower investment spending; antonym, **crowding in**.

cumulative process [16.3.1] with respect to inflation and rates of resource utilization or unemployment, an unstable situation in which a deviation of the real interest rate from the natural rate of interest results in accelerating changes in the same direction in prices and real quantities.

currency [6.1.1] money in its concrete form of banknotes and coins.

current account (of the balance of payments) [2.2.2, 8.2] record of the flows of exports, imports, and income from asset holdings into and out of a country.

current-account balance [3.7, 8.2.2] difference between exports and receipts of income from domestic holdings of foreign assets, on the one hand, and imports and payments of income on foreign holdings of domestic assets, on the other hand.

current-account deficit [2.2.2] negative current-account balance.

current-account surplus [2.2.2] positive current-account balance.

cycle (complete) [5.2.1] period between a peak and the following peak or between a trough and the following trough.

cycle [5.1] synonym, **business cycle**.

cyclical peak [5.1] high point of a business-cycle expansion, marking the end of the expansion and the beginning of a recession.

cyclical trough [5.1] low point of a business-cycle contraction, marking the end of the recession and the beginning of an expansion.

D

debt-financed deficit [16.1.1] government's budget deficit financed by the sale of government bonds.

debtor [6.1.2] a borrower; the holder of a financial liability; compare **use of funds**.

decreasing returns to scale [9.1.1] a characteristic of a production function in which an equi-proportional change in factor inputs results in a change in output of a smaller proportion.

default risk [7.3.1] the risk that the issuer of financial asset (borrower) will default and fail to pay the agreed principal and interest.

deflate [2.4.1] **1.** the process of converting a nominal value into a real value through dividing by the price level or converting to constant dollars; **2.** implementing a policy of **deflation** – a policy action that results in lower aggregate demand.

deflation [2.6.1] **1.** a fall in the general price level; synonym, **disinflation**. **2.** implementation of a policy aimed at reducing aggregate demand.

demand factors [15.1.2] in general, factors related to (aggregate) demand as distinct from (aggregate) supply; particularly with respect to the Phillips curve, factors related to (aggregate) demand, other than the unemployment rate or the rate of resource utilization, that shift the Phillips curve.

demand failure [12.3.1] demand insufficient to maintain full employment of labor or full capacity of capital.

demand-pull inflation [15.1.2] inflation originating in changes in **demand factors** – that is, in government spending or loose monetary policy; compare to **cost-push inflation**.

depreciation (depreciate) 1. [8.3.1] of a foreign exchange rate, a decrease in the value of a currency relative to the value of the currency of another country; **2.** [3.4, 10.3.3] of capital, the amount of capital that is lost during the production process (the process of losing the value of capital through time); synonym, **capital consumption**.

depression [5.2.1] a particularly severe **recession**.

detrended series [G.12.1] time series in which an estimate of the trend has been removed.

diminishing returns to factors of production [9.1.1] a characteristic of a production function in which successive increases in one factor input holding other factor inputs constant result in successively smaller increases in output.

discount [6.2.1] **1.** the act of calculating the present value of a future value using its opportunity cost in determining the appropriate scale factor; of financial assets, the application of discounting in this sense; **2.** to find the market price of a financial asset based on its face value, where the appropriate opportunity cost is given by the yield to maturity of a close substitute asset; **3.** the reduction of the market value of a financial instrument less than its face value in order to generate a positive yield to maturity, as in a *discount bond*; **4.** of a bond, selling at a price less than its face value.

discount bond, pure [6.3.1] a bond with a face value but without coupon (or interest) payments; the yield to maturity arises because the bond is sold at a discount with respect to its face value; for example, a U.S. Treasury bill; synonym, **zero-coupon bond**.

discount loans (or lending) [16.2.2] loans of reserves by the central bank to commercial banks or other regulated financial intermediaries.

discount policy [16.2.3] monetary policy governing the setting of the discount rate or the terms of borrowing from the **Discount Window**.

discount rate [6.2.1, 16.2.3] **1.** opportunity cost used to **discount** a future value when calculating a present value or to calculate a market value from the face value of a bond; **2.** rate of interest charged by the central bank on a discount loan.

Discount Window [16.2.3] institutional mechanism through which the Federal Reserve makes discount loans to banks and other financial intermediaries.

discouraged workers [12.2.3] subset of marginally attached, unemployed workers who offer a job-market related reason for not seeking work, such as believing that current employment prospects are so poor that a search would be fruitless.

discretion [16.5.2] of monetary policy, choosing policy actions as the best response to changing circumstances; contrast **policy rules**.

discretionary (fiscal) policy [13.2, 17.1.1] fiscal policy deliberately chosen to achieve a particular result; compare **automatic (fiscal) policy**.

disinflation [2.6.1] a fall in the general price level; synonym, **deflation**.

disposable income [2.3.2] income available after accounting for taxes and transfers.

disposable-income identity [2.3.2] national-accounting identity that states that disposable income is divided between consumption and saving: $YD \equiv Y - T + TR \equiv C + S$.

dividend yield [6.3.3] rate of return on corporate stock defined as the ratio of the annual dividend paid to the stock price.

dividends [6.3.3] payments of a portion of corporate profits to shareholders in proportion to the number of shares held.

domestic private sector [2.2.2] economy excluding the government and the foreign sector.

double coincidence of wants [6.1.1] necessary condition for *direct* barter: what the first party to a barter transaction wishes to sell, the second party wishes to buy (first coincidence); and what the first party wishes to buy, the second party wishes to sell (second coincidence).

double-entry bookkeeping [6.1.2] practice of recording wealth transactions in such a manner that any changes to wealth must be entered as two (or more changes) to assets, liabilities, or net worth in order to maintain the balance of the account (i.e., the **fundamental identity of accounting** – namely, *assets = liabilities + net worth*).

dynamic [1.3.2] of an economic model, involving time such that the current values of at least some variables depend on the past or expected future values of themselves or other variables.

dynamically inconsistent policy [16.5.2] policy that is optimal when viewed from an earlier time, but is predictably suboptimal when viewed from its actual time of execution; synonym, **time-inconsistent policy**.

E

earnings [6.3.3] revenues remaining to a corporation after payment of expenses; synonym, **profits**.

earnings/price (E/P) ratio [6.3.3] ratio of earnings of a corporation to its share price.

easy monetary policy [16.2.3] monetary policy aimed at increasing aggregate demand; synonyms, **expansionary** or **loose** monetary policy.

economic growth [1.1, 10.1] increase in the size of an economy, especially as measured by GDP.

economic model [1.3.2] representation of the economy, typically in the form of mathematical or graphical relations.

effective-exchange-rate index [8.3.2] index number measuring the appreciation or depreciation of the exchange rate against a basket of currencies, typically weighting changes in individual exchange rates by the importance of each countries' trade to the domestic economy (as a share of its total trade); synonym, **trade-weighted exchange-rate index**.

effective labor [10.4.2] labor measured in units of base-period labor to account for changes in labor productivity (e.g., if labor in period 1 has a productivity of 1, then, in period 2, 10 workers with a productivity of 1.5 are measured as an effective labor force of 15 period-1 workers.)

efficiency-wage hypothesis [12.3.1] general hypothesis that higher wage rates increase worker effort; compare **fair-wage hypothesis, nominal efficiency-wage hypothesis, real efficiency-wage hypothesis**.

efficient-markets hypothesis [7.2.2] hypothesis that there are no *systematically* exploitable arbitrage opportunities based on information that is publicly available to financial markets.

employment rate [9.4.3] fraction of the labor force in paid employment.

endogenous growth [10.5.3] growth that itself causes the technological possibilities to expand; fast growth that begets fast growth.

endogenous technological progress [10.3.1] technological progress that is a function of the economic growth itself.

endogenous variable [1.3.2, 13.1.3] variable determined within a particular system of the economy or within a model that represents that system.

Establishment Survey [12.2.1] part of a survey of firms (establishments) conducted by the Bureau of Labor Statistics to gather statistics related to employment.

ex ante [2.7] Latin for "before"; of economic decisions, taken from a planning or future-oriented perspective and, therefore, necessarily involving expected values of some variables and irreducible uncertainty.

ex ante (or **expected**) **real rate of interest** [6.2.2] market rate of interest adjusted for the rate of inflation expected at the time of making a loan or issuing a bond to obtain over the maturity of the loan or bond: $rr_t^e \approx r_t - \hat{p}_{t+1}^e$.

ex post [2.7] Latin for "after"; of economic decisions, taken from a realized or past-oriented perspective and, therefore, necessarily involving facts that are past and beyond further change (though not necessarily beyond improved measurement).

ex post **real rate of interest** [6.2.2] market rate of interest adjusted for the rate of inflation that actually obtained over the life of the loan or bond: $rr_t \approx r_t - \hat{p}_{t+1}$.

excess capacity [9.4.3] increment of capital redundant at current levels of production; synonyms, **spare capacity**, **unused capacity**.

excess reserves [16.2.3] central-bank reserves held by banks beyond the amount needed to meet statutory reserve requirements.

exchange rate [8.3.1] price of one currency in terms of another currency.

exchange-rate channel (of monetary policy) [16.6.2] mechanism through which changes in monetary policy that result in changes in exchange rates, in turn, affect real economic activity in the domestic economy; contrast **broad credit channel**, **narrow credit channel**, **opportunity-cost (interest-rate) channel**.

exchange-rate risk [8.4.3] risk of a capital loss (measured in the domestic currency) of an unexpected appreciation of the exchange rate.

exchange-rate-risk premium [8.4.3] additional yield required by holders of assets denominated in a foreign currency to compensate for **exchange-rate risk**.

exogenous technological progress [10.3.1] **1.** technological progress, the rate of which is independent of other economic factors; **2.** technological progress modeled as an exogenous variable.

exogenous variable [1.3.2, 13.1.3] variable determined outside a particular system of the economy or outside a model that represents that system.

expansion [5.2.1] the period between the cyclical trough and cyclical peak, when economic activity is rising; synonyms, **boom**, **recovery**.

expansionary monetary policy [16.2.3] monetary policy aimed at increasing aggregate demand; synonyms, **loose** or **easy** monetary policy.

expectations-augmented Phillips curve [15.3.2] an inverse relationship between changes in the rate of inflation and the unemployment rate or a direct relationship between changes in the rate of inflation and a measure of resource utilization; abbreviated **Phillips curve**.

expectations theory of the term structure of interest rates [7.4.2] explanation of the **term structure of interest rates** (i.e., of the pattern of **yields to maturity**) based on arbitrage among current and expected yields on assets of different maturities.

expenditure (or **product**) **method** (of measuring GDP) [3.6.1] measurement of GDP based on adding up the values of all the final goods and services produced in the economy.

export receipts [2.2.2] monetary values received in exchange for exported goods and services.

exports [2.2.2] goods sold to foreigners.

extrapolation [G.10.3] estimates of the value of a variable outside of the observed sample through the projection of a relationship measured or fitted to the observed sample data.

F

face value [6.3.1] the amount paid when a bond comes due or matures.

factor-augmenting technical progress [9.3.2] form of technical progress indistinguishable from simply increasing the quantity of the input of a particular factor of production holding technology constant; compare **capital-augmenting technical progress** and **labor-augmenting technical progress**.

factors of production [2.2.2, 3.2, 9.1.1] inputs to the production process; broadly **capital** and **labor**.

factors payments [2.2.2] incomes earned by owners of factors of production in respect of their use in the production process.

fair-wage hypothesis [12.3.1] version of the **efficiency-wage hypothesis** in which wages that are regarded as "fair" increase worker effort.

fallacy of composition [1.2.1] mistaken inference that what is true of the parts must be true of the whole.

fallacy of division [12.3.1] mistaken inference that what is true of the whole must be true of the parts.

FDI [8.2.2] abbreviation of **foreign direct investment** – for example, investment of a foreign firm in plant and equipment in the domestic economy or acquisition by a foreign firm of substantial ownership interest in domestic firms.

Fed, the [6.1.1] colloquial term for the **Federal Reserve System**.

Federal funds [7.6.1, 16.2.2] in the United States, central-bank reserves, particularly ones involved in overnight loans between commercial banks (the **Federal funds market**).

Federal funds market [7.6.1, 16.2.3] market in which commercial banks borrow central-bank reserves from, or lend central-bank reserves to, another bank (typically a market in overnight loans); synonym, **reserve market**.

Federal-funds rate [7.6.1, 16.2.2] rate of interest charged by one bank to another for the loan of central-bank reserves on the Federal-funds market.

Federal Open Market Committee (FOMC) [16.2.1] committee of the **Federal Reserve System**, consisting of the governors of the **Board of Governors** and a subset of the presidents of the **Federal Reserve Banks**, that determines the policy governing **open-market operations**.

Federal Reserve Bank [6.1.1, 16.2.1] one of twelve regional banks that together with the **Board of Governors** constitute the **Federal Reserve System**.

Federal Reserve System [6.1.1] **central bank** of the United States comprising the **Board of Governors** and twelve regional **Federal Reserve Banks**.

fiat money [6.3.2] money valued not for its material content but because it has been declared legal tender by the government; compare **commodity money**.

final estimates (of the U.S. NIPA accounts) [3.6.2] second revised estimates, released at the end of the third month after the end of the quarter (March, June, September, and December); compare **advance** and **preliminary estimates**.

final goods and services [3.1.2, 2.2.2] any good that leaves the firm sector (crosses the **production boundary**) in the period of measurement; synonym, **final product**.

final product [3.1.2, 2.2.2] any good that leaves the firm sector (crosses the **production boundary**) in the period of measurement; synonym, **final goods and services**.

financial account (of the balance of payments) [8.2.2] transactions recorded on the capital account involving domestic holdings of foreign assets and foreign holdings of domestic assets.

financial instrument [6.1.1] record (paper or electronic) that specifies a claim to a current or future valuable good – for example, to the repayment of a debt or to the privileges of ownership.

financial intermediary [6.1.1] firm whose business is buying and selling financial instruments or, equivalently, matching borrowers to lenders, **sources of funds** to **uses of funds**, or savers to spenders.

financial market [6.1.1] market in which financial instruments are bought and sold.

financial wealth [6.1.2] claims to payment (or transfers) of something valuable at some future time.

firm sector [2.2.2] part of the economy consisting of businesses involved in production or marketing of goods and services; firms may be organized in various ways, including as corporations and proprietorships.

first difference [G.5.2, G.12.1] one-period change in the value of a time-series variable.

fiscal drag [13.2.2] impulse toward lower aggregate demand generated when taxes increase as the result of higher aggregate demand in the face of a fixed tax schedule.

fiscal policy [1.4, 13.2] set of actions that determine the levels of government spending and taxes and that together determine the size of the government's budget deficit.

Fisher effect [7.5.2] point-for-point increase in the market rate of interest that results *ceteris paribus* from an increase in the expected rate of inflation (named for economist Irving Fisher).

Fisher hypothesis [7.5.2] empirical phenomenon in which a change in market rates of interest is associated approximately point for point with a change in the actual rate of inflation (named for economist Irving Fisher).

Fisher-ideal index [4.1.3] price index formed as the geometric average of the Laspeyres (base-weighted) and the Paasche (current-weighted) price indices for the same set of data (named for economist Irving Fisher).

fixed-exchange-rate regime [16.6.2] policy in which the exchange rate is maintained at a constant rate by the willingness of the central bank or treasury to buy or sell freely at that rate or by legal fiat.

flat tax [17.2.5] tax with a constant marginal tax rate.

floating exchange-rate regime [16.6.2] policy in which the exchange rate is determined (with minimal interference) by market forces.

flow [2.2.1, G.1.2] quantity per unit time.

flow of funds [6.1.1] movements of money and financial assets through the economy.

flow of funds account [6.1.2] account tracking the flow of funds.

foreign direct investment [8.2.2] investment of a foreign firm in plant and equipment in the domestic economy or acquisition by a foreign firm of substantial ownership interest in domestic firms; abbreviated **FDI**.

foreign exchange [16.2.2] **1.** market in which the currencies of different nations are traded; **2.** synonym for foreign currencies.

foreign-exchange market [8.3.1] network of banks, brokers, and dealers who trade national currencies against one another (e.g., buy euros for dollars or sell pounds sterling for yen).

foreign sector [2.2.2] part of the world economy (i.e., other countries) engaged in trade or financial exchange with the domestic economy; synonym, **rest of the world**.

foreign-sector deficit [2.3.3] excess of exports over imports; synonyms: **net exports, trade balance**.

frequency distribution [G.4.1] pattern formed by counting the number of instances in which data in a set take each possible value or range of values – for example, the **normal distribution**.

frequency of observation [G.1.2] time period in which data are recorded – for example, daily, weekly, quarterly, annually.

frictional unemployment [12.2.2] unemployment that persists even at the peak of the business cycle.

full employment [12.1] state in which every worker who wants to work at the going wage for work that he is qualified to do has a job.

functional finance [17.2.3] view that government budgets and financing decisions should not be judged by whether or not they balance, but by what effects they have on the economy.

fundamental identity of accounting [6.1.2] most basic relationship in accounting: *Assets ≡ Liabilities + Net Worth*.

fundamentals (, market) [6.3.3, 7.2.1] ideally, considerations that should determine the value of an asset under the unrealistic assumption that people are perfectly informed; factors that are reasonably related to the prospects of the firm to earn profits.

G

GDP [3.2] acronym for **gross domestic product**: the market value of the final goods and services produced by labor and property located within the borders of a country within a definite period.

GDP gap [Box 16.2] actual GDP expressed as a percentage of potential GDP; synonyms, **inflationary gap**, **output gap**.

GDP (implicit price) deflator [2.4.2] price index that converts nominal GDP to real GDP (= *nominal GDP/real GDP*).

general price level [4.1] the central tendency of prices in an economy, usually expressed as a price index.

geometric mean [G.4.2] for a number of data (N), the Nth root of their product.

globalization [8.1] process of increasing economic integration among countries, especially involving financial integration, flows of capital and labor, and trade in intermediate products involved in production.

GNP [3.3] abbreviation of **gross national product** – that is, market value of the final goods and services attributable to the factors of production owned by citizens of a particular country; contrast with **gross domestic product (GDP)**: GDP is produced within a country; GNP may be produced by resources owned by citizens outside of a country.

government budget deficit [2.3.3] excess of government spending on goods and services and transfer payments over revenues.

government expenditure [2.2.2] government spending on real goods and services (excluding transfer payments).

government sector [2.2.2] part of the economy including all levels of government.

government services [2.2.2] services provided by the government, usually economically valued but not priced in the market.

government's budget constraint [16.1.1] financing options for the government budget deficit – issuing bonds or monetary base ("printing money"): $G - (T - TR) = \Delta B^G + \Delta MB$.

gross domestic product [2.1] market value of the final goods and services produced by labor and property located within the borders of a country within a definite period; abbreviated **GDP**.

gross investment [3.4, 10.3.3] portion of GDP that is devoted to maintaining and increasing the stock of capital; compare **net investment**.

gross national income [3.7] total income received by the residents of a particular country.

gross national product [3.3] market value of the final goods and services attributable to the factors of production owned by citizens of a particular country; abbreviated *GNP*; contrast with **gross domestic product (GDP)**: GDP is produced within a country; GNP may be produced by resources owned by citizens outside of a country.

growth rate [G.10.1] proportionate (or percentage) rate of change per unit time.

growth recession [5.2.1, 15.2.3] period of slower-than-trend growth, usually lasting a year or more.

H

histogram [G.4.1] a graph of a **frequency distribution** that counts the number of values in a data set that fall within specific ranges.

holding-period yield [14.4.3] total return on an asset over a period, including both income (interest or dividends) and capital gains expressed as a percentage of the price of the asset at the beginning of the holding period.

homogeneity [G.5.1] of data, situation in which subsets of the data have the same values (to a sufficient close approximation for the purposes) for measures of central tendency and variability.

household sector [2.2.2] part of the economy including workers and consumers.

Household Survey [12.2.1] survey of households conducted by the Bureau of Labor Statistics to gather statistics related to employment and unemployment (part of the *Current Population Survey*).

human capital [3.5.1] acquired education, skills, and social relationships that increase the value of labor.

human wealth [14.2.2] present value of an individual's or group's expected future earnings discounted back to the present.

hyperinflation [17.2.1] very rapid inflation, often defined conventionally as inflation rates of more than 50 percent per month.

I

imperfect competition [9.1.2] market form in which firms (and sometimes workers) are able to choose the prices at which they sell their products (or supply labor), although the amount that they can sell at particular prices is constrained by demand for the product; *monopoly, oligopoly,* and *monopolistic competition* are some of the forms of imperfect competition; contrast **perfect competition**.

imperfectly competitive [15.3] characterized by **imperfect competition**.

implementation lag [16.5.2] delay between the decision to enact a policy and its execution; one element of the **inside lag**.

(implicit) rental rate [9.1.2] price of capital services; *implicit* whenever the capital goods are owned by the user of the services so that no actual payments are made and the rental rate is what the user *would* have to pay if the capital actually had to be rented.

import payments [2.2.2] monetary values paid in exchange for imported goods and services.

imports [2.2.2] goods purchased from a foreign country; compare **exports**.

impulse [5.3.1] in business-cycle analysis, a change in an exogenous variable that initiates a cyclical adjustment.

income effect [11.2.1] in general, change in demand or supply owing to a change in income holding relative prices constant; in labor-market analysis, reduction in the supply of labor as the result of an increase in income holding the real-wage rate constant.

income method (of measuring GDP) [3.6.1] measurement of GDP based on adding up the incomes accruing to the owners of all the factors of production in the economy.

increasing returns to scale [9.1.1] a characteristic of a production function in which an equi-proportional change in factor inputs results in a change in output of a larger proportion.

index number [G.8.1] a number that converts the value of a data set to a proportion of a fixed reference value, typically but not always equal to 100 for a reference period or unit.

index of coincident indicators [5.2.3] average of several time series, converted to an index number, that typically reach their own peaks at or near the business-cycle peak and reach their own troughs at or near the business-cycle trough.

index of industrial production [9.4.3] the ratio of industrial production to capacity converted to an index number.

indices of economic indicators [5.2.3] averages of various time series, grouped into **leading**, **coincident**, and **lagging indicators**, averaged and converted into index numbers.

inflate [2.4.1] **1.** the process of converting a lower nominal value into the higher constant dollars of another year by multiplying by the change in a price index; **2.** implementing a policy of **inflation** – a policy action that results in higher aggregate demand and especially in a higher price level.

inflation [2.6.1] increase in the **general price level**.

inflation-indexed security [Box 6.1] bond in which the face value is adjusted to compensate for inflation over its life.

inflation tax [17.2.1] revenues implicitly earned by the government through reducing private wealth by issuing a new monetary base, possibly increasing the price level, or by allowing inflation to reduce the *real* value of the government's debt.

inflationary gap [Box 16.2] actual GDP expressed as a percentage of potential GDP; synonyms, **GDP gap**, **output gap**.

inflow-outflow identity [2.3.4] national-accounting identity that asserts that value of inflows into the domestic private sector must equal outflows from the domestic private sector: $I + G + TR + EX \equiv S + T + IM$.

inflows [2.3.4] in the circular flow of income and expenditure, expenditures that provide monetary flows to the domestic private sector: investment, government expenditure, transfer payments, and exports.

initial public offering [14.4.3] first-time sale of newly created shares in a corporation; acronym, **IPO**.

input [2.2.2, 9.1.1] real goods or services used up in the production process creating other goods or services for sale (i.e., **output**).

inside lag [16.5.2] the delay in the implementation of an economic policy comprising the **recognition lag** and the **implementation lag**.

insider/outsider model of unemployment [12.3.1] model in which unemployment exists because already employed workers (*insiders* to firms) push for wage rates higher than those that would allow firms to profitably hire unemployed workers (*outsiders*).

intensive form (of a production function) [10.4.2] production function in which input and output quantities are expressed as ratios to one of the factors of production (typically labor) to reduce the function to a simpler relationship.

interest rate [6.2.1] payments for the use of money expressed as a percentage of the purchase price or principal of loan, bond, or other financial instrument; compare **yield**.

interest-rate channel (of monetary policy) [16.4.1] mechanism through which changes in monetary policy result in changes in interest rates that, in turn, induce firms to reevaluate the present value of investment projects and hence to alter their investment spending and aggregate demand; synonym, **opportunity-cost channel**; contrast **broad credit channel**, **exchange-rate channel**.

interest-rate risk [7.3.2] of a bond, the risk of capital gains or losses as a result of changes in interest rates (or bond price) between the point of purchase and the point of sale; synonym, **price risk**.

intermediate goods and services (intermediate product) [2.2.2, 3.1.2] produced good that is used up in the process of producing other goods or services in this period.

internal rate of return [14.4.1] that rate of discount that makes the future stream of income generated by a capital project just equal to its cost of acquisition.

interpolation [G.2.2] calculation of a missing value within a sample based on the relationship of the data available within the sample.

investment [2.2.2, 3.1.2] flow of new physical means of production; the acquisition of newly produced capital goods.

investment accelerator [14.5.2] relationship in which an increase in the capacity to produce GDP requires an increment to the capital stock (investment) *higher* than the desired increase in GDP with the result that the induced investment provides additional (accelerating) stimulus to aggregate demand.

investment function [13.3.1] inverse relationship between the real interest rate and real investment.

investment grade [7.3.1] of bonds, having low default risk (Standard & Poors' ratings BBB or higher and similar ratings for other agencies).

involuntary unemployment [12.1] situation in which a worker is willing and able to work at a job for which he is qualified at the going wage but is not in fact employed; a situation in which an unemployed worker's **reservation wage** is lower than the real-wage rate.

IOU [6.1.1] literally "I owe you"; a general expression of indebtedness or the instrument of indebtedness.

iron law of wages [10.3.2] doctrine in classical political economy that holds that the pressure of population growth will force real-wage rates to the subsistence level.

IS curve [13.3.3] locus of all combinations of real rates of interest and aggregate demand for which plans to invest, given other flows of funds into the domestic private sector, are compatible with plans to save, given other flows of funds away from the domestic private sector.

J

job creation [12.3.3] opening of new workplaces by firms; compare **job destruction**.

job destruction [12.3.3] closing of existing workplaces by firms; compare **job creation**.

junk bond [7.3.1] pejorative term for bonds with a **speculative** rating for default risk – that is, bonds rated below **investment grade**; bonds having a high default risk (Standard & Poors' ratings BB or below and similar ratings for other agencies).

L

labor [9.1.1] human input to production measured in number of workers or worker-hours.

labor-augmenting technical progress [9.3.2] a form of technical progress indistinguishable from simply increasing the quantity of the labor input holding technology constant.

labor demand [11.1.1] need of firms, typically inversely related to the real-wage rate, for a labor input to the production process.

labor-demand curve [11.1.1] inverse relationship between firms' demand for labor and the real-wage rate.

labor force [9.4.3, 11.2.3] the number of people who wish to be in paid employment.

labor-force participation [11.2.2] fraction of the working-age population who are either employed or involuntarily unemployed.

labor hoarding [9.4.2] retention of workers redundant to the production process, typically in anticipation that the costs of firing and then rehiring when demand increases are greater than the costs of using labor inefficiently while demand is slack.

labor productivity [9.3.1] GDP per unit of labor; synonym, **average product of labor**.

labor, scaled [9.5.2] labor in actual use as a fraction of labor available; ratio of labor to the labor force; synonym, **employment rate**.

labor share [9.2.3] portion of income or GDP in a production process attributed to the labor input.

Laffer curve [17.2.5] relationship between tax rates and the revenues that they generate in which, at tax rates of 0 or 100 percent, revenues are zero; while at some tax rate in between, revenues reach a maximum; named for economist Arthur Laffer.

lagging indicator [5.3.2] time series that typically reaches its own peaks after the business-cycle peak and reaches its own troughs after the business-cycle trough.

Laspeyres index [4.1.1] price index in which each rate of change of price of a component good is weighted by the share of expenditure on that good in a base period (so named for statistician Ernst Louis Etienne Laspeyres); synonym, **base-weighted index**.

law of motion [10.3.2] dynamic equation governing the path of a time series.

law of one price [8.4.2] relationship in which the prices of the same good in different locations, measured in a single currency, must differ by no more than the costs (e.g., of transportation) of moving the goods from the market in which they are cheap to the one in which they are dear; in short, the price of any good adjusting for transactions costs is equal everywhere.

leading indicator [5.3.2] time series that typically reaches its own peaks before the business-cycle peak and reaches its own troughs before the business-cycle trough.

"leaning against the wind" [16.5.1] monetary policy of loosening policy when the economy slows and tightening it when the economy booms.

learning-by-doing [10.5.3] situation in which productivity rises with increasing experience of production, holding other things equal.

legal tender [6.3.2] monetary instrument that in law must be accepted to discharge debts denominated in units of that instrument – for example, under U.S. law, the Federal Reserve note is legal tender for debts denominated in dollars.

lender of last resort [16.2.1] function of central banks to maintain liquidity for sound banks when other sources of liquidity are unavailable.

liabilities [6.1.2] debt; things owed; negative wealth; contrast **assets**.

life-cycle hypothesis [14.2.1] theory that consumption is determined by a plan that accounts for the expected pattern of income over a lifetime; closely related to the **permanent-income hypothesis**.

life-cycle wealth [14.2.2] expected present value of all human, real, and financial wealth over a lifetime.

liquidity [6.3.1] ease of buying or selling, especially of financial assets, often implying buying or selling at the current price.

liquidity constraint [14.3] limitation on consumption resulting from an inability to borrow as much as a consumer would like at the current rate of interest; synonym, **borrowing constraint**.

LM curve [7.A.2] locus of all combinations of real rates of interest and aggregate demand for which the demand for money equals the supply of money.

loan [6.1.1] funds given by one party (the lender) to another party (the borrower) to be repaid at a later date, usually with interest.

logarithm [G.11.1] of a number, the power (or exponent) to which a given base must be raised to produce that number; compare **common logarithm**, **natural logarithm**.

logarithmic graph [2.5] graph with one or both axes measured as the logarithm of the root variable.

logarithmic scale [G.11.4] the scale of the axis of a graph measured as the logarithm of the root variable in which equal distances represent the same ratios of values; synonym, **ratio scale**.

loose monetary policy [16.2.3] monetary policy aimed at increasing aggregate demand; synonyms, **expansionary** or **easy** monetary policy.

long run [9.4.1] horizon for economic analysis in which all factors of production are free to adjust and the economy is free to reach equilibrium; the long run is not a specific period of time but a changing state toward which the economy adjusts.

lump-of-labor fallacy [11.3.2] the false belief that increases in labor productivity are detrimental to workers in the long run, because fewer workers can produce the existing output. It is fallacious because it assumes that there is only a fixed amount of work to be done (the lump of labor) rather than noting that increased productivity permits greater new production that can absorb workers made redundant in particular industries.

M

M1 [6.3.2] U.S. monetary aggregate (often with analogue in other countries) the main components of which are currency, checkable deposits at banks, and travelers' checks.

macroeconomic equilibrium [2.7] situation when plans of people to consume are coordinated *ex ante* with plans of firms to produce or, equivalently, when plans of savers are coordinated *ex ante* with plans of investors.

macroeconomic fluctuations [1.1] variations in macroeconomic activity, often identified with the business cycle.

macroeconomics [1.2.1] study of the economy taken as a whole; contrast with **microeconomics**, study of a part of the economy (e.g., particular people, households, firms, markets), taking the remainder as given.

marginal cost [9.1.2] small increase in the cost of the factors of production attributable to a unit increase in output; abbreviated **MC**.

marginal product of capital [9.1.2] small increase in output attributable to a unit increase in the capital input; abbreviated **mpk** (for a single firm) or **mpK** (in aggregate).

marginal product of labor [9.1.2] small increase in output attributable to a unit increase in the labor input; abbreviated **mpl** (for a single firm) or **mpL** (in aggregate).

marginal propensity to consume [13.1.1] rate at which consumption increases when (disposable) income is increased by a small increment; abbreviated **mpc**.

marginal propensity to save [13.1.1] the rate at which savings increases when (disposable) income is increased by a small increment; abbreviated **mps**.

marginal revenue [9.1.2] small increase in revenue attributable to the sale of a unit increase in output; abbreviated **MR**.

marginal tax rate [11.2.1, 13.1.2] fraction of an additional dollar of income that is paid as taxes.

marginally attached workers [12.2.3] people who indicate that they desire to work, are ready to work, and have looked for work sometime in the recent past, but who are not now working or actively seeking work.

market value (of a bond) [6.3.1] actual price a bond commands on the current market; the present value of a bond; synonym, **bond price**.

maturity [6.3.1] of bonds, date at which a bond pays off its face value and ceases to be a liability to its issuer or an asset to its holder.

mean [G.4.2] measure of central tendency in which values are summed and divided by their number; synonyms, **arithmetic mean**, *average*.

means of final payment [6.1.1] characteristic function of money that it terminates indebtedness.

means of transactions [6.1.1] characteristic function of money that it is used as an instrument to buy goods and services.

median [G.4.2] value that divides a set of values for a variable into an equal number above and below; when there are an odd number of values, the median is one of the set; when there are even numbers, the median is conventionally the mean of the highest value in the lower set and the lowest value in the higher set.

median income [2.4.2] income that marks the dividing line at which half the population receives more and half less than this income.

Mercantilism [8.1] economic doctrine dominant before the nineteenth century and frequently echoed in later policy discussions that holds that the object of policy is to enrich a country at the expense of other countries by promoting exports, limiting imports, and amassing precious metals or foreign exchange.

microeconomics [1.2.1] study of a part of the economy (e.g., particular people, households, firms, markets), taking the remainder as given; contrast with **macroeconomics**, study of the economy taken as a whole.

minimum-wage laws [12.2.2] laws specifying that wages must be paid at or above some statutory level.

mixed indicator [5.3.2] time series that when considered in relationship to the business cycle follows a *regular* pattern that is different from a **leading**, **coincident**, or **lagging indicator**.

modified balanced rate of growth [15.2.2] growth rate of GDP sustainable along a balanced growth path modified to account for a changing participation rate; compare **balanced growth**.

monetarism [16.A.1] economic doctrine that, although the supply of money affects only the general price level and no real quantities in the long run, changes in the supply of money are the main source of real fluctuations in the economy in the short run; particularly associated with the economist Milton Friedman.

monetary aggregates [6.3.2] alternative measures of the stock of money in the economy; compare **M1** and **monetary base**.

monetary base [6.3.2, 16.1.1] narrowest monetary aggregate, consisting of **currency** plus **central-bank reserves**; abbreviated **MB**.

monetary-base multiplier [16.A.2] ratio of a wider monetary aggregate (e.g., M1) to the monetary base.

monetary flows [2.2.2] the flows of **monetary instruments** that move in the opposite direction to the flows of real goods and services or **financial instruments** in the circular flow of income and the flow of funds.

monetary instruments [6.1.1] currency or other transactions media recognized as legal tender or other assets closely related to such recognized assets.

monetary policy [1.4, 16.1] government actions that aim to influence macroeconomic performance through the manipulation of financial portfolios and the prices of financial assets (interest rates); policies concerned with the government's financial portfolio and the configuration of interest rates.

monetization of the deficit [16.1.1, 17.2.1] financing government expenditure through the creation of additional monetary base ("printing money").

money illusion [12.3.1, 16.4.1] mistaking a change in a nominal value for a change in a real value.

money market [6.3.1] market for shorter-term financial instruments ("money" here does not refer to currency or monetary aggregates, but to bonds with maturities of usually less than one year).

multifactor productivity [9.2.2, 9.3.1] measure of productivity that accounts for both labor-augmenting and capital-augmenting technical progress; a weighted average of labor and capital productivity; synonym, **total factor productivity (TFP)**.

N

NAIRU [15.3.3] **1.** rate of unemployment that, if maintained, would result in an actual rate of inflation equal to the average expected rate of inflation; rate of unemployment that results in a constant rate of inflation; acronym for **non-accelerating inflation rate of unemployment**; compare **natural rate of unemployment. 2.** rate of resource utilization (e.g., as measured by scaled output) that, if maintained, would result in an actual rate of inflation equal to the average expected rate of inflation; rate of resource utilization that results in a constant rate of inflation; acronym for **non-accelerating inflation rate of resource utilization** (ambiguity of the acronym – "RU" referring to the rate of unemployment *or* resource utilization – is generally resolved by context).

narrow credit channel (of monetary policy) [16.4.1] mechanism through which changes in monetary policy result in changes in balance sheets independently of changes in opportunity costs or interest rates that, in turn, induce banks to ration credit quantitatively to firms or households; contrast **broad credit channel, opportunity-cost (interest-rate) channel, exchange-rate channel.**

national income [3.7] sum of all incomes paid to factors of production net of indirect taxes and subsidies; synonym, **net national income at factor cost**.

national income and product accounts [2.3] system of accounts that record GDP and its components from both the perspective of production and incomes; abbreviated **NIPA**.

natural logarithms [G.11.1] the exponent of e ($= 2.71828\ldots$) needed to express a given number – e.g., natural logarithm of 49, $\log_e(49) = 3.892$, because $e^{3.892} \approx 49$; also written as "log" or "ln"; compare **logarithm, natural logarithm.**

natural rate of growth [10.3.2] the rate of population growth; called "natural" because the rate of population growth determines the rate of growth of the labor force in the long run and a balanced growth path (abstracting from technical progress) cannot exceed the rate of growth of the labor force in the long run.

natural rate of unemployment [15.3.3] rate of unemployment that, if maintained, would result in an actual rate of inflation equal to the average expected rate of inflation; rate of unemployment that results in a constant rate of inflation; compare **NAIRU**.

negative externality [3.5.4] secondary effect of production, such as pollution, that generates a bad outcome for the economy or society outside of market exchanges.

negatively skewed [G.4.2] asymmetrical frequency distribution the mass of which is shifted to the low side; identified when the mean is lower than the median.

negotiable certificates of deposit [16.2.2] type of short-term bond issued by banks and bought and sold on secondary markets.

neoclassical growth model [10.4] a growth model based on a constant-returns-to-scale production function, perfect competition, and full employment.

net acquisition of financial assets [6.1.2] addition to holdings of financial assets that occurs when a sector saves more than it invests.

net exports [2.2.2, 8.1] excess of exports over imports; synonyms, **foreign-sector deficit**, **trade balance**.

net income from abroad [3.3] income receipts from the rest of the world less income payments to the rest of the world; $GNP - GDP = net\ income\ from\ abroad$.

net investment [3.4, 10.3.3] gross investment less depreciation; amount that investment adds to the stock of capital.

net national income at factor cost [3.7] sum of all incomes paid to factors of production net of indirect taxes and subsidies; synonym, **national income**.

net present value [14.4.1] with respect to investment projects, present value of future profits less current costs.

net taxes [2.2.2, 2.3.3] taxes less transfer payments.

net worth [6.1.2] the balance of assets less liabilities; value of a portfolio.

neutral [17.2.5] of taxes, situation in which the average rate of taxation remains constant across taxpayers with increasing incomes, so that the rich and poor pay taxes at the same proportionate rate; compare **progressive** and **regressive**.

new product bias [4.1.1] overstatement of rates of inflation as the result of failing to account for the introduction of new products.

no-arbitrage condition [7.4.2] any relationship of prices or interest rates that presumes that all arbitrage opportunities have been exploited; for example, the **expectations theory of the term structure of interest rates** or the **law of one price**.

nominal [2.4.1] not adjusted for changes in the general price level; contrast **real**.

nominal efficiency-wage hypothesis [12.3.1] version of the **efficiency-wage hypothesis** in which higher nominal wages increase worker effort; contrast **real efficiency-wage hypothesis**.

nominal value [2.4.1] value measured at current market prices; contrast **real value**.

nonaccelerating inflation rate of unemployment [15.3.3] rate of unemployment that, if maintained, would result in an actual rate of inflation equal to the average expected rate of inflation; rate of unemployment that results in a constant rate of inflation; acronym, **NAIRU**; (ambiguity of the acronym – the "RU" may refer either to *rate of unemployment* or to *resource utilization* – is generally resolved by context); compare **natural rate of unemployment**.

non-accelerating inflation rate of resource utilization [15.3.3] rate of resource utilization (e.g., as measured by scaled output) that, if maintained, would result in an actual rate of inflation equal to the average expected rate of inflation; rate of resource utilization that results in a constant rate of inflation; acronym, **NAIRU** (ambiguity of the acronym – the "RU" may refer either to *rate of unemployment* or to *resource utilization* – is generally resolved by context).

nonsense correlation [G.13.1, G.14.1] high measured correlation despite an absence of a genuine relationship between two variables; common in trending or **nonstationary** data.

nonsense regressions [G.15.3] the analogue of nonsense correlation in the regression context, an apparently tightly fitting regression despite the absence of a genuine relationship between variables; common in trending or **nonstationary** data.

nonstationary [G.5.2] of time series, a failure of data to be homogeneous, particularly a failure of the mean to remain stable in different subsamples; examples of nonstationary time series include those with a **trend** and the **random walk**; compare **stationary**.

normal frequency distribution [G.5] frequency distribution with a bell-shaped histogram, which is important because it occurs frequently in statistics since it is the limit of the average of different nonnormal distributions; also called *Gaussian*, after the mathematician Carl Gauss, who studied it.

O

OECD [10.5.1] acronym for the Organization of Economic Cooperation and Development, organization, based in Paris, of countries with highly developed economies.

Okun's law [15.2.3] relationship either between changes in the rate of unemployment or changes in the rate of resource utilization (e.g., scaled output) and the rate of growth of GDP in which there is a critical value of the GDP growth rate such that growth above that value results in falling unemployment rates (or rising rates of resource utilization) and growth below that rate results in the opposite; named for economist Arthur Okun.

Open Market Desk [16.2.3] office of the Federal Reserve Bank of New York that administers open-market operations.

open-market operation [16.2.3] sale or purchase of financial instruments (typically government bonds) in order to reduce or increase the supply of central-bank reserves to the banking system.

open-market purchase [16.2.3] purchase of financial instruments (typically government bonds) in order to increase the supply of central-bank reserves to the banking system; contrast **open-market sale**.

open-market sale [16.2.3] sale of financial instruments (typically government bonds) in order to reduce the supply of central-bank reserves to the banking system; contrast **open-market purchase**.

open-mouth operation [16.2.3] announcement of target for interest rates that becomes a focal point for market trading in bonds and, hence, is achieved without actually engaging in open-market operations.

opportunity cost [3.2, 6.2.1, 11.2.1] the value of the best alternative choice that a particular choice or action forecloses.

opportunity-cost channel (of monetary policy) [16.4.1] mechanism through which changes in monetary policy result in changes in interest rates that, in turn, induce firms to reevaluate the present value of investment projects and hence to alter their investment spending and aggregate demand; synonym, **interest-rate channel**; contrast **broad credit channel, narrow credit channel, exchange-rate channel**.

Organization of Economic Cooperation and Development [10.5.1] organization, based in Paris, of countries with highly developed economies; acronym **OECD**.

outflows [2.3.4] in the circular flow of income and expenditure, expenditures that provide monetary flows away from the domestic private sector: savings, taxes, and imports.

output [2.2.2, 9.1.1] end result of the production process; the product (goods or services) into which inputs have been transformed for sale by the firm.

output gap [Box 16.2] actual GDP expressed as a percentage of potential GDP; synonyms, **GDP gap, inflationary gap**.

output scaled by potential output [9.5.2, 15.1] output expressed as a percentage of potential GDP: $\tilde{Y} = \frac{Y}{Y_{pot}}$; short-form synonym, **scaled output**.

outside lag [16.5.2] delay in the effective operation of a policy action owing to the fact that economic mechanisms in the economy do not work instantly; synonym, **transmission lag**; contrast **inside lag**.

P

Paasche price index [4.1.2] price index in which each rate of change of price of a component good is weighted by the share of expenditure on that good in the current period (named for the statistician Hermann Paasche); synonym, **current-weighted price index**.

par [6.3.1] of a bond, selling at a price equal to its face value.

paradox of thrift [13.4] higher *rates* of savings *ceteris paribus* reduce aggregate demand such that actual *levels* of saving do not increase and, therefore, the resources available for investment do not increase, even though consumption is reduced.

parameter [1.3.2] number that characterizes behavior or the relationship between variables in a model.

participation rate [11.2.3] the labor force as a percentage of the relevant population.

PCE deflator [4.2] acronym for the **personal consumption expenditure deflator**: price index used in the national accounts to convert nominal to real personal consumption expenditures; an alternative measure of consumer prices to the CPI.

P/E ratio [6.3.3] abbreviation of **price/earnings ratio**; an inverse measure of the yield of a stock calculated as the ratio of its price to some measure of its earnings (sometimes averaged over a longer period).

peak, cyclical [5.1] high point of a business-cycle expansion marking the end of the expansion and the beginning of a recession.

percent (percentage) [G.1.2] a value expressed as fraction of another in units of hundredths.

percentage point [G.1.2] unit equal to one hundredth (1/100).

perfect capital market [16.4.1] a market in which anyone may borrow or lend as much as he likes at the current rate of interest; a perfectly competitive financial market.

perfect competition [9.1.2] market form in which firms (and sometimes workers) are able to buy or sell as much as they like at the *market price*, but are unable to set a price different from the market price; firms (or workers) are referred to as "price takers"; contrast **imperfect competition**.

perfect substitutes [7.2.1] goods that are such close substitutes that any small difference in price shifts demand completely to the cheaper good.

permanent income [14.2.2] income stream generated from the earnings of **life-cycle wealth** or equivalently as the maximum amount that can be withdrawn from life-cycle wealth without reducing its value.

permanent-income hypothesis [14.2.1] theory that consumption is based on an estimate of **permanent income**. According to the permanent-income hypothesis, transitory increases in income should be saved, and consumption smoothed over time; closely related to the **life-cycle hypothesis**.

personal consumption expenditure deflator [4.2] price index used in the national accounts to convert nominal to real personal consumption expenditures; an alternative measure of consumer prices to the CPI; acronym, **PCE**.

Phillips curve, expectations-augmented [15.3.2] an inverse relationship between changes in the rate of inflation and the unemployment rate or a direct relationship between changes in the rate of inflation and a measure of resource utilization; abbreviated **Phillips curve**.

policy lag [16.5.2] delay in the execution of policy between the need and final implementation; compare **inside** and **outside lag**.

policy rule [16.5.2] rule relating objective conditions in the economy to particular policy actions; contrast **discretion**.

population, principle of [10.3.2] T. Robert Malthus's principle that, because population, given adequate subsistence, grows exponentially and subsistence grows arithmetically (or, at least, more slowly), population is essentially always at its maximum sustainable level.

portfolio investment [8.2.2] in the international accounts, sale or acquisition of financial assets too small to be considered **foreign direct investment (FDI)**; in U.S. practice, sale or purchase of non-equity foreign financial assets, such as bonds, and shares short of a 10 percent threshold.

portfolio reallocation [6.1.2] shift of funds from one financial instrument to another.

positive externality [17.2.3] secondary effect of production that generates a good outcome for the economy or society outside of market exchanges.

positively skewed [G.4.2] asymmetrical frequency distribution the mass of which is shifted to the high side; identified when the mean is higher than the median.

potential output [9.5.1, Box 16.2] **1.** estimate of the amount of GDP that could be produced if the entire labor force and the entire capital stock were fully employed at their economically optimal levels. **2.** level of GDP consistent with **NAIRU**.

PPI [4.2] acronym for the **producer price index**: base-weighted price index aimed to capture the general level of prices of producers or some subset of producers.

preferred stock [6.3.3] share in a corporation that receives priority in the payment of dividends but that does not provide voting rights to its owner.

preliminary estimates (of the U.S. **NIPA** accounts) [3.6.2] first revised estimates, released at the end of the second month after the end of the quarter (February, May, August, and November); compare **advance** and **final estimates**.

premium [6.3.1] of a bond, selling at a price greater than its face value.

present discounted value [6.2.1] value today of the future benefits or value, given the relevant opportunity cost (interest rate or yield); "discounted" refers to the calculation through discounting the future value by the opportunity cost; synonym, **present value**.

present value [6.2.1] value today of the future benefits or value, given the relevant opportunity cost (interest rate or yield); synonym, **present discounted value**.

price risk [7.3.2] of a bond, the risk of capital gains or losses as a result of changes in interest rates (or bond price) between the point of purchase and the point of sale; synonym, **interest-rate risk**.

price factor [2.4.2, 4.1.1, G.8.2] ratio of price levels in different periods (usually measured by a price index) used to convert nominal monetary values in one period into the monetary values of another period: the price factor used to convert period t prices to those of a reference period is $pf_t = p_{reference}/p_t$.

price index [4] (weighted average) of various prices, typically representative of consumption or production of a group or sector, expressed as an index number; for example, the CPI and the GDP price deflator are price indices.

price setter [9.1.2] an economic actor (particularly a firm) with the power to set its own prices, taking account of the effect on demand for its product; an imperfect competitor; contrast **price taker**.

price taker [9.1.2] an economic actor (particularly a firm) that is able to buy or sell as much as it likes at the market price; a perfect competitor; contrast **price setter**.

price/earnings ratio [6.3.3] an inverse measure of the yield of a stock calculated as the ratio of its price to some measure of its earnings (possibly averaged over a longer period); abbreviation, **P/E ratio**; **earnings/price (E/P) ratio**.

primary deficit [17.2.2] the difference between, on the one hand, government spending on goods, services, and transfer payments, but excluding spending on interest payments and, on the other hand, government revenues.

primary labor markets [11.3.3] usually better-paid and more secure jobs requiring specific skills.

prime-age males [11.2.3] men in their peak working years, ages 24–54.

principle of comparative advantage [8.1] principle that economic output is maximized worldwide if each country specializes in the production of those goods that it is relatively more efficient at producing even if it is not absolutely more efficient than other countries.

principle of population [10.3.2] T. Robert Malthus's principle that, because population, given adequate subsistence, grows exponentially and subsistence grows arithmetically (or, at least, more slowly), population is essentially always at its maximum sustainable level.

principle of similarity and replacement [6.2.1] principle that a good or asset may be valued by finding the replacement cost of a sufficiently similar good or asset.

private-sector deficit [2.3.3] excess of private investment expenditure over savings.

procyclical [5.3.2] of time series, moving in the same direction as the business cycle – rising in expansions, falling in recessions.

producer price index [4.2] base-weighted price index aimed to capture the general level of prices of producers or some subset of producers; acronym, **PPI**.

product-expenditure identity [2.3.1] national-accounting identity that states that the value of production equals the value of expenditure: $Y + M \equiv C + I + G + EX$.

product-real wage [11.3.1] number of units of the good the firm produces that the wage will purchase $(= \frac{w}{price\,of\,product})$.

production boundary [2.2.2] conceptual division between the **firm sector** and the rest of the economy; a good becomes a *final* good when it crosses the production boundary.

production function [9.1.1] mathematical relationship between output (of particular goods or GDP) and the inputs (factors of production) used to produce it.

profits [3.2] excess of revenues of a firm over its costs.

progressive [17.2.5] of taxes, situation in which the average rate of taxation rises across taxpayers with increasing incomes, so that the rich pay taxes at proportionately higher rates; compare **neutral** and **regressive**.

propagation mechanism [5.3.1] in business-cycle analysis, the mechanism through which an exogenous impulse is converted into further endogenous adjustments in the economy, perhaps generating a cycle.

public offering [14.4.3] with respect to stocks, the sale of new shares to the public.

purchasing power of money [2.6.1] the value of money measured in terms of real goods and services.

purchasing-power parity [2.4.2, 8.4.2] situation when the cost of goods or services is equal in different countries once the currency of one country has been converted into the currency of the other; a generalized version of the **law of one price**.

pure discount bond [6.3.1] a bond with a face value but without coupon (or interest) payments; the yield to maturity arises because the bond is sold at discount with respect to its face value; for example, a U.S. Treasury bill; synonym, **zero-coupon bond**.

Q

quality change bias [4.1.2] underestimation of the rate of inflation estimated using a Paasche index, owing to a failure to account for quality change in the goods making up the index.

quid pro quo [3.1.1] Latin for "something for something"; the test of whether or not something is economically a product is quid pro quo – that is, is something given in exchange for it?

R

R^2 [G.15.1] squared correlation coefficient (R); a measure of the goodness of fit of a regression equation equal to the ratio of the variation explained by the equation to the total variation in the explained variable; $0 \leq R^2 \leq 1$ and the closer R^2 to 1, the better the fit; sometimes called the *coefficient of determination*.

R&D [10.3.1] acronym for **research and development**; type of investment expenditure devoted to the discovery and development of new products.

random variable [1.3.2] variable the precise value of which cannot be determined in advance, but the possible values of which may conform to a stable (and known) frequency distribution.

random walk [5.3.1] **1.** time series in which the best expectation of the next value is that it will be the same as the current value; **2.** ... *with a drift*, a time series in which the values form a random walk around a trend growth path.

ratio scale [G.11.4] the scale of the axis of a graph measured as the logarithm of the root variable in which equal distances represent the same ratios of values; synonym, **logarithmic scale**.

real [2.4.1] adjusted for changes in the general price level; contrast **nominal**.

real efficiency-wage hypothesis [12.2.2] version of the **efficiency-wage hypothesis** in which higher real wages increase worker effort; contrast **nominal efficiency-wage hypothesis**.

real exchange rate [8.3.2] that exchange rate that reflects the effective purchasing power of each currency.

real flow [2.2.2] real value of a quantity per unit time.

real rate of interest [6.2.2] **1.** *ex ante* (or **expected**) ..., market rate of interest adjusted for the rate of inflation expected at the time of making a loan or issuing a bond to obtain over the life of the loan or bond: $rr_t^e \approx r_t - \hat{p}_{t+1}^e$. **2. ex post** ..., market rate of interest adjusted for the rate of inflation that actually obtained over the life of the loan or bond: $rr_t \approx r_t - \hat{p}_{t+1}$.

real value [2.4.1] value corrected for changing prices – that is, a value expressed in constant units of money of a particular time.

real-wage rate [9.1.2] value of the wage rate in real terms (either in units of a particular good or in constant monetary units); often written as w/p; compare **consumption-real wage** and **product-real wage**.

real-wage floor [12.2.2] lower bound to how far the real wage can fall.

real wealth [6.1.2] **1.** things owned that provide direct utility or productive services; frequently, but not exclusively tangible; contrast with **financial wealth**; **2.** real value of all forms of wealth.

recession [5.2.1] period between the cyclical peak and the cyclical trough, when economic activity is falling; synonyms, **slump**, **contraction**; compare **depression**, **expansion**.

recognition lag [16.5.2] delay in policy execution owing to the delay between a change in the economic situation and its perception; one element of the **inside lag**.

recovery [5.2.1] **1.** the period between the cyclical trough and cyclical peak, when economic activity is rising; synonyms, **boom**, **expansion**. **2.** sometimes in more limited sense, the period between the trough and when the economy regains either (1) the level of activity experienced at the previous peak or (2) the level it would have experienced had it remained on trend.

reference period [2.4.1, 4.1.1] period (or other economic unit) to which an index number is calibrated by setting it to some arbitrary value – typically, to 100.

reference value [G.8.1] value of a variable in the **reference period**.

regression line [G.15.1] best-fitting (linear or nonlinear) line through a set of data, estimated by choosing coefficient values that minimize the variance of the data around the selected line.

regressive [17.2.5] of taxes, situation in which the average rate of taxation falls across taxpayers with increasing incomes, so that the poor pay taxes at proportionately higher rates; compare **neutral** and **progressive**.

regrettables [3.5.4] goods or services (e.g., security systems) that are purchased not for their intrinsic value but to avoid some cost that we regret having to face.

relative efficiency-wage hypothesis [12.3.1] version of the **nominal efficiency-wage hypothesis** in which wages that are high relative to a norm (e.g., to the wages of other types of workers or to similarly placed workers in other firms or to past wages) increase worker effort.

rental rate [9.1.2] price of capital services; compare **implicit rental rate**.

required reserves [16.2.3] holdings of central-bank reserves needed to meet **reserve requirements**.

research and development [10.3.1] type of investment expenditure devoted to the discovery and development of new products; acronym, **R&D**.

reservation wage [11.2.2] opportunity cost of working compared to not working – that is, the real wage that is high enough to make it just worthwhile for a worker to participate in the labor force.

reserve market [7.6.1, 16.2.3] the market in which commercial banks borrow central-bank reserves from, or lend central-bank reserves to, another bank (typically a market in overnight loans); synonym, **Federal funds market**.

reserve operating procedure [16.A.2] mechanism of implementing monetary policy through targeting a path for the expansion or contraction of central-bank reserves available to the banking system (implemented in the United States 1979–1982).

reserve requirement [16.2.2] regulation requiring banks to hold central-bank reserves equal to some fraction of the value of some particular type of bank liability; for example, in the United States, banks are required to hold reserves equal to 10 percent of their checkable deposits.

reserves, central-bank [16.1.1] credits on the accounts of commercial banks with the central bank.

restrictive monetary policy [16.2.3] monetary policy aimed at reducing aggregate demand; synonyms, **contractionary** or **tight** monetary policy.

retained earnings [6.3.3] earnings of firms that are not distributed as dividends, but reinvested in the firm.

risk premium [7.3.1] increment to the yield required by lenders (bond buyers) to compensate them for the various risks of holding the asset.

Ricardian equivalence [17.2.4] proposition that *ceteris paribus* the pattern of government spending, the mode of finance – taxes or debt finance – has no real effect on the economy; named for the classical economist David Ricardo.

rule of 72 [G.11.3] doubling time of any growing quantity is approximately 72 divided by its growth rate expressed in percentage points (approximations remain good when 68, 69, or 70 replace 72).

rule, policy [16.5.2] rule relating objective conditions in the economy to particular policy actions; contrast **discretion**.

S

savings [2.2.2] income that is not consumed.

savings deposits [16.2.2] interest-bearing bank accounts not subject to transfer by check.

savings function [13.1.1] relationship between savings and (disposable) income or GDP; complement of the **consumption function**.

Say's law [12.3.1] proposition that there is never any barrier to full employment; sometimes rendered as "supply creates its own demand"; named for classical economist Jean-Baptiste Say.

scaled capital [9.5.2] capital in actual use as a fraction of capital available; synonym, **capacity-utilization rate**.

scaled labor [9.5.2] labor in actual use as a fraction of labor available; ratio of labor to the labor force; synonym, **employment rate**.

scaled output [9.5.2, 15.1] short-form synonym for **output scaled by potential output** – that is, output expressed as a percentage of potential GDP: $\tilde{Y} = \frac{Y}{Y_{pot}}$.

scatterplot [G.2.1] relational graph in which each point represents the value that each of two variables takes at a single period or for a single unit; the values of each variable are indicated on one of the two axes; when the data form a time series, the points may be connected by lines indicating their succession in time.

scrap value [14.4.1] residual value of capital when it ceases to be used in the production process.

seasonal factor [G.1.3] number that converts seasonally unadjusted to seasonally adjusted data according (typically) to a multiplicative formula.

seasonally adjusted [3.6.3, G.1.3] of data, transformed to take account of typical seasonal variation comparing the same weeks, months, or quarters in different years to establish a norm; contrast **seasonally unadjusted data**.

seasonally unadjusted [G.1.3] of data, not **seasonally adjusted**.

secondary labor markets [11.3.3] usually more poorly paid and less secure jobs, requiring few skills.

sectoral-deficits identity [2.3.3] national-income-accounting identity that states that the sum of all sectoral deficits is zero: $[G - (T - TR)] + [I - S] + [EX - IM] \equiv 0$

secular [5.1] of the trend, as opposed to the cycle; for example, secular growth is long-term trend growth.

securities [6.3.1] financial instruments traded on organized markets, especially longer-term instruments.

seigniorage [17.2.1] from the French *seigneur* meaning "lord"; profit accruing to the king from the difference in value between the weight of gold (or other precious metal) deposited with the mint and the weight of gold incorporated into the coin given in exchange; by extension, any profit accruing to a government or central bank from issuing new money where the cost of production is below the value of the money.

shares [6.3.3] fractional ownership shares in a corporation (synonyms, **corporate equities, stocks**; compare **common stocks**).

short run [9.4.1] horizon for economic analysis in which some factors of production are fixed and any equilibrium is temporary.

similarity and replacement, principle of [6.2.1] principle that a valuable good or asset may be valued by finding the replacement cost of a sufficiently similar good or asset.

simple annualization [G.10.2] conversion of a rate expressed at a frequency less than or greater than one year by multiplying by an appropriate factor; for example, a monthly rate of interest is simply annualized by multiplying by 12.

slump [5.2.1] period between the cyclical peak and the cyclical trough, when economic activity is falling; synonyms, **contraction, recession**; compare **depression, expansion**.

Solow growth model [10.4.2] parochial American name for the Solow-Swan growth model.

Solow-Swan growth model [10.4.2] particular version of the **neoclassical growth model** characterized by an investment as a fixed proportion of GDP; named for economists Robert Solow and Trevor Swan.

source of funds [6.1.1] lender.

spare capacity [9.4.3] increment of capital redundant at current levels of production; synonyms, **excess capacity, unused capacity**.

speculative grade [7.3.1] of bonds, having high default risk (Standard & Poors' ratings BB or lower and similar ratings for other agencies).

speculative demand for money [7.A.1] portion of the total demand for money sensitive to interest rates; money demanded as part of diversification of a financial portfolio.

stagflation [15.1.1] neologism coined in the 1970s (*stagnation* + in*flation*), meaning a period of both stagnation (based on low real GDP growth rates and high unemployment rates) and high inflation rates.

standard deviation [G.4.3] measure of the variability of data equal to the positive square root of the variance, and having the same units of measurement as the original data.

static [1.3.2] of an economic model, not involving time in any essential way.

stationary [G.5.2] of time series, homogeneous; when every reasonably sized subperiod displays similar descriptive statistics, particularly in the sense that the mean remains stable in different subsamples; compare **nonstationary**.

statistical discrepancy [3.6.1] difference between two methods of counting a quantity that in theory must produce the same value – usually, the result of incompleteness or inaccuracy in measuring some components of the data.

steady state [10.4.2] of a law of motion, when the quantity that it governs stops changing.

sterilized interventions [16.6.1] purchases or sales of foreign exchange whose effect on the outstanding stock of central-bank reserves is offset through a domestic open-market operation of the same size and opposite direction.

stock [2.2.1, G.1.2] **1.** quantity measured in timeless units; as opposed to a **flow**; [6.3.3] **2.** fractional ownership shares in a corporation (synonyms, **corporate equities**, **shares**; compare **common stocks**).

stock price [6.3.3] market price of a corporate share.

store of value [6.1.1] characteristic function of money that it is used as instrument to preserve value through time (to save).

structural unemployment [12.3.2] unemployment that results when jobs remain vacant even though some workers are still unemployed because of a mismatch between the skills needed by firms and the skills possessed by workers or a mismatch in the geographic location of jobs and potential workers.

subsistence wage [10.3.2] wage just sufficient to meet the minimum acceptable standard of living – a partly objective (physiological) and partly subjective (social or psychological) standard.

substitutes (substitution) [4.1.1, 7.2.1] pair of goods such that, when the price of the first good rises, the demand for the first good falls and the demand for the second good rises; typically, substitute goods are ones that can replace each other – raspberry and strawberry jam are substitutes.

substitutes in production [15.1.1] factors of production that are substitutes; a pair of factors of production such that, when if the price of one of them rises, its demand falls, and the demand for the second one rises.

substitution bias [4.1.1] overestimation of the rate of inflation using a base-weighted price index, owing to a failure to account for substitution away from goods with relatively more rapidly rising prices.

substitution effect [11.2.1] in general, change in demand or supply owing to a change in relative prices holding income constant; in labor-market analysis, change in the supply of labor as the result of a change in the real-wage rate, holding income constant.

supply factors [15.1.1] in general, factors related to (aggregate) supply as distinct from (aggregate) demand; particularly with respect to the Phillips curve, factors related to (aggregate) supply (e.g., changes in import prices) that shift the Phillips curve.

supply shocks [15.1.1] exogenous shifts in supply factors.

supply-side economics [11.2.1, 17.2.5] doctrine that lower tax rates substantially promote growth.

T

T-account [6.1.2] balance sheet presented in two columns – one for assets, the other for liabilities and net worth.

tax [2.2.2] fee levied by the government, often on income or the consumption of goods.

tax function [13.1.2] relationship between taxes and GDP.

tax multiplier [13.2.1] ratio of the increase in aggregate-demand changes to an increase in taxes ($\mu_T = \frac{\Delta Y}{\Delta T}$); tax multiplier is negative.

tax wedge [11.2.1] difference between wages paid by employers and wages received by workers after tax.

Taylor rule [16.5.3] family of rules for setting the Federal-funds rate in response to different levels of inflation and the output gap.

technique [9.1.1] knowledge of the process of production; a recipe for production.

technology [9.1.1] the set of available techniques.

temporal aggregation [G.1.2] adding up higher frequency data to form lower frequency data; for example, adding or averaging monthly data to form annual data.

term premium [7.4.3] increment to the yield required by lenders (bond buyers) to compensate them for the additional risk of holding bonds with increasingly long times to maturity.

term structure of interest rates [7.4.1] the pattern of interest rates with different maturities; the shape of the **yield curve**.

TFP [9.2.2, 9.3.1] abbreviation of **total factor productivity**; measure of productivity that accounts for both labor-augmenting and capital-augmenting technical progress; a weighted average of labor and capital productivity; synonym, **multifactor productivity**.

tight monetary policy [16.2.3] monetary policy aimed at reducing aggregate demand (synonyms, **contractionary** or **restrictive** monetary policy).

time deposits [16.2.2] bank deposits (e.g., small certificates of deposit) that have a definite holding period.

time-inconsistent policy [16.5.2] policy that is optimal when viewed from an earlier time, but is predictably suboptimal when viewed from its actual time of execution; synonym, **dynamically inconsistent policy**.

time series [G.1.1] data ordered in time.

time-series plot [G.2.2] graph of a time series.

time to maturity [6.3.1] period until a bond matures.

Tobin's *q* [14.4.3] ratio of the market value of a firm (measured by the value of its outstanding shares) to the replacement cost of its physical assets; named for economist James Tobin.

total factor productivity [9.2.2, 9.3.1] measure of productivity that accounts for both labor-augmenting and capital-augmenting technical progress; a weighted average of labor and capital productivity; abbreviated **TFP**; synonym, **multifactor productivity**.

trade balance [3.7, 8.2.1] exports less imports; synonyms, **foreign-sector deficit**, **net exports**.

trade-weighted exchange-rate index [8.3.2] index number measuring the appreciation or depreciation of the exchange rate against a basket of currencies, typically weighting changes in individual exchange rates by the importance of each country's trade to the domestic economy (as a share of its total trade); synonym, **effective-exchange-rate index**.

transactions accounts [16.2.2] bank accounts used for conducting transactions, including demand deposits (i.e., checking accounts).

transactions costs [8.4.2] of trade, costs such as the cost of transportation and insurance that limit the effectiveness of arbitrage among real goods.

transactions demand for money [7.A.1] money held to facilitate purchases of goods and services.

transfer payment [2.2.2, 3.1.1] payments for which nothing of equal value is given in return; contribution of valuable goods, services, or assets to another party without quid pro quo (e.g., welfare payments, interest payments).

transitional unemployment [12.2.2] unemployment that results inevitably from the fact that it takes time to move between jobs.

transitory income [14.2.3] nonpersistent changes in income; current income less **permanent income**.

transmission lag [16.5.2] delay in the effective operation of a policy action owing to the fact that economic mechanisms in the economy do not work instantly; synonym, **outside lag**; contrast **inside lag**.

trend [5.1] dominant path of a time series, around which the actual values may fluctuate or cycle.

trough, cyclical [5.1] low point of a business-cycle expansion marking the end of the recession and the beginning of an expansion.

turning point [3.6.2] period at which a cyclical series changes from expansion to contraction or from contraction to expansion.

type I error [G.7] in statistics, treating as false that which is true.

type II error [G.7] in statistics, treating as true that which is false.

U

uncovered interest-parity condition [8.4.3] in the foreign exchanges, no-arbitrage condition in which the expected appreciation of the exchange rate is approximately equal to the difference between yields on foreign and domestic assets.

underemployment [12.2.3] situation in which workers are employed in jobs below their ability and their potential value-added – particularly, when workers qualified for **primary labor market** are employed in the **secondary labor market**.

unemployment [9.4.2] **1.** in general, not working for whatever reason; **2.** frequently, equivalent to **involuntary unemployment** – that is, a situation in which a worker is willing and able to work at a job for which he is qualified at the going wage but is not, in fact, employed.

unemployment rate [9.4.3, 12.2.2] the fraction of the labor force not employed.

unit labor costs [15.3.4] real wage (and other compensation and benefits) per unit of output.

unit of account [6.1.1] characteristic function of money that it provides the units in which prices and values are measured.

unused capacity [9.4.3] increment of capital redundant at current levels of production; synonyms. **excess capacity**, **spare capacity**.

use of funds [6.1.1] borrower.

V

value-added [3.1.2] excess of value of the output of a production process over the cost of its inputs.

value-added method (of measuring GDP) [3.6.1] measurement of GDP based on adding up the value added at each stage of production.

variable [1.3.2] concept, represented in a model by a symbol such as a letter, to which a variety of numbers corresponding to measured quantities may be assigned.

variance [G.4.3] measure of the variability of a set of data formed by averaging the squared deviations from the sample mean.

vault cash [16.2.2] currency held by banks in anticipation of withdrawals through human and automatic tellers; a component of central-bank reserves.

voluntary unemployment [12.1] people who choose not to work in the current conditions; people not currently working whose **reservation wage** is greater than the current market wage for work that they are qualified to do.

W

wage [2.2.2] factor payment to suppliers of labor.

wage-price spiral [15.3.4] pattern in which increases in wages encourage firms to raise prices and increases in prices encourage workers and their unions to push for higher wages; an aspect of **cost-push inflation**.

wealth [2.2.1] stock of things owned; value of that stock.

weighted (arithmetic) mean [G.4.2] arithmetic mean in which components are magnified in proportion to their frequency or importance expressed in the form of multiplicative weights.

weighted geometric mean [G.4.2] geometric mean in which components are magnified in proportion to their frequency or importance expressed in the form of exponential weights.

weighted-median CPI [4.3.2] version of the consumer price index in which the component inflation rates are weighted by their expenditure shares and the index is formed from the median value of the components, as opposed to the mean value in the ordinary CPI; proposed as an alternative to the **core rate of inflation**.

Y

yield [6.2.1] income earned on a bond, loan, or other financial asset expressed as a percentage of its purchase price; compare **interest rate**.

yield curve [7.4.1] graph of the term structure of interest rates in which the yields of bonds of different maturities are plotted with the time to maturity measured on the horizontal axis and the yield to maturity on the vertical axis.

yield to maturity [6.3.1] rate of return earned if a bond is bought at the current market price and held until it matures and its face value is paid off.

Z

zero-coupon bond [6.3.1] a bond with a face value but without coupon (or interest) payments; the yield to maturity arises because the bond is sold at discount with respect to its face value; for example, a U.S. Treasury bill; synonym, **pure discount bond**.

zero-sum crowding out [17.2.3] form of **crowding out** in a fully employed economy: any time the government takes more resources, those available to the private sector must fall.

Guide to Online Resources

Source	Web Address	Data Coverage[a]
Online support for the textbook: *Applied Intermediate Macroeconomics*		
Applied Intermediate Macroeconomics	www.appliedmacroeconomics.com	Many links and resources useful to the book and courses based on it; all the data needed for end-of-chapter exercises (updated regularly)
U.S. Government Agencies		
Board of Governors of the Federal Reserve System	www.federalreserve.gov	Interest rates, monetary, bank reserve, and credit data; flow of funds; foreign-exchange rates; industrial production and capacity utilization
Bureau of Economics Analysis	www.bea.gov	U.S. national-accounting data
Bureau of Labor Statistics	www.bls.gov	Data on employment, unemployment, wages, hours, working conditions, CPI and PPI price indices
Bureau of the Census	www.census.gov	U.S. population statistics; socioeconomic data on U.S. population

(*continued*)

(continued)

Source	Web Address	Data Coverage[a]
Central Intelligence Agency	www.cia.gov/library/ publications/ the-world-factbook/ index.html	*World Factbook* – economic and other data on individual countries and cross-country comparative data
Congressional Budget Office	www.cbo.gov/	Federal budget projections, historical budget data, real-time data for potential GDP and NAIRU
Federal Reserve Bank of Cleveland	www.clevelandfed.org/ research/data/	Selection of economic indicators consolidated from a variety of sources; median CPI data
Federal Reserve Bank of Philadelphia	www.philadelphiafed.org/ research-and-data/	Livingston Survey of expectations of economic data; real-time economic data; Survey of Professional Forecasters
Federal Reserve Bank of San Francisco	www.frbsf.org/publications/ fedinprint/index.html	Search engine for publications of the entire Federal Reserve System
Federal Reserve Bank of San Francisco	www.frbsf.org/publications/ economics/index.php	*Economic Letter* (accessible short articles on current economic issues), *FedViews* (analysis of current economic events)
Federal Reserve Bank of St. Louis's *ALFRED* database	alfred.stlouisfed.org	Database of historical ("real-time") data
Federal Reserve Bank of St. Louis's *FRED* database	research.stlouisfed.org/fred2	Easy-to-use database consolidated from U.S. government, Federal Reserve, and private sources

Source	Web Address	Data Coverage[a]
President's Council of Economic Advisers	www.whitehouse.gov/ administration/eop/cea	*Economic Report of the President*, U.S. economic data consolidated from various sources
International Agencies		
Bank of International Settlements	www.bis.org	International finance and exchange-rate data
International Labor Organization	www.ilo.org	*LABORSTA –* database of international labor statistics; *Key Indicators of the Labor Market*
International Monetary Fund	www.imf.org/external/ data.htm	Wide range of data for most countries, particularly national-accounting, balance-of-payments, and financial statistics
Organization of Economic Cooperation and Development (OECD)	www.oecd.org/statsportal	Wide range of standardized data for OECD countries
United Nations Human Development Indicators	hdr.undp.org/en/statistics	International data on comparative well-being
World Bank	www.worldbank.org	International data, World Bank Development Indicators
Other Resources		
American Economic Association Resources for Economists on the Internet	www.aeaweb.org/RFE	Includes links to a variety of data sources, economic dictionaries, software, and other resources
Conference Board	www.conference-board.org/ economics	Consumer confidence and economic indicator data

(*continued*)

(continued)

Source	Web Address	Data Coverage[a]
Measuring Worth	www.measuringworth.com	Variety of historical databases and calculators for making historical comparisons of the value of money using various methods
National Bureau of Economic Research (NBER)	www.nber.org	U.S. business-cycle dates; links to a variety of other data, including the *Economic Report of the President*
Penn World Tables	pwt.econ.upenn.edu/php_site/ pwt_index.php	Many data series on a consistent purchasing-power parity basis, useful for cross-country comparisons of economic growth
Robert Shiller Online Data	www.econ.yale.edu/~shiller/ data.htm	Data on stock markets, housing prices, historical consumption, and historical financial markets

[a] Descriptions of data coverage are only partial; many sites contain much richer resources than documented here.

Index

CPSIA information can be obtained
at www.ICGtesting.com
Printed in the USA
LVHW101505100821
694994LV00005B/164